Gambero Rosso®
Slow Food Editore

italianwines 2009

ITALIAN WINES 2009
GAMBERO ROSSO® - SLOW FOOD EDITORE

EDITORIAL STAFF FOR THE ORIGINAL EDITION
DANIELE CERNILLI AND GIGI PIUMATTI

SENIOR EDITORS
GIANNI FABRIZIO, TIZIANO GAIA, ELEONORA GUERINI, MARCO SABELLICO

TECHNICAL SUPERVISION
GILBERTO ARRU, DARIO CAPPELLONI, GIUSEPPE CARRUS, NICOLA FRASSON, GIANCARLO GARIGLIO,
FABIO GIAVEDONI, VITTORIO MANGANELLI, RICCARDO VISCARDI, PAOLO ZACCARIA

OTHER MEMBERS OF FINAL TASTING PANELS
ALESSANDRO BOCCHETTI, ANTONIO BOCO, GIULIO COLOMBA, GOFFREDO D'ANDREA,
PAOLO DE CRISTOFARO, EGIDIO FEDELE DELL'OSTE, GIACOMO MOJOLI, LEONARDO ROMANELLI

CONTRIBUTORS
NINO AIELLO, GILBERTO ARRU, LORENZO AMAT, STEFANO ASARO, ANTONELLA BAMPA, VITTORIO BARBIERI,
PAOLO BATTIMELLI, ENRICO BATTISTELLA, FRANCESCO BEGHI, FRANCESCA BIDASIO DEGLI IMBERTI,
ALESSANDRO BOCCHETTI, ANTONIO BOCO, SERGIO BONANNO, MICHELE BRESSAN, PASQUALE BUFFA,
PAOLO CAMOZZI, DARIO CAPPELLONI, GIUSEPPE CARRUS, DIONISIO CASTELLO, DANIELE CERNILLI,
ROBERTO CHECCHETTO, GIULIO COLOMBA, PAOLO DE CRISTOFARO, FILIPPO DE GRANDI,
GIANNI FABRIZIO, EGIDIO FEDELE DELL'OSTE, DARIO FERRO, FAUSTO FERRONI, CARLO FIORANI,
NICOLA FRASSON, FABIO FUSINA, TIZIANO GAIA, PIETRO GARIBBO, GIANCARLO GARIGLIO, JONATHAN GEBSER,
FABIO GIAVEDONI, ELEONORA GUERINI, VITO LACERENZA, MASSIMO LANZA, EUGENIO MAILLER,
PATRIZIO MASTROCOLA, GIORGIO MELANDRI, GIACOMO MOJOLI, GIOVANNI NORESE, FRANCO PALLINI,
DAVIDE PANZIERI, NEREO PEDERZOLLI, ONORIO PERON, NICOLA PICCININI, DANIELA PIRANI,
GUIDO PIRAZZOLI, GIGI PIUMATTI, MARIO PLAZIO, MAX PLETT, FABIO PRACCHIA, FRANCESCO QUERCETTI,
PIERPAOLO RASTELLI, LEONARDO ROMANELLI, MARCO SABELLICO, DIEGO SORACCO, MAURIZIO STAGNITTO,
HERBERT TASCHLER, RENATO TEDESCO, MASSIMO TOFFOLO, ANDREA VANNELLI, RICCARDO VISCARDI,
MASSIMO VOLPARI, PAOLO ZACCARIA

MEMBERS OF REGIONAL TASTING PANELS
ANTONELLA AMODIO, ARTEMIO ASSIRI, EMIDIO BACHETTI, SALVATORE BASTA, ALBERTO BETTINI, DENNY BINI,
TEODOSIO BUONGIORNO, REMO CAMURANI, SERGIO CECCARELLI, ANTONIO CIMINELLI, ENZO CODOGNO,
LORENZO COLOMBO, CLAUDIO CORBA, MARIO DEMATTÈ, MARINO DEL CURTO, RICCARDO FERRANTE,
PIERO FIORENTINI, NATALE FIORINO, FRANCESCA GAMBERINI, LAURA GIORGI, DARIO LAURENZI,
CRISTIANA LAURO, MARCO LEONARDO, MIRCO MARCONI, MINO MARTUCCI, NICOLA MASSA,
GIACOMO MAZZAVILLANI, ENZO MERZ, FABIO MONGARETTO, VANNI MURARO, UGO ONGARETTO,
LIANO PETROZZI, RENZO PRIORI, VALENTINO RAMELLI, HELMUT RIEBSCHLÄGER, MAURIZIO ROSSI,
ALESSANDRA RUGGI, BARBARA SCHIFFINI, PAOLO VALDASTRI, VINCENZO VERRASTRO,
MASSIMO ZECCHIN, SIMONE ZOLI

EDITING
DARIO CAPPELLONI, VITTORIO MANGANELLI, EUGENIO SIGNORONI, PAOLO ZACCARIA

EDITORIAL COORDINATOR
GIORGIO ACCASCINA

LAYOUT
GIANNA PETRUCCI

TRANSLATIONS COORDINATED AND EDITED BY
GILES WATSON

TRANSLATORS
ANGELA ARNONE, MAUREEN ASHLEY, HELEN DONALD, RACHEL FELL, DAVE HENDERSON,
STEPHEN JACKSON, SARAH PONTING, SIMON TANNER, GILES WATSON, AILSA WOOD

PUBLISHER
GAMBERO ROSSO, INC.
PRESIDENT SERGIO CELLINI
636 BROADWAY – SUITE 111 – NEW YORK, NY 10012
TEL. +1-212-253-5653 FAX +1-212-253-8349 – E-MAIL: GAMBEROUSA@AOL.COM

DISTRIBUTION
USA AND CANADA BY ANTIQUE COLLECTORS' CLUB, EASTWORKS, 116 PLEASANT ST # 18
EASTHAMPTON, MA 010207, USA;
UK ANBD AUSTRALIA BY ANTIQUE COLLECTORS' CLUB LTD – SANDY LANE, OLD MARTLESHAM
WOODBRIDGE, SUFFOLK IP12 4SD – UNITED KINGDOM
TEL. +44-1394-389950 – FAX +44-1394-389999

ITALIAN WINES 2009 WAS CLOSED ON 20 SEPTEMBER 2008

PRINTED IN ITALY FOR G. R. H. SPA IN JANUARY 2009
BY PFG GRAFICHE SPA – VIA CANCELLERIA, 62 – 00040 ARICCIA - ROME

3

CONTENTS

THE REGIONS

INDEXES

INTRODUCTION

Here we are again, this time with the 2009 edition of Italian Wines, our 22nd. Over the years and the wines, we have made more than 150,000 tastings. For this edition alone, our experts tasted upwards of 25,000 wines to select the 18,000, released by 2,250 wineries up and down Italy, that are actually reviewed here. This vast sensory inquiry was carried out by more than 100 tasters and contributing reviewers at tasting panels set up all over the country. Once again, it was an enormous effort. It all started in May, when the various regional tasting panels began to collect samples for evaluation at blind comparative tastings. We tried, wherever possible, to involve protection consortia, chambers of commerce and anyone else who could act as neutral guarantors for the collection of wines and the organization of tasting sessions. Around 70,000 bottles were collected all over Italy for this edition. They had to be sourced, conserved and masked for tasting after being divided into groups of similar wines. Readers can imagine how much work this involved. We also believe that the supervision of this phase by independent institutions is a very positive factor. Such bodies represent all the producers and scrutinize our operations to ensure they are carried out properly, safeguarding the interests of consumers and monitoring what we do, for which we are very grateful. We will thank all of them, in the hope that none are inadvertently omitted: the consortia of Chianti Classico, Brunello and Rosso di Montalcino, Vino Nobile di Montepulciano, Vernaccia di San Gimignano, Chianti Rufina, Morellino di Scansano, Montecucco, Monteregio di Massa Marittima, Franciacorta, Oltrepò Pavese, Valtellina, Soave and Valpolicella, the Enoteca Regionale del Roero, the Enoteca Regionale at Dozza, the Enoteca Regionale at Gattinara, the Istituto Agronomico Mediterraneo at Valenzano, Centro Agroalimentare Umbro at Foligno, the Bolzano Chamber of Commerce, the Avellino Chamber of Commerce, the Trento Chamber of Commerce, the Arezzo Chamber of Commerce, Assivip at Majolati Spontini, Vinea at Offida and the Anteprima group at Lucca. Then there are the Strada del Vino associations of Carmignano and Costa degli Etruschi, Unioncamere at Matera and the Museo del Vino at Planargia, Magomadas. Private bodies include the Marina at Cala de' Medici, the Réserve at Caramanico, the Vineria della Signora in Rosso at Nizza Monferrato, the Enoteca Grapes at Isernia and the Le Due Sorelle restaurant at Messina. For the first stage, we adopted scores out of 100 and selected about 1,500 wines that went through to the Three Glass finals. These wines were awarded at least Two red Glasses. At the conclusion of this huge effort, the final awards committee met to assign the Three Glass prizes. Selected from prominent tasters on local panels, the committee scrutinized all the wines sent to the finals. Again, all tastings were blind. The judgement here was more drastic: a yes or a no. Each decision was carefully justified. Every wine was discussed and analysed by all the members of the commission, whose votes had equal weight. For this Guide, the following panellists joined Daniele Cernilli, Gigi Piumatti, Gianni Fabrizio, Marco Sabellico, Eleonora Guerini and Tiziano Gaia for at least one of the three final taste-offs over a total of 15 days: Vittorio Manganelli, Dario Cappelloni, Nicola Frasson, Giulio Colomba,

INTRODUCTION

Giacomo Mojoli, Egidio Fedele dell'Oste, Leonardo Romanelli, Paolo Zaccaria, Fabio Giavedoni, Riccardo Viscardi, Giancarlo Gariglio, Antonio Boco, Paolo De Cristofaro and Alessandro Bocchetti. Tastings were held at Città del Gusto in Rome, the Università del Gusto at Pollenzo and the Là di Petros restaurant at Colloredo di Monte Albano. But what are the criteria used to reach a decision? Well, they are above all more humanistic, cultural and hedonistic than strictly scientific. This is why we prefer to use a classification by bands instead of by marks out of 100, which may look more precise but are less easy to justify. While it is fairly unlikely that a wine will move from one band to another at different tastings, it is highly probable that its mark out of 100 will change, albeit only slightly. There are also factors that cannot be evaluated in merely sensory terms. Concepts like a wine's conformity with, or representativeness of, its type, or with concepts of oenological correctness, are quite hard to codify. There are wines we could call emotional, which rise above any minor defects of execution or colour in the same way that the music of jazz masters such as Louis Armstrong or Billie Holliday does. To claim that tasters should restrict themselves to what is in the glass, and refrain from reflection or criticism, is an attitude as blinkered as it is regrettable. Of course, wine should be good but it should also be representative and environmentally friendly. Nor should it bend the knee to fashions in taste or the international market. We believe that the wines of the future will have to take these factors into account and on this point, Gambero Rosso and Slow Food's representatives are in full agreement. This year's Special Awards were largely inspired by this broader vision of wine. Fattoria di Felsina, a stronghold of Cianti's modern tradition, is our Winery of the Year. The Barbaresco Asili Riserva '04 from Bruno Giacosa, a monument of Langhe winemaking, is the Red of the Year. Our White of the Year award goes to Les Crêtes, the winery of that sensitive winemaker, Costantino Charrère, for the Valle d'Aosta Chardonnay Cuvée Bois '06. The Sparkler of the Year, Alto Adige Metodo Classico Hausmannhof Riserva '97, is from Haderburg, a winery that today is biodynamic. Sweet Wine of the Year is Luigi Viola's Moscato Passito '07, a Calabrian white made using ancient traditional techniques. The Best-priced Wine is Giordano Sirch's COF Friulano '07. Our Up-and-Coming Winery is Rocca del Principe in Irpinia. Celestino Lucin, the Kellermeister of Abbazia di Novacella, is out Oenologist of the Year. The Award for Sustainable Viticulture goes to Sicilian agronomist and oenologist Salvo Foti, a passionate advocate of bush training. And the Grower of the Year is Marinella Camerani, from Corte Sant'Alda, a winery that has embraced the philosophy of organic farming. And that's all for this year.

Daniele Cernilli and Gigi Piumatti

THREE GLASS AWARDS 2009

VALLE D'AOSTA

Référence '06	Brégy & Gillioz - Podium	18
Valle d'Aosta Chardonnay Cuvée Bois '06	Les Crêtes	21
Valle d'Aosta Chardonnay Élevé en Fût de Chêne '07	Anselmet	18
Valle d'Aosta Fumin '06	F.lli Grosjean	20

PIEDMONT

Barbaresco Asili Ris. '04	Bruno Giacosa	95
Barbaresco Bric Balin '05	Moccagatta	117
Barbaresco Cottà '05	Sottimano	156
Barbaresco Gaiun '04	Tenute Cisa Asinari dei Marchesi di Grésy	73
Barbaresco Maria Adelaide '04	Bruno Rocca	142
Barbaresco Pora '04	Ca' del Baio	55
Barbaresco Rombone '05	Fiorenzo Nada	123
Barbaresco Sorì Burdin '05	Fontanabianca	89
Barbaresco Sorì Paitin Vecchie Vigne '04	Paitin	128
Barbaresco V. Erte '04	F.lli Cigliuti	72
Barbaresco Vign. Brich Ronchi '05	Albino Rocca	141
Barbaresco Vign. Starderi '05	La Spinetta	157
Barbera d'Asti Bricco della Bigotta '06	Braida	48
Barbera d'Asti Sup. Montruc '06	Franco M. Martinetti	114
Barbera d'Asti Sup. Nizza A Luigi Veronelli '06	Brema	48
Barbera del M.to Sup. Barabba '04	Iuli	105
Barolo Bricco Boschis '04	F.lli Cavallotto Tenuta Bricco Boschis	69
Barolo Bricco Luciani '04	Silvio Grasso	101
Barolo Broglio '04	Schiavenza	152
Barolo Brunate '04	Mario Marengo	113
Barolo Cannubi '04	Michele Chiarlo	70
Barolo Cannubi '04	Damilano	83
Barolo Cannubi Boschis '04	Luciano Sandrone	148
Barolo Cannubi S. Lorenzo-Ravera '04	Giuseppe Rinaldi	140
Barolo Cascina Francia '04	Giacomo Conterno	77
Barolo Case Nere '04	Enzo Boglietti	44
Barolo Ciabot Mentin Ginestra '04	Domenico Clerico	73
Barolo Enrico VI '04	Monfalletto Cordero di Montezemolo	119
Barolo Falletto '04	Bruno Giacosa	95
Barolo Ginestra Ris. '01	Paolo Conterno	77
Barolo Ginestra V. Casa Maté '04	Elio Grasso	100
Barolo Lazzarito '04	Vietti	166
Barolo Le Gramolere '04	Giovanni Manzone	110
Barolo Monfortino Ris. '01	Giacomo Conterno	77
Barolo Parafada '04	Vigna Rionda - Massolino	167
Barolo Prapò '04	Ettore Germano	94
Barolo Ravera '04	Elvio Cogno	74
Barolo Rocche dell'Annunziata '04	Rocche Costamagna	142
Barolo Romirasco '04	Aldo Conterno	76
Barolo S. Giovanni '04	Gianfranco Alessandria	29
Barolo S. Lorenzo '04	F.lli Alessandria	29
Barolo Sarmassa '04	Giacomo Brezza & Figli	49
Barolo V. del Gris '04	Conterno Fantino	78
Barolo V. La Rosa '04	Fontanafredda	89
Barolo V. Rionda '04	Luigi Pira	134
Barolo Vign. La Villa '04	F.lli Seghesio	154
Barolo Vign. Rocche '04	Renato Corino	80
Boca '04	Le Piane	132
Colli Tortonesi Bianco Pitasso '06	Claudio Mariotto	113
Colli Tortonesi Timorasso Derthona '06	Vigneti Massa	169
Colli Tortonesi Timorasso Il Montino '06	La Colombera	75
Dogliani Papà Celso '06	Abbona	26
Dogliani Sirì d'Jermu '06	Pecchenino	130
Dogliani V. Tecc '06	Einaudi	86
Dolcetto d'Alba Barturot '07	Ca' Viola	57
Dolcetto di Dogliani Briccolero '07	Quinto Chionetti & Figlio	71
Gattinara Tre Vigne '04	Giancarlo Travaglini	161

THREE GLASS AWARDS 2009

Gattinara Vign. Osso S. Grato '04	Antoniolo	32
Gavi del Comune di Gavi Bruno Broglia '07	Gian Piero Broglia	52
Ghemme '04	Torraccia del Piantavigna	161
Langhe La Villa '06	Elio Altare - Cascina Nuova	31
Langhe Nebbiolo Costa Russi '05	Gaja	91
Langhe Nebbiolo Sperss '04	Gaja	91
Lessona S. Sebastiano allo Zoppo '04	Sella	154
M.to Rosso Pin '06	La Spinetta	157
Nebbiolo d'Alba '06	Hilberg - Pasquero	104
Piemonte Chardonnay Monteriolo '05	Coppo	79
Roero '06	Filippo Gallino	91
Roero Audinaggio '06	Cascina Ca' Rossa	56
Roero Mombeltramo Ris. '05	Malvirà	109
Roero Srü '06	Monchiero Carbone	118

LIGURIA

Riviera Ligure di Ponente Pigato U Baccan '06	Bruna	189
Riviera Ligure di Ponente Vermentino '07	Maria Donata Bianchi	188

LOMBARDY

Franciacorta Au Contraire Pas Dosé '01	Cavalleri	214
Franciacorta Brut Cabochon '04	Monte Rossa	225
Franciacorta Cuvée Annamaria Clementi '01	Ca' del Bosco	210
Franciacorta Dosage Zéro '04	Ca' del Bosco	210
Franciacorta Extra Brut '04	Monzio Compagnoni	227
Franciacorta Extra Brut Comarì del Salem '03	Uberti	236
Franciacorta Gran Cuvée Brut '04	Bellavista	206
Franciacorta Satèn '04	Ferghettina	218
Lugana Sel. Fabio Contato '07	Provenza	231
OP Barbera Poggio Della Maga '05	Castello di Cigognola	215
OP Pinot Nero Brut Cl. Nature Écru '03	Anteo	205
OP Pinot Nero Cl. Nature	Monsupello	225
OP Pinot Nero Giorgio Odero '05	Frecciarossa	219
Valtellina Sforzato Albareda '06	Mamete Prevostini	230
Valtellina Sfursat '05	Nino Negri	228

TRENTINO

Rosso Faye '05	Pojer & Sandri	267
San Leonardo '04	Tenuta San Leonardo	269
Teroldego Armilo '06	Bolognani	257
Trento Altemasi Graal Brut Ris. '01	Cavit	258
Trento Brut Cuvée dell'Abate Ris. '03	Abate Nero	256
Trento Giulio Ferrari		
Riserva del Fondatore Brut '99	Ferrari	261
Trento Methius Brut Ris. '02	F.lli Dorigati	260

ALTO ADIGE

A. A. Bianco Beyond the Clouds '06	Elena Walch	283
A. A. Cabernet Sauvignon Lafòa '04	Cantina Produttori Colterenzio	281
A. A. Gewürztraminer Kastelaz '07	Elena Walch	283
A. A. Gewürztraminer Nussbaumer '07	Cantina Termeno	303
A. A. Gewürztraminer Passito Terminum V. T. '06	Cantina Termeno	303
A. A. Lagrein Abtei Ris. '05	Cantina Convento Muri-Gries	294
A. A. Lagrein Scuro Prestige Line Ris. '06	Cantina Gries/Cantina di Bolzano	286
A. A. Lagrein Scuro Ris. '05	Erbhof Unterganzner	
	Josephus Mayr	283
A. A. Moscato Giallo Passito Serenade '05	Cantina di Caldaro	280
A. A. Pinot Bianco Dellago '07	Cantina Produttori	
	Santa Maddalena/Cantina di Bolzano	300
A. A. Pinot Bianco Sirmian '07	Cantina Nals Margreid	295
A. A. Pinot Nero Ris. '05	Stroblhof	301
A. A. Sauvignon Praesulis '07	Gumphof - Markus Prackwieser	287
A. A. Sauvignon St. Valentin '07	Cantina Produttori	
	San Michele Appiano	299
A. A. Spumante Hausmannhof Ris. '97	Haderburg	288
A. A. Terlano Pinot Bianco Vorberg Ris. '05	Cantina Terlano	302

THREE GLASS AWARDS 2009

A. A. Valle Isarco Riesling Kaiton '07	Kuenhof - Peter Pliger	291
A. A. Valle Isarco Riesling Praepositus '06	Abbazia di Novacella	278
A. A. Valle Isarco Sylvaner Praepositus '07	Abbazia di Novacella	278
A. A. Valle Isarco Sylvaner R '07	Köfererhof - Günther Kershbaumer	290
A. A. Valle Isarco Veltliner '07	Garlider - Christian Kerchbaumer	285
A. A. Valle Isarco Veltliner '07	Hoandlhof - Manfred Nössing	289
A. A. Valle Venosta Pinot Bianco '07	Falkenstein - Franz Pratzner	284
A. A. Valle Venosta Pinot Bianco '07	Tenuta Unterortl - Castel Juval	305
A. A. Valle Venosta Riesling '07	Falkenstein - Franz Pratzner	284
A. A. Valle Venosta Riesling '07	Tenuta Unterortl - Castel Juval	305

VENETO

Amarone della Valpolicella '03	Marion	347
Amarone della Valpolicella '04	Trabucchi	370
Amarone della Valpolicella Campo dei Gigli '04	Tenuta Sant'Antonio	364
Amarone della Valpolicella Cl. '04	Allegrini	315
Amarone della Valpolicella Cl. '01	Cav. G. B. Bertani	319
Amarone della Valpolicella Cl. Caterina Zardini '04	Giuseppe Campagnola	327
Amarone della Valpolicella Cl. Sergio Zenato '03	Zenato	377
Amarone della Valpolicella Cl. Terre di Cariano '04	Cecilia Beretta	318
Amarone della Valpolicella Cl. Vign. Monte Ca' Bianca '03	Lorenzo Begali	318
Amarone della Valpolicella Cl. Vign. Monte Sant'Urbano '04	F.lli Speri	367
Amarone della Valpolicella Cl. Villa Rizzardi '04	Guerrieri Rizzardi	343
Amarone della Valpolicella Proemio '05	Santi	365
Capitel Croce '06	Roberto Anselmi	316
Colli di Conegliano Rosso Ser Bele '05	Sorelle Bronca	323
Colli Euganei Cabernet Girapoggio '05	Ca' Lustra	325
Colli Euganei Fior d'Arancio Passito Donna Daria '06	Giordano Emo Capodilista	329
Colli Euganei Rosso Arquà '04	Vignalta	373
Custoza Sup. Amedeo '06	Cavalchina - La Prendina	331
Gambellara Cl. Riva del Molino '07	Luigino Dal Maso	338
Montello e Colli Asolani Il Rosso dell'Abazia '05	Serafini & Vidotto	366
Refolà Cabernet Sauvignon '04	Le Vigne di San Pietro	374
Relógio '06	Ca' Orologio	326
Soave Cl. Calvarino '06	Leonildo Pieropan	358
Soave Cl. Le Bine de Costjola '06	Tamellini	368
Soave Cl. Monte Carbonare '07	Suavia	368
Soave Cl. Monte Fiorentine '07	Ca' Rugate	326
Soave Cl. Staforte '06	Prà	359
Soave Sup. Il Casale '07	Agostino Vicentini	372
Valpolicella Cl. Sup. Campo Morar '05	Viviani	377
Valpolicella Sup. Mithas '04	Corte Sant'Alda	336
Valpolicella Sup. Vign. di Monte Lodoletta '04	Romano Dal Forno	338

FRIULI VENEZIA GIULIA

Blanc des Rosis '07	Schiopetto	443
Carso Malvasia '05	Kante	419
Carso Malvasia '06	Zidarich	463
COF BiancoSesto '07	La Tunella	451
COF Friulano '07	Giordano Sirch	445
COF Merlot Filip '04	Miani	425
COF Pinot Bianco Zuc di Volpe '07	Volpe Pasini	462
COF Rosazzo Bianco Terre Alte '06	Livio Felluga	413
COF Tocai Friulano V. Cinquant'Anni '06	Le Vigne di Zamò	457
Collio Bianco '07	Colle Duga	405
Collio Bianco Broy '07	Eugenio Collavini	404
Collio Bianco Fosarin '07	Ronco dei Tassi	438
Collio Bianco Ronco della Chiesa '06	Borgo del Tiglio	393
Collio Bianco Zuani Vigne '07	Zuani	464
Collio Friulano Vigna del Rolat '07	Dario Raccaro	434
Collio Pinot Bianco '07	Isidoro Polencic	432
Collio Pinot Bianco '07	Doro Princic	433
Collio Pinot Bianco '07	Russiz Superiore	440
Collio Pinot Bianco '07	Franco Toros	450

THREE GLASS AWARDS
2009

Collio Pinot Bianco '07	Villa Russiz	459
Collio Pinot Grigio '07	Branko	396
Collio Sauvignon Ronco delle Mele '07	Venica & Venica	452
Collio Tocai Friulano '07	Edi Keber	420
Friuli Grave Merlot Vistorta '06	Vistorta	461
Friuli Isonzo Friulano '07	Mauro Drius	411
Friuli Isonzo Malvasia Istriana Dis Cumieris '06	Vie di Romans	454
Refosco P. R. Morus Nigra '06	Vignai da Duline	456
Ribolla Anfora '04	Gravner	417
Sauvignon Picol '06	Lis Neris	421
W.... Dreams... ...... '06	Jermann	419
Winter Rosso '04	Casa Zuliani	401

EMILIA ROMAGNA

C. B. Cabernet Sauvignon Bonzarone '05	Tenuta Bonzara	472
C. P. Cabernet Sauvignon Luna Selvatica '06	La Tosa	495
C. P. Malvasia Passito '06	Il Negrese	488
C. P. Malvasia Passito V. del Volta '06	La Stoppa	493
Marzieno '04	Fattoria Zerbina	500
Sangiovese di Romagna Sup. Avi Ris. '05	San Patrignano	491
Sangiovese di Romagna Sup. Michelangiolo Ris. '05	Calonga	473
Sangiovese di Romagna Sup. Terra di Covignano Ris. '05	San Valentino	491
Sangiovese di Romagna V. del Generale Ris. '05	Casetto dei Mandorli	475

TUSCANY

Amor Costante '05	Brunelli - Le Chiuse di Sotto	524
Avvoltore '06	Moris Farms	578
Bolgheri Rosso Sup. Grattamacco '05	Podere Grattamacco	559
Bolgheri Sassicaia '05	Tenuta San Guido	611
Bolgheri Sup. Argentiera '05	Argentiera	513
Bolgheri Sup. Ornellaia '05	Tenuta dell' Ornellaia	580
Brancaia Il Blu '06	Brancaia	523
Brunello di Montalcino '03	Biondi Santi S.p.A.	519
Caberlot '05	Podere Il Carnasciale	531
Cabreo Il Borgo '06	Tenute Ambrogio e Giovanni Folonari	552
Camartina '05	Querciabella	599
Carmignano Villa di Capezzana '05	Tenuta di Capezzana	530
Casalferro '05	Barone Ricasoli	517
Cepparello '05	Isole e Olena	562
Chianti Cl. '06	Badia a Coltibuono	514
Chianti Cl. Castello di Ama '05	Castello di Ama	511
Chianti Cl. Cortevecchia Ris. '05	Fattoria Le Corti	546
Chianti Cl. Il Margone Ris. '05	Il Molino di Grace	575
Chianti Cl. Montegiachi Ris. '05	Agricoltori del Chianti Geografico	509
Chianti Cl. Rancia Ris. '05	Fattoria di Felsina	551
Chianti Cl. Ris. Ducale Oro '04	Tenimenti Ruffino	606
Chianti Cl. Tenuta di Capraia Ris. '05	Rocca di Castagnoli	604
Colline Lucchesi Tenuta di Valgiano '05	Tenuta di Valgiano	630
Flaccianello della Pieve '05	Tenuta Fontodi	554
Fontalloro '05	Fattoria di Felsina	551
Galatrona '06	Fattoria Petrolo	586
I Sodi di San Niccolò '04	Castellare di Castellina	534
Il Carbonaione '05	Podere Poggio Scalette	593
Il Corzano '05	Fattoria Corzano e Paterno	547
Kepos '06	Ampeleia	512
Livernano '05	Livernano	565
Lupicaia '05	Castello del Terriccio	623
Montecucco Sangiovese Lombrone Ris. '04	Colle Massari	543
Mormoreto '05	Marchesi de' Frescobaldi	571
Nambrot '05	Tenuta di Ghizzano	558
Nobile di Montepulciano Asinone '05	Poliziano	595
Nobile di Montepulciano Bossona Ris. '04	Maria Caterina Dei	548
Nobile di Montepulciano Ris. '04	La Calonica	526
Pietradonice '05	Casanova di Neri	533
Poggiassai '06	Poggio Bonelli	591

THREE GLASS AWARDS
2009

Pugnitello '06	San Felice	609
Redigaffi '06	Tua Rita	628
Rocca di Frassinello '06	Rocca di Frassinello	604
Saffredi '05	Fattoria Le Pupille	596
Sammarco '05	Castello dei Rampolla	600
Siepi '05	Castello di Fonterutoli	553
Tignanello '05	Marchesi Antinori	512
Vignamaggio '05	Villa Vignamaggio	634
Vin Santo '96	Avignonesi	513

MARCHE

Barricadiero '06	Aurora	666
Conero Rossini Ris. '05	Piantate Lunghe	686
Erasmo Castelli '06	Maria Pia Castelli	670
Fedus Sangiovese '06	San Savino - Poderi Capecci	690
Regina del Bosco '05	Fattoria Dezi	676
Rosso Piceno Sup. Roggio del Filare '05	Velenosi	697
Verdicchio dei Castelli di Jesi Cl. Misco Ris. '05	Tenuta di Tavignano	694
Verdicchio dei Castelli di Jesi Cl. Plenio Ris. '05	Umani Ronchi	695
Verdicchio dei Castelli di Jesi Cl. San Sisto Ris. '05	Fazi Battaglia	677
Verdicchio dei Castelli di Jesi Cl. Stefano Antonucci Ris. '06	Santa Barbara	691
Verdicchio dei Castelli di Jesi Cl. Sup. Podium '06	Gioacchino Garofoli	678
Verdicchio dei Castelli di Jesi Cl. Sup. S. Michele '06	Vallerosa Bonci	696
Verdicchio dei Castelli di Jesi Cl. Villa Bucci Ris. '06	Bucci	667
Verdicchio di Matelica Collestefano '07	Collestefano	672
Verdicchio di Matelica Mirum Ris. '06	La Monacesca	683

UMBRIA

Cervaro della Sala '06	Castello della Sala	718
Lago di Corbara Rosso Villa Monticelli '04	Barberani - Vallesanta	705
Montefalco Sagrantino '05	Perticaia	716
Montefalco Sagrantino 25 Anni '05	Arnaldo Caprai	706
Montefalco Sagrantino Colle delle Allodole '05	Fattoria Colle Allodole	708
Montefalco Sagrantino Gold '04	Còlpetrone	709
Torgiano Rosso Vigna Monticchio Ris. '04	Lungarotti	712

LAZIO

Grechetto Latour a Civitella '06	Sergio Mottura	733
Montiano '06	Falesco	710

ABRUZZO

Montepulciano d'Abruzzo '98	Emidio Pepe	753
Montepulciano d'Abruzzo '06	Villa Medoro	759
Montepulciano d'Abruzzo Bellovedere '05	La Valentina	757
Montepulciano d'Abruzzo Cerasuolo '06	Valentini	757
Montepulciano d'Abruzzo Colline Teramane Zanna Ris. '05	Dino Illuminati	751
Montepulciano d'Abruzzo Malandrino '06	Luigi Cataldi Madonna	746
Montepulciano d'Abruzzo Marina Cvetic '05	Masciarelli	751
Montepulciano d'Abruzzo Solàrea '03	Agriverde	744
Montepulciano d'Abruzzo Valle Reale '06	Valle Reale	758
Montepulciano d'Abruzzo Villa Gemma '05	Masciarelli	751
Pecorino '06	Luigi Cataldi Madonna	746
Trebbiano d'Abruzzo '05	Valentini	757

MOLISE

Molise Don Luigi Ris. '06	Di Majo Norante	765

CAMPANIA

Ambruco '06	Terre del Principe	782
Costa d'Amalfi Fiorduva '07	Marisa Cuomo	771
Falerno del Massico Camarato '04	Villa Matilde	785
Fiano di Avellino '07	Colli di Lapio	770
Fiano di Avellino '07	Rocca del Principe	780

THREE GLASS AWARDS 2009

Fiano di Avellino Vigna della Congregazione '06	Villa Diamante	784
Gladius '06	Tenuta Adolfo Spada	781
Greco di Tufo '07	Pietracupa	779
Greco di Tufo Cutizzi '07	Feudi di San Gregorio	774
Greco di Tufo Novaserra '07	Mastroberardino	777
Montevetrano '06	Montevetrano	778
Taburno Aglianico Bue Apis '04	Cantina del Taburno	782
Taurasi '04	Contrade di Taurasi	770
Taurasi Naturalis Historia '04	Mastroberardino	777
Taurasi Vigna Cinque Querce '04	Salvatore Molettieri	778
Terra di Lavoro '06	Galardi	775

PUGLIA

Artas '06	Castello Monaci	814
Castel del Monte Rosso V. Pedale Ris. '05	Torrevento	817
Lui '06	Cantina Albea	807
Masseria Maime '06	Tormaresca	817
Primitivo di Manduria Es '06	Gianfranco Fino	811
Primitivo di Manduria Zinfandel Sinfarosa '06	Accademia dei Racemi	806
Salice Salentino Rosso Selvarossa Ris. '05	Cantina Due Palme	810

BASILICATA

Aglianico del Vulture Gudarrà '05	Bisceglia	796
Aglianico del Vulture Re Manfredi '05	Terre degli Svevi	801
Aglianico del Vulture Titolo '06	Elena Fucci	799

CALABRIA

Cirò Rosso Cl. Duca Sanfelice Ris. '05	Librandi	828
Moscato Passito '07	Luigi Viola	831

SICILY

Cerasuolo di Vittoria V. Para Para '05	Poggio di Bortolone	847
Chardonnay '06	Tasca d'Almerita	850
Contea di Sclafani Rosso del Conte '05	Tasca d'Almerita	850
Contessa Entellina Milleunanotte '05	Donnafugata	841
Deliella '05	Feudo Principi di Butera	842
Don Antonio '06	Morgante	845
Etna Bianco Sup. Pietramarina '04	Benanti	837
Etna Rosso '05	Cottanera	839
Etna Rosso Outis '05	Vini Biondi	837
Etna Rosso Prephilloxera La V. di Don Peppino '06	Tenuta delle Terre Nere	851
Faro Palari '06	Palari	845
Harmonium '06	Firriato	843
Mandrarossa Cartagho '06	Settesoli	849
Nerosanloré '05	Gulfi	844
Sàgana '06	Cusumano	840
Saia '06	Feudo Maccari	842
Santa Cecilia '06	Planeta	847

SARDINIA

Alghero Marchese di Villamarina '03	Tenute Sella & Mosca	874
Alghero Torbato Terre Bianche Cuvée 161 '07	Tenute Sella & Mosca	874
Barrua '05	Agricola Punica	862
Cannonau di Sardegna Dule Ris. '05	Giuseppe Gabbas	867
Cannonau di Sardegna Josto Miglior Ris. '05	Antichi Poderi Jerzu	868
Cannonau di Sardegna Keramos Ris. '04	Tenute Soletta	874
Carignano del Sulcis Arenas Ris. '05	Sardus Pater	873
Carignano del Sulcis Sup. Terre Brune '04	Cantina Sociale di Santadi	872
Dettori Bianco Un anno dopo '06	Tenute Dettori	865
Malvasia di Bosa '05	F.lli Porcu	871
Turriga '04	Antonio Argiolas	862
Vernaccia di Oristano Antico Gregori	Attilio Contini	864

THE YEAR'S BEST WINES

THE SPARKLER
ALTO ADIGE METODO CLASSICO HAUSMANNHOF RIS. '97 — HADERBURG

THE WHITE
VALLE D'AOSTA CHARDONNAY CUVÉE BOIS '06 — LES CRETES

THE RED
BARBARESCO ASILI RIS. '04 — BRUNO GIACOSA

THE SWEET
MOSCATO PASSITO '07 — VIOLA

WINERY OF THE YEAR

FATTORIA DI FELSINA

OENOLOGIST OF THE YEAR

CELESTINO LUCIN

UP-AND-COMING WINERY

ROCCA DEL PRINCIPE

BEST PRICED WINE

COF FRIULANO '07 — SIRCH

GROWER OF THE YEAR

MARINELLA CAMERANI

AWARD FOR SUSTAINABLE VITICULTURE

SALVO FOTI

FIRST-TIME THREE GLASS WINNERS

VALLE D'AOSTA

Référence	Brégy & Gillioz - Podium	18
Valle d'Aosta Fumin	F.lli Grosjean	20

PIEDMONT

Barbera d'Asti Sup. Nizza A Luigi Veronelli	Brema	48
Barbera del M.to Sup. Barabba	Iuli	105
Barolo Broglio	Schiavenza	152
Barolo Brunate	Mario Marengo	113
Barolo Ginestra Ris.	Paolo Conterno	77
Barolo Rocche dell'Annunziata	Rocche Costamagna	142
Colli Tortonesi Timorasso Il Montino	La Colombera	75
Gavi del Comune di Gavi Bruno Broglia	Gian Piero Broglia	52
Ghemme	Torraccia del Piantavigna	161

LIGURIA

Riviera Ligure di Ponente Vermentino	Maria Donata Bianchi	188

LOMBARDY

Lugana Sel. Fabio Contato	Provenza	231
OP Barbera Poggio Della Maga	Castello di Cigognola	215
OP Pinot Nero Brut Cl. Nature Écru	Anteo	205
OP Pinot Nero Giorgio Odero	Frecciarossa	219

TRENTINO

Teroldego Armilo	Bolognani	257

ALTO ADIGE

A. A. Pinot Nero Ris.	Stroblhof	301

VENETO

Colli di Conegliano Rosso Ser Bele	Sorelle Bronca	323
Colli Euganei Fior d'Arancio Passito Donna Daria	Giordano Emo Capodilista	329
Gambellara Cl. Riva del Molino	Luigino Dal Maso	338
Soave Sup. Il Casale	Agostino Vicentini	372

FRIULI VENEZIA GIULIA

Carso Malvasia	Zidarich	463
COF Friulano	Giordano Sirch	445
Collio Bianco Zuani Vigne	Zuani	464
Winter Rosso	Casa Zuliani	401

EMILIA ROMAGNA

C. P. Malvasia Passito	Il Negrese	488
Sangiovese di Romagna V. del Generale Ris.	Casetto dei Mandorli	475

TUSCANY

Amor Costante	Brunelli - Le Chiuse di Sotto	524
Chianti Cl. Montegiachi Ris.	Agricoltori del Chianti Geografico	509
Kepos	Ampeleia	512
Montecucco Sangiovese Lombrone Ris.	Colle Massari	543
Nobile di Montepulciano Bossona Ris.	Maria Caterina Dei	548
Nobile di Montepulciano Ris.	La Calonica	526

MARCHE

Conero Rossini Ris.	Piantate Lunghe	686
Erasmo Castelli	Maria Pia Castelli	670

UMBRIA

Lago di Corbara Rosso Villa Monticelli	Barberani - Vallesanta	705
Montefalco Sagrantino Colle delle Allodole	Fattoria Colle Allodole	708

ABRUZZO

Montepulciano d'Abruzzo	Emidio Pepe	753
Montepulciano d'Abruzzo Bellovedere	La Valentina	757

CAMPANIA

Ambruco	Terre del Principe	782
Fiano di Avellino	Rocca del Principe	780
Gladius	Tenuta Adolfo Spada	781
Taurasi	Contrade di Taurasi	770

PUGLIA

Primitivo di Manduria Es	Gianfranco Fino	811

CALABRIA

Moscato Passito	Luigi Viola	831

SICILY

Cerasuolo di Vittoria V. Para Para	Poggio di Bortolone	847
Etna Rosso Outis	Vini Biondi	837
Mandrarossa Cartagho	Settesoli	849
Saia	Feudo Maccari	842

SARDINIA

Barrua	Agricola Punica	862
Cannonau di Sardegna Dule Ris.	Giuseppe Gabbas	867
Cannonau di Sardegna Keramos Ris.	Tenute Soletta	874
Carignano del Sulcis Arenas Ris.	Sardus Pater	873
Malvasia di Bosa	F.lli Porcu	871

THE STARS

In the 22 editions of Italian Wines, a total of 108 wineries, in effect the elite of Italian winemaking, have won at least ten Three Glass awards. Heading the list is Angelo Gaja, with a stunning 43 awards. Two other wineries, La Spinetta in Piedmont and Lombardy's Ca' del Bosco, have won three Stars. Two Star wineries have risen in number from six to 14 and, gratifyingly, 18 cellars appear on this page for the first time with ten or 11 awards. Meanwhile, many other producers, now close to inclusion with eight or nine Three Glass prizes, are destined to join this exclusive club.

★★★★
43
Gaja (Piedmont)

★★★
34
La Spinetta (Piedmont)
32
Ca' del Bosco (Lombardy)

★★
27
Elio Altare - Cascina Nuova (Piedmont)
24
Allegrini (Veneto)
Castello di Fonterutoli (Tuscany)
23
Castello di Ama (Tuscany)
Fattoria di Felsina (Tuscany)
22
Valentini (Abruzzo)
20
Marchesi Antinori (Tuscany)
Domenico Clerico (Piedmont)
Feudi di San Gregorio (Campania)
Poliziano (Tuscany)
C. P. San Michele Appiano (Alto Adige)
Villa Russiz (Friuli Venezia Giulia)
Jermann (Friuli Venezia Giulia)

★
19
Castello della Sala (Umbria)
Giacomo Conterno (Piedmont)
Girolamo Dorigo (Friuli Venezia Giulia)
Gravner (Friuli Venezia Giulia)
Masciarelli (Abruzzo)
Planeta (Sicily)
Tenuta San Guido (Tuscany)
18
Bellavista (Lombardy)
Ferrari (Trentino)
Vie di Romans (Friuli Venezia Giulia)
17
Castello Banfi (Tuscany)
Livio Felluga (Friuli Venezia Giulia)
Tenuta Fontodi (Tuscany)
Tenuta dell'Ornellaia (Tuscany)
Tenimenti Ruffino (Tuscany)
Schiopetto (Friuli Venezia Giulia)
Tasca d'Almerita (Sicily)
Cantina Termeno (Alto Adige)
16
Cascina La Barbatella (Piedmont)
Romano Dal Forno (Veneto)
Isole e Olena (Tuscany)
Leonildo Pieropan (Veneto)
Paolo Scavino (Piedmont)
15
C. P. Colterenzio (Alto Adige)
Matteo Correggia (Piedmont)
Bruno Giacosa (Piedmont)
Miani (Friuli Venezia Giulia)
Querciabella (Tuscany)
14
Roberto Anselmi (Veneto)
Antonio Argiolas (Sardinia)
Barone Ricasoli (Tuscany)

14
Arnaldo Caprai (Umbria)
Aldo Conterno (Piedmont)
Conterno Fantino (Piedmont)
Nino Negri (Lombardy)
Castello del Terriccio (Tuscany)
Roberto Voerzio (Piedmont)
13
Elena Walch (Alto Adige)
Maculan (Veneto)
Montevetrano (Campania)
Ronco del Gelso (Friuli Venezia Giulia)
Tenuta San Leonardo (Trentino)
C. P. Santa Maddalena/Cantina di Bolzano (Alto Adige)
Uberti (Lombardy)
Le Vigne di Zamò (Friuli Venezia Giulia)
12
Ca' Viola (Piedmont)
Cantina di Caldaro (Alto Adige)
Casanova di Neri (Tuscany)
Michele Chiarlo (Piedmont)
Falesco (Umbria)
Les Crêtes (Valle d'Aosta)
Mastroberardino (Campania)
Montevertine (Tuscany)
Castello dei Rampolla (Tuscany)
Luciano Sandrone (Piedmont)
Serafini & Vidotto (Veneto)
Venica & Venica (Friuli Venezia Giulia)
Fattoria Zerbina (Emilia Romagna)
11
Avignonesi (Tuscany)
Bricco Rocche - Bricco Asili (Piedmont)
Foradori (Trentino)
Gioacchino Garofoli (Marche)
Elio Grasso (Piedmont)
Lis Neris (Friuli Venezia Giulia)
La Massa (Tuscany)
Prunotto (Piedmont)
Fattoria Le Pupille (Tuscany)
Giuseppe Quintarelli (Veneto)
Bruno Rocca (Piedmont)
Podere Rocche dei Manzoni (Piedmont)
Tenute Sella & Mosca (Sardinia)
Tua Rita (Tuscany)
Vietti (Piedmont)
10
Abbazia di Novacella (Alto Adige)
Gianfranco Alessandria (Piedmont)
Brancaia (Tuscany)
Castellare di Castellina (Tuscany)
Tenuta Col d'Orcia (Tuscany)
Còlpetrone (Umbria)
Cusumano (Sicily)
Les Crêtes (Valle d'Aosta)
Marchesi de' Frescobaldi (Tuscany)
Tenute Ambrogio e Giovanni Folonari (Tuscany)
Tenuta J. Hofstätter (Alto Adige)
Edi Keber (Friuli Venezia Giulia)
Le Macchiole (Tuscany)
Franco M. Martinetti (Piedmont)
Cantina Convento Muri-Gries (Alto Adige)
Cantina Sociale di Santadi (Sardinia)
Cantina Terlano (Alto Adige)
Franco Toros (Friuli Venezia Giulia)
Vigna Rionda - Massolino (Piedmont)

A GUIDE TO VINTAGES 1971-2006

	BARBARESCO	BRUNELLO DI MONTALCINO	BAROLO	CHIANTI CLASSICO	NOBILE DI MONTEPULCIANO	AMARONE
1971	●●●●	●●●	●●●●● (circled)	●●●●●	●●●●	●●●●
1974	●●●●	●●	●●●●	●●●	●●●	●●●●
1975	●●	●●●●●	●●	●●●●	●●●●	●●●●
1977	●●	●●●●	●●	●●●●	●●●●	●●●●
1978	●●●●●	●●●●	●●●●● (circled)	●●●●●	●●●●●	●●●●
1979	●●●●	●●●●	●●●●	●●●●	●●●●	●●●●
1980	●●●●	●●●●	●●●●	●●●●	●●	●●●
1981	●●●	●●●	●●●	●●●	●●●	●●●
1982	●●●●●	●●●●●	●●●●● (circled)	●●●●●	●●●●	●
1983	●●●●	●●●●	●●●●	●●●●	●●●●	●●●●●
1985	●●●●●	●●●●●	●●●●● (circled)	●●●●●	●●●●●	●●●●●
1986	●●●	●●●	●●●	●●●●	●●●●	●●●●
1988	●●●●●	●●●●●	●●●●● (circled)	●●●●●	●●●●●	●●●●●
1989	●●●●●	●●	●●●●● (circled)	●	●	●●
1990	●●●●●	●●●●●	●●●●● (circled)	●●●●●	●●●●●	●●●●●
1991	●●●	●●●	●●●	●●●	●●●	●●
1993	●●●	●●●●	●●●	●●●●	●●●●●	●●●●
1995	●●●●	●●●●●	●●●●	●●●●●	●●●●●	●●●●
1996	●●●●●●	●●●	●●●●● (circled)	●●●	●●●	●●●
1997	●●●●	●●●●●	●●●●	●●●●●	●●●●●	●●●●●
1998	●●●●	●●●●	●●●●	●●●●	●●●	●●●
1999	●●●●●	●●●●●	●●●●● (circled)	●●●●●	●●●●●	●●●●●
2000	●●●●	●●●	●●●● (circled)	●●●	●●●	●●●●
2001	●●●●●	●●●●●	●●●●● (circled)	●●●●●	●●●●●	●●●●●
2002	●●	●	●	●	●	●●
2003	●●●	●●●	●●●	●●●●	●●●	●●●
2004	●●●●●	●●●●●	●●●●● (circled)	●●●●●	●●●●●	●●●●
2005	●●●●	●●●●	●●●●	●●●	●●●	●●●
2006	●●●●●	●●●●●	●●●●● (circled)	●●●●●	●●●●●	●●●●

HOW TO USE THE GUIDE

WINERY FIGURES
ANNUAL PRODUCTION
HECTARES UNDER VINE
VITICULTURE METHOD

KEY
O WHITE WINES
⊙ ROSÉ WINES
● RED WINES

RATINGS
LISTING WITHOUT A GLASS SYMBOL:
A WELL-MADE WINE OF AVERAGE QUALITY IN ITS CATEGORY

Ÿ
ABOVE AVERAGE TO GOOD IN ITS CATEGORY, EQUIVALENT TO 70-79/100

ŸŸ
VERY GOOD TO EXCELLENT IN ITS CATEGORY, EQUIVALENT TO 80-89/100

ŸŸ
VERY GOOD TO EXCELLENT WINE SELECTED FOR FINAL TASTINGS

ŸŸŸ
EXCELLENT WINE IN ITS CATEGORY, EQUIVALENT TO 90-99/100

WINES RATED IN PREVIOUS EDITIONS OF THE GUIDE ARE INDICATED
BY WHITE GLASSES (Ÿ, ŸŸ, ŸŸŸ), PROVIDED THEY ARE STILL DRINKING
AT THE LEVEL FOR WHICH THE ORIGINAL AWARD WAS MADE

STAR ★
INDICATES WINERIES THAT HAVE WON
TEN THREE GLASS AWARDS FOR EACH STAR

price ranges (1) (2)
1 up to $4.20 and up to £2.45
2 from $4.21 to $6.00 and from £2.46 to £3.50
3 from $6.01 to $9.00 and from £3.51 to £5.25
4 from $9.01 to $15.60 and from £5.26 to £9.10
5 from $15.61 to $24.00 and from £9.11 to £14.00
6 from $24.01 to $36.00 and from £14.01 to £21.00
7 from $36.01 to $48.00 and from £21.01 to £28.00
8 more than $48.01 and more than £28.01
(1) Approx. retail prices in USA and UK (2) €1,00 = $1.20 = £0.70

ASTERISK *
INDICATES ESPECIALLY GOOD VALUE FOR MONEY

NOTE PRICES INDICATED REFER TO RETAIL AVERAGES. INDICATIONS OF PRICE NEXT
TO WINES ASSIGNED WHITE GLASSES (AWARDS MADE IN PREVIOUS EDITIONS)
TAKE INTO ACCOUNT APPRECIATION OVER TIME WHERE APPROPRIATE

ABBREVIATIONS
A. A.	Alto Adige
C.	Colli
Cl.	Classico
C.S.	Cantina Sociale
Cant.	Cantina
CEV	Colli Etruschi Viterbesi
Cast.	Castello
COF	Colli Orientali del Friuli
Cons.	Consorzio
Coop.Agr.	Cooperativa Agricola
C. B.	Colli Bolognesi
C. P.	Colli Piacentini
Et.	Etichetta
M.	Metodo
M.to	Monferrato
OP	Oltrepò Pavese
P.R.	Peduncolo Rosso
P.	Prosecco
Rif. Agr.	Riforma Agraria
Ris.	Riserva
Sel.	Selezione
Sup.	Superiore
TdF	Terre di Franciacorta
V.	Vigna
Vign.	Vigneto
V. T.	Vendemmia Tardiva

VALLE D'AOSTA

Valle d'Aosta started out as the Cinderella of northern Italy, largely because of its small size and the obvious difficulties of its mountainous territory. Now, however, the region is no longer the runt of the Italian viticultural litter. That said, no one could have imagined the extraordinary results we have seen this year: four Three Glass awards in three different wine types. Although one came as no surprise, given the dazzling performances we are used to from Costantino Charrère's Chardonnay Cuvée Bois over the last decade, the others came out of the blue. The Grosjean brothers' Fumin is the second red from the region to pick up our prize and Référence is a brand new thoroughbred champ from Swiss partners Bregy and Gillioz. It's a different story for the Anselmet family, whose barrique-matured Chardonnay is fast becoming a banker and hasn't fumbled a vintage. We'd like to give a very quick overview of each of these producers who scored so highly. Loud praises have already been sung of Charrère but we believe we'll be seeing a lot more in print about him because Costantino is constantly on the quest for new challenges. One of the most recent is the Italian Federation of Independent Winemakers that he helped to set up and has chaired since summer 2008. The Grosjean brothers' cellar, headed by patriarch Dauphin, presented a red of enormous character and elegant spiciness that confirms the potential of the indigenous fumin grape. The Swiss producers' sweet wine is a real eye-opener, changing both its name and its style, which is sweeter and richer yet marvellously elegant and distinctly acidic. The Anselmets, Giorgio and his father Renato, have finally completed the new cellar that will enable them to lavish even more attention on maturing their various labels in glass. But the entire valley is in growth mode and we also have several new estates that came very close indeed to taking home our top prize: Michel Vallet gave us two reds of enormous character, La Vrille has produced a first-class dried-grape Muscat and we were bowled over by newcomer Les Granges with their Nus Malvoisie and Fumin. And finally a word on the co-operatives, to which Val d'Aosta winemaking owes so much. They have recently shown a new burst of energy and an ability to create some very interesting labels. Morgex spumantes have taken giant strides forward and we expect to see great things from Gianluca Telloli and Mauro Jaccod. Crotta di Vegneron's dried-grape Moscato is but a whisker away from Three Glasses and the Cave des Onze Communes put on a solid performance with laudable consistency. Something is afoot in the lower part of the valley, where Donnas and Kiuva are producing full, complex nebbiolos. Promises are being fulfilled.

Anselmet

FRAZ. LA CRÊTE, 194
11018 VILLENEUVE [AO]
TEL. 3484127121
www.maisonanselmet.vievini.it

ANNUAL PRODUCTION	35,000 bottles
HECTARES UNDER VINE	5
VITICULTURE METHOD	Conventional

Giorgio and Renato Anselmet have a new cellar! They couldn't wait any longer as the old one was too small for comfort. As usual, the range presented this year includes a series of wines brimming with character and personality. The barrique-aged Chardonnay is superb, offering aromas of grapefruit, wild flowers, thyme and butter. The palate reprises the nose over acidity and pleasant, refreshing tanginess. If they delay its release now that they have the space to cellar it, we are convinced it will be one of Italy's superlative whites. Meanwhile, it again took home Three well-deserved Glasses. The lingering Pinot Gris excels itself, showing fruity, deep, lemony and almost salty. The basic Chardonnay is released in 1,800 bottles and we are most impressed by its fragrance, fruit and thrilling nose, backed up by body and energy. Traminer enthusiasts will love the Stéphanie with its lively aromas of lychee and wild roses. The new Merlot is produced in just 500 magnums while from the other reds, Prisonnier, from overripe petit rouge, fumin, mayolet and cornalin, and the Henri are slightly disappointing.

Brégy & Gillioz - Podium

VIA VERGNOD, 7
11010 SAINT-PIERRE [AO]
TEL. 0041763786668
www.grain-noble.ch

ANNUAL PRODUCTION	10,000 bottles
HECTARES UNDER VINE	3.2
VITICULTURE METHOD	Conventional

This estate started as a hobby and is now transforming itself into something more important. It is run by friends André Brégy and Pierre-André Gilloz, two Swiss who came to Val d'Aosta to pursue their passion for petite arvine. A few years ago, they invested in a three-hectare plot of vines planted at 10,000 plants per hectare, where they installed a drip-feed irrigation system, a must given the wonderful south-facing position and very low rainfall in the zone. They produce just one wine, a dried-grape Passito. Not that they have much choice, living too far away to follow the estate on a daily basis. André, a professional oenologist at the Swiss Federal Centre for Viticulture Research at Changinis, is responsible for winemaking and vineyard management. Two years ago, their wine changed its name from Podium to Référence and the 2006 is the best version we have ever tasted. Its definition is also slightly different, as it presents sweeter, rich, full, and very fragrant with aromas running from liquorice to candied citrus peel. The palate shows perfect harmony of acid and sugar. Three unexpected but fully deserved Glasses.

O Valle d'Aosta Chardonnay Élevé en Fût de Chêne '07	♈♈♈	6
O Valle d'Aosta Chardonnay '07	♈♈	4*
O Valle d'Aosta Pinot Gris '07	♈♈	5
O Stéphanie '07	♈♈	4*
● Valle d'Aosta Cornalin Boblan '07	♈♈	6
● Valle d'Aosta Merlot '06	♈♈	8
● Valle d'Aosta Pinot Noir '07	♈♈	5
● Le Prisonnier '06	♈	7
● Valle d'Aosta Petit Rouge '07	♈	4
● Valle d'Aosta Syrah Henri '06	♈	6
● Valle d'Aosta Torrette '07	♈	5
O Valle d'Aosta Chardonnay Élevé en Fût de Chêne '06	♉♉♉	6
O Valle d'Aosta Chardonnay Élevé en Fût de Chêne '05	♉♉♉	6
O Valle d'Aosta Chardonnay Élevé en Fût de Chêne '04	♉♉♉	5

O Référence '06	♈♈♈	6
O Référence '05	♉♉	6
O Podium '04	♉♉	6
O Podium '03	♉♉	6

La Crotta di Vegneron

P.ZZA RONCAS, 2
11023 CHAMBAVE [AO]
TEL. 016646670
www.lacrotta.it

ANNUAL PRODUCTION 320,000 bottles
HECTARES UNDER VINE 37
VITICULTURE METHOD Conventional

An ambitious project is under way in Val d'Aosta's oenological heartland. The Chambave, Morgex and Arvier co-operatives are forging a strategic partnership. These three big wineries have combined to produce the Quatremille mètres line, more proof of just how dynamic this sector of Val d'Aosta winemaking is. Crotta di Vegneron's organization remains the same, however, with Andrea Costa running things in both the vineyard and the cellar and Elio Cornaz as president. The dry and sweet Moscatos that are the flagship products of this part of the region are on top form. The former is refined and elegant with clean aromas of fruit and stands out for its deep, fruity palate. The second, the jewel in the estate's crown, has a very intense nose with nuances of orange, grapefruit and figs, ending rather closed on notes of medicinal herbs. The palate is sweet, complex and very leisurely. The rest of this impressive range presents peaks of quality in the Fumin and Quatre Vignobles reds, the juicy, harmonious and splendidly drinkable white Nus Malvoisie and the dried-grape Nus Malvoisie Flétri. The Ancestrale, a sparkling red, is unusual and enjoyable.

○ Valle d'Aosta Chambave Moscato Passito Prieuré '06	🍷🍷	6
○ Valle d'Aosta Chambave Muscat '07	🍷🍷	4*
○ Valle d'Aosta Nus Malvoisie '07	🍷🍷	4*
○ Valle d'Aosta Nus Malvoisie Flétri Nonus '06	🍷🍷	6
● Valle d'Aosta Chambave Sup. Quatre Vignobles '06	🍷🍷	4*
● Valle d'Aosta Fumin Esprit Follet '06	🍷🍷	5
⊙ Ancestrale Rougeffervescence	🍷	4
● Valle d'Aosta Chambave '07	🍷	4
● Valle d'Aosta Cornalin '07	🍷	4
● Valle d'Aosta Nus '07	🍷	4
● Valle d'Aosta Nus Sup. Crème '06	🍷	4

Di Barrò

LOC. CHÂTEAU FEUILLET, 8
11010 SAINT-PIERRE [AO]
TEL. 0165903671
www.vievini.it

ANNUAL PRODUCTION 17,000 bottles
HECTARES UNDER VINE 2.5
VITICULTURE METHOD Natural

The wines produced by Andrea Barmaz and his wife Elvira Rini are bursting with personality. They probably have more body than most in Valle d'Aosta and we like the close attention this duo pays to environmentally friendly farming techniques. It's a pity that sometimes the nose of these wines is not altogether convincing. But they may just need more time, a theory borne out by our excellent retasting of the Vigne de Torrette '05 one year after it entered the Guide. Despite the odd imperfection, the overall consensus was very encouraging and we are convinced that if a few issues are resolved, these wines will scale the oenological heights of Valle d'Aosta oenology. Take the '06 Fumin, a full, fruity, mouthfilling wine with very elegant tannins and gamey nuances of saddle leather and sweet tobacco. We enjoyed the intriguing '07 version of Mayolet Vigne de Toule, one of the best ever made. Lo Bien Flapì, a sweet wine obtained from pinot grigio, is superb, as is the basic Torrette. Both the muscular Chardonnay and the Torrette Supérieur need a more time in bottle to achieve perfect balance in the glass.

○ Lo Bien Flapì '06	🍷🍷	7
● Valle d'Aosta Fumin '06	🍷🍷	5
● Valle d'Aosta Mayolet V. de Toule '07	🍷🍷	4*
● Valle d'Aosta Petit Rouge '07	🍷	4
● Valle d'Aosta Torrette Sup. Clos de Château Feuillet '06	🍷	5
○ Valle d'Aosta Chardonnay '07	🍷	4
● Valle d'Aosta Fumin '05	🍷🍷 (white)	5
● Valle d'Aosta Fumin '04	🍷🍷 (white)	5
● Valle d'Aosta Torrette Sup. Clos de Château Feuillet '04	🍷🍷 (white)	5

Feudo di San Maurizio

FRAZ. MAILLOD, 44
11010 SARRE [AO]
TEL. 3383186831
www.feudo.vievini.it

ANNUAL PRODUCTION	30,000 bottles
HECTARES UNDER VINE	6
VITICULTURE METHOD	Conventional

Michel Vallet has made a much anticipated, very rapid leap in quality. His impressive range stunned us. We were expecting great things from him but were astonished by the speed with which he achieved them. Michel has all he needs to be a top winemaker: determination, dedication, and a strong – some would say tetchy – character and absolute dedication to his cellar. Michel has also increased his vine stock while keeping output at previous levels. His Fumin '06 has balance, just the right amount of concentration, and a very complex nose of spices and warm fruity sensations. His Mayolet is a surprise, obtained from a local variety that until a few years ago was used exclusively for blends. Thanks to the work of a handful of viticulturists, it is now revealing its huge potential when vinified alone. Fresh, fruity and elegant yet full-bodied, it is a classy everyday wine. The Grapillon, from traminer, reveals its varietal aromas without losing any of the minerality and acidity that sustain it. The Pierrots from partially dried fumin and petit rouge is unusual, the typical Torrette wins Two Glasses, and the Chardonnay, Müller and Saro Djablo are nice.

F.lli Grosjean

VILLAGGIO OLLIGNAN, 1
11020 QUART [AO]
TEL. 0165775791
www.grosjean.vievini.it

ANNUAL PRODUCTION	80,000 bottles
HECTARES UNDER VINE	8
VITICULTURE METHOD	Conventional

Leafing through old Guides, it is clear that the Grosjeans' serious consistency has paid off. This beautiful estate set among vineyards and orchards is run by a solid, close-knit family headed by Dauphin, who directs the efforts of his sons Eraldo, Fernando, Marco, Piergiorgio and Vincent. For the last two years, the genial Vincent has been president of the Valle d'Aosta Viticulteurs Encaveurs association. The Grosjeans' Fumin '06 is a show-stopper and the best they have ever made. It retains the rustic, peasant base – in the noblest sense of the word – that distinguishes their production but this wine is a miniature masterpiece. Spicy and elegant in its aromas of ripe red berry fruit, it shows harmonious yet gutsy on a palate with a long, satisfying finish . It earned a first well-deserved Three Glass prize for the Grosjeans. We also liked the Pinot Gris Vigne Creton for its distinct pears and enviable drinkability. Another Two Glasses went to the territory-based Pinot Noir with its raspberry aromas. The Blanc de Dauphinis is not quite up to its usual standards, its palate being less juicy than in recent versions. The rest of the range is good.

● Valle d'Aosta Fumin '06	♟♟ 5
● Valle d'Aosta Mayolet '07	♟♟ 5
● Pierrots '06	♟♟ 6
● Valle d'Aosta Torrette '07	♟♟ 4*
○ Grapillon '07	♟♟ 4
○ Valle d'Aosta Chardonnay '07	♟ 4
○ Valle d'Aosta Müller Thurgau '07	♟ 4
● Saro Djablo '06	♟ 4
● Saro Djablo '04	♟♟ 4*
● Valle d'Aosta Fumin '04	♟♟ 4*
● Valle d'Aosta Mayolet '06	♟♟ 4*

● Valle d'Aosta Fumin '06	♟♟♟ 5
● Valle d'Aosta Cornalin V. Rovettaz '06	♟♟ 4*
○ Valle d'Aosta Pinot Gris V. Creton '07	♟♟ 5
● Valle d'Aosta Pinot Noir V. Tzeriat '06	♟♟ 4
○ Blanc de Dauphin '07	♟ 4
○ Valle d'Aosta Petite Arvine V. Rovettaz '07	♟ 5
● Valle d'Aosta Torrette '07	♟ 4
● Valle d'Aosta Fumin '05	♟♟ 5
● Valle d'Aosta Fumin '04	♟♟ 5
● Valle d'Aosta Fumin '03	♟♟ 4

★ Les Crêtes

LOC. VILLETOS, 50
11010 AYMAVILLES [AO]
TEL. 0165902274
www.lescretesvins.it

Lo Triolet

LOC. JUNOD, 7
11010 INTROD [AO]
TEL. 016595437
www.lotriolet.vievini.it

ANNUAL PRODUCTION	230,000 bottles
HECTARES UNDER VINE	25
VITICULTURE METHOD	Conventional

ANNUAL PRODUCTION	30,000 bottles
HECTARES UNDER VINE	3
VITICULTURE METHOD	Conventional

Ten consecutive Three Glass prizes for the same wine is something few estates can boast. Chardonnay Cuvée Bois has earned its place among Italy's elite. Credit goes to Costantino Charrère, a highly regarded grower and a man of extraordinary charisma. Turning to the wines, the prizewinner is the '06 Cuvée Bois, one of the best versions ever produced. It has a very elegant, intriguing nose of citrus fruit, butter and balanced vanilla while the warm palate is lifted by gratifying acidity and minerality. The Pinot Gris is absent this year as it will no longer be produced by the cellar but we consoled ourselves with a Fumin that repeated last year's performance, presenting spicy, rounded and modern in style. La Sabla '06 is captivating, showing subtle but never weak, thanks to elegant tannins and spiciness that are rare in other labels. The rest of the range shows character, a territorial stamp and overall elegance, from the varietal Coteau La Tour from 100 per cent syrah to the dried-grape Les Abeilles that is sweet but never cloys and the fine Torrette. The Petite Arvine Su wasn't quite up to recent versions.

Marco Martin is the king of pinot grigio, a variety that arrived in Valle d'Aosta ten years ago and which he has helped to make great. He is aided by his mother Emilia and father Renato in the vineyards, while his wife runs the family's charming agriturismo. Again this year, Marco's wines stand out for their class and character. The barrique-aged Pinot Gris is back on top form, although a few months in bottle wouldn't go amiss. Sooner or later, we expect Marco will delay its release by a year. Despite its youth and still dominant oak, it shows potential in its power and extraordinary length. The stainless steel-conditioned Pinot Gris is excellent, offering warm pears and golden delicious apples, spicy with hints of thyme and a juicy, acidity-veined palate that closes on a sweetish note. The Coteau Barrage from syrah and fumin is well structured, if too young. It has marked ripe red berry fruit and relaxed, harmonious pulp. The very fragrant MonAtout from 100 per cent traminer is superb, as is the Mistigri, which has just the right sweetness. The Pinot Noir and Gamay are notable for their freshness and drinkability.

○ Valle d'Aosta Chardonnay Cuvée Bois '06	♛♛♛	7
● La Sabla '06	♛♛	4*
● Valle d'Aosta Fumin V. La Tour '06	♛♛	6
● Coteau La Tour '06	♛♛	5
● Valle d'Aosta Torrette V. Les Toules '07	♛♛	4*
○ Les Abeilles '06	♛♛	6
○ Valle d'Aosta Chardonnay V. Frissonnière '07	♛♛	4*
○ Valle d'Aosta Petite Arvine V. Champorette '07	♛	4
● Valle d'Aosta Pinot Noir V. La Tour '07	♛	4
○ Valle d'Aosta Chardonnay Cuvée Frissonnière Les Crêtes Cuvée Bois '05	♛♛♛	7
○ Valle d'Aosta Chardonnay Cuvée Frissonnière Les Crêtes Cuvée Bois '04	♛♛♛	6
○ Valle d'Aosta Chardonnay Cuvée Frissonnière Les Crêtes Cuvée Bois '03	♛♛♛	6

○ Valle d'Aosta Pinot Gris '07	♛	4*
○ Valle d'Aosta Pinot Gris Élevé en Barriques '07	♛♛	5
○ Mistigri '06	♛♛	6
○ MonAtout '07	♛♛	4*
● Valle d'Aosta Rouge Coteau Barrage '07	♛♛	5
● Valle d'Aosta Gamay '07	♛	4
● Valle d'Aosta Pinot Noir '07	♛	4
○ Valle d'Aosta Pinot Gris '05	♛♛♛	4
○ Valle d'Aosta Pinot Gris Élevé en Fût de Chêne '05	♛♛	5
○ Valle d'Aosta Pinot Gris Élevé en Fût de Chêne '04	♛♛	5
● Valle d'Aosta Coteau Barrage '05	♛♛	5
● Valle d'Aosta Coteau Barrage '04	♛♛	5

Cave des Onze Communes

LOC. URBAINS, 14
11010 AYMAVILLES [AO]
TEL. 0165902912
www.caveonzecommunes.it

ANNUAL PRODUCTION **450,000 bottles**
HECTARES UNDER VINE **N.A.**
VITICULTURE METHOD **Natural**

Consistent quality is the key strength of the wines presented by Cave des Onze Communes, the largest co-operative in Valle d'Aosta. Its 220 members are scattered across 11 municipalities located to the left and right of the Dora Baltea. The wines never disappoint. They have loads of personality and fully reflect the characteristics of their territory of origin. Much of the credit for success at our tastings goes to the steady hand of president Dino Darensod and the two technicians who coordinate work in the vineyards and cellar, Massimo Bellocchia and Luciano Vada. From the wide range of wines, we liked the Chardonnay '07 for its notes of peach and golden delicious apple, the mineral, never banal Müller Thurgau and the juicy, leisurely Petite Arvine. The reds are many and good, starting with the Ancien Cépage '06, which displays spicy, delicately smoky aromas and develops on the palate into a pleasant, lingering flesh. The Fumin '06 meets expectations, showing nuances of pepper, Virginia tobacco, raspberry and currants. The Torrette Superiore is very typical with its sensations of wild berries and leather.

Cave du Vin Blanc de Morgex et de La Salle

FRAZ. LA RUINE
CHEMIN DES ÎLES, 19
11017 MORGEX [AO]
TEL. 0165800331
www.caveduvinblanc.com

ANNUAL PRODUCTION **170,000 bottles**
HECTARES UNDER VINE **20**
VITICULTURE METHOD **Conventional**

Last year, we reported some new developments. This year, there are so many that they would take up the space dedicated to the whole of the region. Gianluca Telloli, the dynamic technical director of this major estate, served up a line-up that is finally showing its potential after muddling along for a few years. The time and money invested in sparkling winemaking have yielded great results. Take the gutsy, fragrant Metodo Classico Extreme '06 with its notes of tart apple and pear, and pleasant palate showing acid backbone and character. The Brut Cuvée du Prince '03 is released in small numbers for now and promises well for the future. The nose brims with aromas of yeast and mineral tones of white-fleshed apple-like fruit while the palate is warm, far from lean and supported by the finest and most elegant texture the wine has had to date. The highly enjoyable Rayon '07 is on top form thanks to its very typical nose. The same goes for Blanc del Morgex La Piagne, from organically grown grapes that the estate aims to convert to a biodynamic system. Its unusual, closed notes open out in the glass. The rest of the range has loads of character.

○ Valle d'Aosta Chardonnay '07	▼▼ 3 *
○ Valle d'Aosta Müller Thurgau '07	▼▼ 3 *
○ Valle d'Aosta Petite Arvine '07	▼▼ 4
● Valle d'Aosta Fumin '06	▼▼ 4
● Valle d'Aosta Rosso L'Ancien Cépage '06	▼▼ 5
● Valle d'Aosta Torrette Sup. '06	▼▼ 4
○ Valle d'Aosta Chardonnay V. T. Le Chapiteau '06	▼ 4
○ Valle d'Aosta Pinot Gris '07	▼ 3
● Valle d'Aosta Cornalin '07	▼ 3
● Valle d'Aosta Gamay '07	▼ 4
● Valle d'Aosta Pinot Noir '06	▼ 3
● Valle d'Aosta Fumin '05	▼▼ 4
● Valle d'Aosta Fumin '04	▼▼ 4

○ Valle d'Aosta Blanc de Morgex et de La Salle M. Cl. Brut Extreme '06	▼▼ 5
○ Valle d'Aosta Blanc de Morgex et de La Salle M. Cl. Brut Cuvée du Prince '03	▼▼ 6
○ Valle d'Aosta Blanc de Morgex et de La Salle M. Cl. Extra Brut '06	▼▼ 5
○ Valle d'Aosta Blanc de Morgex et de La Salle Rayon '07	▼▼ 4*
○ Valle d'Aosta Blanc de Morgex et de La Salle '07	▼ 3
○ Valle d'Aosta Blanc de Morgex et de La Salle La Piagne '07	▼ 4
○ Valle d'Aosta Blanc de Morgex et de La Salle M. Cl. Brut '06	▼ 4
○ Valle d'Aosta Blanc de Morgex et de La Salle Vini Estremi '07	▼ 4
● Ancestrale Rougeffervescence	▼ 4

OTHER WINERIES

L'Atoueyo

LOC. URBAINS, 8
11010 AYMAVILLES [AO]
TEL. 0165902550
www.atoueyo.vievini.it

This small estate offers well-styled, impeccably made wines thanks to the great work of Fernanda Saraillon and son Omar Jerusel. As usual, the stainless steel-aged Chardonnay is one of the best. The Fumin is also good, vigorous and full with a lovely finish. The Torrette and fruity Gamay are just behind.

○ Valle d'Aosta Chardonnay '07	♟♟	4*
● Valle d'Aosta Fumin '06	♟♟	5
● Valle d'Aosta Gamay '07	♟	4
● Valle d'Aosta Torrette '07	♟	4

Le Château Feuillet

LOC. CHÂTEAU FEUILLET
11010 SAINT-PIERRE [AO]
TEL. 0165903905
www.chateaufeuillet.vievini.it

Maurizio Fiorano's wines have made a leap in quality and they rarely win less than Two Glasses. This year's Torrette Supérieur 2006 was stunning and came within a whisker of our finals. The fruity, juicy Fumin was every bit its equal. The Chardonnay is always superb.

○ Valle d'Aosta Chardonnay '07	♟♟	4*
● Valle d'Aosta Fumin '06	♟♟	4*
● Valle d'Aosta Torrette Sup. '06	♟♟	4*
● Valle d'Aosta Torrette '07	♟	4

Coopérative de l'Enfer

VIA CORRADO GEX, 65
11011 ARVIER [AO]
TEL. 016599238
www.coenfer.it

Last year, we began to see the hand of Gianluca Telloli in Enfer's wines and this year it is even more evident. All the reds presented showed cleaner red berry fruit aromas and more defined character, especially a Mayolet that could go the full distance. The Enfer and Clos showed well.

● Valle d'Aosta Enfer d'Arvier '06	♟♟	4*
● Valle d'Aosta Mayolet Vins de Seigneurs '07	♟♟	4*
● Valle d'Aosta Enfer d'Arvier Clos de L'Enfer '06	♟	5

Diego Curtaz

FRAZ. VISERAN, 61
11020 GRESSAN [AO]
TEL. 0165251079
www.diegocurtazvini.it

Diego Curtaz surprised us. This year's selection is very interesting, with a Torrette '07 that reflects all the characteristics of the petit rouge variety. The Dï Meun '07 from petit rouge and vuillermin, vien de Nus, gamay and mayolet, is good, a neck ahead of the Petit Rouge 2007.

● Dï Meun '07	♟♟	4*
● Valle d'Aosta Torrette '07	♟♟	4*
● Valle d'Aosta Petit Rouge '07	♟	4

Caves Cooperatives de Donnas

VIA ROMA, 97
11020 DONNAS [AO]
TEL. 0125807096
www.donnasvini.it

This lower valley operation did well. The Cave di Donnas range is worthy of its huge potential. This is the northernmost bastion of nebbiolo, and we have not always been convinced, but the Cavour selection has depth and structure. The '03 Napoleone from a much hotter year is also good.

● Valle d'Aosta Donnas Sup. Vielles Vignes Cavour '04	♟♟	5
● Valle d'Aosta Donnas Sup. Napoleone '03	♟♟	5

Les Granges

FRAZ. LES GRANGES, 8
11020 NUS [AO]
TEL. 0165767229
www.vievini.it

Gualtiero Crea and his wife Liana sent us samples for the first time. The estate was launched a few years ago but promises very well indeed. We were particularly impressed by two of their wines, the Fumin and Nus Malvoisie, which could be one of the most interesting Pinot Grigios in the region.

○ Valle d'Aosta Nus Malvoisie '07	♟♟	4*
● Valle d'Aosta Fumin '06	♟♟	5
● Valle d'Aosta Cornalin '07	♟	4

OTHER WINERIES

Institut Agricole Régional

RÉGION LA ROCHÈRE, 1A
11100 AOSTA
TEL. 0165215811
www.iaraosta.it

We have high hopes that very soon the wines from an operation that has written the story of Valle d'Aosta wine will recapture their previous glory. The Chardonnay is a step in the right direction, with its notes of hazelnut, thyme and apple-like fruit. The Fumin and Petite Arvine are a tad disappointing.

○ Valle d'Aosta Chardonnay '07	▼▼	4*
○ Valle d'Aosta Petite Arvine '07	▼	4
● Valle d'Aosta Fumin '06	▼	5

Cooperativa La Kiuva

FRAZ. PIED DE VILLE, 42
11020 ARNAD [AO]
TEL. 0125966351
lakiuva@libero.it

Change is afoot at Kiuva, until now seemingly immune to the changes sweeping the Valle d'Aosta co-operative scene. The wines received bear out this impression. Arnad-Montjovet '06 offers aromas of red berry fruit and typical spicy notes, and the Chardonnay '07 is pleasant.

● Valle d'Aosta Arnad-Montjovet '06	▼▼	3*
○ Valle d'Aosta Chardonnay '07	▼	4

Vigneti Rosset

LOC. TORRENT DE MAILLOUD, 4
11020 QUART [AO]
TEL. 0165774111
rosanna.ferro@saintroch.it

This lovely estate improved on the excellent impression it made last year. This time, we found the Chardonnay to be very well-made with pleasing minerality and crisp fruit. The Syrah has elegant spicy aromas and nuances of currant and raspberry. The Cornalin comes a step below.

○ Valle d'Aosta Chardonnay '07	▼▼	4*
● Valle d'Aosta Syrah '07	▼▼	4*
● Valle d'Aosta Cornalin '07	▼	4

La Source

LOC. BUSSAN DESSOUS, 1
11010 SAINT-PIERRE [AO]
TEL. 0165904038

Born in 1971, Stefano Celi is a skilled producer who crafts a very decent series of wines. His estate consists of six and a half hectares with a highly unusual combination of terrains. Two of his wines earned Two Glasses, the Petite Arvine and Torrette Superiore. The basic Torrette is just behind.

○ Valle d'Aosta Petite Arvine '07	▼▼	4*
● Valle d'Aosta Torrette Sup. '06	▼▼	4*
● Valle d'Aosta Torrette '07	▼	4

Maison Albert Vevey

FRAZ. VILLAIR
S.DA DEL VILLAIR, 67
11017 MORGEX [AO]
TEL. 0165808930
www.vievini.it

This tiny estate is run by brothers Vevey, Mirko and Mario who carry on the family tradition of skilfully vinifying prié blanc. Their 2007 edition has temptingly flavoursome sensations with nuances of stone, spring water and subtle Alpine flowers, finishing long and tangy.

○ Valle d'Aosta Blanc de Morgex et de La Salle '07	▼▼	4*

La Vrille

LOC. GRANGEON, 1
11020 VERRAYES [AO]
TEL. 0166543018
www.lavrille-agritourisme.com

The zone of Chambave has a new superstar. In this edition of the Guide, Hervé and Luciana Deguillame wowed us with a range that is finally complete and a truly amazing Chambave Muscat Flètrì that is released in just 500 bottles. The Fumin '06 almost made our finals, and the dry Muscat is good.

○ Valle d'Aosta Chambave Muscat Flètrì Passito '06	▼▼	5
○ Valle d'Aosta Chambave Muscat '07	▼▼	4*
● Valle d'Aosta Fumin '06	▼▼	5

PIEDMONT

Piedmont is wonderful wine country. For us, who each year face the arduous task of tasting hundreds of bottles, it is a source of immense satisfaction. More than any other region in Italy, Piedmont offers us cross-vintage tastings that span at least seven growing years. Still, this is no more than you would expect from a region with so many DOC and DOCG designated areas. All over Piedmont, one variety – nebbiolo – reigns supreme, yielding classy wines that are much sought after in markets at home and abroad. From Gattinara to Ghemme, Carema, Roero, Barbaresco and Barolo, nebbiolo-based wines are everywhere, each with its own style, sensory profile and claim to greatness. The variety is important but the crucial element is the accumulated skill of the growers. And to conserve that heritage, investment is needed in vineyards, in cellars, which have be functional and frippery-free, and in the increasingly fragmented market. Luckily, Piedmont's winemakers have been able to link together all the stages in the production chain while keeping standards high in the wines released. This year, we applaud a fine performance from northern Piedmont, which involves several designations. There was a fine showing from Boca, made by Le Piane, which is almost a corner of Burgundy transplanted to the province of Novara. Antoniolo and Travaglini keep the Gattinara flag flying and Sella continues to release fine wines from the Sesia area, including an impressively structured Lessona. As well as all these repeats, there was a welcome new development. Thanks in part to help from Langhe-born oenologist Beppe Caviola, Torraccia del Piantavigna won our top award with a powerful yet elegant Ghemme. South of the Po, Roero is nebbiolo's first stronghold. These monovarietal Nebbiolos are subtler and more approachable than Langhe wines and grow on sandy soil that gives them a stylish, fragrance. Four Roeros and a Nebbiolo d'Alba won Three Glasses, showing that these zones are keen to keep up with larger, more prestigious areas. Barbaresco forges steadily on, even with a fairly modest vintage in 2005, and managed to place a good number of wines in our list of Three Glass winners. But the biggest haul of Glassware went to Barolo, which was fielding a fabulous vintage in 2004. The wines confirmed the quality of a year that will reach its peak of maturation only in a few years' time, when the characteristic edginess of the youthful, rich wines has been smoothed out. On the white front, the province of Alessandria is still the leader. Timorasso and Gavi can stand comparison with the best in Italy while Asti defended the honour of Barbera. Next year, Barbera d'Asti will be a DOCG. We'll round off with Dolcetto, which is at its most impressive in Dogliani where it performs wonderfully both young, when fruit dominates, and when it has had a few years in the cellar.

Abbona

B.TA SAN LUIGI, 40
12063 DOGLIANI [CN]
TEL. 0173721317
www.abbona.com

ANNUAL PRODUCTION	255,000 bottles
HECTARES UNDER VINE	44
VITICULTURE METHOD	Conventional

We applaud another excellent showing from a small winery, now a beacon for Dogliani. The man behind this is Marziano Abbona but congratulations must go to the entire family team, which has made passion and organization the cellar's hallmarks. The signature Dolcetto Papà Celso is back on form, offering immense gratification to both its maker and its serried ranks of admirers. The wine is released under the new DOCG designation, as just "Dogliani" in the superb 2006 vintage and is truly thrilling. Its dark nose slowly expands into an impressive flower and spice bouquet of complexity and definition. All the pulpy flesh comes out on the well-rounded, nicely tannic palate with its balance and velvety mouthfeel. Welcome back to Three Glasses. The 2007 San Luigi is a splendid foil. From the nebbiolo-based reds, we preferred the powerful but perfectly balanced Barolo Terlo Ravero to the stiffer Barolo Pressenda, both from the fantastic 2004 vintage. The Barbera Rinaldi 2006 vies with the best in its category with beautifully fused grace and balance. The viognier-based Cinerino is very well made and the new Langhe Zerosolfiti is delicious.

Anna Maria Abbona

FRAZ. MONCUCCO, 21
12060 FARIGLIANO [CN]
TEL. 0173797228
www.annamariabbona.it

ANNUAL PRODUCTION	58,000 bottles
HECTARES UNDER VINE	10
VITICULTURE METHOD	Conventional

Anna Maria Abbona's range brims with Dolcetto. Of course, when took over the family land at Farigliano, she was well aware that there were few other options at almost 600 metres above sea level, in hills so near to yet so far from Langhe and its Barolo. Dolcetto is the grape that grows best here and with her husband, Franco Schellino, Anna Maria in less than two decades has created a solid but dynamic wine operation. This year, the cellar presented four Dolcetto selections. The Langhe 2007 is very enjoyable and brimming with fruit. Sorì dij But, another 2007, is making progress with its already concentrated florality on the nose and relaxed expansion in the mouth. The wood-matured Dogliani San Bernardo 2006 has assertive, complex aromatics that give summer flowers, rain-soaked earth and vegetal nuances before unveiling a well-rounded, soft-textured palate with lingering length. The steel-only Maioli is a tad obstreperous and fails to follow up its concentrated fruit with sufficient elegance. Finally, the Langhe Rosso Cadò, from barbera with a splash of dolcetto, is admirably complex and elegant while the Langhe Nebbiolo is tannic and austere.

● Dogliani Papà Celso '06	♛♛♛	5
● Barbera d'Alba Rinaldi '06	♛♛	4*
● Barolo Pressenda '04	♛♛	7
● Barolo Vign. Terlo Ravera '04	♛♛	7
● Dolcetto di Dogliani San Luigi '07	♛♛	4*
● Langhe Rosso Zerosolfiti '07	♛♛	7
● Nebbiolo d'Alba Bricco Barone '06	♛♛	4*
○ Cinerino '07	♛♛	5
● Barolo Pressenda '00	♛♛♛	7
● Dogliani Papà Celso '05	♛♛♛	4
● Dolcetto di Dogliani Papà Celso '04	♛♛♛	4
● Dolcetto di Dogliani Papà Celso '00	♛♛♛	4
● Barbera d'Alba Rinaldi '05	♛♛	4
● Barolo Pressenda '03	♛♛	7
● Barolo Vign. Terlo Ravera '03	♛♛	7

● Dogliani San Bernardo '06	♛♛	5
● Langhe Rosso Cadò '06	♛♛	5
● Dogliani Maioli '06	♛♛	4*
● Dolcetto di Dogliani Sorì dij But '07	♛♛	4*
● Langhe Nebbiolo '06	♛♛	4*
● Langhe Dolcetto '07	♛	3
● Dolcetto di Dogliani Maioli '04	♛♛	4
● Dolcetto di Dogliani Maioli '03	♛♛	4
● Dolcetto di Dogliani Maioli '05	♛♛	4
● Langhe Rosso Cadò '04	♛♛	5
● Langhe Rosso Cadò '03	♛♛	5

F.lli Abrigo

VIA MOGLIA GERLOTTO, 2
12055 DIANO D'ALBA [CN]
TEL. 017369104
www.abrigofratelli.com

ANNUAL PRODUCTION	60,000 bottles
HECTARES UNDER VINE	14
VITICULTURE METHOD	Natural

Dolcetto di Diano combines the elegance of Dolcetto d'Alba with the power and extract of Dolcetto di Dogliani. At Diano, Dolcetto finds impeccable harmony, especially in skilled hands like those of Ernesto and Mariarita, the owners of Fratelli Abrigo. Theirs is a family-run operation, where the accent is on vineyard management using low-impact, low-pollution methods. In the range of wines we tasted – all the Diano d'Alba names have changed – the dolcetto grape plays a fundamental role in three different selections. The one we like most was the purple-flecked ruby Superiore Vigna Pietrìn, which gives morello cherry, plum and strawberry, and then unobtrusive, fine-grained extract that leads into a juicy, subtly bitterish finish. We also like Intreccio, a wine that offers fine value for money. Barbera d'Alba La Galùpa is a very good product, giving intense ripe red fruits and sweet spice. Autumn leaves and tobacco are the themes of the barbera, nebbiolo and cabernet Langhe Tambuss, whose abundant well-honed tannins also impress. A step behind are the Rocche dei Berfi and Nebbiolo d'Alba Tardiss 2006 while the Chardonnay Temp dër Fiù is very nice.

Orlando Abrigo

FRAZ. CAPPELLETTO, 5
12050 TREISO [CN]
TEL. 0173630232
www.orlandoabrigo.it

ANNUAL PRODUCTION	75,000 bottles
HECTARES UNDER VINE	15
VITICULTURE METHOD	Conventional

Giovanni Abrigo, Orlando's son, finished studying in 1988 and joined the family cellar full time. His wines have lashings of territory-driven character. The vines grow high up at Treiso and often present more herbaceous aromas than nebbiolo fruit picked in warmer areas. This year's news is the release of Barbaresco Rocche Meruzzano, from a vineyard halfway between Treiso and Alba. Giovanni has produced a virtuoso version and it replaces the base Barbaresco. The bouquet mingles rich fruit with tertiary notes of dried roses, quinine and pepper. Equally striking are the other Barbaresco selections. Our tasters liked the Montersino for its graceful notes of raspberries and currants, and the Vigna Rongaglio is good. From this year, it can no longer be labelled Rongallo because "Gallo" is legally protected in the United States. Barbera d'Alba Mervisano 2006 put on a fine show, taking advantage of an excellent growing year to offer a savoury, juicy palate. We also liked Langhe Bianco D'Amblè, a pleasingly long varietal Sauvignon. And the rest of the range is great, with a particular word of praise for the Barbera d'Alba Vigna Roreto.

● Barbera d'Alba La Galùpa '06	♼♼ 4*
● Diano d'Alba Intreccio '07	♼♼ 3*
● Diano d'Alba Sup. V. Pietrìn '07	♼♼ 4*
● Langhe Rosso Tambuss '05	♼♼ 5
● Diano d'Alba Rocche dei Berfi '07	♼ 3
● Nebbiolo d'Alba Tardiss '06	♼ 5
○ Langhe Chardonnay Temp dër Fiù '07	♼ 2*
● Diano d'Alba Bric Tumlìn '06	♼♼ 3
● Diano d'Alba Sörì dei Berfi V. Pietrìn '06	♼♼ 4
● Diano d'Alba Sörì dei Berfi V. Pietrìn '05	♼♼ 4

● Barbaresco Montersino '05	♼♼ 6*
● Barbaresco Rocche Meruzzano V. Rongalio '05	♼♼ 6
● Barbaresco Rocche Meruzzano '05	♼♼ 6
● Barbera d'Alba Mervisano '06	♼♼ 5
● Barbera d'Alba V. Roreto '06	♼♼ 4*
○ Langhe Bianco D'Amblè '07	♼♼ 4*
○ Langhe Chardonnay Très '07	♼ 4
● Dolcetto d'Alba V. dell'Erto '07	♼ 4
● Barbaresco V. Rongallo '04	♼♼ 6
● Barbaresco V. Rongallo '03	♼♼ 6
● Barbaresco V. Rongallo '01	♼♼ 6
● Barbaresco V. Rongallo '00	♼♼ 6
● Barbaresco V. Montersino '04	♼♼ 6
● Barbaresco V. Montersino '03	♼♼ 6

Giulio Accornero e Figli

CA' CIMA, 1
15049 VIGNALE MONFERRATO [AL]
TEL. 0142933317
www.accornerovini.it

ANNUAL PRODUCTION	100,000 bottles
HECTARES UNDER VINE	22
VITICULTURE METHOD	Natural

Accornero is a guarantee. Every year, we find its wines on our final tasting table and the range is always good. The sparks this year came from Barbera Bricco Battista, which throws a complex nose of red fruits through to spiciness leading to a sumptuous, long-lingering palate. The Centenario also went through to yet another Three Glass final. This cabernet sauvignon and barbera blend's impenetrable ruby red is flecked with purple, framing intense blackberry and balsam laced with herbaceousness preceding a powerful, fresh-tasting palate. Barbera Superiore Cima is always interesting. The 2003 has impeccable balance on nose and palate, thanks in part to shrewd use of oak. Giulìn is stylish and delicious, as is Bricco del Bosco, one of the best Grignolinos we tasted. Finally, we note two more delicious wines, Brigantino, a dessert wine from malvasia, and a white, Fonsìna. We have not reviewed Girotondo, but you can find it at the cellar. The grapes come from a small nebbiolo vineyard planted by Ermanno with the late Massimo a few years ago. When the vines came onstream, Ermanno made Girotondo for the Associazione Massimo Accornero, to which revenue from sales will go.

● Barbera del M.to Sup. Bricco Battista '05	⚏	6
● M.to Rosso Centenario '05	⚏	6
● Barbera del M.to Giulìn '06	⚏⚏	4*
● Barbera del M.to Sup. Cima Ris. '03	⚏⚏	7
● Casorzo Brigantino '07	⚏⚏	4*
● Grignolino del M.to Casalese Bricco del Bosco '07	⚏⚏	4*
○ M.to Bianco Fonsìna '07	⚏⚏	4*
● Barbera d'Asti Bricco Battista '97	⚏⚏⚏	5
● Barbera del M.to Sup. Bricco Battista '99	⚏⚏⚏	6
● Barbera del M.to Sup. Bricco Battista '98	⚏⚏⚏	6
● Barbera del M.to Sup. Bricco Battista '04	⚏⚏⚏	6
● Barbera del M.to Sup. Cima '01	⚏⚏	7

Claudio Alario

VIA SANTA CROCE, 23
12055 DIANO D'ALBA [CN]
TEL. 0173231808
aziendaalario@tiscali.it

ANNUAL PRODUCTION	45,000 bottles
HECTARES UNDER VINE	12
VITICULTURE METHOD	Conventional

Guide wineries do not always have new wines to unveil. This is right because you cannot rush Nature. But Claudio Alario has actually released two this time. And when two new products are as good as the ones from this Diano-based winemaker, there is plenty to be happy about. Claudio's Barolo Sorano 2004, a selection from the vineyard at Serralunga, reveals complex violets, roses, raspberries and blackcurrants. Elegant on the palate, it foregrounds good extract in a very pleasantly drinkable progression. It rounds off with a long, balanced finish. Dolcetto di Diano d'Alba Superiore Pradurent 2006 deserves a special mention for its superlative potential. This selection is spot on, giving morello cherry, black pepper, plum and a harmonious finale lifted by a grace note of bitter almonds. The two long-established Dianos, Costa Fiore and Montagrillo, are hefty and full of attitude, with exuberant fleshy fruit and superb quality. Barolo Riva, from a vineyard in the municipality of Verduno, stands out for its intrinsic elegance and we gave Two Glasses to the Barbera d'Alba Valletta and Nebbiolo Cascinotto.

● Barolo Sorano '04	⚏⚏	8
● Barbera d'Alba Valletta '06	⚏⚏	5
● Barolo Riva '04	⚏⚏	7
● Diano d'Alba Montagrillo '07	⚏⚏	4*
● Diano d'Alba Pradurent Sup. '06	⚏⚏	4*
● Nebbiolo d'Alba Cascinotto '06	⚏⚏	5
● Diano d'Alba Costa Fiore '07	⚏⚏	4*
● Barolo Riva '99	⚏⚏	7
● Barolo Riva '01	⚏⚏	7
● Diano d'Alba Costa Fiore '06	⚏⚏	4
● Diano d'Alba Montagrillo '06	⚏⚏	4
● Barbera d'Alba Valletta '05	⚏⚏	5
● Barolo Riva '03	⚏⚏	7
● Barolo Riva '00	⚏⚏	7

F.lli Alessandria

VIA B. VALFRÉ, 59
12060 VERDUNO [CN]
TEL. 0172470113
www.fratellialessandria.it

ANNUAL PRODUCTION	60,000 bottles
HECTARES UNDER VINE	12
VITICULTURE METHOD	Conventional

The Alessandria brothers are actually working together as this year, Gian's brother Alessandro joined the staff. Gian had been running the operation with his wife Flavia and son Vittone, who married Katia in the summer of 2008. All of these changes, however, have had no impact on the quality of the wines, which continues to be admirably high. Naturally, the 2004 Barolos take centre stage, in particular Monvigliero and San Lorenzo. The latter is estery, recalling raspberries and strawberries melding with sweet spice. Assertive and not entirely settled tannins on the palate need some more time for there is plenty of substance. This fantastic, traditional-style Barolo easily earned Three Glasses. As always, the Monvigliero is elegant to the point where it might seem lacking in power. Spices and strawberry-led red fruits dominate the nose, with faint smokiness, before the palate reveals attractive flesh and a deliciously juicy texture. The Gramolere and the base Barolo scored well. We also liked the Barbera Superiore and the Pelaverga while the base Dolcetto and Barbera were just a step behind. Langhe Rosso's release has been delayed for a year.

★ Gianfranco Alessandria

LOC. MANZONI, 13
12065 MONFORTE D'ALBA [CN]
TEL. 017378576
www.gianfrancoalessandria.com

ANNUAL PRODUCTION	35,000 bottles
HECTARES UNDER VINE	5.5
VITICULTURE METHOD	Conventional

Gianfranco found an opportunity when in 1986 he set up a small, quality-oriented cellar at Monforte, encouraged by the passion for the land inherited from his father Giuseppe. Today, that is history for year after year, Gianfranco has released wines to public acclaim, confirming that he is on the right track in vineyard and cellar. The two Barolos we tasted are excellent. We just preferred the San Giovanni for its depth and complexity. It offers a dry but not aggressive palate, closing elegantly with a fireworks display of fruit and spice. Congratulations on another Three Glass prize for Gianfranco and his classy champion. The base version is more straightforward but just as elegant, melding flowers with still boisterously youthful extract. Barbera Vittoria is on top form again. Its colour bespeaks its concentration, nose-palate consistency is spot on and the acidity is bracing. Sip and savour. L'Insieme is more international in style. Blended from selections of nebbiolo, barbera and cabernet, it gives a satisfyingly balanced palate. Even the simpler wines are very good indeed. We enjoyed the inviting Nebbiolo, Barbera and Dolcetto.

● Barolo S. Lorenzo '04	▼▼▼	7
● Barolo Monvigliero '04	▼▼	7
● Barbera d'Alba Sup. La Priora '06	▼▼	4*
● Barolo '04	▼▼	6
● Barolo Gramolere '04	▼▼	7
● Verduno Pelaverga '07	▼▼	4*
● Barbera d'Alba '07	▼	4
● Dolcetto d'Alba '07	▼	4
● Barolo Monvigliero '00	♀♀♀	7
● Barolo Monvigliero '95	♀♀♀	7
● Barolo S. Lorenzo '97	♀♀♀	7
● Barolo S. Lorenzo '01	♀♀♀	7
● Barolo Monvigliero '03	♀♀	7
● Barolo S. Lorenzo '03	♀♀	7
● Barolo Gramolere '03	♀♀	7

● Barolo S. Giovanni '04	▼▼▼	8
● Barbera d'Alba Vittoria '06	▼▼	6
● Barbera d'Alba '07	▼▼	4*
● Barolo '04	▼▼	7
● Dolcetto d'Alba '07	▼▼	4*
● L'Insieme '05	▼▼	6
● Langhe Nebbiolo '06	▼▼	5
● Barbera d'Alba Vittoria '98	♀♀♀	6
● Barbera d'Alba Vittoria '97	♀♀♀	6
● Barbera d'Alba Vittoria '96	♀♀♀	5
● Barolo '93	♀♀♀	8
● Barolo S. Giovanni '99	♀♀♀	8
● Barolo S. Giovanni '98	♀♀♀	8
● Barolo S. Giovanni '97	♀♀♀	8
● Barolo S. Giovanni '01	♀♀♀	8
● Barolo S. Giovanni '00	♀♀♀	8

Marchesi Alfieri

P.ZZA ALFIERI, 28
14010 SAN MARTINO ALFIERI [AT]
TEL. 0141976015
www.marchesialfieri.it

ANNUAL PRODUCTION   110,000 bottles
HECTARES UNDER VINE 25
VITICULTURE METHOD   Conventional

The superb Marchesi Alfieri estate extends over 150 hectares – 25 planted to vine – at San Martino Alfieri. The imposing castle is set in an English landscape garden with hospitality facilities, an eatery, vinification and maturation cellars, and a tasting room. Since the 1980s, the complex has belonged to the San Martino di San Germano sisters, who in 2000 brought in the multi-talented oenologist Mario Olivero from Col d'Orcia at Montalcino. Mario has clear ideas and a proven track record. This year, the range is comfortingly good. All the wines earned at least Two Glasses and two went through to the finals: the substantial, earthy Grignolino Sansoero 2007, which mingles varietal spice with red fruits, and the barbera and pinot nero Sostegno 2006, an unpretentious but well made, beautifully balanced wine. San Germano 2006, from pinot nero, is warm with sweet tannins and the nebbiolo Costa Quaglia is intriguing, showing much subtlety on its first outing. Balance and drinkability are the distinguishing features of the 2006 Barbera La Tota while the aristocratic Alfiera 2006, from 70-year-old vines, aged in small wood and offers vanilla-veined power.

● Barbera d'Asti La Tota '06	�	4*
● Barbera d'Asti Sup. Alfiera '06	♟	6
● M.to Rosso Costa Quaglia '05	♟	5
● M.to Rosso S. Germano '06	♟	5
● M.to Rosso Sostegno '06	♟	4
● Piemonte Grignolino Sansoero '07	♟	4
● Barbera d'Asti Sup. Alfiera '99	♟♟♟	6
● Barbera d'Asti Sup. Alfiera '05	♟♟♟	6
● Barbera d'Asti Sup. Alfiera '01	♟♟♟	6
● Barbera d'Asti Sup. Alfiera '00	♟♟♟	6
● Barbera d'Asti La Tota '05	♟♟	4
● Barbera d'Asti La Tota '04	♟♟	4
● Barbera d'Asti Sup. Alfiera '04	♟♟	6
● M.to Rosso S. Germano '05	♟♟	5
● M.to Rosso S. Germano '04	♟♟	5

Giovanni Almondo

VIA SAN ROCCO, 26
12046 MONTÀ [CN]
TEL. 0173975256
www.giovannialmondo.com

ANNUAL PRODUCTION   80,000 bottles
HECTARES UNDER VINE 14
VITICULTURE METHOD   Conventional

Despite his relative youth, Domenico Almondo has done much to promote Roero winemaking. He and a handful of other far-sighted local growers were the first to spot the potential and learn from Langhe to get the most out of their arneis, barbera and nebbiolo, which are the only varieties Domenico grows on his 14 hectares. Much has been said about Domenico's skills with white wines and you only have to uncork a bottle of Arneis Vigne Sparse, or even better, Bricco delle Ciliegie, to see why. Vigne Sparse is taut and ready to drink while its fellow is rounder, more reflective and has definite Three Glass potential. The Barbera takes full advantage of a favourable vintage to give wonderful spice, earthiness and acidity. Nebbiolo is also in the spotlight, especially in Roero Bric Valdiana from sandy vineyards that enhance its fragrance and finesse. In fact, provenance and character prompt Domenico to release his reds slightly earlier than other winemakers in Roero. It's a carefully calculated decision that this year has highlighted vanilla and leaf tobacco-laced fruitiness, a soft, already enjoyable mouthfeel and the variety's excellent ageing potential.

● Barbera d'Alba Valbianchera '06	♟	5
● Roero Bric Valdiana '06	♟	6
○ Roero Arneis Bricco delle Ciliegie '07	♟	4*
○ Roero Arneis V. Sparse '07	♟	4
● Roero '06	♟	5
● Langhe Nebbiolo '06	♟	5
● Roero Bric Valdiana '03	♟♟♟	6
● Roero Bric Valdiana '01	♟♟♟	6
● Roero Bric Valdiana '00	♟♟♟	6
● Barbera d'Alba Valbianchera '05	♟♟	5
● Barbera d'Alba Valbianchera '04	♟♟	5
● Roero Bric Valdiana '05	♟♟	6
● Roero Bric Valdiana '04	♟♟	6

★★ Elio Altare - Cascina Nuova

FRAZ. ANNUNZIATA, 51
12064 LA MORRA [CN]
TEL. 017350835
www.elioaltare.com

ANNUAL PRODUCTION 55,000 bottles
HECTARES UNDER VINE 10
VITICULTURE METHOD Natural

There was a wedding in the Altare home this year. Elio's daughter Elena has married and moved to Germany, although her heart still beats for the gentle hills of Annunziata at La Morra. Elio himself spends some of his time in Cinque Terre, where he owns a superb vineyard perched a sheer cliff at Riomaggiore and tends it with all the care he lavishes on his Langhe rows of nebbiolo and barbera. We were impressed by the Langhe La Villa, which finds an exquisite balance of barbera fruit and the more complex elegance of nebbiolo. Three authoritative Glasses. The textbook Larigi 2006 also came close to top honours, combining lovely body with superb drinkability through to an acidity-braced finish. As ever, the 2004 Barolo Arborina is sophisticated, unveiling dried flowers and violets. The base Barolo is also good and we also tasted one of the few bottles of Elio's superb Barolo Brunate, all of which goes abroad. Another Altare thoroughbred, the nebbiolo Langhe Arborina 2006, was devastated by hail and we'll have to wait until next year for the 2006 L'Insieme 2006. The rest of the range, which now features an attractive Langhe Nebbiolo, is better than good.

● Langhe La Villa '06	▼▼▼	8
● Barolo Vign. Arborina '04	▼▼	8
● Langhe Larigi '06	▼▼	8
● Barbera d'Alba '07	▼▼	5
● Barolo '04	▼▼	6
● Dolcetto d'Alba '07	▼▼	4*
● Langhe Nebbiolo '07	▼▼	5
● Barolo Vign. Arborina '01	▽▽▽	8
● Barolo Vign. Arborina '00	▽▽▽	8
● Barolo Vign. Arborina '99	▽▽▽	8
● Barolo Vign. Arborina '98	▽▽▽	8
● Langhe Arborina '98	▽▽▽	8
● Langhe Arborina '97	▽▽▽	8
● Langhe Arborina '96	▽▽▽	8
● Langhe La Villa '05	▽▽▽	8
● Langhe Larigi '99	▽▽▽	8
● Langhe Larigi '04	▽▽▽	8

Antichi Vigneti di Cantalupo

VIA MICHELANGELO BUONARROTI, 5
28074 GHEMME [NO]
TEL. 0163840041
www.cantalupo.net

ANNUAL PRODUCTION 200,000 bottles
HECTARES UNDER VINE 35
VITICULTURE METHOD Conventional

Winemaking at Ghemme has a long history. The earliest evidence dates from ancient times and admiring references to local wines continue down the centuries as Frederick I Barbarossa, Henry IV, Charles V and Cavour in turn praised the cellars of Ghemme. The Arlunno family has been part of the scene at least since 1550 and has owned vineyards since the 19th century. Today, Alberto Arlunno has row in the finest locations of these morainic hills: ten hectares at Breclema, eight at Carella, four at Livelli and the rest spread over Baraggiola, Valera and Cavenago. Sadly, there was no repeat of last year's exploit as some of the big hitters were missing. For various reasons, including hail, technical problems and soaring sales, the cellar's historic selections were not produced in the memorable 2001 vintage. There was no Ghemme Collis Breclemae or Ghemme Collis Carellae. This left Ghemme Signore di Bayard to defend the winery's colours with its intensely complex white truffle and tobacco, elegant tannins and long-lingering juiciness. The 2004 Ghemme is more austere but still has the finesse of northern-grown nebbiolo while Primigenia 2006 is the stand-out from the standard range.

● Ghemme Signore di Bayard '01	▼▼	6
● Colline Novaresi Primigenia '06	▼▼	3*
● Ghemme '04	▼▼	5
○ Carolus '07	▼	4
● Colline Novaresi Agamium '05	▼	4
⊙ Colline Novaresi Nebbiolo Il Mimo '07	▼	4
● Colline Novaresi Vespolina Villa Horta '06	▼	3
● Ghemme Collis Breclemae '00	▽▽▽	7
● Ghemme Collis Carellae '00	▽▽	6
● Ghemme '03	▽▽	5
● Ghemme Collis Breclemae '99	▽▽	6
● Ghemme Collis Breclemae '98	▽▽	6
● Ghemme Collis Carellae '99	▽▽	6

Antico Borgo dei Cavalli

VIA DANTE, 54
28010 CAVALLIRIO [NO]
TEL. 016380115
www.vinibarbaglia.it

ANNUAL PRODUCTION	20,000 bottles
HECTARES UNDER VINE	3
VITICULTURE METHOD	Conventional

When we met in the summer, Sergio Barbaglia's daughter Silvia brought out an old aerial photograph that shows the hills here were once completely covered by vines, just as the Barolo-growing Langhe in the south is today. Today, the same photograph would reveal a very different picture. Vines have given way to woodland where non-agricultural activities have not moved in. Yet Silvia made it clear that there is a will to bring this area back to the levels if not of production, at least of visibility, that it enjoyed in the past. The task would be less daunting if more wine estates aimed for quality like the Barbaglias. We hope this will be the case and for now we toast the future in the new Brut that Sergio's ever-busy imagination has created. Curticella Caballi Regis is an elegant refermented Erbaluce with a secure future but it was the Boca itself from this pocket handkerchief DOC zone that won our hearts. The 2004 edition is sumptuous, austere and rich in extract. The rest of the range is better than ever with special mentions for the acidic, consistent Vespolina, the enjoyably varietal Uva Rara and the erbaluce-based Bianco Lucino.

Antoniolo

C.SO VALSESIA, 277
13045 GATTINARA [VC]
TEL. 0163833612
antoniolovini@bmm.it

ANNUAL PRODUCTION	60,000 bottles
HECTARES UNDER VINE	12
VITICULTURE METHOD	Conventional

Rosanna's children Lorella and Alberto are the third generation of Antoniolos to run this estate. We remember Rosanna in the 1970s and 1980s, when she was a towering female figure in the mainly male world of Italian wine. Now Lorella and Alberto supervise every stage of winemaking. The vine stock is 30 years old on average and extends over 14 hectares in five plots. The San Francesco, Osso San Grato and Castelle vineyards yield selections and the standard Gattinara while Nebbiolo Juvenia and the Bricco Lorella rosé come from the Borelle and Valferana vineyards. The superb 2004 vintage brought us four fine Gattinaras with great cellar potential. Osso San Grato, aged for three years in 30-hectolitre containers, is majestic, melding its complex rhubarb and quinine with a distinctive tannic weave. The San Francesco matured for 30 months in large wood to emerge with the same classy aromatics and more velvety smoothness. Note, too, that this year the standard-label Gattinara is almost as good as the softer Castelle selection. The Juvenia and Bricco Lorella are also nice but the Erbaluce di Caluso lacks a little lustre.

● Boca '04	♟♟	6
● Colline Novaresi Uva Rara Lea '07	♟♟	3*
● Colline Novaresi Vespolina Ledi '07	♟♟	4
○ Colline Novaresi Bianco Lucino '07	♟♟	4
○ Curticella Caballi Regis Brut M. Cl. '05	♟♟	5
● Colline Novaresi Nebbiolo Il Silente '05	♟	5
● Colline Novaresi Croatina Gli Otri '07	♟	4
● Boca '03	♟♟	6
● Colline Novaresi Vespolina Ledi '06	♟♟	4
● Colline Novaresi Vespolina Ledi '05	♟♟	4

● Gattinara Vign. Osso S. Grato '04	♟♟♟	7
● Gattinara '04	♟♟	6
● Gattinara Vign. Castelle '04	♟♟	7
● Gattinara Vign. S. Francesco '04	♟♟	7
● Coste della Sesia Nebbiolo Juvenia '07	♟♟	4*
☉ Coste della Sesia Rosato Bricco Lorella '07	♟♟	4*
○ Erbaluce di Caluso '07		4
● Gattinara Vign. Castelle '99	♟♟♟	7
● Gattinara Vign. Castelle '00	♟♟♟	7
● Gattinara Vign. Osso S. Grato '01	♟♟♟	7
● Gattinara Vign. S. Francesco '03	♟♟♟	7
● Gattinara Vign. S. Francesco '01	♟♟♟	6
● Gattinara '03	♟♟	6

Anzivino

C.SO VALSESIA, 162
13045 GATTINARA [VC]
TEL. 0163827172
www.anzivino.net

ANNUAL PRODUCTION	90,000 bottles
HECTARES UNDER VINE	14
VITICULTURE METHOD	Conventional

Who knows why construction entrepreneur Emanuele Anzivino moved to Gattinara; perhaps it was for the quiet. At the turn of the millennium, though, a passion for winemaking and business prompted him to set up his own operation. His somewhat over-ambitious initial plan has been scaled back and now cellar and vineyards are nicely in line with Emanuele's new lifestyle and he has almost 14 hectares under vine, half at Gattinara. The cellar has avoided conforming to the schools of thought that dominate Italian winemaking. Modern style table wines from international varieties, like the 50-25-25 nebbiolo, merlot and syrah Nemesi, and Caplegna, from native varieties with a dash of merlot, line up with traditional products from native varieties matured in large wood like the Gattinara and Bramaterra. Although still youthful and austere, the Gattinara 2004 impressed with its great personality. The stiffish, dry character of the 2000 Riserva justifies its late release, a full year after its partner from 2003, and the croatina in the Bramaterra 2004 comes through clearly in the generous fruity flesh and slightly assertive tannins.

Araldica Vini Piemontesi

V.LE LAUDANO, 2
14040 CASTEL BOGLIONE [AT]
TEL. 014176311
www.araldicavini.com

ANNUAL PRODUCTION	6,000,000 bottles
HECTARES UNDER VINE	900
VITICULTURE METHOD	Conventional

Araldica is a major wine estate at Castel Boglione, on the border between Asti and Alessandria, and it releases the classic wines of both zones. For some years now, Barbera, Moscato and Brachetto have been joined by Gavi following the purchase of a lovely estate at Novi Ligure, La Battistina. The wines we tasted are sold to restaurants and wine stores as part of a quality project that started in the mid 1990s. Only about 70 of the 900 hectares supervised by the cellar go into the Il Cascinone selection. Eight wines are made for a total output of fewer than 300,000 bottles a year. There are a further three and a half hectares in Roero, which yield fruit for Langhe Nebbiolo and Roero Arneis. This year, the two main selections were missing. Langhe Nebbiolo Castellero 2006 had still to go into bottle and Barbera d'Asti D'Annona was skipping its second vintage: 2004 and 2005. Barbera Rive 2006 is fruit-forward and intense, giving rain-soaked earth and spice followed by a pervasive, savoury palate. It also comes at a very attractive price. The best white is again Sauvignon Camillona, although we also liked the first release of Riesling Fontanino.

● Gattinara '04	♟♟	5
● Bramaterra '04	♟♟	4*
● Gattinara Ris. '00	♟♟	5
● Caplenga	♟	2*
● Coste della Sesia Il Tarlo '06	♟	4
● Nemesi	♟	3
● Bramaterra '03	♟♟	5
● Bramaterra '01	♟♟	5
● Bramaterra Ris. '03	♟♟	6
● Coste della Sesia Faticato '04	♟♟	7
● Coste della Sesia Faticato '03	♟♟	7
● Gattinara '03	♟♟	6
● Gattinara '01	♟♟	6
● Gattinara Ris. '03	♟♟	6
● Gattinara Ris. '01	♟♟	6

● Barbera d'Asti Sup. Rive '06	♟♟	4*
○ Gavi La Battistina '07	♟♟	4*
○ M.to Bianco Camillona '07	♟♟	4*
○ Gavi Bricco Battistina '07	♟	4
○ M.to Bianco Fontanino '07	♟	4
○ Moscato d'Asti Belvedere '07	♟	4
○ Roero Arneis Sorilaria '07	♟	4
● Brachetto d'Acqui Cavallino '07	♟	4
● Barbera d'Asti Sup. Rive '05	♟♟	4
● Barbera d'Asti Sup. Rive '04	♟♟	4
● Barbera d'Asti Sup. D'Annona '03	♟♟	4
● Langhe Nebbiolo Castellero '05	♟♟	4

Tenuta dell'Arbiola

LOC. ARBIOLA
REG. SALINE, 67
14050 SAN MARZANO OLIVETO [AT]
TEL. 0141856194
www.arbiola.it

ANNUAL PRODUCTION	120,000 bottles
HECTARES UNDER VINE	20
VITICULTURE METHOD	Conventional

In this corner of Asti, Domenico Terzano and his son Riccardo have created a fine winemaking operation but a while ago they also added an attractive restaurant, decorated in a modern style. In contrast with last year's list, there is no Barbera Romilda Riserva del Fondatore, one of the cellar's flag-carriers. We consoled ourselves with the fine 2006 edition of Barbera Romilda XI. Rich and complex on the nose, it unveils everything from ripe strawberry and raspberry red berry fruit to quinine, vanilla and cocoa powder from the small wood where it spent 18 months. Rich pulp emerges reluctantly at first on the palate but the finish shows attractively juicy flesh. The 80-20 sauvignon and chardonnay Monferrato Bianco Arbiola tempts with aromas of white-fleshed fruit, nectarines and sage. Well-gauged acidity is partnered by good length and savouriness in the mouth. The enjoyable Barbera Carlotta is remarkably vibrant and enviably fresh while the Moscato is fruity and the uncomplicated Chardonnay offers depth and balance.

L'Armangia

FRAZ. SAN GIOVANNI, 122
14053 CANELLI [AT]
TEL. 0141824947
www.armangia.it

ANNUAL PRODUCTION	77,000 bottles
HECTARES UNDER VINE	9.5
VITICULTURE METHOD	Conventional

Ignazio Giovine makes classic Asti wines. We were unable to taste one of the main selections, Barbera d'Asti Vignali, as the 2006 version was still maturing so we enjoyed a delightful Titon. An excellent growing year has given depth and complexity laced with quinine, tobacco and plum fragrances before the palate reveals all the acidity needed to bolster a deep palate. Ignazio Giovine is a patient man who takes care of his products. In addition to the splendid Titon, he gave us a very fine Monferrato Rosso Macchiaferro from albarossa that has loads of structure and power. Its complex, intriguing nose precedes a long palate with fruit on the finish and plenty of body. Sopra Berruti is a fresh-tasting, drinkable 2007 Barbera. The peach, citronella, sage and apricot Moscato Il Giai is fine wine with a juicy mouthfilling palate. Also nice is Chardonnay Non 2007 while Pratorotondo 2006, reviewed in error last year, is more complex, giving butter, vanilla and zest of orange. The sweet 2007 Mesicaseu picked up a second Glass and there was One Glass for Monferrato Rosso Pacifico 2005, a blend of nebbiolo, merlot, freisa, barbera and cabernet sauvignon.

● Barbera d'Asti Sup. Nizza Romilda XI '06	♥♥ 6	
O M.to Bianco Arbiola '07	♥♥ 4	
O Moscato d'Asti Ferlingot '07	♥ 4	
O Piemonte Chardonnay '07	♥ 3	
● Barbera d'Asti Carlotta '07	♥ 4	
● Barbera d'Asti Sup. Nizza Romilda VII '01	♥♥ 6	
● Barbera d'Asti Sup. Nizza Romilda X '05	♥♥ 6	
● Barbera d'Asti Sup. Nizza Romilda IX '04	♥♥ 5	
● Barbera d'Asti Sup. Nizza Romilda VIII '03	♥♥ 6	

● Barbera d'Asti Sup. Nizza Titon '06	♥♥ 4*	
● Barbera d'Asti Sopra Berruti '07	♥♥ 3*	
● M.to Rosso Macchiaferro '06	♥♥ 4	
O Mesicaseu '07	♥♥ 4	
O Moscato d'Asti Il Giai '07	♥♥ 3*	
O Piemonte Chardonnay Pratorotondo '06	♥♥ 3*	
● M.to Rosso Pacifico '05	♥ 4	
O Piemonte Chardonnay Non '07	♥ 3	
● Barbera d'Asti Sup. Nizza Titon '04	♥♥ 4	
● Barbera d'Asti Sup. Titon '03	♥♥ 4	
● Barbera d'Asti Sup. Titon '01	♥♥ 4	
● Barbera d'Asti Vignali '04	♥♥ 6	
● Barbera d'Asti Vignali Castello di Calosso '01	♥♥ 6	
● Barbera d'Asti Vignali Castello di Calosso '00	♥♥ 6	

Ascheri

VIA PIUMATI, 23
12042 BRA [CN]
TEL. 0172412394
www.ascherivini.it

ANNUAL PRODUCTION	240,000 bottles
HECTARES UNDER VINE	40
VITICULTURE METHOD	Conventional

In recent years, Bra has become internationally famous. Credit for some part of this must go to Matteo Ascheri, the man whose family runs the only large wine enterprise in the town on the edge of Roero and Langhe. The cellar, with its Muri Vecchi eatery and classy hotel, is a short distance from the town centre and today are an attraction for tourists and architecture buffs. The vines are scattered around Langhe in three important areas: Rivalta at La Morra, Sorano at Serralunga and just outside Bra on the Montelupa hill. And it is from Montelupa that the oenologists, led by Matteo, source two unusual wines that are now Guide fixtures. We refer to the spicy, rustic, syrah-based Langhe Rosso Montalupa and the Langhe Bianco, from viognier. Consistent quality was confirmed this year by a highly satisfactory range. The two wines from Bra are flanked by the big hitters, three 2004 Barolos. We were stunned by the elegance and finesse of the Sorano Coste & Bricco selection. Vigna dei Pola is built on similar lines and the Sorano is a tad rough, although still very young. All the other wines scored well.

Azelia

FRAZ. GARBELLETTO
VIA ALBA-BAROLO, 53
12060 CASTIGLIONE FALLETTO [CN]
TEL. 017362859

ANNUAL PRODUCTION	52,000 bottles
HECTARES UNDER VINE	12
VITICULTURE METHOD	Conventional

This historic winery run by the Scavino family concentrates on quality. The 2002 version of Barolo Voghera Brea Riserva was not presented but we tasted a magnificent Barolo Bricco Fiasco 2004, released in 7,500 bottles. Aged in one quarter new small wood, it is persistent and intense on nose and palate, showing elegance and balance. It's a similar story with the 7,000 bottles of Barolo San Rocco 2004. The difference is in the vineyard but the results are comparable: superb structure and power that are already melding well. You can uncork these marvellous wines now but they have a long future ahead. Only a shade less focused, but with plenty of potential, are the 6,500 bottles of Barolo Margheria 2004, part of which ages in large wood. This is the second release. Another good wine is the standard 2004 Barolo, with 12,000 units available. Small and large wood is used for this full-bodied, long-lingering wine. The 7,000 units of Barbera d'Alba Vigneto Punta 2006 were 90 per cent oak-matured and the wine shows pleasingly intense acidity. Finally, the 15,000 bottles of Dolcetto d'Alba are good and the 2007 Langhe Nebbiolo is well crafted.

● Barolo Sorano Coste & Bricco '04	♟♟ 7	
● Barolo Sorano '04	♟♟ 6*	
● Barolo V. dei Pola '04	♟♟ 6*	
● Langhe Rosso Montalupa '04	♟♟ 5	
● Nebbiolo d'Alba Bricco S. Giacomo '06	♟♟ 4*	
● Verduno Pelaverga Do ut Des '07	♟♟ 4*	
O Langhe Bianco Montalupa '06	♟♟ 5	
O Langhe Arneis Cristina Ascheri '07	♟ 4	
● Barbera d'Alba Fontanelle '07	♟ 4	
● Dolcetto d'Alba Nirane '07	♟ 4	
● Dolcetto d'Alba S. Rocco '07	♟ 4	
● Barolo Sorano '00	♟♟♟ 6	
● Barolo Sorano Coste & Bricco '01	♟♟ 7	
● Barolo Sorano Coste & Bricco '00	♟♟ 7	
● Barolo Sorano '01	♟♟ 6	
● Barolo V. dei Pola '01	♟♟ 6	

● Barolo Bricco Fiasco '04	♟♟ 8	
● Barolo S. Rocco '04	♟♟ 8	
● Barolo Margheria '04	♟♟ 8	
● Barbera d'Alba Vign. Punta '06	♟♟ 5	
● Barolo '04	♟♟ 7	
● Dolcetto d'Alba Bricco dell'Oriolo '07	♟♟ 4*	
● Langhe Nebbiolo '07	♟ 4	
● Barolo '91	♟♟♟ 8	
● Barolo Bricco Fiasco '96	♟♟♟ 8	
● Barolo Bricco Fiasco '95	♟♟♟ 8	
● Barolo Bricco Fiasco '93	♟♟♟ 8	
● Barolo Bricco Fiasco '01	♟♟♟ 8	
● Barolo S. Rocco '99	♟♟♟ 8	
● Barolo Voghera Brea Ris. '01	♟♟♟ 8	

Antonio Baldizzone
Cascina Lana
c.so Acqui, 187
14049 Nizza Monferrato [AT]
tel. 0141726734

ANNUAL PRODUCTION	70,000 bottles
HECTARES UNDER VINE	20
VITICULTURE METHOD	Conventional

Antonio Baldizzone and his wife Graziana Rizzoli own a beautifully situated wine estate facing south-east on the border of the municipalities of Acqui Terme and Nizza Monferrato. Over the years, they have improved the quality of their range to the point where they regularly earn a full profile, which is no small feat in a region as competitive as Piedmont. The top of the range was the Barbera d'Asti Superiore Nizza, which again went through to the Three Glass finals. It may have been let down at our finals by its youth, given that it's a 2006, but it is still an outstanding wine, with great structure and superb balance of rich fruit and spiciness. Barbera d'Asti La Cirimela is more approachable. It has a nice varietal nose, fresh fruit and is deliciously drinkable, not to mention excellent value for money. Monferrato Rosso Vën ëd Michen is from cabernet sauvignon, barbera and nebbiolo.
It's elegant, nicely put together and sumptuously rich without cloying. The rest of the range lives up to the cellar's high standards and marks Baldizzone out as one of the wineries to watch over the next few years.

Produttori del Barbaresco
via Torino, 54
12050 Barbaresco [CN]
tel. 0173635139
www.produttoridelbarbaresco.com

ANNUAL PRODUCTION	420,000 bottles
HECTARES UNDER VINE	100
VITICULTURE METHOD	Conventional

Produttori del Barbaresco is a label that wine lovers all over the world recognize as a guarantee of top quality at very affordable prices. For a co-operative winery, the secret lies in the strategic decisions that have been put in place since the cellar opened in 1958, all focused on achieving the best in quality. Not least of these, was the recent decision to ask member growers to reduce yields by ten per cent over the limits allowed by the zone's production protocol. The management team is led by Aldo Vacca on the commercial side and oenologist Gianni Testa for production. We would like to mention the current project to build a new cellar, starting from the expansion of the fermentation facilities just outside the village of Barbaresco. The range presented was limited, in part by the fact that Riserva wines skipped another vintage. After the 2001s, the next Riservas will be from 2004. The 2006 Nebbiolo is approachable and persuasively appealing while the 2004 Barbaresco has remarkable class, austerity and depth for a wine in this price range released in such numbers: 300,000 bottles.

● Barbera d'Asti Sup. Nizza '06	♈♈	5
● Barbera d'Asti La Cirimela '07	♈♈	3*
● M.to Rosso Vën ëd Michen '06	♈♈	5
O Moscato d'Asti '07	♈	3
● Barbera d'Asti Sup. Nizza '05	♈♈	5
● Barbera d'Asti Sup. Nizza '04	♈♈	5
● Barbera d'Asti La Cirimela '06	♈♈	3
● Barbera d'Asti La Cirimela '05	♈♈	3

● Barbaresco '04	♈♈	5*
● Langhe Nebbiolo '06	♈♈	4*
● Barbaresco '99	♈♈♈	5
● Barbaresco Vign. in Montefico Ris. '00	♈♈♈	6
● Barbaresco Vign. in Montefico Ris. '99	♈♈♈	6
● Barbaresco Vign. in Montestefano Ris. '96	♈♈♈	6
● Barbaresco Vign. in Montestefano Ris. '01	♈♈♈	6
● Barbaresco Vign. in Rio Sordo Ris. '01	♈♈♈	6
● Barbaresco Vign. in Rio Sordo Ris. '97	♈♈♈	6
● Barbaresco Vign. in Pajé Ris. '01	♈♈♈	6
● Barbaresco Vign. in Moccagatta Ris. '01	♈♈	6

★ Cascina La Barbatella

S.DA ANNUNZIATA, 55
14049 NIZZA MONFERRATO [AT]
TEL. 0141701434
sonvico.barbatella@libero.it

ANNUAL PRODUCTION	22,000 bottles
HECTARES UNDER VINE	4
VITICULTURE METHOD	Conventional

Angelo Sonvico, owner of Cascina La Barbatella, made his dream come true some time ago. When in the early 1980s, he and his wife Emiliana were starting out in the world of wine, they knew they would soon achieve success. Angelo's wines have delighted tasters all over the globe thanks to his textbook quality-focused approach. To start with, the vines are grouped around winery in one of the finest wine locations in the hills of Nizza Monferrato. The beautiful, practical cellar is state of the art and run by one of the territory's leading winemaking teams: Giuliano Noè and Beppe Rattazzo. Numbers are kept deliberately low because what counts here is quality. Needless to say, this year's wines confirmed the positive trend. From 2005, we enjoyed the ever-delicious Monferrato Rosso Sonvico, Barbera d'Asti Superiore Nizza Vigna dell'Angelo and Monferrato Rosso Mystère. The barbera and cabernet Sonvico enchants with its ripe fruit and rain-soaked earth aromas followed by an appealingly relaxed palate. The Barbera d'Asti La Barbatella 2007 is straightforward but very successful and the cortese and sauvignon Monferrato Bianco Noè is very nice.

Cascina Barisél

REG. SAN GIOVANNI, 30
14053 CANELLI [AT]
TEL. 0141824848
www.barisel.it

ANNUAL PRODUCTION	35,000 bottles
HECTARES UNDER VINE	4
VITICULTURE METHOD	Natural

Cascina Barisél puts emphasis on natural grape farming under the dedicated, responsible management of Franco Penna. Franco is a tireless wine man who step by step is expanding his cellar by adding more space for barrel ageing. He is a firm believer in the potential of moscato, either as a semi-sparkling or dried-grape wine, but he has also shown that he knows how to handle barbera. La Cappelletta went through to the Three Glass finals by virtue of its beefy structure and remarkable energy. It gives rain-soaked earth, black pepper, sweet spices and ripe strawberry and cherry-led red berry fruit. The attractive acidity on the palate supports the excellent length through to a complex lingering finish. The Barisél also did well thanks to a very good growing year that brought out all its qualities, and to its invitingly juicy flesh. The Enrico Penna Brut from chardonnay and pinot nero impressed, its remarkable supporting acidity lending length to the fresh-tasting palate. The Moscato gives tempting sage and citronella whereas the Avila has dried figs and citrus peel. Finally, One Glass went to the favorita-based Bianco Foravìa.

● M.to Rosso Sonvico '05	♈	6
● Barbera d'Asti Sup. Nizza V. dell'Angelo '05	♈	6
● Barbera d'Asti La Barbatella '07	♈♈	4*
● M.to Rosso Mystère '05	♈♈	6
○ M.to Bianco Noè '07	♈	4
● M.to Rosso Aldar '07	♈	4
● Barbera d'Asti Sup. Nizza V. dell'Angelo '01	♈♈♈	7
● M.to Rosso Mystère '01	♈♈♈	7
● M.to Rosso Sonvico '98	♈♈♈	7
● M.to Rosso Sonvico '97	♈♈♈	7
● M.to Rosso Sonvico '04	♈♈♈	6
● M.to Rosso Sonvico '03	♈♈♈	7
● M.to Rosso Sonvico '00	♈♈♈	7

● Barbera d'Asti Sup. La Cappelletta '05	♈♈	5
● Barbera d'Asti Barisél '06	♈♈	4*
○ Enrico Penna Brut '04	♈♈	4*
○ L'Avìja '06	♈♈	5
○ Moscato d'Asti '07	♈♈	4*
○ M.to Bianco Foravìa '07	♈	3
○ L'Avìja '05	♈♈	5
○ L'Avìja '04	♈♈	5
○ L'Avìja '03	♈♈	5
○ L'Avìja '01	♈♈	5
● Barbera d'Asti Sup. La Cappelletta '04	♈♈	5
● Barbera d'Asti Sup. La Cappelletta '03	♈♈	5
● Barbera d'Asti Sup. La Cappelletta '01	♈♈	5

Barni

VIA FORTE, 63
13862 BRUSNENGO [BI]
TEL. 015985977

ANNUAL PRODUCTION	25,000 bottles
HECTARES UNDER VINE	6
VITICULTURE METHOD	Conventional

Filippo Barni is recovering viticulture in Biella, a part of northern Piedmont that was for long considered marginal. This once-proud winemaking zone gradually contracted to the point where only a few determined producers were left. Filippo is one of them and he has proved his courage many times over. For the past 15 years, he has focused on quality at Mesola, his stunning amphitheatre of vines at Brusnengo. Results are excellent again this year, except for one or two doubts about the performance of Mesolone, the cellar's flagship, which we thought wasn't quite up to the standards of previous vintages. Nevertheless, it is still robust, austere and emblematic of Coste della Sesia. Doss Pilun is better. This tannic, powerful Bramaterra is subtle, elegant and nicely restrained in its echoes of vanilla and toastiness. We loved it. From the reds, we like the integrity and fruit of Torrearsa, again from the great 2004 vintage. Albaciara, in contrast, is a fresh-tasting, flowery mix of erbaluce and chardonnay. Cantagal, a dried-grape Erbaluce, is one of the most successful sweet wines you can find in northern Piedmont.

Batasiolo

FRAZ. ANNUNZIATA, 87
12064 LA MORRA [CN]
TEL. 017350130
www.batasiolo.com

ANNUAL PRODUCTION	2,500,000 bottles
HECTARES UNDER VINE	112
VITICULTURE METHOD	Conventional

The Dogliani family's lovely winery is proof that quality can come in serious numbers. Barbaresco 2005 again surprised us by marrying structure with incredible drinkability thanks to already sweet tannins and a long, clean finale. The 2004 vintage sees all the prestigious Barolo selections firing on all cylinders, from the Corda della Briccolina, with oak and fruit marrying on the nose and extract melding with alcohol, to the elegant, faintly balsamic Cerequio. The Bofani and Boscareto Barolos are convincing but still need to bring the oak into line while the base Barolo may not be very broad but is attractive and well made. Cleanness and appeal are the keynotes of this vast range, from which we would point out the Dolcetto d'Alba Bricco di Vergne 2007 and the excellent range of dry, sweet and refermented whites: the Gavi and Arneis; the aromatic, fresh-tasting Moscato Passito Muscatel Tardì 2006 which ends on dried fruits; and the Metodo Classico Millésimé 2003, which has crusty bread aromas. The less ambitious whites are good, including the Arneis and the Chardonnay Serbato. The Morino, aged in small barrels, is edgier and more challenging.

● Bramaterra V. Doss Pilun '04	🍷🍷 5
○ Cantagal '05	🍷🍷 7
● Coste della Sesia Rosso Mesolone '04	🍷🍷 5
● Coste della Sesia Rosso Torrearsa '04	🍷🍷 5
○ Albaciara Bianco '07	🍷 4
○ Cantagal '04	🍷🍷 7
● Bramaterra V. Doss Pilun '03	🍷🍷 5
● Bramaterra V. Doss Pilun '02	🍷🍷 5
● Coste della Sesia Rosso Mesolone '03	🍷🍷 5
● Coste della Sesia Rosso Torrearsa '03	🍷🍷 5

● Barbaresco '05	🍷🍷 6
● Barolo Cerequio '04	🍷🍷 8
● Barolo Corda della Briccolina '04	🍷🍷 8
● Barolo '04	🍷🍷 6
● Barolo Bofani '04	🍷🍷 8
● Barolo Boscareto '04	🍷🍷 8
● Dolcetto d'Alba Bricco di Vergne '07	🍷🍷 4*
○ Gavi del Comune di Gavi Granée '07	🍷🍷 4*
○ Metodo Classico Millésimé '03	🍷🍷 5
○ Moscato d'Asti Bosc dla Rei '07	🍷🍷 4*
○ Piemonte Moscato Passito Muscatel Tardì '06	🍷🍷 6
○ Langhe Chardonnay Morino '07	🍷 6
○ Langhe Chardonnay Serbato '07	🍷 4
○ Roero Arneis '07	🍷 5
● Barolo Corda della Briccolina '90	🍷🍷🍷 8

Luigi Baudana

FRAZ. BAUDANA, 43
12050 SERRALUNGA D'ALBA [CN]
TEL. 0173613354
www.baudanaluigi.com

ANNUAL PRODUCTION	25,000 bottles
HECTARES UNDER VINE	4.50
VITICULTURE METHOD	Conventional

Luigi and his wife Fiorina run this small family business for quality. Of course, the Baudana estate is at Serralunga, one of Langhe's finest wine spots. The range confirmed the cellar's high standards, particularly with its two Barolos. Cerretta Piani is more outgoing, giving plum and vanilla before the palate shows off its balance, and the Baudana, which stands out for its cherry and pepper aromas, length and attractive freshness. At present, Cerretta Piani is readier for drinking while the Baudana's acidity augurs well for the future. The excellent vintage also produced two other reds that caught our tasters' attention. We were especially enamoured of the Dolcetto d'Alba Baudana 2006, which shows its maker's hand in the way it combines elegance and power in the true manner of Dolcetto from Serralunga. Barbera d'Alba Donatella 2006 is in the same style, although it fails to achieve the balance that made the previous vintage's edition so impressive. Langhe Rosso Lorenso from nebbiolo, barbera and merlot is austere and deep while the Langhe Chardonnay, the only white, caught our panel's attention with its florality and full-bodied palate.

Bava

S.DA MONFERRATO, 2
14023 COCCONATO [AT]
TEL. 0141907083
www.bava.com

ANNUAL PRODUCTION	580,000 bottles
HECTARES UNDER VINE	57
VITICULTURE METHOD	Conventional

Roberto, Giulio and Paolo Bava run a tight ship. Giulio and Paolo are in charge of the wines while Roberto, the eldest, has a flair for marketing. For more than 15 years, the Bavas have been managing one of Piedmont's most successful sparkling winemakers, Asti-based Giulio Cocchi. The cellar is part of the Case Spumantistiche Piemontesi and has contributed to the new Alta Langa project. There are three sparklers from the Alta Langa DOC, the pinot nero and chardonnay Toto Corde, the chardonnay-only Bianc 'd Bianc and the Rösa, from 100 per cent pinot nero. The first has complex aromas of crusty bread and hazelnut, with a creamy, slightly over-rich palate. Bianc 'd Bianc is delicate and savoury while Rösa is fruit-led and complex. As we wait for the Barolos from the new holding at Castiglione Falletto, we enjoyed three lovely Barberas. The Piano Alto selection is ethereal and mouthfilling, despite coming from the tricky 2003 vintage, while Libera 2006 is full bodied, dynamic and braced by nice acidity. Stradivario is sincere while peaches and citrus theme the Moscato d'Asti Bass Tuba and the Chardonnay Thou Bianc gives damson and green apple.

● Barolo Baudana '04	♥♥	7
● Barolo Cerretta Piani '04	♥♥	7
● Barbera d'Alba Donatella '06	♥♥	5
● Dolcetto d'Alba Baudana '06	♥♥	4*
● Langhe Rosso Lorenso '05	♥♥	5
● Dolcetto d'Alba '07	♥	4
○ Langhe Chardonnay '07	♥	4
● Barbera d'Alba Donatella '05	♀♀	5
● Barbera d'Alba Donatella '04	♀♀	5
● Barolo Baudana '03	♀♀	7
● Barolo Baudana '01	♀♀	7
● Barolo Baudana '00	♀♀	7
● Barolo Cerretta Piani '03	♀♀	7
● Barolo Cerretta Piani '01	♀♀	7
● Barolo Cerretta Piani '00	♀♀	7
● Barolo Cerretta Piani '99	♀♀	7

○ Alta Langa Brut Bianc 'd Bianc Giulio Cocchi '04	♥♥	6
○ Alta Langa Brut Toto Corde Giulio Cocchi '05	♥♥	5
⊙ Alta Langa Brut Rösa Giulio Cocchi '04	♥♥	6
● Barbera d'Asti Libera '06	♥♥	4*
● Barbera d'Asti Sup. Nizza Piano Alto '03	♥♥	6
● Barbera d'Asti Sup. Stradivario '03	♥♥	7
● M.to Rosso Vigneti di Cadodo '07	♥	4
○ Moscato d'Asti Bass Tuba '07	♥	4
○ Piemonte Chardonnay Thou Bianc '07	♥	4
● Barbera d'Asti Sup. Stradivario '01	♀♀	7
● Barbera d'Asti Sup. Nizza Piano Alto '01	♀♀	6

Bel Colle

FRAZ. CASTAGNI, 56
12060 VERDUNO [CN]
TEL. 0172470196
www.belcolle.it

Bera

VIA CASTELLERO, 12
12050 NEVIGLIE [CN]
TEL. 0173630194
www.bera.it

ANNUAL PRODUCTION	150,000 bottles
HECTARES UNDER VINE	5
VITICULTURE METHOD	Conventional

ANNUAL PRODUCTION	120,000 bottles
HECTARES UNDER VINE	20
VITICULTURE METHOD	Conventional

Bel Colle is a winery with excellent potential. Over the years, it has released reliable wines with clean fragrances and an impeccably clear style. Credit must go mainly to the in-house oenologist, Paolo Torchio, who knows all about selecting grapes. The range includes some of the most emblematic wines from the left bank of the Tanaro. We enjoyed the subtle, fruity Roero Arneis, which takes its leave with attractive savouriness. But the big hitters are hefty reds like Barolo and Barbaresco. Boscato proffers raspberry and blueberry fruit over dried flowers and quinine before the energy of the juicy palate takes you through to an appealingly long finale. Monvigliero, from the celebrated Verduno vineyard, has more elegance while lacking the power and pulpy flesh of the previous wine. Despite a less than memorable vintage, the Roncaglie reveals depth on nose and palate. One wine that went through to the finals was Barbera d'Alba Le Masche, which has ripe blackcurrant and strawberry fruit introducing a tempting and very appealing, acidity-lifted palate. The Verduno Pelaverga is valid, the Favorita leads with fruit and the Dolcetto is youthfully alcoholic.

It hasn't taken Bera long to assert itself as one of the best-known names in Moscato and Asti. Walter is one of the most competent interpreters of the popular native Piedmont vine, which he also releases in a sparkling version, something not many producers attempt. But man does not live by sweet wines alone and this year Walter also gave us an intriguing range of reds, like the Barbaresco 2004 with its ripe red fruit and pepper to cinnamon sweet spices. Extract on the palate is soft, juicy and restrained. Walter's signature wine is Moscato d'Asti Su Reimond, a selection from a one and a half hectare vineyard with 40-year-old vines. Fragrances range from citronella to nectarine and the palate has plenty of thrust, leading to a long, sweet finish. The Asti Spumante nicely offsets its aromatic sensations and mousse, which is never excessive. Croissants and crusty bread are the themes of the invitingly upfront Alta Langa Brut 2005. Two effortless Glasses went to the cellar's reds, Barbera La Lena and the barbera, nebbiolo and merlot Langhe Sassisto, whereas the Chardonnay was not quite up to its usual standard. The Dolcetto is nice.

● Barolo Boscato '04	♟♟	6*
● Barbera d'Alba Le Masche '06	♟♟	4*
● Barbaresco Roncaglie '05	♟♟	6
● Barolo Monvigliero '04	♟♟	6
○ Roero Arneis '07	♟♟	4
○ Langhe Favorita '07	♟	4
● Dolcetto d'Alba '07	♟	4
● Verduno Pelaverga '07	♟	4
● Barolo Monvigliero '03	♟♟	6
● Barolo Monvigliero '01	♟♟	6
● Barolo Monvigliero '00	♟♟	6
● Barolo Monvigliero '99	♟♟	6
● Barolo Monvigliero '98	♟♟	6
● Barolo Monvigliero '97	♟♟	6

○ Asti '07	♟♟	4*
● Barbaresco '04	♟♟	5*
● Barbera d'Alba Sup. La Lena '05	♟♟	4*
● Langhe Sassisto '05	♟♟	5
○ Moscato d'Asti '07	♟♟	4*
○ Moscato d'Asti Su Reimond '07	♟♟	4*
○ Alta Langa M. Cl. Brut Bera '05	♟	5
○ Langhe Chardonnay '07	♟	3
● Dolcetto d'Alba '07	♟	4
● Barbera d'Alba Sup. La Lena '04	♟♟	4
● Barbera d'Alba Sup. La Lena '03	♟♟	4
● Barbera d'Alba Sup. La Lena '01	♟♟	4
● Barbaresco '01	♟♟	5
● Barbaresco '00	♟♟	6

Cinzia Bergaglio

VIA GAVI, 29
15060 TASSAROLO [AL]
TEL. 0143342203
la.fornace@virgilio.it

ANNUAL PRODUCTION 20,000 bottles
HECTARES UNDER VINE 7.2
VITICULTURE METHOD Conventional

Cinzia has been running the family winery for some years now, helped by her parents and husband Massimo, a team that manages to obtain particularly high-quality cortese grapes from its vineyards and, with input from consultant Agostino Berruti, turn them into excellent Gavi wines. It is just reward for the courageous decision some time ago to vinify the grapes, which had previously been sold, on the estate and distribute the wine directly. There are two labels from vineyards at Rovereto and Tassarolo. Gavi Grifone delle Roveri 2007 went through to our finals thanks mainly to its outstanding balance in the mouth, where acidity is well reined in by the power of the body. On the nose, it gives tropical fruits and lingering minerality. The Fornaci label did equally well. The differences in the wines come from the location of the vineyards, at a spot on the clayey soil of Tassarolo where a brick factory once stood. Its deep straw yellow and broad fruit and flower aromas are followed by attractively intense flavour, where fresh acidity perks up the very drinkable palate.

O Gavi del Comune di Gavi Grifone delle Roveri '07	🍷🍷 3*
O Gavi del Comune di Tassarolo Fornaci '07	🍷🍷 2*
O Gavi del Comune di Gavi Grifone delle Roveri '06	♀♀ 3
O Gavi del Comune di Gavi Grifone delle Roveri '05	♀♀ 3
O Gavi del Comune di Tassarolo Fornaci '06	♀♀ 2

Nicola Bergaglio

FRAZ. ROVERETO
LOC. PEDAGGERI, 59
15066 GAVI [AL]
TEL. 0143682195

ANNUAL PRODUCTION 120,000 bottles
HECTARES UNDER VINE 15
VITICULTURE METHOD Conventional

This is one of the wineries that has been included in the Guide since the earliest editions and over the intervening years it has kept its Gavis at the top of the designation. Gianluigi and his family, especially his son Diego, manage to give their wines personality without altering the sensory profile of the cortese grapes grown on the 15 hectares of estate-owned vineyards. In the case of the 2007 vintage, we very much liked the both labels released, the classic Gavi and the cellar's Minaia selection: both went through to the Three Glass finals. We'll start with Minaia. The vines stand in an excellent location that has been productive for several decades. What is outstanding about it is the balance of acidity and structure on the palate but the attractively intense, lingering nose is also very good, giving varietal florality that shades into the balsamic sensations characteristic of this Gavi. Excellence is a word we are also inclined to use about the base Gavi. The straw yellow is flecked with green, the aromas are distinct and wide-ranging and the fresh-tasting palate signs off with a varietal twist of bitterness.

O Gavi del Comune di Gavi '07	🍷🍷 3*
O Gavi del Comune di Gavi Minaia '07	🍷🍷 4*
O Gavi del Comune di Gavi Minaia '06	♀♀ 4
O Gavi del Comune di Gavi Minaia '05	♀♀ 4
O Gavi del Comune di Gavi Minaia '04	♀♀ 4
O Gavi del Comune di Gavi '06	♀♀ 3

Guido Berta

LOC. SALINE, 53
14050 SAN MARZANO OLIVETO [AT]
TEL. 0141856193
bgpm@inwind.it

ANNUAL PRODUCTION	30,000 bottles
HECTARES UNDER VINE	12
VITICULTURE METHOD	Natural

The most important news this year from Guido Berta has little to do with wine and more to do with the arrival of his new daughter, Alessia. The two standard-label versions of Barbera and Chardonnay were missing from the line-up as production was low in 2007 and the range was rationalized as a result. In other respects, Guido's winning team has not been changed and his father Giuseppe is still working with him. When we tasted the wines, we were impressed by Barbera Canto di Luna 2005, which underwent 18 months of ageing in once and twice-used small barrels. Its complex nose hints at pencil lead, quinine and Virginia tobacco before the palate lives up to expectations, revealing length and body on its way to a juicy finish. Guido released 6,000 bottles of its little sister, the Barbera Superiore, which matured for eight months in large wood, emerging approachably full-bodied and harmonious. The minerally, smoke-veined Chardonnay was a nice surprise for its striking elegance and overall harmony. The Moscato d'Asti is moreish.

Bertelli

VIA SAN CARLO
14055 COSTIGLIOLE D'ASTI [AT]
TEL. 0258314153

ANNUAL PRODUCTION	30,000 bottles
HECTARES UNDER VINE	7
VITICULTURE METHOD	Conventional

Some people might ask why we give space in the Guide to such a small winery that makes so many wines in tiny quantities and fails to offer its clientele regular selections. The answer is actually very simple and can be summed up in the word "genius". There is genius in this cellar. There is the genius of Alberto Bertelli, who shuns fashion and has always let his vineyards do their own talking. There is also the genius of Elisabetta, who had the courage to let Alberto make wine his way while increasing the number of bottles available, and with them Alberto's reputation. Finally, there is the genius of the terroir, without which there can be no great wine. This time, Bertelli presented us with three characterful whites: San Marsan Bianco 2004, Plissé Traminer 2004 and Piemonte Chardonnay Giarone 2006. The 2006 version of Giarone brings to mind the great vintages of the past. Its luscious aromas of hazelnut and gunflint accompany a wine that brings together texture and richness with taut freshness. Explosive aromas and opulence in the mouth are the keynotes of the Plissé while the San Marsan has complexity, power and a soft, generous finish.

● Barbera d'Asti Sup. Canto di Luna '05	� 4*
● Barbera d'Asti Sup. '05	� 4
○ Piemonte Chardonnay '07	� 4*
○ Moscato d'Asti '07	� 4
● Barbera d'Asti Sup. Canto di Luna '04	� 4
● Barbera d'Asti Le Rondini '05	� 3
● Barbera d'Asti Sup. Canto di Luna '03	� 4

○ Piemonte Chardonnay Giarone '06	� 6
○ Plissé Traminer '04	� 6
○ San Marsan Bianco '04	� 6
● Barbera d'Asti S. Antonio Vieilles Vignes '01	� 6
● Barbera d'Asti S. Antonio Vieilles Vignes '00	� 6
○ Piemonte Chardonnay Giarone '04	� 6
● Barbera d'Asti Giarone '01	� 6
● Barbera d'Asti Montetusa '01	� 6
● Barbera d'Asti S. Antonio Vieilles Vignes '99	� 6
● M.to Rosso Mon Mayor '01	� 6

Eugenio Bocchino

FRAZ. SANTA MARIA
LOC. SERRA, 2
12064 LA MORRA [CN]
TEL. 0173364226
laperucca@libero.it

ANNUAL PRODUCTION	20,000 bottles
HECTARES UNDER VINE	6
VITICULTURE METHOD	Conventional

It's only just over a decade since they started making wine but Eugenio and Cinzia Bocchino turn out excellent wines nicely in line with tradition while incorporating new technology functionally into the production process. We'll start with the 2,000 bottles of Barolo Lu, aged for 24 months in half new small barrels. The broad, well-defined nose precedes a long-lingering palate with a remarkable harmonious, elegant finish. Barolo La Serra 2004 is more austere, giving tobacco and spices, a powerful, extract-rich palate and a satisfyingly well-balanced finale. The 2,000 bottles of Nebbiolo d'Alba La Perucca are very classy. The cellar's most emblematic wine spent 24 months in new and used small barrels, which lent it spicy, velvety aromas, a pervasive mouthfeel and soft, harmonious finish. There are just 1,200 bottles of the excellent riesling-based Langhe Sas 2006. On its first release, it shows aromatics with varietal minerality and attractive acidity that will conserve its freshness for a long time to come.

Alfiero Boffa

VIA LEISO, 50
14050 SAN MARZANO OLIVETO [AT]
TEL. 0141856115
www.alfieroboffa.com

ANNUAL PRODUCTION	100,000 bottles
HECTARES UNDER VINE	25
VITICULTURE METHOD	Conventional

In just a few years, Alfiero Boffa has made his name as one of the finest interpreters of barbera. For some time, he has been working alongside his sons Rossano and Simone, who help out in cellar and vineyard. There list of labels is long and Alfiero's favourite Asti variety features prominently. Thanks to the more interesting growing year, the 2006 versions are more complex. Muntrivé aged in 700-litre barrels for 12 months and then the same again in bottle. Its distinctly inviting ruby red ushers in a nose of ripe cherry and currant-like fruit laced with cocoa and coffee. Powerful and juicy on the palate, it signs off with impressive balance. Vigna La Riva also ages in large wood, where it spends six months more than Muntrivé. The unusual thing about this wine is that the grapes come from a vineyard planted in 1930, which seems to have brought out the best in the modest 2005 growing year. The rich colour, the perfect balance of fruit and spice and the gutsy, juicy palate are all excellent. La More spent 12 months in 700-litre oak casks, emerging deliciously drinkable. Collina della Vedova is savoury and Cua Longa is as good as ever.

● Barolo Lu '04	ŸŸ 7
● Nebbiolo d'Alba La Perucca '04	ŸŸ 6
● Barolo La Serra '04	ŸŸ 7
O Langhe Sas '06	ŸŸ 4
● Barolo '01	ŸŸ 7
● Barolo '00	ŸŸ 7
● Barolo La Serra '03	ŸŸ 7
● Barolo Lu '03	ŸŸ 7
● Langhe Rosso Suo di Giacomo '04	ŸŸ 6
● Langhe Rosso Suo di Giacomo '03	ŸŸ 6
● Langhe Rosso Suo di Giacomo '02	ŸŸ 5
● Langhe Rosso Suo di Giacomo '00	ŸŸ 6

● Barbera d'Asti Sup. Nizza V. La Riva '05	ŸŸ 5
● Barbera d'Asti Sup. V. Cua Longa '06	ŸŸ 5
● Barbera d'Asti Sup. More '06	ŸŸ 5
● Barbera d'Asti Sup. V. Muntrivé '06	ŸŸ 5
● Barbera d'Asti Sup. Collina della Vedova '05	Ÿ 5
● Barbera d'Asti Sup. Collina della Vedova '04	ŸŸ 5
● Barbera d'Asti Sup. Collina della Vedova '03	ŸŸ 5
● Barbera d'Asti Sup. V. Cua Longa '05	ŸŸ 5
● Barbera d'Asti Sup. V. Muntrivé '05	ŸŸ 5
● Barbera d'Asti Sup. V. Muntrivé '04	ŸŸ 5

Enzo Boglietti

VIA ROMA, 37
12064 LA MORRA [CN]
TEL. 017350330
www.langhe.net/enzoboglietti

ANNUAL PRODUCTION	100,000 bottles
HECTARES UNDER VINE	22
VITICULTURE METHOD	Conventional

Don't be fooled by Enzo Boglietti's distracted air. He and his brother Gianni take scrupulous care over their wines and the winemaking style is generous, sincere and closely bound up with the territory. We liked three in particular. The opulent Barolo Case Nere 2004 gives penetrating black berry fruit and subtle spice, a thrilling flavour and a sublime finale that won it Three Glasses. Langhe Buio 2006, an intriguing blend of nebbiolo and barbera, has elegant morello cherry and tobacco theming a long, flavoursome palate. Barbera Vigna dei Romani 2005 caresses the nose with quinine and briary fruit then unveils a full-bodied palate that skips from varietal notes to tertiary hints and a sumptuous finish. The other Barolos are also good. Brunate 2004 stands out for its legendary personality, Arione from Serralunga has well-defined appeal and a mouthfilling texture and the subtly unfolding Fossati has a drier character. Barbera Roscaleto 2006 earned a special mention for its dark, intense plum aromas and complexity, pulp and persistence. All the other wines are interesting, the Langhe and Dolcetto bottles showing elegant and generously expressive.

Bondi

S.DA CAPPELLETTE, 73
15076 OVADA [AL]
TEL. 0143821369
www.bondivini.it

ANNUAL PRODUCTION	20,000 bottles
HECTARES UNDER VINE	7
VITICULTURE METHOD	Conventional

For many years, the Bondi family has run the Locanda dell'Olmo at Bosco Marengo and a few years ago, they decided to purchase Cascina Banaia, a farm at Cappellette in the hills of Ovada. This is wonderful wine country and dolcetto in particular thrives here. It took a lot of hard work, much of it carried out by Domenico with the help of the younger generation of Bondis, but the operation is now up and running. With each passing year, the cellar confirms its ability to turn out premium-quality wines. The roughly seven hectares under vine are well exposed and the vines are the native dolcetto and barbera varieties. With technical input from Giovanni Bailo, the Bondis were able to present us with some excellent wines. We recommend the well-structured Dolcetto di Ovada Nani, a very easy-drinking wine with impressive length on the palate. The aromas are discreetly intense and it impressed our panel enough to go through to the finals. The intense, berry fruit-led Dolcetto Du'ien did well and we also found two good Barberas on the Bondi list. Banaiotta has a convincing, balanced palate and the slightly edgy Ruvrin 2005 needs more cellar time.

● Barolo Case Nere '04	▼▼▼	8
● Barolo Brunate '04	▼▼	8
● Barbera d'Alba V. dei Romani '05	▼▼	7
● Langhe Rosso Buio '06	▼▼	6
● Barbera d'Alba Roscaleto '06	▼▼	5
● Barolo Arione '04	▼▼	8
● Barolo Fossati '04	▼▼	8
● Dolcetto d'Alba Tigli Neri '07	▼▼	4
● Langhe Cabernet V. Talpone '05	▼▼	6
● Langhe Merlot V. Talpone '05	▼▼	6
● Langhe Nebbiolo '07	▼▼	5
● Barbera d'Alba '07	▼	4
● Dolcetto d'Alba '07	▼	4
● Barolo Brunate '97	▽▽▽	8
● Barolo Brunate '01	▽▽▽	8
● Barolo Fossati '96	▽▽▽	7
● Barolo Case Nere '99	▽▽▽	8

● Dolcetto di Ovada Nani '06	▼▼	3*
● Barbera del M.to Banaiotta '06	▼▼	3*
● Dolcetto di Ovada Sup. Du'ien '06	▼▼	4
● Barbera del M.to Ruvrin '05	▼	4
● Dolcetto di Ovada Sup. Du'ien '05	▽▽	4
● Barbera del M.to Banaiotta '05	▽▽	5
● Barbera del M.to Ruvrin '04	▽▽	5

Borgo Maragliano

REG. SAN SEBASTIANO, 2
14050 LOAZZOLO [AT]
TEL. 014487132
www.borgomaragliano.com

ANNUAL PRODUCTION	210,000 bottles
HECTARES UNDER VINE	21
VITICULTURE METHOD	Conventional

This year, we were struck by Carlo Galliano's metronome-steady quality. The cellar has come to terms with the vineyard conditions at Loazzolo, from 350 to 450 metres above sea level, where the special site climate lends the wines freshness and finesse. There is an exciting newcomer, Francesco Galliano Brut 2005, which spends 18 months on the lees, is a creamy, fresh-tasting Blanc de Blancs with a wealth of white-fleshed fruit sensations. The poised, full, pinot nero-only Giovanni Galliano Brut Rosé 2005 spends 20 months on the lees. The complexity and power of the Giuseppe Galliano Brut 2004, from 80 per cent steel-fermented pinot nero and 20 per cent oak-fermented chardonnay with 36 months on the lees, took it very close to Three Glasses. The other wine vying for top honours was the elegant Moscato d'Asti La Caliera, closely followed by its sweeter but equally refined partner, El Calié. The 2005 version of the cellar's flag-carrier Loazzolo is richer than usual but lacks the harmony of the finest vintages. Simpler, but attractive and affordable, are the Chardonnay Crevoglio and the Charmat method sparkler, Giuseppe Galliano Chardonnay Brut.

Giacomo Borgogno & Figli

VIA GIOBERTI, 1
12060 BAROLO [CN]
TEL. 017356108
www.borgogno-wine.com

ANNUAL PRODUCTION	130,000 bottles
HECTARES UNDER VINE	15
VITICULTURE METHOD	Conventional

Borgogno is one of Barolo's historic wineries so when it changed hands, the move was unlikely to go unobserved. On 1 January 2008, control passed to Oscar Farinetti, a noted food and wine entrepreneur. Few changes are planned as day-to-day decisions will still be taken by Cesare and Giorgio Boschis, ensuring continuity in production. The house style has always been classic. Wines are moderately structured but austere and very much built for the long haul. As you might expect, the Barolos presented were those from the less than wonderful 2003 vintage. As ever, Borgogno releases wines with maturations that exceed the production protocol minimums. The standard Barolo shows the limits of the growing year, presenting decently fresh but with roughish extract and slightly halting progression on the palate. Classico has greater depth, nicely handled warmth, taut, firm structure and a rather unbending finish. Liste is nicely gauged, showing warm with balsam nuances and florality as well as good breadth. The restrained entry on the faintly clenched palate reveals vibrant extract and promises well for the future. All the other wines are well up to snuff.

O Giuseppe Galliano Brut M. Cl. '04	♥♥	5
O Moscato d'Asti La Caliera '07	♥♥	3*
⊙ Giovanni Galliano Brut Rosé M. Cl. '05	♥♥	5
O El Calié '07	♥♥	3*
O Francesco Galliano Blanc de Blancs M. Cl. '05	♥♥	5
O Loazzolo Borgo Maragliano V. T. '05	♥♥	6
O Piemonte Chardonnay Crevoglio '07	♥♥	3*
O Giuseppe Galliano Chardonnay Brut	♥	3
O Loazzolo Borgo Maragliano V. T. '04	♈♈	6
O Loazzolo Borgo Maragliano V. T. '01	♈♈	6
O Loazzolo Borgo Maragliano V. T. '03	♈♈	6

● Barolo Cl. '03	♥♥	8
● Barolo Liste '03	♥♥	8
● Barbera d'Alba '07	♥♥	4*
● Barolo '03	♥♥	8
● Dolcetto d'Alba '07	♥♥	4*
● Barolo Cl. '98	♈♈♈	8
● Barolo Cl. '99	♈♈	8
● Barolo Cl. '01	♈♈	8
● Barolo Cl. '00	♈♈	8
● Barolo Liste '01	♈♈	8
● Barolo Liste '00	♈♈	8
● Barolo '98	♈♈	8
● Barolo '99	♈♈	7
● Barolo '01	♈♈	8

Boroli

LOC. MADONNA DI COMO, 34
12051 ALBA [CN]
TEL. 0173365477
www.boroli.it

ANNUAL PRODUCTION	180,000 bottles
HECTARES UNDER VINE	31
VITICULTURE METHOD	Conventional

Wines from this territory-focused cellar are always impressive. The Boroli family is committed to a project that includes an attractive hotel and restaurant. In Enzo Alluvione, they have also found a seriously good oenologist who can cope with challenging growing years and turn plans into products. This year, the Barolo Villero Riserva 2000 has a stunningly rich, complex nose of delicate spice, plums and quince followed by velvety extract and a long, pervasive finish whose harmony suggest this wine will age virtually forever. The Barolo Villero 2004 impresses with its depth and character. Although still youthful and boisterous, it is already aristocratically generous in its development. There is entrancing structure and balance in the Barolo Cerequio 2004, where terroir-related notes emerge with attractive complexity. Roundness and appeal are the strong suits of the elegantly fluid Barolo 2004. The rest of the range is as good as you would expect and there are two stand-outs: the wonderfully characterful Barbera Fagiani 2005; and the Langhe Rosso Anna 2006, a muscular, dynamic wine with a well-defined tannic weave.

Francesco Boschis

FRAZ. SAN MARTINO DI PIANEZZO, 57
12063 DOGLIANI [CN]
TEL. 017370574
www.marcdegrazia.com

ANNUAL PRODUCTION	40,000 bottles
HECTARES UNDER VINE	11
VITICULTURE METHOD	Conventional

The Boschis cellar is just outside Dogliani, and as you can see from the table below, Dolcetto di Dogliani is the cellar's workhorse, although other varieties are also on the traditional-style list. There is a very varietal Grignolino, which is spicy, fruity and tannic. There's a Freisa with a flower-laced spectrum of aromatics that offers good weight and thrust on the palate. Also present is a sauvignon-based white with summer flowers and varietal minerality ushering in a long, well-balanced palate. But as we said, Dolcetto is the star. Pianezzo is a very successful classic standard-label wine, putting the accent on headily alcoholic aromas and attractive drinkability. The two 2006 Doglianis raise the stakes, having spent an extra year in the cellar to comply with the DOCG production protocol. Vigna dei Prey is excellent, opening on earthiness and then spice and summer flowers before the assertive palate gives savouriness, length and balance. Sorì San Martino has even wider-ranging aromatics, with forest fruits and jam coming through. On the palate, the extract is soft and mouthfilling and the finish is harmonious.

● Barolo Villero '04	❦❦	8
● Barolo Villero Ris. '00	❦❦	8
● Barolo Cerequio '04	❦❦	8
● Barbera d'Alba Sup. Fagiani '05	❦❦	6
● Barolo '04	❦❦	7
● Dolcetto d'Alba Madonna di Como '07	❦❦	4*
● Langhe Rosso Anna '06	❦❦	4*
O Moscato d'Asti Aureum '07	❦❦	4*
O Langhe Chardonnay Bel Amì '07	❦	4
● Nebbiolo d'Alba '06	❦	5
● Barolo Villero '01	❦❦❦	8
● Barolo Villero '00	❦❦❦	8
● Barolo Cerequio '03	❦❦	8
● Barolo Villero '03	❦❦	8
● Barolo Villero Ris. '99	❦❦	8

● Dogliani V. dei Prey '06	❦❦	4*
● Dogliani Sorì S. Martino '06	❦❦	4*
● Dolcetto di Dogliani Pianezzo '07	❦❦	4*
O Langhe Bianco V. dei Garisin '07	❦	4
● Langhe Freisa Bosco delle Cicale '07	❦	4
● Piemonte Grignolino '07	❦	4
● Barbera d'Alba Le Masserie '05	❦❦	5
● Dolcetto di Dogliani V. dei Prey '05	❦❦	4
● Dolcetto di Dogliani V. dei Prey '04	❦❦	4
● Dogliani V. del Ciliegio '05	❦❦	4
● Dolcetto di Dogliani Sup. V. del Ciliegio '04	❦❦	4

Luigi Boveri

LOC. MONTALE CELLI
VIA XX SETTEMBRE, 6
15050 COSTA VESCOVATO [AL]
TEL. 0131838165
www.boveriluigi.com

ANNUAL PRODUCTION	60,000 bottles
HECTARES UNDER VINE	15
VITICULTURE METHOD	Conventional

If you ever go to Montale Celli, combine the pleasure of your trip into the hills of Valle Ossona with a little business. Recently, several fine winemakers have emerged in this part of the Colli Tortonesi so it won't be hard to stock up on good wine. And the first to make his mark here, where soils vary considerably even on the same hill, was Luigi Boveri. Luigi's Barbera Vignalunga was one of the first from the zone to make a name for itself outside Piedmont. Sadly, the 2005 growing year wasn't up to the level of recent vintages but Luigi made no attempt to tweak the year's poorish fruit in the cellar. Still, his cask-conditioned Barbera is balanced and well-structured, giving vegetality before shifting to chocolate-like notes. Barbera Poggio delle Amarene 2006 is as good as ever. Aged in steel, it stands out for drinkability. The 2006 vintage favoured Timorasso Filari, one of Luigi's best bottles with impressive minerality leading into subtle sweet almonds and remarkable persistence. The croatina-based Sensazioni red did well on its first outing and both the Barbera Boccanera and the 2007 Cortese Vigna del Prete are good-value easy-drinkers.

O Colli Tortonesi Timorasso Filari di Timorasso '06		♀ 5
● Colli Tortonesi Barbera Poggio delle Amarene '06		♀♀ 6
● Colli Tortonesi Barbera Vignalunga '05		♀♀ 6
● Colli Tortonesi Barbera Boccanera '07		♀ 3*
● Colli Tortonesi Croatina Sensazioni '06		♀ 4
O Colli Tortonesi Cortese Vigna del Prete '07		♀ 3*
O Colli Tortonesi Bianco Filari di Timorasso '05		♀♀ 5
● Colli Tortonesi Barbera Vignalunga '04		♀♀ 6

Gianfranco Bovio

FRAZ. ANNUNZIATA
B.TA CIOTTO, 63
12064 LA MORRA [CN]
TEL. 017350667
www.boviogianfranco.com

ANNUAL PRODUCTION	55,000 bottles
HECTARES UNDER VINE	13
VITICULTURE METHOD	Conventional

Even without the Castiglione Falletto-sourced Barolo Bricco Parussi, which like all the cellar's other top wines was not produced in 2002, Gianfranco Bovio, Walter Porasso and consultant Beppe Caviola gave us a fine range. We start with Langhe Bianco La Villa 2007, a 50-50 blend of sauvignon and chardonnay vinified together without malolactic fermentation. The aromatics are very sauvignon-like and the fresh-tasting palate skips vibrantly through to a long, well-defined finale. The three 2004 Barolos scored well. Rocchettevino has subtly attractive florality with a dynamic, juicy palate. Barolo Arborina, matured for 20 months in small barrels, some new, has more character. Sweetness and spice pervade the nose before the assertive extract melds nicely with the fruit. Barolo Gattera, from vines an average of 70 years old, aged for 30 months in 15 to 20-hectolitre barrels and has a spectacular fruit-lifted nose of rose and violet-led florality. The austere palate has sweet but beefy tannins, good flesh and a lingering finish. Barbera Regiaveja is still maturing and skips a year. The fruity Dolcetto and standard Barbera are both very well crafted.

● Barolo V. Arborina '04		♀♀ 7
● Barolo V. Gattera '04		♀♀ 7
● Barolo Rocchettevino '04		♀♀ 6
● Dolcetto d'Alba Dabbene '07		♀♀ 3*
O Langhe Bianco V. La Villa '07		♀♀ 3*
● Barbera d'Alba Il Ciotto '07		♀ 4
● Barolo Bricco Parussi Ris. '01		♀♀♀ 7
● Barolo V. Arborina '90		♀♀♀ 8
● Barolo Bricco Parussi Ris. '00		♀♀ 7
● Barolo Rocchettevino '00		♀♀ 7
● Barolo V. Arborina '03		♀♀ 7
● Barolo V. Arborina '01		♀♀ 7
● Barolo V. Arborina '00		♀♀ 7
● Barolo V. Gattera '03		♀♀ 7
● Barolo V. Gattera '01		♀♀ 7
● Barolo V. Gattera '00		♀♀ 7

Braida

S.DA PROVINCIALE, 9
14030 ROCCHETTA TANARO [AT]
TEL. 0141644113
www.braida.it

Brema

VIA POZZOMAGNA, 9
14045 INCISA SCAPACCINO [AT]
TEL. 014174019
vinibrema@inwind.it

ANNUAL PRODUCTION	520,000 bottles
HECTARES UNDER VINE	53
VITICULTURE METHOD	Natural

ANNUAL PRODUCTION	140,000 bottles
HECTARES UNDER VINE	20
VITICULTURE METHOD	Conventional

Barbera, and Barbera d'Asti in particular, is the Bologna family's business. In charge now after the sad death of Giacomo is his wife Anna, with children Beppe and Raffaella, and Austrian-born son-in-law Norbert. After missing a year, Ai Suma is back and all three Barbera selections are great. Ai Suma, from slightly raisined grapes, has nice plum, coffee, sweet spice and rain-soaked earth. Substance and a tight-knit tannic weave grace the long, velvety palate. Bricco dell'Uccellone is in one of its best-ever versions, showing great finesse and elegance on the well-structured, juicy, complex palate. But this year, it was Barbera Bricco della Bigotta that stood out for its rich oak-derived aromas of sweet spices and vanilla, ending with coffee-veined toastiness. The acidity-braced palate is stunning and we gave it Three unanimous Glasses. Montebruna is another seriously good, fruity wine with depth and well-defined strawberries and raspberries. Finally, the three whites from the Serra dei Fiori estate owned by the Bolognas with Neive-based Giacosa Fratelli did well. The Riesling and Chardonnay are good and the other wines in the range are well crafted.

At Nizza Monferrato, Brema means Barbera d'Asti from Carlo and his children Ermanno and Alessandro. Barbera Superiore Nizza A Luigi Veronelli 2006 is superb. The dense lustrous colour introduces elegant, intense ripe black fruits and sweet spices followed by a hefty, rich-textured palate and a long, savoury finish. The bottle, dedicated to a great wine journalist, justly won Three Glasses. Close behind is another 2006, the more austere Bricco della Volpettona, with fresh aromas of red berry fruit, varietal quinine and earthiness, acidity slightly hardening a palate has still to absorb its oak. Monferrato Rosso Il Fulvo 2006, a Bordeaux-type blend, is very good. The dark garnet precedes redcurrant and bell peppers with estery nuances and a savoury palate. Barbera Ai Cruss 2007 is good, a fruity, fresh-tasting wine with hints of earth and minerality that flow over the palate. The best reds are two Dolcettos, Montera 2007 and Vigna Impagnato 2006, and the flowery, extract-rich Grignolino Le Roche. We preferred the stylish Moscato with honey and yellow-fleshed fruits, creamy texture and good balance to the straightforward strawberry-themed Brachetto.

● Barbera d'Asti Bricco della Bigotta '06	♈♈♈	7
● Barbera d'Asti Ai Suma '06	♈♈	8
● Barbera d'Asti Bricco dell'Uccellone '06	♈♈	7
● Barbera d'Asti Montebruna '06	♈♈	4*
● Grignolino d'Asti '07	♈♈	4*
● M.to Rosso Il Bacialé '06	♈♈	4*
○ Langhe Bianco Riesling Re di Fiori '07	♈♈	5
○ Langhe Chardonnay Asso di Fiori '06	♈♈	5
○ Langhe Bianco Il Fiore '07	♈	4
● Brachetto d'Acqui '07	♈	4
● Barbera d'Asti Bricco dell'Uccellone '05	♈♈♈	7
● Barbera d'Asti Bricco dell'Uccellone '01	♈♈♈	7

● Barbera d'Asti Sup. Nizza A Luigi Veronelli '06	♈♈♈	5
● Barbera d'Asti Sup. Bricco della Volpettona '06	♈♈	5
● Barbera d'Asti Ai Cruss '07	♈♈	4*
● M.to Rosso Il Fulvo '06	♈♈	5
○ Piemonte Moscato Mariasole '07	♈♈	4*
● Dolcetto d'Asti Montera '07	♈	4
● Dolcetto d'Asti V. Impagnato '06	♈	4
● Grignolino d'Asti Le Roche '07	♈	3
● Piemonte Brachetto Carlotta '07	♈	4
● Barbera d'Asti Sup. Bricco della Volpettona '03	♈♈	6
● Barbera d'Asti Sup. Bricco della Volpettona '01	♈♈	6
● Barbera d'Asti Sup. Bricco della Volpettona '05	♈♈	6
● Barbera d'Asti Sup. Bricconizza '05	♈♈	6

Giacomo Brezza & Figli

VIA LOMONDO, 4
12060 BAROLO [CN]
TEL. 0173560921
www.brezza.it

Bric Cenciurio

VIA ROMA, 24
12060 BAROLO [CN]
TEL. 017356317
www.briccenciurio.com

ANNUAL PRODUCTION	80,000 bottles
HECTARES UNDER VINE	16.5
VITICULTURE METHOD	Conventional

The Brezza family has been quietly running a major winemaking, restaurant and hotel complex in the town of Barolo for several generations. Vinfication, under Enzo Brezza, is very traditional with long maceration, large wood for unhurried ageing, a non-invasive winemaking policy and total respect for the grapes. There is space for new developments but only if they enhance the territorial character of the wines. The ones we tasted are all whistle-clean and full of personality, from the upfront 2007 Dolcetto San Lorenzo to the two Barberas. Santa Rosalia 2007 is more immediate and enjoyable, Cannubi Muscatel 2006 is deep, savoury and meaty while the fragrant, coherent Nebbiolo Santa Rosalia 2006 is a fine introduction to the 2004 Barolos, of which there are only two, Sarmassa and Bricco Sarmassa. Sarmassa is a sumptuous Three Glass winner with a ripe, earthy flavour and robust extract nicely offset by acid backbone. Don't be in a hurry to uncork this massive wine. Its partner has broader, more approachably nuanced aromatics where flowers and spices come through. A tad slimmer, it has elegance, variety and lashings of charm.

ANNUAL PRODUCTION	35,000 bottles
HECTARES UNDER VINE	12
VITICULTURE METHOD	Conventional

The Pittatore and Sacchetto families own 12 hectares at Barolo and Castellinaldo. We'll start with Barolo Costa di Rose 2004, from 40-year-old vines. Its intense red is flecked with garnet, the aromatics embrace red fruits and spices and the pulpy palate flaunts silky tannins lifted by intriguing cocoa powder and liquorice. Barbera Naunda 2006 is vibrantly intense, its cherry and spice leading to varietal acidity nicely offset by fruit on a very drinkable palate. It all adds up to a wine that will be at the top of its maturation curve in a few years' time. Sito dei Fossili Vendemmia Tardiva 2006 is intriguing. Barrique-aged, its vibrant copper-flecked yellow offers rich ripe fruit and vanilla aromatics and a sweet but not cloying palate that is kept in check by substantial acidity. Rosso di Caialupo is from cabernet sauvignon only. Beautifully made, it is an object lesson in the variety's sensory profile, giving understated vegetality, red berry fruits and soft tannins. Roero Arneis Sito dei Fossili is all fruit and flowers with a hint of vanilla. Finally, the standard-label Roero Arneis and the brachetto-based Birbét are deliciously drinkable.

● Barolo Sarmassa '04	♟♟♟ 7
● Barolo Bricco Sarmassa '04	♟♟ 8
● Barbera d'Alba Cannubi Muscatel '06	♟♟ 5
● Barbera d'Alba Santa Rosalia '07	♟♟ 4*
● Dolcetto d'Alba S. Lorenzo '07	♟♟ 4*
● Nebbiolo d'Alba Santa Rosalia '06	♟♟ 4
● Barolo Cannubi '96	♟♟♟ 7
● Barolo Cannubi '01	♟♟♟ 7
● Barolo Sarmassa '03	♟♟♟ 7
● Barolo Bricco Sarmassa '01	♟♟ 8
● Barolo Sarmassa '00	♟♟ 7
● Barolo Bricco Sarmassa '03	♟♟ 8
● Barolo Cannubi '99	♟♟ 7
● Barolo Sarmassa '01	♟♟ 7

● Barolo Costa di Rose '04	♟♟ 7
● Barbera d'Alba Sup. Naunda '06	♟♟ 5
● Langhe Rosso Rosso di Caialupo '05	♟♟ 5
○ Roero Arneis Sito dei Fossili '06	♟♟ 4*
○ Sito dei Fossili V. T. '06	♟♟ 6
● Birbét '07	♟ 4
○ Roero Arneis '07	♟ 4
● Barolo Costa di Rose '01	♟♟ 6
● Barolo Costa di Rose '03	♟♟ 6
● Barolo Costa di Rose Ris. '01	♟♟ 7
● Barbera d'Alba Sup. Naunda '05	♟♟ 5
● Barbera d'Alba Sup. Naunda '04	♟♟ 5
○ Sito dei Fossili V. T. '05	♟♟ 6

Bricco del Cucù

LOC. BRICCO, 10
12060 BASTIA MONDOVÌ [CN]
TEL. 017460153
www.briccocucu.com

ANNUAL PRODUCTION	50,000 bottles
HECTARES UNDER VINE	10
VITICULTURE METHOD	Conventional

Welcome to the other Langhe. Dario Sciolla will take you somewhere very different from the glossy Langhe of nearby Barolo. The passionate, competent Dario will take you through a harsher, darker landscape where vines alternate with hazelnut woods, the soil is less generous and results less predictable. Take your choice. Dario's wines are certainly distinctive. They may sometimes be less than perfect – this year, we were tasting them too early – but they have great personality. As we wait for the range to regain two Langhe Dolcettos and the Langhe Rosso Superbum, we enjoyed a Dolcetto di Dogliani Bricco San Bernardo that was on top form. A few more days in glass would have improved it but even so, it is earthy, spicy and fruity on the nose and pervades the palate with a rather attractive rustic hint. The base Dolcetto is slightly insubstantial, although its fruit and flower aromas are appealing. There was also a fine performance from the multi-faceted, mouthfilling, dolcetto and merlot Diavolisanti while the arneis and sauvignon white is pleasing.

● Dolcetto di Dogliani '07	❦❦	4*
● Dolcetto di Dogliani Sup. Bricco S. Bernardo '06	❦❦	4*
● Langhe Rosso Diavolisanti '05	❦❦	4*
○ Langhe Bianco '07	❦	3
● Dolcetto di Dogliani Sup. Bricco S. Bernardo '05	❦❦	4
● Dolcetto di Dogliani Sup. Bricco S. Bernardo '04	❦❦	4
● Langhe Rosso Diavolisanti '04	❦❦	4
● Langhe Rosso Superboum '05	❦❦	4

Bricco Maiolica

FRAZ. RICCA
VIA BOLANGINO, 7
12055 DIANO D'ALBA [CN]
TEL. 0173612049
www.briccomaiolica.it

ANNUAL PRODUCTION	90,000 bottles
HECTARES UNDER VINE	20
VITICULTURE METHOD	Conventional

Beppe Accomo is always talking about what the territory has to do if it wants to feature on the wine tourism map. Our hero has plenty of ideas so it is a pity that he doesn't always get the support he deserves from the local community, or even from some other winemakers. On the wine front, this year's range has recovered a prize that was missing last time, the celebrated Bricco Maiolica, which had been kept back for a year. We think this new interpretation of the variety is intriguing and irresistible. Its rich ruby red is flecked with purple in the glass and the nose gives plums, cinnamon, raspberries and liquorice before revealing the complexity and depth of the rich-textured palate. The 2005 Barbera Vigna Vigia is remarkably intense, juicy and well-balanced. The merlot-only Langhe Rosso Filius is back in the line-up, combining the variety's signature vegetality with red berry fruits and the warmth of these hills. Finally, the chardonnay and sauvignon Rolando is excellent and the pinot nero-only Lorié is valid, despite still showing a tad too much oak.

● Diano d'Alba Sup. Sörì Bricco Maiolica '06	❦❦	4*
● Barbera d'Alba Sup. V. Vigia '05	❦❦	5
○ Langhe Bianco Rolando '07	❦❦	4
● Dolcetto di Diano d'Alba '07	❦❦	4
● Langhe Rosso Filius '04	❦❦	6
● Nebbiolo d'Alba Cumot '05	❦❦	5
● Barbera d'Alba '06	❦	4
● Langhe Rosso Lorié '04	❦	6
● Barbera d'Alba V. Vigia '98	❦❦❦	5
● Barbera d'Alba V. Vigia '04	❦❦	5
● Barbera d'Alba V. Vigia '03	❦❦	5
● Barbera d'Alba V. Vigia '01	❦❦	5
● Diano d'Alba Sörì Bricco Maiolica '06	❦❦	4
● Diano d'Alba Sörì Bricco Maiolica '05	❦❦	4

Bricco Mondalino

REG. MONDALINO, 5
15049 VIGNALE MONFERRATO [AL]
TEL. 0142933204
www.briccomondalino.it

ANNUAL PRODUCTION	80,000 bottles
HECTARES UNDER VINE	13
VITICULTURE METHOD	Conventional

Bricco Mondalino is one of the best-known producers in the Alessandria part of Monferrato. Over the years, Mauro Gaudio has focused on recovering traditional-style Grignolino, trying various ways of vinifying this rough-edged, rebarbative grape. He offers two versions, both valid, but very different, expressions. The basic version adheres to tradition. It's fairly light in colour, quite tannic and redolent of spices, with plenty of black pepper. The 2007 vintage hews to this profile, showing pleasurable and tasty. In the early 1990s, Gaudio went down the path of riper fruit to see if he could reduce the acids and tannins and render the wine both smoother and better structured. Here too he was successful, coming out with a deep-coloured Bricco Mondalino giving fragrances of ripe fruit and appeal on the warmly alcoholic palate. The Bergantino selection is missing this year from the Barberas. Gaudio was also a Barbera pioneer, making the wine from riper grapes but without losing fruit or crucial acidity. Zerolegno performs well while lovely hints of roses adorn Malvasia di Casorzo. Cortese is a well-executed white.

★ Bricco Rocche - Bricco Asili

VIA MONFORTE, 63
12060 CASTIGLIONE FALLETTO [CN]
TEL. 0173282582
www.ceretto.com

ANNUAL PRODUCTION	50,000 bottles
HECTARES UNDER VINE	18.5
VITICULTURE METHOD	Conventional

The Ceretto brothers' winery has a striking view and the traditional values inside are equally impressive, even when assisted by modern technology. We tasted five wines this year, all fermented in steel then aged in new barriques. Soon, we will see fruit from a new plot recently acquired in the historic Cannubi vineyard at Barolo. Barbaresco Bricco Asili 2005 is immediately entrancing with its colour and rich nose. Steady, powerful development already shows good balance but fine acidity and extractive mass promise an impressive future. Equally fine is Barbaresco Bernardot 2005, with very graceful tannins and good length from first to last. The 2004 edition of Barolo Brunate is outstanding, opening with complexity on the nose and laying out lengthy, already enjoyable development. Noble structure and good length fuel a good performance by Barolo Bricco Rocche 2004, nor does the complex nose disappoint. Barolo Prapò 2004 shines even brighter, coming from an excellent harvest and the superb vineyard of Serralunga. All the virtues of nebbiolo are on glorious display here, in an alluring duet of power and elegance.

● Barbera del M.to Zerolegno '06	♥♥	4*
● Grignolino del M.to Casalese Bricco Mondalino '07	♥♥	4*
● Malvasia di Casorzo d'Asti Molignano '07	♥♥	4*
● Grignolino del M.to Casalese '07	♥	4
○ M.to Casalese Cortese '07	♥	3
● Barbera d'Asti Il Bergantino '01	♥♥	4
● Barbera d'Asti Il Bergantino '00	♥♥	4
● Barbera del M.to Sup. '05	♥♥	3
● Barbera del M.to Zerolegno '05	♥♥	4
● Barbera M.to Sel. Gaudium Magnum '00	♥♥	5
● Grignolino del M.to Casalese Bricco Mondalino '06	♥♥	4

● Barbaresco Bricco Asili '05	♥♥	8
● Barolo Prapò '04	♥♥	8
● Barbaresco Bernardot '05	♥♥	8
● Barolo Bricco Rocche '04	♥♥	8
● Barolo Brunate '04	♥♥	8
● Barbaresco Bricco Asili '99	♥♥♥	8
● Barbaresco Bricco Asili '97	♥♥♥	8
● Barbaresco Bricco Asili '96	♥♥♥	8
● Barbaresco Bricco Asili '89	♥♥♥	8
● Barbaresco Bricco Asili '88	♥♥♥	8
● Barbaresco Bricco Asili '86	♥♥♥	8
● Barbaresco Bricco Asili '85	♥♥♥	8
● Barolo Bricco Rocche '89	♥♥♥	8
● Barolo Brunate '90	♥♥♥	8
● Barbaresco Bernardot '04	♥♥	8
● Barolo Brunate '03	♥♥	8

Gian Piero Broglia

LOC. LOMELLINA, 22
TENUTA LA MEIRANA
15066 GAVI [AL]
TEL. 0143642998
www.broglia.eu

ANNUAL PRODUCTION	N.A.
HECTARES UNDER VINE	47
VITICULTURE METHOD	Conventional

Gian Piero Broglia's Cascina Meirana occupies a gorgeous position in the centre of 47 hectares of vineyards. His long-running success at producing outstanding Gavis continues with the 2007 vintage. The winery's top cru selection is Gavi Bruno Broglia, dedicated to Broglia's father. Sourced from cortese vineyards with very low yields, thanks to specific vineyard practices as well as to the vines' average age of 60 years. With the latest Gavi vintages, maturation is no longer in oak and the wines are released in the year following harvest. In consequence, we tasted two successive vintages this year. Bruno Broglia 2006 is excellent but the 2007 is magnificent. Showing a lovely, gold-flecked straw yellow, it lays out a wondrously lavish nose, with prominent floral and fruit notes, plus hints of balsam, then struts a very firm structure bolstered by emphatic acidity. Here is a great Gavi that brought Broglia our Three Glasses for the first time. La Meirana, the other Gavi, adds a bright shimmer to its straw yellow, then yields a nice florality on the way to a delicious palate, which shows zesty acidity and a harmonious finish with subtle bitter almond.

Brovia

VIA ALBA-BAROLO, 54
12060 CASTIGLIONE FALLETTO [CN]
TEL. 017362852
www.brovia.net

ANNUAL PRODUCTION	60,000 bottles
HECTARES UNDER VINE	18
VITICULTURE METHOD	Conventional

First of all, we welcome Livia, the latest addition to the Brovia family and obviously the best news of the year. We also report a development in the family's Rocche vineyard, which needed terracing. The vines will be in full production in the next few years. Brovia's wines are, as always, thrilling. The 2004 Barolos are each better than the last yet each is unique. Ca' Mia di Serralunga is powerful and almost domineering, with the classic earthiness that smoothes out the wine's lengthy finish. Unsurpassed elegance marks Rocche di Castiglione Falletto, whose glossy tannins seduce every bit as much as the delicate finesse of its dried rose petals. Still-incisive tannins and slaty minerality set off Garblèt Sué, as well as vibrant fruit, which continues juicy and smooth into the finish. The basic Barolo is superb, with vivacious, driving fruit. The 2006 grapes destined for Dolcetto Solatio were not deemed fine enough for this Brovia classic so they found a home in Ciabot del Re, where they are appealingly succulent. Dolcetto Vignavillej is youthful, minerally and alcohol rich, an icon of its category.

O Gavi del Comune di Gavi Bruno Broglia '07	♛♛♛ 5
O Gavi del Comune di Gavi Bruno Broglia '06	♛♛ 5
O Gavi del Comune di Gavi La Meirana '07	♛♛ 4*
● M.to Rosso Le Pernici '07	♛ 4
O Gavi del Comune di Gavi Bruno Broglia '05	♛♛ 5
O Gavi del Comune di Gavi Bruno Broglia '04	♛♛ 5
O Gavi del Comune di Gavi Bruno Broglia '03	♛♛ 5
O Gavi del Comune di Gavi Bruno Broglia '02	♛♛ 5
O Gavi del Comune di Gavi La Meirana '06	♛♛ 4

● Barolo Ca' Mia '04	♛♛ 8
● Barolo Garblèt Sué '04	♛♛ 7
● Barolo Rocche dei Brovia '04	♛♛ 8
● Barolo '04	♛♛ 6
● Dolcetto d'Alba Ciabot del Re '06	♛♛ 5
● Dolcetto d'Alba Vignavillej '06	♛♛ 4*
● Barolo Ca' Mia '96	♛♛♛ 8
● Barolo Ca' Mia '00	♛♛♛ 8
● Barolo Monprivato '90	♛♛♛ 8
● Barolo Ca' Mia '03	♛♛ 8
● Barolo Ca' Mia '01	♛♛ 8
● Barolo Rocche dei Brovia '03	♛♛ 8
● Barolo Rocche dei Brovia '01	♛♛ 8
● Barolo Villero '03	♛♛ 8
● Barolo Villero '01	♛♛ 8
● Barolo Villero '00	♛♛ 8

G. B. Burlotto

VIA VITTORIO EMANUELE, 28
12060 VERDUNO [CN]
TEL. 0172470122
www.burlotto.com

ANNUAL PRODUCTION	60,000 bottles
HECTARES UNDER VINE	12
VITICULTURE METHOD	Conventional

Marina Burlotto, assisted by her son Fabio Alessandria, manages this historic cellar with singular bravura and energy that every year yield a world-class line-up of wines. Some time ago, they also launched a terrific agriturismo, the Locanda dell'Orso Bevitore, managed with the same mixture of panache and professionalism. From this year's wines, the 2004 Barolos were top-notch, particularly Acclivi, which gives elegant spice refined by overtones of ripe fruit. Almost neck and neck is the noble Cannubi da Barolo, with savoury, juicy fruit and fine-grained tannins well tucked in. We were thrilled by the whites, both from sauvignon. Dives 2006 is given some cask ageing while Viridis 2007 shows more crisp and mineral-rich. Rosato Teres, made from barbera and nebbiolo, is both intriguing and very successful. Many in the Langhe are closely watching this style. Both the standard-label Barolo and Barbera d'Alba Aves 2006 gained Two Glasses, as did the barbera and nebbiolo Langhe Mores 2005. The spicy, deliciously inviting Pelaverga gets an honourable mention and the remaining wines are all worthy of the G.B. Burlotto name.

Piero Busso

VIA ALBESANI, 8
12052 NEIVE [CN]
TEL. 017367156
www.bussopiero.com

ANNUAL PRODUCTION	35,000 bottles
HECTARES UNDER VINE	8
VITICULTURE METHOD	Conventional

Piero and Lucia Busso, with their children Pier and Emanuela, run a fine operation. They didn't quite reach the top this year but the wines are first-rate. Barbaresco San Stunet Santo Stefanetto 2005 may not quite display the volume of recent editions but it has a hallmark rich, emphatic nose and long-driving progression, with tannins already well integrated. A whisker behind is Barbaresco Borgese 2005, an effortlessly elegant image of the DOCG. Its lengthy, crisp-edged finish is the perfect foil to a nicely evolved, floral nose. Similar in style but less complex is Mondino 2005, while Gallina 2004 shows saddle leather and forest floor tertiary impressions. Its tannins need time to mellow. The debut of Barbera d'Alba Santo Stefanetto 2005 will get your friends talking. It's unusual but appealing, full of roasted espresso, topsoil, and oak. With Barbera d'Alba Majano 2006, we return to orthodoxy while Langhe Nebbiolo 2006 and Dolcetto d'Alba Majano 2007 are very varietal in their purity of expression and appeal. Finally, we salute the chardonnay and sauvignon Langhe Bianco 2007, which has sage and blossoms then crisp, rich flavours.

● Barolo Acclivi '04	♥♥	7
○ Langhe Bianco Dives '06	♥♥	4*
○ Langhe Bianco Viridis '07	♥♥	4*
☉ Rosato Teres '07	♥♥	4*
● Barbera d'Alba Aves '06	♥♥	5
● Barolo '04	♥♥	7
● Barolo Vign. Cannubi '04	♥♥	7
● Langhe Mores '05	♥♥	5
● Langhe Nebbiolo '06	♥♥	4*
● Verduno Pelaverga '07	♥♥	4*
● Dolcetto d'Alba '07	♥	4
● Langhe Freisa '06	♥	4
● Barolo Vign. Cannubi '03	♥♥	7
● Barolo Vign. Cannubi '00	♥♥	7
● Barolo Vign. Cannubi '01	♥♥	7
● Barolo Vign. Monvigliero '03	♥♥	7

● Barbaresco Borgese '05	♥♥	7
● Barbaresco S. Stunet S. Stefanetto '05	♥♥	8
● Barbaresco Mondino '05	♥♥	6
● Barbaresco Gallina '04	♥♥	8
● Barbera d'Alba S. Stefanetto '05	♥♥	4*
● Barbera d'Alba V. Majano '06	♥♥	5
● Dolcetto d'Alba V. Majano '07	♥♥	4*
● Langhe Nebbiolo '06	♥♥	5
○ Langhe Bianco '07	♥♥	4*
● Barbaresco S. Stefanetto '04	♥♥♥	8
● Barbaresco S. Stefanetto '03	♥♥♥	8
● Barbaresco S. Stefanetto '01	♥♥♥	8
● Barbaresco S. Stefanetto '00	♥♥♥	8
● Barbaresco V. Borgese '97	♥♥♥	7
● Barbaresco Borgese '01	♥♥	7
● Barbaresco Gallina '01	♥♥	8

Ca' Bianca

REG. SPAGNA, 58
15010 ALICE BEL COLLE [AL]
TEL. 0144745420
www.cantinacabianca.it

ANNUAL PRODUCTION 550,000 bottles
HECTARES UNDER VINE 39
VITICULTURE METHOD Conventional

Ca' Bianca, Gruppo Italiano Vini's main operation in Piedmont, produces a wide variety of styles from the region's traditional grapes. Barbera, dolcetto and moscato vineyards surround the winery while the Gavi is sourced from the Novi area and the Barolo from La Morra. But the lion's share of the list is based on barbera. We tasted three. Ca' Bianca's main cru selection is Barbera d'Asti Chersì. The fruit comes from the Polsino property vineyards and the wine matures 12 months in barriques. Forthright aromas convey red berry fruit and subtle balsam before the palate displays fine structure, decent length and character. Overall, it's an outstanding, complex, well balanced wine. We were also impressed by the delicious Barbera Antè, where tasty acidity rounds off a lusty palate. Worthy of note is Teis, a standard-label Barbera with refreshing acidity and dense texture. The Barolo is soundly made, giving smooth tannins, but the nose is absolutely splendid, bursting with ripe morello, spice and tertiary notes of rich tanned leather. Dolcetto d'Acqui and Gavi easily merit One Glass.

● Barbera d'Asti Sup. Chersì '06	▼▼	5
● Barbera d'Asti Antè '06	▼▼	4*
● Barbera d'Asti Teis '07	▼▼	4*
● Barolo '04	▼▼	6
● Dolcetto d'Acqui '07	▼	4
○ Gavi '07	▼	4
● Barbera d'Asti Sup. Chersì '05	▽▽	5
● Barbera d'Asti Sup. Chersì '04	▽▽	5
● Barbera d'Asti Sup. Chersì '03	▽▽	5
● Barbera d'Asti Antè '05	▽▽	4
● Barbera d'Asti Antè '04	▽▽	4

Ca' d' Gal

FRAZ. VALDIVILLA
S.DA VECCHIA DI VALDIVILLA, 1
12058 SANTO STEFANO BELBO [CN]
TEL. 0141847103
www.ca-d-gal.com

ANNUAL PRODUCTION 60,000 bottles
HECTARES UNDER VINE 10
VITICULTURE METHOD Conventional

Who says that moscato doesn't hold up over the years? Practically everyone. With the exception, that is, of Alessandro Boido, who in both word and deed is waging a battle that seemed lost before it even began. Believing tenaciously in this ancient noble variety, he held back older vintages of his Vigna Vecchia, from 1998 on, and he is now organizing tastings that are, to say the least, eye-opening. Among the wines he gave us for this year's tastings, Alessandro inserted a 2000 and a 2001 Vigna Vecchia, vintages that we had reviewed in past editions, of course, and thus could not review again. Well, what we discovered were very alluring wines, releasing emphatic tertiary impressions of dried tea leaves and apricot. These bottlings were in no way tired nor in the least oxidized, which was quite a surprise. The 2007s are more than pleasant, above all Vigna Vecchia, which shows warm, rounded, succulent and finishes long. Lumine is more straightforward but refreshing and a pleasure. Asti is superlative, complex through and through. Dolcetto was not ready at this time, nor did we taste Pian del Gaje, which is undergoing a stylistic makeover.

○ Moscato d'Asti V. Vecchia '07	▼▼	5
○ Asti '07	▼▼	4*
○ Moscato d'Asti Lumine '07	▼▼	4*
○ Moscato d'Asti V. Vecchia '06	▽▽	5

Ca' del Baio

VIA FERRERE, 33
12050 TREISO [CN]
TEL. 0173638219
www.cadelbaio.com

ANNUAL PRODUCTION	100,000 bottles
HECTARES UNDER VINE	25
VITICULTURE METHOD	Conventional

Giulio Grasso, now joined by his eldest daughter Paola, has a fine operation. The cellar is efficient and up-to-date, the use of oak large and small masterful and the wines are flawless. All the bottles tasted were good and some were fabulous. This year's most big news is Barbaresco Pora 2004. Produced in 1,000 bottles and the same number of magnums, only a small amount was matured in new oak. The nose offers delicate fruit and hints of underbrush but the palate is loaded with power and succulent, herb-infused fruit. It closes long with enchanting complexity and persuaded our panel that it deserved Three Glasses. Of the Barbaresco 2005 cru selections, Valgrande is elegant and multi-faceted, with pungent, juicy fruit and good progression while Asili boasts rich aromatic fruit, smooth tannins on the already fine palate and an energy-laden finish. Intriguing notes of earth and spice characterize Marcarini, plus pulpy fruit and a savoury finale. Barbera Giardin 2005 is fruity and approachable, as is Nebbiolo Bric del Baio 2006. Dolcetto and Barbera Paolina are well executed, even more so Langhe Bianco, Langhe Chardonnay and Moscato, all 2007s.

La Ca' Növa

S.DA OVELLO, 4
12050 BARBARESCO [CN]
TEL. 0173635123
lacanova@libero.it

ANNUAL PRODUCTION	50,000 bottles
HECTARES UNDER VINE	13.50
VITICULTURE METHOD	Conventional

Marco and Ivano Rocca direct this well-known family operation. The vineyards, located in Barbaresco, are planted exclusively to red grapes, three quarters nebbiolo. Traditional macerations and ageing are used: dolcetto in steel, and barbera and nebbiolo in large Slavonian wood. The wines that emerge, never too concentrated, are refined and elegant. We liked this year's Barbarescos, perfect images of their vintage, whose key characteristic is immediate appeal. The standard label shows elegant and fruity, more nebbiolo-like than Barbarescoesque. Bric Mentina is exuberant and energy-laden, lavish on the nose and relaxed and open on the balanced, pleasurable palate. Montestefano, which the great Beppe Colla called "the most Baroloesque Barbaresco vineyard", is a grand cru for its exceptional exposure, soils and elevation. As usual, the wine is rough and undeveloped now but it always emerges down the road. Earth and spice are plentiful, and incisive tannins must still integrate into its superb structure, but the conclusion is all thoroughbred, long, lean and austere. We liked the fruity, dense Barbera Loreto 2006 and Dolcetto is very fine.

● Barbaresco Pora '04	♟♟♟	7
● Barbaresco Asili '05	♟♟	6
● Barbaresco Marcarini '05	♟♟	6
● Barbaresco Valgrande '05	♟♟	6
● Barbera d'Alba Giardin '05	♟♟	4*
● Barbera d'Alba Paolina '06	♟♟	4*
● Dolcetto d'Alba Lodoli '07	♟♟	4*
● Langhe Nebbiolo Bric del Baio '06	♟♟	4*
O Langhe Bianco '07	♟♟	4*
O Langhe Chardonnay Sermine '07	♟♟	5
O Moscato d'Asti '07	♟♟	4*
● Barbaresco Valgrande '99	♟♟♟	6
● Barbaresco Valgrande '04	♟♟♟	6
● Barbaresco Asili '04	♟♟	6
● Barbaresco Asili '03	♟♟	6
● Barbaresco Marcarini '03	♟♟	6

● Barbaresco Bric Mentina '05	♟♟	5*
● Barbaresco '05	♟♟	5*
● Barbaresco Montestefano '05	♟♟	5*
● Barbera d'Alba Loreto '06	♟♟	4*
● Dolcetto d'Alba '07	♟	3
● Barbaresco Bric Mentina '01	♟♟♟	6
● Barbaresco Bric Mentina '04	♟♟	5
● Barbaresco Bric Mentina '03	♟♟	6
● Barbaresco Montestefano '04	♟♟	5
● Barbaresco Montestefano '03	♟♟	6
● Barbaresco Montestefano '01	♟♟	6
● Barbera d'Alba Loreto '05	♟♟	4

Ca' Rome' - Romano Marengo

S.DA RABAJÀ, 86/88
12050 BARBARESCO [CN]
TEL. 0173635126
www.carome.com

ANNUAL PRODUCTION	30,000 bottles
HECTARES UNDER VINE	5
VITICULTURE METHOD	Conventional

Romano Marengo decided in 1980 to build his dream, a modest winery in his beloved Langhe making wines of absolute quality, with no Dolcetto, no sparklers and certainly no whites. He started with barbera, then expanded to a wealth of nebbiolos from Barbaresco and Serralunga. Romano's wines found a place in our Guide right from the start. His children Giuseppe and Paola are now taking over in Marengo's efficient cellar. We tasted some fascinating wine reflecting different terroirs, thanks to vinifications that remain quite traditional. We liked the approachability and gorgeous fruit of the standard Barbaresco 2005, and the finesse and character of Sorì Rio Sordo, which builds an impressively lengthy conclusion, lean but juicy. The cru selection Maria di Brun has both power and elegance, its mouth rich, warm and sapid. Barolo Rapet, from Bricco del Cerretta di Serralunga, comes across still somewhat stiff and closed but redolent of earth and leather. Vigna Cerretta 2004 seems better with lavish, fine-tuned spice, ample volume in the mouth, smooth tannins and a long finish. A great terroir wine. Barbera, from Serralunga, got One very full Glass.

Cascina Ca' Rossa

LOC. CASCINA CA' ROSSA, 56
12043 CANALE [CN]
TEL. 017398348
www.cascinacarossa.com

ANNUAL PRODUCTION	60,000 bottles
HECTARES UNDER VINE	15
VITICULTURE METHOD	Natural

We have come to appreciate Angelo Ferrio for his warm openness, his talents as a winemaker, and, most recently, his conception of viticulture to yield wines with natural, genuine characteristics. He is focusing increasing attention on non-invasive organic practices, dedicating his efforts to wide-ranging experimentation in this area. The results are in the glass. Improved vineyards and sounder fruit have considerably boosted the average quality of Angelo's wines and his three most ambitious reds are all outstanding. Starting at the bottom, on our scoresheet, 2005 did not yield the most interesting version of Roero Riserva Mompissano but it still gave us a fine, austerely powerful Nebbiolo. On a higher rung is Barbera Mulassa, superb, elegant and lengthy, with a backbone of firm acidity. Audinaggio crowns Cascina Ca' Rossa's pyramid once again. It's a magisterial example of a youthful Roero already fine enough to win Three Glasses and enthuse with its complex bouquet, tannic yet velvet palate, and unsurpassed balance. The rest of the line is superb, from Langhe Nebbiolo to Arneis and the basic Barbera.

● Barolo V. Cerretta '04	⏣⏣	7
● Barbaresco '05	⏣⏣	7
● Barbaresco Maria di Brun '05	⏣⏣	8
● Barbaresco Sorì Rio Sordo '05	⏣⏣	7
● Barolo Rapet '04	⏣⏣	7
● Barbera d'Alba La Gamberaja '06	⏣	5
● Barolo Rapet '03	⏲⏲	7
● Barolo V. Cerretta '01	⏲⏲	7
● Barbaresco Maria di Brun '04	⏲⏲	8
● Barbaresco Maria di Brun '03	⏲⏲	8
● Barbaresco Maria di Brun '01	⏲⏲	8
● Barbaresco Sorì Rio Sordo '04	⏲⏲	7
● Barbaresco Sorì Rio Sordo '03	⏲⏲	7
● Barbaresco Sorì Rio Sordo Ris. '01	⏲⏲	7
● Barolo Rapet '01	⏲⏲	7
● Barolo V. Cerretta '03	⏲⏲	7

● Roero Audinaggio '06	⏣⏣⏣	6
● Barbera d'Alba Mulassa '06	⏣⏣	6
● Roero Mompissano Ris. '05	⏣⏣	6
● Langhe Nebbiolo '07	⏣⏣	4*
O Roero Arneis Merica '07	⏣⏣	4*
● Barbera d'Alba '07	⏣	4
● Birbét '07	⏣	4
● Barbera d'Alba Mulassa '99	⏲⏲⏲	6
● Barbera d'Alba Mulassa '04	⏲⏲⏲	6
● Roero Audinaggio '01	⏲⏲⏲	6
● Roero V. Audinaggio '96	⏲⏲⏲	6
● Roero Audinaggio '05	⏲⏲	6
● Roero Audinaggio '04	⏲⏲	6
● Roero Mompissano '04	⏲⏲	6
● Roero Mompissano '03	⏲⏲	6

★ Ca' Viola

B.TA SAN LUIGI, 11
12063 DOGLIANI [CN]
TEL. 017370547
www.caviola.com

Marco Canato

FRAZ. FONS SALERA
LOC. CA' BALDEA, 18/2
15049 VIGNALE MONFERRATO [AL]
TEL. 0142933653
www.canatovini.it

ANNUAL PRODUCTION	50,000 bottles
HECTARES UNDER VINE	11
VITICULTURE METHOD	Conventional

Beppe Caviola and his wife Simonetta have created a tidy complex on their hill behind Dogliani. Caviola vinifies the grapes from their estate vineyards and he also has a laboratory for his consulting and research. They have also opened a modest Relais bed and breakfast with three charming rooms. Despite all this, the wines were all up to our expectations. Langhe Nebbiolo Sotto Castello 2006 astonished our tasting panels, decisively raising the quality bar for a denomination usually considered marginal. Instead, Caviola's painstaking selection of fruit and his winemaking talents have given us a truly great wine, with spice, wild berry fruit and tobacco leaf on a multi-faceted nose, tannic yet velvety in the mouth, elegant and lengthy. There was even a chance that it would overshadow the renowned Bric du Luv but the latter's customary finesse and harmony enabled it to hold onto the sceptre of Ca' Viola's Langhe reds. Three Glasses went to Dolcetto Barturot 2007, which is an exhibition piece. It shows clean, intense and rich on the nose, then consistent and rounded in the mouth, where it builds massive structure.

ANNUAL PRODUCTION	30,000 bottles
HECTARES UNDER VINE	11
VITICULTURE METHOD	Conventional

The line-up of wines that Marco Canato presented this year can only be described as great. All of his usual stars received high marks at our tastings. Barbera del Monferrato Rapet, after 14 months' maturation in oak, emerged in fine form, with nose and palate in perfect proportion and unleashing a triumphant finish. Barbera Superiore La Baldea never disappoints its fans and this 2006 flaunts dense aromatic blackberry and redcurrant perfectly matched by the lively acidity and fragrance in the mouth. Gambaloita 2007 is thrilling, certainly one of the finest standard Barberas we tasted this year. Grignolino del Monferrato Casalese Celio, showing well-integrated tannins and delicate spice on nose and palate, is another fine bargain for consumers. Chardonnay Piasì, matured in steel, should not be overlooked, nor Bric di Bric, with six months in oak. Overall, Canato presents a fine team of bottlings. If he still lacks that trophy-winning performance, his continuous quality improvement tells us it will come.

● Dolcetto d'Alba Barturot '07	▼▼▼	5
● Langhe Nebbiolo Sotto Castello '06	▼▼	5
● Langhe Rosso Bric du Luv '06	▼▼	6
● Barbera d'Alba Brichet '07	▼▼	5
● Dolcetto d'Alba Vilot '07	▼▼	4*
● L'Insieme '05	▼▼	7
● Dolcetto d'Alba Barturot '05	♔♔♔	5
● Dolcetto d'Alba Barturot '01	♔♔♔	5
● Dolcetto d'Alba Barturot '98	♔♔♔	5
● Dolcetto d'Alba Barturot '96	♔♔♔	5
● Langhe Rosso Bric du Luv '05	♔♔♔	6
● Langhe Rosso Bric du Luv '03	♔♔♔	6
● Langhe Rosso Bric du Luv '01	♔♔♔	6
● Langhe Rosso Bric du Luv '99	♔♔♔	6
● Langhe Rosso Bric du Luv '98	♔♔♔	6
● Langhe Rosso Bric du Luv '96	♔♔♔	6
● Langhe Rosso Bric du Luv '95	♔♔♔	6

● Barbera del M.to Sup. Rapet '05	▼▼	4*
● Barbera del M.to Gambaloita '07	▼▼	3*
● Barbera del M.to Sup. La Baldea '06	▼▼	4
● Grignolino del M.to Casalese Celio '07	▼▼	4
○ Piemonte Chardonnay Bric di Bric '06	▼	4
○ Piemonte Chardonnay Piasì '07	▼	4
● Barbera del M.to Sup. La Baldea '05	♔♔	4
● Barbera del M.to Sup. La Baldea '04	♔♔	3

Cantina del Pino

VIA OVELLO, 31
12050 BARBARESCO [CN]
TEL. 0173635147
www.cantinadelpino.com

ANNUAL PRODUCTION	35,000 bottles
HECTARES UNDER VINE	7
VITICULTURE METHOD	Conventional

Renato Vacca presides over a modern, efficient facility with plenty of oak barrels large and small. Although his first wines date only from 1997, his competence, and the reliability of his excellent wines, suggest an older tradition. We found Dolcetto 2007 light in body and colour but delicious and well-balanced, from its fragrant candied fruit and roses through to a classic bitter-almond finale. The young Gallina and Ovello vineyards yield Langhe Nebbiolo 2006. After fragrant spice and cocoa powder, the mouth is crisp and appealingly tannic yet with fine texture. It's a modern wine of admirable evenness and character. The usual high marks go to the two Barbarescos, the classic 2005 and Ovello 2004, both great and distinguished only by nuances. The first, still closed but showing good fruit and mineral, and hints of cocoa, opens expansive and succulent in the mouth and closes lean. Ovello, from 70-year-old vineyards, has more refinement, with spicy liquorice and vanilla, a heady, emphatic palate with well-built tannins and a lengthy development. A fine expression of a great terroir. Freisa is lively and Barbera 2006 fragrant.

● Barbaresco '05	▼▼	6*
● Barbaresco Ovello '04	▼▼	7
● Dolcetto d'Alba '07	▼▼	4*
● Langhe Nebbiolo '06	▼▼	4*
● Barbera d'Alba '06	▼	5
● Langhe Freisa '07	▼	4
● Barbaresco '04	▼▼▼	6
● Barbaresco '03	▼▼▼	5
● Barbaresco Ovello '99	▼▼▼	6
● Barbaresco '02	▼▼	5
● Barbaresco Ovello '03	▼▼	7
● Barbaresco Ovello '02	▼▼	6
● Barbaresco Ovello '01	▼▼	6
● Barbera d'Alba '05	▼▼	5

Casalone

VIA MARCONI, 100
15040 LU [AL]
TEL. 0131741280
www.casalone.it

ANNUAL PRODUCTION	50,000 bottles
HECTARES UNDER VINE	10
VITICULTURE METHOD	Conventional

We recorded a performance with flying colours for the Casalone family, who brought out wines of impressive character. Take the fine Bricco Morlantino, a 2006 Barbera del Monferrato that is a sensory jewel. After a very dark ruby red, it foregrounds fine fruit over judiciously integrated notes of oak. The attack is most impressive, and a crisp acidity laces superb, pulpy fruit, propelling an almost endless finale. Rubermillo, a remarkable Barbera d'Asti that matures for about a year in oak, preserves glorious fruit on the nose and exhibits a palate of admirable proportion. Barbera, merlot and pinot nero combine in Rus to create a wine that has become iconic for Casalone for several years now. The varieties are kept separate though some 15 months in barriques then assembled into the final wine just before bottling. We close with Monemvasia, an aromatic white from malvasia greca, which also yields Monemvasia Vendemmia Tardiva.

● Barbera d'Asti Rubermillo '05	▼▼	4*
● Barbera del M.to Bricco Morlantino Sup. '06	▼▼	4*
● M.to Rosso Rus '06	▼▼	4
O Monemvasia '07	▼	4
O Monemvasia V. T.	▼	5
● Barbera d'Asti Rubermillo '04	▼▼	4
● M.to Rosso Rus '05	▼▼	4
● M.to Rosso Rus '04	▼▼	4
● M.to Rosso Rus '03	▼▼	4
● M.to Rosso Rus '01	▼▼	4

Cascina Adelaide

VIA AIE SOTTANE, 14
12060 BAROLO [CN]
TEL. 0173560503
www.cascinaadelaide.com

ANNUAL PRODUCTION	50,000 bottles
HECTARES UNDER VINE	8
VITICULTURE METHOD	Conventional

Again, Amabile Drocco's Cascina Adelaide gave us a battery of enviable labels. The staff here is as dedicated in vineyard and cellar as the owner. The Barolos are superlative but the simpler wines also did well at our tastings, evidence of a house style aiming at elegance and balance. We found Barolo Preda the most impressive. It draws from 2004 luscious blossoms and fruit on the nose, particularly rose petals and raspberry, which act as an intriguing foil to the mint and tobacco leaf on the finish, supported by sturdy structure and caressed by smooth tannins. We thought Barolo Cannubi had the most refined aromatics while Fossati relies on emphatic, pulpy fruit beautifully enriched with liquorice and cocoa. Measured acidity infuses the fruit and tannins of Barbera Preda. Barbera Amabilin, enhanced with ten per cent nebbiolo, presents dark ruby and a nose of red berry fruit and spice, then fine acidity and expressive tannins. Dolcetto Costa Fiore, from Diano d'Alba fruit, conjoins a sturdy body and supple, delicious flavours, making it a terrific wine for most dishes. The standard Barolo shows impressive finesse and Langhe Nebbiolo is delightful.

Cascina Ballarin

FRAZ. ANNUNZIATA, 115
12064 LA MORRA [CN]
TEL. 017350365
www.cascinaballarin.it

ANNUAL PRODUCTION	40,000 bottles
HECTARES UNDER VINE	7
VITICULTURE METHOD	Conventional

There's plenty at Cascina Ballarin to keep Gianni and Giorgio Viberti, their parents and their wives busy. In addition to managing their lovely agriturismo, there are more than ten wines to look after, all getting better all the time. The Barolos lead the way, relying on fabulous fruit from some of the denomination's most prestigious crus. Barolo Bussia, from the celebrated vineyard at Monforte, again stands out with a 2004 that went to the national finals. Masterfully calibrated oak lends a smooth glossiness to its overall harmony of nose and palate. La Morra, on the other hand, yields Barolo Bricco Rocca 2004. Matured in large wood, it offers red berry fruit foregrounding florality hinting of blossoms on the cusp of fresh and dry, and already integrating tannins in the mouth. Barolo I Tre Ciabot 2004 is pre-eminently a blend, both of vineyards and of small and large cooperage. It offers clean-edged fruit but its volume is a tad modest. From the other, admirably clean wines, Langhe Bianco Ballarin 2007 deserves mention. It's a successful mosaic of chardonnay, favorita and white-fermented pinot nero.

● Barolo Preda '04	▼▼ 8
● Barbera d'Alba Sup. Amabilin '06	▼▼ 6
● Barbera d'Alba Sup. V. Preda '06	▼▼ 5
● Barolo Cannubi '04	▼▼ 8
● Barolo Fossati '04	▼▼ 8
● Dolcetto di Diano d'Alba Costa Fiore '07	▼▼ 4*
● Barolo '04	▼ 7
● Langhe Nebbiolo '05	▼ 5
● Barolo '03	♀♀ 7
● Barolo '01	♀♀ 7
● Barolo Per Elen Ris. '01	♀♀ 8
● Barolo Per Elen Ris. '00	♀♀ 8
● Barolo Cannubi '03	♀♀ 7
● Barolo Cannubi '01	♀♀ 7
● Barolo Preda '03	♀♀ 8
● Barolo Preda '01	♀♀ 8

● Barolo Bussia '04	▼▼ 8
● Barbera d'Alba Giuli '06	▼▼ 6
● Barbera d'Alba Pilade '06	▼▼ 4*
● Barolo Bricco Rocca '04	▼▼ 8
● Barolo I Tre Ciabot '04	▼▼ 6
● Dolcetto d'Alba Bussia '07	▼▼ 4*
● Langhe Rosso Ballarin '05	▼▼ 5
○ Langhe Bianco Ballarin '07	▼▼ 4*
● Dolcetto d'Alba Pilade '07	▼ 4
● Langhe Rosso Cino '07	▼ 3
● Barolo Bricco Rocca '00	♀♀ 7
● Barolo Bricco Rocca '01	♀♀ 7
● Barolo Bussia '03	♀♀ 8
● Barolo Bussia '01	♀♀ 7
● Barolo Bussia '00	♀♀ 7
● Barolo I Tre Ciabot '00	♀♀ 7

Cascina Bongiovanni

FRAZ. UCCELLACCIO
VIA ALBA BAROLO, 4
12060 CASTIGLIONE FALLETTO [CN]
TEL. 0173262184
www.cascinabongiovanni.com

ANNUAL PRODUCTION	35,000 bottles
HECTARES UNDER VINE	6.2
VITICULTURE METHOD	Conventional

Davide Mozzone, who directs this small operation with considerable passion, once again rolled out a range of well-executed wines. We always notice their admirable cleanness but they also evidence Mozzone's desire for faithful typicity. A vineyard 45-50 years old yields Barolo Pernanno 2004, in a run of 4,000 bottles. Aged in new casks, the colour is deep and the nose modernish, with plenty of delicate violets while a crisp palate exhibits sturdy tannins and juicy, balsam-edged fruit. The standard Barolo is more straightforward and already temptingly approachable. Barbera 2006 is delicious, with magnificent freshness and sound fruit after a floral and fruit nose. We were impressed by Langhe Rosso Faletto 2006, from 60 per cent cabernet sauvignon plus barbera and nebbiolo. It shows scents of wild red berries followed by elegant succulence and solid weight. Of the two 2007 Dolcettos, Diano is naturally the more structured and cautious, conveying tasty well-ripened fruit, whereas Dolcetto d'Alba is more linear and readier for the corkscrew. Langhe Arneis 2007 is well made.

● Barolo Pernanno '04	▼▼	7
● Langhe Rosso Faletto '06	▼▼	5
● Barbera d'Alba '06	▼▼	5
● Barolo '04	▼▼	6
● Dolcetto di Diano d'Alba '07	▼▼	4*
● Dolcetto d'Alba '07	▼	4
○ Langhe Arneis '07	▼	4
● Barolo Pernanno '01	♈♈♈	7
● Barolo Pernanno '00	♈♈	7
● Barolo Pernanno '99	♈♈	7
● Barolo Pernanno '98	♈♈	7
● Barolo '03	♈♈	6
● Barolo '01	♈♈	6
● Barbera d'Alba '05	♈♈	5
● Langhe Rosso Faletto '05	♈♈	5

Cascina Bruciata

S.DA RIO SORDO, 46
12050 BARBARESCO [CN]
TEL. 0173638826
cascina.bruciata@tiscali.it

ANNUAL PRODUCTION	40,000 bottles
HECTARES UNDER VINE	7
VITICULTURE METHOD	Conventional

In the heart of Barbaresco, Rio Sordo is an enduring powerhouse of a cru, its fruit long vinified by most of the best producers in the Langhe. We recently tasted Rio Sordo 2001 made by Cesare Balbo, his first bottling in fact, and it embodies what this piece of earth is capable of giving over time: harmony, power, length and beautifully tamed tannins. We mention again the family's recent modernization of the cellar and their efforts on behalf of the area. Superlative fruit and careful vinifications gift us sturdy wines, a tad rough and stiffish, their only fault, perhaps, being they are released and tasted too soon after bottling, which penalizes younger bottles. In a word, be patient until the tannins of the two Barbarescos smooth out and proffer the thrilling impressions we found with the 200. We will surely enjoy again the warmth, the silkiness and the fabulous length of that cru, along with the fruit and rich flavours of the standard version, formerly Vigneto Balbo. The same goes for the two 2007 Dolcettos. Rian is more approachable and ductile; Vigneti in Rio Sordo sturdy, rich and long. Nebbiolo 2006 is edgy but only needs time.

● Barbaresco '05	▼▼	6
● Barbaresco Rio Sordo '05	▼▼	6
● Dolcetto d'Alba Rian '07	▼▼	4*
● Dolcetto d'Alba Vign. in Rio Sordo '07	▼▼	4*
● Langhe Nebbiolo Vign. dell'Usignolo '06	▼	4
● Barbaresco '04	♈♈	6
● Barbaresco Rio Sordo '04	♈♈	6
● Barbaresco Rio Sordo '03	♈♈	6
● Barbaresco Rio Sordo '01	♈♈	6
● Barbaresco Vign. Balbo '03	♈♈	6
● Barbaresco Vign. Balbo '01	♈♈	6

Cascina Castlet

S.DA CASTELLETTO, 6
14055 COSTIGLIOLE D'ASTI [AT]
TEL. 0141966651
www.cascinacastlet.com

ANNUAL PRODUCTION	170,000 bottles
HECTARES UNDER VINE	18
VITICULTURE METHOD	Natural

Mariuccia Borio, Cascina Castlet's strong-willed owner, has created a model operation in her corner of the Asti area, thanks to a new facility with low environmental impact. She has also been carrying out vineyard experiments in recent years, the most interesting focusing on the uvalino grape variety. As far as her wines go, Passsum continues to impress, as have its past editions. The nose yields up rich ripe fruit, cinchona and citrus zest while the mouth displays power and terrific grip, thanks to a magisterial acidity. Borio's decision to hold back release of Monferrato Rosso Policalpo and Barbera d'Asti Litina was right on the money. Litina 2005 gave a gorgeous performance, with nuances of morello and wild strawberry, followed by vibrant energy and emphatic fruit. Policalpo 2004, made of 70 per cent barbera and the rest cabernet sauvignon, is remarkably powerful with a compelling progression that fuels a wonderfully long, thrilling finish. Moscato Passito Avié receives high marks for its candied citrus zest, dried figs and grapefruit. Barbera La Vespa 2007 is crisply fruited while Moscato d'Asti, Barbera Goj and Chardonnay A Taj are all delicious.

Cascina Corte

B.TA VALDIBERTI, 33
12063 DOGLIANI [CN]
TEL. 0172411641
www.cascinacorte.it

ANNUAL PRODUCTION	30,000 bottles
HECTARES UNDER VINE	5.5
VITICULTURE METHOD	Certified organic

Sandro Barosi has begun his wine adventure, which sounds the right word for leaving a prestigious job, purchasing a farm in the Langhe near Doglio, planting a vineyard, going organic immediately, building a winemaking cellar and setting up distribution for his wines. So even today, such adventurers exist and there are even those, like Barosi, whose spouses, in this case Amalia, share the same aspirations. Let's turn to their wines, first to Dolcetto di Dogliani – or just plain "Dogliani" as it says on the label – Vigna Pirochetta. It stayed a year longer in the cellar, in compliance with the new production code. Lavish spice and earth theme a fine nose, which then lays out a broad, even-handed progression capped by a long, well-proportioned finish, nicely laden with the aromas we savoured previously. Also fine is Dolcetto di Dogliani – with the full name – briefly aged and showing crisp and straightforward. We have always appreciated the Barbera for its effective, vivacious acidity. Finally, the lean, austere Nebbiolo, its acid in nice balance with the tannins, finishes long for a splendid effort.

● Barbera d'Asti Sup. Passum '05		5
● Barbera d'Asti La Vespa '07		4*
● Barbera d'Asti Sup. Litina '05		5
● M.to Rosso Policalpo '04		5
O Piemonte Moscato Passito Avié '06		5
O Moscato d'Asti '07		4
O Piemonte Chardonnay A Taj '07		4
● Barbera del M.to Goj '07		4
● Barbera d'Asti Sup. Passum '05		5
● Barbera d'Asti Sup. Passum '04		5
● Barbera d'Asti Sup. Passum '03		5
● Barbera d'Asti Sup. Passum '01		5
● M.to Rosso Policalpo '03		5
● M.to Rosso Policalpo '01		5
● M.to Rosso Policalpo '00		5
● Barbera d'Asti Sup. Litina '04		5

● Dogliani V. Pirochetta '06		4*
● Dolcetto di Dogliani '07		3*
● Langhe Nebbiolo '06		5
● Piemonte Barbera '07		4
● Dolcetto di Dogliani V. Pirochetta '05		4
● Dolcetto di Dogliani V. Pirochetta '04		4
● Dolcetto di Dogliani V. Pirochetta '03		4
● Dolcetto di Dogliani '06		4
● Langhe Nebbiolo '05		4

Cascina Cucco

LOC. CUCCO
VIA MAZZINI, 10
12050 SERRALUNGA D'ALBA [CN]
TEL. 0173613003
www.cascinacucco.com

ANNUAL PRODUCTION	60,000 bottles
HECTARES UNDER VINE	12
VITICULTURE METHOD	Conventional

Cascina Cucco, a splendid farm sensitively restructured by the Stroppiana family, lies just outside Serralunga. You can gaze over the vineyards to the castle with its huddle of three time-battered towers overlooking the town. The family has made important progress since 1999, and their investments have brought high quality and the respect of other local producers. At the top of the class is Barolo Cucco, named after a small block inside the Cerrati cru vineyard. Heady aromas meld together with notes of mint and rosemary, and it vaunts powerful structure, full tannins and alcohol in the mouth but smooth, supple fruit as well, concluding long and smooth. The other Barolo is also sourced from Cerrati. Less complex than its elder brother, its stay in oak and emphatic fruit keep incisive extract in its place. The standard Barolo, simpler but still stylish, is the readiest of the three. Not to be overlooked is Rosso Mondo, a Langhe blend with a bit of cabernet that drinks international and appealing. Both Barberas, from 2006 and 2007, are excellent, as is Dolcetto Vughera while the floral and tropical-infused Chardonnay is quite successful.

Cascina degli Ulivi

S.DA MAZZOLA, 14
15067 NOVI LIGURE [AL]
TEL. 0143744598
www.cascinadegliulivi.it

ANNUAL PRODUCTION	100,000 bottles
HECTARES UNDER VINE	22
VITICULTURE METHOD	Certified biodynamic

Wine is not political but sadly its variegated band of practitioners sometimes splits into two camps. On one side are the fierce promoters of biodynamics; on the other those who seek simply genuineness in a wine, holding stylistic purity more important than issues like natural management of the vineyards. But we recommend wines based on their sensory qualities and we liked Stefano Bellotti's wines this year. Bellotti was one of the first in Italy to speak of organics and biodynamics. It was an uphill task in times when natural viticultural practices were not the marketing tool they are today. Stefano's wines are unusual and they need more time and patient attention than is usually accorded at hurried tasting sessions. Gavi Filagnotti 2007 performed well, exuding lemon and citrus and finishing with enviable succulence. Another winery star is the minerally Montemarino, here with a spicy, complex opening. We were impressed by Nibiô Terre Rosse. Tight and closed in its first moments, it then opens up and reveals rich hints of fruit and cinchona. Barbera Mounbé is on a par, whereas Nibiô Montemarino and the standard Gavi run a length behind.

● Barolo V. Cucco '04	🍷🍷 7
● Barbera d'Alba Sup. '06	🍷🍷 5
● Barolo '04	🍷🍷 6
● Barolo Cerrati '04	🍷🍷 6
● Dolcetto d'Alba Vughera '07	🍷🍷 4*
○ Langhe Chardonnay '07	🍷🍷 4*
● Langhe Rosso Mondo '06	🍷🍷 5
● Barbera d'Alba '07	🍷 4
● Barolo V. Cerrati '01	🍷🍷 7
● Barolo V. Cerrati '00	🍷🍷 7
● Barolo V. Cucco '01	🍷🍷 7
● Barolo V. Cucco '00	🍷🍷 7
● Barbera d'Alba Sup. '04	🍷🍷 5
● Barolo '01	🍷🍷 7
● Barolo V. Cerrati '99	🍷🍷 7
● Barolo V. Cucco '99	🍷🍷 7

○ Gavi del Comune di Tassarolo Filagnotti '07	🍷🍷 4*
○ M.to Bianco Montemarino '06	🍷🍷 4*
● M.to Dolcetto Nibiô Terre Rosse '06	🍷🍷 4*
● Piemonte Barbera Mounbé '06	🍷🍷 5
● M.to Dolcetto Nibiô Montemarino '06	🍷 4
○ Gavi '07	🍷 4
● M.to Dolcetto Nibiô Terre Rosse '05	🍷🍷 4

Cascina Fonda

LOC. CASCINA FONDA, 45
12056 MANGO [CN]
TEL. 0173677156
www.cascinafonda.com

ANNUAL PRODUCTION	120,000 bottles
HECTARES UNDER VINE	2
VITICULTURE METHOD	Conventional

For 20 years now, Marco and Massimo Barbero have been looking after their family operation near Mango. Since they specialize in whites, production essentially revolves around the grape classic to the area, moscato. Fonda wines have always been high quality and this reliability has won them a faithful band of aficionados who appreciate their freshness and balance. In exceptional vintages, the highest quality fruit goes to produce limited quantities of special selection wines, which are often both unusual and impressive. Driveri is one of the best of these. It is an Asti Spumante that undergoes traditional bottle refermentation and is disgorged after 18 months. There's also a Brut Metodo Classico from pinot nero and chardonnay, a Moscato passito cask aged for two years, and a Moscato from ultra-ripe fruit. While waiting for the newer vintages of these bottlings, we enjoyed a fine Moscato d'Asti Del Piano, subtly redolent of blossoms and gooseberry and showing classic moscato aromas and sweetness on the palate. The Asti Spumante is enjoyable, the Brachetto and Dolcetto 2007 sound.

Cascina Garitina

VIA GIANOLA, 20
14040 CASTEL BOGLIONE [AT]
TEL. 0141762162
www.cascinagaritina.it

ANNUAL PRODUCTION	180,000 bottles
HECTARES UNDER VINE	26
VITICULTURE METHOD	Conventional

Gianluca Morino is an emerging Asti producer. With help from his parents, Assunta and Pasquale, he tends several hectares planted largely to the main local variety, barbera. Morino also does well with the other local varieties. In fact, he brought out an unexpected Monferrato Rosso Alfero 2004, made exclusively from pinot nero sourced from a 1991 vineyard whose grapes had previously gone to enrich Amis. This first vintage matured for ten months in once-used barriques and a further year in glass. After a shimmering red, it unveils a delicate medley of cocoa powder and raspberry preserves, followed by finely tuned tannins and a succulent finale. Barbera Superiore Nizza Neuvsent 2005 is the stable thoroughbred, thanks to dense fruit and smooth pencil lead on the nose, its massive dimensions and the incredible length of its development on the palate. Barbera Caranti 2006 is a pleasure in every way and well up to past editions. Monferrato Amis 2004 did not hit the ball quite as far as we expected. The Vera and Bricco Garitta Barberas are crisp and tasty, Dolcetto d'Asti Caranzano shows heft and warmth, and Brachetto ton of fruit. All are 2007s.

O Asti '07	♥♥ 4*
O Moscato d'Asti Del Piano '07	♥♥ 4*
● Dolcetto d'Alba Brusalino '07	♥ 4
● Piemonte Brachetto '07	♥ 4
O Asti Driveri M. Cl. '05	♀♀ 5
O Brut M. Cl. '04	♀♀ 5
● Barbaresco Bertola '04	♀♀ 6

● Barbera d'Asti Sup. Nizza Neuvsent '05	♥♥ 5
● Barbera d'Asti Sup. Caranti '06	♥♥ 4*
● M.to Rosso Alfero '04	♥♥ 5
● Barbera d'Asti Bricco Garitta '07	♥ 4
● Barbera d'Asti Vera '07	♥ 4
● Brachetto d'Acqui Niades '07	♥ 4
● Dolcetto d'Asti Caranzano '07	♥ 4
● M.to Rosso Amis '04	♥ 5
● Barbera d'Asti Sup. Nizza Neuvsent '04	♀♀ 5
● Barbera d'Asti Sup. Nizza Neuvsent '03	♀♀ 5
● Barbera d'Asti Sup. Nizza Neuvsent '01	♀♀ 5
● Barbera d'Asti Sup. Nizza Neuvsent '00	♀♀ 5

Cascina Gilli

VIA NEVISSANO, 36
14022 CASTELNUOVO DON BOSCO [AT]
TEL. 0119876984
www.cascinagilli.it

ANNUAL PRODUCTION 140,000 bottles
HECTARES UNDER VINE 23
VITICULTURE METHOD Conventional

Specializing in native varieties the critics snub is an improbable road to fame but Gianni Vergnano has taken it. He and his experienced team, which includes Bruno Tamagnone, Giovanni Matteis, Marco Piovano and Germana Rosa Clot, are constantly experimenting. The news in this edition of the Guide is Freisa d'Asti Arbi 2004. After a 30-month stay in barriques, it gives incisive vanilla and toastiness, and a powerful palate that needs to find perfect balance. Vigna del Forno 2006 is a fragrant Freisa that lays out strawberry, black pepper and much more besides, closing with liqueur fruit. In the mouth, there are full flavours, pulpy fruit and a fine progression that rises to an exuberant conclusion. We found the usual fine performances by the young Freisa d'Asti Luna di Maggio and Barbera d'Asti Vigna delle More, the latter marked by crisp, delicious readiness, and the same goes for Dlicà, from late-harvested malvasia. Bonarda Sernù was not ready yet to be tasted, nor was Freisa Arlevé, for which Arbi was the stand-in. Malvasia di Castelnuovo Don Bosco, Bonarda Vivace Moyé, Barbera d'Asti Sebrì and Freisa Vivace are all well executed.

● Barbera d'Asti V. delle More '06	🍷🍷 4*
● Dlicà	🍷🍷 5
● Freisa d'Asti Arbi '04	🍷🍷 6
● Freisa d'Asti Luna di Maggio '07	🍷🍷 3*
● Freisa d'Asti V. del Forno '06	🍷🍷 4*
● Malvasia di Castelnuovo Don Bosco '07	🍷🍷 4*
● Barbera d'Asti Sebrì '06	🍷🍷 6
● Freisa d'Asti Vivace '07	🍷 3
● Piemonte Bonarda Vivace Moyé '07	🍷 3
● Barbera d'Asti Sebrì '05	♀♀ 4
● Barbera d'Asti V. delle More '05	♀♀ 4
● Freisa d'Asti V. del Forno '05	♀♀ 4

Cascina La Maddalena

FRAZ. SAN GIACOMO
LOC. PIANI DEL PADRONE, 257
15078 ROCCA GRIMALDA [AL]
TEL. 0143876074
www.cascina-maddalena.com

ANNUAL PRODUCTION 25,000 bottles
HECTARES UNDER VINE 5
VITICULTURE METHOD Conventional

Cascina La Maddalena has been a reliable producer in the Ovada area for more than ten years, and recently enlarged its bed and breakfast accommodation. The last few harvests have seen good quality rise further. A small parcel of merlot recently came into production but most of the five hectares is planted to local varieties, in particular dolcetto and barbera, testifying to La Maddalena's commitment to the area's traditions. On the occasion of their tenth harvest, in 2006, they produced Monferrato Rosso La Decima Vendemmia, which we tasted as a preview of its official release. A masterful assemblage of barbera, dolcetto and merlot, it offers fine fruit and a subtle herbaceousness on the nose then outstanding complexity and length in the mouth. No less fine is Dolcetto Bricco del Bagatto, where nuances of fruit and hints of spice compose a very graceful nose, and the palate is built around fine-grained, tasty tannins and steady length. Barbera Rossa d'Ocra is a bit short but shows crisp and fresh while both Barbera and the standard Dolcetto di Ovada are impeccably executed.

● Dolcetto di Ovada Bricco del Bagatto '06	🍷🍷 4*
● M.to Rosso La Decima Vendemmia '06	🍷🍷 6
● Dolcetto di Ovada '07	🍷🍷 3
● Barbera del M.to '07	🍷 3
● Barbera del M.to Rossa d'Ocra '06	🍷 4
● Dolcetto di Ovada Bricco del Bagatto '05	♀♀ 4
● M.to Rosso Bricco della Maddalena '04	♀♀ 5
● M.to Rosso Bricco della Maddalena '03	♀♀ 5

Cascina Roera

FRAZ. BIONZO
VIA BIONZO, 32
14055 COSTIGLIOLE D'ASTI [AT]
TEL. 0141968437

ANNUAL PRODUCTION 20,000 bottles
HECTARES UNDER VINE 4
VITICULTURE METHOD Conventional

Seven years ago, Carlo Rosso and Piero Nebiolo launched Cascina Roera, and their considerable progress has been marked by wines that have acquired distinctive stylistic features. They rooted their winemaking in the Asti-area traditions, and since they are located at Costigliole d'Asti, home of the barbera grape, it is no wonder that their iconic bottlings are Barbera d'Asti. But first a glance at Freisa, where the favourable 2006 vintage created aromatic complexity and a fragrant, nicely rounded palate. Turning to the three versions of Barbera, you might think Roera 2006 was the standard version but, far from being an uncomplicated wine, it vaunts superlative acidity that both drives and enlivens a fine development. The two principal Barberas are from the distant 2004 vintage. Cardin's nose showcases an entrancing harmony of fruit, spice and earth, reflected on the equally harmonious finish with its long-lingering balance of alcohol and acidity. The palate is expansive and still as vibrant as you could wish. Fruit very carefully selected in the vineyard goes to produce Cardin Selezione, which is then given slightly longer maturation in oak.

● Barbera d'Asti Sup. Cardin '04	🍷🍷 4*
● Barbera d'Asti Sup. Cardin Sel. '04	🍷🍷 5
● Barbera d'Asti La Roera '06	🍷🍷 3*
● Freisa d'Asti '06	🍷 3
● Barbera d'Asti Sup. S. Martino '04	🍷🍷 4
● Barbera d'Asti Sup. Cardin '03	🍷🍷 4
● Barbera d'Asti Sup. Cardin '01	🍷🍷 4
● Barbera d'Asti Sup. Cardin Sel. '03	🍷🍷 5
● Barbera d'Asti Sup. Cardin Sel. '01	🍷🍷 5
● M.to Rosso V. Piva '03	🍷🍷 4

Renzo Castella

VIA ALBA, 15
12055 DIANO D'ALBA [CN]
TEL. 017369203
renzocastella@virgilio.it

ANNUAL PRODUCTION 28,000 bottles
HECTARES UNDER VINE 10
VITICULTURE METHOD Conventional

Renzo Castella is passionate about his task of crafting wine from his family's vineyards, which he regards as a true privilege. Growing in Diano d'Alba is not simple though, because the market does not currently place any great value on this type of red, which is a shame, since Dolcettos are generally enviable value for money. Castella, as usual, presented two selections of Dolcetto di Diano d'Alba, each quite distinct. Rivolia – the word "Vigna" has disappeared – is the more powerful and concentrated of the pair, showing intense, warm aromas and a palate notable for its fine-grained tannins and juicy acidity. Elegance and readiness are more the style of Vigna Piadvenza, although it is far from uncomplicated as the nose makes clear, with an amalgam of morello cherry, violets and wild strawberries. Nebbiolo d'Alba Vigna Madonnina, which matures for 12 months in ten-hectolitre barrels, is distinctive for its undertones of dried flowers, cinchona and raspberry. Barbera Vigna Sarcat spends a year in twice-used barriques and acquires appreciable balance of its fruit component and generous nuances of toasty spice.

● Dolcetto di Diano d'Alba Rivolia '07	🍷🍷 3*
● Dolcetto di Diano d'Alba V. della Piadvenza '07	🍷🍷 3*
● Nebbiolo d'Alba V. Madonnina '06	🍷🍷 4
● Barbera d'Alba V. Sarcat '06	🍷🍷 3*
● Dolcetto di Diano d'Alba V. della Rivolia '06	🍷🍷 3
● Dolcetto di Diano d'Alba V. della Rivolia '05	🍷🍷 3
● Dolcetto di Diano d'Alba V. della Piadvenza '06	🍷🍷 3

Castellari Bergaglio

FRAZ. ROVERETO, 136
15066 GAVI [AL]
TEL. 0143644000
www.castellaribergaglio.it

ANNUAL PRODUCTION	80,000 bottles
HECTARES UNDER VINE	11
VITICULTURE METHOD	Conventional

The production philosophy of Castellari Bergaglio, right from its beginning, has been to focus on growing just one grape and that grape is cortese. The fact that Marco Bergaglio and his family pour true passion into their work and into their cortese, combined with the fact that their vineyards are located in Rovereto, the cru par excellence of the denomination, goes a long way to explaining the reason for the constant improvement in quality of the Bergaglio Gavis. Turning to the wines we tasted, Rovereto stood out, its fruit coming from a long-established vineyard now over 80 years old. The bouquet is fairly intense, with blossoms and a subtle pungency, but the palate is superb, laced with tasty acidity that delivers great drinking pleasure. Fornaci, too, gained high marks for its good florality and white-fleshed fruit on the nose, and appreciable savouriness in the mouth enhanced by an emphatic vein of acidity that integrates nicely with the structure. We also liked Rolona, a crisp, refreshing quaffer with an insistent yet graceful bouquet.

O Gavi del Comune di Gavi Rovereto Vignavecchia '07		♚♚ 4*
O Gavi del Comune di Gavi Rolona '07		♚♚ 4
O Gavi del Comune di Tassarolo Fornaci '07		♚♚ 4
O Gavi del Comune di Tassarolo Fornaci '06		♛♛ 4
O Gavi del Comune di Tassarolo Fornaci '05		♛♛ 4
O Gavi del Comune di Gavi Rovereto Vignavecchia '05		♛♛ 4

Castello di Neive

VIA CASTELBORGO, 1
12052 NEIVE [CN]
TEL. 017367171
neive.castello@tin.it

ANNUAL PRODUCTION	150,000 bottles
HECTARES UNDER VINE	26
VITICULTURE METHOD	Conventional

Italo Stupino, Castello di Neive's cultured owner, and Claudio Roggero, its talented winemaker, are the star team that keeps the cellar's flag flying, helped by star consultant Gianfranco Cordero. They are meticulous about every wine but aim to become one of the driving forces in Barbaresco, aware that they enjoy a monopoly on Santo Stefano di Neive, one of the finest crus in the entire denomination. Sadly, we must wait for the release of Riserva del Barbaresco Santo Stefano 2004, since it needs more time. Instead we tasted the 2003 edition, which embodies all of the characteristics typical of an untypical vintage. The garnet hue is already showing signs of evolving, heady scents of strawberry preserves, and a tannic roughness in the mouth. This is a good Barbaresco to enjoy at table over the next five years. We preferred the fresh bouquet and stylish elegance of Santo Stefano 2005. From a line-up of wines that shows no sign of faltering – all are delicious and beautifully typed – we would single out the richly flavoured Barbera Santo Stefano 2007 and above all Pinot Nero Brut 2004, an incisive, rich Piedmontese sparkler.

● Barbaresco S. Stefano '05		♚♚ 6
● Barbaresco S. Stefano Ris. '03		♚♚ 8
● Barbera d'Alba Mattarello '06		♚♚ 5
● Barbera d'Alba S. Stefano '07		♚♚ 4*
● Dolcetto d'Alba Basarin '07		♚♚ 4*
● Dolcetto d'Alba Messoirano '07		♚♚ 4*
O Castello di Neive Passito '06		♚♚ 6
O Piemonte Spumante M. Cl. Castello di Neive '04		♚♚ 5
O Langhe Arneis Montebertotto '07		♚ 4
● Barbaresco S. Stefano Ris. '99		♛♛♛ 8
● Barbaresco S. Stefano Ris. '01		♛♛♛ 8
● Barbaresco S. Stefano '04		♛♛ 6
● Barbaresco S. Stefano '03		♛♛ 7
● Barbaresco S. Stefano '01		♛♛ 6
● Barbaresco S. Stefano '00		♛♛ 7

Tenuta Castello di Razzano

FRAZ. CASARELLO
LOC. RAZZANO, 2
15021 ALFIANO NATTA [AL]
TEL. 0141922124
www.castellodirazzano.it

ANNUAL PRODUCTION	200,000 bottles
HECTARES UNDER VINE	38
VITICULTURE METHOD	Conventional

The quality of the Oleari family's wines has soared. We were used in past years to a fine overall level of quality but the outstanding results from this year's line-up means that Castello di Razzano is taking its place in the select top ranks of Alexandria-area producers. Barbera del Monferrato Superiore Eugenea 2005 is in fine fettle, the lovely fruit on the nose barely caressed by well-measured oak resulting in beautifully complex aromatics. Barbera d'Asti Beneficio, too, showed extremely well, sporting an almost opaque ruby red and wild strawberry on the nose as a fitting prelude to a harmonious, long-lingering palate. Making its first appearance in the Guide is Monferrato Munfrà, an impressive young wine marked by depth on the nose followed by a bright, tasty acidity. Completing the team is Chardonnay Costa al Sole, masterfully crafted, delicious and well proportioned throughout. All in all, it's a fascinating group of labels that ever more convincingly demonstrates the distinctiveness that will make Castello di Razzano one of the region's top producers.

Castello di Tassarolo

CASCINA ALBORINA, 1
15060 TASSAROLO [AL]
TEL. 0143342248
www.castelloditassarolo.it

ANNUAL PRODUCTION	100,000 bottles
HECTARES UNDER VINE	20
VITICULTURE METHOD	Natural

Massimiliana Spinola, in charge of this historic Gavi producer for a few years now, has taken things in a new direction by converting vineyard practices to biodynamic, assisted by agronomist Vincenzo Munì. The process will be completed over the next few harvests. Castello di Tassarolo's output puts it on the top rung of the denomination. That is particularly true of the main winery selection, Gavi Vigneto Alborina. A glimpse of the shimmering straw yellow flecked with gold in the glass tells you it is stellar. Subtle floral notes and scents of citrus compose an extremely elegant, lengthy bouquet and luscious, acid-enriched structure accentuates its sensory richness in the mouth. It easily went on to our final taste-offs. Castello di Tassarolo is a worthy exemplar of all that is best in classic cortese. We also found the overall balance to be superb in S, with its finesse on the nose. The winery's new philosophy has led to the introduction of a new designation, NS, for "no sulphites". The first such wine, Monferrato Rosso Cuvée dei Marchesi Spinola, is a well-executed blend of barbera and cabernet.

● Barbera d'Asti Sup. Eugenea '05	🍷🍷 4*
● Barbera d'Asti Sup. Beneficio '06	🍷🍷 5
● Barbera del M.to Munfrà '07	🍷🍷 3*
O M.to Bianco Costa al Sole '07	🍷 3
● Barbera d'Asti Sup. V. Valentino Caligaris '05	🍷🍷 5
● Barbera d'Asti Sup. V. Valentino Caligaris '04	🍷🍷 5
● Barbera d'Asti Sup. Campasso '04	🍷🍷 3
● Barbera d'Asti Sup. Eugenea '04	🍷🍷 4
● Barbera d'Asti Sup. Beneficio '04	🍷🍷 4

O Gavi del Comune di Tassarolo Vign. Alborina '06	🍷🍷 5
O Gavi del Comune di Tassarolo Castello di Tassarolo '07	🍷🍷 4
O Gavi del Comune di Tassarolo S '07	🍷🍷 3*
● M.to Rosso Cuvée dei Marchesi Spinola '06	🍷🍷 4
O Gavi del Comune di Tassarolo NS '07	🍷 3
O Gavi del Comune di Tassarolo Vign. Alborina '05	🍷🍷 5
O Gavi del Comune di Tassarolo Castello di Tassarolo '06	🍷🍷 4
O Gavi del Comune di Tassarolo S '06	🍷🍷 3

Castello di Verduno

VIA UMBERTO I, 9
12060 VERDUNO [CN]
TEL. 0172470284
www.castellodiverduno.com

ANNUAL PRODUCTION	47,000 bottles
HECTARES UNDER VINE	8
VITICULTURE METHOD	Conventional

Castello di Verduno has always stood apart from the hurly-burly of Langhe, perhaps because of its secluded position, perhaps because of Franco Bianco's retiring temperament. But two decades of history and a myriad admirers underline the quality of the wines and its benchmark role in the area. When a glance at the map reveals estate plots in vineyards like of Massara and Monvigliero in Barolo, and Faset and Rabajà in Barbaresco, and when you see Bianco's winemaking skills, then the reasons for the success are clear. The 2003 vintage was challenging, of course, for Castello di Verduno as for others. Barolo Massara 2003, however, is smooth and harmonious, with hints of dried flowers, and seems to have dodged the bullet but the two Barbarescos, Faset and Rabajà, still display drying tannins, which make them more suitable for food than for tasting on their own. The standard Barbaresco 2004 is less rich than in the past but it has already achieved better balance. This year's champion performance was turned in by Barolo Riserva Massara 1999, which is complex and simply extraordinary. Both Pelaverga Basadone and Barbera are excellent.

La Caudrina

S.DA BROSIA, 21
12053 CASTIGLIONE TINELLA [CN]
TEL. 0141855126
www.caudrina.it

ANNUAL PRODUCTION	200,000 bottles
HECTARES UNDER VINE	30
VITICULTURE METHOD	Conventional

With 40 years of making moscato under his belt, Romano Dogliotti is one of the iconic producers for moscatophiles and fellow winemakers. Only the finest lots of moscato grapes will leave the vineyards, destined for his bottlings of Asti or Moscato, and they are then subjected to a strict production protocol designed to ensure consistent high quality. This year brought few new wines, which means that we found ourselves again with wines of long-proved character. Of the two Moscatos, La Caudrina is the stand-out, and went to the taste-offs. After prodigal aromas of apricot and blossoms, the palate opens rich and dense, well balanced and very lengthy. La Galeisa is its expected fine self again, refreshing and redolent of crisp citrus and aniseed. Asti La Selvatica is one of the finest wines we tasted this year in its category. Both Barberas are magisterially crafted, sourced from vineyards in the prestigious Nizza area. Montevenere 2005, aged in barriques, displays dense mouthfeel and smooth tannins after evolved aromas edged with spice. Less complex but by no means simple is the steel-aged Solista 2006, nicely crisp and fruited.

● Barolo Massara Ris. '99	♥♥ 7
● Barbaresco '04	♥♥ 6
● Barbaresco Rabajà '03	♥♥ 6
● Barbera d'Alba Bricco del Cuculo '06	♥♥ 4*
● Barolo Massara '03	♥♥ 7
● Verduno Basadone '07	♥♥ 4*
● Barbaresco Faset '03	♥ 6
● Dolcetto d'Alba Campot '07	♥ 4
● Barolo Massara '01	♥♥♥ 7
● Barbaresco Rabajà '01	♥♥ 6
● Barbaresco Rabajà '00	♥♥ 7
● Barbaresco Rabajà Ris. '99	♥♥ 7
● Barbaresco Faset '01	♥♥ 6
● Barolo Massara '99	♥♥ 7
● Barolo Monvigliero '01	♥♥ 6
● Barolo Monvigliero '00	♥♥ 6

○ Moscato d'Asti La Caudrina '07	♥♥ 4*
○ Moscato d'Asti La Galeisa '07	♥♥ 4
○ Asti La Selvatica '07	♥♥ 4
● Barbera d'Asti La Solista '06	♥♥ 4
● Barbera d'Asti Sup. Montevenere '05	♥♥ 5
● Barbera d'Asti La Solista '05	♥♥ 4
● Barbera d'Asti Sup. Montevenere '04	♥♥ 5
● Barbera d'Asti Sup. Montevenere '00	♥♥ 5
● Barbera d'Asti Sup. Montevenere '99	♥♥ 5

F.lli Cavallotto
Tenuta Bricco Boschis

LOC. BRICCO BOSCHIS
S.DA ALBA-MONFORTE
12060 CASTIGLIONE FALLETTO [CN]
TEL. 017362814
www.cavallotto.com

ANNUAL PRODUCTION	100,000 bottles
HECTARES UNDER VINE	23
VITICULTURE METHOD	Natural

Cavallotto is a producer that exudes reassurance. Visiting the cellar, you see straight away many of the qualities shared by Langhe's best producers: tradition, excellent growing conditions, vineyards of considerable maturity, meticulous vineyard and cellar practices and a warm, genuine sense of hospitality. Classic is the term to describe the winery philosophy, with a natural approach in the vineyard, lengthy macerations and maturation in large oak casks but these practices are supported by carefully chosen, appropriate modern technology. The new generation, represented by siblings Alfio, Giuseppe and Laura, has the reins solidly in hand and they are driving nicely. Although we were unable to taste the two Barolo Riservas, the other wines are outstanding. The nose on Barolo Bricco Boschis 2004, with blossoms and earth, shows elegant, stylish and cleanly delineated while the palate is solidly built, clean-edged and linear. It's a classic well worth its Three Glasses. Barbera Vigna del Cuculo 2005 is terrific, nervy and crisp. It may not be powerful but it's certainly full and utterly delicious. The remaining reds worthily fill out a noble line-up.

Ceretto

LOC. SAN CASSIANO, 34
12051 ALBA [CN]
TEL. 0173282582
www.ceretto.com

ANNUAL PRODUCTION	900,000 bottles
HECTARES UNDER VINE	87
VITICULTURE METHOD	Conventional

Arbarei, a Riesling from Albaretto della Torre, is a great white again in 2006. Luscious opening fruit bears the imprint of emerging petrol notes, which carries over onto a seductive palate and a full-flavoured, heady finale. This Riesling can only get better. Obviously, Cerretto does not live by Riesling alone. This year, there is a thrilling Barolo Zonchera 2004. Multi-layered aromas range from ripe fruit to spice and tobacco leaf before dense, tight tannins caress succulent fruit in the mouth and it lays out an alluring finish. Equally interesting is Monsordo 2005, made of cabernet, merlot, syrah and nebbiolo, a mainly international mosaic that speaks the Langhe dialect. A wine of appreciable finesse, it leaves impressions of moist earth and graphite with subtle hints of capsicum and blackberry before continuing graceful on the palate and concluding lengthy and balanced. Both Barbaresco Asij and Nebbiolo d'Alba display evolved characteristics while the standard Barbera Piana is fragrantly fruity. Dolcetto d'Alba 2007 drinks beautifully, with a hallmark bitter-almond finish. Finally, Blangé is a slightly fizzy Langhe Arneis to enjoy everyday.

● Barolo Bricco Boschis '04	♀♀♀	8
● Barbera d'Alba V. del Cuculo '05	♀♀	5
● Dolcetto d'Alba V. Melera '06	♀♀	4*
● Dolcetto d'Alba V. Scot '07	♀♀	4*
● Langhe Freisa '07	♀♀	4*
● Barolo Bricco Boschis V. S. Giuseppe Ris. '99	♀♀♀	8
● Barolo Bricco Boschis V. S. Giuseppe Ris. '01	♀♀♀	8
● Barolo Bricco Boschis V. S. Giuseppe Ris. '00	♀♀♀	8
● Barolo V. S. Giuseppe Ris. '89	♀♀♀	8
● Barolo Vignolo Ris. '01	♀♀	8
● Barolo Vignolo Ris. '00	♀♀	8
● Barbera d'Alba V. del Cuculo '04	♀♀	5
● Langhe Nebbiolo '05	♀♀	5

○ Langhe Bianco Arbarei '06	♀♀	5
● Langhe Rosso Monsordo '05	♀♀	5
◑ Barolo Zonchera '04	♀♀	6
● Barbaresco Asij '05	♀	6
● Barbera d'Alba Piana '07	♀	4
● Dolcetto d'Alba Rossana '07	♀	4
● Nebbiolo d'Alba Bernardina '06	♀	5
○ Langhe Arneis Blangé '07	♀	5
○ Langhe Bianco Arbarei '05	♀♀	5
○ Langhe Bianco Arbarei '04	♀♀	6
○ Langhe Bianco Arbarei '03	♀♀	5
● Langhe Rosso Monsordo '04	♀♀	5
● Langhe Rosso Monsordo '03	♀♀	6
● Langhe Rosso Monsordo '01	♀♀	6

Erede di Armando Chiappone

S.DA SAN MICHELE, 51
14049 NIZZA MONFERRATO [AT]
TEL. 0141721424
www.eredechiappone.com

★ ## Michele Chiarlo

S.DA NIZZA-CANELLI, 99
14042 CALAMANDRANA [AT]
TEL. 0141769030
www.chiarlo.it

ANNUAL PRODUCTION	30,000 bottles
HECTARES UNDER VINE	10
VITICULTURE METHOD	Conventional

ANNUAL PRODUCTION	950,000 bottles
HECTARES UNDER VINE	100
VITICULTURE METHOD	Conventional

Barbera d'Asti Superiore Nizza is not just the most majestic Barbera in the Asti area. Nizza is also an extraordinarily close-knit group of growers who, focusing ambitiously on one area and on one wine, have splendidly developed the rich potential of this corner of the denomination. Among them is Daniele Chiappone, and his wines do the group honour. Like so many in the area, his is a family operation and he has worked hard over the years to raise quality both in his cellar operations and in each of his vineyards, to which the few wines he produces bear ample testimony. His star is Ru 2005, a fruit-filled Barbera d'Asti Superiore Nizza with fine structure and overall balance. Top marks also go to Freisa d'Asti Sanpedra 2004 and to Barbera d'Asti Brentura 2006, which shows rich fruit and a full-flavoured finish. Dolcetto d'Asti Mandola 2006 and Monferrato Bianco Valbeccara 2006, a blend of cortese and favorita, are both well made, and the Rosato from barbera and dolcetto is very tasty.

Michele Chiarlo's Barbera d'Astis are a credit to the area. Two selections impressed us, each a classic. Barbera Cipressi della Court 2006 is fresh but not simple. It gains complexity from its rich fruit and whiffs of moist earth before showing power on the palate accompanied by lively fruit and acid through the finish. Barbera La Court, from the Nizza subzone, is a rung higher in complexity. Deep ruby precedes an equally impressive nose of wild red berry, cinchona and spice with delicate toastiness in the background. Spice returns on the palate and the balance is exemplary. Staying in the Monferrato area, Montemareto Countacc! 2005 is an excellent blend of barbera, syrah and cabernet sauvignon, and an Albarossa, Montald, makes its debut. Awaiting us in Langhe are superb Barolos. The finest, which strolled off with our Three Glasses, is Cannubi 2004. Elegant spice, tobacco leaf and cinchona create appeal on a multi-layered nose while fine-grained, complex tannins and an enviable follow-through complete a fine Barolo. Barolo Brunate, Cerequio 2004 and a complex Barbaresco Asili 2005 end the list. Gavi Rovereto 2007 is great.

● Barbera d'Asti Sup. Nizza Ru '05	♈♈	5
● Dolcetto d'Asti Mandola '06	♈♈	4
● Freisa d'Asti Sanpedra '04	♈♈	3*
● Barbera d'Asti Brentura '06	♈♈	4
○ M.to Bianco Valbeccara '06	♈	3
⊙ Rosita '07	♈	3
● Barbera d'Asti Sup. Nizza Ru '04	♈♈	5
● Barbera d'Asti Sup. Nizza Ru '03	♈♈	5
● Barbera d'Asti Sup. Nizza Ru '01	♈♈	5
● Barbera d'Asti Brentura '05	♈♈	4

● Barolo Cannubi '04	♈♈♈	8
● Barbera d'Asti Sup. Nizza La Court '05	♈♈	6
● Barolo Cerequio '04	♈♈	8
● M.to Rosso Montemareto Countacc! '05	♈♈	6
● Barbera d'Asti Sup. Cipressi della Court '06	♈♈	4*
● Barolo Brunate '04	♈♈	8
● Barbaresco Asili '05	♈♈	7
● M.to Rosso Montald '06	♈♈	5
○ Gavi del Comune di Gavi Rovereto '07	♈♈	4*
○ Moscato d'Asti Nivole '07	♈	3
● Barbera d'Asti Sup. Nizza La Court '01	♈♈♈	6

Cascina Chicco

VIA VALENTINO, 144
12043 CANALE [CN]
TEL. 0173979411
www.cascinachicco.com

ANNUAL PRODUCTION	230,000 bottles
HECTARES UNDER VINE	28
VITICULTURE METHOD	Conventional

The Faccenda family is building, a sign of their determination to grow their operation, already one of the Roero area's finest. Their judicious growth encompasses purchase of new vineyards, largely on the left bank of the Tanaro, but also recently, for the first time, in Barolo country in the Langhe. Respect to far-sighted brothers Enrico and Marco, well assisted by their wives and by their charismatic father, Federico. The wines we tasted were, as usual, terrific. The standard Arneis and Barbera Granera Alta were fruity and refreshing. Up a step and practically on an equal footing were Roero Montespinato and Nebbiolo Mompissano, the first a tad tannic, the second smooth and velvety. The favourable 2006 vintage gave Barbera Bric Loira a lush, complex nose and opulence and harmony on the palate. Roero Valmaggiore 2005 is today the flagship wine, here with a nose of rich spice and fruit, then sumptuous, elegant and endless in the mouth. The Passito, always one of the best, is as good as ever, with measured sweetness and fine balance.

Quinto Chionetti & Figlio

B.TA VALDIBERTI, 44
12063 DOGLIANI [CN]
TEL. 017371179
www.chionettiquinto.com

ANNUAL PRODUCTION	73,000 bottles
HECTARES UNDER VINE	14
VITICULTURE METHOD	Conventional

Quinto Chionetti is a benchmark amid all the changes over the years to both culture and countryside in the Langhe, that genuine and, to quote Cesare Pavese, mythical corner of earth. We will reprise the history of this spry, 80-something grower so attached to Dogliani and to his profession, nor recall his history and event-filled memory. Here we wish to discuss only the winemaker. Listed here are two wines, the usual two Dolcettos that Chionetti has been making since time immemorial, sticking to the fundamentals, focusing on cru vineyards and to his determination to coax out of his beloved dolcetto grape all, and only, what it can give. Fragrances above all, then impressive tannic structure, a stiffness that is judicious but still felt, and a smoothness that depends on the vintage. Vinifications in steel are required to avoid blunting the expression of the fruit, which is always unblemished, crisp and vibrant in both versions. We prefer Briccolero, and awarded it the Three Glasses for its clean nose, rounded volume in the mouth, its length and harmony. San Luigi is outstanding as well, showing succulent, dynamic and long-lingering.

O Arcàss Passito '06	♟♟	5
● Roero Valmaggiore '05	♟♟	5
● Barbera d'Alba Bric Loira '06	♟♟	5
● Nebbiolo d'Alba Mompissano '06	♟♟	5
● Roero Montespinato '06	♟♟	4*
O Roero Arneis Anterisio '07	♟♟	4*
● Barbera d'Alba Granera Alta '07	♟	4
O Arcàss Passito '04	♟♟♟	5
● Barbera d'Alba Bric Loira '98	♟♟♟	5
● Barbera d'Alba Bric Loira '97	♟♟♟	5
● Nebbiolo d'Alba Mompissano '99	♟♟♟	5
● Barbera d'Alba Bric Loira '05	♟♟	5
● Barbera d'Alba Bric Loira '04	♟♟	5
● Roero Valmaggiore '04	♟♟	5
● Roero Valmaggiore '03	♟♟	5
● Roero Valmaggiore '01	♟♟	5

● Dolcetto di Dogliani Briccolero '07	♟♟♟	4*
● Dolcetto di Dogliani S. Luigi '07	♟♟	4*
● Dolcetto di Dogliani Briccolero '04	♟♟♟	4
● Dolcetto di Dogliani Briccolero '06	♟♟	4
● Dolcetto di Dogliani Briccolero '05	♟♟	4
● Dolcetto di Dogliani Briccolero '03	♟♟	4
● Dolcetto di Dogliani Briccolero '01	♟♟	4
● Dolcetto di Dogliani S. Luigi '06	♟♟	4
● Dolcetto di Dogliani S. Luigi '05	♟♟	4

Cieck

FRAZ. SAN GRATO
VIA BARDESONO
10011 AGLIÈ [TO]
TEL. 0124330522
www.cieck.it

ANNUAL PRODUCTION 100,000 bottles
HECTARES UNDER VINE 20
VITICULTURE METHOD Conventional

Although Cieck dates back only to 1985, it already seems one of Piedmont's old-timers. Domenico Caretto has recently joined the Bardesono and Falconieri families, but Remo Falconieri is often in the cellar on a daily basis and little has changed. What distinguishes Cieck is its ability to make so many kinds of wines, whether sparkling or passito, dry white or red. The estate vineyards are planted mainly to erbaluce, whose acidity makes it ideal for sparklers, such as the long-respected San Giorgio and Calliope, both fermented in the bottle. Now comes a Brut Rosé, which has some neretto with the erbaluce. In these 2004 editions, our preference went, as usual, to the graceful San Giorgio over the fuller Calliope. Rosé, though crisp and tasty enough, lacks depth. Erbaluce T 2005 is quite distinctive and complex, testifying to the cellarability of Ivrea-area whites. Misobolo 2007 already augurs well, and Nebbiolo 2005 impresses with the austerity of its tannins while Cieck Neretto, from the somewhat down-market neretto di Bairo grape, possesses a kind of no-nonsense charm. Alladium Passito, though showing rich and dense, is still too youthful.

○ Erbaluce di Caluso Spumante Brut S. Giorgio '04	TT	5*
○ Caluso Passito Alladium '03	TT	5
○ Erbaluce di Caluso Spumante Brut Calliope '04	TT	5
○ Erbaluce di Caluso T '05	TT	4
○ Erbaluce di Caluso Misobolo '07	TT	4
⊙ Rosé Brut	TT	4
● Canavese Nebbiolo '05	TT	4
● Canavese Rosso Cieck Neretto '05	TT	3*
○ Erbaluce di Caluso Spumante Brut S. Giorgio '02	YY	4
○ Caluso Passito Alladium '02	YY	5
● Canavese Nebbiolo '04	YY	4
○ Erbaluce di Caluso Spumante Brut Calliope '02	YY	5

F.lli Cigliuti

VIA SERRABOELLA, 17
12052 NEIVE [CN]
TEL. 0173677185
www.cigliuti.it

ANNUAL PRODUCTION 35,000 bottles
HECTARES UNDER VINE 6.5
VITICULTURE METHOD Conventional

The venerable Cigliuti cellar gave us two Barbarescos, 2004 and 2005. The superb Barbaresco Vigne Erte 2004, whose 6,000 bottles were matured 26 months in large oak casks, merits Three Glasses. After a pungent medley of spice and underbrush, it looms powerful on the palate but classy tannins and lengthy development help to create enviable harmony. Barbaresco Serraboella 2004 matured in casks of varying sizes and shows luscious aromatics and a good balance. The 2005 Barbarescos exhibited more finesse and readiness at the time of our tastings. Barbaresco Vigne Erte 2005 largely mirrors last year's style but a bit less powerful, although with velvety tannins and excellent length. Barbaresco Serraboella 2005 was sourced from 30-year-old vines, which seems to attenuate the characteristics of the vintage. The nose is compelling and it achieves a fine state of proportion on the finish. Barbera d'Alba Serraboella 2006, which stayed 15 months in twice-used barriques, shows well scented and crisp throughout. We liked Barbera Campass 2006. Cask-aged for 15 months, it exhibits pronounced spice, a sturdy structure and an extremely impressive conclusion.

● Barbaresco V. Erte '04	TTT	7
● Barbaresco Serraboella '04	TT	7
● Barbaresco V. Erte '05	TT	7
● Barbaresco Serraboella '05	TT	7
● Barbera d'Alba Campass '06	TT	5
● Barbera d'Alba Serraboella '06	TT	5
● Barbaresco '83	YYY	7
● Barbaresco Serraboella '97	YYY	8
● Barbaresco Serraboella '96	YYY	8
● Barbaresco Serraboella '90	YYY	8
● Barbaresco Serraboella '01	YYY	7
● Barbaresco Serraboella '00	YYY	7
● Barbaresco Serraboella '03	YY	7
● Barbaresco V. Erte '03	YY	6
● Barbaresco V. Erte '01	YY	6
● Barbaresco V. Erte '00	YY	6
● Langhe Rosso Briccoserra '04	YY	6

Tenute Cisa Asinari dei Marchesi di Grésy

S.DA DELLA STAZIONE, 21
12050 BARBARESCO [CN]
TEL. 0173635222
www.marchesidigresy.com

ANNUAL PRODUCTION	200,000 bottles
HECTARES UNDER VINE	35
VITICULTURE METHOD	Conventional

The vineyard at Martinenga, a steep horseshoe facing south, could hardly be more striking, and as a terroir few areas can compete. Alberto di Grésy was sensitive to these surroundings when he enlarged his facility, sparing no expense to preserve their fascination. Environmental considerations led to major results, such as solar panels to provide extra power during the harvest. Tenute Cisa Asinari's vineyards are divided into three separate entities. The Barbaresco property yields Barbaresco and dry whites, Treiso produces Dolcetto and dry whites, while Cassine, in the province of Alessandria makes Barberas and Moscatos. This year, Three Glasses go to Gaiun 2004, which releases beguiling tobacco leaf, raspberry and dried flowers, followed by a well-proportioned palate and dynamic finale. Close behind is Camp Gros, perhaps a little less approachable and with more assertive extract that slows progression. Although from a minor vintage, Martinenga 2005 is already enjoyable. Among the whites, Chardonnay Grésy 2004 pulls ahead, its bright acidity is a tasty foil to an opulent, fat palate. Marco Dotta continues to ensure outstanding overall quality.

★★ Domenico Clerico

LOC. MANZONI, 67
12065 MONFORTE D'ALBA [CN]
TEL. 017378171
domenicoclerico@libero.it

ANNUAL PRODUCTION	95,000 bottles
HECTARES UNDER VINE	21
VITICULTURE METHOD	Conventional

Domenico Clerico is a volcano. The site of his new facility, to be ready in two or three years, is equally active. Also in the offing is a new Barolo from Serralunga but performances continue to be superb. The two Barolos strove for pre-eminence and Ciabot Mentin Ginestra 2004 claimed Three Glasses. Classic garnet is followed by a truly thrilling bouquet that unfolds slowly to infuse the palate, although the pungent balsam does nothing to hinder the pure expression of its fruit. This is a noble wine that will deliver a myriad impressions in the future but which already shows rich and harmonious. Barolo Pajana 2004 is another jewel, starting with beautifully proportioned fruit and oak, with some evolved nuances, all mirrored admirably on the palate, itself is a model of balanced tannins and fine length. Langhe Rosso Arte 2006 is, as always, classy. Despite maturation in all new oak, its fruit remains dense and succulent, and ten per cent barbera adds a nice tot of freshness to the nebbiolo. The youthful and delicious Langhe Dolcetto Visadì 2007 and the elegant and full-bodied Barbera d'Alba Trevigne 2006 are among the finest of their vintages.

● Barbaresco Gaiun '04	▼▼▼	8
● Barbaresco Camp Gros '04	▼▼	8
● Barbaresco Martinenga '05	▼▼	8
● Barbera d'Asti '06	▼▼	4*
● Barbera d'Asti Monte Colombo '05	▼▼	6
● M.to Rosso Merlotdasolo '04	▼▼	6
○ Langhe Bianco Villa Giulia '07	▼▼	4*
○ Langhe Chardonnay Grésy '04	▼▼	6
○ Piemonte Moscato Passito L'Altro Moscato '05	▼▼	6
○ Langhe Chardonnay '07	▼	4
○ Langhe Sauvignon '07	▼	4
○ Moscato d'Asti La Serra '07	▼	4
● Dolcetto d'Alba Monte Aribaldo '07	▼	4
● Barbaresco Camp Gros '01	�♀♀	8
● Barbaresco Camp Gros '00	♀♀♀	8
● Barbaresco Gaiun '97	♀♀♀	8

● Barolo Ciabot Mentin Ginestra '04	▼▼▼	8
● Barolo Pajana '04	▼▼	8
● Langhe Rosso Arte '06	▼▼	6
● Barbera d'Alba Trevigne '06	▼▼	5
● Langhe Dolcetto Visadì '07	▼▼	4*
● Barolo Percristina '01	♀♀♀	8
● Barolo Percristina '99	♀♀♀	8
● Barolo Percristina '98	♀♀♀	8
● Barolo Percristina '97	♀♀♀	8
● Barolo Percristina '96	♀♀♀	8
● Barolo Percristina '95	♀♀♀	8
● Barolo Ciabot Mentin Ginestra '01	♀♀♀	8
● Barolo Ciabot Mentin Ginestra '99	♀♀♀	8
● Barolo Ciabot Mentin Ginestra '89	♀♀♀	8
● Barolo Pajana '95	♀♀♀	8
● Barolo Pajana '90	♀♀♀	8

Elvio Cogno

VIA RAVERA, 2
12060 NOVELLO [CN]
TEL. 0173744006
www.elviocogno.com

ANNUAL PRODUCTION	70,000 bottles
HECTARES UNDER VINE	11
VITICULTURE METHOD	Conventional

Walter Fissore and Nadia Cogno continue to assert their role in Novello as one of the Langhe's finest. As to the future, Bricco Pernice, a two-hectare, south-facing parcel in Ravera, will soon be yielding a new bottling. The 2003 vintage sees Barolo Vigna Elena return, showing richness and finesse with noble spice on the nose and lush fruit. Barolo Ravera 2004, an extraordinary Barolo from an exceptional vintage, fully merits Three Glasses. The nose parades the subtlest impressions of mint and cinchona, followed by a magisterial palate and proportioned finish, the quintessence of Barolo. The well-crafted Barolo 2004 is classic in its expression. Langhe Montegrilli 2006, an impressive blend of half nebbiolo and half barbera, offers complexity and approachability. Barbera Bricco dei Merli 2006 pleases and intrigues. Aged in large casks, it is redolent of forest floor and its tannins are well integrated. Dolcetto Vigna del Mandorlo 2007 surprises with extractive weight and long-lingering scents of blackberry and pomegranate. Langhe Anas-cëtta 2007 is a white that marries firm structure and pronounced aromatics with refined flavours and character.

● Barolo Ravera '04	♟♟♟	7
● Barolo V. Elena '03	♟♟	8
○ Langhe Bianco Anas-cëtta '07	♟♟	4*
● Barbera d'Alba Bricco dei Merli '06	♟♟	5
● Barolo '04	♟♟	6
● Dolcetto d'Alba V. del Mandorlo '07	♟♟	4*
● Langhe Rosso Montegrilli '06	♟♟	5
● Barolo Ravera '01	♟♟♟	7
● Barolo V. Elena '01	♟♟♟	8
● Barolo V. Elena '99	♟♟♟	8
● Barolo V. Elena '00	♟♟	8
● Barolo V. Elena '98	♟♟	8
● Barolo Ravera '03	♟♟	7
● Barolo Ravera '00	♟♟	7
● Barolo Ravera '99	♟♟	7
○ Langhe Bianco Anas-cëtta '06	♟♟	4

Colle Manora

S.DA BOZZOLE, 5
15044 QUARGNENTO [AL]
TEL. 0131219252
www.collemanora.it

ANNUAL PRODUCTION	70,000 bottles
HECTARES UNDER VINE	20
VITICULTURE METHOD	Conventional

No one could accuse Colle Manora of lacking consistency, since it has been performing at a high level for some years now, thanks to the fine efforts of Mauro Burighel and Valter Piccinino. The winery standard-bearer remains Barbera del Monferrato Superiore Manora, which shows the deepest red, then reveals rich red berry fruit and pungent balsam followed by excellent balance and length in the mouth. Barbera Pais gains its considerable delight from the refreshing crispness of its fruit and its lively acidic grip. Rosso Barchetta, a melange of cabernet sauvignon, merlot and barbera with a ruby red hue, delivers berry fruit and subtle notes of fresh greens before entering smoothly onto a palate marked by alcoholic warmth and plenty of length. For years now, we have considered the all-sauvignon Monferrato Bianco Mimosa one of the most impressive whites made in the province of Alessandria, fermented and aged in steel, and released two years after the harvest. Mila is a partnering of sauvignon blanc and chardonnay that receives some six months' cask-ageing, and boasts a graceful yet rich nose.

● Barbera del M.to Manora '05	♟♟	5
● Barbera del M.to Pais '06	♟♟	4*
● M.to Rosso Barchetta '05	♟♟	6
○ M.to Bianco Mimosa '06	♟♟	4*
○ Mila Bianco '06	♟	6
○ M.to Bianco Mimosa '05	♟♟	4
● Barbera del M.to Manora '04	♟♟	5
● Barbera del M.to Manora '01	♟♟	5
● M.to Rosso Palo Alto '04	♟♟	6
● M.to Rosso Palo Alto '03	♟♟	6
● M.to Rosso Palo Alto '01	♟♟	6
● M.to Rosso Palo Alto '00	♟♟	6

Collina Serragrilli

VIA SERRAGRILLI, 30
12057 NEIVE [CN]
TEL. 0173677010
www.serragrilli.it

ANNUAL PRODUCTION	120,000 bottles
HECTARES UNDER VINE	15
VITICULTURE METHOD	Conventional

The Lequio family and winemaker Gianfranco Cordero craft the wines here, which over a very brief span of time have won enviable results. The 15 hectares of vineyards are planted in exceptional locations in the municipalities of Neive and Barbaresco, making possible the creation of powerful yet well-balanced wines. Barbaresco Serragrilli unleashed a terrific performance. Sourced from 50-year-old vines and barrique-aged, it yields notes of spice and red berry fruit, and then opens up a broad palate with silky tannins and crisp acidity, concluding impressively long. Barbera Grillaia leads with very dark ruby and needs time to open but flaunts, on both nose and mouth, an ambitious range of floral and fruit impressions, matched on the palate by an exuberant acidity and glossy tannins. High marks too for Barbaresco Basarin, with its fragrant rose petals and wild forest berries, plus considerable structure and emphatic tannins. Langhe Grillorosso is 60 per cent nebbiolo, with the rest barbera and cabernet, and the result is powerful, spicy, and finely fruited. Both Dolcetto and the standard Barbera d'Alba are very fine examples of their category.

● Barbaresco Serragrilli '05	♟♟ 6*
● Barbera d'Alba Grillaia '06	♟♟ 4*
● Barbaresco Basarin '04	♟♟ 6
● Langhe Grillorosso '05	♟♟ 4*
● Barbera d'Alba '06	♟ 4
● Dolcetto d'Alba '07	♟ 4
● Barbaresco Serragrilli '04	♟♟ 6
● Barbaresco Basarin '03	♟♟ 6
● Barbaresco Serragrilli '03	♟♟ 6
● Barbaresco Serragrilli '01	♟♟ 6
● Barbera d'Alba Grillaia '05	♟♟ 4

La Colombera

S.DA COMUNALE VHO, 7
15057 TORTONA [AL]
TEL. 0131867795
www.lacolomberavini.it

ANNUAL PRODUCTION	50,000 bottles
HECTARES UNDER VINE	22
VITICULTURE METHOD	Conventional

We stated in last year's Guide that La Colombera could no longer be considered a surprise in the Tortona area. As proof, this year brings a series of outstanding wines, fully three of which went to our national taste-offs. After some name changes in recent years for their Timorasso, Piercarlo and Elisa have finally settled on Il Montino for the selection and the more classic name Derthona for the second label. We consider the pair to be among the finest from the category that we tasted this year. The latter privileges finesse and a tasty vein of acidity, whereas Il Montino exhibits a splendid minerality, extractive weight and just-ripe fruit. This was the wine that brought Three Glasses for the first time to La Colombera. The 2005 growing year was a far from prodigious vintage for some but brought Elisa back to its accustomed high quality. It shows measured depth, outstanding balance and a thrilling elegance. The remaining labels are all impressive, including the croatina Arché and Vegia Rampana, a barbera vinified in steel. The cortese Bricco Bartolomeo and Freisa Colle del Grillo 2007 are ready now and flaunt reasonable price tags.

○ Colli Tortonesi Timorasso Il Montino '06	♟♟♟ 5
○ Colli Tortonesi Timorasso Derthona '06	♟♟ 5
● Piemonte Barbera Elisa '05	♟♟ 4
● Colli Tortonesi Rosso Arché '05	♟♟ 4
● Colli Tortonesi Freisa Colle del Grillo '07	♟ 4
● Colli Tortonesi Rosso Vegia Rampana '06	♟ 4
○ Colli Tortonesi Bianco Bricco Bartolomeo '07	♟ 3
○ Colli Tortonesi Timorasso '05	♟♟ 5
● Colli Tortonesi Rosso Suciaja '04	♟♟ 5
● Colli Tortonesi Rosso Suciaja '03	♟♟ 5
● Colli Tortonesi Rosso Suciaja '01	♟♟ 5
● Piemonte Barbera Elisa '04	♟♟ 4

Il Colombo - Barone Riccati

VIA DEI SENT, 2
12084 MONDOVÌ [CN]
TEL. 017441607
www.ilcolombo.com

ANNUAL PRODUCTION 15,000 bottles
HECTARES UNDER VINE 3.3
VITICULTURE METHOD Natural

Il Colombo is another dimension, in landscape and culture as well as winemaking. It's light years from the picture-postcard Langhe of Barolo, tourists thronging wineries and restaurants, and the exploitation of the territory and its resources. Time flows more slowly and the ever-present woodland, nearby mountains and the views over Mondovì have a certain flavour of yesteryear. But Bruno Chionetti, the multi-tasking manager of this beautiful winery, owned by the Norwegian Holm family. Aided by his wife Sabina, Bruno enthusiastically promotes an area wrongly considered marginal. This year we tasted two excellent examples of Dolcetto delle Langhe Monregalesi and a Langhe Rosso. Il Colombo 2006 is at the top of its game: dark, concentrated ruby red introduces a harmonious bouquet of complex spicy and earthy notes. On the palate it is tannic, rounded, mouthfilling and elegant. La Chiesetta is just a touch more simple, but attractive for its linearity, the linear progression of the body and the overall harmony. The Langhe Rosso is a blend of dolcetto and merlot which still needs to settle down. The winery is in the process of converting to organic methods.

● Dolcetto delle Langhe Monregalesi Sup. Il Colombo '06	YY	4*
● Dolcetto delle Langhe Monregalesi La Chiesetta '07	YY	3*
● Langhe Rosso Monteregale '05	Y	5
● Dolcetto delle Langhe Monregalesi Il Colombo '98	YYY	4
● Dolcetto delle Langhe Monregalesi Il Colombo '97	YYY	4
● Dolcetto delle Langhe Monregalesi Sup. Il Colombo '05	YY	4
● Dolcetto delle Langhe Monregalesi Sup. Il Colombo '04	YY	4
● Dolcetto delle Langhe Monregalesi Sup. Il Colombo '03	YY	4
● Langhe Monteregale '03	YY	5

★ Aldo Conterno

LOC. BUSSIA, 48
12065 MONFORTE D'ALBA [CN]
TEL. 017378150
www.poderialdoconterno.com

ANNUAL PRODUCTION 120,000 bottles
HECTARES UNDER VINE 25
VITICULTURE METHOD Conventional

Is hail ever a godsend? Well in 2004, hail hit the Cicala vineyard, crucial to Barolo Gran Bussia, while the Romirasco grapes also used in the blend were untouched. Unperturbed, Franco, Giacomo and Stefano Conterno vinified the grapes separately and the results were good. So good that Romirasco will continue to be produced when Gran Bussia comes back in 2011. It throws an elegant bouquet of fruit and leather, followed by a long, clean tannic weave in a warm, mouthfilling structure. This superb wine is, however, matched by the more closed but very complex Barolo Colonnello 2004 and the 2004 Barolo – formerly Barolo Bussia, but now partly sourced from new Barolo vineyards – which is ready for drinking. Three Glasses went to the superlative Romirasco, which confirms the Games' Barolo skills. Il Favot 2005 combines red berry fruits and spice while the drinkable Langhe Rosso 2005 is now a blend based on 80 per cent freisa topped up with cabernet and merlot. The Bussiador 2005 is charming. A Chardonnay aged in new barriques, it gives tobacco and apricots then a fresh, well-balanced palate with a very long finish.

● Barolo Romirasco '04	YYY	8
● Barolo '04	YY	8
● Barolo Colonnello '04	YY	8
● Barbera d'Alba Conca Tre Pile '05	YY	6
● Langhe Nebbiolo Il Favot '05	YY	7
● Langhe Rosso '05	YY	5
O Langhe Bianco Bussiador '05	YY	6
● Langhe Dolcetto Il Masante '07	Y	4
● Barbera d'Alba Conca Tre Pile '89	YYY	6
● Barolo Gran Bussia Ris. '01	YYY	8
● Barolo Gran Bussia Ris. '95	YYY	8
● Barolo Gran Bussia Ris. '90	YYY	8
● Barolo Gran Bussia Ris. '89	YYY	8
● Barolo Gran Bussia Ris. '88	YYY	8
● Barolo Gran Bussia Ris. '82	YYY	8
● Barolo Bussia Soprana '86	YYY	8
● Barolo V. del Colonnello '90	YYY	8

★ Giacomo Conterno

Loc. Ornati, 2
12065 Monforte d'Alba [CN]
tel. 017378221

ANNUAL PRODUCTION 50,000 bottles
HECTARES UNDER VINE 14
VITICULTURE METHOD Conventional

The Conterno winery is not for trend-seekers or indeed admirers of tradition. The wines soon tell that this is a vibrant operation and the aristocratic style is indicative of rigorous viticulture practices that transcend time. Roberto Conterno thoughtfully discusses Langhe wine and his words hint that after seven years in wood, he thinks there is little to add to his ageworthy Monfortino Riserva 2001. Excellently made, it mingles rich aromas of morello cherry, blackcurrant and walnut, accompanied by fine scents of elderflower. The assertively appealing palate is mouthfilling and attractively structured with a full-flavoured and harmonious finish of outstanding length. This is a wine of character and personality. But don't expect Barolo Cascina Francia 2004 to play second fiddle. In fact, it has a generously spacious bouquet, combining austerity and fruit on the palate, and judiciously balancing the tannins with acidity to provide a flavoursome finish that reprises the aromas. Both of these Barolos are Three Glass standard. The range is rounded off by an excellent Barbera 2006.

● Barolo Cascina Francia '04	▼▼▼	8
● Barolo Monfortino Ris. '01	▼▼▼	8
● Barbera d'Alba Cascina Francia '06	▼▼	6
● Barolo Cascina Francia '97	▽▽▽	8
● Barolo Cascina Francia '90	▽▽▽	8
● Barolo Cascina Francia '89	▽▽▽	8
● Barolo Cascina Francia '87	▽▽▽	8
● Barolo Cascina Francia '85	▽▽▽	8
● Barolo Cascina Francia '01	▽▽▽	8
● Barolo Monfortino Ris. '00	▽▽▽	8
● Barolo Monfortino Ris. '99	▽▽▽	8
● Barolo Monfortino Ris. '97	▽▽▽	8
● Barolo Monfortino Ris. '96	▽▽▽	8
● Barolo Monfortino Ris. '90	▽▽▽	8
● Barolo Monfortino Ris. '88	▽▽▽	8
● Barolo Monfortino Ris. '87	▽▽▽	8

Paolo Conterno

via Ginestra, 34
12065 Monforte d'Alba [CN]
tel. 017378415
www.paoloconterno.com

ANNUAL PRODUCTION 50,000 bottles
HECTARES UNDER VINE 11
VITICULTURE METHOD Conventional

The Conterno's classic winery is in a fine growing area at Monforte. This year, 6,000 bottles of Barolo Ginestra Riserva 2001 were on show. The selection is made only in excellent years (the next will be 2004). It is steel-fermented and aged for five and a half years in large wood, then 18 months in bottle. This gem's intense, orange-edged garnet ushers in spices, tobacco and a hint of tar. Powerful, elegant and refined, the beautifully balanced palate signs off long finish. Three effortless Glasses. The Barolo Ginestra 2004, in 12,000 bottles, aged in large barrels and has an intense nose with a good follow-through. The 6,000 bottles of basic 2004 Barolo, matured like the Ginestra. They give violet and fruit that lead into a full-flavoured, structured palate. The Barbera Ginestra 2006, in 10,000 bottles, is superb after a year's ageing in steel and pre-used barriques, proffering elegant aromas lifted by firm acidity to a harmonious finish. Similar but with less complexity is the Barbera Bricco Sant'Ambrogio 2007, in 7,000 bottles, matured for six months in large barrels. The Langhe Nebbiolo 2006 and Dolcetto d'Alba Ginestra 2007 pass muster.

● Barolo Ginestra Ris. '01	▼▼▼	8
● Barbera d'Alba Ginestra '06	▼▼	5
● Barolo '04	▼▼	7
● Barolo Ginestra '04	▼▼	8
● Barbera d'Alba Bricco Sant'Ambrogio '07	▼▼	4*
● Dolcetto d'Alba Ginestra '07	▼	4
● Langhe Nebbiolo '06	▼	5
● Barolo Ginestra Ris. '99	▽▽	8
● Barolo Ginestra Ris. '98	▽▽	8
● Barolo Ginestra Ris. '97	▽▽	8
● Barbera d'Alba Ginestra '05	▽▽	5
● Barolo Ginestra '03	▽▽	8
● Barolo Ginestra '01	▽▽	8
● Barolo Ginestra '00	▽▽	8
● Barolo Ginestra '99	▽▽	8

★ Conterno Fantino

VIA GINESTRA, 1
12065 MONFORTE D'ALBA [CN]
TEL. 017378204
www.conternofantino.it

ANNUAL PRODUCTION	140,000 bottles
HECTARES UNDER VINE	25
VITICULTURE METHOD	Conventional

For over 20 years, Claudio Conterno and Guido Fantino have been a successful team. Claudio in the vineyard and Guido at the winery have achieved in record time results that might take other wineries decades of hard work. Success breeds confidence and the two partners thrive. Conterno Fantino is like a fashion designer who crafts hand-sewn items for the select few. Thanks to the 2004 harvest, which is fulfilling the potential everyone was talking about, the cellar is showing that its reputation is well founded. The two best-known Barolos, Sorì Ginestra and Vigna del Gris, sailed into our finals. The fact that only the Vigna del Gris earned top honours is due to the form displayed by the wine at that precise moment in time. It has everything you could wish from a great Barolo: finesse, power, complexity, length and close-woven tannins. When we tasted, Sorì Ginestra struck us as a touch more clenched and less open. The Mosconi, from a superb vineyard, is currently a tad austere. The 2005 Monprà was a pleasant surprise and seems to be right back on form.

Contratto

VIA G. B. GIULIANI, 56
14053 CANELLI [AT]
TEL. 0141823349
www.contratto.it

ANNUAL PRODUCTION	290,000 bottles
HECTARES UNDER VINE	55
VITICULTURE METHOD	Conventional

The great classics of the Contratto winery are still the same despite line-up changes. Production remains anchored to sparklers but there are excursions into the world of still wines, starting with Barolo. And it was Barolo Cerequio 2004 that topped the bill. Mid garnet introduces dried flowers and tobacco layered with ripe red berry fruits and the elegant, caressing palate reveals youthful but already smooth tannins. This is a good interpretation of Cerequio, one of the finest vineyards in the entire DOCG. Asti De Miranda, the first made using the classic method, is superb as always. The iconic bouquet has clear tropical fruit boosted by the natural aromatic sensations of moscato. A sumptuous palate is seductive in its non-sweet sweetness. Among the classic method sparklers, we liked the Giuseppe Contratto Riserva 2004, a fine example of elegance, although just a touch too forthright. The For England Rosé 2005 is pleasantly fruity whereas the For England 2005 was less convincing, and lacked complexity. The selection is rounded off with a full-flavoured, robust current Barbera aged for a few months in barrique.

● Barolo V. del Gris '04	♥♥♥	8
● Barolo Mosconi '04	♥♥	8
● Barolo Sorì Ginestra '04	♥♥	8
● Langhe Rosso Monprà '05	♥♥	6
● Barbera d'Alba Vignota '07	♥♥	5
● Dolcetto d'Alba Bricco Bastia '07	♥♥	4*
○ Langhe Chardonnay Bastia '06	♥♥	6
● Langhe Nebbiolo Ginestrino '07	♥	5
● Barolo Sorì Ginestra '99	♥♥♥	8
● Barolo Sorì Ginestra '98	♥♥♥	8
● Barolo Sorì Ginestra '00	♥♥♥	8
● Barolo V. del Gris '97	♥♥♥	8
● Barolo V. del Gris '96	♥♥♥	8
● Barolo V. del Gris '01	♥♥♥	8
● Langhe Rosso Monprà '98	♥♥♥	8
● Langhe Rosso Monprà '97	♥♥♥	8

○ Asti De Miranda M. Cl. '05	♥♥	6
● Barolo Cerequio '04	♥♥	8
● Barbera d'Asti Panta Rei '07	♥♥	5
⊙ For England Rosé '05	♥♥	6
○ Spumante M. Cl. Brut Ris. Giuseppe Contratto '04	♥♥	6
○ For England Pas Dosé '05	♥	6
○ Asti De Miranda M. Cl. '97	♥♥♥	6
○ Asti De Miranda M. Cl. '96	♥♥♥	6
● Barolo Cerequio '99	♥♥♥	8
● Barolo Cerequio Tenuta Secolo '97	♥♥♥	8
● Barolo Cerequio '03	♥♥	8
○ Asti De Miranda M. Cl. '04	♥♥	6
○ Spumante M. Cl. Brut Ris. Giuseppe Contratto '99	♥♥	6

Coppo

VIA ALBA, 68
14053 CANELLI [AT]
TEL. 0141823146
www.coppo.it

ANNUAL PRODUCTION	420,000 bottles
HECTARES UNDER VINE	56
VITICULTURE METHOD	Conventional

Third-generation winemakers, the Coppo brothers, own a beautiful winery hewn out of the tufa hill and, with other Canelli wineries, is waiting to become a UNESCO Heritage Site. It is difficult to find weak points in the Coppo range but there are many peaks of quality. This year, three wines were up for Three Glasses: Chardonnay Monteriolo 2005, Freisa Mondaccione 2004 and Barbera Pomorossso 2006. The first two exploited their extra year's ageing to the full, having softened their edges or excessive oakiness, and were on brilliant form. The power and class of Monteriolo gives it a Burgundyesque feel that we rewarded with Three Glasses. Mondaccione has all splendid distinctiveness of freisa: well-defined spice on the nose and tannic richness in the mouth. True to form, Pomorosso reveals ripe and crisp fruit behind a layer of delightfully toasty wood. A special mention also went to the still explosive Barbera Riserva della Famiglia 2003, the powerful Piero Coppo Riserva del Fondatore 1998, disgorged after around nine years on the lees, and the international Alterego 2005. Younger Gavi, Moscato d'Asti and Barbera wines complete the superlative range.

O Piemonte Chardonnay Monteriolo '05	♥♥♥	6
● Barbera d'Asti Pomorosso '06	♥♥	7
● Langhe Freisa V. Vecchie Mondaccione '04	♥♥	6
● Barbera d'Asti Camp du Rouss '06	♥♥	4*
● Barbera d'Asti L'Avvocata '07	♥♥	4*
● Barbera d'Asti Sup. Nizza Riserva della Famiglia '03	♥♥	8
● M.to Alterego '05	♥♥	6
O Piero Coppo Ris. del Fondatore Brut '98	♥♥	8
O Gavi La Rocca '07	♥♥	4*
O Moscato d'Asti La Rocca '07	♥	4
O Piemonte Chardonnay Costebianche '07	♥	4

Giovanni Corino

FRAZ. ANNUNZIATA, 24B
12064 LA MORRA [CN]
TEL. 0173509452

ANNUAL PRODUCTION	40,000 bottles
HECTARES UNDER VINE	8
VITICULTURE METHOD	Conventional

Giuliano Corino runs his small winery with excellent results, producing wines that faithfully reflect their provenance, always embodying the balance and reserve typical of Langhe folk. Making the most of a favourable year, Giuliano presented a Barolo Giachini 2004 in fine form, complex and balsamic on the nose, powerful on the palate, with smooth tannins and the velvety mouthfeel that distinguishes Barolo from La Morra. The finish shows fine verve. It's a fantastically cellarable wine. Barolo Arborina 2004 goes all out for elegance, showing floral notes in a layered, truly seductive bouquet. The palate displays a good balance of tannins and succulent fruit with good length. The Barolo 2004 is less complex but has convincing balance and is anything but banal. The Barolo Vecchie Vigne 2003 is from a less successful harvest but is well-made. Luscious ripe fruit on the nose opens onto a sweet warm palate, with slightly raw tannins and a juicy finish. The Dolcetto 2007 is highly drinkable. Heady, fruity and lively in the mouth, it is rounded and impeccably clean. The Barbera d'Alba 2007, meanwhile, is well typed, fresh and fruity.

● Barolo Vign. Arborina '04	♥♥	8
● Barolo V. Giachini '04	♥♥	8
● Barbera d'Alba '07	♥♥	4*
● Barolo '04	♥♥	7
● Barolo Vecchie Vigne '03	♥♥	8
● Dolcetto d'Alba '07	♥♥	4*
● Barolo Rocche '01	♥♥♥	8
● Barolo Rocche '90	♥♥♥	8
● Barolo Vecchie Vigne '99	♥♥♥	8
● Barolo Vecchie Vigne '98	♥♥♥	8
● Barolo V. Giachini '03	♥♥	8
● Barolo V. Giachini '01	♥♥	7

Renato Corino

B.TA POZZO, 49A
12064 LA MORRA [CN]
TEL. 0173500349

ANNUAL PRODUCTION	30,000 bottles
HECTARES UNDER VINE	6
VITICULTURE METHOD	Conventional

In a new winery amid famous vineyards with views over the whole of La Morra, Renato Corino concentrates on quality, with over 20 years of experience and ideal terroir for classic Langhe wines. With the help of the excellent 2004 growing year, he gave us a great Barolo Rocche with a vibrant profile and violet-led aromas integrated with the French oak. Despite its youth, it is succulent on the elegant, complex palate with its soft tannins. A classy Three Glasses. The Barolo Arborina 2004 offers attractive spice and florality, and a palate with extract that is still marked but soft and beautifully elegant. The finish lingers. The Barolo 2004 is a success thanks to Renato's decision to source it from the Roncaglie vineyard, and is linear, clean and agreeably complex. The Barolo Vecchie Vigne 2003 reflects the growing year in its warm notes and ripe fruit. The Barbera Vigna Pozzo 2005 has a tad too much wood but as always is fruit-driven and lively, with good length and balance. The 2007 Dolcetto and Barbera are well executed and well typed, and the Nebbiolo d'Alba 2006, sourced from a vineyard in Vezza d'Alba, is also attractive.

Cornarea

VIA VALENTINO, 150
12043 CANALE [CN]
TEL. 017365636

ANNUAL PRODUCTION	75,000 bottles
HECTARES UNDER VINE	14
VITICULTURE METHOD	Conventional

Last year, the Cornarea profile began: "There is always a lot of Arneis in the range of wines released by the Bovone family…". This year, there is even more, because, together with Andrè, their classic late-harvest Roero Arneis table wine, and the Tarasco Passito, the winery has brought out a Charmat method sparkler. We'll look at it next year but initial tastings show that arneis stands up well as a sparkling wine, yet another string to the bow of a generous local variety that is little known, or at least little exploited. Moving on to the estate classics, pride of place as usual goes to the dry and dried-grape versions. The former is complex, richly aromatic, velvety and well balanced, one of the year's best Arneis wines, and a candidate for top honours. The passito is, as usual, divine, with notes of dried fruit on the palate combined with the richness and harmony of a real thoroughbred. The Andrè 2005 is also surprisingly good, offering subtle exotic fruit, dried flowers and musk. The reds are on the up. Nebbiolo d'Alba 2005 is austere and tannic while the deep, dry, well-balanced Roero 2005 has never been so convincing.

● Barolo Vign. Rocche '04	▼▼▼ 8
● Barolo Vign. Arborina '04	▼▼ 8
● Barbera d'Alba V. Pozzo '05	▼▼ 6
● Barbera d'Alba '07	▼▼ 4*
● Barolo '04	▼▼ 6
● Barolo Vecchie Vigne '03	▼▼ 8
● Dolcetto d'Alba '07	▼▼ 4*
● Nebbiolo d'Alba '06	▼ 5
● Barolo Vign. Rocche '04	♈♈♈ 8
● Barbera d'Alba V. Pozzo '04	♈♈ 6
● Barolo Vecchie Vigne '01	♈♈ 8
● Barolo Vign. Arborina '03	♈♈ 8

○ Roero Arneis '07	▼▼ 4*
○ Tarasco Passito '04	▼▼ 6
○ Andrè '05	▼▼ 5
● Nebbiolo d'Alba '05	▼▼ 4
● Roero '05	▼▼ 4
○ Tarasco Passito '03	♈♈ 6
○ Tarasco Passito '01	♈♈ 6
○ Tarasco Passito '00	♈♈ 6
● Roero '04	♈♈ 4
● Roero '03	♈♈ 4
● Roero Sup. '01	♈♈ 5

★ Matteo Correggia

LOC. GARBINETTO
VIA S. STEFANO ROERO, 124
12043 CANALE [CN]
TEL. 0173978009
www.matteocorreggia.com

ANNUAL PRODUCTION	120,000 bottles
HECTARES UNDER VINE	20
VITICULTURE METHOD	Natural

The Correggia winery continues to set the pace for other wineries in the area, providing topics for discussion and food for thought. This is the way of things ever since the much-mourned Matteo showed just how much potential there was in an apparently marginal area. Today, Ornella and her exceptional staff, who were preparing the wedding reception of their young oenologist, Luca Rostagno, when we visited, is a champion of sustainable viticulture. Correggia's natural approach means working the land in the full awareness of the surrounding environment. It's another field in which Correggia is leading the way, sensibly and without ostentation. The other great investment in the future regards the signature wine not only of the winery but in a sense of the whole of Roero. The iconic Ròche d'Ampsèj 2005, which is not being released this year, will be presented for tasting in 2009, after almost four years' ageing. Without its star player, and also lacking Le Marne Grigie 2005, the winery can console itself with an outstanding trio: Barbera Marun 2006, the classic Nebbiolo d'Alba 2006 and Langhe Bianco 2006. All the other wines are first-rate.

● Barbera d'Alba Marun '06	♟	6
O Langhe Bianco Matteo Correggia '06	♟	6
● Nebbiolo d'Alba La Val dei Preti '06	♟	6
● Anthos Passito '07	♟	5
● Barbera d'Alba '06	♟	4*
● Roero '06	♟	4*
● Anthos '07	♟	4*
O Roero Arneis '07	♟	4*
● Barbera d'Alba Marun '04	♟♟♟	6
● Roero Ròche d'Ampsèj '99	♟♟♟	8
● Roero Ròche d'Ampsèj '98	♟♟♟	8
● Roero Ròche d'Ampsèj '97	♟♟♟	8
● Roero Ròche d'Ampsèj '96	♟♟♟	8
● Roero Ròche d'Ampsèj '04	♟♟♟	7
● Roero Ròche d'Ampsèj '01	♟♟♟	8
● Roero Ròche d'Ampsèj '00	♟♟♟	8
● Roero Ròche d'Ampsèj '03	♟♟	8

Giuseppe Cortese

S.DA RABAJÀ, 80
12050 BARBARESCO [CN]
TEL. 0173635131
www.cortesegiuseppe.it

ANNUAL PRODUCTION	50,000 bottles
HECTARES UNDER VINE	8
VITICULTURE METHOD	Conventional

The Cortese winery is in the heart of the Rabajà vineyard and in 2009 will also be offering bed and breakfast facilities with panoramic views. Production is driven by care in the vineyard and traditional winemaking. The quality of the wines is great, from the fresh and attractive Dolcetto Trifolera 2007 to the two Barberas. The steel-aged 2006 is meaty and forthright, while Morassina 2005, darker and more intense, has aromatics from ageing in small oak barrels. The Nebbiolo 2006 is interesting, with marked, rose-themed aromas. Barbaresco Rabajà 2005 is intense, powerful and earthy with fruit tones over crushed flowers and herbs. Flavoursome and mouthfilling, it manages to maintain elegance and depth in its assertive tannic structure. After leisurely maturation, Barbaresco Rabajà Riserva 2001 emerged to join excellent vintages from the past, such as the outstanding 1996. It's well rounded, austere and mature as tertiary aromas begin to come through in hints of tobacco, plum, medicinal herbs and cocoa, accompanied by a warm, reassuring mouthfeel. Robust and deep, with imposing yet already smoothish tannins, it can only improve with further ageing.

● Barbaresco Rabajà '05	♟	6*
● Barbaresco Rabajà Ris. '01	♟	8
● Barbera d'Alba '06	♟	4*
● Barbera d'Alba Morassina '05	♟	5
● Dolcetto d'Alba Trifolera '07	♟	4*
● Langhe Nebbiolo '06	♟	5
● Barbaresco Rabajà Ris. '96	♟♟♟	8
● Barbaresco Rabajà Ris. '99	♟♟	8
● Barbaresco Rabajà '04	♟♟	6
● Barbaresco Rabajà '03	♟♟	6
● Barbaresco Rabajà '01	♟♟	6
● Barbaresco Rabajà '00	♟♟	6
● Barbaresco Rabajà '99	♟♟	6
● Barbaresco Rabajà '98	♟	6

Costa Olmo

VIA SAN MICHELE, 18
14040 VINCHIO [AT]
TEL. 0141950423
www.costaolmo.com

ANNUAL PRODUCTION	50,000 bottles
HECTARES UNDER VINE	5
VITICULTURE METHOD	Conventional

We'll try not to call these wines "gems". Their maker, Vittorio Limone, is a former Turin jeweller. With his Treviso-born wife Paola, he moved 30 years ago to Asti to make wine and they eventually settled on the area of Vinchio and Vaglio: in other words, barbera country. Skipping the early days, we pick up the story exactly ten years ago when the family bottled their first harvest under the Costa Olmo brand. Since then, with the painstaking precision of the real craftsman and the assistance of oenologist Roberto Olivieri, Paola and Vittorio have built up a small range of wines with great territorial character, except for their floral, varietal Chardonnay. Moving on to the two Barberas, we liked the enjoyable acidity and mouthfeel of La Madrina 2006, which is extremely well textured, partly by reason of one of the best vintages in recent years. The winery's star is Barbera Superiore Costa Olmo 2005, dark ruby red, concentrated, and almost impenetrable. On the nose, scents of morello cherry, rain-soaked earth, sweet spice and blackcurrant emerge while the palate is warm, mellow and well defined, matching power with elegance.

Daniele Coutandin

B.TA CIABOT, 12
10063 PEROSA ARGENTINA [TO]
TEL. 0121803473
ramie.countadin@alpimedia.it

ANNUAL PRODUCTION	4,000 bottles
HECTARES UNDER VINE	0.8
VITICULTURE METHOD	Conventional

The big news this year is the change in ownership. The winery has passed from Giuliano Coutandin to his son, Daniele. This is encouraging because, as his mother Laura says, "Everyone talks about mountain viticulture but very few actually do it". Yet here we have a young man who has made the decision to stay in his home countryside and commit himself to the complicated and difficult craft of grape growing in extreme conditions. The difficulties involved are not just the steep slopes, the climate and the loneliness. The estate itself is extremely small, which makes it impossible to exploit economies of scale. Nevertheless, the Coutandins are not giving up and have installed new systems aimed at increasing their modest current output. This year, they presented an excellent Ramìe 2006 – from avanà, avarengo, neretto and bequet grapes – that shows marked spiciness and delicate fruit. With the 2004 harvest, we see the return of the important barbera and bequet Barbichè with its velvety tannins and refreshing acidity. The current Gagin is as attractive as usual.

● Barbera d'Asti La Madrina '06	♟♟	4*
● Barbera d'Asti Sup. Costa Olmo '05	♟♟	5
○ Piemonte Chardonnay A Paola '07	♟♟	4*
● Barbera d'Asti La Madrina '04	♟♟	4
● Barbera d'Asti Sup. '04	♟♟	5
● Barbera d'Asti Sup. '03	♟♟	5

● Barbichè '04	♟♟	4*
● Pinerolese Ramìe '06	♟♟	5
● Gagin '07	♟	4
● Barbichè '03	♟♟	4
● Pinerolese Ramìe '05	♟♟	5
● Pinerolese Ramìe '04	♟♟	5
● Pinerolese Ramìe '03	♟♟	5

Dacapo

S.DA ASTI MARE, 4
14040 AGLIANO TERME [AT]
TEL. 0141964921
www.dacapo.it

ANNUAL PRODUCTION	45,000 bottles
HECTARES UNDER VINE	7
VITICULTURE METHOD	Conventional

Paolo Dania and Dino Riccomagno set up this winery 11 years ago to make top-quality wines and bring out the best of their vineyards of Agliano Terme for Barbera. These, then, are wines rooted in their terroir but with a modern style and the duo should take credit for the results achieved, which are exceptional. This year the wines were good but did not scale the heights of previous vintages. Having said that, we should acknowledge that the leading wines had to grapple with a harvest that was good but not exceptional. The Monferrato Rosso Tre 2005, a blend of merlot, barbera and nebbiolo, is elegant and well-balanced, spacious on the nose and attractively long on the palate. The Barbera Nizza Dacapo 2005 is nothing short of sumptuous, with aromas ranging from blackcurrant to cocoa powder, showing warm, intense and long in the mouth. The Barbera Sanbastiàn from the fine 2006 harvest presents well-defined, ripe plum-jammy fruit and a typically floral nose with violet-led aromas. Ruché Bric Majoli again has all the appeal and drinkability that have so often charmed us in the past.

Damilano

VIA ROMA, 31
12060 BAROLO [CN]
TEL. 017356265
www.cantinedamilano.it

ANNUAL PRODUCTION	350,000 bottles
HECTARES UNDER VINE	32
VITICULTURE METHOD	Conventional

Guido and Margherita Damilano, with their cousins Paolo and Mario, can look back on a 2008 full of news: the reorganization of the commercial department, a fantastic new tasting room, which completes the restructuring of the winery and, above all, the addition of eight hectares in the prestigious Cannubi vineyard to go with their selection from the no less prestigious Brunate since the 2005 harvest. As we wait for greater quantities, let's enjoy the quality of the Cannubi 2004, one of the best versions ever and a Three Glass wine of real elegance. Consultant oenologist Beppe Caviola can also feel satisfied, having produced a wine with perfect fruit-balsamic balance and fine-grained tannins echoed in the clean, lingering finish. Not far behind are Liste 2004, more austere in its development but no less complex, and Lecinquevigne 2004, more traditional both in that it ages in large wood and in blending grapes from several vineyards. The rest of the wines are good, especially the two Barbera d'Albas. The basic 2007 has typical freshness and the complex, flavoursome La Blu 2006, from 40-year-old vines.

● Barbera d'Asti Sanbastiàn '06	▼▼ 4*
● Barbera d'Asti Sup. Nizza V. Dacapo '05	▼ 5
● M.to Rosso Tre '05	▼▼ 6
● Ruché di Castagnole M.to Bric Majoli '07	▼ 4
● M.to Rosso Tre '04	♀♀ 6
● Barbera d'Asti Sanbastiàn '05	♀♀ 4
● Barbera d'Asti Sanbastiàn '04	♀♀ 4
● Barbera d'Asti Sup. Nizza V. Dacapo '04	♀♀ 5
● Barbera d'Asti Sup. Nizza V. Dacapo '01	♀♀ 5
● Ruché di Castagnole M.to Bric Majoli '06	♀♀ 4

● Barolo Cannubi '04	▼▼▼ 8
● Barolo Liste '04	▼▼ 8
● Barolo Lecinquevigne '04	▼▼ 7
● Barbera d'Alba '07	▼▼ 4*
● Barbera d'Alba La Blu '06	▼▼ 5
● Nebbiolo d'Alba '06	▼▼ 5
● Dolcetto d'Alba '07	▼ 4
O Langhe Arneis '07	▼ 4
● Barolo Cannubi '01	♀♀♀ 8
● Barolo Cannubi '00	♀♀♀ 8
● Barolo Cannubi '03	♀♀ 8
● Barolo Cannubi '99	♀♀ 8
● Barolo Liste '03	♀♀ 8
● Barolo Liste '01	♀♀ 8
● Barolo Liste '00	♀♀ 8

Sergio Degiorgis

VIA CIRCONVALLAZIONE, 3
12056 MANGO [CN]
TEL. 014189107
www.degiorgis-sergio.com

ANNUAL PRODUCTION	70,000 bottles
HECTARES UNDER VINE	9.5
VITICULTURE METHOD	Conventional

Among the splendid hills at Mango, this small family winery bottles the very essence of terroir year after year. Sergio Degiorgis, who runs the show with his determined, energetic wife Patrizia, has managed to show just how well moscato grows here and again, the results are more than satisfying. Two wines made it to the final round, the base Moscato d'Asti 2007 and the Sorì del Re 2007 selection. The former has a fresh, well-rounded aromatic profile, showing attractive fresh notes ranging from sage to green tea. On the palate it is sumptuous, elegant, full flavoured and long. The selection is similarly elegant and harmonious, giving flowers and hazelnuts that give way to inviting citrussy freshness. The Passito Essenza 2005 does credit to its name, showing an intense bouquet of spring flowers and summer fruit leading into a generous, almost honeyed palate nicely offset by attractive acidity. The finish is long and persistent, with an intriguing fresh aftertaste. The range is rounded off by two superb Barberas. We particularly liked the Barbera d'Alba 2006 with its balance and spiciness.

O Moscato d'Asti '07	ŸŸ	4*
O Moscato d'Asti Sorì del Re '07	ŸŸ	4*
O Piemonte Moscato Passito Essenza '05	ŸŸ	5
● Barbera d'Alba '06	ŸŸ	4
● Barbera d'Alba Luna Nuova '07	Ÿ	3
● Dolcetto d'Alba Bricco Peso '07	Ÿ	3
O Piemonte Moscato Passito Essenza '04	ŸŸ	5
● Barbera d'Alba '05	ŸŸ	4
● Barbera d'Alba '04	ŸŸ	4
● Langhe Rosso Riella '01	ŸŸ	5

Deltetto

C.SO ALBA, 43
12043 CANALE [CN]
TEL. 0173979383
www.deltetto.com

ANNUAL PRODUCTION	150,000 bottles
HECTARES UNDER VINE	20
VITICULTURE METHOD	Conventional

Tonino Deltetto, the man who has been in the forefront of the Roero winemaking renaissance, surges on. He improved quality, brought his winery facilities up to speed and then pushed up production and expanded the range. When we think about the new wines, the first that spring to mind are the sparklers, a field in which Deltetto is now the recognized local leader. What started out almost as a game has become a serious commitment, with three versions produced: Rosé, Brut and Extra Brut Riserva, listed in this year's rising order of merit in our opinion. These are now produced in such large quantities that further operational improvements and extensions have had to be made to the premises. The Deltettos do not neglect the territory, though. Far from it, for their classic products are evidently inspired by awareness of terroir. These range from the consistently top-notch Arneis wines – San Michele in particular, but Daivej is hard on its heels – to the Barbera Bramé and the Barbera Rocca delle Marasche 2006, as invigorating as ever, and the complex, elegant Roero, which has benefited from an extra year's ageing.

● Barbera d'Alba Sup. Rocca delle Marasche '06	ŸŸ	6
● Barbera d'Alba Sup. Bramé '06	ŸŸ	4*
● Roero Braja '05	ŸŸ	5
O Deltetto M. Cl. Brut	ŸŸ	5
O Deltetto M. Cl. Extra Brut Ris. '05	ŸŸ	5
O Roero Arneis S. Michele '07	ŸŸ	4*
⊙ Deltetto M. Cl. Extra Brut Rosé	Ÿ	5
O Langhe Favorita Sarvai '07	Ÿ	4
O Roero Arneis Daivej '07	Ÿ	4
● Barbera d'Alba Sup. Rocca delle Marasche '04	ŸŸŸ	6
● Barbera d'Alba Sup. Rocca delle Marasche '05	ŸŸ	6
● Roero Braja '04	ŸŸ	5
● Barbera d'Alba Sup. Bramé '05	ŸŸ	4

Luigi Dessilani e Figlio

VIA CESARE BATTISTI, 21
28073 FARA NOVARESE [NO]
TEL. 0321829252
www.dessilani.it

ANNUAL PRODUCTION	250,000 bottles
HECTARES UNDER VINE	35
VITICULTURE METHOD	Conventional

The wines from the Dessilani winery exude terroir. And terroir is the driving force behind the plans of Nicola Lucca, heir to the dynasty that started with Luigi Dessilani and has reached us in the capable hands of Nicola's father, Enzo. It is clear from Nicola's remarks that he wants this strip of Piedmont's wine country to stop being seen as a future promise and become once and for all simply a reality. The sensations conveyed by the wines presented this year are equally real and tangible. We were amazed at how the powerful, austere body of the Fara Vecchie Vigne selection has been tamed in a successful quest for refined elegance. Not far behind we find the other Fara, the Lochera, which harmoniously brings together nebbiolo and vespolina, exploiting the combination to produce a wine that exudes mellowness and well-balanced tannins. Ghemme and Sizzano have their own respective styles, and are just a touch below excellence. The Nebbiolo has a slightly rugged first impact on the nose and shows a little reticent before it unfolds with faultless development and remembers it comes from one of the noblest, most generous varieties in Italy.

Destefanis

VIA MORTIZZO, 8
12050 MONTELUPO ALBESE [CN]
TEL. 0173617189
www.marcodestefanis.it

ANNUAL PRODUCTION	60,000 bottles
HECTARES UNDER VINE	12
VITICULTURE METHOD	Conventional

We like Marco Destefanis' cellar because it is typical Langhe: family-run, small and traditional in its winemaking. Here nothing is forced. Growing and vinification are carried out with respect for the grapes that the vineyards around Montelupo, and now extending over a dozen hectares, always give. This year, standards are very high after a couple of good growing seasons. Dolcetto Vigna Monia is no longer a newcomer. It's been at the top of its category for years. The 2007 is bursting with well-defined, impeccably intense aromas followed by a tannic palate that signs off with a lingering, full-flavoured finale. Bricco Galluccio has the none-too-easy role of second wine, which it performs well, presenting spacious on the nose and enjoyably supple in the mouth. We also liked the extremely drinkable Barbera Bricco Galluccio, which made the most of the good 2006 vintage, smoothly unfolding with good acidity and roundness. The latest version passed muster. Nebbiolo 2006 is somewhat austere, with faint vegetal notes, but unveils soft tannins on the palate. Last off is a basic Chardonnay that is floral, taut on the palate and lingering on the finish.

● Fara Lochera '05	▓▓ 6
● Fara Vecchie Vigne '04	▓▓ 7
● Colline Novaresi Nebbiolo '05	▓▓ 4*
● Ghemme '04	▓▓ 6
● Sizzano '04	▓▓ 5
● Fara Caramino '99	▓▓▓ 6
● Fara Caramino '04	▓▓ 6
● Fara Caramino '03	▓▓ 5
● Fara Caramino '01	▓▓ 5
● Fara Caramino '00	▓▓ 6
● Fara Lochera '04	▓▓ 6
● Fara Lochera '03	▓▓ 5
● Colline Novaresi Nebbiolo '04	▓▓ 4
● Ghemme '03	▓▓ 6
● Ghemme '00	▓▓ 6

● Dolcetto d'Alba V. Monia Bassa '07	▓▓ 4*
● Barbera d'Alba Bricco Galluccio '06	▓▓ 4
● Dolcetto d'Alba Bricco Galluccio '07	▓▓ 3*
● Nebbiolo d'Alba '06	▓▓ 4
● Barbera d'Alba '07	▓ 3
O Langhe Chardonnay '07	▓ 2
● Dolcetto d'Alba V. Monia Bassa '06	▓▓ 3
● Dolcetto d'Alba V. Monia Bassa '05	▓▓ 3
● Dolcetto d'Alba V. Monia Bassa '04	▓▓ 3
● Nebbiolo d'Alba '05	▓▓ 4

Einaudi

B.TA GOMBE, 31/32
12063 DOGLIANI [CN]
TEL. 017370191
www.poderieinaudi.com

ANNUAL PRODUCTION 220,000 bottles
HECTARES UNDER VINE 50
VITICULTURE METHOD Conventional

The Einaudi range continues to expand but it is the quality that impresses. We'll start with an unusual white from pinot grigio introduced from Alsace in 1897. It's fruity and fresh, with decent complexity and minerality. The Dolcettos are good. From the simpler 2007, we shift up a gear to Filari 2006, which is bright, spicy and tannic, and Vigna Tecc from the same year. This is a splendid interpretation that offers elegance, lovely aromatics, velvet smoothness and length after an extra year in bottle. Three Glasses. Moving on to the nebbiolo-based reds, we tasted an austere, dynamic Langhe and three Barolos that comprise a crescendo of complexity and territorial expression. The basic version, Costa Grimaldi, is appealing and well made with tones of rain-soaked earth and tobacco leaves before moving into a warm, caressing palate. The Cannubi is even better, almost citrussy on the nose with its well-layered aromas sprinkled with sweet spice. On the palate, vigorous tannins are offset by its underlying elegance. To close, we uncorked Langhe Rosso Luigi Einaudi, a cellar classic. The 2005 is superb but a tad less juicy than the previous vintage.

● Dogliani V. Tecc '06	▼▼▼	5
● Barolo nei Cannubi '04	▼▼	8
● Dogliani I Filari '06	▼▼	6
● Langhe Rosso Luigi Einaudi '05	▼▼	7
● Barolo '04	▼▼	8
● Barolo Costa Grimaldi '04	▼▼	8
○ Langhe V. Meira '07	▼▼	6
● Dolcetto di Dogliani '07	▼	5
● Langhe Nebbiolo '06	▼	5
● Barolo Costa Grimaldi '01	▽▽▽	8
● Barolo nei Cannubi '99	▽▽▽	8
● Barolo nei Cannubi '98	▽▽▽	8
● Barolo nei Cannubi '00	▽▽▽	8
● Langhe Rosso Luigi Einaudi '04	▽▽▽	6
● Langhe Rosso Luigi Einaudi '99	▽▽▽	6
● Langhe Rosso Luigi Einaudi '98	▽▽▽	6
● Langhe Rosso Luigi Einaudi '97	▽▽▽	6

Tenuta Il Falchetto

FRAZ. CIOMBI
VIA VALLE TINELLA, 16
12058 SANTO STEFANO BELBO [CN]
TEL. 0141840344
www.ilfalchetto.com

ANNUAL PRODUCTION 190,000 bottles
HECTARES UNDER VINE 33.5
VITICULTURE METHOD Conventional

Standard-cork moscato has only emerged in the last few years as smaller wineries concentrated more on yields and grape quality. Public and critics have responded and output has increased. Tenuta Il Falchetto, owned by brothers Giorgio, Roberto, Adriano and Fabrizio Forno, rides this success with attractive, characterful wines. The two Moscatos we tasted are great. Tenuta del Fant is the stand-out, with nuances of chlorophyll, peach and wild flowers, wrapped up in sensations of finesse. Ciombi is slightly simpler but extremely aromatic, with hints of lemon, orange zest and sage. The palate is full-flavoured, with a sustained, extremely long finish. As in the past, pride of place among the reds went to Barbera Bricco Paradiso, which, despite the difficult 2005 growing year, conveys intense, harmoniously succulent fruit of rare finesse. An absolute innovation for the winery is the meatily varietal Monferrato Rosso Solo 2006, from pinot nero. The Passito was not presented while the Monferrato La Mora 2005, from barbera and cabernet, and the Barbera d'Asti Pian Scorrone 2007, performed well.

● Barbera d'Asti Sup. Bricco Paradiso '05	▼▼	6
○ Moscato d'Asti Tenuta del Fant '07	▼▼	4*
○ Moscato d'Asti Ciombi '07	▼▼	4
● M.to Rosso La Mora '05	▼▼	5
● M.to Rosso Solo '06	▼▼	6
● Barbera d'Asti Pian Scorrone '07	▼	3
● Barbera d'Asti Sup. Bricco Paradiso '03	▽▽	4
● Barbera d'Asti Sup. Bricco Paradiso '04	▽▽	4
○ Piemonte Moscato Passito '04	▽▽	6

Alessandro e Gian Natale Fantino

VIA G. SILVANO, 18
12065 MONFORTE D'ALBA [CN]
TEL. 017378253

ANNUAL PRODUCTION	50,000 bottles
HECTARES UNDER VINE	10
VITICULTURE METHOD	Natural

The small, attractive winery of the Fantino brothers is in the underground rooms of a 17th-century palazzo in the old town of Monforte. It's ideal for the traditional vinification and ageing of wines from Dardi, in the prestigious Bussia Soprana vineyard. Viticulture respects the environment and focuses on nebbiolo and barbera, which give us a Barolo Riserva, a classic Barolo, a Barbera and an unusual nebbiolo-based dried-grape wine. This year, there was no Riserva and attention focused on Barolo Vigna dei Dardi. Warm, fruity aromas open onto a dry palate showing lean, elegant, never aggressive structure and a long appealing finish. Very old vines in the same area bring us Barbera. Deep-coloured, with sweet fruit, it's well typed on the palate and attractively drinkable. Nepas 2000 is made from nebbiolo grapes loft-dried for three months and shows concentrated, offering a rich bouquet of mature aromas. The palate, softened by robust alcohol, is not oversweet while the tannins and acidity underpin impressive structure and the extremely long finish of coffee and chocolate.

Ferrando

VIA TORINO, 599
10015 IVREA [TO]
TEL. 0125633550
www.ferrandovini.it

ANNUAL PRODUCTION	50,000 bottles
HECTARES UNDER VINE	7
VITICULTURE METHOD	Conventional

This corner of Piedmont, similar to the neighbouring Valle d'Aosta in climate, has in the Ferrando family a proud champion of its wines. For over a century, the Ferrandos have been active wine as growers, bottlers and even wine merchants. Their shop at Ivrea and their work as selectors – especially of Carema and Erbaluce di Caluso – has saved many an excellent but difficult vineyard and boosted the reputation of local wines. Where else could our assessment of the wines begin if not with the Carema Etichetta Nera, the winery's standard-bearer, released for the first time over 30 years ago. The only thing stopping the 2003 from repeating the success of the 2001 was the very hot vintage. As usual, the nose is impressive and the wine's strength is its complexity, although the tannins unfold with less orchestration than in cooler years. The finesse of the Etichetta Bianca 2004 bodes extremely well for the future of its elder brother, due to be released next year. Among the other wines, we particularly liked the Erbaluce from the Cariola vineyard, especially the dried-grape version made famous by Vittorio Boratto, and the Canavese Rosso La Torrazza.

● Barolo V. dei Dardi '04	♙♙	6
● Barbera d'Alba V. dei Dardi '06	♙♙	4 *
● Nepas Rosso '00	♙♙	6
● Barolo V. dei Dardi Ris. '00	♙♙♙	7
● Barolo V. dei Dardi Ris. '99	♙♙	7
● Barolo V. dei Dardi Ris. '98	♙♙	7
● Barolo V. dei Dardi Ris. '97	♙♙	7
● Barolo V. dei Dardi Ris. '01	♙♙	7
● Barolo V. dei Dardi '99	♙♙	6
● Barolo V. dei Dardi '98	♙♙	6
● Barolo V. dei Dardi '97	♙♙	6

○ Caluso Passito Vign. Cariola '03	♙♙	6
● Carema Et. Nera '03	♙♙	7
● Canavese Rosso La Torrazza '06	♙♙	4*
● Carema Et. Bianca '04	♙♙	5
○ Erbaluce di Caluso Cariola '07	♙	4
○ Solativo V. T. '06	♙	5
○ Erbaluce di Caluso La Torrazza '07		4
● Carema Et. Nera '01	♙♙♙	6
● Carema Et. Nera '00	♙♙	6
● Carema Et. Nera '99	♙♙	6
● Carema Et. Nera '98	♙♙	6
● Carema Et. Bianca '03	♙♙	5
● Carema Et. Bianca '01	♙♙	5
○ Caluso Passito Vign. Cariola '02	♙♙	6
○ Caluso Passito Vign. Cariola '01	♙♙	6

Roberto Ferraris

FRAZ. DOGLIANO, 33
14041 AGLIANO TERME [AT]
TEL. 0141954234
az.ferraris@virgilio.it

ANNUAL PRODUCTION   35,000 bottles
HECTARES UNDER VINE 9
VITICULTURE METHOD   Conventional

Roberto Ferraris is a standard bearer of Barbera d'Asti crafted with skill, traditional farming methods and the spark of genius that makes the difference. Roberto's good fortune is being in Agliano Terme, a town synonymous with Barbera. The hills around here yield superb grapes and Roberto Ferraris exploits their characteristics to the full. The winery is small and prices are equally modest. With the 2006 vintage, one of the best of the new century, Roberto is on cracking form with three superb interpretations of Barbera. The most seductive is the Nobbio selection, from a vineyard 80 years old, still on Vitis rupestris rootstock. It elegantly unfolds notes of rain-soaked earth and ripe fruit before the close-knit, harmonious palate reveals well-integrated components. We were impressed by the tonneau-aged Riserva del Bisavolo, characterized by marked notes of spice and chocolate. On the palate, the fruitiness is complemented by forthright richness of flavour. La Cricca, obtained from the best-aspected vines, is more ethery, with fruit sensations a little reluctant to open up. The basic Barbera is earthy and succulent.

F.lli Ferrero

FRAZ. ANNUNZIATA, 12
12064 LA MORRA [CN]
TEL. 017350691
www.baroloferrero.com

ANNUAL PRODUCTION   30,000 bottles
HECTARES UNDER VINE 4
VITICULTURE METHOD   Conventional

We have been watching this small family-run winery, managed by Renato Ferrero and his wife Nina Rasmussen, for some years. Just over four hectares yield on average 30,000 bottles a year of Barbera and Barolo from excellent plots at La Morra. You won't find any Dolcetto here as it isn't one of Renato's favourite wines. For this edition of the Guide, we tasted a full-flavoured Barbera d'Alba Goretta 2006. After brief aeration in the glass, forest fruits come through, backed up by spice and the toast-and-vanilla aromas of barrique ageing. The palate displays bright acidity, imposing structure and assertive tannins. A particular success was the Barolo Manzoni 2004, with its bright ruby and intense aromas of blackberry, spice and dried roses, rounded off by hints of leather, cocoa powder and liquorice. These persist on the palate, underpinned by boisterous tannins and good acidity, and contribution of new oak is well gauged. Almost as outstanding is the well-balanced, elegant Barolo Gattera e Luciani, partly aged in barriques and partly in large barrels, which gives fresh fruit, florality and impressive length.

● Barbera d'Asti Nobbio '06	♟♟ 4*
● Barbera d'Asti Sup. Riserva del Bisavolo '06	♟♟ 5
● Barbera d'Asti '06	♟♟ 3*
● Barbera d'Asti Sup. La Cricca '06	♟♟ 4
● Barbera d'Asti Nobbio '05	♟♟ 4
● Barbera d'Asti Nobbio '04	♟♟ 4
● Barbera d'Asti Sup. La Cricca '05	♟♟ 4
● Barbera d'Asti Sup. La Cricca '04	♟♟ 5
● Barbera d'Asti Sup. Riserva del Bisavolo '05	♟♟ 5

● Barolo Manzoni '04	♟♟ 7
● Barbera d'Alba Goretta '06	♟♟ 5
● Barolo Gattera e Luciani '04	♟♟ 6
● Barbera d'Alba Goretta '04	♟♟ 5
● Barbera d'Alba Goretta '05	♟♟ 5
● Barolo Gattera e Luciani '03	♟♟ 6
● Barolo Gattera e Luciani '01	♟♟ 6
● Barolo Gattera e Luciani '00	♟♟ 6
● Barolo Manzoni '03	♟♟ 7
● Barolo Manzoni '00	♟♟ 7
● Barolo Manzoni '99	♟♟ 7

Fontanabianca

VIA BORDINI, 15
12057 NEIVE [CN]
TEL. 017367195
www.fontanabianca.it

ANNUAL PRODUCTION	50,000 bottles
HECTARES UNDER VINE	14
VITICULTURE METHOD	Natural

Just how good this winery is clear from the fact that the standard Barbaresco 2005 went to our finals along with the more prestigious Sorì Burdin. The latter has accustomed us to excellence but we were struck by the complexity of the Barbaresco with its fruit and flower aromas, liquorice-led spiciness, seductive drinkability and glossy tannins. Burdin 2005 is a more austere and polished wine, a Three Glass performer showing notes of dried flowers, leather, red berry fruits, mint and cocoa powder. Still somewhat closed, it will benefit from further ageing. The two big hitters are joined by a series of attractive wines created by Aldo Pola and Bruno Ferro with consultancy from Beppe Caviola. Langhe Arneis is fresh and fragrant, with a slightly bitterish finish, while the Dolcetto is purplish in colour, fruity and tannic. The current Barbera d'Alba gives hints of spice and red berry fruits, progressing in the mouth with well-balanced acidity and tannins. The dark ruby Barbera Brunet 2006 needs time and aeration to express itself to the full but offers pleasant fruit lifted by spice and cocoa powder. Acidity on the palate promises good ageing potential.

Fontanafredda

VIA ALBA, 15
12050 SERRALUNGA D'ALBA [CN]
TEL. 0173626111
www.fontanafredda.it

ANNUAL PRODUCTION	6,000,000 bottles
HECTARES UNDER VINE	90
VITICULTURE METHOD	Conventional

The Monte dei Paschi bank has been joined by the Eataly group here and this iconic winery looks well placed for the future. The terroir, style and personality of the range are, and will continue to be, crafted by oenologist Danilo Drocco. The 2004 La Rosa Barolo has an aristocratic nose of ripe liquorice and fine-cut tobacco, wrapped up by a generous, harmonious finish that all adds up to Three Glasses. The Serralunga 2004 is elegant and shows seductive notes of autumn leaves, offsetting the elegance against muscle and enhancing the variety's austerity with appeal. Paiagallo La Villa 2004 opens on roses and spice, echoed on the palate, assertive tannins and an aromatic finish. Nebbiolo Marne Brune 2006 is deep and complex, giving tobacco, morello cherry and walnut. Barbaresco Coste Rubin 2005 is convincing and generous, with upfront mushroom and plum framed in a subtle, expressive profile. Contessa Rosa 2005, an Alta Langa Brut with great finesse and a lingering finish of spring flowers and tart apple, is also worthy of merit and we also liked Moscato d'Asti Moncucco 2007, clean on the palate with well-judged caressing sweetness.

● Barbaresco Sorì Burdin '05	🍷🍷🍷	7
● Barbaresco '05	🍷🍷	6
● Barbera d'Alba '07	🍷🍷	4*
● Barbera d'Alba Brunet '06	🍷🍷	5
● Dolcetto d'Alba Bordini '07	🍷🍷	4*
○ Langhe Arneis '07	🍷	4
● Barbaresco Sorì Burdin '04	🍷🍷🍷	7
● Barbaresco Sorì Burdin '01	🍷🍷🍷	7
● Barbaresco Sorì Burdin '98	🍷🍷🍷	7
● Barbaresco Sorì Burdin '03	🍷🍷	7
● Barbaresco Sorì Burdin '00	🍷🍷	8
● Barbaresco '04	🍷🍷	6
● Barbera d'Alba Brunet '05	🍷🍷	5
● Barbera d'Alba Brunet '04	🍷🍷	5

● Barolo V. La Rosa '04	🍷🍷🍷	8
● Barolo Paiagallo V. La Villa '04	🍷🍷	7
● Barolo Serralunga '04	🍷🍷	6*
● Barbaresco Coste Rubin '05	🍷🍷	6
● Barbera d'Alba Raimonda '06	🍷🍷	3*
● Diano d'Alba La Lepre '07	🍷🍷	4*
● Nebbiolo d'Alba Marne Brune '06	🍷🍷	4*
○ Alta Langa Brut Contessa Rosa '05	🍷🍷	5
○ Moscato d'Asti Moncucco '07	🍷🍷	4*
○ Roero Arneis Pradalupo '07	🍷	4
● Barolo Lazzarito V. La Delizia '01	🍷🍷🍷	8
● Barolo Lazzarito V. La Delizia '99	🍷🍷🍷	8
● Barolo V. La Rosa '00	🍷🍷🍷	8
● Barolo V. La Rosa '98	🍷🍷🍷	8
● Barolo V. La Rosa '01	🍷🍷	8
● Barolo Serralunga '03	🍷🍷	6

Forteto della Luja

REG. CANDELETTE, 4
14051 LOAZZOLO [AT]
TEL. 014487197
www.fortetodellaluja.it

ANNUAL PRODUCTION	60,000 bottles
HECTARES UNDER VINE	8.5
VITICULTURE METHOD	Certified biodynamic

Silvia and Gianni Scaglione's estate includes much of the small unspoilt valley below the winery, which has become a WWF oasis. To ensure harmony with the environment, the vines are cultivated using non-invasive methods. The cool site climate of the hills, which act as a watershed between the Belbo and Bormida valleys, gives wines of finesse. The late-harvested moscato bianco in particular, has shown that it can give such exclusive character to dessert wines from part-dried grapes to merit its own DOC zone, one of the smallest in Italy. Forteto della Luja has supported the DOC zone since the very beginning. Loazzolo Piasa Rischei 2005 uses two types of grapes – late-harvested and part-dried – and stayed for over 20 months in French oak barriques. This wine is an excellent example of Moscato Passito, drinking sweet, lingering and coherent. Brachetto Pian dei Sogni aims for non-sweet sweetness and shows bags of character as well as original flower and spice aromas. The 2006 harvest has brought us and aristocratic Le Grive, from barbera and a splash of pinot nero, whose best qualities are balance and elegance.

Gabutti - Franco Boasso

B.TA GABUTTI, 3A
12050 SERRALUNGA D'ALBA [CN]
TEL. 0173613165
www.gabuttiboasso.com

ANNUAL PRODUCTION	25,000 bottles
HECTARES UNDER VINE	5
VITICULTURE METHOD	Conventional

Franco Boasso's winery is family run. He, his wife Marina and their sons Claudio and Ezio cultivate five hectares of vineyards and run the I Grappoli agriturismo, situated round the corner from the winery at Gabutti, one of Serralunga's most representative vineyards. The top Barolo is Gabutti, which displays full-fruit aromas and hints of leather then an interesting palate, whose tannins still require some smoothing. The structure is only moderate and the long finish offers tannin and fruity notes. The other selection is Margheria, more overtly fruit-driven but still showing its youth overall, which offers notes of chocolate and a certain spiciness. Barolo Serralunga, obtained from the grapes of both vineyards, is the freshest of the three and, apart from a certain roughness in the tannins, typical of the area, it is complex and distinctive with fruitiness and spice. The Grappoli Red, meanwhile, is an interesting classic nebbiolo-heavy Langhe blend with character and sinew. The Meriame area gives us the interesting, warm and fruity Dolcetto, for early drinking. Last up are the Grappoli White, a nice fruity Chardonnay, and a sweet, heady Moscato.

O Loazzolo Piasa Rischei '05	▼▼ 7
● M.to Rosso Le Grive '06	▼▼ 5
● Piemonte Brachetto Pian dei Sogni '06	▼▼ 6
O Loazzolo Piasa Rischei '97	▼▼▼ 7
O Loazzolo Piasa Rischei '96	▼▼▼ 7
O Loazzolo Piasa Rischei '95	▼▼▼ 7
O Loazzolo Piasa Rischei '94	▼▼▼ 7
O Loazzolo Piasa Rischei '93	▼▼▼ 7
O Loazzolo Piasa Rischei '04	▼▼ 7
O Loazzolo Piasa Rischei '03	▼▼ 7
O Loazzolo Piasa Rischei '01	▼▼ 7
O Loazzolo Piasa Rischei '00	▼▼ 7

● Barolo Gabutti '04	▼▼ 8
● Barolo Margheria '04	▼▼ 7
● Barolo Serralunga '04	▼▼ 6
● Dolcetto d'Alba Meriame '07	▼▼ 4*
● Grappoli Red '06	▼▼ 4
O Grappoli White '07	▼ 3
O Moscato d'Asti Grappoli '07	▼ 4
● Barolo Gabutti '04	▼▼ 8
● Barolo Gabutti '01	▼▼ 7
● Barolo Gabutti '00	▼▼ 7
● Barolo Gabutti '99	▼▼ 7
● Barolo Gabutti '98	▼▼ 7
● Barolo Serralunga '00	▼▼ 7
● Barolo Serralunga '99	▼▼ 7

★★★★ Gaja

VIA TORINO, 18
12050 BARBARESCO [CN]
TEL. 0173635158
info@gajawines.com

ANNUAL PRODUCTION	300,000 bottles
HECTARES UNDER VINE	92
VITICULTURE METHOD	Conventional

Last year, Gaja was our Winery of the Year. Two wines earned Three Glasses while the other five all made the finals. The Barbaresco and the three selections, Sorì Tildin, Costa Russi and San Lorenzo, were from the excellent 2004 vintage while the rest of the range came from the hot 2003 harvest. A year on, we are again singing Gaja's praises. Not even work on the winery has distracted Angelo Gaja, who is helped by his wife Lucia and now also by daughter Gaia. As usual, we restricted our tastings to the nebbiolo-based reds and Darmagi, from cabernet. Sorì Tildin, Costa Russi and San Lorenzo have cult status and the 2005 vintage is no exception. Elegant and less powerful than the 2004s, they flaunt assertive yet restrained tannins. This year, our top award went to Costa Russi for its fruit superbly lifted by oak. The first-rate Barbaresco sailed into the finals, although it missed top honours. Even better was the lovely Sperss, a Langhe Nebbiolo from Serralunga. A superlative bouquet of youthful fruit nuanced with tobacco precedes a powerful, well-behaved palate that also took home Three Glasses. Darmagi and Conteisa are only a whisker behind.

Filippo Gallino

FRAZ. VALLE DEL POZZO, 63
12043 CANALE [CN]
TEL. 017398112
www.filippogallino.com

ANNUAL PRODUCTION	70,000 bottles
HECTARES UNDER VINE	13.5
VITICULTURE METHOD	Conventional

When visited last time, the Gallino family were in the vineyard. It was a splendid summer day with a blue sky setting off the lush green hills of Roero covered with vineyards kept like window boxes. The essence of this strip of Piedmont is to be found in meticulous vineyard work and direct contact with the land and its fruits. It might not seem possible but this philosophy is clearly reflected in the wines. Let's take the Roero 2006 by Filippo and Gianni Gallino. Austere on the nose, it broods a little, reluctant to open up, but then shows layered and complex with earthy and fruit notes. The palate is a marvel of almost husky structure were the overwhelming flesh not enveloped in an elegant, silkily mellow profile. Three Glasses, yet again. In the Barbera Superiore 2006, we found the same development of sensations, from initial surprise over the sumptuousness of the fruit to the pleasant finish with fresh and spicy hints. Two real gems. The vintage reds are a lower-key but similar hymn to the terroir which produced them and the Arneis is noteworthy for its florality and hint of bitterness.

● Langhe Nebbiolo Sperss '04	▼▼▼ 8
● Langhe Nebbiolo Costa Russi '05	▼▼▼ 8
● Barbaresco '05	▼▼ 8
● Langhe Darmagi '05	▼▼ 8
● Langhe Nebbiolo Conteisa '04	▼▼ 8
● Langhe Nebbiolo Sorì S. Lorenzo '05	▼▼ 8
● Langhe Nebbiolo Sorì Tildin '05	▼▼ 8
● Barbaresco '04	♀♀♀ 8
● Barbaresco '01	♀♀♀ 8
● Langhe Nebbiolo Conteisa '01	♀♀♀ 8
● Langhe Nebbiolo Costa Russi '05	♀♀♀ 8
● Langhe Nebbiolo Costa Russi '04	♀♀♀ 8
● Langhe Nebbiolo Costa Russi '03	♀♀♀ 8
● Langhe Nebbiolo Sorì S. Lorenzo '03	♀♀♀ 8
● Langhe Nebbiolo Sorì Tildin '00	♀♀♀ 8

● Roero '06	▼▼▼ 6
● Barbera d'Alba Sup. '06	▼▼ 5
● Barbera d'Alba '07	▼▼ 4*
● Langhe Nebbiolo '07	▼▼ 4*
● Birbét '07	▼ 4
○ Roero Arneis '07	▼ 4
● Barbera d'Alba Sup. '05	♀♀♀ 5
● Barbera d'Alba Sup. '04	♀♀♀ 5
● Barbera d'Alba Sup. '97	♀♀♀ 5
● Roero Sup. '03	♀♀♀ 6
● Roero Sup. '01	♀♀♀ 6
● Roero Sup. '99	♀♀♀ 6
● Roero Sup. '98	♀♀♀ 6
● Barbera d'Alba Sup. '03	♀♀ 5
● Roero '05	♀♀ 6

Gancia

c.so Libertà, 66
14053 Canelli [AT]
tel. 01418301
www.gancia.it

ANNUAL PRODUCTION 30,000,000 bottles
HECTARES UNDER VINE N.A.
VITICULTURE METHOD Conventional

Gancia has been working in Canelli for over 150 years. The statistics are awe-inspiring: over 2000 hectares of controlled vineyards, over 5,000,000 kilograms of grapes vinified, almost 30,000,000 bottles a year and a market of no fewer than 60 countries. These impressive figures make Gancia a leading brand in Italy and one of the top producers of sparkling wine. Sparklers have always been in the family's DNA since founder Carlo Gancia brought to Canelli the art of bottle fermentation he had learned in Champagne. Today, the company, run by Edoardo and his cousins Lamberto and Max, bases the range on quality sparkling wines. The ones tasted were well executed and are reaping the benefits of technical innovations that the Gancias introduced in the late 1990s. The 2004 vintage was good and the powerful Integral Riserva del Fondatore took advantage. Gold, in contrast, is a simpler affair. From the sweet wines, Modonovo is impressive, aromatic and full-flavoured on the not too sweet palate. As always, the 2006 Asti Camillo Gancia Metodo Classico is outstanding, with grape-like aromas followed by a sweet, full palate with contrasting acidity.

○ Asti Camillo Gancia M. Cl. '06	🍷🍷 6
○ Alta Langa Vintage Integral M. Cl. Riserva del Fondatore '04	🍷🍷 6
○ Asti Modonovo '07	🍷🍷 4*
○ Piemonte Gold Integral M. Cl.	🍷🍷 5
⊙ Carlo Gancia M. Cl. Brut Rosé Integral	🍷 5
○ Asti Camillo Gancia M. Cl. '05	YY 6
○ Alta Langa Vintage Integral M. Cl. Riserva del Fondatore '03	YY 6

Garetto

s.da Asti Mare, 30
14041 Agliano Terme [AT]
tel. 0141954068
www.garetto.it

ANNUAL PRODUCTION 100,000 bottles
HECTARES UNDER VINE 20
VITICULTURE METHOD Conventional

Agliano is in the so-called golden triangle of Barbera. The wedge-shaped area between the Tanaro and Belbo rivers is home to the best Barberas of the Asti denomination and Agliano is at its heart. The hills around the town yield fine selections and the Garetto family presented three, all excellent. Alessandro Garetto, the last generation of this fine family of farmers, has, with the support of oenologist Enzo Quinterno, created a small range of successful wines, all hinging around Barbera. After last year's success with the great 2004 Favà, Alessandro presented a superb 2005 that came close to winning Three more Glasses. Complex, elegant and well-balanced with red berry fruit and spices, it is succulent, long and full-flavoured on the palate. In short, a wine of great class. An excellent score also went to the Superiore In Pectore, showing notes of rain-soaked earth and quinine. Lastly, the vintage selection Tra Neuit e Dì, with intense fruit and good progression on the palate, was nice. The winery leaves some room for whites, with the Chardonnay Diversamente ahead of a straightforward yet drinkable Cortese Le Due Cioche.

● Barbera d'Asti Sup. In Pectore '06	🍷🍷 4*
● Barbera d'Asti Sup. Nizza Favà '05	🍷🍷 5
● Barbera d'Asti Tra Neuit e Dì '07	🍷🍷 3*
○ Piemonte Chardonnay Diversamente '07	🍷🍷 4
○ Cortese dell'Alto M.to Le Due Cioche '07	🍷 3
● Barbera d'Asti Sup. Nizza Favà '04	YYY 5
● Barbera d'Asti Sup. Favà '03	YY 5
● Barbera d'Asti Sup. Favà '01	YY 5
● Barbera d'Asti Sup. In Pectore '05	YY 4
● Barbera d'Asti Sup. In Pectore '04	YY 4

Gastaldi

VIA ALBESANI, 20
12057 NEIVE [CN]
TEL. 0173677400

ANNUAL PRODUCTION	20,000 bottles
HECTARES UNDER VINE	14
VITICULTURE METHOD	Conventional

In last year's profile, we called the unpredictable Dino Gastaldi an "absent-minded professor". A year later, Dino is still one of a kind but there is substance behind his apparent caprice. That substance comes from the exceptional vine stock located in the best-aspected sites of the area. Grapes for the Barbaresco come from Albesani di Neive – the 2004 is still maturing and no release date has been set – while fruit from Coste di Monforte d'Alba goes into the Barolo, of which no vintage has been released since the 2001. The Moriolo area of Rodello provided the grapes for the Dolcetto d'Alba and the Langhe Bianco, from chardonnay and sauvignon. The former was the first Dolcetto to be awarded Three Glasses by the Guide for the 1990 vintage. Only two selections were presented for this edition of the Guide, and both perfectly embody Dino's philosophy. Langhe Bianco Gastaldi is from 2003 and, despite the very hot harvest, manages to express itself coherently. On the nose it shows ripe, almost tropical fruit while the palate it is heavier than usual but with loads of personality. The Dolcetto 2006 is superb and will benefit from further ageing.

O Langhe Bianco Gastaldi '03	♟♟	6
● Dolcetto d'Alba Moriolo '06	♟♟	4*
● Dolcetto d'Alba Sup. Moriolo '90	♟♟♟	5
● Gastaldi Rosso '89	♟♟♟	8
● Gastaldi Rosso '88	♟♟♟	8
● Langhe Rosso Gastaldi '98	♟♟	7
● Barbaresco '03	♟♟	7
● Barbaresco '01	♟♟	7
● Barbaresco '99	♟♟	7
● Barolo '01	♟♟	8
O Langhe Bianco Gastaldi '02	♟♟	6
O Langhe Bianco Gastaldi '01	♟♟	6
O Langhe Bianco Gastaldi '00	♟♟	6

Piero Gatti

LOC. MONCUCCO, 28
12058 SANTO STEFANO BELBO [CN]
TEL. 0141840918
www.vinigatti.it

ANNUAL PRODUCTION	60,000 bottles
HECTARES UNDER VINE	8
VITICULTURE METHOD	Conventional

This small winery was established in 1988 by Piero Gatti, who sadly died a few years ago. His legacy was taken up by his wife Rita and daughter Barbara. The winery and the majority of the vines are found on Moncucco, without doubt one of the best-suited hilltops for growing moscato. And it is no coincidence that the Gattis' main, and most successful wine, is Moscato. Highly complex on the nose, with notes of lemon zest, peach tea, sage and apricot, on the palate it offers succulence and a refreshing attack. The cellar's new product is Vignot 2006, a sweet wine from part-dried moscato grapes, of which only 800 bottles were released. The grapes are loft-dried for 18 months and the wine offers stunning sensory characteristics, showing warm notes of candied citrus fruit, apricots and dried figs. The palate has energy and vitality thanks refreshing undertones of acidity. The Gattis' also do a fine interpretation of freisa, vinified both as a rose petal and cherry-themed monovarietal and in tandem with barbera, as is the case with Verbeia 2006. The Piemonte Brachetto is also pleasant.

O Piemonte Moscato '07	♟♟	4*
● Langhe Freisa La Violetta '07	♟♟	4*
●·Verbeia '06	♟♟	4*
O Vignot V. T. '06	♟♟	5
● Piemonte Brachetto '07	♟	4
● Verbeia '05	♟♟	4
● Verbeia '04	♟♟	4

Ettore Germano

LOC. CERRETTA, 1
12050 SERRALUNGA D'ALBA [CN]
TEL. 0173613528
www.germanoettore.com

ANNUAL PRODUCTION	70,000 bottles
HECTARES UNDER VINE	13.5
VITICULTURE METHOD	Conventional

Who said that Serralunga d'Alba always sees red? Sergio Germano disagrees, having planted white varieties at Cigliè, over 30 kilometres from the winery. Today, he has two separate holdings. The main Serralunga property is planted to traditional Langhe red nebbiolo, barbera and dolcetto with some merlot, plus a little chardonnay in the more sheltered spots, and Cigliè, where a few hectares at 500 metres are entirely planted to white varieties, above all riesling renano and chardonnnay. Sergio has achieved success with both types but he has Barolo in his blood. He has three Barolos and we preferred the austere finesse of Prapò to the softer, fuller Cerretta but were equally impressed by the Serralunga, simpler, yet long and well orchestrated. The Three Glasses, however, went to Prapò. From the whites, Hérzu, with all the variety's hydrocarbon minerality and crispness, is fast becoming one of Italy's best Rieslings. The Chardonnay and the riesling and chardonnay Binel are first-rate. The rest of the wines are excellently made, starting with the Barbera and the Langhe Rosso Balàu. Sergio also has some sparklers in the pipeline.

La Ghibellina

FRAZ. MONTEROTONDO, 61
15066 GAVI [AL]
TEL. 0143686257
www.laghibellina.it

ANNUAL PRODUCTION	60,000 bottles
HECTARES UNDER VINE	8
VITICULTURE METHOD	Conventional

La Ghibellina is situated in Monterotondo, in perfect cortese country. The estate extends over 18 hectares, with eight under vine planted to 90 per cent cortese and the rest barbera. Alberto and Marina Ghibellini run the operation, which they took over some years ago, and avail themselves of the technical consultancy of Beppe Caviola. Every year, they manage to improve the quality of the wines and the 2007 vintage is no exception. Particularly noteworthy was the Gavi Mainìn, its bright straw yellow introducing lingering floral and fruit aromas, freshness on the palate and a satisfyingly long finish. Gavi Altius is a wine of great character, which is partially aged in small oak barrels. The floral aromas are offset by citrus and balsamic notes, and the palate shows good structure with upfront, refreshing acidity and a classic bitterish finish, qualities that took the wine into the final taste-offs for Three Glasses. The barbera Monferrato Rosso Nero del Montone also has lots of personality, with intense aromas and hints of red berry fruits on the harmonious, lingering palate.

● Barolo Prapò '04	♟♟♟ 7
● Barolo Cerretta '04	♟♟ 7
○ Langhe Bianco Hérzu '06	♟♟ 5
○ Langhe Bianco Binel '06	♟♟ 4*
○ Langhe Chardonnay '07	♟♟ 4*
● Barbera d'Alba V. della Madre '06	♟♟ 5
● Barolo Serralunga '04	♟♟ 6
● Dolcetto d'Alba Vign. Pra di Pò '07	♟♟ 4*
● Langhe Nebbiolo '06	♟♟ 4
● Langhe Rosso Balàu '06	♟♟ 5
● Dolcetto d'Alba Vign. Lorenzino '07	♟ 4
● Barolo Cerretta '98	♟♟♟ 7
● Barolo Cerretta '01	♟♟♟ 7
● Barolo Cerretta '99	♟♟ 8
● Barolo Prapò '01	♟♟ 7
○ Langhe Bianco Hérzu '05	♟♟ 5

○ Gavi del Comune di Gavi Altius '06	♟♟ 5
○ Gavi del Comune di Gavi Mainìn '07	♟♟ 4*
● M.to Rosso Nero del Montone '06	♟♟ 5
○ Gavi del Comune di Gavi Altius '05	♟♟ 4
○ Gavi del Comune di Gavi Mainìn '06	♟♟ 4

Attilio Ghisolfi

LOC. BUSSIA, 27
12065 MONFORTE D'ALBA [CN]
TEL. 017378345
www.ghisolfi.com

ANNUAL PRODUCTION	45,000 bottles
HECTARES UNDER VINE	6.5
VITICULTURE METHOD	Conventional

This profile confirms the high quality of Gianmarco Ghisolfi's winery but there are significant absences. We will have to wait until 2011 for the Fantini Riserva 2005, which skipped the 2002 to 2004 vintages, while release has also been delayed for Alta Bussia, Carlin and Barbera Vigna Lisi, all from 2006, to give them time to mature. So let's have a look at what is on offer, starting with the Barolo Bricco Visette 2004. This has an impressive, well-developed nose, with tertiary aromas starting to come through, and on the palate shows smooth if evident tannins, good length and well-balanced oakiness, thanks to 30 per cent used barriques. The Barolo 2004, aged only in large wood, has crisp, clean aromas and a sensation of youthfulness. The fresh, well-typed Barbera d'Alba Maggiora 2006 comes from a vineyard in its first production year and can only get better. Another newcomer is Langhe Nebbiolo 2007, from vineyards in Montelupo, with attractive cherry overtones and an appealing palate that invites early drinking. We liked Pinay 2006, a Pinot Nero that compensates for limited structure with its approachability and elegance.

★ Bruno Giacosa

VIA XX SETTEMBRE, 52
12057 NEIVE [CN]
TEL. 017367027
www.brunogiacosa.it

ANNUAL PRODUCTION	400,000 bottles
HECTARES UNDER VINE	20
VITICULTURE METHOD	Conventional

We welcome to the Bruno Giacosa cellar a new oenologist, Giorgio Lavagna, and wish Bruna all the best for her involvement with the family business. As for Bruno himself, it's always a pleasure to talk to him. His matchless knowledge of Langhe, and his humility and calm in imparting it, are quite awesome. This year, Bruno decided to surprise his fans with nebbiolo-based wines from 2004 that are more convincing than ever. The red-label Barbaresco Asili was nothing short of spectacular, with floral aromas, mellow tannins, sumptuous richness and a lingering finish. Three Glasses to cherish and our special award for Red of the Year. The Barbaresco Rabajà is, as always, a little more rugged with powerful tannins and great cellar prospects. The extremely elegant Barbaresco Santo Stefano displays good acidity and ripe tannins. Lastly, another wine for connoisseurs is Barolo Falletto 2004, surprisingly drinkable despite its power, and a classic Serralunga Barolo for the cellar. The Three Glasses were never in doubt. And there will be other wines from that 2004 nebbiolo harvest. All the other wines tasted range from good to excellent.

● Barolo Bricco Visette '04	♈♈	7
● Barolo '04	♈♈	6
● Langhe Nebbiolo '07	♈♈	4*
● Langhe Rosso Pinay '06	♈♈	4*
● Barbera d'Alba Maggiora '06	♈	4
● Barolo Bricco Visette '01	♈♈♈	7
● Barolo Fantini Ris. '01	♈♈♈	8
● Langhe Rosso Alta Bussia '01	♈♈♈	6
● Langhe Rosso Alta Bussia '00	♈♈♈	6
● Langhe Rosso Alta Bussia '99	♈♈♈	6
● Barolo Bricco Visette '03	♈♈	7
● Barolo Fantini Ris. '00	♈♈	7
● Langhe Rosso Alta Bussia '05	♈♈	5
● Langhe Rosso Carlin '05	♈♈	5
● Langhe Rosso Carlin '02	♈♈	5

● Barbaresco Asili Ris. '04	♈♈♈	8
● Barolo Falletto '04	♈♈♈	8
● Barbaresco Rabajà '04	♈♈	8
● Barbaresco Santo Stefano '04	♈♈	8
● Barbera d'Alba Sup. Falletto '06	♈♈	7
● Dolcetto d'Alba Sorano '07	♈♈	5
O Bruno Giacosa Extra Brut '04	♈♈	6
O Roero Arneis '07	♈♈	5
● Barbaresco Asili Ris. '96	♈♈♈	8
● Barbaresco Asili '99	♈♈♈	8
● Barbaresco Rabajà Ris. '01	♈♈♈	8
● Barbaresco Santo Stefano '01	♈♈♈	8
● Barbaresco Santo Stefano '00	♈♈♈	8
● Barolo Falletto '01	♈♈♈	8
● Barolo Le Rocche del Falletto Ris. '01	♈♈♈	8

Carlo Giacosa

S.DA OVELLO, 9
12050 BARBARESCO [CN]
TEL. 0173635116
www.carlogiacosa.it

ANNUAL PRODUCTION 45,000 bottles
HECTARES UNDER VINE 4
VITICULTURE METHOD Conventional

The small winery is one to watch closely. Run by the determined Maria Grazia, backed by her parents Carlo and Carla, and the enthusiasm of the young Darko, the four hectares yield forthright wines made with minimum intervention and utmost respect for the raw materials. Our attention focused on the two Barbarescos, both first-rate yet different. Montefico 2005 is a classic austere, territory-focused wine with a still somewhat closed, veiled profile offering marked florality and mineral hints. Long and lingering on the palate, it progresses attractively and has good ageing potential. Narin 2005, from grapes from the top Asili, Cole and Ovello vineyards, matures in small wood of various ages, unlike the previous wine. Full and well-balanced, with a soft, caressing entry and well-structured tannins, it has a rich aromatic profile, opening to red berry fruit, flowers and spices, revealing judicious use of oak. Apart from the two Barbera d'Albas – Mucin 2007, fresher and more immediate, and the fleshier, richer Lina 2006 – and an attractive Nebbiolo Maria Grazia 2007, we also liked the full-flavoured Dolcetto Cuchet 2007.

● Barbaresco Narin '05	🍷🍷 6*
● Barbaresco Montefico '05	🍷🍷 6
● Barbera d'Alba Lina '06	🍷🍷 4*
● Barbera d'Alba Mucin '07	🍷🍷 4*
● Dolcetto d'Alba Cuchet '07	🍷🍷 4*
● Langhe Nebbiolo Maria Grazia '07	🍷 4
● Barbaresco Carla '03	♀♀ 6
● Barbaresco Montefico '04	♀♀ 6
● Barbaresco Montefico '03	♀♀ 6
● Barbaresco Montefico '01	♀♀ 6
● Barbaresco Montefico '00	♀♀ 6
● Barbaresco Narin '04	♀♀ 6
● Barbaresco Narin '01	♀♀ 6
● Barbaresco Narin '03	♀♀ 6
● Barbaresco Narin '00	♀♀ 6

F.lli Giacosa

VIA XX SETTEMBRE, 64
12057 NEIVE [CN]
TEL. 017367013
www.giacosa.it

ANNUAL PRODUCTION 600,000 bottles
HECTARES UNDER VINE 40
VITICULTURE METHOD Conventional

There are barriques and solar panels, which provide half the winery's energy, as well as cement vats, some of them built on site, at this family business that by Langhe standards is large. It's a mixture of old and new that works perfectly. This year, like last time, we were particularly convinced by the Barbaresco Gian Matè 2005. Elegant and modern on the nose, it has a succulent palate, tannins that are sweet but still need softening and a satisfying long minty finish. The Barbaresco Basarin 2005 is floral and nicely fresh, with tannins a touch harsher than the Gian Matè. From the three 2004 Barolos, the Vigna Mandorlo, from the Castiglione Falletto vineyard, stands out for its dried roses and firmly structured palate. The Bussia offers balsamic notes and good energy on the palate. It will benefit from further ageing. The basic Barolo has intact fruit, a clean palate and a succulent finish. We also liked the Barbera Maria Gioana 2005, which is fresh and fruity, and will be able to age, and the almondy, fruity Dolcetto. The whites are simple but well made. The barrel-aged Ca' Lunga is still young looking for greater balance.

● Barbaresco Basarin V. Gian Matè '05	🍷🍷 6*
● Barolo V. Mandorlo '04	🍷🍷 7
● Barbaresco Basarin '05	🍷🍷 6
● Barbera d'Alba Maria Gioana '05	🍷🍷 5
● Barolo '04	🍷🍷 5*
● Barolo Bussia '04	🍷🍷 6
● Dolcetto d'Alba Madonna di Como '07	🍷🍷 4*
○ Langhe Chardonnay Ca' Lunga '06	🍷 5
○ Langhe Chardonnay Rorea '07	🍷 4
○ Roero Arneis '07	🍷 4
● Barbaresco Gian Matè '04	♀♀ 6
● Barbaresco Basarin '04	♀♀ 6
● Barbera d'Alba Maria Gioana '04	♀♀ 5
● Barolo Bussia '01	♀♀ 7
● Barolo V. Mandorlo '03	♀♀ 6
● Barolo V. Mandorlo '01	♀♀ 6

Raffaele Gili

Loc. Pautasso, 7
12050 Castellinaldo [CN]
tel. 0173639011

ANNUAL PRODUCTION 46,000 bottles
HECTARES UNDER VINE 8
VITICULTURE METHOD Conventional

Raffaele Gili's range is back at full strength. After a couple of years of settling down, with the wines kept back to mature further and work being completed on the new winery, we were able to review some major reds: Barbera di Castellinaldo, Nebbiolo Sansivé and Roero Bric Angelino, all from the 2005 vintage. The Barbera is on form, having shuffled off its woody notes after long barrel ageing while keeping its background acidity. The aromatics are complex and intense, providing a good example of how well-suited the Castellinaldo terroir is to this type of wine. The Nebbiolo is still extremely tannic but not without finesse or elegance. Above all, it is satisfyingly drinkable. The Roero is also good, showing fragrant and layered on the nose of red berry fruit, forest floor and rain-soaked earth, and powerful and lingering on the palate. Coming up behind these three terrific wines we have a full house of well-executed labels: another two reds – the youthful, easy-drinking Barbera Pautasso 2006 and the firmly structured 2005 blend of nebbiolo, barbera and cabernet sauvignon – and two well-styled whites, Arneis and Favorita.

● Castellinaldo Barbera d'Alba '05	**YY**	5
● Nebbiolo d'Alba Sansivé '05	**YY**	5
● Roero Bric Angelino '05	**YY**	5
● Barbera d'Alba Pautasso '06	**Y**	4
O Langhe Arneis '07	**Y**	3
O Langhe Favorita '07	**Y**	3
● Langhe Rosso L'Assemblato '05	**Y**	5
● Castellinaldo Barbera d'Alba '01	YY	5
● Castellinaldo Barbera d'Alba '04	YY	5
● Castellinaldo Barbera d'Alba '00	YY	5
● Roero Bric Angelino '04	YY	5
● Roero Bric Angelino '03	YY	5
● Roero Bric Angelino '01	YY	5

Giovanni Battista Gillardi

Cascina Corsaletto, 69
12060 Farigliano [CN]
tel. 017376306

ANNUAL PRODUCTION 35,000 bottles
HECTARES UNDER VINE 7
VITICULTURE METHOD Conventional

Giacolino Gillardi must have been thinking of us when he introduced a raft of innovations. There's no shortage of material for his profile! First, we visited his splendid new winery, a gem of efficiency in the old family farmhouse. The only aesthetic quirk visible from outside is a building with something of the Guggenheim about it, which will be used as a warehouse. Moving on to the wines, a well-crafted Merlot made its Guide debut showing varietal, well balanced, soft and lingering. We reviewed the 2006 but we also tasted the 2005 and 2004, both of which impressed. We decided to leave out the new Granaccio, produced from grenache grapes. This full-bodied, expressive wine is produced in too limited a quantity to justify inclusion. We hope that fans of the variety, typical of the south of France, can go and buy a few bottles at the winery itself. Moving on to the classics, everything is as it should be: exceptional. The Dolcetto Cursalet is powerful, tannic and smooth while the Maestra is fruitier. Yeta, from dolcetto and a splash of cabernet, is an intriguing, balsamic wine and Harys, from syrah grapes, is deep and well orchestrated.

● Dolcetto di Dogliani Cursalet '07	**YY**	4*
● Langhe Rosso Harys '06	**YY**	7
● Dolcetto di Dogliani Vign. Maestra '07	**YY**	4*
● Langhe Rosso Merlo '06	**YY**	6
● Langhe Rosso Yeta '06	**YY**	5
● Harys '00	YYY	7
● Harys '99	YYY	7
● Harys '98	YYY	7
● Dolcetto di Dogliani Cursalet '06	YY	4
● Dolcetto di Dogliani Cursalet '05	YY	4
● Dolcetto di Dogliani Vign. Maestra '06	YY	4
● Langhe Rosso Yeta '05	YY	5
● Langhe Rosso Harys '05	YY	7
● Harys '04	YY	7

Cascina Giovinale

S.DA SAN NICOLAO, 102
14049 NIZZA MONFERRATO [AT]
TEL. 0141793005
www.cascinagiovinale.com

ANNUAL PRODUCTION	25,000 bottles
HECTARES UNDER VINE	7
VITICULTURE METHOD	Conventional

Bruno Ciocca and his wife Anna have a fine winery. In Nizza Monferrato, on the hill of San Nicolao, in the heart of the DOC zone most famous for barbera, their small operation has for ten years now been producing a selection of highly respectable wines. The oenological expertise of the highly professional Giuliano Noè and his team, who take scrupulous care of the vines, underlines the intention to pursue absolute quality throughout the production process. The wines tasted proved to be well made and consistent. Our tasting panel complimented all the wines presented, starting, as we do every year, with the Anssèma selection, an extremely well-crafted Superiore Nizza from the 2005 vintage. Concentration and power ensure good ageing potential. The well-fruited and nicely acidic Barbera d'Asti Superiore 2006 is superb, and also excellent value for money, which doesn't hurt. The Moscato is appealingly approachable.

● Barbera d'Asti Sup. Nizza Anssèma '05	♟	5
● Barbera d'Asti Sup. '06	♟♟	4*
O Moscato d'Asti '07	♟	4
● Barbera d'Asti Sup. Nizza Anssèma '04	♟♟	5
● Barbera d'Asti Sup. Nizza Anssèma '03	♟♟	5
● M.to Trinum '04	♟♟	5
● M.to Trinum '03	♟♟	5

La Giribaldina

REG. SAN VITO, 39
14042 CALAMANDRANA [AT]
TEL. 0141718043
www.giribaldina.com

ANNUAL PRODUCTION	55,000 bottles
HECTARES UNDER VINE	10
VITICULTURE METHOD	Conventional

This Calamandrana winery confirmed its quality. La Giribaldina is owned by the Colombo family from Varese, who moved to the hills of Monferrato in the mid 1990s to grow barbera and moscato, with which they make a sweet wine from part-dried grapes. These two varieties are the raw materials for a winery which has conceded little to fashion or international taste, except for some sauvignon for the house white. This year, the Barberas are on top form, starting with the simplest, the current Barbera del Monferrato Vivace. We move up the scale with the Barbera d'Astis, which are released in three versions. The Monte del Mare selection shows richly intense cherry with underlying hints of spice before the palate powerful progression reveals is a highly drinkable current Barbera with great promise. There were also fine performances from the full-bodied, ethery Superiore Nizza Cala delle Mandrie 2005. Less complex on the nose, yet rich and caressing, is Barbera Vigneti della Val Sarmassa 2006, sourced from vineyards in the Val Sarmassa nature park at Vaglio Serra. The Monferrato Bianco Ferro di Cavallo is full flavoured with pineapple and peach fruit.

● Barbera d'Asti Monte del Mare '07	♟♟	3*
● Barbera d'Asti Sup. Nizza Cala delle Mandrie '05	♟♟	5
● Barbera d'Asti Sup. Vign. della Val Sarmassa '06	♟♟	4*
O M.to Bianco Ferro di Cavallo '07	♟♟	4*
● Barbera del M.to Vivace Pavonessa '07	♟	3
● Barbera d'Asti Sup. Cala delle Mandrie '04	♟♟	5
● Barbera d'Asti Sup. Cala delle Mandrie '01	♟♟	5
● Barbera d'Asti Sup. Vign. della Val Sarmassa '05	♟♟	4

La Gironda

S.DA BRICCO, 12
14049 NIZZA MONFERRATO [AT]
TEL. 0141701013
www.lagironda.com

ANNUAL PRODUCTION	28,000 bottles
HECTARES UNDER VINE	8
VITICULTURE METHOD	Conventional

Situated in Bricco Cremosina, one of the great Nizza Monferrato crus, La Gironda has given us characterful Barberas over the years. The Barbera Superiore Nizza Le Nicchie 2005, with noticeable but well-integrated wood, red berry fruit and a note of spice that highlights its length, went to our finals but Barbera d'Asti La Gena 2006 is also extremely good was close behind, flaunting a bouquet of violets and freshness that underlines its persistence and rounded fruit. The Barbera d'Asti La Lippa makes a virtue of simplicity. It's an excellent Barbera, easy drinking but far from banal. These are three great Barberas, each with its own style, and confirm that Susanna Galandrino and her husband Alberto Adamo have clear ideas about where they want to go. They have already come a good long way, and although they have not yet achieved the highest accolade, they are clearly on the right track. This is a fine object lesson, and thankfully not the only one, in how to express the qualities and characteristics of the Nizza Monferrato area to the full.

La Giustiniana

FRAZ. ROVERETO, 5
15066 GAVI [AL]
TEL. 0143682132
www.lagiustiniana.it

ANNUAL PRODUCTION	200,000 bottles
HECTARES UNDER VINE	40
VITICULTURE METHOD	Conventional

La Giustiniana is one of the longest-standing Gavi estates. As far back as the 17th century, cortese grapes for white wines to be sold in the markets of nearby Liguria were grown here. Today, the estate extends over roughly 120 hectares, about 40 of which are under vine. The property belongs to the Lombardini family, who rely on the estate management skills of Enrico Tomalino, who has ensured constant level of excellence over the years, without neglecting experimentation. One example is the vineyard planted last year with 12 different clones of cortese. As for the wines, Gavi Il Nostro Gavi is once more at the top of its class. The nose shows intense scents of spring flowers with slight mineral hints before the palate unfolds zesty yet at the same time sumptuous, with excellent length. The Lugarara was also extremely good this year, in fact one of the best ever tasted, as was the Montessora, and Just Bianco is delicious. On the red front, we were impressed by Grangiarossa, with its beautifully elegant ruby red ushering in berry fruit aromas and a stunning velvety mouthfeel.

● Barbera d'Asti Sup. Nizza Le Nicchie '05	♀♀ 5
● Barbera d'Asti La Gena '06	♀♀ 4*
● Barbera d'Asti La Lippa '07	♀♀ 3*
● Barbera d'Asti Sup. Nizza Le Nicchie '04	♀♀ 5
● Barbera d'Asti Sup. Nizza Le Nicchie '03	♀♀ 5
● Barbera d'Asti La Gena '05	♀♀ 4
● Barbera d'Asti La Gena '04	♀♀ 4
● Barbera d'Asti La Lippa '06	♀♀ 3

○ Gavi del Comune di Gavi Il Nostro Gavi '06	♀♀ 5
○ Gavi del Comune di Gavi Lugarara '07	♀♀ 4
○ Gavi del Comune di Gavi Montessora '07	♀♀ 5
● Piemonte Barbera Grangiarossa '05	♀♀ 3*
○ Just Bianco '05	♀ 6
○ Gavi del Comune di Gavi Il Nostro Gavi '04	♀♀ 5
○ Gavi del Comune di Gavi Montessora '06	♀♀ 5
○ Gavi del Comune di Gavi Montessora '05	♀♀ 5

Cantina del Glicine

VIA GIULIO CESARE, 1
12052 NEIVE [CN]
TEL. 017367215
www.cantinadelglicine.it

ANNUAL PRODUCTION	45,000 bottles
HECTARES UNDER VINE	4
VITICULTURE METHOD	Natural

Cantina del Glicine was on form. The Barbarescos from Adriana Mazzi and Roberto Bruno convince with their elegance and mouthfeel. The most interesting is still Marcorino, from the wonderfully aspected Neive vineyard. Right from its orange-edged ruby hue, its firmness is evident. The bouquet gives youthful fruit aromas already shifting to more ethery sensations of quinine and tobacco. In the mouth, succulent elegance enshrouds well-honed tannins and a lingering, almost silky finish. Not far behind is Curà, from another of designation's best vineyards, with tannins only a tad more clenched and a little less structure than its stablemate. The well-made Barberas are La Sconsolata, which has ten per cent Barbaresco nebbiolo, and the barrique-aged Dormiosa. We liked La Sconsolata's cherry-like bouquet, rounded off by liquorice and tobacco, while the harmonious palate has an acidulous vein that lends vibrancy to the long finish. La Dormiosa has riper, more succulent fruit and is still dominated by oak. This powerful young Barbera will benefit from ageing. The simpler wines are also well made, from the Dolcetto d'Alba Olmiolo to the Roero Arneis Il Mandolo.

★ Elio Grasso

LOC. GINESTRA, 40
12065 MONFORTE D'ALBA [CN]
TEL. 017378491
www.eliograsso.it

ANNUAL PRODUCTION	80,000 bottles
HECTARES UNDER VINE	14
VITICULTURE METHOD	Conventional

Elio Grasso is a Langhe character. Shy, but open and affable, Elio will stop working to chat about farming. The winery is beautifully situated, with a fantastic view over the vineyards, impressing on visitors just how important it is to keep it unspoilt. But let's move get to the wines. We'll start with a real thoroughbred, the Three Glass Barolo Ginestra Vigna Casa Maté 2004, of which 13,000 bottles were released. Aged for two years in large wood, it proffers a deep nose followed by velvety elegance on the palate and a lingering, seductive finish. The Barolo Gavarini Vigna Chiniera 2004, in 12,000 bottles, is more austere and still closed but has power and cellarability. It just needs more ageing. Barbera d'Alba Vigna Martina 2005, in 14,000 bottles, steel-vinified and aged in new and used wood, is very nice, with marked acidity and length. The interesting Langhe Chardonnay Educato 2007, in 6,000 bottles, fermented part in steel and part in barrique. Well-balanced and harmonious, it is a fine expression of its variety. Dolcetto d'Alba dei Grassi 2007 and Langhe Nebbiolo Gavarini 2007 are also well worth uncorking.

● Barbaresco Marcorino '05	▼▼	6*
● Barbaresco Curà '05	▼▼	6
● Barbera d'Alba Sup. La Dormiosa '05	▼▼	5
● Barbera d'Alba La Sconsolata '06	▼▼	4*
● Dolcetto d'Alba Olmiolo '07	▼	4
○ Moscato d'Asti '07	▼	4
○ Roero Arneis Il Mandolo '07	▼	4
● Barbaresco Marcorino '04	▼▼	6
● Barbaresco Marcorino '03	▼▼	6
● Barbaresco Curà '04	▼▼	6
● Barbaresco Curà '03	▼▼	6

● Barolo Ginestra V. Casa Maté '04	▼▼▼	8
● Barolo Gavarini V. Chiniera '04	▼▼	8
● Barbera d'Alba V. Martina '05	▼▼	5
● Dolcetto d'Alba dei Grassi '07	▼▼	4*
● Langhe Nebbiolo Gavarini '07	▼▼	5
○ Langhe Chardonnay Educato '07	▼▼	5
● Barolo Gavarini V. Chiniera '01	▼▼▼	8
● Barolo Gavarini V. Chiniera '00	▼▼▼	8
● Barolo Gavarini V. Chiniera '99	▼▼▼	8
● Barolo Gavarini V. Chiniera '98	▼▼▼	8
● Barolo Ginestra V. Casa Maté '03	▼▼▼	8
● Barolo Runcot '01	▼▼▼	8
● Barolo Runcot '00	▼▼▼	8
● Barolo Runcot '99	▼▼▼	8
● Barolo Runcot '98	▼▼▼	8
● Barolo Runcot '96	▼▼▼	8

Silvio Grasso

FRAZ. ANNUNZIATA
CASCINA LUCIANI, 112
12064 LA MORRA [CN]
TEL. 017350322

ANNUAL PRODUCTION	70,000 bottles
HECTARES UNDER VINE	11
VITICULTURE METHOD	Conventional

The tempo of wine is not always in step with Guide's schedule so this edition is unable to describe the Dolcetto, Nebbiolo or Barberas from Marilena and Silvio Grasso, not yet in bottle when we went to print. But we can report on L'Insieme and the six – six! – Barolos from 2004. L'Insieme is a project involving several small producers to raise funds for charitable and environmental programmes. The Grassos' 2004 version is an appealing blend of nebbiolo, barbera, cabernet and merlot with soft tannins and vibrant aromas of fruit, spices and cocoa powder. Moving on to the cellar's thoroughbreds, we enjoyed the balanced, flavoursome basic Barolo Pì Vigne and in particular, the Bricco Luciani, a classic Grasso Barolo that shows complex and elegant with fruity, ethery aromas and hints of spice, tobacco and leather supported nicely by silky tannins. Three Glasses. The Manzoni and L'André, aged in large wood, were almost as good while the sophisticated Giachini and powerful Plicotti impressed.

Bruna Grimaldi

VIA RODDINO
12050 SERRALUNGA D'ALBA [CN]
TEL. 0173262094
www.grimaldibruna.it

ANNUAL PRODUCTION	47,000 bottles
HECTARES UNDER VINE	10
VITICULTURE METHOD	Conventional

Bruna Grimaldi and Franco Fiorino's estate comprises several plots in Roero, Serralunga and Diano d'Alba and two working wineries at Serralunga and nearby Gallo Grinzane. The fact that two new Barolo vineyard selections will be released over the next three years shows that estate is forward-looking. This year, Barolo Badarina Vigna Regnola again leads the pack, with subtle and stylish aromas in the 2004 version. The fruit is enhanced by aromatic star anise-like spice while the palate is nicely drinkable and very harmonious. Grapes from an old vineyard are used for the Nebbiolo d'Alba Briccola 2006, which has impeccable acid backbone and a rounded, well-balanced finish. Another mature vineyard shapes the character of Barbera d'Alba Superiore Scassa 2006, with hints of black cherries and a lightly grassiness, both echoed nicely in the finish. The remaining two wines are both enjoyably fragrant. Langhe Chardonnay Valscura 2007 has distinct, upfront mineral sensations while the tannic, slightly tangy Dolcetto d'Alba Vigna San Martino 2007 reflects the varietal features of the grape.

● Barolo Bricco Luciani '04	♀♀♀ 8
● Barolo Ciabot Manzoni '04	♀♀ 8
● Barolo L'André '04	♀♀ 7
● Barolo Giachini '04	♀♀ 7
● Barolo Pì Vigne '04	♀♀ 6
● Barolo V. Plicotti '04	♀♀ 7
● L'Insieme '04	♀♀ 5
● Barolo Bricco Luciani '01	♀♀♀ 8
● Barolo Bricco Luciani '96	♀♀♀ 8
● Barolo Bricco Luciani '95	♀♀♀ 8
● Barolo Bricco Luciani '90	♀♀♀ 8
● Barolo Bricco Luciani '03	♀♀ 8
● Barolo Ciabot Manzoni '03	♀♀ 8
● Barolo Giachini '03	♀♀ 7
● Barolo L'André '03	♀♀ 7
● Barolo V. Plicotti '03	♀♀ 7

● Barolo Badarina V. Regnola '04	♀♀ 7
● Barbera d'Alba Sup. Scassa '06	♀♀ 4*
● Nebbiolo d'Alba Briccola '06	♀♀ 4*
● Dolcetto d'Alba V. S. Martino '07	♀ 3
O Langhe Chardonnay Valscura '07	♀ 3
● Barolo Badarina V. Regnola '03	♀♀ 6
● Barolo Badarina V. Regnola '01	♀♀ 6
● Barbera d'Alba Sup. Scassa '05	♀♀ 4
● Barbera d'Alba Sup. Scassa '04	♀♀ 4
● Nebbiolo d'Alba Briccola '04	♀♀ 4

Giacomo Grimaldi

VIA LUIGI EINAUDI, 8
12060 BAROLO [CN]
TEL. 0173560536
ferruccio.grimaldi@libero.it

ANNUAL PRODUCTION	50,000 bottles
HECTARES UNDER VINE	10
VITICULTURE METHOD	Conventional

It was another year of progress for Ferruccio Grimaldi at his family farmhouse on the hill that rises from the centre of Barolo towards Novello. His clean, efficient style combining the varietal with elegant drinkability is absolutely respected throughout the range. The best wine is an exemplary Barolo Le Coste 2004. Beautifully mature and vigorous, it gives a rounded, enfolding nose packed with fruit and spice leading into a spacious, harmonious palate with an appealing finish. Barolo Sotto Castello di Novello 2004 has generous aromas and a youthful, dynamic flavour. Making its debut, the new Barolo 2004 did well with classic aromatics and a taut palate supported by expertly gauged tannin. The other wines are forthright and very interesting, particularly the Barberas. The Pistin 2007 is a fine example of varietal fleshy fruit supported by acidity. Fornaci 2006 shows more generous body and broad black berry fruit with appealing hints of resin. The Dolcetto 2007 and the Nebbiolo Valmaggiore 2006 both give an attractive interpretation of their varietal characteristics. Lastly, we must emphasize the winery's admirably balanced pricing policy.

Sergio Grimaldi - Ca' du Sindic

LOC. SAN GRATO, 15
12058 SANTO STEFANO BELBO [CN]
TEL. 0141840341
grimaldi.sergio@virgilio.it

ANNUAL PRODUCTION	45,000 bottles
HECTARES UNDER VINE	10
VITICULTURE METHOD	Conventional

If you fancy a pleasantly complex and very fresh dessert wine, you can't do better than Moscato d'Asti. Sergio Grimaldi is one of its most skilled exponents, managing this little winery with the help of his wife Angela and son Paolo, who now works there full-time. The two Moscatos are very enjoyable for their territory focus and strong character. Capsula Oro is the standard-bearer, obtained from grapes grown in a very steep vineyard planted with vines that are more than 50 years old. They yield a generous wine with complex aromas ranging from ripe peaches to apricots, citronella and sage and a sweet but never cloying palate braced by a harmonious and well-judged backbone of acidity. The Capsula Argento, sourced from the vineyards growing near the winery, is fresher and simpler but not banal. The palate is mouthwatering and satisfying with a long, not excessively sweet finish. The Barbera d'Asti San Grato returns to the line-up in a 2005 version with excellent fruit, hints of raspberries and blueberries and a subtle, stylish entry on the palate. The aromatic Brachetto and the fresh-tasting basic Barbera are very pleasant.

● Barbera d'Alba Fornaci '06	♆♆	5
● Barolo Le Coste '04	♆♆	7
● Barbera d'Alba Pistìn '07	♆♆	4*
● Barolo '04	♆♆	6
● Barolo Sotto Castello di Novello '04	♆♆	6
● Dolcetto d'Alba '07	♆♆	3*
● Nebbiolo d'Alba Valmaggiore '06	♆♆	4*
● Barbera d'Alba Fornaci '05	♆♆	5
● Barbera d'Alba Fornaci '04	♆♆	5
● Barolo Le Coste '03	♆♆	7
● Barolo Le Coste '01	♆♆	7
● Barolo Le Coste '00	♆♆	8
● Barolo Le Coste '99	♆♆	8
● Barolo Sotto Castello di Novello '03	♆♆	6
● Barolo Sotto Castello di Novello '01	♆♆	6
● Barolo Sotto Castello di Novello '00	♆♆	7

O Moscato d'Asti Ca' du Sindic Capsula Oro '07	♆♆	4*
O Moscato d'Asti Ca' du Sindic Capsula Argento '07	♆♆	3*
● Barbera d'Asti San Grato '05	♆♆	4*
● Barbera d'Asti '06	♆	4
● Piemonte Brachetto Ca' du Sindic '07	♆	3
O Moscato d'Asti Ca' du Sindic Capsula Oro '06	♆♆	4
● Barbera d'Asti San Grato '04	♆♆	4

La Guardia

PODERE LA GUARDIA, 74
15010 MORSASCO [AL]
TEL. 014473076

ANNUAL PRODUCTION	**150,000 bottles**
HECTARES UNDER VINE	**40**
VITICULTURE METHOD	**Conventional**

La Guardia is a benchmark for Dolcetto di Ovada. The Priarone family has always experimented, as many of their wines confirm. The estate's 40 hectares are planted to native grapes like dolcetto, barbera and cortese as well as international varieties like chardonnay, sauvignon, cabernet and merlot. The Priarones' love of dolcetto is particularly evident in the Bricco Riccardo selection, the only one presented this year: the others, Villa Delfini and Gamondino, will be tasted next year after further ageing. Bricco Riccardo delivers enthralling aromas and a mouthwatering palate lifted by lively tannin. There are three Barberas: the Ornovo is the freshest and most drinkable; Vigna di Dante has fruity aromas with light balsamic hints and the newest, Ultimo Caffè, is simpler but still mouthfilling with an austere, well-balanced palate. The Monferrato Rosso Innominato, from dolcetto and cabernet, is good and Monferrato Rosso Leone is an interesting blend of pinot noir, dolcetto and cabernet. We also recommend the Sacro e Profano, a well-made blend of barbera and cabernet, the 805 based on merlot and cabernet, and the Chardonnay Butàs.

● Barbera del M.to Ornovo '06	♟♟ 4*
● Barbera del M.to V. di Dante '05	♟♟ 5
● Dolcetto di Ovada Sup. Bricco Riccardo '05	♟♟ 4*
● M.to Rosso Innominato '05	♟♟ 5
● M.to Rosso Sacro e Profano '04	♟ 5
○ Piemonte Chardonnay Butàs '06	♟ 5
● Barbera del M.to Ultimo Caffè '06	♟ 4
● M.to Rosso 805 '06	♟ 5
● M.to Rosso Leone '05	♟ 4
● Barbera del M.to Ornovo '05	♟♟ 4
● M.to Rosso Leone '04	♟♟ 4

Clemente Guasti

C.SO IV NOVEMBRE, 80
14049 NIZZA MONFERRATO [AT]
TEL. 0141721350
www.clemente.guasti.it

ANNUAL PRODUCTION	**200,000 bottles**
HECTARES UNDER VINE	**35**
VITICULTURE METHOD	**Conventional**

This classic Nizza Monferrato operation founded in 1946 is situated in the town centre, as wineries traditionally were when country folk only made wine for their own consumption. But don't imagine that Clemente Guasti is stuck in the past. Far from it. The winery has done much to promote the area. It was one of the first to bottle back in the 1950s and is still among the most interesting here. Barbera Barcarato 2005, the only wine aged in barriques, delivers cherries and leather followed by nice, elegant structure although longer maturation will make it more expressive. The more impressive Barbera Cascina Fonda San Nicolao has a slightly husky nose but very enjoyable palate with a lingering mineral finish. Barbera d'Asti Superiore Boschetto Vecchio is less austere with morello cherries on the expressive nose and a nice tangy finish. The Barbera d'Asti Desideria is a fine combination of approachable healthy fresh fruit and earthy, gamey aromas. The Barbera d'Asti Superiore has distinctive ripe fruit and jam on the nose and a nicely balanced palate, although it has less personality than the others. The Grignolino has nice black pepper and spices.

● Barbera d'Asti Desideria '07	♟♟ 4*
● Barbera d'Asti Sup. Cascina Boschetto Vecchio '05	♟♟ 5
● Barbera d'Asti Sup. Cascina Fonda San Nicolao '05	♟♟ 5
● Barbera d'Asti Sup. Nizza Barcarato '05	♟♟ 6
● Barbera d'Asti Sup. '05	♟ 4
● Grignolino d'Asti '07	♟ 4
● Barbera d'Asti Sup. Nizza Barcarato '04	♟♟ 6
● Barbera d'Asti Sup. Nizza Barcarato '01	♟♟ 6
● Barbera d'Asti Sup. Cascina Boschetto Vecchio '04	♟♟ 5
● Barbera d'Asti Sup. Cascina Fonda San Nicolao '04	♟♟ 5

Hilberg - Pasquero

VIA BRICCO GATTI, 16
12040 PRIOCCA [CN]
TEL. 0173616197
www.hilberg-pasquero.com

ANNUAL PRODUCTION	21,000 bottles
HECTARES UNDER VINE	5
VITICULTURE METHOD	Natural

Much has been written about this gem of a winery clinging to the vine-clad top of a gentle hill just outside Priocca. We have already discussed the estate's natural farming techniques, the range of only reds, although not Roero yet, and restrict quantities of the selections. This enables the cellar to lavish care on each individual bottle, making the winery an anomaly in an increasingly quantity-focused sector. News for this year is that Michelangelo "Miclo" Pasquero and Annette Hilberg are more determined than ever to pursue biodynamic viticulture. Not the trendy, media-friendly version but the quiet, hard-won result of daily labours among the rows, much trial and occasional error, and a visceral passion for the land. The wines that emerge are extraordinarily good. On their way to even greater heights are the classic acidity-and-fruit Barbera, the unusual barbera and brachetto Vareij, the Langhe Nebbiolo, and the two feathers in the winery's cap: the warm, rounded, earthy Barbera Superiore 2006 and the extract-rich Nebbiolo d'Alba 2006, an austere, close-knit masterpiece with great depth that again won Three Glasses.

Icardi

LOC. SAN LAZZARO
VIA BALBI, 30
12053 CASTIGLIONE TINELLA [CN]
TEL. 0141855159
icardivini@libero.it

ANNUAL PRODUCTION	351,000 bottles
HECTARES UNDER VINE	75
VITICULTURE METHOD	Natural

Claudio Icardi is at the helm here with his sister Maria Grazia, who shares his clear vision, dynamic spirit and great tenacity. Claudio puts territory and vintage first in winemaking, playing down human intervention. In his vineyards there is absolute respect for the natural balance of the fragile ecosystem and no chemical products are used. This philosophy extends to the cellar, where the light touch never neglects traditional techniques. Thanks to the diversity of the vineyards, spread over prestigious growing zones in Langhe and Monferrato, the range of wines is interesting and varied, each with its own distinct personality. Outstanding in this year's tastings is the heady, dark-skinned fruit-themed Barolo Parej 2004. The full-bodied, concentrated palate is supported and refreshed by the acidity and tannic structure. Monferrato Rosso Cascina Bricco del Sole is a striking wine again, this time in the spicy, weightily balanced 2006 version. Monferrato Bianco Pafoj 2007, from sauvignon and chardonnay, is very interesting and unusually powerful on both nose and palate. The fresh, citrussy Moscato La Rosa Selvatica is also good.

● Nebbiolo d'Alba '06	♟♟♟	6
● Barbera d'Alba Sup. '06	♟	6
● Barbera d'Alba '07	♟♟	4*
● Langhe Nebbiolo '06	♟♟	5
● Vareij Rosso '07	♟♟	4*
● Barbera d'Alba Sup. '98	♟♟♟	6
● Barbera d'Alba Sup. '97	♟♟♟	6
● Nebbiolo d'Alba '05	♟♟♟	6
● Nebbiolo d'Alba '04	♟♟♟	6
● Nebbiolo d'Alba '03	♟♟♟	6
● Nebbiolo d'Alba '01	♟♟♟	6
● Nebbiolo d'Alba '00	♟♟♟	6
● Nebbiolo d'Alba '99	♟♟♟	6
● Barbera d'Alba Sup. '05	♟♟	6

● Barolo Parej '04	♟♟	8
● Barbera d'Asti Nuj Suj '06	♟♟	5
● Langhe Nebbiolo Surìsjvan '06	♟♟	5
● Langhe Rosso Nej '06	♟♟	5
● M.to Rosso Cascina Bricco del Sole '06	♟♟	6
○ M.to Bianco Pafoj '07	♟♟	5
○ Moscato d'Asti La Rosa Selvatica '07	♟♟	4
● Barbaresco Montubert '05	♟	6
● Barbera d'Alba Surì di Mù '06	♟	5
● Barbera d'Asti Tabaren '07	♟	4
● Dolcetto d'Alba Rousori '07	♟	4
○ Piemonte Moscato Passito Sara d'Oro '04	♟	5
● Barbaresco Montubert '04	♟♟	6

Isabella

FRAZ. CORTERANZO
VIA GIANOLI, 64
15020 MURISENGO [AL]
TEL. 0141693000
info@isabellavini.com

ANNUAL PRODUCTION	120,000 bottles
HECTARES UNDER VINE	25.5
VITICULTURE METHOD	Conventional

This dynamic Monferrato winery near Alessandria keeps its full profile even though the Barbera d'Asti Truccone selection was not among the wines presented, having been left in the cellar for further maturation. Gabriele Calvo has finished work on the beautiful accommodation facility next to the cellar so now he can focus on his prestigious wines. Turning to the wines tasted this year, we were extremely impressed with the other Barbera selection, Bric Stupui, which skipped last year's edition of the Guide. The character and personality of the 2004 are certainly worthy of the denomination. In this earthy Barbera d'Asti, ripe fruit aromas are followed by enthralling sensations of spice and cocoa powder. The generous, austere palate has a hint of acidity in the finish. The Grignolino del Monferrato Casalese is impressive. It has a pale ruby red colour, black pepper and dried flowers on the nose and an approachable palate with a somewhat gutsy, extract and acidity-boosted finish. The Barbera Montemà and Freisa Sobric sparkling wines are simpler but well made.

Iuli

FRAZ. MONTALDO
VIA CENTRALE, 27
15020 CERRINA MONFERRATO [AL]
TEL. 0142946657
www.iuli.it

ANNUAL PRODUCTION	35,000 bottles
HECTARES UNDER VINE	9
VITICULTURE METHOD	Natural

Fabrizio Iuli is convinced that leaving his wines to mature for much longer than normal enhances texture and character. We noticed a certain affectionate concern on the part of his closest companions in this venture – his sister Cristina, the Lerner team consisting of Gad, Umberta and Dan, and Fabrizio's girlfriend Lella – who have faith in Fabrizio but were anxious about the delayed release times, which entail challenging and often painful winery choices. However the Barbera del Monferrato Superiore Barabba 2004 sweeps aside all remaining doubts with its best ever performance, earning Three Glasses. It is concentrated without losing finesse, delivering complex aromas of fruit, spices and flowers, and a dynamic, rounded palate with good acidity and endless length. It's a monument to the variety, the frontier-like land and a courageous, patient winery. The name may mean "Barabas" but the wine is no pariah. To the contrary, it intrigues. The other Barbera selections presented seem to pale in comparison, but that is just an impression. Even the standard-label Umberta and, above all, the Rossore 2005 are commendable products.

● Barbera d'Asti Bric Stupui '04	♟♟ 5
● Barbera del M.to Vivace Bricco Montemà '07	♟ 3
● Grignolino del M.to Casalese Montecastello '07	♟ 4
● M.to Freisa Vivace Sobric '07	♟ 3
● Barbera d'Asti Bric Stupui '03	♟♟ 5
● Barbera d'Asti Bric Stupui '01	♟♟ 5
● Barbera d'Asti Truccone '04	♟♟ 4
● Barbera d'Asti Truccone '03	♟♟ 4
● Barbera del M.to Bricco Montemà Tardivo '05	♟♟ 4

● Barbera del M.to Sup. Barabba '04	♟♟♟ 6
● Barbera del M.to Sup. Rossore '05	♟♟ 5
● Barbera del M.to Sup. Umberta '07	♟♟ 4*
● Barbera del M.to Rossore '03	♟♟ 4
● Barbera del M.to Sup. Barabba '03	♟♟ 6
● Barbera del M.to Sup. Barabba '01	♟♟ 6
● Barbera del M.to Rossore '04	♟♟ 4
● Barbera del M.to Sup. Umberta '06	♟♟ 4
● M.to Rosso Malidea '04	♟♟ 6
● M.to Rosso Nino '05	♟♟ 5

Tenuta La Volta - Cabutto

VIA SAN PIETRO, 13
12060 BAROLO [CN]
TEL. 017356168
www.cabuttolavolta.com

ANNUAL PRODUCTION	100,000 bottles
HECTARES UNDER VINE	18
VITICULTURE METHOD	Conventional

Osvaldo and Bruno Cabutto's lovely winery presented two wines this year for a number of reasons, including the non-production of Barolo Riserva del Fondatore 2002 – a year when no Barolos were – and the removal of the Dolcetto d'Alba from the winery's list. So there were only wines from nebbiolo and barbera but all of an excellent standard. In fact, the Barbera d'Alba Superiore 2006, in 12,000 bottles, is the best of all in this very well-made version, its lovely bright red preceding a vibrant nose with good upfront fruit. The well-judged use of wood, after ageing in used barriques, never intrudes. The palate is broad and typically fresh-tasting with a nice finish. The Barolo La Volta 2004, in 50,000 bottles after almost a month on the skins and ageing for over three years in 100-hectolitre casks, is a good garnet-red with a trim edge, giving red berry fruit with faint tertiary aromas. The palate shows the right amount of dryness with sweetish tannins in the finish. Despite less than huge structure and robust alcohol, it is balanced, stylish and already pleasantly drinkable.

Gianluigi Lano

FRAZ. SAN ROCCO SENO D'ELVIO
S.DA BASSO, 38
12051 ALBA [CN]
TEL. 0173286958
lano.vini@tiscali.it

ANNUAL PRODUCTION	40,000 bottles
HECTARES UNDER VINE	6
VITICULTURE METHOD	Conventional

This small family winery, founded 15 years ago by Gianluigi Lano, is consolidating its presence in the Guide. Motivated by self-belief and wisdom, Gianluigi has been aided by the unwavering care of winemaker Gianfranco Cordero since the start. The vineyards are distributed around the house in the quiet hills in the quietest, but no less charming, corners of Alba. In the wide range of wines presented, the Barbaresco 2005 stands out for its depth, classic aromas and nicely tangy impact on the palate with well-judged extract. This lends an elegant imprint of the terroir and a very pleasant finish. Of the two leading Barberas, Altavilla 2006 shows more harmonious, stimulating texture nicely supported in the flavour while the Fondo Prà 2006 is sourced from older vineyards and shows fruitier and warm with a soft finish that reprises the nose. We salute a remarkable debut from Langhe Rosso Samuele 2006, from barbera and freisa in equal quantities with a little cabernet, after a year ageing in tonneaux. Fruity, piquant aromas precede a firm palate that finishes dry. The other wines are all good, with a clean, pleasant style and very reasonable prices.

● Barbera d'Alba Sup. '06	¶¶ 5
● Barolo La Volta '04	¶¶ 7
● Barolo La Volta '03	♀♀ 7
● Barolo La Volta '01	♀♀ 7
● Barolo Ris. del Fondatore '99	♀♀ 7
● Barolo Ris. del Fondatore '98	♀♀ 7
● Barolo Ris. del Fondatore '97	♀♀ 7
● Barolo Ris. del Fondatore '96	♀♀ 7
● Barolo Ris. del Fondatore '90	♀♀ 7
● Barolo Ris. del Fondatore V. Sarmassa '01	♀♀ 8
● Barolo Ris. del Fondatore V. Sarmassa '00	♀♀ 8

● Barbaresco '05	¶¶ 6
● Barbera d'Alba Fondo Prà '06	¶¶ 4*
● Langhe Rosso Samuele '06	¶¶ 4*
● Barbera d'Alba Altavilla '06	¶¶ 4*
● Barbera d'Alba '06	¶ 3
● Dolcetto d'Alba '07	¶ 3
● Dolcetto d'Alba Ronchella '06	¶ 4
● Langhe Freisa Vivace '07	¶ 3
O Langhe Favorita '07	¶ 3
● Barbaresco '04	♀♀ 6
● Barbaresco '03	♀♀ 6
● Barbaresco '01	♀♀ 6
● Barbera d'Alba Fondo Prà '05	♀♀ 4
● Barbera d'Alba Fondo Prà '04	♀♀ 4
● Barbera d'Alba Fondo Prà '03	♀♀ 5

Ugo Lequio

VIA DEL MOLINO, 10
12057 NEIVE [CN]
TEL. 0173677224
www.ugolequio.it

ANNUAL PRODUCTION 25,000 bottles
HECTARES UNDER VINE N.A.
VITICULTURE METHOD Conventional

Ugo Lequio releases not many bottles but quality is high. With no vineyards of his own, Ugo's main skill is selection, but then he is from Langhe and knows the best crus of Langhe and Neive, in particular, like the back of his hand. The selections hail from Gallina, one of the two "grand crus" of Neive Barbaresco (the other is Santo Stefano). Located on beautifully aspected hillsides along the road from Neive down to the Tanaro, Gallina provides Ugo with grapes for his Barbaresco and Barbera d'Alba Superiore. This year, the Barbaresco Gallina 2005 and 2004 were released together. The former shows finesse and elegance in a slender body, reflecting the vintage year perfectly. The 2004 has benefited from an extra year's ageing to gain even more complexity. It's a great Barbaresco with a bouquet of dried flowers, liquorice and quinine preceding a juicy, mouthfilling palate with silkily streamlined tannins. The basic wines are fresh, fruity and very good. The preview tasting of Barbera d'Alba Gallina 2006, just bottled now and to be released next year, convinced us of the wisdom of Ugo's wise decision to age it for at least a year in glass.

● Barbaresco Gallina '05	🍷🍷 6*
● Barbaresco Gallina '04	🍷🍷 6*
● Barbera d'Alba '07	🍷 4
O Langhe Arneis '07	🍷 4
● Barbaresco Gallina '01	🍷🍷 6
● Barbaresco Gallina '00	🍷🍷 6
● Barbaresco Gallina Ris. '01	🍷🍷 7
● Barbaresco Gallina Ris. '99	🍷🍷 7
● Barbera d'Alba Sup. Gallina '05	🍷🍷 4

Cascina Luisin

S.DA RABAJÀ, 34
12050 BARBARESCO [CN]
TEL. 0173635154
cascinaluisin@tiscali.it

ANNUAL PRODUCTION 30,000 bottles
HECTARES UNDER VINE 7
VITICULTURE METHOD Conventional

This classic Barbaresco winery is run in traditional style by Luigi Minuto and his energetic son Roberto, now increasingly involved in the vineyards and cellar. The wines are made with nature-friendly methods, usually emerging not particularly soft and needing plenty of maturing time. A good example is the Barbaresco Rabajà 2004. It has the cru's trademark strength and austerity, plus encouragingly warm, ripe fruit and a taut, edgy palate with a huge but nicely distributed tannic structure that augurs well for the future. Barbaresco Sorì Paolin 2004 is broad, warm and mellow with nice balsamic hints of iodine and aromatic herbs, and a stylish, spacious palate with a good firm structure. Barolo Leon 2004, which originates from a small vineyard at Serralunga, is very expressive of the terroir with aromas of cherries, leather and red berries, and gives exuberant tannin on a palate that is mouthfilling and broad, rather than lingering. The Barbera Asili 2005, from a seriously good vineyard with plots over 50 years old, is weighty, generous and juicy but also offers depth and well-handled savouriness and mineral sensations. The other wines are all good.

● Barbaresco Rabajà '04	🍷🍷 7
● Barbaresco Sorì Paolin '04	🍷🍷 7
● Barbera d'Alba Asili '06	🍷🍷 5
● Barbera d'Alba Maggiur '07	🍷🍷 4*
● Barolo Leon '04	🍷🍷 7
● Dolcetto d'Alba Bric Trifüla '07	🍷 4
● Langhe Nebbiolo Maggiur '07	🍷 4
● Barbera d'Alba Asili '99	🍷🍷🍷 6
● Barbera d'Alba Asili '00	🍷🍷🍷 6
● Barbera d'Alba Asili Barrique '97	🍷🍷🍷 6
● Barbaresco Rabajà '02	🍷🍷 5
● Barbaresco Rabajà '01	🍷🍷 7
● Barbaresco Rabajà '99	🍷🍷 6
● Barbaresco Sorì Paolin '03	🍷🍷 7
● Barbaresco Sorì Paolin '01	🍷🍷 7
● Barbaresco Sorì Paolin '00	🍷🍷 7

La Luna del Rospo

FRAZ. SALERE, 38
14041 AGLIANO TERME [AT]
TEL. 0141954222
www.lalunadelrospo.it

ANNUAL PRODUCTION	45,000 bottles
HECTARES UNDER VINE	9.5
VITICULTURE METHOD	Certified biodynamic

Asti is certainly no Chiantishire full of northern Europeans in search of nature but during the 1990s, many estates were up for sale and some Swiss and Germans decided to move to here. In 1994, Bavarian wine enthusiasts Michael Schaffer and Renate Schütz bought a lovely farmhouse surrounded by vineyards and over time their mastery of viticulture grew as did the quality of their products. The vineyards are organically farmed with vines averaging more than 40 years old. The oldest vineyards yield grapes for Barbera d'Asti Solo Per Laura, a characterful wine that made it through to the final tastings. Some of the wine is aged for 12 months in new barriques and the rest in small barrels after malolactic fermentation. The resulting selection is modern with complex aromas of ripe red berries and sweet spice. Bric Rocche is more traditional in style after maturation exclusively in large barrels. Two Glasses went to Monferrato Rosso Gli Storni, a blend of nebbiolo and barbera that hints at vanilla and cocoa powder. The Grignolino is spicy with black pepper and cinnamon and the Cortese is nice.

● Barbera d'Asti Solo per Laura '05	♈♈	5
● Barbera d'Asti Bric Rocche '05	♈♈	4
● Grignolino d'Asti '07	♈♈	3*
● M.to Rosso Gli Storni '04	♈♈	5
○ Piemonte Cortese '07	♈	3
● Barbera d'Asti Bric Rocche '04	♈♈	4
● Barbera d'Asti Solo per Laura '04	♈♈	5

Malabaila di Canale

FRAZ. MADONNA DEI CAVALLI, 19
12043 CANALE [CN]
TEL. 017398381
www.malabaila.com

ANNUAL PRODUCTION	80,000 bottles
HECTARES UNDER VINE	22
VITICULTURE METHOD	Conventional

When the estate owned by Conti Malabaila di Canale earned a full profile last year, we talked about the winery's history and beautiful location. This year, we will focus on the range because it is now complete and we can make a global assessment. The two whites are both very sound, the Arneis being fresh and tangy and the Favorita, from a variety perhaps wrongly neglected in this area, gives captivatingly clean aromas. There is a subtle distinction to be made regarding the reds. The two Barberas, both from 2006 and with the same name, differ in the harvesting strategy and, especially, ageing procedures used. The standard Mezzavilla aged exclusively in stainless steel while the other aged in barriques, as it says on the label, which has left it softer and more structured. We can reveal that the names will shortly be distinguished. Finally, the 2005 Roeros: Bric Volta delivers aromas of red berry fruit, earth and leather, with an austere palate, and Castelletto Riserva is even better, with generous tertiary aromas, a mouthfilling flavour and memorable overall harmony.

● Barbera d'Alba Mezzavilla Barrique '06	♈♈	4*
● Roero Bric Volta '05	♈♈	5
● Roero Castelletto Ris. '05	♈♈	5
● Barbera d'Alba Mezzavilla '06	♈	4
○ Langhe Favorita '07	♈	4
○ Roero Arneis Pradvaj '07	♈	4
● Barbera d'Alba Mezzavilla '05	♈♈	4
● Roero Sup. Bric Volta '04	♈♈	5
● Roero Sup. Castelletto '04	♈♈	5
● Roero Sup. Castelletto '03	♈♈	5
● Roero Sup. Castelletto '01	♈♈	5
● Roero Sup. Castelletto '00	♈♈	5

Malgrà

LOC. BAZZANA
VIA NIZZA, 8
14046 MOMBARUZZO [AT]
TEL. 0141725055
www.malgra.it

ANNUAL PRODUCTION	950,000 bottles
HECTARES UNDER VINE	140
VITICULTURE METHOD	Conventional

Having rejuvenated Bersano, the traditional Nizza Monferrato winery famous worldwide since the 1950s, Nico Conta and Massimiliano Diotto went into business at the start of the new century and purchased part of the Chiarle estate, creating the new Malgrà brand. With Ezio and Giorgio Chiarle, they have set up a dynamic winery that has made its name internationally in just a few years and impressed critics everywhere. Back in spring 2005, they created the new Malgrà project and opened a wine group that has expanded into northern Piedmont, in a joint venture with the Gattinara-based Nervi winery, and Tuscany with Giunti of Poggibonsi. We tasted a reliable range of Barbera d'Astis for the new edition of the Guide but the top wine was the Nizza Mora di Sassi 2005. Its fruity nose is laced with spice and quinine and the balanced, richly textured palate takes you through to a stylish, lingering finish with nicely handled wood. The Superiore Gaiana 2005 is tangier and more approachable. Barbera Fornace di Cerreto 2006 is still young but quite appetizing with fruity sensations while the standard-label Barbera, Briga della Mora, is uncomplicated.

Malvirà

LOC. CANOVA
VIA CASE SPARSE, 144
12043 CANALE [CN]
TEL. 0173978145
www.malvira.com

ANNUAL PRODUCTION	350,000 bottles
HECTARES UNDER VINE	40
VITICULTURE METHOD	Natural

The Malvirà beacon continues to show Roero the way forward. Helped by their families and assistants, Roberto and Massimo Damonte press on both in the winery, situated in the centre of an amphitheatre of tidy vineyards, and in their scenic hilltop guest accommodation. But beyond aesthetics, you need to sit down at the Villa Tiboldi restaurant and taste the wines to discover the spirit of this winery. The many wines are better than ever, thrusting Malvirà up among the most illustrious names in oenological Piedmont. The Roero Trinità and Mombeltramo, both 2005, are miracles of grace and elegance in perfect Malvirà style. We just preferred the Riserva Mombeltramo, which walked away with Three Glasses. But another red we liked very much was the soft yet acidic Barbera Superiore 2005. The Damontes are acknowledged experts with whites in so the choice of a favourite from the three Arneis vineyard selections is a matter of personal taste. In our opinion, Saglietto is the best. The two white Langhe wines are excellent. The monovarietal Sauvignon is beautifully drinkable and the Treuve, from chardonnay, sauvignon and arneis, is harmonious.

● Barbera d'Asti Sup. Nizza Mora di Sassi '05	♥♥	6
● Barbera d'Asti Sup. Gaiana '05	♥♥	4*
● Barbera d'Asti Sup. Fornace di Cerreto '06	♥♥	4*
● Barbera d'Asti Briga della Mora '07	♥	3
O Gavi del Comune di Gavi Poggio Basco '07	♥	4
● Barbera d'Asti Sup. Nizza Mora di Sassi '04	♥♥	6
● Barbera d'Asti Sup. Nizza Mora di Sassi '03	♥♥	6
● Barbera d'Asti Sup. Nizza Mora di Sassi '01	♥♥	6
O Col dei Ronchi Brut M. Cl. Cuvée Malgrà '03	♥♥	5
● M.to Rosso Treviri '05	♥♥	5

● Roero Mombeltramo Ris. '05	♥♥♥	6
● Barbera d'Alba Sup. S. Michele '05	♥♥	5
● Roero Trinità Ris. '05	♥♥	6
O Roero Arneis Saglietto '07	♥♥	4*
O Langhe Bianco '07	♥♥	4
O Langhe Bianco Tre Uve '06	♥♥	4
O Roero Arneis Renesio '07	♥♥	4
O Roero Arneis Trinità '07	♥♥	4
● Barbera d'Alba S. Michele '06	♥♥	4
● Langhe Nebbiolo '06	♥♥	4
● Langhe Rosso S. Guglielmo '05	♥♥	5
O Roero Arneis '07	♥	4
● Roero Sup. Mombeltramo '04	♥♥♥	6
● Roero Sup. Mombeltramo '00	♥♥♥	6
● Roero Sup. Trinità '03	♥♥♥	6
● Roero Sup. Trinità '01	♥♥♥	6

Giovanni Manzone

VIA CASTELLETTO, 9
12065 MONFORTE D'ALBA [CN]
TEL. 017378114
www.manzonegiovanni.com

ANNUAL PRODUCTION	**40,000 bottles**
HECTARES UNDER VINE	**8**
VITICULTURE METHOD	**Conventional**

Extension work continues and during our visit, Giovanni's likeable son Mauro Manzone showed us where the ageing cellar and tasting rooms will be located. Mauro has worked with his father since 2005, continuing the family tradition that began in 1925 when his great-grandfather bought the Ciabot del Preve. Today, the eight hectares of vineyards in prestigious locations produce territory-focused wines. Top of the class is Barolo Le Gramolere, which has a broad, subtle nose and juicy, very stylish palate with complex aromas of tobacco and ripe, mellow tannins. Three Glasses confirm its absolute class. Bricat is more concentrated with black berry fruit, mint melding with the alcohol, nice structure and a liquorice note in the warm aftertaste. Making its debut, the Barolo Castelletto is the simplest of the three with a dry palate, lean-bodied structure and fruity, alcoholic finish. Nebbiolo Il Crutin, from Gramolere, the Barbera and the Dolcetto from La Serra all attracted our attention. Finally, there's a white from rossese, a variety saved from oblivion to delight our palates with its strong, lingering aromas and balanced, savoury flavour.

Paolo Manzone

LOC. MERIAME, 1
12050 SERRALUNGA D'ALBA [CN]
TEL. 0173613113
www.barolomeriame.com

ANNUAL PRODUCTION	**60,000 bottles**
HECTARES UNDER VINE	**10**
VITICULTURE METHOD	**Conventional**

One of Paolo Manzone's two wineries is at Meriame near Serralunga, in a magnificent natural amphitheatre of nebbiolo vines. The fully restored farmhouse is also used as guest accommodation, offering five bedrooms and a swimming pool overlooking the estate. Barolo Meriame, made from a selection of the best grapes from the Meriame vineyard, has a sweet, warm nose with upfront oak before soft tannins blend in the spacious structure without clashing with the fruity sensations. The finish is long and lingering with sweet toasty hints. The Barolo Serralunga is slender and more typical, revealing a palate vibrant with tannins that require softening, as well as fresh fruit and a muted hint of oak leading into a warm finish. Grapes for the Nebbiolo Mirinè come from the Sinio vineyards. Aged in Barolo barrels, it is still youthful with a forward mouth-drying sensation, fresh flavour and appealing palate. Lastly, approachability is the strongpoint of two very distinctive wines: Barbera Fiorenza and Dolcetto Magna.

● Barolo Le Gramolere '04	♟♟♟	7
● Barolo Bricat '04	♟♟	7
● Barbera d'Alba '07	♟♟	5
● Barbera d'Alba Sup. La Serra '06	♟♟	5
● Barolo Castelletto '04	♟♟	6
● Dolcetto d'Alba La Serra '07	♟♟	4*
● Langhe Nebbiolo Il Crutin '07	♟♟	5
○ Langhe Bianco Rosserto '06	♟♟	4*
● Dolcetto d'Alba Le Ciliegie '07	♟	3
● Barolo Le Gramolere Ris. '01	♟♟♟	8
● Barolo Le Gramolere Ris. '00	♟♟♟	8
● Barolo Le Gramolere Ris. '99	♟♟♟	8
● Barolo Bricat '03	♟♟	7
● Barolo Bricat '01	♟♟	7
● Barolo Le Gramolere '01	♟♟	7
● Barolo Le Gramolere '00	♟♟	7
● Barolo Le Gramolere '99	♟♟	5

● Barbera d'Alba Fiorenza '07	♟♟	4*
● Barolo Meriame '04	♟♟	7
● Nebbiolo d'Alba Mirinè '06	♟♟	5
● Barolo Serralunga '04	♟	6
● Dolcetto d'Alba Magna '07	♟	3
● Barolo Meriame '01	♟♟	7
● Barolo Meriame '00	♟♟	7
● Barolo Meriame '99	♟♟	7
● Barolo Serralunga '01	♟♟	6

Poderi Marcarini

P.zza Martiri, 2
12064 La Morra [CN]
tel. 017350222
www.marcarini.it

ANNUAL PRODUCTION	110,000 bottles
HECTARES UNDER VINE	20
VITICULTURE METHOD	Conventional

The lovely, long-established La Morra winery owned by Luisa and Manuel Marchetti could not let the opportunity of 2004's excellent growing year slip through its fingers so there are two great Barolos from that year. The lively Barolo La Serra has pale colour and balsamic hints on the nose with a touch of sage on a floral background. The palate is alluring, sophisticated, stylish and harmonious. It's good to drink now although a few years in bottle will undoubtedly improve it further. The Barolo Brunate, like the La Serra, underwent protracted skin contact and again shows the class and depth of a grand cru with typical dried roses on the nose, a hint of spice, and a palate that is sweet, austere, powerful and stylish, with distinctive hints of liquorice in a long finish. The other wines presented this year are also in good shape, from the fresh, juicy Barbera Ciabot Camerano 2006 to the enjoyable Nebbiolo Lasarin 2007, the delicious barbera, nebbiolo and syrah Langhe Rosso 2005 and the ever-unique Dolcetto Boschi di Berri 2007, from ungrafted vines. The Dolcetto Fontanazza 2007, the well-typed Arneis and the Moscato d'Asti are all very sound.

Marchesi di Barolo

via Alba, 12
12060 Barolo [CN]
tel. 0173564400
www.marchesibarolo.com

ANNUAL PRODUCTION	1,350,000 bottles
HECTARES UNDER VINE	117
VITICULTURE METHOD	Conventional

Marchesi di Barolo is a juggernaut and like all juggernauts is rarely unprepared for action. This year, the winery owned by the Abbona and Scarzello families presented a series of wines that were rich in personality and showed very high average quality. For purely incidental reasons – the unfavourable 2002 growing year – one of the most interesting Marchesi wines was missing. There was no Barolo Riserva Grande Annata. Still, we consoled ourselves with an excellent 2004 version of Barolo Cannubi. This wine perfectly reflects its terroir, one of the most famous vineyards in the DOCG zone, with a range of particularly stylish aromatics: roses, violets, quinine and balsam. The palate shows sweet tannins, with a slight hint of oak, and a very long, mouthfilling finish. The Barolo Sarmassa is very good indeed with hints of leather and spices, as is Coste di Rose, which delivers tobacco, strawberries and dried flowers. Both are from 2004. The rest of the well-stocked range is very enjoyable, with special mentions for the Barolo Vigneti di Proprietà 2004, the Barbaresco Creja 2005 and the Barbera d'Alba Ruvei 2006.

● Barolo Brunate '04	▼▼ 7
● Barolo La Serra '04	▼▼ 7
● Dolcetto d'Alba Boschi di Berri '07	▼▼ 4*
● Barbera d'Alba Ciabot Camerano '06	▼ 4*
● Langhe Nebbiolo Lasarin '07	▼▼ 4*
● Langhe Rosso '05	▼▼ 5
● Dolcetto d'Alba Fontanazza '07	▼ 4
○ Moscato d'Asti '07	▼ 4
○ Roero Arneis '07	▼ 4
● Barolo Brunate '03	▼▼▼ 8
● Barolo Brunate '01	▼▼▼ 7
● Barolo Brunate '99	▼▼▼ 7
● Barolo Brunate '96	▼▼▼ 7
● Barolo Brunate Ris. '85	▼▼▼ 7
● Dolcetto d'Alba Boschi di Berri '96	▼▼▼ 5

● Barolo Cannubi '04	▼▼ 7
● Barolo Sarmassa '04	▼▼ 7
● Barbaresco Creja '05	▼▼ 6
● Barbera d'Alba Ruvei '06	▼▼ 4*
● Barolo Coste di Rose '04	▼▼ 7
● Barolo Vign. di Proprietà in Barolo '04	▼▼ 7
● Barbaresco Ris. Grande Annata '03	▼▼ 6
● Dolcetto d'Alba Madonna di Como '07	▼▼ 4*
● Nebbiolo d'Alba Michet '06	▼ 5
○ Moscato d'Asti Zagara '07	▼ 4
○ Roero Arneis '07	▼ 4
● Barolo Estate Vineyard '97	▼▼▼ 8
● Barolo Ris. Grande Annata '99	▼▼▼ 7
● Barolo Vign. di Proprietà in Barolo '98	▼▼▼ 8

Marchesi Incisa della Rocchetta

VIA ROMA, 66
14030 ROCCHETTA TANARO [AT]
TEL. 0141644647
www.lacortechiusa.it

Marenco

P.ZZA VITTORIO EMANUELE, 10
15019 STREVI [AL]
TEL. 0144363133
www.marencovini.com

ANNUAL PRODUCTION	50,000 bottles
HECTARES UNDER VINE	17
VITICULTURE METHOD	Conventional

Angelus Novus is the name of the new barbera and merlot-based Monferrato Rosso from this lovely Rocchetta Tanaro estate, which Barbara Incisa della Rocchetta and her son Filiberto Massone, who runs the estate with her. Their consultant winemaker is Donato Lanati. Let's start with that Angelus Novus 2006. Pleasant raspberry and strawberry fruit on the nose introduces a powerful structure supported by good freshness on a palate free of bitter tannins and rich in aromas. It was an excellent debut. The more traditional wines also gave a good account of themselves, both Barberas earning very flattering results. The Sant'Emiliano 2005 delivers complex aromas with perfect balance of sweet spice and red berries, followed by a powerful, harmonious entry on the palate. There's also probably the most impressive version ever of Valmorena 2006, whose beautifully drinkable palate combines with enviably forthright, clean aromas. The two Monferratos were up to snuff. Rollone 2006 is a blend of pinot noir and barbera while the Leopoldo 2007 is a monovarietal Pinot Noir, from this year aged for a much shorter time. The Grignolino is very pleasant.

ANNUAL PRODUCTION	300,000 bottles
HECTARES UNDER VINE	90
VITICULTURE METHOD	Conventional

Marenco confirms that Strevi is outstanding wine country. The estate's extensive vineyards grow typical local grape varieties: barbera, dolcetto, moscato and brachetto. The last two, in particular, are the area's strong suit and Marenco produces very sound examples in Moscato Scrapona and Brachetto Pineto. The former has a lovely bright golden colour and distinctive varietal sensations of peach and apricot fruit and cakes, followed by a good entry on the palate, where creamy sensations enhance the harmonious sweetness. The Brachetto is also good, giving elegance and finesse on the nose and a weighty, generous palate. Turning to the other wines, the pleasant ruby red Barbera d'Asti Bassina has a fresh palate and very bright aromas including red berries, damp earth and spices. Also enjoyable is the Dolcetto d'Acqui Marchesa, which gives vibrant ripe red berries and grassy hints while the lightly tannic palate lingers. The new albarossa-based wine, Red Sunrise, is interesting. This year's dry Moscato, MaMu – a conflation of Marenco Muscatè – is well typed. Also worth mentioning is Carialoso, from the rare native caricalasino variety.

● Barbera d'Asti Sup. Sant'Emiliano '05	🍷🍷 5
● Barbera d'Asti Valmorena '06	🍷🍷 4*
● M.to Rosso Angelus Novus '06	🍷🍷 7
● M.to Rosso Marchese Leopoldo '07	🍷🍷 5
● M.to Rosso Rollone '06	🍷🍷 4*
● Grignolino d'Asti '07	🍷 4
● Barbera d'Asti Sup. Sant'Emiliano '04	🍷🍷 5
● Barbera d'Asti Sup. Sant'Emiliano '03	🍷🍷 5
● M.to Rosso Marchese Leopoldo '03	🍷🍷 5
● M.to Rosso Marchese Leopoldo '01	🍷🍷 5

● Barbera d'Asti Bassina '06	🍷🍷 4*
● Brachetto d'Acqui Pineto '07	🍷🍷 4*
● Dolcetto d'Acqui Marchesa '07	🍷🍷 4*
○ MaMu '07	🍷🍷 6
○ Moscato d'Asti Scrapona '07	🍷🍷 4*
○ Carialoso '07	🍷 4
● M.to Albarossa Red Sunrise '06	🍷 5
● Barbera d'Asti Bassina '05	🍷🍷 4
● Barbera d'Asti Ciresa '04	🍷🍷 6
● Barbera d'Asti Ciresa '03	🍷🍷 6

Mario Marengo

VIA XX SETTEMBRE, 34
12064 LA MORRA [CN]
TEL. 017350127
marengo1964@libero.it

Claudio Mariotto

S.DA PER SAREZZANO, 29
15057 TORTONA [AL]
www.claudiomariotto.it

ANNUAL PRODUCTION	20,000 bottles
HECTARES UNDER VINE	4
VITICULTURE METHOD	Conventional

ANNUAL PRODUCTION	90,000 bottles
HECTARES UNDER VINE	26
VITICULTURE METHOD	Conventional

At last, Three Glasses have come to this small La Morra winery. Marco Marengo is the latest in a long line of growers at the estate named after his father. In Mario's day, growing was a secondary business, and the vineyards were a hobby cultivated to maintain a link with the family's ancestors. The winery is certainly not be one of the area's largest but the four hectares of vineyards in some of the most favourable positions in Langhe and Roero are enough to sustain a family. A few years ago, Marco's friend Elio Altare helped him to become a full-time grower-producer. As the cellar is small, they opted for barrique ageing, with 40 per cent new barrels, for the more ambitious wines. Bricco delle Viole 2004, a Barolo, aims for finesse with plenty of fruity aromas and an alcohol-rich structure held in place by vigorous acidity. But the real winery champion is the Brunate. Its incomparably elegant aromas and flavours derive from the terroir, while the old vines, on average 60 years old, endow it with weight and outstanding length. The rest of the wines all lived up to our expectations.

Again, Claudio Mariotto presented a high-scoring raft of wines. We were all expecting 2006 to produce another breathtaking Pitasso but the Derthona also sailed into the finals with effortless flamboyance. Pitasso has striking aromas starting with minerality and benzene that open into fruitier sensations. With the nicely concentrated palate and juicy flavour, they earned a compelling Three Glasses. The Derthona is softer and more accessible. We preferred Vho 2006 to the Poggio del Rosso 2005. Both are made from barbera and aged in oak, the former presenting more balanced and drinkable than its elder brother, which is robustly concentrated with very weighty structure. In this limited space, we can't list all the wines on offer from this estate but we should certainly mention the steel-aged Barbera, Territorio, which is interesting and reasonably priced. The cortese-heavy white Profilo and the debuting Montemirano, from croatina, are both very sound. There's also something for fans of semi-sparkling wines in the red Martirella and white Coccalina. Lastly, a mention for another new wine, the freisa-based Braghè 2007.

● Barolo Brunate '04	♟♟♟ 7
● Barolo Bricco Viole '04	♟ 7
● Dolcetto d'Alba '07	♟♟ 4*
● Nebbiolo d'Alba Valmaggiore '06	♟♟ 4*
● Barolo Brunate '03	♟♟ 7
● Barolo Brunate '01	♟♟ 7
● Barolo Brunate '00	♟♟ 7
● Barolo Brunate '99	♟♟ 7
● Barolo Brunate '97	♟♟ 7
● Barolo Brunate '96	♟♟ 7
● Barolo Bricco Viole '03	♟♟ 8
● Barolo Bricco Viole '01	♟♟ 8
● Barolo Bricco Viole '98	♟♟ 8
● Barolo Bricco Viole '97	♟♟ 8

○ Colli Tortonesi Bianco Pitasso '06	♟♟♟ 6
○ Colli Tortonesi Bianco Derthona '06	♟♟ 5
● Colli Tortonesi Rosso Vho '06	♟♟ 5
● Colli Tortonesi Rosso Montemirano '06	♟♟ 5
● Colli Tortonesi Rosso Poggio del Rosso '05	♟♟ 6
○ Colli Tortonesi Bianco Profilo '07	♟♟ 4*
● Colli Tortonesi Rosso Territorio '07	♟♟ 4*
○ Colli Tortonesi Bianco Coccalina '07	♟ 4
● Colli Tortonesi Rosso Braghè '07	♟ 4
● Colli Tortonesi Rosso Martirella '07	♟ 4
○ Colli Tortonesi Bianco Pitasso '05	♟♟♟ 5
○ Colli Tortonesi Bianco Pitasso '04	♟♟♟ 5
○ Colli Tortonesi Bianco Derthona '05	♟♟ 5
● Colli Tortonesi Rosso Vho '05	♟♟ 5
● Colli Tortonesi Rosso Vho '04	♟♟ 5

Marsaglia

VIA MADAMA MUSSONE, 2
12050 CASTELLINALDO [CN]
TEL. 0173213048
www.cantinamarsaglia.it

ANNUAL PRODUCTION	70,000 bottles
HECTARES UNDER VINE	15
VITICULTURE METHOD	Conventional

We are glad we believed in the Marsaglia family's Castellinaldo-based winery. Over the years, it has improved, first earning a place among the full profiles, and now flattering marks for all the wines in the range, which include some of the most dependable in the area. The Roero Arneis is excellent, presenting fruity and acidic, streaked with minerality and lingering in the mouth. The San Servasio vineyard brings us a floral, sage-themed Langhe Arneis. The two Barberas are very different, for obvious reasons. The approachable freshness of the 2007 San Cristoforo is complemented by a 2005 Castellinaldo that is vigorous and almost austere, were it not tempered by shrewd use of small oak. Both are excellent in their respective categories and food matchings. The Nebbiolo 2006 provides a robust example of the variety's value while the Roero 2005 is a happy medley of fruit, tertiary aromas, strength and finesse with a long, harmonious finish. The range, reflecting the direction taken by the winery, closes with a sweet but not cloying arneis-based Passito.

★ Franco M. Martinetti

VIA SAN FRANCESCO DA PAOLA, 18
10123 TORINO [TO]
TEL. 0118395937
www.francomartinetti.it

ANNUAL PRODUCTION	150,000 bottles
HECTARES UNDER VINE	4
VITICULTURE METHOD	Conventional

Franco and his sons Michele and Guido have further extended the Martinetti range with two excellent steel-aged whites, a Gavi and a Timorasso, now flanking the much-respected selections. But the Martinettis' fame is built primarily on the great Piedmontese reds, of which Franco is a leading exponent as he scours the region selecting fruit from the best areas to make three very good wines: the fresh-tasting Barolo Marasco 2004 with smooth tannins; the soft, heady Monferrato Sul Bric 2006; and Barbera d'Asti Montruc 2004, a soft, silky wine with perfectly judged acidity that takes advantage of the excellent growing year. Franco's unremitting work was rewarded by his tenth Three Glass prize. A word about the two leading whites, both gems: Minaia has elegant aromas and Martin is complex with a long-lingering palate. From the rest of the range, we liked the well-established Brut Quarantatre and the new Langhe Nebbiolo, as drinkable as it is weighty. But the less ambitious wines are also well typed, making Martinetti one of Piedmont's most reliable wineries.

● Barbera d'Alba S. Cristoforo '07	♟♟ 4*
● Castellinaldo Barbera d'Alba '05	♟♟ 5
● Nebbiolo d'Alba San Pietro '06	♟♟ 4*
● Roero Brich d'America '05	♟♟ 5
○ Roero Arneis Serramiana '07	♟♟ 4*
○ Arsicà	♟ 5
○ Langhe Arneis San Servasio '07	♟ 4
● Castellinaldo Barbera d'Alba '04	♟♟ 5
● Castellinaldo Barbera d'Alba '03	♟♟ 5
● Castellinaldo Barbera d'Alba '01	♟♟ 5
● Castellinaldo Barbera d'Alba '00	♟♟ 5
● Roero Sup. Brich d'America '04	♟♟ 5
● Roero Sup. Brich d'America '03	♟♟ 5
● Roero Sup. Brich d'America '02	♟♟ 5
● Roero Sup. Brich d'America '01	♟♟ 5

● Barbera d'Asti Sup. Montruc '06	♟♟♟ 6
● Barolo Marasco '04	♟♟ 8
● M.to Rosso Sul Bric '06	♟♟ 7
○ Gavi Minaia '07	♟♟ 6
○ Colli Tortonesi Bianco Martin '06	♟♟ 7
○ Brut M. Cl. Quarantatre '04	♟♟ 6
○ Colli Tortonesi Timorasso Biancofranco '07	♟♟ 4*
○ Gavi del Comune di Gavi '07	♟♟ 5
● Barbera d'Asti Bric dei Banditi '07	♟♟ 4*
● Colli Tortonesi Rosso Lauren '06	♟♟ 6
● Langhe Nebbiolo Siccis Omnia Dura Deus Proposuit '06	♟♟ 5
● Colli Tortonesi Rosso Georgette '06	♟ 6
○ Alcedo '04	♟ 7
● Barolo Marasco '01	♟♟♟ 8

Bartolo Mascarello

VIA ROMA, 15
12060 BAROLO [CN]
TEL. 017356125

ANNUAL PRODUCTION	30,000 bottles
HECTARES UNDER VINE	5
VITICULTURE METHOD	Conventional

If you are looking for dark, intense wines with broad fruit and powerful explosive structure, this is not the winery for you. If, on the other hand, you love complex, slightly rustic wines rich in sensations, that need to open slowly to reveal all their generous qualities, you're sure to enjoy the range from Maria Teresa Mascarello, who follows in her father's footsteps and hews to the most sincere Langhe tradition. The 2004 is on great form. A blend of grapes from the Rocche, Cannubi, San Lorenzo and Ruè vineyards, it presents ruby red with a garnet edge, opening on the nose with faintly fruity, floral aromas picked up on the palate and lifted with leather, tobacco and liquorice, nicely evident tannin combining with perceptible acidity. We expect this wine to improve for many years. The Dolcetto 2007 is purplish in colour with generous fruit aromas of raspberries and cherries, good structure and prominent extract. The Barbera 2006 reveals its youth with lively acidity backing up the fruit and spices evident on nose and palate. The nebbiolo-style Freisa needs aeration to release its typical fruity aromas.

Giuseppe Mascarello e Figlio

S.DA DEL GROSSO, 1
12060 MONCHIERO [CN]
TEL. 0173792126
www.mascarello1881.com

ANNUAL PRODUCTION	50,000 bottles
HECTARES UNDER VINE	17
VITICULTURE METHOD	Conventional

Tradition, austerity and character are the words that best sum up the winery managed by Mauro Mascarello and his son Giuseppe. The wines all stick to tradition: austere, husky and edgy when young, they are absolute jewels when they eventually release their aromas as they develop in elegance for those who have the patience to wait for them. In fact, they are released to market only when the cellar feels the moment is right. Contrary to what we wrote last year, the Barolos from 2003 were produced and are excellent. Although they tend to be broader and warmer on both nose and palate, and may have less ageing potential than more classic vintages, they are distinctively fresh with surprisingly ripe tannins given the year. Of the three, Monprivato stands out for its broad, varied aromas and balanced, elegant palate while the tangy, linear S. Stefano di Perno has distinctive character and austerity. Villero is more balsamic but stiffer and less deep. From the other wines, we particularly liked the depth and sophisticated definition of the Barbera S. Stefano 2005.

● Barolo '04	♥♥	8
● Barbera d'Alba Vign. S. Lorenzo '06	♥♥	5
● Dolcetto d'Alba Monrobiolo e Ruè '07	♥♥	4*
● Langhe Freisa '06	♥♥	4*
● Barolo '01	♥♥♥	8
● Barolo '99	♥♥♥	8
● Barolo '98	♥♥♥	8
● Barolo '89	♥♥♥	8
● Barolo '85	♥♥♥	8
● Barolo '84	♥♥♥	8
● Barolo '83	♥♥♥	8
● Barbera d'Alba Vign. S. Lorenzo '05	♥♥	5

● Barbera d'Alba Sup. S. Stefano di Perno '05	♥♥	6
● Barolo Monprivato '03	♥♥	8
● Barolo S. Stefano di Perno '03	♥♥	8
● Barbera d'Alba Sup. Scudetto '04	♥♥	6
● Barolo Villero '03	♥♥	8
● Langhe Freisa Toetto '04	♥♥	5
● Barolo Monprivato '85	♥♥♥	8
● Barolo Monprivato '01	♥♥♥	8
● Barolo S. Stefano di Perno '98	♥♥♥	8
● Barolo Villero '96	♥♥♥	8
● Barbera d'Alba Sup. Codana '04	♥♥	7
● Barolo Monprivato '00	♥♥	8
● Barolo Monprivato '99	♥♥	8
● Barolo Monprivato '98	♥♥	8
● Barolo S. Stefano di Perno '01	♥♥	8

Tenuta La Meridiana

via Tana Bassa, 5
14048 Montegrosso d'Asti [AT]
tel. 0141956172
www.tenutalameridiana.com

ANNUAL PRODUCTION 85,000 bottles
HECTARES UNDER VINE 12
VITICULTURE METHOD Conventional

The winery dates from 1999 but wine has been produced at Meridiana for four generations, as Giampiero Bianco points out, proud of his roots and passionate about Barbera. Who are we to disagree? The basic steel-aged version, Vitis 2006, is good, simple and fresh. Le Gagie 2006, which aged in 30-hectolitre barrels, is more minerally, presenting deep, fruity and warm. The Superiore Bricco Sereno 2006, sourced from vines almost 70 years old that Giampiero inherited from his mother, aged in new and pre-used barriques. Wonderfully harmonious, it has a spicy, earthy nose and caresses the palate with firm tannins and a dry tangy finish. Saving the best for last, Superiore Tra La Terra e Il Cielo 2005, from a selection of riper grapes and aged for 12 months in new barriques, is dark and powerful, if perhaps a little extreme with its jam and vanilla aromas and warm, buttery, very soft palate. Two Glasses for the Rivaia 2005, reviewed in error last year instead of the 2004, a blend of nebbiolo, barbera and cabernet with a rounded palate, raspberry aromas and nice extract. Finally, the sweet Malaga is aroma-rich and similar to brachetto.

● Barbera d'Asti Sup. Nizza Tra La Terra e Il Cielo '05	🍷🍷	5
● Barbera d'Asti Le Gagie '06	🍷🍷	4
● Barbera d'Asti Sup. Bricco Sereno '06	🍷🍷	4
● Barbera d'Asti Vitis '06	🍷🍷	3*
● M.to Rosso Rivaia '05	🍷🍷	5
● La Malaga '07	🍷	4
○ M.to Bianco Puntet '07	🍷	4
● Barbera d'Asti Sup. Nizza Tra La Terra e Il Cielo '04	YY	5
● Barbera d'Asti Sup. Nizza Tra La Terra e Il Cielo '03	YY	5
● Barbera d'Asti Sup. Nizza Tra La Terra e Il Cielo '01	YY	5
● M.to Rosso Rivaia '03	YY	5

Noceto Michelotti

s.da Bogliona, 15/17
14040 Castel Boglione [AT]
tel. 0141762170
www.nocetomichelotti.com

ANNUAL PRODUCTION 160,000 bottles
HECTARES UNDER VINE 32
VITICULTURE METHOD Conventional

Any list of the most dynamic terroir in Piedmont should include Asti. New wineries, expansion or profound organizational changes in traditional labels, ambitious emerging producers and, unique to the area, substantial input from non-Italian management all abound. Noceto Michelotti personifies this trend. Owned by Graham Kresfelder and Margret Schratt-Kresfelder, it has quickly built up a solid image quickly thanks to the intelligent choice of a first-class technical team: oenologist Beppe Caviola, agronomist Federico Curtaz and general manager Giovanni Conte. Under these conditions, results were bound to come along and here they are: prompt, authoritative and classy. There are three Barbera d'Astis and we preferred the Montecanta 2005, a selection that delivers broad, well-coordinated aromas and a fragrant, acidic palate. The Strada del Sole 2006 is leaner-bodied while the classic Barbera focuses on delicious freshness. Of the two Monferratos, the Oro from barbera, nebbiolo, merlot and freisa has satisfyingly complex aromas and a mouthfilling flavour. Monferrato Rosso is a well-made blend of barbera and freisa. The Chardonnay is enjoyable.

● Barbera d'Asti Sup. Montecanta '05	🍷🍷	5
● Barbera d'Asti '06	🍷🍷	4*
● Barbera d'Asti Strada del Sole '06	🍷🍷	4*
● M.to Rosso Oro '04	🍷🍷	6
● M.to Rosso '06	🍷	4
○ Piemonte Chardonnay Montecanta '06	🍷	4
● Barbera d'Asti '05	YY	4
● Barbera d'Asti Strada del Sole '05	YY	4

Moccagatta

S.DA RABAJÀ, 46
12050 BARBARESCO [CN]
TEL. 0173635228

ANNUAL PRODUCTION	60,000 bottles
HECTARES UNDER VINE	12
VITICULTURE METHOD	Conventional

It's hard to choose from the three Barbarescos presented by brothers Franco and Sergio Minuto, who did a great job with the uneven 2005 vintage. Right now the most appealing is Basarin: its ruby red ushers in wild berries, dried roses, leather and liquorice, vigorous but elegant tannins and a very lingering finish. But Three Glasses went to Bric Balin, thanks to weighty structure with excellent ageing prospects, fruit and flower aromas with faint spice and mint, and unusual complexity. Cole focuses more on elegance and balance. These three outstanding wines are the peak of the estate's output but the other wines are also high achiever. The Langhe Chardonnay 2007 has aromas of bananas and spring flowers and a freshly acidic flavour. Chardonnay Buschet 2006 has ripe fruit and vanilla aromas lent complexity by ageing in oak. The Dolcetto is one of the best 2007 wines, combining impressive structure with a nicely drinkable palate. The fruity, spicy Barbera d'Alba aged for six months in used barriques, the powerful palate closing with captivating smoky sensations. The Langhe Nebbiolo is actually an impressive little Barbaresco with vigorous tannins.

F.lli Molino

LOC. AUSARIO
VIA AUSARIO, 5
12050 TREISO [CN]
TEL. 0173638384
tommy58@libero.it

ANNUAL PRODUCTION	75,000 bottles
HECTARES UNDER VINE	12
VITICULTURE METHOD	Conventional

The three brothers, Dario, Franco and Tommaso, earned another full profile. Although they have very little space, they present clean, well-made wines that reflect their terroir. When we talked, Dario stressed the care taken over all stages of production, the curiosity and the desire to continue working towards quality. The winery is situated on a hilltop above the subzone of Ausario where the vineyards are planted with nebbiolo, barbera or dolcetto according to their aspect. The Barbaresco Ausario 2005, aged for 22 months in small and large oak, has lively colour, vibrant floral aromas with a hint of spice and a firmly structured, lingering palate with no bitterness in the tannin. The Barbaresco Teorema 2005, a blend of grapes from two different areas, is already quite enjoyable with nice lively fruit and well-balanced tannin in the finish. The Barbera Ausario 2006 is deliciously fruity, juicy, tangy and thirst-quenching, with a minty finish. Turning to the two 2007 Dolcettos, Le Querce is heady and approachable while Ausario is more structured with nice fresh fruit. The Langhe Arneis is very appetizing.

● Barbaresco Bric Balin '05	♛♛♛	7
● Barbaresco Basarin '05	♛♛	7
● Barbaresco Cole '05	♛♛	7
● Barbera d'Alba '07	♛♛	4*
● Dolcetto d'Alba '07	♛♛	4*
● Langhe Nebbiolo '07	♛♛	5
O Langhe Chardonnay Buschet '06	♛♛	6
O Langhe Chardonnay '07	♛	4
● Barbaresco Bric Balin '04	♛♛♛	7
● Barbaresco Bric Balin '01	♛♛♛	8
● Barbaresco Bric Balin '90	♛♛♛	8
● Barbaresco Cole '97	♛♛♛	8
● Barbaresco Basarin '04	♛♛	7
● Barbaresco Bric Balin '03	♛♛	7
● Barbaresco Cole '04	♛♛	7

● Barbaresco Ausario '05	♛♛	6
● Barbaresco Teorema '05	♛♛	6
● Barbera d'Alba Ausario '06	♛♛	5
● Dolcetto d'Alba Ausario '07	♛♛	4*
● Dolcetto d'Alba Le Quercie '07	♛	3
O Langhe Arneis '07	♛	4
● Barbaresco Ausario '04	♛♛	6
● Barbaresco Ausario '01	♛♛	6
● Barbaresco Teorema '04	♛♛	6

Mauro Molino

FRAZ. ANNUNZIATA
B.TA GANCIA, 111
12064 LA MORRA [CN]
TEL. 017350814
www.mauromolino.it

ANNUAL PRODUCTION   50,000 bottles
HECTARES UNDER VINE 10
VITICULTURE METHOD   Conventional

This year, there is news from the winery team. The tried and tested pairing of father Mauro and his son Matteo has become a threesome now that daughter Martina has brought fresh blood into this already dynamic winery. The range presented in 2008 is varied with good performances from the four 2004 Barolos. Top of the class is the elegant, complex Conca with developing tannins present in the long finish among the hints of fruit and spices. Just a step below is the distinctively harmonious and enviably drinkable Vigna Gancia. The powerful Vigna Gallinotto is still closed with unripe sensations softened by alcohol and the nicely marked spice. Last in the series is the linear, lean-bodied basic Barolo, with a fresh phenolic sensation enhancing the nicely drinkable palate. The Barbera Vigna Gattere is also first-rate, showing complex and structured with fruitiness sweetened by a hint of oak. Lastly, the standard-label steel-fermented Barbera has distinctive juicy fruit supported by nice acidity and the barrique-aged Chardonnay is warm and tropical.

Monchiero Carbone

VIA SANTO STEFANO ROERO, 2
12043 CANALE [CN]
TEL. 017395568
www.monchierocarbone.com

ANNUAL PRODUCTION   90,000 bottles
HECTARES UNDER VINE 11
VITICULTURE METHOD   Conventional

Several years ago, we met Francesco Monchiero when he was finding his feet in the family business, then run by his father Marco. Francesco has since acquired experience, taking important decisions with his father and later taking up the reins of this winery in the centre of Canale. Marco can now dedicate himself to viticulture, secure in the knowledge that Francesco is managing things. The range of wines is typical of a local vision of wine: two Arneis, one Barbera and two nebbiolo wines with a territorial bent. This winery is committed to promoting a dynamic image of the left bank of the Tanaro. Re Cit and Cecu d'la Biunda are two distinct versions of Arneis, the former being fresher and more accessible while the second is more complex and coordinated. The Barbera 2006 is juicy and long with vibrant fruit whereas the two Roeros repeat the white formula: Srü 2006 focuses on finesse and elegance while the Printi 2005 is dynamic, voluptuous and very generous. This year we preferred Srü, which comes from a better growing year, so Three Glasses. The only slight digression from the pattern is an impressive Langhe Bianco, from arneis and chardonnay.

● Barbera d'Alba V. Gattere '06	♟ 6
● Barolo V. Conca '04	♟♟ 8
● Barolo V. Gancia '04	♟♟ 8
● Barolo V. Gallinotto '04	♟♟ 7
● Barbera d'Alba '07	♟ 4
● Barolo '04	♟♟ 6
● Langhe Nebbiolo '07	♟♟ 4*
○ Langhe Chardonnay Livrot '07	♟ 4
● Barbera d'Alba V. Gattere '00	♟♟♟ 6
● Barbera d'Alba V. Gattere '97	♟♟♟ 6
● Barbera d'Alba V. Gattere '96	♟♟♟ 6
● Barolo V. Conca '00	♟♟♟ 8
● Barolo V. Conca '97	♟♟♟ 8
● Barolo V. Conca '96	♟♟♟ 8
● Barolo V. Gallinotto '01	♟♟♟ 8
● Barolo V. Gallinotto '03	♟♟♟ 8

● Roero Srü '06	♟♟♟ 5
● Roero Printi Ris. '05	♟♟ 6
○ Roero Arneis Cecu d'la Biunda '07	♟♟ 4*
○ Langhe Bianco Tamardì '06	♟♟ 4
○ Roero Arneis Re Cit '07	♟♟ 4
● Barbera d'Alba MonBirone '06	♟♟ 5
● Roero Printi '99	♟♟♟ 6
● Roero Printi '04	♟♟♟ 6
● Roero Printi '00	♟♟♟ 6
● Roero Printi '01	♟♟ 6
● Roero Srü '05	♟♟ 5
● Roero Srü '04	♟♟ 5
● Barbera d'Alba MonBirone '05	♟♟ 5

Monfalletto
Cordero di Montezemolo
FRAZ. ANNUNZIATA, 67
12064 LA MORRA [CN]
TEL. 017350344
www.corderodimontezemolo.com

ANNUAL PRODUCTION	220,000 bottles
HECTARES UNDER VINE	35
VITICULTURE METHOD	Conventional

Administration has been reorganized and the winery has been made over, including the reception area veranda overlooking the vineyards and legendary cedar tree. Focus is now on consolidating results worthy of the label. Three very different Barolos, all good, top a fine range. Bricco Gattera 2004 delivers approachable aromas of elderflower and morello cherries in a strong, spacious expression of the vineyard leading to an exciting finish. Even better, thanks to its flawless harmony, is the Enrico VI 2004. Hints of ripe fruit blend with roses and are softly reprised on the palate. Sweet, robust tannins accompany the long expressive structure through to the finish for Three Glasses. The Monfalletto 2004 refuses to play second fiddle, showing enchantingly silky, mouthfilling and harmonious on the palate with youthful hints of forest floor and subtly austere, flavoursome sensations typical of the grape. The excellent Barbera Funtani 2006 delivers generous, stylish aromas of almonds and plums while the equally good Langhe Nebbiolo 2007 is well balanced with clear, varietal extract and good depth. The other wines are all very good.

Montaribaldi
FRAZ. TRE STELLE
S.DA NICOLINI ALTO, 12
12050 BARBARESCO [CN]
TEL. 0173638220
www.montaribaldi.com

ANNUAL PRODUCTION	70,000 bottles
HECTARES UNDER VINE	29
VITICULTURE METHOD	Conventional

Brothers Luciano and Roberto Taliano, with their parents Carla and Giuseppe and their wives Antonella and Franca, present a large number of wines. This year, the one we liked best was Barbera d'Alba dü Gir, which went through to the finals with its purple-tinged dark ruby red, plums and wild berries laced with spice, tobacco, vanilla and cocoa powder and a very enjoyable palate, despite the weighty structure. The Barbaresco selections are excellent, especially the 2005 Söri Montaribaldi and Palazzina whose generous floral and fruity aromas blend with saddle leather, black pepper, vanilla and tobacco and preceding the powerful but silky extract and good acidity. Dolcetto Vagnona delivers distinctive cherries and raspberries while red berries also characterize the nose of the Langhe Rosso Nicolini 2007, a single-variety Dolcetto. Barbera d'Asti La Consolina is fresh, captivating, soft and fruity. The Nebbiolo Gambarin is pale ruby red with red berry aromas and a robust body with slightly dry tannins. Among the whites, we enjoyed the Chardonnay and Arneis while the Moscato d'Asti is sweet but not cloying.

● Barolo Enrico VI '04	♀♀♀ 8
● Barolo V. Bricco Gattera '04	♀♀ 8
● Barolo Monfalletto '04	♀♀ 7
● Barbera d'Alba '07	♀♀ 4*
● Barbera d'Alba Sup. Funtanì '06	♀♀ 6
● Dolcetto d'Alba '07	♀♀ 4*
● Langhe Nebbiolo '07	♀♀ 5
● Langhe Rosso Curdè '04	♀♀ 5
○ Langhe Arneis '07	♀ 4
○ Langhe Chardonnay Elioro '06	♀ 5
● Barolo Enrico VI '03	♀♀♀ 8
● Barolo V. Enrico VI '00	♀♀♀ 8
● Barolo V. Enrico VI '97	♀♀♀ 8
● Barolo V. Enrico VI '96	♀♀♀ 8
● Barolo V. Bricco Gattera '99	♀♀♀ 8

● Barbera d'Alba dü Gir '06	♀♀ 5
● Barbaresco Palazzina '05	♀♀ 5*
● Barbaresco Söri Montaribaldi '05	♀♀ 6
● Barbera d'Asti La Consolina '07	♀♀ 3*
● Dolcetto d'Alba Vagnona '07	♀♀ 3*
● Langhe Rosso Nicolini '07	♀♀ 4
○ Langhe Chardonnay Stissa d'le Favole '07	♀ 3
● Langhe Nebbiolo Gambarin '06	♀ 4
○ Moscato d'Asti Righey '07	♀ 4
○ Roero Arneis Capural '07	♀ 4
● Barbaresco Söri Montaribaldi '04	♀♀ 6
● Barbaresco Söri Montaribaldi '03	♀♀ 6
● Barbaresco Söri Montaribaldi '01	♀♀ 6
● Barbaresco Söri Montaribaldi '00	♀♀ 6
● Barbaresco Palazzina '04	♀♀ 5

Monti

LOC. SAN SEBASTIANO, 39
12065 MONFORTE D'ALBA [CN]
TEL. 017378391
www.paolomonti.com

ANNUAL PRODUCTION	50,000 bottles
HECTARES UNDER VINE	11
VITICULTURE METHOD	Conventional

This dynamic winery, managed by Paolo Monti, has been in business for just over ten years. Missing this year are the new versions of Langhe Rosso Dossi Rossi, Langhe Bianco L'Aura and the Barbera. Barolo Bussia 2004, in 7,000 units, did well after ageing for 15 months in once-used barriques and a further 15 months in large barrels. The grapes from the six small plots are fermented separately before blending. Vanilla and fruit aromas precede a powerful front palate with well-gauged extract and a long-lingering finish. The basic 2004 Barolo, in 10,000 bottles, is a 75-25 blend of grapes from the Bussia and Le Coste vineyards. The must is fermented in stainless steel for ten days and the result is an alluring nose and generous palate with a nicely balanced, harmonious finish. The very sound Nebbiolo d'Alba 2006 in 5,000 bottles was vinified for the second year with just five days of maceration followed by 12 months in small once-used oak barrels. Violets and wild berries on the nose usher in pleasant acidity and a persistent body with a clean, enjoyable finish.

La Morandina

LOC. MORANDINI, 11
12053 CASTIGLIONE TINELLA [CN]
TEL. 0141855261
www.lamorandina.com

ANNUAL PRODUCTION	100,000 bottles
HECTARES UNDER VINE	20
VITICULTURE METHOD	Natural

Few families can boast such a long winemaking tradition as the Morandos. Work in the vineyards under Paolo Morando is the starting point but much else has to be done. The route to characterful, fine quality wines continues throughout fermentation and ageing, which are skilfully supervised by his brother Giulio. Environmental issues are always to the fore with natural procedures in the vineyards, a new bioheating system and plans for a photovoltaic facility to produce clean energy. The family has a considerable commitment to social projects like L'Insieme and others programmes. Outstanding in the tastings this year was Barbera Varmant 2006, sourced from vineyards over 80 years old and aged in barriques. Very low yields make this an unusually concentrated wine with a broad range of dark fruit aromas and light hints of spice. The palate is mouthfilling and full bodied with plenty of typical Barbera freshness. Zucchetto 2007, aged in large barrels, is a good choice for fans of less challenging wines. The Barbera d'Asti Cinque Vigne 2007 is also enjoyable and fresh with red berry fruit aromas. The aromatic Moscato d'Asti is nicely put together.

● Barolo Bussia '04	▼▼ 8
● Barolo '04	▼▼ 7
● Nebbiolo d'Alba '06	▼▼ 5
● Barolo Bussia '03	♀♀ 8
● Barolo Bussia '01	♀♀ 8
● Barolo Bussia '00	♀♀ 8
● Barolo '03	♀♀ 7
● Barbera d'Alba '05	♀♀ 6
● Barbera d'Alba '04	♀♀ 6
● Langhe Rosso Dossi Rossi '04	♀♀ 6
● Langhe Rosso Dossi Rossi '03	♀♀ 6
○ Langhe Bianco L'Aura '06	♀♀ 5
○ Langhe Bianco L'Aura '05	♀♀ 5

● Barbera d'Asti Varmat '06	▼▼ 5
● Barbera d'Asti Cinque Vigne '07	▼▼ 4*
● Barbera d'Asti Zucchetto '07	▼▼ 4*
● L'Insieme '05	▼▼ 8
○ Moscato d'Asti '07	▼▼ 4*
● Barbaresco Bricco Spessa '05	▼ 7
○ Langhe Chardonnay '07	▼ 4
○ Costa del Sole Passito '04	♀♀ 5
● Barbera d'Asti Varmat '05	♀♀ 5
● Barbera d'Asti Varmat '04	♀♀ 6
● Barbera d'Asti Varmat '01	♀♀ 6
● Barbaresco Bricco Spessa '04	♀♀ 7
● L'Insieme '04	♀♀ 8

Cascina Morassino

s.da Bernino, 10
12050 Barbaresco [CN]
tel. 0173635149

ANNUAL PRODUCTION   **20,000 bottles**
HECTARES UNDER VINE   **3.8**
VITICULTURE METHOD   **Conventional**

After much sacrifice, Roberto Bianco and his father Mauro have completed the new, more spacious and impressively equipped winery and it will now be easier to maintain the high quality that has always been a feature of their bottles. The two Barbaresco selections demonstrate this. Ovello 2005 stands out for its luminous garnet colour, nicely coordinated nose, free of any balsam from the 70 per cent new barriques used for ageing, and a broad, warm palate with well-judged tannins and a long, very clean finish. Morassino 2005 is also sound, distinctly less complex but already more evolved with well-honed tannins. The 700 bottles of Langhe Rosso Vigna del Merlo 2006, made almost for fun, might be cited as an excellent example of Langa's vocation for growing merlot. In contrast, territory focus is the keynote of the Barbera d'Alba Vignot 2006, with its pleasantly vibrant red berry fruit and drinkable palate, the Langhe Nebbiolo 2006, with its hints of plums and spices, and the Dolcetto d'Alba 2007, whose flowers and cherries precede a fresh and pleasant, if not broad, palate.

Stefanino Morra

via Castagnito, 50
12050 Castellinaldo [CN]
tel. 0173213489
www.morravini.it

ANNUAL PRODUCTION   **65,000 bottles**
HECTARES UNDER VINE   **10**
VITICULTURE METHOD   **Conventional**

The range of wines presented this year by Stefanino Morra of Castellinaldo has been shaken up. We would not hesitate to call some of his choices courageous. The whites are on show on the red front, quite a few have been stopped in their tracks. So our review begins in an unusual way by describing what we didn't taste. Castellinaldo Barbera, to name one leading wine, was not produced in the year we should be tasting now, 2005. The same applies to the other Barbera selection, Castlè, but both will be back next year. Roero Srai, the winery's leading Nebbiolo, wasn't produced in 2005 either, since Stefanino did not consider it a year for making great wines and by now, we believe him. The remaining wines confirm the Morras' skill as grower-producers. We loved the standard Arneis, one of the freshest and fruitiest ever tasted, even more than the Vigneto San Pietro, which is soft and richly extracted. The Barbera 2006 is anything but a basic wine, giving bags of acidity with enviably fruity, harmonious aromas. The Roero is all succulence, earth and extract in a precious nectar. Lastly, the Favorita is very enjoyable.

● Barbaresco Morassino '05	🍷🍷 7
● Barbaresco Ovello '05	🍷🍷 7
● Barbera d'Alba Vignot '06	🍷🍷 5
● Langhe Nebbiolo '06	🍷🍷 5
● Langhe Rosso V. del Merlo '06	🍷🍷 5
● Dolcetto d'Alba '07	🍷 4
● Barbaresco Ovello '04	🍷🍷 7
● Barbaresco Ovello '03	🍷🍷 7
● Barbaresco Ovello '02	🍷🍷 7
● Barbaresco Ovello '01	🍷🍷 7
● Barbaresco Ovello '00	🍷🍷 7
● Barbaresco Ovello '99	🍷🍷 7
● Barbaresco Morassino '04	🍷🍷 6
● Barbaresco Morassino '03	🍷🍷 6
● Barbaresco Morassino '01	🍷🍷 6

● Barbera d'Alba '06	🍷🍷 4*
● Roero '05	🍷🍷 5
○ Roero Arneis '07	🍷🍷 4*
○ Langhe Favorita '07	🍷 3
○ Roero Arneis Vign. S. Pietro '06	🍷 4
● Castellinaldo Barbera d'Alba '04	🍷🍷 5
● Castellinaldo Barbera d'Alba '03	🍷🍷 5
● Castellinaldo Barbera d'Alba '01	🍷🍷 5
● Roero Srai '04	🍷🍷 6
● Roero Srai '03	🍷🍷 6
● Roero Srai '01	🍷🍷 6
● Roero Sup. '04	🍷🍷 4
● Roero Sup. '03	🍷🍷 4
● Roero Sup. '01	🍷🍷 4

F.lli Mossio

VIA MONTÀ, 12
12050 RODELLO [CN]
TEL. 0173617149
www.mossio.com

ANNUAL PRODUCTION	50,000 bottles
HECTARES UNDER VINE	10
VITICULTURE METHOD	Conventional

Mauro Mossio would have liked this year's profile. He kept us up to date and would have been proud to tell us about the cellar's 40th anniversary and the tenth harvest of Dolcetto Bricco Caramelli. It's a shame he is no longer with us. We admit that a couple of seasons on from his demise – a true countryman, he liked to measure time in seasons rather than years – his warm personality is still sadly missed. The Mossio family – Valerio, Remo, Claudio and Guido – have done amazingly well to keep up the name and image of this little Langhe winery above Alba. Dolcetto is the main grape and growing it is considered an art. What is Bricco Caramelli 2007, if not a masterpiece? Very subtle aromas accompany a substantial palate where the elegant texture is backed up by marked but nicely controlled extract. Let's remember that from 2008 on, the winery will tend to keep the wines back for an extra year so we will have to wait a while before we taste it again. The Piano delli Perdoni plays the role of second wine to perfection. The 2006 Barbera, Langhe Nebbiolo and Langhe Rosso are still ageing in the cellar. We'll talk about them in our next Guide.

Mutti

LOC. SAN RUFFINO, 49
15050 SAREZZANO [AL]
TEL. 0131884119

ANNUAL PRODUCTION	55,000 bottles
HECTARES UNDER VINE	15
VITICULTURE METHOD	Conventional

If the timorasso is so well known and appreciated, some of the credit must go to Andrea Mutti. While Walter Massa is unanimously acknowledged as the rediscoverer of the variety, Andrea provided him with confirmation of its quality by successfully flanking him in his challenging project. Andrea has always made a Timorasso, Castagnoli, which differs from those normally presented in the area because it never has the concentration or explosive character often found in similar wines. Instead, it has balance of structure and finesse without losing the grape's own special features. The 2006 version is another version for the cellar. The San Ruffino 2005 is equally sound. A Barbera aged in small barrels, it requires a few minutes' aeration to release its aromatics. The sauvignon-based Sull'Aia is also good, opening on fresh aromas of sage and white peaches to close on distinctively lingering sweet almonds. The cortese-based Noceto, also 2007, is fresher with subtle acidic sensations and offers particularly good value for money. The heady Zerba Soprana, from dolcetto and the forthright barbera Boscobarona are also worth uncorking.

● Dolcetto d'Alba Bricco Caramelli '07	♍♍ 4*
● Dolcetto d'Alba Piano delli Perdoni '07	♍♍ 4*
● Dolcetto d'Alba Bricco Caramelli '00	♍♍♍ 4
● Dolcetto d'Alba Bricco Caramelli '06	♍♍ 4
● Dolcetto d'Alba Bricco Caramelli '05	♍♍ 4
● Dolcetto d'Alba Piano delli Perdoni '06	♍♍ 4
● Langhe Nebbiolo '05	♍♍ 5
● Langhe Rosso '05	♍♍ 5
● Langhe Rosso '03	♍♍ 5

○ Colli Tortonesi Bianco Castagnoli '06	♍ 5
● Colli Tortonesi Rosso S. Ruffino '05	♍♍ 5
○ Colli Tortonesi Bianco Noceto '07	♍♍ 3*
○ Colli Tortonesi Bianco Sull'Aia '07	♍♍ 4
● Colli Tortonesi Rosso Boscobarona '07	♍ 3
● Colli Tortonesi Rosso Zerba Soprana '07	♍ 3
○ Colli Tortonesi Bianco Castagnoli '05	♍♍ 5
● Colli Tortonesi Rosso S. Ruffino '04	♍♍ 5
● Colli Tortonesi Rosso S. Ruffino '03	♍♍ 5

Ada Nada

LOC. ROMBONE
VIA AUSARIO, 12B
12050 TREISO [CN]
TEL. 0173638127
www.adanada.it

ANNUAL PRODUCTION	45,000 bottles
HECTARES UNDER VINE	10
VITICULTURE METHOD	Conventional

Visit this captivating family winery just before lunchtime and you can taste the wines with – excellent – bread, cheese and salami in the company of the Nada family, consisting of father Giancarlo, daughter Annalisa and her husband Elvio. The winery's future is guaranteed by their two little girls, but they have plenty of time! Coming up soon from this red wine estate is a new sauvignon blanc-based white. Turning to the wines themselves, the Barbaresco Elisa 2004, from a very old vineyard at Valeirano area, has vibrant, clearly defined fruity aromas and a lingering, juicy palate with sweet tannins on the firm finish. The Barbaresco Cichin 2005, still austere on the nose, is juicy and beautifully lingering with a final hint of liquorice. The Barbaresco Valeirano 2005 delivers vibrant raspberry aromas on the nose with a floral touch while the palate is already nicely drinkable and lingers on the back palate. The Barbera 2006 is fruity and mouthwatering with refreshing acidity to complement the softness and the Dolcetto Autinot 2007 is heady, with nice fruit. Release of the Langhe Rosso La Bisbetica has been postponed for a year.

Fiorenzo Nada

LOC. ROMBONE
VIA AUSARIO, 12C
12050 TREISO [CN]
TEL. 0173638254
www.nada.it

ANNUAL PRODUCTION	30,000 bottles
HECTARES UNDER VINE	6.5
VITICULTURE METHOD	Conventional

Bruno Nada promotes the territory through his splendid wines as well as in his role as Treiso town councillor for culture. This takes up a fair bit of his time but he does the work with pride. In 2008, the basic Barbaresco was named Vigna Manzola after the subzone where the grapes are grown, a few hundred metres from the winery. It is both powerful and sophisticated with raspberries and morello cherry-like red berry fruit, intriguingly nuanced with tobacco and quinine. For the time being, Rombone stays in pole position, thanks to considerable but never overpowering structure and sustained depth and elegance. Red berries and dried flowers on the nose with sweet tannins on the excitingly drinkable palate earned an effortless Three Glasses. There was another towering performance from the Langhe Rosso Seifile, from barbera with a small percentage of nebbiolo, which gives very clean, crisp fruit on the captivating nose. Bruno is also very skilled at making less ambitious wines like the fresh and very enjoyably drinkable Barbera and the Dolcetto, a pleasant blend of initial sweetness and a bitterish finish.

● Barbaresco Elisa '04	¶¶ 7
● Barbaresco Cichin '05	¶¶ 7
● Barbaresco Valeirano '05	¶¶ 7
● Barbera d'Alba V. 'd Pierin '06	¶¶ 5
● Dolcetto d'Alba Autinot '07	¶¶ 4*
● Barbaresco Cichin '01	♈♈ 7
● Barbaresco Valeirano '04	♈♈ 7
● Barbaresco Valeirano '03	♈♈ 7
● Barbaresco Valeirano '01	♈♈ 7
● Barbaresco Valeirano '00	♈♈ 7

● Barbaresco Rombone '05	¶¶¶ 8
● Barbaresco V. Manzola '04	¶¶ 8
● Langhe Rosso Seifile '05	¶¶ 8
● Barbera d'Alba '06	¶¶ 5
● Dolcetto d'Alba '07	¶¶ 4*
● Barbaresco '01	♈♈♈ 7
● Barbaresco Rombone '04	♈♈♈ 8
● Barbaresco Rombone '99	♈♈♈ 8
● Barbaresco Rombone '97	♈♈♈ 8
● Langhe Rosso Seifile '96	♈♈♈ 8
● Langhe Rosso Seifile '95	♈♈♈ 8
● Langhe Rosso Seifile '01	♈♈♈ 8
● Seifile '93	♈♈♈ 8
● Barbaresco Rombone '03	♈♈ 8
● Barbaresco Rombone '01	♈♈ 8

Cantina dei Produttori Nebbiolo di Carema

VIA NAZIONALE, 32
10010 CAREMA [TO]
TEL. 0125811160
www.saporipiemontesi.it

ANNUAL PRODUCTION	65,000 bottles
HECTARES UNDER VINE	N.A.
VITICULTURE METHOD	Conventional

Carema is one of Italy's smallest DOC zones, on the left bank of the Dora Baltea on the border with Valle d'Aosta. In this south to southwest-facing terraced hollow less than 18 hectares of pergola-trained vineyards grow over 600 metres above sea level. This heroic situation has been saved by the Cantina which allows its 45, often elderly, members to earn money part-time from these tiny plots, preventing this ancient activity from falling into neglect. The cellar is strictly traditional and only produces two wines, both made entirely from nebbiolo. The basic Carema, with its distinctive black label, is partnered by the white label Carema Riserva. The wines undergo long ageing in large oak barrels – 24 months for the basic and 30 for the Riserva – although in some years, the cellar releases a few bottles of a barrique-aged version. Two Caremas were presented this year and we preferred the 2004, from a growing year with better weather. The Riserva 2004 was more impressive than the 2003, which has distinctive coffee and bottled fruit aromas, thanks to fresh aromas of flowers and liquorice on nose and palate.

Angelo Negro & Figli

FRAZ. SANT'ANNA, 1
12040 MONTEU ROERO [CN]
TEL. 017390252
www.negroangelo.it

ANNUAL PRODUCTION	250,000 bottles
HECTARES UNDER VINE	54
VITICULTURE METHOD	Conventional

Leading wineries maintain high quality year after year, overcoming or buffering the positive or negative impact of individual vintages. And Negri is a leader, having grown steadily over the years thanks to investments in the vineyard and cellar, to reach a podium of excellence, where it has remained ever since. The solid, skilled family team now has a new addition, Angelo's baby daughter Francesca. Turning to the wines, the leading reds are on fine form. Of the two 2006 Barberas we again preferred the Bertu selection. All acidity and elegance, it has the edge over the very well-made Nicolon. The two 2005 Roeros battle it out with soft tannins and strength. We loved both but we gave a higher score goes again to the Sudisfà, which tempers an austere grape variety with the finesse acquired from well-judged use of wood. The Barbaresco is just a step behind but very good. The rest of the range focuses on arneis. The Negris have always been sophisticated interpreters of this grape, as is shown by the freshness of the sparkler and the perfect varietal imprint of the two dry, still versions and the warm, fruity dried-grape Passito.

● Carema '04	♟♟ 4*
● Carema Ris. '03	♟ 4
● Carema Barricato '01	♟♟ 5
● Carema Barricato '00	♟♟ 5
● Carema Et. Bianca Barricato '98	♟♟ 4
● Carema Et. Bianca Ris. '99	♟♟ 4
● Carema Et. Nera '01	♟♟ 4
● Carema Ris. '02	♟♟ 4
● Carema Ris. '01	♟♟ 4

● Barbera d'Alba Bertu '06	♟♟ 5
● Roero Sudisfà Ris. '05	♟♟ 6
● Barbaresco Basarin '05	♟♟ 6
● Barbera d'Alba Nicolon '06	♟♟ 4*
● Roero Prachiosso '05	♟♟ 5
O Perdaudin Passito '06	♟♟ 6
O Roero Arneis '07	♟♟ 4*
O Roero Arneis Perdaudin '07	♟♟ 4*
O Roero Arneis Brut M. Cl. Giovanni Negro '06	♟♟ 5
● Roero Sudisfà '04	♟♟♟ 6
● Roero Sudisfà '03	♟♟♟ 6
● Roero Prachiosso '04	♟♟ 5
● Roero Sudisfà '01	♟♟ 6
● Roero Sudisfà '00	♟♟ 6
● Roero Prachiosso '03	♟♟ 5

Nervi

C.SO VERCELLI, 117
13045 GATTINARA [VC]
TEL. 0163833228
www.gattinara-nervi.it

ANNUAL PRODUCTION **100,000 bottles**
HECTARES UNDER VINE **33**
VITICULTURE METHOD **Conventional**

Time stands still at this traditional Gattinara winery, where Giorgio Aliata welcomes visitors to his wood-panelled offices. Nervi presents its wines in dribs and drabs. One year, it's Gattinara Vigneto Molsino, then it's Gattinara Podere di Ginepri while Coste della Sesia never seems to be available. Having reviewed Molsino 2003 last year, we tasted Podere dei Ginepri from the same vintage. Compared to Vigneto Molsino, which debuted in 1978, it's quite a new wine, bottled separately since the 2001 vintage. The vineyard that produces Podere dei Ginepri is situated next to Molsino, in a south-southwest facing location at an altitude of about 300 metres. The wines stay in the cellar for three years, with mixed ageing techniques: part in large Slavonian oak barrels, part in 700-litre tonneaux and part in barriques. Sadly, the 2003 did not follow in the footsteps of its illustrious predecessor for reasons related to the very difficult growing year. The colour and nose show signs of evolution with nicely forward hints of quinine and medicinal herbs lifted by forest floor. A soft, mouthfilling palate reveals its tannins only in the finish.

Andrea Oberto

B.TA SIMANE, 11
12064 LA MORRA [CN]
TEL. 017350104
obertoandrea@libero.it

ANNUAL PRODUCTION **100,000 bottles**
HECTARES UNDER VINE **16**
VITICULTURE METHOD **Conventional**

This estate run by father and son Andrea and Fabio has vineyards scattered across Barolo country. The 2004 products are complemented by the debuting barrique-aged Barolo Brunate, in 3,500 units, with intense colour, vibrant aromas and good structure. Vigneto Barolo Rocche dell'Annunziata 2004, in 4,500 bottles, aged the same way and shows complex and elegant with a lingering finish. The 6,500 bottles of Barolo Vigneto Albarella from the Cannubi vineyard also aged in small oak barrels and give vibrant varietal aromas, structure and good balance. The excellent basic Barolo 2004, in 11,000 bottles, is a blend of fruit from three vineyards aged in different types of oak. Barbera Giada 2005 performed wonderfully. Aged for 18 months in new barriques, it has a well-structured, powerful palate with impressive length. Langhe Rosso Fabio 2005 is a well-made, lingering blend of nebbiolo and barbera aged for 18 months in new oak. The 2007 wines are all very sound. The Barbera and Langhe Nebbiolo aged in once-used oak while the gutsy Dolcetto is steel-aged.

● Gattinara Podere dei Ginepri '03	🍷🍷	6
● Gattinara Podere dei Ginepri '01	🍷🍷🍷	6
● Gattinara Vign. Molsino '00	🍷🍷🍷	6
● Gattinara Vign. Molsino '03	🍷🍷	6
● Gattinara Vign. Molsino '01	🍷🍷	6
● Gattinara Vign. Molsino '99	🍷🍷	6

● Barbera d'Alba Giada '05	🍷🍷	6
● Barolo Vign. Rocche dell'Annunziara '04	🍷🍷	8
● Barolo Vign. Albarella '04	🍷🍷	8
● Barbera d'Alba '07	🍷🍷	4*
● Barolo '04	🍷🍷	7
● Barolo Brunate '04	🍷🍷	8
● Dolcetto d'Alba '07	🍷🍷	4*
● Langhe Nebbiolo '07	🍷🍷	4*
● Langhe Rosso Fabio '05	🍷🍷	6
● Barbera d'Alba Giada '00	🍷🍷🍷	6
● Barbera d'Alba Giada '97	🍷🍷🍷	6
● Barbera d'Alba Giada '96	🍷🍷🍷	6
● Barolo Vign. Rocche dell'Annunziata '96	🍷🍷🍷	8
● Barolo Vign. Albarella '01	🍷🍷🍷	8

Oddero

FRAZ. SANTA MARIA
VIA TETTI, 28
12064 LA MORRA [CN]
TEL. 017350618
www.oddero.it

ANNUAL PRODUCTION	110,000 bottles
HECTARES UNDER VINE	35
VITICULTURE METHOD	Conventional

Oddero is a historic name and an impressively large estate for the area with 35 hectares in various municipalities. The range is wide and varied, combining high quality with firm roots in tradition and territory its classic, cleanly elegant, no-nonsense wines. There is news on the Barolo front with the release of two new wines from 2004, Villero and Brunate. The first is still rather undeveloped, stiff and earthy with rather leanish structure but the Brunate is in a class of its own, showing style, depth, serious extract and terrific quality in a broad yet subtle, ever-changing taste profile. Among the other Barolos, Mondoca di Bussia Soprana 2004 is absent as it needs further ageing. The basic 2004 version is reliable and while the hot summer made Vigna Rionda 2003 less dynamic and deep than usual, it is still charming. Rocche di Castiglione 2004 is quite outstanding, showing subtle minerality and elegance. The Barbaresco Gallina 2005, from a marvellous location at Neive, was very convincing with well-focused crisp fruit and tannins that are still young, spirited and tight. Its wonderful density and depth make it well worth investigating.

Tenuta Olim Bauda

REG. PRATA, 50
14045 INCISA SCAPACCINO [AT]
TEL. 0141702171
www.tenutaolimbauda.it

ANNUAL PRODUCTION	120,000 bottles
HECTARES UNDER VINE	27
VITICULTURE METHOD	Conventional

In the 1960s, the Bertolino family acquired 100 hectares with Villa Bauda di Incisa and its farms in the municipalities of Isola d'Asti, Nizza and Fontanile. Currently, there are 27 hectares under vine. The cellar was made over in 1998 and, with help from Beppe Caviola, siblings Diana, Dino and Gianni taken it to the front rank of Nizza winemaking in a decade. The sweet wines are very sound. Moscato Centive 2007, in 55,000 bottles, from the Fontanile vineyard, is full, fat and almost tangy with honey and peach fragrances. The dried-grape San Giovanni 2003 is very sweet with 200 grams of sugar per litre, tropical aromas and nice structure. There's a sound Chardonnay, with ripe fruit and a caressing mouthfeel. The simpler but well-made Gavi 2007 is soft and flowery. Then there are three great Barberas from the vines at the cellar: the steel-aged La Villa 2007, in 45,000 units, which captures barbera's immediacy; the deep, silk-soft, earth and tobacco-themed Superiore 2006 from the Rocchette vineyard at Isola d'Asti; and the impressive dark Barbera Nizza 2005, which gives vanillaed aromas of spice and chocolate, with a warm, caressing palate.

● Barbaresco Gallina '05	♛♛	7
● Barolo Brunate '04	♛♛	8
● Barolo Rocche di Castiglione '04	♛♛	8
● Barolo V. Rionda '03	♛♛	8
● Barbera d'Alba '06	♛♛	4*
● Barbera d'Asti Vinchio '06	♛♛	4*
● Barolo '04	♛♛	6
● Barolo Villero '04	♛♛	7
● Langhe Furesté '07	♛♛	4*
○ Langhe Chardonnay Collaretto '07	♛♛	4*
● Dolcetto d'Alba '07	♛	4
○ Moscato d'Asti Cascina Fiori '07	♛	4
● Barbaresco Gallina '04	♛♛♛	7
● Barolo V. Rionda '01	♛♛♛	8
● Barolo V. Rionda '00	♛♛♛	8
● Barolo V. Rionda '98	♛♛♛	8

● Barbera d'Asti Sup. Le Rocchette '06	♛♛	5
● Barbera d'Asti Sup. Nizza '05	♛♛	5
● Barbera d'Asti La Villa '07	♛♛	4*
○ Moscato d'Asti Centive '07	♛♛	4*
○ Piemonte Chardonnay I Boschi '06	♛♛	4*
○ Piemonte Moscato Passito S. Giovanni '03	♛	7
○ Gavi del Comune di Gavi '07	♛	4
● Barbera d'Asti Sup. '04	♛♛	5
● Barbera d'Asti Sup. '03	♛♛	5
● Barbera d'Asti Sup. '01	♛♛	5
● Barbera d'Asti Sup. Nizza '04	♛♛	5
● Barbera d'Asti Sup. Nizza '03	♛♛	5
● Barbera d'Asti Sup. Nizza '01	♛♛	6

Orsolani

via Michele Chiesa, 12
10090 San Giorgio Canavese [TO]
tel. 012432386
www.orsolani.it

ANNUAL PRODUCTION 150,000 bottles
HECTARES UNDER VINE 20
VITICULTURE METHOD Conventional

Gigi Orsolani's winery is beacon for the Canavese area. It may not be particularly famous but the family has always worked well, selecting vineyards in the best locations. Despite working with supposedly second-string denominations, Orsolani came close to top honours with two wines but we admired the overall standard of quality. Most of raw material is provided by the versatile erbaluce grape, which can give exquisite classic method spumantes, excellent dry whites and fine dried-grape passitos. It's hard to choose between the two Caluso Spumantes. Brut 2004 is more zesty and refined while the Brut Gran Riserva 2003, which underwent its first fermentation in oak, is more powerful and complex. The oak-fermented Vignot Sant'Antonio 2006 takes still Erbaluce into a new dimension. It reveals whiffs of chlorophyll and a refreshing, firm palate leading on to a minerally, lingering finish. La Rustìa is only a couple of points behind it in terms of richness. Sulé, still very young, seemed less well-orchestrated than usual. The two reds, Acini Sparsi and Le Tabbie, are a tad grassy. Le Tabbie, in particular, will be at its best in a few years' time.

○ Caluso Spumante Brut Cuvée Tradizione Gran Ris. '03	▼▼	6
○ Caluso Bianco Vignot S. Antonio '06	▼▼	5
○ Caluso Passito Sulé '03	▼▼	6
○ Caluso Spumante Brut Cuvée Tradizione '04	▼▼	5
○ Erbaluce di Caluso La Rustìa '07	▼▼	4*
● Carema Le Tabbie '04	▼▼	5
● Canavese Rosso Acini Sparsi '06	▼	4
○ Caluso Passito Sulé '98	▽▽▽	6
○ Caluso Passito Sulé '02	▽▽	6
○ Caluso Passito Sulé '00	▽▽	6
● Carema Le Tabbie '03	▽▽	5
● Carema Le Tabbie '01	▽▽	6

Pace

fraz. Madonna di Loreto
Cascina Pace, 52
12043 Canale [CN]
tel. 0173979544
aziendapace@infinito.it

ANNUAL PRODUCTION 30,000 bottles
HECTARES UNDER VINE 20
VITICULTURE METHOD Conventional

Brothers Dino and Pietro Negro continue on their upward quality path, matching that of Roero in general. This family farm has about 20 hectares under vine and a strong tradition of selling grapes and unbottled wine so there has been a sea change towards bottles and quality. Pace is emblematic of Roero. Actually, every winery is different so even the Negro brothers have their own specific style. Personality is transferred to the wine, which is a mirror reflecting the winemaker. The wines this year from Pace are few in number because bottling and release times for some of the range were later than usual. The rest show how hard the family has been working in the cellar. The Arneis, the currently vey popular native white variety, is among the best we tasted this year, showing fresh, fruity, dense on the palate and in no hurry to sign off. The greater structure of the Superiore 2006 sets it apart from its stablemate Barbera but both are decent. The Roero Riserva 2005 throws a nose of fruit and spice before the generous, caressing palate reveals its tannins and long, well-balanced finish.

● Barbera d'Alba Sup. '06	▼▼	5
○ Roero Arneis '07	▼▼	4*
● Roero Ris. '05	▼▼	5
● Barbera d'Alba '06	▼	3
● Barbera d'Alba '05	▽▽	4
● Barbera d'Alba Sup. '05	▽▽	5
● Barbera d'Alba Sup. '04	▽▽	4
● Roero '05	▽▽	4
● Roero '04	▽▽	4

Paitin

LOC. BRICCO
VIA SERRA BOELLA, 20
12052 NEIVE [CN]
TEL. 017367343
www.paitin.it

ANNUAL PRODUCTION	60,000 bottles
HECTARES UNDER VINE	17
VITICULTURE METHOD	Natural

There's nothing to add here. Every year, the Pasquero family shows that it deserves a place in the front rank at Barbaresco, occasionally venturing out of the zone with a wine like the rich, complex Barbera d'Alba Campolive 2006. This year, the 2004 Barbaresco Sorì Paitin Vecchie Vigne is the top wine after ageing for three months in large barrels to emerge brimming with red berry fruit, accompanied by hints of spice and tertiary aromas, near perfect tannins and fabulous length. It's a wine from another age that earned Three unhesitating Glasses. It is flanked by Barbaresco Sorì Paitin 2005, younger on the nose and in its tannins, but equally complex and well structured. The rest of the range is also worthwhile, starting with the excellent Langhe Paitin 2006, from nebbiolo and barbera grown at Alba and aged in large wood. Next up are the Barbera d'Alba Serra Boella 2007, with refreshing cherries and red berries; Nebbiolo d'Alba Ca Veja 2006, with lovely cleanliness, especially in the mouth; the young, fruity Dolcetto d'Alba Sorì Paitin 2007 with its good nose-palate harmony; and, finally, the Langhe Arneis Elisa 2007, which gives pear and banana.

Armando Parusso

LOC. BUSSIA, 55
12065 MONFORTE D'ALBA [CN]
TEL. 017378257
www.parusso.com

ANNUAL PRODUCTION	125,000 bottles
HECTARES UNDER VINE	22
VITICULTURE METHOD	Natural

The aim here is to make wines from healthy grapes, gathered at the right stage of ripeness and handled with maximum respect for their natural state. This translates into fruit-forward, layered wines that can be enjoyed straight away but will improve with age. We saw this when we tasted some bottles uncorked then and there and others which had been open for four days. These were even better, with more fragrance and greater balance. We tasted many wines, including two lovely, succulent whites from sauvignon. The Dolcetto is approachable, with raspberry aromas, and gives satisfyingly sweet tannins. The Barbera Ornati 2007 is very varietal while the Ornati Superiore 2006 gives charming fruit and spice aromas with acidity and tannins in evidence. The basic Barolo is good and those from 2004 are excellent. Mariondino is generous, revealing spice, vanilla, wild berries and balsam. The Bussia is more austere and minerally with good structure and length. Dried flowers, vanilla and coffee characterize the Coste Mosconi while the Langhe Nebbiolo 2006 is agreeable and convincing.

● Barbaresco Sorì Paitin Vecchie Vigne '04	▼▼▼ 8
● Barbaresco Sorì Paitin '05	▼▼ 6*
● Barbera d'Alba Campolive '06	▼▼ 5
● Barbera d'Alba Serra Boella '07	▼▼ 4*
O Langhe Arneis Elisa '07	▼▼ 4*
● Langhe Paitin '06	▼▼ 4*
● Nebbiolo d'Alba Ca Veja '06	▼▼ 5
● Dolcetto d'Alba Sorì Paitin '07	▼ 4
● Barbaresco Sorì Paitin '04	♈♈♈ 6
● Barbaresco Sorì Paitin '95	♈♈♈ 7
● Barbaresco Sorì Paitin Vecchie Vigne '99	♈♈♈ 8
● Barbaresco Sorì Paitin Vecchie Vigne '01	♈♈♈ 8
● Barbaresco Sorì Paitin '01	♈♈ 6

● Barolo Bussia '04	▼▼ 8
● Barolo Le Coste Mosconi '04	▼▼ 8
● Barolo Mariondino '04	▼▼ 7
● Barbera d'Alba Sup. Ornati '06	▼▼ 6
● Barolo '04	▼▼ 7
● Dolcetto d'Alba Piani Noci '07	▼▼ 4*
● Langhe Nebbiolo '06	▼▼ 5
O Langhe Bianco '07	▼▼ 4*
O Langhe Bianco Bricco Rovella '06	▼▼ 6
● Barbera d'Alba Ornati '07	▼ 4
● Barolo Bussia V. Munie '99	♈♈♈ 8
● Barolo Bussia V. Munie '97	♈♈♈ 8
● Barolo Bussia V. Munie '96	♈♈♈ 8
● Barolo Le Coste Mosconi '03	♈♈♈ 8
● Barolo Vecchie V. in Mariondino Ris. '99	♈♈♈ 8

Massimo Pastura - Cascina Ghersa

VIA SAN GIUSEPPE, 19
14050 MOASCA [AT]
TEL. 0141856012
www.laghersa.it

ANNUAL PRODUCTION	185,000 bottles
HECTARES UNDER VINE	22
VITICULTURE METHOD	Conventional

This winery began with Uncle Barbero's wine business in Turin in the 1930s and ends, for now, with the current winery in Moasca. We'll tell it another day because we have four new wines in the generous range. The newcomers are named after the proprietor, Massimo Pastura, and comprise a selection of only 10,000 bottles of the great Piedmontese grapes: cortese, timorasso and barbera. There's a soft Gavi Il Poggio 2007 and a warm, leisurely Timorasso Timian 2006, which is as good as any, and two Barbera Superiores. Le Cave 2005 is subtle, elegant and fruity while the 2004 Muascae – the ancient name for Moasca – is balanced, juicy and beautifully extracted. We sent it to the finals. Vignassa 2005 is convincingly full and savoury and the Camparò 2006, the winery workhorse with its production run of 70,000 bottles, is a warm, soft Barbera redolent of liquorice and cocoa powder. The white Sivoy 2007 from cortese, chardonnay and sauvignon is attractive. Its fruit is ripe, its softness remarkable and its sauvignon stands out. The Piagè 2007 series is very decent. Finally, the creamy Moscato Giorgia 2007 is nicely aromatic, with warm notes of peach.

● Barbera d'Asti Sup. Muascae Massimo Pastura '04		㉎㉎ 7
● Barbera d'Asti Sup. Nizza Vignassa '05		㉎㉎ 5
● Barbera d'Asti Sup. Camparò '06		㉎㉎ 4*
● Barbera d'Asti Sup. Le Cave Massimo Pastura '05		㉎㉎ 4*
● M.to Rosso La Ghersa '05		㉎㉎ 5
○ Colli Tortonesi Timorasso Timian Massimo Pastura '06		㉎㉎ 5
○ M.to Bianco Sivoy '07		㉎㉎ 4*
○ Moscato d'Asti Giorgia '07		㉎㉎ 4*
○ Gavi Il Poggio Massimo Pastura '07		㉎ 4
○ M.to Bianco Piagè '07		㉎ 3
☉ M.to Chiaretto Piagè '07		㉎ 3
● Barbera d'Asti Piagè '07		㉎ 3

Agostino Pavia e Figli

FRAZ. BOLOGNA, 33
14041 AGLIANO TERME [AT]
TEL. 0141954125
mauro.pavia@crasti.it

ANNUAL PRODUCTION	75,000 bottles
HECTARES UNDER VINE	7.5
VITICULTURE METHOD	Conventional

This small, dynamic winery, run by Mauro and Giuseppe Pavia with the help of their father Agostino, has vineyards about 50 years old. This venerable age tells you that the family knows how to handle vines without exhausting them in pursuit of excessive yields, which damages the health and longevity of the plants. The wines we tasted bore out all the positive things we have said in previous editions of the Guide. This is an emerging estate that stands out for a style in which tradition and modernity find a happy balance. As to the wines, the Barbera Superiore La Marescialla from the 2005 vintage is opulent, with some oak still detectable, but the fruit is intact and there's stylish balance. La Moliss from the same vintage has a lovely, violet-led floral nose, a tighter palate and lovely, refreshing length. The Barbera Bricco Blina has a nice varietal nose, an outgoing character and good acidity. The balance of the Monferrato Talin, made with barbera and syrah grapes, is still rather uncertain but more bottle time should resolve this. Finally, the Grignolino d'Asti is very pleasant, with a fresh, intriguing peppery note.

● Barbera d'Asti Bricco Blina '06		㉎㉎ 4*
● Barbera d'Asti Sup. La Marescialla '05		㉎㉎ 5
● Barbera d'Asti Sup. Moliss '05		㉎㉎ 4*
● Grignolino d'Asti '07		㉎㉎ 3*
● M.to Rosso Talin '05		㉎ 5
● Barbera d'Asti Bricco Blina '05		㉎㉎ 4
● Barbera d'Asti Sup. La Marescialla '04		㉎㉎ 4
● Barbera d'Asti Sup. La Marescialla '03		㉎㉎ 4
● Barbera d'Asti Sup. La Marescialla '01		㉎㉎ 5
● Barbera d'Asti La Marescialla '00		㉎㉎ 5
● Barbera d'Asti Sup. Moliss '04		㉎㉎ 4

Pecchenino

B.TA VALDIBERTI, 59
12063 DOGLIANI [CN]
TEL. 017370686
www.pecchenino.com

ANNUAL PRODUCTION	90,000 bottles
HECTARES UNDER VINE	24
VITICULTURE METHOD	Conventional

This has been a memorable year for Attilio and Orlando Pecchenino, the two Dogliani-based brothers who have created one of the iconic wineries of this corner of the Langhe. Theirs is a typical story of the countryside, yet unusual in the ambition that has driven them to emerge, supported by their parents, on the winemaking panorama. On reaching the front rank, they gradually took the lead among the small Dogliani producers who make the emblematic Dolcetto di Dogliani. It has been a decade full of challenges and results with more ahead in a future that has already begun. Barolo is the next step. The princes of Dolcetto have crossed the border into Langhe to make a new wine that is superb in its first year. The Peccheninos' Le Coste 2004 is amazingly good, showing tannic, mouthfilling and harmonious. We love it, as have the critics and wine lovers who have followed its first steps. All the rest is Dolcetto. The spicy Jermu 2006 is among the very best, showing clear, invigorating and rounded on the palate, with an aristocratic finish pleasantly supported by acidity. The San Luigi is a youngster, no bad thing for it is nearly perfect already.

Pelissero

VIA FERRERE, 10
12050 TREISO [CN]
TEL. 0173638430
www.pelissero.com

ANNUAL PRODUCTION	250,000 bottles
HECTARES UNDER VINE	35
VITICULTURE METHOD	Conventional

Giorgio Pelissero's wines are impeccably clean, precisely vinified and carefully aged. The already functional winery will eventually be extended to make work easier and more efficient. The 2005 Barbarescos stood out among the wines presented. Vanotu is stupendous, with intense notes of dried roses, power and marvellous fullness on the palate, where sweet tannins blend very nicely with the fruit. Tulin doesn't give much away on the nose but has plenty of verve on the juicy palate, which has a rising finish and assertive tannins. Nubiola, a blend of various vineyards, has violet-led florality and more extract in the mouth than the other two. We liked the Langhe Rosso Long Now, a 50-50 blend of nebbiolo and barbera in which, as usual when this wine is young, the fresh, fruity notes of barbera predominate. The current Barbera Piani is concentrated, juicy and full flavoured. There's also a white. Langhe Favorita is well handled, flowery and nicely assertive. The two Dolcettos and the Langhe Nebbiolo deserve praise for their typicity and faultless execution while the Freisa is perfect for drinking chilled on a hot summer's afternoon.

● Dogliani Sirì d'Jermu '06	♈♈♈	5
● Barolo Le Coste '04	♈♈	7
● Barbera d'Alba Quass '06	♈♈	5
● Dolcetto di Dogliani S. Luigi '07	♈♈	4*
● Langhe Nebbiolo V. Botti '06	♈♈	5
O Langhe V. Maestro '07	♈	5
● Dolcetto di Dogliani Sirì d'Jermu '03	♉♉♉	5
● Dolcetto di Dogliani Sirì d'Jermu '01	♉♉♉	5
● Dolcetto di Dogliani Sirì d'Jermu '99	♉♉♉	5
● Dolcetto di Dogliani Sup. Bricco Botti '04	♉♉♉	5
● Dogliani Sirì d'Jermu '05	♉♉	5

● Barbaresco Tulin '05	♈♈	7
● Barbaresco Vanotu '05	♈♈	8
● Langhe Rosso Long Now '06	♈♈	6
● Barbaresco Nubiola '05	♈♈	6
● Barbera d'Alba Piani '07	♈♈	4*
● Dolcetto d'Alba Augenta '07	♈♈	4*
● Dolcetto d'Alba Munfrina '07	♈♈	4*
● Langhe Nebbiolo '07	♈♈	5
O Langhe Favorita '07	♈	3
● Langhe Freisa '07	♈	3
● Barbaresco Vanotu '99	♉♉♉	8
● Barbaresco Vanotu '97	♉♉♉	8
● Barbaresco Vanotu '95	♉♉♉	8
● Barbaresco Vanotu '01	♉♉♉	8
● Barbaresco Vanotu '04	♉♉	8
● Langhe Rosso Long Now '05	♉♉	6

Cascina Pellerino

LOC. SANT'ANNA, 93
12040 MONTEU ROERO [CN]
TEL. 0173978171
www.cascinapellerino.com

ANNUAL PRODUCTION   80,000 bottles
HECTARES UNDER VINE   10
VITICULTURE METHOD   Conventional

For the past few years, Cristian Bono has been restructuring the winery. He began when Roberto Ghione joined the firm and continued with the acquisition of new vineyards. This translated into a more extensive and varied range of wines, capable of catering for a range of tastes. The newer wines, from the Rosé to the Brut, Arneis Desiré and Barbera Diletta, are all extremely drinkable and the result of extremely skilful handling of the raw materials coming into the winery. Moreover, we continue – and we're not alone here – to focus our attention on the traditional bottles, which are again earning the winery plaudits this year. Barbera Gran Madre 2006 has taken full advantage of a great vintage, proffering intense aromas around a fruit and spice body. Acidity on the palate is enhanced but not altered by the small wood in which it aged, to show long and well balanced. The Vicot 2005 is even better, the extra year of ageing lending texture and austerity while the swath of aromatics is worthy of champion. Roero André 2006 focuses more on softness. The René, a blend of nebbiolo, barbera and cabernet, has good structure.

Elio Perrone

S.DA SAN MARTINO, 3BIS
12053 CASTIGLIONE TINELLA [CN]
TEL. 0141855803
www.elioperrone.it

ANNUAL PRODUCTION   140,000 bottles
HECTARES UNDER VINE   12
VITICULTURE METHOD   Conventional

This family winery deploys its different skills intelligently and to good effect in every stage of production. In the vineyard, the enthusiastic Stefano can count on his parents' long experience. On the administrative side, he is helped by his wife Giulia, who uses her artistic talents to look after the winery's image and labels. All their efforts focus on a small range, and are reflected in the quality of the wines. The aim of preserving all the freshness of the moscato grapes, and finding just the right balance in the bottle, has been achieved in Sourgal 2007, which has delicate floral and citrussy notes, great harmony, elegance and a lovely, lingering finish. The three Barberas are all fine ambassadors for their type. Mongovone 2006, from old vines and aged in small barrels, is intense and stylish, with complex notes of dark fruit, cocoa powder and spices, lots of body and softness tempered by attractive freshness. The Tasmorcan 2007 is up to snuff, presenting fresh and appealing in a pure expression of young Barbera. Aged in large barrels, it gives subtle aromas of berry fruit and red rose petals. The Grivò 2006 is a nice compromise.

● Roero Vicot '05	♥♥ 5
● Barbera d'Alba Diletta '06	♥♥ 4*
● Barbera d'Alba Sup. Gran Madre '06	♥♥ 5
● Langhe Rosso René '06	♥♥ 6
● Roero André '06	♥♥ 4*
O Roero Arneis Boneur '07	♥♥ 4*
O Poch ma Bon Passito '06	♥ 6
O Roero Arneis Desiré '07	♥ 4
⊙ Enrì '07	♥ 4
● Barbera d'Alba Sup. Gran Madre '05	♀♀ 5
● Roero Leoni '04	♀♀ 6
● Roero Leoni '01	♀♀ 6
● Roero Vicot '04	♀♀ 5

● Barbera d'Asti Sup. Mongovone '06	♥♥ 6
● Barbera d'Asti Grivò '06	♥♥ 4*
● Barbera d'Asti Tasmorcan '07	♥♥ 4*
O Moscato d'Asti Sourgal '07	♥♥ 4*
● Barbera d'Asti Grivò '05	♀♀ 4
● Barbera d'Asti Grivò '04	♀♀ 4
● Barbera d'Asti Sup. Mongovone '05	♀♀ 6
● Barbera d'Asti Sup. Mongovone '04	♀♀ 6
● Barbera d'Asti Sup. Mongovone '01	♀♀ 6
● Barbera d'Asti Tasmorcan '05	♀♀ 4

Le Piane

LOC. LE PIANE
VIA CERRI, 10
28010 BOCA [NO]
TEL. 3483354185
www.bocapiane.com

ANNUAL PRODUCTION **20,000 bottles**
HECTARES UNDER VINE **7**
VITICULTURE METHOD **Conventional**

When Christoph Künzli visited Antonio Cerri, the soon-to-retire grower who gave him his old vineyards in the Monte Fenera nature park, he must have seen their potential. After planting new vineyards and reorganizing existing ones, Christoph achieved an enviably secure position as a winemaker. If we add to this viticulture-friendly porphyritic hills, so similar to those of Côte Rôtie, we see why Le Piane has had such rapid success. The owner's philosophy is to seek out varieties that grow well here, plain and simple. The winery produces just three wine types for a total of 20,000 bottles, using only native grapes. Boca, a blend of 85 per cent nebbiolo and 15 per cent vespolina aged for three years in barrels of Slavonian oak, effortlessly repeated last year's performance. Its minerally, iodine-laced nose leads into an aristocratic, leisurely palate. Le Piane, from croatina grapes, expresses the variety's indomitable character, which not even small French wood manages to tame. The youthful vigour lets you know that it is destined to age for a very long time. The refreshing, complex Maggiorina is one of the finest easy-drinking reds we tasted in Piedmont.

Fabrizio Pinsoglio

FRAZ. MADONNA DEI CAVALLI, 31BIS
12050 CANALE [CN]
TEL. 0173968401
fabriziopinsoglio@libero.it

ANNUAL PRODUCTION **40,000 bottles**
HECTARES UNDER VINE **9**
VITICULTURE METHOD **Conventional**

Fabrizio Pinsoglio, Canale's new resident – the transfer of the new winery, just a few metres from the old one, involved moving from Castellinaldo to Canale – sticks to quality. His winery is geared for minimum intervention and maximum quality in all his wines. Fabrizio is aware of the potential of the area in which he works. Not for him easy successes or flattering write-ups at any cost. He gives us his wines to taste when they are good and ready. If a bottle needs more time to mature, Fabrizio leaves it until the following year. This year's was a fair selection, with some serious wines on show. The Arneis is again one of the best in Roero, verging on excellence. The distance between the two Barberas has shrunk, not because of an inferior performance by the renowned Rondolina but because of the improvement in the Giaconi 2007, a standard-label wine with splendid character. There's an austere, tannin-rich Nebbiolo in the Riserva di Roero 2005, which has never been so attractive, thanks to its seductive weave on the nose and depth, elegance and balance on the palate.

● Boca '04	▼▼▼ 7
● Colline Novaresi Le Piane '06	▼▼ 6
● Colline Novaresi La Maggiorina '06	▼▼ 3*
● Boca '03	♀♀♀ 7
● Boca '01	♀♀ 7
● Boca '00	♀♀ 5
● Colline Novaresi La Maggiorina '05	♀♀ 3
● Colline Novaresi Le Piane '05	♀♀ 6
● Colline Novaresi Le Piane '04	♀♀ 6
● Colline Novaresi Le Piane '03	♀♀ 4

● Barbera d'Alba Bric La Rondolina '06	▼▼ 5
● Barbera d'Alba Vign. Giaconi '07	▼▼ 4*
● Roero Ris. '05	▼▼ 5
O Roero Arneis Vign. Malinat '07	▼▼ 3*
● Nebbiolo d'Alba '06	▼ 4
● Barbera d'Alba Bric La Rondolina '05	♀♀ 5
● Barbera d'Alba Bric La Rondolina '04	♀♀ 5
● Barbera d'Alba Bric La Rondolina '01	♀♀ 5
● Roero Sup. '03	♀♀ 5
● Roero Sup. '01	♀♀ 5
● Roero Sup. '04	♀♀ 5

Pio Cesare

VIA CESARE BALBO, 6
12051 ALBA [CN]
TEL. 0173440386
www.piocesare.it

ANNUAL PRODUCTION	370,000 bottles
HECTARES UNDER VINE	52
VITICULTURE METHOD	Conventional

A short distance from the imposing cathedral of Alba is Pio Cesare's winery, one of the longest-established operations in Langhe. In charge is Pio Boffa, assisted by oenologist Paolo Fenocchio, who has been here since 1981, and vineyard manager Claudio Pirra who has been supervising the estate's and its outside growers' vines 2001. The recent makeover of the production spaces is an indication of the constant drive for improvement as the winery maintains its links with tradition. The selection of wines presented reflects the history of the estate, starting with L'Altro 2007, from chardonnay partly fermented in wood, which has attractive structure backed by perceptible acidity and delicious tanginess. The Barolo 2004 is very classy. A wine of terrific character, it gives ripe fruit and powerful tannins to support the structure. The Barbaresco Il Bricco 2004 also has plenty of body, slightly in thrall to the oak but still eminently enjoyable. Finally, Barbera Fides 2006 is decent, revealing great body, nice extract and acidity in the finish that enhances drinkability.

Pioiero

CASCINA PIOIERO, 1
12040 VEZZA D'ALBA [CN]
TEL. 017365492
www.pioiero.com

ANNUAL PRODUCTION	30,000 bottles
HECTARES UNDER VINE	5.5
VITICULTURE METHOD	Conventional

Arneis, Favorita, Barbera d'Alba in two versions, Nebbiolo and Roero. Everything is in place this year in the range from the Rabino family's quality operation. The language spoken here is the local Roero dialect of Roero; there's no need of any other. The vines are the traditional varieties, the rows are long and sun-kissed, neatly lined up behind the large farmhouse in the hills. The approach to vinification is to tease out of the raw material whatever it has to give: aromas, flavours, evocations and stories. Here's this year's report. A refreshingly quaffable Favorita flanks a flavoursome Arneis that shows fragrant, complex and long. It was one of the best versions we tasted, and not just at Poiero but in the entire area. The two Barberas vying with each other in acidity and fruit, which are very much in evidence in the traditional 2006 version but more subtle in the Superiore 2005, which has great elegance and bearing. Finally, while the Nebbiolo is austere and tannic, the Roero 2006 is blessed with softness and harmony; a hymn to the finest characteristics of the noble nebbiolo grape in Roero.

● Barbaresco Il Bricco '04	♀♀ 8
● Barolo '04	♀♀ 8
● Barbaresco '04	♀♀ 8
● Barbera d'Alba Fides '06	♀♀ 6
● Barolo Ornato '04	♀♀ 8
○ Piemonte Chardonnay L'Altro '07	♀♀ 4
○ Langhe Arneis '07	♀ 4
● Barbera d'Alba '06	♀ 6
● Nebbiolo d'Alba '05	♀ 4
● Barbaresco Il Bricco '97	♀♀♀ 8
● Barolo Ornato '89	♀♀♀ 8
● Barolo Ornato '85	♀♀♀ 8
● Barbaresco Il Bricco '01	♀♀ 8
● Barbaresco Il Bricco '00	♀♀ 8
● Barolo Ornato '01	♀♀ 8
● Barolo Ornato '00	♀♀ 8

○ Roero Arneis '07	♀♀ 3*
● Barbera d'Alba '06	♀♀ 3*
● Barbera d'Alba Sup. '05	♀♀ 4
● Roero '06	♀♀ 4
● Nebbiolo d'Alba '06	♀ 4
○ Langhe Favorita '07	♀ 3
● Roero '05	♀♀ 4
● Roero Sup. '04	♀♀ 4
● Roero Sup. '03	♀♀ 4
● Roero Sup. '01	♀♀ 4
● Nebbiolo d'Alba '05	♀♀ 4

E. Pira & Figli

VIA VITTORIO VENETO, 1
12060 BAROLO [CN]
TEL. 017356247
www.pira-chiaraboschis.com

Luigi Pira

VIA XX SETTEMBRE, 9
12050 SERRALUNGA D'ALBA [CN]
TEL. 0173613106

ANNUAL PRODUCTION	20,000 bottles
HECTARES UNDER VINE	3.5
VITICULTURE METHOD	Certified biodynamic

Chiara Boschis is like a river in full flood when she talks about her wines. She tells you about the attention she gives vineyards and nature in general; getting the grapes to just the right degree of ripeness; the winemaking techniques she uses to bring out variety and terroir. Her passion is again reflected in this year's wines. The Barolo Cannubi 2004 is a superb expression of the celebrated vineyard with broad aromatics and elegance. Its ruby hue is rimmed with garnet and the nose offers red berries, roses and balsam before silky tannins accompany sensations of mint and tobacco to a beautifully long finish. Barolo Via Nuova also impressed. Its slower to reveal itself, its austere structure braced by vigorous tannins and fruit aromas lifted by liquorice and tobacco. The Dolcetto d'Alba 2007 marries drinkability and texture, fragrances of cherry and raspberry framing the assertive, mouthfilling tannins. The Barbera d'Alba 2006 offers forest fruits and spices in the nose and caresses the palate with fleshy fruit and notes of chocolate, together with faint tannins that mingle perfectly with the typical acidity of the vine.

ANNUAL PRODUCTION	50,000 bottles
HECTARES UNDER VINE	10
VITICULTURE METHOD	Conventional

This Langhe wine producer's history goes back several generations. It still bears the name of Luigi Pira, who used to sell much of his production to bottlers in Alba, but its modern history began in the early 1990s, when his son Giampaolo took over, to be joined later by his brother Romolo. At that point, the family's fine Serralunga plots in Vigna Rionda, Marenca and Margheria started living up to their status. Sound vineyard management and painstaking work in the cellar, with its new and used barriques and assorted large wood, have taken the winery into the Barolo elite. Luigi Pira obtained fine results from the great 2004 growing year. A well-earned Three Glasses went to Barolo Vigna Rionda, which matches a nose themed on an enviable harmony of sweet spices and red fruit with a full, velvet-textured palate. As so often, Vigneto Marenca is more complex, giving truffles and cloves, but also harder for its tannins are still rather rough-edged. The Vigneto Margheria's tannins do not show the same finesse but it too has a brilliant future. The basic Barolo is more straightforward, with simpler fruit-like aromas and a less demanding palate.

● Barolo Cannubi '04	♟♟	8
● Barbera d'Alba '06	♟♟	6
● Barolo Via Nuova '04	♟♟	8
● Dolcetto d'Alba '07	♟♟	5
● Barolo '94	♟♟♟	8
● Barolo Cannubi '00	♟♟♟	8
● Barolo Cannubi '97	♟♟♟	8
● Barolo Cannubi '96	♟♟♟	8
● Barolo Ris. '90	♟♟♟	8
● Barolo Cannubi '99	♟♟	8
● Barolo Cannubi '98	♟♟	8
● Barolo Cannubi '03	♟♟	8
● Barolo Cannubi '01	♟♟	8
● Barolo Via Nuova '03	♟♟	8
● Barolo Via Nuova '01	♟♟	8
● Barolo Via Nuova '00	♟♟	8

● Barolo V. Rionda '04	♟♟♟	8
● Barolo Vign. Marenca '04	♟♟	8
● Barolo Vign. Margheria '04	♟♟	7
● Barbera d'Alba '06	♟♟	5
● Barolo '04	♟♟	7
● Langhe Nebbiolo '06	♟♟	5
● Dolcetto d'Alba '07	♟	4
● Barolo V. Rionda '00	♟♟♟	8
● Barolo Vign. Marenca '97	♟♟♟	8
● Barolo Vign. Marenca '01	♟♟♟	8
● Barolo V. Rionda '03	♟♟	8
● Barolo V. Rionda '01	♟♟	8
● Barolo Vign. Marenca '03	♟♟	8
● Barolo Vign. Margheria '03	♟♟	7

Poderi Colla

LOC. SAN ROCCO SENO D'ELVIO, 82
12051 ALBA [CN]
TEL. 0173290148
www.podericolla.it

ANNUAL PRODUCTION	150,000 bottles
HECTARES UNDER VINE	27
VITICULTURE METHOD	Conventional

Over many years, the Collas have made a great contribution to wine in Langhe. Today, they are creating a prestigious range. Federica now adds a very competent extra pair of hands to the rigorous estate management, which is transparent and respectful of the terroir. We tasted one of the most exciting Barolos of the year here, Bussia Dardi Le Rose 2004. A compendium of excellence, it gives the vineyard's classic, distinctive aromas, opening full and velvety on both nose and palate, with subtle elegance, and refined tannins and a long, well-balanced finale that echoes the nose. Barbaresco Roncaglie 2005 is also very well executed. Assertive fruit precedes an enfolding, velvety mouthfeel on the austere palate. Langhe Bricco del Drago 2005 has deep scents of blackberry and fine tobacco leading into a full, wonderfully balanced palate. The other wines in the range are very convincing. A special mention goes to the deliciously varietal Langhe Bianco Riesling 2007 from a very old vineyard, and to the Metodo Classico Pietro Colla Extra Bru, a successful spumante that does the family honour with its palate-caressing fragrances, finesse and structure.

Paolo Poggio

VIA ROMA, 67
15050 BRIGNANO FRASCATA [AL]
TEL. 0131784929
cantinapoggio@tiscali.it

ANNUAL PRODUCTION	17,000 bottles
HECTARES UNDER VINE	3
VITICULTURE METHOD	Conventional

Paolo Poggio will no doubt be happy to seeing that his Timorasso Ronchetto has earned the same high mark it obtained in the last edition of the Guide. It is no small thing for a small, family-run winery, which has had its difficulties, to achieve a certain continuity in the lines it offers. So let's celebrate this Timorasso 2006, which offers lightly vanillaed aromas and progresses over fruit in syrup while retaining the minerality typical of the variety. After a year's absence, the 2004 Derio is back and picked up Two Glasses straight away, presenting itself as an affordable version of good quality wood-aged Barbera. The 2006 version of the croatina-based Prosone is also very pleasant, with good structure and delicious aromas reminiscent of liquorice and green peppers. On the palate, the tannins are still a little unripe but by no means unpleasant. The white Campogallo, made from cortese grapes, is refreshing and lemony. Take a glance at the price tag and you'll see that it's an astonishing bargain.

● Barolo Bussia Dardi Le Rose '04	♟♟ 7
● Barbaresco Roncaglie '05	♟♟ 7
○ Langhe Bianco Riesling '07	♟♟ 4*
○ Langhe Bianco Sanrocco '07	♟♟ 4*
○ Pietro Colla M. Cl. Extra Brut	♟♟ 5
● Langhe Bricco del Drago '05	♟♟ 5
● Dolcetto d'Alba Pian Balbo '07	♟ 4
● Nebbiolo d'Alba '06	♟ 5
● Barolo Bussia Dardi Le Rose '99	♟♟♟ 7
● Barolo Bussia Dardi Le Rose '01	♟♟ 7
● Barolo Bussia Dardi Le Rose '00	♟♟ 7
● Langhe Bricco del Drago '04	♟♟ 5
● Barbaresco Roncaglie '04	♟♟ 7
● Barbaresco Roncaglie '01	♟♟ 7

○ Colli Tortonesi Ronchetto '06	♟♟ 3*
● Colli Tortonesi Barbera Derio '04	♟♟ 4
● Colli Tortonesi Rosso Prosone '06	♟♟ 2*
○ Colli Tortonesi Bianco Campogallo '07	♟ 2
○ Colli Tortonesi Ronchetto '05	♟♟ 3
○ Colli Tortonesi Ronchetto '04	♟♟ 3
○ Colli Tortonesi Ronchetto '05	♟♟ 3
● Colli Tortonesi Barbera Derio '99	♟♟ 4
● Colli Tortonesi Barbera Derio '98	♟♟ 4

Porello

C.SO ALBA, 71
12043 CANALE [CN]
TEL. 0173979324
www.porellovini.it

Ferdinando Principiano

VIA ALBA, 19
12065 MONFORTE D'ALBA [CN]
TEL. 0173787158
www.ferdinandoprincipiano.it

ANNUAL PRODUCTION	70,000 bottles
HECTARES UNDER VINE	15
VITICULTURE METHOD	Conventional

ANNUAL PRODUCTION	30,000 bottles
HECTARES UNDER VINE	7.5
VITICULTURE METHOD	Conventional

The news is that there's no Roero 2006 this year. Marco Porello took the decision he had been pondering for some time and left the top wine in his range to mature for longer. Roero Torretta, which won Three Glasses for the 2004 edition, focused the wine world's attention on this small, dynamic estate on the left bank of the Tanaro. When Marco told us about his decision, we realized just how serious this young winemaker with his clearly set out ideas actually is about making seriously good Roero that can be drunk young – a fine quality this, not a sign of weakness – but equally capable of acquiring the characteristics of a great wine with appropriate cellar time. There are plenty of other wines, though. Briefly, there's the Favorita, the current Barbera and the Nebbiolo 2006, all three very convincing in their respective categories. Next come the stars of the range with two bottles tying for first place: the soft, juicy Barbera Filatura 2006 and the 2007 Arneis, the best and most fragrant ever, and a wine that has never before come this close to absolute excellence.

Careful vineyard management, grape selection and monitoring with scant use of invasive or diversity-threatening techniques mark out Ferdinando Principiano's style. He makes territorial wines that reflect their varieties and the range for this year's Guide is first class. Barbera Laura is pleasantly refreshing and fruity while Dolcetto Sant'Anna is fragrant and food-friendly, as tradition decrees. Nebbiolo Coste is more serious. Ruby red with a garnet edge, it unveils ethery aromas, robust body with evident tannins and wafts of liquorice and tobacco. The alcohol in Barbera Romualda is offset by good structure. A charming dark ruby, it offers forest fruits and spice aromas, a silky palate and acids and tannins in harmony ushering in a very classy, flavoursome finish laced with cocoa powder and mint. The Barolo Serralunga's restrained elegance frames a still-young wine in need of ageing. Very low yields from vines for 40 years yielded a great Barolo Boscareto 2004, a fine example of generous, cellarable nebbiolo fruit with spacious fragrances of fruit and minerality with tertiary overtones. This stunning wine can only improve over the years.

● Barbera d'Alba Filatura '06	♥♥	5
○ Roero Arneis Camestrì '07	♥♥	4*
● Barbera d'Alba Mommiano '07	♥♥	4
● Nebbiolo d'Alba '06	♥♥	4
○ Langhe Favorita '07	♥	4
● Roero Torretta '04	♥♥♥	5
● Barbera d'Alba Filatura '05	♥♥	5
● Barbera d'Alba Filatura '04	♥♥	5
● Roero Torretta '05	♥♥	5
● Roero Torretta '03	♥♥	5
● Roero Torretta '02	♥♥	5
● Roero Torretta '01	♥♥	4
● Barbera d'Alba Filatura '03	♥♥	5
● Nebbiolo d'Alba '05	♥♥	4

● Barbera d'Alba La Romualda '06	♥♥	6
● Barolo Boscareto '04	♥♥	8
● Barolo Serralunga '04	♥♥	7
● Dolcetto d'Alba S. Anna '07	♥♥	4*
● Langhe Nebbiolo Coste '07	♥♥	4
● Barbera d'Alba Laura '07	♥	4
● Barolo Boscareto '93	♥♥♥	8
● Barbera d'Alba La Romualda '05	♥♥	6
● Barbera d'Alba La Romualda '04	♥♥	6
● Barolo Boscareto '99	♥♥	8
● Barolo Boscareto '01	♥♥	8
● Barbera d'Alba La Romualda '03	♥♥	5
● Barolo Boscareto '00	♥♥	8

★ Prunotto

REG. SAN CASSIANO, 4G
12051 ALBA [CN]
TEL. 0173280017
www.prunotto.it

ANNUAL PRODUCTION	600,000 bottles
HECTARES UNDER VINE	55
VITICULTURE METHOD	Conventional

Since 1989, Prunotto has been part of the Antinori group. Recently, it has bought some of the land that yields the grapes and it now has 55 hectares. The goal for the next few years is to increase the stock of 50-hectolitre barrels and separate the wines strictly by provenance for improved quality control. The range released is wide and all the wines are impressive, starting with the very aromatic, refreshing Arneis 2007. The Dolcetto d'Alba Mosesco 2006 is full flavoured, with ethery red berries reprised intensely in the mouth. New this year is the Monferrato Bricco Colma 2005, made from albarossa grapes, a hybrid of nebbiolo and barbera created by Professor Dalmasso in 1934. The grape is grown at Calliano near Asti and yields an intensely coloured wine in which the dominant acidity and tannin are a little too aggressive. The Barolo Bussia 2004 is powerful and warm, proffering soft, stylish texture. The Barbaresco Bric Turot 2004 is also wonderful and very elegant, with a fine structure and intense fruit, though its tannins are still a little young. The Barbera Nizza Costamiòle is excellent, scoring a few marks more than Pian Romualdo.

Carlo Quarello

VIA MARCONI, 3
14020 COSSOMBRATO [AT]
TEL. 0141905204
valerio.quarello@libero.it

ANNUAL PRODUCTION	20,000 bottles
HECTARES UNDER VINE	5.5
VITICULTURE METHOD	Conventional

When you sip Quarello's Grignolino, you wonder why so few people appreciate the variety. Valerio Quarello, who helps his father Carlo out these days, explains that it is not well known because often it is blended with barbera and other varieties, even white grapes! Planting grignolino was a real challenge. Carlo started in 1963 when, after years working on cruise ships, he decided to make wine. This was in the days of bulk unbottled wine and he embarked on grignolino growing in tandem with his new job as a school teacher. Production was sold in demijohns until the 1980s, when Carlo started bottling, encouraged by requests from local restaurateurs. This was the last hurdle for the wine on its path to quality and its current status as a benchmark for the wine type today. This year's news is the completion of the cellar at Cardona, where the vineyards are located. The new facility will be operative before the next harvest. The only wine presented, Grignolino Marcaleone 2007, is excellent, with a rich nose of berry fruit and light spice, an elegantly peppery palate and assertive but not aggressive tannins.

● Barbera d'Asti Sup. Nizza Costamiòle '04	🍷🍷	7
● Barolo Bussia '04	🍷🍷	8
● Barbaresco '05	🍷🍷	7
● Barbaresco Bric Turot '04	🍷🍷	8
● Barbera d'Alba Pian Romualdo '05	🍷🍷	6
● Barolo '04	🍷🍷	7
● Dolcetto d'Alba Mosesco '06	🍷🍷	5
● M.to Bricco Colma '05	🍷🍷	5
● Nebbiolo d'Alba Occhetti '05	🍷🍷	5
● Barbera d'Alba '06	🍷	4
● Barbera d'Asti Fiulòt '07	🍷	4
● Dolcetto d'Alba '07	🍷	4
● M.to Mompertone '06	🍷	5
O Roero Arneis '07	🍷	5
● Barolo Bussia '01	🍷🍷🍷	8

● Grignolino del M.to Casalese Cré Marcaleone '07	🍷🍷	4*
● Grignolino del M.to Casalese Cré Marcaleone '06	🍷🍷	4
● Grignolino del M.to Casalese Cré Marcaleone '05	🍷🍷	4
● Grignolino del M.to Casalese Cré Marcaleone '04	🍷🍷	4
● Grignolino del M.to Casalese Cré Marcaleone '03	🍷🍷	4

Renato Ratti

FRAZ. ANNUNZIATA, 7
12064 LA MORRA [CN]
TEL. 017350185
www.renatoratti.com

ANNUAL PRODUCTION	300,000 bottles
HECTARES UNDER VINE	35
VITICULTURE METHOD	Conventional

Pietro Ratti's wines are a good compromise between tradition and modernity. They reflect their areas of provenance, and could hardly do otherwise. The winery bears the name of the man who, more than anyone, promoted Barolo's subzones, Pietro's father the late Renato Ratti. The wines are clean, well focused and true to type, as well as technically impeccable. Such definition can sometimes limit personality but it is appropriate for a winery that deals in large quantities and big numbers. From the wines we tasted, the 2004 Barolos are outstanding for their nobility and the excellent vintage, the first vinified in the beautiful, impressive new cellar. The Marcenasco is clean in its fruit, with suffused florality, showing attractive and reliable with a reassuringly soft impact. Conca is still young and very complex but suggests nice balsamic fragrances with citrus peel before the rich, caressing palate unveils its well-honed tannins. The nobility of the vineyard is in your glass with the Rocche. A generously complex nose proffers aromas of dark fruit, violets, spice and herbs preceding a precise, measured palate of elegance, savouriness and depth.

Ressia

VIA CANOVA, 28
12052 NEIVE [CN]
TEL. 0173677305
www.ressia.com

ANNUAL PRODUCTION	30,000 bottles
HECTARES UNDER VINE	4.5
VITICULTURE METHOD	Natural

In just over ten years in business, the winery run by Fabrizio Ressia has reached an excellent standard. Fabrizio is nice, friendly and understands viticulture in the traditional way, with respect for the environment around him. The Barbaresco Canova 2005, in 4,300 bottles, is fantastic. Three years in 900-litre casks and large barrels lend austerity and elegance to nose and palate, and the lingering finish is wonderful. The Barbera d'Alba Superiore Canova 2006, in 1,000 bottles, aged in 900-litre casks for a year. Already balanced, it is surprisingly generous. The Dolcetto d'Alba Superiore Canova 2006, in 1,500 bottles, aged in stainless steel and casks, and shows fresh but with some complexity on the nose. The Evien Oro 2006 is special, a Moscato vinified to dryness and aged in barrique for a year. It's fragrant, velvety and has a dry, lingering aftertaste. The Langhe Nebbiolo Gepù 2006, is 2,000 bottles, is good with fruit and spice aromas and nice balance. The more approachable base wines are also good, with the Langhe Favorita, Dolcetto d'Alba Canova and Barbera d'Alba Canova completing an estimable range.

● Barolo Conca Marcenasco '04	▼▼ 8
● Barolo Rocche Marcenasco '04	▼▼ 8
● Barbera d'Alba Torriglione '07	▼▼ 4*
● Barolo Marcenasco '04	▼▼ 7
● Nebbiolo d'Alba Ochetti '06	▼▼ 5
● Dolcetto d'Alba Colombè '07	▼ 4
● Barolo Rocche Marcenasco '84	▼▼▼ 8
● Barolo Rocche Marcenasco '83	▼▼▼ 8
● Barolo Conca Marcenasco '03	▼▼ 8
● Barolo Conca Marcenasco '01	▼▼ 8
● Barolo Rocche Marcenasco '99	▼▼ 8
● Barolo Rocche Marcenasco '03	▼▼ 8
● Barolo Rocche Marcenasco '00	▼▼ 8
● Piedolo Conca Marcenasco '99	▼▼ 8
● Barolo Marcenasco '03	▼▼ 7
● Barolo Rocche Marcenasco '01	▼▼ 8

● Barbaresco Canova '05	▼▼ 6
● Barbera d'Alba Sup. Canova '06	▼▼ 4
● Dolcetto d'Alba Sup. Canova '06	▼▼ 3*
O Evien Oro '06	▼▼ 4
● Langhe Nebbiolo Gepù '06	▼▼ 5
● Barbera d'Alba Canova '06	▼ 4
● Dolcetto d'Alba Canova '06	▼ 4
O Langhe Favorita La Miranda '07	▼ 3
● Barbaresco Canova '04	▼▼ 6
● Barbera d'Alba Sup. Canova '05	▼▼ 4
● Dolcetto d'Alba Sup. Canova '05	▼▼ 4
● Langhe Rosso Resiot '05	▼▼ 5
● Langhe Rosso Resiot '04	▼▼ 5

F.lli Revello

FRAZ. ANNUNZIATA, 103
12064 LA MORRA [CN]
TEL. 017350276
www.revellofratelli.it

ANNUAL PRODUCTION	65,000 bottles
HECTARES UNDER VINE	12
VITICULTURE METHOD	Natural

Carlo and Enzo Revello's 2004 vintage is summarized below. Rocche dell'Annunziata, in only 1,000 bottles, aged for 24 months in half-new small barrels. Intense on the nose, it is powerful in the mouth and finishes long. Autumn leaves and spices theme Vigna Conca, in 5,300 bottles, aged in the same way as the previous wine. Vigna Giachini, in 4,700 bottles, offers fruit and violets, a velvety, lingering palate and nice harmony. Vigna Gattera, in 6,500 bottles, spent 24 months in 15-hectolitre casks. Closed on the nose, it has a complex, balanced palate. Even the basic Barolo 2004 is impressive. In 12,000 bottles, it matured for 24 months in 80 per cent used barrels and has forest floor and violets followed by an intense, lingering palate. The splendid Barbera d'Alba Ciabot du Re 2006, in 5,000 bottles, matured for 18 months in new small oak. Vanillaed morello cherry is backed up by robust alcohol and extract, and it finishes dry. L'Insieme 2006, in only 1,000 bottles, is from barbera, nebbiolo and cabernet sauvignon aged for 18 months in oak and a further 12 in bottle. The Dolcetto, the Nebbiolo and the tasty basic Barbera, all 2007, are very decent.

Michele Reverdito

B.TA GARASSINI, 74B
12064 LA MORRA [CN]
TEL. 017350336
www.reverdito.it

ANNUAL PRODUCTION	60,000 bottles
HECTARES UNDER VINE	18
VITICULTURE METHOD	Conventional

The Reverdito family's efforts take this winery on by leaps and bounds. Michele, the owner, can now offer wine lovers some top-quality bottles. The winery first vinified in 2000, and is currently expanding, an indication of the desire to keep growing. As for the wines, Barolo Serralunga 2004 deserves an honourable mention for its power and elegance. There are hints of dried flowers, coffee and well-balanced wood on the nose, while austere tannin mingles with nuances of ripe berries on the palate. The same goes for the Barolo Codane 2004. An intense, citrussy wine, it is very potent but a little dry from the oak. Barolo Bricco Cogni 2003 is evolved, with tannins still rather rough-edged after the indifferent growing year. The Barbera d'Alba Butti 2006 is fruity with toasty wood notes and clear balsamic notes in the finish while the Delia 2005 is leaner in comparison. The rest of the range is of a high standard. Particularly good is Verduno Pelaverga 2007, from the native pelaverga variety, which has spicy sensations on the nose and a convincing follow-through in the mouth.

● Barbera d'Alba Ciabot du Re '06	▼▼ 6
● Barolo V. Conca '04	▼▼ 8
● Barolo V. Gattera '04	▼▼ 8
● Barolo Rocche dell'Annunziata '04	▼▼ 8
● Barbera d'Alba '07	▼▼ 4*
● Barolo '04	▼▼ 6
● Barolo V. Giachini '04	▼▼ 7
● Langhe Rosso L'Insieme '05	▼▼ 7
● Dolcetto d'Alba '07	▼▼ 4*
● Langhe Nebbiolo '07	▼ 5
● Barbera d'Alba Ciabot du Re '05	▼▼▼ 6
● Barbera d'Alba Ciabot du Re '00	▼▼▼ 7
● Barolo Rocche dell'Annunziata '97	▼▼▼ 8
● Barolo Rocche dell'Annunziata '01	▼▼▼ 8
● Barolo Rocche dell'Annunziata '00	▼▼▼ 8
● Barolo V. Conca '99	▼▼▼ 8

● Barolo Serralunga '04	▼▼ 6
● Barbera d'Alba Butti '06	▼▼ 4*
● Barbera d'Alba Delia '05	▼▼ 5
● Barolo Bricco Cogni '03	▼▼ 7
● Barolo Codane '04	▼▼ 6
● Verduno Pelaverga '07	▼▼ 4*
● Dolcetto d'Alba Sup. Formica '06	▼ 4
● Langhe Nebbiolo Simane '06	▼ 4
● Barolo Moncucco '03	♈♈ 5
● Barolo Moncucco '02	♈♈ 5
● Barolo Serralunga '03	♈♈ 5
● Barolo Serralunga '02	♈♈ 5

Carlo Daniele Ricci
VIA MONTALE CELLI, 9
15050 COSTA VESCOVATO [AL]
TEL. 0131838115

Giuseppe Rinaldi
VIA MONFORTE, 3
12060 BAROLO [CN]
TEL. 017356156

ANNUAL PRODUCTION	30,000 bottles
HECTARES UNDER VINE	8
VITICULTURE METHOD	Conventional

Daniele Ricci is stubborn and strong-willed, with a firm belief in the territory and the results to be obtained by working its soil. Having put huge effort into upgrading and enhancing his winery, elsewhere in the estate Daniele has decided to open a genuine agriturismo. He only opens it at weekends, serving simple food and wines from his cellar. Nothing more than this, in the original spirit of the agriturismo concept. This year's wines also did very well indeed, even though the Timorasso Terre del Timorasso just missed reaching our finals, in contrast to the last two editions of the Guide. Ricci's is still an excellent version of this indigenous white wine; it's just that there's rather too noticeable a vein of acidity. The Castellania is an excellent interpretation of a barbera-based red. It takes its name from the plots located in the area of that name. At first, the nose has oaky notes but then opens up into aromas of red fruit and cocoa powder. But this is a wine that is at its best on the palate, where its structure and well-handled acidity stand out. The Elso, from croatina, is also attractive while Bonarda 'L Mat is attractively alcoholic.

ANNUAL PRODUCTION	30,000 bottles
HECTARES UNDER VINE	6.5
VITICULTURE METHOD	Natural

Among the huge maturing casks and historic, still functioning wooden fermentation vat in Giuseppe Rinaldi's cellar, beneath his superb early 20th-century house, there is a sense of a world still in touch with tradition and peasant farming, in the noblest sense of the term. Beppe is a man of wit and culture. He'll tell you about Barolo and Barolo wine, events of times past and the results of his enthusiastic researches. He presented only the two Barolos from the great 2004 vintage. Traditional in type, classic and austere, they were obtained through bringing together fruit from four different, very prestigious vineyards in pairs. The Brunate-Le Coste, like an unbroken horse, is rich and full-blooded, with a spacious range of subtle, earthy aromas with cocoa powder and mint. It has tremendous structure, rich flavour, depth, firm tannin and a rising finish. Tuck it away in the cellar. The Cannubi S. Lorenzo-Ravera is smoother, showing long and relaxed with elegant florality. It's readier to drink and better able to absorb impressive tannic structure. This spectacular Langhe classic earned Three Glasses.

● Colli Tortonesi Barbera Castellania '06		🍷🍷 5
● Colli Tortonesi Rosso Elso '05		🍷🍷 4*
○ Colli Tortonesi Terre del Timorasso '06		🍷🍷 4*
● Piemonte Bonarda 'L Matt '06		🍷 4
○ Colli Tortonesi Terre del Timorasso '05		🍷🍷 4
○ Colli Tortonesi Terre del Timorasso '04		🍷🍷 4
○ Colli Tortonesi Terre del Timorasso '03		🍷🍷 4
○ Colli Tortonesi Terre del Timorasso '02		🍷🍷 4

● Barolo Cannubi S. Lorenzo-Ravera '04		🍷🍷🍷 7
● Barolo Brunate-Le Coste '04		🍷🍷 7
● Barolo Brunate-Le Coste '01		🍷🍷🍷 7
● Barolo Brunate-Le Coste '00		🍷🍷🍷 7
● Barolo Brunate-Le Coste '97		🍷🍷🍷 7
● Barolo Brunate-Le Coste '99		🍷🍷 7
● Barolo Brunate-Le Coste '03		🍷🍷 7
● Barolo Cannubi S. Lorenzo-Ravera '04		🍷🍷 7
● Barolo Cannubi S. Lorenzo-Ravera '03		🍷🍷 7
● Barolo Cannubi S. Lorenzo-Ravera '01		🍷🍷 7
● Barolo Cannubi S. Lorenzo-Ravera '00		🍷🍷 7

Rizzi

VIA RIZZI, 15
12050 TREISO [CN]
TEL. 0173638161
www.cantinarizzi.it

ANNUAL PRODUCTION	40,000 bottles
HECTARES UNDER VINE	35
VITICULTURE METHOD	Conventional

This lovely winery has 28 hectares in a block on the Rizzi hill, one of the best areas of Barbaresco for growing nebbiolo. Founded in 1974 by Ernesto Dellapiana, it has incorporated adjoining plots to reach its current shape and Ernesto is helped on the estate by his two children, Jole and Enrico. The style is precise and traditional with ageing in large oak casks and long maceration of the grapes. There are four different selections of Barbaresco, very different from one another and rich in character. Our favourite is Nervo Fondetta, an austere, frill-free wine with fragrances of raspberries, violets, cinchona and dried roses. The tannin is well-structured and soft on the palate, and the finish is stylish. The Pajorè is also very classy. It comes from a plot in the vineyard of the same name recently acquired by the Dellapianas. Two Glasses also went to Rizzi Boito, which is captivating in its rich, complex aromas of liquorice, mint, rain-soaked earth, saddle leather and tobacco. The basic Barbaresco is lovely and the Barbera is very decent. The Dolcetto is youthfully alcoholic and fruity while the Chardonnay is refreshing and very drinkable.

Albino Rocca

S.DA RONCHI, 18
12050 BARBARESCO [CN]
TEL. 0173635145
www.roccaalbino.com

ANNUAL PRODUCTION	108,000 bottles
HECTARES UNDER VINE	18
VITICULTURE METHOD	Conventional

Paola Rocca is expanding the winery she took over from her father and grandfather. For example, her husband's vineyards yield an excellent basic Barbaresco 2005 and a lovely Moscato d'Asti Fiordaliso 2007. Barbera d'Alba Gepin 2006 is textbook stuff and, as always, one of the year's finest. While we await the new Brich Ronchi Riserva 2004, the two Barberescos are outstanding. Brich Ronchi 2005 is serious, generous and complex, but at the same time well balanced, elegant and ready for the corkscrew now. Its oak – 90 per cent new small wood – gives roundness and this Barbaresco with a distinctly promising future earned our Three Glass award. The Loreto 2005, which ages only in large barrels, also reached the finals. It's a little younger and less developed but as in so many previous years, it will evolve very positively with time. For now, it has good astringency, minerality and breadth. The nose-palate harmony on the fruity Dolcetto d'Alba Vignalunga 2007 is appealing while, of the two whites, we prefer the tangy freshness of the cortese Langhe Bianco La Rocca 2007 to the racy Langhe Chardonnay da Bertü 2007. The Moscato d'Asti is excellent.

● Barbaresco Nervo Fondetta '05	♟♟ 6
● Barbaresco '05	♟♟ 6
● Barbaresco Pajorè '05	♟♟ 6
● Barbaresco Rizzi Boito '05	♟♟ 6
● Barbera d'Alba '06	♟♟ 4*
● Dolcetto d'Alba '07	♟ 4
O Langhe Chardonnay '07	♟ 4
● Barbaresco Boito '04	♟♟ 6
● Barbaresco Nervo Fondetta '04	♟♟ 6
● Barbaresco Pajorè Suran '04	♟♟ 6

● Barbaresco Vign. Brich Ronchi '05	♟♟♟ 7
● Barbaresco Vign. Loreto '05	♟♟ 7
● Barbera d'Alba Gepin '06	♟♟ 5
● Barbaresco '05	♟♟ 6
● Dolcetto d'Alba Vignalunga '07	♟♟ 4*
O Langhe Bianco La Rocca '07	♟♟ 5
O Moscato d'Asti Fiordaliso '07	♟♟ 4*
O Langhe Chardonnay da Bertü '07	♟ 4
● Barbaresco Vign. Brich Ronchi '97	♟♟♟ 7
● Barbaresco Vign. Brich Ronchi '96	♟♟♟ 7
● Barbaresco Vign. Brich Ronchi '93	♟♟♟ 7
● Barbaresco Vign. Brich Ronchi '03	♟♟♟ 7
● Barbaresco Vign. Brich Ronchi '00	♟♟♟ 7
● Barbaresco Vign. Loreto '98	♟♟♟ 7
● Barbaresco Vign. Loreto '95	♟♟♟ 7
● Barbaresco Vign. Brich Ronchi '01	♟♟ 7

★ Bruno Rocca

S.DA RABAJÀ, 60
12050 BARBARESCO [CN]
TEL. 0173635112
www.brunorocca.it

ANNUAL PRODUCTION 60,000 bottles
HECTARES UNDER VINE 15
VITICULTURE METHOD Conventional

Everything is in place here. First, there's Rabajà, considered by experts one of the five great vineyards of Barbaresco and capable of harmonizing opposites like power and elegance. Second, there's Bruno Rocca, one of the most gifted winemakers of his generation, a man who is already considered a veteran. His 20 years' experience, with the youthful input of his children, is the key to understanding the winery's uninterrupted success. The stars of the range are the Barbarescos but the others are all out of the top drawer and just as widely praised. This year sees the release of Barbaresco Maria Adelaide 2004, a selection of the estate's best grapes dedicated to his mother. Its ruby hue introduces clove-like punctuating the oak-derived aromas and fruit. It is extraordinarily rounded on the palate and shows sumptuous density of fruit. Three exemplary Glasses to a wine that made the most of the excellent growing year. The Rabajà 2005 is a lovely modern Barbaresco, rich in spice and sweet sensations from the oak, which combines extractive power with the vineyard's refined tannic weave. The Langhe Rosso and two Barberas are well up to scratch.

Rocche Costamagna

VIA VITTORIO EMANUELE, 8
12064 LA MORRA [CN]
TEL. 0173509225
www.rocchecostamagna.it

ANNUAL PRODUCTION 85,000 bottles
HECTARES UNDER VINE 15
VITICULTURE METHOD Conventional

This estate in the centre of La Morra is run by Alessandro Locatelli and has four guest rooms, as well as a splendid terrace with wonderful views over Barolo and Langhe. The many wines made from the 15 hectares are sourced mainly from the Rocche dell'Annunziata vineyard. This is the origin the crowning glory, or rather Barolo Rocche dell'Annunziata 2004, which has never before been so austere, complete and fragrant as in this editing, combining earthy minerality notes with powerful extract. Three terrific Glasses. The Barolo Rocche dell'Annunziata Bricco Francesco 2004 is equally excellently made, if slightly less lingering, with lovely leather-like notes. The same vineyard provides grapes for both the Barbera d'Alba Superiore Rocche delle Rocche 2006, which we prefer for its soft notes of ripe fruit, and the Annunziata 2006 with its floral overtones. The two Dolcettos are also good. Rùbis 2007 has wonderfully full notes of woodland, damson and cherry, and a well-balanced finish. All the other wines are good, including a Langhe Arneis 2007 with scents of fresh-cut flowers and yellow-fleshed fruit.

● Barbaresco Maria Adelaide '04	▼▼▼ 8
● Barbaresco Rabajà '05	▼▼ 8
● Barbera d'Alba '06	▼▼ 6
● Barbera d'Asti '06	▼▼ 5
● Dolcetto d'Alba V. Trifolè '07	▼▼ 4*
○ Langhe Chardonnay Cadet '07	▼▼ 5
● Langhe Rosso Rabajolo '06	▼▼ 6
● Barbaresco Coparossa '97	♈♈♈ 8
● Barbaresco Coparossa '04	♈♈♈ 8
● Barbaresco Maria Adelaide '01	♈♈♈ 8
● Barbaresco Rabajà '98	♈♈♈ 8
● Barbaresco Rabajà '96	♈♈♈ 8
● Barbaresco Rabajà '93	♈♈♈ 8
● Barbaresco Rabajà '89	♈♈♈ 6
● Barbaresco Rabajà '01	♈♈♈ 8
● Barbaresco Rabajà '00	♈♈♈ 8

● Barolo Rocche dell'Annunziata '04	▼▼▼ 6
● Barolo Bricco Francesco Rocche dell'Annunziata '04	▼▼ 7
● Barbera d'Alba Annunziata '06	▼▼ 4*
● Barbera d'Alba Sup. Rocche delle Rocche '06	▼▼ 5
● Dolcetto d'Alba Murrae '07	▼▼ 4*
● Dolcetto d'Alba Rùbis '07	▼▼ 4*
○ Langhe Arneis '07	▼ 4
● Langhe Nebbiolo Roccardo '07	▼ 4
● Langhe Novis '05	▼ 5
● Barolo Bricco Francesco Rocche dell'Annunziata '03	♈♈ 7
● Barolo Bricco Francesco Rocche dell'Annunziata '01	♈♈ 7
● Barolo Rocche dell'Annunziata '01	♈♈ 7

★ Podere Rocche dei Manzoni

LOC. MANZONI SOPRANI, 3
12065 MONFORTE D'ALBA [CN]
TEL. 017378421
www.rocchedeimanzoni.it

ANNUAL PRODUCTION	250,000 bottles
HECTARES UNDER VINE	40
VITICULTURE METHOD	Conventional

One of the most beautiful wineries in Langhe, set up in the early 1970s by Valentino Migliorini and his wife Jolanda, has had a dreadful year. After Jolanda passed away in March 2007, in December it was Valentino's turn and a few months later their eldest child died. Originally from Caorso near Piacenza, the Migliorinis achieved much in Italy and internationally in just under 30 years, earning their reputation through meticulous work, targeted investments and the smiling figure of Valentino. Today, control has passed to his determined son Rodolfo, who is the spitting image of his father. Rodolfo's philosophy on production involves low environmental impact farming and traditional vinification with some innovation and ageing in small barrels, all with the aim of not wasting the wonderful raw material obtained from all that hard work in the rows. The Rocche dei Manzoni Barolos express their terroir to perfection, especially after a few years' ageing. The Cappella di Santo Stefano is excellent. Vigna d'la Roul and the Big 'd Big, both from 2004, are first-rate. The Bricco Manzoni, made from 80 per cent nebbiolo and the remainder barbera, is terrific.

Flavio Roddolo

FRAZ. BRICCO APPIANI
LOC. SANT'ANNA, 5
12065 MONFORTE D'ALBA [CN]
TEL. 017378535

ANNUAL PRODUCTION	22,500 bottles
HECTARES UNDER VINE	6
VITICULTURE METHOD	Natural

Flavio Roddolo's estate is at Sant'Anna, at the top of Bricco Appiani, on the border between the lower and upper parts of Langhe. The farmhouse-cum-winery has been extended in the last few years to make room for the selections of Barolo which need to age in bottle. The location is at the edge of the Langhe designation, just a few hundred metres from the Barolo DOCG zone. Flavio is a genuine grower-producer, painstaking about his vines and the ageing of his wines, employing environmentally sound practices in the vineyard and watching the phases of the moon for all cellar operations, especially bottling. That was why Flavio decided to postpone release this year of the Barolo and the Bricco Appiani, which is monovarietal Cabernet and was still awaiting bottling at the time of our tastings. We settled for the simpler wines. The Dolcetto d'Alba Superiore – Flavio is one of the few people in Langhe who uses the term – is earthy and well structured. The Nebbiolo, Baroloesque and palate-pervading, falls within the Alba DOC here. The 2004 Barbera Superiore is rustic and savoury with the exemplary acidity characteristic of the vine.

● Barolo V. Big 'd Big '04	⚑⚑ 8
● Barolo V. Cappella di S. Stefano '04	⚑⚑ 8
● Langhe Bricco Manzoni '04	⚑⚑ 8
● Barolo V. d'la Roul '04	⚑⚑ 8
● Langhe Quatr Nas '04	⚑⚑ 8
○ Valentino Brut Ris. Elena '04	⚑⚑ 6
● Barolo V. Big Ris. '89	⚑⚑⚑ 8
● Barolo V. Cappella di S. Stefano '96	⚑⚑⚑ 8
● Barolo V. Cappella di S. Stefano '01	⚑⚑⚑ 8
● Barolo V. d'la Roul Ris. '90	⚑⚑⚑ 8
● Barolo Vigna Big Ris. '90	⚑⚑⚑ 6
● Langhe Rosso Quatr Nas '99	⚑⚑⚑ 8
● Langhe Rosso Quatr Nas '96	⚑⚑⚑ 8
○ Valentino Brut Zero Ris. '98	⚑⚑⚑ 6

● Barbera d'Alba Sup. '04	⚑⚑ 5
● Dolcetto d'Alba '07	⚑⚑ 3*
● Dolcetto d'Alba Sup. '06	⚑⚑ 4*
● Nebbiolo d'Alba '05	⚑⚑ 5
● Barolo Ravera '97	⚑⚑⚑ 6
● Barolo Ravera '01	⚑⚑⚑ 6
● Bricco Appiani '99	⚑⚑⚑ 6
● Barolo Ravera '99	⚑⚑ 6
● Barolo Ravera '03	⚑⚑ 6
● Barolo Ravera '00	⚑⚑ 6
● Langhe Rosso Bricco Appiani '04	⚑⚑ 6
● Langhe Rosso Bricco Appiani '03	⚑⚑ 6

Ronchi

S.DA RONCHI, 23
12050 BARBARESCO [CN]
TEL. 0173635156
az.ronchi@libero.it

ANNUAL PRODUCTION	30,000 bottles
HECTARES UNDER VINE	6
VITICULTURE METHOD	Conventional

The Ronchi farm has recently been converted into a spacious winery. The man behind the wheel is Giancarlo Rocca, ably assisted by his father, Alfonso. The Ronchi vineyard is one of the largest in the municipality. It's a "sorì del mattino", or east and south-east facing slope extending across the whole valley side overlooking the villages of Tetti and Cottà. Moderate altitudes and plenty of sun mean grapes with lots of ripe sugar that make robust, generous wines whose only limitations concern elegance and finesse. None of the wines we tasted managed to repeat the success of last year's Barbaresco Ronchi, although this year's edition is still a classy Barbaresco. The nose gives ripe red fruits, violets and balsam while the palate it progresses with tannins that are still a little edgy. The basic Barbaresco is a worthy second label. Compared with the Ronchi, it lacks concentration and richness of flavour. We preferred the fresh 2007 version of the Dolcetto for its agreeable, well-balanced character to the oak-aged Dolcetto Rosario 2006. The powerful Barbera 2006, generous Chardonnay 2006 and slightly bitter Freisa 2007 are all good.

Giovanni Rosso

LOC. BAUDANA, 6
12050 SERRALUNGA D'ALBA [CN]
TEL. 0173613340
www.giovannirosso.com

ANNUAL PRODUCTION	55,000 bottles
HECTARES UNDER VINE	10
VITICULTURE METHOD	Natural

Everything depends on the vineyard and territory, according to Davide Rosso. His method involves meticulous care for the vines, and respect for their delicate, interdependent relationship with the environment. This means natural techniques at every stage of production to bring about the transformation of the year's best grapes. In the cellar, Davide uses ambient yeasts and ageing in cement and large barrels. He makes a territory-dedicated Barolo from the Ceretta vineyard that shows stiff and tannic, with a complex, muscular flavour. Mint and fruit mingle to give intriguing sensations for a lingering finish. Grapes from the La Serra vineyard, first used in the Barolo Serralunga, go to make the new house Barolo, which differs from its elder brother not in its less austere, more approachable palate. The Barolo Serralunga, a blend of five vines fermented separately and then blended, is not bad at all. Its flavour is genuine Serralunga in the way it reflects the hardness and minerality of its origins. The Barbera Margherita and the Dolcetto are both attractive and we liked the varietal, extremely drinkable Sauvignon with its succulent structure.

● Barbaresco Ronchi '05	▼▼ 6
● Barbaresco '05	▼▼ 6
● Barbera d'Alba Terlé '06	▼▼ 4
● Dolcetto d'Alba '07	▼▼ 5
● Dolcetto d'Alba Rosario '06	▼ 4
○ Langhe Chardonnay '06	▼ 4
● Langhe Freisa '07	▼ 4
● Barbaresco Ronchi '04	▼▼▼ 7
● Barbaresco Ronchi '03	▼▼ 6
● Barbaresco '04	▼▼ 6
● Barbera d'Alba Terlé '05	▼▼ 4

● Barolo Cerretta '04	▼▼ 8
● Barolo La Serra '04	▼▼ 8
● Barbera d'Alba Donna Margherita '06	▼▼ 4*
● Barolo Serralunga '04	▼▼ 6
● Dolcetto d'Alba Le Quattro Vigne '07	▼▼ 4*
○ Langhe Bianco '07	▼▼ 4*
● Barolo Cerretta '01	▼▼ 7
● Barbera d'Alba Donna Margherita '04	▼▼ 4
● Barbera d'Alba Donna Margherita '01	▼▼ 5
● Barolo Cerretta '00	▼▼ 7
● Barolo Serralunga '01	▼▼ 6
● Barolo Serralunga '00	▼▼ 6

Rovellotti

INTERNO CASTELLO, 22
28074 GHEMME [NO]
TEL. 0163841781
www.rovellotti.it

ANNUAL PRODUCTION	60,000 bottles
HECTARES UNDER VINE	15
VITICULTURE METHOD	Conventional

The Rovellotti family is lucky enough to own one of the most beautiful wineries in Italy, set inside the 14th-century walled citadel known as the Ricetto. Such good fortune does present problems in terms of the organization of work. If we have to make a criticism, it is that energy is wasted on too many wines. As a result, even if the overall result is impressive, there are no high notes. Antonello handles nebbiolo and vespolina well, whether vinified separately as monovarietals from the Novara hills or blended together to make Ghemme. The Ghemme Chioso dei Pomi 2003, which has strong steak tartare and sea salt aromatics, remains the cellar's leading wine. Nebbiolo Valplazza 2007 and Vespolina Ronco al Maso 2007 are enjoyable because they are so satisfying and very easy to drink, in fact they are ideal for everyday drinking. Also good is Sciatò Muloeta, a firm, no-nonsense red in which all the estate's non-indigenous grapes, merlot, pinot noir and cabernet sauvignon, mingle in the vespolina. Just behind are the dry white Criccone and the dried-grape Valdenrico, from greco, the local name for erbaluce.

● Colline Novaresi Nebbiolo Valplazza '07		Ÿ 4
● Colline Novaresi Vespolina Ronco al Maso '07		ŸŸ 3*
● Ghemme Chioso dei Pomi '03		ŸŸ 6
● Sciatò Muloeta '04		ŸŸ 5
○ Valdenrico Passito '05		Ÿ 7
○ Colline Novaresi Bianco Il Criccone '07		Ÿ 4
● Colline Novaresi Uva Rara La Paganella '07		3
● Ghemme Ris. '98		♈ 6
● Ghemme Chioso dei Pomi '01		♈ 6
● Ghemme Costa del Salmino Ris. '01	♈ 6	
● Ghemme Ris. '99		♈ 6
● Ghemme Ris. '01		♈ 6

Podere Ruggeri Corsini

LOC. BUSSIA CORSINI, 106
12065 MONFORTE D'ALBA [CN]
TEL. 017378625
www.ruggericorsini.com

ANNUAL PRODUCTION	58,000 bottles
HECTARES UNDER VINE	7
VITICULTURE METHOD	Conventional

Nicola Argamante and Loredana Addari's small winery, founded in 1995, is thriving, with some small young vineyards not yet in production, good exports and high-quality, well-priced wines. The prize this year goes to the Barolo Corsini 2004 for its delightful fragrances of lavender, dark berry fruit and tobacco, fused in an intense bouquet, well-gauged tannins and clean typicity on the palate. The traditional-style ripeness of Barolo San Pietro 2004 earned extra marks for its aristocratically lingering finale. The Langhe Nebbiolo 2006 is excellent, showing slender but with appealing tannins backed by a long, convincing palate. The two vineyards planted in the late 1940s that yield the 2006 Barbera d'Alba Armujan 2006 proved their worth. The wine is full and generous, with intense, lasting character that will offer satisfaction over time. The other wines are all good, well made and expressive. Langhe Bianco 2007 is made from four types of grape and sees only steel, emerging aromatic and pungent. The Dolcetto d'Alba 2007 has luscious, lip-smacking fruit and the Barbera d'Alba 2007 is vigorous, with pleasing freshness.

● Barbera d'Alba Sup. Armujan '06	ŸŸ 5
● Barolo Corsini '04	ŸŸ 6
● Barolo San Pietro '04	ŸŸ 6
● Langhe Nebbiolo '06	ŸŸ 4*
● Barbera d'Alba '07	Ÿ 4
● Dolcetto d'Alba '07	Ÿ 4
○ Langhe Bianco '07	Ÿ 4
● Barolo Corsini '03	♈ 6
● Barolo Corsini '02	♈ 6
● Barolo Corsini '01	♈ 6

Josetta Saffirio

LOC. CASTELLETTO, 32
12065 MONFORTE D'ALBA [CN]
TEL. 017378660
www.josettasaffirio.com

ANNUAL PRODUCTION	16,000 bottles
HECTARES UNDER VINE	5
VITICULTURE METHOD	Conventional

The winery that lived twice. We could take our inspiration from the Hitchcock for the title to our notes from this small estate. At the end of the 1980s, Josetta Saffirio gave us two wonderful versions of Barolo – 1988 and 1989 – that won Three Glasses, but in 1992 she decided to give up winemaking to look after her two children, Alessia and Sara. Then, at the age of 19, Sara decided that her future lay in the vineyard. It didn't take her long to put some new drive into this small but beautiful estate, with help from her oenologist father, Roberto Vezza, and her mother. Since the 2008 harvest, she has had a new fermentation and ageing cellar. The winery's forte is still Barolo, produced in two versions. The Persiera, from a plot in the Castelletto vineyard, releases aromas of raspberry and currant-like red berry fruit but also has nuances of dried flowers, cinchona and liquorice. The basic Barolo is agreeable, and so too is the juicy Barbera d'Alba. There is remarkable tone and texture in the Langhe Rosso Alna Rosso, made from merlot with a little barbera. Finally, the Langhe Nebbiolo is also decent.

Cascina Salicetti

VIA CASCINA SALICETTI, 2
15050 MONTEGIOCO [AL]
TEL. 0131875192

ANNUAL PRODUCTION	25,000 bottles
HECTARES UNDER VINE	16
VITICULTURE METHOD	Conventional

Anselmo Franzosi took over the reins of this winery a few years ago, looking after both the grape growing side and, since he is an oenologist, taking care of the cellar. After the flattering results achieved in the last edition of the Guide, Anselmo gave us another fine set of wines. In the absence of Barbera Punta del Sole, which has been left to rest for another year to give it time to reach a peak of maturity, the steel-aged Morganti Barbera made up for it with fresh fruity fragrances and a delicate vein of balsam. Its structure is not exactly massive but it is an extremely drinkable, pleasant Barbera. The Dolcetto Rugras didn't quite manage Two Glasses. It probably needs a few months in bottle to be at its best. The other two reds, Dolcetto Di Marzi and Bonarda Caminari, are both very drinkable. There were no surprises on the white front, where both the Timorasso Ombra della Luna and the Cortese Montarlino easily picked up Two Glasses. The Timorasso has impressive great minerality, warmth and full aromas of fruit in syrup whereas Montarlino is fresh with an acid vein that sits well in this well-structured wine.

● Barolo Persiera '04	⟡⟡ 8
● Barbera d'Alba '06	⟡⟡ 4*
● Barolo '04	⟡⟡ 6
● Langhe Rosso Alna Rosso '06	⟡⟡ 5
● Langhe Nebbiolo '06	⟡ 5
● Barolo '03	⟡⟡ 6
● Barolo Persiera '03	⟡⟡ 7

● Colli Tortonesi Barbera Morganti '06	⟡⟡ 4*
○ Colli Tortonesi Cortese Montarlino '07	⟡⟡ 4*
○ Colli Tortonesi Timorasso Ombra della Luna '06	⟡⟡ 5
● Colli Tortonesi Dolcetto Di Marzi '06	⟡ 3
● Colli Tortonesi Dolcetto Rugras '06	⟡ 5
● Piemonte Bonarda Caminari '06	⟡ 3
● Colli Tortonesi Rosso Morganti '05	⟡⟡ 4
○ Colli Tortonesi Timorasso Ombra della Luna '05	⟡⟡ 3
● Colli Tortonesi Rosso Punta del Sole '05	⟡ 4

San Fereolo

LOC. SAN FEREOLO
B.TA VALDIBÀ, 59
12063 DOGLIANI [CN]
TEL. 0173742075
www.sanfereolo.com

ANNUAL PRODUCTION	46,000 bottles
HECTARES UNDER VINE	12
VITICULTURE METHOD	Certified biodynamic

The nebbiolo Langhe Rosso Provinciale will be back on Nicoletta Bocca's list in 2009. But the trio of Dolcettos makes up for any other absences. Nicoletta has put together a trio of gems. The fresh-tasting 2007 Valdibà is big on body and approachability The 2006 Dolcetto di Dogliani does full justice to the DOCG in which Nicoletta had and continues to have such faith. An extra year's ageing has made it more supply aromatic, densely fruity, packed with florality and spiciness, and explosive on the palate. But if we're talking about longer ageing for the Dogliani, what can we say about the Dolcetto 1593? It hails from a vintage that looks ancient, but not to Nicoletta. She presented it after five years' ageing. This wine from the hardly glorious 2003 vintage still has vibrant aromatics and great thrust on the palate while the finale gloriously encores the fruit. There's not much room left for the Langhe Austri, which is a pity, because the 2006 is one of the best of all time, showing wonderful harmony at all stages of tasting. The riesling renano Coste di Riavolo is now a taut, pleasantly minerally table wine.

San Romano

B.TA GIACHELLI, 8
12063 DOGLIANI [CN]
TEL. 017376289
www.sanromano.com

ANNUAL PRODUCTION	50,000 bottles
HECTARES UNDER VINE	8
VITICULTURE METHOD	Conventional

This winery's recent admission into the galaxy of Eataly, the new wine and food concept created by Oscar Farinetti whose Turin outlet is its most prestigious showcase, ends a period of renovation that the far-sighted, capable owner, Giulio Napoli, was so keen to set in motion. Company matters only interest us so far, or rather, they are important to understand a winery's strategic future but only in relation to what counts most: the quality of the wine. The Bricco delle Lepri 2007 opens with very lively, captivating hints of cinchona and rhubarb. After moving through more earthy aromas, the nose then discloses more spice and dried flowers. On the palate it is soft at first before expanding swiftly and developing a serious tannic weave, though this is always held well in check. The finish is lingering and harmonious. Vigna del Pilone, a great Dolcetto di Dogliani, is even better. Dark in appearance, it tempts the nose with scents of sweet spices, tobacco and gunflint. Powerful on the front palate, it fills the mouth without compromising on finesse or elegance until the finish triumphantly reprises the fruit on the nose.

● Dogliani '06	♈♈ 4*
● Langhe Rosso Austri '06	♈♈ 5
○ Coste di Riavolo '06	♈♈ 4
● Dolcetto di Dogliani Sup. 1593 '03	♈♈ 5
● Dolcetto di Dogliani Valdibà '07	♈♈ 4
● Dolcetto di Dogliani S. Fereolo '99	♈♈♈ 4
● Dolcetto di Dogliani S. Fereolo '97	♈♈♈ 4
● Langhe Rosso Austri '03	♈♈♈ 5
● Langhe Rosso Brumaio '97	♈♈♈ 5
● Dogliani '05	♈♈ 4
● Langhe Rosso Austri '05	♈♈ 5
● Langhe Rosso Austri '04	♈♈ 5

● Dolcetto di Dogliani V. del Pilone '07	♈♈ 4*
● Dolcetto di Dogliani Bricco delle Lepri '07	♈♈ 3*
● Dolcetto di Dogliani V. del Pilone '99	♈♈♈ 4
● Dolcetto di Dogliani V. del Pilone '98	♈♈♈ 4
● Dolcetto di Dogliani V. del Pilone '97	♈♈♈ 4
● Dolcetto di Dogliani Sup. Dolianum '01	♈♈ 5
● Dolcetto di Dogliani Sup. Dolianum '00	♈♈ 5
● Dolcetto di Dogliani V. del Pilone '04	♈♈ 4

Tenuta San Sebastiano

CASCINA SAN SEBASTIANO, 41
15040 LU [AL]
TEL. 0131741353
www.dealessi.it

ANNUAL PRODUCTION	80,000 bottles
HECTARES UNDER VINE	10
VITICULTURE METHOD	Conventional

The San Sebastiano winery is surrounded by beautifully tended rows. Owner Roberto De Alessi respects tradition, seeking to minimize environmental impact. He cultivates the traditional varieties of the area, especially barbera and grignolino. The small but functional cellar is a gem, with all the right technology for winemaking and an equally small but lovely maturation area Roberto uses for ageing the most flagship wines. Normally, Barbera Mepari leads the field. The 2006 edition was still ageing at the time of our tastings and in its absence, the two Monferrato Rossos made up the difference. The Sol-Do is a very varietal pinot nero on the nose and palate. Its initial impact on the nose is laced with spiciness and the terrific structure in the mouth is impressive. The merlot and cabernet sauvignon Monferrato Dalera is every bit as good, showing very rounded and soft. Three wines that are very well styled for their categories remain. As usual, the Grignolino is one of the best in the denomination while LV, a dried-grape Moscato, gives fine display of the variety's aromatics. The current Barbera is pleasant and focuses on freshness.

★ Luciano Sandrone

VIA PUGNANE, 4
12060 BAROLO [CN]
TEL. 0173560023
www.sandroneluciano.com

ANNUAL PRODUCTION	100,000 bottles
HECTARES UNDER VINE	26
VITICULTURE METHOD	Conventional

Every year and every bottle tells the story of a dream come true: the young cellarman who became one of Barolo's emblematic figures. Luciano remains convinced that excellence is born in the vineyard. Painstaking care in the rows, meticulous selection in the cellar and vinification that enhances what nature has provided: all this is sums up how he works. It's easy enough to describe but harder to do. The Barolo Cannubi Boschis has proved its worth again this year, presenting generous, stylish and layered on the nose before opening nicely tannic on the palate and expanding with style through to a long, complex finish. This great Barolo which brings out the best in its vineyard of origin and wins an elegant Three Glasses. Barolo Le Vigne is sourced from vineyards at Barolo, Monforte and Novello. Traditionally, it has less complexity than its stablemate but shows good overall balance. The Nebbiolo Valmaggiore is excellent, as always, and elegantly appealing drinking. The juicy, varietally acidic Barbera is also successful and last but not least, there is a very well-made Dolcetto.

● Grignolino del M.to Casalese '07	♟♟	3*
● M.to Rosso Sol-Do '06	♟♟	4
● M.to Rosso Dalera '04	♟♟	4
● Barbera del M.to '07	♟	3
○ LV Passito '06	♟	4
● Barbera del M.to Mepari '04	♟♟	4
● Barbera del M.to Mepari '03	♟♟	4
● Barbera del M.to Sup. Mepari '05	♟♟	4
● M.to Rosso Sol-Do '05	♟♟	4
● Barbera del M.to Mepari '01	♟♟	4
○ LV Passito '05	♟♟	4
● M.to Rosso Dalera '03	♟♟	6
● M.to Rosso Dalera '01	♟♟	6

● Barolo Cannubi Boschis '04	♟♟♟	8
● Barolo Le Vigne '04	♟♟	8
● Barbera d'Alba '06	♟♟	5
● Dolcetto d'Alba '07	♟♟	4
● Nebbiolo d'Alba Valmaggiore '06	♟♟	6
● Barolo Cannubi Boschis '90	♟♟♟	8
● Barolo Cannubi Boschis '89	♟♟♟	8
● Barolo Cannubi Boschis '87	♟♟♟	8
● Barolo Cannubi Boschis '86	♟♟♟	8
● Barolo Cannubi Boschis '01	♟♟♟	8
● Barolo Cannubi Boschis '00	♟♟♟	8
● Barolo Le Vigne '99	♟♟♟	8
● Barolo Le Vigne '00	♟♟	8

Cantine Sant'Agata

REG. MEZZENA, 19
14030 SCURZOLENGO [AT]
TEL. 0141203186
www.santagata.com

ANNUAL PRODUCTION	150,000 bottles
HECTARES UNDER VINE	11
VITICULTURE METHOD	Conventional

The Cavallero siblings are increasingly well-known as ruché growers. This aromatic grape hails from the municipality of Castagnole Monferrato but is very much at home in Scurzolengo, where the chalky soil gives if distinctive character. Four versions are produced, of which we tasted three this year. Il Cavaliere is an easy drinker with extract and pepper-like spice. The 9.99, released with a glass stopper, gives candied peel and is softer. Going up a notch, 'Na Vota – 30,000 bottles in 2007 – is dark, dense and flowery with hints of dried roses and spices, then soft, warm and juicy in the mouth. A wine in a class of its own. Ruché Pro Nobis 2007, the estate's flag-bearer, will be released with a year's delay to mature further. We loved the two Barbera Superiores. Altea 2006 is more traditional, earthy, fruity and elegant while Cavalé is softer, potent and generous, presenting savoury with a liquorice and vanilla-themed finish. Monterovere 2006 is still rather closed, Barbera Baby 2007 is good and Grignolino Miravalle 2007 is again seriously good, hinting at roses and peach stone.

Paolo Saracco

VIA CIRCONVALLAZIONE, 6
12053 CASTIGLIONE TINELLA [CN]
TEL. 0141855113
info@paolosaracco.it

ANNUAL PRODUCTION	380,000 bottles
HECTARES UNDER VINE	35
VITICULTURE METHOD	Conventional

Paolo Saracco is a true believer in the moscato grape. He has been campaigning for some time to raise the profile of its limited production within the Asti wine consortium, which has historically been dominated by big wineries. To this end, with about 70 other producers, Paolo has created the Muscatellum association. The range of characterful wines he presented is an excellent illustration of what his vineyards can offer. Moscato d'Autunno is a strong performer, with complex, rich aromas nuanced with sage, tomato leaves, camomile and citrus. Succulent on the palate, it is naturally sweet but braced and enriched by satisfyingly refreshing acidity. It misses out on a top prize by the merest whisker. The basic Moscato is a little lighter on the palate but still deliciously enjoyable and appealing. The Chardonnay Prasuè is excellent. The nose opens up after it has been in the glass for a few minutes. Polished sensations emerge enhanced by elegant, complex aromas of peach, spring flowers and grapefruit. The Pinot Nero is well executed. The Riesling 2007 was not ready at the time of going to press so we'll be tasting it next year.

● Barbera d'Asti Sup. Altea '06	♟♟	4*
● Barbera d'Asti Sup. Cavalé '06	♟♟	5
● Grignolino d'Asti Miravalle '07	♟♟	4*
● M.to Rosso Monterovere '06	♟♟	5
● Ruché di Castagnole M.to 'Na Vota '07	♟♟	4*
● Barbera d'Asti Baby '07	♟	3
● Ruché di Castagnole M.to 9.99 '07	♟	4
● Ruché di Castagnole M.to Il Cavaliere '07	♟	4
● Ruché di Castagnole M.to Pro Nobis '06	♟♟	5
● Barbera d'Asti Sup. Altea '05	♟♟	4
● Barbera d'Asti Sup. Cavalé '05	♟♟	5
● Ruché di Castagnole M.to 'Na Vota '06	♟♟	4

○ Piemonte Moscato d'Autunno '07	♟♟	4*
○ Langhe Chardonnay Prasuè '07	♟♟	4
● M.to Rosso Pinot Nero '05	♟♟	5
○ Moscato d'Asti '07	♟♟	4
○ Piemonte Moscato d'Autunno '06	♟♟	4
○ Piemonte Moscato d'Autunno '05	♟♟	4
○ Piemonte Moscato d'Autunno '04	♟♟	4
● M.to Rosso Pinot Nero '04	♟♟	5

Roberto Sarotto

VIA RONCONUOVO, 13
12050 NEVIGLIE [CN]
TEL. 0173630228
www.robertosarotto.com

ANNUAL PRODUCTION	150,000 bottles
HECTARES UNDER VINE	50
VITICULTURE METHOD	Conventional

Neviglie mayor Roberto Sarotto presented a range from grapes from four different properties scattered across southern Piedmont. The style is very precise, especially in the simpler wines, and not as rich in character as we might have hoped. This year, the wine that we liked best was Barolo Bricco Bergera 2004, from vineyards at Novello and Barolo, which tempts the nostrils with raspberry and blueberry-like red fruit sensations, as well as cinchona, dried flowers and saddle leather. Energy and drive on the palate are backed up by tannins that never intrude. The Barbaresco Gaia Principe is also very classy, succeeding in making the most of a good but less than excellent year. On the nose there are perceptible aromas of autumn leaves, dried roses, sweet tobacco and blueberries before a sound entry takes you through to a lingering finish. The cabernet sauvignon and nebbiolo Langhe Rosso Enrico I is up to expectations with good body and an international style. Gavi di Gavi Bric Sassi 2007 is zesty and fruity while Moscato d'Asti Sorì Ciabot 2007 is wonderfully smooth and fragrant. The rest of the range is appealing and stylistically flawless.

Scagliola

VIA SAN SIRO, 42
14052 CALOSSO [AT]
TEL. 0141853183
scagliola@libero.it

ANNUAL PRODUCTION	135,000 bottles
HECTARES UNDER VINE	23
VITICULTURE METHOD	Conventional

Barbera and Moscato have long been associated with this estate, which has stayed a genuine farming operation. Work here goes on to the rhythms of the seasons and the moon. Calosso is turning out to be a wonderful barbera vineyard, on a par with other subzones nearby. And it is from this classic Asti grape that the Scagliolas get their best results. This year, Barbera Selezione SanSì 2005 is an almost impenetrable ruby red wine, with aromas of spice, ripe berry fruit, cocoa and oak. The palate is compact, with nice oak, pulp and good acidity. SanSì 2006 is almost as good, showing spice and berry fruit. The powerful palate is sound and savoury. The Barbera Frem 2007 is also very pleasant, foregrounding fruit and approachability. Moscato d'Asti Volo di Farfalle convinces again with citrus and a refreshingly stylish palate, despite overall sweetness. We thought the better of the internationals was the fresh Chardonnay Casot dan Vian 2007, in preference to the ethery nebbiolo, barbera and cabernet sauvignon 2006 Azörd.

● Barbaresco Gaia Principe '05	❡❡	6
● Barolo Bricco Bergera '04	❡❡	6
○ Gavi del Comune di Gavi Bric Sassi '07	❡❡	4*
○ Langhe Chardonnay Briccomoro '07	❡❡	4*
● Langhe Rosso Enrico I '04	❡❡	5
● Barbera d'Alba Briccomacchia '06	❡	4
● Barbera d'Alba Elena '06	❡	4
● Barolo Audace '04	❡	6
○ Gavi del Comune di Gavi L'Aurora '07	❡	4
○ Langhe Arneis Runcneuv '07	❡	4
○ Moscato d'Asti Sorì Ciabot '07	❡	4
● Piemonte Brachetto '07	❡	4
● Barolo Audace '00	❡❡	6
● Barolo Audace Ris. '01	❡❡	7
● Barolo Bricco Bergera '00	❡❡	6

● Barbera d'Asti Sup. SanSì '06	❡❡	7
● Barbera d'Asti Sup. SanSì Sel. '05	❡❡	8
● Barbera d'Asti Frem '07	❡❡	5
○ Moscato d'Asti Volo di Farfalle '07	❡❡	4*
○ Piemonte Chardonnay Casot dan Vian '07	❡❡	4*
● M.to Dolcetto Busiord '07	❡	4
● M.to Rosso Azörd '06	❡	6
● Barbera d'Asti Sup. SanSì Sel. '99	❡❡❡	7
● Barbera d'Asti Sup. SanSì Sel. '01	❡❡❡	7
● Barbera d'Asti Sup. SanSì Sel. '00	❡❡❡	7
● Barbera d'Asti Sup. SanSì '05	❡❡	5

Giorgio Scarzello e Figli

VIA ALBA, 29
12060 BAROLO [CN]
TEL. 017356170
www.barolodibarolo.com

ANNUAL PRODUCTION	25,000 bottles
HECTARES UNDER VINE	5.5
VITICULTURE METHOD	Conventional

The Scarzello family's Barolo estate may be small in size, but it's big in substance. Federico plays an increasingly important role in the management of the winery, assisted by the rest of the family. It's always a pleasure to discuss wine and other matters with this enthusiastic, inquisitive and competent wine man. The estate's plots are situated in the fine Sarmassa, Terlo and Paiagallo vineyards. This year's list is as good as ever, commencing with the captivating Barolo '04, which is supple, balanced easy drinker with excellent continuity and good length. Vigna Merenda '04, from a plot in Sarmassa, is a superior wine that shows classic and austere with a very floral nose and a dense palate with fine-grained tannins that are more elegant than powerful. It's a highly alluring traditional Barolo, which opens leisurely before revealing its full splendour. Nebbiolo '06 is warm, soft and fruity, while the characterful Barbera Superiore '05 is rather closed and edgy, suggesting that further bottle ageing is required to express its full potential. Dolcetto '06 is rich, soft and fresh.

★ Paolo Scavino

FRAZ. GARBELLETTO
VIA ALBA-BAROLO, 59
12060 CASTIGLIONE FALLETTO [CN]
TEL. 017362850
e.scavino@libero.it

ANNUAL PRODUCTION	100,000 bottles
HECTARES UNDER VINE	20
VITICULTURE METHOD	Conventional

Enrico Scavino is one of the greatest virtuosos of the nebbiolo grape. Some of the finest Barolos that we've ever tasted were from his lovely winery in Castiglione Falletto. For several years now, Enrico has been aided by his two daughters Enrica and Elisa, as well as his wife Anna Maria. This year, we had the good fortune to taste an impressive array of the estate's wines, which missed our Three Glass award by a hair. Bric dël Fiasc '04, aged for 12 months in small oak casks and for a further 12 months in barrels, has a nose of berry fruit laced with vanilla and coffee spice. The excellent Cannubi '04 is elegant, balanced and very juicy. Barolo Bricco Ambrogio '04, from a vineyard in the less well-known municipality of Roddi, throws a very intense nose and the long back palate signs off with a lingering finish. Barolo Carobric 2004 is a blend of three of the estate's great crus – Rocche di Castiglione, Cannubi and Fiasco – and proffers ethery notes and attractive hints of cinchona. The basic Barolo is also pleasant, as is Langhe Sorriso '06, a well-made aromatic white from viognier grapes.

● Barolo V. Merenda '04	♟♟	7
● Barbera d'Alba Sup. '05	♟♟	5
● Barolo '04	♟♟	6
● Dolcetto d'Alba '06	♟♟	4*
● Langhe Nebbiolo '06	♟♟	4*
● Barolo V. Merenda '99	♟♟♟	6
● Barolo V. Merenda '01	♟♟	7
● Barolo V. Merenda '98	♟♟	6
● Barolo '99	♟♟	6
● Barolo '97	♟♟	6
● Barolo '96	♟♟	6
● Barolo '01	♟♟	6

● Barolo Bric dël Fiasc '04	♟♟	8
● Barolo Cannubi '04	♟♟	8
● Barolo '04	♟♟	8
● Barolo Bricco Ambrogio '04	♟♟	8
● Barolo Carobric '04	♟♟	8
○ Langhe Sorriso '06	♟♟	6
● Barolo Bric dël Fiasc '96	♟♟♟	8
● Barolo Bric dël Fiasc '95	♟♟♟	8
● Barolo Bric del Fiasc '89	♟♟♟	8
● Barolo Bric del Fiasc '85	♟♟♟	6
● Barolo Rocche dell'Annunziata Ris. '97	♟♟♟	8
● Barolo Rocche dell'Annunziata Ris. '96	♟♟♟	8
● Barolo Rocche dell'Annunziata Ris. '01	♟♟♟	8

Schiavenza

VIA MAZZINI, 4A
12050 SERRALUNGA D'ALBA [CN]
TEL. 0173613115
www.schiavenza.com

ANNUAL PRODUCTION	30,000 bottles
HECTARES UNDER VINE	8
VITICULTURE METHOD	Conventional

This year, the Serralunga-based Schiavenza estate did tremendously well, winning Three Glasses for the first time with the big-hitting Barolo Broglio '04. Behind this excellent result are Luciano Pira and Walter Anselma, a pair of retiring grower producers, a world apart from the Langhe jet set. Their family has also long owned a charming restaurant that serves traditional Piedmont fare. The menu reflects the region and the wines bespeak a terroir with great potential. Cellar processes are kept to a minimum, with long maceration and ageing in large barrels only. The result is a range of characterful Barolos that clearly reflect their vineyards of provenance. Our Three Glass winner with its elegance and wonderfully intense bouquet comes from a less celebrated subzone. The Broglio vineyard is situated immediately below the estate's cellar, with an ideal south-eastern aspect. But the other two selections also performed very well. Ceretta is powerful and intense while Prapò shows juicy and complex. This year, the Perno was not released because the grapes were damaged by hail. The well-typed Barbera Perno took Two Glasses and the Dolcetto is pleasant.

Sciorio

VIA ASTI-NIZZA, 87
14055 COSTIGLIOLE D'ASTI [AT]
TEL. 0141966610

ANNUAL PRODUCTION	18,000 bottles
HECTARES UNDER VINE	8
VITICULTURE METHOD	Conventional

The estate owned by the Gozzelino brothers has a short but excellent list with two Barberas, a cabernet-based Monferrato Rosso and a sauvignon-based Monferrato Bianco. Barbera, of course, is the star for Costigliole is its acknowledged home. Local growers often affectionately refer to the grape as the "lady in red". The two Monferratos reflect a legitimate, but cautious, move to open up to the outside world. The DOC production protocol is fairly loose and producers can take a few liberties using international varieties, sometimes with pleasing results. But now let's set theory aside and take a look at the results of this year's tastings. Barbera Vigna Beneficio '04 is on top form. Its deep ruby accompanies a nose that has coped well with long ageing in oak and a dense, full-bodied palate that is potent but not overpowering and finishes in style. Scorio, another '04, is almost as good as its stablemate, showing similarly fragrant but less balanced overall. Monferrato Rosso, from cabernet, displays varietal vegetal and spicy notes while the sauvignon Monferrato Bianco S is well typed and refreshing, with mineral aromas.

● Barolo Broglio '04	♈♈♈	7
● Barolo Prapò '04	♈♈	6*
● Barbera d'Alba Perno '05	♈♈	4*
● Barolo '04	♈♈	6
● Barolo Bricco Cerretta '04	♈♈	6
● Dolcetto d'Alba Vughera '07	♈	4
● Barolo Bricco Cerretta '03	♉♉	6
● Barolo Broglio Ris. '01	♉♉	6
● Barolo Perno '03	♉♉	6

● Barbera d'Asti Sup. V. Beneficio '04	♈♈	5
● Barbera d'Asti Sup. Sciorio '04	♈♈	4*
○ M.to Bianco S '07	♈	3
● M.to Rosso Antico Vitigno '03	♈	5
● Barbera d'Asti Sup. Sciorio '01	♉♉	4
● Barbera d'Asti Sup. Vigna Beneficio '03	♉♉	5
● Barbera d'Asti Sup. Sciorio '03	♉♉	4
● Barbera d'Asti Sup. Sciorio '00	♉♉	4
● Barbera d'Asti Sup. V. Beneficio '01	♉♉	5
● M.to Rosso Antico Vitigno '01	♉♉	5

Franco e Mario Scrimaglio

S.DA ALESSANDRIA, 67
14049 NIZZA MONFERRATO [AT]
TEL. 0141721385
www.scrimaglio.it

ANNUAL PRODUCTION	700,000 bottles
HECTARES UNDER VINE	18
VITICULTURE METHOD	Certified biodynamic

This leading estate, headed by the enterprising brothers Giorgio and Francesco Scrimaglio, is located in the village of Scrimaglio just outside Nizza Monferrato. There's an extensive, nicely diversified list covering many Piedmont designations, with prices for all pockets. In recent years, Scrimaglio has also achieved great success with its labels dedicated to great "Made in Italy" brands, including Fiat and Alfa Romeo. Its flagship wines are still territory focused, however, with particular emphasis on Barbera d'Asti. This year's tasters were very pleased with the labels presented, commencing with the excellent Barbera d'Asti Superiore Crôutin '06, which is exceptionally elegant and powerful, perfectly reflecting its grape variety. The highly enjoyable, full-bodied Nizza Acsé '05 is almost as good. While simpler, Rocca Nivo and Sant'Ippolito '06, are also delicious. Monferrato Rosso Tantra '06, from cabernet sauvignon and barbera, performed well, as did the two No Cork '07 selections, a Barbera and a Sauvignon.

Mauro Sebaste

FRAZ. GALLO
VIA GARIBALDI, 222BIS
12051 ALBA [CN]
TEL. 0173262148
www.maurosebaste.it

ANNUAL PRODUCTION	150,000 bottles
HECTARES UNDER VINE	25
VITICULTURE METHOD	Conventional

Mauro Sebaste founded this operation in 1991 after leaving the family estate run until 1985 by his mother Sylla, one of the first women producers in Langhe. Mauro set up at Gallo d'Alba, near his father-in-law's winery. Most of the grapes that he uses come from trusted growers, who are assisted by agronomist Domenico Franco. This ensures uniform harvest for Domenico insists on extensive crop thinning not only for the most important wines but also for the whites and the Moscato. The most important new wine this year is the white Langhe Centobricchi '07, a monovarietal Sauvignon vinified for the first time exclusively in steel, making it fresher and truer to type. Another new development is the winery's decision to stop producing Freisa, at least for the moment, because of low market demand. The three '04 Barolos performed very well. Monvigliero is exceptionally elegant on the palate, with particularly soft tannins while Brunate vaunts a balsamic, floral nose and prominent but well-integrated tannins. Prapò is on similar lines, although slightly longer and more balsamic than the other two, and with more assertive tannins.

● Barbera d'Asti Sup. Crôutin '06		♟♟ 6
● Barbera d'Asti Sup. Nizza Acsé '05		♟♟ 6
● Barbera d'Asti Sup. Bricco S. Ippolito '06		♟♟ 5
● Barbera d'Asti Sup. Vign. Rocca Nivo '06		♟♟ 4*
● M.to Rosso Tantra '06		♟♟ 6
● Barbera d'Asti No Cork '07		♟ 4
● Barbera d'Asti Nowood '07		♟ 4
○ M.to Bianco No Cork '07		♟ 3
● Barbera d'Asti Sup. Nizza Acsé '04		♟♟ 6
● Barbera d'Asti Sup. Nizza Acsé '01		♟♟ 6
● Barbera d'Asti Sup. Crôutin '04		♟♟ 6

● Barolo Monvigliero '04		♟♟ 7
● Barolo Prapò '04		♟♟ 8
● Barolo Brunate '04		♟♟ 8
○ Langhe Bianco Centobricchi '07		♟♟ 4*
● Langhe Rosso Centobricchi '06		♟♟ 6
● Nebbiolo d'Alba Parigi '06		♟♟ 5
● Barbera d'Alba S. Rosalia '07		♟ 4
● Dolcetto d'Alba S. Rosalia '07		♟ 4
○ Moscato d'Asti '07		♟ 4
○ Roero Arneis '07		♟ 4
● Barolo Brunate '03		♟♟ 7
● Barolo Brunate '01		♟♟ 7
● Barolo Monvigliero '03		♟♟ 7
● Barolo Monvigliero '01		♟♟ 7
● Barolo Prapò '03		♟♟ 7
● Barolo Prapò '01		♟♟ 7

F.lli Seghesio

LOC. CASTELLETTO, 19
12065 MONFORTE D'ALBA [CN]
TEL. 017378108
az.agricolaseghesio@libero.it

ANNUAL PRODUCTION	60,000 bottles
HECTARES UNDER VINE	10
VITICULTURE METHOD	Conventional

Aldo and Riccardo Seghesio's winery dominates the eastern slope of Monforte, where the splendid La Villa vineyard is situated. The south-facing portion is the ideal site for nebbiolo while the other side is planted to barbera and dolcetto. Aldo and Riccardo focus on terroir, grape variety and ripening times in order to interpret the vintage to best effect, ensuring quality and typicity. They certainly achieved the feat with Barolo La Villa '04, which is simply spectacular. It flaunts powerful, ripe tannins elegantly offset by the complex body. Barrique and barrel ageing lend it roundness and hints of spice, and the long finish unveils notes of autumn leaves. It is an exemplary wine, which deservedly won Three Glasses. But the basic labels are also good and include a Barbera '07 with big fruit and a refreshing, juicy alcoholic palate; a livelier, very easy-drinking Dolcetto; and an austere current Langhe Nebbiolo. The estate's other important wines, which we tasted soon after bottling, are Barbera Vigneto della Chiesa '06 and Langhe Rosso Bouquet '06, both of which are outstanding and destined to get even better.

● Barolo Vign. La Villa '04	∅∅∅ 7
● Barbera d'Alba Vign. della Chiesa '06	∅∅ 5
● Barbera d'Alba '07	∅∅ 4*
● Dolcetto d'Alba Vign. della Chiesa '07	∅∅ 4*
● Langhe Rosso Bouquet '06	∅∅ 6
● Langhe Nebbiolo '07	∅ 4
● Barbera d'Alba Vign. della Chiesa '97	∅∅∅ 6
● Barbera d'Alba Vign. della Chiesa '00	∅∅∅ 6
● Barolo Vign. La Villa '99	∅∅∅ 7
● Barolo Vign. La Villa '91	∅∅∅ 7
● Barolo Vign. La Villa '01	∅∅ 7
● Barolo Vign. La Villa '00	∅∅ 7
● Langhe Rosso Bouquet '05	∅∅ 6

Sella

VIA IV NOVEMBRE
13060 LESSONA [BI]
TEL. 01599455
aziendeagricolesella@virgilio.it

ANNUAL PRODUCTION	80,000 bottles
HECTARES UNDER VINE	20
VITICULTURE METHOD	Conventional

Sella has been an important name for Italian history and a benchmark in the country's wine production since 1671. Today, Gioacchino Sella and his competent young team are busy implementing new projects. The most recent of these is Coste della Sesia Casteltorto, which strays from the estate's usual classic style with a wine of exceptional fruit integrity and fullness, achieved by using a higher proportion of croatina – up to 35 per cent – shorter maceration times, greater use of the fine lees and ageing reduced to 12 months, exclusively in tonneaux and barriques. In the absence of Lessona Omaggio a Quintino Sella, Lessona San Sebastiano allo Zoppo '04 steals the limelight. This red from nebbiolo with a tiny amount of vespolina shows great depth on a nose dominated by notes of spice and minerals, and a supremely elegant palate with caressing tannins. Bramaterra I Porfidi '04 is only a step behind the '03 but, for the moment, is overshadowed by the Three Glass-winning Lessona San Sebastiano. "Enduring classic quality" sums up the basic Bramaterra and Lessona. Vignaluce has been replaced by La Doranda, from erbaluce two days on the skins.

● Lessona S. Sebastiano allo Zoppo '04	∅∅∅ 6
● Bramaterra I Porfidi '04	∅∅ 6
● Coste della Sesia Rosso Casteltorto '06	∅∅ 5
● Bramaterra '05	∅∅ 5
● Coste della Sesia Rosso Orbello '07	∅∅ 4*
● Lessona '05	∅∅ 5
○ Coste della Sesia Bianco La Doranda '07	∅ 4
⊙ Coste della Sesia Rosato Majoli '07	∅ 4
● Bramaterra I Porfidi '03	∅∅∅ 6
● Lessona S. Sebastiano allo Zoppo '01	∅∅∅ 6
● Lessona S. Sebastiano allo Zoppo '00	∅∅ 6

Enrico Serafino

c.so Asti, 5
12043 Canale [CN]
tel. 0173979485
www.enricoserafino.it

ANNUAL PRODUCTION	450,000 bottles
HECTARES UNDER VINE	13
VITICULTURE METHOD	Conventional

It always takes time for businesses to settle down after any kind of major upheaval. This is also true for the Enrico Serafino estate, which has experienced a thorough shake-up and a drastic change of direction over the past few years. This year's tastings allow us to confirm that the transition is now complete. The characterful wines are released under two clearly distinguished labels, a classic line and the Cantina Maestra range of Roero products. The entire estate, from the cellar management to the public relations office, having worked hard and well is now reaping the rewards. The Serafino name has recovered its prestige both locally and further afield: the splendours of the past have returned. But let's take a look at the wines. Barbera Parduné and Roero Pasiunà have never been this good. The first is acidic, fruity and earthy while Pasiunà is austere, muscular and elegant. Alta Langa is much improved. The wager has been won and it offers a clear vision of what this particular terroir can offer: fragrance, freshness, softness and silky smoothness. The two Arneis wines are among the best in their class and the rest of the list is very good.

Poderi Sinaglio

fraz. Ricca
via Sinaglio, 5
12055 Diano d'Alba [CN]
tel. 0173612209
www.poderisinaglio.it

ANNUAL PRODUCTION	44,000 bottles
HECTARES UNDER VINE	13
VITICULTURE METHOD	Conventional

Brothers Bruno and Silvano Accomo run their estate with dedicated skill, releasing wines with a well-defined, recognizable style. The list focuses on dolcetto but also features other classic Piedmont grape varieties, such as barbera, nebbiolo and moscato, in both standard-cork and dried-grape versions. We'll start with the Diano d'Albas, which merit particular attention. Bric Maiolica has high ambitions and expresses them in a nose of berries and bitter almonds. On the palate, it's very full and heady, with an elegant, complex finish. Its little brother, Dolcetto di Diano d'Alba, is simpler but by no means banal. A fine everyday wine, it presents fresh, easy drinking, complex and highly enjoyable. We were also impressed by Barbera Vigna Erta, aged in small oak casks for 12 months, which boasts hints of cocoa powder, cherries and coffee. Moscato d'Asti La Mimosa is tasty with attractive acidity while Langhe Rosso Sinaij, from barbera, nebbiolo, and freisa, is nicely complex. Boccabarile, a sauvignon and chardonnay blend, is still rather marked by oak, Piemonte Moscato Passito Le Monache is very sweet, and Nebbiolo d'Alba Giachét '06 is well made.

● Barbera d'Alba Sup. Parduné Cantina Maestra '05	♥♥ 5
● Roero Pasiunà Cantina Maestra '05	♥♥ 5
● Barbera d'Alba Bacajè Cantina Maestra '07	♥♥ 4*
● Roero '05	♥♥ 4*
○ Alta Langa M. Cl. '04	♥♥ 5
○ Roero Arneis '07	♥♥ 4*
○ Roero Arneis Canteiò Cantina Maestra '07	♥♥ 4*
○ Moscato d'Asti '07	♥ 4
● Barbera d'Alba Sup. Parduné '04	♀♀ 4
● Barbera d'Alba Sup. Parduné '03	♀♀ 4
● Roero Sup. Pasiunà '04	♀♀ 4
● Roero Sup. Pasiunà '01	♀♀ 4

● Barbera d'Alba V. Erta '06	♥♥ 4*
● Diano d'Alba Sörì Bric Maiolica '07	♥♥ 4*
● Dolcetto di Diano d'Alba '07	♥♥ 3*
● Langhe Rosso Sinaij '05	♥♥ 5
○ Piemonte Moscato Passito Le Monache '06	♥♥ 5
○ Langhe Bianco Boccabarile '06	♥ 4
● Nebbiolo d'Alba Giachét '06	♥ 5
○ Moscato d'Asti La Mimosa '07	♥ 4
● Barbera d'Alba V. Erta '05	♀♀ 4
● Barbera d'Alba V. Erta '04	♀♀ 4
● Diano d'Alba Sörì Bric Maiolica '06	♀♀ 4
● Diano d'Alba Sorì Bric Maiolica '05	♀♀ 4

Sottimano

FRAZ. COTTÀ, 21
12052 NEIVE [CN]
TEL. 0173635186
www.sottimano.it

ANNUAL PRODUCTION	65,000 bottles
HECTARES UNDER VINE	15
VITICULTURE METHOD	Conventional

This year the well-located estate owned by the Sottimano family since 1975 presented such a wide range of Barbarescos we had difficulty choosing a favourite. The vineyards used for selections have an average age of 35 to 55 years and the wine is fermented in steel before ageing for 20 to 22 months in part-new barrels. Barbaresco Currà '05 is chewy with great structure and notes of violet and wild berries while Barbaresco Fausoni '05 focuses more on elegance and minerality, proffering evolved, spicy aromas and a long, caressing finish. Barbaresco Pajoré '05 has soft, elegant notes on nose and palate, which are echoed in the finale. Barbaresco Cottà shows full and dense in the mouth, with impressive length and a well-orchestrated finish worthy of a great wine. It is our favourite Barbaresco, winning Three Glasses for its excellent complexity. We also liked Barbera d'Alba Pairolero '06, which aged for 16 months in 20 per cent new barrels. The same maturation process was also used for Langhe Nebbiolo '06 from young vineyards. Maté '07, a dry Brachetto, is as good as ever and Dolcetto d'Alba Bric del Salto '07 is equally impressive.

Luigi Spertino

VIA LEA, 505
14047 MOMBERCELLI [AT]
TEL. 0141959098
www.luigispertino.it

ANNUAL PRODUCTION	40,000 bottles
HECTARES UNDER VINE	6
VITICULTURE METHOD	Conventional

We have run out of words to describe Luigi Spertino's enthusiasm after more than half a century. When and his son Mauro take journalists round the cellar to taste the new wines, he stands to one side, listening out for every positive remark. Then his eyes light up. Luigi's greatest achievement has been to convey the same enthusiasm for good wine and hard work to his son. However, there is an important difference between the two men. Luigi has long been a champion of Grignolino d'Asti while Spertino Jr is a diehard defender of Barbera. And it was the estate's new Barbera, La Mandorla, that scored highest in our tastings. This hefty cask-aged wine is made from only the estate's ripest and soundest grapes, some subsequently partially dried. It shows dark ruby, with a nose of rain-soaked earth and plum jam, and an explosive palate whose natural refreshing acidity counters the warm caressing alcohol. The basic Barbera is an excellent and well-priced alternative for those preferring a more conventional wine. We also tasted a well-typed Grignolino and a Monferrato Rosso, from pinot nero, with gamey aromas and well-behaved, Burgundy-like extract.

● Barbaresco Cottà '05	♆♆♆ 8
● Barbaresco Currà '05	♆♆ 8
● Barbaresco Fausoni '05	♆♆ 8
● Barbaresco Pajoré '05	♆♆ 8
● Barbera d'Alba Pairolero '06	♆♆ 5
● Dolcetto d'Alba Bric del Salto '07	♆♆ 4
● Langhe Nebbiolo '06	♆♆ 5
● Maté '07	♆♆ 4*
● Barbaresco Cottà '99	♉♉♉ 7
● Barbaresco Cottà '98	♉♉♉ 7
● Barbaresco Cottà V. Brichet '97	♉♉♉ 7
● Barbaresco Currà '04	♉♉♉ 7
● Barbaresco Fausoni V. del Salto '96	♉♉♉ 7
● Barbaresco Pajoré '98	♉♉♉ 7
● Barbaresco Pajoré '01	♉♉♉ 7
● Barbaresco Pajoré '00	♉♉♉ 7

● Barbera d'Asti '06	♆♆ 4*
● Barbera d'Asti Sup. La Mandorla '06	♆♆ 6
● Grignolino d'Asti '07	♆♆ 4
● M.to Rosso La Mandorla '05	♆♆ 6
● Barbera d'Asti '05	♉♉ 4
● Barbera d'Asti '04	♉♉ 4
● Barbera d'Asti '03	♉♉ 4
● M.to Rosso La Mandorla '04	♉♉ 6
● M.to Rosso La Mandorla '01	♉♉ 6

★★★ La Spinetta

VIA ANNUNZIATA, 17
14054 CASTAGNOLE DELLE LANZE [AT]
TEL. 0141877396
www.la-spinetta.com

ANNUAL PRODUCTION	600,000 bottles
HECTARES UNDER VINE	100
VITICULTURE METHOD	Conventional

The Rivetti brothers' fine winery has Barolo, Barbaresco and Asti DOCGs, as well as the Langhe and Monferrato DOCs, on its list. Their scrupulous care ensures consistently high quality. Maturation for the three Barbaresco selections is almost identical, starting with 18 months in new barriques. The classic-style Vigneto Gallina, from Neive, gives berries and a weighty palate while the refined Vigneto Starderi, also from Neive, won Three Glasses for a nose of cherries and intense balsam, and a structured, elegant palate. Vigneto Valeirano, from Treiso, is all fruit and spice with prominent alcohol and tannins. Barolo Campè '04, aged in new wood for 24 months, offers wild berries and spices, a powerful entry with good acidity and a lingering finish. Three Glasses went to the magnificently balanced Monferrato Rosso Pin '06, from nebbiolo and barbera. Barbera d'Asti Superiore Bionzo '06 is spicy, mouthfilling and delicious. The rest of the '06 reds – Barbera d'Asti Ca' di Pian, Barbera d'Alba Vigneto Gallina and Langhe Nebbiolo – are outstanding. Moscato d'Asti Bricco Quaglia is always good but the '07 vintage is particularly fresh and fruity.

Luigi Tacchino

VIA MARTIRI DELLA BENEDICTA, 26
15060 CASTELLETTO D'ORBA [AL]
TEL. 0143830115
www.luigitacchino.it

ANNUAL PRODUCTION	120,000 bottles
HECTARES UNDER VINE	10
VITICULTURE METHOD	Conventional

Over the years, this family-run estate has made a name for itself as one of the area's leading wineries. Each harvest confirms the quality of its wines and brings continuous developments, which fully respect both tradition and the terroir. This is underscored by the decision not to release the Du Riva Dolcetto selection, which will age for another year. We'll be able to give our verdict in the next edition of the Guide. The two current wines performed very well, particularly the Barbera, which shows concentrated and forthright on the nose, with alcohol-rich notes, and fresh and juicy on the pleasantly ripe palate. Its high quality combined with a reasonable price tag makes it one of the best of its kind. The Dolcetto isn't quite such good value but does have attractive tannins and nice complexity. Its aromas are upfront but not very intense. Barbera Albarola also put on a good performance, showing ruby red with a concentrated nose of berries and nicely balanced body and acidity. The refreshing Gavi is captivating and deliciously tangy. Cortese Marsenca and Monferrato Di Fatto, from barbera, dolcetto and cabernet, took One Glass each.

● Barbaresco Vign. Starderi '05	♟♟♟	8
● M.to Rosso Pin '06	♟♟♟	7
● Barbaresco Vign. Gallina '05	♟♟	8
● Barbaresco Vign. Valeirano '05	♟♟	8
● Barbera d'Asti Sup. Bionzo '06	♟♟	7
● Barolo Campè '04	♟♟	8
○ Moscato d'Asti Bricco Quaglia '07	♟♟	4*
● Barbera d'Alba Vign. Gallina '06	♟♟	7
● Barbera d'Asti Ca' di Pian '06	♟♟	5
● Langhe Nebbiolo '06	♟♟	6
● Barbaresco Vign. Starderi '04	♟♟♟	8
● Barbaresco Vign. Starderi '01	♟♟♟	8
● Barbaresco Vign. Starderi '00	♟♟♟	8
● Barbaresco Vign. Valeirano '04	♟♟♟	8
● Barolo Campè '01	♟♟♟	8
● Barolo Campè '00	♟♟♟	8

● Barbera del M.to '07	♟	4*
● Barbera del M.to Albarola '06	♟♟	4
● Dolcetto di Ovada '07	♟♟	4
○ Gavi del Comune di Gavi '07	♟♟	4
○ Cortese dell'Alto M.to Marsenca '07	♟	3
● M.to Rosso Di Fatto '04	♟	5
● Barbera del M.to '06	♟♟	3
● Barbera del M.to Albarola '04	♟♟	4
● Dolcetto di Ovada '06	♟♟	4
○ Gavi del Comune di Gavi '06	♟♟	4

Michele Taliano

c.so A. Manzoni, 24
12046 Montà [CN]
TEL. 0173976512
www.talianomichele.com

ANNUAL PRODUCTION **60,000 bottles**
HECTARES UNDER VINE **12**
VITICULTURE METHOD **Conventional**

Alberto and Ezio Taliano continue to
consolidate their excellent, very varied list
of wines. While several more modern-style
wines have been added over the years,
including a Langhe Bianco and a Langhe
Rosso made from a blend of local and
international varieties, the estate hews to
the traditions of the Roero area. The sole
exception is Barbaresco Ad Altiora, from
Langhe, with which the Talianos have
historical and sentimental ties as a branch
of the family has a winery in Barbaresco.
Langhe Rosso '05 is convincing, showing
young and fruity, with plenty of tannins.
Roero '05 and Barbera Laboriosa '05
are the estate's top wines. The Roero
has a deep nose and a long, balanced,
flavoursome palate while the Barbera
displays complex aromas of spice, berries
and leaves followed by a full but seductively
elegant palate. The current Barbera,
predictably enough, focuses on freshness
and exemplary fruit while the pleasant
Arneis reveals the variety's characteristic
twist of bitterness. Both the Langhe
Nebbiolo and the Dolcetto are well made.

Tenuta La Tenaglia

s.da Santuario di Crea, 5c
15020 Serralunga di Crea [AL]
TEL. 0142940252
www.latenaglia.com

ANNUAL PRODUCTION **100,000 bottles**
HECTARES UNDER VINE **30**
VITICULTURE METHOD **Conventional**

Alois Ehrmann is a German who fell in love
with Italy. In 2001, after having explored
the entire country, he decided to purchase
the splendid Tenuta La Tenaglia. Alois
chose Monferrato because he particularly
liked the area, preferring it to the more
celebrated Tuscany. The estate that he
bought has a great history of winemaking
and is situated in one of the most beautiful
areas of southern Piedmont, directly
beneath the spectacular shrine of Crea.
From the very outset, the venture involved
Alois's daughter Sabine, a long-time Italian
resident, who rose enthusiastically to the
challenge. It didn't take long for the wines
to become seriously good. The estate's
labels are classic Piedmont, with emphasis
on the region's native vines. We were
most impressed by Barbera d'Asti Giorgio
Tenaglia '06, which proffers rich sensations
of ripe berries, with hints of cinchona and
cocoa powder. Barbera d'Asti Emozioni '06
is also very interesting, showing powerful
and juicy with a long, complex finish, while
Grignolino del Monferrato Casalese '07 is
spicy and full bodied. Barbera Tenaglia è...
also earned Two Glasses and the rest of
the list is well made.

● Roero Ròche dra Bòssora '05	♟♟	5
● Barbaresco Ad Altiora '05	♟♟	6
● Barbera d'Alba A Bon Rendre '07	♟♟	4*
● Barbera d'Alba Laboriosa '05	♟♟	4
● Langhe Nebbiolo Blagheur '07	♟♟	4*
● Dolcetto d'Alba Ciabot Vigna '07	♟	4
● Langhe Rosso '05	♟	4
○ Langhe Bianco '06	♟	4
○ Roero Arneis Sernì '07	♟	4
● Barbaresco Ad Altiora '01	♟♟	6
● Roero Ròche dra Bòssora '04	♟♟	5
● Roero Ròche dra Bòssora '03	♟♟	5
● Barbaresco Ad Altiora '04	♟♟	6
● Barbera d'Alba Laboriosa '04	♟♟	4

● Barbera d'Asti Emozioni '06	♟♟	6
● Barbera d'Asti Giorgio Tenaglia '06	♟♟	5
● Barbera del M.to Sup. Tenaglia è... '06	♟♟	4*
● Grignolino del M.to Casalese '07	♟♟	4*
● Barbera d'Asti Bricco Crea '07	♟	4
● Monferrrato Paradiso '07	♟	4
● Barbera del M.to Sup. Tenaglia è... '03	♟♟	4
● Barbera del M.to Sup. Tenaglia è... '04	♟♟	4

Tenuta dei Fiori

FRAZ. RODOTIGLIA
VIA VALCALOSSO, 3
14052 CALOSSO [AT]
TEL. 0141853819
www.tenutadeifiori.com

ANNUAL PRODUCTION	20,000 bottles
HECTARES UNDER VINE	4.5
VITICULTURE METHOD	Conventional

The winemaking philosophy of owner Walter Bosticardo has two focuses: the terroir and the certainty that patience is a fundamental requirement for making good wine. Strolling around the estate's cellar, located in Calosso among the scenic hills of the Asti countryside on the border between Langhe and Monferrato, you might find bottles of '99 Cabernet that have only just been released for sale. However, this excellent wine, which is still very youthful and fresh on the palate despite its age, is hardly emblematic of Walter's production. Gamba di Pernice, however, is. The grape variety, native to Calosso, was traditionally used to make sweet semi-sparkling wine and had gradually disappeared until it was revived by this estate in 1985. Today, Walter uses it to make a hefty still dry wine, which was not presented this year. Barbera Rusticardi '05 is excellent, showing very intense and full bodied, with pleasing acidity that makes it highly drinkable. Finally, there's the estate's new wine, which we did not assess. Pensiero is a very personal interpretation of the traditional Asti Metodo Classico, left on the lees for 12 years.

Terralba

FRAZ. INSELMINA
15050 BERZANO DI TORTONA [AL]
TEL. 013180403
www.terralbavini.com

ANNUAL PRODUCTION	50,000 bottles
HECTARES UNDER VINE	15
VITICULTURE METHOD	Conventional

Stefano Daffonchio's estate performed admirably and found a few surprises in store for us. This year the best Timorasso wasn't Stato, the flagship wine, which nonetheless easily earned Two Glasses, but the simpler Derthona. The term "simple", however, is misleading because all Terralba's wines are very concentrated with impressive structure. It may have been Timorasso Stato's excessive quest for structure that made us prefer Derthona, packed with balsamic and mineral notes and with a fruitier finale. On the palate, it finds an excellent balance of structure and acidity. Barbera Terralba also performed very well, almost making it to our finals. It's another wine with great structure and an impenetrable hue, combined with well-integrated acidity, which allows it to express itself to the full. Croatina Montegrande is a similarly high-quality offering that is already great but will probably be at its best in a few years. Vigna di Mezzo, from barbera with 30 per cent croatina, is also spot on.

● Barbera d'Asti Sup. Rusticardi 1933 Castello di Calosso '05	♥♥ 6
○ Moscato d'Asti Rairì '07	♥♥ 3
○ Piemonte Chardonnay Il Vento '06	♥♥ 3*
● Barbera d'Asti Tulipanonero '05	♥ 6
● Barbera d'Asti Sup. Rusticardi 1933 Castello di Calosso '04	♥♥ 6
● M.to Rosso Cinque File '03	♥♥ 5
● Barbera d'Asti Tulipanonero '03	♥♥ 6
● M.to Rosso Cinque File '04	♥♥ 5
● Gamba di Pernice '04	♥ 4

○ Colli Tortonesi Timorasso Derthona '06	♥♥ 5
○ Colli Tortonesi Bianco Stato '06	♥♥ 6
● Colli Tortonesi Rosso Montegrande '05	♥♥ 5
● Colli Tortonesi Rosso Terralba '05	♥♥ 6
● Colli Tortonesi Rosso Vigna di Mezzo '05	♥♥ 5
○ Colli Tortonesi Bianco Stato '05	♥♥ 6
○ Colli Tortonesi Bianco Stato '04	♥♥ 6
○ Colli Tortonesi Bianco Stato '03	♥♥ 5
● Colli Tortonesi Rosso Terralba '04	♥♥ 6

Terre da Vino

VIA BERGESIA, 6
12060 BAROLO [CN]
TEL. 0173564611
www.terredavino.it

ANNUAL PRODUCTION	5,500,000 bottles
HECTARES UNDER VINE	4.600
VITICULTURE METHOD	Conventional

This large consortium, whose Barolo base is being extended, has labels covering almost all the Piedmont designations, buying in wine from associated co-operatives and monitoring its member growers. The range caters for all segments of the Italian and international market. Managed by Piero Quadrumolo, with oenologist Bruno Cordero, Terre da Vino offers several lines, all very good, including one for the on-trade, to which the wines we tasted belong, one for supermarkets and one for budget wines. The sheer scale of operations makes careful selection possible and the cellar brings out the characteristics of each type. We were impressed by the classy Barolo Essenze '04, which presents a dense garnet ruby with a citrus fruit nose laced with notes of tobacco, dried flowers and spices. The palate is estery and caressing, with a slightly dry finish. Other Langhe wines include the excellent Barbaresco La Casa in Collina '05 and the similarly convincing Barbera d'Alba Croere '06, which shows fruity, powerful and spicy with a long, full-flavoured finish. The Barbera Nizza Martlet '06 is stylish and dynamic while the rest of the list is well made.

Terre del Barolo

VIA ALBA-BAROLO, 5
12060 CASTIGLIONE FALLETTO [CN]
TEL. 0173262053
www.terredelbarolo.com

ANNUAL PRODUCTION	2,500,000 bottles
HECTARES UNDER VINE	800
VITICULTURE METHOD	Conventional

Langhe's international image and fine reputation as wine country undoubtedly derive from the ceaseless work of the area's many producers. One of these is Terre del Barolo, one of the few co-operative wineries that have been benchmarks for many growers since the 1950s. Although located in an area of small family-owned estates, the consortium headed by Matteo Bosco boasts impressive figures: over 400 members, 800 hectares under vine and an annual production of 2,500,000 bottles. The wines are the classics of the area and form a nicely diverse list. Once again this year, we tasted several Barolo Riservas. We particularly liked the Barolo Castello Riserva '00 and '01 selections, although our favourite wine was the basic Barolo '04, which shows pleasant, fresh and balanced. Dogliani '06 and the two '06 Barbera d'Albas, Valdisera and Superiore, are also very good, particularly in terms of value for money. The rest of the extensive list is characterized by easy-drinking wines in the traditional style.

● Barolo Essenze '04	♟♟ 7
● Barbera d'Alba Sup. Croere '06	♟♟ 5
● Barbera d'Asti Sup. Nizza Martlet '06	♟♟ 5
● Barolo Scarrone '03	♟♟ 8
● Barbaresco La Casa in Collina '05	♟♟ 6*
● Barbera d'Asti Sup. La Luna e i Falò '06	♟♟ 5
● Langhe Nebbiolo La Malora '05	♟♟ 5
O M.to Bianco Tra Donne Sole '07	♟♟ 4*
● Barolo Paesi Tuoi '04	♟ 6
O Roero Arneis La Villa '07	♟ 4
O Gavi del Comune di Gavi Masseria dei Carmelitani '07	♟ 4
O Piemonte Moscato Passito La Bella Estate '06	♟ 5
● Barolo Essenze '01	♟♟ 7

● Barbera d'Alba Sup. '06	♟♟ 3*
● Barbera d'Alba Valdisera '06	♟♟ 3*
● Barolo '04	♟♟ 6
● Barolo Castello Ris. '01	♟♟ 7
● Barolo Castello Ris. '00	♟♟ 7
● Barolo Rocche Ris. '00	♟♟ 6
● Dogliani '06	♟♟ 4*
● Barbera d'Alba '07	♟ 3
● Barolo Cannubi '03	♟ 7
● Barolo Monvigliero '03	♟ 6
● Dolcetto d'Alba '07	♟ 3
● Dolcetto di Diano d'Alba '07	♟ 3
O Langhe Favorita '07	♟ 3
● Nebbiolo d'Alba '06	♟ 4
● Verduno Pelaverga '07	♟ 4
● Barolo Rocche Ris. '99	♟♟ 6

Torraccia del Piantavigna

VIA ROMAGNANO, 69A
28074 GHEMME [NO]
TEL. 0163840040
www.torracciadelpiantavigna.it

ANNUAL PRODUCTION	90,000 bottles
HECTARES UNDER VINE	40
VITICULTURE METHOD	Conventional

What started almost as a hobby for the Francoli family from Lombardy – their main activity is as owners of one Italy's most famous distilleries – has slowly grown in importance. Perhaps the surname of Alessandro Francoli's maternal grandmother's, Piantavigna ("vineyard planter") and his love for these hills, were signs of destiny that could not be ignored. What is certain is that the estate's current manager has a passion for grape growing. Starting with the estate's many vineyards, and fine-tuning the cellar as wine quality improved, Torraccia del Piantavigna has worked its way up through the Guide to top honours this year. It's hard to choose between its two leading wines, Ghemme and Gattinara. They share an impressively complex nose, with more tobacco and citrus notes in the Ghemme, and themed to cinchona and iodine in the Gattinara. Both show considerable length on the palate but different tactile sensations, with the Ghemme fuller and the Gattinara more austere and almost crisp. We prefer the Ghemme, which won our Three Glasses for the first time. The rest of the range is extremely reliable, particularly the flavoursome Nebbiolo Ramale.

Giancarlo Travaglini

VIA DELLE VIGNE, 36
13045 GATTINARA [VC]
TEL. 0163833588
www.travaglinigattinara.it

ANNUAL PRODUCTION	250,000 bottles
HECTARES UNDER VINE	42
VITICULTURE METHOD	Conventional

In the last edition of the Guide, we highlighted the work of Giancarlo Travaglini, son, grandson and great-grandson of Gattinara winegrowers, who in 45 years of toil transformed a modest farm, like many others in Piedmont, into one of the most prestigious wineries in Italy with a large slice of the vineyards in the Gattinara designation. This year, we want to focus on Giancarlo's moral legacy. Before his death after the 2004 harvest, Travaglini had an idea for a new wine, made from part-dried nebbiolo grapes, using the same principle as Amarone. Prior to the start of the harvest, the smallest loose-packed bunches were carefully selected, picked and laid on racks to dry until the end of December. After long ageing, Giancarlo's dream has been unveiled: Il Suo Sogno, an amazingly powerful red with subtle hints of oak, which has preserved all the aromatic freshness and flavour of the terroir. The estate deservedly returns to Three Glass status with the spectacular Tre Vigne '04, which combines an elegant nose of rhubarb and dried flowers with a juicy, well-balanced palate and fine-grained tannins. Gattinara '04 is aristocratic and very classy.

● Ghemme '04	♛♛♛ 6
● Gattinara '04	♛♛ 6
○ Colline Novaresi Bianco Erbavoglio '07	♛♛ 4
● Colline Novaresi Nebbiolo Ramale '05	♛♛ 5
● Colline Novaresi Vespolina La Mostella '06	♛♛ 4
● Colline Novaresi Nebbiolo Tre Confini '06	♛ 4
⊙ Colline Novaresi Nebbiolo Rosato Barlàn '07	4
● Gattinara '03	♛♛ 6
● Gattinara '01	♛♛ 6
● Colline Novaresi Nebbiolo Ramale '04	♛♛ 5
● Gattinara '00	♛♛ 6

● Gattinara Tre Vigne '04	♛♛♛ 6
● Gattinara '04	♛♛ 5*
● Il Suo Sogno '04	♛♛ 7
● Gattinara Ris. '01	♛♛♛ 6
● Gattinara '03	♛♛ 5
● Gattinara '01	♛♛ 5
● Gattinara Ris. '99	♛♛ 6
● Gattinara Ris. '97	♛♛ 6
● Gattinara Ris. '00	♛♛ 6
● Gattinara Tre Vigne '01	♛♛ 6
● Gattinara '00	♛♛ 5
● Gattinara Ris. '98	♛♛ 6
● Gattinara Tre Vigne '00	♛♛ 6

Castello di Uviglie

VIA CASTELLO DI UVIGLIE, 73
15030 ROSIGNANO MONFERRATO [AL]
TEL. 0142488132
www.castellodiuviglie.com

ANNUAL PRODUCTION	70,000 bottles
HECTARES UNDER VINE	25
VITICULTURE METHOD	Conventional

Castello di Uviglie was built between 1239 and 1271 by the Paucaparte di Celle family and in 1491 became the property of the Conti Pico-Gonzaga, who started to farm the land. Over the centuries, the castle has had a series of other owners, including the Conti Callori di Vignale from 1820 to 1879, who sold the estate to Conte Cacherano di Bricherasio, one of the founders of the Fiat automobile company. The castle finally became the property of the current owners in 1992. Today, the estate's 25 hectares of vineyards are enough for an annual production of 70,000 bottles, with ten or so different labels made chiefly from grape varieties native to Monferrato. The star of the list is a great vintage of Le Cave, which ages only briefly in oak and vaunts a concentrated nose and a confident, leisurely palate. After 15 months in wood, Pico Gonzaga displays aromas of red berry fruit with well-integrated oak and a long, forceful palate. The current Barbera Bricco del Conte, Grignolino San Bastiano and Piemonte Chardonnay Ninfea are all well executed.

● Barbera del M.to Sup. Le Cave '05	♟♟	4*
● Barbera del M.to Sup. Pico Gonzaga '04	♟♟	5
● Barbera del M.to Bricco del Conte '07	♟	4
● Grignolino del M.to Casalese San Bastiano '07	♟	4
○ Piemonte Chardonnay Ninfea '07	♟	4
● Barbera del M.to Sup. Le Cave '04	♟♟	4
● Barbera del M.to Sup. Pico Gonzaga '03	♟♟	5

G. D. Vajra

LOC. VERGNE
VIA DELLE VIOLE, 25
12060 BAROLO [CN]
TEL. 017356257
gdvajra@tin.it

ANNUAL PRODUCTION	200,000 bottles
HECTARES UNDER VINE	45
VITICULTURE METHOD	Conventional

Aldo and Milena Vaira have created a prestigious estate in the highest hills of Barolo. Their professionalism and warmth are also in the wines, which reflect the terroir and the Vairas' infinite passion. The estate's leading Barolo comes from the Bricco delle Viole vineyard in the Vergne area of Barolo. Low yields and judicious ageing in large barrels produce a full, elegant wine whose complex notes of fruit and flowers are integrated into a tannic structure that puts elegance ahead of weight. The finish is long and spicy. Almost as good is Barolo Albe, sourced from three vineyards, which shows powerful and complex with notes of liquorice and brandied fruit. Barbera Superiore '06 and Dolcetto Coste & Fossati '07, always among the best of their kind, deserve a special mention. Freisa Kyè '05, which we reviewed last year by error, is very attractive and distinctive, showing character, balance and freshness despite its long ageing. The excellent Langhe Bianco '07, a Riesling Renano from 21-year-old vineyards, is big, zesty, mineral, elegant and powerful. Moscato d'Asti is also impressive, with a varietal nose and a sweet, but not cloying, palate.

● Barbera d'Alba Sup. '06	♟♟	5
● Barolo Bricco delle Viole '04	♟♟	8
● Dolcetto d'Alba Coste & Fossati '07	♟♟	5
○ Langhe Bianco '07	♟♟	5
● Barbera d'Alba '06	♟♟	4*
● Barolo Albe '04	♟♟	7
● Langhe Freisa Kyè '05	♟♟	5
● Langhe Nebbiolo '06	♟♟	5
○ Moscato d'Asti '07	♟♟	4
● Dolcetto d'Alba '07	♟	4
● Barbera d'Alba Sup. '01	♟♟♟	5
● Barbera d'Alba Sup. '00	♟♟♟	6
● Barolo Bricco delle Viole '99	♟♟♟	8
● Barolo Bricco delle Viole '01	♟♟♟	8
● Barolo Bricco delle Viole '00	♟♟♟	8
○ Langhe Bianco '02	♟♟♟	5
○ Langhe Bianco '06	♟♟	5

Cascina Val del Prete

S.DA SANTUARIO, 2
12040 PRIOCCA [CN]
TEL. 0173616534
valdelprete@tiscali.it

ANNUAL PRODUCTION	40,000 bottles
HECTARES UNDER VINE	13
VITICULTURE METHOD	Natural

Simplicity, as we always say, is the key to success with arneis, barbera and nebbiolo. There's no need for flights of fancy when you can count on three varieties of rock-solid consistency. Mario Roagna is well aware of this and puts most of his efforts into enhancing the qualities of these grape varieties to the full. Instead of expending his creative energies on new wines, Mario prefers to focus it on experiments with well-established selections. The results are impressive, even though this approach inevitably involves a period of waiting for the new personality of the wines to settle down. This is very true of Roero Arneis, the wine that Mario considers his flagship and whose recent makeover has given it even greater charisma. For the moment, we can enjoy its depth and structure, while awaiting its finesse to emerge. Regarding the two Barberas, we liked the fresh, easy-drinking vintage Serra de' Gatti and the complexity of Carolina '06, which remains at the top of its category. Nebbiolo d'Alba '06 is excellent and the best possible foil for the Roero '05, again soft, elegant, firm and well behaved in every respect.

Tenute dei Vallarino

REG. VALLE ASINARI, 20
14050 SAN MARZANO OLIVETO [AT]
TEL. 0141823048

ANNUAL PRODUCTION	150,000 bottles
HECTARES UNDER VINE	38
VITICULTURE METHOD	Conventional

Tenute dei Vallarino is the Gancia still wine operation. Its latest label is Albarossa '06, from the red variety of that name from a crossing made by Giovanni Dalmasso in 1938. His aim was to create a variety with the qualities of nebbiolo and the hardiness of barbera. Recent studies have shown that the crossing did not use nebbiolo at all, but chatus, aka nebbiolo di Dronero. This estate's version stands out for its full nose, with currants and raspberries with black pepper spice. On the palate, it shows good acidity and nicely developed tannins. Barbera Bricco Asinari '05 was back this year, proffering warm fruit laced with hints of cocoa powder, vanilla and coffee. The palate shows deep and slightly tannic, with a round, juicy finish. We were impressed by the captivating Moscato d'Asti Castello Gancia, with its notes of citrus fruit and peach blossom. Two Glasses also went to the highly refreshing, fruity Barbera d'Asti La Ladra. The list of whites is very good. It's topped by Pèpero, a powerful, floral, zesty Sauvignon. Not far behind is Unisono, a single-variety Chardonnay, and La Ciò, from bussanello, an old Piedmont grape variety.

● Barbera d'Alba Sup. Carolina '06	♟♟ 6
● Roero '05	♟♟ 7
● Barbera d'Alba Serra de' Gatti '07	♟♟ 4*
● Nebbiolo d'Alba V. di Lino '06	♟♟ 6
○ Roero Arneis Luet '07	♟ 4
● Nebbiolo d'Alba V. di Lino '00	♟♟♟ 5
● Roero '04	♟♟♟ 7
● Roero '03	♟♟♟ 7
● Roero '01	♟♟♟ 7
● Roero '00	♟♟♟ 6
● Barbera d'Alba Sup. Carolina '05	♟♟ 6
● Barbera d'Alba Sup. Carolina '04	♟♟ 6

● Barbera d'Asti Sup. Nizza Bricco Asinari '05	♟♟ 6
● Barbera d'Asti Sup. La Ladra '06	♟♟ 4*
○ M.to Bianco Pèpero '07	♟♟ 4*
● M.to Rosso Albarossa '06	♟♟ 5
● M.to Rosso Dialogo '06	♟♟ 6
○ Moscato d'Asti Castello Gancia '07	♟♟ 4*
○ M.to Bianco La Ciò '07	♟ 4
○ M.to Bianco Unisono '07	♟ 4
● Barbera d'Asti Sup. Nizza Bricco Asinari '04	♟♟ 6
● Barbera d'Asti Sup. Nizza Bricco Asinari '03	♟♟ 6
● M.to Rosso Dialogo '05	♟♟ 6
● M.to Rosso Dialogo '04	♟♟ 6
● Barbera d'Asti Sup. La Ladra '05	♟♟ 4

Rino Varaldo

VIA SECONDINE, 2
12050 BARBARESCO [CN]
TEL. 0173635160
varaldo@varaldo.com

ANNUAL PRODUCTION 40,000 bottles
HECTARES UNDER VINE 7
VITICULTURE METHOD Conventional

The Varaldo brothers' estate, situated in the centre of the village of Barbaresco, boasts seven hectares of vineyards in the municipalities of Barbaresco, Neive and Treiso, as well as in the Terlo area of Barolo for the production of its Vigna di Aldo. The '04 vintage of the latter strolled into our tasting finals thanks to its elegance and weight. Elegant and fruity, it displays well-integrated hints of wood. Barbaresco Sorì Loreto '05 was just a hair's-breadth behind, with typical aromas of tobacco and dried flowers. On the palate it shows soft and velvety, but with refreshing acidity. One step down is Bricco Libero '05, the biggest and most powerful of the three, with minty notes on a base of ripe fruit. La Gemma '05, from the Treiso vineyard, still displays prominent oak and a fresher, simpler palate. The younger wines also have good character, with marked acidity and tannins. Dolcetto '07 is very nice, showing powerful with notes of jam and liquorice and a soft but striking palate. Nebbiolo '06 vaunts splendid aromas but is still rather hard on the palate. Finally, we liked the two fresh, full-flavoured Barberas and Fantasia 4.20, from nebbiolo, barbera, cabernet and merlot.

● Barbaresco Sorì Loreto '05	TT	7
● Barolo V. di Aldo '04	TT	8
● Barbaresco Bricco Libero '05	TT	7
● Barbaresco La Gemma '05	TT	7
● Dolcetto d'Alba '07	TT	4*
● Langhe Nebbiolo '06	TT	4*
● Langhe Rosso Fantasia 4.20 '06	TT	5
● Barbera d'Alba '07	T	4
● Barbera d'Alba V. delle Fate '06	T	5
● Barbaresco Bricco Libero '97	YYY	7
● Barbaresco Bricco Libero '04	YY	7
● Barbaresco Bricco Libero '01	YY	7
● Barbaresco Sorì Loreto '04	YY	7
● Barolo V. di Aldo '01	YY	8
● Barolo V. di Aldo '00	YY	8
● Langhe Rosso Fantasia 4.20 '05	YY	5

Mauro Veglio

FRAZ. ANNUNZIATA
CASCINA NUOVA, 50
12064 LA MORRA [CN]
TEL. 0173509212
www.mauroveglio.com

ANNUAL PRODUCTION 60,000 bottles
HECTARES UNDER VINE 12
VITICULTURE METHOD Conventional

The loving care lavished on the estate's vineyards and cellar work, such as the use of native yeasts and the elimination of filtration, is reflected in results of which Mauro and Daniela can be proud. This year, the '04 Barolo selections, to be flanked by a basic version from the '06 vintage, were the tops. Our favourite was Arborina, which has an estery, nicely balsamic nose and a warm, long, elegant palate with well-balanced tannins. It's followed by the impressive, cellarable Rocche dell'Annunziata and a Gattera with well-calibrated red berry fruit and spice. Castelletto is sourced from the Monforte vineyards and has greater structure but currently also displays more prominent tannins. Barbera d'Alba Cascina Nuova '06 is as good as ever. It comes from vineyards almost 60 years old and has acquired a unique blend of elegance and power after ageing in small oak casks for 18 months. L'Insieme '05 is an attractive blend of cabernet, barbera and nebbiolo while Langhe Nebbiolo Angelo '06 sports pleasant young tannins. The absence of wood in '07 Dolcetto and Barbera d'Alba makes both wines juicy and approachable.

● Barbera d'Alba Cascina Nuova '06	TT	6
● Barolo Vign. Arborina '04	TT	7
● Barolo Vign. Rocche dell'Annunziata '04	TT	7
● Barbera d'Alba '07	TT	4*
● Barolo Castelletto '04	TT	7
● Barolo V. Gattera '04	TT	7
● Dolcetto d'Alba '07	TT	4*
● Langhe Nebbiolo Angelo '06	TT	5
● Langhe Rosso L'Insieme '05	TT	7
● Barbera d'Alba Cascina Nuova '99	YYY	5
● Barolo V. Rocche '96	YYY	7
● Barolo Vign. Arborina '01	YYY	7
● Barolo Vign. Arborina '00	YYY	7

Eraldo Viberti

FRAZ. SANTA MARIA
BORGATA TETTI, 53
12064 LA MORRA [CN]
TEL. 017350308
eraldoviberti@libero.it

ANNUAL PRODUCTION	25,000 bottles
HECTARES UNDER VINE	4
VITICULTURE METHOD	Conventional

They say that good things come in small parcels and this is very true of Eraldo Viberti, owner and oenologist of an estate whose three hectares of vineyards, plus one rented, yield a modest number of labels and bottles. This year, we didn't taste the Langhe Nebbiolo, which Eraldo has decided requires further ageing. The Barolo '04 comes from the Santa Maria vineyards in the eastern part of the municipality of La Morra. It's very well made and well able to compete with the other great wines of its type. This Barolo convinced us with its nose of cherry jam and its bracingly fresh palate. It shows soft and round, with well-calibrated oak and a long, lingering finish. It's destined to improve further over the coming years. Barbera d'Alba Vigna Clara '05 boasts an impressively concentrated nose of fruit and spices. These notes are faithfully echoed on a palate characterized by impressive acidity that makes it exceptionally drinkable. The last wine, Dolcetto d'Alba '07 is a successful, well-calibrated expression of the grape, displaying varietal notes of cherry, raspberry and blackberry.

Vicara

CASCINA MADONNA DELLE GRAZIE, 5
15030 ROSIGNANO MONFERRATO [AL]
TEL. 0142488054
www.vicara.it

ANNUAL PRODUCTION	200,000 bottles
HECTARES UNDER VINE	37
VITICULTURE METHOD	Biodinamico certificato

This winery has an interesting history. Diego Visconti, Carlo Cassinis and Domenico Ravizza, who owned different farms and had different experiences, joined forces and pooled their 37 hectares to form an estate with more potential in terms of both quality and market. Last year, the top wines were missing and their entry in the Guide suffered somewhat. However, this edition sees the return of Vicara's flagships: Barbera Vadmò '04 – mistakenly reviewed in last year's edition of the Guide – stands out for its rich notes of ripe berry fruit, including morello cherry and raspberry. It shows nicely acidic on the palate with a balanced finish. We awarded an enthusiastic Two Glasses to Cantico della Crosia, aged for 12 months in small casks, which boasts warm aromas of vanilla and pepper-led spice and a complex, inviting palate. Grignolino del Monferrato Casalese was our favourite from the current wines, impressing us with its austerity and excellent balance. Barbera Volpuva is a step below but it's still very young. The rather impressive list is completed by a pleasantly fruity Airales and the simple, but not banal, Monferrato Freisa.

● Barolo '04		🍷🍷 7
● Barbera d'Alba V. Clara '05		🍷🍷 6
● Dolcetto d'Alba '07		🍷🍷 3*
● Barbera d'Alba V. Clara '04		🍷🍷 6
● Barbera d'Alba V. Clara '03		🍷🍷 6
● Barolo '01		🍷🍷 7
● Barolo '00		🍷🍷 7
● Langhe Nebbiolo '06		🍷🍷 5

● Barbera del M.to Sup. Cantico della Crosia '05		🍷🍷 5
● Barbera del M.to Sup. Vadmò '04		🍷🍷 4*
● Grignolino del M.to Casalese '07		🍷🍷 4*
● Barbera del M.to Volpuva '07		🍷 4
O M.to Bianco Airales '07		🍷 4
● M.to Freisa '07		🍷 4
● Barbera del M.to Sup. Cantico della Crosia '03		🍷🍷 5
● Barbera del M.to Sup. Cantico della Crosia '01		🍷🍷 5
● Barbera del M.to Sup. Cantico della Crosia '04		🍷🍷 5

Vielmin

VIA MAGLIANO ALFIERI, 13A
12050 CASTELLINALDO [CN]
TEL. 0173611248
ivan.gili@tin.it

ANNUAL PRODUCTION	30,000 bottles
HECTARES UNDER VINE	5
VITICULTURE METHOD	Conventional

Ivan Gili presented an unusual array of wines at our tastings. Some of the small estate's old favourites were missing, replaced by wines that we hadn't tasted for years, which allowed us to form an even clearer idea of the cellar's potential. Ivan is now able to call on his new winery, situated on the slopes that rise up from Castellinaldo towards Magliano Alfieri. The estate's vineyards extend for several hectares around the new premises. Both the whites are pleasant and fruity, although we slightly preferred the Arneis. Dolcetto '07 shows forthright on the nose and tannic on the palate, with a leisurely finish. This year the estate's flagship reds, Castellinaldo Barbera and Roero La Rocca, have been replaced by an '06 and an '07 Barbera, as well as a '05 Nebbiolo, all of which are outstanding. The Nebbiolo shows austere, beefy and perfectly balanced after ageing in large barrels, which has given it impressive body. The Barbera '07 is highly drinkable while the Barbera Srëi '06 is acidic, fragrant and taut.

★ Vietti

P.ZZA VITTORIO VENETO, 8
12060 CASTIGLIONE FALLETTO [CN]
TEL. 017362825
www.vietti.com

ANNUAL PRODUCTION	250,000 bottles
HECTARES UNDER VINE	35
VITICULTURE METHOD	Conventional

Vietti is one of the best producers in Langhe. Luca Currado and his brother-in-law Mario Cordero have carried on the work begun in the early 1950s by Alfredo Currado and his wife Luciana, expanding the estate and establishing a style that reconciles tradition with modern tastes. There are many labels, from Arneis del Roero to Barbaresco, but it is the Barolo and Barbera selections that typify the estate. There are several Barolo selections: Villero and Rocche from Castiglione Falletto, Brunate from La Morra, Lazzarito from Serralunga d'Alba and Ravera from Novello. The Barberas hail from Langhe and Monferrato, with Scarrone representing Alba and La Crena and Tre Vigne Asti. Villero Riserva, made only in great vintages, was absent this time but we tasted an excellent Barolo Lazzarito '04 from Serralunga d'Alba, with a deep nose of ripe fruit lifted by estery notes and spice, and a nice, assertively tannic palate. This great wine won Three Glasses. Three other Barolos, Rocche, with a slightly dry finish, Brunate and Castiglione, came very close behind. From the Barberas, we liked the fullness and elegance of Scarrone Vigna Vecchia and La Crena.

● Barbera d'Alba '07	🍷🍷 3*
● Barbera d'Alba Srëi '06	🍷🍷 4*
● Nebbiolo d'Alba '05	🍷🍷 5
● Langhe Dolcetto '07	🍷 3
O Langhe Arneis '07	🍷 3
O Langhe Favorita '07	🍷 3
● Castellinaldo Barbera d'Alba '05	🍷🍷 5
● Castellinaldo Barbera d'Alba '04	🍷🍷 5
● Castellinaldo Barbera d'Alba '01	🍷🍷 5
● Roero La Rocca '05	🍷🍷 5
● Roero La Rocca '04	🍷🍷 5
● Roero La Rocca '03	🍷🍷 5
● Roero La Rocca '01	🍷🍷 5

● Barolo Lazzarito '04	🍷🍷🍷 8
● Barbera d'Alba Scarrone V. Vecchia '06	🍷🍷 7
● Barbera d'Asti Sup. Nizza La Crena '05	🍷🍷 6
● Barolo Castiglione '04	🍷🍷 7
● Barolo Rocche '04	🍷🍷 8
● Barbaresco Masseria '05	🍷🍷 8
● Barbera d'Alba Scarrone '06	🍷🍷 6
● Barbera d'Alba Tre Vigne '06	🍷🍷 5
● Barbera d'Asti Tre Vigne '06	🍷🍷 5
● Barolo Brunate '04	🍷🍷 8
● Dolcetto d'Alba Tre Vigne '07	🍷 4
O Roero Arneis '07	🍷 4
● Barolo Rocche '01	🍷🍷🍷 8
● Barolo Villero Ris. '01	🍷🍷🍷 8

★ Vigna Rionda - Massolino

P.ZZA CAPPELLANO, 8
12050 SERRALUNGA D'ALBA [CN]
TEL. 0173613138
www.massolino.it

ANNUAL PRODUCTION	100,000 bottles
HECTARES UNDER VINE	19
VITICULTURE METHOD	Conventional

This historic cellar under the main square embodies the spirit of Serralunga. The Barolo selections are back this year. These reflect the work of Franco Massolino and his family, worthy heirs to an estate set up by their great-grandfather in 1896. The list offers three versions of Barolo, showcasing the distinctive traits of the most prestigious vineyards. Vigna Rionda Riserva '02 captivated us with fresh, complex notes of cinchona and dried roses, followed by a harmonious, velvety palate, good follow-thorough and an exemplary finish. Parafada '04 is more potent and fuller flavoured, with marked tannins and a dynamic character, while Margheria '04 has a stimulating, open nose dominated by aniseed and tobacco, and a long, balanced finish. All three are excellent and Parafada won our top accolade. Barbera Gisep '06 is another remarkably expressive wine, from three small, old vineyards. Its blackberry and pungent spices are accompanied by attractive, well-balanced acidity. All the other wines are good, if not excellent. Our favourites were Dolcetto '07, with soft, caressing fruit, and Barbera '07, is varietal, clean and well structured.

I Vignaioli di Santo Stefano

LOC. MARINI, 26
12058 SANTO STEFANO BELBO [CN]
TEL. 0141840419
www.ceretto.com

ANNUAL PRODUCTION	290,000 bottles
HECTARES UNDER VINE	35
VITICULTURE METHOD	Conventional

A handful of labels and utmost care in vineyards and cellar are the criteria underpinning the work of the partners who established this splendid estate at Santo Stefano Belbo. Over the years, the founders have been joined by the Ceretto family, who handle the distribution of the products. The winery was one of the first to vinify moscato grapes on a small scale, demonstrating that it was possible to achieve exceptional results without the mass production that – both then and now – has dominated the Asti Spumante market. Asti remains one of Vignaioli's finest labels, offering refined, elegant aromas ranging from citron through to peach blossom. On the palate it's sweet, but never cloys and has a pleasant, slightly bitterish finish. The Moscato d'Asti is also very good, with citrus-like aromas and hints of passion fruit and pineapple. The palate intrigues with its stunning freshness and an attractive finish with nicely balanced acidity and sweetness. Finally, the Moscato Passito is warm, smooth and caressing, thanks to a hefty, but not excessive, dose of sugar.

● Barolo Parafada '04	♟♟♟	8
● Barolo Margheria '04	♟♟	8
● Barolo V. Rionda Ris. '02	♟♟	8
● Barbera d'Alba '07	♟♟	4*
● Barbera d'Alba Gisep '06	♟♟	6
● Barolo '04	♟♟	6
● Dolcetto d'Alba '07	♟♟	4*
● Langhe Nebbiolo '05	♟♟	5
○ Langhe Chardonnay '07	♟♟	4*
○ Moscato d'Asti di Serralunga '07	♟	4
● Barolo Margheria '97	♟♟♟	7
● Barolo Parafada '96	♟♟♟	8
● Barolo V. Rionda Ris. '99	♟♟♟	8
● Barolo V. Rionda Ris. '98	♟♟♟	8
● Barolo V. Rionda Ris. '97	♟♟♟	8
● Barolo V. Rionda Ris. '01	♟♟♟	8

○ Asti '07	♟♟	4
○ Moscato d'Asti '07	♟♟	4
○ Piemonte Moscato Passito IL '04	♟♟	5
○ Asti '06	♟♟	4
○ Piemonte Moscato Passito IL '03	♟♟	5
○ Piemonte Moscato Passito IL '02	♟♟	5

Vignaioli Elvio Pertinace

LOC. PERTINACE, 2
12050 TREISO [CN]
TEL. 0173442238
www.pertinace.it

ANNUAL PRODUCTION 200,000 bottles
HECTARES UNDER VINE 60
VITICULTURE METHOD Conventional

Vignaioli Pertinace is a small co-operative winery that vinifies the grapes of 15 member growers with a total of 70 hectares of vines. The wines put on an interesting performance, although the use of oak in the Barbarescos was not perfectly calibrated this time. One of the great strengths of all the winery's bottles is their very competitive price tags, which applies to the most prestigious selections and the so-called basic wines alike. Let's start with the wines from nebbiolo, which is the estate's emblematic variety. As we mentioned earlier, Barbaresco Castellizzano suffers from rather too prominent oak, which prevented it from obtaining more than One Glass. Marcarini performed better, with its notes of dried flowers and saddle leather, as did the fruity, well-orchestrated Nervo. Barbera d'Asti Gratia Plena '06 is terrific, flaunting aromas of rain-soaked earth, black pepper, raspberries and cassis. The palate reveals good acidity and a fresh, sweet finish. Dolcetto d'Alba Castellizzano and Vigneto Nervo both have plenty of character and structure while the rest of the extensive list is a succession of good, high-quality, refreshing wines.

● Barbaresco Marcarini '05	🍷🍷	6
● Barbaresco Nervo '05	🍷🍷	6
● Barbera d'Asti Gratia Plena '06	🍷🍷	4*
● Dolcetto d'Alba Castellizzano '07	🍷🍷	4*
● Dolcetto d'Alba Vign. Nervo '07	🍷🍷	4*
● Barbaresco '05	🍷	6
● Barbaresco Castellizzano '05	🍷	6
● Barbera d'Alba '07	🍷	4
● Dolcetto d'Alba '07	🍷	4
O Langhe Chardonnay '07	🍷	4
O Roero Arneis '07	🍷	4
● Langhe Nebbiolo '06	🍷	4
● Langhe Rosso Pertinace '05	🍷	5
● Barbaresco Castellizzano '04	YY	6
● Barbaresco Marcarini '04	YY	6
● Barbaresco Nervo '04	YY	6

Il Vignale

LOC. LOMELLINA
VIA GAVI, 130
15067 NOVI LIGURE [AL]
TEL. 014372715
www.ilvignale.it

ANNUAL PRODUCTION 45,000 bottles
HECTARES UNDER VINE 12
VITICULTURE METHOD Conventional

Il Vignale is situated in the middle of an area particularly suited to the cultivation of cortese grapes, where the municipalities of Novi Ligure and Gavi meet. Piero and Vilma Cappelletti have owned the estate for about a decade. Although they come from different professional backgrounds, their enthusiasm and determination have enabled the estate to achieve the highest quality levels in the denomination. This year, they presented three versions of Gavi: the Vilma Cappelletti Etichetta Verde '07 selection, Vilma Cappelletti Etichetta Nera '06, which is partly aged in wood, and Vigne Alte '06. Again this year, Vilma Cappelletti reached our tasting finals.
It shows an attractive straw yellow with intense, typically floral aromas and fruity overtones. In the mouth it offers good, refreshing acidity and nice structure. Vigne Alte is slightly less complex, presenting a floral nose and a very fresh, zesty palate with a faintly bitter finish. Rosso di Malì wasn't presented as it hadn't been bottled at the time of our tastings.

O Gavi Vilma Cappelletti Et. Verde '07	🍷🍷	4*
O Gavi Vigne Alte '07	🍷🍷	4
O Gavi Vilma Cappelletti Et. Nera '06	🍷🍷	4
O Gavi Vilma Cappelletti '06	YY	4
O Gavi Vigne Alte '06	YY	4
● M.to Rosso Rosso di Malì '04	YY	4

Vigne Regali

VIA VITTORIO VENETO, 76
15019 STREVI [AL]
TEL. 0144362600
www.castellobanfi.it

ANNUAL PRODUCTION	1,900,000 bottles
HECTARES UNDER VINE	75
VITICULTURE METHOD	Conventional

Vigne Regali is a Banfi group winery. Many different grape varieties are grown on its 75 hectares, from international cultivars used for the estate's sparkling wines, to traditional local ones, like barbera, dolcetto and the aromatic brachetto and moscato. Cortese, another Piedmont grape, is grown around Gavi on the plots belonging to the Principessa Gavia estate. There were plenty of labels at our tastings. Barbera Banin is excellent, with a clean, complex nose of overripe fruit, cakes and faint hints of balsam. The full, harmonious palate is terrific, with enough acidity to support its almost opulent body. Dolcetto L'Ardì is also captivating, with nicely rounded tannins and impressive structure and length. The Gavi presents pale straw with a rather underdeveloped nose. The palate is very refreshing and moreish. From the aromatic wines, we liked the very drinkable Brachetto Vigneto La Rosa, with elegant varietal aromas and a delicate finish. Moscato Strevi is moderately intense on the nose and refreshing but not too sweet on the palate. The sparklers include the interesting Banfi Brut Talento, Tener and the Cuvée Aurora.

Vigneti Massa

P.ZZA G. CAPSONI, 10
15059 MONLEALE [AL]
TEL. 013180302

ANNUAL PRODUCTION	80,000 bottles
HECTARES UNDER VINE	19.5
VITICULTURE METHOD	Natural

A glance at the table below shows how well this winery performed, thanks to the skills of Walter Massa. Walter spends his days in the cellar or among the rows and his evenings in Italy's best restaurants proposing his wines. He manages and farms in the same dogged spirit. We duly note the fine results with timorasso from the man who rediscovered this native vine. This year, Derthona '06 joined its senior partners Costa del Vento and Sterpi in our finals and actually took our top accolade. Its perfect style outclassed the estate's two star wines. Derthona has a generous nose and a palate perked up by dynamic minerality and full, but not excessive, body. The other two wines are initially closed before opening into a charming fruit bouquet. This time we preferred Sterpo to Costa del Vento, which needs further ageing. Last year, we celebrated the return of Bigolla, one of the best Barberas around, but this time it is joined by Monleale '07 vying for the title of the estate's best red. Bigolla is concentrated and opulent while Monleale is softer and fresher. We also correct a mistake in last year's Guide. Croatina Pertichetta was the '04 and not the '05.

Wine	Rating
● Barbera d'Asti Vign. Banin '05	🍷🍷 6
○ Alta Langa Cuvée Aurora '03	🍷🍷 6
○ Banfi Brut Talento N. M.	🍷🍷 4
● Dolcetto d'Acqui L'Ardì '07	🍷🍷 4
○ Moscato d'Asti Strevi '07	🍷 4
⊙ Alta Langa Cuvée Aurora Rosé '05	🍷 6
● Brachetto d'Acqui Vign. La Rosa '07	🍷 5
○ Gavi Principessa Gavia '07	🍷 4
○ Tener Brut	🍷 4
● Barbera d'Asti Vign. Banin '04	🍷🍷 6
● Dolcetto d'Aqui Argusto '04	🍷🍷 4

Wine	Rating
○ Colli Tortonesi Timorasso Derthona '06	🍷🍷🍷 6
● Colli Tortonesi Monleale Bigolla '05	🍷🍷 7
● Colli Tortonesi Monleale '05	🍷🍷 6
○ Colli Tortonesi Timorasso Sterpi '06	🍷🍷 7
○ Colli Tortonesi Timorasso Costa del Vento '06	🍷🍷 7
● Colli Tortonesi Croatina Pertichetta '05	🍷🍷 5
● Colli Tortonesi Barbera Sentieri '07	🍷🍷 5
○ Colli Tortonesi Moscato Muscatè '07	🍷🍷 3*
● Colli Tortonesi Rosso Pietra del Gallo '07	🍷 4
○ Colli Tortonesi Bianco Costa del Vento '05	🍷🍷🍷 8
○ Colli Tortonesi Bianco Sterpi '04	🍷🍷🍷 7

Villa Fiorita

VIA CASE SPARSE, 2
14034 CASTELLO DI ANNONE [AT]
TEL. 0141401231
www.villafiorita-wines.com

ANNUAL PRODUCTION	80,000 bottles
HECTARES UNDER VINE	12
VITICULTURE METHOD	Conventional

Francesco Rondolino is the man behind this handsome estate. Over the years, he has put together a good team with agronomist Sergio Carpignano and oenologist Piero Ballario. This year, several labels that performed well in the past are missing. Consequently, we were unable to taste Monferrato Bianco Sovrano and Monferrato Rosso Nero di Villa Riserva, neither of which was considered ready. However, there was an excellent Barbera d'Asti Superiore Il Giorgione '06, which deservedly returned to our finals. It shows deep ruby with hints of purple. The palate has enormous energy and power, accompanied by impressive acidity. The nose is heady, showing well-balanced fruit and tertiary aromas. Barbera d'Asti Superiore '06, a wine of character and texture, performed well. Monferrato Rosso Abaco '06, from pinot nero vinified in steel and large barrels, is very young with good ageing prospects, as is the impressive, spicy Grignolino Pian delle Querce '07. The most exciting new feature this year is a highly drinkable, enjoyable Freisa d'Asti Vivace, of which just 5,000 bottles were produced. Chardonnay Le Tavole '07 is uncomplicated but interesting.

Villa Giada

REG. CEIROLE, 4
14053 CANELLI [AT]
TEL. 0141831100
www.andreafaccio.it

ANNUAL PRODUCTION	238,000 bottles
HECTARES UNDER VINE	25
VITICULTURE METHOD	Conventional

Andrea Faccio and his team run this fine estate at Ceirole, near Canelli, where the Moscato is produced, and another two properties in the surrounding hills, the four-hectare Cascina del Parroco and the 12-hectare Cascina Dani, at Agliano Terme. The wines are traditional, with a few international reds and whites, such as Merlot and Chardonnay. The estate philosophy is rooted in the terroir, which it fully conveys, and up-to-date technology ensures consistent results during vinification. A wide range of wines was submitted, although this year the most important selection, Barbera d'Asti Bricco Dani '06, was absent, as it is ageing for another year. Instead, the estate presented a valid Barbera d'Asti Nizza, dedicated to Andrea's son Federico, which has a balsamic nose and a powerful palate. La Quercia '06 is less concentrated with fresher, fuller-flavoured fruit. The current Barberas Ajan and Surì – the latter from naturally farmed vineyards – are pleasant and easy drinking. From the Monferrato DOC reds, Treponti, from nebbiolo and barbera, is austere and a tad dried while the brand new Novenove Merlot focuses on finesse rather than weight.

● Barbera d'Asti Sup. Il Giorgione '06	♟♟	5
● Barbera d'Asti Sup. '06	♟♟	4
● Grignolino d'Asti Pian delle Querce '07	♟♟	3*
● M.to Rosso Abaco '06	♟♟	3*
● Freisa d'Asti Vivace '07	♟	3
O Piemonte Chardonnay Le Tavole '07	♟	4
● Barbera d'Asti Sup. Il Giorgione '03	♟♟	5
● Barbera d'Asti Sup. Il Giorgione '01	♟♟	6
● Barbera d'Asti Sup. Il Giorgione '00	♟♟	6
● M.to Rosso Maniero '04	♟♟	5
● M.to Rosso Nero di Villa Ris. di Famiglia '05	♟♟	6

● Barbera d'Asti Sup. La Quercia '06	♟♟	5
● Barbera d'Asti Sup. Nizza Dedicato a Federico '04	♟♟	6
● PrimoVolo '05	♟♟	6
● Barbera d'Asti Ajan '07	♟	4
● Barbera d'Asti I Surì '07	♟	3
O M.to Bianco I Surì '07	♟	3
● M.to Rosso Novenove '05	♟	3
● M.to Rosso Treponti '06	♟	4
O Moscato d'Asti Ceirole '07	♟	4
● Barbera d'Asti Sup. Nizza Bricco Dani '04	♟♟	5
● Barbera d'Asti Sup. Nizza Bricco Dani '05	♟♟	5

Villa Sparina

FRAZ. MONTEROTONDO, 56
15066 GAVI [AL]
TEL. 0143633835
www.villasparina.it

ANNUAL PRODUCTION 480,000 bottles
HECTARES UNDER VINE 56
VITICULTURE METHOD Conventional

The Moccagatta family has always believed in this area, maximizing its potential first with great wine and then with their Relais Ostelliere and adjoining La Gallina restaurant. They have been aided by the beauty and climate of this part of Gavi – the Monterotondo hill – but the Moccagattas identified its potential. Again this year, the two selections, Gavi Monterotondo and Monferrato Rosso Rivalta, achieved excellent results. Monterotondo is bright straw yellow with golden flecks, giving delicate nose of fruit and spring flowers, and a balanced, nicely acidic palate with a long, very distinctive finish. Monferrato Rosso Rivalta, from barbera with a dash of merlot, has a very elegant nose of fruit and subtle spiciness, and a long, balanced palate. The current Gavi is also great, particularly in the mouth, where good structure is supported by nice acidity and balance. Brut Metodo Classico, from cortese grapes, is impressive, revealing yeasty aromas and a fine, persistent bead. Montej has fuller body of the two Barberas. Monferrato Bianco Montej, from chardonnay, müller thurgau and sauvignon bianco, and Dolcetto Maioli both earned One Glass.

O Gavi del Comune di Gavi Monterotondo '06	🍷🍷	6
● M.to Rosso Rivalta '05	🍷🍷	6
● Barbera del M.to '05	🍷🍷	4*
● Barbera del M.to Montej '06	🍷🍷	4*
O Brut M. Cl.	🍷🍷	5
O Gavi del Comune di Gavi '07	🍷🍷	4*
● Dolcetto di Ovada Maioli '06	🍷	4
O M.to Bianco Montej '07	🍷	4
● M.to Rosso Rivalta '99	🍷🍷🍷	6
● M.to Rosso Rivalta '04	🍷🍷🍷	6
● M.to Rosso Rivalta '00	🍷🍷🍷	6
● M.to Rosso Rivalta '03	🍷🍷	6
● M.to Rosso Rivalta '02	🍷🍷	6
● M.to Rosso Rivalta '01	🍷🍷	6

Cantina Sociale di Vinchio Vaglio Serra

REGIONE SAN PANCRAZIO, 1
14040 VINCHIO [AT]
TEL. 0141950903
www.vinchio.com

ANNUAL PRODUCTION 1,000,000 bottles
HECTARES UNDER VINE 320
VITICULTURE METHOD Conventional

On 26 February 2009, this co-operative winery will celebrate its 50th anniversary. The half century has been punctuated by successes that have accompanied, and in many cases driven, the improvement of Barbera d'Asti. Over this period, the number of member growers has risen from 19 to 224. There are 320 hectares under vine, yielding almost a million bottles. This year, some of the most interesting wines were missing. Barbera Sei Vigne Insynthesis was not made in the poor 2005 vintage. Similarly, Barbera Vigne Vecchie '06 had not been bottled at the time of printing and our tasting has been deferred to next year, as it has for Monferrato Tutti per Uno. Despite the gaps in this year's list, Vinchio Vaglio Serra's less ambitious wines put on a fine performance, reminding us of their underlying quality. Barbera I Tre Vescovi has fruit with hints of cocoa powder and vanilla after eight months in barrique. The palate is full bodied with nice acidity on the finish. The basic Barbera d'Asti is very attractive. Piemonte Chardonnay '07 and Grignolino d'Asti Le Nocche are both well made.

● Barbera d'Asti '07	🍷🍷	4
● Barbera d'Asti Sup. I Tre Vescovi '06	🍷🍷	4
● Grignolino d'Asti Le Nocche '07	🍷	3
O Piemonte Chardonnay '07	🍷	3
● Barbera d'Asti Sup. Sei Vigne Insynthesis '01	🍷🍷🍷	7
● Barbera d'Asti Sup. Sei Vigne Insynthesis '04	🍷🍷	7
● Barbera d'Asti Sup. Sei Vigne Insynthesis '03	🍷🍷	7
● Barbera d'Asti Sup. I Tre Vescovi '05	🍷🍷	4
● Barbera d'Asti Sup. I Tre Vescovi '04	🍷🍷	4

Gianni Voerzio

S.DA LORETO, 1
12064 LA MORRA [CN]
TEL. 0173509194
voerzio.gianni@tiscali.it

ANNUAL PRODUCTION	66,000 bottles
HECTARES UNDER VINE	12.5
VITICULTURE METHOD	Natural

This estate's products are closely associated with Langhe. Gianni applies a blend of tradition and technology to his wines, paying meticulous attention to grape selection and using the very latest cellar equipment to ensure consistently high quality. The La Serra vineyard selection yields an impeccable Barolo with an intense, full, spicy nose and a concentrated palate full of youthful tannins that reveals tobacco and brandied fruit as it progresses. Barbera Ciabot della Luna '06 is another vineyard selection, which shows powerful and fruity before the flavoursome palate unveils its warm, spicy body. We were impressed by the elegant Langhe Nebbiolo '06, aged in new 500-litre barrels, and Langhe Serrapiù '06, a barrique-aged nebbiolo and barbera blend, which is the most feminine wine on the list, with its grace, elegance and style. The selection of reds is completed by an interesting Dolcetto and an unusual slightly sparkling Freisa, which is very drinkable. A dry, zesty Arneis and a sweet, delicately aromatic Moscato d'Asti are the estate's whites.

★ Roberto Voerzio

LOC. CERRETO, 1
12064 LA MORRA [CN]
TEL. 0173509196

ANNUAL PRODUCTION	35,000 bottles
HECTARES UNDER VINE	17
VITICULTURE METHOD	Natural

Roberto Voerzio's philosophy is simple. Meticulous work in the vineyard will produce characterful wines. The results are impressive, thanks in part to the very limited yields that Roberto obtains from each hectare under vine. As no more than 35,000 bottles are produced from the 12 estate-owned and five rented hectares each year, each hectare effectively yields just over 2,000 bottles. It's not just limited production that drives quality, though, for the vineyards from which the grapes are sourced is also crucial. All are superb vineyards in the La Morra area, plus one in Barolo territory. Cerequio, Brunate and La Serra are on the slopes overlooking the municipality of Barolo, Rocche and Torriglione are situated at the village of Annunziata, and I Capalot is on the road from La Morra to Santa Maria. Sarmassa is located in the municipality of Barolo. All the Barolos that we tasted were very good and complex, with the slightly raisined note that is the estate's signature. While this feature is nicely offset by tannins and balanced acidity in the excellent 2004 vintage, the wines produced in the warmer 2003 season unfold less gracefully.

● Barbera d'Alba Ciabot della Luna '06	￥￥	5
● Barolo La Serra '04	￥￥	8
● Dolcetto d'Alba Rocchettevino '07	￥￥	4*
● Langhe Freisa Sotto I Bastioni '07	￥￥	4*
● Langhe Nebbiolo Ciabot della Luna '06	￥￥	6
● Langhe Rosso Serrapiù '06	￥￥	6
O Moscato d'Asti Vignasergente '07	￥￥	5
O Langhe Arneis Bricco Cappellina '07	￥	5
● Barolo La Serra '98	￥￥￥	8
● Barolo La Serra '97	￥￥￥	8
● Barolo La Serra '96	￥￥￥	8
● Barolo La Serra '01	￥￥	8
● Barolo La Serra '00	￥￥	8

● Barolo Brunate '04	￥￥	8
● Barolo Cerequio '04	￥￥	8
● Barolo La Serra '04	￥￥	8
● Barolo Rocche dell'Annunziata Torriglione '04	￥￥	8
● Barolo Sarmassa di Barolo '04	￥￥	8
● Barolo Vecchie Viti dei Capalot e delle Brunate Ris. '03	￥￥	8
● Barolo Brunate '99	￥￥￥	8
● Barolo Brunate '98	￥￥￥	8
● Barolo Brunate '96	￥￥￥	8
● Barolo Brunate '93	￥￥￥	8
● Barolo Brunate '90	￥￥￥	6
● Barolo Brunate '89	￥￥￥	6
● Barolo Cerequio '96	￥￥￥	8
● Barolo Cerequio '91	￥￥￥	6

OTHER WINERIES

Marco e Vittorio Adriano

Fraz. San Rocco Seno d'Elvio, 13a
12051 Alba [CN]
tel. 0173362294
www.adrianovini.it

Brothers Marco and Vittorio Adriano run this fine estate at San Rocco Seno d'Elvio, focusing on the classic Langhe grapes. The two Barbarescos are very good but we slightly preferred the rich, complex Basarin. Sanadaive is exceptionally elegant and Barbera d'Alba Superiore '06 is first rate.

● Barbaresco Basarin '05	🍷🍷 6
● Barbaresco Sanadaive '05	🍷🍷 6
● Barbera d'Alba Superiore '06	🍷🍷 4*

Valerio Aloi

via Pietro Fissore, 6
12046 Montà [CN]
tel. 0173975604
nico.bono@libero.it

The estate founded by the late Valerio Aloi continues to make great wines. Nicoletta is determined to carry on her husband's work. The Arneis has been one of best for years. Roero '06 has intriguing spicy aromas and a warm, rounded palate with an attractive liquorice finish.

O Roero Arneis '07	🍷🍷 4*
● Roero Bricco Morinaldo '06	🍷🍷 5

Osvaldo Barberis

b.ta Valdibà, 42
12063 Dogliani [CN]
tel. 017370054

Dolcetto is the main variety at Dogliani and Osvaldo is skilled at interpreting it. This year, he presented two selections: the complex, firm Dogliamo Puncin '06; and the fresher, easier drinking Dolcetto di Dogliani Valdibà '07. Barbera Castella is impressive while Barbera Brichat '07 is a rung down.

● Barbera d'Alba Castella '06	🍷🍷 4*
● Dogliani Puncin '06	🍷🍷 4*
● Dolcetto di Dogliani Valdibà '07	🍷🍷 3*
● Piemonte Barbera Brichat '07	🍷 3

Beccaria

via Giovanni Bianco, 3
15039 Ozzano Monferrato [AL]
tel. 0142487321
www.beccaria-vini.it

Beccaria did well even without the flagship Convivium, whose release has been postponed by a year. The attractive, fresh Barbera Evoè came close to Two Glasses while the balanced, well-typed Grignolino and the almost aromatic still Freisa, with its fruits and herbs fragrances, also did well.

● Grignolino del M.to Casalese Grignò '07	🍷🍷 3*
● M.to Freisa Lilàn '07	🍷🍷 3*
● Barbera del M.to Evoè '06	🍷 4

Benotto

via San Carlo, 52
14055 Costigliole d'Asti [AT]
tel. 0141966406
benottovini@virgilio.it

The house speciality is Barbera, which the Benotto brothers presented in three convincing versions. The '06 stands out for its alluring fruit nose with hints of rain-soaked earth and sweet spices. Vigneto Casot '04 is impressively fresh while Superiore Balau is just behind.

● Barbera d'Asti '06	🍷🍷 2*
● Barbera d'Asti Sup. Vign. Casot '04	🍷🍷 3*
● Barbera d'Asti Sup. Balau '04	🍷 4

Bersano

p.zza Dante, 21
14049 Nizza Monferrato [AT]
tel. 0141720211
www.bersano.it

This large Nizza Monferrato winery gave us two very convincing wines: Barbera La Generala, with notes of cocoa powder and sweet spices, and the characterful, fruit-forward Barbera Cremosina '06. The Gavi from the Raggio estate is piquant and fruity.

● Barbera d'Asti Sup. Cremosina '06	🍷🍷 4*
● Barbera d'Asti Sup. Generala '06	🍷🍷 6
O Gavi del Comune di Gavi Raggio '07	🍷 5

OTHER WINERIES

Bianchi

VIA ROMA, 37
28070 SIZZANO [NO]
TEL. 0321810004
www.bianchibiowine.it

Bianchi's list is increasingly impressive and this year featured several gems. The most interesting is the spicy Sizzano '03 with its sweet tannins and subtle background fruit. Ghemme '04 is firm, powerful and notably long. Luminae, a single-variety Erbaluce, is first rate and the Nebbiolo is well made.

● Ghemme '04	♥♥	5
● Sizzano '03	♥♥	4*
O Colline Novaresi Bianco Luminae '07	♥♥	4*
● Colline Novaresi Nebbiolo '07	♥	3

Massimo Bo

FRAZ. SANT'ANNA
VIA SANT'ANNA, 19
14055 COSTIGLIOLE D'ASTI [AT]
TEL. 0141961891
bo.massimo@hotmail.com

Massimo Bo is the last in a long line of grower producers. He and his parents Armando and Marcella run a ten-hectare estate in the heart of Barbera country. Arbuc, aged in steel, embodies the fruity, young style of the grape while Costiliolae, aged in barriques and tonneaux, is more complex.

● Barbera d'Asti Arbuc '07	♥♥	4*
● Barbera d'Asti Sup. Costiliolae '05	♥♥	4*

Renato Boveri

VIA XXV APRILE, 1
15059 MONLEALE [AL]
TEL. 013180560

The Boveri estate has always made interesting wines and this year was no exception. The cream of the crop is Croatina Costa, which won Two Glasses for its fruity nose and alluring palate. Sant'Ambrogio is a little short on structure. Dolcetto La Cereta is good.

● Colli Tortonesi Rosso Costa '06	♥♥	5
● Colli Tortonesi Barbera S. Ambrogio '06	♥	4
● Colli Tortonesi Rosso La Cereta '06	♥	4

Cantina del Bricchetto

VIA BRICCHETTO, 4
12057 NEIVE [CN]
TEL. 0173677307

Franco Rocca's wines are forthright and rustic in style, occasionally with the odd flaw. This year, Barbera Bricco Sterpone is slightly cramped by oak and the appealing, moderately concentrated Barbaresco Albesani shows well-amalgamated tannins. Sernì Sörì Alessia, from barbera and nebbiolo, is well made.

● Barbaresco Albesani '05	♥♥	5
● Barbera d'Alba Bricco Sterpone '05	♥	5
● Sernì Sörì Alessia '06	♥	5

Francesco Brigatti

VIA OLMI, 31
28019 SUNO [NO]
TEL. 032285037
www.vinibrigatti.it

This estate's list is long and features many interesting wines. We were pleasantly surprised by Colline Novaresi Barbera '06, which gives fruit against a background of sweet spices and leather. MötZiflon is rich and complex, with sensations of tobacco and cinchona. Mötfrei '05 earned One Glass.

● Colline Novaresi V. MötZiflon '05	♥♥	4*
● Colline Novaresi Barbera '06	♥♥	4*
● Colline Novaresi Nebbiolo V. Mötfrei '05	♥	4

Renato Buganza

LOC. CASCINA GARBINOTTO, 4
12040 PIOBESI D'ALBA [CN]
TEL. 0173619370
rbuganza@tin.it

This small family-run estate performed well again this year, with a trio of well-crafted, characterful wines. Despite its hefty body, the Arneis is very fruity and refreshing. The Barbera has an acidity-led palate and the Roero is pleasantly tannic with a rounded palate and leisurely finish.

O Roero Arneis dla Trifula '07	♥♥	4*
● Roero Bric Paradis '05	♥♥	5
● Barbera d'Alba V. Veja '05	♥	4

OTHER WINERIES

Ca' dei Mandorli

VIA IV NOVEMBRE, 15
14010 CASTEL ROCCHERO [AT]
TEL. 0141760131
www.cadeimandorli.com

This large estate aims to make approachable, easy-drinking wines. That goal is achieved in spades by the captivatingly juicy Brachetto d'Acqui, which shows sweet, but not cloying, on the finish. Moscato d'Asti is fragrant and Dolcetto d'Acqui Il Ruja is well made.

● Brachetto d'Acqui Le Donne dei Boschi '07	♥♥ 4*
● Dolcetto d'Acqui Il Ruja' '07	♥ 4
O Moscato d'Asti Dei Giari '07	♥ 4

Ca' Nova

VIA SAN ISIDORO, 1
28020 BOGOGNO [NO]
TEL. 0322863406
www.cascinacanova.it

In 1996, Giada Codecasa gave up law to start making wine on her Bogogno estate. Her ten hectares of vineyards at Bogogno and Romagnano Sesia are planted mainly to nebbiolo. The list is headed by a Ghemme with a fine tannic weave, followed by an austere Vigna San Quirico and the fragrant Bocciòlo.

● Colline Novaresi Nebbiolo V. San Quirico '04	♥♥ 5
● Ghemme '04	♥♥ 5
● Colline Novaresi Nebbiolo Bocciòlo '06	♥ 3

Cantina Sociale del Canavese

VIA MONTALENGHE, 9
10090 CUCEGLIO [TO]
TEL. 012432034
www.cantinacanavese.it

This co-operative winery performed well at our tastings, particularly with the excellent Canavese Rosso, which combines considerable elegance with grip and powerful tannins. Erbaluce di Caluso Elisa is less impressive than last year. It's still fresh and fruity but not as complex.

● Canavese Rosso '06	♥♥ 3*
O Erbaluce di Caluso Elisa '07	♥ 3

La Caplana

VIA CIRCONVALLAZIONE, 4
15060 BOSIO [AL]
TEL. 0143684182
lacaplana@libero.it

Gavi Vigna Vecchia '07 is one of the best of its kind and Natalino Guido must be proud of this impressive result. His big hitter proffers notes of apples and pears with spring flowers on the nose. The rest of the list is also excellent, particularly Gavi di Gavi and Narciso.

O Gavi del Comune di Gavi V. Vecchia '07	♥♥ 3*
● Barbera d'Asti Rubis '05	♥♥ 3*
● Dolcetto di Ovada Narciso '06	♥♥ 3*
O Gavi del Comune di Gavi '07	♥♥ 4

Carlotta

VIA CONDOVE, 61
10050 BORGONE SUSA [TO]
TEL. 0119646150
rfrancesca@libero.it

Carla Cometto grows grapes in the hills in an area long abandoned by most farmers. She handles the difficulties competently and determinedly. We were impressed by Costa Oro, from neretta cuneese, ciliegiolo and barbera, and Vigna Combe, from rare local grapes. Rocca del Lupo, from avanà and barbera, earned One Glass.

● Valsusa Costa Oro '07	♥♥ 4*
● Valsusa V. Combe '07	♥♥ 4*
● Valsusa Rocca del Lupo '07	♥ 4
● Valsusa Costa Oro '06	♥♥ 4

Tenuta Carretta

LOC. CARRETTA, 2
12040 PIOBESI D'ALBA [CN]
TEL. 0173619119
www.tenutacarretta.it

This large estate is recovering from recent restructuring. Some of the wines still have a way to go but quality is the goal that in mind. Arneis Canorei and Arneis Cayega are very good with the former showing greater structure. The Barbaresco focuses on softness while the Barolo is austere and well rounded.

● Barbaresco Cascina Bordino '05	♥♥ 7
● Barolo Vign. in Cannubi '04	♥♥ 8
O Roero Arneis V. Canorei '07	♥♥ 5
O Roero Arneis Cayega '07	♥ 4

OTHER WINERIES

Carussin

REG. MARIANO, 27
14050 SAN MARZANO OLIVETO [AT]
TEL. 0141831358
www.carussin.it

Bruna Ferro believes in her work and invests a lot of energy in the many activities of her fine estate. Bruna's personality is reflected in her wines and some achieved excellent results. Her Barbera Ferro Carlo is juicy and complex, and La Tranquilla is first rate, while Lia Vì and Filari Corti are not far behind.

● Barbera d'Asti La Tranquilla '04	ŸŸ	4*
● Barbera d'Asti Sup. Nizza Ferro Carlo '04	ŸŸ	5
● Barbera d'Asti Lia Vì '07	Ÿ	4
○ Moscato d'Asti Filari Corti '07	Ÿ	3

La Casaccia

VIA BARBANO DANTE, 10
15034 CELLA MONTE [AL]
TEL. 0142489986

Giovanni Rava works well, which enabled him to present an impressive list of wines again this year. Barbera del Monferrato is concentrated and long, Barbera d'Asti may be young but is already drinking deliciously and Grignolino is one of the best around, with an impressive follow-though on the palate.

● Grignolino del M.to Casalese Poggetto '07	ŸŸ	4*
● Barbera d'Asti V. Sant'Anna '07	ŸŸ	4*
● Barbera del M.to Sup. Bricco del Bosco '06	ŸŸ	5

Casavecchia

VIA ROMA, 2
12055 DIANO D'ALBA [CN]
TEL. 017369321
cantinacasavecchia@casavecchiasergio.191.it

The list from the Casavecchia brothers features some of the most typical wines of southern Piedmont. Barolo Piantà is powerful, with perfectly balanced acidity and tannins, while Diano d'Alba Sörì Bruni is still closed on the nose. The Nebbiolo '06 and Langhe Rosso Pian del Lupo '04 also earned Two Glasses.

● Barolo Piantà '04	ŸŸ	6*
● Diano d'Alba Sörì Bruni '07	ŸŸ	4*
● Langhe Rosso Pian del Lupo '04	ŸŸ	5
● Nebbiolo d'Alba Piadvenza '06	ŸŸ	4*
● Barbera d'Alba San Quirico '06	Ÿ	4

Cascina Flino

VIA ABELLONI, 7
12055 DIANO D'ALBA [CN]
TEL. 017369231
flino@flino.com

The splendid 2004 growing year enabled Cascina Flino to present a terrific version of Barolo San Lorenzo. Its complex nose of berries and sweet spices precedes a juicy palate with a lingering finish. Diano d'Alba '07 is as attractive as ever, like the spicy Barbera Flin '06.

● Barbera d'Alba Flin '06	ŸŸ	4*
● Barolo San Lorenzo '04	ŸŸ	6*
● Diano d'Alba V. Vecchia '07	ŸŸ	3*

Cascina Montagnola

S.DA MONTAGNOLA, 1
15058 VIGUZZOLO [AL]
TEL. 0131898558
www.cascinamontagnola.com

This Viguzzolo estate's decision to produce a Timorasso was right on the money and the cellar's Barbera Rodeo also impressed, coming close to a Three Glass prize.
The Timorasso is first rate, despite a few rough edges and Chardonnay Risveglio is pleasant.

● Colli Tortonesi Barbera Sup. Rodeo '05	ŸŸ	6
○ Colli Tortonesi Bianco Morasso '06	ŸŸ	5
○ Colli Tortonesi Bianco Risveglio '07	Ÿ	5

Castello del Poggio

LOC. POGGIO, 9
14100 PORTACOMARO [AT]
TEL. 0141202543
www.poggio.it

Some of Castello del Poggio's most interesting labels were missing from the list this year and in consequence we tasted only three wines. The most convincing was the caressing Barbera d'Asti '05 with its full-flavoured finish. Moscato and Monferrato Dolcetto are both charming.

● Barbera d'Asti '05	ŸŸ	4*
● M.to Dolcetto '07	Ÿ	4
○ Moscato d'Asti '07	Ÿ	4

OTHER WINERIES

Castello di Tagliolo

VIA CASTELLO, 1
15070 TAGLIOLO MONFERRATO [AL]
TEL. 014389195
www.castelloditagliolo.com

Oberto Pinelli Gentile and his son Luca's wines did very well. Dolcetto La Peira is excellent, giving fruit and spice that lead to a complex finale. Monferrato Rosso Nobile, from barbera and cabernet sauvignon, mingles vegetality with notes of morello cherry. La Castagnola is pleasant.

● Dolcetto di Ovada La Peira '05	♟♟ 4*
● M.to Rosso Nobile '04	♟♟ 4*
● Dolcetto di Ovada La Castagnola '03	♟ 4

Cave di Moleto

REG. MOLETO, 4
15038 OTTIGLIO [AL]
TEL. 0142921468
www.moleto.it

This year, Cave di Moleto failed to present many of its leading labels and so we were unable to give it a full profile. The only wine that we tasted for this edition of the Guide was the Grignolino, which showed very well, earning Two Glasses for its spicy finish.

● Grignolino del M.to Casalese '07	♟♟ 3*
● Barbera del M.to '05	♟♟ 3
● M.to Rosso Pieve di San Michele '05	♟♟ 4

Le Cecche

VIA MOGLIA GERLOTTO, 10
12055 DIANO D'ALBA [CN]
TEL. 017369323
www.lececche.com

Non-Italians who decide to make wine often do so for the sheer fun of it, not from any natural bent. But not Jan Jules De Bruyne and his wife Paola, who make seriously good wines. Le Cecche is powerful and fruity, the basic Diano d'Alba is exciting and the Barbera shows full flavoured, juicy and alcoholic.

● Diano d'Alba '07	♟♟ 3*
● Diano d'Alba Sörì Le Cecche '07	♟♟ 4*
● Barbera d'Alba '06	♟ 4

La Chiara

LOC. VALLEGGE, 24
15066 GAVI [AL]
TEL. 0143642293
www.lachiara.it

La Chiara presented us with an excellent Gavi del Comune di Gavi, which shows bright straw yellow with a nose of apples and pears, a nicely acidic palate and a very long, juicy finish. There was One Glass for the Vigneto Gropella selection.

○ Gavi del Comune di Gavi '07	♟♟ 3*
○ Gavi del Comune di Gavi Vign. Gropella '06	♟ 4

Cocito

LOC. MICCA, 25
12057 NEIVE [CN]
TEL. 017367052
ezio.cocito@tiscali.it

Ezio Cocito produces just one wine, Barbaresco Baluchin Riserva. The '04 vintage proffers a complex nose with notes of truffle, hazelnut, black olives, raspberries and currants. There's good continuity on the palate but the finish is penalized by slightly green tannins.

● Barbaresco Baluchin Ris. '04	♟♟ 8
● Barbaresco Baluchin Ris. '03	♟♟ 8
● Barbaresco Baluchin '03	♟♟ 8

Vigne Marina Coppi

VIA SANT'ANDREA, 5
15051 CASTELLANIA [AL]
TEL. 3385360111
www.vignemarinacoppi.com

Francesco Bellocchio's mainly Barbera estate is named after his mother, the daughter of Italian cycling legend Fausto Coppi. It did well again this year. Sant'Andrea is captivating, showing fresher and more drinkable than the nonetheless convincing I Grop. Marine, from favorita, has taut mineral notes.

● Colli Tortonesi Barbera I Grop '06	♟♟ 5
● Colli Tortonesi Barbera Sant'Andrea '07	♟♟ 4*
○ Colli Tortonesi Favorita Marine '07	♟♟ 5
● Colli Tortonesi Barbera Castellania '06	♟ 4

OTHER WINERIES

Clemente Cossetti

VIA GUARDIE, 1
14043 CASTELNUOVO BELBO [AT]
TEL. 0141799803
www.cossetti.it

This interesting large winery, with an annual production of 600,000 bottles, put on an impressive show. Barbera Superiore Nizza has raspberry and blueberry-like fruit and delicate spiciness. La Vigna Vecchia is very pleasant drinking, while VentidiMarzo is simpler but not banal.

● Barbera d'Asti La Vigna Vecchia '06	♟♟	3*
● Barbera d'Asti Sup. Nizza '04	♟♟	5
● Barbera d'Asti VentidiMarzo '07	♟	3

Giovanni Daglio

VIA MONTALE CELLI, 10
15050 COSTA VESCOVATO [AL]
TEL. 0131838262
giovanni.daglio@tiscali.it

This estate did well, although Barbera Basinas '05 suffered from a less fortunate growing year than the previous one. We preferred the basic Pias, which is warm and fruity. Timorasso Cantico was the top scorer, with prominent mineral notes, concentrated aromas and a long finish. Cortese is simple and fruity.

○ Colli Tortonesi Timorasso Cantico '06	♟♟	5
● Colli Tortonesi Barbera Pias '06	♟♟	4*
● Colli Tortonesi Barbera Basinas '05	♟	4
○ Colli Tortonesi Cortese V. del Re '07	♟	3

Gianni Doglia

FRAZ. ANNUNZIATA, 56
14054 CASTAGNOLE DELLE LANZE [AT]
TEL. 0141878359
wine-doglia@libero.it

Young Gianni Doglia is an acknowledged maestro of moscato. His '07 vintage has a nose of sage, citronella, citrus fruit and peaches. It's sweet and juicy on the palate with a fresh, acidic finish. Barbera d'Alba Superiore '06 is also great, with intriguing notes of rain-soaked earth.

● M.to Rosso "!" '05	♟♟	5
● Barbera d'Asti Sup. '06	♟♟	5
○ Moscato d'Asti '07	♟♟	4*
● Barbera d'Asti Boscodonne '07	♟	4

Favaro

S.DA CHIUSURE, 1BIS
10010 PIVERONE [TO]
TEL. 012572606
www.cantinafavaro.it

This year, several of the most distinguished labels are missing from the winery's list, as they weren't ready at the time of going to press. We still managed to taste two very interesting wines: Erbaluce di Caluso and Basy '06, a barbera and syrah blend.

● Basy '06	♟♟	4
○ Erbaluce di Caluso Le Chiusure '07	♟	4

Cascina Ferro

VIA NOSSERIO, 14
14055 COSTIGLIOLE D'ASTI [AT]
TEL. 0141966693

Cascina Ferro is among the Other Wineries this year, not because of any slip in quality but simply because it presented too few wines – just one – to merit a full profile. Barbera Bric is spot on, proffering a layered nose of fruit and spice followed by a fragrant palate that attractively reprises the fruit.

● Barbera d'Asti Bric '06	♟♟	5
● Barbera d'Asti Bric '04	♟♟	4
● Barbera d'Asti Sup. Vanet '04	♟♟	6

Fabio Fidanza

VIA RODOTIGLIA, 55
14052 CALOSSO [AT]
TEL. 0141826921
www.castellodicalosso.it

Fabio Fidanza has confirmed his talent for barbera. Sterlino Castello di Calosso has great character and personality, showing warm and soft with a deep, juicy finish. Barbera d'Asti is fresh and fruity, with a well-orchestrated finish, while Monferrato Rosso Que Duàn is very decent.

● Barbera d'Asti '06	♟♟	3*
● Barbera d'Asti Sterlino Castello di Calosso '05	♟♟	5
● M.to Rosso Que Duàn '06	♟	4

OTHER WINERIES

Funtanin

VIA TORINO, 191
12043 CANALE [CN]
TEL. 0173979488

The Sperone brothers' estate is a Roero stalwart for it has grown with the region's recent success. Both reds are excellent, showing concentrated and earthy. From the two Arneis, we preferred the selection, which is more mouthfilling than the nonetheless pleasant basic version.

● Barbera d'Alba Ciabot Pierin '06	♟♟	5
○ Roero Arneis Pierin di Soc '07	♟♟	4*
● Roero Bricco Barbisa '05	♟♟	5
○ Roero Arneis '07	♟	3

Gaggino

S.DA S. EVASIO, 29
15076 OVADA [AL]
TEL. 0143822345
vinigaggino@libero.it

Gabriele Gaggino gave a rather lacklustre performance and didn't manage to repeat last year's success with his Barbera del Monferrato. He made amends with the terrific Dolcetto di Ovada Il Convivio, which flaunts confident, gutsy body and considerable energy. Sant'Evasio earns One Glass.

● Dolcetto di Ovada Il Convivio '07	♟♟	3*
● Barbera del M.to La Zarina '07	♟	3
● Dolcetto di Ovada Sup. S. Evasio '06	♟	4

Gianni Gagliardo

B.TA SERRA DEI TURCHI, 88
12064 LA MORRA [CN]
TEL. 017350829
www.gagliardo.it

This fine La Morra estate gave us to high-scoring Barolos. Barolo Serre '04 is impeccable, with a nose of raspberries and strawberries and a palate that gives ripe tannins and a complex finish. Cannubi '04 has an exceptionally elegant bouquet and a rounded palate with perfectly gauged tannins.

● Barolo Cannubi '04	♟♟	8
● Barolo Serre '04	♟♟	7

Incisiana

VIA SANT'AGATA, 10/12
14045 INCISA SCAPACCINO [AT]
TEL. 0141747113
www.incisiana.com

Florian Oelssner moved to Piedmont to farm five hectares of vineyards with his friend Eckhard Fischer. The barbera vines yield two wines: a splendid Barbera d'Asti '06, with complex rain-soaked earth and cherry, then a powerful palate, and the austere, slightly oaky Zerosso '03. The Merlot is harmonious.

● Barbera d'Asti '06	♟♟	4*
● M.to Rosso Merlotone '05	♟♟	6
● Barbera d'Asti Sup. Zerosso '03	♟	6

Ioppa

VIA OTTAVIANO TRINCHERI, 12
28078 ROMAGNANO SESIA [NO]
TEL. 0163833079
www.viniioppa.it

The Ioppa family's tradition as growers in Ghemme has not prevented brothers Gianpiero and Giorgio from keeping up with the times. The house style favours highly extracted wines softened by oak. Both the Vespolina and Ghemme Bricco Balsina outclass the basic Ghemme, which has slightly too much wood.

● Colline Novaresi Vespolina '05	♟♟	5
● Ghemme Bricco Balsina '04	♟♟	6
● Ghemme '04	♟	5

Isolabella della Croce

VIA CAFFI, 3
14051 LOAZZOLO [AT]
TEL. 014487166
www.borgoisolabella.com

This fine estate performed well. We were impressed by Barbera d'Asti Giuliano '05's enchanting aromas of berries, sweet spices and cinchona. Monferrato Le Marne and the white Solum also earned Two Glasses. Moscato d'Asti Valdiserre is sweet, but never cloys, while Loazzolo is slightly disappointing.

● Barbera d'Asti Sup. Giuliano '05	♟♟	5
● M.to Le Marne '06	♟♟	4*
○ M.to Bianco Solum '07	♟♟	4*
○ Loazzolo Solìo '04	♟	6
○ Moscato d'Asti Valdiserre '07	♟	4

OTHER WINERIES

Tenuta Langasco

FRAZ. MADONNA DI COMO, 10
12051 ALBA [CN]
TEL. 0173286972
www.tenutalangasco.it

In recent years, owner Claudio Sacco has given us consistently high-quality wines at interesting prices. Barbera d'Alba Madonna di Como is very attractive, giving ripe berries and sweet spices. The Nebbiolo is also impressive while the alcohol-rich Vigna Miclet is worth One Glass.

● Barbera d'Alba Madonna di Como '06	▼▼ 4*
● Nebbiolo d'Alba Sorì Coppa '06	▼▼ 5
● Dolcetto d'Alba Madonna di Como V. Miclet '07	▼ 3

Castello di Lignano

VIA LIGNANO, 1
15035 FRASSINELLO MONFERRATO [AL]
TEL. 0142925326
www.castellodilignano.com

Castello di Lignano is currently in a transitional period in terms of quality. Very good selections are flanked by somewhat less successful labels but the overall level is high. Barbera Vigna Stramba, for example, is excellent, showing rounded and fragrant. Monferrato Blasonato earned One Glass.

● Barbera d'Asti Sup. V. Stramba '05	▼▼ 4*
● M.to Rosso Blasonato '05	5

Le Marie

VIA CARDÉ, 5
12032 BARGE [CN]
TEL. 0175345159
raviolobeltramo@tiscali.it

This little winery is still the exclusive property of Valerio Raviolo, who once again presented an impressive list. Barbera Colombè is very attractive. Debàrges, from nebbiolo, barbera and other local varieties, is rich and complex while the basic Barbera and chardonnay-based white are easy drinking.

● Pinerolese Barbera Colombè '06	▼▼ 4*
● Pinerolese Debàrges '06	▼▼ 4*
● Pinerolese Barbera '07	▼ 3
O Blaçnonnay	▼ 4

Franco Mondo

REG. MARIANO, 33
14050 SAN MARZANO OLIVETO [AT]
TEL. 0141834096
francomondo@inwind.it

This small estate has 13 hectares under vine and an annual output of 60,000 bottles. Barbera is king, and all three selections did very well. The most interesting is Vigna delle Rose, which is juicy with a long finish. Vigna del Salice also won Two Glasses while the basic Barbera is a rung below.

● Barbera d'Asti Sup. V. delle Rose Sel. '05	▼▼ 5
● Barbera d'Asti V. del Salice '06	▼▼ 4*
● Barbera d'Asti '07	▼ 3

Cecilia Monte

VIA SERRACAPELLI, 17
12052 NEIVE [CN]
TEL. 017367454
cecilia.monte@libero.it

Cecilia Monte's continue to improve and she gave us a good Barbaresco '05, despite the difficult vintage. Serracapelli mingles tertiary aromas with roses, cinchona, liquorice and raspberries. The soft tannins are well calibrated, accompanying the wine's progression. Dolcetto is fruity, pleasant and enjoyable.

● Barbaresco Serracapelli '05	▼▼ 6
● Dolcetto d'Alba Montubert '07	▼ 4
● Barbaresco Serracapelli '04	▽▽ 6

Morgassi Superiore

CASE SPARSE SERMORIA, 7
15066 GAVI [AL]
TEL. 0143642007
www.morgassisuperiore.it

This estate, run by the Piacitelli family, has a good range of Gavis. The basic Gavi '07 stands out for its zestiness, which contrasts nicely with rich fruit. The Etichetto Oro line, which has benefited from an extra year's ageing, displays more complex development on the palate.

O Gavi del Comune di Gavi '07	▼▼ 4*
O Gavi del Comune di Gavi Et. Oro '06	▼▼ 5

OTHER WINERIES

Cantina Sociale di Nizza

VIA ALESSANDRIA, 57
14049 NIZZA MONFERRATO [AT]
TEL. 0141721348
www.nizza.it

This co-operative has played an important role in Barbera d'Asti's recent growth in quality. Again this year, it presented a truly impressive list. Ceppi Vecchi is classy, showing powerful and complex with a juicy, well-orchestrated finish, while 50 Vendemmie is impressively complex. Magister is nice.

● Barbera d'Asti Sup. 50 Vendemmie '06	🍷🍷 4*
● Barbera d'Asti Sup. Ceppi Vecchi '06	🍷🍷 4*
● Barbera d'Asti Sup. Magister '06	🍷 4

Podere Macellio

VIA ROMA, 18
10014 CALUSO [TO]
TEL. 0119833511
www.erbaluce-bianco.it

Daniele Bianco and his father Renato gave us three interesting, well-made wines. Spumante Brut has a nose of crusty bread, croissant and spring flowers with perfect acidity and freshness on the palate. Erbaluce has citrus notes and good structure while Caluso Passito gives candied peel and honey.

○ Caluso Passito '04	🍷🍷 5
○ Erbaluce di Caluso '07	🍷🍷 3*
○ Erbaluce di Caluso Brut	🍷🍷 5

Pomodolce

VIA IV NOVEMBRE, 7
15050 MONTEMARZINO [AL]
TEL. 0131878135
www.pomodolce.it

Full marks for this estate, which presented a first-rate Timorasso for the second year running. It has mineral notes and a very long, soft finish. Barbera '05, which we mistakenly reviewed last year, is also top notch while Croatina Fontanino is pleasant.

● Colli Tortonesi Barbera '05	🍷🍷 4*
○ Colli Tortonesi Bianco Diletto '06	🍷🍷 4*
● Colli Tortonesi Croatina Fontanino '06	🍷 4

Prinsi

VIA GAIA, 5
12052 NEIVE [CN]
TEL. 017367192
www.prinsi.it

Gaia Principe '05 is outstanding, on a par with the estate's generally high level. Its complex nose introduces an austere palate with prominent tannins. The other Barbaresco, Fausone '03, has suffered from the overly warm vintage and the tannins are bitterish. Barbera Vigneto Much '05 is good.

● Barbaresco Gaia Principe '05	🍷🍷 6
● Barbaresco Fausone Ris. '03	🍷 6
● Barbera d'Alba Sup. Vign. Much '05	🍷 5

Produttori del Gavi

VIA CAVALIERI DI VITTORIO VENETO, 45
15066 GAVI [AL]
TEL. 0143642786
cantina.prodgavi@libero.it

This co-operative winery gave us some remarkable wines. It focuses on the cortese grape, using it for three very convincing selections. Gavi del Comune di Gavi GG reached our finals with its very fruity citrus nose and zesty finish. Gavi G and the basic Gavi di Gavi both won Two Glasses.

○ Gavi del Comune di Gavi GG '07	🍷🍷 4*
○ Gavi del Comune di Gavi '07	🍷🍷 3*
○ Gavi G '07	🍷🍷 4*

La Raia

S.DA MONTEROTONDO, 79
15067 NOVI LIGURE [AL]
TEL. 0143743685
www.la-raia.it

La Raia, acquired by the Rossi Contini family several years ago, has converted to biodynamic farming and is affiliated to the Demeter brand. The few wines presented are very good, particularly Gavi Pisè. Fruity sensations are followed by hazelnut on the nose while the palate shows attractive tanginess.

○ Gavi Pisè '07	🍷🍷 4
○ Gavi '07	🍷 4

OTHER WINERIES

F.lli Rovero

LOC. VALDONATA
FRAZ. SAN MARZANOTTO, 218
14100 ASTI [AT]
TEL. 0141592460
www.rovero.it

The wines from Claudio, Franco and Michele Rovero showed a few problems on the nose because of the excessive youth of the samples tasted. However, we're sure that a few months in bottle will improve matters. Gustin '05 is firm and powerful while Sanpansè is refreshing. Lajetto is very convincing.

● M.to Rosso Lajetto '06	¶¶ 4*
● Barbera d'Asti Sanpansè '07	¶ 3
● Barbera d'Asti Sup. Vign. Gustin '05	¶ 4

San Pietro

LOC. SAN PIETRO, 2
15067 TASSAROLO [AL]
TEL. 0143342422
www.tenutasanpietro.it

The '07 vintage confirms the return to excellence of this historic estate following its acquisition a few years ago by the Alotta family. Gavi Il Mandorlo is classy, showing full and pleasant on the palate where good body is braced by acidity. Gorrina is multi-faceted and San Pietro a little simpler.

○ Gavi del Comune di Tassarolo Il Mandorlo '07	¶¶ 5
○ Gavi del Comune di Tassarolo Gorrina '06	¶¶ 6
○ Gavi di Tassarolo San Pietro '07	¶¶ 4*

Simone Scaletta

LOC. MANZONI, 61
12065 MONFORTE D'ALBA [CN]
TEL. 3484912733
www.viniscaletta.com

It's not wise to praise young growers as success may go to their heads but we'll take the risk with Simone Scaletta. We're sure his head is firmly on his shoulders. The Barolo shows exceptional character and made it into our finals. The Barbera is excellent and the Nebbiolo is concentrated.

● Barolo Chirlet '04	¶¶ 7
● Barbera d'Alba Sarsera '06	¶¶ 4*
● Langhe Nebbiolo Autin 'd Madama '06	¶¶ 5

Daniele Saccoletto

S.S. CASALE-ASTI, 82
15020 SAN GIORGIO MONFERRATO [AL]
TEL. 0142806509
www.saccolettovini.com

Daniele Saccoletto's relentlessly meticulous work comes through in his reliable wines. The fruity, ethery Barbera has a heady nose and a long, balanced palate with a finish perked up by nice acidity. Grignolino '07 is very varietal with a spicy nose echoed on the palate.

● Barbera del M.to Vigna Minerva '06	¶¶ 4*
● Grignolino del M.to Casalese Vigna in Cornalasca '07	¶¶ 3*

Giacomo Scagliola e Figlio

REG. SANTA LIBERA, 20
14053 CANELLI [AT]
TEL. 0141831146
www.scagliolagiacomo.it

This year marked the return of the outstanding Moscato d'Asti Santa Libera. The '07 proffers rich notes of peaches, sage, citronella and apricots while the palate is supported and enhanced by refreshing acidity. Vigna dei Mandorli is tremendous while La Faia '05 is good.

● Barbera d'Asti V. dei Mandorli '04	¶¶ 4*
○ Moscato d'Asti Santa Libera '07	¶¶ 3*
● Barbera d'Asti La Faia '05	¶ 5

La Scamuzza

CASCINA POMINA, 17
15049 VIGNALE MONFERRATO [AL]
TEL. 0142926214
www.lascamuzza.it

Vigneto della Amorosa is on top form, with notes of ripe fruit and aromatic herbs. Grignolino del Monferrato Casalese Tumas '07 is one of the best tasted this year. The current Barbera Baciamisubito and Monferrato Rosso Bricco San Tomaso are also nice.

● Barbera del M.to Sup. Vign. della Amorosa '05	¶¶ 6
● Grignolino del M.to Casalese Tumas '07	¶¶ 4*
● Barbera del M.to Baciamisubito '07	¶ 4
● M.to Rosso Bricco S. Tomaso '06	¶ 5

OTHER WINERIES

Antica Casa Vinicola Scarpa

VIA MONTEGRAPPA, 6
14049 NIZZA MONFERRATO [AT]
TEL. 0141721331
www.scarpavini.it

This historic estate returns to the Guide after a year's absence. The wines are marked by more personality, particularly in the case of the best-known selections. Oenologist Gianfranco Cordero's work is evident in a list that maintains its links with tradition but is now more focused.

● Barbera d'Asti La Bogliona '05	￼	6
● M.to Rosso Rouchet Briccorosa '07	￼	6
● M.to Rosso Super '06	￼	6
● La Selva di Moirano '03	￼	6

La Smilla

VIA GARIBALDI, 7
15060 BOSIO [AL]
TEL. 0143684245
www.lasmilla.it

This small family-run estate makes characterful wines. All are from the Bosio district and show exceptional finesse and fragrance. Gavi '07 is great, with impressive fruit and acidity, and the I Bergi selection is also terrific. The Dolcetto is well typed and the Barbera flavoursome.

O Gavi del Comune di Gavi '07	￼	3*
● Dolcetto di Ovada Nsè Pesa '06	￼	4
O Gavi I Bergi '06	￼	4
● Barbera del M.to Scarlatta '06	￼	3

Giuseppe Stella

S.DA BOSSOLA, 8
14055 COSTIGLIOLE D'ASTI [AT]
TEL. 0141966142
stellavini@libero.it

This winery put on a chequered performance. Barbera Bricco Fubine '06 is impressive, earning Two Glasses for its berries and rain-soaked earth laced with black pepper and vanilla. But Gaiet is not as harmonious as it could be and seems very young. The Grignolino has pleasing acidity and tannins.

● Barbera d'Asti Bricco Fubine Il Vino del Maestro '06	￼	5
● Barbera d'Asti Giaiet '06	￼	5
● Grignolino d'Asti Vign. Sufragio '07	￼	3

Traversa - Cascina Bertolotto

VIA PIETRO PORRO, 70
15018 SPIGNO MONFERRATO [AL]
TEL. 014491223

The approachable semi-sparkling Brachetto d'Acqui Il Virginio is excellent, showing sweet but not cloying. Dolcetto La Cresta has good balance. Il Barigi, from favorita and cortese grapes, is also pleasing on the palate. The list is completed by Surì di Bertoletto, from part-dried moscato grapes.

● Brachetto d'Acqui Il Virginio '07	￼	4*
● Dolcetto d'Acqui La Cresta '07	￼	4
O M.to Bianco Il Barigi '07	￼	4
O Surì di Bertolotto	￼	6

Laura Valditerra

S.DA MONTEROTONDO, 75
15067 NOVI LIGURE [AL]
TEL. 0143321451
laura@valditerra.it

Laura Valditerra's wines performed impeccably. The new Gavi Tenuta Merlassino did very well, showing full bodied on the palate with nicely balanced acidity. Vigna del Lago also impressed, flaunting a concentrated nose with exceptional finesse. The red FiorDesAr is nice.

O Gavi Tenuta Merlassino '07	￼	4*
O Gavi V. del Lago '07	￼	4*
● M.to Rosso FiorDesAri '06	￼	4

Valfieri

S.DA LORETO, 5
14055 COSTIGLIOLE D'ASTI [AT]
TEL. 0141966881
www.valfieri.it

This estate, founded in 1961, has been releasing nice wines, particularly from barbera, for several years. Barbera d'Asti '07 is drinkable with concentrated fruit while the monovarietal merlot Monferrato Matot '05 is juicy and approachable. The Barbera Superiore has done better in the past.

● Barbera d'Asti '07	￼	4*
● M.to Rosso Matot '05	￼	5
● Barbera d'Asti Sup. '06	￼	4

OTHER WINERIES

Cantine Valpane

CASCINA VALPANE, 10/1
15039 OZZANO MONFERRATO [AL]
TEL. 0142486713
www.cantinevalpane.com

Pietro Arditi has produced another excellent vintage of Barbera Valpane. The '04 version shows deep ruby with a complex nose and a long, confident palate. Barbera Perlydia and Freisa Canone Inverso, at its debut in the Guide with the '05 vintage, are also good.

● Barbera del M.to Sup. Valpane '04	▼▼ 5
● Barbera del M.to Perlydia '05	▼ 4
● M.to Freisa Canone Inverso '05	▼ 4

Vecchia Posta

VIA MONTEBELLO, 2
15050 AVOLASCA [AL]
TEL. 0131876254
lavecchiaposta@virgilio.it

While our favourite wine last year was Rebelot but this year Timorasso was the top scorer. The '06 vintage is characterized by marked balsamic notes, which are very evident on the nose. Rebelot needs time to breathe if you want to enjoy its fruit to the full.

O Colli Tortonesi Bianco Il Selvaggio '06	▼▼ 4*
● Colli Tortonesi Barbera Languia '05	▼ 4
● Colli Tortonesi Rosso Rebelot '06	▼ 3

Osvaldo Viberti

FRAZ. SANTA MARIA
B.TA SERRA DEI TURCHI, 95
12064 LA MORRA [CN]
TEL. 017350374
www.vibertiosvaldo.it

Following a disappointing '03, Barolo Serra dei Turchi is back on form, showing convincing notes of cinchona, liquorice, dried flowers and currants. On the palate, the tannins are extremely soft, balanced and elegant. Barbera Mancine is excellent while Dolcetto Galletto is fresh, fruity and heady.

● Barolo Serra dei Turchi '04	▼▼ 6*
● Barbera d'Alba Mancine '06	▼▼ 4*
● Dolcetto d'Alba Galletto '07	▼▼ 3*

Vietto

LOC. PANEROLE
12060 NOVELLO [CN]
TEL. 0173731379
www.vietto-panerole.it

Although this estate has a long viticultural tradition, it has only been bottling its own selections since 2000. Brothers Davide and Luigi Vietto run the handsome winery at Panerole. Their Barolo '04 is very interesting, showing complex and lingering. The Barbera is fresh and the Dolcetto is pleasant.

● Barolo Panerole '04	▼▼ 6*
● Barbera d'Alba Panerole '07	▼▼ 3*
● Dolcetto d'Alba Panerole '07	▼ 3

Virna

VIA ALBA, 73
12060 BAROLO [CN]
TEL. 017356120
www.virnabarolo.it

This small Barolo estate focuses on nebbiolo, which it makes in a traditional style. Our favourite is the Cannubi Boschis, which is deep, austere and easy drinking thanks to supple tannins. Preda Sarmassa won Two Glasses, showing austere and multi-layered on the palate. The basic Barolo is also great.

● Barolo Cannubi Boschis '04	▼▼ 6
● Barolo '04	▼▼ 6
● Barolo Preda Sarmassa '04	▼▼ 6

La Zerba

S.DA PER FRANCAVILLA, 1
15060 TASSAROLO [AL]
TEL. 0143342259
www.la-zerba.it

The Lorenzi family's La Zerba estate presented two excellent Gavis. We particularly liked Terrarossa, which has a very elegant, concentrated nose with hawthorn-like florality and a satisfying palate that balances body and freshness impressively. Gavi La Zerba is also exciting.

O Gavi Terrarossa '07	▼▼ 3*
O Gavi La Zerba '07	▼▼ 3*

LIGURIA

As usual, Liguria's production embraces a generous number of interesting wines. Most are made from traditional local grapes but we also find the internationals, which have been present for a few years now and have a particularly positive contribution to the region's reds. Granaccia, the local grenache, has been planted for more than a century around Quiliano and expanded along the western coast, to be followed by syrah, cabernet sauvignon, merlot and others. But the area's foundation grapes, those with the most marked typicity, remain ormeasco in the west, ciliegiolo and sangiovese in the east, and of course rossese di Dolceacqua. We enjoyed this in a number of fine versions, ample proof of the quality of its practitioners and evidence that they have worked through recent problems posed by erratic styles. Almost all of the wineries that appear in the following pages exhibit praiseworthy consistency of quality, crucial for building long-term rapport with wine consumers, and there is every reason to believe that this reliability will grow. Not that all problems have been solved, though. There is still a lack of effective communication among producers, still a tendency to address only local markets and consumers, and still a lack of attention to the wine sector by regional authorities. Today's extremely competitive wine world has no place for producers who rest on one's laurels. This has motivated some winemakers to focus on the distinctive characteristics of their own vineyards and local varieties, a philosophy that is paying off handsomely, and on finely tuned winemaking practices that yield wines of truly striking character. This year's Guide reports some ground-breaking results for Liguria, including the region's very first Three Glass award, as well as 11 that went through to the national finals. Bruna's Pigato Baccan is, for the fourth time running, the stand-out: the 2006 edition is a minor, terroir-focused winemaking miracle. And to demonstrate that excellence in Liguria is not isolated, there are other top-notch producers, too. Fill a glass with Emanuele Trevia's brilliant Vermentino 2007, an elegantly intense offering that crowns a decade of unceasing commitment and hard labour. To the top awards, moreover, must be added the fine performances recorded by other producers. Vladimiro Galluzzo of Terre Rosse, continuing his superb run, still amazes with the captivating character of his products, and the near 80-year-old dean of Dolceacqua reds, Mandino Cane, is no nearer to letting up. And keep a sharp eye on the likes of Alessandri, Durin, Bianchi Carenzo and Poggio dei Gorleri while the western coast boasts Bisson, Buranco, Santa Caterina, Walter De Battè and Heydi Bonanini. The trend is encouraging and gauntlet seems to have been picked up. We look forward to future results.

A Maccia

FRAZ. BORGO
VIA UMBERTO I, 54
18020 RANZO [IM]
TEL. 0183318003
www.amaccia.it

ANNUAL PRODUCTION	20,000 bottles
HECTARES UNDER VINE	3
VITICULTURE METHOD	Conventional

Grower Loredana Faraldi has maintained high quality in the wines from her family's historic operation at Ranzo, which dates from 1850. She shows a fine sense for terroir and each of her vintages exhibits distinctive hallmarks. The respect she has won is a tribute to her energy and passionate commitment to the family heritage. Faraldi's daughter Carlotta, now with a degree from agricultural school, has just joined her, which augurs well for the future. We were impressed by Loredana's Pigato. It's an intriguing wine with a well-defined, multi-layered nose releasing alluring notes of Mediterranean scrubland and well-ripened fruit, an elegant prelude to a fine performance on the palate, which shows warm and smooth, with just a hint of sweetness. This is a delicate wine overall but with marked character. The Rossese also bespeaks skill, showing pungent balsam and subtle, white pepper-like spice. Supple and aromatic in the mouth, it is a delicious, well-balanced quaffer, with warm tones and lovely length. A Maccia produces a fine extra virgin olive oil. The most recent bottling can stand with the region's best.

Massimo Alessandri

VIA COSTA PARROCCHIA
18020 RANZO [IM]
TEL. 018253458
www.massimoalessandri.it

ANNUAL PRODUCTION	30,000 bottles
HECTARES UNDER VINE	6
VITICULTURE METHOD	Conventional

Owner Massimo Alessandri has poured technical and human investment into his vineyards and tradition-respecting winemaking practices. The results are visible in his splendid wines. Generously aromatic, Pigato Vigne Vegie 2006 is a stand-out from first to last. Savoury flavours unfold over a bitter almond background as it develops steadily into a lengthy, impressive finish. Costa de Vigne 2007 is equally fine. Ripe fruit, pungent moss and autumn leaves compose a well-defined nose, contributing to a wine that will please those who prize refreshing, pleasant, easy-drinking bottles. Viorus was a true surprise. This roussanne and viognier blend ferments in six-hectolitre casks then remains in oak, with bâtonnage, for a further eight months. The result is a rich, multi-layered nose displaying citrus fruit, blossoms and slate-like minerality followed by a sumptuous, full-flavoured palate of power and balance. Seiana, largely merlot with some cabernet sauvignon, is rich and classy, with mint and white pepper enlivening smooth balsam. Ligustico is a fruity blend of granaccia and syrah with sweet tannins and lively development.

O Riviera Ligure di Ponente Pigato '07	♟♟ 4*
● Riviera Ligure di Ponente Rossese '07	♟♟ 4*
O Riviera Ligure di Ponente Pigato '06	♟♟ 4

O Viorus '07	♟♟ 5
O Riviera Ligure di Ponente Pigato Vigne Vegie '06	♟♟ 5
● A' Seiana '06	♟♟ 6
● Ligustico '06	♟♟ 6
O Riviera Ligure di Ponente Pigato Costa de Vigne '07	♟ 4
● Ligustico '05	♟♟ 6
● Ligustico '04	♟♟ 6

Alta Via

LOC. ARCAGNA
18035 DOLCEACQUA [IM]
TEL. 0184488230

ANNUAL PRODUCTION	40,000 bottles
HECTARES UNDER VINE	5
VITICULTURE METHOD	Conventional

Dolceacqua is a striking medieval village in Val Nervia, close to France and a few kilometres from the sea. Producing wine in these unpromising hills is not easy but Savino Formentini and Gianni Arlotti are up to the job. A few years ago, they built their modern wine facility here, siting it to blend into the surroundings. Oenologist Federico Curtaz consults. The wine style here is contemporary but the wines maintain a strong link with tradition and reflect their intriguing terroir. A compelling example is Noname, from vermentino and viognier. The broom blossom and Mediterranean scrubland bouquet segues into lively, crisp succulence in the mouth and a long-lingering finale. Our favourite red again was Skip Intro, from syrah grapes grown at Sanremo. Rich impressions of blackberry preserves and wild cherry lead off, complemented on the palate by fine-grained tannins and judicious acidity that support impressive structure and complete a very satisfying wine. The Rossese turn also turned in a fine performance, showcasing crisp, aromatic sage and thyme plus a palate brimming with refreshing flavours. Finally, Rosarosae is well made and tasty.

○ Noname '07	♈♈	5
● Rossese di Dolceacqua Sup. '07	♈♈	5
● Skip Intro '05	♈♈	5
⊙ Rosarosae '07	♈	4
● Rossese di Dolceacqua Sup. '06	♈♈	5
● Rossese di Dolceacqua Sup. '05	♈♈	5
● Rossese di Dolceacqua Sup. '04	♈♈	5
● Skip Intro '04	♈♈	5

Laura Aschero

P.ZZA V. EMANUELE, 7
18027 PONTEDASSIO [IM]
TEL. 0183710307
lauraaschero@uno.it

ANNUAL PRODUCTION	60,000 bottles
HECTARES UNDER VINE	2.8
VITICULTURE METHOD	Conventional

We confess our fondness for this producer. Located at Pontedassio, it is owned by Marco Rizzo, who learned his trade while the winery was still directed by his mother, Laura Aschero. Rizzo has shown himself a master at blending tradition with modernity, the happy result being an impressively equipped cellar where solid vineyard management practices feed into state-of-the-art winemaking. The marriage yields wines that get better and better. Vermentino, an ancient grape variety, left Spain for Liguria, passing through Corsica and southern France along the way. It is the grape Marco loves to work with most and Vermentino has become the iconic Aschero wine. Wonderful complexity and delicacy mark the nose, which displays a broad varietal medley of apricot, citrus and pungent herbs. Fullness in the mouth combines with vivacious acidity, ensuring energy-laden development. The Rossese is equally good. Its silky texture is impressive as is its clean, rich fruit, admirable balance, and long-lingering conclusion. Pigato is an alluring display of pungent balsam and Mediterranean scrubland, developing smoothly despite slightly assertive alcohol.

● Riviera Ligure di Ponente Rossese '07	♈♈	4*
○ Riviera Ligure di Ponente Vermentino '07	♈♈	4*
○ Riviera Ligure di Ponente Pigato '07	♈	4
○ Riviera Ligure di Ponente Vermentino '06	♈♈	4
○ Riviera Ligure di Ponente Vermentino '05	♈♈	4
○ Riviera Ligure di Ponente Vermentino '04	♈♈	4

Maria Donata Bianchi

LOC. VAL CROSA
18013 DIANO CASTELLO [IM]
TEL. 0183498233

ANNUAL PRODUCTION	35,000 bottles
HECTARES UNDER VINE	4.5
VITICULTURE METHOD	Natural

Visiting this lovely facility is a pleasure, as is a conversation with that able grower, Emanuele Trevia. He believes in painstaking attention in the cellar but without excess and tasting his wines immediately reveals their consistently high quality. Top of the range is the Vermentino 2007. An eloquent expression of terroir and grape, it leads with an elegant medley of crisp medicinal herbs, blossoms and varietal fruit before opening to impressive volume and savoury expression, considerably assisted by tangy acidity. This fine performance deservedly won Three Glasses. Pigato also earned very high marks. Peppery scrub and balsam enliven the mineral-edged fruit on the nose. The fleshy, fruit-laden palate is as lively and succulent as one could wish. Antico Sfizio lags, though, a heavyish nose and a tad too much alcohol on the finish, despite a vibrant, full palate. The reds performed nicely. The grenache and syrah Mattana 2006 in particular stood out for the sharp detail of its components, offering dense but classy draughts of spicy and balsam, and then a seductive, ultra-mouthfilling palate. Bormano 2007 is well layered and delicious.

O Riviera Ligure di Ponente		
Vermentino '07	♥♥♥	4*
● La Mattana '06	♥♥	6
● Bormano '07	♥♥	5
O Riviera Ligure di Ponente Pigato '07	♥♥	5
O Antico Sfizio '07	♥	4
O Antico Sfizio '04	♀♀	4
O Antico Sfizio '05	♀♀	4
O Riviera Ligure di Ponente Pigato '06	♀♀	5
O Riviera Ligure di Ponente		
Vermentino '06	♀♀	4
● La Mattana '04	♀♀	6

BioVio

FRAZ. BASTIA
VIA CROCIATA, 24
17031 ALBENGA [SV]
TEL. 018220776
www.biovio.it

ANNUAL PRODUCTION	40,000 bottles
HECTARES UNDER VINE	4
VITICULTURE METHOD	Certified biodynamic

Aimone Vio and his wife Chiara direct the winery that Aimone's grandfather, Giobatta, launched in the early 1900s. Located in the Albenga plain, this totally organic operation complements its wine production with extra virgin olive oil and aromatic herbs. We were particularly struck by the Vermentino, which is made in a style that showcases fine-textured aromas of scrumptious fruit. Its vivacious acidity is an effective foil to dense fruit and warm alcohol while tasty apricot accompanies the lengthy finale. We liked Rossese as well, which offers intriguing notes of geranium along with the more expected red berry fruit. The palate is well contained yet crisp and nicely layered, with spiciness that carries through to a pleasantly almondy finish. Vio offers two Pigatos, Marixe and Bon in da Bon. Subtle citrus and pungent autumn leaves characterize the former, along with graceful development and Mediterranean scrubland aromas in the mouth. Bon in da Bon is more fruit-driven, showing rich and dense on the nose with plenty of peach and ripe plum. Bacilò is a well-executed, expansive red with a balsam theme.

● Riviera Ligure di Ponente Rossese		
Bastiò '07	♥♥	4*
O Riviera Ligure di Ponente		
Vermentino '07	♥♥	4*
O Riviera Ligure di Ponente Pigato		
Bon in da Bon '07	♥	4
O Riviera Ligure di Ponente Pigato		
Marixe '07	♥	4
● Bacilò '07	♥	4

Enoteca Bisson

c.so GIANELLI, 28
16043 CHIAVARI [GE]
TEL. 0185314462
www.bissonvini.it

ANNUAL PRODUCTION	80,000 bottles
HECTARES UNDER VINE	12
VITICULTURE METHOD	Natural

Piero Lugano's background is more in fishing than making wine but he made a well-justified act of faith in the potential of Liguria's eastern coast for quality wine. Piero's winemaking is in constant evolution but we can always be sure of tasting characterful wines, even if there are occasionally one or two rough edges. Lugano's line-up is extensive, and his manner of handling the varieties almost maverick with respect to the conventions of the area, but there's no gainsaying what is in the bottle. Take the complex, ruby-hued Braccorosso, which follows classy ripe red berry fruit with judiciously extracted tannins, progressing steadily into a well-balanced, warm conclusion. Il Granaccio, on the other hand, shows subtle notes of tree sap and resin over a floor of generous red berry fruit, which layer through into the finish, concluding a wine that impresses for its lean crispness and fine delineation. The Vermentinos are also impressive, showing vibrant, clean, well balanced and as tasty as you could wish. The crisp, well-focused Marea is finely crafted throughout.

Bruna

FRAZ. BORGO
VIA UMBERTO I, 81
18020 RANZO [IM]
TEL. 0183318082
aziendaagricolabruna@libero.it

ANNUAL PRODUCTION	45,000 bottles
HECTARES UNDER VINE	6.2
VITICULTURE METHOD	Conventional

Few producers can equal Riccardo Bruna's passion, a trait now passed on to daughter Francesca. A leader in the Pigato renaissance, Bruna did much to give the variety wider appeal, using his talents to capture the soul of the grape. Riccardo coaxes equally impressive results out of his reds, particularly Pulin, which wasn't ready for us to taste. Still, the Rossese shows a dense nose of alluring raspberry and white pepper, and its succulent palate unfolds attractively. The delicious Colline Savonesi Rosso 2007 has a liquorice-laden palate, after the crisp balsam of the nose, with mellow tannins and good structure completing the picture. Pigato Baccan 2006 was again the star of the show, winning Three Glasses. Apricot, white pepper and a nice minerally edge contribute to its rich, sensuous bouquet and the palate is a masterful exposition of energy, crispness, elegance, depth, complexity and unalloyed pleasure. The tasty Torrachetta shows aromatic and fruity throughout its rising progression, capped by an almond-laced finish. Finally, Le Russeghine is a well-structured, smooth-textured Pigato with considerable elegance and length.

● Braccorosso Granaccia Barrique '07	▼▼ 5
● Il Granaccio '06	▼▼ 5
○ Golfo del Tigullio Vermentino Vigna Intrigoso '07	▼▼ 4*
○ Cinque Terre Marea '07	▼ 4
○ Cinque Terre Sciacchetrà '05	▼ 8
○ Pigato '07	▼ 4
○ Mosaico '06	▼ 4
○ Golfo del Tigullio Bianchetta Genovese Ü Pastine '07	▼ 4
○ Golfo del Tigullio Moscato Passito '06	▼ 5
○ Golfo del Tigullio Vermentino Vigna Erta '07	▼ 4
● Makallé Il Granaccia '06	♈♈ 5

○ Riviera Ligure di Ponente Pigato U Baccan '06	▼▼▼ 5
● Rosso '07	▼▼ 4*
● Riviera Ligure di Ponente Rossese '07	▼▼ 4*
○ Riviera Ligure di Ponente Pigato Le Russeghine '07	▼▼ 4*
○ Riviera Ligure di Ponente Pigato Villa Torrachetta '07	▼▼ 4*
○ Riviera Ligure di Ponente Pigato U Baccan '05	♈♈♈ 5
○ Riviera Ligure di Ponente Pigato U Baccan '04	♈♈♈ 5
○ Riviera Ligure di Ponente Pigato U Baccan '03	♈♈♈ 5
○ Riviera Ligure di Ponente Pigato U Baccan '00	♈♈ 5
○ Riviera Ligure di Ponente Pigato Le Russeghine '06	♈♈ 4
○ Riviera Ligure di Ponente Pigato Le Russeghine '05	♈♈ 4

Buranco

VIA BURANCO, 72
19016 MONTEROSSO AL MARE [SP]
TEL. 0187817677
www.buranco.info

ANNUAL PRODUCTION	9,000 bottles
HECTARES UNDER VINE	1
VITICULTURE METHOD	Conventional

This is the Grillo family's second harvest after the change in ownership two years ago and we can attest that the wines are improving in quality. With oenologist Sergio Pappalardo completing the team, the Grillos are making steady but determined progress. In particular, the terraces that were lost when farming ceased are being laboriously recuperated. Buranco's impressive array of Two Glasses awards shows that the Grillos are determined to produce distinctive, complex wines that reflect their terroir. The amber-hued Sciacchetrà lays out intriguing impressions of dried fruit and Mediterranean scrub; attractively warm and utterly seductive, it shows silk smooth on the palate, with fine acidity that keeps cloy at bay. The two Cinque Terres communicate the character of a challenging territory where nature rules. Leading with fruit and clean citrus, they are marked by full flavours, dense weave and fine structure, rounding off with lengthy, well-delineated finishes. Buranco is their equal. It's a red with fairly dense aromas of berry fruit and resin, then a sturdy structure undergirds the emphatic palate.

Calleri

LOC. SALEA
REG. FRATTI, 2
17031 ALBENGA [SV]
TEL. 018220085
postmaster@cantinecalleri.com

ANNUAL PRODUCTION	90,000 bottles
HECTARES UNDER VINE	N.A.
VITICULTURE METHOD	Conventional

Year after year, Marcello Calleri's wines are models of reliability. We know that they will always do well at our tastings. One of the reasons is the painstaking care he exercises in selecting his grapes from long-time growers and the other is his mastery in the cellar. Hence the performance of Pigato 2007, which opens with a lovely weave of balsam-laced peach and pear, followed by succulent, fleshy fruit supporting a tempting aromatic medley that goes on almost forever. Vermentino I Muzazzi also received high marks for its intriguing, citrussy nose and supple acidity that guides the steady development on the palate and contributes to an appreciable complexity. Delicate, crisp hints of broom and almond blossoms infuse Vermentino 2007, nicely matched by a markedly savoury and graceful palate, though this is no lightweight, and the finish signs off with tangy bitter almond. Pigato Saleasco merits attention. Notes of mown grass and pungent scrub enliven subtle nuances of fruit, and its lively palate is a fine display of fleshy fruit and zesty acidity. Ormeasco is heady and youthful but perhaps a tad too husky.

● Buranco '06	▼▼ 6
○ Cinque Terre '07	▼▼ 5
○ Cinque Terre Mangioa '07	▼▼ 6
○ Cinque Terre Sciacchetrà '06	▼▼ 8
○ Cinque Terre Sciacchetrà '04	♈ 8
○ Cinque Terre Sciacchetrà '03	♈ 8
○ Cinque Terre '05	♈ 5
● Buranco '05	♈ 6

○ Riviera Ligure di Ponente Pigato '07	▼▼ 4*
○ Riviera Ligure di Ponente Pigato Saleasco '07	▼ 4
○ Riviera Ligure di Ponente Vermentino '07	▼ 4
○ Riviera Ligure di Ponente Vermentino I Muzazzi '07	▼ 4
● Ormeasco di Pornassio '06	▼ 4

Giobatta Mandino Cane

VIA ROMA, 21
18035 DOLCEACQUA [IM]
TEL. 0184206120

ANNUAL PRODUCTION	6,000 bottles
HECTARES UNDER VINE	1
VITICULTURE METHOD	Conventional

Rossese grows here in a harsh and unforgiving terroir of small terraces clinging to frighteningly steep cliffs, conditions that do not daunt the dynamic Mandino Cane, now 80 years old. One of the first to believe in high quality Rossese, Mandino resists the temptation to sell off his operation, preferring to regale us with tradition-rich wines of great fascination. L'Intruso 2006, mistakenly reviewed last year instead of the 2005, is a fine example. This is a Syrah of great character, with a full, complex nose composed of dark fruit, tar and cocoa powder. Its powerful palate is held under control by a suite of fine-grained tannins and solid acidity, segueing into a dynamic, lengthy conclusion. As usual, the two Rosseses are among the region's best. Vigneto Arcagna offers supple, alluring aromas emanating from rich fruit and graceful florality, which go on to infuse the palate, where a fine-textured mouthfeel, soft alcohol and impressive overall harmony emerge. Both the bouquet and palate of Vigneto Morghe, on the other hand, foreground raspberry and wild berry fruit lifted by balsam, carrying through to a clean, crisp and refreshing finale.

● L'Intruso '06	♈♈	5
● Rossese di Dolceacqua Sup. Vigneto Arcagna '07	♈♈	5
● Rossese di Dolceacqua Sup. Vigneto Morghe '07	♈♈	5
● Rossese di Dolceacqua Sup. Vigneto Arcagna '06	♈♈	5
● Rossese di Dolceacqua Sup. Vigneto Arcagna '05	♈♈	5
● Rossese di Dolceacqua Sup. Vigneto Arcagna '04	♈♈	5
● Rossese di Dolceacqua Sup. Vigneto Morghe '06	♈♈	5
● Rossese di Dolceacqua Sup. Vigneto Morghe '05	♈♈	5

Cascina Praié

S.DA CASTELLO, 20
17051 ANDORA [SV]
TEL. 019602377
m_viglietti@tin.it

ANNUAL PRODUCTION	35,000 bottles
HECTARES UNDER VINE	8
VITICULTURE METHOD	Conventional

Cascina Praié, owned by Massimo Viglietti and his wife Anna Maria Corrent, is located in the venerable hilltop village of Colla Micheri, which overlooks Andora and Laigueglia. Like Norwegian anthropologist Thor Heyerdhal, who lived here, Viglietti loves to challenge reigning paradigms, and is always trying out new grape varieties, winemaking techniques and eco-friendly practices, while not turning his back on time-tested local methods. In this year's generous line-up of offerings, Vermentino Colla Micheri particularly impressed us. A lavish nose presents aromatic herbs and pungent scrub nicely rounded by glossy mineral notes, and the palate displays decent heft and a tasty blend of a zesty acidity and fresh greens. Ardesia, too, is good, showing rich fruit preserves on the nose, supple mouthfeel and plenty of individuality. Ripe, spice-veined fruit characterizes Vermentino Le Cicale, made from late-harvested grapes. Pigato Il Canneto is somewhat less complex but balanced and pleasurable nonetheless while Cervo Rosso, from rossese and syrah, and the rosé Ros' é are both well executed.

● Ardesia '06	♈♈	5
○ Riviera Ligure di Ponente Vermentino Colla Micheri '07	♈♈	5
○ Riviera Ligure di Ponente Pigato Il Canneto '07	♈	4
○ Riviera Ligure di Ponente Vermentino Le Cicale '06	♈	4
☉ Ros' é '07	♈	4
● Cervo Rosso '07	♈	4
● Ardesia '05	♈♈	5
● Ardesia '04	♈♈	5
● Sciurbì '05	♈♈	4
● Sciurbì '04	♈♈	4

Walter De Batté

VIA TRARCANTU, 25
19017 RIOMAGGIORE [SP]
TEL. 0187920127

ANNUAL PRODUCTION	15,000 bottles
HECTARES UNDER VINE	5
VITICULTURE METHOD	Natural

Walter De Batté was one of the first around here to realize the potential of native grapes, a renaissance that gave a burst of winemaking energy to the Cinque Terre. Growers here have a myriad daily challenges: soils barely fit for cultivation, crumbling terraces and wild animals in the vineyards but De Batté held fast, imposing his will on a piece of earth as picturesque as it is hostile to viticulture. His Cinque Terre is a wine of stupendous character, seducing with draughts of dried fruit and honey, then following through with energetic development and sapid, full flavours. De Batté and other partners launched a new project, Prima Terra, at Campiglia. The vineyards, located in Val di Vara and Val di Magra, bordering Tuscany, are yielding wines of marked distinctiveness. Viasso, a blend of albarola, vermentino, chardonnay and traminer, is fruity, smooth and savoury while Çerico is a spicy, pungent pairing of granaccia and syrah, supple in the mouth, with an alcoholic warmth that contributes to its smoothness and balance. Equally fine are Tonos, a melange of ten varieties; Bozòlo, from dolcetto and merlot; and the vermentino Carlaz.

Durin

VIA ROMA, 202
17037 ORTOVERO [SV]
TEL. 0182547007
www.durin.it

ANNUAL PRODUCTION	140,000 bottles
HECTARES UNDER VINE	16
VITICULTURE METHOD	Conventional

Our tastings confirm that this historic family winery in the hills over the Albenga plain and Valle Arroscia, has succeeded in making top quality wines. Over the past 25 years, owner Antonio Basso, ably assisted by his wife Laura, has left behind the promiscuous viticulture of the past, and heavy investment has enabled him to maximize the sensory qualities of the fruit. The Durin line of wines, relying on local varieties, is good. The standard Vermentino is outstanding, bursting with rich fruit fragrances, whose palate is distinctive for its volume, balance, crisp character and fine mouthfeel. I Matti is on the same quality rung. This red boasts wonderfully dense fruit on the nose, with an intriguing balsam-mineral filigree and hints of liquorice and tar that carry over effectively onto the palate. Here there is elegant, steadily building progression, admirable proportion, and as much expansiveness and aromatic depth as one could wish for: a magisterial offering. No less stellar are the two Pigatos and the two Rossos. All are fine exemplars of their class, displaying fine character and flawless rapport between colour and acidity.

O Cinque Terre '07	♈♈	5
O Viasso '06	♈♈	5
● Çerico '05	♈♈	5
● Bozòlo '06	♈	5
● Tonos '06	♈	5
O Carlaz '06	♈	5
O Cinque Terre Sciacchetrà '03	♈♈	8
O Cinque Terre Sciacchetrà '01	♈♈	8
O Cinque Terre Sciacchetrà '04	♈♈	8

● I Matti '06	♈♈	5
O Riviera Ligure di Ponente Vermentino '07	♈♈	4*
O Riviera Ligure di Ponente Pigato '07	♈♈	4
O Riviera Ligure di Ponente Pigato I S-cianchi '07	♈♈	4
O Riviera Ligure di Ponente Vermentino Lunghèra '07	♈♈	4
● Ormeasco di Pornassio Sup. '06	♈♈	4
● Riviera Ligure di Ponente Rossese '07	♈♈	4
O Riviera Ligure di Ponente Pigato V. Braie '07	♈	4
● Granaccia '06	♈♈	4
● Ormeasco di Pornassio Sup. '05	♈♈	4
O Riviera Ligure di Ponente Vermentino Lunghera '06	♈♈	4

Tenuta Giuncheo

LOC. GIUNCHEO
18033 CAMPOROSSO [IM]
TEL. 0184288639
www.tenutagiuncheo.it

ANNUAL PRODUCTION 35,000 bottles
HECTARES UNDER VINE 7
VITICULTURE METHOD Conventional

Tenuta Giuncheo, one of the western coast's older operations, is set in a peaceful landscape dense with scrub, vines and olive trees high on the slopes of Camporosso. Acquired years ago by architect Arnold Schweizer, it is now directed by Marco Romagnoli, a talented wine craftsman who succeeds in combining intuitive brilliance with high quality production, and the rich experience of oenologist Donato Lanati is a valuable additional resource. Strange as it may seem, Romagnoli is rarely completely satisfied with his wines, not out of false modesty but because he is relentlessly in search of perfection. We continue to be impressed with Giuncheo's offerings, beginning with elegant Rossese Pian del Vescovo, which shows nicely varietal fruit and balsam impressions and supple progression. The more assertive Selezione 2006 is a mix of syrah, cabernet sauvignon and merlot that spends 15 months in barriques. It is a large, vigorous wine at every moment – bouquet, attack and development – although the tannins are still very powerful. Vermentino 2007 on the other hand is all grace, in particular on the nose of sweet ripe peach and apple.

● Rossese di Dolceacqua Vigneto Pian del Vescovo '06	🍷🍷	5
● Selezione '06	🍷🍷	5
○ Riviera Ligure di Ponente Vermentino '07	🍷	4
● Rossese di Dolceacqua Vigneto Pian del Vescovo '02	YY	5
● Sirius '03	YY	7
● Rossese di Dolceacqua Vigneto Pian del Vescovo '05	YY	5
● Rossese di Dolceacqua Vigneto Pian del Vescovo '04	YY	5
● Rossese di Dolceacqua Vigneto Pian del Vescovo '03	YY	5

Ottaviano Lambruschi

VIA OLMARELLO, 28
19030 CASTELNUOVO MAGRA [SP]
TEL. 0187674261
ottavianolambruschi@libero.it

ANNUAL PRODUCTION 30,000 bottles
HECTARES UNDER VINE 5
VITICULTURE METHOD Conventional

Lambruschi's winery has become an institution in Lunigiana. Its origins go back to the 1970s, when Ottaviano decided to leave the marble quarries of Carrara and then purchased two wooded hectares near Costa Marina. Gradually, determinedly, he acquired other vineyard properties, such as the legendary Sarticola, which was celebrated even in Roman times. With the help of his son Fabio, Lambruschi's long labours in vineyard and cellar have brought forth fine wines indeed. Costa Marina, for example, is a fascinating Vermentino that shows barrique contribution on the nose and markedly sweet fruit in the mouth, plus fine texture and balance. Very smooth progression flows into a well-focused, warm finish. Sarticola is equally delightful, releasing a lightly oak-scented medley of citrus, fruit and fresh vegetables, and an almondy finish that concludes with toasty nuances. Balance and body more than decent. Alessandro comes across as less complex but is appealingly supple with a lively acidity and a clean, lean-edged finale.

○ Colli di Luni Vermentino Costa Marina '07	🍷🍷	4*
○ Colli di Luni Vermentino Alessandro '07	🍷	4
○ Colli di Luni Vermentino Sarticola '07	🍷	4
○ Colli di Luni Vermentino Costa Marina '06	YY	4
○ Colli di Luni Vermentino Costa Marina '05	YY	4

La Pietra del Focolare

FRAZ. ISOLA DI ORTONOVO
VIA DOGANA, 209
19034 ORTONOVO [SP]
TEL. 0187662129
www.lapietradelfocolare.it

ANNUAL PRODUCTION	30,000 bottles
HECTARES UNDER VINE	7
VITICULTURE METHOD	Conventional

La Pietra del Focolare boasts 11 vineyards, all fairly close to each other on various sites in Val di Vara and Val di Magra. The setting has a character all its own, enjoying superb vistas over the valley and out to the Mediterranean. One of the top operations on Liguria's eastern coast, La Pietra del Focolare certainly doesn't lack the means to instil even more quality into the already admirable wines, since the Vermentinos show ample evidence of sound fruit and good winemaking practices. We found Solarancio a forthright wine with lengthy progression, good weight and close-woven texture. We liked the clean, crisp fruit that shines through on the nose, as well as in its rich, warm finale. Herbaceous and floral notes are initially somewhat blurred in Villa Linda but it is an approachable, delicious offering nonetheless, with a winning, supple body. Viva Luce displays lovely fruit subtly enhanced with wood resin, then a delicate, well-delineated palate where zesty acidity modulates the structure. Although Rosso Saltamasso comes across as a tad rustic, its wild berry fruit and slight mineral edge more than redeem its sensory impact.

O Colli di Luni Vermentino Solarancio '07	♀♀ 5
O Colli di Luni Vermentino Augusto '07	♀ 4
O Colli di Luni Vermentino Villa Linda '07	♀ 5
O Colli di Luni Vermentino Viva Luce '07	♀ 2
● Colli di Luni Rosso Saltamasso '07	♀ 5
O Colli di Luni Vermentino Solarancio '06	♀♀ 5

Poggio dei Gorleri

FRAZ. GORLERI
VIA SAN LEONARDO
18013 DIANO MARINA [IM]
TEL. 0183495207
www.poggiodeigorleri.com

ANNUAL PRODUCTION	60,000 bottles
HECTARES UNDER VINE	8
VITICULTURE METHOD	Conventional

The Merano family prides itself on sustained research and experimentation married to a passionate enthusiasm for wine. Hence their introduction, over the years, of ever more innovative procedures and equipment, such as must chilling and automatic washing of the picking bins, all with the goal of unceasingly ratcheting up wine quality. They have also opened a charming farmstay, which enjoys a stunning view out over the gulf of Diano. On the wine front, Vermentino Apricus unfolds gorgeous fruit caressed by smooth hints of honey while the warmly alcoholic palate presents even richer aromatic complexity. The impressively structured Pigato Cycnus displays character and fine progression but its forte is its ultra-refined fruit, with classic ripe peach and ethereal forest floor. Both Vermentinos are worthy of full respect, Vigna Sorì graceful and well proportioned, and the standard version savoury and harmonious. Albium 2007, a Pigato briefly macerated on the skins, is promising. A deep straw yellow, it releases rich aniseed and hazelnut, then develops energetically in the mouth, where succulent fruit and powerful structure offset nervy acidity.

O Riviera Ligure di Ponente Pigato Albium '07	♀♀ 5
O Riviera Ligure di Ponente Vermentino Apricus '07	♀♀ 5
O Riviera Ligure di Ponente Pigato Cycnus '07	♀♀ 4*
O Riviera Ligure di Ponente Vermentino V. Sorì '07	♀♀ 4*
O Riviera Ligure di Ponente Vermentino '07	♀ 4
O Riviera Ligure di Ponente Pigato Albium '06	♀♀ 5
O Riviera Ligure di Ponente Pigato Cycnus '06	♀♀ 4
O Riviera Ligure di Ponente Pigato Cycnus '05	♀♀ 4
O Riviera Ligure di Ponente Vermentino Apricus '06	♀♀ 5
O Riviera Ligure di Ponente Vermentino Apricus '05	♀♀ 5

La Rocca di San Nicolao

FRAZ. GAZZELLI
VIA DANTE, 10
18027 CHIUSANICO [IM]
TEL. 018352850
www.roccasannicolao.com

ANNUAL PRODUCTION   38,000 bottles
HECTARES UNDER VINE   4
VITICULTURE METHOD   Conventional

Marco Della Valle directs Rocca di San Nicolau's vineyards and cellar, and his wines have won high marks for some years now. The vineyards, planted in Gazzelli, in the municipality of Chiusanico, at elevations between 300 and 650 metres, enjoy generous sun as well as an exceptional aspect facing the sea, where rising breezes create conditions ideal for superb vine growth. Della Valle's Pigato Vigna Proxi showed well this year. Rich scents of citrus and ripe peach compose an emphatic, lingering bouquet, enlivened with pungent hints of basil. The palate's aromatics are enthralling as is its even, consistent finish with a hint of bitter almond. Full marks for Vermentino, which gives generous ripe melon and apricot with a touch of herbs. The aromas continue temptingly onto the palate, which revels in firm, well-balanced structure that finishes savoury. Vermentino Vigna Proxi, with a rather lightweight nose, has crisp acidity that makes it a delicious quaffer. The standard Pigato is also good. Intriguing elderflower and tomato leaf make for a striking bouquet while more varietal notes of fresh fruit and slate-like minerality emerge on the palate.

Le Rocche del Gatto

FRAZ. SALEA
REG. RUATO, 4
17031 ALBENGA [SV]
TEL. 3355223547
www.lerocchedelgatto.it

ANNUAL PRODUCTION   80,000 bottles
HECTARES UNDER VINE   7
VITICULTURE METHOD   Conventional

Fausto De Andreis' experience plus Gigi and Chiara Crosa di Vergagni's enthusiasm led to the birth of Le Rocche del Gatto in 2002. While observing tradition and taking advantage of up-to-date vineyard and cellar practices, they have created complex, evolved wines of distinctive character. Specialized fermenters permit slow, cool whole-berry fermentation, which maximizes extraction of pigato and vermentino's varietal aromatics. Spigau Crociata, a vigorous Pigato brimming with character, is made from rigorously selected fruit. The bouquet is a medley of balsam, herbs and ripe fruit, which yield to citrus and mineral in the mouth. The smooth but firm palate shows alcoholic warmth that also infuses the lengthy finish. Rossese is notably complex, opening with well-delineated wild berry fruit, a tad on the sweet side. The palate is smooth, balanced and savoury, with decent structure and pleasing aromatic richness, and it concludes clean and dry. Both Vermentino and Pigato exhibit a verve and freshness that help them stand out. Rather simple liqueur cherries open Macajolo but it develops more dynamic fruit in the mouth and a velvety, warm finish.

O Riviera Ligure di Ponente Pigato Vigna Proxi '07	₸₸ 5
O Riviera Ligure di Ponente Vermentino '07	₸₸ 4*
O Riviera Ligure di Ponente Pigato '07	₸ 4
O Riviera Ligure di Ponente Vermentino Vigna Proxi '07	₸ 5
O Riviera Ligure di Ponente Pigato Vigna Proxi '06	♈♈ 5
O Riviera Ligure di Ponente Pigato Vigna Proxi '05	♈♈ 4*

O Spigau Crociata '06	₸₸ 4*
O Riviera Ligure di Ponente Pigato '07	₸ 4
O Riviera Ligure di Ponente Vermentino '07	₸ 4
● Macajolo '06	₸ 4
● Riviera Ligure di Ponente Rossese '07	₸ 4
● Macaiolo '04	♈♈ 4
● Macajolo '05	♈♈ 4
O Spigau Crociata '05	♈♈ 4
O Spigau Crociata '04	♈♈ 4

Sancio

VIA LAIOLO, 73
17028 SPOTORNO [SV]
TEL. 019743255
cantinasancio@libero.it

ANNUAL PRODUCTION **60,000 bottles**
HECTARES UNDER VINE **4.5**
VITICULTURE METHOD **Conventional**

The Sancio family has dedicated itself for 40 years to winegrowing. With one of the brothers now elsewhere, Riccardo directs operations. His declared goal is to raise the quality bar still higher but always within the ambit of local traditions. One of his products is Cappellania, a fine Pigato that has become the winery's icon. The ripe fruit, balsam and minerality that compose its multi-layered bouquet glide beautifully onto the palate, which shows supple texture and full, sapid flavours before the almond-edged finale. The standard Pigato is a fine teammate, offering finesse of fruit on the nose and an almond-rich palate with steady progression. Vermentino 2007 is back a length or two, showing uncomplicated, fruity and tasty enough. Lumassina is a difficult grape to handle well but Sancio succeeds here. We liked its crisp florality and fresh-cut grass on the nose, as well as its impressively supple palate enlivened by delicious, tangy acidity. The reds are well crafted. Granaccia 2006 is not as firm as one might like but it shows nice balsam and subtle spice. Rossese 2007 lacks aromatic depth but is fruity and easy drinking.

Terre Bianche

LOC. ARCAGNA
18035 DOLCEACQUA [IM]
TEL. 018431426
www.terrebianche.com

ANNUAL PRODUCTION **57,000 bottles**
HECTARES UNDER VINE **8**
VITICULTURE METHOD **Conventional**

Both the characterful wines and the beautiful setting of Terre Bianche richly deserve a visit. Filippo Rondelli and Franco Laconi have worked hard, focusing on painstaking vineyard practices, such as drastic cluster thinning and ultra-rigorous grape selection, as well as on important changes in winemaking and ageing protocols in the cellar. Bricco Arcagna 2006 crowns these efforts. A luscious mosaic of red berry fruit, wild herbs and pine resin precedes a palate that offers juicy, supple fruit and impressive forcefulness. The standard Rossese is also fine, with herb-infused fruit on the nose and good volume in the mouth, where vivacious acidity and a vein of bitterish almond characterize long, steady progression. Arcana Rosso 2005, from cabernet sauvignon with a bit of rossese, is huge on both nose and palate, showing balance and appeal at every stage. The pigato and vermentino Arcana Bianco 2006 put on a fine performance too, with complex aromatics, smooth, rounded fruit and textbook development. The Vermentino offers attractive impressions, while the Pigato, though somewhat warm, releases tasty honey and ripe fruit.

○ Riviera Ligure di Ponente Pigato '07	♈♈ 4*
○ Riviera Ligure di Ponente Pigato Cappellania '07	♈♈ 4*
○ Riviera Ligure di Ponente Lumassina '07	♈ 3
○ Riviera Ligure di Ponente Vermentino '07	♈ 4
● Granaccia Edoardo I '06	♈ 5
● Riviera Ligure di Ponente Rossese '07	♈ 4
○ Riviera Ligure di Ponente Pigato '06	♈♈ 4
○ Riviera Ligure di Ponente Pigato Cappellania '06	♈♈ 5
● Riviera Ligure di Ponente Rossese '06	♈♈ 4

● Rossese di Dolceacqua Bricco Arcagna '06	♈♈ 5
● Arcana Rosso '05	♈♈ 6
● Rossese di Dolceacqua '07	♈♈ 4*
○ Arcana Bianco '06	♈♈ 5
○ Riviera Ligure di Ponente Vermentino '07	♈♈ 4*
○ Riviera Ligure di Ponente Pigato '07	♈ 4
○ Riviera Ligure di Ponente Vermentino '06	♈♈ 4
● Arcana Rosso '03	♈♈ 5
● Arcana Rosso '04	♈♈ 6
● Rossese di Dolceacqua '06	♈♈ 4
● Rossese di Dolceacqua Bricco Arcagna '05	♈♈ 5
● Rossese di Dolceacqua Bricco Arcagna '01	♈♈ 5

Cascina delle Terre Rosse

VIA MANIE, 3
17024 FINALE LIGURE [SV]
TEL. 019698782

ANNUAL PRODUCTION	32,000 bottles
HECTARES UNDER VINE	5.5
VITICULTURE METHOD	Conventional

Vladimiro Galluzzo's magical kingdom is the Manie plateau in Liguria's interior. Galluzzo, who is passionately professional about his work, has long been turning out exceptional wines, with assistance from talented consultant Giuliano Noè. Cascina delle Terre Rosse wines, all of them long-lived, are led by the winery's iconic Pigatos. The standard version Pigato is actually the most impressive. It releases a lavish array of apricot, melon, citrus and wild herbs, whose impact is fully matched by the elegant, leisurely flow of the progression and its ample yet refreshing palate. Apogeo 2007 shows an equally fine, if more rounded palate, introducing a delicate toasty note layered into its mineral and fruit. Le Banche furnishes another interpretation of the variety, with admirable equilibrium of fruit and oak, sober development and seductive, sapid flavours. Solitario is becoming increasingly refined and shows an ever-surer winemaking hand. The subtly spiced 2006 version showcases magnificent fruit on nose and palate, admirable energy and silky texture. The Vermentino is fresh and varietal, as is the alluring Acerbina.

Il Torchio

VIA PROVINCIALE, 202
19030 CASTELNUOVO MAGRA [SP]
TEL. 0187674075

ANNUAL PRODUCTION	36,000 bottles
HECTARES UNDER VINE	5
VITICULTURE METHOD	Conventional

Giorgio Tendola calls a spade a spade, and he is just as natural and unfeigned as his wines. He refers to himself as a "product" of the land he was born to, and even his wines seem to take on the character of this diamond in the rough. Giorgio's family mainly grew and pressed olives, and their wine went largely to their own table and to local eateries. Tendola never ceases to surprise us with the unfailing quality and value for money of his wines. He has always been inspired by Alsatian wines and has focused on the utilization of cool temperatures to maximize aromatic extraction, particularly in his Vermentino, Il Torchio's standard-bearer. The 2007 version demonstrates that extractive richness, with captivating tropical fragrances of pineapple and citrus notes on both nose and palate. It is crisp and well balanced, and drives through the gears with determination. Rosso also displays fine fruit, particularly sweet and smooth yet subtle red berry. A good medium-weight body is supported by fine-grained, supple tannins and capped by a fluid conclusion with appreciable length.

O Riviera Ligure di Ponente Pigato '07	♟♟	5
O Apogeo '07	♟♟	5
O Le Banche '07	♟♟	5
● Solitario '06	♟♟	6
O L'Acerbina '07	♟	4
O Riviera Ligure di Ponente Vermentino '07	♟	5
O Riviera Ligure di Ponente Pigato '99	♟♟♟	5
O Riviera Ligure di Ponente Pigato '05	♟♟	5
O Riviera Ligure di Ponente Pigato '06	♟♟	5
● Solitario '05	♟♟	6
● Solitario '04	♟♟	6
● Solitario '03	♟♟	6
● Solitario '01	♟♟	7

O Colli di Luni Vermentino '07	♟♟	4*
● Colli di Luni Rosso '07	♟	4
O Colli di Luni Vermentino '06	♟♟	4

La Vecchia Cantina

FRAZ. SALEA
VIA CORTA, 3
17031 ALBENGA [SV]
TEL. 0182559881

ANNUAL PRODUCTION	18,000 bottles
HECTARES UNDER VINE	4
VITICULTURE METHOD	Conventional

Umberto Calleri, legendary grower and owner of Vecchia Cantina di Salea in Albenga, is a man of few words but strong convictions. With a wealth of experience gleaned over 40 years of activity, he is loath to delegate anything of importance, tending his vines daily in vineyards scattered through Scuea, Cianboschi and the Frati area, and personally labouring in his modest but up-to-date winemaking cellar. He is proud of the wines he produces, and they certainly more than justify his production philosophy: always soundly made, impressive and easy drinking but far from simple. Vermentino is a perfect example. It opens to a rich, pungent spectrum of balsam, pine resin and wild herbs, which continue generously through entry in the mouth, where firm structure, plenty of energy and sapid, pulpy fruit come through. Pigato also scored well. It is an accessible but classic varietal with hedonistic, well-ripened peach and apricot that yield to fresh herbaceousness in the mouth. The palate is masterful, building a fine progression through to a warm, smooth finish and displays excellent texture, well-calibrated equilibrium and appreciable overall finesse.

O Riviera Ligure di Ponente Pigato '07	♥♥	4*
O Riviera Ligure di Ponente Vermentino '07	♥♥	4*
O Riviera Ligure di Ponente Pigato '07	♀♀	4
O Riviera Ligure di Ponente Pigato '06	♀♀	4
O Riviera Ligure di Ponente Pigato '05	♀♀	4

Claudio Vio

FRAZ. CROSA, 16
17032 VENDONE [SV]
TEL. 018276338

ANNUAL PRODUCTION	12,500 bottles
HECTARES UNDER VINE	2
VITICULTURE METHOD	Conventional

The adage "slow and steady..." fits Claudio Vio like a glove. Exuding a farmer's love for his earth, Vio spends entire days working the vine rows and uses all his professional experience to draw out the finest qualities from his fruit in the cellar. U Grottu, in its second release this year, is a worthy reflection of this philosophy. The pigato grapes spend an extra three weeks on the vine and the must is given a five-day maceration on the skins. The wine matures on the fine lees, with periodic bâtonnage. These procedures yield a huge bouquet packed with fruit and blossoms, nicely edged with slate-like minerality that becomes more prominent on the palate, where it contributes to bright sapidity. Equally impressive are U Grottu's fine mouthfeel and disciplined overall focus. Pigato is no less successful, the finesse achieved by cleanly delineated peach and citron being fully matched by succulent fruit, fine balance and admirable length. Vermentino shows less complex, with graceful impressions of fruit and subtle herbs, but refreshing and tasty on the palate. Runcu Brujau shows similar characteristics. It's a clean, uncomplicated yet very enjoyable offering.

O Riviera Ligure di Ponente Pigato '07	♥♥	4*
O U Grottu '07	♥♥	4*
O Riviera Ligure di Ponente Vermentino '07	♀	4
● Runcu Brujau '07	♀	4
O U Grottu '06	♀♀	4

OTHER WINERIES

Cooperativa Agricoltori della Vallata di Levanto

LOC. GHIARE - VIA S. MATTEO, 20
19015 LEVANTO [SP]
TEL. 0187800867
www.levanto.com/cooperativa

Consistently reliable wines from this cooperative keep it in the editions of this Guide. Their well-balanced Costa di Mattelun offers a lovely mix of toasty oak notes and hints of green apple. We found newly introduced Passito Lievàntu impressive and well balanced, with intriguing apricot, but not too complex.

● Colline di Levanto Canuet '07	♟	4
● Passito Rosso Lievàntu '05	♟	6
○ Colline di Levanto Costa di Mattelun '07	♟	4
○ Colline di Levanto Lievàntu '07	♟	3

Anfossi

FRAZ. BASTIA
VIA PACCINI, 39
17031 ALBENGA [SV]
TEL. 018220024
www.aziendaagrariaanfossi.it

A project of the region of Liguria has recently helped the environment-friendly Anfossi to install two photovoltaic panels with 30 kilowatt capacity. Their Vermentino is superlative, its crisp aromas the perfect complement to a lean, delicious palate. The Pigato offers fine citrus impressions.

○ Riviera Ligure di Ponente Vermentino '07	♟♟	4*
○ Riviera Ligure di Ponente Pigato '07	♟	4

Alessandro Anfosso

C.SO VERBONE, 175
18036 SOLDANO [IM]
TEL. 3383116590

Marisa Perotti and husband Alessandro Anfosso launched their wine adventure in 2002 and have achieved outstanding results, assisted by oenologist Walter Bonetti. We were impressed by their standard Rossese and by Luvaira, as well as by Poggio I Pini, sourced from a vineyard over 100 years old.

● Rossese di Dolceacqua '07	♟♟	4*
● Rossese di Dolceacqua Luvaira '07	♟♟	5
● Rossese di Dolceacqua Sup. Poggio I Pini '06	♟♟	5

Luigi Bianchi Carenzo

VIA LANTERO, 19
18013 DIANO SAN PIETRO [IM]
TEL. 0183429072

Luigi Bianchi Carenzo's modest enterprise always amazes. His Vermentino, one of the best wines tasted this year, offers rich, spot-on varietal aromas of wild herbs, followed by an alluring, splendidly solid palate with plenty of length. The Pigato is beautifully proportioned, with ripe fruit and delicious balsam.

○ Riviera Ligure di Ponente Vermentino '07	♟♟	4*
○ Riviera Ligure di Ponente Pigato '07	♟♟	4*
● Riviera Ligure di Ponente Rossese '07	♟	4

Samuele Heydi Bonanini

VIA DI LOCA, 189
19017 RIOMAGGIORE [SP]
TEL. 3483162470

Heydi Bonanini produces very few bottles but their performance is top-notch, particularly on the nose. The star, Sciacchetrà, releases well-delineated dried apricot and honeyed impressions, lifted by tangy acidity. Cinque Terre is offers crisp, refreshing florality.

○ Cinque Terre '07	♟♟	5
○ Cinque Terre Sciacchetrà '06	♟♟	8
● U Neigru	♟	5

Enoteca Andrea Bruzzone

VIA BOLZANETO, 94/96
16162 GENOVA
TEL. 0107455157
www.andreabruzzonevini.it

This hard-working producer is small, but a powerhouse in the Val Polcevera. Bruzzone has restored to production small, long-abandoned parcels, and they yield him first-class wines, such as this well-fruited, refreshing Vermentino, his admirably distinctive Coronata, and a delicious red, Pellandrun.

○ Val Polcevera Coronata '07	♟	4
○ Val Polcevera Vermentino '07	♟	3
● Pellandrun	♟	4

OTHER WINERIES

Luciano Capellini

VIA MONTELLO, 240B
19017 RIOMAGGIORE [SP]
TEL. 0187920632
www.vinbun.it

Luciano Capellini crowns seven generations of growers in Volastra. His two wines beautifully conjure up a remarkable terroir. Generous draughts of balsam and spice open Sciacchetrà, which lays out judiciously complex honey, while the lively acidity in his Cinque Terre is the perfect foil to its warm alcohol.

O Cinque Terre '07	♟ 6
O Cinque Terre Sciacchetrà '06	♟ 8

La Colombiera

LOC. MONTECCHIO, 92
19030 CASTELNUOVO MAGRA [SP]
TEL. 0187674265

Piero Ferro, located in the Castelnuovo Magra area, produces wines that exhibit good expression of their terroir. His Vermentino displays generous, ultra-ripe fruit on both nose and palate while Terrizzo shows more evolved, rounded yet still crisp and refreshing in the mouth.

● Colli di Luni Rosso Terrizzo '06	♟ 4
O Colli di Luni Vermentino '07	♟ 4

La Felce

VIA BOZZI, 36
19034 ORTONOVO [SP]
TEL. 018766789
www.picedibenettini.it

Andrea Marcesini runs this fairly new operation on the eastern coast. Pian di Sabbia is full bodied and the nose showing a complex herbaceousness elegantly enriched with a touch of sweet oak. His Vermentino, flaunting a crisp medley of fragrances, shows admirable structure and steady progression.

● Pian di Sabbia Rosso '07	♟♟ 4*
O Colli di Luni Vermentino '07	♟ 4
O Passito 739 '07	♟ 5

Colle dei Bardellini

LOC. BARDELLINI
VIA FONTANAROSA, 12
18100 IMPERIA
TEL. 0183291370
www.colledeibardellini.it

Colle dei Bardellini's four-hectare estate vineyard is sited on a sunny hill behind Oneglia, where it yields the vermentino for U Munte and Pigato La Torretta. The former is straightforward and supple, while the latter releases marked impressions of crisp citrus.

O Riviera Ligure di Ponente Vermentino V. U Munte '07	♟♟ 4*
O Riviera Ligure di Ponente Pigato V. La Torretta '07	♟ 5

Conte Picedi

VIA SOMMOVIGO
19038 ARCOLA [SP]
TEL. 0187625147
www.picedibenettini.it

Conte Picedi is a solid eastern Liguria producer. We liked the generosity and full body of Gran Baccano, with its lovely aromatic interplay between vanilla and red berry fruit, then good development and a lengthy, warm finale. Both Vermentinos are judiciously executed, sapid and varietal.

● Colli di Luni Rosso Gran Baccano '07	♟♟ 4*
O Colli di Luni Vermentino Stemma '07	♟♟ 4*
O Colli di Luni Vermentino '07	♟ 4
● Colli di Luni Rosso Villa II Chioso '07	♟ 4

Fontanacota

VIA DOLCEDO, 121
18100 IMPERIA
TEL. 0183293456
viniberta@tiscali.it

Marina Antonella Berta's wines are finely crafted and appealingly distinctive. Alluring draughts of emphatic, well-ripened fruit pervade Pigato. Ormeasco Superiore offers inviting, fragrant cherry and good supporting tannins while the standard Ormeasco is younger, warm and heady. The Vermentino is sound.

● Ormeasco di Pornassio '07	♟♟ 4*
● Ormeasco di Pornassio Sup. '06	♟♟ 4*
O Riviera Ligure di Ponente Pigato '07	♟♟ 4*
O Riviera Ligure di Ponente Vermentino '07	♟ 4

OTHER WINERIES

Forlini Cappellini

LOC. MANAROLA
VIA RICCOBALDI, 45
19010 RIOMAGGIORE [SP]
TEL. 0187920496
forlinicappellini@libero.it

A veritable icon of heroic viticulture, this historic winery knows how to infuse its offerings with its intriguing terroir. Self confidence and admirable character mark Cinque Terre. Stylish elegance on the nose is followed by delicious fruit, whose smoothness characterizes the wine's entire development.

○ Cinque Terre '07	▼ 5

Giacomelli

VIA PALVOTRISIA, 134
19030 CASTELNUOVO MAGRA [SP]
TEL. 0187674155

Young Roberto Petacchi dedicates his efforts to the native varieties of Lunigiana and his Vermentinos are valuable glimpses into the classic traditions of the area. Boboli is subtle, refined and deliciously fruity while the standard Vermentino offers green notes among subtle fruit and a full-flavoured finish.

○ Colli di Luni Vermentino '07	▼ 5
○ Colli di Luni Vermentino Boboli '07	▼ 5

Ka Manciné

FRAZ. SAN MARTINO
PIAZZA OTTO LUOGHI, 36
18036 SOLDANO [IM]
TEL. 0184289089

Maurizio Anfosso's winery makes a fine Guide debut. Launched in 1998, its first release was just last year. He produces two wines, both Rosseses. In Beragna, nuances of wild berry fruit alternate with notes of rose petals while Galeae shows generous fragrances of pungent balsam and wild herbs.

● Rossese di Dolceacqua Beragna '07	▼▼ 4*
● Rossese di Dolceacqua Galeae '07	▼ 5

Il Monticello

VIA GROPPOLO, 7
19038 SARZANA [SP]
TEL. 0187621432
www.ilmonticello.tin.it

The Neri brothers are determined to stand out from other producers on the eastern coast. Their wines, made in styles unusual for the area, are gaining high marks. Poggio dei Magni is an emphatically self-confident wine, yet shows elegance and smooth mouthfeel, and Poggio Paterno is outstanding.

● Colli di Luni Rosso Poggio dei Magni '05	▼▼ 4*
○ Colli di Luni Vermentino Poggio Paterno '06	▼▼ 4*
○ Colli di Luni Vermentino '07	▼ 4
● Colli di Luni Rosso Rupestro '07	▼ 4

Nirasca

FRAZ. NIRASCA
VIA ALPI, 3
18026 PIEVE DI TECO [IM]
TEL. 0183368067
www.cascinanirasca.com

Marco Temesio and Gabriele Maglio put out a wide variety of top quality bottlings. The stand-out is Ormeasco Superiore, which exhibits multi-layered fruit and mineral on the nose. The generous, very aromatic Vermentino is superb and Pigato and Ormeasco are both delicious.

● Ormeasco di Pornassio Sup. '06	▼▼ 4*
○ Riviera Ligure di Ponente Vermentino '07	▼▼ 4*
● Ormeasco di Pornassio '07	▼ 4
○ Riviera Ligure di Ponente Pigato '07	▼ 4

Antonio Perrino

18035 DOLCEACQUA [IM]
TEL. 0184206267

Antonio Perrino, or "Testalonga" (Longhead), a nickname he inherited from an ancestor, avoids over-manipulation in the cellar and sticks to the old ways. His wines may not be perfect but they display impressive character. Rossese 2007 is all ripe fruit and its palate bursts with crisp, delicious flavours.

● Rossese di Dolceacqua '07	▼▼ 5

OTHER WINERIES

Poggi dell'Elmo
C.SO VERBONE, 135
18036 SOLDANO [IM]
TEL. 3384736742

Giovanni Gugliemi's vineyards are at Pini di Soldano, one of the area's best spots for rossese. We found his wines extremely well made. A fine varietal nose opens the standard Rossese, which is lithe and well balanced. The well-structured Superiore releases wild red berry and builds up smoothly across the palate.

- ● Rossese di Dolceacqua '07 🍷🍷 4*
- ● Rossese di Dolceacqua Sup. '06 🍷🍷 4*

Lorenzo Ramò
VIA S. ANTONIO, 9
18020 PORNASSIO [IM]
TEL. 018333097

The distinctive varietal characteristics of ormeasco come to the fore in Gian Paolo Ramò's wines. The 2007 flaunts gorgeous fruit and intriguing spice nuances on the nose, followed by a velvety palate and a delicious, nicely almond-laced finale. Sciactrà, with ultra-savoury flavours, is a delight to drink.

- ● Ormeasco di Pornassio '07 🍷🍷 4*
- ⊙ Ormeasco di Pornassio Sciac-trà '07 🍷 4

La Ricolla
VIA GARIBALDI, 12/2
16040 NE [GE]
TEL. 0185337087
laricolla@alice.it

Daniele Parma puts a vigorous imprint on his wines and they reflect Valgraveglia, a challenging terroir. Fliscano is fruity and aromatic with vivacious acidity while the nose on Çimixâ verges on the tropical.

- O Golfo Del Tigullio Vermentino Fliscano '07 🍷🍷 4*
- O Çimixâ Casottana Vign. Rivara '07 🍷 5
- O Golfo del Tigullio Vermentino Tolceto '07 🍷 4

Santa Caterina
VIA SANTA CATERINA, 6
19038 SARZANA [SP]
TEL. 0187629429
akih@libero.it

Deeply rooted grower Andrea Kihlgren has been at the helm of Santa Caterina since 1990 and always puts out impressive wines. His two Vermentinos, both superb, are sensorially diverse. The standard version shows off smooth, rich melon and apricot while Poggi Alti is more restrained.

- O Colli di Luni Vermentino '07 🍷🍷 4*
- O Colli di Luni Vermentino Poggi Alti '07 🍷🍷 4*
- O Giuncaro '07 🍷 4
- ● Ghiaretolo '05 🍷 4

Terre dei Doria
C.SO VERBONE, 135
18036 SOLDANO [IM]
TEL. 3356957956
terredeidoria@aol.com

Terre dei Doria puts out only 4,000 bottles but it deserves close attention. It is run by three friends, and Jo Sergi, an authority on the French denomination of Bellet, manages the winemaking. The Rossese is impressive all the way through, the Rosé is alluring and the Vermentino well balanced.

- ⊙ Rosé '07 🍷🍷 5
- ● Rossese di Dolceacqua Sup. '07 🍷🍷 6
- O Riviera Ligure di Ponente Vermentino '07 🍷 5

Vis Amoris
LOC. CARAMAGNA - S.DA MOLINO JAVÈ, 23
18100 IMPERIA
TEL. 3483959569
visamoris@libero.it

Roberto Tozzi and Rossana Zappa are soon to do more planting and build a new cellar. Their current production is limited but quality is very high. Vigna Domè conveys seductive nuances of peach and citrus on the nose, and the palate keeps that very much alive, adding lovely balsam notes.

- O Riviera Ligure di Ponente Pigato V. Domè '07 🍷🍷 5*

LOMBARDY

When we stated in the last Guide progress in Lombardy winemaking was huge, we didn't expect to see the results, glass in hand, quite so quickly. But with the speed characteristic of other business sectors in Lombardy, wine has forged ahead and our judges awarded Three Glasses to 15 wines, the best result in the Guide's 22 years in existence. More importantly, and before we go into detail, we should say that we believe this to be more of a starting point than a final destination for Lombard winemakers. Top of the class among the zones is Franciacorta, the first designated zone to establish years ago tough regulations and ambitious objectives, and then put in place all the necessary resources to reach those objectives. A flag-bearer for top quality Italian wine worldwide, Ca' del Bosco won two awards for two excellent Franciacortas, the Cuvée Annamaria Clementi '01, with its rarefied elegance, and the timeless classic Dosage Zéro, again a stand-out in the '04 vintage. Following these come the deep, highly individual Cabochon '04 from Monte Rossa, the elegant Grand Cuvée '04 from Bellavista, another label with a major international presence, the irresistible Satèn '04 from Ferghettina, the formidable Comarì del Salem '03 from Uberti, the Extra Brut '04 from Monzio Compagnoni, established as a top-quality estate, and the spectacular Extra Brut Au Contraire '01 from Cavalleri. But there could be even more. In the last Guide, we mentioned the vast latent potential of Oltrepò Pavese, which this year has shown itself to be fundamental for the region. It has continued to grow and collected three new awards alongside the established star Monsupello, hitherto in its own. Although the Pinot Nero Nature confirms this estate's high quality, Pinot Nero is the type making the fortune of the designated area. Aside from the new DOCG regulations, this is also shown by the Nature Écru '03 from Anteo and excellent Pinot Nero Giorgio Odero '05 from historic Frecciarossa, which testifies to the bright prospects of a territory that is emerging as a second home in Italy for this challenging grape. Sealing this success, driven by the Oltrepò protection consortium's efforts to point out the way forward, is the excellent Barbera Poggio della Maga '05 from Castello di Cigognola, owned by the Moratti family. Another excellent wine area, Valtellina, contributed two more prizewinning wines, the classic Sfursat '05 from Nino Negri and Sfursat Albareda '06 from Mamete Prevostini. Only testing growing years held the other excellent estates back from higher scores. We'll close with Garda and the success of Lugana Fabio Contato '07 from Provenza. It's a wine of great class from excellent wine country that will continue to give its producers great satisfaction, as will Valtenesi, we believe, with its Groppellos.

Marchese Adorno

VIA CORIASSA, 4
27050 RETORBIDO [PV]
TEL. 0383374404
www.marcheseadorno-wines.it

ANNUAL PRODUCTION	200,000 bottles
HECTARES UNDER VINE	80
VITICULTURE METHOD	Conventional

Recent progress at this estate owned by Marchese Marcello Cattaneo Adorno has involved major investment, a lovely cellar and some emerging wines. The best is the deep ruby coloured Barbera Vigna del Re '05, which offers spice, fruit and balsam, well-handled oak, structure, backbone, depth and a chocolate-like finish. Chocolate also dominates the aromas in the Cliviano '06, a spicy Bordeaux blend with a soft, rather ingratiating style. While the Bonarda Frizzante '07 is fragrant and agreeable, with nice wild berries up front, the Rugla '05 still can't quite express itself as it should and could. This, too, is a Bordeaux blend, like the Cliviano, but rather more serious in its fundamental conception. The wine itself still has to find its identity and for the time being gives rather marked vegetal sensations and rigid tannins. Perhaps it will benefit from more bottle ageing. The simple Pinot Grigio '07 is fresh and well executed, the Pinot Nero '06 is varietal, the Barbera '06 has nice substance, and the IGT Arcolaio '06, from cortese and chardonnay, shows citrus and tropical fruit aromas.

● Cliviano '06	♙♙	4
● OP Barbera V. del Re '05	♙♙	6
● OP Bonarda Frizzante '07	♙♙	4*
O Arcolaio '06	♙	4
● OP Barbera '06	♙	4
O OP Pinot Grigio '07	♙	4
● OP Pinot Nero '06	♙	5
● Rugla '05	♙	6
O Arcolaio '05	♟♟	4*
● Cliviano '05	♟♟	4
● OP Barbera V. del Re '04	♟♟	6
● OP Bonarda Frizzante '06	♟♟	4

Agnes

VIA CAMPO DEL MONTE, 1
27040 ROVESCALA [PV]
TEL. 038575206
www.fratelliagnes.it

ANNUAL PRODUCTION	70,000 bottles
HECTARES UNDER VINE	16
VITICULTURE METHOD	Conventional

We repeat ourselves every year but we do so gladly because this Oltrepò estate is where the croatina variety, and Bonarda wine, are at their absolute best in every possible form. The barrique-aged Poculum is as excellent as ever, the '06 showing still young with oak still predominant, but this fails to cover the wild berries and enhances an imposing structure. The Bonarda Millennium '05 is cask-conditioned with an extra year's ageing. At the moment, it has more of a balance of fruit, flowers and oak-derived spiciness and powers vibrantly through to a long, precise finish. From the sparkling '07 Bonardas, we just preferred Cresta del Ghiffi, which is balanced, fragrant and deep starting from its impenetrable colour. Other Two Glass winners are Campo del Monte, which proffers darker notes with hints of forest floor and Possessione del Console, which unveils blueberry notes against a remarkably harmonious framework. The Loghetto Ammandorlato '07 is rather sweet and pleasant while Vignazzo, although attractive with balanced tannins, has a fairly pronounced vegetal note.

● OP Bonarda Campo del Monte '07	♙♙	3*
● OP Bonarda Cresta del Ghiffi '07	♙♙	3*
● OP Bonarda Millenium '05	♙♙	5
● OP Bonarda Possessione del Console '07	♙♙	3*
● Rosso Poculum '06	♙♙	5
● Loghetto Ammandorlato '07	♙	4
● Rosso Vignazzo '07	♙	4
● OP Bonarda Campo del Monte '06	♟♟	3*
● Rosso Poculum '05	♟♟	5
● Rosso Vignazzo '04	♟♟	4

Anteo

LOC. CHIESA
27040 ROCCA DE' GIORGI [PV]
TEL. 038599073
www.anteovini.it

ANNUAL PRODUCTION	240,000 bottles
HECTARES UNDER VINE	26
VITICULTURE METHOD	Conventional

We welcome Piero and Antonella Cribellati's estate into the Three Glass club. The prize went to the best version ever of the Nature Écru. Alongside its usual elegant aromas of flowers, wild berries and aromatic herbs, the confident attack, balance, tanginess, depth and clear acid backbone, the '03 vintage also has not insignificant structure that further enhances the wine without making it seem heavy. Also in the finals was the Rosé, which has always been the stand-out in a zone where this wine type is making more and more headway. Deep in colour, it explodes on the nose with wild berries that linger onto the clean, soft, fragrant palate. Just as good is the Riserva del Poeta '01, which nearly ended up in the finals. The whirlwind of aromatic herbs on the complex nose mingles perfectly with the aromas of fruit and cakes before the palate offers minerality, balance and a long-lingering finish. Proof of Anteo's skill with the classic method comes in the base Brut, which strolled off with Two Glasses. The Bonarda and Moscato are both varietal and well made. The two cuve close sparklers, a white and a rosé from Pinot Nero, are pleasant and soft.

Barone Pizzini

LOC. TIMOLINE
VIA BRESCIA, 3A
25050 CORTE FRANCA [BS]
TEL. 0309848311
www.baronepizzini.it

ANNUAL PRODUCTION	380,000 bottles
HECTARES UNDER VINE	36
VITICULTURE METHOD	Certified organic

Barone Pizzini is owned by Brescia-based businessmen who years ago appointed Silvano Brescianini to manage it. Silvano turned it into a model estate, now farmed organically. This led to other operations with Tenuta del Barco in Puglia, Podere Ghiaccioforte in the Tuscan Maremma and Pievalta in Marche, all run with natural methods to bring out the best in the territorial varieties. Barone Pizzini's top cuvée is Franciacorta Nature Bagnadore, from equal parts of Chardonnay and Pinot Nero. The '03 shows a lovely, deep straw with copper highlights, a fine bead and complex aromas of ripe fruit and citrus with winning minerality. The palate is solid and powerful yet balanced, with caressing effervescence and a long fruit finish. The Satèn '04 is also sound, with lovely coffee and charred oak preceding a supple palate. The same goes for the Extra Dry, which shows a happy balance between sweet fruity notes and acid backbone. The other labels are also reliable. From the Puglia list, a special mention goes to the soft, full-bodied Pezza delle Case '06, from negroamaro, malvasia nera and merlot. Wines from Tenuta del Barco in Puglia are sound.

○ OP Pinot Nero Brut Cl. Nature Écru '03	♟♟♟	5
⊙ OP Pinot Nero Extra Dry Cl. Rosé	♟♟	5
● OP Bonarda Staffolo '07	♟♟	4*
⊙ OP Moscato La Volpe e L'Uva '07	♟♟	4*
○ OP Pinot Nero Brut Cl.	♟♟	5
○ OP Pinot Nero Brut Cl. Riserva del Poeta '01	♟♟	6
○ OP Pinot Nero Brut Martinotti	♟	4
⊙ OP Pinot Nero Brut Martinotti Rosé	♟	4
○ OP Pinot Nero Brut Cl. Nature Ecru '99	♟♟	5
○ OP Pinot Nero Brut Cl. Nature Écru '02	♟♟	5
○ OP Pinot Nero Brut Cl. Nature Ecru '00	♟♟	5
○ OP Pinot Nero Brut Cl. Riserva del Poeta '99	♟♟	6
● OP Bonarda Staffolo '06	♟♟	4*

○ Franciacorta Extra Brut Bagnadore '03	♟♟	6
○ Franciacorta Extra Dry	♟♟	6
○ Franciacorta Satèn '04	♟♟	6
● Tenuta del Barco Pezza delle Case '06	♟♟	3*
○ Franciacorta Brut	♟	5
⊙ Franciacorta Rosé Brut	♟	6
● San Carlo '04	♟	6
○ TdF Bianco Curtefranca '07	♟	4
● TdF Rosso Curtefranca '06	♟	4
○ Tenuta del Barco Scoglio del Tonno '07	♟	3
○ Franciacorta Extra Brut Bagnadore '02	♟♟	6
○ Franciacorta Satèn '01	♟♟	6
● San Carlo '01	♟♟	6

Bellaria

FRAZ. MAIRANO
VIA CASTEL DEL LUPO, 28
27045 CASTEGGIO [PV]
TEL. 038383203
www.vinibellaria.it

ANNUAL PRODUCTION	50,000 bottles
HECTARES UNDER VINE	19.5
VITICULTURE METHOD	Conventional

This year Paolo Massone's estate sent two wines to our finals. The Bricco Sturnèl '04, from 80-20 cabernet sauvignon and barbera, presents a deep ruby with aromas of ripe wild black berry fruit, hay, spice and balsam. There is a nice attack on the palate where smooth tannins introduce a compact, solid structure with fruity pulp and a remarkably long, deep finish. The Barbera Olmetto '05, one of the best from Oltrepò, also scored high. Showing a brilliant ruby colour with purple highlights, this wine has distinctive aromas with recognizable chocolate and chestnut flour meshing well with the cherry typical of the variety. The palate reveals substance, good backbone and commendable balance. The merlot-only La Macchia '04 is also very good. Varietal notes of pepper, bell pepper and blueberry emerge upfront, and structure, softness and elegance make the palate very attractive indeed. The well executed, slightly sparkling Bonarda Bria '07 has an impenetrable dark colour as well as a nose of black berry fruit and forest floor, balanced on the palate by excellently gauged tannins.

● Bricco Sturnèl '04	♙♙	5
● OP Barbera Olmetto '05	♙♙	4*
● La Macchia '04	♙♙	5
● OP Bornarda Vivace La Bria '07	♙♙	4*
● Bricco Sturnèl '01	♙♙	5
● La Macchia '01	♙♙	5
● La Macchia '00	♙♙	5
● OP Barbera Olmetto '04	♙♙	4
● OP Barbera Olmetto '03	♙♙	4
● OP Bornarda Vivace La Bria '06	♙♙	4*

★ Bellavista

VIA BELLAVISTA, 5
25030 ERBUSCO [BS]
TEL. 0307762000
www.bellavistawine.it

ANNUAL PRODUCTION	1,300,000 bottles
HECTARES UNDER VINE	184
VITICULTURE METHOD	Conventional

We are always keen to taste the wines from the famous flagship estate of the Terra Moretti group. Owner Vittorio made an excellent choice when he entrusted estate management to Mattia Vezzola around 20 years ago. The 18th Three Glass award arrived at the door in tribute to the delightful charms of Franciacorta Gran Cuvée Brut '04 with its bright, straw yellow lit up by classic greenish highlights. Aromas range from ripe white-fleshed fruit to flowers, citrus peel and delicate vanilla notes in a swath that is more than elegant. On the palate, you find fresh, full sensations, extraordinary elegance and spectacular balance that close in a lingering, fresh, fruity finish. Terre di Franciacorta Bianco Convento dell'Annunciata is as excellent as ever in the '05 vintage, which has soft opulence and overall harmony. If the complex, apple and pear-crisp Satèn embodies the archetype of this wine then the Rosé '04, among the best from the vintage, and the Pas Operé '02, redolent of aromatic herbs, are both just as sound. The Terre di Franciacorta Uccellanda '05, Curtefranca Bianco '07 and standard Franciacorta Brut are well up to snuff.

○ Franciacorta Gran Cuvée Brut '04	♙♙♙	7
○ Franciacorta Gran Cuvée Satèn	♙♙	7
○ TdF Bianco Convento dell'Annunciata '05	♙♙	6
○ Franciacorta Cuvée Brut	♙♙	6
⊙ Franciacorta Gran Cuvée Brut Rosé '04	♙♙	7
○ Franciacorta Gran Cuvée Pas Operé '02	♙♙	8
○ TdF Bianco Uccellanda '05	♙♙	6
○ TdF Curtefranca Bianco '07	♙♙	4
○ Franciacorta Extra Brut Vittorio Moretti '01	♙♙♙	8
○ Franciacorta Gran Cuvée Brut '99	♙♙♙	6
○ Franciacorta Gran Cuvée Brut '98	♙♙♙	6
○ Franciacorta Gran Cuvée Brut '02	♙♙♙	7
○ Franciacorta Gran Cuvée Pas Operé '00	♙♙♙	7

Cantina Sociale Bergamasca

VIA BERGAMO, 10
24060 SAN PAOLO D'ARGON [BG]
TEL. 035951098
www.cantinabergamasca.it

ANNUAL PRODUCTION	650,000 bottles
HECTARES UNDER VINE	90
VITICULTURE METHOD	Conventional

Every year, Cantina Sociale Bergamasca submits a good series of wines offering, among other things, excellent value for money. This year, we liked the Sogno '07, an Incrocio Manzoni with forthright aromas of flowers and tropical fruit that has balance and remarkable appeal. The Valcalepio Rosso Riserva Akros '04 initially shows a perplexingly noticeable note of alcohol but then the bouquet emerges as well made as ever, unfolding blackberry, bell pepper and chestnut flour. It has good density, though it is still quite young and in need of further bottle ageing, and we awarded Two Glasses for its future prospects. Varietal, fresh and balanced, the Valcalepio Rosso Orologio '06 is one of the cellar's banner wines, a lovely red at an extremely competitive price. A good score also goes to the Schiava della Bergamasca '07 for its deep cherry colour, good wild berry aromas, nicely gauged acidity and agreeable finish. A bit under par, the Riserva Vigna del Conte '05 hasn't been in bottle long enough for an objective judgement so patience is in order. The rest of the range is well made.

F.lli Berlucchi

LOC. BORGONATO
VIA BROLETTO, 2
25040 CORTE FRANCA [BS]
TEL. 030984451
www.berlucchifranciacorta.it

ANNUAL PRODUCTION	400,000 bottles
HECTARES UNDER VINE	70
VITICULTURE METHOD	Conventional

Pia Donata Berlucchi, with the valuable support of daughter Tilli Rizzo and oenologist Cesare Ferrari, enthusiastically manages the family's historic estate, which has 70 hectares under vine in the best-suited areas of the DOC zone such as Torbiato in Adro and Borgonato in Corte Franca. The wines are their usual high quality with a Franciacorta Brut '04 in the lead. It has a bright, greenish straw-yellow colour, creamy mousse and fresh, elegant nose marked by hedgerow, apricot and damson, with a hint of vanilla and citrus. The palate shows full body and soft freshness, healthy fruit, backbone and length. The Satèn from the same vintage is also excellent with notes of torrefaction and vanilla on the nose and a dense, caressing palate. The pale pink, rich, juicy Rosé '04 unveils lovely notes of red berries. The Franciacorta Casa delle Colonne Brut '01, Chardonnay with 20 per cent Pinot Nero, has mouthfilling structure and medicinal herbs. The red Casa delle Colonne is a non-vintage Bordeaux blend with sound body and soft tannins. The DOC Dossi delle Querce Bianco '05 shows lovely structure and harmony, and the other labels are all interesting.

○ Manzoni Bianco Sogno '07	♈♈ 3*
☉ Schiava '07	♈♈ 3*
● Valcalepio Rosso Akros Ris. '04	♈♈ 4
● Valcalepio Rosso Orologio '06	♈♈ 3*
○ Bianco della Bergamasca '07	♈ 3
● Rosso della Bergamasca '07	♈ 3
○ Valcalepio Bianco Orologio '07	♈ 3
● Valcalepio Rosso V. del Conte Ris. '05	♈ 5
● Valcalepio Rosso Akros Ris. '03	♉♉ 4*
● Valcalepio Rosso Akros Ris. '02	♉♉ 4
● Valcalepio Rosso Orologio '04	♉♉ 3*
● Valcalepio Rosso V. del Conte Ris. '04	♉♉ 5
● Valcalepio Rosso V. del Conte Ris. '03	♉♉ 5

○ Franciacorta Brut '04	♈♈ 5
● Casa delle Colonne	♈♈ 8
○ Franciacorta Casa delle Colonne '01	♈♈ 7
☉ Franciacorta Rosé Brut '04	♈♈ 5
○ Franciacorta Satèn '04	♈♈ 6
○ TdF Bianco Dossi delle Querce '05	♈♈ 4
○ Franciacorta Pas Dosé '04	♈ 6
● TdF Rosso '06	♈ 3
○ Franciacorta Satèn '03	♉♉ 6
○ Franciacorta Brut '03	♉♉ 5
○ Franciacorta Casa delle Colonne '00	♉♉ 6
○ Franciacorta Pas Dosé '03	♉♉ 6
☉ Franciacorta Rosé Brut '03	♉♉ 5

Guido Berlucchi & C.

LOC. BORGONATO
P.ZZA DURANTI, 4
25040 CORTE FRANCA [BS]
TEL. 030984381
www.berlucchi.it

ANNUAL PRODUCTION   5,000,000 bottles
HECTARES UNDER VINE 590
VITICULTURE METHOD   Conventional

At 5,000,000 units a year sold worldwide, the Ziliani family's Guido Berlucchi & C. is one of the most successful brands in Italian wine. It all started with Franco Ziliani, a Franciacorta pioneer, who in the early 1960s began to make a classic method that would have overwhelming success. His children are at the helm nowadays –oenologist Arturo, sales director Paolo, and Cristina in charge of public relations – and, after years of great success with the Cuvée Imperiale, they have again focused on Franciacorta. So here in its debut edition is the Franciacorta Satèn '04 that made a good showing in our finals. It is a lovely, bright straw yellow with refined white-fleshed fruit and floral aromas. The juicy, rich palate has clear tones of fruit, vanilla and gingerbread. An excellent showing was also made by the creamily soft, assertive Franciacorta Brut, and the two Cellarius '04s, the zesty, elegant white and the Rosé with ringing wild berry echoes. And a special mention goes to the base wine, released in millions of units: Cuvée Imperiale Brut is still the best quality icon made on this estate in the past few years.

Bersi Serlini

LOC. CERETO
VIA CERETO, 7
25050 PROVAGLIO D'ISEO [BS]
TEL. 0309823338
www.bersiserlini.it

ANNUAL PRODUCTION   220,000 bottles
HECTARES UNDER VINE 32
VITICULTURE METHOD   Conventional

The Bersi Serlini family from Provaglio is one of the historic names in this DOCG. Today, the winery is among the area's most beautiful and modern, built around a medieval building that belonged to the monks of San Pietro in Lamosa and reminds us how life here has ancient rhythms. The Franciacorta Brut Vintage '01 has soft aromas of barley sugar and vanilla but the palate reveals backbone and grip, closing out long on mineral and citrus notes with remarkable charm. The Satèn has apparently more developed tones, at least the nose, while the palate recovers youthful vigour and shows off a comfortable fullness. From Chardonnay with 30 per cent Pinot Nero, the Rosé is also quite sound with a pale colour and refined aromas of red berry fruit and forest floor. The Demi Sec Nuvola has pleasant tones of honey and exotic fruit, and a well-balanced palate. The Extra Brut '03 and two Bruts, the base and the Cuvée n. 4, Blanc de Blancs, pleasant and well executed.

O Franciacorta Satèn Brut '04	🍷🍷	6
O Cellarius Brut '04	🍷🍷	6
⊙ Cellarius Brut Rosé '04	🍷🍷	6
O Cuvée Imperiale Brut	🍷🍷	5
O Cuvée Imperiale Brut Vintage '02	🍷🍷	7
O Franciacorta Brut Cuvée Storica	🍷🍷	5
O Gavi La Bollina '07	🍷🍷	4*
O Gavi V. Il Beneficio '06	🍷🍷	5
O Cuvée Imperiale Brut Extrême	🍷	5
⊙ Cuvée Imperiale Max Rosé	🍷	5
O TdF Curtefranca Bianco '07	🍷	4
O Cuvée Imperiale Brut Vintage '01	🍷🍷	7
O Gavi V. Il Beneficio '05	🍷🍷	5

⊙ Franciacorta Brut Rosa Rosae	🍷🍷	6
O Franciacorta Brut Vintage '01	🍷🍷	6
O Franciacorta Satèn	🍷🍷	6
O Franciacorta Brut	🍷	6
O Franciacorta Brut Cuvée n. 4	🍷	6
O Franciacorta Demi Sec Nuvola	🍷	6
O Franciacorta Extra Brut '03	🍷	7
O Franciacorta Extra Brut '02	🍷🍷	6

Bisi

LOC. CASCINA SAN MICHELE
FRAZ. VILLA MARONE, 70
27040 SAN DAMIANO AL COLLE [PV]
TEL. 038575037
www.aziendagricolabisi.it

ANNUAL PRODUCTION 100,000 bottles
HECTARES UNDER VINE 30
VITICULTURE METHOD Conventional

The best, most consistent Barbera in the entire territory again swept into our finals. The '05 version of Roncolongo has its usual sensory profile: an almost impenetrable ruby red colour; a broad, varied bouquet that runs from wild berries to spice, cherry and balsam and then a clean attack in the mouth that combines structure, depth and considerable acid backbone. Tasting previous vintages confirms this wine's marked propensity for ageing. In the excellent quality Cabernet Primm, from the same '05 vintage, the primary vegetal aromas move to the background behind the exuberance of overripe fruit that returns on the fleshy palate till the long, lingering finish. The equally remarkable Villa Marone '05 is a dried-grape wine from an old vineyard of malvasia that displays a bright golden colour and a bouquet that embraces orange peel, nuts – walnutskin in particular – and florality that precedes a lovely balance of sweetness and acidity. The Bonarda Frizzante '07 is juicy and flavoursome while the Riesling '07 gives ripe melon and lovely minerality.

● OP Barbera Roncolongo '05	🍷🍷	5
○ Bianco Passito Villa Marone '05	🍷🍷	5
● OP Bonarda La Peccatrice '07	🍷🍷	3
○ OP Riesling '07	🍷🍷	3*
● Primm '05	🍷🍷	5
● OP Barbera Roncolongo '04	🍷🍷	5
● OP Barbera Roncolongo '03	🍷🍷	5
● OP Barbera Roncolongo '01	🍷🍷	5
○ OP Riesling '06	🍷🍷	3*
● Primm '04	🍷🍷	5

Bonomi - Tenuta Castellino

VIA SAN PIETRO, 46
25030 COCCAGLIO [BS]
TEL. 0307721015
www.tenutabonomi.it

ANNUAL PRODUCTION 148,000 bottles
HECTARES UNDER VINE 17
VITICULTURE METHOD Conventional

Vineyards on the Bonomi family estate surround the lovely Art Nouveau villa at Coccaglio, in the extreme south of Franciacorta, with beautiful exposure in the natural amphitheatre of Monte Orfano. These are high density, low yield plantings, most of them on terraced plots that rise to nearly 300 metres above sea level and are surrounded by woods. This is ideal terroir for vines that yield excellent base wines for Franciacortas and especially still wines. The most interesting bottle at our tasting was the Extra Brut Lucrezia '01 with tiny bubbles and a fruit-led bouquet that tends to fresh citrus and vanilla notes. The palate has substance, freshness and balance. The red Cordelio '05 is a dark ruby with blueberry and raspberry aromas, introducing structure and well-gauged new oak. The very good white Solicano '06 has nuances of apricot and vanilla on the nose and a full, balanced palate with caressingly fresh fruit tones. A step below this are the fresh and floral Satèn '04, the slightly lean Franciacorta Brut with biscuity tones, the delicately vanillaed Satèn and the bright, deep coloured Rosé that shows cherry on nose and palate.

○ Franciacorta Extra Brut Lucrezia '01	🍷🍷	8
○ TdF Bianco Curtefranca Solicano '06	🍷🍷	4
● TdF Rosso Curtefranca Cordelio '05	🍷🍷	5
○ Franciacorta Brut	🍷	6
⊙ Franciacorta Rosé	🍷	6
○ Franciacorta Satèn '04	🍷	6
○ Franciacorta Satèn	🍷	6
○ Franciacorta Extra Brut Lucrezia '99	🍷🍷	8
○ TdF Bianco Curtefranca Solicano '04	🍷🍷	4
● TdF Rosso Curtefranca Cordelio '04	🍷🍷	5

Ca' dei Frati

FRAZ. LUGANA
VIA FRATI, 22
25019 SIRMIONE [BS]
TEL. 030919468
www.cadeifrati.it

ANNUAL PRODUCTION	700,000 bottles
HECTARES UNDER VINE	110
VITICULTURE METHOD	Conventional

That Lugana is one of the most cellarable Italian whites has always been a fundamental tenet here at the Dal Cero winery. What is more, those few bottles from outstanding vintages of the past that repose in the cellar show just how drinkable they still are. Now Igino Dal Cero has decide to go further and release to market selections from the best recent vintages that he set aside to demonstrate the soundness over time of this wine from the clay soils of Garda. Igino's first release is Lugana I Frati Selezione Vecchie Annate '03, which shows respectable fruit richness, plenty of spice and a captivating mineral vein. The Lugana I Frati and Brolettino, in the '07 and '06 versions respectively, are as well made as ever with notes of flowers, peaches and apricots. The sweet Tre Filer, from part-dried trebbiano di Lugana, chardonnay and sauvignon blanc, boasts excellent balance of fruity sweetness and acidity. The rest of the wines are excellent, as usual.

★★★ Ca' del Bosco

VIA ALBANO ZANELLA, 13
25030 ERBUSCO [BS]
TEL. 0307766111
www.cadelbosco.it

ANNUAL PRODUCTION	1,100,000 bottles
HECTARES UNDER VINE	154
VITICULTURE METHOD	Conventional

A state of the art cellar, that increasingly resembles an art gallery, and 150 hectares under vine in one of the finest wine areas in Franciacorta are the starting points every year for Maurizio Zanella to produce a series of top quality labels, beginning with the excellent new Cuvée Prestige Franciacorta. In this edition of the Guide, we gave Three Glasses to the Cuvée Annamaria Clementi '01 for its extraordinary finesse. It brims with elegance from the bright greenish straw yellow to the crystal-clear apricot and white-fleshed fruit with complex mineral shades leading into a harmonious, structured palate that closes stylishly on echoes of Mediterranean herbs. Three Glasses also went to the Dosage Zéro '04 with its irresistible fruitiness, perfectly balanced palate and extraordinarily pleasant, refined back palate redolent of damson, yeasts and hints of vanilla and minerals. The rest of the range is similarly excellent. We'd mention a Chardonnay '05 with great vigour and French-style complexity, an '04 Pinot Nero Pinèro that is one of the most interesting ever and a Brut '04 with great balance and depth.

O Lugana I Frati Sel. Vecchie Annate '03	♈♈ 5
O Lugana Brolettino '06	♈♈ 4
O Lugana I Frati '07	♈♈ 4*
O Pratto '06	♈♈ 5
⊙ Riviera del Garda Bresciano I Frati Chiaretto '07	♈ 4*
● Ronchedone '05	♈♈ 5
O Tre Filer '05	♈♈ 5
O Pratto '96	♈♈♈ 4
O Lugana Brolettino Grande Annata '99	♈♈ 6
O Lugana I Frati '06	♈♈ 4*
O Pratto '02	♈♈ 5
O Lugana Brolettino '05	♈♈ 4
O Lugana Brolettino Grande Annata '02	♈♈ 5
● Ronchedone '04	♈♈ 4

O Franciacorta Cuvée Annamaria Clementi '01	♈♈♈ 8
O Franciacorta Dosage Zéro '04	♈♈♈ 7
O Franciacorta Brut '04	♈♈ 7
O Franciacorta Satèn '03	♈♈ 7
O TdF Chardonnay '05	♈♈ 8
● Carmenèro '03	♈♈ 7
O Franciacorta Brut Cuvée Prestige	♈♈ 6
⊙ Franciacorta Cuvée Prestige Rosè	♈♈ 7
● Maurizio Zanella '03	♈♈ 8
● Pinèro '04	♈♈ 8
O TdF Bianco Curtefranca '07	♈♈ 5
● TdF Rosso Curtefranca '05	♈♈ 5
O Franciacorta Cuvée Annamaria Clementi '99	♈♈♈ 8
O Franciacorta Cuvée Annamaria Clementi '98	♈♈♈ 8
O Franciacorta Cuvée Annamaria Clementi '97	♈♈♈ 8
O Franciacorta Dosage Zéro '03	♈♈♈ 7
O Franciacorta Satèn '02	♈♈♈ 7

Ca' di Frara

VIA CASA FERRARI, 1
27040 MORNICO LOSANA [PV]
TEL. 0383892299
www.cadifrara.it

ANNUAL PRODUCTION	260,000 bottles
HECTARES UNDER VINE	48
VITICULTURE METHOD	Conventional

It's no surprise Ca' di Frara wines always win high scores in our tastings but the Bellani family always a surprise for us. The most important news is the Oltre il Classico project for classic method sparklers that for now has seen the release of only two versions, a Rosé from pinot nero only and a Blanc de Blancs, but other labels with more time on the yeasts are on their way. We preferred the Rosé, which has broader, more complex aromas, to the well-made but simpler white. The trend in the still wines is towards greater elegance. Significant for this are the two late-harvest wines, the Riesling and Pinot Grigio from the '07 vintage, which share remarkable floral finesse and exemplary balance on the palate. The Riesling has more thrust to go with its elegant melon aroma and gave it a place in our finals. With its broad nose, sweet tannins and careful use of oak, the Bonarda La Casetta '07 better than ever. The Io Bianco '07, from chardonnay, riesling and malvasia, is intense, balanced, fresh and clean. Finally, the new steel-fermented and aged Nero Pinot '07 is very varietal.

Ca' Lojera

LOC. ROVIZZA
VIA 1886, 19
25019 SIRMIONE [BS]
TEL. 0457551901
www.calojera.com

ANNUAL PRODUCTION	160,000 bottles
HECTARES UNDER VINE	18
VITICULTURE METHOD	Conventional

Having blown out his 70th candle some time ago, Franco Tiraboschi is a paragon of youthful determination when you watch him bustle about his vineyards or cellar. In fact, you almost immediately identify him with that wolf on the label of his showcase wine, á Lugana capable of defying the years. The '06 edition of the Lugana del Lupo comes back with the vibrant personality we enjoyed so much in the '03 version, which is still dynamic and spirited even today. The dense, ripe fruit is shot through with typical minerally veins as refreshing nuances of chlorophyll emerge from the background. Another white capable of soaring above the passage of time is the Lugana Superiore '05, which hinges on soft, chewy tones of peaches and apricots. In any case, Franco and Ambra Tiraboschi are never in a hurry to release their wines and keep a good supply of old vintages in their cellar for enthusiasts. The Lugana '07 is more rustic and immediate. The pleasantly fresh Ravel '05 is a sweet, white, dried-grape wine and the merlot and cabernet Rosato '07 is as powerful as ever. The reds are good.

○ OP Riesling Renano Apogeo Raccolta Tardiva '07	▼ 4*
○ Io Bianco '07	▼▼ 5
● OP Bonarda La Casetta '07	▼▼ 4
○ OP Pinot Grigio Raccolta Tardiva '07	▼▼ 4
⊙ OP Pinot Nero Brut Oltre il Classico Rosé	▼▼ 5
● OP Pinot Nero Pinot '07	▼▼ 5
○ Oltre il Classico	▼ 5
● OP Pinot Nero Il Raro '01	▽▽ 5
○ OP Riesling Renano Apogeo Raccolta Tardiva '06	▽▽ 4*
● OP Rosso Il Frater Ris. '03	▽▽ 6
● Io Rosso '04	▽▽ 5
○ OP Pinot Grigio Raccolta Tardiva '06	▽▽ 4

○ Lugana Riserva del Lupo '06	▼▼ 5
○ Lugana Sup. '05	▼▼ 5
○ Ravel '05	▼▼ 5
● Garda Cabernet '06	▼ 4
○ Garda Chardonnay '06	▼ 4
● Garda Merlot '06	▼ 4
○ Lugana '07	▼ 4
⊙ Monte della Guardia Rosato '07	▼ 3
○ Lugana Sup. '04	▽▽ 5
○ Lugana Riserva del Lupo '04	▽▽ 5
○ Lugana Sup. '03	▽▽ 5
○ Ravel '04	▽▽ 5

Il Calepino

VIA SURRIPE, 1
24060 CASTELLI CALEPIO [BG]
TEL. 035847178
www.ilcalepino.it

ANNUAL PRODUCTION	200,000 bottles
HECTARES UNDER VINE	15
VITICULTURE METHOD	Conventional

This estate specializes in high-scoring classic method sparklers, although we should not forget the rest of the very complete range. As always, the most convincing is the historic Riserva dedicated to Fra' Ambrogio, nicknamed "Il Calepino". Once again in the '02 vintage, it has a golden colour and broad, intense nose with noticeable oak and touches of cakes and dried fruits. The palate is fresh and balanced with a long, clear, precise finish. The full, elegant Brut '04 is also good if simpler with aromas of fresh fruit and Sicilian cannolo cakes. Sweet and spirited at the same time, the dried-grape Chardonnay Epias features notes of orange flowers and overripe tropical fruit. The Trentesima Cuvée '03 is a Nature with a lovely bouquet of flowers and honey, nice impact on the palate, good fullness and marked citrus-free acidity. Recently bottled, the Valcalepio Rosso Surìe Riserva '04 has yet to express all its potential and needs at least a year in bottle but the raw material is all there. The Brut Rosé is pleasant and clean while the Valcalepio Bianco '07 and Rosso '06 are well made, although we preferred the latter.

Cantrina

FRAZ. CANTRINA
VIA COLOMBERA, 7
25081 BEDIZZOLE [BS]
TEL. 0306871052
www.cantrina.it

ANNUAL PRODUCTION	25,000 bottles
HECTARES UNDER VINE	5.8
VITICULTURE METHOD	Conventional

We applaud another great showing from Nepomuceno, the Merlot made by Cristina Inganni and Diego Lavo, with consultancy from Celestino Gaspari. It's sourced from vineyards at Cantrina, a small village in the deepest hinterland of Garda. It has nice texture with good freshness and in fact is one of the best examples from Valtenesi. It won us over again with the '04 edition, which has hints of berries, veined with light vegetal expressions and a pepper-like nuance. While waiting on the sweet wine front for the new vintage of the white dried-grape Sole di Dario to be released, we were amazed by the '05 Eretico. It's an unusual Pinot Nero from part-dried grapes, released for the first time with the sweltering '03 growing year and now rereleased in an version even more redolent of berry preserves, melding convincingly with intriguing spice. The other Pinot Nero, Corteccio '04, is a solid product while the white Rinè '06, from sauvignon, sémillon and riesling, delivers the usual aromatics themed by tropical fruit and summer flowers.

O Brut Cl. Fra' Ambrogio Ris. '02	♟♟	5
O Brut Cl. Il Calepino '04	♟♟	5
O Chardonnay Epias	♟♟	6
O Trentesima Cuvée Non Dosato '03	♟♟	5
☉ Brut Cl. Rosé Il Calepino '03	♟	5
O Valcalepio Bianco '07	♟	3
● Valcalepio Rosso '06	♟	4
● Valcalepio Rosso Surìe Ris. '04	♟	4
O Brut Cl. Fra' Ambrogio Ris. '00	♟♟	5
O Extra Brut Cl. Il Calepino '01	♟♟	5
● Kalòs '04	♟♟	7

● Nepomuceno '04	♟♟	6
● Corteccio '04	♟♟	5
● Eretico '05	♟♟	6
O Rinè '06	♟♟	4
● Nepomuceno '03	♟♟	6
● Nepomuceno '01	♟♟	5
● Corteccio '01	♟♟	5
● Eretico '03	♟♟	6
O Rinè '05	♟♟	4
O Sole di Dario '03	♟♟	6
O Sole di Dario '01	♟♟	6
● Zerdì '05	♟♟	4

Caseo

FRAZ. CASEO, 9
27040 CANEVINO [PV]
TEL. 038599937
www.caseowines.com

ANNUAL PRODUCTION 280,000 bottles
HECTARES UNDER VINE 47
VITICULTURE METHOD Conventional

This year, several labels were missing at this estate managed by Marco Goia but Caseo wines are always interesting. In this edition of the Guide, the lion's share goes to the classic method sparklers. But let's take things in order, beginning with the only red submitted, Bonarda Vivace Costa delle More '07, which is a lovely deep purple with violet and rose-like floral sensations lifted by camomile, well-gauged tannins and a nice final thrust. The sparkling Gioiacaseo spumante has a lovely bead and rather mature tones while showing fresh and pleasant in the mouth. Grande Cuvée Pas Dosé '01 is more complex, marked as it is by oaky notes from the first fermentation of part of the base but has plenty of freshness, filling the mouth with substantial structure: a classic through-the-meal sparkler. The Brut Rosé shades into orange, revealing varietal berry perceptions with notes of citrus and cakes on the nicely balanced palate. The Blanc de Blancs has a good base. With a touch more finesse, would have scored much higher. Lastly, the Naro Bianco '07 blend is fresh and pleasant.

○ Gioiacaseo Brut Cl.	▼▼	5
● OP Bonarda Vivace Costa delle More '07	▼▼	4
○ OP Grande Cuvée Pas Dosé '01	▼▼	5
⊙ OP Pinot Nero Spumante Cl. Rosé	▼▼	5
○ Extra Dry Cl. Blanc de Blancs	▼	5
○ Naro Bianco '07	▼	3
○ OP Grande Cuvée Pas Dosé '00	▽▽	5
○ OP Moscato Passito Soleggia '03	▽▽	6
○ OP Riesling Renano Le Segrete '06	▽▽	4

Cantina di Casteggio

VIA TORINO, 96
27045 CASTEGGIO [PV]
TEL. 0383806311
www.cantinacasteggio.it

ANNUAL PRODUCTION 2,500,000 bottles
HECTARES UNDER VINE 950
VITICULTURE METHOD Conventional

Fresh from the merger with Cantina Sociale Intercomunale di Broni, Cantina di Casteggio presented a fine array of wines, as it has since the start of Progetto Qualità. Again in the '06 vintage, Barbera Console Marcello is outstanding. Introduced by an impenetrable ruby, it takes time to open but then reveals a broad fruity range of fairly overripe tones with lovely spiciness, remarkable structure and a rising finish. The Longobardo is almost as good. This IGT from croatina, barbera, pinot nero and cabernet sauvignon shows convincing elegance and balance with fine-grained tannins and intact pulp. The other Barbera, Autari '06, is good and varietal. It's fragrant and more of an early drinker. Also as excellent as ever is the Riesling Italico Clefi '07, which presents a deep, straw yellow with elegant fruit and flower notes, good structure and a lingering finish. The trio of Metodo Classico Postumio sparklers impresses. Our preference is for the persuasive red berries of the Rosé over the two whites, which are elegant yet fairly simple. The three current whites, Malvasia, Pinot Grigio and Sauvignon, are well made, varietal and pleasant.

● OP Barbera Console Marcello '06	▼▼	4*
● Il Longobardo '06	▼▼	6
● OP Barbera Autari '06	▼▼	4*
⊙ OP Pinot Nero Brut Postumio Rosè	▼▼	4
○ OP Riesling Italico Clefi '07	▼▼	4*
○ OP Malvasia '07	▼	4
○ OP Pinot Grigio '07	▼	4
○ OP Pinot Nero Brut Postumio	▼	4
○ OP Sauvignon '07	▼	4
○ Postumio Brut 100° Anniversario	▼	4
● OP Barbera Autari '05	▽▽	4
● OP Barbera Autari '04	▽▽	3*
● OP Barbera Autari '03	▽▽	3*
● OP Barbera Console Marcello '05	▽▽	4*
● OP Barbera Console Marcello '04	▽▽	4*
● Il Longobardo '05	▽▽	6

CastelFaglia

FRAZ. CALINO
LOC. BOSCHI, 3
25046 CAZZAGO SAN MARTINO [BS]
TEL. 059812411
www.cavicchioli.it

ANNUAL PRODUCTION 250,000 bottles
HECTARES UNDER VINE 20
VITICULTURE METHOD Conventional

It has been ten years since the sparkler-loving Cavicchioli family from Modena – they also own Bellei Spumanti – gave life to this estate. CastelFaglia now boasts serious production in quantity as well as quality, entirely sourced from their own vineyards in Cazzago San Martino. The range of labels is vast – perhaps too vast! – but every cuvée from the estate offers excellent value for money. Opening the series of Franciacortas, here is an excellent Satèn with elegant, floral tones and a clear, juicy palate. These qualities are shared with an excellent Extra Brut which reveals enthralling nuances of aromatic herbs and exemplary bottle fermentation. The Blanc de Blancs Monogram has bright acidity, freshness and balance marked by fruity, citrus-like tones. The Brut is enjoyable for its floral tones and the juiciness on the palate. The Monogram Brut Cuvée Giunone brims with freshness, structure and balance, and shows a round, balanced back palate. The Satèn Monogram has rich tones of ripe white-fleshed fruit and softness, closing out on pleasant vanilla and oak tones. The other labels are sound.

○ Franciacorta Blanc de Blancs Monogram	TT 5
○ Franciacorta Brut	TT 5
○ Franciacorta Extra Brut	TT 5
○ Franciacorta Monogram Brut Cuvée Giunone	TT 6
○ Franciacorta Satèn	TT 6
○ Franciacorta Satèn Monogram	TT 6
⊙ Franciacorta Rosé Brut	T 6
○ TdF Bianco '06	T 4
○ TdF Bianco Prestigio '07	T 4
● TdF Campo Lungo '04	T 6
● TdF Rosso Prestigio '06	T 4
○ Franciacorta Brut Monogram '98	YY 7

Cavalleri

VIA PROVINCIALE, 96
25030 ERBUSCO [BS]
TEL. 0307760217
www.cavalleri.it

ANNUAL PRODUCTION 250,000 bottles
HECTARES UNDER VINE 43
VITICULTURE METHOD Conventional

After receiving the prestigious Sparkler of the Year award for its Collezione Esclusiva '99 last year, Cavalleri amazed us again with another extraordinary Cuvée that waltzed off with Three Glasses. We refer to Franciacorta Pas Dosé Au Contraire '01, a cuvée of Chardonnay and Pinot Nero, the reverse of the other wines, from the excellent '01 growing year. After spending more than six years on the yeasts, it presents a bright, golden straw with extra-fine bubbles. Though initially reduced, the bouquet opens into complex breadth with elegant notes of red and white berries laced with iodine-nuanced medicinal herbs, minerals and attractive oak. The palate has incredible freshness and youthful harmony, closing out long and caressing. This minor miracle confirms the potential of the terroir at Erbusco and the exceptional talent of Giulia Cavalleri and her skilled staff. From the Pas Dosé '04 to the still wines, the rest of the range offers the same excellent quality.

○ Franciacorta Au Contraire Pas Dosé '01	TTT 8
○ Franciacorta Pas Dosé '04	TT 6
○ Franciacorta Brut Blanc de Blancs	TT 6
○ Franciacorta Collezione Brut '02	TT 6
⊙ Franciacorta Collezione Rosé '02	TT 6
○ Franciacorta Satèn	TT 6
○ TdF Bianco '07	TT 4
○ TdF Bianco Rampaneto '06	TT 5
● TdF Rosso '05	T 4
○ Franciacorta Collezione Brut '99	YYY 6
○ Franciacorta Collezione Brut '94	YYY 6
○ Franciacorta Collezione Esclusiva Brut '99	YYY 8
○ Franciacorta Collezione Brut '01	YY 6
○ Franciacorta Collezione Esclusiva Brut '97	YY 7
○ TdF Bianco Rampaneto '05	YY 4*

Castello di Cigognola

P.ZZA CASTELLO, 1
27040 CIGOGNOLA [PV]
TEL. 038585601
www.castellodicigognola

ANNUAL PRODUCTION 40,000 bottles
HECTARES UNDER VINE 25
VITICULTURE METHOD Conventional

With its centuries of history, Castello di Cigognola has also become a winemaking estate since its purchase by Gianmarco Moratti. Major investments here are only now showing their great potential. With the supervision of Riccardo Cotarella and the efforts of skilled wine man Emilio Defilippi, till now the estate has only presented Barbera, this year in two versions. But the project also envisages the introduction of Pinot Nero and the production of a classic method sparkler. In the meantime, we enjoyed the Barbera from the '05 vintage called Poggio della Maga. Although the '03 and '04 vintages reached our finals, it was the '05 vintage that won Three Glasses. Sure, the style is not exactly Oltrepò but it's hard not to appreciate the deep ruby colour with its still purplish rim, the perfectly dosed oak, the clarity and integrity of the wild berries, the balance between structure and acidity, and the great length on the palate. The Barbera Dodicidodici '06 is also excellent, winning us over at once with its persuasive chocolate-like notes, nice acidity and overall harmony.

● OP Barbera Poggio Della Maga '05	🍷🍷🍷	8
● OP Barbera DodiciDodici '06	🍷🍷	5
● OP Barbera '04	ΥΥ	6
● OP Barbera '03	ΥΥ	6

Comincioli

LOC. CASTELLO
VIA ROMA, 10
25080 PUEGNAGO SUL GARDA [BS]
TEL. 0365651141
www.comincioli.it

ANNUAL PRODUCTION 45,000 bottles
HECTARES UNDER VINE 9
VITICULTURE METHOD Conventional

Defender of biodiversity in Garda and extreme experimenter in both winemaking and olive growing, Gianfranco Comincioli, one of the last champions of the old Riviera del Garda Bresciano DOC, is considered a benchmark producer in Valtenesi agriculture. Constantly striving to tease out the potential of the territory and its main variety, groppello, Gianfranco gave his wines a new direction with the last harvest, placing less emphasis on ripening the grapes and ageing the wine, and more on vinifying the new Groppello Zephiro '07, whose first release charms with its clean fruit, freshness and elegance. The Sulèr '04 is the other side of the coin, where concentrated fruit and extract encouraged by part-drying the grapes and leisurely ageing in oak. In the Pedemut '04, the groppello variety is blended with barbera, marzemino and sangiovese in the traditional style. The white Perlì '07, made from the rare local erbamat and trebbiano varieties, is spirited, citrussy and vegetal. The Chiaretto is as powerful and spicy as ever.

○ Perlì '07	🍷🍷	4
⊙ Riviera del Garda Bresciano Chiaretto '07	🍷🍷	4
● Riviera del Garda Bresciano Groppello Sulèr '04	🍷🍷	7
● Riviera del Garda Bresciano Groppello Zephiro '07	🍷🍷	4
● Riviera del Garda Bresciano Pedemut '04	🍷🍷	4
○ Perlì '06	ΥΥ	4
○ Perlì '05	ΥΥ	4
● Riviera del Garda Bresciano Gropèl '04	ΥΥ	5
● Riviera del Garda Bresciano Gropèl '03	ΥΥ	5
● Riviera del Garda Bresciano Sulèr '03	ΥΥ	7

Contadi Castaldi

LOC. FORNACE BIASCA
VIA COLZANO, 32
25030 ADRO [BS]
TEL. 0307450126
www.contadicastaldi.it

ANNUAL PRODUCTION	750,000 bottles
HECTARES UNDER VINE	100
VITICULTURE METHOD	Conventional

Again this year, good tasting scores went to wines from Contadi Castaldi, wine merchants for Terra Moretti, the group of winemaking estates created by Vittorio Moretti with Bellavista as its flagship. While waiting for the new vintage of its excellent Satèn Soul, we tasted two exceptional Rosés, a 2004 vintage and a sound base. The first has a lovely pale pink colour and fine bead that puts the accent on elegant tones. The complex bouquet of dried roses and raspberry swirls around notes of vanilla and oak but always stays fresh with crunchy fruit upfront. The palate is clear and caressing. The base Rosé has a simpler, more confident style and makes wild berry tones and structure its strong points. The zesty, fruity Terre di Franciacorta Bianco '07 and delicately sweet, long Pinodisé '01, a dessert wine from chardonnay with a splash of wine spirit, both scores seriously well. The Satèn '04 was slightly below our expectations but the other labels are good.

Costaripa

VIA COSTA, 1A
25080 MONIGA DEL GARDA [BS]
TEL. 0365502010
www.costaripa.it

ANNUAL PRODUCTION	330,000 bottles
HECTARES UNDER VINE	36
VITICULTURE METHOD	Conventional

The Groppello Maim gets better and better. Sourced from the family vineyards at Moniga del Garda by Mattia Vezzola, renowned for his sparkling winemaking in Franciacorta, with his brother Imer, the '05 edition has elegant fresh, juicy notes of fruit and pleasant spicy veining that lift this indigenous Valtenesi variety to the level of a Garda-side Pinot Nero. It's a red that offers a template for the relaunch of production in a territory with clear wine potential. Another lovely interpretation of Groppello, this time in a classic cuvée with dashes of barbera, marzemino and sangiovese, is Campostarne '06, a wine with good structure that remains eminently drinkable. The young Groppello Vigneto Le Castelline '07 is juicy and pleasant. Marzemino is the main actor in another characterful red, Mazane '07. There are two Chiarettos, a fragrant standard-label Rosamara and the spicy Molmenti '05, fermented and finished in oak. It goes without saying that the sparklers are excellent. The Lugana is well made.

⊙ Franciacorta Brut Rosé '04	♟♟	6
⊙ Franciacorta Brut Rosé	♟♟	6
○ Pinodisé '01	♟♟	6
○ TdF Bianco Curtefranca '07	♟♟	4
○ Franciacorta Brut	♟	5
○ Franciacorta Satèn '04	♟	6
○ Franciacorta Zéro '04	♟	6
● TdF Rosso Curtefranca '05	♟	4
○ Franciacorta Satèn '01	♟♟	6
○ Franciacorta Soul Satèn '00	♟♟	7
○ TdF Bianco Curtefranca '06	♟♟	4*
● TdF Rosso Curtefranca '04	♟♟	4*

● Garda Cl. Groppello Maim '05	♟♟	5
○ Brut Cl. Costaripa '01	♟♟	6
○ Costaripa Brut	♟♟	5
⊙ Garda Cl. Chiaretto Molmenti '05	♟♟	5
● Garda Cl. Groppello Vign. Le Castelline '07	♟♟	4
● Garda Cl. Rosso Campostarne '06	♟♟	4
○ Lugana Pievecroce '07	♟♟	4
● Marzemino Le Mazane '07	♟♟	4
⊙ Brut Rosé Costaripa	♟	5
⊙ Garda Cl. Chiaretto Rosamara '07	♟	4
● Garda Cl. Groppello Maim '04	♟♟	5
● Garda Cl. Groppello Maim '01	♟♟	5
● Garda Cl. Rosso Campostarne '05	♟♟	4

Doria

LOC. CASA TACCONI, 3
27040 MONTALTO PAVESE [PV]
TEL. 0383870143
www.vinidoria.com

ANNUAL PRODUCTION	140,000 bottles
HECTARES UNDER VINE	30
VITICULTURE METHOD	Conventional

The Doria winery has always been reliable and is now managed by Lazio-born Daniele Manini. Daniele's efforts to bring back chestnut barrels is producing good results, so much so that year after year the chestnut-matured Barbera AD is carving out a significant niche on the vast panorama of Oltrepò wine and beyond. Special notes from the chestnut give even the '05 vintage unique characteristics, above all in its bouquet, which discloses notes of spice and, as you might expect, chestnut. With its lovely minerality and camomile-like aromas, the Riesling Roncobianco '05 has taken full advantage from a well-judged period in oak. The winery's historic nebbiolo-based IGT, AD Memorial '05, is good, although not quite as impressive as the previous versions, which went to our finals. The wine is all there but it's still too young and the tannins have to mature. We gave Two Glasses for potential since we know how this wine develops over time. Interesting, although again still behind in its development, is the Pinot Nero Querciolo '05, which has nice fruit but still needs to absorb the oak. Finally, the Bonarda Vivace '07 is pleasant.

Sandro Fay

LOC. SAN GIACOMO DI TEGLIO
VIA PILA CASELLI, 1
23030 TEGLIO [SO]
TEL. 0342786071
elefay@tin.it

ANNUAL PRODUCTION	38,000 bottles
HECTARES UNDER VINE	13
VITICULTURE METHOD	Conventional

The Fay family, led by father Sandro, is synonymous with quality wine. They deserve credit for having always believed in Valgella, bringing out its best and safeguarding it with sacrifices and courageous investments. A good example is Cartería '05, a very personal wine with intense aromas of red berries and a complex palate supported by good acidity. The classic Ca' Morei '05 shows shades of ripe fruit, cinchona and spice. The warm palate is caressing, dry and full flavoured with a sustained body. The well-executed La Faya, from nebbiolo, merlot and syrah, is austere with spicy aromas, well-developed tannins and good progression. The distinctive Nebbiolo '06 has a varied bouquet of violet-led florality followed by a supple palate. Sassella Il Glicine '05 is very good and gives varietal aromatics, enhanced by balsamic notes. The palate is soft with a pleasant, full-flavoured finish. In closing, we salute the Sforzato Ronco del Picchio '05 with its rich, complex aromas of spice, red berries and alcohol warmth, preceding an elegant palate with stylish extract and a long-lingering finish.

● OP Barbera A.D. '05	♈♈ 5
● OP Pinot Nero Querciolo '05	♈♈ 6
○ OP Riesling Renano Roncobianco '05	♈♈ 4
● Rosso A.D. Memorial '05	♈♈ 6
● OP Bonarda Vivace '07	♈ 4
● Rosso A.D. '99	♈♈ 6
● Rosso A.D. '98	♈♈ 6
● Rosso A.D. '97	♈♈ 5
● OP Barbera A.D. '04	♈♈ 5
● OP Bonarda Vivace '06	♈♈ 4*
○ OP Riesling Renano Roncobianco '04	♈♈ 4
● Rosso A.D. Memorial '04	♈♈ 6

● Valtellina Sforzato Ronco del Picchio '05	♈♈ 7
● La Faya '05	♈♈ 5
● Valtellina Sup. Sassella Il Glicine '05	♈♈ 5
● Valtellina Sup. Valgella Ca' Morèi '05	♈♈ 5
● Valtellina Sup. Valgella Cartería '05	♈♈ 5
● Nebbiolo '06	♈ 4
● Valtellina Sforzato Ronco del Picchio '02	♈♈♈ 7
● Valtellina Sforzato Ronco del Picchio '99	♈♈ 6
● Valtellina Sforzato Ronco del Picchio '04	♈♈ 7
● Valtellina Sforzato Ronco del Picchio '03	♈♈ 7
● Valtellina Sforzato Ronco del Picchio '01	♈♈ 6
● Valtellina Sup. Valgella Cartería '04	♈♈ 5
● Valtellina Sup. Valgella Cartería '03	♈♈ 5

Ferghettina

VIA SALINE, 11
25030 ADRO [BS]
TEL. 0307451212
www.ferghettina.it

ANNUAL PRODUCTION	350,000 bottles
HECTARES UNDER VINE	120
VITICULTURE METHOD	Conventional

The Gatti family's Ferghettina is one of the most interesting producers in the designation. Roberto and Andreina, with children Laura, oenologist, and Matteo, oenology student, now manage 120 hectares of lovely vineyards in six different municipalities in the DOCG zone and make their wine in a new, well-equipped cellar at Adro. Again this year, the estate gave us a textbook version of the Satèn. The '04 vintage again earned Three Glasses. We loved its bright, greenish straw yellow, customary fine bubbles and elegant, complex aromas of just ripened white-fleshed fruit and vanilla laced with subtle flowers. The palate of this Blanc de Blancs has pulp, a soft, fruit-led attack and supple freshness, singing off with a rich, long finish. The Rosé from the same vintage, mostly pinot nero, was one of the best tasted this year, giving delicate tones of wild strawberry, raspberry, blueberry and fuji apples, lovely structure and zesty suppleness. We also enjoyed the Extra Brut '01 for its soft, ripe tones and nice minerality. The Terre di Franciacorta Bianco '07 is great but we also felt the Terre Rosso '06 and base Franciacorta Brut were very good.

Le Fracce

FRAZ. MAIRANO
VIA CASTEL DEL LUPO, 5
27045 CASTEGGIO [PV]
TEL. 038382526
info@le-fracce.it

ANNUAL PRODUCTION	200,000 bottles
HECTARES UNDER VINE	40
VITICULTURE METHOD	Conventional

The flagship Bohemi from Roberto Gerbino's estate is back. The '03 version felt the year's extreme heat, showing overripeness in its wild berries, but without excess, and a good dose of oak that translates into sweet spice and coffee. There's a lovely, fruity texture on the balanced palate and the finish lingers. The nice finesse and floral aromas of the Riesling Landò '07 introduce a clear, fresh palate. Minerality will emerge over the next few years if you have the patience to wait. Among the best Bonardas from Oltrepò this year, La Rubiosa '07 has impenetrable colour, forthright, elegant raspberry and strawberry aromas and good balance of tannins and residual sugar. The OP Pinot Nero Extra Brut Martinotti Cuvée Bussolera '06 is one of the area's best Martinotti method sparklers. After around 12 months on the yeasts under pressure, it is fragrant, pleasant, harmonious and elegant, showing melon and tropical fruit aromas. The well-made IGT Garboso from barbera is fresh simple and flavourful. The varietal, nicely centred Pinot Nero '04 is sourced from a recently planted vineyard and the Pinot Grigio Levriere '07 shows citrus and spring flowers.

○ Franciacorta Satèn '04	♟♟♟	6
☉ Franciacorta Rosé '04	♟♟	6
○ Franciacorta Extra Brut '01	♟♟	6
○ TdF Curtefranca Bianco '07	♟♟	4*
○ Franciacorta Brut	♟	5
● TdF Curtefranca Rosso '06	♟	4
○ Franciacorta Extra Brut '98	♟♟♟	6
○ Franciacorta Satèn '99	♟♟♟	6
○ Franciacorta Satèn '97	♟♟♟	5*

● Garboso '06	♟♟	4*
● OP Bonarda La Rubiosa '07	♟♟	4*
○ OP Pinot Nero Cuvée Bussolera Extra Brut '06	♟♟	4
○ OP Riesling Landò '07	♟♟	4
● OP Rosso Bohemi '03	♟♟	6
○ OP Pinot Grigio Levriere '07	♟	4
● OP Pinot Nero '04	♟	6
● OP Rosso Bohemi '01	♟♟	6
● Garboso '05	♟♟	4*
● Garboso '04	♟♟	4*
● OP Bonarda La Rubiosa '06	♟♟	4*
● OP Pinot Nero '03	♟♟	6
○ OP Pinot Nero Cuvée Bussolera Extra Brut '05	♟♟	4
○ OP Pinot Nero Cuvée Bussolera Extra Brut '04	♟♟	4
○ OP Riesling Landò '06	♟♟	4

Antica Cantina Fratta

VIA FONTANA, 11
25040 MONTICELLI BRUSATI [BS]
TEL. 030652068
www.anticafratta.it

ANNUAL PRODUCTION	250,000 bottles
HECTARES UNDER VINE	N.A.
VITICULTURE METHOD	Conventional

While Berlucchi made its historic journey that only recently brought it back to its original designation, Antica Fratta, part of Berlucchi since 1979, never abandoned production of Franciacorta. Run by Cristina Ziliani with a separate staff and vineyard holding from the parent company, Antica Fratta today estate shines with its own light. After a series of encouraging performances, the estate reached our finals this time with an elegant, pale pink Franciacorta Rosé with dense, continuous bubbles. The nose opens on inviting aromas of red berry fruit and vanilla. The palate is juicy, refined, elegant, spirited and long, signing off with gratifying, delicately tannic notes laced with fruit. The Satèn shows pleasant tones of citrus and white-fleshed fruit on the nose before the palate gives enjoyable expressive finesse and vanilla tones on the fresh back palate. We also thought the Brut was excellent, with clear echoes of flowers and rennet apple on both the nose and a palate that is structured and supple at the same time. Finally, the Terre di Franciacorta Rosso Ragnoli '06 is very good, proffering blackberry aromas and solid structure.

Frecciarossa

VIA VIGORELLI, 141
27045 CASTEGGIO [PV]
TEL. 0383804465
www.frecciarossa.com

ANNUAL PRODUCTION	150,000 bottles
HECTARES UNDER VINE	20
VITICULTURE METHOD	Conventional

Three Glasses have finally been awarded to the first Pinot Nero from Oltrepò Pavese. It is no coincidence that Frecciarossa achieved this distinction. It's one of the estates that has been dedicating more time and attention to this difficult, fascinating wine type. The Giorgio Odero '05 shows typical ruby shading into garnet and a broad bouquet of currants, ripe wild berries and spice. The palate has nice impact, exemplary balance and a great finish with remarkable elegance. Already good, it will improve further over the years along the lines of the recently tasted and quite spectacular '00. The merlot-heavy IGT Francigeno is very good, showing intensity on the nose and full pulpy flesh. The zesty Riesling Gli Orti '07 has great backbone and a bouquet of peach, apricot and medicinal herbs. The IGT Praielle '05 shows off its barbera base in outstanding acidity and red berry aromas. The pleasant Bonarda Vivace Dardo '07 shows wild berry aromas, but lacks a bit of length in the finish. The Uva Rara '07 has a typical huskiness and the white, semi-sparkling Nai, an IGT from riesling renano and pinot nero, is pleasant.

⊙ Franciacorta Rosé	▼▼ 5
O Franciacorta Antica Fratta Brut	▼▼ 5
O Franciacorta Satèn	▼▼ 6
● TdF Rosso Ragnoli '06	▼▼ 4*
O Franciacorta Brut '03	▽▽ 5
O Franciacorta Brut '00	▽▽ 7
● TdF Rosso Ragnoli '05	▽▽ 5

● OP Pinot Nero Giorgio Odero '05	▼▼▼ 6
● Francigeno '04	▼▼ 5
O OP Riesling Renano Gli Orti '07	▼▼ 4*
● Le Praielle '05	▼ 4
O Nai '07	▼ 4
● OP Bonarda Vivace Dardo '07	▼ 4
● Uva Rara '07	▼ 4
● OP Pinot Nero Giorgio Odero '03	▽▽ 5
● OP Pinot Nero Giorgio Odero '00	▽▽ 5
● Francigeno '03	▽▽ 5
● OP Bonarda Vivace Dardo '06	▽▽ 4*
● OP Pinot Nero Giorgio Odero '04	▽▽ 5

Enrico Gatti

via Metelli, 9
25030 Erbusco [BS]
tel. 0307267999
www.enricogatti.it

ANNUAL PRODUCTION 120,000 bottles
HECTARES UNDER VINE 17
VITICULTURE METHOD Conventional

It is a real pity the Gattis' Satèn '04 came up short and broke its four-vintage winning streak. It's not a disaster, though, because this dynamic estate run by brother and sister Lorenzo and Paola, along with her husband Enzo Balzarini, enjoys excellent health and has ambitious projects for the future. Proof is there in the soft, sensual, juicy Satèn, with stylish aromas of lavender and crusty bread preceding a solid, minerally palate. We also enjoyed the newcomer, the Brut '02, rich in complex notes of ripe fruit, antique wood and oriental spices. The palate is structured, tangy and vital with a slightly astringent back palate. The Nature is as good as ever and evokes acacia and mixed-flower honey on the nose. The palate offers up almost austere structure and a finish that drifts into softer, more satisfying tones. We thought the Rosé was also pleasant, with its nice, bright, pale pink colour, a lovely bouquet of red berries and a palate that closes long, fresh and harmonious. The non-vintage Franciacorta Brut is pleasant and well made although we might have expected a pinch more structure.

○ Franciacorta Satèn '04	🍷🍷	6
○ Franciacorta Brut '02	🍷🍷	7
○ Franciacorta Nature	🍷🍷	6
⊙ Franciacorta Rosè	🍷🍷	6
○ Franciacorta Brut	🍷	5
○ Franciacorta Satèn '03	🍷🍷🍷	6
○ Franciacorta Satèn '02	🍷🍷🍷	6
○ Franciacorta Satèn '01	🍷🍷🍷	5
○ Franciacorta Satèn '00	🍷🍷🍷	6

F.lli Giorgi

fraz. Camponoce, 39a
27044 Canneto Pavese [PV]
tel. 0385262151
www.giorgi-wines.it

ANNUAL PRODUCTION 1,600,000 bottles
HECTARES UNDER VINE 30
VITICULTURE METHOD Conventional

Every year, step by step, the Giorgi family's historic Oltrepò estate improves its results, thanks in particular to the enthusiasm of Fabiano, a young man with clear ideas about quality. And for the first time, it sent a wine to the finals. The bottle in question is Pinot Nero Brut 1870 '04, a classic method sparkler with broad aromas of cakes and citrus, a complex, elegant palate and a great finish. The hand of Alberto Musatti is noticeable. Almost as good is the dense Brut Gianfranco Giorgi Selezione '03 with its great backbone and lovely verve on the finish. The '04 version shows Buttafuoco Storico Casa del Corno is one of the best of this type, thanks to its structure, aromas and velvety tannins from part-drying the grapes. In its first release, the Riesling Il Bandito '07 reveals minerality and aromatic herbs and the Sangue di Giuda '07 is as good as ever. The dried-grape Zimmolo from malvasia is interesting and balanced. And the rest of the range is good with a special mention for Vigalòn, a blend of barbera, croatina and uva rara that offers excellent value for money.

○ OP Pinot Nero Brut Cl. 1870 '04	🍷🍷	6
● OP Buttafuoco Storico Casa del Corno '04	🍷🍷	4
○ OP Pinot Nero Brut Cl. Gianfranco Giorgi Sel. '03	🍷🍷	6
○ OP Riesling Il Bandito '07	🍷🍷	5
● OP Sangue di Giuda Frizzante '07	🍷🍷	4*
○ Zimmolo	🍷🍷	5
● OP Bonarda Vivace La Brughera '07	🍷	4
○ OP Pinot Nero Extra Dry Cuvée Eleonor '06	🍷	4
⊙ OP Pinot Nero Extra Dry Cuvée Eleonor Rosé	🍷	4
⊙ OP Pinot Nero Gianfranco Giorgi Rosé Pas Dosé '05	🍷	6
● OP Pinot Nero Monteroso '06	🍷	5
● Vigalòn '07	🍷	3*
● OP Buttafuoco Storico Casa del Corno '03	🍷🍷	4

Conte Carlo Giorgi di Vistarino

VILLA FORNACE
27040 ROCCA DE' GIORGI [PV]
TEL. 038585117
www.contevistarino.it

ANNUAL PRODUCTION	550,000 bottles
HECTARES UNDER VINE	180
VITICULTURE METHOD	Conventional

Ottavia Giorgi di Vistarino has not set herself simplest of tasks. She intends to bring this estate up to the level of quality it deserves. But year after year, albeit with some false steps, the improvements are starting to show. The croatina-based IGT Sorbe '06 is always good quality, though not as explosive as on other occasions and still a bit behind. It needs a few more months in bottle to find its proper balance but the raw material is there. The Riesling 7 Giugno '07 has a nice, almost aromatic bouquet, interesting minerality and good overall balance. The Pinot Nero Pernice '05 has more or less the same problems as the Sorbe. The raw material is all there, with varietal aromas and refined tannins, but the wine is still too young. We gave it Two Glasses anyway for its prospects. The readier-to-drink Pinot Nero, Costa del Nero '06, is crafted in a simpler, fresher style. Bonarda Vivace L'Alcova '07 has forthright wild berry aromas and well-gauged tannins and the Brut Metodo Classico shows nice elegance but lacks a bit of length. The other wines in the range are all decent.

Isimbarda

LOC. CASTELLO
CASCINA ISIMBARDA
27046 SANTA GIULETTA [PV]
TEL. 0383899256
www.tenutaisimbarda.com

ANNUAL PRODUCTION	100,000 bottles
HECTARES UNDER VINE	30
VITICULTURE METHOD	Conventional

Under the guidance of oenologist Daniele Zangelmi, after a lacklustre period Isimbarda is making such a good comeback it earned a full entry in the Guide. We gave an excellent score went to the OP Rosso Riserva Montezavo '05. Its nearly impenetrable dark ruby leads to a lovely bouquet of ripe fruit, spices, hay and coffee with echoes of balsam. The palate has substance, smooth tannins and decent length with an almondy finish. From renano only, the Riesling Vigna Martina '07 has a golden colour and lovely elderflower, honeysuckle, and robinia florality. The palate hits the spot with barely suggested mineral notes and a precise finish. The well-made Bonarda Vivace '07 shows nicely upfront ripe wild berries, elegant tannins and is fairly soft. We also liked the OP Rosso Monplò with its rather accented notes of barbera, nicely measured tannins and acidity, and good substance, as well as a certain elegance. The Pinot Nero Vigna del Cardinale '05 also came close to a second Glass, showing garnet-shaded ruby with nice, if slightly evolved, aromas of black berry fruit. The standard label Barbera Vivace is pleasant and fresh.

● OP Pinot Nero Costa del Nero '06	♟♟ 3*
● OP Pinot Nero Pernice '05	♟♟ 5
○ OP Riesling 7 Giugno '07	♟♟ 4
● Sorbe '06	♟♟ 4
● OP Bonarda L'Alcova '07	♟ 3
● OP Buttafuoco Monte Selva '06	♟ 4
○ OP Pinot Nero Brut Cl.	♟ 3
○ OP Pinot Nero Brut Martinotti Cuvée della Rocca	♟ 3
● OP Sangue di Giuda Costiolo '07	♟ 3
● OP Pinot Nero Pernice '04	♟♟ 5
● OP Pinot Nero Pernice '03	♟♟ 4
● Sorbe '05	♟♟ 4
● Sorbe '04	♟♟ 4

● OP Bonarda Vivace '07	♟♟ 4*
○ OP Riesling Renano Vigna Martina '07	♟♟ 4*
● OP Rosso Monplò '05	♟♟ 4*
● OP Rosso Montezavo Ris. '05	♟♟ 5
● OP Barbera Vivace '07	♟ 4
● OP Pinot Nero V. del Cardinale '05	♟ 4
○ OP Riesling Renano Vigna Martina '06	♟♟ 4

Cantina Sociale La Versa

VIA F. CRISPI, 15
27047 SANTA MARIA DELLA VERSA [PV]
TEL. 0385798411
www.laversa.it

ANNUAL PRODUCTION	6,000,000 bottles
HECTARES UNDER VINE	1300
VITICULTURE METHOD	Conventional

Francesco Cervetti has added another brick to the edifice of this historic estate's renaissance. The Testarossa Principio '01 burst into the finals and came close to Three Glasses. Complex and elegant, it has a broad range of aromas leading into a full, nicely evolved palate with freshness and great length. Also in the finals was the Testarossa Rosé '04, which has pleasant wild berry aromas and is elegant, balanced and long. Another high score also went to the Testarossa Brut '03, an elegant, taut wine with style, cleanliness and length. The ever excellent Pinot Nero Brut Carta Oro spent 36 months on the yeasts and may well be the best value Italian sparkler there is. The great Moscato passito Lacrimae Vitis '04 has a bouquet of citrus, aromatic herbs and barley sugar, and shows balanced and long. The Buttafuoco Roccolo delle Viole '05 is fragrant and typically husky. The Sangue di Giuda and Bonarda Ca' Bella '07 are equally fragrant and clean, proffering crisp wild berry fruit and the Riesling Roccolo delle Fate '07 is typical, well structured and fragrant. The rest of the range is good.

Lantieri de Paratico

LOC. COLZANO
VIA SIMEONE PARATICO, 50
25031 CAPRIOLO [BS]
TEL. 030736151
www.lantierideparatico.it

ANNUAL PRODUCTION	150,000 bottles
HECTARES UNDER VINE	17
VITICULTURE METHOD	Conventional

This property at Capriolo has been in the family for centuries and is now skilfully and enthusiastically managed by Fabio Lantieri. Over the past few years, Fabio has clearly begun to shift the estate's focus towards higher quality wines and cuvées. For example, the Brut Arcadia '04 made a good showing in the final taste-offs thanks to its lovely, bright greenish straw-yellow colour, a complex bouquet where you perceive ripe fruit and floral tones, shades of cakes and vanilla, and citrussy hints. The wine spreads across the palate, showing fresh, caressing and harmonious before it signs off in leisurely fashion on mineral and citrus nuances with lovely finesse. While the promising new Arcadia Rosé is still maturing in the cellar, we tasted an excellent Terre di Franciacorta Bianco Colzano '06 with a vanilla-laced nose, good structure and acidity, and a sound Terre di Franciacorta Rosso Colzano '05 which offers solid body and soft tannins. Finally, the three Brut, Extra Brut and Satèn non-vintage Franciacortas are good.

○ Cuvée Testarossa Principio '01	♉	8
☉ OP Pinot Nero Rosé Cuvée Testarossa Brut '04	♉	8
● OP Bonarda Frizzante Ca' Bella '07	♉	4*
● OP Buttafuoco Roccolo delle Viole '05	♉	4*
○ OP Moscato Passito Lacrimae Vitis '04	♉	6
○ OP Pinot Nero Brut Carta Oro	♉	4*
○ OP Pinot Nero Cuvée Testarossa Brut '03	♉	8
○ OP Riesling Roccolo delle Fate '07	♉	4
● OP Sangue di Giuda '07	♉	4
● OP Bonarda Frizzante Terre d'Alteni '07	♉	3
○ OP Moscato di Volpara Frizzante I Roccoli '07	♉	4
○ OP Pinot Nero Brut Cuvée Storica	♉	4
☉ OP Pinot Nero Brut Cuvée Storica Rosé	♉	4
○ OP Pinot Nero MonteCalvo	♉	4

○ Franciacorta Brut Arcadia '04	♉	6
○ TdF Bianco Colzano '06	♉	5
● TdF Rosso Colzano '05	♉	5
○ Franciacorta Brut	♉	5
○ Franciacorta Extra Brut	♉	4
○ Franciacorta Satèn	♉	5
○ Franciacorta Brut Arcadia '02	♉♉	6
○ Franciacorta Brut Arcadia '01	♉♉	6
○ TdF Bianco Colzano '05	♉♉	5
● TdF Rosso Colzano '04	♉♉	5

Majolini

LOC. VALLE
VIA MANZONI, 3
25050 OME [BS]
TEL. 0306527378
www.majolini.it

ANNUAL PRODUCTION	160,000 bottles
HECTARES UNDER VINE	20
VITICULTURE METHOD	Conventional

Ezio Majolini, administrator of the family estate and president of the Franciacorta consortium, runs both with equal passion and enthusiasm. This entry only deals with the family estate, which over the past ten years has been among the best on the DOCG zone's crowded landscape. Only a Three Glass high note was lacking this year to frame the high quality performance of all these wines. We felt the Satèn Ante Omnia was the year's most successful cuvée and is certainly one of the finest incarnations of this type of wine. The 2003 has an elegant, pervasive nose that at first gives biscuit and honey tones before these slowly give way to white-fleshed fruit, yeasts and a hint of Alpine herbs. Then comes a solid, well-polished palate with creamy effervescence and a vanillaed apricot finish. The full, rich Pas Dosé Aligi Sassu '04 has intense yeast and toasted bread aromas, and a lovely acid backbone in the mouth. The enjoyable Brut Electo '04 shows overall soft harmony and fleshy texture supported by the fresh vein of acidity. Rosé Altera is among the best we tasted of its type and the same goes for the dense, well-balanced base Brut.

Le Marchesine

VIA VALLOSA, 31
25050 PASSIRANO [BS]
TEL. 030657005
www.lemarchesine.it

ANNUAL PRODUCTION	320,000 bottles
HECTARES UNDER VINE	40
VITICULTURE METHOD	Conventional

Loris Biatta skilfully manages this estate founded in the mid 1980s by his father Giovanni. Grapes from the estate's 30 hectares of vineyards are vinified in the cellar at Passirano with consultancy from Jean Pierre Valade, an oenologist based in France. Again this year, a Biatta family vintage sparkler, the Brut '01, is one of the best in the DOCG. It has a nice, bright straw-yellow colour, tiny bubbles and a complex bouquet where floral and vanilla tones seem at first to dominate but then give way to deeper, fresher sensations of white-fleshed fruit and citrus. The palate is broad, juicy, rich in acid backbone and not too ripe fruit. There is solid structure and the aromas are lifted by fascinating nuances of sage, mint and apricot pulp. Nearly as good is the Satèn '04, which gives elegant floral tones, soft, rich fullness and a spicy, balsamic finish. The Secolo Novo '02, from chardonnay grown in a vineyard on the La Santissima hill at Gussago, shows complex tertiary and oak tones leading into a palate with remarkable harmony and freshness. Outstanding among the other sound labels is a Rosé '04, one of the best of its type.

O Franciacorta Satèn Ante Omnia '03	♟♟	8
O Franciacorta Aligi Sassu Pas Dosé '04	♟♟	8
O Franciacorta Brut	♟♟	7
O Franciacorta Brut Electo '04	♟♟	8
⊙ Franciacorta Rosé Altera Brut	♟♟	6
O Franciacorta Brut Electo '99	♟♟♟	6
O Franciacorta Brut Electo '97	♟♟♟	6
O Franciacorta Brut Electo '00	♟♟♟	7
O Franciacorta Aligi Sassu Pas Dosé '03	♟♟	8
O Franciacorta Brut Electo '03	♟	8

O Franciacorta Brut '01	♟♟	6
⊙ Franciacorta Brut Rosé '04	♟♟	6
O Franciacorta Brut Secolo Novo '02	♟♟	8
O Franciacorta Satèn '04	♟♟	6
● Il Podere Pinot Nero '03	♟♟	6
● Cabernet Sauvignon Alice '03	♟	6
O Franciacorta Brut	♟	5
O Franciacorta Extra Brut	♟	6
O TdF Bianco Curtefranca '07	♟	4
O Franciacorta Brut Secolo Novo '00	♟♟	7
O Franciacorta Satèn '02	♟♟	6
O Franciacorta Brut Secolo Novo '99	♟♟	7
O Franciacorta Satèn '03	♟♟	6

Tenuta Mazzolino

VIA MAZZOLINO, 26
27050 CORVINO SAN QUIRICO [PV]
TEL. 0383876122
www.tenuta-mazzolino.com

ANNUAL PRODUCTION	100,000 bottles
HECTARES UNDER VINE	22
VITICULTURE METHOD	Conventional

There was a place in the finals for the Pinot Nero Noir '05 from Tenuta Mazzolino, mistakenly included in the Guide last year when bottling was not yet definitive. Its mid garnet colour precedes upfront aromas of wild berries and elegance on both nose and palate, with remarkable balance of tannins and fruit, nice backbone and impressive energy driving to a lingering finish. This wine is an important indication of the potential for pinot nero in Oltrepò. The nicely varietal Bonarda Mazzolino '07 has fragrant aromas and a satisfyingly tannic palate with a pleasant, almondy finish. The Chardonnay Blanc '06 is also good. In comparison with the past, the oak is less invasive and clear notes of ripe tropical fruit emerge while freshness in the mouth enhances drinkability without diminishing complexity. The Mazzolino Brut is a Blanc de Blancs, as you can tell from the pineapple and banana notes that vein the nice bouquet along with aromas of cakes. The palate is well defined and spirited with citrussy notes. The two base IGTs, the chardonnay-based white Camarà and the pinot nero-only red Terrazze, are decent.

Mirabella

VIA CANTARANE, 2
25050 RODENGO SAIANO [BS]
TEL. 030611197
www.mirabellavini.it

ANNUAL PRODUCTION	500,000 bottles
HECTARES UNDER VINE	60
VITICULTURE METHOD	Conventional

Although the estate's showcase vintage wine, the Non Dosato, was missing, all the wines from this winery, managed by Francesco Bracchi, put on an absolutely outstanding performance. We really like the Satèn with its supporting acidity, structure and fresh soft aromas of cakes, vanilla and golden apples with a sweet note of baked apples. The palate is fresh, lively and juicy. Despite its simplicity, the Rosé is also good with a lovely pale pink colour and toasted oak on the nose that precede exuberant tones of black and red berries. The palate shows good acidity, freshness and length, even more than the Cuvée Demetra Rosé, which is slightly too evolved and weighed down by oak. In contrast, the Cuvée Demetra fermented off the skins has enjoyable toastiness and oaky notes. Here again, a pinch more freshness would in our opinion have been an overall improvement. Finally, the good cabernet, merlot and nebbiolo-based red, Nero d'Ombra '04, gives blueberry aromas and a palate that shows soft tannins and structure.

● OP Pinot Nero Noir '05	♟♟	6
● OP Bonarda Mazzolino '07	♟♟	4*
○ OP Chardonnay Blanc '06	♟♟	4*
○ OP Mazzolino Brut	♟♟	5
○ Camarà '07	♟	3
● Terrazze '07	♟	3
● OP Pinot Nero Noir '00	♟♟	6
● OP Cabernet Sauvignon Corvino '05	♟♟	4
● OP Pinot Nero Noir '04	♟♟	6
● OP Pinot Nero Noir '02	♟♟	6

○ Franciacorta Brut Cuvée Demetra	♟♟	5
⊙ Franciacorta Rosé Brut	♟♟	5*
○ Franciacorta Satèn	♟♟	5*
● Nero d'Ombra '04	♟♟	6
○ Franciacorta Brut	♟	5
⊙ Franciacorta Brut Rosé Cuvée Demetra	♟	5
⊙ Ibisco '07	♟	4
○ Passito Incanto '05	♟	6
○ Franciacorta Non Dosato '98	♟♟	5*
○ Franciacorta Non Dosato '00	♟♟	5

Monsupello

VIA SAN LAZZARO, 5
27050 TORRICELLA VERZATE [PV]
TEL. 0383896043
www.monsupello.it

ANNUAL PRODUCTION	280,000 bottles
HECTARES UNDER VINE	48
VITICULTURE METHOD	Conventional

The Boatti family manages Monsupello with marvellous skill. Successive acquisitions have enabled them to control almost 50 hectares of vineyards in the best wine areas of this large DOC zone. Every year, they submit a vast range of excellent wines and sparklers. Again in this edition of the Guide, the top honours go to the Pinot Nero Nature, by now a classic of Oltrepò winemaking. It has the colour of a real Blanc de Noirs, a golden straw yellow with copper highlights, and opens brightly on the nose vital with complex tones of red berries, delicate shades of medicinal herbs, vanilla and spice. The palate has backbone and structure, features extraordinary harmony and freshness, and closes long on elegant hints of mineral and oak. This minor masterpiece is also one of the best-value wines in its sector you can find. The Cuvée Ca' del Tava is a blend of equal parts of Chardonnay and Pinot Nero with wonderfully opulent fullness and also went forward to our finals with the new Merlot '05, which is rich, juicy and varietal. But from the extremely pleasant Pinot Nero Junior '07 to the current whites, every bottle is worth uncorking.

Monte Rossa

FRAZ. BORNATO
VIA MONTE ROSSA, 1
25040 CAZZAGO SAN MARTINO [BS]
TEL. 030725066
www.monterossa.com

ANNUAL PRODUCTION	500,000 bottles
HECTARES UNDER VINE	70
VITICULTURE METHOD	Conventional

The Rabotti family estate, founded by Paolo and Paola Rovetta in the 1970s and now managed by their son Emanuele, is one of the major names in the history of this young, prestigious DOCG. The Rabottis are always in the front rank and again this year won Three Glasses, the ninth such award in the cellar's history thanks to their prestige cuvée, Cabochon. The '04 vintage confirms it is one of the most interesting Franciacorta cuvées and faithful to a personal style that sees the wine closed on release despite many years spent on the yeasts. Then it slowly but surely opens with the passing years to expresses the great qualities of its native terroir. Structure, elegance and complex minerality are its distinctive features, and make it a great wine every year. With its buttery, vanillaed tones, the Satèn is an excellent Blanc de Blancs. Prima Cuvée will seduce you with the fresh, overwhelming vitality of its fruity tones and the Brut P.R. presents overall balance, crisp fruit and elegant floral nuances. This excellent list of wines closes with a Rosé in a subtle, elegant style themed to crystal-clear blueberry notes.

O OP Pinot Nero Cl. Nature	♟♟♟ 5*
● Merlot '05	♟♟ 6
O OP Brut Cl. Cuvée Ca' del Tava	♟♟ 7
O Chardonnay '07	♟♟ 4*
● OP Barbera I Gelsi '05	♟♟ 4*
● OP Bonarda Vivace Vaiolet '07	♟♟ 4*
● OP Pinot Nero 3309 '05	♟♟ 6
O OP Pinot Nero Brut Cl.	♟♟ 5
O OP Pinot Nero Brut Classese '03	♟♟ 5
O Pinot Grigio '07	♟♟ 4
● Pinot Nero Junior '07	♟♟ 4*
O Riesling Renano '07	♟♟ 4*
● Rosso Great Ruby Vivace '07	♟♟ 4*
O Sauvignon '07	♟♟ 4*
● OP Barbera Vivace Magenga '07	♟ 4
O OP Brut Cl. Cuvée Ca' del Tava	♟♟♟ 7
O OP Pinot Nero Cl. Nature	♟♟♟ 5*

O Franciacorta Brut Cabochon '04	♟♟♟ 7
O Franciacorta Brut P. R.	♟♟ 6
O Franciacorta Prima Cuvée Brut	♟♟ 5
⊙ Franciacorta Rosé	♟♟ 6
O Franciacorta Satèn Brut	♟♟ 6
O Franciacorta Brut Cabochon '99	♟♟♟ 8
O Franciacorta Brut Cabochon '98	♟♟♟ 6
O Franciacorta Brut Cabochon '97	♟♟♟ 6
O Franciacorta Brut Cabochon '03	♟♟♟ 7
O Franciacorta Brut Cabochon '01	♟♟♟ 7
O Franciacorta Extra Brut Cabochon '93	♟♟♟ 6
O Franciacorta Satèn	♟♟♟ 6

Montelio

VIA D. MAZZA, 1
27050 CODEVILLA [PV]
TEL. 0383373090
montelio.gio@alice.it

ANNUAL PRODUCTION	130,000 bottles
HECTARES UNDER VINE	27
VITICULTURE METHOD	Conventional

Montelio, an established Oltrepò Pavese estate, has long been owned by the Brazzola family. Now, it is managed by Mario Maffi, an oenologist who knows the territory well. The Pinot Nero Costarsa '03 emerged in decent shape from the blistering growing season. It has a certain freshness and still rather abundant fine tannins, aromas of spice, coffee, chocolate and wild berries with interesting balsamic notes. Giostra '06 is a white from barrique-fermented müller thurgau. The oak is less marked than in the past, boosting freshness and drinkability, not to mention its complexity on the nose and depth on the palate. With the merlot-only Comprino Mirosa '05 missing because it is not yet ready, the base Comprino '06 makes a nice impression with pepper and blueberry, good structure, remarkable balance and tempting drinkability. The very good Bonarda Frizzante '07 is one of the best from the vintage, showing fragrant with intense wild black berries and balanced tannins. The OP Rosso Solarolo Riserva '04 earned Two Glasses for its chewy pulp and long finish, although it has still to mature. The other wines submitted were well typed and varietal.

La Montina

VIA BAIANA, 17
25040 MONTICELLI BRUSATI [BS]
TEL. 030653278
www.lamontina.it

ANNUAL PRODUCTION	500,000 bottles
HECTARES UNDER VINE	62
VITICULTURE METHOD	Conventional

The Bozza brothers' estate offers a wide range of top quality labels. Cesare Ferrari, oenologist, Alceo Totò and Rocco Marino for agronomy, and Michele Bozza who co-ordinates sales, make up a close-knit team that over the past few years has boosted winery production in both numbers and quality. The Brut '04 has a nice, bright, golden straw-yellow colour, a complex nose of ripe fruit and shades of dried fruit and coffee that swirl around the soft tones of yeast and toasted bread. The palate offers rich, creamily persistent effervescence. As always, the Satèn is zesty and juicy, with clear fruit and vanilla tones, and satisfyingly long on the palate. The Curtefranca Bianco Palanca '07 is enjoyable thanks to overall freshness, good body and floral tones. The red Barbour is to be a Bordeaux blend with a solid framework. The rest of the wines are good even though we expected greater definition and fuller structure from the Brut and Extra Brut. We believe the estate could aspire to more ambitious goals.

● Comprino Rosso '06	♛♛	3*
○ Müller Thurgau La Giostra '06	♛♛	3*
● OP Bonarda Frizzante '07	♛♛	3*
● OP Pinot Nero Costarsa '03	♛♛	5
● OP Rosso Solarolo Ris. '04	♛♛	5
○ Müller Thurgau '07	♛	3
○ OP Cortese '07	♛	3
○ OP Riesling Italico '07	♛	3
⊙ OP Rosato '07	♛	3
● Comprino Mirosa '04	♛♛	6
● Comprino Mirosa '03	♛♛	6
● Comprino Mirosa '01	♛♛	6
● OP Pinot Nero Costarsa '01	♛♛	5
● OP Rosso Solarolo Ris. '01	♛♛	5

○ Franciacorta Brut '04	♛♛	5
○ Franciacorta Satèn '05	♛♛	6
○ TdF Bianco Palanca '07	♛♛	3*
● Barbour	♛	5
○ Franciacorta Brut	♛	5
○ Franciacorta Extra Brut '05	♛	5
⊙ Franciacorta Rosé Demi Sec	♛	5
● TdF Rosso dei Dossi '05	♛	4
○ Franciacorta Brut '00	♛♛	6
○ Franciacorta Extra Brut '02	♛♛	5
○ Franciacorta Extra Brut '01	♛♛	5

Monzio Compagnoni

VIA NIGOLINE, 18
25030 ADRO [BS]
TEL. 0307457803
www.monziocompagnoni.com

ANNUAL PRODUCTION	250,000 bottles
HECTARES UNDER VINE	30
VITICULTURE METHOD	Conventional

It's time for celebration again at the house of Monzio Compagnoni. Three well-deserved Glasses go to the Franciacorta Extra Brut '04 on the heels of the success of the previous vintage. All this confirms the good work of Marcello Monzio Compagnoni, who over the past ten years has moved permanently to Franciacorta from Valcalepìo, where a branch of the operation continues to turn out excellent results. These have been years of sacrifice, investment, work and experimentation but the results are there before the eyes – and noses – of us all. Today the new, modern cellar at Adro releases a range of praiseworthy wines. Getting back to the Extra Brut, you will be surprised at how elegant this wine is on the nose as well as the palate, while at the same time unveiling power and intense, fruit and minerality-themed character. It has worthy companions in the Satèn '04, with its marked juiciness and fullness, a Brut from the same vintage with floral aromas and a lively backbone, compact fruit, and a complex, stylish, elegant, deep Rosé. The other labels run from good to excellent.

Il Mosnel

LOC. CAMIGNONE
VIA BARBOGLIO, 14
25040 PASSIRANO [BS]
TEL. 030653117
www.ilmosnel.com

ANNUAL PRODUCTION	250,000 bottles
HECTARES UNDER VINE	39
VITICULTURE METHOD	Conventional

Giulio and Lucia Barzanò manage this family estate, which has been producing excellent wine since the 1960s. The base is a perfectly restructured 16th-century building, fitted out with up-to-date cellar equipment, at Passirano near Camignone. Around it are the vineyards in a single 40-hectare plot, which is unusual in these parts. The vines yield top-quality grapes that the cellar transforms into a wide range of still wines and Franciacortas. This year, three cuvées reached our finals, confirming the estate's excellent quality. The Brut Emanuela Barboglio '04 shows floral aromas with notes of lavender and fruit, and the palate offers a solid, elegant structure and caressing effervescence. The Rosé Pas Dosè Parosé '04, from mostly pinot nero, has delicate touches of raspberry and cherry, a lean, graceful body and pale, bright colour. Finally, the Pas Dosé has floral tones, harmony, fresh citrussy hints and a long finish. Special mention goes to the Brut QdE '98, a sort of chardonnay and pinot bianco-based recently disgorged sparkler released in a few hundred magnums. This is a subtle, elegant wine with great charm and minerality.

O Franciacorta Extra Brut '04	♙♙♙	6
O Franciacorta Satèn Brut '04	♙♙	6
O Franciacorta Brut '04	♙♙	5
⊙ Franciacorta Brut Rosé '04	♙♙	6
O TdF Bianco della Seta '06	♙♙	5
● Valcalepio Rosso di Luna '05	♙♙	5
● Rosso di Nero '06	♙	5
O TdF Bianco Ronco della Seta '07	♙	4
O Valcalepio Bianco Colle della Luna '07	♙	3
O Franciacorta Extra Brut '03	♟♟♟	6
O Franciacorta Brut '02	♟♟	6
O Franciacorta Extra Brut '01	♟♟	5
O Franciacorta Satèn '03	♟♟	6
O Franciacorta Satèn '01	♟♟	6

O Franciacorta Brut Emanuela Barboglio '04	♙♙	6
O Franciacorta Pas Dosé	♙♙	5
⊙ Franciacorta Pas Dosé Parosé '04	♙♙	6
O Franciacorta Brut QdE '98	♙♙	
O Franciacorta Satèn '04	♙♙	6
O Sebino Passito '06	♙♙	6
O Franciacorta Brut	♙	5
O TdF Bianco '07	♙	4
O Franciacorta Brut Emanuela Barboglio '03	♟♟	6
O Franciacorta Pas Dosé	♟♟	5
⊙ Franciacorta Pas Dosé Parosé '03	♟♟	6
O Franciacorta Satèn '02	♟♟	6
O Sebino Passito '05	♟♟	6

★ Nino Negri

VIA GHIBELLINI
23030 CHIURO [SO]
TEL. 0342485211
www.ninonegri.it

Pasini - San Giovanni

FRAZ. RAFFA
VIA VIDELLE, 2
25080 PUEGNAGO SUL GARDA [BS]
TEL. 0365651419
www.pasiniproduttori.it

ANNUAL PRODUCTION	830,000 bottles
HECTARES UNDER VINE	36
VITICULTURE METHOD	Natural

The Three Glass race between Sfursat 5 Stelle and Negri's traditional Sfursat is neck and neck. The difference could be less than a single mark in a hundred. In the end, the Sfursat '05 won this year because of that touch more elegance, coupled with the complex bouquet, with wild berries and cyclamen, and the progression on the dry palate refreshed by acidity. Following intense, clear ripe fruit, and healthy, rustic notes of leather, the 5 Stelle '05 unveils a dense palate with nice extract and balanced acidity. The Vigneto Fracia '05 ranges across notes of spice and dried flowers. The palate is warm and savoury with balanced oak and echoes of red berry fruit. The characteristic, dynamic Sassella Le Tense '05 shows great finesse and a palate with an admirable balance of tannins and acidity. The Mazer '05 has a fruit-led nose and a warm, silky palate. The Grumello '05 has spicy tones on the nose and an original palate with almond shades in the finish. The Ca' Brione '07, from sauvignon, chardonnay and incrocio Manzoni, put on a good performance with its intense, fruity aromas, structured, savoury palate and slightly dubious vanillaed backdrop.

ANNUAL PRODUCTION	300,000 bottles
HECTARES UNDER VINE	36
VITICULTURE METHOD	Conventional

The San Giovanni estate winery, until a short while ago known as Pasini Produttori, celebrates half a century in business by confirming its excellent quality, showing how well old and new generations work together. Beppe, Diego, Paolo and Luca Pasini work side by side on their 40 or so hectares of vineyards on Lake Garda. Groppello, the indigenous variety in Valtenesi, offers the best wines. It's a single-variety wine in the Groppello Riserva Vigneto Arzane '04, aged in small wood, which has intense red berries and varietal strawberries as well as spice. Then there's a traditional blend with barbera, marzemino and sangiovese in the Rosso Superiore Cap del Priù '05. We perceived ripe fruity sensations veined with fresh medicinal notes. Groppello is again the star, but with cabernet this time, in San Gioan '04. Scores for the two Luganas were good, the white from the '07 vintage and the new, very dry Busocaldo '06. Both give a classic mix of peaches and apricots lifted by a mineral, salt-nuanced freshness. The sparkling wines are interesting.

● Valtellina Sfursat '05	♟♟♟	8
● Valtellina Sfursat 5 Stelle '05	♟♟	8
● Valtellina Sup. Vign. Fracia '05	♟♟	8
○ Ca' Brione '07	♟♟	7
● Valtellina Sup. Grumello V. Sassorosso '05	♟♟	6
● Valtellina Sup. Mazer '05	♟♟	6
● Valtellina Sup. Sassella Le Tense '05	♟♟	6
● Valtellina Sfursat '04	♟♟♟	7
● Valtellina Sfursat '03	♟♟♟	7
● Valtellina Sfursat '02	♟♟♟	6
● Valtellina Sfursat 5 Stelle '99	♟♟♟	6
● Valtellina Sfursat 5 Stelle '98	♟♟♟	6
● Valtellina Sfursat 5 Stelle '97	♟♟♟	6
● Valtellina Sfursat 5 Stelle '03	♟♟♟	8
● Valtellina Sfursat 5 Stelle '02	♟♟♟	7
● Valtellina Sfursat 5 Stelle '01	♟♟♟	7

● Garda Cl. Groppello Vign. Arzane Ris. '04	♟♟	4*
● Garda Cl. Rosso Sup. Cap del Priù '05	♟♟	4*
○ Lugana Il Lugana '07	♟♟	4*
● San Gioan Rosso I Carati '04	♟♟	4*
○ Brut Cl. Ceppo 326	♟	5
○ Extra Brut Cl. Ceppo 326 Ex Trentacarati '03	♟	5
⊙ Garda Cl. Chiaretto '07	♟	4
● Garda Cl. Groppello Il Groppello '07	♟	4
○ Lugana Brut	♟	4
○ Lugana Busocaldo '06	♟	4
● Garda Cl. Groppello Vign. Arzane Ris. '03	♟♟	4
● Garda Cl. Groppello Vign. Arzane Ris. '01	♟♟	4
● Garda Cl. Groppello Vign. Arzane Ris. '01	♟♟	4

Cascina La Pertica

LOC. PICEDO
VIA ROSARIO, 44
25080 POLPENAZZE DEL GARDA [BS]
TEL. 0365651471
www.cascinalapertica.it

ANNUAL PRODUCTION	60,000 bottles
HECTARES UNDER VINE	16
VITICULTURE METHOD	Natural

Ruggero Brunori and Andrea Salvetti run a benchmark winemaking operation for the entire territory of Lombardy along the Brescia shores of Lake Garda, in the heart of Valtenesi. Fifteen or so hectares of organically managed vines sprawl out across the morainic hills of Polpenazze facing the lake. Cabernet Le Zalte is the finest product of these vineyards, a wine capable of uniting and enhancing varietal characteristics as well as the features imbued by the terroir. These emerge right on time in the '06 version, which is a bit under par by reason of its prematurely evolved character compared to previous Three Glass-winning vintages. The other two reds from the Garda DOC zone, the Groppello Il Colombaio '07 and Garda Classico Rosso are marked out by classic territoriality. The Sincette '05, also essentially based on the indigenous groppello, proffers crunchy, dense, strawberry-led fruit combined with varietal echoes of spic. The Chiaretto '07 is fresh-tasting and spirited.

Andrea Picchioni

LOC. CAMPONOCE, 8
27044 CANNETO PAVESE [PV]
TEL. 0385262139
www.picchioniandrea.it

ANNUAL PRODUCTION	60,000 bottles
HECTARES UNDER VINE	8
VITICULTURE METHOD	Natural

Picchioni does it again! Last year, we gave him a first full profile in the Guide as a reward for his passionate work and great consistency in the style and quality of his wines. And what does he do this year? He pulls out of his hat a Metodo Classico that, after ten years on the yeasts, swept into the Three Glass finals. Profilo '97 is a Pinot Nero with a golden, straw yellow colour, an evolved, complex nose with recognizable aromas of toasted hazelnuts and small cakes followed by an intense in the attack on the palate that heads into a clean, remarkably long finish. Not bad for a first try. The croatina-heavy Rosso d'Asia '04 is as excellent as ever, showing balsamic, structured and warm with ripe tannins. The Buttafuoco Riva Bianca '04 is dense, slightly overripe and very deep. Another new item is the Pinot Nero Bricco Arfena '06, which is typical in both colour and bouquet. It's an IGT because of an incomprehensible decision by the DOC commission to reject it. The '07 Bonarda is one of the best from Oltrepò with its crunchy, meaty fruit. The croatina and merlot Monnalisa '04 is soft and the Sangue di Giuda '07 well typed.

● Garda Cabernet Le Zalte '06	♀♀	7
● Garda Cl. Groppello Il Colombaio '07	♀♀	4*
● Garda Cl. Rosso Le Sincette '05	♀♀	5
⊙ Garda Cl. Chiaretto Le Sincette '07	♀	4
● Il Rosso '06	♀	4
○ Le Sincette Bianco '07	♀	4
● Garda Cabernet Le Zalte '99	♀♀♀	5
● Garda Cabernet Le Zalte '05	♀♀♀	7
● Garda Cabernet Le Zalte '04	♀♀♀	7
● Garda Cabernet Le Zalte '03	♀♀♀	7
● Garda Cabernet Le Zalte '01	♀♀♀	7
● Garda Cabernet Le Zalte '00	♀♀♀	7
● Garda Cl. Groppello Il Colombaio '06	♀♀	4

○ OP Profilo Brut Nature M. Cl. '97	♀♀	6
● Monnalisa '04	♀♀	5
● OP Bonarda '07	♀♀	3*
● OP Buttafuoco Bricco Riva Bianca '04	♀♀	5
● Pinot Nero Bricco Arfena '06	♀♀	5
● Rosso d'Asia '04	♀♀	5
● OP Sangue di Giuda '07	♀	3
● Monnalisa '03	♀♀	5
● OP Buttafuoco Bricco Riva Bianca '03	♀♀	5
● OP Sangue di Giuda '06	♀♀	3*
● Rosso d'Asia '03	♀♀	5
● Rosso d'Asia '01	♀♀	4

Plozza

VIA SAN GIACOMO, 22
23037 TIRANO [SO]
TEL. 0342701297
www.plozza.com

ANNUAL PRODUCTION	450,000 bottles
HECTARES UNDER VINE	28
VITICULTURE METHOD	Conventional

Year after year, the wines from the Zanolari family put on laudably reliable performances. In the front row representing elegance is the nebbiolo-based Numero Uno '04, which shows striking complexity on the intense, fruity nose. The palate is compact and juicy with iodine sensations and a long finish. Passione '03 is perfectly, perhaps even too perfectly, executed giving a spice and ripe fruit nose ushering in a powerful, warm, silky palate. Sfursat Vin da Ca' '04 is a wine of exemplary class, its spicy nose laced with mineral notes, before the palate shows a sharp edge, tautened by supporting acidity. The varietal Riserva Grumello '04 has stylish aromas and a round, graceful palate. The '04 version of the Sassella Riserva La Scala has slightly green aromas but the palate is confident, intense and warm with good length. Finally, the red berry fruit and flowers Inferno Riserva '04 is soft on the palate, unfurling tannins with good finesse.

Mamete Prevostini

VIA LUCCHINETTI, 63
23020 MESE [SO]
TEL. 034341003
www.mameteprevostini.com

ANNUAL PRODUCTION	130,000 bottles
HECTARES UNDER VINE	15
VITICULTURE METHOD	Conventional

As well as making good bottles, Mamete Prevostini has a knack of interpreting the trends that are constantly sweeping through the wine world. It enables him to see the way forward, for example by eliminating some excesses in the cellar such as the muscular wines so much in vogue a few years ago. Now he has released a splendidly elegant Sforzato Albareda '06, probably his best ever. Perceptions of fruit and spice come through on the complex nose, the taut palate shows no excess and progresses tonic and austere with lively acidity. There is still some work to be done on the use of oak but the Sforzato Corte di Cama '06 is already interesting the way it is, with notes of tar, a dynamic palate and almost gamey nuances. The Sassella Sommarovina '06 is a bit short yet supple. The Sassella San Lorenzo has intense aromas with oak upfront, and a soft, warm palate. The Sassella '06 is gutsy and fruity with good acidity. Grumello '06 nicely made and drinkable. Santarita '07 and Botonero '07, both from nebbiolo, boast alcohol-rich aromas and round palates. Finally, Opera '07, from chardonnay, sauvignon and müller thurgau, is fresh and fruity.

● Valtellina Numero Uno '04	♥♥ 8
● Valtellina Sforzato Vin da Ca' '04	♥♥ 6
● Passione Barrique '03	♥♥ 7
● Valtellina Sup. Grumello Ris. '04	♥♥ 4*
● Valtellina Sup. Inferno Ris. '04	♥♥ 5
● Valtellina Sup. Sassella La Scala Ris. '04	♥♥ 4*
● Valtellina Sforzato Vin da Ca' '03	♀♀ 6
● Valtellina Sup. Sassella La Scala Ris. '03	♀♀ 4
● Passione Barrique '02	♀♀ 7
● Valtellina Sforzato Vin da Ca' '02	♀♀ 6
● Valtellina Sup. Grumello Ris. '03	♀♀ 4

● Valtellina Sforzato Albareda '06	♥♥♥ 7
● Valtellina Sup. Corte di Cama '06	♥♥ 6
● Valtellina Sup. Sassella '06	♥♥ 4*
● Valtellina Sup. Sassella San Lorenzo '05	♥♥ 6
● Botonero '07	♥ 3
○ Opera Bianco '07	♥ 5
● Valtellina Santarita '07	♥ 4
● Valtellina Sup. Grumello '06	♥ 4
● Valtellina Sup. Sassella Sommarovina '06	♥ 5
● Valtellina Sforzato Albareda '05	♀♀♀ 7
● Valtellina Sforzato Albareda '04	♀♀♀ 7
● Valtellina Sforzato Albareda '03	♀♀♀ 7
● Valtellina Sforzato Albareda '00	♀♀♀ 7
● Valtellina Sup. Corte di Cama '05	♀♀ 6
● Valtellina Sup. Corte di Cama '04	♀♀ 6

Provenza

VIA DEI COLLI STORICI
25015 DESENZANO DEL GARDA [BS]
TEL. 0309910006
www.provenzacantine.it

ANNUAL PRODUCTION	1,000,000 bottles
HECTARES UNDER VINE	100
VITICULTURE METHOD	Conventional

There are times in life when you need to have the courage to change. Fabio Contato understood this and has made some critical adjustments in his otherwise successful production of whites from the Lugana DOC. He has almost totally given up oak in a search for greater freshness, supporting the character of the trebbiano variety grown in the clay soil around Lake Garda and abandoning the Superiore type. His results deserve a hearty round of applause and the Lugana selection that carries his name won our Three Glasses this year. The Fabio Contato '06 is racy, spirited, slightly salty and rich in crunchy pears and apples, yet also already shot through with subtle hints of minerality. The Molin '07 selection and base Lugana from Tenuta Maiolo '07 are both also very good. The sparkling versions of Lugana are equally good and a special mention goes to the classic method product. The selection of Garda Classico Rosso '05 is as elegant and fruit-forward as ever and the pleasant Groppello '07 comes from vineyards recently acquired in Valtenesi. The rest of the production is exemplary.

Quaquarini

LOC. MONTEVENEROSO
VIA CASA ZAMBIANCHI, 26
27044 CANNETO PAVESE [PV]
TEL. 038560152
www.quaquarinifrancesco.it

ANNUAL PRODUCTION	650,000 bottles
HECTARES UNDER VINE	60
VITICULTURE METHOD	Certified organic

After a few years' absence, the Quaquarini estate is back with a full profile with an array of convincing wines, including the outstanding Pinot Nero Blau '05 that went into the Three Glass finals for of its extremely clean, clear fruit, compact nose and palate, typicity and lovely length without attempting any particular complexity. Given its vintage, the Buttafuoco Storico Vigna Pregana '02 does not have that much power but the good fruity texture makes up for this with overripe hints, smooth tannins and energy on the palate. The good quality Classese is a sparkler with attitude and potential, although we tasted too soon after disgorgement. The two '07 Sangue di Giudas are good, both leading with nice intact blueberry and raspberry, and both showing balance between the extract and the residual sugar. We just preferred Vigna Acqua Calda because of its greater structure. The Bonarda Frizzante '07 is also well made with typical vegetal notes supporting the fruit. The rest of the range includes four well-executed, pleasant reds offering good value for money. We thought the best of these was Buttafuoco Vigna La Guasca '06.

○ Lugana Sel. Fabio Contato '07	▼▼▼ 6
● Garda Cl. Groppello Tenuta Maiolo '07	▼▼ 4*
● Garda Cl. Rosso Negresco '06	▼▼ 5
● Garda Cl. Rosso Sel. Fabio Contato '05	▼▼ 6
○ Lugana Brut Cl. Ca' Maiol '04	▼▼ 5
○ Lugana Sup. Molin '07	▼▼ 4*
○ Lugana Tenuta Maiolo '07	▼▼ 4*
○ Sol Doré '06	▼▼ 6
⊙ Garda Cl. Chiaretto Tenuta Maiolo '07	▼ 4
● Giomè '07	▼ 4
○ Lugana Brut Sebastian '07	▼ 4
⊙ Sebastian Rosè '07	▼ 4
○ Lugana Sup. Sel. Fabio Contato '05	♀♀ 5
○ Lugana Sup. Sel. Fabio Contato '04	♀♀ 6
● Garda Cl. Rosso Sel. Fabio Contato '04	♀♀ 6

● OP Pinot Nero Blau '05	▼▼ 4*
● OP Bonarda Frizzante '07	▼▼ 3*
● OP Buttafuoco V. Pregana '02	▼▼ 6
○ OP Classese Brut	▼▼ 4*
● OP Sangue di Giuda '07	▼▼ 3*
● OP Sangue di Giuda V. Acqua Calda '06	▼▼ 4*
● Grandesco '07	▼ 4
● OP Barbera Poggio Anna '06	▼ 4
● OP Buttafuoco V. La Guasca '06	▼ 4
● OP Rosso Magister '06	▼ 4
● OP Sangue di Giuda '06	♀♀ 3*

Aldo Rainoldi

VIA STELVIO, 128
23030 CHIURO [SO]
TEL. 0342482225
www.rainoldi.com

ANNUAL PRODUCTION   220,000 bottles
HECTARES UNDER VINE   10
VITICULTURE METHOD   Conventional

Again Peppino Rainoldi and his nephew Aldo presented us a series of top quality wines, starting with the Sfursat Ca' Rizzieri '04. Even though still a bit closed, the nose tempts with elegant spiciness and notes of tobacco with balsamic shades. The palate is taut, continuous and gutsy, the finish long and sustained by good acidity. The '04 Sfursat has concentrated aromas with light hints of gaminess. It's a bit more rustic than in the past, endowed with strong personality, confident flavours, clear acidity and iodine tones. After a deep, tar-veined nose, the Sassella Riserva '04 presents a tannin-rich palate with good acidity that will guarantee untrammelled ageing. Although slightly green in its aromas, the Inferno Riserva '04 still has full flavour and soft tannins that mesh well into the structure. From sauvignon with a splash of nebbiolo fermented off the skins, Ghibellino '07 has stylish aromas, good structure and strikingly vibrant savouriness. We close with a new item, the classic method '04 vintage Rosé Brut from nebbiolo grapes. After 30 months on the yeasts, it flaunts well-supported fruit.

Ricci Curbastro

VIA ADRO, 37
25031 CAPRIOLO [BS]
TEL. 030736094
www.riccicurbastro.it

ANNUAL PRODUCTION   240,000 bottles
HECTARES UNDER VINE   28.5
VITICULTURE METHOD   Conventional

The enthusiastic, skilled Riccardo Ricci Curbastro manages a family estate that now boasts almost 30 hectares of vineyards and a lovely cellar in the historic villa at Capriolo. This year, two of his cuvées, produced with oenological consultancy from Alberto Musatti, reached our finals. We refer to the Satèn '03, a complex, opulent wine, rich on the nose with tones of ripe fruit and oak laced with remarkably subtle shades of minerals and balsam. The palate is juicy and full yet fresh with great balance and closes out long and elegant. The Rosé has a nice, bright, pale pinkish complexion and expresses elegant notes of wild berries and Alpine herbs. The palate shows no nonsense character and imposing structure. Dosage Zero Gualberto '03 has complex tones and elegant minerality while the Satèn has presence, soft fruit and lovely freshness. The Extra Brut, Brut and Demi Sec are just a step behind. Other decent wines on the list include the tangy, invigorating Bianco Vigna Bosco Alto '05 and the rest are interesting and well made.

● Valtellina Sfursat Fruttaio Ca' Rizzieri '04	♈ 7	
○ Bianco Ghibellino '07	♈ 5	
⊙ Brut Rosé '04	♈ 5	
● Valtellina Sfursat '04	♈ 6	
● Valtellina Sup. Inferno Ris. '04	♈ 6	
● Valtellina Sup. Sassella Ris. '04	♈ 5	
● Valtellina Sfursat Fruttaio Ca' Rizzieri '98	♈♈♈ 6	
● Valtellina Sfursat Fruttaio Ca' Rizzieri '97	♈♈♈ 6	
● Valtellina Sfursat Fruttaio Ca' Rizzieri '95	♈♈♈ 5	
● Valtellina Sfursat Fruttaio Ca' Rizzieri '02	♈♈♈ 7	
● Valtellina Sfursat Fruttaio Ca' Rizzieri '00	♈♈♈ 7	
● Valtellina Sfursat '03	♈♈ 6	
● Valtellina Sup. Sassella Ris. '01	♈♈ 5	

⊙ Franciacorta Brut Rosé	♈ 6	
○ Franciacorta Satèn Brut '03	♈ 6	
○ Franciacorta Brut Satèn	♈ 5	
○ Franciacorta Dosaggio Zero Gualberto '03	♈ 6	
○ TdF Bianco V. Bosco Alto '05	♈ 4*	
○ TdF Bianco Curtefranca '07	♈ 3	
○ Franciacorta Brut	♈ 5	
○ Franciacorta Demi Sec	♈ 5	
○ Franciacorta Extra Brut '04	♈ 5	
● Sebino Rosso '06	♈ 3	
● TdF Rosso Curtefranca '06	♈ 3	
○ Franciacorta Extra Brut '03	♈♈ 5*	
○ Franciacorta Dosaggio Zero Gualberto '01	♈♈ 6	
○ Franciacorta Satèn Brut '02	♈♈ 6	
○ TdF Bianco V. Bosco Alto '04	♈♈ 4*	

Ronco Calino

FRAZ. TORBIATO
LOC. QUATTRO CAMINI
VIA FENICE, 45
25030 ADRO [BS]
TEL. 0307451073
www.roncocalino.it

ANNUAL PRODUCTION	40,000 bottles
HECTARES UNDER VINE	10
VITICULTURE METHOD	Conventional

Several years ago, Paolo Radici decided to purchase the lovely villa at Torbiato that once belonged to the pianist Benedetti Michelangeli. The surrounding vineyards produce the raw material for a small but scrupulously made range from the new, modern cellar. This year, we particularly enjoyed the Franciacorta Rosé Radijan, a Pinot Nero cuvée Paolo dedicated to his father Gianni. It has an elegant antique rose colour and complex red berry and oak notes on the nose. The full, elegant palate is well sustained by acid backbone and fades out on vivid notes of wild strawberry and raspberry. The Satèn is equally excellent, with engaging notes of aromatic herbs and ripe pears and apples before the palate develops harmonious and rich in fresh, lively fruity tones. The Franciacorta Brut is also good, with ripe apple and apricot on the nose and a compact, caressing and juicy palate. Finally, the sound Terre di Franciacorta Rosso '04 has a bouquet of forest floor and blueberry preceding a soft, structured palate. The other labels are all reliable.

Tenuta Roveglia

LOC. ROVEGLIA, 1
25010 POZZOLENGO [BS]
TEL. 030918663
www.tenutaroveglia.it

ANNUAL PRODUCTION	200,000 bottles
HECTARES UNDER VINE	61
VITICULTURE METHOD	Conventional

The step change at Tenuta Roveglia, owned by the Zweifel Azzone family, was confirmed this year by one of the best Luganas we have tasted recently. From late-harvested trebbiano from the oldest vines in the 60 hectares of vineyards, Filo di Arianna Superiore '05 aged long on the lees in large, oak barrels and flaunts a juicily dense, engaging array of apricots and peaches weaving into a charming spicy texture that gives a glimpse of further interesting developments with a more time in bottle. With this white, Paolo Fabiani and consultant Flavio Prà seem to have begun exploring a new way of interpreting Lugana to flank with the traditional approach aimed more at fresh, immediate drinkability, which finds great expression in the Lugana '07. The Lugana Superiore Vigne di Catullo '06, again on great form, is a happy medium between the two stylistic choices. The cuve close method Lugana is also good and the Cabernet Sauvignon '05 well made.

O Franciacorta Brut	♈♈	5
⊙ Franciacorta Brut Rosé Radijan	♈♈	6
O Franciacorta Satèn	♈♈	5
● TdF Rosso '04	♈♈	5
O Franciacorta Brut '04	♈	6
O TdF Bianco '07	♈	4
O Franciacorta Brut '01	♈♈	6
● Pinot Nero L'Arturo '03	♈♈	6
● Pinot Nero L'Arturo '01	♈♈	7
O TdF Bianco '06	♈♈	4*
● TdF Rosso '03	♈♈	5

O Lugana Sup. Filo di Arianna '05	♈♈	5
O Lugana '07	♈♈	4*
O Lugana Brut	♈♈	4*
O Lugana Sup. Vigne di Catullo '06	♈♈	4*
● Garda Cabernet Sauvignon '05	♈	4
⊙ Garda Cl. Chiaretto '07	♈	4
O Lugana Sup. Vigne di Catullo '05	♈♈	4
O Lugana '06	♈♈	4
O Lugana Sup. Filo di Arianna '04	♈♈	5

San Cristoforo

VIA VILLANUOVA, 2
25030 ERBUSCO [BS]
TEL. 0307760482
www.sancristoforo.eu

ANNUAL PRODUCTION	80,000 bottles
HECTARES UNDER VINE	12
VITICULTURE METHOD	Conventional

Bruno Dotti and his wife Claudia Cavalleri are passionate about the Erbusco estate they purchased in 1992 and subsequently expanded and improved. Over the past few years there have been a few uncertainties but we have always enjoyed the cuvées from these winemakers. We are especially happy to have voted the Pas Dosé '04 into our finals on its debut release. It's a first step that bodes well for the future. This vintage has a lovely bright greenish straw-yellow colour and intense fresh aromas of apricot and white-fleshed fruit with elegant shades of Alpine hay and flowers before the palate shows solid, tangy, full and harmonious. We felt the Brut '04 was very sound, with its tones of tropical fruit typical of Chardonnay from Erbusco and caressing, vanilla-laced palate. The non-vintage Brut keeps its place in that restricted group of the best, offering a welter of soft apple and white peach and then a zesty, fresh palate. The other labels are all sound.

O Franciacorta Pas Dosé '04	▼▼ 6
O Franciacorta Brut '04	▼▼ 6
O Franciacorta Brut	▼▼ 5
● San Cristoforo Uno '04	▼ 6
O TdF Curtefranca Bianco '06	▼ 4
● TdF Curtefranca Rosso '05	▼ 4
O Franciacorta Brut '03	♀♀ 6
● Re Probus '03	♀♀ 8

Conti Sertoli Salis

VIA STELVIO, 18
23037 TIRANO [SO]
TEL. 0342710404
www.sertolisalis.com

ANNUAL PRODUCTION	250,000 bottles
HECTARES UNDER VINE	8
VITICULTURE METHOD	Conventional

Management at this beautiful, influential estate is in the hands of Roberta Dotti, the single administrator, who is an executive from Milan with origins in Valtellina. Working alongside her in vineyard and cellar is the celebrated Vittorio Fiore while Fabio Romegialli is the agronomist. The new Sforzato label, Feudo del Conte '04, has good body but is still a little masked by the oak. The spicy nose has notes of cocoa powder and the dense palate is concentrated, opening out attractively on the finish. Cherry-themed fruit and notes of dried flowers waft from the Sassella '05, heralding a round palate supported by good acidity. The Inferno '05 has good texture, clear notes of ripe red berries emerging on the nose before the soft palate progresses through to a finish enhanced by a delicious harmony of acidity and extract. Fresh floral aromas grace the Torre della Sirena, a white from pignola and rossola, has a supple palate with savoury notes.

● Valtellina Sforzato Feudo dei Conti '04	▼▼ 8
● Valtellina Sup. Inferno '05	▼▼ 5
● Valtellina Sup. Sassella '05	▼▼ 4*
O Torre della Sirena '07	▼ 4
● Valtellina Sforzato Canua '99	♀♀♀ 6
● Valtellina Sforzato Canua '97	♀♀♀ 6
● Valtellina Sforzato Canua '02	♀♀♀ 7
● Valtellina Sforzato Canua '01	♀♀♀ 7
● Valtellina Sforzato Canua '00	♀♀♀ 6
● Valtellina Sup. Sassella '03	♀♀ 4

Lo Sparviere

VIA COSTA, 2
25040 MONTICELLI BRUSATI [BS]
TEL. 030652382
www.losparviere.com

ANNUAL PRODUCTION	120,000 bottles
HECTARES UNDER VINE	30
VITICULTURE METHOD	Conventional

The Gussalli Beretta family, one of the oldest industrial dynasties in Europe, owns this beautiful estate in Monticelli Brusati, where it has 30 hectares under vine. Oenologist Francesco Polastri again this year presented us with some fine wines and cuvées. The most interesting of these in our tastings was the Franciacorta Brut '04. If the greenish straw colour and tiny, continuous bubbles already tell you that this is a seriously good wine, then the complex nose you find in the glass will cancel any remaining doubt. Lemon blossom, pears, apples, faint vegetality vein and an intriguing touch of fresh oregano all go into a complex, vivid bouquet that finds its perfect match in a rich, solid palate, with appealing freshness and graceful fruit tones as well as a long vanillaed finish. The Rosé has a pale rosy flesh complexion and a palate with youthful energy and rich black and red berry pulp. Among the best Curtefrancas from '05 is Cacciatore, which has intense red berry fruit, pleasant structure and plenty of well-honed extract. The other wines are well made and up to par for this designation.

Travaglino

LOC. TRAVAGLINO, 6A
27040 CALVIGNANO [PV]
TEL. 0383872222
www.travaglino.it

ANNUAL PRODUCTION	220,000 bottles
HECTARES UNDER VINE	80
VITICULTURE METHOD	Conventional

Fabrizio Marzi's Classese '04 is very good indeed. It tempts right from the luscious gold hue and bright tiny bubbles in the glass. There are aromas of baking, Sicilian cannolo cakes and fruit leading into a ripe, balanced palate with a fresh attack and lingering finish. This is a great example of a classic method Pinot Nero from Oltrepò. The Riesling Campo della Fojada '07 is as good as ever. Calvignano lies in the heart of the newly created Valle del Riesling, a zone with white soil well suited to this variety, and the '07 expresses the usual, unmistakable aromas of sage, mint and rosemary. It has a nice minerality, plenty of backbone and structure and shows a quality finish. Also excellent is the Brut Rosé Monteceresino shows, which presents a typical deep onionskin hue with an unmistakable pinot nero nose and a meaty, fresh palate. The Poggio della Buttinera '03 missed on the flesh and freshness as this Pinot Nero fermented on the skins has good structure but suffered somewhat from the hot growing year. The Pinot Nero Pernero '07 is good, fresh and varietal while the Brut Grand Cuvée is pleasant and well made but lacks a little length.

○ Franciacorta Brut '04	♉♉ 5
⊙ Franciacorta Rosé Brut	♉♉ 6
● TdF Rosso Il Cacciatore '05	♉♉ 4*
○ Franciacorta Satèn	♉ 5
○ Passito Esperidio	♉ 6
○ TdF Curtefranca Bianco '07	♉ 4
● TdF Curtefranca Rosso '06	♉ 4
○ Franciacorta Extra Brut '01	♈♈ 6
○ Franciacorta Brut '03	♈♈ 5

○ OP Pinot Nero Brut Classese '04	♉♉ 5
⊙ OP Pinot Nero Brut Rosé Monteceresino	♉♉ 5
○ OP Riesling Campo della Fojada '07	♉♉ 4
○ OP Pinot Nero Grand Cuvée	♉ 5
● OP Pinot Nero Pernero '07	♉ 4
● OP Pinot Nero Poggio della Buttinera '03	♉ 6
○ OP Pinot Nero Brut Classese '03	♈♈ 5
○ OP Pinot Nero Brut Classese '01	♈♈ 5
○ OP Riesling Campo della Fojada '06	♈♈ 4
○ OP Riesling Campo della Fojada '05	♈♈ 4

Triacca

VIA NAZIONALE, 121
23030 VILLA DI TIRANO [SO]
TEL. 0342701352
www.triacca.com

ANNUAL PRODUCTION	700,000 bottles
HECTARES UNDER VINE	47
VITICULTURE METHOD	Conventional

We were impressed by Prestigio '04. One of the finest examples of a nebbiolo-based wine here in the variety's Valtellina enclave, it has elegance and a clear sense of place. Made by drying the grapes directly on cut canes, it unveils spicy, violet and floral aromas on the nose before the palate delivers harmonious flavour, fragrant acidity and a long finish. The Sforzato San Domenico '04 shows classic pepper and saddle leather while the palate is elegant with soft, velvety tannins. The Riserva La Gatta '03 has dried fruit with tobacco sensations on the nose and a well-rounded palate with balanced acidity. Sassella '05 has fruity, clean aromas, slightly grassy tones on the palate and signs off with a hint of almondiness. The down to earth, fruit-forward nose of Casa La Gatta '05 introduces a supple palate of medium intensity. The Grumello '05's elegant, characteristic aromas precede a palate with a confident attack and long, spirited finish. The nice Inferno '05 has notes of tobacco and tar leading into a soft palate with well-integrated acidity. The sauvignon-based white Del Frate '06 gives fragrant aromas and savouriness in the mouth.

● Valtellina Sup. Prestigio '04	♟♟	7
○ Sauvignon Del Frate '06	♟♟	6
● Valtellina Sforzato San Domenico '04	♟♟	7
● Valtellina Sup. Grumello '05	♟♟	5
● Valtellina Sup. Inferno '05	♟♟	5
● Valtellina Sup. La Gatta Ris. '03	♟♟	6
● Valtellina Sup. Casa La Gatta '05	♟	5
● Valtellina Sup. Sassella '05	♟	5
● Valtellina Prestigio Millennium '97	♟♟♟	5
● Valtellina Sforzato '99	♟♟♟	6
● Valtellina Sforzato '00	♟♟♟	7
● Valtellina Sforzato San Domenico '03	♟♟♟	7
● Valtellina Sforzato San Domenico '01	♟♟♟	7

★ Uberti

LOC. SALEM
VIA E. FERMI, 2
25030 ERBUSCO [BS]
TEL. 0307267476
www.ubertivini.it

ANNUAL PRODUCTION	170,000 bottles
HECTARES UNDER VINE	24
VITICULTURE METHOD	Conventional

With a well-deserved Three Glasses for the now famous cuvée Comarì del Salem '03, the Ubertis achieved the 13th success of their career, underlining how important this family operation at Erbusco is. With her degree in oenology and significant experience abroad, Agostino and Eleonora's daughter Silvia works alongside her parents and shows she has not just their skill but also their passion for wine and Franciacorta in particular. The Comarì '03 has complex aromas of tropical fruit and soft notes of vanilla and oak on the nose before offering up imposing yet complex structure that makes the palate fresh, supple and enjoyable, supported by an elegant acid note that fades into minerality on the satisfyingly long finish. Non Dosato Sublimis '02 has great finesse, complexity and clarity of fruit and the Magnificentia is again an excellent Blanc de Blancs this year. The Franciacortas from the Francesco I line and the estate's still wines are all very sound.

○ Franciacorta Extra Brut Comarì del Salem '03	♟♟♟	7
○ Franciacorta Non Dosato Sublimis '02	♟♟	7
○ Franciacorta Brut Francesco I	♟♟	6
○ Franciacorta Satèn Magnificentia	♟♟	6
○ TdF Bianco Maria Medici '06	♟♟	5
○ Franciacorta Extra Brut Francesco I	♟	6
☉ Franciacorta Rosé Francesco I	♟	6
● Rosso dei Frati Priori '05	♟	6
○ TdF Bianco '07	♟	4
● TdF Rosso '06	♟	4
○ Franciacorta Brut Comarì del Salem '00	♟♟♟	7
○ Franciacorta Extra Brut Comarì del Salem '02	♟♟♟	7
○ Franciacorta Extra Brut Comarì del Salem '01	♟♟♟	7

Vercesi del Castellazzo

VIA AURELIANO, 36
27040 MONTÙ BECCARIA [PV]
TEL. 038560067
vercesidelcastellazzo@libero.it

ANNUAL PRODUCTION	80,000 bottles
HECTARES UNDER VINE	15
VITICULTURE METHOD	Conventional

The best Bonarda Fatila ever went straight to the Three Glass finals. The '03 version is garnet-tinged ruby with a beautifully complex, elegant nose with ripe wild berries and balsam. All this returns in perfect harmony in the mouth, where the remarkable structure supports a weave of fine-grained tannins through to a great fruity finish. The good-value Pezzalunga '07 is fragrant with nice intact fruit. Even more of this intact fruit is found in the Bonarda Vivace Luogo della Milla '07, one of the best from the vintage with notes of wild berries, balance and length, as well as in the Barbera Clà '06, which struggles more to open but then reveals typicity and drinkability. The Pinot Nero Luogo Dei Monti '98 is a newcomer to the Guide which shows the potential of this variety in Oltrepò. Nearly ten years after the harvest, it is evolved yet still flaunts acid backbone and balance. Fermented exclusively from the indigenous variety called vespolina, Vespolino '07 is simple and pleasant with the upfront spicy notes typical of the variety. The Pinot Nero fermented off the skins Gugiarolo '07 is quite fresh and pleasant.

● OP Bonarda Fatila '03	♙♙	5
● OP Barbera Clà '06	♙♙	4*
● OP Bonarda Luogo della Milla '07	♙♙	3*
● OP Pinot Nero Luogo dei Monti '98	♙♙	4*
● OP Rosso Pezzalunga '07	♙♙	3*
○ OP Pinot Nero in Bianco Gugiarolo '07	♙	3
● Vespolino '07	♙	3
● Rosso del Castellazzo '03	♟♟	5
● OP Bonarda Fatila '00	♟♟	5
● OP Rosso Pezzalunga '06	♟♟	3*
● Vespolino '06	♟♟	3*

Bruno Verdi

VIA VERGOMBERRA, 5
27044 CANNETO PAVESE [PV]
TEL. 038588023
www.verdibruno.it

ANNUAL PRODUCTION	100,000 bottles
HECTARES UNDER VINE	9
VITICULTURE METHOD	Conventional

This is the fourth year in a row that Paolo Verdi's OP Rosso Riserva Cavariola has reached the finals. We may have to invent an award. The '05 is again recognizable for marked balsamic notes that enhance the ripe fruit before the hefty but stylish weave of the tannins takes you through to a balanced finish. It still needs a bit of bottle age to bring out all its great potential. The Barbera Campo del Marrone '06 is as good as ever, with a cherry, spice and chocolate bouquet followed by a taut palate. Since the Vergomberra Brut '05 was not yet ready, we tasted a recently disgorged Jeroboam from '00. Full and balanced, with nice aromas of flowers and cakes, it still has loads of energy. The two sweet wines, Moscato di Volpara and Sangue di Giuda '07, are as well made as ever. The first has touches of meringue and classic citrussy notes whereas the second unearths woodland sensations of berries and truffles. There's the same clean, chewiness on the Bonarda Frizzante '07 and the interesting Pinot Nero '06 is full-flavoured and varietal. The Pinot Grigio '07 has floral fragrances and the Riesling Vigna Costa '07 is better on the palate than the nose.

● OP Rosso Cavariola Ris. '05	♙♙	5
● OP Barbera Campo del Marrone '06	♙♙	4*
● OP Bonarda Vivace Possessione di Vergombera '07	♙♙	4*
○ OP Moscato Volpara '07	♙♙	3*
○ OP Pinot Grigio '07	♙♙	4*
● OP Pinot Nero '06	♙♙	4*
● OP Sangue di Giuda Dolce Paradiso '07	♙♙	3*
○ OP Riesling Renano V. Costa '07	♙	4
● OP Rosso Cavariola Ris. '04	♟♟	5
● OP Rosso Cavariola Ris. '03	♟♟	5
● OP Rosso Cavariola Ris. '02	♟♟	5
○ OP Moscato Volpara '06	♟♟	3*
● OP Pinot Nero '05	♟♟	4
● OP Sangue di Giuda Dolce Paradiso '06	♟♟	3*

Giuseppe Vezzoli

VIA COSTA SOPRA, 22
25030 ERBUSCO [BS]
TEL. 0307267579
eveniogv@libero.it

ANNUAL PRODUCTION 130,000 bottles
HECTARES UNDER VINE 40
VITICULTURE METHOD Conventional

The most interesting cuvée presented this year by Giuseppe Vezzoli was an Extra Brut, Nefertiti Dizeta '02. It has a bright, greenish straw-yellow hue and small, fine bubbles that linger. The nose opens on sensations of ripe white-fleshed fruit like golden apples and peach, swirling into more evolved, almost tertiary, notes of oak and minerals. In contrast, the palate reprises bright, clear fruit that spreads out in a broad structure and closes with attractive youthful hints of mint. The supple, stylish Franciacorta Satèn flaunts juicy tones of ripe fruit on the nose and palate, where it offers up lovely acid backbone that supports the complex, rich structure. The Franciacorta Brut is also excellent, showing slightly reduced on the nose at first but then opening into complex, satisfying aromas of fruits and minerality before the savoury palate expands over good structure. We thought the Nefertiti Brut '02 seemed a bit under par, however, with rather evolved characteristics and fruit that lacked underlying intensity. The Rosé is well typed but not that exciting.

Villa

VIA VILLA, 12
25040 MONTICELLI BRUSATI [BS]
TEL. 030652329
www.villa-franciacorta.it

ANNUAL PRODUCTION 320,000 bottles
HECTARES UNDER VINE 37
VITICULTURE METHOD Conventional

The list from Paolo Bianchi's estate was still quite impressive but the quality of terroir and vineyards, the lovely, modern cellar in its medieval village and the excellent staff make us hope for something more. We think this operation can aspire to greater things but for now we'll console ourselves with the excellent Satèn '04. This delightful bottle offers complex aromas of butter, yeast and white-fleshed fruit wrapped in appealing aromatic herbs. The palate is solid yet restrained, showing harmonious, elegant and well balanced. The Brut from the same vintage has sweet cake and ripe fruit notes introducing a vanillaed palate with juicy fruit. This is supported by a clear acid note that fades out harmonious and elegant on hints of citrus, mint and flowers. The Rosé Demi Sec '04 is one of the few convincing examples of this type and derives its charm from a controlled sweetness that never dulls the fresh notes of blueberry and wild strawberries on both nose and palate. The Brut Cuvette '03 is stylish, mineral and pleasantly harmonious and the red blackberry-themed Gradoni '05 has nice structure and tannins. The other labels are sound.

O Franciacorta Brut '04	▼▼ 6
O Franciacorta Extra Brut Nefertiti Dizeta '02	▼▼ 7
O Franciacorta Satèn '04	▼▼ 6
O Franciacorta Brut Nefertiti '02	▼ 7
⊙ Franciacorta Rosé	▼ 6
O Franciacorta Brut '99	♈♈ 6
O Franciacorta Brut '01	♈♈ 6
O Franciacorta Brut '03	♈♈ 6
O Franciacorta Brut Nefertiti '00	♈♈ 7

O Franciacorta Brut '04	▼▼ 5
O Franciacorta Brut Cuvette '03	▼▼ 6
⊙ Franciacorta Rosé Demi Sec '04	▼▼ 6
O Franciacorta Satèn '04	▼▼ 6
● TdF Rosso Gradoni '05	▼▼ 5
O TdF Bianco '06	▼ 4
O TdF Bianco Pian della Villa '06	▼ 4
● TdF Rosso '05	▼ 4
● TdF Rosso Anno Santo '00	▼ 6
O Franciacorta Extra Brut '98	♈♈♈ 5*
O Franciacorta Brut '02	♈♈ 5*
O Franciacorta Brut '01	♈♈ 5*
O Franciacorta Extra Brut '99	♈♈ 5
O Franciacorta Satèn	♈♈ 6
O TdF Bianco Pian della Villa '05	♈♈ 4

Villa Crespia - F.lli Muratori

VIA VALLI, 11
25030 ADRO [BS]
TEL. 0307451051
www.fratellimuratori.com

ANNUAL PRODUCTION	400,000 bottles
HECTARES UNDER VINE	60
VITICULTURE METHOD	Conventional

The Muratori brothers are entrepreneurs from Brescia with a passion for wine. They have turned that passion into a business by entrusting Professor Francesco Iacono with an ambitious project to set up a chain of top winemaking estates in Lombardy, Tuscany and Campania. Faithful to the principle of "one terroir, one wine", Iacono has dedicated Villa Crespia in Franciacorta exclusively to sparklers he makes in numerous versions from different vineyards planted according to in-depth zoning studies of the area. From the Cisiolo di Adro vineyard comes a Pinot Nero cuvée of refined elegance, which in the '03 vintage has backbone, classic elegance and mineral complexity worthy of the best Blanc de Noirs and went through to our finals. In contrast, the Satèn Brut Cesonato is an excellent Chardonnay with soft, opulent tones. The Extra Brut Brolese is a Rosé with appealing tones of wild strawberries and raspberries on both nose and palate while Numerozero is a Dosage Zero of Chardonnay from vineyards in several locations that gives elegant, intact fruit. The other labels, Brut Miolo and Novalia, are sound. Both are Blanc de Blancs.

○ Franciacorta Dosaggio Zero Cisiolo '03	♈	6
○ Franciacorta Dosaggio Zero Numerozero	♈	6
⊙ Franciacorta Rosé Extra Brut Brolese	♈	7
○ Franciacorta Satèn Brut Cesonato	♈	6
○ Franciacorta Brut Miolo	♈	6
○ Franciacorta Brut Novalia	♈	6
⊙ Franciacorta Brolese Rosé Extra Brut '02	♈♈	8
○ Franciacorta Dosaggio Zero Cisiolo '02	♈♈	5

Chiara Ziliani

VIA FRANCIACORTA, 7
25050 PROVAGLIO D'ISEO [BS]
TEL. 030981661
www.cantinazilianichiara.it

ANNUAL PRODUCTION	210,000 bottles
HECTARES UNDER VINE	22
VITICULTURE METHOD	Conventional

Chiara Ziliani's lovely estate is one of the DOCG's most interesting new operations. Chiara has a fairly small winemaking concern comprising a modern cellar and more than 20 hectares of well-positioned vineyards on a morainic hill at Provaglio d'Iseo. Franciacorta Satèn is the workhorse wine in the stable for Chiara makes three well-crafted versions that merit a full profile in the Guide. The vintage Ziliani C '04 has a lovely bright greenish straw-yellow colour, complex aromas of ripe fruit that shade into antique wood, beeswax and vanilla, and a palate layered with citrus tones that signs off with wispily complex hints of roast coffee beans. The Satèn Conte di Provaglio is clear, fragrant and juicy in its flower and fruit on both nose and palate, where it expands savoury and fresh on notes of apple, white peach and aromatic herbs. Finally, the Satèn Duca d'Iseo has round, soft touches of butter and cakes on the nose, recovers backbone and freshness on the palate and ends crunchy, clear and long on wings of fruit. The two Bruts and Terre di Franciacorta Bianco '07 are good.

○ Franciacorta Satèn Conte di Provaglio	♈	5
○ Franciacorta Satèn Duca d'Iseo	♈	5
○ Franciacorta Satèn Ziliani C '04	♈	5
○ Franciacorta Brut Conte di Provaglio	♈	5
○ Franciacorta Brut Ziliani C	♈	5
○ TdF Bianco '07	♈	4

OTHER WINERIES

Al Rocol

VIA PROVINCIALE, 79
25050 OME [BS]
TEL. 0306852542
www.alrocol.com

From nine hectares under vine at Ome, Gianluigi Vimercati produces various Franciacortas and territory wines. We tasted an excellent Franciacorta Ca' del Luf '04 with vibrant freshness and rich fruit, a Satèn Martignac with soft, slightly evolved tones, and a sound Terre di Franciacorta Rosso Roncat '05.

O Franciacorta Brut Ca' del Luf '04	⟡⟡ 5
● TdF Roncat '05	⟡⟡ 5
O Franciacorta Satèn Martignac	⟡ 5

Riccardo Albani

LOC. CASONA
S.DA SAN BIAGIO, 46
27045 CASTEGGIO [PV]
TEL. 038383622
www.vinialbani.it

The Riesling '06 shows the evolved notes, savouriness, minerality and structure of a classic natural wine. The OP Rosso Costa del Morone '04 has lashings of fruit but lacks a bit of balance. The curious Delibes is a sweet wine from croatina with good length.

O OP Riesling Renano '06	⟡⟡ 4
O Delibes	⟡ 5
● OP Rosso Costa del Morone '04	⟡ 4

Castello degli Angeli

VIA SCALETTE
24060 CAROBBIO DEGLI ANGELI [BG]
TEL. 035951056
www.castellodegliangeli.com

Prescelto is a curious table wine, a dry vinified Moscato Bianco aged in 190-litre barrels. The result is odd yet appealing. Valcalepio Rosso Barbariccia '05 has a fruity body that has difficulty emerging from under the generous oak. The Chardonnay Estereta '06 is good and clean.

O Il Prescelto	⟡⟡ 8
O Estereta '06	⟡ 6
● Valcalepio Rosso Barbariccia '05	⟡ 6

Tenuta degli Angeli

FRAZ. SANTO STEFANO
VIA FARA, 2
24060 CAROBBIO DEGLI ANGELI [BG]
TEL. 035687130
www.tenutadegliangeli.it

Valcalepio Bianco Triplok '07 is well made with a complex, elegant nose and fresh, clean palate. The curious Valcalepio Moscato Passito '05 has clear notes of cakes and stewed prunes. The two classic method sparklers are well executed. We just preferred the slightly more expressive Extra Brut '01.

O Valcalepio Bianco Triplok '07	⟡⟡ 4
● Valcalepio Moscato Passito '05	⟡⟡ 7
O Spumante Brut Cl. degli Angeli '02	⟡ 5
O Spumante Extra Brut Cl. degli Angeli '01	⟡ 5

Antica Tesa

LOC. MATTINA
VIA MERANO, 28
25080 BOTTICINO [BS]
TEL. 0302691500

The Noventa family defends the honour of this small DOC zone with a Botticino Gobbio '04 from old vineyards that shows body, finesse and complexity. Pià della Tesa '05 is also sound with blackberry aromas and good body. We felt Vigna degli Ulivi '05 was decent with a fresher, suppler style.

● Botticino Pià della Tesa '05	⟡⟡ 5
● Botticino Vigna del Gobbio '04	⟡⟡ 6
● Botticino Vigna degli Ulivi '05	⟡ 4

Avanzi

VIA TREVISAGO, 19
25080 MANERBA DEL GARDA [BS]
TEL. 0365551013
www.avanzi.net

The Avanzi family makes excellent Garda wines both in the Lugana DOC, especially the Superiore '06, and Valtenesi, where reds prevail, especially those based on the indigenous groppello. Vigna Bragagna '04, a Cabernet from Garda territory, is enjoyable.

● Garda Cabernet Sauvignon V. Bragagna '04	⟡⟡ 5
● Garda Cl. Groppello Giovanni Avanzi '07	⟡⟡ 4*
O Lugana Sup. Sirmione '06	⟡⟡ 4
● Garda Cl. Sup. Rosso '06	⟡ 4

OTHER WINERIES

Luciano Barberini

VIA EMILIA, 93
27050 REDAVALLE [PV]
TEL. 038574164
www.barberinilucianovini.it

The IGT Castlà '06 is from a croatina base with a small amount of pinot nero that softens its aggressiveness. The La Gatta '05 50-50 blend from cabernet sauvignon and barbera is not that precise on the nose but satisfies in the mouth. Riesling La Morena '07 is varietal and mature.

● Castlà '06	🍷🍷 4
● La Gatta '05	🍷 4
O OP Riesling La Morena '07	🍷 4

Barboglio De Gaioncelli

FRAZ. COLOMBARO
VIA NAZARIO SAURO
25040 CORTE FRANCA [BS]
TEL. 0309826831
www.barbogliodegaioncelli.it

The Costa family's 15 hectares of lovely vineyards at Corte Franca yield good grapes for their cuvées. This year, we liked the Rosé Donna Alberta with fresh wild berry aromas, a Terre di Franciacorta Bianco with good structure and balance, and a fascinating Franciacorta Extra Dry with measured sweetness.

⊙ Franciacorta Rosé Donna Alberta	🍷🍷 4
O TdF Curtefranca Bianco '07	🍷🍷 3*
O Franciacorta Extra Dry	🍷 4

F.lli Bettini

LOC. SAN GIACOMO
VIA NAZIONALE, 4A
23036 TEGLIO [SO]
TEL. 0342786068
bettvini@tin.it

The Sfursat '05 has dried fruit aromas, dense structure and concentration, the extract interweaving with balanced acidity. Inferno Prodigio '04 interprets the territory with clean aromas of violets and flowers, showing round and long in the mouth. The even Sassella Reale '05 shows elegant aromas.

● Valtellina Sfursat '05	🍷🍷 7
● Valtellina Sup. Inferno Prodigio '04	🍷🍷 5
● Valtellina Sup. Sassella Reale '05	🍷 5

Conti Bettoni Cazzago

VIA MARCONI, 6
25046 CAZZAGO SAN MARTINO [BS]
TEL. 0307750875
www.contibettonicazzago.it

The Satèn from Vincenzo Bettoni Cazzago is very good this year. It has elegant florality and a sweet, well-gauged palate, signing off with precise fruit and vanilla. Brut Tetellus '04 is enjoyable for its solid, well-profiled body, complex, evolved aromas and intriguing minerality on the back palate.

O Franciacorta Brut Satèn	🍷🍷 6
O Franciacorta Brut Tetellus '04	🍷🍷 7

Bonaldi - Cascina del Bosco

LOC. PETOSINO
VIA GASPAROTTO, 96
24010 SORISOLE [BG]
TEL. 035571701
www.cascinadelbosco.it

The Valcalepio Rosso Riserva Cantoalto '04 is a great wine with structure, impact, slightly overripe fruit and a long finish. The Metodo Classico sparkler is well crafted, fresh and clean, with crisp acidity. The old style Valcalepio Rosso '06 shows pronounced yet attractively fine-grained tannins.

● Valcalepio Rosso Cantoalto Ris. '04	🍷🍷 5
O Bonaldi Brut M. Cl.	🍷 5
● Valcalepio Rosso '06	🍷 3

Borgo La Caccia

LOC. CACCIA, 1
25010 POZZOLENGO [BS]
TEL. 0309916044
www.borgolacaccia.it

Borgo La Caccia is a new operation on the border between the provinces of Brescia and Mantua. This co-operative farm concentrates on grape growing, prevalently international varieties, and raising horses. The Pinot Nero '05 is the stand-out on the list of wines, all IGT from Alto Mantovano.

● Pinot Nero '05	🍷🍷 6
● Aurelio Merlot '04	🍷 5
● Carmenoire '04	🍷 6
● Nerone Cabernet Sauvignon '03	🍷 6

OTHER WINERIES

Borgo La Gallinaccia

VIA IV NOVEMBRE, 15
25050 RODENGO SAIANO [BS]
TEL. 030611314
www.borgolagallinaccia.it

This small Rodengo Saiano estate makes excellent wines. We noted a Satèn with elegant floral aromas and a fresh, supple palate rich in fruit. The Franciacorta Brut has an enjoyably invigorating structure and overall cleanliness. We also thought the Bordeaux Colmo dei Colmi '05 was good.

● Colmo dei Colmi '05	￥￥	5
○ Franciacorta Satèn	￥￥	5
○ Franciacorta Brut	￥	5

La Boscaiola

VIA RICCAFANA, 19
25033 COLOGNE [BS]
TEL. 0307156386
www.laboscaiola.com

Giuliana Cenci produces excellent wines and Franciacortas at her beautiful family estate in Cologne. We enjoyed a Satèn with clear sensations of white-fleshed fruit and a juicy, vanilla palate, a Brut with comforting complexity, and a pleasant Terre di Franciacorta Bianco Giuliana C. '06.

○ Franciacorta Satén Brut	￥￥	6
○ Franciacorta Brut	￥	5
○ TdF Bianco Giuliana C. '06	￥	4

Boschi

VIA ISEO, 76
25030 ERBUSCO [BS]
TEL. 03077245
www.agricolaboschi.it

The owner and symbol of this Franciacorta winery, Franco Timoteo Metelli presents a wide range of labels with plenty of territory products. This year, we point out a Franciacorta Brut '00, with opulent tropical fruit aromas and a soft palate, and a well-structured Terre di Franciacorta Rosso '04.

○ Franciacorta Brut '00	￥￥	7
● TdF Rosso '04	￥	4

Tenuta Il Bosco

LOC. IL BOSCO
27049 ZENEVREDO [PV]
TEL. 0385245326
www.ilbosco.it

Always one of the best around, the Bonarda Vivace '07 from Tenuta Il Bosco shows perfectly integrated fruit and balance. The Pinot Nero Poggio Pelato '05 has potential but has yet to mature. The two Martinotti-method Philèos are well made with red berry fruit for the Rosé and cake for the white.

● OP Bonarda Vivace '07	￥￥	4*
○ OP Pinot Nero Brut Martinotti Philèo	￥	4
● OP Pinot Nero Poggio Pelato '05	￥	4
⊙ Phileo Rosè Extra Dry	￥	4

Bosio

LOC. TIMOLINE
VIA MARIO GATTI
25040 CORTE FRANCA [BS]
TEL. 030984398
www.bosiofranciacorta.it

Only lack of space prevents us from saying more about Cesare Bosio's 30-hectare estate at Corte Franca and a sound range of products. The best this year was the Extra Brut Boschedòr '04 with complex ripe fruit and citrus peel aromas and a harmonious palate. The Satèn is also sound.

○ Franciacorta Extra Brut		
Boschedòr '04	￥￥	5
○ Franciacorta Satèn	￥￥	5

Bredasole

LOC. BREDASOLE
VIA SAN PIETRO, 44
25030 PARATICO [BS]
TEL. 035910407
www.bredasole.it

The Ferrari brothers produce wines and Franciacortas with consultancy from oenologist Corrado Cugnasco. The sound Pas Dosé '04 is floral on the nose and harmonious on the palate. The pleasant Satèn has delicate fruit and flower hints on the nose and a supple, balanced palate.

○ Franciacorta Pas Dosé '04	￥￥	5
○ Franciacorta Satèn	￥	5

OTHER WINERIES

Luciano Brega

FRAZ. BERGAMASCO, 7
27040 MONTÙ BECCARIA [PV]
TEL. 038560237
www.lucianobrega.it

Bonarda Casapaia '06 has good fruit, well-controlled tannins and flavoursome body. The very drinkable Bonarda Vivace '07 is also good, with fragrant raspberry and blueberry aromas. The Gran Montù Rosé is a classic method with upfront fruit.

● OP Bonarda Casapaia '06	♟♟ 4*
● OP Bonarda Vivace '07	♟♟ 3
⊙ Gran Montù Brut Rosé	♟ 5

Cantina Sociale di Broni

VIA SANSALUTO, 81
27043 BRONI [PV]
TEL. 038551505
cantinasocialebroni@tin.it

The Barbera Bronis Selezione '05 has nice crunch, clean fruit and good overall balance. The Bonarda Bronis Selezione '07 has a raspberry and strawberry bouquet and clean tannins. The two classic method sparklers are also good, although we preferred the Rosé, which reveals backbone and substance.

● OP Barbera Bronis Sel. '05	♟♟ 3*
● OP Bonarda Bronis Sel. '07	♟♟ 3*
O OP Pinot Nero Brut Classese	♟ 4
⊙ OP Pinot Nero Brut Rosè '03	♟ 4

La Brugherata

FRAZ. ROSCIATE
VIA G. MEDOLAGO, 47
24020 SCANZOROSCIATE [BG]
TEL. 035655202
www.labrugherata.it

Moscato di Scanzo Passito Doge '05 is outstanding with its red berries, nice structure and depth. The Valcalepio Bianco Vescovado del Feudo '07 shows minerals and lovely apricots and peaches. The Valcalepio Rosso Doglio Riserva '04 still has to mature. The Valcalepio Rosso Vescovado '06 is well typed.

● Moscato di Scanzo Passito Doge '05	♟♟ 8
O Valcalepio Bianco Vescovado del Feudo '07	♟♟ 4
● Valcalepio Rosso Doglio Ris. '04	♟ 5
● Valcalepio Rosso Vescovado '06	♟ 4

Tenuta Cà Boffenisio

VIA BOFFENISIO, 3
27040 BORGO PRIOLO [PV]
TEL. 0383871149
info@caboffenisio.it

There are still a few things to sort out on Maria Adele Galanti's estate but we are certain that with her energy, good results will surely come. The still Bonarda '04 is well made and spicy. Iperbole '06 is an IGT Pinot Nero with rather evolved notes.

● OP Bonarda '04	♟♟ 4
● Iperbole '06	♟ 5

Ca' del Gè

FRAZ. CA' DEL GÈ, 3
27040 MONTALTO PAVESE [PV]
TEL. 0383870179
www.cadelge.it

Montalto is the land of Riesling. We choose two interpretations from the Padroggi family estate. The Filagn Long '07 is a fragrant, well-made Riesling Italico with structure and length. The base Riesling Italico '07 is also good.

O OP Riesling Italico Filagn Long '07	♟♟ 3*
O OP Riesling Italico '07	♟ 2

Ca' del Santo

LOC. CAMPOLUNGO, 4
27040 MONTALTO PAVESE [PV]
TEL. 0383870545
www.cadelsanto.it

Carlo Saviotti and Laura Bozzi always work well. The Bonarda Vivace Grand Cuvée '07 is balanced and fragrant with violet aromas. The Riesling Rivalunga '06 is zesty, minerally and mature. The dried-grape Muscà '06 Moscato has a lovely fruity base and lacks only a touch of acid thrust.

● OP Bonarda Vivace Grand Cuvée '07	♟♟ 4*
O OP Riesling Italico Rivalunga '06	♟♟ 3*
O Muscà	♟♟ 3

OTHER WINERIES

Ca' Montebello

LOC. MONTEBELLO, 10
27040 CIGOGNOLA [PV]
TEL. 038585182
www.camontebello.it

The Scarani family's Pinot Nero '07 is varietal and fruity. Lovely red berries and balsamic notes emerge on the nose of the Barbera '06 with good backbone and balance on the palate and a fairly sustained finish. The Bonarda Frizzante '07 is pleasant, giving violets and roses as well as well-gauged tannins.

● OP Pinot Nero '07		▼▼ 3*
● OP Barbera '06		▼ 3
● OP Bonarda Frizzante '07		▼ 3

Ca' Tessitori

VIA MATTEOTTI, 15
27043 BRONI [PV]
TEL. 038551495
www.catessitori.it

The Barbera Marona '06 from Luigi Giorgi has solid structure, good backbone and a spectrum of aromatics from wild berries to balsam. The classic method sparkler is pleasing and balanced. Borghesa '07 is simple with excellent drinkability and the varietal Bonarda Frizzante '07 has a wealth of extract.

● OP Barbera Marona '06		▼▼ 4
○ OP Pinot Nero Cl. Brut		▼▼ 5
● OP Bonarda Frizzante '07		▼ 4
● OP Rosso Borghesa '07		▼ 4

Calvi

FRAZ. VIGALONE, 13
27044 CANNETO PAVESE [PV]
TEL. 038560034
www.andreacalvi.it

Andrea Calvi's Bonarda '07 has flower-led perceptions, lovely colour and overall balance. The typical Pinot Grigio '07 shows notes of citron and tangerine. The classic method Pinot Nero Brut has nice bubbles, toasty notes and a citrussy finish.

● OP Bonarda '07		▼ 3
○ OP Pinot Nero Brut		▼ 5
○ Pinot Grigio '07		▼ 3

Caminella

VIA DANTE ALIGHIERI, 13
24069 CENATE SOTTO [BG]
TEL. 035941828
www.caminella.it

Caminella only submitted table wines. Luna Rossa '06 from cabernet, merlot and pinot nero is soft and pleasant. Verde Luna '06, a chardonnay, sauvignon blanc and pinot bianco mix, shows nice oak and good fruit. The Goccio di Sole '06, from part-dried moscato di Scanzo, and sparkling Ripa di Luna '04 are decent.

● Luna Rossa '06		▼▼ 5
○ Verde Luna Bianco '06		▼▼ 4
● Goccio di Sole '06		▼ 6
○ Ripa di Luna Brut '04		▼ 5

Camossi

VIA METELLI, 5
25030 ERBUSCO [BS]
TEL. 0307268022
azvitcamossi@yahoo.it

This lovely Erbusco estate makes its Guide debut with an excellent Satèn. It has a complex, elegant nose of spring flowers, ripe peach and vanilla and a supple, elegant palate. The Franciacorta Brut is fresh, well made, supple and lively.

○ Franciacorta Satèn		▼▼ 4
○ Franciacorta Brut		▼ 5

Carlozadra

VIA GANDOSSI, 13
24064 GRUMELLO DEL MONTE [BG]
TEL. 035830244

The pleasant Extra Dry Liberty by Carlo Zadra shows restrained residual sugar, tropical fruit aromas, freshness and good length. The Brut from the '03 vintage, from chardonnay, pinot bianco and nero sourced from Trentino, has evolved tones as well as backbone and substance.

○ Carlozadra Cl. Brut '03		▼▼ 5
○ Carlozadra Extra Dry Liberty		▼▼ 5

OTHER WINERIES

Cascina Gnocco

FRAZ. LOSANA, 20
27040 MORNICO LOSANA [PV]
TEL. 0383892280
www.cascinagnocco.it

Nino Cuneo chooses to vinify only grapes from Mornico and the facts prove him right. Orione '06 has a unique, complex range of aromas, structure and soft tannins. The Bonarda '07 is built in the traditional style and the decent Moscato Adagetto is varietal.

● Orione '06	♈ 6
○ Moscato Adagetto '07	♈ 3
● OP Bonarda '07	♈ 3

Cascina San Pietro

FRAZ. CALINO DI CAZZAGO SAN MARTINO
VIA SAN PIETRO, 30
25040 CAZZAGO SAN MARTINO [BS]
TEL. 035912448
www.cascinaspietro.it

Giuseppe Pecis delivers good quality and presents a broad range of Franciacortas and wines from the territory. This year, we felt the Satèn was very good with butter, milk and vanilla aromas. The palate shows rich fruity pulp and is, as it should be, soft and harmonious. The Franciacorta Brut is sound.

○ Franciacorta Satèn	♈ 5
○ Franciacorta Brut	♈ 5

Tenimenti Castelrotto - Torti

FRAZ. CASTELROTTO, 6
27047 MONTECALVO VERSIGGIA [PV]
TEL. 0385951000
www.tortiwinepinotnero.com

During the best years, the Torti family manages to produce a remarkably good quality Pinot Nero. The '05 is a case in point with its classic pale garnet colour, wild berry aromas, attack on the palate and balance. The cuve close method Casaleggio from pinot nero is fresh and pleasant.

● OP Pinot Nero '05	♈ 5
○ OP Pinot Nero Brut Casaleggio	♈ 5

Castelveder

VIA BELVEDERE, 4
25040 MONTICELLI BRUSATI [BS]
TEL. 030652308
www.castelveder.it

Renato and Elena Alberti obtain around 100,000 bottles of wines and Franciacortas from their 12 hectares of vineyards.
This year, we liked the Brut's elegance, freshness, harmony and minerality. The sound Satèn shows vanillaed tones and the Rosé has rich notes of red berries but lacks structure.

○ Franciacorta Brut	♈ 5
⊙ Franciacorta Brut Rosè	♈ 5
○ Franciacorta Satèn	♈ 5

Caven Camuna

VIA CAVEN, 1
23036 TEGLIO [SO]
TEL. 0342484330
www.cavencamuna.it

Sforzato Messere '03 has of ripe plum, spice and dried flowers on the nose, concentrated flavour and a fresh, well-integrated acid vein. The elegant Sassella La Priora '03 has a harmonious palate with a long, savoury finish. The Inferno Al Carmine '03 has varietal red berries and a soft, silky palate.

● Valtellina Sforzato Messere '03	♈ 7
● Valtellina Sup. Inferno Al Carmine '03	♈ 6
● Valtellina Sup. Sassella La Priora '03	♈ 6

Le Chiusure

FRAZ. PORTESE
VIA BOSCHETTE, 2
25010 SAN FELICE DEL BENACO [BS]
TEL. 0365626243
www.lechiusure.net

The two IGTs from Alessandro Luzzago, the barbera, marzemino and sangiovese Campei '05 and Mal Borghetto '05, from rebo, merlot and barbera, are among the best Valtenesi reds from the Brescia shore of Lake Garda. The Groppello '06 is rustic and fruity. The Chiaretto '07 is typically salty.

● Campei '05	♈ 4
● Mal Borghetto '05	♈ 5
⊙ Garda Cl. Chiaretto '07	♈ 4
● Garda Cl. Groppello '06	♈ 4

OTHER WINERIES

Il Cipresso

VIA CERRI, 2
24020 SCANZOROSCIATE [BG]
TEL. 0354597005
www.ilcipresso.info

The forthright, balanced Moscato di Scanzo Serafino is always good. Its well-made stablemate, Valcalepio Bianco Melardo '07, has lavender-led aromatics, balanced and length. The Valcalepio Rosso Dionisio '06 is well made and the Riserva Bartolomeo was still in the barrel. We'll be back for it next year.

O Moscato di Scanzo Serafino '05	♟♟	7
O Valcalepio Bianco Melardo '07	♟♟	4*
● Valcalepio Rosso Dionisio '06	♟	4

Battista Cola

VIA INDIPENDENZA, 3
25030 ADRO [BS]
TEL. 0307356195
www.colabattista.it

Restricted space prevents us from giving greater visibility to Stefano Cola's wines, sourced from his terraced vineyards on Monte Alto at Adro. There's an excellent Brut '04 that shows complex, fresh and mineral and a Satèn that offers balance and finesse, taking its leave with floral notes.

O Franciacorta Brut '04	♟♟	6
O Franciacorta Satèn	♟♟	6
O Franciacorta Brut	♟	5

Cornaleto

VIA CORNALETTO, 2
25030 ADRO [BS]
TEL. 0307450507
www.cornaleto.it

Luigi Lancini specializes in vintage Franciacortas and regularly offers us recent disgorgements of former growing years. We enjoyed a '97 with great backbone, rich floral tones and a broad, lively, complex palate. The Brut '99 will surprise you with its soft, red berries, eloquent depth and a long finish.

O Franciacorta Brut '99	♟♟	6
O Franciacorta Brut '97	♟♟	6

La Costa

FRAZ. COSTA
VIA CURONE, 15
22050 PEREGO [LC]
TEL. 0395312218
www.la-costa.it

As we wait for new vintages of San Giobbe and Serìz, the stylish, structured Solesta '07 has improved, thanks to good work in the vineyards where the two grapes – chardonnay and riesling – are grown. Moscato Càlido '07 made a good debut. It's a dried-grape wine with dried figs and honey on the nose.

O Càlido '07	♟♟	5
O Solesta '07	♟♟	4

Tenuta La Costaiola

VIA COSTAIOLA, 25
27054 MONTEBELLO DELLA BATTAGLIA [PV]
TEL. 038383169
www.lacostaiola.it

This has been an interim year for the Rossetti and Scrivani families' estate. The good Riesling Bellarmino '07 is full and fragrant. Bonarda Vivace Giada '07 is fleshy but Barbera Auriga '04 has overripe notes. Vigna Bricca '06, from barbera, croatina, and pinot nero, is simple and drinkable.

O Bellarmino '07	♟♟	4
● Auriga '04	♟	5
● OP Bonarda Vivace Giada '07	♟	3
● Vigna Bricca '06	♟	4*

Delai

VIA MORO, 1
25080 PUEGNAGO SUL GARDA [BS]
TEL. 0365555527

Red wines from Sergio Delai in Valtenesi, inland from Lake Garda, scored well again. The elegant Fronsaga '06 is from barbera. The fresh and fruity Vigna Nobile '07 is a blend of groppello, barbera, marzemino and sangiovese while the personable marzemino-only Sovenigo '07 is husky.

● Fronsaga '06	♟♟	5
● Garda Bresciano Rosso Vigna Nobile '07	♟♟	4
● Garda Bresciano Groppello '07	♟	4
● Sovenigo '07	♟	5

OTHER WINERIES

Lorenzo Faccoli & Figli

VIA CAVA, 7
25030 COCCAGLIO [BS]
TEL. 0307722761
az.faccoli@libero.it

The Faccoli brothers dedicatedly cultivate their vineyards in Coccaglio and submit Franciacortas with a well-crafted style. This year, we enjoyed the Brut with its fresh, floral aromas and a bright, vibrant palate. The Extra Brut is dry and taut in the mouth but not lacking in harmony.

O Franciacorta Brut	♟♟ 5
O Franciacorta Extra Brut	♟ 5

Fiamberti

VIA CHIESA, 17
27044 CANNETO PAVESE [PV]
TEL. 038588019
www.fiambertivini.it

Buttafuoco Storico Vigna Solenga '04 has pulp, abundant tannins and overripe notes. The two classic method sparklers from pinot nero are well typed. We gave the Rosé Two Glasses for its exuberance of fruit. The Bonarda Frizzante Vigna Bricco della Sacca '07 has straightforward fragrances.

⊙ OP Brut Cl. Rosé Fiamberti	♟♟ 5
● OP Buttafuoco Storico V. Solenga '04	♟♟ 5
● OP Bonarda Frizzante Bricco della Sacca '07	♟ 4
O OP Brut Cl. Fiamberti	♟ 5

La Fiòca

FRAZ. NIGOLINE
VIA VILLA, 13B
25040 CORTE FRANCA [BS]
TEL. 0309826313
www.lafioca.com

The Gatti family's La Fiòca makes interesting wines using grapes from their own vineyards. We liked the excellent Brut '03 with its classic, initially reduced, bouquet that opens complex and deep over notes of yeast and oak before showing solid, rich structure with intact fruit upfront. The base Brut is also sound.

O Franciacorta Brut '03	♟♟ 6
O Franciacorta Brut	♟ 5

Fondazione Fojanini

VIA VALERIANA, 32
23100 SONDRIO [SO]
TEL. 0342512654

The still slightly closed Sforzato '02 has good body and a dynamic palate with nice acidity and character. Sassella '03 is complex and fruity with a solid, well co-ordinated palate. There are wild flower and spice fragrances on the Sassella Le Barberine Riserva '02, which has slightly unbending tannins.

● Valtellina Sup. Sassella '03	♟♟ 5
● Valtellina Sup. Sforzato '02	♟♟ 6
● Valtellina Sup. Sassella Le Barberine Ris. '02	♟ 5

Fattoria Gambero

FRAZ. CASE NUOVE
27045 SANTA MARIA DELLA VERSA [PV]
TEL. 038579268
www.fattoriailgambero.it

The Bonarda Frizzante Alborada '07 from Vittorio Ferrario is fragrant, soft, scented and well made. The Pinot Nero Tinterosse '06 is as varietal and pleasant as the Riesling Italico Kafir '06, which is nice and savoury. The Rosso Riserva Bacuco '04 has good fruit but evolved aromas.

● OP Bonarda Frizzante Alborada '07	♟♟ 3*
● OP Pinot Nero Tinterosse '06	♟ 4
O OP Riesling Italico Kafir '06	♟ 4
● OP Rosso Bacuco '04	♟ 4

Gatta

VIA SAN ROCCO, 33
25064 GUSSAGO [BS]
TEL. 0302772950
www.paginegialle.it/agricolagatta

Mario Gatta submits quality wines and Franciacortas with admirable consistency. We liked a sound Extra Brut Molener '00 with elegantly evolved, minerally notes, a zesty, round Satèn '03, with lime blossom and lavender on the nose, and a good Cellatica Negus '01.

O Franciacorta Brut Satèn '03	♟♟ 5
O Franciacorta Extra Brut Molener '00	♟♟ 5
● Cellatica Negus '01	♟ 4

OTHER WINERIES

Castello di Grumello

VIA FOSSE, 11
24064 GRUMELLO DEL MONTE [BG]
TEL. 0354420817
www.castellodigrumello.it

The pleasant Valcalepio Bianco '07 has nice tropical notes. Valcalepio Rosso '05 is enjoyable, especially on the palate where the texture is good and fruity. The Valcalepio Moscato Passito '01 has a garnet hue and evolved tones.

○ Valcalepio Bianco '07	🍷	3
● Valcalepio Moscato Nero Passito '01	🍷	6
● Valcalepio Rosso '05	🍷	3

La Guarda

FRAZ. CASTREZZONE
VIA ZANARDELLI, 49
25080 MUSCOLINE [BS]
TEL. 0365372948
www.laguarda.com

Gigi Negri is faithful to his credo, which means never rushing to market. Alongside fresh wines from the new vintage, like the juicy Groppello '07 and Chiaretto '07, he again released a series of longer aged reds, like the full-flavoured Sabbioso and varietal Marzemino, both from '03.

● Garda Cl. Groppello '07	🍷🍷	3*
● Garda Cl. Rosso Sabbioso '03	🍷🍷	5
☉ Garda Cl. Chiaretto '07	🍷	4
● Garda Marzemino '03	🍷	4

F.lli Guerci

FRAZ. CROTESI, 20
27045 CASTEGGIO [PV]
TEL. 038382725
guerci_flli@libero.it

With its impenetrable purple ruby colour, the Bonarda Vivace '07 from the Guerci brothers has a lovely, deep blueberry and violet nose and precise tannins. The initially muzzy nose of the Barbera Le Vignole '04 gives way to balsam and a good palate. The Pinot Nero Sinté Russ '07 is uncomplicated and varietal.

● OP Bonarda Vivace '07	🍷🍷	3*
● OP Barbera Le Vignole '04	🍷	4
● Sinté Russ '07	🍷	4

Leali di Monteacuto

FRAZ. MONTEACUTO
VIA DOSSO, 5
25080 PUEGNAGO SUL GARDA [BS]
TEL. 0365651291
antonio.leali@genie.it

Simut is a powerful red with concentrated fruit that is also capable of showing the well-gauged freshness typical of wines from the Brescia shore of Lake Garda. From a blend of groppello and marzemino, the '05 again is yet again one of the best examples from the zone. The Groppello '06 is well made.

● Garda Bresciano Groppello '06	🍷🍷	4
● Simut '05	🍷🍷	7
☉ Garda Bresciano Chiaretto '07	🍷	4
● Garda Bresciano Rosso '06	🍷	4

Locatelli Caffi

VIA A. MORO, 6
24060 CHIUDUNO [BG]
TEL. 035838308
www.locatellicaffi.it

The dynamic, well-structured Valcalepio Riserva'04 from Locatelli Caffi is good, deep in colour and fragrant with typical touches of blackberry and bell pepper. Valcalepio Rosso I Pilendrì '06 shows silky tannins and pulp, pity about the short finish. The Valcalepio Rosso '06 is well typed and well made.

● Valcalepio Rosso Ris. '04	🍷🍷	4
● Valcalepio Rosso '06	🍷	3
● Valcalepio Rosso I Pilendrì '06	🍷	3

Lurani Cernuschi

VIA CONVENTO, 3
24031 ALMENNO SAN SALVATORE [BG]
TEL. 035642576
www.luranicernuschi.it

The good Valcalepio Rosso Tornago '05 is elegant and long. Valcalepio Bianco '07 is better on the nicely structured palate than on the inexpressive nose. The Umbriana '06 Cabernet Sauvignon has notes of chocolate and blueberry, and decent length while Incrocio Manzoni Opis '07 is fairly fragrant.

● Valcalepio Rosso Tornago '05	🍷🍷	3*
○ Opis '07	🍷	3
● Umbriana '06	🍷	3
○ Valcalepio Bianco '07	🍷	3

OTHER WINERIES

Castello di Luzzano

LOC. LUZZANO, 5
27040 ROVESCALA [PV]
TEL. 0523863277
www.castelloluzzano.it

The OP Rosso Riserva 270 from '06 has broad aromas and lively vitality. The soft, winning Merlot Merloblù '07 is fruity and forthright. Bonarda Carlino '07 has good integrity and freshness, and a bouquet of cherry and raspberry whereas Pinot Nero Umore Nero '07 is varietal and a bit oaky.

● Merloblù '07	♟♟ 4*
● OP Rosso Luzzano 270 Ris. '06	♟♟ 6
● OP Bonarda Carlino '07	♟ 4
● OP Pinot Nero Umore Nero '07	♟ 4

Eligio Magri

COLLE DEI PASTA, 8/A
24060 TORRE DÈ ROVERI [BG]
TEL. 0354528868
www.eligiomagri.it

The Eligio Magri estate deserves its Guide debut as it presented one of the best Valcalepio Rosso Riservas from the vintage. Patrizio '04 is elegant with lovely spice, excellent oak, fruit with distinct overripeness and a full, well-knit palate. The Valcalepio Rosso '05 has substance and a blueberry bouquet.

● Valcalepio Rosso Patrizio Ris. '04	♟♟ 4
● Valcalepio Rosso '05	♟ 4

Martilde

FRAZ. CROCE, 4A1
27040 ROVESCALA [PV]
TEL. 0385756280
www.martilde.it

Barbera La Strega, la Gazza e il Pioppo is in the finals for the second year. The '05 has structure, wild berry sensations and a lovely finish. The excellent dry Malvasia Dedica '06 is intense on the nose and long on the palate. The other Malvasia, Piume '07, is fresher and the '07 Barbera is an easy drinker.

● OP Barbera La Strega, la Gazza e il Pioppo '05	♟♟ 5
○ OP Malvasia Dedica '06	♟♟ 4
● OP Barbera '07	♟ 4
○ OP Malvasia Piume '07	♟ 4

Montagna

VIA CAIROLI, 67
27043 BRONI [PV]
TEL. 038551028
www.cantinemontagna.it

The wild berry-themed Bonarda Frizzante Viti di Luna '07 is clean and fresh on the palate. The Cabernet Sauvignon Viti di Luna '06 is compact and balanced. Chardonnay Berté & Cordini '05 is fairly intense but it's a pity the finish is softish. Sauvignon Berté & Cordini '07 is simple and varietal.

● OP Bonarda Frizzante Viti di Luna '07	♟♟ 2*
● OP Cabernet Sauvignon Viti di Luna '06	♟ 3
○ OP Chardonnay Berté & Cordini '05	♟ 3
○ OP Sauvignon Berté & Cordini '07	♟ 3

Marchesi di Montalto

LOC. COSTA GALLOTTI, 5
27040 MONTALTO PAVESE [PV]
TEL. 3394982856
www.marchesidimontalto.it

We inspected a double pair of Riesling Italicos and classic method sparklers from pinot nero by Gabriele Marchesi's cellar. Monsaltus '06, a finalist, is richer and more complex than the still good, minerally '05. The Brut '06 is also excellent, full and fresh while the Rosé '04 is good.

○ OP Riesling Italico Monsaltus V. T. '06	♟♟ 5
○ OP Pinot Nero M. Cl. '06	♟♟ 5
○ OP Riesling Italico Monsaltus '05	♟♟ 4
⊙ OP Pinot Nero Rosè M. Cl. '04	♟ 5

Monte Cicogna

VIA DELLE VIGNE, 6
25080 MONIGA DEL GARDA [BS]
TEL. 0365503200
www.montecicogna.it

Don Lisander made another great showing. This is one of the benchmark reds from the Garda Bresciano winemaking tradition. Comprising mainly the indigenous groppello, the '04 version presents ripe, juicy red berry fruit. The Rubinere and current Groppello are varietal with their tones of strawberry and spice.

● Garda Cl. Rosso Sup. Don Lisander '04	♟♟ 5
● Garda Cl. Rosso Sup. Rubinere '05	♟♟ 4
⊙ Garda Cl. Chiaretto Siclì '07	♟ 4
● Garda Cl. Rosso Groppello Beana '06	♟ 4

OTHER WINERIES

Tenuta Monte Delma

LOC. VALENZANO, 23
25050 PASSIRANO [BS]
TEL. 0306546161
www.montedelma.it

Pietro Berardi is committed to this family estate and presents interesting labels. This year, we enjoyed a Satèn with crunchy, intense fruit that melds on the palate with soft tones of vanilla and candied citrus. The Rosé is also interesting with its intense strawberry, cherry and vanilla.

☉ Franciacorta Rosé	♟♟	5
○ Franciacorta Satèn	♟♟	5

Montenisa

FRAZ. CALINO
VIA PAOLO VI, 62
25046 CAZZAGO SAN MARTINO [BS]
TEL. 0307750838
www.antinori.it

While waiting for new releases of the vintage cuvées from the Franciacorta estate of the Antinori family, we report an excellent Franciacorta Brut that has fruit and flower aromas of violets and apricots followed by a fresh, harmonious palate with a note of savouriness.

○ Franciacorta Brut	♟♟	6

Monterucco

VALLE CIMA, 38
27040 CIGOGNOLA [PV]
TEL. 038585151
www.monterucco.it

Barbera Valle Cima '06 throws a broad, fragrant nose of red berry fruit and a fresh, pleasant palate. The Bonarda Frizzante Vigna Il Modello '07 is good with varietal violets and well-controlled tannins. The Brut Classese has fair body that makes up in fullness what it lacks in elegance.

● OP Barbera Valle Cima '06	♟♟	4*
● OP Bonarda Frizzante V. Il Modello '07	♟♟	3*
○ OP Pinot Nero Brut Classese	♟	4

Il Montù

VIA MARCONI, 10
27040 MONTÙ BECCARIA [PV]
TEL. 0385262252
www.ilmontu.com

This historic winery in Montù Beccaria is back in the Guide with three classic method sparklers. The Pinot Rosé Da Noir and Pinot Blanc Da Noir are non-DOC. We just prefer the Rosé for its aromatic complexity. The Classese '03 has substance but lacks a bit of finesse.

○ OP Pinot Nero Brut Cl.		
Classese Il Millesimato '03	♟	6
○ Pinot Blanc Da Noir	♟	5
☉ Pinot Rosè Da Noir	♟	4

Nettare dei Santi

VIA CAPRA, 17
20078 SAN COLOMBANO AL LAMBRO [MI]
TEL. 0371200523
www.nettaredeisanti.it

The Franco Riccardi Selezione Mombrione '04 is a merlot-heavy Bordeaux with classic herbaceous tones of bell pepper mingling with wild berries and good fullness and substance. San Colombano Mombrione Riserva '05 shows overripeness and smooth tannins. The Metodo Classico Domm '02 is pleasant.

● Franco Riccardi Sel. Mombrione '04	♟♟	5
● San Colombano Mombrione Ris. '05	♟	3
○ Spumante Brut Domm '02	♟	4

Olivini

VIA DEL PILANDRO, 1
LOC. DEMESSE VECCHIE
25015 DESENZANO DEL GARDA [BS]
TEL. 0309910268
www.olivini.net

Wines from the house of Olivini are always reliable. The new item this year is the pleasant, fruity Garda Rosé Brut '05, a classic method spumante based on the typical local blend, based on groppello. The same variety goes into the crunchy, tangy Garda Classico Rosso '05. The Luganas are well made.

☉ Garda Rosé Brut '05	♟♟	5
● Garda Rosso Cl. '05	♟♟	3*
○ Lugana '07	♟	4
○ Lugana Sup. Demesse Vecchie '05	♟	4

OTHER WINERIES

Panigada - Banino

VIA DELLA VITTORIA, 13
20078 SAN COLOMBANO AL LAMBRO [MI]
TEL. 037189103
vinobanino@hotmail.com

The pleasant Malvasia Passita Aureum
'05 has clear citrus aromas, good acidity
and length. The San Colombano Vigna
La Merla Riserva '04 never varies: good,
authentically rustic and best drunk after
a few years. The riesling, sauvignon and
chardonnay Banino Bianco '07 is decent.

○ Malvasia Passita Aureum '05	♟♟ 5
● San Colombano Banino V. La Merla Ris. '04	♟♟ 5
○ Banino Bianco '07	♟ 3

Angelo Pecis

SAN PIETRO DELLE PASSERE, 12
24060 SAN PAOLO D'ARGON [BG]
TEL. 035959104

The Laurenzio IGT from part-dried moscato
has a nice honey hue, candied citrus
aromas and good balance in the mouth
where good backbone supports the
sweetness. Valcalepio Rosso della Pezia
Riserva '03 has structure and balanced
tannins. The Valcalepio Rosso San Pietro
delle Passere '04 is fairly typical.

○ Laurenzio	♟♟ 5
● Valcalepio Rosso della Pezia Ris. '03	♟ 4
● Valcalepio Rosso San Pietro delle Passere '04	♟ 4

Percivalle

VIA TORCHI, 9
27040 BORGO PRIOLO [PV]
TEL. 0383871175
www.percivalle.com

The interesting and slightly unusual
Bonarda Frizzante Amanti '07 shows sound
aromas of cut flowers and blackberries.
The Bordeaux blend La Cura '05 has
abundant fruit and decent fruity pulp. The
elegant, fairly simple IGT Triade '07 is from
chardonnay, riesling and pinot nero.

● OP Bonarda Frizzante Amanti '07	♟♟ 3*
● La Cura '05	♟ 4
○ Triade '07	♟ 3

Piccolo Bacco dei Quaroni

FRAZ. COSTAMONTEFEDELE
27040 MONTÙ BECCARIA [PV]
TEL. 038560521
www.piccolobaccodeiquaroni.it

The well-made Buttafuoco Vigneto Ca'
Padroni '04 shows nicely ripened tannins
and good balsamic notes. The Bonarda
Vivace Mons Acutus '07 is fragrant, fleshy
and balanced. Malvasia Passita Elos '06
has lavender and wildflower aromas. The
Pinot Nero Vigneto La Fiocca '05 is varietal
but has still to evolve.

○ Elos '06	♟♟ 4
● OP Bonarda Vivace Mons Acutus '07	♟♟ 3*
● OP Buttafuoco Vign. Ca' Padroni '04	♟♟ 4
● OP Pinot Nero Vign. La Fiocca '05	♟ 4

Podere della Cavaga

VIA GAFFORELLI, 1
24060 FORESTO SPARSO [BG]
TEL. 035930939
www.vinicavaga.it

The intense Valcalepio Bianco Adamante
'07 gives overripe tropical fruit and spring
flowers. The interesting franconia-based
Ol Giopì '05 has mature hay notes and is
soft and balanced. The Valcalepio Rosso
Foresto '05 is spicy with good extract and
the citrussy Brut Clamor has a lovely nose.

○ Valcalepio Bianco Adamante '07	♟♟ 3*
○ Brut Cl. Clamor	♟ 5
● Ol Giopì '05	♟ 4
● Valcalepio Rosso Foresto '05	♟ 4

Quadra

VIA SANT'EUSEBIO, 1
25033 COLOGNE [BS]
TEL. 0307157314
www.quadrafranciacorta.it

The Ghezzi family has many business
interests in Italy and Argentina. Founded
in 2003, this estate proposes an excellent
Rosé with complex aromas and a solid,
rich, structured palate and a Satèn Sodelu
with soft, creamy, oaky tones. The Brut
Cuvée Marzaghi is interesting.

⊙ Franciacorta Rosé	♟♟ 5
○ Franciacorta Satèn Sodelu	♟♟ 5
○ Franciacorta Brut Cuvée Marzaghi	♟ 5

OTHER WINERIES

Riccafana

VIA FACCHETTI, 91
25033 COLOGNE [BS]
TEL. 0307156797
www.riccafana.com

The Fratus family produces Franciacortas and well-crafted wines from the territory. We noted an excellent Dosaggio Zero '04 with lively acid backbone and solid, full body that gives complex minerality, a Satèn with a fresh, pulpy character and a Rosé with wild strawberry and cake notes.

⊙ Franciacorta Rosé	🍷🍷	5
○ Franciacorta Dosaggio Zero '04	🍷🍷	5
○ Franciacorta Satèn	🍷🍷	4

Ricchi

FRAZ. RICCHI
VIA FESTONI, 13D
46040 MONZAMBANO [MN]
TEL. 0376800238
www.cantinaricchi.it

The nice moscato and garganega dried-grape Le Cime has honey and citrus perceptions. The Chardonnay Meridiano has good structure that still has to find balance on the palate. More or less the same goes for the Cabernet Ribò '05, which is spicy with ripe touches and still prominent tannins.

● Garda Cabernet Ribò '05	🍷	4
○ Garda Chardonnay Meridiano '07	🍷	4
○ Passito Le Cime	🍷	5

Riva di Franciacorta

LOC. FANTECOLO
VIA CARLO ALBERTO, 19
25040 PROVAGLIO D'ISEO [BS]
TEL. 030653011
cantina@rivadifranciacorta.it

The Riva family bought more than 30 hectares of vineyards, rebuilt an old house and fitted it with modern winemaking equipment. Outstanding wines include the fresh, citron-fragranced Franciacorta Satèn with its long palate, a Rosé with inviting blackberries and cherries, and a solidly structured Brut.

⊙ Franciacorta Rosé	🍷🍷	5
○ Franciacorta Satèn	🍷🍷	5
○ Franciacorta Brut	🍷	5

Tenuta San Francesco

VIA SCAZZOLINO, 55
27040 ROVESCALA [PV]
TEL. 029085141
www.alziati.it

Wines from Annibale Alziati's farm are intentionally old style and should be judged from this viewpoint. The Barbera '04 has good fruit but is a bit smothered by notes of oak. Gaggiarone Vitigni Giovani is a table wine from croatina with a fairly balanced tannic framework.

● Gaggiarone Vitigni Giovani	🍷	5
● OP Barbera La Barbera '04	🍷	3

San Michele

VIA GARIBALDI, 48-50
25020 CAPRIANO DEL COLLE [BS]
TEL. 0309747329
www.vinisanmichele.it

If the whites stood out last year, this time the reds from San Michele, on the Capriano hill just outside Brescia, were especially convincing. The Rosso Riserva '05 has outstanding personality but the Rosso '06 also impressed. The whites are pleasant.

● Capriano del Colle Rosso '06	🍷🍷	4
● Capriano del Colle Rosso Ris. '05	🍷🍷	5
○ Capriano del Colle Bianco '07	🍷	4
○ Montecorso '07	🍷	4

Tenuta Scarpa Colombi

VIA GROPPALLO, 26
27049 BOSNASCO [PV]
TEL. 0385272081
www.colombiwines.com

The Ariolo '06 is a Pinot Nero with fragrant flowers, good fruit and tannins that still needs to mature, as is normal here in the first hills in eastern Oltrepò. The balanced still Bonarda Marubbio '06 is rather good and the long Martinotti method Cuvée di Famiglia shows ripe melon.

● OP Pinot Nero Ariolo '06	🍷🍷	4
● OP Bonarda Marubbio '06	🍷	4
○ OP Pinot Nero Brut Martinotti Cuvée di Famiglia	🍷	4

OTHER WINERIES

Scuropasso

FRAZ. SCORZOLETTA, 40/42
27043 PIETRA DÈ GIORGI [PV]
TEL. 038585143
www.scuropasso.it

Fabio Marazzi is steering this winery to quality. The excellent Roccapietra, a classic method Pinot Nero, is complex and spirited. Buttafuoco Lunapiena '04 Pieno has close-knit, smooth tannins. The Bonarda Palatinus '07 is flavoursome and frank. Pinot Nero Roccapietra '06 is lively and varietal.

● OP Bonarda Vivace Palatinus '07	♼♼	3*
● OP Buttafuoco Lunapiena '04	♼♼	5
○ OP Pinot Nero Brut Cl. Roccapietra	♼♼	5
● OP Pinot Nero Roccapietra '06	♼	4

Cantine Selva Capuzza

LOC. SELVA CAPUZZA
25010 DESENZANO DEL GARDA [BS]
TEL. 0309910381
www.selvacapuzza.it

The Formentini family's estate did very well this year with good interpretations from all three DOCs along the Brescia shore of Lake Garda. Kudos to the taut Lugana Superiore '06, the elegant Garda Classico Madèr '06, and the unusual, vibrantly floral San Martino della Battaglia Campo del Soglio '07.

● Garda Cl. Sup. Rosso Madèr '06	♼♼	4
○ Lugana Sup. '06	♼♼	5
○ San Martino della Battaglia Campo del Soglio '07	♼♼	4
○ Lugana Selva Capuzza '07	♼	4

Vincenzo Tallarini

VIA FONTANILE, 7/9
24060 GANDOSSO [BG]
TEL. 035834003
www.tallarini.com

The interesting Serafo '05, a well-made Bordeaux blend from overripe grapes, shows good structure. The good Valcalepio Rosso Riserva San Giovannino '04 is soft and velvety. Brut Cuvée Angelo Tallarini is rather full and fragrant but Moscato di Scanzo '05 is less convincing than usual.

● Serafo '05	♼♼	6
● Valcalepio Rosso San Giovannino Ris. '04	♼♼	5
○ Brut Cl. Cuvée Angelo Tallarini	♼	6
● Moscato di Scanzo '05	♼	7

Togni Rebaioli

FRAZ. ERBANNO
VIA ROSSINI, 19
25047 DARFO BOARIO TERME [BS]
TEL. 0364529706

Enrico Togni is a leading light in the tiny mountain IGT of Valcamonica, where a handful of estates are making great headway. Modest quantities force the early of reds that deserve more ageing. The Millesettecentotre '06, from merlot and marzemino, has great fruit.

● Millesettecentotre '06	♼♼	4
● Lambrù '06	♼	4
● Merlot Rebaioli Cav. Enrico '06	♼	5

La Torre

FRAZ. MOCASINA DI CALVAGESE
25080 CALVAGESE DELLA RIVIERA [BS]
TEL. 030601034
www.pasini-latorre.com

Attilio Pasini is a supporter of a particular biotype of the indigenous groppello, mocasina, which takes its name from the village at Calvagese, inland from Lake Garda. The '06 version has a winning mix of red berries and spice. The Chardonnay Brut is well made and the other wines are reliable.

● Garda Cl. Groppello Mocasina '06	♼♼	3
● Garda Cabernet Sauvignon Castagneto '05	♼	5
○ Garda Chardonnay Brut La Torre	♼	5
○ Garda Cl. Bianco Rossetto '07	♼	3

Torrevilla

VIA EMILIA, 4
27050 TORRAZZA COSTE [PV]
TEL. 038377003
www.torrevilla.it

The classic method Rosé from the co-operative winery managed by Guerrino Saviotti is sound with good fruity body. The other two sparklers, Chardonnay La Genisia '05 and Classese, are well crafted, fresh and pleasant. The Bonarda La Genisia '07 is fragrant, especially on the palate.

⊙ OP Pinot Nero Brut Cl. Rosé	♼♼	4
○ Brut Cl. La Genisia	♼	5
● OP Bonarda La Genisia '07	♼	4
○ OP Pinot Nero Brut Classese	♼	4

OTHER WINERIES

Pietro Torti

FRAZ. CASTELROTTO, 9
27047 MONTECALVO VERSIGGIA [PV]
TEL. 038599763
www.pietrotorti.it

Sandro Torti's Bonarda Vivace '07 is one of the best from Oltrepò, showing meaty and fragrant with roses and red berries. The croatina-based IGT Verzello '07 has pleasant, simple fruit. Riesling Italico '07 is fresh and well typed. The Pinot Nero '05 has evolved notes and a lot of fruit but lacks some finesse.

● OP Bonarda Vivace '07	♟♟	3*
● OP Pinot Nero '05	♟	5
○ OP Riesling Italico '07	♟	3
● Verzello '07	♟	3

Cantina Sociale Val San Martino

VIA BERGAMO, 1195
24030 PONTIDA [BG]
TEL. 035795035
www.cantinavalsanmartino.com

Sinew and cake aromas emerge in the Valcalepio Moscato Passito '04 from Cantina Sociale Val San Martino in the area west of Bergamo. The other wines are pleasant and well made, including three IGTs, a red, a white and a rosé from schiava that stand out for cleanliness and value for money.

● Valcalepio Moscato Passito '04	♟♟	6
○ Bianco della Bergamasca '07	♟	3
● Rosso della Bergamasca '07	♟	3
⊙ Schiava della Bergamasca '06	♟	2

La Valle

VIA VALLE, 21
25031 CAPRIOLO [BS]
TEL. 0307461620
www.ripadelbosco.it

Located at Capriolo, Valle makes its Guide debut with some fine wines. The Brut has minerals and medicinal herbs on the nose and a consistent, zesty, rich palate. The Demi Sec is one of the best with soft tones of vanilla and quince.

○ Franciacorta Demi Sec	♟♟	5
○ Franciacorta Brut	♟♟	5
● TdF Rosso '05	♟♟	4

Vanzini

FRAZ. BARBALEONE, 7
27040 SAN DAMIANO AL COLLE [PV]
TEL. 038575019
www.vanzini-wine.com

While waiting for their major wines, we gave a short profile to the Vanzini brothers, producers of traditional products such as their fragrant, well-balanced Bonarda and Sangue di Giuda. Of the two Martinotti method sparklers, we just preferred the fruity pulp of the Rosé but the Extra Dry is also well made.

● OP Bonarda Frizzante '07	♟♟	3*
⊙ OP Pinot Nero Rosé Extra Dry	♟♟	4*
● OP Sangue di Giuda '07	♟♟	4*
○ Pinot Nero Charmat Extra Dry	♟	4

Vigna Dorata

FRAZ. CALINO
VIA SALA, 80
25046 CAZZAGO SAN MARTINO [BS]
TEL. 0307254275
www.vignadorata.it

Luciana Mingotti produces top quality wines and Franciacortas at her cellar in Calino. Proof of this is the Rosé with complex aromas of red berries, toasted bread and oakiness. The palate is solid and supple. Luciana's Runcat '05 red has elegant, spicy aromas and a full body while her Satèn is decent.

⊙ Franciacorta Rosé	♟♟	5
● TdF Rosso Runcat '05	♟♟	4*
○ Franciacorta Satèn	♟	5

Emilio Zuliani

VIA TITO SPERI, 28
25080 PADENGHE SUL GARDA [BS]
TEL. 0309907026
www.vinizuliani.it

Tradition and innovation come together at the Zuliani cellar. The more traditional line, linked with father Emilio's style, is epitomized in the Donna Lucia '04 but there is now a new territory-focused trend, which his daughter Lucia is exploring, for example in the Groppello Balosse '05.

● Garda Cl. Groppello Balosse '05	♟♟	4
⊙ Garda Chiaretto Cl. '07	♟	3
○ Garda Cl. Terre Bianche '07	♟	3
● Garda Sup. Rosso Donna Lucia '04	♟	4

TRENTINO

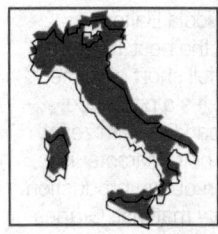

This time things have not gone well. There is no point downplaying it or focusing attention on the usual suspects that have won Three Glasses again this year. Trentino estates and winemaking have not fulfilled the promise predicted by production that is founded on technically well-made wines at good prices plus a number of wonderful stand-outs. We tasted a lot of good, even excellent, wines but these were only special cases, solo high notes and not a choral melody. Results should be more convincing in a region where the mountain community spirit reigns supreme. Practically all farming operations, from animal husbandry to grape growing and winemaking, are run as co-operatives. The project for quality, identity and the future of winemaking seems to lack drive, despite economic incentives and the committed assistance of structures created by the Trento provincial authority and major agricultural research foundations, with the wine school at San Michele all'Adige a leader in the genetic mapping of grape varieties. All these laudable activities may have induced most growers to ease back and exploit the commercial success of Trentino's wine co-operatives. Flourishing vineyards on well-suited plots have such high yields per hectare that Trentino harvests on average 15,000 kilograms of grapes per hectare, which hardly encourages quality, especially since most are at high elevations on hillsides that ought to yield small quantities. This could be another reason for our disappointment. We expected to taste wines redolent of their terroir, the flavours of the Dolomites or the temperament of the winemaker. Instead, many wines revealed limits of personality and territorial identity. The sparklers usually did well and the Teroldegos also held up, one winning Three Glasses. We could say that as usual our Three Glasses went to a small number of significant estates with famous names. From the Lunelli brothers' excellent Giulio Ferrari '99 to the reliable San Leonardo '04 from Guerrieri Gonzaga, these wines have for decades been major players in Italian winemaking. Other great products stand with these big hitters to defend the honour of Trentino wine. We note the Graal Altemasi Brut '01 sparkler from Cavit, the only co-operative with a solo voice capable of lifting the choir, and another two sparklers, the Abate Nero '03 and the return of the Methius in the 2002 vintage. Nor should we forget two magnificent reds: the Teroldego Armilo '06 from Diego Bolognani, cellarman at Lavis, the first to release a truly special Teroldego, in part because it is vinified outside the boundaries of the Campi Rotaliani DOC, or the classic Faye Rosso '05 from Pojer & Sandri.

Abate Nero

FRAZ. GARDOLO
SPONDA TRENTINA, 45
38014 TRENTO
TEL. 0461246566
www.abatenero.it

Nicola Balter

VIA VALLUNGA II, 24
38068 ROVERETO [TN]
TEL. 0464430101
www.balter.it

ANNUAL PRODUCTION	70,000 bottles
HECTARES UNDER VINE	65
VITICULTURE METHOD	Conventional

ANNUAL PRODUCTION	60,000 bottles
HECTARES UNDER VINE	10
VITICULTURE METHOD	Conventional

Oenologist Luciano Lunelli is one of the best sparkling winemakers in Italy and has been major player for decades on the Trentino winemaking scene. He and Eugenio de Castel Terlago several years ago founded this specialist label in Trento that sources fruit from vineyards in the province's best areas. For the third consecutive year, Luciano has presented a cuvée of extraordinary distinction, the Cuvée dell'Abate Riserva '03. The estate, by the way, is dedicated to the Benedictine monk who invented the classic method. From a cuvée of Chardonnay, Pinot Nero and Pinot Bianco, it is a bright, greenish straw yellow with tiny bubbles. The nose opens on fresh apples and pears with clear florality and citrus with a touch of vanilla. On the palate you will find stylish structure and backbone that lead into a long, caressing finale of fruit and mineral aromas. We thought the Trento Extra Dry was nearly as good. Lunelli has interpreted this difficult wine type with style. Rich kiwi and tropical fruit flirt with sweetness but never weigh down the acidity-braced structure. The Trento Bruts are all the usual good quality.

The two versions of Nicola Balter's spumante are among the best Trento, though this time they fell short of some recent performances. It's a pity since these are attractive sparklers with zesty, invigorating palates. Their character is the result of dedication during production and seriously good raw material. Grapes are harvested from the sunniest slopes of the estate above Rovereto in enchanting surroundings of woods and nature parks. This plateau jutting into the valley, perfectly suited for vineyards, is stubbornly protected by the Balter family from building and real estate speculation. An enterprising winemaker and talented entrepreneur, Nicola Balter never loses courage when faced with the whims of growing seasons that have definitely influenced the style of his still wines, above all the cabernet sauvignon, merlot and lagrein Barbanico, which needs more time to express itself to the full after the extremely difficult 2006 vintage in Vallagarina. The other estate wines are always forthright and very drinkable, beginning with the honest, and honestly priced, Lagrein-Merlot '07 through to the fresh-tasting, varietal Sauvignon '07.

O Trento Brut Cuvée dell'Abate Ris. '03	♗♗♗	6
O Trento Abate Nero Brut	♗♗	5
O Trento Abate Nero Extra Dry	♗♗	5
O Trento Brut Cuvée dell'Abate Ris. '02	♗♗♗	6
O Trento Brut Cuvée dell'Abate Ris. '01	♗♗♗	6

O Trento Balter Ris. '02	♗♗	6
● Barbanico '06	♗♗	5
O Trento Balter Brut	♗♗	5
● Lagrein-Merlot '07	♗	4
O Sauvignon '07	♗	4
● Barbanico '97	♗♗♗	5
O Trento Balter Ris. '01	♗♗♗	6
● Barbanico '04	♗♗	5
● Barbanico '03	♗♗	5
● Barbanico '01	♗♗	5
O Trento Brut Ris. '00	♗♗	6

Bellaveder

LOC. MASO BELVEDERE
38010 FAEDO [TN]
TEL. 0461650171
www.bellaveder.it

ANNUAL PRODUCTION	30,000 bottles
HECTARES UNDER VINE	7.40
VITICULTURE METHOD	Conventional

The winemaking insights of Tranquillo Lucchetta and his partners have come up trumps. Despite its relative youth, Bellaveder's wines already show character and a certain complexity. Evidently this fan-shaped zone, running from San Michele all'Adige to Faedo and Valle di Cembra, is especially suited to growing grapes, including – and this is a pleasant surprise – the teroldego variety. It has produced a seriously good wine that presents vigorous with succulent, ripe tannins and length you would never expect from a hillside version of the variety harvested outside the DOC zone. Campo Rotaliano is just below this farm, which enjoys a beautiful panorama over the lush valley vineyards. So the Teroldego '07 earns praise but the other wines are not bad either, including the classic Chardonnay from the same vintage and an equally rich Lagrein '06, in a version that echoes the Teroldego perhaps because the two varieties are close relations. Meanwhile, some promising classic method sparklers are ageing in the cellar, where the tranquil Tranquillo looks after them with the greatest care.

Bolognani

VIA STAZIONE, 19
38015 LAVIS [TN]
TEL. 0461246354
www.bolognani.com

ANNUAL PRODUCTION	70,000 bottles
HECTARES UNDER VINE	4.40
VITICULTURE METHOD	Conventional

Praise to Diego Bolognani and his siblings, though the Three Glasses are dedicated to the estate's founder. Nilo Bolognani passed away years ago but has never been forgotten by his family or by the many farmers who faithfully supplied grapes to what was originally a cellar and slowly turned into a solid winemaking estate. We could call Armilo an off-zone Teroldego since it is produced outside the DOC. It is perhaps unique for this reason, showing dark and varied in its aromas of cherries and ripe fruit, and then fresh and full on the in some respects unique palate. The name Armilo is also special as the Bolognanis dedicated it to their parents, mother Armida and father Nilo. For some time, they have been diversifying their activities as expert cellarmen, applying innovative techniques and personal intuition to the management of their vineyards, some in Val di Cembra where the valley floor plots are planted to red grapes while aromatic varieties ripen in the hills of Trento. The better than good Traminer and flavourful Nosiola are both from '07 and the Gabàn '05, a Bordeaux blend and the Bolognanis' special project, is a sound as ever.

● Teroldego Mas Picol '07	♟♟	4*
○ Trentino Chardonnay '07	♟♟	4*
● Trentino Lagrein '06	♟	5
● Rosso Bellaveder '05	♟♟	4*
● Rosso Bellaveder '04	♟♟	4
○ Trentino Chardonnay '06	♟♟	4*

● Teroldego Armilo '06	♟♟♟	4*
● Gabàn '05	♟♟	6
○ Trentino Traminer Aromatico Sanròc '06	♟♟	4
○ Trentino Müller Thurgau '07	♟	4
○ Trentino Nosiola '07	♟	4
● Gabàn '04	♟♟	6
● Gabàn '03	♟♟	6
● Gabàn '01	♟♟	6
● Gabàn '00	♟♟	6
● Teroldego Armilo '04	♟♟	4

Borgo dei Posseri

LOC. POZZO BASSO, 1
38061 ALA [TN]
TEL. 0464671899
www.borgodeiposseri.com

ANNUAL PRODUCTION   60,000 bottles
HECTARES UNDER VINE 18
VITICULTURE METHOD   Certified organic

It takes a lot of enthusiasm and just as much dedication to obtain results like these in just a few harvests. The estate is high in the hills, located on the sunny side of the last bit of Vallagarina before the area of Verona, where Martin Mainenti and Margherita de Pilati have noticeably improved the quality of their wines. The reds in particular have come on. Merlot and pinot nero vines are planted in their own "campo" to create selections linked to traditional place names above the village of Ala. Merlot Rocol '05 is in a class of its own and provides a pleasant surprise. Intense aromas lead into a rich palate with round tannins, good balance, and great character and expression. The Pinot Nero Paradis '05 is not bad either. This is another variety the estate is betting on, planting clones specially selected for sparkling wine production. The Sauvignon Furiel 2007 is as convincing as usual, showing dry with distinct notes of elderflower, a plant that not coincidentally surrounds the vineyards in Posseri before it gives way to beech, larch and fir trees.

Cavit

VIA PONTE DI RAVINA, 31
38040 TRENTO
TEL. 0461381711
www.cavit.it

ANNUAL PRODUCTION   75,000,000 bottles
HECTARES UNDER VINE 5.700
VITICULTURE METHOD   Conventional

Cavit is convincing right at the top of the range, confirming the status of its prestige classic sparkler, Altemasi Graal Brut 2001, an unrivalled Trento DOC. Three Glasses are inevitable for a sparkler as appealing and elegant as it is dynamic and rich in personality. This wine shows the true worth of this operation – the consortium brings together most of the co-operative wineries in Trentino – as well as sending a strong signal to the more than 5,000 member growers. Invest in grape varieties for sparkling wine production and vinify chardonnay mainly for this purpose. But Cavit means more than just sparklers. Twenty-six wines were submitted to our tastings, a broad range with products that cater for wine types, market segments and consumer tastes in Italy and abroad. All the wines have Trentino territorial character and a Cavit style you can recognize with your eyes shut. Apart from that prodigious Graal, other wines we liked were the Teroldego Maso Cervara '05, which went to the finals, and the nicely bitterish, well-structured Nosiola '07 with its fresh palate and full flavour. But the whole range is excellent.

● Merlot Rocol '05	♥♥	4*
● Pinot Nero Paradis '05	♥♥	5
○ Sauvignon Furiel '07	♥	5
● Merlot Rocol '04	♥♥	4
○ Sauvignon Furiel '06	♥♥	5

○ Trento Altemasi Graal Brut Ris. '01	♥♥♥	7
● Teroldego Rotaliano Maso Cervara '05	♥♥	5
○ Trento Altemasi Brut '01	♥♥	5*
● Teroldego Rotaliano Bottega Vinai '06	♥♥	4
● Trentino Cabernet Sauvignon Bottega Vinai '05	♥♥	4*
○ Trentino Chardonnay Maso Torresella Sup. '06	♥♥	5
● Trentino Lagrein Dunkel Bottega Vinai '05	♥♥	4*
● Trentino Marzemino Bottega Vinai '07	♥♥	4*
● Trentino Marzemino Maso Romani Sup. '06	♥♥	5
○ Trentino Nosiola Bottega Vinai '07	♥♥	3*
○ Trentino Sauvignon Bottega Vinai '07	♥♥	4*
○ Trento Cantus Brut	♥♥	5
○ Trentino Müller Thurgau Bottega Vinai '07	♥	4
○ Trento Altemasi Graal Brut Ris. '00	♥♥♥	6

Cesconi

FRAZ. PRESSANO
VIA MARCONI, 39
38015 LAVIS [TN]
TEL. 0461240355
www.cesconi.it

ANNUAL PRODUCTION	120,000 bottles
HECTARES UNDER VINE	21
VITICULTURE METHOD	Conventional

The wines have always been outstanding, so we were sorry the Cesconis were missing from the Trentino Three Glass club. Two wines went to our finals. The first, Olivar '06 from pinot bianco, pinot grigio and chardonnay is a superior white. Then the surprising Chardonnay '06 is the best from the 40 or so submitted by Trentino cellars. But talented winemakers like the Cesconis never lose heart. The four young siblings are already working on new projects, including one for sparkling wine. Meanwhile, they continue to study, testing new cultivation practices and innovative winemaking solutions. They tend to their vineyards, some located around the modern cellar in Pressano above Lavis, and others, especially for red varieties, in Valle del Sarca between Drò and the hollow of Lake Garda. Speaking of red wines, these splendid white winemakers are showing they can handle merlot, cabernet, teroldego and lagrein. Pivier, from merlot only, had not been bottled so they presented the Cesconi Rosso '05, a lagrein-teroldego blend with great personality, elegance and youthful energy. The other wines are all convincing, above all the Traminer '06.

Marco Donati

VIA CESARE BATTISTI, 41
38016 MEZZOCORONA [TN]
TEL. 0461604141
donatimarcovini@libero.it

ANNUAL PRODUCTION	90,000 bottles
HECTARES UNDER VINE	20
VITICULTURE METHOD	Conventional

Marco Donati has the classic wineman's look about him. He's a country gentleman constantly working his vineyards spread across Trentino, although his main focus is Teroldego for vines of this variety surround the winery built into a 15th-century structure. The ups and downs of the growing years have not done winemakers in Piana Rotaliana many favours, including Marco Donati who was forced to reckon with a 2006 harvest that was not exactly fantastic. His Superteroldego Sangue di Drago shows a few cracks in its usual elegance even though the wine has solid structure and full body. A peculiar mix of teroldego with some lagrein and merlot goes into Vino del Maso '07. Its fruity tones lend movement to the marvellous base, which attractively mingles simplicity and character with lovely notes of fruit and cocoa powder. It's dense and complex on the palate, and surprisingly well priced. Results for the whites were a bit up and down but a well-made Riesling Stellato '07 stands out, showing varietal with attractive concentration.

O Chardonnay '06	🍷🍷	5
O Olivar '06	🍷🍷	5
● Moratel '05	🍷🍷	4*
● Rosso Cesconi '05	🍷🍷	5
O Trentino Traminer Aromatico '06	🍷🍷	5
O Nosiola '06	🍷	4
O Pinot Grigio '06	🍷	5
⊙ Trentino Lagrein Rosato '07	🍷	3
O Olivar '05	🍷🍷🍷	5
O Olivar '01	🍷🍷🍷	5
● Rosso del Pivier '04	🍷🍷	6
● Rosso del Pivier '03	🍷🍷	6
O Chardonnay '05	🍷🍷	5
O Chardonnay '04	🍷🍷	5
● Moratel '04	🍷🍷	4
● Moratel '03	🍷🍷	4

● Teroldego Rotaliano Sangue del Drago '06	🍷🍷	6
O Trentino Riesling Stellato '07	🍷🍷	4*
● Vino del Maso Rosso '07	🍷🍷	4*
● Teroldego Rotaliano Bagolari '07	🍷	5
● Teroldego Rotaliano Sangue del Drago '98	🍷🍷🍷	4
● Teroldego Rotaliano Sangue del Drago '04	🍷🍷	6

F.lli Dorigati

VIA DANTE, 5
38016 MEZZOCORONA [TN]
TEL. 0461605313
www.dorigati.it

ANNUAL PRODUCTION	100,000 bottles
HECTARES UNDER VINE	13
VITICULTURE METHOD	Conventional

We applaud the wines from this estate, which recently celebrated its 150th harvest, toasting a fantastic 2002 vintage spumante Methius Riserva that is back among the serious Stemware. To tell the truth, it has always been good even when it failed to win Three Glasses. Probably the professionalism and craftsmanship of the production system were unable to make up for certain flaws from the growing season and the rush to release this extraordinary sparkler as soon as possible. Citrussy, and almost resin-like in timbre, it shows a whole series of aromatic interweavings that provide the complexity we find again on the palate. It's a wine that reaffirms the Dorigatis' skills as sparkling winemakers, as well as cellarmen. They also demonstrate their talent with the Diedri '05 – from exclusively Teroldego – a serious wine that deservedly reached our finals. But the Dorigatis are equally serious about their other wines: the good Cabernet '06, the interesting Trentino Cabernet Grener '04 from cabernet and carmenère, a base version of Teroldego Rotaliano 2006 and the easy-going rosé Lagrein Kretzer from 2007.

Endrizzi

LOC. MASETTO, 2
38010 SAN MICHELE ALL'ADIGE [TN]
TEL. 0461650129
www.endrizzi.it

ANNUAL PRODUCTION	500,000 bottles
HECTARES UNDER VINE	40
VITICULTURE METHOD	Conventional

On their estate at Faedo, below Castel Monreale, the Endricis – the surname is usually pronounced "Endritsi" in Trentino – have created a garden of fragrances, a trail of the senses to discover the aromas of wine through medicinal plants. They brought back native varieties of vines for a park of viticultural biodiversity and also changed the technical staff – Vito Piffer and Hartmann Donà have arrived as consultants – to relaunch the prestige of this long-standing estate. Results soon arrived. The whites are more vibrant thanks to shrewd vineyard management and the technique of vinifying in nitrogen chambers to protect the aromas. But Paolo Endrici's estate shines especially with two astonishing reds. The better of these is Gran Masetto '05, from teroldego grapes part-dried on special racks Amarone-style. It's a wondrously unusual version of Teroldego that will win you over as soon as you taste it. Masetto Nero Superiore '05, a Bordeaux blend with added teroldego and lagrein, is also rather good. Outstanding among the whites is a fragrant Traminer '07 with elegant structure and pleasant drinkability. The classic Spumante is always sound.

○ Trento Methius Brut Ris. '02	♥♥♥	7
● Teroldego Rotaliano Diedri '05	♥♥	6
● Teroldego Rotaliano '06	♥	4
● Trentino Cabernet '06	♥	4
● Trentino Cabernet Grener '04	♥	6
☉ Trentino Lagrein Kretzer '07	♥	4
○ Trento Methius Brut Ris. '00	♀♀♀	7
○ Trento Methius Brut. Ris. '98	♀♀♀	7
● Teroldego Rotaliano Diedri '04	♀♀	6
● Teroldego Rotaliano Diedri '03	♀♀	6
● Teroldego Rotaliano '05	♀♀	4
● Trentino Cabernet Grener '03	♀♀	6
● Trentino Cabernet Grener '01	♀♀	6

● Gran Masetto '05	♥♥	7
● Masetto Nero Sup. '05	♥♥	4*
● Serpaiolo Serpara '07	♥♥	4*
○ Trentino Nosiola '07	♥♥	4*
○ Trentino Traminer Aromatico '07	♥♥	4*
○ Trento Brut '04	♥♥	5
● Morellino di Scansano Serpaia '06	♥	4
● Teroldego Rotaliano '06	♥	4
● Trentino Moscato Rosa '06	♥	5
● Teroldego Rotaliano Maso Camorz Ris. '04	♀♀	4
○ Masetto Dulcis '05	♀♀	5
● Masetto Nero '04	♀♀	5

Ferrari

VIA PONTE DI RAVINA, 15
38100 TRENTO [TN]
TEL. 0461972311
www.ferrarispumante.it

ANNUAL PRODUCTION	5,200,000 bottles
HECTARES UNDER VINE	120
VITICULTURE METHOD	Conventional

The 1999 edition of the legendary Riserva del Fondatore was well up to expectations. It has a bright greenish straw-yellow hue with faint golden highlights, despite being almost ten years old. The nose opens charming with complex notes of ripe apples and pears, flowers and Alpine herbs with shades of vanilla and citrus. The palate is as sumptuous as ever, rich in backbone and length. In other words, Three Glasses go to this great classic, which closes elegantly on hints of acacia honey and minerals. Worthy counterparts to this wine are a compact, juicy, fruit-rich Perlé '04 with complexity, balance and freshness, and the new Perlé Nero '02, an enchanting copper-flecked deep straw monovarietal Pinot Nero with an intriguingly complex nose of yeasts, medicinal herbs and red berries. The palate shows structure and backbone, finesse and power for an excellent debut. The Lunellis' broad, excellent range of cuvées earned a special mention for the delicious, dark pink Perlé Rosé '04 with an alcohol-rich nose, delicately creamy fizz and vibrant fresh wild berries.

Graziano Fontana

VIA CASE SPARSE, 9
38010 FAEDO [TN]
TEL. 0461650400

ANNUAL PRODUCTION	35,000 bottles
HECTARES UNDER VINE	7
VITICULTURE METHOD	Conventional

Faedo means Müller Thurgau. In fact, during the 1960s these hills jutting towards Valle di Cembra were the site of experiments with the grape variety created at the end of the 19th century in Switzerland by Professor Hermann Müller with encouraging results. Graziano Fontana is one of the great interpreters of Müller Thurgau. His 2007 is the result of patient production that brings out all the peculiarities offered by the climate and soil of Faedo to create a wine with a powerful, elegant identity. It is fresh and fruity with those aromas of spring flowers, lemon verbena and vague hints of absinthe that render it distinctive. But this pleasant, hospitable winemaker of few words also produces an interesting Sauvignon '07, one of the few versions from the region to stand out. The Traminer Aromatico '07 is fresh and deep while on the red front the Lagrein '06 is well balanced with a fragrant bouquet and tasty bitterish vein, in comparison with other wines that are more typically Faedoesque.

O Trento Giulio Ferrari Riserva del Fondatore Brut '99	👑👑👑 8
O Trento Brut Perlé '04	👑👑 6
O Trento Extra Brut Perlé Nero '02	👑👑 8
O Trento Brut	🍷🍷 6
☉ Trento Brut Perlé Rosé '04	🍷🍷 7
O Trento Maximum Brut	🍷🍷 6
O Trento Maximum Démi Sec	🍷🍷 5
O Trentino Chardonnay Villa Margon '06	🍷 5
O Trento Giulio Ferrari '97	🍷🍷🍷 8
O Trento Giulio Ferrari '96	🍷🍷🍷 8
O Trento Giulio Ferrari '95	🍷🍷🍷 8
O Giulio Ferrari '93	🍷🍷🍷 8
O Giulio Ferrari '91	🍷🍷🍷 8
O Trento Brut Perlé '02	🍷🍷🍷 6

● Trentino Lagrein di Faedo '06	🍷🍷 5
O Trentino Müller Thurgau di Faedo '07	🍷🍷 4
O Trentino Sauvignon di Faedo '07	🍷🍷 4
O Trentino Traminer Aromatico di Faedo '07	🍷🍷 4
● Trentino Lagrein di Faedo '04	🍷🍷 5
O Trentino Müller Thurgau di Faedo '05	🍷🍷 4
● Trentino Pinot Nero di Faedo '04	🍷🍷 5
O Trentino Sauvignon di Faedo '05	🍷🍷 4

★ Foradori

VIA DAMIANO CHIESA, 1
38017 MEZZOLOMBARDO [TN]
TEL. 0461601046
www.elisabettaforadori.com

ANNUAL PRODUCTION	200,000 bottles
HECTARES UNDER VINE	24
VITICULTURE METHOD	Certified biodynamic

Elisabetta Foradori's constant experimentation and day to day commitment to wine as a living product make her an exceptional wine woman. Expert at managing every phase of operations, from vineyard to cellar, and at presenting the finished product, Elisabetta puts her heart into everything she does. For some years, she has adopted growing methods that splendidly combine naturalness, biodynamics and feminine grace. The results are on their way and look fascinating. Just taste her last three wines now on the market. Their style and character are irresistible and never banal. At present, they are in transition, still searching for a definitive form, which is perhaps why you will not find the Granato '06 among Trentino's top prizewinners. But this is unimportant since the wine is always characterful, authoritative, graceful and muscular, as only one of the greats can be. The Foradori '06 is quite sound. This well-made single-variety Teroldego Rotaliano is anything but a second wine. It's a top-quality bottle in its own right. The delicate and pleasantly acidulous Myrto '06 is a blend of sauvignon and incrocio Manzoni.

Gaierhof

VIA IV NOVEMBRE, 51
38030 ROVERÈ DELLA LUNA [TN]
TEL. 0461658514
www.gaierhof.com;
www.masopoli.com

ANNUAL PRODUCTION	550,000 bottles
HECTARES UNDER VINE	130
VITICULTURE METHOD	Conventional

We have said in previous Guides that there are two different estates combined in the same entry here. Both belong to Luigi Togn's family. These are wines of great personality, each one representative of the specific qualities of its estate. The headquarters of Vinicola Gaierhof in Roverè della Luna has a great Moscato Rosa '07, an ever more intriguing rarity, a 2007 selection of Müller Thurgau, labelled Settecento or 700 from the altitude of the vineyards, and a 2007 Nosiola. Both are very varietal. There's also a subtle Riesling '07 with zesty minerality. Maso Poli, a modern winemaking estate managed by the newer generations of Togns on the Lavis hillside, amazed us with the Marmoran '05, a red from teroldego and lagrein. This wine is juicy and dense yet outstandingly elegant, with silky tannins and a spicy, minerally finish that shows off the professionalism of Valentina Togn and Goffredo Pasolli, head oenologist at both Gaierhof and Maso Poli. Further confirmation comes from the Pinot Nero '05 and a typical blend from the Lavis area, Sorni '07, a white from nosiola, chardonnay and müller thurgau.

● Granato '06	▼▼	8
○ Myrto '06	▼▼	5
● Teroldego Rotaliano Foradori '06	▼▼	5
● Granato '04	▼▼▼	7
● Granato '03	▼▼▼	7
● Granato '02	▼▼▼	7
● Granato '01	▼▼▼	7
● Granato '00	▼▼▼	7
● Granato '96	▼▼▼	5
● Granato '93	▼▼▼	5
● Granato '91	▼▼▼	5

● Marmoran Maso Poli '05	▼▼	6
● Trentino Moscato Rosa '07	▼▼	6
○ Trentino Müller Thurgau Sup. dei Settecento '07	▼▼	4*
○ Trentino Nosiola '07	▼▼	4*
● Trentino Pinot Nero Maso Poli '05	▼▼	5
○ Trentino Sorni Maso Poli '07	▼▼	4*
● Teroldego Rotaliano '07	▼	4
● Teroldego Rotaliano Ris '06	▼	5
○ Trentino Riesling Italico '07	▼	4
○ Trentino Müller Thurgau Sup. dei Settecento '05	▼▼	4

Grigoletti

VIA GARIBALDI, 12
38060 NOMI [TN]
TEL. 0464834215
www.grigoletti.com

ANNUAL PRODUCTION	60,000 bottles
HECTARES UNDER VINE	7
VITICULTURE METHOD	Conventional

Merlot, Nomi and Grigoletti. A solid bond ties this variety to the village of Nomi, a grape growing town on the right bank of the River Adige near Rovereto, where for generations the Grigolettis have been planting their best plots to merlot. This year, the Antica Vigna di Nomi, the Grigolettis' famous Riserva, turned out to be sound, although the 2006 harvest produced an enjoyable Merlot that is just a bit too simple. To raise morale, there was the Retiko '06, a white from chardonnay and sauvignon. This interesting wine gives notes of aniseed, citrus and pear on the nose and lively vitality on a palate that closes out minerally and deep. Other outstanding wines from this winemaking dynasty include the Cabernet '06, which is traditional in every way with those grassy notes that emerge with such determination only in Trentino. The interesting Maso Federico '04 is from bunches of marzemino, cabernet, lagrein and merlot left to dry slowly before crushing. Only a few bottles are produced of this wine, which is presented by the Grigolettis more as a sign of country hospitality than for commercial purposes.

La Vis/Valle di Cembra

VIA CARMINE, 7
38034 LAVIS [TN]
TEL. 0461440111
www.la-vis.com

ANNUAL PRODUCTION	5,500,000 bottles
HECTARES UNDER VINE	1350
VITICULTURE METHOD	Conventional

We received around 15 wines for tasting, if we count the sparklers from Cesarini Sforza, a group subsidiary, and wines from Valle di Cembra - Cantina di Montagna. This ever-expanding winemaking group operates various sites in the Dolomites, Tuscany and Sicily. Oenological management is in the hands of the experienced Francesco Polastri, assisted by Giorgia Brugnara for the sparklers and Massimo Tarter in the cellar at Cembra. Roberto Giacomoni and Fausto Peratoner are still at the helm. The wines show the usual reliability and great value for money, in line with the La Vis development strategy. The orchestra here plays in harmony but this time the top notes are missing. Good scores went to the enjoyable classic sparkler Aquila Reale Riserva '01 and a nice Sorni '07, a blend of chardonnay, nosiola and pinot bianco from one of the smallest DOC zones in the region. We should also mention wines from the high hills, selected in Valle di Cembra. Among these are a Müller Thurgau Vigna delle Forche '07 and a good Pinot Nero Dos Caslir '06. In the meantime, new riservas are ageing in the cellar. We will say more about them in the future.

○ Retiko '06	♀♀ 5
● Maso Federico Passito Rosso '04	♀ 5
● Trentino Cabernet '06	♀ 4
● Trentino Merlot Antica Vigna di Nomi '06	♀ 5
● Trentino Merlot Antica Vigna di Nomi '05	♀♀ 5
● Trentino Merlot Antica Vigna di Nomi '04	♀♀ 5
● Trentino Merlot Antica Vigna di Nomi '03	♀♀ 5
● Trentino Merlot Antica Vigna di Nomi '02	♀♀ 5
● Maso Federico Passito Rosso '02	♀♀ 5

○ Trento Aquila Reale Ris. '01	♀♀ 8
○ Trentino Bianco dei Sorni '07	♀♀ 4*
○ Trentino Chardonnay Ritratti '07	♀♀ 4*
○ Trentino Müller Thurgau V. delle Forche '07	♀♀ 4
● Trentino Pinot Nero Dos Caslir '06	♀♀ 5
● Trentino Pinot Nero Ritratti '06	♀♀ 5
○ Mandolaia '07	♀ 5
● Ritratto Rosso '06	♀ 5
○ Trentino Müller Thurgau Maso Roncador '07	♀ 4
● Ritratto Rosso '03	♀♀♀ 5
● Ritratto Rosso '04	♀♀ 5
○ Ritratto Bianco '06	♀♀ 5
○ Trentino Chardonnay Ritratti '06	♀♀ 4
○ Trentino Müller Thurgau V. delle Forche '06	♀♀ 4

Letrari

VIA MONTE BALDO, 13/15
38068 ROVERETO [TN]
TEL. 0464480200
www.letrari.it

ANNUAL PRODUCTION	150,000 bottles
HECTARES UNDER VINE	23
VITICULTURE METHOD	Natural

The lion roars again with a new interpretation of spumante, a Riserva del Fondatore 976 '00 with amazing character, bearing, development and distinct versatility. The lion in question is Leonello Letrari who, with almost 70 harvests behind him, is a patriarch of Trentino wine. A few seasons back, he transferred his estate to his children, oenologist Lucia and sales director Paolo, but Leonello is always ready to suggest, change or if necessary criticize. The range of Letrari wines is broad and varied, in some respects perhaps too varied. The family has plans for expanding sparkling wine production with a Rosé and improving vineyard management for Enantio, the red wine from Terra dei Forti south of Vallagarina, original home of the Letraris where they own splendid vineyards. Aside from the classic sparkler, the two versions of Cabernet and a Marzemino are particularly pleasant. This is especially true of the Cabernet Sauvignon '04, one of the best we tasted in Trentino, while the Marzemino Selezione '07 is a perfect example of its wine type.

Longariva

FRAZ. BORGO SACCO
VIA R. ZANDONAI, 6
38068 ROVERETO [TN]
TEL. 0464437200
www.longariva.it

ANNUAL PRODUCTION	100,000 bottles
HECTARES UNDER VINE	22
VITICULTURE METHOD	Natural

The Quartella Riserva '04, a red from cabernet franc, is the wine we feel best represents the production philosophy of Marco and Rosanna Manica, a Rovereto couple who for years have been leading personalities on the Trentino wine scene. Despite the fact the 2004 growing year was not especially favourable, they managed to produce a well-balanced, elegant red with great power, capable of developing to its best in a few years' time. Here at Longariva, the Manicas have never wanted to have it all now. They are accustomed to thinking and acting over the long term so it is no accident that they tend their vineyards like gardens, deliberately planting for drastically reduced yields to produce wines that will last over time. The other estate reds are always good, from the Merlot Tovi Riserva '04 to the Bordeaux Tre Cesure Riserva '04, but the Cabernet Sauvignon Marognon '04 failed to display its customary impact on the nose. The Manicas did not present their Marzemino and wines from white grapes have yet to fully express their vitality. The copper-hued Pinot Grigio Graminè '07 is always a delight.

● Trentino Cabernet Sauvignon '04	▼▼ 5
○ Trento Riserva del Fondatore 976 '00	▼▼ 7
● Trentino Cabernet Franc Ris. '04	▼▼ 5
● Trentino Marzemino Letrari Sel. '07	▼▼ 4*
○ Trento Brut '05	▼▼ 5
● Ballistarius '04	▼ 6
● Ballistarius '01	♉ 6
○ Trento Riserva del Fondatore '98	♉ 6
○ Trento Riserva del Fondatore 976 '99	♉ 7
● Ballistarius '03	♉ 6
● Trentino Marzemino Sel. '05	♉ 5

● Trentino Cabernet Quartella Ris. '04	▼▼ 4*
● Trentino Rosso Tre Cesure Ris. '04	▼▼ 6
● Trentino Cabernet Sauvignon Marognon Ris. '04	▼ 6
● Trentino Merlot Tovi Ris. '04	▼ 4
○ Trentino Pinot Grigio Graminé '07	▼ 5
○ Trentino Sauvignon Cascari '06	▼ 4
● Trentino Cabernet Sauvignon Marognon Ris. '01	♉ 6
● Trentino Cabernet Quartella Ris. '03	♉ 4
● Trentino Rosso Tre Cesure Ris. '03	♉ 6
● Trentino Rosso Tre Cesure Ris. '00	♉ 5

Maso Furli

LOC. FURLI
VIA FURLI, 32
38015 LAVIS [TN]
TEL. 0461240667
masofurli@alice.it

ANNUAL PRODUCTION   18,000 bottles
HECTARES UNDER VINE 4
VITICULTURE METHOD   Natural

Many consider Marco Zanoni one of the finest white winemakers in Trentino. Others think of him as a winemaker skilled at making reds and whites. Either way, Zanoni is an expert. He has one of the smallest estates in the Dolomites, and perhaps in Italy, with beautifully tended vineyards and very advanced winery technology with machines almost all conceived, designed, built and put into operation by Marco himself, inspired by oenologist friends such as Mario Pojer and Fulvio Mattedi. There is technology for crushing in a nitrogen-saturated environment to protect the aromas of the grape, and other devices imitated or copied long ago by various winemaking equipment companies. Marco's wines are absolutely Trentino and show the power of technique when it combines with the gift of simplicity. Again this year, he has a marvellous red, the Furli 2005, that went to our finals. It's very good indeed with typically vegetal aromas and a chewy palate with smooth tannins and a dynamic finish. The juicy, vibrant Incrocio Manzoni '06 is a supple white veined with fragrances, despite substantial alcohol and mouthfilling structure. The Traminer '06 is sound.

Maso Martis

LOC. MARTIGNANO
VIA DELL'ALBERA, 52
38100 TRENTO
TEL. 0461821057
www.masomartis.it

ANNUAL PRODUCTION   60,000 bottles
HECTARES UNDER VINE 12
VITICULTURE METHOD   Conventional

This estate set up by Antonio Stelzer and his wife Roberta Giuriali on the hill at the foot of Mount Calisio, with some of the best-aspected plots around Trento, produces still wines and sparklers with a deliberately soft in style, aroma-led timbre. The family manage the property with a special eye on chardonnay and pinot nero, varieties destined to be transformed into Trento wines, increasingly requested by the market. The attractive Riserva '02, from 70 per cent pinot nero and the remainder chardonnay, shows broad, complex aromas with toasted bread sensations and shades of minerality. The succulent palate signs off with a bay leaf-themed finish. The fresh, juicy Demi Sec is also interesting and the Brut Rosé, from pinot nero with five per cent chardonnay, has a full palate laced with black cherry sensations. There are also plenty of still wines. Among these we mention the Cabernet Sauvignon L'Indaco '04 and a fragrant Chardonnay Incanto '06.

● Maso Furli Rosso '05	♟♟ 5
○ Incrocio Manzoni '06	♟♟ 5
○ Trentino Traminer Aromatico '06	♟ 5
● Maso Furli Rosso '04	♟♟ 5
● Maso Furli Rosso '03	♟♟ 5
○ Trentino Traminer Aromatico '05	♟♟ 5

○ Trento Brut Ris. '02	♟♟ 6
○ Trento Demi Sec	♟♟ 6
● Trentino Cabernet Sauvignon L'Indaco '04	♟ 6
○ Trentino Chardonnay L'Incanto '06	♟ 5
◉ Trento Brut Rosé	♟ 6
● Moscato Rosa '06	♟♟ 6
○ Trentino Chardonnay L'Incanto '04	♟♟ 4

MezzaCorona

VIA DEL TEROLDEGO, 1
38016 MEZZOCORONA [TN]
TEL. 0461616399
www.mezzacorona.it

ANNUAL PRODUCTION	30,000,000 bottles
HECTARES UNDER VINE	3.500
VITICULTURE METHOD	Conventional

This major group, both in vine stock and sales, is ubiquitous on the Italian and international markets. Mezzacorona is a big numbers operation in Trentino and elsewhere: it also has holdings in Sicily. For some years now, the cellar has been releasing a selection of top-quality wines. Accustomed to producing runs of millions of bottles, the cellar treated Teroldego Riserva '05 – around 150,000 units – with craft-like attention that created a wine worthy of the Three Glass finals. It immediately shows off its elegant structure and rich fruit with smooth tannins and perceptions on nose and palate that recall chocolate and liquorice. The finish is deep and enjoyable. Another small, attractive selection, this time a Trento DOC, is Flavio, the '02 Riserva of Rotari. The Teroldego Riserva Nos '04 also put on an excellent performance: this characterful, varietal wine is released in 10,000 units. Other sound wines include the fresh, savoury Müller Thurgau and the lean yet nicely complex Selezione Castel Firmian Chardonnay. The Traminer, the Sauvignon and an outsider – for Mezzacorona – the Marzemino are all sound.

Casata Monfort

VIA CARLO SETTE, 21
38015 LAVIS [TN]
TEL. 0461246353
www.cantinemonfort.it

ANNUAL PRODUCTION	140,000 bottles
HECTARES UNDER VINE	40
VITICULTURE METHOD	Conventional

In time, wines from this estate will show their terroir-driven worth. But the wineries themselves are unique, one in the historic structure in Lavis, the other at Civezzano, at Maso Cantanghel, in the walls of a fortress built at the start of the 20th century by the Hapsburg army. There are many varieties and product images but the philosophy is the same, with Lorenzo Simoni and his relatives always in the front line in the vineyards and cellar. They are also active in recovering old grape varieties threatened with extinction, from wanderbara to lagarino, san lorenzo and portoghese, as well as growing Trentino favourites. It was an indifferent year and the usually excellent wines have either suffered from the weather or may need further ageing. The Teroldego Rotaliano '07, for example, is still slightly clenched on nose and palate. Above all the famous Pinot Nero Maso Cantanghel gave a much more confident performance with the 2005 vintage. The other wines, the Müller Thurgau and Pinot Grigio, both from 2007, the Lagrein '06 and Spumante Classico, are well crafted and drinkable.

● Teroldego Rotaliano Ris. '05	♼♼	5
○ Trento Rotari Flavio Ris. '02	♼♼	7
● Teroldego Rotaliano Nos Ris. '04	♼♼	6
○ Trentino Chardonnay Castel Firmian '07	♼♼	4*
○ Trentino Müller Thurgau Castel Firmian '07	♼♼	4
● Trentino Marzemino Castel Firmian '07	♼	4
○ Trentino Sauvignon Castel Firmian '07	♼	4
○ Trentino Traminer Castel Firmian '07	♼	4
● Teroldego Rotaliano Nos '01	♼♼	6
○ Trento Rotari Flavio '01	♼♼	7
● Teroldego Rotaliano Ris. '01	♼♼	5*

● Teroldego Rotaliano '07	♼	4
● Trentino Lagrein '06	♼	4
○ Trentino Müller Thurgau '07	♼	4
○ Trentino Pinot Grigio '07	♼	4
● Trentino Pinot Nero Maso Cantanghel '05	♼	5
○ Trento Brut Monfort	♼	5
○ Blanc de Sers '06	♼♼	4
○ Blanc de Sers '05	♼♼	4

Pojer & Sandri

LOC. MOLINI, 4
38010 FAEDO [TN]
TEL. 0461650342
www.pojeresandri.it

ANNUAL PRODUCTION	250,000 bottles
HECTARES UNDER VINE	25
VITICULTURE METHOD	Conventional

Mario Pojer and Fiorentino Sandri have won Three Glasses again. The star is Faye Rosso '05, a Bordeaux blend base with lagrein. Always succulent, long and elegantly complexity, this time it has benefited from fine growing season at Faedo. Experimental vinification techniques, from nitrogen-saturated chambers to washing the grapes, are applied as the vineyards in Valle di Cembra are expanded. Our heroes have also restored a splendid farm, built a vinegar house and planted grape varieties for organic cultivation. In short, Pojer and Sandri look to the future. The range includes Essenzia '06, a late harvest of chardonnay, sauvignon, riesling renano, gewürztraminer and kerner, Besler Bianck '04, from pinot bianco, riesling renano, sauvignon, incrocio Manzoni and kerner, and Besler Ross '04, from blends with old native varieties, including zweigelt and negrare. Then there is the classic line-up of 2007 whites, the sparklers, cuvées from different vintages with a juicy Rosé, an estate classic, the chardonnay and pinot bianco Faye Bianco '05 and a curiosity, Merlino, from lagrein must fortified with the brandy Pojer & Sandri have distilled for years.

Pràvis

LOC. LE BIOLCHE, 1
38076 LASINO [TN]
TEL. 0461564305
www.pravis.it

ANNUAL PRODUCTION	200,000 bottles
HECTARES UNDER VINE	32
VITICULTURE METHOD	Conventional

The 2007 harvest was the last entirely co-ordinated by the estate's historic trio, where the Valle dei Laghi vineyards lie at altitudes ranging from the valley floor's olive groves at nearby Lake Garda, to the slopes of Mount Bondone. Now Domenico Pedrini's daughter, Erica, has joined the staff, bringing two degrees in oenology, one from Geisenheim in Germany. Since the last harvest, Domenico's other daughter Giulia and Alessio, oldest son of the farm manager Gianni Chistè, have also been contributing, although both are still students. This gives an insight into an estate that has always operated with country frankness. The wines are special and in a sense obscure, especially those from grapes lightly dried on racks: Stravino di Stravino, from riesling, incrocio Manzoni, chardonnay, kerner and sauvignon, as well as Ora from nosiola and Soliva, beefed up with goldtraminer, a variety from a crossbreeding project by Rebo Rigotti. All have an up-and-down nose-palate profile. So it is the Kerner that reveals the character of these winemakers who look to the future with confidence.

● Rosso Faye '05	ҮҮҮ	6
O Besler Biank '04	ҮҮ	5
O Essenzia Vendemmia Tardiva '06	ҮҮ	5
O Spumante Cuvée '03/'04	ҮҮ	6
● Besler Ross '04	ҮҮ	5
O Bianco Faye '05	ҮҮ	5
☉ Cuvée Rosé	ҮҮ	5
● Merlino	ҮҮ	6
O Müller Thurgau Palai '07	ҮҮ	4*
O Nosiola '07	ҮҮ	4*
● Pinot Nero '07	ҮҮ	5
● Pinot Nero Sel. '04	ҮҮ	5
O Sauvignon '07	Ү	5
☉ Vin dei Molini Rosato '07	Ү	4
O Bianco Faye '01	ҮҮҮ	5
● Rosso Faye '00	ҮҮҮ	6
● Rosso Faye '94	ҮҮҮ	5
● Rosso Faye '93	ҮҮҮ	5

O Kerner '07	ҮҮ	4*
O Stravino di Stravino '05	ҮҮ	5
● Fratagranda '04	Ү	5
O Soliva Gold '05	Ү	6
● Fratagranda '02	ҮҮ	5
O L'Ora '05	ҮҮ	5
O Stravino di Stravino '04	ҮҮ	5
O Stravino di Stravino '03	ҮҮ	6

Eugenio Rosi

VIA TAVERNELLE, 3B
38060 VOLANO [TN]
TEL. 0464461375
www.vignaioli.trentino.it

Cantina Rotaliana

VIA TRENTO, 65B
38017 MEZZOLOMBARDO [TN]
TEL. 0461601010
www.cantinarotaliana.it

ANNUAL PRODUCTION	18,000 bottles
HECTARES UNDER VINE	5.5
VITICULTURE METHOD	Certified organic

ANNUAL PRODUCTION	1,000,000 bottles
HECTARES UNDER VINE	330
VITICULTURE METHOD	Conventional

A few bottles but good ones. Eugenio Rosi doesn't want to change his approach as a self-proclaimed wine artisan. Eugenio wants hands-on control of every stage of winemaking, from field to cellar and on to distribution. For the past few vintages, Rosi has been producing wines to absolutely natural criteria, adopting organic methods in both vineyard and cellar. This year he has broadened the range – if that's the right expression – of his wines, adding to his traditional reds a thousand bottles of wine from pinot bianco, nosiola and chardonnay. He calls the new product Anisos, a unique white made in the style used for red grape varieties. Anisos '07 is off-beat in that it was not filtered, aged in large barrels and made practically without sulphur. Its calling card is delicate white cherry fragrances followed by a savoury, minerally palate with a taut, dynamic finish. The Esegesi '04 is a truly great wine, a complex solid Bordeaux blend with elegant development, silky tannins and great depth. Finally, the unusual, intriguing Dòron comes from marzemino grapes left to part-dry on racks to create a fine meditation wine.

This is the Teroldego winery par excellence, in both quantity – it leads the field – and reliability. The search for quality has spurred this solid co-operative winery to major achievements and the latest harvests to be bottled are impressive. But in contrast to other vintages, they did not win Three Glasses. Clesurae '06 stayed in the cellar to age some more so the Teroldego Riserva '05 took its turn as Rotaliana's flag bearer, a task it performed very well. It shows its usual elegance and is nicely harmonious if slightly less interesting than previous vintages. There was a great performance from the base version of Teroldego, Etichetta Rossa '07, released in more than 600,000 bottles at a fair price for straightforward, satisfying drinkability. The oenologist-manager Leonardo Pilati also shows he is a sound interpreter of the white grapes from member-growers. The most convincing was Traminer Aromatico '07, a full-bodied, minerally wine with good structure and a tangy, pleasantly spirited finish. Other outstanding wines include the Lagrein and the new Groppello di Revò.

● Trentino Rosso Esegesi '04	⟨Ⳑ⟩	5
● Dòron '05	⟨ⳐⳐ⟩	6
O Anisos '07	⟨Ⳑ⟩	5
● Trentino Rosso Esegesi '99	⟨ⳐⳐ⟩	5
● Trentino Rosso Esegesi '03	⟨ⳐⳐ⟩	5
● Trentino Rosso Esegesi '02	⟨ⳐⳐ⟩	5
● Dòron '04	⟨ⳐⳐ⟩	6
● Trentino Marzemino Poiema '04	⟨ⳐⳐ⟩	5
● Trentino Marzemino Poiema Ris. '05	⟨ⳐⳐ⟩	5

● Teroldego Rotaliano Ris. '05	⟨Ⳑ⟩	5
● Teroldego Rotaliano Et. Rossa '07	⟨ⳐⳐ⟩	4*
O Trentino Traminer Aromatico '07	⟨ⳐⳐ⟩	4*
● Groppello di Revò '07	⟨Ⳑ⟩	4
O Thamè Bianco '07	⟨Ⳑ⟩	5
⊙ Thamè Rosato '07	⟨Ⳑ⟩	4
O Trentino Chardonnay '07	⟨Ⳑ⟩	3
● Trentino Lagrein '07	⟨Ⳑ⟩	4
● Trentino Merlot '07	⟨Ⳑ⟩	4
O Trentino Müller Thurgau '07	⟨Ⳑ⟩	3*
● Teroldego Rotaliano Clesurae '99	⟨ⳐⳐⳐ⟩	6
● Teroldego Rotaliano Clesurae '02	⟨ⳐⳐⳐ⟩	6
● Teroldego Rotaliano Clesurae '05	⟨ⳐⳐ⟩	6
● Teroldego Rotaliano Ris. '04	⟨ⳐⳐⳐ⟩	4

★ Tenuta San Leonardo

FRAZ. BORGHETTO ALL'ADIGE
LOC. SAN LEONARDO
38060 AVIO [TN]
TEL. 0464689004
www.sanleonardo.it

ANNUAL PRODUCTION	145,000 bottles
HECTARES UNDER VINE	21
VITICULTURE METHOD	Conventional

Father and son Marchesi Carlo and
Anselmo Guerrieri Gonzaga are used to
the challenges of difficult growing years.
In fact, that is when they strive to show
that once a wine is great, it is always great.
Ties with the land and farming culture are
strong so innovations never alter tradition
and the estate is beautifully tended, with a
couple of hectares of new vines planted in
a strip of parkland. The history of Trentino
wine is here in these orderly rows, the
ancient church, the stately home and the
venerable cellar. In it, Luigino Tinelli and his
enthusiastic staff, the children of farmers
who have worked here for generations,
lavish care on the vineyards and dedication
in the cellar. The San Leonardo '04 soared
effortlessly over the Three Glass hurdle with
its broad range of aromatics that reveal
refined sensations of ripe fruit and bay
leaf before the equally well-defined palate
tempts with velvety structure and elegant
tannins. A step below this is the vigorous
Villa Gresti, which is still agile and complex
despite coming from the 2004 growing
season, not one of the most memorable in
Trentino. But class will out.

Istituto Agrario Provinciale San Michele all'Adige

VIA EDMONDO MACH, 1
38010 SAN MICHELE ALL'ADIGE [TN]
TEL. 0461615252
www.ismaa.it

ANNUAL PRODUCTION	250,000 bottles
HECTARES UNDER VINE	60
VITICULTURE METHOD	Conventional

Seven sound wines honoured this long
established, dynamic wine school. Winery
manager Enrico Paternoster's intuition
can be seen in the style of these bottles,
which have been improving for the past
couple of years. The most representative,
a red Cabernet Franc and a white blend
of sauvignon, chardonnay, pinot grigio,
incrocio Manzoni and riesling renano,
belong to the Monastero line dedicated
to the Augustinian monastery, splendidly
restored by the Trento provincial authority,
which houses the modern cellar, now
transformed into the Edmondo Mach
foundation. The Monastero label '05
Bianco is outstanding. It's one of the best
wines from the category we tasted this year
and deservedly reached our finals. The
Monastero Rosso '05 is good, though still
a bit closed. The other Bordeaux blend, the
Castel San Michele '06, is built on similar
lines and holds a record. In 1964 it was
the first Trentino wine to be fermented in
barrique. Other good showings came from
the fruity Pinot Bianco San Donà '07 to the
late-harvest Prepositura, the elegant Pinot
Nero and a textbook interpretation of Müller
Thurgau.

● San Leonardo '04	♟♟♟	8
● Villa Gresti '04	♟♟	6
● San Leonardo '99	♟♟♟	8
● San Leonardo '97	♟♟♟	5
● San Leonardo '96	♟♟♟	5
● San Leonardo '95	♟♟♟	5
● San Leonardo '94	♟♟♟	5
● San Leonardo '93	♟♟♟	5
● San Leonardo '90	♟♟♟	5
● San Leonardo '88	♟♟♟	5
● San Leonardo '03	♟♟♟	8
● San Leonardo '01	♟♟♟	8
● San Leonardo '00	♟♟♟	8
● Villa Gresti '03	♟♟♟	7

○ Trentino Bianco Monastero '05	♟♟	5
○ Prepositura '07	♟♟	5
○ Trentino Müller Thurgau '07	♟♟	4*
○ Trentino Pinot Bianco Vign. San Donà '07	♟♟	4*
● Trentino Rosso Castel San Michele '06	♟♟	5
● Trentino Rosso Monastero '06	♟♟	6
● Trentino Pinot Nero '06	♟	5
● Trentino Rosso Monastero '04	♟♟	6
● Trentino Rosso Monastero '03	♟♟	6
○ Trento Mach Riserva del Fondatore '02	♟♟	5

Toblino

FRAZ. SARCHE
VIA LONGA, 1
38070 CALAVINO [TN]
TEL. 0461564168
www.toblino.it

ANNUAL PRODUCTION 400,000 bottles
HECTARES UNDER VINE 700
VITICULTURE METHOD Conventional

Things here move quickly. This co-operative winery is perennially busy in winemaking and on the hospitality front, with groups of tourists and wine aficionados wandering through the nearby vineyards, among the fermentation silos or sitting in the comfortable restaurant and tasting room with more than 400 wines. Few other co-operative wineries can offer so much. Credit goes to the president, Carlo Filiberto Bleggi, and a staff always ready to tackle new challenges. But at Toblino, the focus is mainly on wine and experiments are under way with varieties never grown in the Valle dei Laghi between Garda and the Brenta Dolomites. The most exciting surprise came from an unusual variety for the valley, teroldego. Made in a fresh, approachable style and sold at an affordable price, it is complex and drinkable, revealing character and frankness that would shame some more ambitious wines. Ora '05, a wine from part-dried nosiola grapes, is also thought-provoking and rather good. The traditional Nosiola is also sound, as is a Kerner that gets more convincing every year. Toblino, and the Valle dei Laghi's, pride and joy, Vino Santo '98 is still austere.

● Teroldego '06	TT	3*
○ Kerner '07	TT	4*
○ Trentino Traminer Aromatico '07	TT	4*
○ Trentino Vino Santo Puro Sel. '98	TT	7
○ L'Ora '05	T	5
○ Trentino Müller Thurgau '07	T	3
○ Trentino Nosiola '07	T	3
○ L'Ora '04	YY	5
○ Trentino Vino Santo Puro Sel. '97	YY	6
○ Trentino Vino Santo Puro Sel. '96	YY	6
○ L'Ora '04	YY	5
○ Trentino Traminer Aromatico '02	YY	3*

Vallarom

FRAZ. MASI, 21
38063 AVIO [TN]
TEL. 0464684297
www.vallarom.it

ANNUAL PRODUCTION 48,000 bottles
HECTARES UNDER VINE 8
VITICULTURE METHOD Natural

Barbara and Filippo Scienza are two of the most active winemakers in Trentino. They experiment with vineyard and cellar techniques aimed more at respecting nature than exploiting technology and they can do so thanks to their know-how and personal experience in the vineyards. On their splendid farm opposite the dramatic Castello d'Avio in the heart of the Campi Sarni, an excellent wine area mentioned in medieval documents, the Vallarom vineyards are producing excellent results. The Bordeaux-style red Campi Sarni '05 shows intense aromatics, its close-woven palate is fleshy with clear minerality, elegantly textured tannins and a complex, layered finish. The Chardonnay Vigneto Casetta '06 is also complex. This rich white wine is concentrated throughout and promises well for the future. It should be said that this fine brace is accompanied by a range of very respectable products, from the Syrah '06 to the Merlot Vigneto Belvedere '07 and sauvignon, riesling, pinot bianco and chardonnay Vadum Caesaris '07. All are excellent value for the money.

● Campi Sarni Rosso '05	TT	5
○ Chardonnay Vigneto Casetta '06	TT	5
○ Vadum Caesaris '07	TT	4*
● Merlot Vigneto Belvedere '07	T	4
● Syrah '06	T	6
● Syrah '04	YY	6
● Syrah '05	YY	6

Vigneti delle Meridiane

LOC. CASTELLER, 6
38100 TRENTO
TEL. 0464419393
www.vignetimeridiane.it

Vilàr

VIA CAVOLAVILLA, 35
38060 VILLA LAGARINA [TN]
TEL. 0464409028
www.vilar.it

ANNUAL PRODUCTION 250,000 bottles
HECTARES UNDER VINE 50
VITICULTURE METHOD Conventional

The 2009 harvest will be the first at the new headquarters, a modern, wood and steel structure not far from Trentino airport, of this long-established co-operative city winery, which has been called Le Meridiane for the past few years. Silently, but with great determination, this co-operative has always worked in tandem with other wineries – Concilio di Volano – to expand their market. The new structure can only be beneficial for the quality of the already convincing products. Member growers in this co-operative farm a whole series of magnificent hillside vineyards typical of the Trento landscape, extending across Mounts Calisio, Marzola and Bondone, at altitudes in some places over 700 metres, as well as valley floor holdings on alluvial soil along the Adige. Here is the line-up, Pinot Nero Riserva '06, Teroldego Cernidor '06 and Müller Thurgau '07, all wines of character and great technical quality, accompanied by a Merlot '06, Sauvignon '07 and Traminer '07, as well as a Marzemino '06 from grapes sourced from neighbouring Vallagarina.

ANNUAL PRODUCTION 22,000 bottles
HECTARES UNDER VINE 4.5
VITICULTURE METHOD Natural

Luigi Spagnolli did not exactly rush into winemaking. He decided some time ago to transfer his experience as an oenologist to the country and look after every phase of work himself through exhaustion, obstacles and successes. Luigi is working away – he says he will be ready in a couple of years, growing years permitting – to present international style and territory-focused wines. His vineyards are on the hills of Villalagarina, from where this tiny estate takes its name, farmed with the most natural agricultural practices possible, though Luigi never takes sides as a supporter of organic or biodynamic methods. But recent harvests have certainly not made his job easier. He has had to face a whole series of difficult weather factors and further reduce his already small yields. He has produced wines that are perhaps a bit less complex than other vintages but still made with dedication and precision. His Cabernet Sauvignon '05 has intensely fruity aromas, the palate showing balance and juiciness with ripe, sweet tannins and an elegant finish. The Marzemino '07 is in the usual mould with a lovely nose but a rather severe palate.

● Teroldego Cernidor '06	▾▾	4*
○ Trentino Müller Thurgau '07	▾▾	4*
● Trentino Pinot Nero Ris. '06	▾▾	4*
○ Trentino Chardonnay '07	▾	4
○ Trentino Gewürztraminer '07	▾	4
● Trentino Marzemino '06	▾	4
● Trentino Merlot '06	▾	4
○ Trentino Sauvignon '07	▾	4

● Cabernet Sauvignon '05	▾▾	4*
● Trentino Marzemino '07	▾	4
● Morela '03	▾▾	6
● Cabernet Sauvignon '04	▾▾	4
● Cabernet Sauvignon '03	▾▾	4
● Morela '04	▾▾	6

Vivallis

VIA VALENTINI, 37
38060 CALLIANO [TN]
TEL. 0464834113
www.vivallis.it

ANNUAL PRODUCTION	1,000,000 bottles
HECTARES UNDER VINE	730
VITICULTURE METHOD	Conventional

Many co-operative wineries in Trentino seek visibility by almost arrogantly flaunting their production figures. This winery has taken a diametrically opposed strategy. Despite being one of the largest growing and winemaking co-operatives in the Dolomites, it has chosen to only present excellent quality products under its own name. Adriano Orsi is the president, as he is of Cavit, assisted by manager Mauro Baldessari and oenologist Flavio Cristoforetti, who is increasingly expert at interpreting the emblematic local variety, marzemino. In fact, all three Marzeminos racked up excellent scores, although we just preferred the Ziresi '06 over the Isera '06 and Vigna Fornas '06. But this winery is more than just Marzemino. Its range has a dozen or so wines, all carefully selected from the zoned "campi", or fields, of Vallagarina. Each vineyard has its own variety. The Merlot Vigna Borgosacco '06 is nicely made and has shown fine character and elegance for some years now. Lagrein Vigna Costa '06, a variety rarely grown in south Trentino, is also well crafted.

Roberto Zeni

FRAZ. GRUMO
VIA STRETTA, 2
38010 SAN MICHELE ALL'ADIGE [TN]
TEL. 0461650456
www.zeni.tn.it

ANNUAL PRODUCTION	189,000 bottles
HECTARES UNDER VINE	20
VITICULTURE METHOD	Conventional

If small Trentino producers are joining the emerging Italian Independent Winemakers Federation, credit goes in part to Roberto Zeni. He has been president of the local organization for years. His estate has been active for 30 years and experiments constantly. At the moment, Roberto is giving the cellar an extensive makeover and expanding the vineyards around his farmhouse high in the hills, where he produces several thousand bottles of an excellent, chardonnay-only classic sparkler with long lees ageing. Zeni also vinifies a forgotten native variety, rossara, and has not abandoned his red vineyards. The Teroldego comes in various versions, depending on the vintage. The youngest, Le Albere '06, again this year has plenty of backbone, a broad red berry bouquet and obvious longevity. As on other estates, the 2007 vintage was not great for whites. Not even skill can repair nature's defects and the whites from the Zeni family – Roberto works alongside his brother Andrea, children and grandchildren – are not always convincing. But the pinot bianco, riesling, sauvignon and chardonnay Bianco Sortì is very pleasant.

● Trentino Lagrein V. Costa '06	4*
● Trentino Marzemino dei Ziresi Sup. '06	5
● Trentino Marzemino V. Fornas '06	4*
● Trentino Merlot V. Borgosacco '06	4*
● Trentino Cabernet Sauvignon V. Carbonera '06	4
● Trentino Marzemino di Isera Sup. '06	4
○ Trentino Pinot Grigio V. Reselé '07	4
● Trentino Marzemino dei Ziresi Sup. '04	5
● Trentino Marzemino di Isera Sup. '05	4*
● Trentino Marzemino dei Ziresi Sup. '05	5

○ Trento Zeni Brut '03	6
⊙ Rossara '07	4*
○ Sortì '07	5
● Teroldego Rotaliano Vign. Le Albere '06	4*
○ Pinot Grigio Ramato '07	4
⊙ Pinot Nero Vign. Broili '07	4
○ Trentino Müller Thurgau Le Croci '07	4
○ Sortì '05	5
● Teroldego Rotaliano Pini '99	6
● Teroldego Rotaliano Pini '01	7
○ Sortì '06	5

OTHER WINERIES

Albino Armani
VIA CERADELLO, 401
37020 DOLCÈ [TN]
TEL. 0457290033
www.albinoarmani.com

For years, Albino Armani has been a landmark for aficionados of foja tonda, a little known variety given a second chance by this estate. The decent '05 version has floral and aromatic herb aromas and a fruity, juicy palate. The Pinot Grigio Vigneto Corvara '07 and Chardonnay Piccola Botte '06 are interesting.

● Foja Tonda Rosso '05　　　　　　　♀ 4
○ Valdadige Chardonnay
　　Piccola Botte '06　　　　　　　　♀ 4
○ Valdadige Pinot Grigio Vign. Corvara '07 ♀ 4

Athesia Vini
VIA DANTE, 14
38063 AVIO [TN]
TEL. 0464834195
www.athesiavini.it

Two famous Trentino co-operative wineries, Avio and Nomi, set up Athesia Vini to combine forces while respecting the two lines. A dozen or so wines are on show at the new sales outlet in Nomi, all great value for money. Outstanding wines include the Bordeaux from Avio '05 and Marzemino Le Fornas di Nomi '06.

● Trentino Rosso Avio '05　　　　　♀♀ 4*
● Trentino Marzemino Le Fornas Nomi '06　♀ 4

Riccardo Battistotti
VIA 3 NOVEMBRE, 21
38060 NOMI [TN]
TEL. 0464834145
www.battistotti.com

Marzemino has always been the keynote wine at this small Vallagarina estate run by expert oenologist and skilled grower Riccardo Battistotti. There are two versions of the symbolic product: one for immediate consumption, the other, Verdini, designed to enable the Marzemino to mature further in the cellar.

● Trentino Marzemino '07　　　　　♀♀ 4*
● Trentino Marzemino Verdini '07　　♀ 4
○ Trentino Nosiola '07　　　　　　　♀ 4

Conti Bossi Fedrigotti
VIA UNIONE, 43
38068 ROVERETO [TN]
TEL. 0464439250
www.bossifedrigotti.com

Masi Agricola, the famous Verona-based wine enterprise, has managed the vineyards, cellar and sales since the 2007 harvest. The Conti Bossi Fedrigotti family took this step to relaunch the image of their wines. Marzemino and Fojaneghe are two house jewels.

● Fojaneghe Rosso '05　　　　　　　♀ 6
● Trentino Marzemino '07　　　　　　♀ 4

Campo Maseri
VIA ROTALIANA, 27A
38017 MEZZOLOMBARDO [TN]
TEL. 0461601486
www.villadevarda.com

Oenologist and shrewd connoisseur of Trentino wines Luigi Dolzan presents a dozen different labels each year, all distinctive and good value for money. Particularly well-crafted wines include the two versions of Teroldego, the Merlot '06 and the Müller Thurgau '07.

● Teroldego Rotaliano Ris. '05　　　♀♀ 5
● Teroldego Rotaliano Broilet '06　　♀ 4*
● Trentino Merlot Lenticlar '06　　　♀ 4
○ Trentino Müller Thurgau Roncola '07 ♀ 4

Cantina d'Isera
VIA AL PONTE, 1
38060 ISERA [TN]
TEL. 0464433795
www.cantinaisera.it

Wines from this solid co-operative winery are coming on in quality after the makeover of the facilities and vineyards. The Marzemino '07, released in 400,000 bottles, is as reliable as ever. The other wines may perhaps be less exciting but they are still well made and very attractively priced.

● Trentino Marzemino '07　　　　　♀♀ 3*
● Trentino Cabernet '06　　　　　　♀ 3*
○ Trentino Müller Thurgau '07　　　♀ 3*

OTHER WINERIES

De Tarczal

FRAZ. MARANO D'ISERA
VIA G. B. MIORI, 4
38060 ISERA [TN]
TEL. 0464409134
www.detarczal.com

A prominent place in the history of Trentino wine goes to this noble winemaking dynasty. Ruggero de Tarczal is a skilled entrepreneur, even though the latest harvests at Isera have not been a great help. The Merlot '04 and Cabernet Sauvignon from the same vintage are both sound.

● Trentino Merlot '04	🍷🍷	4
● Trentino Cabernet Sauvignon '04	🍷	4

Francesco Moser

LOC. GARDOLO DI MEZZO
38040 TRENTO
TEL. 0461990786
www.cantinemoser.com

Il Checco, as cycling tourists call him, no longer cycles competitively but he continues to tend his vast vineyards in areas near his native Valle di Cembra. The rows are currently undergoing conversion to yield appealing, territory-focused Trentino wines.

O Chardonnay '07	🍷	4
O Müller Thurgau '07	🍷	4

Madonna delle Vittorie

VIA LINFANO, 81
38062 ARCO [TN]
TEL. 0464505432
www.madonnadellevittorie.it

The rows run alongside the olive groves on the Trentino shore of Lake Garda. Both olives and grapes ripen in this Mediterranean climate and results are interesting. The oil is excellent but the wines are also intriguing. Top bottles include the Cabernet Sauvignon '06 and Nosiola '07.

● Trentino Cabernet Sauvignon '06	🍷🍷	4*
O Trentino Nosiola '07	🍷🍷	3*
O Trentino Chardonnay '07	🍷	4
● Trentino Rebo '06	🍷	4

Maso Bastie

LOC. BASTIE, 1
38060 VOLANO
TEL. 0464412747
www.masobastie.it

In one of the most beautiful grape growing corners of Trentino, Giuseppe and Patrizia Torelli tend splendid vineyards and make wines in the lovely cellar installed in their old farm. The few bottles of very special wines include the outstanding Moscato Rosa '06.

● Moscato Rosa '06	🍷🍷	6

Mori - Colli Zugna

VIA DEL GARDA, 35
38065 MORI [TN]
TEL. 0464918154
www.cantinamoricollizugna.it

This major co-operative winery in Vallagarina deserves a full profile. It produces 15 or so wines, all convincing, from the sparkler to Marzemino and Teroldego Vigna del Gelso '06, made outside the zone but deliciously approachable.

● Terodelgo V. del Gelso '06	🍷🍷	4*
● Trentino Lagrein Sup. Terra di San Mauro '05	🍷	4
O Trentino Moscato Giallo '07	🍷	4
O Trento Terra di San Mauro	🍷	5

Gino Pedrotti

FRAZ. LAGO DI CAVEDINE
VIA CAVEDINE, 7
38073 CAVEDINE [TN]
TEL. 0461564123
www.ginopedrotti.it

Pedrottis have been growing grapes for generations. The fruit comes from the family vineyards in Valle dei Laghi, part of which is currently being converted to biodynamic and organic methods. It goes into forthright wines like the hard-to-find Vino Santo '97. The Rebo and Nosiola are always flavourful.

O Trentino Vino Santo '97	🍷🍷	7
O Nosiola '07	🍷	4
● Rebo '05	🍷	4

OTHER WINERIES

Pelz & Piffer

VIA CAVADE
38034 CEMBRA [TN]
TEL. 0461683051
piffervito@tin.it

It is nice to watch the development of this tiny Cembra estate, energetically managed by Diego Pelz and Vito Piffer. The duo produce wines with backbone and character in their splendid cellar, starting with a splendid Riesling '04.

○ Trentino Riesling '04		3*

Pisoni

FRAZ. PERGOLESE DI LASINO
VIA SAN SIRO, 7A
38070 LASINO [TN]
TEL. 0461564106
www.pisoni.net

The Pisonis are a winemaking dynasty committed to making sparklers and distilling pomace. Above all, they are inveterate experimenters. They have opted to convert their vineyards to natural cultivation methods and while we wait for the results, they only submitted three sparklers.

○ Trento Extra Brut Ris. '03	5
○ Trento Brut	4
⊙ Trento Brut Rosé	5

Redondèl

VIA ROMA, 28
38017 MEZZOLOMBARDO [TN]
TEL. 0461601618
www.redondel.it

This estate makes very little wine from its vineyards in the heart of Campo Rotaliano at Redondèl, an area that features on 14th-century maps. A few thousand well-crafted bottles of two interpretations of Teroldego emerge from the cellar, although this year only one, the '06, was submitted for tasting.

● Teroldego Rotaliano '06		4*

Arcangelo Sandri

VIA VANEGGE, 4
38010 FAEDO [TN]
TEL. 0461650935
www.arcangelosandri.it

Arcangelo Sandri and his daughters, Nadia and Sonia, are expanding the tiny vineyards in the high hills of Faedo. Recent harvests have shown ups and downs in the well-made wines, among which the nicely aromatic Traminer Razer '07 is the stand-out.

○ Trentino Traminer Razer '07	4
○ Trentino Müller Thurgau Cosler '07	4

Alessandro Secchi

FRAZ. SERRAVALLE DI ALA
LOC. COLERI, 10
38061 ALA [TN]
TEL. 0464696647
www.secchivini.it

On the valley floor, which is well suited to growing red grapes, the Secchi family looks after the vineyards that yield a blend of marzemino and lagrein, Realgar '06, as well as their Bordeauxesque blend, Corindone '05.

● Corindone Rosso '05	5
● Realgar '06	4

Armando Simoncelli

VIA NAVICELLO, 7
38068 ROVERETO [TN]
TEL. 0464432373

These vineyards stand where once there was a river port that served the city of Rovereto, at Navicello on the river Adige. Armando Simoncelli shows all his skill as a master winemaker with the Bordeaux blend dedicated to the old port, Navesèl '05. The spumante is also good.

● Trentino Rosso Navesèl '05	4
○ Trento Brut	4
○ Trentino Chardonnay '07	3

OTHER WINERIES

Spagnolli

VIA G. B. ROSINA, 4A
38060 ISERA [TN]
TEL. 0464409054
www.vinispagnolli.it

Wines from Spagnolli are always reliable and fairly priced. The family has worked these vineyards for generations and the convincing current range includes the outstanding Tebro '04, a traditional blend of cabernet and merlot, Merlot '06 and Nosiola '07.

● Rosso Tebro '04	♥ 5
● Trentino Merlot '06	♥ 4
○ Trentino Nosiola '07	♥ 4

Villa Corniole

FRAZ. VERLA
VIA AL GREC', 23
38030 GIOVO [TN]
TEL. 0461695067
www.villacorniole.com

The four Pellegrini siblings built their cellar right in the heart of the porphyry area at Verla, near Giovo. Their traditional version Teroldego '06 convinced us for its freshness and elegance. Other good wines include the Chardonnay Lukin '04 and the Cimbro '06, a blend of teroldego, lagrein and merlot.

● Cimbro '06	♥♥ 4
● Teroldego Rotaliano '06	♥♥ 4*
○ Trentino Chardonnay Lukin '04	♥♥ 5
○ Trentino Chardonnay '07	♥ 4

Conti Wallenburg

LOC. MARTIGNANO
VIA BASSANO, 3
38100 TRENTO
TEL. 045913399
www.masowallenburg.it

Created by the historic Veneto-based Montresor wine company on the Martignano side of the hill of Trento, this estate can look back on only a few harvests. Nevertheless, the already outstanding range shows that the original intention, to set up a Trento estate for sparklers, is the right one.

○ Trento Corte Imperiale Brut	♥♥ 5
☉ Cuvée Costantinopoli Rosé	♥ 5
● Marquardo '06	♥ 6
○ Trentino Traminer Maria Adelaide '07	♥ 6

Elio e F.lli Zanotelli

V.LE 4 NOVEMBRE, 52
38034 CEMBRA [TN]
TEL. 0461683131
aa.zanotelli@inwind.it

Brother and sister team, Orietta and Dino Zanotelli are enthusiastic about the family estate. The bottles are crafted by genuine winemakers who are convinced that Pinot Nero can thrive at altitude. The 2005 harvest proves this with an elegant, juicy wine. The two whites are well typed.

● Trentino Pinot Nero Le Strope '05	♥♥ 4*
○ Trentino Müller Thurgau '07	♥ 4
○ Trentino Pinot Grigio '07	♥ 4

ALTO ADIGE

 This has been a five-star year for producers in Alto Adige. The number of Three Glass prizes has risen from 22 last year to 26 in the 2009 Guide. But there is more good news to show the sector's great energy, creativity and professional maturity. Let's start with the first Three Glass sparkler from Alto Adige, a splendid Brut Hausmannhof Riserva 1997 from Haderburg that has no equals. In fact, we nominated it Sparkler of the Year. What we think is one of the most interesting whites here, Pinot Bianco, continues to reap success. Five awards demonstrate that producers, too, believe in the potential of a variety that is particularly distinctive in the province of Bolzano. But the most sensational outcome is the number of Three Glass awards from two subzones that are small in terms of bottles produced but big in quality: Valle Isarco and Valle Venosta totted up ten award-winning wines. The former may no longer be news since its skilled small producers include the double Three Glass award-winner Abbazia di Novacella, whose Kellermeister, Celestino Lucin, is our Oenologist of the Year, but Valle Venosta has surprised even those who have loved and appreciated its wines for years. Two Three Glass Awards for Riesling and Pinot Bianco, both with screw caps like the rest of their wines, pay tribute to two emblematic Valle Venosta producers, Franz Prazner and Martin Aurich, proving that international quality wines can come from a valley where viticulture seems almost intrusive. Another small yet important news item is that five wines have screw tops, testifying to their producers' courage and willingness to innovate. Naturally, there are the usual serial winners. Elena Walch appears to have a yearly subscription to the Three Glass Award, as do Cantina di Bolzano (Gries and Santa Maddalena) and Termeno with two gewürztraminer-based wines. Naturally, there list includes Terlano, Colterenzio, Nals, Caldaro and San Michele Appiano for co-operative wineries along with Muri-Gries, Gumphof, Josephus Mayr and new entry, Stroblhof, with a characteristically Alto Adige-style Pinot Nero. Another small news item is that this year 14 schiava-based wines reached our finals and we have never been closer to awarding a top prize to at least one of them. Lagrein, one of the most widely planted wines in the province of Bolzano, Lagrein is now showing signs of stylistic maturity while the 2007 vintage for Gewürztraminer and Sauvignon shows that aromatic wine quality is good but not outstanding. The only sad note here is the rise in prices. While this may be indicative of Alto Adige's robust commercial health, we are unsure whether it is particularly far-sighted.

★ Abbazia di Novacella

FRAZ. NOVACELLA
VIA DELL'ABBAZIA, 1
39040 VARNA/VAHRN [BZ]
TEL. 0472836189
www.abbazianovacella.it

ANNUAL PRODUCTION	500,000 bottles
HECTARES UNDER VINE	20
VITICULTURE METHOD	Conventional

With seven wines in the finals, two Three Glass awards, the Oenologist of the Year and a range of high quality wines, the profile for Abbazia di Novacella and the team of oenologist Lucin and manager von Klebelsberg team could end here. The advance towards absolute excellence of this Valle Isarco estate has few equals on the Italian winemaking scene. Among the stand-outs this year are two new products, the Riesling '06 and Veltliner '07, both from the Praepositus line. The first, with a 30 per cent of its fruit harvested late at the beginning of December 2006, won Three Glasses on its first outing thanks to complex citrus, aromatic herb and spice aromas followed by a meaty palate where minerality, fullness and suppleness vie with each other through to a long, deep finish. The Veltliner fell short of winning the same prize only because it was trumped by the Sylvaner Praepositus '07, which won by a nose for its usual fragrant tropical fruit attack laced with clear mineral notes and an almost salty, vibrantly savoury palate. As far as the rest of the wines are concerned, just read the chart below.

Cantina Produttori Andriano

VIA DELLA CHIESA, 2
39010 ANDRIANO/ANDRIAN [BZ]
TEL. 0471510137
www.andrianer-kellerei.it

ANNUAL PRODUCTION	300,000 bottles
HECTARES UNDER VINE	85
VITICULTURE METHOD	Conventional

The most important news from here has to be the merger of this co-operative winery, the oldest in the province of Bolzano, with one of the most popular labels in Alto Adige winemaking, Cantina Terlano. The two brands will remain distinct but cellar and agronomic management will be placed in the capable hands of Rudi Kofler. New vintages will all be bottled at Terlano. Having said this, the wines from Andriano convinced us starting with a great winery classic, Lagrein Tor di Lupo '06, aged for two years in large and small barrels. Its caressing aromas of ripe blackberry mingle with varietal spiciness. The palate is chewy but nicely supple with lovely, well-honed tannins. The two Terlano Sauvignons, the Tor di Lupo version and the classic line, both from the 2007 vintage, are well balanced although we had a slight preference for the latter and its lean, dynamic profile. The Terlano Pinot Bianco '07 is fresh and well typed.

○ A. A. Valle Isarco Riesling Praepositus '06	♛♛♛	5
○ A. A. Valle Isarco Sylvaner Praepositus '07	♛♛♛	5
● A. A. Moscato Rosa Praepositus '07	♛♛	6
○ A. A. Valle Isarco Gewürztraminer Praepositus '07	♛♛	5
○ A. A. Valle Isarco Kerner Praepositus '07	♛♛	5
○ A. A. Valle Isarco Sylvaner '07	♛♛	4*
○ A. A. Valle Isarco Veltliner Praepositus '07	♛♛	5
● A. A. Lagrein Praepositus Ris. '05	♟♟	6
● A. A. Pinot Nero Praepositus Ris. '05	♟♟	6
○ A. A. Valle Isarco Kerner '07	♟♟	4
○ A. A. Valle Isarco Kerner Praepositus Passito '06	♟♟	6
○ A. A. Valle Isarco Pinot Grigio '07	♟♟	4
○ A. A. Valle Isarco Gewürztraminer '07	♟	5
○ A. A. Valle Isarco Kerner Praepositus '05	♛♛♛	5*
○ A. A. Valle Isarco Sylvaner Praepositus '06	♛♛♛	4*

● A. A. Lagrein Scuro Tor di Lupo '06	♟♟	6
○ A. A. Terlano Pinot Bianco Cl. '07	♟♟	3*
○ A. A. Terlano Sauvignon Cl. '07	♟♟	4*
○ A. A. Terlano Sauvignon Tor di Lupo '07	♟♟	4*
● A. A. Lagrein Scuro Tor di Lupo '00	♛♛♛	5
○ A. A. Gewürztraminer Sel. Tor di Lupo '04	♛♛	6
● A. A. Lagrein Scuro Tor di Lupo '05	♛♛	6
● A. A. Lagrein Scuro Tor di Lupo '02	♛♛	6
○ A. A. Terlano Sauvignon Tor di Lupo '06	♛♛	4

Baron Widmann

ENDERGASSE, 3
39040 CORTACCIA/KURTATSCH [BZ]
TEL. 0471880092
www.baron-widmann.it

ANNUAL PRODUCTION	35,000 bottles
HECTARES UNDER VINE	15
VITICULTURE METHOD	Conventional

Andreas Widmann's wines are sketched in light and shade rather than flashy colours. These very discreet wines run the risk of being overlooked at comparative tastings when up against with products that flaunt a showier profile. Nonetheless, these are wines that are not just impeccably made: they have a well-defined style and loads of personality. One taste of the standard Schiava '07 clearly confirms what we have just said. Graceful aromas of flowers and fruit mingle gracefully with spice and tobacco as they lead into a soft, fresh, delicately almond-like palate. In short, a delight. Elegant in its aromas of fruit and nettles, the Sauvignon '07 has a flamboyantly juicy, dynamic palate. Finally, we mention two very good and distinctly elegant : the Weiss '07, from 70 per cent pinot bianco and the rest chardonnay, and Rot '06, which stands out for its juicy, fragrant palate with lively grip.

● A. A. Schiava '07	♈♈	4*
○ A. A. Sauvignon '07	♈♈	4*
○ A. A. Weiss '07	♈♈	4*
● Rot '06	♈♈	5
● A. A. Cabernet Feld '91	♈♈♈	5
● A. A. Cabernet-Merlot Auhof '97	♈♈♈	5
● A. A. Merlot '93	♈♈♈	5
● A. A. Cabernet-Merlot Rot '04	♈♈	5
● A. A. Schiava '06	♈♈	3*
○ A. A. Weiss '06	♈♈	4*
○ A. A. Weiss '05	♈♈	4*

Josef Brigl

LOC. SAN MICHELE
VIA MADONNA DEL RIPOSO, 3
39057 APPIANO/EPPAN [BZ]
TEL. 0471662419
www.brigl.com

ANNUAL PRODUCTION	2,000,000 bottles
HECTARES UNDER VINE	50
VITICULTURE METHOD	Conventional

Ignaz and Josef Brigl own some of the most beautiful vineyards in all Alto Adige and a winemaking estate with a heritage over a century old. Wines produced here are consistently good and well crafted but we have the impression that even more could be achieved, especially from the standpoint of personality and stylistic definition, considering the huge potential. We were most convinced this year by the Sauvignon '07 above all for its juicy, full palate that also has minerality and savouriness with a dynamic finish. The Pinot Bianco Haselhof '07 is fresh and typical but we thought one of the flagship wines, the Lagrein Briglhof Riserva '05, was slightly dried out by the oak, although it is concentrated and full. The rest of the range is admirable with our preference just going to the special character and elegance of the Schiava Grigia Kaltenburg '07.

○ A. A. Sauvignon '07	♈♈	4*
○ A. A. Gewürztraminer Windegg '07	♈♈	4*
● A. A. Lagrein Briglhof Ris. '05	♈♈	5
○ A. A. Pinot Bianco Haselhof '07	♈♈	4*
● A. A. Pinot Nero Kreuzbichler Ris. '05	♈♈	5
● A. A. Riesling Kreuzbichler '07	♈♈	5
● A. A. Schiava Grigia Kaltenburg '07	♈♈	4*
● A. A. Lagrein Briglhof Ris. '03	♈♈	5
● A. A. Lagrein Scuro Briglhof '04	♈♈	5
○ A. A. Pinot Bianco Haselhof '06	♈♈	4*
● A. A. Pinot Nero Briglhof Ris. '04	♈♈	5
● A. A. Pinot Nero Kreuzbichler '04	♈♈	5
○ A. A. Sauvignon '06	♈♈	4

Cantina Produttori Burggräfler

via Palade, 64
39020 Marlengo/Marling [BZ]
tel. 0473447137
www.burggraefler.it

ANNUAL PRODUCTION 1,220,000 bottles
HECTARES UNDER VINE 140
VITICULTURE METHOD Conventional

The Merano area is known worldwide for its therapeutic hot springs but this area also produces high quality wines. Mild temperatures year round and regular precipitation mean the zone has a balanced climate, which is ideal for grape production. The Burggräfler co-operative winery has always been noted for products that provide consumers with excellent value for money and this year is no exception. Among the most convincing wines is the Pinot Bianco Privat '07, which has fresh aromas of flowers, white-fleshed fruit and aromatic herbs. The palate is full and chewy yet well balanced by fresh acidity. Fruit-forward, with subtle, typical smoky notes, the schiava-based Meranese Schickenburg '07 offers frank, appealing drinkability. Other good quality wines include the fresh, elegant Gewürztraminer MerVin '07 and the Bianco Vendemmia Tardiva MerVin '07 from 60 per cent pinot bianco and the rest equal parts chardonnay and sauvignon.

● A. A. Meranese Schickenburg '07	🍷🍷 4*
○ A. A. Pinot Bianco Privat '07	🍷🍷 4*
● A. A. Bianco V. T. MerVin '07	🍷🍷 6
○ A. A. Gewürztraminer MerVin '07	🍷🍷 5
● A. A. Merlot MerVin '05	🍷🍷 6
● A. A. Merlot-Lagrein Privat '06	🍷🍷 5
○ A. A. Moscato Giallo Schickenburg Privat '07	🍷🍷 4*
○ A. A. Chardonnay Privat '07	🍷 4
● A. A. Lagrein-Cabernet MerVin '06	🍷 6
○ Cuvée Wais '07	🍷 4
○ A. A. Gewürztraminer MerVin '06	YY 5
● A. A. Merlot-Lagrein Privat '04	YY 5
● A. A. Merlot MerVin '04	YY 6
○ A. A. Pinot Bianco Privat '06	YY 4*

★ Cantina di Caldaro

via Cantine, 12
39052 Caldaro/Kaltern [BZ]
tel. 0471963149
www.kellereikaltern.com

ANNUAL PRODUCTION 1,700,000 bottles
HECTARES UNDER VINE 295
VITICULTURE METHOD Conventional

Cantina di Caldaro starts over with Andreas Prast. Having arrived from the Manincor estate, this young oenologist faces the huge responsibility of replacing historic Caldaro Kellermeister Helmuth Zozin, who has moved to Manincor in a curious game of musical chairs. It is no surprise that the Moscato Giallo Passito Serenade once again wins Three Glasses with the '05 vintage. This sweet wine has by now become one of the most reliable in its category anywhere in Italy. The product of a rather cool growing season, it lacks the concentration of other recent versions but is already showing all its complex citrus, flower and saffron aromas. Saffron in particular returns on the rich, creamy palate, which is resplendent with crystal-clear acidity that gives the wine a long, fresh finish. Another winery classic, the juicy, varietal Pinot Bianco Vial '07, also went to the finals, as did the certified biodynamic Lago di Caldaro Solos '07. But this whole range offers fantastic quality.

○ A. A. Moscato Giallo Passito Serenade '05	🍷🍷🍷 6
● A. A. Lago di Caldaro Solos '07	🍷🍷 4*
○ A. A. Pinot Bianco Vial '07	🍷🍷 4*
○ A. A. Chardonnay Castel Giovanelli '06	🍷🍷 6
○ A. A. Gewürztraminer Campaner '07	🍷🍷 5
● A. A. Lago di Caldaro Scelto Pfarrhof '07	🍷🍷 4*
● A. A. Cabernet Sauvignon Ris. '95	YYY 5
● A. A. Cabernet Sauvignon Ris. '93	YYY 5
● A. A. Cabernet Sauvignon Ris. '92	YYY 5
○ A. A. Gewürztraminer Campaner '99	YYY 4
○ A. A. Moscato Giallo Passito Serenade '99	YYY 6
○ A. A. Moscato Giallo Passito Serenade '04	YYY 6
○ A. A. Moscato Giallo Passito Serenade '03	YYY 6
○ A. A. Sauvignon Castel Giovanelli '02	YYY 6

★ Cantina Produttori Colterenzio

LOC. CORNAIANO/GIRLAN
S.DA DEL VINO, 8
39057 APPIANO/EPPAN [BZ]
TEL. 0471664246
www.colterenzio.it

ANNUAL PRODUCTION	1,600,000 bottles
HECTARES UNDER VINE	315
VITICULTURE METHOD	Conventional

What is impressive about the results achieved by Schreckbichl/Colterenzio is not just yet another Three Glass award for Cabernet Sauvignon Lafòa, this time the '04 vintage, or the other three wines that reached our finals, but the average scores earned by the wines submitted for tasting. This is a sign of robust technical and commercial health in the face of market challenges are becoming increasingly difficult all the time, which means that quality at all levels is a necessity, not an option. This year's Three Glass winner is introduced by ripe fruit, pencil lead, spices and subtle smoky notes followed by a dense, minerally, still austere palate with solid, powerful tannins, the whole framed with balance and elegance. Also among the best versions ever is the Sauvignon Lafòa '07, which shows the usual fullness but at the same time more care with the use of oak. We would also like to mention two especially outstanding reds, the concentrated, elegant Merlot Siebeneich Praedium Riserva '05 and the Pinot Nero Villa Nigra from the same vintage, which has great finesse and depth.

Cantina Produttori Cornaiano

LOC. CORNAIANO/GIRLAN
VIA SAN MARTINO, 24
39050 APPIANO/EPPAN [BZ]
TEL. 0471662403
www.girlan.it

ANNUAL PRODUCTION	1,150,000 bottles
HECTARES UNDER VINE	205
VITICULTURE METHOD	Conventional

One more time, a bumper crop of wines – six in total – from this historic winery at Cornaiano made it to our finals. Although a big winner didn't emerge, the overall result is one to frame. This operation has clearly made great strides in terms of quality and the arrival on the team as sales manager of an old acquaintance like Oscar Lorandi can only accelerate this laudable process. The wines all have great depth, confident technique and personality. One example for all is the Schiava Gschleier '07 in which the skills of Kellermeister Gherard Kofler have been deployed to good effect. The intense, inebriating aromas include delicate smoky notes accompanied by cinchona and spice. The austere palate is still quite young, its juicy, tannin-rich, minerally structure showing the quality of the growing year, and progression is vibrant. This is a wine that can age for a long time and now is only partly revealing its complexity. The Pinot Bianco Plattenriegl '07 is varietal and fragrant while the Gewürztraminer Pasithea Oro '06 is concentrated and particularly assertive. The rest of the list collected a raft of Glassware.

● A. A. Cabernet Sauvignon Lafòa '04	♙♙♙ 7
● A. A. Merlot Siebeneich Ris. '05	♙♙ 5
○ A. A. Pinot Bianco Cornell Acclivis '06	♙♙ 5
○ A. A. Sauvignon Lafòa '07	♙♙ 6
○ A. A. Chardonnay Altkirch '07	♙♙ 4*
○ A. A. Gewürztraminer '07	♙♙ 4*
○ A. A. Gewürztraminer Cornell Atisis '07	♙♙ 5
● A. A. Lagrein Cornell Sigis Mundus '04	♙♙ 6
● A. A. Merlot-Cabernet Sauvignon Cornelius '05	♙♙ 6
○ A. A. Pinot Bianco Thurner '07	♙♙ 4*
○ A. A. Pinot Bianco Weisshaus '07	♙♙ 4
○ A. A. Pinot Grigio '07	♙♙ 4*
○ A. A. Pinot Grigio Puiten '07	♙♙ 4*
● A. A. Pinot Nero Villa Nigra Cornell '05	♙♙ 6
○ A. A. Sauvignon Prail '07	♙♙ 4*
● A. A. Cabernet Sauvignon Lafòa '03	♟♟♟ 8
● A. A. Cabernet Sauvignon Lafòa '01	♟♟♟ 8
○ A. A. Gewürztraminer Cornell '05	♟♟♟ 5

● A. A. Lagrein SelectArt Flora Ris. '05	♙♙ 5
○ A. A. Pinot Bianco Plattenriegl '07	♙♙ 4*
○ A. A. Sauvignon Indra '07	♙♙ 4*
○ A. A. Sauvignon SelectArt Flora '07	♙♙ 5
● A. A. Schiava Gschleier SelectArt Flora '07	♙♙ 4*
○ Pasithea Oro '06	♙♙ 6
● A. A. Cabernet Sauvignon SelectArt Flora Ris. '05	♙♙ 5
○ A. A. Gewürztraminer SelectArt Flora '07	♙♙ 5
● A. A. Moscato Rosa Passito Pasithea Rosa '06	♙♙ 6
○ A. A. Pinot Bianco '07	♙♙ 4*
● A. A. Santa Maddalena Bischofhof '07	♙♙ 4*
● A. A. Schiava Fass N. 9 '07	♙♙ 4*
○ A. A. Pinot Bianco Plattenriegl '06	♟♟ 4*
○ A. A. Sauvignon SelectArt Flora '06	♟♟ 5
● A. A. Schiava Gschleier SelectArt Flora '06	♟♟ 4*
● A. A. Schiava Gschleier SelectArt Flora '05	♟♟ 4*

Cantina Produttori Cortaccia

S.DA DEL VINO, 23
39040 CORTACCIA/KURTATSCH [BZ]
TEL. 0471880115
www.kellerei-kurtatsch.it

Egger-Ramer

VIA GUNCINA, 5
39100 BOLZANO/BOZEN
TEL. 0471280541
www.egger-ramer.com

ANNUAL PRODUCTION   1,000,000 bottles
HECTARES UNDER VINE 200
VITICULTURE METHOD   Conventional

ANNUAL PRODUCTION   100,000 bottles
HECTARES UNDER VINE 14
VITICULTURE METHOD   Conventional

Here's some news that marks the passage of an epoch. Arnold Terzer, the long-serving president and major personality over the past decade of Alto Adige winemaking, has retired. Given his influence, changes are inevitable. In the meantime, we can report the usual series of well-crafted wines typical of the lower Adige valley. Full and rich, these are wines that can be a bit heavy but always have great character. It is no coincidence that the three wines with the best scores are the winery's historic showcase products, beginning with the Gewürztraminer Brenntal '07, which is as concentrated and full-bodied as ever with a fairly dynamic development. Merlot Brenntal '05 is one of the best in its category, presenting full-textured and fresh with particularly refined tannins. The intense Bianco Freienfeld '06, from 70 per cent chardonnay, 15 per cent sauvignon, ten per cent pinot bianco and a touch of gewürztraminer, has fruity, juicy aromas and a fragrant palate.

Toni and Peter Egger are a skilled winemaking couple who manage this long-established Bolzano estate with confidence. Over the past few years, their wines have experienced an impressive rise in quality while fortunately prices have remained at reasonable levels, earning our heroes more visibility in the Guide. Their production of around 100,000 bottles includes all the most typical wine types from the zone so of course this means Lagrein and Santa Maddalena, with an unexpected excursion into Valle Isarco for a splendid Müller Thurgau '07. This intense wine with fruity aromas has a savoury, taut, mineral-veined and surprisingly deep palate. Returning to more typically Bolzano wines, two classic Lagreins, the Tenuta Kristan '06 and Riserva '05, reached our finals where they offered excellent interpretations of their respective vintages. The first shows a modern style, combining a full, chewy texture with elegance and harmony. The second is still a bit marked by oak but shows concentrated and dynamic. The Santa Maddalena Reiseggerhof '07 is simply delicious.

O A. A. Gewürztraminer Brenntal '07	♀♀	6
O A. A. Bianco Freienfeld '06	♀♀	5
● A. A. Lagrein Freienfeld '05	♀♀	5
● A. A. Merlot Brenntal '05	♀♀	6
O A. A. Pinot Grigio Penòner '07	♀♀	4*
O A. A. Sauvignon Fohrhof '07	♀♀	4*
O A. A. Chardonnay Felsenhof '07	♀	4
O Bianco Freienfeld V. T. '06	♀	6
O A. A. Gewürztraminer Brenntal '02	♀♀♀	6
O A. A. Gewürztraminer Brenntal '00	♀♀♀	5
● A. A. Merlot Brenntal '97	♀♀♀	5

● A. A. Lagrein Gries Tenuta Kristan Ris. '05	♀♀	5
● A. A. Lagrein Scuro Gries Tenuta Kristan '06	♀♀	4*
O A. A. Valle Isarco Müller Thurgau '07	♀♀	4*
● A. A. Santa Maddalena Cl. Reiseggerhof '07	♀♀	4*
● A. A. Lagrein Gries Tenuta Kristan Ris. '04	♀♀	5
● A. A. Lagrein Scuro Gries Kristan '04	♀♀	4*
● A. A. Santa Maddalena Cl. Reiseggerhof '06	♀♀	4*
● A. A. Lagrein Gries '05	♀♀	4*
● A. A. Lagrein Gries '03	♀♀	4*
● A. A. Lagrein Gries Tenuta Kristan Ris. '03	♀♀	5

★ Elena Walch

VIA A. HOFER, 1
39040 TERMENO/TRAMIN [BZ]
TEL. 0471860172
www.elenawalch.com

ANNUAL PRODUCTION	350,000 bottles
HECTARES UNDER VINE	30
VITICULTURE METHOD	Conventional

We thought winning a double Three Glass award two years running was already an impressive accomplishment. This year, the task was made more difficult since the award-winning Lagrein Castel Ringberg was not released to market. Despite everything, Elena Walch and her almost entirely female team did themselves proud with the usual Gewürztraminer Kastelaz '07 as well as the Bianco Beyond the Clouds '06. In the first case, we are speaking about a wine that has for years been consistently among the best in its type because of a typicity coupled with elegance that makes it unmistakable. The second, from mostly chardonnay with dashes of aromatic varieties, after a few years of stylistic indecision, seems to have found the right path. It's evidently rich and concentrated yet also has harmony and nice drinkability. The curious red Kermesse '05 – "curious" because the blend contains cabernet sauvignon, cabernet franc, merlot, lagrein and syrah – also made an excellent impression with its ripe fruit and lean, elegant palate. The rest of the wines are of a quality befitting one of the finest estates in Alto Adige.

Erbhof Unterganzner Josephus Mayr

FRAZ. CARDANO
VIA CAMPIGLIO, 15
39053 BOLZANO/BOZEN
TEL. 0471365582
mayr.unterganzner@dnet.it

ANNUAL PRODUCTION	65,000 bottles
HECTARES UNDER VINE	8.5
VITICULTURE METHOD	Conventional

Josephus Mayr is more than just a great winemaker with a passion that has never faded over the years. He also produces several hundred – for the time being – bottles of splendid olive oil. That's right, olive oil north of Bolzano. To round things off, he generates energy from a small hydroelectric facility. This year, Mayr's Unterganzner farm put on an unprecedented performance with five wines in the finals and a Three Glass Award for the Lagrein Riserva '05. It's a wine that has acquired classic stature and stylistic definition, leaving behind all showy excess. The Lamarein '06 is powerful yet balanced and harmonious while the Santa Maddalena Classico '06 is spicy and fragrant. The dense, austere Composition Reif '05 comes from mostly cabernet with some added lagrein. The surprise is the Sauvignon Platt & Pignat '07 which has great elegance right from the aromas of bell pepper and nettles to its lean, spirited structure with solid integrity and clear progression. All Mayr's wines have the mark of greatness.

○ A. A. Bianco Beyond the Clouds '06	¶¶¶	7
○ A. A. Gewürztraminer Kastelaz '07	¶¶¶	6
● Kermesse '05	¶¶	7
○ A. A. Cashmere Passito '06	¶¶	7
⊙ Rosé 20/26 '07	¶¶	4*
● A. A. Merlot Kastelaz Ris. '04	¶	7
○ A. A. Bianco Beyond the Clouds '02	♀♀♀	6
○ A. A. Bianco Beyond the Clouds '01	♀♀♀	6
● A. A. Cabernet Sauvignon Castel Ringberg Ris. '97	♀♀♀	5
○ A. A. Gewürztraminer Kastelaz '97	♀♀♀	4
○ A. A. Gewürztraminer Kastelaz '06	♀♀♀	6
○ A. A. Gewürztraminer Kastelaz '05	♀♀♀	6
⊙ A. A. Gewürztraminer Kastelaz '04	♀♀♀	6
○ A. A. Gewürztraminer Kastelaz '00	♀♀♀	5
● A. A. Lagrein Castel Ringberg Ris. '04	♀♀♀	6
● A. A. Lagrein Castel Ringberg Ris. '03	♀♀♀	6

● A. A. Lagrein Scuro Ris. '05	¶¶¶	5
● A. A. Santa Maddalena Cl. '06	¶¶	4*
○ A. A. Sauvignon Platt & Pignat '07	¶¶	4*
● Composition Reif '05	¶¶	7
● Lamarein '06	¶¶	7
● A. A. Cabernet Ris. '05	¶¶	6
○ A. A. Chardonnay Platt&Pignat '07	¶¶	4*
⊙ A. A. Lagrein Rosato '07	¶¶	4*
● A. A. Lagrein Scuro Ris. '99	♀♀♀	5
● A. A. Lagrein Scuro Ris. '98	♀♀♀	5
● A. A. Lagrein Scuro Ris. '97	♀♀♀	5
● A. A. Lagrein Scuro Ris. '01	♀♀♀	5
● A. A. Lagrein Scuro Ris. '00	♀♀♀	5
● Lamarein '05	♀♀♀	7

Cantina Sociale Erste & Neue

VIA DELLE CANTINE, 5/10
39052 CALDARO/KALTERN [BZ]
TEL. 0471963122
www.erste-neue.it

ANNUAL PRODUCTION	1,000,000 bottles
HECTARES UNDER VINE	320
VITICULTURE METHOD	Conventional

A new wind is blowing at Erste & Neue, Prima & Nuova in Caldaro, one of the oldest co-operative wineries in Alto Adige. The new, young management team has achieved remarkable results. President Manfred Schullian, head cellarman Gerhard Sanin and sales manager Hannes Durnwalder have boosted the winery's image in short order with high quality wines. The Puntay line represents the top of their production and brings together their best grapes, selected by the oenologist in the vineyards. The following wines went through to the Three Glass finals this year: Pinot Bianco Puntay '07, which is fruity, fragrant, fresh, tangy and structured; the savoury, aromatic Sauvignon Puntay '07 with its full body and great length; and the Lago di Caldaro Scelto Puntay '07, a soft, fresh, varietal wine with surprising length. The classic line, released at remarkably reasonable prices, sells on typicity and freshness while the cru line presents structured, characterful wines. Special mention goes to the Pinot Bianco Prunar '07, Sauvignon Stern '07, Moscato Giallo Barleit '07 and Lago di Caldaro Scelto Leuchtenburg '07.

Falkenstein - Franz Pratzner

VIA CASTELLO, 15
39025 NATURNO/NATURNS [BZ]
TEL. 0473666054
www.falkenstein.bz

ANNUAL PRODUCTION	45,000 bottles
HECTARES UNDER VINE	7
VITICULTURE METHOD	Natural

This year's tastings were irrefutable proof that Franz Pratzner's wines are carving themselves a niche, and not just here in Italy. It's not so much because of the two Three Glass awards as the depth and stylistic maturity they have achieved and above all the future prospects for this mountain winemaker. The subtle, passionate Pinot Bianco and Riesling, both from '07, are unmistakable, indeed almost feline in their display of quick, nervous energy. The first was a relative surprise, a very Valle Venosta-style Pinot Bianco because of its smoky, peppery notes, and also very Falkenstein in style because of its citrussy vein and imposing yet vibrant structure with firm, perfectly gauged acid backbone. The Riesling brings us back to our initial comments. We are convinced this '07 could easily stand up to its more noble relatives from across the Alps. The aromas of thyme, citrus and gunflint are already complex, the palate is meaty and almost sensual in its light, residual sweetness that balances the clear acidity, and the finish marries elegance with a depth that is hard to achieve. Note that all these wines are sold with screw caps.

● A. A. Lago di Caldaro Scelto Puntay '07	🍷🍷	4*
○ A. A. Pinot Bianco Puntay '07	🍷🍷	4*
○ A. A. Sauvignon Puntay '07	🍷🍷	5
○ A. A. Gewürztraminer Puntay '07	🍷🍷	5
● A. A. Lago di Caldaro Scelto Leuchtenburg '07	🍷🍷	4*
● A. A. Lagrein Puntay Ris. '05	🍷🍷	5
○ A. A. Moscato Giallo Secco Barleit '07	🍷🍷	4*
○ A. A. Pinot Bianco Prunar '07	🍷🍷	4*
● A. A. Santa Maddalena Gröbnerhof '07	🍷🍷	4*
○ A. A. Sauvignon Stern '07	🍷🍷	5
○ A. A. Chardonnay Salt '07	🍷	4
○ A. A. Pinot Bianco '07	🍷	4
○ A. A. Gewürztraminer Puntay '01	🍷🍷🍷	5
● A. A. Lago di Caldaro Scelto Puntay '06	🍷🍷	4*
○ A. A. Pinot Bianco Puntay '06	🍷🍷	4*

○ A. A. Valle Venosta Pinot Bianco '07	🍷🍷🍷	5
○ A. A. Valle Venosta Riesling '07	🍷🍷🍷	6
○ A. A. Valle Venosta Sauvignon '07	🍷🍷	5
○ A. A. Valle Venosta Gewürztramlner '07	🍷🍷	5
○ A. A. Valle Venosta Riesling '98	🍷🍷🍷	5
○ A. A. Valle Venosta Riesling '06	🍷🍷🍷	6
○ A. A. Valle Venosta Riesling '05	🍷🍷🍷	6
○ A. A. Valle Venosta Riesling '00	🍷🍷🍷	5
○ A. A. Valle Venosta Gewürztramlner '06	🍷🍷	5
○ A. A. Valle Venosta Pinot Bianco '06	🍷🍷	5
○ A. A. Valle Venosta Pinot Bianco '05	🍷🍷	5
○ A. A. Valle Venosta Sauvignon '06	🍷🍷	5

Garlider - Christian Kerchbaumer

VIA UNTRUM, 20
39040 VELTURNO/FELDTHURNS [BZ]
TEL. 0472847296
www.garlider.it

ANNUAL PRODUCTION	16,000 bottles
HECTARES UNDER VINE	3.5
VITICULTURE METHOD	Natural

The small Garlider estate, managed by Christian Kerschbaumer, picked up Three Glasses once again. This result is embellished by a series of very convincing wines with well-defined personality. We are in Valle Isarco so the characteristics of the wines tend to follow the style of the zone even though Garlider wines have more southern, warmer shades. This is, after all, Velturno in the extreme south of the valley. The still very young Veltliner '07 has a full, meaty palate with great richness of flavour accented by an ash-like vein and acidity that refreshes this very southern structure. The Sylvaner '07 is probably still too young to fully express all its potential. Then there are two surprises: an at last convincing Pinot Nero '06 and a full yet balanced Pinot Grigio '07. In the meantime, the talented Christian is establishing small vineyards to boost production at least a little and above all he continues, with a farmer's caution, to experiment with fermentation without cultured yeasts with whites as well as reds. Up till now the results seem better than good.

Glögglhof - Franz Gojer

FRAZ. SANTA MADDALENA
VIA RIVELLONE, 1
39100 BOLZANO/BOZEN
TEL. 0471978775
www.gojer.it

ANNUAL PRODUCTION	40,000 bottles
HECTARES UNDER VINE	4.3
VITICULTURE METHOD	Conventional

This has been a bit of an in-between vintage year for Glögglhof, the estate run by likeable, insightful winemaker Franz Gojer. Since 1982, the year he inherited the estate, Franz has produced some of the most territory-focused wines in the Bolzano area. In fact, Glögglhof is located on the distinctive hill of Santa Maddalena north of Bolzano. And it turns out that the wine we scored highest this year was the Santa Maddalena Rondell '07. The estate's historic selection always shows a little more complexity without ever compromising the fragrances or appealing drinkability. The same goes for the simpler version of the Lagrein Riserva '06 which is built along similar lines. Our man Franz has decided to let it age for another year in his cellar. Full-bodied and balanced with nicely smoothed tannins, the still austere Merlot Spitz '06 flaunts a decidedly Bordeauxesque style.

○ A. A. Valle Isarco Veltliner '07	▼▼▼ 5
○ A. A. Valle Isarco Pinot Grigio '07	▼▼ 5
○ A. A. Valle Isarco Sylvaner '07	▼▼ 4*
● A. A. Pinot Nero '06	▼▼ 5
○ A. A. Valle Isarco Gewürztraminer '07	▼▼ 5
○ A. A. Valle Isarco Müller Thurgau '07	▼▼ 4*
○ A. A. Valle Isarco Veltliner '05	▽▽▽ 4*
○ A. A. Valle Isarco Müller Thurgau '06	▽▽ 4*
○ A. A. Valle Isarco Sylvaner '06	▽▽ 4*
○ A. A. Valle Isarco Veltliner '06	▽▽ 5
● A. A. Pinot Nero '05	▽▽ 5
○ A. A. Valle Isarco Gewürztraminer '06	▽▽ 5
○ A. A. Valle Isarco Pinot Grigio '06	▽▽ 4

● A. A. Santa Maddalena Rondell '07	▼▼ 4*
● A. A. Merlot Spitz '06	▼▼ 5
● A. A. Santa Maddalena Cl. '07	▼▼ 4*
● A. A. Lagrein Scuro Ris. '04	▽▽ 5
● A. A. Lagrein Scuro Ris. '03	▽▽ 5
● A. A. Lagrein Scuro Ris. '05	▽▽ 5
● A. A. Merlot Spitz '05	▽▽ 5
● A. A. Merlot Spitz '04	▽▽ 5
● A. A. Santa Maddalena Rondell '06	▽▽ 4*

Cantina Gries/Cantina di Bolzano

FRAZ. GRIES
P.ZZA GRIES, 2
39100 BOLZANO/BOZEN
TEL. 0471270909
www.cantinabolzano.com

ANNUAL PRODUCTION 1,100,000 bottles
HECTARES UNDER VINE 170
VITICULTURE METHOD Conventional

Last year, we chided Stefan Filippi a little for the unconvincing scores by red wines from this winery. And here to embarrass us is an unprecedented version of the Lagrein Prestige Line Riserva '06 that was voted Three Glasses without a dissenting voice. On the nose, this wine breaks down the entire aromatic range of a lagrein: flowers, spices, ripe blackberry and cinchona. The creamy, caressing palate shows an acidity that contributes freshness and suppleness. The tannins are so silky they erase all memories of certain rough, edgy Lagreins from a few years ago. The more traditional version of Lagrein, the Collection Baron Carl Eyrl '06, also made it to our finals and even the simplest wine, a simply delicious Grieser '07, came quite close. Moscato Giallo Vinalia is always one of the best and the '06 shows delicate notes of citron and dried apricot followed by a sweet, concentrated palate perked up by vivid freshness and signing off with a long, dynamic finish. In short, these wines are so good you could frame them.

● A. A. Lagrein Scuro Prestige Line Ris. '06	🍷🍷🍷 6
● A. A. Lagrein Grieser Baron Carl Eyrl '06	🍷🍷 5
○ A. A. Moscato Giallo Vinalia '06	🍷🍷 8
● A. A. Cabernet Collection Otto Graf Huyn Ris. '06	🍷🍷 5
● A. A. Lagrein Grieser '07	🍷🍷 4*
● A. A. Lagrein Merlot Mauritius '06	🍷🍷 7
⊙ A. A. Lagrein Rosato Pischl '07	🍷🍷 4*
● A. A. Merlot Collection Otto Graf Huyn '06	🍷🍷 5
● A. A. Lagrein Scuro Prestige Line Ris. '99	🍸🍸🍸 6
● A. A. Lagrein Scuro Prestige Line Ris. '00	🍸🍸🍸 6
○ A. A. Moscato Giallo Vinalia '99	🍸🍸🍸 5
○ A. A. Moscato Giallo Vinalia '03	🍸🍸🍸 6
○ A. A. Pinot Bianco Collection Dellago '06	🍸🍸🍸 4*

Griesbauerhof - Georg Mumelter

VIA RENCIO, 66
39100 BOLZANO/BOZEN
TEL. 0471973090
www.tirolensisarsvini.it

ANNUAL PRODUCTION 25,000 bottles
HECTARES UNDER VINE 3.3
VITICULTURE METHOD Conventional

For the reserved Georg Mumelter, the only place to be is his vineyard and winery near Rencio, where he produces a limited number of bottles of austere – like their maker – well-crafted wines with lots of charm and personality. A man of few words, Georg lets his wines speak for him and they regularly tell the tale of territory and types. These wines are the real deal, never embellished or artificial. They may not always be perfect but there's no denying their typicity or craftsmanship. All the characteristic wine types of Bolzano are represented, starting with Lagrein and moving on to Santa Maddalena, which in fact were the ones we found most convincing. The splendid Lagrein '06 mirrors the man who makes it. Austere to the point of severity, this red is still very characterful with a very traditional style. One unmissable classic is the Santa Maddalena '07, which makes the most of the favourable growing season in the completeness of its spectrum of aromatics and impeccable palate. The Cabernet Sauvignon Riserva '05, Lagrein Riserva '05 and Pinot Grigio '07 are as reliable as ever.

● A. A. Lagrein '06	🍷🍷 4*
● A. A. Cabernet Sauvignon Ris. '05	🍷🍷 5
● A. A. Lagrein Scuro Ris. '05	🍷🍷 5
○ A. A. Pinot Grigio '07	🍷🍷 4*
● A. A. Santa Maddalena Cl. '07	🍷🍷 3*
● A. A. Lagrein Scuro Ris. '04	🍸🍸 5
● A. A. Lagrein '05	🍸🍸 4*
● A. A. Santa Maddalena Cl. '06	🍸🍸 3*

Gummerhof - R. Malojer

VIA WEGGESTEIN, 36
39100 BOLZANO/BOZEN
TEL. 0471972885
www.malojer.it

ANNUAL PRODUCTION	100,000 bottles
HECTARES UNDER VINE	6
VITICULTURE METHOD	Conventional

This is an excellent performance by Gummerhof, the estate north of Bolzano managed with passion and skill by Elisabeth, Urban and Alfred Malojer. Two wines landed in the finals. Lagrein Riserva '05 and Sauvignon Gur Zur Sand '07 have never been this good and they are accompanied by a well-made range of wines at popular prices. The Lagrein is one of the zone's great classics, outstanding for exceptional elegance that expresses itself right from the fruity, delicately spicy aromas. The palate is creamy yet lean and minerally with light, soft tannins and a finish that has plenty of heft. The positive surprise is the Sauvignon '07 with its refined aromas, rich, vigorously mineral structure and fresh, tangy finish. The Müller Thurgau '07 is also very convincing, presenting more typical than many with its pleasant, fruity notes. Drinking deliciously as usual, the Santa Maddalena Classico from the '07 vintage, a very favourable growing year for the wine type, offers varietal typicity and pleasant drinkability.

Gumphof - Markus Prackwieser

LOC. NOVALE DI PRESULE, 8
39050 FIÈ ALLO SCILIAR/
VÖLS AM SCHLERN [BZ]
TEL. 0471601190
www.gumphof.it

ANNUAL PRODUCTION	36,000 bottles
HECTARES UNDER VINE	4.5
VITICULTURE METHOD	Conventional

Clinging to the side of a ridge at the southern edge of Valle Isarco, Markus Prackwieser's Gumphof estate periodically serves us up a nice surprise. This year, it is called Sauvignon Praesulis '07, in our opinion the best ever produced at Gumphof. It's a Sauvignon with well-defined fragrances of aromatic herbs and nettles, mingling with gunflint and citrus. The palate has great dynamism and integrity as the citrus returns in force accompanied by distinct salty, even iodine sensations. It was a shoo-in for Three Glasses. But then the Gewürztraminer Praesulis '07 has never been this good and makes elegance combined with a lean profile its stylistic trademark. A certain character is starting to show in the Pinot Nero, an old obsession of Markus's, which is rather convincing in the '06 version. An estate classic also turned out to be very successful this year: the Pinot Bianco Praesulis '07 is full and tangy, lacking perhaps only a pinch of freshness for a better score in our finals. The Schiava is always extremely good and is on top form in the 2007 vintage.

● A. A. Lagrein Scuro Ris. '05	♟♟	5
○ A. A. Sauvignon Gur zur Sand '07	♟♟	4*
● A. A. Lagrein Scuro Gummerhof zu Gries '06	♟♟	4*
○ A. A. Müller Thurgau '07	♟♟	3*
● A. A. Santa Maddalena Cl. '07	♟♟	4*
● A. A. Cabernet-Lagrein Bautzanum Ris. '05	♟	5
○ A. A. Chardonnay Justina '07	♟	4
● A. A. Lagrein Scuro Ris. '04	♟♟	5
● A. A. Cabernet-Lagrein Bautzanum Ris. '04	♟♟	5
● A. A. Lagrein Scuro Gummerhof zu Gries '05	♟♟	4*
● A. A. Lagrein Scuro Ris. '03	♟♟	5
● A. A. Lagrein Scuro Ris. '02	♟♟	5
○ A. A. Pinot Bianco '06	♟♟	4*
○ A. A. Sauvignon Gur zur Sand Classic '06	♟♟	4*

○ A. A. Sauvignon Praesulis '07	♟♟♟	5*
○ A. A. Gewürztraminer Praesulis '07	♟♟	5
○ A. A. Pinot Bianco Praesulis '07	♟♟	4*
○ A. A. Pinot Bianco '07	♟♟	4*
● A. A. Pinot Nero '06	♟♟	5
● A. A. Schiava '07	♟♟	3*
○ A. A. Pinot Bianco Praesulis '06	♟♟♟	4*
○ A. A. Sauvignon Praesulis '04	♟♟♟	5*
○ A. A. Pinot Bianco Praesulis '04	♟♟	4*
○ A. A. Sauvignon Praesulis '06	♟♟	4*
○ A. A. Sauvignon Praesulis '05	♟♟	5
○ A. A. Gewürztraminer Praesulis '06	♟♟	5
○ A. A. Pinot Bianco '06	♟♟	4*
● A. A. Pinot Nero '05	♟♟	5

Franz Haas

VIA VILLA, 6
39040 MONTAGNA/MONTAN [BZ]
TEL. 0471812280
www.franz-haas.it

ANNUAL PRODUCTION	290,000 bottles
HECTARES UNDER VINE	35
VITICULTURE METHOD	Conventional

Having almost come to the end of the long-standing project to create his new, and quite beautiful, cellar, the award winning Haas-Manna company presented its usual bumper crop of top-quality wines. All that was missing was a top note to take Three Glasses, perhaps because the Schweizer selection of Pinot Nero wasn't released this time and the white Manna was still a little bit rigid in the '06 version, which didn't express itself to the full. At any rate, we should point out the usual Moscato Rosa '06, one of the most typical and elegant produced in the region, and an excellent Gewürztraminer '07, which shows particularly tangy and harmonious in the mouth with an elegant, rising finish. The very interesting red Istante, a Bordeaux blend that was firing on all cylinders in the 2004 vintage, is elegantly balanced on the dynamically progressive palate. In a word, the usual date with Three Glasses has only been postponed.

Haderburg

FRAZ. BUCHOLZ
LOC. POCHI, 30
39040 SALORNO/SALURN [BZ]
TEL. 0471889097
www.haderburg.it

ANNUAL PRODUCTION	80,000 bottles
HECTARES UNDER VINE	12
VITICULTURE METHOD	Certified biodynamic

This Hausmannhof Riserva 1997 is great. The first Three Glass award for a sparkler from Alto Adige would be enough to make news but add to this the prize for Sparkler of the Year. And what really left us with our mouths open was the authority with which it won. The Hausmannhof is an extraordinary vintage from chardonnay with small amounts of pinot nero, disgorged after ten years on the yeasts. It shows its age with apparently decadent, almost faded touches but comes back to life caressing the palate with energy and freshness accompanied by a complexity shown only by very great wines. The vineyards that produced the cuvées for Haderburg are located on the hill above Salorno in the idyllic location of I Pochi, or Buchholz, one of the great crus of Alto Adige winemaking. As if this were not enough, Alois Ochsenreiter, estate oenologist and owner, cultivates these to biodynamic standards. Alongside this real gem, we'll add a splendid Gewürztraminer Blaspichl '07, which is concentrated, fresh and dynamic.

O A. A. Gewürztraminer '07	♟♟	5
● A. A. Moscato Rosa '06	♟♟	6
● Istante '04	♟♟	6
O Manna '06	♟♟	5
● A. A. Lagrein '06	♟♟	5
O A. A. Pinot Bianco '07	♟♟	5
O A. A. Pinot Nero '06	♟♟	5
O A. A. Müller Thurgau '07	♟	4
● A. A. Moscato Rosa Schweizer '00	♟♟♟	5
● A. A. Pinot Nero Schweizer '02	♟♟♟	6
● A. A. Pinot Nero Schweizer '01	♟♟♟	6
O Manna '05	♟♟♟	5
O Manna '04	♟♟♟	5
● A. A. Moscato Rosa '05	♟♟	6
● A. A. Pinot Nero '05	♟♟	5

O A. A. Spumante Hausmannhof Ris. '97	♟♟♟	7
O A. A. Chardonnay Hausmannhof '07	♟♟	4*
● A. A. Erah '04	♟♟	6
O A. A. Gewürztraminer Blaspichl '07	♟♟	5
● A. A. Pinot Nero Hausmannhof '06	♟♟	5
O A. A. Spumante Pas Dosé '03	♟♟	6
O A. A. Valle Isarco Sylvaner Obermairlhof '05	♟♟♟	4*
● A. A. Erah '03	♟♟	6
O A. A. Spumante Hausmannhof Ris. '93	♟♟	7
O A. A. Spumante Pas Dosé '01	♟♟	5
● A. A. Pinot Nero Hausmannhof '05	♟♟	5

Hoandlhof - Manfred Nössing

FRAZ. KRANEBIH
VIA DEI VIGNETI, 66
39042 BRESSANONE/BRIXEN [BZ]
TEL. 0472832672
www.manninoessing.com

ANNUAL PRODUCTION	17,000 bottles
HECTARES UNDER VINE	4.3
VITICULTURE METHOD	Conventional

Those of us who work for the Guide never risk boredom with Manni Nössing. This year, considering the great success of his wines with press and public, Manni decided not to send us any for tasting. But we are patient and stubborn, and above all feel we must provide a service to our readers, and so we bought and tasted the Hoandlhof wines. They are fantastic. In fact, we can say that with the 2007 vintage, wines by Nössing, now collaborating with Sicilian oenologist Nicola Centonze, have lost some of their more baroque qualities. Now they are drier and more stylized, having acquired complexity and purity. Shining proof of this is the Veltliner '07, a wine perhaps not that close to Manni's heart but one we liked so much we gave it Three Glasses. Sorry Manni. It has intense aromas of citrus and damson. The palate marries savouriness with minerality and almost cutting acidity that is tamed by black berry fruit. The finish is expansive and vibrant. The other two winery classics are also great. We just preferred the Sylvaner to the Kerner.

★ Tenuta J. Hofstätter

P.ZZA MUNICIPIO, 7
39040 TERMENO/TRAMIN [BZ]
TEL. 0471860161
www.hofstatter.com

ANNUAL PRODUCTION	720,000 bottles
HECTARES UNDER VINE	53.5
VITICULTURE METHOD	Conventional

Great attention to work in the vineyard and cellar, special care for traditional varieties without losing sight of market requirements, and aggressive marketing strategies with a wide range of initiatives are the points in favour of this estate managed by Martin Foradori. One of the most modern and dynamic cellars in the province of Bolzano, it sent three wines to our finals. They are perhaps the most representative wines from an estate that, in the case of the Gewürztraminer Kolbenhof and Pinot Nero Barthenau Vigna Sant'Urbano, has written the history of the wine type. Alongside these big hitters is the Lagrein Steinraffler that for some years now has been firmly established among the variety's elite. As usual, youth does not become the '07 Kolbenhof. It's more of a middle-distance runner than a sprinter and takes its time to reveal all its complexity, which for the time being is only partly revealed. The Pinot Nero '05 is still slightly clenched and the Lagrein Steinraffler from the same vintage is varietal, full-bodied and gutsy.

O A. A. Valle Isarco Veltliner '07	♟♟♟	5
O A. A. Valle Isarco Kerner '07	♟♟	4*
O A. A. Valle Isarco Sylvaner '07	♟♟	4*
O A. A. Valle Isarco Kerner '06	♟♟♟	4*
O A. A. Valle Isarco Kerner '05	♟♟♟	4*
O A. A. Valle Isarco Kerner '03	♟♟♟	4*
O A. A. Valle Isarco Kerner '02	♟♟♟	4
O A. A. Valle Isarco Sylvaner '04	♟♟♟	4*
O A. A. Valle Isarco Gewürztraminer '01	♟♟	4*
O A. A. Valle Isarco Sylvaner '06	♟♟	4*
O A. A. Valle Isarco Sylvaner '05	♟♟	4*
O A. A. Valle Isarco Veltliner '05	♟♟	4*

O A. A. Gewürztraminer Kolbenhof '07	♟♟	6
● A. A. Lagrein Scuro Steinraffler '05	♟♟	6
● A. A. Pinot Nero Barthenau V. S. Urbano '05	♟♟	8
O A. A. Gewürztraminer '07	♟♟	5
● A. A. Lagrein '07	♟♟	4*
O A. A. Pinot Bianco '07	♟♟	4*
● A. A. Pinot Nero Ris. '05	♟♟	6
O A. A. Riesling '07	♟♟	4*
O De Vite '07	♟♟	4*
● Yngram '05	♟♟	7
O A. A. Gewürztraminer Kolbenhof '99	♟♟♟	4
O A. A. Gewürztraminer Kolbenhof '04	♟♟♟	5
O A. A. Gewürztraminer Kolbenhof '03	♟♟♟	5
O A. A. Gewürztraminer Kolbenhof '01	♟♟♟	6
● A. A. Pinot Nero S. Urbano '95	♟♟♟	7
● Yngram '00	♟♟♟	7
● A. A. Pinot Nero Barthenau V. S. Urbano '04	♟♟	8

Köfererhof
Günther Kershbaumer

FRAZ. NOVACELLA
VIA PUSTERIA, 3
39040 VARNA/VAHRN [BZ]
TEL. 0472836649
info@koefererhof.it

ANNUAL PRODUCTION	48,000 bottles
HECTARES UNDER VINE	5.5
VITICULTURE METHOD	Conventional

Over the past four or five years, Valle Isarco has established itself as one of the best areas in Italy for white wines, which have consequently become much sought after. One of the main actors in this renaissance is without Günther Kershbaumer and his Köfererhof estate, located a few kilometres north of Bressanone. In just a few years, Günther's wines have developed stylistically, which has taken them to the forefront in a zone where competition has now become fierce. Three Glasses go to the splendid Sylvaner R '07 which, in spite of its usual extreme youth, already shows powerful complexity that melds iodine, gunflint and aromatic herbs. The palate cuts like a knife, showing deep, smoky and overwhelming. We would also put money on the future of the Riesling '07 that Günther still can't bring himself to release two years after the harvest. The substantial concentration, power and acidity are kept well in check and framed by tangy hints of the sea. But all the wines that come out of Köfererhof have character to burn. If anyone has any doubts about this, just taste the basic Müller Thurgau '07.

Tenuta Kornell

FRAZ. SETTEQUERCE
VIA BOLZANO, 23
39018 TERLANO/TERLAN [BZ]
TEL. 0471917507
www.kornell.it

ANNUAL PRODUCTION	60,000 bottles
HECTARES UNDER VINE	14.5
VITICULTURE METHOD	Conventional

The wine world needs more people like Florian Brigl, who is serious, passionate, modest and attentive to details. For further details, pay a brief visit to his splendid estate in Settequerce, on the road from Bolzano to Terlano. Observe the care taken in organizing the cellar, including the traditional straw insulation on the door, and vineyards that look like gardens. It's really no surprise that this estate has become a small gem over the past few years. Having said this, we would also add that the wines are good and above all constantly developing in terms of personality and stylistic definition. Certain naive practices, like the occasionally excessive use of new oak, are slowly disappearing. We are also happy to note improvement in the only, for now, white produced, Sauvignon Cosmas '07, which reached our finals thanks to its elegance and freshness. But the reds are also flavourful and typical, and above all delightfully drinkable without sacrificing richness or complexity. We rather like the juicy Merlot Staves '05 and the fresh, spicy Lagrein Greif '07.

O A. A. Valle Isarco Sylvaner R '07	♟♟♟	5
O A. A. Valle Isarco Kerner '07	♟♟	5
O A. A. Valle Isarco Riesling '07	♟♟	5
O A. A. Valle Isarco Veltliner '07	♟♟	4*
O A. A. Valle Isarco Gewürztraminer '07	♟♟	5
O A. A. Valle Isarco Müller Thurgau '07	♟♟	4*
O A. A. Valle Isarco Pinot Grigio '07	♟♟	4*
O A. A. Valle Isarco Sylvaner '07	♟♟	4*
O A. A. Valle Isarco Sylvaner R '06	♟♟♟	5
O A. A. Valle Isarco Kerner '06	♟♟	5
O A. A. Valle Isarco Pinot Grigio '06	♟♟	4*
O A. A. Valle Isarco Riesling '06	♟♟	5
O A. A. Valle Isarco Riesling '05	♟♟	5
O A. A. Valle Isarco Riesling '04	♟♟	5
O A. A. Valle Isarco Sylvaner '06	♟♟	4*
O A. A. Valle Isarco Müller Thurgau '06	♟♟	4*

O A. A. Sauvignon Cosmas '07	♟♟	4*
● A. A. Cabernet Sauvignon Staves '05	♟♟	6
● A. A. Lagrein Greif '07	♟♟	4*
● A. A. Merlot Staves '05	♟♟	6
● A. A. Cabernet Sauvignon Staves '04	♟♟	6
● A. A. Cabernet Sauvignon Staves '03	♟♟	6
● A. A. Cabernet Sauvignon Staves '02	♟♟	6
● A. A. Lagrein Greif '04	♟♟	4*
● A. A. Merlot Staves '03	♟♟	6
● A. A. Zeder '05	♟♟	4*

Tenuta Kränzl - Graf Franz Pfeil

VIA PALADE, 1
39010 CERMES/TSCHERMS [BZ]
TEL. 0473564549
www.labyrinth.bz

Kuenhof - Peter Pliger

LOC. MARA, 110
39042 BRESSANONE/BRIXEN [BZ]
TEL. 0472850546
pliger.kuenhof@rolmail.net

ANNUAL PRODUCTION	35,000 bottles
HECTARES UNDER VINE	6
VITICULTURE METHOD	Certified organic

As usual, wines from Franz Pfeil caught the Guide's various tasting panels off balance. These wines have a rather complex personality that cannot be traced back to any fashion or cultural trend. They are mature and warm, at times evanescent but indisputably charming. We are so convinced of the value of wines from Tenuta Kränzl that we sent three of them to our finals. We should say right off we have a certain liking for Schiava Baslan, which in the 2007 version flaunts a truly unique character with sensual aromas of tobacco and spice followed by a palate so mineral-rich it is almost earthy yet has fresh, caressing fruit and a soft, silky, elegantly almondy finish. The rich, mature version of the Pinot Bianco Helios '07 presents a meaty, slightly alcoholic palate with salty nuances and uncommon length. The '05 Sagittarius is one of the best versions ever. From 80 per cent cabernet sauvignon and the rest merlot, it opens on elegant aromas of cinchona, graphite and black berries that are faithfully reprised on the full, dynamic palate.

ANNUAL PRODUCTION	23,000 bottles
HECTARES UNDER VINE	6
VITICULTURE METHOD	Natural

After years of titanic labour, which is no exaggeration if you consider the masses of rock moved to create the traditional terraces, the new vineyards above Kuenhof are practically finished and even the small track designed by Peter Pliger to move around those tight spaces is finally in place. In the meantime, we report the release of a wonderfully pure version of the Riesling Kaiton. This is a very elegant white, a little stylized but solid and as spirited as a ballet dancer. It gives aromas of damson and gunflint, refined by light spice, before the typically Kuenhof, apparently evanescent, palate but with relentless energy and grip. A Three Glass wine without question. Although still too young, the Sylvaner '07 has unmistakable finesse and harmonious expansion while the Veltliner grows year by year in character and definition. Wines from Peter and Brigitte Pliger follow the growing seasons and diligently reflect the differences, reproducing them faithfully in the glass. One final note: from this year, all Kuenhof wines have screw caps.

O Pinot Bianco Helios '07	▼▼	5
● Sagittarius '05	▼▼	6
● Schiava Baslan '07	▼▼	4*
O Corona '07	▼▼	6
O A. A. Gewürztraminer Passito Dorado '04	♈♈	6
● A. A. Meranese Hügel Baslan Ris. '05	♈♈	4*
O A. A. Pinot Bianco Helios '02	♈♈	5
O A. A. Gewürztraminer Passito Dorado '03	♈♈	6
O A. A. Pinot Bianco Helios '06	♈♈	5
● A. A. Pinot Nero Ris. '04	♈♈	5
● A. A. Pinot Nero Ris. '02	♈♈	5

O A. A. Valle Isarco Riesling Kaiton '07	▼▼▼	5*
O A. A. Valle Isarco Sylvaner '07	▼▼	5
O A. A. Valle Isarco Veltliner '07	▼▼	5
O A. A. Valle Isarco Gewürztraminer '07	▼▼	5
O A. A. Valle Isarco Riesling Kaiton '05	♈♈♈	4*
O A. A. Valle Isarco Sylvaner '06	♈♈♈	4*
O A. A. Valle Isarco Sylvaner '03	♈♈♈	4*
O A. A. Valle Isarco Sylvaner '02	♈♈♈	4*
O A. A. Valle Isarco Sylvaner V.T. '04	♈♈♈	4*
O Kaiton '99	♈♈♈	4
O Kaiton '01	♈♈♈	4
O A. A. Valle Isarco Gewürztraminer '06	♈♈	4*
O A. A. Valle Isarco Veltliner '06	♈♈	4*

Cantina Laimburg

LOC. LAIMBURG, 6
39040 VADENA/PFATTEN [BZ]
TEL. 0471969700
www.laimburg.bz.it

ANNUAL PRODUCTION 180,000 bottles
HECTARES UNDER VINE 45
VITICULTURE METHOD Natural

Staff at the experimental agricultural institute in Laimburg did well this year. It has been some time since the range of wines submitted for tasting has shown such consistency and quality. A high note was missing but the overall result was very convincing. Three wines tasted are in the finals but if you look at the scores there are few differences with the others. As well as technical perfection, which can sometimes be a limit, we noticed there is more character emerging, something that has now become indispensable for big hitters in the ever more difficult wine market. The Gewürztraminer Elyònd '07 is indisputably one of the best wines in its category, showing fleshy and full on the palate yet at the same time offering rather easy-going drinkability. Still austere, yet already convincing, the Cabernet Sauvignon Sass Roà Riserva '04 is lean and expansive on the palate, which has a taut, minerally finish. The Col de Réy '04, from (50 per cent lagrein, 30 per cent petit verdot and the rest tannat, is still young but dense with confident acid backbone. Lagrein Barbagòl Riserva '05, one of the estate's historic wines, is rich and caressing.

● A. A. Cabernet Sauvignon Sass Roà Ris. '04	TT	6
○ A. A. Gewürztraminer Elyònd '07	TT	5
● Col de Réy '04	TT	7
● A. A. Lagrein Scuro Barbagòl Ris. '05	TT	6
○ A. A. Sauvignon Oyèll '07	TT	5
○ A. A. Sauvignon Passito Saphir '06	TT	8
○ Dòa De '06	TT	5
○ A. A. Pinot Bianco Rayèt '07	T	5
● A. A. Lagrein Scuro Barbagòl Ris. '00	YYY	6
● A. A. Lagrein Scuro Barbagòl Ris. '03	YY	6
● A. A. Lagrein Scuro Barbagòl Ris. '01	YY	6
○ A. A. Gewürztraminer Elyònd '05	YY	5

Loacker Schwarhof

LOC. SANTA GIUSTINA, 3
39100 BOLZANO/BOZEN
TEL. 0471365125
www.loacker.net

ANNUAL PRODUCTION 60,000 bottles
HECTARES UNDER VINE 7
VITICULTURE METHOD Certified biodynamic

The Loacker estate celebrates its 30th birthday with an unparalleled performance in quality and consistency, lacking only a Three Glass winner. Rainer Loacker was a pioneer, one of the first in Alto Adige to use organic farming methods in his vineyards. He later introduced homeopathy to the estate and today, alongside his sons Hayo, the oenologist, and sales manager Franz Josef, he runs the entire estate to the precepts of biodynamic agriculture. The wines, which have great personality, are very varietal, characteristic representatives of their territory, distinguished by what we might call their positive energy. Many of the 60,000 bottles produced have glass caps. Three truly extraordinary labels landed in the Three Glass finals: the particularly fragrant, spicy Santa Maddalena Morit '07; the Chardonnay Ateyon '06; and the Pinot Nero Norital '06, which is absolutely one of the best in its category from Alto Adige.

○ A. A. Chardonnay Ateyon '06	TT	5
● A. A. Pinot Nero Norital '06	TT	5
● A. A. Santa Maddalena Cl. Morit '07	TT	4*
● A. A. Cabernet Lagrein Kastlet '05	TT	5
● A. A. Lagrein Gran Lareyn '06	TT	5
● A. A. Merlot Ywain '06	TT	5
○ A. A. Sauvignon Blanc Tasnim '07	TT	5
○ A. A. Valle Isarco Gewürztraminer Atagis '07	TT	5
○ A. A. Valle Isarco Sylvaner Ysac '07	TT	4*
● A. A. Merlot Ywain '04	YYY	5*
● A. A. Pinot Nero Norital '05	YY	5
● A. A. Pinot Nero Norital '04	YY	5
● A. A. Santa Maddalena Cl. Morit '06	YY	4
○ A. A. Sauvignon Blanc Tasnim '06	YY	5

H. Lun

VIA VILLA, 22/24
39044 EGNA/NEUMARKT [BZ]
TEL. 0471813256
www.lun.it

ANNUAL PRODUCTION 300,000 bottles
HECTARES UNDER VINE 35
VITICULTURE METHOD Conventional

One of the oldest and most famous wineries in the province of Bolzano continues its rise to the top of wine production in Alto Adige. Credit goes to the new technical staff that has brought this Egna/Neumarkt estate back on track in no time at all. This year, three wines made it to our finals but the difference comes from a series of well-made products that are respectful of varietal typicity. The list begins with a Gewürztraminer '07 that foregrounds finesse and fresh drinkability that accompanies every stage of tasting. One of the best in its category, the Moscato Giallo Passito '06 shows distinct dried apricot aromas that we find again on the full, concentrated palate perked up by well-balanced acidity. Also well crafted is the Bianco Sandbichler '07, from 40 per cent each chardonnay and pinot bianco with 15 per cent sauvignon and a splash of riesling, which shows fruity and juicy. The Santa Maddalena '07 is simply delicious.

○ A. A. Bianco Sandbichler '07	🍷🍷	4*
○ A. A. Gewürztraminer Sandbichler '07	🍷🍷	5
○ A. A. Moscato Giallo Sandbichler Passito '06	🍷🍷	6
● A. A. Cabernet Sauvignon Ris. '05	🍷🍷	4*
○ A. A. Chardonnay '07	🍷🍷	4*
● A. A. Lagrein Sandbichler Ris. '05	🍷🍷	6
○ A. A. Pinot Bianco '07	🍷🍷	4*
● A. A. Santa Maddalena '07	🍷🍷	4*
○ A. A. Sauvignon Sandbichler '07	🍷🍷	5
○ A. A. Riesling '07	🍷	4
● A. A. Lagrein Scuro Albertus Ris. '04	🍷🍷 (white)	5
○ A. A. Bianco Sandbichler '06	🍷🍷 (white)	4

Manincor

SAN GIUSEPPE AL LAGO, 4
39052 CALDARO/KALTERN [BZ]
TEL. 0471960230
www.manincor.com

ANNUAL PRODUCTION 200,000 bottles
HECTARES UNDER VINE 48
VITICULTURE METHOD Natural

A major change has taken place at Manincor in Caldaro. Though young, this estate, which was started in 1996, has a history that goes back to the early 17th century. Owner Conte Michael Goëss-Enzenberg has appointed a star as his winery manager. Helmuth Zozin did rather well at Cantina di Caldaro and now finds himself on the same wavelength as Goëss-Enzenberg regarding the choice of biodynamic viticulture methods. The importance of this change could begin to show next year but for now we report a series of wines with a discreet style, elegant enough but lacking that pinch of character to lift them to the status of great. One finalist was the stylish red Cassiano '05, from over half merlot, 30 per cent cabernet franc and a touch of syrah and petit verdot, is creamy and minerally with smooth tannins and a taut, mouthfilling finish. Also interesting is the Pinot Nero Mason di Mason '05, which offers floral aromas and a soft palate with tannins of rare smoothness. The sweet Le Petit de Manincor '06, from the petit manseng variety, is delicious.

● Cassiano '05	🍷🍷	6
● A. A. Lago di Caldaro Cl. Sup. '07	🍷🍷	4*
○ A. A. Moscato Giallo '07	🍷🍷	4*
● A. A. Pinot Nero Mason di Mason '05	🍷🍷	8
● Castel Campan '04	🍷🍷	8
○ Le Petit de Manincor '06	🍷🍷	6
○ Sophie '06	🍷🍷	5
● Cassiano '04	🍷🍷 (white)	6
● A. A. Pinot Nero Mason di Mason '03	🍷🍷 (white)	8
● Castel Campan '03	🍷🍷 (white)	8
○ Sophie '05	🍷🍷 (white)	5

Cantina Vini Merano

LOC. MAIA BASSA
VIA SAN MARCO, 11
39012 MERANO/MERAN [BZ]
TEL. 0473235544
www.meranerkellerei.com

★ Cantina Convento Muri-Gries

FRAZ. GRIES
P.ZZA GRIES, 21
39100 BOLZANO/BOZEN
TEL. 0471282287
www.muri-gries.com

ANNUAL PRODUCTION	450,000 bottles
HECTARES UNDER VINE	140
VITICULTURE METHOD	Conventional

ANNUAL PRODUCTION	450,000 bottles
HECTARES UNDER VINE	30
VITICULTURE METHOD	Conventional

This small co-operative winery in Merano finds itself in a slightly curious situation. Every year, it presents a series of very good, typical wines with some excellent high points but it has still not been able to win our highest award. This is too bad, especially this year when the skilled estate oenologist Stefan Kapfinger pulled various well-aimed arrows from his quiver. First off is the estate classic Moscato Giallo Passito Sissi from 80 per cent moscato giallo and 20 per cent gewürztraminer. It's great in the '06 version with complex aromas of citrus, dates and barley sugar followed by a concentrated, nicely sweet palate well supported by acidity. Another unmissable estate wine is the excellent Gewürztraminer Graf Von Meran '07, which shows how well they make this type of wine here. In fact, the basic version is not far behind for definition and typicity. The Valle Venosta-style Pinot Bianco Sonnenberg '07 lacks just a pinch of complexity. As usual, the schiava-based wines are very successful, although our favourite is the Sonnenberg '07.

For decades, the Werth family has been involved in the fortunes of this ancient estate-cum-monastery. The current Kellermeister Christian seems to live in a sort of symbiosis with lagrein, particularly the Riserva Abtei that has become a flag-carrier for this wine type. The '05 version holds no particular surprises in the sense that this wine is as great as usual and strode off with Three Glasses for the tenth time, picking up a first Star for Cantina Convento Muri-Gries. In keeping with the vintage year, this Lagrein puts the accent more on freshness and elegance than concentration. Spice, tobacco and black berry fruits characterize its well-defined aromas and the palate is lean, with aristocratic tannins and great length. Above all, it embodies Lagrein. Showing balanced and varietal, in other words better than ever, the Moscato Rosa '06 comes from one of the most difficult varieties to manage but the sure hand of Christian Werth makes it seem almost malleable. All the other wines are irreproachable, with a special mention for the Santa Maddalena.

○ A. A. Gewürztraminer Graf Von Meran '07	🍷🍷	5
○ A. A. Sissi Passito '06	🍷🍷	6
○ A. A. Val Venosta Pinot Bianco Sonnenberg '07	🍷🍷	4*
○ A. A. Amadeus V. T. '06	🍷🍷	6
○ A. A. Gewürztraminer '07	🍷🍷	4*
● A. A. Meraner Eines Fürsten Traum '07	🍷🍷	4*
● A. A. Meraner St. Valentin '07	🍷🍷	3*
○ A. A. Pinot Bianco Graf von Meran '07	🍷🍷	4*
● A. A. Pinot Nero Zeno Ris. '05	🍷🍷	5
○ A. A. Riesling Graf von Meran '07	🍷🍷	5
● A. A. Santa Maddalena '07	🍷🍷	3*
○ A. A. Sauvignon '07	🍷🍷	4*
○ A. A. Sauvignon Graf Von Meran '07	🍷🍷	5
● A. A. Val Venosta Schiava Sonnenberg '07	🍷🍷	3*
○ A. A. Gewürztraminer Graf Von Meran '05	🍷🍷	5
○ A. A. Gewürztraminer Graf Von Meran '04	🍷🍷	5

● A. A. Lagrein Abtei Ris. '05	🍷🍷🍷	5
● A. A. Moscato Rosa Abtei '06	🍷🍷	6
○ A. A. Bianco Abtei Muri '06	🍷🍷	4*
● A. A. Lagrein '07	🍷🍷	4*
● A. A. Pinot Nero Abtei Muri Ris. '05	🍷🍷	5
● A. A. Santa Maddalena '07	🍷🍷	3*
○ A. A. Pinot Bianco '07	🍷	4
● A. A. Lagrein Abtei Ris. '04	🍷🍷🍷	5
● A. A. Lagrein Abtei Ris. '03	🍷🍷🍷	5
● A. A. Lagrein Abtei Ris. '02	🍷🍷🍷	5
● A. A. Lagrein Abtei Ris. '01	🍷🍷🍷	5
● A. A. Lagrein Abtei Ris. '00	🍷🍷🍷	5

Cantina Nals Margreid

VIA HEILIGENBERG, 2
39010 NALLES/NALS [BZ]
TEL. 0471678626
www.kellerei.it

ANNUAL PRODUCTION	850,000 bottles
HECTARES UNDER VINE	150
VITICULTURE METHOD	Conventional

It's no surprise Cantina Nals Margreid has won Three Glasses for the second consecutive year with the Pinot Bianco Sirmian '07 and sent another four wines to our finals. The estate seems to have found near perfect organization and technical maturity so the 140 member-growers in the co-operative can rest easy. Once again kudos goes to the Sirmian that despite its youth offers florality and damson aromas followed by a palate with imposing structure and great energy, confident progression and a mineral finish enhanced by delicate spice. Regarding the Schiava Galea '07, sourced from a vineyard over 100 years old, we can only say that this year it won the prize in its category at the Vernatsch Cup and is so good even those who are most sceptical about the variety should now be convinced. Alongside these two champions is a series of wines that range across all the Alto Adige types, showing consistently high quality in a list that has few equals even in a territory as competitive as the province of Bolzano.

Niklaserhof - Josef Sölva

LOC. SAN NICOLÒ
VIA DELLE FONTANE, 31A
39052 CALDARO/KALTERN [BZ]
TEL. 0471963432
www.niklaserhof.it

ANNUAL PRODUCTION	45,000 bottles
HECTARES UNDER VINE	5.5
VITICULTURE METHOD	Conventional

Original wines with convincing quality might sum up the most significant characteristics of the Niklaserhof estate in the small village of San Nicolò above the town of Caldaro. From the five hectares under vine on their family property, Josef and Dieter Sölva produce around 50,000 bottles each year. On this small estate, long tradition blends particularly well with the winemaker's innovative personal style. Special attention is paid to whites beginning with Pinot Bianco in three versions: the Classico '07, Mondevinum, which has 30 per cent sauvignon and ten per cent chardonnay, and Klaser, both from the '06 vintage. We prefer the '07 for its richness, which is nicely paired with confident minerality and tension in the mouth. The Kerner '07 is pleasant and easy drinking while the Lago di Caldaro Scelto '07 is as usual one of the best of this type.

○ A. A. Pinot Bianco Sirmian '07	🍷🍷🍷 4*
○ A. A. Gewürztraminer Baron Salvadori '07	🍷🍷 5
○ A. A. Pinot Grigio Punggl '07	🍷🍷 4*
● A. A. Schiava Galea '07	🍷🍷 4*
○ Baronesse Baron Salvadori Passito '06	🍷🍷 7
● A. A. Cabernet Sauvignon Baron Salvadori Ris. '05	🍷🍷 6
● A. A. Lagrein Baron Salvadori Ris. '05	🍷🍷 5
● A. A. Merlot Anticus Baron Salvadori Ris. '05	🍷🍷 6
○ A. A. Pinot Bianco Penon '07	🍷🍷 4*
● A. A. Pinot Nero Mazzon '06	🍷🍷 5
● A. A. Santa Maddalena Cl. Rieserhof '07	🍷🍷 4*
○ A. A. Sauvignon Mantele '07	🍷🍷 5
● A. A. Schiava Grigia '07	🍷🍷 3*
○ A. A. Pinot Bianco Sirmian '06	🍷🍷🍷 4*
○ A. A. Moscato Giallo Passito Baronesse '05	🍷🍷 6
● A. A. Schiava Galea '06	🍷🍷 4*

○ A. A. Bianco Mondevinum '06	🍷🍷 5
● A. A. Lago di Caldaro Scelto Cl. '07	🍷🍷 3*
○ A. A. Pinot Bianco '07	🍷🍷 4*
○ A. A. Pinot Bianco Klaser '06	🍷🍷 4*
○ A. A. Kerner '07	🍷 4
○ A. A. Bianco Mondevinum '05	🍷🍷 5
○ A. A. Pinot Bianco Klaser R '05	🍷🍷 4*
○ A. A. Pinot Bianco '06	🍷🍷 4*
○ A. A. Sauvignon '06	🍷🍷 4*

Nusserhof - Heinrich Mayr

VIA MAYR NUSSER, 72
39100 BOLZANO/BOZEN
TEL. 0471978388

ANNUAL PRODUCTION	15,000 bottles
HECTARES UNDER VINE	2.5
VITICULTURE METHOD	Certified organic

You can say a lot of things about Heinrich Mayr's wines but not that they are ingratiating or specially tailored for the market. On the contrary, if possible, they have acquired even more austerity that in some cases verges on severity. Having said that, the wines show unique character and are eminently cellarable yet they pay for this by risking incomprehension when young. Anyway, we still like Heinrich's wines very much starting with the Tyroldego '05, an Alto Adige version of Trentino's Teroldego with great concentration. It's a touch rustic but has plenty of grip thanks to confident acidity and minerality. As usual, the Lagrein Riserva '05 is one of a kind. At this stage, it is still a bit edgy but knowing its proverbial ageing ability, it should give great satisfaction over the next few years to lovers of the variety because of pressure and dynamism that cool growing season has enhanced to the maximum. We would add the usual floral and vibrant white Blaterle '07, from the variety of the same name, and the delicious Lagrein Rosato '07 in one of its best versions ever. In short, a visit to the "Hazelnut Estate" is well worth the detour.

Pacherhof - Andreas Huber

FRAZ. NOVACELLA
V.LO PACHER, 1
39040 VARNA/VAHRN [BZ]
TEL. 0472835717
www.pacherhof.com

ANNUAL PRODUCTION	50,000 bottles
HECTARES UNDER VINE	6.5
VITICULTURE METHOD	Natural

Andreas Huber is one of Italy's most promising younger producers. His whites are very northern in style. They are vigorous, light-bodied wines that need time to unfold the full breath of their aromatics. This is true for all of them, starting with the Sylvaner Alte Reben '07 from the oldest vineyard planted to this variety in Valle Isarco. Although its aromas are slightly compressed, white-fleshed fruit and delicate minerality are already showing and the lean palate has well-supported progression. The Riesling '07 just needs some bottle ageing but early signs indicate that this is a great wine, presenting floral and mineral on the nose. It is almost overpowering on the palate, gunflint shades into hints of iodine notes. The estate, currently in the process of converting to biodynamic farming, is simply splendid. Andreas works in the cellar, with help from his father Josef, while his sisters run the lovely, hotel-restaurant on the premises. All the wines from here have character in spades.

● A. A. Lagrein Scuro Ris. '05	♥♥	5
● Tyroldego '05	♥♥	5
○ A. A. Blaterle '07	♥♥	4*
⊙ A. A. Lagrein Rosato '07	♥♥	4*
● Tyroldego '06	♥♥	5
● A. A. Lagrein Scuro Ris. '04	♀♀	4*
● A. A. Lagrein Scuro Ris. '01	♀♀	4*
○ A. A. Blaterle '06	♀♀	3*
● Tyroldego	♀♀	4*

○ A. A. Valle Isarco Riesling '07	♥♥	5
○ A. A. Valle Isarco Sylvaner Alte Reben '07	♥♥	5
○ A. A. Valle Isarco Kerner '07	♥♥	5
○ A. A. Valle Isarco Müller Thurgau '07	♥♥	4*
○ A. A. Valle Isarco Pinot Grigio '07	♥♥	4*
○ A. A. Valle Isarco Sylvaner '07	♥♥	5
○ A. A. Valle Isarco Riesling '04	♀♀♀	5
○ A. A. Valle Isarco Sylvaner Alte Reben '05	♀♀♀	5
○ A. A. Valle Isarco Riesling '06	♀♀	5
○ A. A. Valle Isarco Riesling '05	♀♀	5
○ A. A. Valle Isarco Sylvaner Alte Reben '06	♀♀	5

Pfannenstielhof
Johannes Pfeifer

VIA PFANNESTIEL, 9
39100 BOLZANO/BOZEN
TEL. 0471970884
www.pfannenstielhof.it

ANNUAL PRODUCTION	38,000 bottles
HECTARES UNDER VINE	4
VITICULTURE METHOD	Conventional

Pfannenstielhof wines closely resemble Johannes and Margareth Pfeifer, the likeable owners. They are communicative and sincere: in a word, real. These wines diligently reflect the progress and vagaries of the growing seasons and the Lagrein Riserva '05 is a snapshot of its year: a red that is full yet not that concentrated, showing fresh fruit and confident, spirited acidity for a varietal, fragrant Lagrein. Regularly among the best for years, the '07 version Santa Maddalena fully exploits the ideal growing year for schiava and reveals its best with caressing floral and spice aromas followed by a deliciously juicy, fruity palate. The standard label Lagrein is fresh and forthright in a version that drinks as if it had been specially made to accompany dishes from Alto Adige.

● A. A. Lagrein Scuro '07	♥♥	4*
● A. A. Lagrein Scuro Ris. '05	♥♥	5
● A. A. Pinot Nero '05	♥♥	5
● A. A. Santa Maddalena Cl. '07	♥♥	3*
● A. A. Santa Maddalena Cl. '06	♀♀	3*
● A. A. Lagrein Scuro Ris. '04	♀♀	5
● A. A. Lagrein Scuro Ris. '03	♀♀	5
● A. A. Pinot Nero '04	♀♀	5

Tenuta Pfitscherhof
Klaus Pfitscher

VIA GLENO, 9
39040 MONTAGNA/MONTAN [BZ]
TEL. 0471819773
www.pfitscher.it

ANNUAL PRODUCTION	50,000 bottles
HECTARES UNDER VINE	5.5
VITICULTURE METHOD	Conventional

Ansiz Pfitscher earns a more than well-deserved debut among the full profiles for this small family estate in Montagna that for years has delivered high quality. Once again, it is an old family operation, begun in 1861, that has been carried on and is currently managed by the able Klaus Pfitscher. This zone is among the best for Pinot Nero and one of the estate warhorses is in fact the Matan '05, with delicately floral aromas and shades of golden leaf tobacco and spices. The palate is lean and soft, cosseted by elegant tannins. But we were most convinced by the Gewürztraminer Stoass '07, which has never been this complex or balanced right from the aromas, where tropical fruits overlay citrus notes and minerality. The palate is vibrant, taut and nicely sweet with enjoyable freshness. Also well made is the red Cortazo '06, from lagrein, merlot and syrah, which is fruity, floral and juicy. All the wines produced here bear the signs of an ongoing search for an individual style focused on typicity and drinkability.

○ A. A. Gewürztraminer Stoass '07	♥♥	5
● A. A. Cuvée Cortazo '06	♥♥	6
● A. A. Lagrein Kotznloater '06	♥♥	5
● A. A. Pinot Nero Matan '05	♥♥	6
○ A. A. Sauvignon Blanc Langefeld '07	♀	4
● A. A. Lagrein Kotznloater '04	♀♀	5
● A. A. Pinot Nero Matan '04	♀♀	5
● A. A. Cuvée Cortazo '03	♀♀	5
● A. A. Lagrein Kotznloater '05	♀♀	5
● Cortazo '04	♀♀	5

Tenuta Ritterhof

S.DA DEL VINO, 1
39052 CALDARO/KALTERN [BZ]
TEL. 0471963298
www.ritterhof.it

ANNUAL PRODUCTION	290,000 bottles
HECTARES UNDER VINE	7.5
VITICULTURE METHOD	Conventional

It is a genuine pleasure to taste wines from Tenuta Ritterhof, at number one on the Caldaro Wine Trail. Year after year, these wines show even more varietal and territorial character. Oenologist Hannes Bernard and manager Ludwig Kaneppele know their craft well and the owners, the Roner family, should be more than satisfied with the results achieved. The estate produces two lines. Ritterhof includes all the classic Alto Adige whites and reds, with better than convincing typicity and quality. The Pinot Bianco, Sauvignon, Gewürztraminer and Santa Maddalena from this line are all well worth tasting. The Crescendo line is from a selection of grapes sourced from the best-aspected plots and bottled only in the best vintages. In our Three Glass finals this year was the spectacular Gewürztraminer Crescendo '07, which gives caressing floral and tropical fruit aromas ushering in a zesty, spicy palate with a long, fresh finish. The remarkably drinkable Lagrein Riserva Crescendo '05 is structured, full, velvety, spicy and elegant.

Hans Rottensteiner

VIA SARENTINO, 1A
39100 BOLZANO/BOZEN
TEL. 0471282015
www.rottensteiner-weine.com

ANNUAL PRODUCTION	400,000 bottles
HECTARES UNDER VINE	10
VITICULTURE METHOD	Conventional

Founded in 1956 by Hans Rottensteiner, this winemaking estate at the entrance to Val Sarentino is now managed by Anton Rottensteiner and his son Hannes. Special attention is focused on grapes from the ten hectares of vineyards on their property in the heart of the classic zone for Lagrein and Santa Maddalena Classico. The splendid '06 version of the Gewürztraminer Passito Cresta is an extraordinary sweet wine that ranks as one of the best in its type from Alto Adige. It is complex with notes of tropical fruit and citrus, showing a concentrated, minerally palate enlivened by fresh acidity. For years now, we have been accustomed to the Lagrein Grieser Select Riserva '05 being one of the best. It's powerful and creamy yet at the same time expansive with great length. A timeless classic, the '07 version of the Santa Maddalena Premstallerhof went straight through to our finals. The Valle Isarco Sylvaner '07 shows surprising freshness and typicity.

O A. A. Gewürztraminer Crescendo '07	♟♟ 5
O A. A. Gewürztraminer '07	♟♟ 4*
● A. A. Lagrein Crescendo Ris. '05	♟♟ 5
O A. A. Pinot Bianco '07	♟♟ 4*
● A. A. Santa Maddalena '07	♟♟ 4*
O A. A. Sauvignon '07	♟♟ 4*
● A. A. Cabernet Merlot Crescendo Ris. '05	♟ 5
O A. A. Chardonnay '07	♟ 4
O A. A. Müller Thurgau '07	♟ 4
O A. A. Pinot Grigio '07	♟ 4
O A. A. Gewürztraminer Crescendo '05	♟♟ 5
O A. A. Sauvignon '05	♟♟ 4*
● A. A. Lagrein Crescendo Ris. '04	♟♟ 5

O A. A. Gewürztraminer Passito Cresta '06	♟♟ 6
● A. A. Lagrein Grieser Select Ris. '05	♟♟ 5
● A. A. Santa Maddalena Cl. Premstallerhof '07	♟♟ 4*
O A. A. Gewürztraminer Cancenai '07	♟♟ 4
O A. A. Valle Isarco Sylvaner '07	♟♟ 4*
O A. A. Müller Thurgau '07	♟ 4
O A. A. Pinot Grigio '07	♟ 4
O A. A. Gewürztraminer Cresta '01	♟♟ 7
O A. A. Gewürztraminer Passito Cresta '04	♟♟ 6
● A. A. Lagrein Grieser Select Ris. '04	♟♟ 5
O A. A. Gewürztraminer Cancenai '06	♟♟ 4
● Prem '06	♟♟ 4

Castel Sallegg

V.LO DI SOTTO, 15
39052 CALDARO/KALTERN [BZ]
TEL. 0471963132
www.castelsallegg.it

ANNUAL PRODUCTION	120,000 bottles
HECTARES UNDER VINE	31
VITICULTURE METHOD	Conventional

The Castel Sallegg estate of the noble Kuenburg family at Caldaro gets better every year. Although once among the benchmark wineries in the area, it remained in the shadows for too many years. A long history, rich tradition, a beautiful castle with old cellars and above all vineyards in the best areas around Lake Caldaro are all prerequisites for making great wines. The new oenologist Matthias Hauser has clear ideas and knows his craft well. Georg Kuenburg seems persuaded and is satisfied with the results. Wines submitted by Castel Sallegg this year reflect this wave of positive energy. Outstanding among them are the Pinot Nero '05, Merlot Riserva '04 and Merlot Nussleiten Riserva '04, three reds with great quality and character. However, the two whites that landed in our finals showed even more self-confidence: the Pinot Bianco '07 and Pinot Grigio '07 are both elegantly fresh, fruity and savoury wines. Nor should we forget the special estate wine, the legendary Moscato Rosa. The latest vintage, the '01, is one of the best from the past few years.

★★ Cantina Produttori San Michele Appiano

VIA CIRCONVALLAZIONE, 17/19
39057 APPIANO/EPPAN [BZ]
TEL. 0471664466
www.stmichael.it

ANNUAL PRODUCTION	2,300,000 bottles
HECTARES UNDER VINE	370
VITICULTURE METHOD	Conventional

Hans Terzer may be tired of his reputation as the specialist in Sauvignon and white wines in general. So for a few years now, he has also been giving us reds of growing stature and assertiveness. The only criticism we could make about his Merlot Sanct Valentin '05 is its youth. It has a very Bordeauxesque style of minerality, concentration and elegance. From the same Sanct Valentin line, the Lagrein '05 is dense and still austere with a careful use of oak that gives it depth, freshness and a complexity establishing it as one of the best from the vintage. This Lagrein will hold some nice surprises for those with the patience to wait for another few years. A recent tasting of the '00 vintage convinced us that this variety has considerable ageing potential. We almost forgot to say that the Sauvignon Sanct Valentin '07 has once again taken Three Glasses with a version that is particularly vibrant, taut and juicy. But perhaps the real news would have been it had failed to win. The rest of the range earned the usual embarrassing raft of Glassware.

● A. A. Moscato Rosa '01	♟♟	7
○ A. A. Pinot Bianco '07	♟♟	4*
○ A. A. Pinot Grigio '07	♟♟	4*
● A. A. Lago di Caldaro Scelto Bischofsleiten '07	♟♟	4*
● A. A. Merlot Nussleiten Ris. '04	♟♟	7
● A. A. Merlot Ris. '04	♟♟	5
○ A. A. Moscato Giallo Secco '07	♟♟	4*
● A. A. Pinot Nero '05	♟♟	5
● A. A. Cabernet Ris. '05	♟	5
● A. A. Lagrein Ris. '04	♟	5
○ A. A. Sauvignon '07	♟	4
● A. A. Merlot Nussleiten Ris. '03	♟♟	7
● A. A. Merlot Ris. '03	♟♟	5
○ A. A. Pinot Grigio '06	♟♟	4*

○ A. A. Sauvignon St. Valentin '07	♟♟♟	6
○ A. A. Bianco Passito Comtess '06	♟♟	6
● A. A. Lagrein St. Valentin '05	♟♟	6
● A. A. Merlot St. Valentin '05	♟♟	6
○ A. A. Pinot Grigio St. Valentin '06	♟♟	6
● A. A. Cabernet St. Valentin '05	♟♟	6
○ A. A. Chardonnay Merol '07	♟♟	4*
○ A. A. Gewürztraminer St. Valentin '07	♟♟	6
● A. A. Merlot Ris. '05	♟♟	5
○ A. A. Pinot Bianco Schulthauser '07	♟♟	4*
○ A. A. Pinot Bianco St. Valentin '06	♟♟	6
○ A. A. Pinot Grigio Anger '07	♟♟	4*
● A. A. Pinot Nero Ris. '05	♟♟	5
● A. A. Pinot Nero St. Valentin '05	♟♟	6
○ A. A. Riesling Montiggl '07	♟♟	4*
○ A. A. Sauvignon Lahn '07	♟♟	4*
● A. A. Schiava Pagis '07	♟♟	4*
○ A. A. Sauvignon St. Valentin '06	♟♟♟	5

Cantina Sociale San Paolo

LOC. SAN PAOLO
VIA CASTEL GUARDIA, 21
39050 APPIANO/EPPAN [BZ]
TEL. 0471662183
www.kellereistpauls.com

ANNUAL PRODUCTION	1,000,000 bottles
HECTARES UNDER VINE	170
VITICULTURE METHOD	Conventional

It's been an up and down year for this historic co-operative winery at Appiano. Some of the wines we tasted were utterly convincing whereas others seemed to show rather more uncertain progress, although the recent handover in technical management permits us to look forward to rapid improvement. The typical, creamy Lagrein DiVinus Riserva '05 shows outstanding personality and only slightly excessive new oak compromises its energy. Still, it is a solid red with a secure future. The floral and intensely fruity Gewürztraminer Passion '07 presents a harmonious, full, solid structure while the Spumante Praeclarus Noblesse Riserva '04 is well crafted and fragrant. Another two wines are also particularly interesting, the Sauvignon Passion '07 and the fresh, elegant Pinot Nero Luziafeld Exclusiv '06.

★ Cantina Produttori Santa Maddalena/Cantina di Bolzano

VIA BRENNERO, 15
39100 BOLZANO/BOZEN
TEL. 0471270909
www.cantinabolzano.com

ANNUAL PRODUCTION	1,300,000 bottles
HECTARES UNDER VINE	130
VITICULTURE METHOD	Conventional

After eight consecutive Three Glass awards, this year the Taber decided to take a break. Although it only missed by a hair, the '06 vintage didn't quite make it this time. But don't misunderstand us. This wine is great, with caressing spice and tobacco aromas and a creamy palate that shows minerally and fresh with a hint of cocoa powder but by now we expect only the best from it so this was not enough. Proof that Lagrein is deeply rooted in Kellermeister Stefan Filippi's conscience can be found in the presence in our finals of the deliciously cheeky Perl '06. Naturally, Three Glasses went to the '07 Pinot Bianco Dellago, which encored last year's success with an even more convincing version, thanks to a spectrum of aromatics that runs from white-fleshed fruit to spice and a palate on which juicy, full fruit mingles with almost salty savouriness and the depth of a great wine. The rest of the line-up comprises good, typical wines with two Santa Maddalenas in the lead, the Classico and the legendary Huck am Bach, both from the '07 vintage.

○ A. A. Gewürztraminer Passion '07	♥♥	5
● A. A. Lagrein Scuro DiVinus Ris. '05	♥♥	6
● A. A. Pinot Nero Luziafeld Exclusiv '06	♥♥	5
○ A. A. Praeclarus Noblesse Ris. '04	♥♥	6
○ A. A. Sauvignon Passion '07	♥♥	5
● A. A. Schiava Passion '07	♥♥	4*
○ A. A. Pinot Bianco Exclusiv Plötzner '07	♥	4
○ A. A. Pinot Bianco Passion '07	♥	5
○ A. A. Pinot Grigio Exclusiv Egg Leiten '07	♥	4
○ A. A. Sauvignon Exclusiv Gfillhof '07	♥	5
● A. A. Lagrein Scuro DiVinus Ris. '04	♥♥	6
○ A. A. Pinot Grigio Exclusiv Egg Leiten '06	♥♥	4*
○ A. A. Pinot Bianco Exclusiv Plötzner '05	♥♥	4*

○ A. A. Pinot Bianco Dellago '07	♥♥♥	5
● A. A. Lagrein Scuro Perl '06	♥♥	5
● A. A. Lagrein Scuro Taber Ris. '06	♥♥	7
● A. A. Cabernet Mumelter Ris. '05	♥♥	6
○ A. A. Chardonnay Kleinstein '07	♥♥	5
○ A. A. Gewürztramier Kleinstein '07	♥♥	6
○ A. A. Gewürztraminer '07	♥♥	5
● A. A. Merlot Siebeneich Ris. '06	♥♥	6
● A. A. Santa Maddalena Cl. '07	♥♥	4*
● A. A. Santa Maddalena Cl. Huck am Bach '07	♥♥	4*
○ A. A. Sauvignon Mock '07	♥♥	5
● A. A. Lagrein Scuro Taber Ris. '05	♥♥♥	6
● A. A. Lagrein Scuro Taber Ris. '04	♥♥♥	6
● A. A. Lagrein Scuro Taber Ris. '01	♥♥♥	6

Peter Sölva & Söhne

VIA DELL'ORO, 33
39052 CALDARO/KALTERN [BZ]
TEL. 0471964650
www.soelva.com

ANNUAL PRODUCTION	75,000 bottles
HECTARES UNDER VINE	11
VITICULTURE METHOD	Conventional

The Peter Sölva & Söhne estate is one of the oldest winemaking operations in Caldaro. The estate's activities have been documented as far back as 1731. Today, bottles are released under two labels, Desilvas and Amistar, and the wines show good typicity, character and impeccable technique. Credit for the oenological and commercial success of this estate goes to the oenologist Christian Belutti and the dynamic owner Stefan Sölva, who have for some time being striding firmly along the path to quality. Among the best in its category is the Terlano Pinot Bianco Desilvas '07, which is still slightly austere but shows juicy and zesty as it expands brightly in the mouth. The Amistar Edizione '05, from cabernet, merlot and lagrein, is a table wine with caressing balsamic aromas mingling with wild berries and pencil lead before its rich, creamy palate offers harmonious, confident progression. The rest of the range is equally sound, showing just how confident winemaking at this cellar has become.

○ A. A. Terlano Pinot Bianco Desilvas '07	♥♥	5
● Amistar Edizione '05	♥♥	7
● A. A. Cabernet Franc Amistar '05	♥♥	6
● A. A. Lago di Caldaro Scelto Cl. Sup. Desilvas Peterleiten '07	♥♥	4*
○ A. A. Sauvignon Desilvas '07	♥	5
● Amistar Rosso '05	♥	6
○ A. A. Gewürztramimer Amistar '04	♡♡	5
● A. A. Lagrein Scuro Desilvas '05	♡♡	4
○ A. A. Sauvignon Desilvas '06	♡♡	5
○ A. A. Terlano Pinot Bianco Desilvas '06	♡♡	5
● Amistar Rosso '04	♡♡	6
● A. A. Cabernet Franc Amistar '04	♡♡	6

Stroblhof

LOC. SAN MICHELE
VIA PIGANÒ, 25
39057 APPIANO/EPPAN [BZ]
TEL. 0471662250
www.stroblhof.it

ANNUAL PRODUCTION	30,000 bottles
HECTARES UNDER VINE	3.7
VITICULTURE METHOD	Conventional

Andreas Nicolussi-Leck has been close to Three Glasses for a few years now. It was a toss-up between his Pinot Bianco Strahler and one of his Pinot Neros for the privilege. For years, Andreas's Pinot Neros have been among the best with a taut, spirited style that recalls the proprietor, who uses the consultancy of emerging winemaker Hans Terzer. All the wines show this mineral and acidity-forward style: the Gewürztraminer declares more than six grams per litre. There are no secrets to this success. A visit to the vineyards reveals dark, volcanic soil, completely different from the norm in the zone. Surprisingly, the winner is the Pinot Nero Riserva '05, despite our tasting panel's deep distrust of wine of this type from outside Burgundy, making it an even greater honour. This red has fruity, floral aromas as well as a touch of liquorice. The supple palate gives smooth yet gutsy tannins and above all great thrust in its progression. The Pinot Bianco Strahler '07 cuts like a knife with its minerality and vibrant acid grip while for the time being the Pinot Nero Pigeno '06 is a step behind the Riserva. The Gewürztraminer Pigeno '07 shows surprising freshness and a gutsy palate.

● A. A. Pinot Nero Ris. '05	♥♥♥	6
○ A. A. Gewürztraminer Pigeno '07	♥♥	5
○ A. A. Pinot Bianco Strahler '07	♥♥	4*
○ A. A. Chardonnay Schwarzhaus '07	♥♥	4
● A. A. Pinot Nero Pigeno '06	♥♥	5
○ A. A. Sauvignon Nico '07	♥♥	5
○ A. A. Pinot Bianco Strahler '06	♡♡	4*
● A. A. Pinot Nero Pigeno '04	♡♡	5
● A. A. Pinot Nero Ris. '04	♡♡	6
● A. A. Pinot Nero Ris. '02	♡♡	6
○ A. A. Sauvignon Nico '06	♡♡	5

Taschlerhof - Peter Wachtler

LOC. MARA, 107
39042 BRESSANONE/BRIXEN [BZ]
TEL. 0472851091
www.taschlerhof.com

ANNUAL PRODUCTION	19,000 bottles
HECTARES UNDER VINE	3.5
VITICULTURE METHOD	Natural

We believe the talented Peter Wachtler has for the past couple of years been finding a good length for his wines, after a brief period in the shadows that coincided with the construction of the new cellar. Now that everything is set, our winemaker can fully concentrate on his range and the results are better than good. Considering his skill and the terrain, we remain convinced Peter could do even better but he is young and has time on his side. It is difficult to establish a classification for Peter's wines. They are all varietal, very well made, very redolent of the Valle Isarco territory and comprise a range that is missing only a top quality high point. This year, we particularly appreciated a Kerner '07 with outstanding personality, balanced fruit and citrus aromas and a savoury, minerally palate with depth and length we have rarely encountered in wines from Taschlerhof. The Sylvaner '07 shows aromatic herbs and white-fleshed fruit upfront before the palate expands supple and dynamic. But the entire range of wines presented here manages to embody all those characteristics that make Valle Isarco wines famous.

★ Cantina Terlano

VIA SILBERLEITEN, 7
39018 TERLANO/TERLAN [BZ]
TEL. 0471257135
www.cantina-terlano.com

ANNUAL PRODUCTION	1,000,000 bottles
HECTARES UNDER VINE	140
VITICULTURE METHOD	Conventional

While waiting to see how the merger with Cantina di Andriano develops, Cantina Terlano sent seven wines to our finals, turning in an average score that could well be without equal in Italy. The amazing thing is not only are the most famous wines as good as ever but the so-called second lines keep improving in quality. This is the sign of highly professional winemaking management with clear objectives. One example is the Cabernet Siemegg Riserva '04, which puts grip and elegance at the service of a rich-textured wine with juicy tannins. Three Glasses were the reward for a great estate classic, the Pinot Bianco Vorberg Riserva '05, a wine that has now become emblematic of white wine production in Alto Adige. It has complex aromas of white-fleshed fruit interweaving with spiciness and restrained smoky notes. The savoury palate shows almost aggressive dynamism with iodine and mineral notes underpinned by vibrant grip. The extraordinarily fresh, complex Pinot Bianco 1996 is sumptuous and aristocratic with notes of oriental spices and saffron. The only problem is that very few bottles are released. The chart below is eloquent.

○ A. A. Valle Isarco Kerner '07	▼▼	5
○ A. A. Valle Isarco Gewürztraminer '07	▼▼	5
○ A. A. Valle Isarco Sylvaner '07	▼▼	4*
○ A. A. Valle Isarco Sylvaner Lahner '07	▼▼	5
○ A. A. Valle Isarco Kerner '05	♈♈	4*
○ A. A. Valle Isarco Gewürztraminer '06	♈♈	5
○ A. A. Valle Isarco Sylvaner '06	♈♈	4*
○ A. A. Valle Isarco Sylvaner Lahner '06	♈♈	4*

○ A. A. Terlano Pinot Bianco Vorberg Ris. '05	▼▼▼	4*
● A. A. Cabernet Siemegg Ris. '04	▼▼	4*
○ A. A. Gewürztraminer Lunare '06	▼▼	6
● A. A. Lagrein Porphyr Ris. '05	▼▼	6
○ A. A. Terlano Chardonnay Kreuth '06	▼▼	4*
○ A. A. Terlano Pinot Bianco 1996 '96	▼▼	8
○ A. A. Terlano Sauvignon Quarz '06	▼▼	6
○ A. A. Chardonnay Cl. '07	▼▼	4*
● A. A. Lagrein Gries Ris. '05	▼▼	5
● A. A. Merlot Siebeneich Ris. '05	▼▼	5
○ A. A. Pinot Grigio '07	▼▼	4
● A. A. Pinot Nero Montigl Ris. '05	▼▼	5
○ A. A. Terlano Cl. '07	▼▼	4*
○ A. A. Terlano Nova Domus Ris. '05	▼▼	6
○ A. A. Terlano Pinot Bianco Cl. '07	▼▼	4*
○ A. A. Terlano Sauvignon Winkl '07	▼▼	4
○ A. A. Terlano Pinot Bianco Vorberg Ris. '02	♈♈♈	4*

★ Cantina Termeno

S.DA DEL VINO, 144
39040 TERMENO/TRAMIN [BZ]
TEL. 0471860126
www.tramin-wine.it

ANNUAL PRODUCTION	1,400,000 bottles
HECTARES UNDER VINE	220
VITICULTURE METHOD	Conventional

Whether Willi Stürzt's Gewürztraminers will win Three Glasses or not is no longer an issue. The question is whether they are better than the previous vintage. Our impression is that the Nussbaumer '07 is slightly better than the '06 in its overall dynamism. It's concentrated, yet more spirited and racy with clear citrussy notes that accompany each phase of tasting up to a finish of rare poise. The complexity of the Terminum '06 recalls the legendary 1998 edition with an aromatic range of great breadth that shifts from citrus to thyme, marjoram and spice. The palate is stylish and elegant, with 200 grams of sugar per litre perfectly offset by acidity that tops eight grams per litre. The citron peel is reprised deliciously alongside apricot and saffron. The interesting, gutsy Pinot Grigio Unterebner '07 is the result of Willi's experiment with harvesting the grapes on the stalks. The Schiava Freisinger '07 is as usual one of the best. We should also mention Willi's efforts at reducing the use of herbicides, to be completely eliminated by all members of the co-operative during the next growing season.

Thurnhof - Andreas Berger

LOC. ASLAGO
VIA CASTEL FLAVON, 7
39100 BOLZANO/BOZEN
TEL. 0471288460
www.thurnhof.com

ANNUAL PRODUCTION	25,000 bottles
HECTARES UNDER VINE	3.5
VITICULTURE METHOD	Natural

Andreas Berger lives with his lovely family on their small estate, currently under conversion to organic production, on the edge of Bolzano in one of the warmest zones in the province. His modern-style wines bear more than just a slight resemblance to the man who makes them. They are reserved to the point of timidity but after a while they show all their gutsy character. This year, we tasted a series of balanced, well-made wines with outstanding personality. At the top of our list is a particularly well-crafted Lagrein Riserva '05. The wine is concentrated and balanced with nicely textured tannins and lovely freshness that give it captivating drinkability. Above all, we note that the use of oak is better balanced, something we could say about all the reds. As usual, the vintage Lagrein, the Merlau '07, is fresh and perky. The Sauvignon '07 is better than ever, revealing caressing aromas of nettles and white-fleshed fruit, along with a zesty, gutsy, supple palate that lingers attractively. The rest of the range is as good as usual.

○ A. A. Gewürztraminer Nussbaumer '07 ♟♟♟ 5	
○ A. A. Gewürztraminer Passito	
Terminum V. T. '06	♟♟♟ 8
○ A. A. Pinot Bianco Tauris '06	♟♟ 5
○ A. A. Sauvignon Montan '07	♟♟ 5
○ A. A. Gewürztraminer '07	♟♟ 4*
● A. A. Lagrein Urban '06	♟♟ 6
● A. A. Loam '05	♟♟ 6
● A. A. Pinot Grigio Unterebner '07	♟♟ 5
● A. A. Schiava Freisinger '07	♟♟ 4*
● A. A. Schiava Grigia '07	♟♟ 4*
○ A. A. Stoan '07	♟♟ 5
○ A. A. Gewürztraminer Nussbaumer '06 ♟♟♟ 5	
○ A. A. Gewürztraminer Nussbaumer '05 ♟♟♟ 5	
○ A. A. Gewürztraminer	
Passito Terminum '98	♟♟♟ 6
○ A. A. Gewürztraminer	
Passito Terminum V. T. '04	♟♟♟ 8

● A. A. Lagrein Scuro Merlau '07	♟♟ 4*
● A. A. Lagrein Scuro Ris. '05	♟♟ 5
○ A. A. Moscato Giallo	
Passito Passaurum '06	♟♟ 6
● A. A. Santa Maddalena '07	♟♟ 4*
○ A. A. Sauvignon '07	♟♟ 4*
○ A. A. Moscato Giallo '07	♟ 4
● A. A. Lagrein Scuro Ris. '04	♟♟ 5
● A. A. Lagrein Scuro Ris. '02	♟♟ 5
● A. A. Cabernet Sauvignon Ris. '04	♟♟ 5
● A. A. Lagrein Scuro Merlau '06	♟♟ 4*
● A. A. Santa Maddalena '06	♟♟ 4*

Tiefenbrunner

FRAZ. NICLARA
VIA CASTELLO, 4
39040 CORTACCIA/KURTATSCH [BZ]
TEL. 0471880122
www.tiefenbrunner.com

ANNUAL PRODUCTION	700,000 bottles
HECTARES UNDER VINE	20.5
VITICULTURE METHOD	Conventional

We should just give Three Glasses automatically to the Tiefenbrunner estate every year. Few producers are capable of presenting a range of wines at this level of quality with such consistency. There are five finalists but tasting scores were so close that there could have been more, or different wines. But that final touch was lacking, which we regret because over the past few years Christof Tiefenbrunner has made a huge effort to bring this venerable old estate to the front rank of Alto Adige and Italian winemaking. Moving on to the wines, we must confess to a passion for the Feldmarschall. Although it is a simple Müller Thurgau, this extraordinary white from the mountains has distinctive style and personality. The introduction of a screw cap is big news this year, and says a lot about Christof's vision. The wine is a delicious as ever with hints of white pepper and a palate that is supple, tangy, complex, long and pure. As usual, the Gewürztraminer '07 is one of the best, showing complexity, harmony and restraint, which could well be the cellar's trademark.

Untermoserhof - Georg Ramoser

VIA SANTA MADDALENA, 36
39100 BOLZANO/BOZEN
TEL. 0471975481
untermoserhof@rolmail.net

ANNUAL PRODUCTION	40,000 bottles
HECTARES UNDER VINE	4.5
VITICULTURE METHOD	Conventional

Untermoserhof only submitted three wines but they were well made and typical, although we always expect the best from a skilled winemaker like Georg Ramoser. Untermoserhof has been located on the lovely hill of Santa Maddalena since the 17th century and managed by three generations of the Ramoser family, which makes wines in the classic styles of the zone. These have a fairly modern spin but maintain exemplary typicity and faithfully reflect the characteristics of the terroir. Perhaps the growing year was not the most favourable, or perhaps the wine is still too young, but we were not completely convinced by the Lagrein Riserva '05. Although fresh and concentrated, it seems a bit rigid and clenched for the time being and the contribution of new oak is still a bit too noticeable. The pleasant, standard label Lagrein is simpler yet dense with moderate structure and satisfying drinkability. Simply exquisite, and not for the first time, the Santa Maddalena '07 is a varietal, full wine with refined spicy notes and fresh, caressing finish. We'll be back next year and we are certain that Georg will be on hand to amaze us.

○ A. A. Chardonnay Castel Turmhof '07	♈♈ 4*
○ A. A. Chardonnay Linticlarus '06	♈♈ 5
○ A. A. Cuvée Anna Castel Turmhof '07	♈♈ 4*
○ A. A. Gewürztraminer Castel Turmhof '07	♈♈ 5
○ Feldmarschall von Fenner zu Fennberg '07	♈♈ 5
● A. A. Lagrein Linticlarus Ris. '05	♈♈ 5
● A. A. Pinot Nero Linticlarus Ris. '05	♈♈ 5
○ A. A. Sauvignon Kirchleiten '07	♈♈ 4*
● A. A. Schiava Grigia Castel Turmhof '07	♈♈ 4*
○ Feldmarschall von Fenner zu Fennberg '05	♈♈♈ 5
● A. A. Cabernet Sauvignon Linticlarus Ris. '04	♈♈ 6
○ A. A. Cuvée Anna Castel Turmhof '06	♈♈ 4*
○ A. A. Sauvignon Kirchleiten '06	♈♈ 4*
● A. A. Lagrein Linticlarus Ris. '04	♈♈ 5

● A. A. Lagrein Scuro '07	♈♈ 4*
● A. A. Lagrein Scuro Ris. '05	♈♈ 5
● A. A. Santa Maddalena Cl. '07	♈♈ 4*
● A. A. Lagrein Scuro Ris. '03	♈♈♈ 5*
● A. A. Lagrein Scuro '06	♈♈ 4*
● A. A. Lagrein Scuro Ris. '04	♈♈ 5
● A. A. Merlot Ris. '04	♈♈ 5

Tenuta Unterortl - Castel Juval

FRAZ. JUVAL, 1B
39020 CASTELBELLO CIARDES/
KASTELBELL TSCHARS [BZ]
TEL. 0473667580
www.unterortl.it

ANNUAL PRODUCTION	30,000 bottles
HECTARES UNDER VINE	4
VITICULTURE METHOD	Conventional

Castel Juval is very much part of this year's Valle Venosta renaissance. Then again, Martin and Gisela Aurich have been working since 1992 on this amazing terroir, a word that may be inflated but is justified in this case. They have remarkable, dizzyingly beautiful, plots but the terroir's contribution is obvious in the rare style and personality of the wines. Here for the second time in Valle Venosta, we applaud the minor miracle of a double Three Glass Award. But choosing only one from the '07 Riesling and Pinot Bianco would have devalued the other. What can we say about the Riesling '07? It fulfils all its potential showing aromas of fruit, white pepper and a flash of iodine. The palate expands supple and savoury with an interminable sea salt-tinged. Never before has the Pinot Bianco '07 been so complex with its notes of white-fleshed fruit, aromatic herbs, spice and a minerally palate with extraordinary dynamism and purity. The surprise is the red Gneis '06, from pinot nero, zweigelt, St. Laurent, gamaret and garanoir, a big little red wine from the mountains. There's another little revolution: all the bottles have screw caps.

Cantina Produttori Valle Isarco

VIA COSTE, 50
39043 CHIUSA/KLAUSEN [BZ]
TEL. 0472847553
www.cantinavalleisarco.it

ANNUAL PRODUCTION	750,000 bottles
HECTARES UNDER VINE	130
VITICULTURE METHOD	Conventional

If you are in a restaurant or wine bar and happen on a bottle from Cantina Produttori Valle Isarco, whether it's a standard bottle or an Aristos selection, whatever the type, you are not going to be disappointed. These are all well-made wines that reflect a territory now considered a sort of Eldorado for Italian white winemaking. Honours go to one of the passions of the talented Kellermeister Thomas Dorfmann, a Riesling Aristos '07 with rare elegance and complexity. It's in the estate style, concentrated and full yet with plenty of energy and freshness through to the deep, complex finish. The Veltliner Aristos '07 is here to show the potential of this variety, shamefully neglected till a few years ago. Peach and citron peel come through clearly on the nose before the dense palate reveals a distinct touch of acidity and great development. These two wines reached our finals but the rest of the range hot on their heels.

○ A. A. Valle Venosta Pinot Bianco '07	♆♆♆ 4*
○ A. A. Valle Venosta Riesling '07	♆♆♆ 5*
● Juval Gneis '06	♆♆ 4*
○ Juval Glimmet '07	♆♆ 4*
○ A. A. Valle Venosta Riesling '04	♆♆♆ 5*
○ A. A. Valle Venosta Riesling '03	♆♆♆ 5*
○ A. A. Valle Venosta Riesling '00	♆♆♆ 4
○ A. A. Valle Venosta Riesling Windbichel '05	♆♆♆ 5
○ A. A. Valle Venosta Riesling '06	♆♆ 5*
○ A. A. Valle Venosta Pinot Bianco '06	♆♆ 4*
● A. A. Valle Venosta Pinot Nero '05	♆♆ 5
○ A. A. Valle Venosta Riesling Windbichel '04	♆♆ 5

○ A. A. Valle Isarco Riesling Aristos '07	♆♆ 5
○ A. A. Valle Isarco Veltliner Aristos '07	♆♆ 5
○ A. A. Sauvignon Aristos '07	♆♆ 5
○ A. A. Valle Isarco Gewürztraminer Aristos '07	♆♆ 5
○ A. A. Valle Isarco Kerner Aristos '07	♆♆ 5
● A. A. Valle Isarco Klausener Laitacher '07	♆♆ 4*
○ A. A. Valle Isarco Pinot Grigio Aristos '07	♆♆ 5
○ A. A. Valle Isarco Sylvaner '07	♆♆ 4*
○ A. A. Valle Isarco Sylvaner Aristos '07	♆♆ 5
○ A. A. Valle Isarco Veltliner '07	♆♆ 4*
○ A. A. Valle Isarco Kerner Aristos '05	♆♆♆ 4*
○ A. A. Valle Isarco Riesling Aristos '06	♆♆ 4*
○ A. A. Valle Isarco Riesling Aristos '04	♆♆ 4*
○ A. A. Valle Isarco Sylvaner Aristos '06	♆♆ 4*
○ A. A. Valle Isarco Veltliner Aristos '06	♆♆ 4*

Vivaldi - Arunda

VIA PAESE, 53
39010 MELTINA/MÖLTEN [BZ]
TEL. 0471668033
www.arundavivaldi.it

ANNUAL PRODUCTION	85,000 bottles
HECTARES UNDER VINE	N.A.
VITICULTURE METHOD	Conventional

The unquestionably great talent of sparkling winemaker Joseph Reiterer has made him a role model for anyone producing classic method cuvées in Alto Adige. The Reiterers own no vineyards but select their chardonnay, pinot bianco and pinot nero grapes from trusted growers in the best-suited areas of the province. At the top of our list this year is a new label, Excellor Rosé, a delicious Brut from pinot nero only with a lovely bright pink colour and fresh, intensely absorbing aromas of blueberry, raspberry and wild strawberries that swirl around vanilla and white chocolate. The solid, well-constructed palate stays pleasant and fruity through the long, caressing finish. The Cuvée Marianna, an Extra Brut, from mostly chardonnay with some pinot nero, is savoury and fresh yet at the same time complex with elegant minerality. The Arunda Brut is even more convincing this year with its fresh fullness and tones of golden apple and citrus peel lifted by tropical fruit and a spirited, savoury that fulfils all expectations. The Reiterers' other cuvées are excellent.

Tenuta Waldgries
Christian Plattner

LOC. SANTA GIUSTINA, 2
39100 BOLZANO/BOZEN
TEL. 0471323603
www.waldgries.it

ANNUAL PRODUCTION	50,000 bottles
HECTARES UNDER VINE	5.1
VITICULTURE METHOD	Conventional

Dare we say it? The Santa Maddalena '07 from Christian Plattner may be the greatest ever produced in the past few years in Alto Adige. It is nothing new for this wine to be among the best in its type but this year it is really something special. Typicity, elegance, balance, complexity and delicious drinkability combine into the stylistic signature of a splendid wine that soars beyond the limits of its category. Moving on to the Lagreins, the other branch of the splendid Tenuta Waldgries production, we noticed that the progressive reduction in the use of new barriques is giving wines greater expressivity and definition. We especially like the Lagrein Mirell '06, which is redolent of intense fruit and liquorice leading into a full, creamy palate with harmonious development. The oaky notes are still slightly too prominent but the Riserva '06 is still a lovely Lagrein that only needs a little time in bottle to harmonize its powerful structure. In our humble opinion, the talented Christian seems to be on the right track.

○ A. A. Spumante Arunda Brut		5
○ A. A. Spumante Blanc de Blancs Arunda		6
○ A. A. Spumante Extra Brut Arunda		6
○ A. A. Spumante Extra Brut Arunda Ris. '04		6
○ A. A. Spumante Extra Brut Cuvée Marianna		6
⊙ A. A. Spumante Rosé Brut		6
⊙ Arunda Reiterer & Reiterer		6
⊙ Excellor Rosé Brut		6
○ A. A. Spumante Extra Brut Arunda Ris. '98		6
○ A. A. Spumante Extra Brut Arunda Ris. '03		6

● A. A. Lagrein Scuro Mirell '06		7
● A. A. Santa Maddalena Cl. '07		4*
● A. A. Lagrein Scuro Ris. '06		6
● A. A. Laurenz '06		6
● A. A. Moscato Rosa '06		6
● A. A. Cabernet Sauvignon '99		6
● A. A. Lagrein Scuro Mirell '01		7
● A. A. Lagrein Scuro Mirell '03		7
● A. A. Lagrein Scuro Ris. '05		6
● A. A. Santa Maddalena Cl. '06		4*

OTHER WINERIES

Baron Di Pauli

VIA CANTINE, 12
39052 CALDARO/KALTERN [BZ]
TEL. 0471963696
www.barondipauli.com

Baron di Pauli has released an interesting new item, Exilissi Ice '04, a drinkable Eiswein with great concentration and complexity. The Lago di Caldaro Kalkofen '07 is excellent and juicy while Lagrein Carano '06 is well typed and elegant.

● A. A. Lago di Caldaro Cl. Sup.	
Kalkofen '07	♟♟ 4*
○ Exilissi Ice '04	♟♟ 7
● A. A. Carano Lagrein '06	♟♟ 5

Bessererhof - Otmar Mair

NOVALE DI PRESULE, 10
39050 FIÈ ALLO SCILIAR/
VÖLS AM SCHLERN [BZ]
TEL. 0471601011
www.bessererhof.it

Otmar Mair's wines are varietal and well crafted. Particularly outstanding this year is the minerally Chardonnay '05 with its delicate oaky notes and tangy, vibrant finish. The Schiava '07 and Pinot Bianco '07 are excellent.

○ A. A. Chardonnay '05	♟♟ 4*
○ A. A. Pinot Bianco '07	♟♟ 4*
● A. A. Schiava '07	♟♟ 3*

Braunbach

LOC. SETTEQUERCE
VIA PADRE ROMEDIUS, 5
39018 TERLANO/TERLAN [BZ]
TEL. 0471910184
www.braunbach.it

Maso Braunbach's beautiful vineyards are splendidly positioned at San Genesio, in the heart of the Santa Maddalena Classico zone. The Sauvignon Calldiv '07, Lagrein Calldiv '06 and Merlot Calldiv Siebeneich from the same vintage are all convincing.

● A. A. Lagrein Scuro Calldiv '06	♟♟ 4*
● A. A. Merlot Calldiv Siebeneich '06	♟♟ 5
○ A. A. Sauvignon Calldiv '07	♟♟ 4*

Brunnenhof - Kurt Rottensteiner

LOC. MAZZON
VIA DEGLI ALPINI, 5
39044 EGNA/NEUMARKT [BZ]
TEL. 0471820687
www.brunnenhof-mazzon.it

Kurt Rottensteiner is a real winemaker and works in one of the finest zones for Pinot Nero. Austere and still very young, perhaps too young, the Riserva '06 is a bit closed. The Gewürztraminer '07 is typical and austere.

● A. A. Pinot Nero Ris. '06	♟♟ 6
○ A. A. Gewürztraminer '07	♟♟ 5

Ferruccio Carlotto

VIA CLAUSER, 19
39040 ORA/AUER [BZ]
TEL. 0471810407
michelacarlotto@virgilio.it

Michela Carlotto is a young but expert oenologist who works alongside that famous wine man, her father Ferruccio. The wines tasted were excellent, starting with the Pinot Nero Filari di Mazzon '06 and Lagrein Di Ora in Ora '06. The Schiava Krenzl '07 is crisp and delicious.

● A. A. Pinot Nero Filari di Mazzon '06	♟♟ 5
● A. A. Lagrein Di Ora in Ora '06	♟♟ 4
● A. A. Schiava Krenzl '07	♟♟ 4*

Castelfeder

VIA FRANZ HARPF, 15
39040 CORTINA/KURTINIG [BZ]
TEL. 0471820420
www.castelfeder.it

Lack of space in the Guide prevents us from giving this estate a full profile. Gewürztraminer Passito Endidae '05 is the high point in this impressive series of fine wines. The most successful bottles include the two Lagreins, the '06 and the Riserva Burgum Novum '05, and the Pinot Bianco '07.

○ A. A. Gewürztraminer	
Endidae Passito '05	♟♟ 6
● A. A. Lagrein '06	♟♟ 4*
● A. A. Lagrein Burgum Novum Ris. '05	♟♟ 5
○ A. A. Pinot Bianco '07	♟♟ 4*

OTHER WINERIES

Peter Dipoli

LOC. EGNA/NEUMARKT
VIA VILLA, 5
39055 EGNA/NEUMARKT [BZ]
TEL. 0471813400
vino@finewines.it

That explosive producer, driving spirit of
the Alto Adige winemakers' association
and distributor of Italian and non-domestic
wines, Peter Dipoli makes his Guide debut.
We tasted three wines, preferring the juicy,
elegantly long Sauvignon Voglar '06. The
other wines are decent.

○ A. A. Sauvignon Voglar '06	♥♥ 5
● A. A. Merlot Fihl '04	♥ 5
● A. A. Merlot-Cabernet Sauvignon Yugum '04	♥ 5

Ebnerhof - Johannes Plattner

FRAZ. CARDANO - LOC. RENON
LASTE BASSE, 21
39053 BOLZANO/BOZEN
TEL. 0471365120
www.ebnerhof.it

Wines from this small, certified organic
estate are as juicy and fragrant as usual.
The Santa Maddalena '07, by now
established as one of the best in the
category, went to the finals. The Sauvignon
'07 is elegant and full-bodied, and the Pinot
Nero '06, stylish.

● A. A. Santa Maddalena '07	♥♥ 4*
○ A. A. Sauvignon '07	♥♥ 4*
● A. A. Pinot Nero '06	♥♥ 5

Gottardi

LOC. MAZZON
VIA DEGLI ALPINI, 17
39044 EGNA/NEUMARKT [BZ]
TEL. 0471812773
www.gottardi-mazzon.com

Bruno Gottardi's nine-hectare estate
turns out 50,000 bottles a year. An air of
legend cloaks the cellar, partly because the
wines are hard to find and partly because
his Pinot Nero is outstanding. The fresh,
coherent '06 vintage shows fine-grained
tannins.

● A. A. Pinot Nero '06	♥♥ 5

Kettmeir

VIA DELLE CANTINE, 4
39052 CALDARO/KALTERN [BZ]
TEL. 0471963135
www.kettmeir.com

Owned by Gruppo Marzotto/Santa
Margherita, Kettmeier is historically one of
the most famous labels in Alto Adige. The
most interesting wines this year include
the Pinot Bianco, the fresh and typical
Sauvignon and the Chardonnay Reinerhof,
all from the '07 vintage.

○ A. A. Chardonnay Reinerhof '07	♥♥ 4*
○ A. A. Pinot Bianco '07	♥♥ 4*
○ A. A. Sauvignon '07	♥♥ 4*

Tenuta Klosterhof
Oskar Andergassen

LOC. CLAVENZ, 40
39052 CALDARO/KALTERN [BZ]
TEL. 0471961046
www.garni-klosterhof.com

Oskar Andergassen makes only a handful
of wines from his two hectares under
vine but the quality is beyond doubt. The
Moscato Giallo, Gewürztraminer and Lago
di Caldaro Plantaditsch, all from the '07
vintage, are typical and elegant.

○ A. A. Gewürztraminer '07	♥♥ 4*
● A. A. Lago di Caldaro Plantaditsch '07	♥♥ 3*
○ A. A. Moscato Giallo '07	♥♥ 4*

Köfelgut - Martin Pohl

RIONE AI TRE CANTI, 12
39020 CASTELBELLO CIARDES/
KASTELBELL TSCHARS [BZ]
TEL. 0473624634
pohlmartinfofelgut@dnet.it

With the fantastic success this year of Valle
Venosta, Martin Pohl's Gewürztraminer
'07 had to be in on the action, thanks to
the elegance and depth of this great wine.
Another very elegant wine is the Pinot
Bianco '07, also good and fragrant.

○ A. A. Valle Venosta Gewürztraminer '07	♥♥ 5
○ A. A. Valle Venosta Pinot Bianco '07	♥♥ 4*

OTHER WINERIES

Kössler

VIA CASTEL GUARDIA, 21
39050 APPIANO/EPPAN [BZ]
TEL. 0471662183
www.koessler.it

Now owned by Cantina Sociale di San
Paolo, Kössler produces around 200,000
bottles to good overall standards of
quality. Top wines include the Chardonnay
Kreuzstein '07, Lagrein Larcherhof '06 and
Santa Maddalena '07.

○ A. A. Chardonnay Kreuzstein '07	♟♟	4*
● A. A. Lagrein Larcherhof '06	♟♟	4*
● A. A. Santa Maddalena Cl. '07	♟♟	4*

Kupelwieser

S.DA DEL VINO, 24
39040 CORTINA/KURTINIG [BZ]
TEL. 0471809240
www.kupelwieser.it

Skilfully managed by Peter Zemmer, this
winery is eminently reliable. Ten hectares
yield 100,000 bottles that include the
outstanding Müller Thurgau '07, Lagrein '06
and Sauvignon '07, all from the Intenditore
line.

● A. A. Lagrein Intenditore '06	♟♟	5
○ A. A. Müller Thurgau Intenditore '07	♟♟	4*
○ A. A. Sauvignon Intenditore '07	♟♟	5

Lieselehof - Werner Morandell

VIA KARDATSCH, 6
39052 CALDARO/KALTERN [BZ]
TEL. 0471965060
www.lieselehof.com

Werner Morandell's small organic estate,
producing just over 10,000 bottles a
year, has had an up and down year. From
schiava grapes, the convincing Amadeus
'07 red is particularly fresh and minerally.

● Amadeus '07	♟♟	4*
○ A. A. Pinot Bianco '07	♟	4

Marinushof - Heinrich Pohl

S.DA VECCHIA 9B
39020 CASTELBELLO CIARDES/
KASTELBELL TSCHARS [BZ]
TEL. 0473624717
www.marinushof.it

Sabrina and Heiner Pohl own the tiny
Marinus farm. Less than one hectare under
vine produces only 5,000 bottles. The two
wines produced are very much in the Valle
Venosta idiom: an elegant, smoky Pinot
Nero '06 and a decent Pinot Grigio '07.

○ A.A. Valle Venosta Pinot Grigio '07	♟♟	4*
● A.A. Valle Venosta Pinot Nero '06	♟♟	5

Messnerhof - Bernhard Pichler

LOC. SAN PIETRO, 7
39100 BOLZANO/BOZEN
TEL. 0471977162
www.messnerhof.net

We had no difficulty predicting the steady
improvement at Bernard Pichler's small
estate. The splendid Lagrein Riserva '06 is
full-textured, powerful and deep so we sent
it to our finals. The Santa Maddalena '07 is
delicious.

● A. A. Lagrein Ris. '06	♟♟	4*
● A. A. Santa Maddalena '07	♟♟	4*

Josef Niedermayr

LOC. CORNAIANO/GIRLAN
VIA CASA DI GESÙ, 15
39050 APPIANO/EPPAN [BZ]
TEL. 0471662451
www.niedermayr.it

There have been big changes at this long-
standing Cornaiano winery, which will now
vinify only estate-grown grapes. Awaiting
the new products, we note the usual great
Passito Aureus '06 and a series of well-
made wines: the Sauvignon Lage Naun '07,
Lagrein Aus Gries Riserva '06 and Pinot
Nero Riserva '06.

○ A. A. Aureus '06	♟♟	7
● A. A. Lagrein Aus Gries Ris. '06	♟♟	6
● A. A. Pinot Nero Ris. '06	♟♟	6
○ A. A. Sauvignon Lage Naun '07	♟	5

OTHER WINERIES

Obermoser - H. & T. Rottensteiner

FRAZ. RENCIO
VIA SANTA MADDALENA, 35
39100 BOLZANO/BOZEN
TEL. 0471973549
www.obermoser.it

The Obermoser estate of Heinrich Rottensteiner and his son Thomas did well. All four wines submitted earned better than good scores. Outstanding bottles include the Santa Maddalena, the Sauvignon and the very juicy Lagrein, all from the '07 vintage. The Cabernet-Merlot Riserva Putz '05 is also good.

● A. A. Cabernet-Merlot Putz Ris. '05	♟♟	5
● A. A. Lagrein '07	♟♟	4*
● A. A. Santa Maddalena Cl. '07	♟♟	4*
○ A. A. Sauvignon '07	♟♟	4*

Oberrautner - Anton Schmid

FRAZ. GRIES
VIA M. PACHER, 3
39100 BOLZANO/BOZEN
TEL. 0471281440
www.schmid.bz

Schmid Oberrautner is at Gries on the outskirts of Bolzano. Andreas Schmid works alongside his son Florian and sent to our finals the fragrant Lagrein Villa Schmid '06, rich in ripe fruit and spice aromas with a generous, gutsy palate. The Chardonnay Vormas '07 is good.

● A. A. Lagrein Scuro Villa Schmid '06	♟♟	4*
○ A. A. Chardonnay Vormas '07	♟♟	4*
● A. A. Lagrein Scuro Grieser Oro Ris. '05	♟	5

Thomas Pichler

VIA DELLE VIGNE, 4
39052 CALDARO/KALTERN [BZ]
TEL. 0471963094
pichler.thomas@dnet.it

This tiny estate in the Caldaro area must be the smallest of all small producers. Less than a hectare under vine produces around 7,000 bottles. The Lago di Caldaro Alte Reben '07 and Lagrein Sond Riserva '06 are both excellent.

● A. A. Lago di Caldaro Alte Reben '07	♟♟	4*
● A. A. Lagrein Sond Ris. '06	♟♟	5

Popphof - Andreas Menz

VIA TERZO DI MEZZO, 5
39020 MARLENGO/MARLING [BZ]
TEL. 0473447180
www.popphof.com

We are rather pleased about the return to the Guide of Andreas Menz's estate after too long an absence. The well-crafted Cabernet Merlot '04 is still austere and shows cinchona and pencil lead aromas leading into a generously meaty palate that expands nicely. The deep finish shows good acid-extract balance.

● A. A. Cabernet Merlot '04	♟♟	5

Castello Rametz

LOC. MAIA ALTA
VIA LABERS, 4
39012 MERANO/MERAN [BZ]
TEL. 0473211011
www.rametz.com

This Merano estate made an excellent showing. In first place, the Riesling '07 is so convincing it reached our finals while the two Chardonnays, the Cèsuret '05 and '07 from the classic line, are also both well executed.

○ A. A. Riesling '07	♟♟	4*
○ A. A. Chardonnay '07	♟♟	3*
○ Cèsuret '05	♟♟	5

Röckhof - Konrad Augschöll

VIA SAN VALENTINO, 9
39040 VILLANDRO/VILLANDERS [BZ]
TEL. 0472847130

The Augshöll family has a small estate and beautiful family farm. Their wines have been coming on nicely, starting with the wine that made Röckhof famous, Müller Thurgau. The '07 version is zesty, crunchy and deliciously drinkable. The Riesling from the same vintage is also very fine.

○ A. A. Valle Isarco Müller Thurgau '07	♟♟	4*
○ A. A. Valle Isarco Riesling '07	♟♟	4*
○ Caruess '07	♟♟	4*

OTHER WINERIES

Castello Schwanburg

VIA SCHWANBURG, 16
39010 NALLES/NALS [BZ]
TEL. 0471678622
www.schwanburg.it

Dieter Rudolph's early passing threw more than a shadow over the future of one of the most renowned winemaking estates in Italy. We hope his heirs will carry on the great heritage of Castello Schwamburg. The Terlano Pinot Bianco Sonnenberg, Riesling Bacher and Chardonnay Dreieck are all from '07 and all good.

○ A. A. Chardonnay Dreieck '07	▼▼ 4*
○ A. A. Riesling Bacher '07	▼▼ 4*
○ A. A. Terlano Pinot Bianco Sonnenberg '07	▼▼ 5

Stachlburg - Baron von Kripp

VIA MITTERHOFER, 2
39020 PARCINES/PARTSCHINS [BZ]
TEL. 0473968014
www.stachlburg.com

Wines from Barone Von Kripp's Stachlburg estate are always characterful, starting with the stylish, territory-focused Valle Venosta Pinot Nero '06, which has smoky notes and a delicate palate. The Pinot Bianco '07 is almost as good.

● A. A. Valle Venosta Pinot Nero '06	▼▼ 5
○ A. A. Valle Venosta Pinot Bianco '07	▼▼ 4*

Strasserhof - Hannes Baumgartner

FRAZ. NOVACELLA
UNTERRAIN, 8
39040 VARNA/VAHRN [BZ]
TEL. 0472830804
www.strasserhof.info

Hannes Baungartner is a promising producer from Valle Isarco. His wines are well made and fairly typical, starting with the Gewürztraminer, Sylvaner and Müller Thurgau from '07. Our only suggestion might be to take a few more risks.

○ A. A. Valle Isarco Gewürztraminer '07	▼▼ 4*
○ A. A. Valle Isarco Sylvaner '07	▼▼ 4
○ A. A. Valle Isarco Müller Thurgau '07	▼ 4*

Villscheiderhof - Florian Hilpold

PIAN DI SOTTO, 13
39042 BRESSANONE/BRIXEN [BZ]
TEL. 0472832037
villscheider@akfree.it

Valle Isarco never ceases to amaze us. We thought the area was full to the brim with winemakers but here to prove us wrong are the Sylvaner and Kerner '07 from this tiny winemaking estate, immersed in the woods a few kilometres from Brixen. The operation is run by the Hilpold family.

○ A. A. Valle Isarco Kerner '07	▼▼ 5
○ A. A. Valle Isarco Sylvaner '07	▼▼ 4*

Karl Vonklausner

VIA CASTELLANO, 30A
39042 BRESSANONE/BRIXEN [BZ]
TEL. 0472833700
www.vonklausner.it

Christian Vonklausner's small estate confirms its Guide status with a couple of fresh, well-made wines that show the typical tones of Valle Isarco. We felt the more convincing was the Kerner '07, full bodied and minerally with nice grip. The Gewürztraminer '07 is decent.

○ A.A. Valle Isarco Kerner '07	▼▼ 4*
○ A.A. Valle Isarco Gewürztraminer '07	▼ 4

Wilhelm Walch

VIA A. HOFER, 1
39040 TERMENO/TRAMIN [BZ]
TEL. 0471860103
www.walch.it

Wines from Wilhelm Walch's winery at Termeno are always well made and attractively priced. Kudos goes this year to the Chardonnay Pilat '07, which shows remarkable intensity of aromas and flavours. The Schiava Grigia Plattensteig '07 is splendidly varietal.

○ A. A. Chardonnay Pilat '07	▼▼ 4*
● A. A. Schiava Plattensteig '07	▼▼ 4*
○ A. A. Müller Thurgau '07	▼ 3

OTHER WINERIES

Alois Warasin

LOC. CORNAIANO/GIRLAN
VIA COLTERENZIO, 1
39047 APPIANO/EPPAN [BZ]
TEL. 0471662462
weine.a.warasin@rolmail.net

We received only two wines from this small Cornaiano estate whose four hectares yield only about 10,000 bottles. The usual excellent Sauvignon completely convinced us with its fresh, coherent style and good drinkability. The Schiava '07 is savoury and juicy.

O A.A. Sauvignon '07	♟♟	3*
O A.A. Schiava '07	♟♟	3*

Josef Weger

LOC. CORNAIANO
VIA CASA DEL GESÙ, 17
39050 APPIANO/EPPAN [BZ]
TEL. 0471662416
www.wegerhof.it

This long-standing Cornaiano estate impressed again and sent to our finals its dried-grape Rodon Maso delle Rose '04, from gewürztraminer, sauvignon, pinot bianco and grigio. But the red Joanni '04, from merlot, cabernet and lagrein, and the Pinot Grigio '05 are also very good.

O Rodon '04	♟♟	6
O A. A. Pinot Grigio '05	♟♟	4*
● Joanni '04	♟♟	5

Peter Zemmer

S.DA DEL VINO, 24
39040 CORTINA/KURTINIG [BZ]
TEL. 0471817143
www.zemmer.com

This estate managed by Helmuth and Günther Zemmer keeps quality high across the entire range of wines produced. The Bianco Cortinie '07, from chardonnay and pinot grigio with some sauvignon and gewürztraminer, and the Pinot Bianco La Lot '07 are particularly well executed.

O A. A. Pinot Bianco La Lot '07	♟♟	4*
O Cortinie Bianco '07	♟♟	5
O A. A. Chardonnay '07	♟	4

Zohlhof
Josef Michael Unterfrauner

ZOHLHOF, 60
39040 VELTURNO/FELDTHURNS [BZ]
TEL. 0472847400
www.zoehlhof.it

Josef Michael Unterfrauner's small, organically run estate amazed us this year by coming very close to a Three Glass award. Both wines produced reached our finals by virtue of their impressive typicity, density and acid backbone.

O A.A. Gewürztraminer '07	♟♟	4*
O A.A. Sylvaner '07	♟♟	4*

VENETO

An incredible 1,900 wines tasted, 31 Three Glass awards and over 100 wines that just fell short of the highest accolade say it all about Veneto's harvest after the steady improvements of the last few years. Of course, as in every other year, Valpolicella took the lion's share, this time thanks to the excellent 2004 vintage, but the Colli Euganei zone has improved exponentially in quality, and consequently in awards. Here, success is driven by the growers' labours rather than the quality of the growing years. This is borne out by the predictable presence of Luciano and Franco Piona's Custoza and the consecration of the Gambellara Riva del Molino, bringing honour to the Dal Maso winery and to a DOC that has what it takes. The Colli di Conegliano DOC zone received our highest accolade for a very classy Ser Bele to crown the efforts and passion of Piero Balcon and the Sorelle Bronca. The distribution of the Three Glass awards is the clearest demonstration of the whole region's development. Veneto has become a benchmark for Italian winemaking thanks to products that are so often superb value for money. The awards, for vintages from 2001 to 2007, also demonstrate how good wine areas are able to compensate for temperamental weather conditions and how producers have learned to roll with the meteorological punches, alternately emphasizing subtlety and strength in products that embody fine quality and respect for terroir and climate. Soave had a slight drop in the number of Glasses awarded but the quality remains very high with a series of wines that have become classics of Italian winemaking. Calvarino, Monte Fiorentine, Monte Carbonare, to name the most reliable wines, are never disappointing and are joined for the first time by Agostino Vicentini's solid, gutsy Casale. There are no new entries in Valpolicella but many welcome returns, from Cecilia Beretta's Terre di Cariano to Speri's Sant'Urbano and Santi's Proemio, as well as the classics from Allegrini and Begali, with the marvellous 2003 Riserva, Sergio Zenato's legacy. Marinella Camerani, who won the Grower of the Year prize, leads the array of excellent Valpolicellas, followed by Claudio Viviani and Romano Dal Forno. Meanwhile, in the Colli Euganei, Vignalta, Ca' Lustra and Ca' Orologio all give memorable performances and are joined for the first time by Giordano Emo Capodilista with an unusually complex, harmonious Fior d'Arancio dried-grape wine. Lastly, two reds made from the same grapes but from two very different areas: Serafini & Vidotto in Montello with an outstandingly elegant Rosso dell'Abazia, and Carlo Nerozzi of Vigne di San Pietro, both use cabernet grape to highlight the generous diversity of the Verona area.

Stefano Accordini

LOC. PEDEMONTE
VIA ALBERTO BOLLA, 9
37020 SAN PIETRO IN CARIANO [VR]
TEL. 04537029
www.accordinistefano.it

ANNUAL PRODUCTION	40,000 bottles
HECTARES UNDER VINE	11
VITICULTURE METHOD	Conventional

Work on the new cellar has begun at last at the Pedemonte winery, which will make it possible to work directly below the hillside vineyards planted at Mazzurega and Caval. Viticulture in these two locations had been abandoned until about ten years ago but today they are attracting the attention of far-sighted producers prepared to go above 400 metres in their pursuit of grapes with elegant aromas. The range of wines is well-established, like the winery's style, which pursues strength and generosity with aromatic integrity and good grip. This approach is evident when you taste the Recioto 2005, a wine which more than any other brims with sumptuous ebullience. The fruit in Accordini wines is very ripe but also firm, crisp and nicely reflected on the palate, where sweetness, acidity and tannin blend together in beautiful harmony. The powerful but fresh-tasting Amarone 2004 is even more compelling, revealing a distinctively dry, confident finish. The Valpolicella Ripasso 2006 keeps up this style although a suppler body makes it more approachably drinkable. The pleasant red Passo 2006 and the standard-label Valpolicella are both sound wines.

Adami

FRAZ. COLBERTALDO
VIA ROVEDE, 27
31020 VIDOR [TV]
TEL. 0423982110
www.adamispumanti.it

ANNUAL PRODUCTION	550,000 bottles
HECTARES UNDER VINE	10
VITICULTURE METHOD	Conventional

Once again Franco Adami, who runs the winery with his brother Armando, has succeeded in matching production standards with the reputation his wines have earned. This continuity is an integral part of the long family tradition that began in 1920 with grandfather Abele and has become a benchmark in the Prosecco zone today, a tradition backed up by technical skill and territorial focus. The Prosecco Dry Giardino 2007 holds a secure place among the best versions of this type we have tasted. Clear, outstandingly delicate aromas from a broad spectrum of fruit and creamy, delicate fizz highlight the typical flavours of the prosecco grape with a subtle almondy finish to enhance and prolong the progression. The Cartizze has very appealing floral aromas alongside hints of fruit with nicely integrated sweetness on a stylish dynamic palate. Not far behind these two big hitters are the Brut Bosco di Gica and the Extra Dry dei Casel, which both present the winery's trademark distinctively full, elegant aromas and generous, well-made palate supported by creamy mousse.

● Amarone della Valpolicella Cl. Acinatico '04	▼▼ 8
● Valpolicella Cl. Sup. Ripasso Acinatico '06	▼▼ 5
● Passo Rosso '06	▼▼ 6
● Recioto della Valpolicella Cl. Acinatico '05	▼▼ 7
● Valpolicella Cl. '07	▼ 4
● Amarone della Valpolicella Cl. Vign. Il Fornetto '95	▼▼▼ 8
● Amarone della Valpolicella Cl. Vign. Il Fornetto '93	▼▼▼ 8
● Recioto della Valpolicella Cl. Acinatico '00	▼▼▼ 7
● Amarone della Valpolicella Vign. Il Fornetto '01	▼▼ 8
● Amarone della Valpolicella Cl. Acinatico '98	▼▼ 7

○ P. di Valdobbiadene Dry Vign. Giardino '07	▼▼ 4*
○ Cartizze Dry	▼▼ 5
○ P. di Valdobbiadene Bosco di Gica Brut	▼▼ 4*
○ P. di Valdobbiadene Extra Dry dei Casel	▼▼ 4*
○ P. di Valdobbiadene Tranquillo Giardino '07	▼ 4
○ Waldaz Brut Ris.	▼ 4
○ P. di Valdobbiadene Dry Vign. Giardino '06	▼▼ 4

Ida Agnoletti

LOC. SELVA DEL MONTELLO
VIA SACCARDO, 55
31040 VOLPAGO DEL MONTELLO [TV]
TEL. 0423620947
ettore.agnoletti@virgilio.it

ANNUAL PRODUCTION	50,000 bottles
HECTARES UNDER VINE	13
VITICULTURE METHOD	Conventional

Montello is a vast and still largely unknown hillside area situated between the Treviso plain and the foothills of the mountains. The soil and weather are excellent for grapes and the land endows the wines with a strong identity. In fact, they offer impressive expressions of the terroir despite the international image of merlot and cabernet grapes. This is naturally also true of Ida Agnoletti's winery in Selva del Montello, where this strong-willed producer has worked for years on the production of a fine range of upfront, flavoursome wines as well as two excellent selections, Seneca and Ludwy. The Seneca 2005 comes from a 50-year-old vineyard planted to merlot with some cabernet. The wine is striking in its expression of subtle aromas, with fruit appearing alongside Alpine herbs and spices, and its tangy, dry palate supported by the area's trademark good acidity. The proportions of the grape varieties are reversed in the Ludwy 2005, which has a less developed range of aromas but a more ebullient and pleasantly husky palate. Among the younger reds, we liked the Cabernet 2006 for its very firm palate. The Manzoni Bianco is a mature, succulent wine.

★★ Allegrini

VIA GIARE, 5
37022 FUMANE [VR]
TEL. 0456832011
www.allegrini.it

ANNUAL PRODUCTION	800,000 bottles
HECTARES UNDER VINE	70
VITICULTURE METHOD	Conventional

Poja, Amarone and Recioto are quintessentially territorial, blending classic and modern features. Credit goes to the Allegrinis for their sensitivity to a recent past that still inspires them. Poja originated from the vineyard of the same name in 1983 when the family saw the possibility of producing a great terroir-dedicated wine without drying the grapes. The 2004 version is one of the most sophisticated yet. It's dynamic and precise to the point of austerity in its impeccable progression but just too young to drink, so leave it in the cellar for at least five or six years before uncorking it. In the opulent Amarone 2004, minerally aromas alternate with ripe fruit and Alpine herbs while the perfectly balanced, soft, dry palate is infused with beautifully blended, captivatingly tangy tannins. Another fine version of a classic Three Glass wine. The Recioto Giovanni Allegrini 2005 is one of the area's benchmark bottles, gradually giving controlled sweetness with lovely hints of basil and juicy fruit and unusual finesse in the finish. The enthralling Grola 2005 stands out for its charming, rangy profile. A splendid performance overall.

● Ludwy '05	♟♟ 4*
● Seneca '05	♟♟ 4*
● Montello e Colli Asolani Cabernet Sauvignon '06	♟ 3
● Montello e Colli Asolani Merlot '06	♟ 3
O Manzoni Bianco '06	♟ 3
O Prosecco Frizzante P.S.L.	♟ 3
● Seneca '04	♟♟ 4*
● Seneca '03	♟♟ 4*

● Amarone della Valpolicella Cl. '04	♟♟♟ 8
● La Poja '04	♟♟ 8
● Recioto della Valpolicella Cl. Giovanni Allegrini '05	♟♟ 7
● La Grola '05	♟♟ 5
● Palazzo della Torre '05	♟♟ 5
● Valpolicella Cl. '07	♟♟ 4*
O Soave '07	♟♟ 4*
● Amarone della Valpolicella Cl. '03	♟♟♟ 8
● Amarone della Valpolicella Cl. '01	♟♟♟ 8
● Amarone della Valpolicella Cl. '00	♟♟♟ 8
● Amarone della Valpolicella Cl. '98	♟♟♟ 8
● Amarone della Valpolicella Cl. '97	♟♟♟ 8
● Amarone della Valpolicella Cl. '96	♟♟♟ 8
● Amarone della Valpolicella Cl. '95	♟♟♟ 8
● La Poja '01	♟♟♟ 8
● Recioto della Valpolicella Cl. Giovanni Allegrini '00	♟♟♟ 6

Andreola Orsola

LOC. COL SAN MARTINO
VIA CAL LONGA, 52
31010 FARRA DI SOLIGO [TV]
TEL. 0438989379
www.andreolaorsola.it

ANNUAL PRODUCTION	400,000 bottles
HECTARES UNDER VINE	20
VITICULTURE METHOD	Conventional

The strip of hills stretching from Valdobbiadene to Conegliano is almost entirely dedicated to growing Treviso's most famous grape variety, prosecco. Although Andreola Orsola operates in the heart of these hills and devotes the greater part of its attention to Prosecco in all its permutations – still, semi-sparkling, sparkling and even a dried-grape version – the winery also makes room for reds and verdiso, a lesser known variety usually employed in sparkling Proseccos but produced here produced as a monovarietal. The Brut Dirupo is excellent. Fruity on the nose with tropical hints, it offers a strikingly dry palate to close on a pleasant almondy note. The Cartizze is of the same standard, mouthfilling and exuberant thanks to higher residual sugar. The uncomplicatedly gutsy, very drinkable Extra Dry Dirupo is a step away from its second Glass. Among the less ambitious wines, we liked the pleasantly husky, assertive Verdiso for its fresh acidity and from the reds, we found the Cabernet Franc 2007 simple yet moreish in comparison to the more structured, challenging Valbone 2005.

★ Roberto Anselmi

VIA SAN CARLO, 46
37032 MONTEFORTE D'ALPONE [VR]
TEL. 0457611488
www.anselmi.eu

ANNUAL PRODUCTION	700,000 bottles
HECTARES UNDER VINE	70
VITICULTURE METHOD	Conventional

This year as every year, there was a whirlwind of activity at Anselmi, with ongoing modifications to the cellar and plans for new plantations. Roberto is in the control room, directing all the activities from vineyard management to sales and marketing. In recent years, his two children have come to his aid: Lisa on the administrative and commercial front line, and Tommaso behind the scenes in the cellar. The range of wines presented this year is absolutely outstanding and the house champ, Capitel Croce, shares the limelight with the most compelling Capitel Foscarino 2007 ever. Well-defined, appealing fruity aromas and perfectly harmonious sensations lead to a very classy finish. The Croce 2006 unfolds more gradually and subtly, the fruit embracing floral and mineral sensations with a tangy, sophisticated palate. We gave it Three classy Glasses for its sheer flavour. As usual, we saw an excellent performance from the '07 San Vincenzo, a wine for all seasons that will impress both occasional drinkers and expert tasters. The dried-grape I Capitelli 2006 is excellent, showing beautiful definition and balance.

O Cartizze	♟♟	5
O P. di Valdobbiadene Brut Vign. Dirupo	♟♟	4
● Cabernet Franc '07	♟	3
● Valbone Rosso '05	♟	4
O P. di Valdobbiadene Dry Mill. '07	♟	4
O P. di Valdobbiadene Extra Dry Vign. Dirupo	♟	4
O P. Passito Pensieri '05	♟	6
O Verdiso '07	♟	3
O P. di Valdobbiadene Tranquillo Romit '07		3
O P. Frizzante Sur Lie '07		3
● Refosco '07		3

O Capitel Croce '06	♟♟♟	5
O Capitel Foscarino '07	♟♟	4*
O I Capitelli '06	♟♟	7
O San Vincenzo '07	♟♟	4*
O Capitel Croce '99	♟♟♟	5
O Capitel Croce '00	♟♟♟	5
O Capitel Croce '01	♟♟♟	5
O Capitel Croce '02	♟♟♟	5
O Capitel Croce '03	♟♟♟	5
O Capitel Croce '04	♟♟♟	5
O Capitel Croce '05	♟♟♟	5
O Capitel Foscarino '06	♟♟	4
O Capitel Foscarino '05	♟♟	4
O I Capitelli '04	♟♟	6
O I Capitelli '03	♟♟	7

Balestri Valda

VIA MONTI, 44
37038 SOAVE [VR]
TEL. 0457675393
www.vinibalestrivalda.com

ANNUAL PRODUCTION	45,000 bottles
HECTARES UNDER VINE	13
VITICULTURE METHOD	Conventional

There's good news from Guido Rizzotto's winery. Without alterations to the range of labels, the 2006 and 2007 vintages have managed to provide greater balance and focus down a list that includes three Soaves, a Recioto and a red that is not released every year. Since it was founded just a few years ago, Balestri Valda has been noted for the production of a good, subtle Soave Classico with bags of finesse, as well as two selections aged in wood that did not entirely impress. Today, the Classico has become a very approachable wine, without losing the finesse and restraint endowed by grapes grown on the slopes of Castelcerino, while the two selections, Lunalonga and Sengialta, have improved considerably. The former is aged in small oak barrels and expresses ripe fruit aromas laced with hints of oak and a full, generous palate. The Sengialta is even better, characterized by the typical garganega aromas of flowers, fresh fruit and vegetal hints. The palate is firm but supple, tangy, beautifully lingering nicely balanced. The Recioto 2003 is pleasantly Mediterranean.

Cantina Beato Bartolomeo da Breganze

VIA ROMA, 100
36042 BREGANZE [VI]
TEL. 0445873112
www.cantinabreganze.it

ANNUAL PRODUCTION	3,500,000 bottles
HECTARES UNDER VINE	850
VITICULTURE METHOD	Conventional

Since it was set up in the middle of the last century, Cantina di Breganze has been a benchmark for the area without dominating local winemaking, as has happened in nearby areas. Today, it represents about 70 per cent of the territory, with 850 hectares divided among as many producers, indicating a widespread attachment to the land. The turnover in the management of the Cantina in recent years has brought in new enthusiasm and a desire to do well, a change that has already come through in products we tasted recently. The excellent flagship Breganze Cabernet Kilò Riserva was presented in both 2004 and 2005 versions. The '04 has clearly defined fruit and spice aromas and a firm but supple, gutsy palate. The 2005 is not quite so classy but its soft sensations are enjoyable. The two Torcolatos both performed well. One is pleasantly husky and traditional while the other, Bosco Grande, is rangier and more modern in style. Quality across the rest of the range is very sound.

O Soave Cl. Sengialta '07	▼▼	4*
O Soave Cl. '07	▼▼	3*
O Soave Cl. Lunalonga '06	▼▼	4
O Recioto di Soave Cl. '03	▼	6
O Soave Cl. '06	♈♈	4
O Soave Cl. '05	♈♈	3

● Breganze Cabernet Kilò Ris. '04	▼▼	5
O Breganze Torcolato '05	▼▼	6
● Merlot Bosco Grande '05	▼▼	5
O Breganze Torcolato Bosco Grande '05	▼▼	5
O Breganze Bianco Sup. Savardo '07	▼	4
O Breganze Vespaiolo Sup. Savardo '07	▼	4
O Spumante Vespaiolo Extra Dry	▼	4
● Breganze Cabernet Kilò Ris. '05	▼	5
● Breganze Cabernet Sup. Bosco Grande '05	▼	5
● Breganze Cabernet Sup. Savardo '06	▼	4
● Breganze Cabernet Kilò Ris. '03	♈♈	5

Lorenzo Begali

VIA CENGIA, 10
37020 SAN PIETRO IN CARIANO [VR]
TEL. 0457725148
www.begaliwine.it

ANNUAL PRODUCTION	60,000 bottles
HECTARES UNDER VINE	8
VITICULTURE METHOD	Conventional

Castelrotto is a major Valpolicella Classico hillslope vineyard. The small district of Cengia, where the Begali winery is located, takes its name from the area's distinctive rocky ledges, or "cenge". The estate has always aimed to bring excellent grapes into the cellar and over the years the wines have shown increasing elegance and concentration. To show that excellence is there even in the basic wines, the Amarone Classico 2004 has fresh floral and orange aromas mingling with more traditional hints of ripe fruit and cocoa powder, and a succulent, expressively husky palate. The Ca' Bianca vineyard yields an Amarone which, despite the heat of 2003, is a brilliant modern interpretation. This mouthwatering, lingering wine will stand the test of time and strolled off with Three effortless Glasses. The other jewel in the winery's crown is the Recioto, of which the founder and soul of the winery, Lorenzo, is particularly fond. The 2005 is weighty with heady aromas of fruit preserve and herbs, lingering with well-controlled sweetness. The Tigiolo, the standard-label Valpolicella and the Superiore all show dependable quality and excellent stature.

Cecilia Beretta

LOC. SAN FELICE EXTRA
VIA BELVEDERE, 135
37131 VERONA
TEL. 0458432111
www.ceciliaberetta.it

ANNUAL PRODUCTION	200,000 bottles
HECTARES UNDER VINE	89
VITICULTURE METHOD	Conventional

Last year's good impression by Cecilia Beretta was confirmed thanks to wines that were unanimously praised at our tasting. The dependable reds come from the large estate vineyard. The style is distinctive, mixing a cleanly harmonious modern approach with maturity and tradition. The whites come from the Soave area and are uncomplicated but beautifully balanced. As ever, the Amarone Terre di Cariano beat the competition thanks to clearly defined aromas with ripe, juicy red fruit lifted by minerally hints and aromatic herbs in the 2004 vintage. The well-structured palate is supported by acidity and sweet tannins that create lovely integrity. This splendid wine went home with Three Glasses. The two 2005 Valpolicellas are only slightly behind. Roccolo di Mizzole is intensely peppery and mouth-watering while the Ripasso is still very young but impressive nonetheless. The Amarone 2005 from the non-Classico area is well up to snuff and the Picàie 2004, a red made from corvina, cabernet sauvignon and merlot, is full-bodied and mature thanks to the ripasso technique of adding unpressed Amarone skins to the fermented wine.

● Amarone della Valpolicella Cl. Vign. Monte Ca' Bianca '03	▼▼▼ 8
● Amarone della Valpolicella Cl. '04	▼▼ 7
● Recioto della Valpolicella Cl. '05	▼▼ 7
● Tigiolo '05	▼▼ 6
● Valpolicella Cl. Sup. Ripasso Vign. La Cengia '06	▼▼ 4*
● Valpolicella Cl. '07	▼ 3
● Amarone della Valpolicella Cl. '03	♈♈♈ 7
● Amarone della Valpolicella Cl. Vign. Monte Ca' Bianca '01	♈♈♈ 7
● Amarone della Valpolicella Cl. Vign. Monte Ca' Bianca '00	♈♈♈ 8
● Amarone della Valpolicella Cl. Vign. Monte Ca' Bianca '99	♈♈♈ 8
● Amarone della Valpolicella Cl. Vign. Monte Ca' Bianca '97	♈♈♈ 8
● Recioto della Valpolicella Cl. '00	♈♈♈ 7

● Amarone della Valpolicella Cl. Terre di Cariano '04	▼▼▼ 8
● Amarone della Valpolicella '05	▼▼ 7
● Picàie '04	▼▼ 6
● Valpolicella Sup. Ripasso '05	▼▼ 5
● Valpolicella Sup. Roccolo di Mizzole '05	▼▼ 3*
○ Recioto di Soave Case Vecie '05	▼ 6
○ Soave Cl. Brognoligo '07	▼ 4
● Amarone della Valpolicella Cl. Terre di Cariano '99	♈♈♈ 7
● Amarone della Valpolicella Cl. Terre di Cariano '03	♈♈ 8
● Amarone della Valpolicella Cl. Terre di Cariano '01	♈♈ 8
● Amarone della Valpolicella Cl. Terre di Cariano '00	♈♈ 7

Cav. G. B. Bertani

VIA ASIAGO,1
37023 GREZZANA [VR]
TEL. 0458658444
www.bertani.net

ANNUAL PRODUCTION	2,000,000 bottles
HECTARES UNDER VINE	180
VITICULTURE METHOD	Conventional

Bertani wines are reassuring. Their modern yet traditional character comes across in the balance of the type's fullness with the lightness and elegance brought by the winery's experience. The range of wines has been revised but the leading labels are unaffected and their class remains intact. Let's begin with the Soave Sereole, a wine which has achieved more definition and integrity in recent years. The fruit is fresh and the palate is so harmonious and sophisticated that the wine seems almost simple, although it actually has bags of character and personality. On the palate, the Amarone 2001 shows the usual blend of strength and silkiness but this year more distinctive ripe fruit and raisining earned it Three Glasses. The Valpolicella Ognisanti 2005 has lost the over-evolved profile typical of recent versions and gives the fresh peppery aromas typical of corvina and a firm palate nicely backed up with acidity. Lastly, the Secco 2005 is splendid. This, more than any other wine, is emblematic of the estate. It's a generously fruity, peppery and fresh bottle with excellent grip. The other products are reliably good.

La Biancara

FRAZ. SORIO
C.DA BIANCARA, 14
36053 GAMBELLARA [VI]
TEL. 0444444244
www.biancaravini.it

ANNUAL PRODUCTION	50,000 bottles
HECTARES UNDER VINE	12
VITICULTURE METHOD	Natural

Agniolino Maule's decision to take a challenging path has had a tangible effect on La Biancara's wine production in recent years. Well aware that when one door closes another opens, Maule is rethinking again, especially in the vineyard. The aim is to obtain healthy, balanced grapes, the only fruit that can express the intimate nuances of the terroir without the aid of chemicals. While the Masieri Bianco 2007 is growing in personality, Sassaia, on the other hand, is particularly introspective and even a tad careworn. The excellent mouthfeel struggles to find expression initially as it is almost compressed by the yeasty sensations covering the ripe juicy fruit but a little aeration brings out the wine's intense, characterful aromas. The excellent dry, mouth-watering palate is deliciously moreish. The Recioto di Gambellara 2004 is even more extreme. Aromas of iodine and ginger frame an unusual balance of sweetness and extract on the palate. The So San 2006 made from tocai rosso grapes is fruity, racy and gutsy on the palate, while the Merlot from the same vintage is firmer and more austere. Pico skips a year as it continues to age.

● Amarone della Valpolicella Cl. '01	♙♙♙	8
○ Soave Sereole '07	♙♙	4*
● Valpolicella Cl. Sup. Vigneto Ognisanti '05	♙♙	4
● Amarone della Valpolicella Valpantena Villa Arvedi '04	♙♙	7
● Recioto della Valpolicella Valpantena '06	♙♙	5
● Valpolicella Valpantena Secco Bertani '05	♙♙	4
● Valpolicella Cl. Sup. Ripasso '06	♙♙	5
○ Le Lave '06	♙	4
● Amarone della Valpolicella Cl. '99	♙♙♙	8
● Amarone della Valpolicella Cl. '98	♙♙♙	8
● Amarone della Valpolicella Cl. '97	♙♙♙	8
● Amarone della Valpolicella Cl. '00	♙♙♙	8

○ Sassaia '07	♙♙	4
○ Masieri Bianco '07	♙♙	3*
○ Recioto di Gambellara '04	♙♙	6
● Merlot '06	♙♙	5
● So San '06	♙♙	5
● Canà Rosso '06	♙	4
● Masieri Rosso '07	♙	4
○ Pico '02	♙♙♙	4
○ Pico '04	♙♙	5
○ Pico '03	♙♙	4
○ Sassaia '06	♙♙	4
○ Sassaia '05	♙♙	4
○ Sassaia '04	♙♙	4
○ Recioto di Gambellara '03	♙♙	6
● Merlot '04	♙♙	5

Desiderio Bisol & Figli

FRAZ. SANTO STEFANO
VIA FOLLO, 33
31049 VALDOBBIADENE [TV]
TEL. 0423900138
www.bisol.it

ANNUAL PRODUCTION	1,300,000 bottles
HECTARES UNDER VINE	100
VITICULTURE METHOD	Natural

The Bisol family's estate has one of the largest vineyards in the whole DOC zone and is always one of the benchmarks for the area, indicative of where the world of Prosecco is going. The very wide range of wines might be confusing but it is actually organized into two lines. Jeio, which is the simpler, more characteristically Prosecco-like in style, is dedicated to wines made from grapes grown all over the area. The wines in the other line, Bisol, bear a mention of the specific area of origin of the grapes and usually show the place-name or soil type, as is the case with Crede. The Garnei 2006 is a very good Dry released one year after the harvest. Intensely fruity and citrussy, with complex flavour, it is quite unusual for a wine type that is usually very approachable in style. The sparkling Fol 2007, from the site of the same name, shows its usual pedigree, presenting subtle, floral and rich in apple and peach aromas, with impressively silky fizz and harmony. Cartizze and Crede 2007 keep up the standard and we are delighted to note the improvements of the Cartizze and Colmei in the Jeio line.

O Cartizze '07	♟♟ 6
O Cartizze Jeio	♟♟ 5
O P. di Valdobbiadene Brut Crede '07	♟♟ 4*
O P. di Valdobbiadene Dry Garnei '06	♟♟ 5
O P. di Valdobbiadene Extra Dry Colmei Jeio	♟♟ 4*
O P. di Valdobbiadene Extra Dry Vigneti del Fol '07	♟♟ 5
O P. di Valdobbiadene Dry Salis '07	♟ 4
O P. di Valdobbiadene Passito Duca di Dolle	♟ 7
O P. di Valdobbiadene Tranquillo Molera '07	♟ 4

F.lli Bolla

FRAZ. PEDEMONTE
VIA ALBERTO BOLLA, 3
37029 SAN PIETRO IN CARIANO [VR]
TEL. 0458090911
www.bolla.it

ANNUAL PRODUCTION	15,000,000 bottles
HECTARES UNDER VINE	350
VITICULTURE METHOD	Conventional

Bolla products have not suffered in the slightest from the change in ownership, and the wine upgrading process continues under the watchful technical direction of Giampaolo Vaona, with valuable input from Cristian Scrinzi, the Gruppo Italiano Vini's leading winemaker. An amazing three Amarones were presented, each with its own production style and equally distinctive commercial profile. The 2005 Amarone is aimed at the broad public of wine lovers and highlights the simplest, best-known feature of this type, raisining, with jammy aromas and a full, soft palate. The Capo di Torbe 2004 from the upper Valpolicella area is a modern-style wine with well-expressed fresh fruit and floral aromas and an impressively rigorous palate. Lastly, the Le Origini 2004 is the most traditional of the three. Enthrallingly broad and evolved on the nose, it opens with aristocratic restraint on the palate, proceeding through to end with a dry finale. Also from the village of Torbe is the gutsy, taut and beautifully characterful Valpolicella Superiore 2004. The Ripasso 2005 and the Soave Tufaie 2007 are harmonious and rich in texture.

● Amarone della Valpolicella Cl. '05	♟♟ 7
● Amarone della Valpolicella Cl. Capo di Torbe '04	♟♟ 8
● Amarone della Valpolicella Cl. Le Origini '04	♟♟ 8
● Valpolicella Cl. Sup. Capo di Torbe '04	♟♟ 5
● Valpolicella Cl. Sup. Le Pojane Ripasso '05	♟ 5
O Soave Cl. Tufaie '07	♟ 4
● Amarone della Valpolicella Cl. Le Origini '03	♟♟ 7
● Amarone della Valpolicella Cl. Capo di Torbe '01	♟♟ 8
● Valpolicella Cl. Sup. Capo di Torbe '03	♟♟ 5

Borin Vini & Vigne

FRAZ. MONTICELLI
VIA DEI COLLI, 5
35043 MONSELICE [PD]
TEL. 042974384
www.viniborin.it

ANNUAL PRODUCTION	140,000 bottles
HECTARES UNDER VINE	28
VITICULTURE METHOD	Conventional

The new generations are working hard at Borin. They're not out to replace their father Gianni, who remains firmly at the helm, but contribute to the estate's business: Francesco is particularly involved in production while Giampaolo is more concerned with marketing. Naturally, their watchful mother, Teresa, keeps an eye on everything. All the wines have a specific place in the range of products, in terms of quality, price and style. At the top of the pyramid is the most recent wine, Zuan 2006, a cabernet sauvignon-based Bordeaux blend. Vibrant red fruit and spice introduce a deftly handled but solid body with a sophisticated finish. Of the two Riservas, Rocca Chiara 2006 and Mons Silicis 2005, we preferred the former, which is a Merlot. It arrays floral and fruity aromas introducing a lively, beautifully supple body. The Mons Silicis, in contrast, expresses ripe aromas of Cabernet Sauvignon with grace and texture. Among the whites, the tangy moscato Fiore di Gaia gave an excellent performance, as did the Corte Borin, a flavoursome Manzoni Bianco with excellent grip. Fans of the Fior d'Arancio Passito will have to wait till next year.

F.lli Bortolin Spumanti

FRAZ. SANTO STEFANO
VIA MENEGAZZI, 5
31049 VALDOBBIADENE [TV]
TEL. 0423900135
www.bortolin.com

ANNUAL PRODUCTION	350,000 bottles
HECTARES UNDER VINE	20
VITICULTURE METHOD	Conventional

Valeriano Bortolin is part of the generation who invented the Prosecco phenomenon and today, now that his children have started working in the winery, his colleagues point to his operation as a beacon for quality and continuity in the he designated area. Although Prosecco has made the fortune of this winery and the whole area, Fratelli Bortolin has always chosen to stay mainly family run, shunning big numbers and capping production at 300-400,000 bottles. This is a long way short of some of its local competitors but guarantees enviable quality. The winery's war-horse Cartizze is on top form. Generous fruit and flower aromas and impressively creamy fizz, precede a perfect blend of acidity and sweetness. The Dry version of the Prosecco is also very good, with mature fruity aromas and a tangy, vivaciously drinkable palate. The Brut is lean in its apple and pear aromas and in the acidic, gutsy flavour. The two Extra Drys are enjoyable and well put together while the Extra Brut Vigneto del Convento is balanced and well typed.

● Zuan '06	▼▼	6
● Colli Euganei Cabernet Sauvignon Mons Silicis Ris. '05	▼▼	5
● Colli Euganei Cabernet Sauvignon V. Costa '06	▼▼	4*
● Colli Euganei Merlot Rocca Chiara Ris. '06	▼▼	5
○ Corte Borin '07	▼▼	4*
○ Fiore di Gaia '07	▼▼	4*
○ Colli Euganei Pinot Bianco Monte Archino '07	▼	3
○ Colli Euganei Chardonnay Vigna Bianca '06	▼	4
● Colli Euganei Merlot V. del Foscolo '06	▼	4
● Zuan '04	▼▼	6

○ Cartizze '07	▼▼	5
○ P. di Valdobbiadene Brut	▼▼	4*
○ P. di Valdobbiadene Dry	▼▼	4*
○ P. di Valdobbiadene Extra Dry	▼	4
○ P. di Valdobbiadene Extra Dry Rù	▼	4
○ Vigneto del Convento Extra Brut	▼	4

Bortolomiol

VIA GARIBALDI, 142
31049 VALDOBBIADENE [TV]
TEL. 0423974911
www.bortolomiol.com

ANNUAL PRODUCTION	2,200,000 bottles
HECTARES UNDER VINE	5
VITICULTURE METHOD	Conventional

The Bortolomiol family own one of the classic wineries in the Valdobbiadene zone, run on the same lines as the great maisons of Champagne, which own very little land and purchase grapes from independent growers to make their wine. As always tends to happen around here, the range is split across the classic types, based on residual sugar content. Bortolomiol has also expanded its range with different labels according to demand. The fresh Cartizze performed well with florality and apple-like aromas on the nose and a harmonious palate perked up by attractive prickle. Equally good is the Extra Dry Senior, a Prosecco with pleasantly husky apple and pear fruit on the nose and a dry palate of unquestionable personality. The remaining products are well typed and enjoyable in style, exploiting the approachable aromas typical of Treviso's subtle local grape variety and play on the balance of acidity, sugars and fizz.

Bosco del Merlo

VIA POSTUMIA, 14
30020 ANNONE VENETO [VE]
TEL. 0422768167
www.boscodelmerlo.it

ANNUAL PRODUCTION	430,000 bottles
HECTARES UNDER VINE	128
VITICULTURE METHOD	Natural

For years now, the pages of this Guide have revealed how results obtained by their red wines have proved the Paladin brothers right as they have managed to turn around the quality of their products in just a few vintages. But this year, we are delighted to put the spotlight on the whites, which have never been so impressive, especially the Turranio, a Sauvignon which stands up to comparison with its fellows in neighbouring Friuli. It has strikingly intense, generous aromas ranging from classic green apple-like hints to tropical fruit and spices before it reveals dry body and a long-lingering palate. Also excellent are the two pedigree 2005 reds. The Roggio dei Roveri is a fragrant Refosco leaning more towards elegance than strength while the 360, a delightful blend with merlot as the principal variety, is tangy and harmoniously drinkable. The Lison Juti is always dependable, stylish and elegant while the Priné 2006 seems to have achieved the perfect balance of fruit and oak. The 2007 version of the Pinot Grigio is lovely and the Merlot Campo Camino 2005 and Vineargenti 2004 are full bodied and focus more on structure than finesse.

○ Cartizze	♈♈ 6
○ P. di Valdobbiadene Extra Dry Senior	♈♈ 4
○ P. di Valdobbiadene Brut Motus Vitae mill. '06	♈ 5
○ P. di Valdobbiadene Brut Prior	♈ 4
○ P. di Valdobbiadene Demi Sec Suavis	♈ 4
○ P. di Valdobbiadene Extra Dry Sel. Banda Rossa '07	♈ 4
○ P. di Valdobbiadene Frizzante Il Ponteggio	♈ 4
○ P. di Valdobbiadene Tranquillo Canto Fermo '07	♈ 4
○ Ris. del Governatore Extra Brut	♈ 4
☉ Filanda Rosé Brut Ris.	♈ 4
● Piave Cabernet Sauvignon Mormorò '05	♈ 4

● Lison-Pramaggiore Refosco P. R. Roggio dei Roveri '05	♈♈ 6
○ Lison-Pramaggiore Sauvignon Turranio '07	♈♈ 4*
○ Lison-Pramaggiore Lison Cl. Juti '06	♈♈ 4
○ Priné '06	♈♈ 5
● 360 Ruber Capitae Rosso '05	♈♈ 5
● Vineargenti Plessi '04	♈♈ 6
● Lison-Pramaggiore Merlot Campo Camino '05	♈ 4
○ Lison-Pramaggiore Pinot Grigio '07	♈ 4
○ Verduzzo Soandre '06	♈ 4
● 360 Ruber Capitae Rosso '04	♈♈ 5
● Lison-Pramaggiore Refosco P. R. Roggio dei Roveri '04	♈♈ 6

Brigaldara

FRAZ. SAN FLORIANO
VIA BRIGALDARA, 20
37020 SAN PIETRO IN CARIANO [VR]
TEL. 0457701055
www.valpolicella.it/brigaldara

ANNUAL PRODUCTION	200,000 bottles
HECTARES UNDER VINE	45
VITICULTURE METHOD	Conventional

While the genuine, healthily rustic nature farming is central to winemaking, which risks over-exposure in the media on a daily basis, people like Stefano Cesari are equally precious for their lucid ability to see beyond the horizon and bring into focus apparently distant problems that may already be affecting the present. The superficially straightforward decision to delay release of the Amarone Case Vecie 2004 was born not of convenience or market demand but from an awareness that the designated area has been rushing ahead and now needs to go back to slower rhythms. Given the performance of the '04 Amarone Classico, the situation is not desperate. Vibrant fresh fruit aromas, caressed with minerally and floral streaks preface the stylish, gentle palate which is enjoyably silky and light. The Ripasso Il Vegro 2005 is well typed and emphasizes this type of wine's huskier, more spontaneous nature, while the Valpolicella 2006 is more spicy and subtle. The Garganega, and especially the rosé made from dindarella grapes, are both dry and fragrant with an excellent weight on the palate.

Sorelle Bronca

FRAZ. COLBERTALDO
VIA MARTIRI, 20
31020 VIDOR [TV]
TEL. 0423987201
www.sorellebronca.com

ANNUAL PRODUCTION	250,000 bottles
HECTARES UNDER VINE	20
VITICULTURE METHOD	Certified organic

Ersiliana and Antonella Bronca's winery is just outside the Prosecco di Valdobbiadene zone. Some of the vineyards fall inside it and others are situated further east, where red varieties are traditionally grown alongside prosecco in the Colli di Congeliano DOC zone, of which the winery is a leading exponent. The Ser Bele, from cabernet franc, cabernet sauvignon, merlot and a little marzemino, is a deep wine with ripe fruit and vegetal hints, a juicy palate with sweet tannins and a long finish. It is drinking well now and will be even better after ageing, like the previous version we sampled. This excellent wine earned the lovely Treviso winery Three Glasses. The Prosecco did well in all its versions starting with the assertive, tropical Brut, the clearly defined, succulent and moreish Extra Dry and lastly the thoroughbred Particella 68, named after the land registry code for the plot it is sourced from. The wine has vibrant aromas, creamy foam and a dry finish. The Colli Bianco Delico 2006 is subtly aromatic, emphasizing elegance rather than structure, while the Difetto Perfetto 2005 is a very nice cask-conditioned Pinot Bianco aged in oak.

● Amarone della Valpolicella Cl. '04	♟♟	7
● Valpolicella Cl. '06	♟♟	4*
● Valpolicella Cl. Sup. Ripasso Il Vegro '04	♟♟	5
☉ Dindarella '07	♟	4
○ Garda Garganega '07	♟	4
● Amarone della Valpolicella Case Vecie '03	♟♟♟	8
● Amarone della Valpolicella Case Vecie '00	♟♟♟	7
● Amarone della Valpolicella Cl. '99	♟♟♟	7
● Amarone della Valpolicella Cl. '98	♟♟♟	7
● Amarone della Valpolicella Cl. '97	♟♟♟	7
● Amarone della Valpolicella Case Vecie '99	♟♟	7
● Amarone della Valpolicella Case Vecie '01	♟♟	7
● Amarone della Valpolicella Cl. '95	♟♟	6

● Colli di Conegliano Rosso Ser Bele '05	♟♟♟	6
○ P. di Valdobbiadene Extra Dry Particella 68 '07	♟♟	5
○ Colli di Conegliano Bianco Delico '06	♟♟	5
○ P. di Valdobbiadene Brut '07	♟♟	4*
○ P. di Valdobbiadene Extra Dry '07	♟♟	4*
○ Difetto Perfetto '05	♟	6
● Colli di Conegliano Rosso Ser Bele '04	♟♟	6
● Colli di Conegliano Rosso Ser Bele '03	♟♟	6
● Colli di Conegliano Rosso Ser Bele '02	♟♟	6
● Colli di Conegliano Rosso Ser Bele '01	♟♟	6

Luigi Brunelli

VIA CARIANO, 10
37029 SAN PIETRO IN CARIANO [VR]
TEL. 0457701118
www.brunelliwine.com

Tommaso Bussola

LOC. SAN PERETTO
VIA MOLINO TURRI, 30
37024 NEGRAR [VR]
TEL. 0457501740
www.bussolavini.com

ANNUAL PRODUCTION	100,000 bottles
HECTARES UNDER VINE	12
VITICULTURE METHOD	Conventional

ANNUAL PRODUCTION	80,000 bottles
HECTARES UNDER VINE	9.5
VITICULTURE METHOD	Conventional

The superbly restored Corte Cariano is immersed in green vineyards. Visitors take a step backwards in time to a farming civilization that enjoyed a simple, respectful relationship with nature through farming. Leaving the house for the cellar brings us back to the modern day, with up-to-date technology and a well-stocked barrel cellar where barriques rub shoulders with larger oak barrels. The usual range of traditional wines is joined this year by a generous, fruity red based on corvina, named after the Corte. Three Amarones were presented: a simple, harmonious basic 2004; the Campo Inferi 2003 aged in large oak barrels, which has fresh aromas and a delicate palate; and Campo del Titari 2003, a generously structured version aged in small oak barrels, with a supple, elegant profile. The Recioto 2006 is particularly well typed, with a complex nose and juicy, moreish palate with perfectly integrated sugar. Of the two 2006 Valpolicella Superiores, we preferred the Pa' Riondo for its greater finesse.

Extension work on the cellars at Bussola is proceeding quickly affecting the wines, indeed we noticed a turn towards a less extreme, more clearly defined style. While last year only Reciotos were presented – all of a high standard we might add – this year the San Peretto-based Bussolas presented us with three Amarones and a Valpolicella Superiore, all from the 2004 vintage. Tommaso's style is unchanged, featuring full body, strength and clean, sound, crunchy fruit in the Amarones. The deep, intensely fruity Amarone Classico gave an outstanding performance with aromatic herbs and a good solid palate with perfectly fused acidity and tannins. The even more generous and fruity Vigneto Alto is almost intoxicating, giving substantial texture, sweetness and a long clean finish. The TB, however, shows unquestionable quality but fails to keep up with its two stablemates because of rather excessive sweetness. The Valpolicella has considerable potential in its weighty structure but still needs time to find more harmony.

● Amarone della Valpolicella Cl. Campo del Titari Ris. '03	♟♟ 8
● Amarone della Valpolicella Cl. Campo Inferi Ris. '03	♟♟ 8
● Recioto della Valpolicella Cl. '06	♟♟ 6
● Valpolicella Cl. Sup. Ripasso Pa' Riondo '06	♟♟ 4*
● Amarone della Valpolicella Cl. '04	♟ 7
● Corte Cariano Rosso '06	♟ 4
● Valpolicella Cl. '07	♟ 4
● Valpolicella Cl. Sup. Campo Praesel '06	♟ 4
● Amarone della Valpolicella Cl. Campo del Titari '97	♟♟♟ 8
● Amarone della Valpolicella Cl. Campo del Titari '96	♟♟♟ 8
● Amarone della Valpolicella Cl. '03	♟♟ 7

● Amarone della Valpolicella Cl. '04	♟♟ 8
● Amarone della Valpolicella Cl. TB '04	♟♟ 8
● Amarone della Valpolicella Cl. TB Vign. Alto '04	♟♟ 8
● Valpolicella Cl. Sup. '04	♟ 6
● Recioto della Valpolicella Cl. BG '03	♟♟♟ 7
● Recioto della Valpolicella Cl. TB '99	♟♟♟ 8
● Recioto della Valpolicella Cl. TB '98	♟♟♟ 8
● Recioto della Valpolicella Cl. TB '97	♟♟♟ 8
● Recioto della Valpolicella Cl. TB '95	♟♟♟ 8

Ca' La Bionda

FRAZ. VALGATARA
LOC. BIONDA, 4
37020 MARANO DI VALPOLICELLA [VR]
TEL. 0456801198
www.calabionda.it

ANNUAL PRODUCTION	110,000 bottles
HECTARES UNDER VINE	29
VITICULTURE METHOD	Natural

The beautiful, recently restored cellar next to the old Castellani family home, with its magnificent views of the Marano valley, prepares visitors nicely for the winery's production philosophy. Everything suggests a winery where every process is carried out with scrupulous professionalism. In recent years, attention in the cellar and vineyard has increasingly focused on natural farming and the abandonment of chemicals. The wines are very good, flaunting a character that offers a few rough edges for the sake of authenticity and flavour that makes them perfect with food. We particularly liked the Valpolicella Campo Casal Vegri 2006, made from chilled grapes, for its traditional aromas and a palate than handles its considerable texture very smoothly. The Amarone Ravazzol and the 2004 Classico have both succeeded in contrasting slightly rustic aromas with an interestingly supple, generous palate. The Valpolicella Ravazzol 2006 is also well made.

Ca' Lustra

LOC. FAEDO
VIA SAN PIETRO, 50
35030 CINTO EUGANEO [PD]
TEL. 042994128
www.calustra.it

ANNUAL PRODUCTION	190,000 bottles
HECTARES UNDER VINE	38
VITICULTURE METHOD	Conventional

Franco Zanovello has become sole owner, as well as driving spirit, of the winery. Today Ca' Lustra is an integral part of Colli Euganei, giving quality throughout the range and value for money, with some peaks of excellence among the selections. The vineyards are located in highly favourable areas like Faedo, Arquà Petrarca and Monte Versa, which guarantee top-quality fruit. Leading the range of wines is the Cabernet Girapoggio 2005, with strong, stylish grassy aromas and a complex palate of blackcurrants and pencil lead over an assertive tannic weave. The performance was enough to pick up our highest accolade, Three Glasses. Merlot Sassonero 2006 unfolds with cherry and plum aromas into a rounded, luscious palate. Lay this one down and enjoy it in the future. Rosso Natio 2006 is a classic Bordeaux blend aged in oak barrels for five months, with aromas of violets, cherries and blackberries. The subtle, stylish Manzoni Bianco 2007 is good again, as is the flower and spice Moscato Secco 'A Cengia. The Fior D'Arancio dried-grape wine is excellent and the basic 2006 Cabernet and Merlot are wines to buy by the case.

● Amarone della Valpolicella Cl. '04	♟♟ 6
● Amarone della Valpolicella Cl. Vign. di Ravazzol '04	♟♟ 7
● Valpolicella Cl. Sup. Campo Casal Vegri '06	♟♟ 5
● Valpolicella Cl. Sup. Vign. di Ravazzol '06	♟♟ 4
● Amarone della Valpolicella Cl. Vign. di Ravazzol '03	♙♙ 7
● Amarone della Valpolicella Cl. Vign. di Ravazzol '00	♙♙ 7
● Amarone della Valpolicella Cl. '03	♙♙ 6
● Valpolicella Cl. Sup. Campo Casal Vegri '04	♙♙ 5
● Valpolicella Cl. Sup. Campo Casal Vegri '03	♙♙ 5

● Colli Euganei Cabernet Girapoggio '05	♟♟♟ 5
● Colli Euganei Cabernet '06	♟♟ 4*
● Colli Euganei Merlot '06	♟♟ 3*
● Colli Euganei Merlot Sassonero '06	♟♟ 5
● Colli Euganei Rosso Natio '06	♟♟ 5
O Colli Euganei Fior d'Arancio Passito '06	♟♟ 5
O Manzoni Bianco Pedevenda '07	♟♟ 4*
O Moscato Secco 'A Cengia '07	♟♟ 4*
O Colli Euganei Bianco '07	♟ 3
O Colli Euganei Chardonnay Villa Alessi '06	♟ 4
O Colli Euganei Pinot Bianco '07	♟ 3
O Sauvignon Olivetani '07	♟ 4
● Marzemino Belvedere '07	♟ 4
● Colli Euganei Merlot Sassonero Villa Alessi '05	♙♙♙ 5

Ca' Orologio

VIA CA' OROLOGIO, 7A
35030 BAONE [PD]
TEL. 042950099
www.caorologio.com

ANNUAL PRODUCTION	27,800 bottles
HECTARES UNDER VINE	12
VITICULTURE METHOD	Certified organic

In an area like Colli Euganei, which has experienced unprecedented turmoil recently, the Ca' Orologio winery has rocketed ahead. Judging by the recognition obtained in just a few years, it might seem that grower Mariagioia Rosellini has been smiled on by the sort of good fortune often enjoyed by those who experiment in a new area. However if we dig deeper, we find a reserved, determined and curious woman, motivated by a passion for the land, vineyards and wine that perforce involves endless, gratifying hard work. Our tastings confirmed this consistent quality, starting with the Colli Euganei Rosso Calaóne 2006, which won us over with its balanced aromas and strong palate. Ripe fruit gives way to enticing hints of aromatic herbs and spices while the palate is succulent with nice sweet tannins. The Relógio of the same vintage is of a very high standard. From carmenère grapes with a splash of cabernet sauvignon, it is firm-textured, powerful and dreamily aromatic, all of which earned it Three Glasses. The white Salaróla 2007, from tocai and moscato with a small proportion of riesling, is stylish and dry with a long, elegant palate.

Ca' Rugate

VIA PERGOLA, 72
37030 MONTECCHIA DI CROSARA [VR]
TEL. 0456176328
www.carugate.it

ANNUAL PRODUCTION	450,000 bottles
HECTARES UNDER VINE	50
VITICULTURE METHOD	Conventional

Ca' Rugate strides on. Commitment to becoming a high-profile winery through scrupulous care and experimentation is flanked by exemplary attention to clients, a beautiful wine museum and the rediscovery of the old Vin Santo di Brognoligo dried-grape wine, which officially does not exist. Credit for this goes to the team of Amedeo, Gianni and Michele Tessari. The quality of the two Soave selections continues to astonish. Monte Alto 2006 is sophisticated with a generous nose and palate of pure silk, where oak is a mere detail, while Monte Fiorentine 2007's vibrant aromas and impeccable palate swept up Three Glasses. Sadly for its many admirers, Bucciato has disappeared but the fragrant San Michele is some consolation. Turning to the reds, the well-defined, mouth-wateringly elegant Campo Lavei 2006 is practically perfect, like the Amarone 2004 with its beautifully handled body. La Perlara shows exemplary harmony and finesse while L'Eremita is a paragon of fruity exuberance. Lastly, a lucky few will have a chance to taste Corte Durlo, an extraordinary oxidized dried-grape wine that we did not mark because of its extremely limited availability.

● Relógio '06	▼▼▼	5
● Colli Euganei Rosso Calaóne '06	▼▼	5
○ Salaróla '07	▼▼	4*
● Colli Euganei Rosso Calaóne '05	♈♈♈	5
● Relógio '04	♈♈♈	5
● Colli Euganei Rosso Calaóne '04	♈♈	5
● Colli Euganei Rosso Calaóne '03	♈♈	5
● Lunisóle '05	♈♈	5
● Relógio '03	♈♈	5

○ Soave Cl. Monte Fiorentine '07	▼▼▼	4*
○ Recioto di Soave La Perlara '06	▼▼	6
○ Soave Cl. Monte Alto '06	▼▼	4*
● Valpolicella Sup. Campo Lavei '06	▼▼	5
● Amarone della Valpolicella '04	▼▼	8
● Recioto della Valpolicella L'Eremita '06	▼▼	6
○ Soave Cl. San Michele '07	▼▼	3*
● Valpolicella Rio Albo '07	▼	3
○ Soave Cl. Monte Fiorentine '06	♈♈♈	4
○ Soave Cl. Monte Fiorentine '05	♈♈♈	4
○ Soave Cl. Monte Fiorentine '04	♈♈♈	4
○ Soave Cl. Sup. Bucciato '99	♈♈♈	4
○ Soave Cl. Sup. Monte Alto '96	♈♈♈	4
○ Soave Cl. Sup. Monte Alto '00	♈♈♈	4
○ Bucciato '05	♈♈	4
○ Soave Cl. Monte Alto '05	♈♈	4

Cambrago

FRAZ. SAN ZENO
VIA CAMBRAGO, 7
37030 COLOGNOLA AI COLLI [VR]
TEL. 0457650745
www.cambrago.it

ANNUAL PRODUCTION	120,000 bottles
HECTARES UNDER VINE	14
VITICULTURE METHOD	Conventional

Bruno Fasali has been the winery's driving force since he took over in 1977, first managing the vineyards and now also the cellar, with winemaker Flavio Prà. But the land remains his real passion, where the vines, as he loves to say, need to be looked after, educated and protected from adversity just like children. The perfectly tended vineyards still use the pergoletta training system, which Bruno believes should be maintained because it provides the right measure of cool shade to produce well-balanced grapes. If the weather makes it possible to take time over the harvest, the results are excellent, as we saw from the products of the latest vintage. Vigne Maiores, grown on gravelly soil, has approachable aromas and an uncomplicated, enjoyable palate. The Classico I Cerceni, which originates from the slopes leading to Costeggiola, is deeper in colour and reveals ripe fruit and spicy aromas. The palate is classier, well structured and tangy with acidity, and in the end it nearly went through to our finals. The mouth-watering, nicely harmonious red Cerceni 2004 comes from an old vineyard where cabernet and merlot grow side by side.

O Soave Cl. I Cerceni '07	♟♟	4*
O Soave Vigne Maiores '07	♟♟	3*
● I Cerceni '04	♟	5
O Recioto di Soave I Cerceni '04	♟♟	6
O Soave Cl. I Cerceni '06	♟♟	3*
O Soave Cl. I Cerceni '05	♟♟	4

Giuseppe Campagnola

FRAZ. VALGATARA
VIA AGNELLA, 9
37020 MARANO DI VALPOLICELLA [VR]
TEL. 0457703900
www.campagnola.com

ANNUAL PRODUCTION	4,800,000 bottles
HECTARES UNDER VINE	85
VITICULTURE METHOD	Conventional

Campagnola cannot really be described as a farm, yet the tangible connection to the land is clear both from chatting to Giuseppe and from examining the wine types produced here. Although the quantities are high, most of the red Valpolicellas come from Purano and the rest of the Marano valley, a further very firm link with their roots. Of the two most important selections, dedicated to grandmother Caterina, we particularly enjoyed the Amarone 2004, with its wild berry and mint aromas and supple, racy palate, despite considerable body. Again, it won Three Glasses. The Caterina Zardini Valpolicella 2006 is similar but more restrained, while the Amarone Classico 2005 is surprisingly elegant and balanced for a wine released in such quantity. The Recioto Casotto del Merlo 2006 is well-made, rounded and sweet yet very quaffable. Lastly, the winery is showing interest in the Lake Garda area, as the new release of a very decent Bardolino demonstrates.

● Amarone della Valpolicella Cl. Caterina Zardini '04	♟♟♟	7
● Valpolicella Cl. Sup. Caterina Zardini '06	♟♟	5
● Amarone della Valpolicella Cl. '05	♟♟	6
● Recioto della Valpolicella Cl. Casotto del Merlo '06	♟♟	6
O Soave Cl. Vign. Monte Foscarino Le Bine '07	♟♟	4
● Bardolino Roccolo del Lago Cl. '07	♟	4
● Valpolicella Cl. Sup. Ripasso Vign. di Purano Le Bine '06	♟	4
● Amarone della Valpolicella Cl. Caterina Zardini '99	♟♟♟	7
● Amarone della Valpolicella Cl. Caterina Zardini '01	♟♟♟	7
● Valpolicella Cl. Sup. Caterina Zardini '05	♟♟♟	4

I Campi

VIA SARMAZZA, 29 A
37032 MONTEFORTE D'ALPONE [VR]
TEL. 0456175915
www.icampi.it

ANNUAL PRODUCTION	20,000 bottles
HECTARES UNDER VINE	12
VITICULTURE METHOD	Conventional

After many years consulting for other wineries, Flavio Prà has taken the plunge and become a producer, purchasing a dozen hectares in the Soave and Valpolicella DOC zones. The estate's name, which means "The Fields", announces his links with the local area, where every plot corresponds to a different grape variety, indicated on the labels. For now, the cellar is just a project waiting for the green light, so fermentation facilities have been rented, but the winery's strength lies in its vines, which are located in seriously good wine areas. The bottles we tasted were all good but the best was Soave Campo Vulcano 2007, a white from 85 per cent garganega and the rest trebbiano di Soave. The nose is subtle and piquant, with prominent fruit and light hints of aromatic herbs and minerals. The palate is confident, elegant and rounded but dry, its uncomplicated drinkability backed up nicely by acidity. The two reds – Amarone Campo Marna 2003 and Valpolicella Campo Prognare 2004 – are much more rounded and energetic. Rich fruit on the mouthfilling palate is lifted by a dense tannic weave and rather forward oak. Time will tame these youthful excesses.

Canevel Spumanti

LOC. SACCOL
VIA ROCCAT E FERRARI, 17
31049 VALDOBBIADENE [TV]
TEL. 0423975940
www.canevel.it

ANNUAL PRODUCTION	600,000 bottles
HECTARES UNDER VINE	12
VITICULTURE METHOD	Conventional

The prosecco grape is aroma-rich but lacks the explosive qualities of sauvignon or traminer. It is more like a bunch of spring flowers: subtle and elegant, with faint aromas of apples and pears. The wine owes its strikingly fresh aromatic quality to care in the vineyards and expertise in the cellar, where the choice is between favouring aroma or flavour. Oenologist Roberto De Lucchi, the man behind the winery, was among those who built up the Prosecco phenomenon around the world and continues to make good wines. There are two stand-outs: Cartizze, from a great terroir, and Millesimato, from a great winemaker. The former has a healthy rusticity, offering golden delicious apples and wisteria on the nose, and an unexpectedly solid flavour. The Millesimato, in contrast, gives firm body backed up by a dense, creamy fizz. The other sparklers in the range differ in their levels of residual sugar but share the winery's signature style, which seeks a well-rounded palate rather than especially pungent aromatics.

○ Soave Cl. Campo Vulcano '07	♀♀	5
● Amarone della Valpolicella Campo Marna '03	♀♀	8
● Valpolicella Cl. Campo Prognare '04	♀♀	8

○ Cartizze	♀♀	6
○ P. di Valdobbiadene Extra Dry Il Millesimato '07	♀♀	5
○ P. di Conegliano Valdobbiadene Brut	♀	4
○ P. di Valdobbiadene Demi Sec	♀	4
○ P. di Valdobbiadene Extra Dry	♀	4
○ P. di Valdobbiadene Extra Dry Vign. del Faé '07	♀	4
○ P. di Valdobbiadene Tranquillo '07	♀	4
○ P. di Valdobbiadene Frizzante Vign. S. Biagio '07		4

Giordano Emo Capodilista

VIA VILLA RITA
35030 BAONE [PD]
TEL. 049637294
www.classica.it

ANNUAL PRODUCTION	14,000 bottles
HECTARES UNDER VINE	10
VITICULTURE METHOD	Conventional

Fewer than 20,000 bottles from ten hectares of vineyards should be enough to explain the aspirations of Giordano Emo Capodilista, who has worked in the Colli Euganei for years. The winery, situated in the south of the DOC zone on Monte Castello, produces just two wines: a cabernet sauvignon-based red and a Fiori d'Arancio Passito made from the area's most interesting white grape variety. Both are from the excellent 2006 vintage and neither disappoints – to the contrary, the Ireneo has never been so good. This wine has finally found a way to bring together the personality of the Colli Euganei in exuberant aromas and warmth with the rigour demanded of a pedigree red. The palate is tangy, harmonious and lingering, making it one of the most interesting labels in the entire DOC zone. The Passito is tropical and rich in aromatic herbs with a very light vein of oxidation lending depth and character. A wine of sheer class, it swept up Three emphatic Glasses. Explosive sweetness on the palate is reined in by acidity through to the fresh, dry finish with its hints of rosemary.

La Cappuccina

FRAZ. COSTALUNGA
VIA SAN BRIZIO, 125
37032 MONTEFORTE D'ALPONE [VR]
TEL. 0456175036
www.lacappuccina.it

ANNUAL PRODUCTION	267,000 bottles
HECTARES UNDER VINE	33
VITICULTURE METHOD	Certified organic

After a year in which Soave production took a rest, the Tessari brothers promptly redeemed themselves with an impressive and well-balanced range. Now that the new cellar is finished, they have turned their attention to the vineyards, which are being replanted. The leading wine this year is in fact a Soave, San Brizio 2006, which has found the right balance of oak over the years. Flowers and fruit are echoed on the gutsy palate with bags of class. The Arzìmo from the same vintage is a white garganega-based dried-grape wine which expresses the sunny Mediterranean character of the type while maintaining an austere profile and dry palate. The Campo Buri 2005 is also very good. This wine started life as a single-variety Cabernet Franc a few decades ago, but is now a strong, austere wine made from part-dried carmenère and oseleta grapes. The sweet dried-grape wine from the same blend, Carmenos 2006, is also well typed and harmonious, like the 2007 Soave and Sauvignon which both reveal very approachable sensations. The sophisticated, tangy Soave Fontégo 2007 came close to a second Glass.

O Colli Euganei Fior d'Arancio Passito Donna Daria '06	▼▼▼ 6
● Colli Euganei Cabernet Sauvignon Ireneo '06	▼▼ 6
● Colli Euganei Cabernet Sauvignon Ireneo '05	♀♀ 6
● Colli Euganei Cabernet Sauvignon Ireneo '04	♀♀ 6
● Colli Euganei Cabernet Sauvignon Ireneo '03	♀♀ 6
● Colli Euganei Cabernet Sauvignon Ireneo '01	♀♀ 6
O Colli Euganei Fior d'Arancio Passito Donna Daria '05	♀♀ 6
O Colli Euganei Fior d'Arancio Passito Donna Daria '04	♀♀ 6
O Colli Euganei Fior d'Arancio Passito Donna Daria '02	♀♀ 6

O Soave San Brizio '06	▼▼ 4*
O Arzìmo Passito '06	▼▼ 5
● Campo Buri '05	▼▼ 5
● Carmenos Passito '06	▼▼ 5
● Madégo '07	▼ 4
O Sauvignon '07	▼ 4
O Soave '07	▼ 3
O Soave Fontégo '07	▼ 4
● Campo Buri '04	♀♀ 5
● Campo Buri '02	♀♀ 5
O Soave Fontégo '05	♀♀ 4
O Soave Fontégo '04	♀♀ 4
O Soave Fontégo '03	♀♀ 4
O Soave San Brizio '04	♀♀ 4*
O Soave San Brizio '03	♀♀ 4
O Soave San Brizio '02	♀♀ 4

Casa Roma

VIA ORMELLE, 19
31020 SAN POLO DI PIAVE [TV]
TEL. 0422855339
www.casaroma.com

ANNUAL PRODUCTION	200,000 bottles
HECTARES UNDER VINE	28.15
VITICULTURE METHOD	Conventional

The Piave area traditionally offers wines that are enjoyable rather than particularly ambitious and offer very good value for money. Credit goes to cousins Adriano and Luigi Perruzzetto for succeeding in this apparently simple but actually challenging task with the greatest professionalism. Their well-stocked range often goes beyond merely well-typed basic wines, leaving the impression that the pair is driven by a desire to do more than just rely on technology. For a few years now, the cellar's most prestigious wine has been Raboso. Recovering this wine type is the self-appointed task of an increasingly large group of young local producers. The 2004 is fresher than the previous vintage, showing lovely delicate aromas, particularly nice red berry fruit laced with hints of oak. The rounded, full-bodied palate has good grip and well-balanced acidity and tannin. There's a nice surprise in Vinegia, from marzemino bianco, another local grape variety that has recently been relaunched. Deliciously mineral, it gives a good taut, tangy palate. The San Dordi, from Manzoni bianco, is more than sound, as ever.

● Piave Raboso '04	♟♟ 5
○ San Dordi '07	♟♟ 4*
○ Vinegia '07	♟♟ 3*
○ Manzoni Bianco '07	♟ 3
○ Piave Chardonnay '07	♟ 3
○ Piave Pinot Grigio '07	♟ 3
○ Sauvignon '07	♟ 3
◉ Manzoni Rosato Spumante Dolce	♟ 4
● Cabernet Franc '07	♟ 3
● Piave Cabernet Sauvignon '07	♟ 3
● Piave Merlot '07	♟ 3
● Piave Raboso '03	♟♟ 5
● Piave Raboso '02	♟♟ 5
● Piave Raboso '01	♟♟ 5
● Piave Raboso '00	♟♟ 5
● Piave Raboso '99	♟♟ 5

Michele Castellani

FRAZ. VALGATARA
VIA GRANDA, 1
37020 MARANO DI VALPOLICELLA [VR]
TEL. 0457701253
www.castellanimichele.it

ANNUAL PRODUCTION	300,000 bottles
HECTARES UNDER VINE	48
VITICULTURE METHOD	Conventional

In the Valpolicella area, wine has always been a beacon. Production can expand in favourable times and diminish in more problematic periods, bringing various hilly areas in and out of the spotlight. At the moment, the trend is favourable to expansion and local wineries, including this one, are looking for more space for their vineyards. Sergio is the driving force behind the winery, located at Valgatara at the foothills leading to the Marano valley. The range of wines is quite extensive so we will limit our assessment to the leading products. There are two well-established lines, Castei and Ca' del Pipa, named after the vineyards extending over the hills behind the winery. In both cases, the trend is for full-bodied, fruity, solid wines. We preferred the Amarone Ca' del Pipa 2004, with its vibrant, clearly defined aromas of red berry fruit and aromatic herbs, and creamy palate, well-sustained by acidity and tannins. A step behind is the Recioto 2005 from the same line, which successfully reins in its exuberant sugary sweetness. The same wines from the Castei line are enjoyable and dependable, if a little less exciting.

● Amarone della Valpolicella Cl. Le Vigne Ca' del Pipa '04	♟♟ 7
● Amarone della Valpolicella Cl. Campo Casalin I Castei '04	♟♟ 7
● Recioto della Valpolicella Cl. Le Vigne Ca' del Pipa '05	♟♟ 7
● Recioto della Valpolicella Cl. Monte Fasenara I Castei '06	♟♟ 7
● Valpolicella Cl. Sup. Ripasso Costamaran I Castei '06	♟ 5
● Recioto della Valpolicella Cl. Le Vigne Ca' del Pipa '99	♟♟♟ 7
● Recioto della Valpolicella Cl. Le Vigne Ca' del Pipa '04	♟♟ 7
● Amarone della Valpolicella Cl. Le Vigne Ca' del Pipa '03	♟♟ 7

Cantina del Castello

CORTE PITTORA, 5
37038 SOAVE [VR]
TEL. 0457680093
www.cantinacastello.it

ANNUAL PRODUCTION	130,000 bottles
HECTARES UNDER VINE	12
VITICULTURE METHOD	Conventional

Cantina del Castello is a key point for the Soave area and its owner, Arturo Stocchetti, who chairs the consortium, skilfully caters for both the small wineries that have made Soave great and the huge co-operatives. For years now, the guiding principle of Cantina del Castello for Soave has been to preserve a really smooth profile, favouring lightness, fragrance and subtlety over structure. Arturo's connection with the local area, which goes beyond the winemaking, have turned him an enlightened producer who is perfectly able to combine the demands of his own winery with those of the DOC zone. Soave Castello 2007 is one of the most popular in the area, with approachable floral aromas, a beautifully drinkable palate and plenty of appeal for traditional Soave drinkers. Pressoni is aimed at a more open-minded drinker who is able to grasp the finer, deeper features of the garganega grape, the principal component of the blend, including its distinctive fresh aromas and taut flavour. We'll have to wait another year for the other two selections, Acini Soavi and Carniga.

Cavalchina - La Prendina

FRAZ. CUSTOZA
LOC. CAVALCHINA
VIA SOMMACAMPAGNA, 7
37066 SOMMACAMPAGNA [VR]
TEL. 045516002
www.cavalchina.com

ANNUAL PRODUCTION	500,000 bottles
HECTARES UNDER VINE	75
VITICULTURE METHOD	Conventional

Winemaking near Lake Garda offers various options. Tradition, image and plenty of tourists guarantee easy commercial success whereas dedication to notoriously light wine types can be an obstacle to critical acclaim. However, Franco and Luciano Piona are managing to square that particular circle by offering wines that are uncomplicated but not commonplace, and light yet firm-bodied and characterful. It's easy enough to say this but it's another matter to make good Bardolino and Custoza. Flanking these wines and those from nearby Monzambano is the first Valpolicella, Superiore Morari 2006. A fruity, weighty red, it gives a cheeky nod to Amarone. From the whites, we preferred the well-structured and gutsy Garganega Paroni. Sauvignon Valbruna is approachable and fragrant but the most impressive wine, which won Three Glasses, is the now classic, sophisticated and very long-lingering Amedeo. The reds also did brilliantly. Faial 2005 has its usual muscle, the subtler, more individual Falcone 2005 is nice and the Santa Lucia 2006 is as good as it has been for some time. Lastly, a special mention for the peppery, succulent Corvina 2006.

○ Soave Cl. Pressoni '07	🍷🍷 4*
○ Soave Cl. Castello '07	🍷🍷 4*
○ Soave Cl. Sup. Monte Pressoni '01	🍷🍷🍷 4
○ Soave Cl. Pressoni '06	🍷🍷 4
○ Soave Cl. Pressoni '05	🍷🍷 4
○ Soave Cl. Pressoni '04	🍷🍷 4
○ Soave Cl. Pressoni '03	🍷🍷 4
○ Soave Cl. Carniga '04	🍷🍷 4
○ Soave Cl. Acini Soavi '05	🍷🍷 5

○ Custoza Sup. Amedeo '06	🍷🍷🍷 4*
○ Garda Garganega Paroni La Prendina '06	🍷🍷 4*
● Bardolino Sup. S. Lucia '06	🍷🍷 4
● Garda Cabernet Sauvignon Vign. Il Falcone La Prendina '05	🍷🍷 5
● Garda Corvina La Prendina '06	🍷🍷 4
● Garda Merlot Faial La Prendina '05	🍷🍷 6
○ Garda Sauvignon Valbruna La Prendina '06	🍷🍷 4
● Valpolicella Sup. Morari Terre d'Orti '06	🍷🍷 5
● Bardolino '07	🍷 4
○ Bianco di Custoza '07	🍷 4
○ Bianco di Custoza Sup. Amedeo '05	🍷🍷🍷 4
○ Bianco di Custoza Sup. Amedeo '04	🍷🍷🍷 4

Domenico Cavazza & F.lli

C.DA SELVA, 22
36054 MONTEBELLO VICENTINO [VI]
TEL. 0444649166
www.cavazzawine.com

ANNUAL PRODUCTION   1,000,000 bottles
HECTARES UNDER VINE   150
VITICULTURE METHOD   Conventional

Without a shadow of doubt, buying Cavazza wines is a classic example of "intelligent shopping". These are well-made, very drinkable bottles with no pointless elaboration or vulgar dressing-up, and sold at very fair prices. Nowadays that's hard to find. The most outstanding wine is missing this year from the compact, well-stocked range but while the Creari 2007 finishes ageing, we have focused on the reds. Let's start with Fornetto 2006, a blend of merlot, syrah and tocai rosso with an intriguing palate and no little complexity. From the Cicogna estate we prefer the Merlot 2006, which is still very young but subtle and complex. It stands out from the crowd with its elegant handling of its substantial texture. Cabernet Cicogna is more austere and restrained, and needs further ageing. The Corallo, a Tocai Rosso with a seamless profile, is promising but still a little predictable. The Dulcis Cicogna is fragrant and enthralling while the Recioto di Gambellara 2006 is more finely tuned, with vibrant candied fruit and dried flower aromas, as well as perfect balance.

Giorgio Cecchetto

FRAZ. TEZZE DI PIAVE
VIA PIAVE, 67
31020 VAZZOLA [TV]
TEL. 043828598
www.rabosopiave.com

ANNUAL PRODUCTION   220,000 bottles
HECTARES UNDER VINE   60
VITICULTURE METHOD   Conventional

Often the products of wineries in the Piave DOC are limited to typically approachable and accessible standard wines. This is to some extent also true of Giorgio Cecchetto's winery, which has a range of enjoyably well-made varietal wines. But this more basic line is flanked by Giorgio's great passion, Raboso with a capital "R", to emphasize his love for this very hard to handle variety. There are three versions, all of them interesting. The first is the classic version with aromas of morello cherries and vegetal hints, followed by a rugged palate where acidity and extract bring out all the variety's rage (rabbia). The second version, Gelsaia, is the prototype of Rabosos made with part-dried grapes, and was the forerunner for the DOCG project. The 2005 has riper aromas and a fuller, more rounded palate. Finally, the dried-grape version produces a sweet, fruity wine supported by taut acidity. Finally, Merlot Sante 2006 is quite a generous, smoothly drinkable wine.

● Colli Berici Cabernet Cicogna '06	♥♥	5
● Colli Berici Merlot Cicogna '06	♥♥	5
● Il Fornetto '06	♥♥	4*
○ Recioto di Gambellara Cl. Capitel S. Libera '06	♥♥	6
○ Gambellara Cl. La Bocara '07	♥♥	4
○ Dulcis Cicogna '07	♥	5
○ Pinot Grigio Campo Corì '07	♥	4
● Colli Berici Cabernet Costiera '06	♥	4
● Colli Berici Tocai Rosso Corallo '06	♥	5
● Colli Berici Cabernet Cicogna '03	♀♀	5
● Colli Berici Merlot Cicogna '05	♀♀	5
● Colli Berici Merlot Cicogna '04	♀♀	5
● Colli Berici Merlot Cicogna '03	♀♀	5

● Piave Raboso '04	♥♥	5
● Piave Raboso Gelsaia '05	♥♥	6
● Cabernet Franc '07	♥	3
● Piave Cabernet Sauvignon '07	♥	3
● Piave Merlot Sante '06	♥	4
● Piave Raboso Passito	♥	6
○ Piave Pinot Grigio '07		3
● Piave Merlot Sante '05	♀♀	4
● Piave Merlot Sante '03	♀♀	5
● Piave Raboso '03	♀♀	5
● Piave Raboso Gelsaia '03	♀♀	6

Italo Cescon

FRAZ. RONCADELLE
P.ZZA DEI CADUTI, 3
31024 ORMELLE [TV]
TEL. 0422851033
www.cesconitalo.it

ANNUAL PRODUCTION	800,000 bottles
HECTARES UNDER VINE	115
VITICULTURE METHOD	Conventional

Domenico, Gloria and Graziella are tenaciously making progress with the winery founded by their father, aiming for high quality released under the La Cesura label. But they stay true to the origins of the winery itself, which is known in many parts of Italy for the Tralcetto line, with its signature "tralcio", or cane, tied near the neck of the bottles. These are well-typed, enjoyable wines but the more ambitious line is much more satisfying. The Rabìa Riserva 2003 made an explosive debut. There are only a few bottles of this Raboso with profound, vibrantly fruity aromas and light vegetal hints expressing the grape variety's distinctively "rabid" character. The usual acidity, restrained on the palate by firm structure, lightens the wine and makes it very drinkable. The 2005 Merlot and Cabernet show that they come from the Piave area, which produces remarkably weighty wines while sacrificing a touch of elegance. Both are rounded and mouth-wateringly moreish. Among the whites, there was a good performance from the Manzoni La Cesura, Sauvignon and Chardonnay while the '05 Amaranto 72 seemed less impressive than the previous version.

Coffele

VIA ROMA, 5
37038 SOAVE [VR]
TEL. 0457680007
www.coffele.it

ANNUAL PRODUCTION	110,000 bottles
HECTARES UNDER VINE	25
VITICULTURE METHOD	Conventional

Castelcerino is one of the best-sited vineyards in Soave. Garganega grapes grow and ripen perfectly on this limestone soil with its extraordinary potential at altitudes of 200 to 350 metres, and the soil enriches the wines with elegance and finesse. Excellent fruit is a basic requirement for making great wines but it is more difficult to maintain continuity and style year after year. Alberto shows he can read and make the best of the growing year. He lets the wines express their identity and character. His Soave Ca' Visco 2007 has very subtle, stylish aromas with hints of ripe fruit and flowers before delicate minerally sensations, which return on the outstandingly taut palate. Recioto di Soave Le Sponde 2006 is an outstanding example of the type, an explosion of excitingly fresh citrus and dried fruit that follows through delightfully on the palate, where the sugars and acidity come together in harmony. The Soave Classico 2007 is solid, unpretentious and nicely characterized by the healthy huskiness of the garganega grape, while the Alzari 2006 reveals garganega's more generous, mouthfilling features.

● Piave Cabernet La Cesura Ris. '05	▼▼ 5
● Piave Merlot La Cesura Ris. '05	▼▼ 5
● Piave Raboso Rabìa Ris. '03	▼▼ 6
● Amaranto 72 '05	▼ 6
● Piave Raboso La Cesura '04	▼ 5
O Manzoni Bianco Elmeceo '07	▼ 5
O Manzoni Bianco La Cesura '07	▼ 4
O Müller Thurgau La Cesura '07	▼ 4
O P. di Valdobbiadene Extra Dry '07	▼ 4
O Piave Chardonnay La Cesura '07	▼ 4
O Sauvignon La Cesura '07	▼ 4
O Italo 06 '06	5
● Piave Cabernet La Cesura Ris. '04	♀♀ 5
● Piave Cabernet La Cesura Ris. '03	♀♀ 5
● Piave Cabernet La Cesura Ris. '02	♀♀ 4
● Piave Merlot La Cesura Ris. '05	♀ 5

O Recioto di Soave Cl. Le Sponde '06	▼▼ 6
O Soave Cl. Ca' Visco '07	▼▼ 4*
O Soave Cl. '07	▼▼ 4*
O Soave Cl. Alzari '06	▼▼ 5
O Soave Cl. Ca' Visco '05	♀♀♀ 4
O Soave Cl. Ca' Visco '04	♀♀♀ 4
O Soave Cl. Ca' Visco '03	♀♀♀ 4
O Recioto di Soave Cl. Le Sponde '05	♀♀ 6
O Recioto di Soave Cl. Le Sponde '04	♀♀ 6
O Soave Cl. Alzari '05	♀♀ 5
O Soave Cl. Alzari '04	♀♀ 5

Col Vetoraz

FRAZ. SANTO STEFANO
S.DA DELLE TRESIESE, 1
31040 VALDOBBIADENE [TV]
TEL. 0423975291
www.colvetoraz.it

ANNUAL PRODUCTION   800,000 bottles
HECTARES UNDER VINE   12
VITICULTURE METHOD   Conventional

In a year like 2007, with its long, hot summer, prosecco grapes ripened to a sugary, aromatic maturity we had not seen for years. Under the expert technical direction of Loris Dell'Acqua, Col Vetoraz masterfully handled the exceptional sweetness of these grapes to produce wines that are less penetrating and citrussy than usual, but fruitier and more rounded on the palate with quite remarkable depth. The wine which emphasizes this difference more than any other is Millesimato 2007, a Dry which had us expecting heady aromatic performances. This year, it is more accommodating and delicate with aromas of apples, pears and sugared almonds and a very rounded palate that handles the sugar with style. The Cartizze and Prosecco Extra Dry are excellent, floral and fruity, their creamy foam holding up through the palate. In contrast, the Brut is flawlessly made but lacks its usual aromatic verve and gutsy grip, even though it is still very moreish.

Conte Collalto

VIA 24 MAGGIO, 1
31058 SUSEGANA [TV]
TEL. 0438738241
www.collalto.it

ANNUAL PRODUCTION   800,000 bottles
HECTARES UNDER VINE   135
VITICULTURE METHOD   Conventional

During the last year, there has been a change at the helm of this traditional Susegana winery. Since last summer, it has been run personally by Isabella Collalto de Croy, the owner of the estate and, with her son, of the entire village. Isabella's long-standing colleagues have stayed with her, notably Adriano Cenedese whose knack for continuity has enabled the change to take place without affecting the wines. The range is better than just good, with some very interesting peaks. Leading the pack is Torrai Riserva 2003, a Cabernet which has modern qualities while retaining a more traditional profile in which the fruit is never explosive but reveals streaks of vegetality, flowers and spices. The palate is relaxed, supple and racy. The Prosecco put on an excellent performance and the Brut has floral, as well as white-fleshed fruit, aromas while the creamy palate is edgy and tangy. The Dry Millesimato, in its first release, gives lovely peach and acacia flower aromas and a fresh-tasting, quite lingering palate. The Wildbacher and the Incrocio Manzoni 2.15, both from 2006, are straightforward, mouth-watering and very enjoyable.

O Cartizze	🍷🍷 6
O P. di Valdobbiadene Dry Millesimato '07	🍷🍷 4*
O P. di Valdobbiadene Extra Dry	🍷🍷 4*
O P. di Valdobbiadene Brut	🍷 4

● Incrocio Manzoni 2.15 '06	🍷🍷 4*
● Piave Cabernet Torrai Ris. '03	🍷🍷 5
O P. di Conegliano Brut	🍷🍷 4*
O P. di Conegliano Dry Millesimato	🍷🍷 4*
O Chardonnay '07	🍷 3
O Colli di Conegliano Bianco Schenella I '07	🍷 4
O Manzoni Bianco '07	🍷 3
O P. di Conegliano Extra Dry	🍷 4
O Pinot Grigio '07	🍷 3
O Verdiso '07	🍷 3
● Piave Cabernet '06	🍷 3
● Wildbacher '06	🍷 4
● Piave Cabernet Torrai Ris. '00	🍷🍷 5
● Rambaldo VIII '03	🍷🍷 5

Le Colture

FRAZ. SANTO STEFANO
VIA FOLLO, 5
31049 VALDOBBIADENE [TV]
TEL. 0423900192
www.lecolture.it

ANNUAL PRODUCTION	520,000 bottles
HECTARES UNDER VINE	50
VITICULTURE METHOD	Conventional

In Champagne, large wineries with no vineyards which are supplied with grapes by outside growers are flanked by other estates that make wines from start to finish, from berry to bottle, as it were. Valdobbiadene, too, is a place where some wineries work primarily with estate-grown grapes, which is what happens chez Ruggeri. Since the vineyards also extend over about 50 hectares, this is very much a one-off. There you have Le Colture, an estate with deep roots in the Valdobbiadene area. New purchases may have thrust the Montello area into the spotlight, but Renato and Cesare's hearts and heads remain in Via Follo. Production focuses on four sparklers, three of which are named for their sugar content while the other comes from the DOC zone's leading and best-known vineyard, Cartizze. This wine has generous aromas of flowers and apple and pear fruit and a creamy palate where the sugars, acidity and fizz blend harmoniously Brut Fagher is even more impressive, with its understated aromas and confident, gutsy palate. Cruner and Pianer are two nice, unchallenging wines with beautifully harmonious palates.

Corte Gardoni

LOC. GARDONI, 5
37067 VALEGGIO SUL MINCIO [VR]
TEL. 0457950382
www.cortegardoni.it

ANNUAL PRODUCTION	200,000 bottles
HECTARES UNDER VINE	25
VITICULTURE METHOD	Conventional

Although the quite well-stocked range includes international elements, a result of Gianni and his family's passion for French wine rather than any tip of the hat to fashion, the heart of this lovely winery beats for the traditional local wines, Custoza and Bardolino. We have always preferred Bardolino, which is masterfully interpreted here in three very valid wines. The Chiaretto is tangy, fresh and drinkable, the Le Fontane emphasizes the fruitier, more joyful side of Bardolino and finally there is the Superiore 2006. This red succeeds in expressing corvina's potential for delicacy and complexity with wild berries, pepper, flowers and minerally hints preceding a dry and light but very gutsy palate. Becco Rosso 2006 and Rosso di Corte 2005 both put on an excellent performance while maintaining slender, stylish profiles. On the Custoza front, we enjoyed the firm Mael as well as the more predictable, fragrant Custoza while Fenili 2006 is ripe and sunny with beautifully handled sugar. This very positive overall picture is completed by the tidy, silky Merlot Validium 2005.

O Cartizze	♟♟ 5
O P. di Valdobbiadene Brut Fagher	♟♟ 4
O P. di Valdobbiadene Dry Cruner	♟ 4
O P. di Valdobbiadene Extra Dry Pianer	♟ 4

● Bardolino Sup. '06	♟♟ 4*
● Bardolino Le Fontane '07	♟♟ 3*
● Becco Rosso '06	♟♟ 4
● Rosso di Corte '05	♟♟ 5
O Bianco di Custoza '07	♟♟ 3*
O Bianco di Custoza Mael '07	♟♟ 4
O Bianco di Custoza Passito Fenili '06	♟♟ 6
☉ Bardolino Chiaretto '07	♟ 3
● Garda Merlot Vallidium '05	♟ 5
● Bardolino Sup. '04	♟♟ 4
● Bardolino Sup. '03	♟♟ 4
● Bardolino Sup. '02	♟♟ 4
● Rosso di Corte '04	♟♟ 5

Corte Rugolin

FRAZ. VALGATARA
LOC. RUGOLIN
37020 MARANO DI VALPOLICELLA [VR]
TEL. 0457702153
www.corterugolin.it

ANNUAL PRODUCTION 60,000 bottles
HECTARES UNDER VINE 11
VITICULTURE METHOD Conventional

The Coati family is profoundly attached
to the Valpolicella area, where they have
been growing since time immemorial, first
as tenant farmers and now as the owners
of their estate. This background underlines
the characteristic features of all the wines,
which tend to be huskily elegant without
losing sight of modern style. Showing
nice and light without excessive muscle,
the range aims primarily for freshness
and well-gauged oak. Amarone Monte
Danieli 2003, sourced from the hills near
Castelrotto, demonstrates the winery
style with appealing if not particularly
concentrated colour, and oak-laced vanilla
and chocolate aromas on the nose melding
into a generous range of fresh red berry
fruit sensations. The juicy, mouth-watering
palate is harmonious and balanced. The
rest of the range is equally impressive,
starting with the very enjoyable youngest
Amarone, Crosara de Le Strie 2004, and
the Valpolicella Superiore Ripasso 2005,
which promises interesting development
in the cellar. The Recioto 2005 is very
good and the standard-label Valpolicella
dependably appealing.

Corte Sant'Alda

LOC. FIOI
VIA CAPOVILLA, 28
37030 MEZZANE DI SOTTO [VR]
TEL. 0458880006
www.cortesantalda.it

ANNUAL PRODUCTION 82,000 bottles
HECTARES UNDER VINE 16.8
VITICULTURE METHOD Certified organic

We have praised Marinella Camerani in
the past for her organic farming and today
we have further reason to congratulate
her for the high quality of all the wines,
which are more inviting than ever before.
The difference in style between the
Mithas wines and the rest of the products
is more apparent, showing where the
winery is going. Valpolicella Campi Magri
2005 is a magnificent wine full of spicy
freshness, with a taut, mouth-watering
palate extended and enhanced by acidity.
Valpolicella Mithas 2004 is more generous
and fruity, although the spice is still there,
and its firmer palate with a dry finish earned
it Three well-deserved Glasses. There is a
similar relationship between the two 2004
Amarones. While the Corte S. Alda version
is fruity and approachable, the Mithas is
deeper and more austere, shot with very
subtle sensations of aromatic herbs and
flowers, showing dry yet mouthfilling.
Finally, there is a special mention for
the Valpolicella Ca' Fiui 2007, which is
uncomplicated and accessible but not
predictable. For Marinella, there were Three
Glasses this time and also our special prize
for Grower of the Year.

● Amarone della Valpolicella Cl. Monte Danieli '03	🍷🍷 7
● Amarone della Valpolicella Cl. Crosara de le Strie '04	🍷🍷 6
● Recioto della Valpolicella Cl. '05	🍷🍷 6
● Valpolicella Cl. Sup. Ripasso '05	🍷🍷 5
● Valpolicella Cl. '07	🍷 3
● Amarone della Valpolicella Cl. Monte Danieli '01	♀♀ 7
● Amarone della Valpolicella Cl. Monte Danieli '00	♀♀ 7
● Amarone della Valpolicella Cl. Monte Danieli '99	♀♀ 7
● Amarone della Valpolicella Cl. Crosara de le Strie '03	♀♀ 6
● Valpolicella Cl. Sup. Ripasso '04	♀♀ 5
● Valpolicella Cl. Sup. Ripasso '03	♀♀ 5

● Valpolicella Sup. Mithas '04	🍷🍷🍷 7
● Amarone della Valpolicella '04	🍷🍷 8
● Amarone della Valpolicella Mithas '04	🍷🍷 8
● Valpolicella Sup. Ripasso Campi Magri '05	🍷🍷 5
● Recioto della Valpolicella '06	🍷🍷 7
● Valpolicella Ca' Fiui '07	🍷🍷 4*
○ Soave V. di Mezzane '07	🍷 4
● Amarone della Valpolicella '90	♀♀♀ 8
● Amarone della Valpolicella '95	♀♀♀ 8
● Amarone della Valpolicella '98	♀♀♀ 8
● Amarone della Valpolicella '00	♀♀♀ 8
● Amarone della Valpolicella Mithas '95	♀♀♀ 8
● Valpolicella Sup. '03	♀♀♀ 6
● Amarone della Valpolicella Mithas '00	♀♀ 8
● Valpolicella Sup. Mithas '03	♀♀ 7

Casa Coste Piane

FRAZ. SANTO STEFANO
VIA COSTE PIANE, 2
31040 VALDOBBIADENE [TV]
TEL. 0423900219
casacostepiane@libero.it

ANNUAL PRODUCTION	50,000 bottles
HECTARES UNDER VINE	6
VITICULTURE METHOD	Conventional

If Prosecco is the king of Valdobbiadene, its most loyal equerry is Loris Follador. At a time when no one in Italy or abroad would have risked money on an area that is now so important, Follador continued to produce Prosecco wines using the spontaneous bottle fermentation method, better known as sur lies. This Champagne-style method is the essence of Valdobbiadene. Today, Follador's wines have achieved semi-cult status and the few bottles released are much sought after by enthusiasts, wine shops and the best restaurants. The estate is situated in the heart of Prosecco at Fol, a superb vineyard near Santo Stefano di Valdobbiadene. For years, the vine stock has been managed by non-invasive farming methods to respect the land and the grapes. The best features of the wine are its forthright frankness and drinkability, with typical aromas of apples, wisteria and acacia flowers. The palate is fresh, stimulating and mineral. Note that the wine is made without additional sulphur dioxide. The Tranquillo still version is one of the purest expressions in the whole DOC zone. San Venanzio is pleasantly fragrant.

O P. di Valdobbiadene Frizzante Sur Lie		▼▼ 4*
O P. di Valdobbiadene Extra Dry San Venanzio		▼ 4
O P. di Valdobbiadene Tranquillo '07		▼ 4

Costozza

FRAZ. COSTOZZA
P.ZZA DA SCHIO, 4
36023 LONGARE [VI]
TEL. 0444555099
www.costozza-villadaschio.it

ANNUAL PRODUCTION	20,000 bottles
HECTARES UNDER VINE	12
VITICULTURE METHOD	Conventional

Giulio da Schio's estate is located on the Riviera Berica, the strip of hills over the Po valley that looks east towards the Colli Euganei hills, so near yet so very different in soil and farming history. The Conti da Schio family has plenty of history but it is thanks to Giulio's work that the winery has claimed a leading place in Vicenza in recent years. The vineyards are all located in hilly areas and are primarily planted to the red varieties used to make two cabernet-based reds, a Pinot Noir and one white wine, a Pinot. The most interesting wine in the range is the '06 Cabernet, a spicy red with wild berry aromas and the typical peppery, subtly vegetal hints of the predominant cabernet franc grape. The palate shows good but not excessive structure, supported by good acidity and sweet tannins with a long dry finish. The Cabernet Sauvignon from the same vintage is simpler and very drinkable while the Pinot Bianco 2007 has apple and pear fruit set off against a smoky background, with a tangy palate and good weight.

● Colli Berici Cabernet '06		▼▼ 4
● Cabernet Sauvignon '06		▼ 5
● Pinot Nero '07		▼ 3
O Colli Berici Pinot Bianco '07		▼ 3
● Rosso Costozza '04		▼▼ 5
● Rosso Costozza '03		▼▼ 5
● Colli Berici Cabernet '04		▼▼ 4
● Colli Berici Cabernet '03		▼▼ 5

★ Romano Dal Forno

FRAZ. CELLORE
LOC. LODOLETTA, 1
37030 ILLASI [VR]
TEL. 0457834923
www.dalforno.net

ANNUAL PRODUCTION	45,000 bottles
HECTARES UNDER VINE	25
VITICULTURE METHOD	Conventional

Last year, this Cellore winery's performance was penalized by two wines from less than memorable years, the rainy, chilly 2002 and the extremely hot, dry 2003. No matter how much commitment and passion is lavished on these situations – and Romano is by no means the sort of man to give up – nature always gains the upper hand, which means great wines in great vintages and lesser wines from lesser years. This time, it was a different story, with a very deep 2004 Valpolicella and a 2003 Amarone which rolled with the punches of a challenging growing year more successfully than last year's Valpolicella. The 2004 is vibrantly fruity and rich in fines herbes on the nose, in true Dal Forno style, the granite-solid palate revealing all the class of the vintage in its acid backbone and tautness. The excellent Valpolicella picked up Three Glasses. The Amarone, on the other hand is a hymn to full body. The nose is still closed but the well-rounded palate gives fruit, aromatic herbs and spices in massive structure where the extract is kept in check by soft alcohol.

Luigino Dal Maso

LOC. SELVA
C.DA SELVA, 62
36054 MONTEBELLO VICENTINO [VI]
TEL. 0444649104
www.dalmasovini.com

ANNUAL PRODUCTION	500,000 bottles
HECTARES UNDER VINE	35
VITICULTURE METHOD	Conventional

Now that the cellar extension is complete, the estate run by Nicola Dal Maso with his sisters Anna and Silvia, has found a point of balance for Gambellara and Colli Berici wines. Their father Luigino, who founded the winery, still oversees everything. Flavio Prà's collaboration has resulted in a remarkable change of pace in the whites. There is a memorable Riva del Molino 2007, whose vibrant aromas range from flowers to ripe fruit, streaked with spices and minerally hints, leading into a generous, tangy and long-lingering palate that won the cellar's first Three Glasses. The Ca' Fischele 2007 is just a little less challenging but very sound while the basic Gambellara is approachable and enjoyable. The reds are all sourced in the nearby Colli Berici hills and we enjoyed the refreshing, enthralling Colpizzarda 2006. The tocai rosso vines are reaching maturity and the wine has gained in depth both on the nose and on the palate, which is excellent with bags of personality. The Bordeaux Terra dei Rovi 2006, the Merlot and the Cabernet Casara Roveri 2005 are all outstandingly deep and vibrant, although we preferred the first two.

● Valpolicella Sup. Vign. di Monte Lodoletta '04	▼▼▼ 8
● Amarone della Valpolicella Vign. di Monte Lodoletta '03	▼▼ 8
● Amarone della Valpolicella Vign. di Monte Lodoletta '01	♀♀♀ 8
● Amarone della Valpolicella Vign. di Monte Lodoletta '00	♀♀♀ 8
● Amarone della Valpolicella Vign. di Monte Lodoletta '99	♀♀♀ 8
● Amarone della Valpolicella Vign. di Monte Lodoletta '98	♀♀♀ 8
● Amarone della Valpolicella Vign. di Monte Lodoletta '97	♀♀♀ 8
● Amarone della Valpolicella Vign. di Monte Lodoletta '96	♀♀♀ 8
● Amarone della Valpolicella Vign. di Monte Lodoletta '95	♀♀♀ 8

○ Gambellara Cl. Riva del Molino '07	▼▼▼ 4*
● Colli Berici Merlot Casara Roveri '05	▼▼ 5
● Colli Berici Tocai Rosso Colpizzarda '06	▼▼ 5
● Colli Berici Cabernet Casara Roveri '05	▼▼ 5
● Terra dei Rovi Rosso '06	▼▼ 6
○ Gambellara Cl. Ca' Fischele '07	▼▼ 3*
○ Recioto di Gambellara Cl. Riva dei Perari '06	▼▼ 6
○ Gambellara Cl. '07	▼ 2
● Colli Berici Cabernet Montebelvedere '06	▼ 4
● Colli Berici Tocai Rosso Colpizzarda '05	♀♀ 5
● Colli Berici Tocai Rosso Colpizzarda '04	♀♀ 4

F.lli Degani

FRAZ. VALGATARA
VIA TOBELE, 3A
37020 MARANO DI VALPOLICELLA [VR]
TEL. 0457701850
aldo.degani@tin.it

ANNUAL PRODUCTION 55,000 bottles
HECTARES UNDER VINE 4
VITICULTURE METHOD Conventional

Renovation continues on the Degani cellar and the whole family is involved. Most of the production work will now be transferred further down the valley, away from the winery and residence, to a small, convenient building which will soon have a tasting room and warehouse. New stainless steel vats have already been purchased for the new premises, and the old ones thrown out. The standard-label Valpolicella is breezily drinkable, mouthwatering and gutsy while the Superiore 2005 starts with a burst of pulpy fruit and ends on a dry note. The Cicilio 2005 has a modern feel on the nose and the palate but lacks a little definition and elegance. The two 2005 Amarones are interesting. La Rosta is concentrated and powerful while the Classico is lighter and tangier on the palate. Out of the two 2006 Reciotos, the La Rosta prevails in structure, where the barrique ageing clearly shows through, while the basic steel-aged version is one of the cleanest and most drinkable of its type, after it has been allowed to breathe. The Passito Bianco 2006 label has changed but the wine remains uncomplicated and enjoyable.

● Amarone della Valpolicella Cl. '05	🍷🍷	6
● Amarone della Valpolicella Cl. La Rosta '05	🍷🍷	6
● Recioto della Valpolicella Cl. '06	🍷🍷	5
● Recioto della Valpolicella Cl. La Rosta '06	🍷🍷	5
○ Passito Bianco '06	🍷	5
● Valpolicella Cl. '07	🍷	3
● Valpolicella Cl. Sup. '05	🍷	4
● Valpolicella Cl. Sup. Cicilio Ripasso '05	🍷	4
● Amarone della Valpolicella Cl. '04	🍸🍸	5
● Amarone della Valpolicella Cl. '03	🍸🍸	5
● Amarone della Valpolicella Cl. '01	🍸🍸	6
● Amarone della Valpolicella Cl. La Rosta '04	🍸🍸	6

Il Filò delle Vigne

VIA TERRALBA, 14
35030 BAONE [PD]
TEL. 042956243
www.ilfilodellevigne.it

ANNUAL PRODUCTION 40,000 bottles
HECTARES UNDER VINE 18
VITICULTURE METHOD Conventional

Il Filò delle Vigne is the southernmost winery in the Colli Euganei zone, not just in location but also in the warmth of its sunny, powerful, weighty wines. The owners, Carlo Giordani and Nicolò Voltan, have had the good sense to seek assistance from people who know the local area, so Matteo Zanaica, who is in charge of the technical side, has been joined by Filippo Giannone and Andrea Boaretti as consultant agronomist and oenologist, respectively. Thanks to the local climate, the grapes ripen very easily so the main problems are preserving the freshness of aromas and acidity in the wines. This has been successfully accomplished in the Cabernet Borgo delle Casette 2004. Vibrant blackberry, blueberry and mint aromas preface the weighty palate, stylishly handled with acidity and fine-grained tannins. The Pinot Bianco Vigna delle Acacie 2007 also gave an excellent performance, with apple and pear fruit and jasmine on the nose, and a pleasantly tangy palate. The Luna del Parco 2006 is a late-harvested Fior d'Arancio offering subtle, penetrating aromas and perfectly balanced sweetness on a supple, drinkable palate.

● Colli Euganei Cabernet Borgo delle Casette Ris. '04	🍷🍷	6
○ Colli Euganei Fior d'Arancio Luna del Parco '06	🍷🍷	6
○ Colli Euganei Pinot Bianco Vigna delle Acacie '07	🍷🍷	5
○ Il Calto delle Fate '06	🍷	6
● Colli Euganei Cabernet Borgo delle Casette Ris. '03	🍸🍸	5
● Colli Euganei Cabernet Borgo delle Casette Ris. '02	🍸🍸	5
● Colli Euganei Cabernet Borgo delle Casette Ris. '01	🍸🍸	5
● Colli Euganei Cabernet Borgo delle Casette Ris. '00	🍸🍸	5
● Colli Euganei Cabernet Vigna Cecilia di Baone Ris. '03	🍸🍸	5

Silvano Follador

FRAZ. SANTO STEFANO
LOC. FOLLO
VIA CALLONGA, 11
31040 VALDOBBIADENE [TV]
TEL. 0423900295
www.silvanofollador.it

ANNUAL PRODUCTION 45,000 bottles
HECTARES UNDER VINE 4
VITICULTURE METHOD Natural

The densely farmed area of Conegliano Valdobbiadene comprises mainly small and medium-sized wineries that follow the whole winemaking process from vineyard to bottle. In contrast, the large wine houses bottle wines they make with grapes purchased from outside growers. What these different types of business all have in common, apart from the grape variety, is the range of wines they offer. Most are sparklers released under various labels according to their residual sugar level. Usually, these wineries offer five or six labels, sometimes up to a dozen. So in this context it is unusual enough to find a producer that concentrates on just two different labels. If you bear in mind that the Follador approach to the whole process is based on interfering as little as possible, it becomes a true rarity. Brother and sister team Silvano and Alberta Follador have achieved memorable results. Their basic, pleasantly husky Cartizze is perfectly in tune with the expression of prosecco from these hills while the Brut is fresh, dry and floral.

O Cartizze	▼▼ 5
O P. di Valdobbiadene Brut	▼▼ 4*

Le Fraghe

LOC. COLOMBARA, 3
37010 CAVAION VERONESE [VR]
TEL. 0457236832
www.fraghe.it

ANNUAL PRODUCTION 90,000 bottles
HECTARES UNDER VINE 28
VITICULTURE METHOD Conventional

Le Fraghe, surrounded by the main Lake Garda roads, has an enchanting appearance, with its dovecot and farmhouse among the vineyards bearing witness to its significant agricultural history. For some time now, Matilde Poggi has kept two donkeys, Piergiorgio and Clemente, who graze in the vineyards, carrying out the necessary task of trimming the grass among the rows. Matilde runs the winery rationally, focusing on the local land, a decision that is amply justified by the exemplary quality of her Bardolino. The 2007 version is clear, appetizing ruby red in colour with crisp red berries and pepper on the nose. It shuns fireworks and keeps its feet are firmly planted in the terroir. Ròdon, made from corvina and molinara which undergo brief maceration, is an agreeably drinkable Chiaretto thanks to its lightness and considerable charm, backed up by with good solid flavours. The Garganega Camporengo has never been so good. Striking fruit and flowers on the nose precede a tangy, beautifully gutsy palate and a long, mouthwatering finish. The Sover Pinot Grigio is well typed, light and enjoyable.

● Bardolino '07	▼▼ 3*
O Garganega Camporengo '07	▼▼ 4*
O Sover Pinot Grigio '07	▼ 3
⊙ Bardolino Chiaretto Ròdon '07	▼ 4
● Bardolino '06	▽▽ 3
● Quaiare Cabernet '03	▽▽ 4
● Quaiare Cabernet '01	▽▽ 5
● Quaiare Cabernet '00	▽▽ 5
● Quaiare Cabernet '98	▽▽ 5
● Quaiare Cabernet '97	▽▽ 5
● Quaiare Cabernet '96	▽▽ 5

Tenute Galtarossa

VIA ANDREA MONGA, 9
37029 SAN PIETRO IN CARIANO [VR]
TEL. 0456838307
www.tenutegaltarossa.com

ANNUAL PRODUCTION	50,000 bottles
HECTARES UNDER VINE	80
VITICULTURE METHOD	Conventional

Since it first broke into the market a few years ago, Giacomo Galtarossa's winery has worked with GIV with more than impressive results. Production is currently partly based on the large estate's own vineyards and the range is divided into three labels, two of which adhere to denomination protocols. The other, a specialty wine named Massabò, is missing from the line-up this year so we focused on the Amarone 2005 and Valpolicella 2006. From the very first harvest, the winery's style has focused on perfectly expressed fruity aromas with elegant flavour rather than excessively weighty structure. That mission is perfectly accomplished by the Valpolicella Corte Colombara, which delivers raisining aromas on the nose but the palate is its strong point. The delicate entry opens into a light, tangy palate kept in check by sweet, sophisticated tannins. The Amarone inevitably aims for greater power while maintaining a rigorous style with aromas of jam and bitter chocolate on the nose and a rounded, nicely taut palate. In a couple of years, the overall balance is sure to be even more impressive.

Fattoria Garbole

LOC. GARBOLE
VIA FRACANZANA, 6
37039 TREGNAGO [VR]
TEL. 0457809020
www.fattoriagarbole.it

ANNUAL PRODUCTION	15,000 bottles
HECTARES UNDER VINE	6
VITICULTURE METHOD	Conventional

Fattoria Garbole was founded recently, in 2000, by Ettore and Filippo Finetto who began this adventure with the vineyards they inherited from their grandmother. All the vineyards are situated on hillsides, and most are newly planted, but the youth of the vines is compensated by the training and planting systems, which are oriented towards high quality production. Inside the recently completed cellar are the wines destined for the three labels produced, Valpolicella, Amarone and Recioto, although the last has not yet been presented. The style might be defined as modern with characteristically clear aromas and a solid, substantial structure. The Valpolicella 2005, made from part-dried grapes, delivers vibrant aromas of stewed red berries and a firm-bodied, dry palate. The Amarone 2004 yields its aromas a little more reluctantly, slowly releasing hints of Alpine herbs and dried flowers alongside the fruit. The powerful palate is also dry and beautifully balanced while the considerable body is handled with striking elegance.

● Valpolicella Cl. Sup. Corte Colombara '06	♥♥	6
● Amarone della Valpolicella Cl. '05	♥♥	8
● Amarone della Valpolicella Cl. '04	♥♥	7
● Amarone della Valpolicella Cl. '03	♥♥	7
● Amarone della Valpolicella Cl. '01	♥♥	7
● Valpolicella Cl. Sup. Corte Colombara '04	♥♥	5
● Valpolicella Cl. Sup. Corte Colombara '03	♥♥	5
● Valpolicella Cl. Sup. Corte Colombara '02	♥♥	5

● Amarone della Valpolicella '04	♥♥	8
● Valpolicella Sup. '05	♥♥	6
● Amarone della Valpolicella '03	♥♥	7

Gini

VIA MATTEOTTI, 42
37032 MONTEFORTE D'ALPONE [VR]
TEL. 0457611908
www.ginivini.com

ANNUAL PRODUCTION 200,000 bottles
HECTARES UNDER VINE 30
VITICULTURE METHOD Conventional

Olinto Gini is one of the most fundamentally significant figures for modern Soave, a true pioneer and one of the first to focus on monovarietal garganega-based wines, bottling individual vineyard selections and standing firm on quality. Today, this beautiful winery is run by Claudio and Sandro who have been open to new ideas while not compromising on the winery's principles. Campo alle More, a rarely made Pinot Noir, is exemplary and the 2004 has crisp fruit and a sophisticated flavour. But the winery's roots are in Soave, starting with a dependable, complex basic version. A great deal of care was necessary in the vineyards in 2007 and the selection has paid off with a La Froscà that delivers a mature profile enhanced by the usual minerally sensations and tangy palate. The Salvarenza Vecchie Vigne 2006 is one of the most balanced and successful that we can remember. Salty and almost austere, it has memorable, incredibly subtle progression. We recommend a few years' cellaring for both. The Reciotos both show exemplary harmony and fragrance. Renobilis 2004 is complex and Col Foscarin 2006 is simpler, more exuberant.

Gregoletto

FRAZ. PREMAOR
VIA SAN MARTINO, 83
31050 MIANE [TV]
TEL. 0438970463
www.gregoletto.com

ANNUAL PRODUCTION N.A.
HECTARES UNDER VINE 15
VITICULTURE METHOD Conventional

Luigi Gregoletto's long list of wines is a rainbow with the succession of bottles as its colours, constantly shifting to create new sensations and emotions. All this takes place against the noble backdrop of prosecco, among the hills of the Conegliano and Valdobbiadene DOC zone. The shrewd Luigi exploits this great terroir to make excellent still wines so we'll start with those. The Colli di Conegliano Rosso 2004 shows intense garnet, delivering delicious aromas of grass, forest floor and mushrooms on the nose with a full-bodied, lingering palate. The core aromas of the pleasant Merlot 2006 are sweet pipe tobacco, blackberries and plums while the Cabernet delivers shrubs, pencil lead, liquorice and red berries. Turning to the whites, we liked the Manzoni Bianco best. Historically linked to the researches of Professor Manzoni at the Conegliano Oenology Institute in the last century, it has deep links with this area. The Albio is very sound. As ever, the Prosecco Tranquillo is one of the best while the Prosecco and Verdiso sur lie, naturally fermented in the bottles, are both captivating.

O Soave Cl. Contrada Salvarenza Vecchie Vigne '06	♟♟ 5
O Soave Cl. La Froscà '07	♟♟ 5
● Campo alle More Pinot Nero '04	♟♟ 6
O Recioto di Soave Renobilis '04	♟♟ 6
O Soave Cl. '07	♟♟ 4*
O Recioto di Soave Col Foscarin '06	♟ 6
O Soave Cl. La Froscà '06	♟♟♟ 5
O Soave Cl. La Froscà '05	♟♟♟ 5
O Soave Cl. Sup. La Froscà '99	♟♟♟ 5
O Soave Cl. Sup. La Froscà '97	♟♟♟ 5
O Soave Cl. Sup. Contrada Salvarenza Vecchie Vigne '00	♟♟♟ 6
O Soave Cl. Sup. Contrada Salvarenza Vecchie Vigne '98	♟♟♟ 6
O Soave Cl. Contrada Salvarenza Vecchie Vigne '05	♟♟ 5

● Cabernet '06	♟♟ 4
● Colli di Conegliano Rosso '04	♟♟ 6
● Merlot '06	♟♟ 4
O Chardonnay '07	♟♟ 4
O Colli di Conegliano Bianco Albio '07	♟♟ 4
O Manzoni Bianco '07	♟♟ 4
O Pinot Bianco '07	♟♟ 4
O P. di Conegliano Valdobbiadene Extra Dry	♟ 4
O P. di Conegliano Valdobbiadene Tranquillo '07	♟ 4
O Prosecco Frizzante '07	♟ 4
O Verdiso Frizzante '07	♟ 4
O Colli di Conegliano Bianco Albio '06	♟♟ 4
● Merlot '05	♟♟ 3

Guerrieri Rizzardi

VIA VERDI, 4
37011 BARDOLINO [VR]
TEL. 0457210028
www.guerrieri-rizzardi.it

ANNUAL PRODUCTION	600,000 bottles
HECTARES UNDER VINE	100
VITICULTURE METHOD	Conventional

Last year we praised Bardolino Tacchetto. This time, Superiore Munus 2006 demonstrates the Rizzardi focus on the modern appeal of that classic Garda wine, Bardolino. Corvina is the uncontested leader among Veronese red grapes and interpreting it in the pinot noir style endows Munus with beautifully expressive aromas of wild berries and black pepper before the light, tangy palate reveals its grip and acidity. This is a wine with attitude. Valpolicella Superiore Pojega 2006 is on the same lines, rich in fruit and spice aromas with a fuller, more rounded palate. The first release of the Clos Roareti 2006, a monovarietal Merlot, is interesting. Giuseppe Rizzardi's experience in France helps to enhance this very Valpolicellaesque wine with finesse and complexity on the nose. Last come the two house champs, both from 2004. As usual, Calcarole shows greater strength but also perfectly handled texture, courageously taking the same path as the Bardolino Munus. Villa Rizzardi still has a rather uncomplicated nose but the palate is light with perfectly blended components, and this overall harmony won a well-deserved Three Glass prize.

● Amarone della Valpolicella Cl. Villa Rizzardi '04	♟♟♟ 7
● Amarone della Valpolicella Cl. Calcarole '04	♟♟ 8
● Bardolino Cl. Sup. Munus '06	♟♟ 5
● Castello Guerrieri Rosso '05	♟♟ 5
● Clos Roareti '06	♟♟ 6
● Valpolicella Cl. Sup. Ripasso Poiega '06	♟♟ 4
○ Soave Cl. '07	♟♟ 3*
○ Soave Cl. Costeggiola '07	♟♟ 4
○ Recioto di Soave '05	♟ 5
☉ Rosa Rosae '07	♟ 4
● Bardolino Cl. '07	♟ 3
● Bardolino Cl. Tacchetto '07	♟ 4
● Amarone della Valpolicella Cl. Villa Rizzardi '01	♟♟♟ 7

Inama

LOC. BIACCHE, 50
37047 SAN BONIFACIO [VR]
TEL. 0456104343
www.inamaaziendaagricola.it

ANNUAL PRODUCTION	300,000 bottles
HECTARES UNDER VINE	45
VITICULTURE METHOD	Conventional

Inama is an international winery, as many of its wines are sold on foreign markets. This is reflected in the estate's style, which pays particular attention to the palates of consumers from different cultural and dietary traditions. The aim is quality that can be shared as universally as possible. Nonetheless, Inama wines also succeed in the difficult task of interpreting their strong links to the local area, highlighting the particular features of the noble garganega grape and the prestigious terroir in the hills around Soave. Soave Vigneto Du Lot 2006 provides confirmation in a very classy presentation. On the nose there are distinct hints of skilfully used oak blending with the wine and a range of very subtle fruity and floral aromas. The palate is rounded and mature with lovely grip. Quality is dependably good throughout the range of wines but we would like to mention a new arrival, Oratorio di San Lorenzo 2004. This monovarietal Carmenère is sourced from the Colli Berici and already shows marked personality with remarkably powerful flavour.

○ Soave Cl. Vign. Du Lot '06	♟♟ 5
● Oratorio di San Lorenzo '04	♟♟ 7
● Bradisismo '04	♟♟ 6
● Carmenere Più '06	♟♟ 4
○ Soave Cl. Vign. di Foscarino '06	♟♟ 5
○ Soave Cl. Vin Soave '07	♟♟ 4
○ Vulcaia Après '06	♟♟ 5
○ Chardonnay '07	♟ 4
○ Vulcaia '07	♟ 4
○ Vulcaia Fumé '06	♟ 6
○ Soave Cl. Vign. Du Lot '99	♟♟♟ 5
○ Soave Cl. Vign. Du Lot '96	♟♟♟ 5
○ Soave Cl. Vign. Du Lot '05	♟♟♟ 5
○ Soave Cl. Vign. Du Lot '01	♟♟♟ 5
○ Soave Cl. Vign. Du Lot '00	♟♟♟ 5
○ Soave Cl. Vign. di Foscarino '05	♟♟ 5

Castello di Lispida

VIA IV NOVEMBRE, 4
35043 MONSELICE [PD]
TEL. 0429780530
www.lispida.com

ANNUAL PRODUCTION 18,000 bottles
HECTARES UNDER VINE 8
VITICULTURE METHOD Natural

As well as reorganizing the cellar and vineyards, Alessandro Sgaravatti has carried forward a project for accommodation at Castello di Lispida which includes making use of the thermal spas typical of the central and northern parts of the Colli Euganei. Release of almost all the estate's leading wines has been delayed this year so we were unable to taste the full range. However, we consoled ourselves with the excellent Terralba 2004, a white based mainly on tocai which is macerated at length on the skins and aged in oak barrels. The colour is almost amber and the decently complex aromas are full of personality, starting out with strong hints of iodine and Mediterranean scrubland and opening into minerally sensations with aromas of apricots and dried flowers. The entry on the palate is confident and austere, with striking structure and a complete absence of sugar. This wine is bound to gain overall harmony after more bottle age. The two Charmat method sparkling wines, on the other hand, left us a little perplexed. The Brut is dry and husky in style while the Rosé is a little uninteresting and inexpressive.

Conte Loredan Gasparini

FRAZ. VENEGAZZÙ
VIA MARTIGNAGO ALTO, 23
31040 VOLPAGO DEL MONTELLO [TV]
TEL. 0438492250
www.venegazzu.com

ANNUAL PRODUCTION 300,000 bottles
HECTARES UNDER VINE 80
VITICULTURE METHOD Natural

Lorenzo Palla has made a very distinctive mark on this estate, while respecting tradition and the professional skills of all his colleagues. The results can be seen in both the character of the products and the basic quality that derives from very professional work in the vineyards, followed through in the cellar. The 2005 version of Capo di Stato, which has always been the estate's leading wine, gave a very high calibre performance and ascends the Olympian heights of the Veneto wine firmament. This classic Bordeaux blend delivers complex but still very youthful aromas with fruit nicely blended in a well-coordinated and elegant bouquet. Refreshing acidity and fine-grained tannins follow on the palate, where the nicely ripe flavours and tertiary hints fuse in an impressive whole. Venegazzù della Casa 2005 is a little more accessible and uncomplicated, while the Falconera Rosso 2006 is also interesting, with a fruity nose, characterful palate and dry, robust progression. The short-term plan is to make this a monovarietal Merlot. The Manzoni Bianco 2007 and the Prosecco Brut are dependable, if not outstanding.

○ Terralba '04	♟♟ 6
○ H Brut '07	♟ 5
☉ H Rosé Brut '07	5
○ Terralba '03	♟♟ 6
○ Terralba '02	♟♟ 6
○ Terralba '01	♟♟ 7
○ Terralba '00	♟♟ 7

● Capo di Stato '05	♟♟ 6
● Falconera Rosso '06	♟♟ 4*
● Venegazzù della Casa '05	♟♟ 5
○ Manzoni Bianco '07	♟ 4
○ Montello e Colli Asolani Prosecco Brut	♟ 4
● Capo di Stato '04	♟♟ 6
● Capo di Stato '02	♟♟ 6
● Capo di Stato '03	♟♟ 6
● Capo di Stato '00	♟♟ 6
● Venegazzù della Casa '04	♟♟ 5
● Venegazzù della Casa '03	♟♟ 5
● Venegazzù della Casa '02	♟♟ 5

★ Maculan

VIA CASTELLETTO, 3
36042 BREGANZE [VI]
TEL. 0445873733
www.maculan.net

ANNUAL PRODUCTION	850,000 bottles
HECTARES UNDER VINE	39
VITICULTURE METHOD	Conventional

The technical and commercial profile of this renovated Breganze estate is complete with the arrival of Fausto's daughter Maria Vittoria, fresh from her degree in oenology. A great deal has changed since Fausto Maculan's neighbours used to think he was from outer space. What has not changed is his self-discipline, his desire to experiment or his inexhaustible energy. Let's start with an outstanding edition of a wine particularly close to Fausto's heart. Acininobili 2004 is back on top form with a sumptuous, brilliant version free of excessive concentration and, in short, quite perfect. Standing out among the reds are the Breganze Cabernet Sauvignon Palazzotto and the Fratta, both from the 2006 vintage. The former is weighty and creamy with plenty of vigorous fruit as well as hints of oak that need time to tone down. The Fratta is tidier and more austere, halfway between California and Bordeaux. The concentration is there, flanked by verve and a refreshing finish. Lastly, an honourable mention for Brentino, a reasonably priced merlot and cabernet sauvignon-based red that never disappoints.

Manara

FRAZ. SAN FLORIANO
VIA DON CESARE BIASI, 53
37020 SAN PIETRO IN CARIANO [VR]
TEL. 0457701086
www.manaravini.it

ANNUAL PRODUCTION	75,000 bottles
HECTARES UNDER VINE	11
VITICULTURE METHOD	Conventional

This family estate owned by the Manara brothers consists of around a dozen hectares in the hills dedicated mainly to traditional wines, the classic types covered by the denomination protocols, while also taking the opportunity to present bottles in a slightly different style. This is the case with the Amarone Classico and the Postera 2004. The former adheres scrupulously to tradition, delivering raisined fruit alongside vegetal hints, aromatic herbs and medium body with a subtle flavour. Postera, in contrast, aims at greater concentration, with weighty fruit on the nose and a rounded palate. Both are satisfying wines and the choice of one or the other is up to the consumer. The Valpolicella Superiore and the Le Morete 2005 also represent contrasting styles, less concentrated of course but both pleasant and harmonious. The Recioto 2005 is even more impressive with an explosive front palate of substantial, pulpy fruit bursting with sweetness and a long finish. The white dried-grape wine, Strinà 2005, is uncomplicated and pleasantly husky.

○ Acininobili '04		♟♟ 8
● Breganze Cabernet Sauvignon Palazzotto '06		♟♟ 5
● Fratta '06		♟♟ 8
● Brentino '06		♟♟ 4*
● Speaia '06		♟♟ 4*
○ Bidibi '07		♟ 4
○ Breganze Vespaiolo '07		♟ 4
○ Dindarello '07		♟ 5
○ Ferrata '07		♟ 5
○ Pino & Toi '07		♟ 3
☉ Costadolio '07		♟ 4
● Breganze Cabernet '06		♟ 4
● Breganze Cabernet Sauvignon Palazzotto '05		♟♟♟ 5
● Breganze Cabernet Sauvignon Palazzotto '04		♟♟♟ 5
● Fratta '01		♟♟♟ 8

● Amarone della Valpolicella Cl. '04		♟♟ 6
● Amarone della Valpolicella Cl. Postera '04		♟♟ 6
● Recioto della Valpolicella Cl. El Rocolo '05		♟♟ 5
● Valpolicella Cl. Sup. '05		♟ 3
● Valpolicella Cl. Sup. Le Morete Ripasso '05		♟ 4
○ Strinà Passito '05		♟ 5
● Amarone della Valpolicella Cl. '00		♟♟♟ 6
● Amarone della Valpolicella Cl. '03		♟♟ 6
● Amarone della Valpolicella Cl. '01		♟♟ 6
● Guido Manara '04		♟♟ 6
● Guido Manara '03		♟♟ 6

Le Mandolare

LOC. BROGNOLIGO
VIA SAMBUCO, 180
37030 MONTEFORTE D'ALPONE [VR]
TEL. 0456175083
www.cantinalemandolare.com

ANNUAL PRODUCTION	60,000 bottles
HECTARES UNDER VINE	20
VITICULTURE METHOD	Conventional

Renzo Rodighiero and his wife Germana have a new, functional cellar a little off the beaten track for the usual Soave DOC wineries. It's not luxurious but practical and well-organized almost as if the external appearance is proclaiming the message that substance is more important than form. You get the same feeling when you taste the wines. The impression is that the products focus on the versatility of the garganega grape rather than on absolute top quality. Don't come to Le Mandolare looking for perfection or opulence. Enjoy a journey of discovery through this great denomination. We'll start with the simple, fragrant Corte Menini 2007, which is light and drinkable, to continue with Il Roccolo 2007, less fruity and flaunting an enviably firm palate that combines body and suppleness. Finally, the estate's most ambitious wine is Monte Stella 2006, named after the area where the grapes are grown. It is designed to impress with its remarkable fullness. Mission accomplished, despite the consequent loss of lightness and drinkability.

Marcato

VIA PRANDI, 10
37030 RONCÀ [VR]
TEL. 0457460070
www.marcatovini.it

ANNUAL PRODUCTION	400,000 bottles
HECTARES UNDER VINE	50
VITICULTURE METHOD	Conventional

The Marcato family estate is quite large, with about 50 hectares of cultivated land in various designated areas, particularly Soave and – with even more impressive results – the Colli Berici zone, whose potential is as vast as it is untapped. The Marcato winery made its debut in the Guide last year and after waiting to judge the new products we have to admit there were no surprises. The wide, well-balanced range consists of good quality, fairly priced wines and includes some peaks of interest. The Tirso 2006 from the Soave vineyards has a mature nose with dried flowers and minerally sensations alongside the ripe fruit. The palate is confidently rounded and juicy, although the oak has not yet been fully absorbed. The Recioto di Soave Il Duello 2005 is fresh and mouthwatering while the Soave Le Barche 2007 is very pleasant. From the Colli Berici comes the Pian Alto, a Cabernet Riserva made partly with lightly dried grapes. The hot 2003 growing year has endowed it with powerful structure but at the cost of lightness.

O Soave Cl. Il Roccolo '07		♟♟ 3*
O Soave Cl. Sup. Monte Sella '06		♟♟ 4*
O Il Vignale '06		♟ 5
O Soave Cl. Corte Menini '07		♟ 3
O Soave Cl. Il Roccolo '06		♟♟ 3
O Soave Cl. Sup. Monte Sella '05		♟♟ 4
O Soave Cl. Sup. Monte Sella '04		♟♟ 4
O Recioto di Soave Cl. Le Schiavette '05		♟♟ 5
O Recioto di Soave Cl. Le Schiavette '04		♟♟ 5

O Soave Sup. Il Tirso '06		♟♟ 5
● Baraldo '04		♟ 6
● Colli Berici Cabernet '06		♟ 3
● Colli Berici Cabernet Pianalto Ris. '03		♟ 7
● Palladiano '06		♟ 4
O Lessini Durello Brut I Prandi		♟ 3
O Lessini Durello Brut M. Cl. '03		♟ 5
O Recioto di Soave Il Duello '05		♟ 6
O Soave Cl. Le Barche '07		♟ 4
O Colli Berici Sauvignon Sel. '06		4
● Colli Berici Cabernet Pianalto Ris. '02		♟♟ 7
● Colli Berici Cabernet Pianalto Ris. '01		♟♟ 7

Marion

FRAZ. MARCELLISE
VIA BORGO, 2
37036 SAN MARTINO BUON ALBERGO [VR]
TEL. 0458740021
www.marionvini.it

ANNUAL PRODUCTION	40,000 bottles
HECTARES UNDER VINE	14
VITICULTURE METHOD	Conventional

The Valpolicella growing zone embraces prestigious valley areas like Marcellise, which is a delightful cameo east of the Classico zone. The soil here gives the wines layered complexity and potential, which unfold over the years. Stefano Campedelli tells us quite openly that his and Nicoletta's secret begins with the land. The decision to plant teroldego came about almost by chance but the adoption of clones selected by Elisabetta Foradori, protectress of the variety, was deliberate. Today, the wine delivers enjoyably generous aromas and good solid flavour. The Cabernet Sauvignon, made from another grape variety not traditionally grown locally, is crafted from overripe grapes that are part-dried after picking. The 2003 is mouthfilling and ready to drink now but with a little patience it has a lot more to offer. The Valpolicella 2004 is racy, with enthralling, well-defined aromas of fruit and spices, exciting in all phases of the tasting and a true shining jewel in Marion's crown. The Amarone from the torrid 2003 vintage is vibrantly fruity, with cocoa powder and spice on the nose and an extraordinarily generous, beautifully managed palate. Three warm, powerful Glasses.

Masari

LOC. MAGLIO DI SOPRA
VIA BEVILACQUA, 2 A
36078 VALDAGNO [VI]
TEL. 0445410780
www.masari.it

ANNUAL PRODUCTION	25,000 bottles
HECTARES UNDER VINE	4
VITICULTURE METHOD	Natural

The Masari estate was founded because Massimo Dal Lago and Arianna Tessari believed in an area widely reckoned to be of little interest. Viticulture in the Valle dell'Agno is documented but it was abandoned at the beginning of the last century, rather like the rest of the valley's farming sector. Our determined heroes, however, have rediscovered the area's underrated riches. The Agnobianco 2007, a blend of garganega and durella, is making reassuring progress. Fragrant aromas of flowers with apple and pear fruit on the nose precede a palate whose sharp acidity is now balanced by more concentrated, lingering flavours. The Passito Doro 2005, from a similar blend, has predominantly tropical fruits and citrus aromas and an extremely elegant palate, thanks to confident acidity and enthralling minerality. Masari 2006, the only red wine presented, has bags of personality and underwent lengthy skin contact to enhance its ageing potential. This weighty, mouthfilling wine will need appropriate ageing to acquire greater finesse and poise on the nose. San Martino's release has been postponed because even less ambitious products need to mature.

● Amarone della Valpolicella '03	♟♟♟	8
● Valpolicella Sup. '04	♟♟	5
● Cabernet Sauvignon '03	♟♟	5
● Teroldego '04	♟♟	6
● Amarone della Valpolicella '01	♟♟♟	8
● Amarone della Valpolicella '00	♟♟	8
● Cabernet Sauvignon '01	♟♟	6
● Valpolicella Sup. '03	♟♟	6
● Valpolicella Sup. '02	♟♟	6
● Valpolicella Sup. '01	♟♟	6
● Teroldego '03	♟♟	6

○ Doro Passito Bianco '05	♟♟	5
● Masari '06	♟♟	6
○ Agnobianco '07	♟♟	4*
○ Doro Passito Bianco '04	♟♟	5
○ Doro Passito Bianco '03	♟♟	5
○ Doro Passito Bianco '02	♟♟	5
○ Doro Passito Bianco '01	♟♟	5
● Masari '05	♟♟	6
● Masari '04	♟♟	6
● Masari '03	♟♟	6

Masi

FRAZ. GARGAGNAGO
VIA MONTELEONE, 26
37015 SANT'AMBROGIO DI VALPOLICELLA [VR]
TEL. 0456832511
www.masi.it

ANNUAL PRODUCTION	4,100,000 bottles
HECTARES UNDER VINE	520
VITICULTURE METHOD	Conventional

It's difficult to find something new to say about the estate run by Sandro Boscaini, which has been a beacon and a constant presence in the sector's publications for decades. Yet if you taste the wines, you note a minor revolution taking place. It's one of those quiet revolutions that usually has lasting effects. The change can be seen in the style of the wines, especially the Amarone, which have moved away from being symbols of tradition and are now more impressively modern, delivering greater clarity and integrity. The three big hitters are all from 2003: Mazzano, Campolongo di Torbe and Costasera Riserva, making its debut. While the first two are from the production areas of the same name, the third is a selection from several vineyards, which from now on will only be made in outstanding vintages. The first two both deliver red fruit jam on the nose. The Mazzano has a complex palate while the Campolongo is powerful and the Costasera shows better defined identity, with well-developed aromas and a textured palate. Finally, we should mention the excellent performance of Toar 2005, a blend of traditional grapes.

Masottina

LOC. CASTELLO ROGANZUOLO
VIA BRADOLINI, 54
31020 SAN FIOR [TV]
TEL. 0438400775
www.masottina.it

ANNUAL PRODUCTION	2,000,000 bottles
HECTARES UNDER VINE	44
VITICULTURE METHOD	Conventional

After a year in which it slid into the Other Wineries, the Dal Bianco family's winery has returned to full visibility thanks to a range of excellent wines. The very extensive range consists of a selection of standard-label wines from the Piave area, all very enjoyable and favourably priced, and a series of more ambitious products called Ai Palazzi, which includes some very interesting labels. Then, of course, there's Prosecco, one of the leading wines in this area, and the wines of the Colli di Conegliano DOC. As usual, the most striking wine was the Merlot Ai Palazzi Riserva 2006, a red with approachable but not ordinary fruitiness, streaked through with aromatic herbs and spices. Taut and tangy on the palate, it reveals good texture and beautifully sweet tannins. The Colli di Conegliano Rosso Montesco 2006 gave an excellent performance, offering vibrant fruit with oak aromas tucked away at the back of the nose and a gutsy, juicy palate. From the Proseccos, we liked the subtle, penetrating Extra Dry and the creamy, nicely poised Cartizze.

● Amarone della Valpolicella Cl. Campolongo di Torbe '03		♟♟ 8
● Amarone della Valpolicella Cl. Costasera Ris. '03		♟♟ 8
● Amarone della Valpolicella Cl. Costasera '05		♟♟ 7
● Amarone della Valpolicella Cl. Mazzano '03		♟♟ 8
● Toar '05		♟♟ 5
● Valpolicella Cl. Sup. Anniversario 650 anni Serego Alighieri '05		♟♟ 6
● Amarone della Valpolicella Cl. Vaio Armaron '04		♟ 8
● Campofiorin '05		♟ 5
● Grandarella '05		♟ 6
● Il Brolo di Campofiorin '05		♟ 5
● Amarone della Valpolicella Cl. Mazzano '01		♟♟♟ 8

○ Cartizze		♟♟ 6
○ P. di Conegliano Valdobbiadene Extra Dry		♟♟ 4
● Colli di Conegliano Rosso Montesco '05		♟♟ 6
● Piave Merlot Vign. ai Palazzi Ris. '05		♟♟ 5
● Piave Cabernet '07		♟ 3
● Piave Cabernet Vign. ai Palazzi Ris. '05		♟ 5
○ Colli di Conegliano Bianco Rizzardo '06		♟ 5
○ Incrocio Manzoni 6.0.13 '07		♟ 4
○ Piave Chardonnay '07		♟ 3
○ Piave Chardonnay Vign. ai Palazzi '07		♟ 4
○ Piave Pinot Grigio '07		♟ 3
○ Piave Pinot Grigio Vign. ai Palazzi '07		♟ 4
● Piave Merlot Vign. ai Palazzi Ris. '04		♟♟ 5

Roberto Mazzi

LOC. SAN PERETTO
VIA CROSETTA, 8
37024 NEGRAR [VR]
TEL. 0457502072
www.robertomazzi.it

ANNUAL PRODUCTION	50,000 bottles
HECTARES UNDER VINE	8
VITICULTURE METHOD	Conventional

Antonio and Stefano Mazzi are no-nonsense growers, men of few words who prefer to let their wines do the talking. Their products often manage to find the delicate balance of genuine territorial expression with, at the same time, a well-judged contemporary feel. The Mazzis have put together a range of very high quality wines from the beautifully aspected hillside vineyards at Calcarole: Castel, Poiega and San Peretto. In particular, we'd like to focus on the lively interpretation of Poiega 2005, a convincingly essential Valpolicella Superiore with good grip, a generous nose with enthralling hints of crushed fruit alternating with pepper and fines herbes and a broad, tangy palate with practically perfect tannic weave and balance. The Amarone Punta di Villa 2004 is modern in style with very ripe, mouthfilling fruit, offset by a taut, tangy, mouthwatering palate free of any excessive softness. Once again, the 2005 Recioto Le Calcarole is quite excellent, its explosion of wild berries blending with spiciness and a rounded, juicy, very concentrated palate. The Valpolicella Superiore 2006 is well defined, savoury, nicely acidic and favourably priced.

Merotto

LOC. COL SAN MARTINO
VIA SCANDOLERA, 21
31010 FARRA DI SOLIGO [TV]
TEL. 0438989000
www.merotto.it

ANNUAL PRODUCTION	400,000 bottles
HECTARES UNDER VINE	12
VITICULTURE METHOD	Conventional

Col San Martino is situated along the ridge joining Conegliano Veneto to Valdobbiadene, the strip of foothills which has for centuries been dedicated primarily to prosecco. It is here that Graziano Merotto runs his estate with skill and passion. Some of the vineyards surround the winery buildings and others are located further away. The cellar is simple but well equipped and organized, indispensable qualities for dealing with a grape as delicate as prosecco. The range of wines consists mainly of sparkling wines distinguished by provenance and residual sugar content. The Cartizze delivers subtle, captivating aromas of flowers and white-fleshed fruit while the palate shows a near-perfect balance of acidity, sugar and fizz. The Brut Barreta and the Extra Dry Colbelo are on the same level. The Brut is vibrant and racily drinkable while the Extra Dry is more generous and mouthwatering. Finally, an honourable mention for the La Primavera di Barbara, one of the first selections from the area. It has delicious aromas of apples, pears and wisteria, just as a Prosecco should, and drinks rounded and mouthfilling, with unusually fine bubbles.

● Amarone della Valpolicella Cl. Punta di Villa '04	▼▼ 8
● Valpolicella Cl. Sup. Vign. Poiega '05	▼▼ 5
● Recioto della Valpolicella Cl. Le Calcarole '05	▼▼ 6
● Valpolicella Cl. Sup. '06	▼▼ 4*
● Amarone della Valpolicella Cl. Castel '03	♀♀ 8
● Amarone della Valpolicella Cl. Punta di Villa '03	♀♀ 8
● Amarone della Valpolicella Cl. Punta di Villa '01	♀♀ 7
● Amarone della Valpolicella Cl. Punta di Villa '00	♀♀ 7
● Amarone della Valpolicella Cl. Punta di Villa '99	♀♀ 6
● Valpolicella Cl. Sup. Vign. Poiega '04	♀♀ 5
● Valpolicella Cl. Sup. Vign. Poiega '03	♀♀ 5

○ Cartizze	▼▼ 6
○ P. di Valdobbiadene Brut Barreta	▼▼ 4
○ P. di Valdobbiadene Dry La Primavera di Barbara	▼▼ 4
○ P. di Valdobbiadene Extra Dry Colbelo	▼▼ 4
◉ Grani Rosa di Nero	▼ 4
○ P. di Valdobbiadene Dry Colle Molina '07	▼ 4
○ P. di Valdobbiadene Tranquillo Olchera '07	▼ 4
○ Prosecco Passito Royam '07	▼ 6

Firmino Miotti

VIA BROGLIATI CONTRO, 53
36042 BREGANZE [VI]
TEL. 0445873006
www.firminomiotti.it

ANNUAL PRODUCTION	25,000 bottles
HECTARES UNDER VINE	5
VITICULTURE METHOD	Conventional

Breganze is a small DOC zone extending along the strip of foothills between Bassano to the east and Breganze to the west. The classic Bordeaux red varieties are grown here, as they are in all of Veneto, while from the whites we should mention vespaiolo, which is not a particularly fragrant grape but one that can yield excellent acidity and is very resistant to drying. Needless to say, the most interesting wine, and one that has helped to make the zone's name, is Torcolato, made from part-dried vespaiolo. Torcolato has been an emblematic wine for this estate, run today by Franca Miotti, since the days when her father Firmino produced memorable versions of this wine. The 2005 reflects the usual style. It is extraordinarily rich and luscious delivering aromas of candied fruit, vegetality, spices and camomile leading into a palate whose marked sweetness is balanced beautifully by acidity. In the absence of the red Valletta, which was not produced because of the difficult harvest in 2005, our tasting continued with a range of accessible, enjoyable whites and more structured reds.

Ornella Molon Traverso

FRAZ. CAMPO DI PIETRA
VIA RISORGIMENTO, 40
31040 SALGAREDA [TV]
TEL. 0422804807
www.ornellamolon.it

ANNUAL PRODUCTION	350,000 bottles
HECTARES UNDER VINE	42
VITICULTURE METHOD	Conventional

For years, this Campo di Pietra winery was considered the most representative in the Piave DOC, although it never really hit the heights. Despite increasingly determined competition in the area, the estate appears even sounder this year with renewed freshness and elegance throughout a range that now flaunts a new, more assertively attractive label. There are many impressive wines, starting with a silky version of the Vite Rossa 2004, a classic Bordeaux blend with strikingly well-defined aromas and a tangy palate with excellent grip. The winery's thoroughbred Merlot 2005 is in fine form while the Cabernet has become lighter and more supple, which comes through in elegance and mouthwatering drinkability. For years, we thought the Raboso too husky and heavy but the 2004 vintage has lent it wonderful balance, toning down the edginess typical of this variety. The estate's leading wine, Rosso di Villa 2005, is very well made and nicely embodies the depth and structure of the local terroir. From the whites, we particularly liked the Traminer Ornella 2007 with its vibrant aromas and delicious palate.

O Breganze Torcolato '05	♈♈ 7
O Breganze Pinot Bianco '07	♈ 3
O Breganze Vespaiolo '07	♈ 3
O Le Colombare '07	♈ 3
O Pedevendo '07	♈ 3
● Breganze Cabernet '06	♈ 4
● Groppello '07	♈ 4
● Gruajo '07	♈ 4
O Breganze Torcolato '04	♈♈ 7
O Breganze Torcolato '03	♈♈ 7
O Breganze Torcolato '02	♈♈ 7
● Rosso Valletta '04	♈♈ 6
● Rosso Valletta '03	♈♈ 6
● Rosso Valletta '01	♈♈ 6
● Rosso Valletta '00	♈♈ 6

● Piave Merlot Rosso di Villa '05	♈♈ 6
● Piave Cabernet Ornella '05	♈♈ 5
● Piave Merlot Ornella '05	♈♈ 5
● Piave Raboso Ornella '04	♈♈ 5
● Vite Rossa Ornella '04	♈♈ 5
O Traminer Ornella '07	♈♈ 4*
O Piave Chardonnay Ornella '07	♈ 4
O Sauvignon Ornella '07	♈ 4
O Vite Bianca Ornella '06	♈ 4
● Piave Merlot Rosso di Villa '04	♈♈ 6
● Piave Merlot Rosso di Villa '03	♈♈ 6
● Piave Merlot Rosso di Villa '02	♈♈ 6
● Piave Merlot Rosso di Villa '01	♈♈ 6
● Piave Merlot Rosso di Villa '00	♈♈ 6

Monte del Frà

S.DA PER CUSTOZA, 35
37066 SOMMACAMPAGNA [VR]
TEL. 045510490
www.montedelfra.it

ANNUAL PRODUCTION	1,000,000 bottles
HECTARES UNDER VINE	143
VITICULTURE METHOD	Conventional

The Bonomo family's estate has transformed its approach in recent years, from a very fragmented range of well-typed, low-priced products to a line-up that focuses on quality. This abrupt change in direction coincided with the arrival of Marica on the winery's team, alongside her father Eligio and uncle Claudio. Later additions were prestigious Valtellina winemaker Claudio Introini and, last January, Gianpiero Romana, a very sound agronomist. A good 70 per cent of the considerable production is devoted to the two leading wines of this part of Veneto, Bardolino and Custoza, with increasingly impressive results. The Bardolino is fruity and approachable with a lovely flavour and Custoza comes in two versions, one fragrant and approachable and the other more expressive on the nose and weightier on the palate. The most interesting wines, though, come from the new Valpolicella estate, starting with the 2004 Amarone, which delivers clearly defined fruity aromas and a juicy palate supported by densely woven tannins and excellent acidity. The Valpolicella Ripasso 2006 is more than sound, with upfront aromas and a beautifully supple flavour.

Monte Fasolo

LOC. FAEDO
VIA MONTE FASOLO, 2
35030 CINTO EUGANEO [PD]
TEL. 0429634030
www.montefasolo.com

ANNUAL PRODUCTION	200,000 bottles
HECTARES UNDER VINE	72
VITICULTURE METHOD	Conventional

The beautiful Colli Euganei area has suddenly come to life. In just a few harvests, a number of seriously good wineries have emerged and one of these belongs to the Mazzuccato family. Although it has been operative for many years, the cellar started to steer a new course towards higher quality at the beginning of the new millennium. Despite the extensive vine stock, the range of wines presented is quite limited, demonstrating a desire to focus on a few dependable types rather than waste time and attention on a myriad of different labels. Le Tavole 2006, a Cabernet from the vineyards located in the south of the DOC zone, is on top form. This unusually elegant red delivers vibrant red berry, floral and aromatic herb aromas and a juicy palate which is rounded and harmonious without excessive muscle. Only just behind it is the Solone 2005, an intoxicatingly aromatic dried-grape wine with citrus and tropical fruit, well-balanced sweetness and a long finish. The white Milante 2007 is interesting and subtly aromatic. Although the red Rusta 2006 has been a little less impressive in recent years, the new Rosato 2007 put on a very good performance.

● Amarone della Valpolicella Cl. Tenuta Lena di Mezzo '04	♟♟ 7
● Valpolicella Cl. Sup. Ripasso Tenuta Lena di Mezzo '06	♟♟ 4
○ Bianco di Custoza '07	♟♟ 3*
○ Bianco di Custoza Sup. Ca' del Magro '06	♟♟ 3*
○ Garda Garganega Vign. Colombara '06	♟ 4
☉ Bardolino Chiaretto '07	♟ 3
● Bardolino '07	♟ 3
● Valpolicella Cl. '07	♟ 3
● Valpolicella Cl. Sup. Tenuta Lena di Mezzo '06	♟ 4
● Valpolicella Cl. Sup. Ripasso '03	♟♟ 5

● Colli Euganei Cabernet Podere Le Tavole '06	♟♟ 4*
○ Colli Euganei Fior d'Arancio Passito Solone '05	♟♟ 5
○ Milante '07	♟♟ 4
○ Colli Euganei Fior d'Arancio Spumante Dolce '07	♟ 4
☉ Rosato '07	♟ 3
● Colli Euganei Rosso Rusta '06	♟ 4
● Colli Euganei Cabernet Podere Le Tavole '05	♟♟ 4
● Colli Euganei Cabernet Podere Le Tavole '04	♟♟ 4
● Colli Euganei Rosso Rusta '05	♟♟ 3
● Colli Euganei Rosso Rusta '04	♟♟ 3

Monte Tondo

LOC. MONTE TONDO
VIA S. LORENZO, 89
37038 SOAVE [VR]
TEL. 0457680347
www.montetondo.it

ANNUAL PRODUCTION 160,000 bottles
HECTARES UNDER VINE 28
VITICULTURE METHOD Conventional

Hard work and passion have made forthright, strong-minded grower Gino Magnabosco's dream come true. He has created a major Soave operation from virtually nothing. You need to visit the vineyards with Gino himself and climb up daunting slopes, to understand his drive and energy over recent years as he has tended vineyards that were either abandoned or problematic, but located in favourable areas like Monte Foscarino. The series of wines Gino regaled us with shows that hard work pays off. The Monte Tondo 2007, a monovarietal Garganega aged in stainless steel, might be described as unfussy with stylish floral aromas leading into a dry, gutsy palate. Foscarin Slavinus 2005, on the other hand, makes a softer, mature impact with confident fruit opening into mineral sensations that enhance the mouthfeel. The other winery selection, Casette Foscarin 2005, is made from garganega with a small percentage of trebbiano di Soave. It aged in oak and delivers enjoyably complex aromas with a beautifully harmonious palate.

La Montecchia

VIA MONTECCHIA, 16
35030 SELVAZZANO DENTRO [PD]
TEL. 049637294
www.lamontecchia.it

ANNUAL PRODUCTION 110,000 bottles
HECTARES UNDER VINE 23
VITICULTURE METHOD Conventional

They say that an estate's worth is revealed in leaner years but we think it is shown even more when the proprietors reluctantly decide that the grapes are not good enough and the wines are not released. This can involve flagship wines, and much more rarely basic wines, when it is an even greater sacrifice. But that is precisely what Giordano Emo Capodilista did in 2005. He did not consider the grapes from his La Montecchia estate good enough for Villa Capodilista or Fior d'Arancio Passito. So we focused on the excellent Fior d'Arancio Spumante 2007, with its lively nose and palate, and the even more impressive Ca' Emo 2006, a merlot-heavy Bordeaux blend that delivers fresh fruit and forest floor on the nose and a mid-bodied, juicy, gutsy and drinkable palate. The Godimondo 2007 has doubled up this time with a new cabernet franc-only version that shows approachable, juicy and supple as well as the quieter, subtler version from the many old carmenère vines growing on the estate. Finally, we liked the new Piùchebello, a dry and enthrallingly aromatic Moscato, and the good performance of the Pinot Bianco 2007.

O Soave Cl. Casette Foscarin '05	♟♟ 4*
O Soave Cl. Monte Tondo '07	♟♟ 4*
O Soave Cl. Sup. Foscarin Slavinus '05	♟♟ 5
O Recioto di Soave '05	♟ 5
O Soave Cl. Monte Tondo '06	♟♟♟ 4
O Soave Cl. Casette Foscarin '04	♟♟ 4
O Soave Cl. Casette Foscarin '03	♟♟ 4
O Soave Cl. Sup. Foscarin Slavinus '04	♟♟ 5
O Soave Cl. Sup. Foscarin Slavinus '03	♟♟ 5

O Colli Euganei Moscato Fior d'Arancio Spumante '07	♟♟ 4
● Colli Euganei Rosso Ca' Emo '06	♟♟ 3*
● Godimondo Cabernet Franc '07	♟♟ 4
● Godimondo Carmenère '07	♟ 4
O Colli Euganei Pinot Bianco '07	♟ 3
O Piùchebello '07	♟ 4
O Colli Euganei Moscato Fior d'Arancio Passito '03	♟♟ 6
● Colli Euganei Rosso Villa Capodilista '04	♟♟ 6
● Colli Euganei Rosso Villa Capodilista '03	♟♟ 6
● Colli Euganei Rosso Villa Capodilista '01	♟♟ 6
● Colli Euganei Rosso Villa Capodilista '00	♟♟ 6

Cantina Sociale di Monteforte d'Alpone

VIA XX SETTEMBRE, 24
37032 MONTEFORTE D'ALPONE [VR]
TEL. 0457610110
www.cantinadimonteforte.it

ANNUAL PRODUCTION	300,000 bottles
HECTARES UNDER VINE	1500
VITICULTURE METHOD	Conventional

Although the winery run by Gaetano Tobin has an enormous expanse of vineyards, it actually releases a very limited number of bottles, passing most of its production to other bottlers. This means its direct presence on the market is very restricted but on the other hand it enables the technical staff to carry out ultra-scrupulous selection of the grapes for their own labels. For this reason we are extremely happy to confirm a perceptible improvement in the quality of the Soave Clivus and the Vicario, although these wines are not aiming for the top of the market. The former is striking, uncomplicated and very enjoyable while the Vicario delivers lovely fruity aromas reflected on the firm, nicely harmonious palate. Vigneti di Castellaro 2006 is only slightly inferior, favouring generosity over suppleness in style. The Amarone 2005 gave a good account of itself, coming close to a second Glass, as did the Recioto di Soave and the Valpolicella from the same vintage. Credit also goes to the winery for its attention to durello grape, which is the base for a sound Metodo Classico and deserves greater visibility.

Montegrande

VIA TORRE, 2
35030 ROVOLON [PD]
TEL. 0495226276
www.vinimontegrande.it

ANNUAL PRODUCTION	250,000 bottles
HECTARES UNDER VINE	23
VITICULTURE METHOD	Conventional

The wines presented by the Cristofanon family are increasingly impressive and while the good 2006 growing year was a big help for the leading selections, the basic wines reveal how well the winery works. The estate presents a very well-stocked, balanced range of wines that are sold at attractive prices. Top of the list for us is the Cabernet Sereo 2005, a red which puts strength before finesse but still delivers strikingly vibrant fruit aromas reflected nicely on the rounded, mouthwateringly drinkable palate. Vigna delle Roche 2006 is quite different, with a subtle, penetrating bouquet accentuating the fresh sensations of pepper and fines herbes that accompany wild berries and a medium-bodied palate backed up by taut acidity and a silky tannic weave. The Castearo 2007 is an interesting moscato-based white with enjoyably fresh aromas and a tangy flavour. An honourable mention goes to the basic Merlot, which is impressively uncomplicated in its forthright red berry and spice aromas and approachably rounded, juicy palate.

O Soave Cl. Clivus '07	♈♈ 3*
O Soave Cl. Il Vicario '07	♈♈ 3*
● Amarone della Valpolicella Re Teodorico '05	♈ 6
● Recioto della Valpolicella I Vini del Chiostro '05	♈ 5
O Lessini Durello Brut M. Cl.	♈ 4
O Recioto di Soave Cl. Il Sigillo I Vini del Chiostro '05	♈ 5
O Soave Cl. Sup. Vign. di Castellaro '06	♈ 4
O Soave Cl. Clivus '06	♈♈ 3
O Soave Cl. Sup. Vign. di Castellaro '05	♈♈ 4
O Soave Cl. Sup. Vign. di Castellaro '04	♈♈ 4

● Colli Euganei Cabernet Sereo '05	♈♈ 4*
● Colli Euganei Merlot '07	♈♈ 3*
● Colli Euganei Rosso V. delle Roche '06	♈♈ 4*
O Castearo '07	♈ 3
O Colli Euganei Bianco '07	♈ 3
O Colli Euganei Fior d'Arancio Passito '05	♈ 5
O Colli Euganei Fior d'Arancio Spumante Dolce	♈ 3
● Colli Euganei Cabernet '07	♈ 3
● Colli Euganei Rosso '07	♈ 3
● Colli Euganei Rosso V. delle Roche '06	♈♈ 4
● Colli Euganei Rosso V. delle Roche '05	♈♈ 4
● Colli Euganei Rosso V. delle Roche '04	♈♈ 4

Giacomo Montresor

VIA CA' DI COZZI, 16
37124 VERONA
TEL. 045913399
www.vinimontresor.it

ANNUAL PRODUCTION	3,500,000 bottles
HECTARES UNDER VINE	152
VITICULTURE METHOD	Conventional

A breath of fresh air has entered the winery's technical management with Alberto Marchisio and Corrado Eridani, and it is perceptible in the wines themselves. Owner Paolo Montresor has always had a knack for choosing colleagues and if it's true that you can see the way things will end from how they begin, he has hit the bull's eye this time. Amarone Castelliere delle Guaite 2004 is back on form, showing fresher and more sophisticated than in the past and going through to our final tastings. Floral aromas accompany the fresh, fruity sensations with hints of fines herbes and spice and the even more impressive palate is mouthwatering with beautifully handled texture. The Capitel della Crosara 2004 behaves like a younger brother, showing excellent quality and harmony but lacking the personality of the more ambitious wine. Once again, the Valpolicella Castelliere delle Guaite 2005 is characterful with excellent structure and strength. The three 2007 whites are more approachable than complex, and our favourite was the Lugana Gran Guardia with uncomplicated fruity aromas and a satisfyingly rounded, nicely balanced palate.

Mosole

FRAZ. CORBOLONE
VIA ANNONE VENETO, 60
30029 SANTO STINO DI LIVENZA [VE]
TEL. 0421310404
www.mosole.com

ANNUAL PRODUCTION	220,000 bottles
HECTARES UNDER VINE	29.5
VITICULTURE METHOD	Conventional

As this DOC zone struggles to recover its former greatness, a few wineries are trying hard to emerge, including Mosole. Lucio is always ready for a challenge and has faced many related to quality. Above all, there is vineyard management and his attempts to make great wines in an area that has always focused on standard-label products. From the start, he has believed in the merlot grape. The basic 2007 version shows interesting character but the Ad Nonam 2006 achieves rather more. This Merlot is very much a child of its terroir and one with ambitions. The complex nose gives vibrant fruit, spice and flower aromas, reflected on the creamy, lingering palate. The Hora Sexta 2006, a full, beautifully balanced Cabernet, keeps up a smart pace as does its white namesake, a monovarietal Chardonnay, also from 2006, which is very varietal with a good follow-through on the palate. Both versions of Eleo are sound, especially the Bianco, a nicely made Tocai. The nose opens with fresh aromas giving way to mature sensations and edgy acidity, complemented by good firm body on the tangy, lingering palate.

● Amarone della Valpolicella Cl. Castelliere delle Guaite '04	¶¶ 8
● Amarone della Valpolicella Cl. Capitel della Crosara '04	¶¶ 8
● Valpolicella Cl. Primo Ripasso Castelliere delle Guaite '05	¶¶ 6
○ Lugana Gran Guardia '07	¶¶ 5
○ Bianco di Custoza Vign. Monte Fiera '07	¶ 5
○ Soave Cl. Capitel Alto '07	¶ 4
● Amarone della Valpolicella Cl. Castelliere delle Guaite '99	¶¶ 8
● Amarone della Valpolicella Cl. Castelliere delle Guaite '00	¶¶ 8
● Amarone della Valpolicella Cl. Castelliere delle Guaite '01	¶¶ 8
● Valpolicella Cl. Primo Ripasso Castelliere delle Guaite '04	¶¶ 6

○ Hora Sexta '06	¶¶ 4*
● Lison-Pramaggiore Cabernet Hora Sexta '06	¶¶ 4*
● Lison-Pramaggiore Merlot Ad Nonam '06	¶¶ 5
● Lison-Pramaggiore Cabernet Franc '07	¶ 3
● Lison-Pramaggiore Eleo Rosso '07	¶ 4
● Lison-Pramaggiore Merlot '07	¶ 3
● Lison-Pramaggiore Refosco P. R. '07	¶ 3
○ Lison-Pramaggiore Chardonnay '07	¶ 3
○ Lison-Pramaggiore Eleo Bianco '07	¶ 4
○ Lison-Pramaggiore Sauvignon '07	¶ 3
○ Pinot Grigio '07	¶ 3
● Lison-Pramaggiore Merlot Ad Nonam '04	¶¶ 5

Il Mottolo

LOC. LE CONTARINE
VIA COMEZZARE
35030 BAONE [PD]
TEL. 049632185

ANNUAL PRODUCTION 15,000 bottles
HECTARES UNDER VINE 5
VITICULTURE METHOD Conventional

Il Mottolo is a fairly new estate in the Colli Euganei and shows its potential year after year. The winery is located in the southern part of the DOC zone, in the municipality of Baone, a great area for red wines. Owners Sergio Fortin and Roberto Dalla Libera are busily working to fine-tune their production structure, from the vineyards to the cellar, aided by the experience of wine man Franco Zanovello and the professionalism of agronomist Filippo Giannone. This year, the release of the leading wine Serro, a Colli Euganei Rosso made from Bordeaux grapes, has been brought forward. The excellent 2006 harvest has made this necessary and the barrel tasting confirmed its high potential. But the other wines also performed well. The Cabernet 2006 opens subtly with black pepper, balsamic hints and floral aromas followed by a confident yet graceful palate, with elegant handling of the considerable texture. The Merlot has fines herbes and forest floor aromas nicely reflected on a rounded, mouthfilling palate. Le Contarine 2007 is fresh and floral, while the Fior d'Arancio Passito 2006 made an impressive debut.

● Colli Euganei Cabernet V. Marè '06	2 black glasses	3*
● Colli Euganei Merlot Comezzara '06	2 black glasses	3*
○ Colli Euganei Fior d'Arancio Passito Vigna del Pozzo '06	2 black glasses	5
○ Le Contarine '07	1 black glass	3
● Colli Euganei Cabernet V. Marè '05	2 white glasses	3
● Colli Euganei Merlot Comezzara '05	2 white glasses	3
● Colli Euganei Rosso Serro '05	2 white glasses	4
● Colli Euganei Rosso Serro '04	2 white glasses	4

Musella

VIA FERRAZZETTE, 2
37036 SAN MARTINO BUON ALBERGO [VR]
TEL. 045973385
www.musella.it

ANNUAL PRODUCTION 120,000 bottles
HECTARES UNDER VINE 31
VITICULTURE METHOD Conventional

When we see such impressive wines showing such high quality year after year, we realize that the project begun by Emilio and his daughter Maddalena Pasqua was ambitious from the start. The aim was to make the most of the vineyards with new high-density plantings on greatly differing soils to tease out the greatest possible potential from different vine types. This is backed up by great care in the cellar and patience over the time needed by the wines. Two wines stood out as particularly distinctive at our tasting: the Amarone 2004 Riserva and the Valpolicella Superiore Ripasso 2005. The former delivers profound aromas of ripe fruit mingling and layering over mineral and spicy sensations. The palate is generous and silky with very fine-grained tannins and extraordinary length thanks to the acid backbone. The Valpolicella astounded us with its effortless handling of the considerable structure on a supple, nicely dynamic palate. The other Superiore, Vigne Nuove di Musella 2006, is also very well typed, offering a fresh, elegant interpretation of subtle vegetal sensations and aromatic herbs with a firm, tangy and very gutsy palate.

● Amarone della Valpolicella Ris. '04	2 black glasses	7
● Monte del Drago Rosso '04	2 black glasses	6
● Valpolicella Sup. Ripasso '05	2 black glasses	4*
● Valpolicella Sup. Vigne Nuove di Musella '06	2 black glasses	4*
○ Bianco del Drago '05	1 black glass	4
● Amarone della Valpolicella '03	2 white glasses	6
● Amarone della Valpolicella '01	2 white glasses	7
● Amarone della Valpolicella '00	2 white glasses	7
● Amarone della Valpolicella '99	2 white glasses	7
● Monte del Drago Rosso '03	2 white glasses	6
● Monte del Drago Rosso '02	2 white glasses	6
● Monte del Drago Rosso '01	2 white glasses	6
● Valpolicella Sup. Ripasso '04	2 white glasses	4

Angelo Nicolis e Figli

VIA VILLA GIRARDI, 29
37029 SAN PIETRO IN CARIANO [VR]
TEL. 0457701261
www.vininicolis.com

ANNUAL PRODUCTION	200,000 bottles
HECTARES UNDER VINE	42
VITICULTURE METHOD	Conventional

The Nicolis brothers are putting a great deal of energy into building the new cellar and gradually reorganizing the vineyards at Maso, and they follow each stage of the work very carefully. The vineyards are situated at over 400 metres, allowing the grapes to benefit greatly from temperature variations and breezes. Judging by the quality of the wines presented in 2008, the Nicolis' intense efforts have borne fruit. Let's start with a particularly impressive version of the Valpolicella Seccal 2005. It won us over with its harmonious blend of fruit and spicy elements, and subtle sensations of aromatic herbs. The palate stays well in step, presenting appearing sophisticated and dry with a supple flavour progression. The other thoroughbred, the Amarone Ambrosan 2003 is just as good. Generous, powerful and almost exuberant with lively ripe fruit, it unveils a nicely taut, dynamic palate. The Recioto 2005 is fresher and more approachable with a very sweet but juicy and harmonious palate. The Testal 2004, made from corvina with some cabernet and merlot, is worth uncorking, as are the standard-label Valpolicella and the Superiore 2006.

Nino Franco

VIA GARIBALDI, 147
31049 VALDOBBIADENE [TV]
TEL. 0423972051
www.ninofranco.it

ANNUAL PRODUCTION	1,000,000 bottles
HECTARES UNDER VINE	2.5
VITICULTURE METHOD	Conventional

Grave di Stecca is a walled vineyard above Valdobbiadene where the hills meet the mountains. From this newly replanted "clos", Primo Franco has produced a surprisingly delicate Prosecco with unusually vibrant aromas and generous flavour that offers a magnificent expression of the territory. Early ripening in the 2007 growing year prompted the cellar to deploy its legendary technical skill and present a range of the usual high standard. Its emblematic wine, Primo Franco, is again the leading exemplar. A wealth of sugar lends suppleness to accompany florality, smooth mousse and a distinctive hint of juniper. The Rive di S. Floriano is its opposite in style as it has less residual sugar and drinks subtle, taut and citrus-fresh. The Prosecco Brut is fragrant with aromatic herbs, rennet apples and spices, and an excellent accompaniment for Venetian "moeche frite", fried soft-shell crabs. Cartizze is the deep soul of Prosecco, an eloquent dialogue of elegance and fragrance. The Rustico is always reliably good. Finally, the Brut Rosé Faìve from 2007 is sound.

● Amarone della Valpolicella Cl. Ambrosan '03		8
● Valpolicella Cl. Sup. Seccal '05		5
● Recioto della Valpolicella Cl. '05		6
● Testal '04		5
● Valpolicella Cl. '07		4
● Valpolicella Cl. Sup. '06		4
● Amarone della Valpolicella Cl. Ambrosan '98		8
● Amarone della Valpolicella Cl. Ambrosan '93		8
● Amarone della Valpolicella Cl. '03		7
● Amarone della Valpolicella Cl. '01		7
● Amarone della Valpolicella Cl. Ambrosan '01		8
● Amarone della Valpolicella Cl. Ambrosan '00		8
● Valpolicella Cl. Sup. Seccal '04		5

○ P. di Valdobbiadene Dry Primo Franco '07		4*
○ Cartizze '07		5
○ P. di Valdobbiadene Brut		.4
○ P. di Valdobbiadene Brut Rive di S. Floriano '07		4
○ P. di Valdobbiadene Brut Rustico		4
○ Valdobbiadene Grave di Stecca Brut '07		4
⊙ Brut Rosé Faìve '07		5
○ P. di Valdobbiadene Brut Rive di S. Floriano '06		4*
○ P. di Valdobbiadene Dry Primo Franco '06		4

Novaia

VIA NOVAIA, 1
37020 MARANO DI VALPOLICELLA [VR]
TEL. 0457755129
www.novaia.it

ANNUAL PRODUCTION	30,000 bottles
HECTARES UNDER VINE	7
VITICULTURE METHOD	Conventional

The Marano valley has perhaps more than any other maintained its natural profile of vineyards, olive groves and woodlands. As you approach the town, this impression is confirmed by the old houses and courtyards. In fact, the absence of new buildings is almost surprising, as if you could no longer find valleys unscarred by construction work. The vineyards line the roadside, or sometimes disappear from view into a fold in the slopes, like those belonging to the Vaona family, which can only be discovered by following a country lane to the magnificent courtyard where the winery is situated. Although production quantities are limited, there are six wines, subdivided into three made from a single vineyard and the other three from the whole estate. From the first trio we enjoyed the mouthwatering, compact Amarone Le Balze Riserva 2003, made in the same distinctive style as the Valpolicella I Cantoni 2005, while the Recioto Le Novaje 2005 delivers gamey aromas and well-measured sweetness. The basic wines are also dependably good, especially the Amarone Corte Vaona 2004 and the Valpolicella Classico 2006.

Ottella

FRAZ. S. BENEDETTO DI LUGANA
LOC. OTTELLA
37019 PESCHIERA DEL GARDA [VR]
TEL. 0457551950
www.ottella.it

ANNUAL PRODUCTION	200,000 bottles
HECTARES UNDER VINE	30
VITICULTURE METHOD	Conventional

The Lugana area divides the southern Garda basin in two to form the DOC zone of the same name. For many years, wine played second fiddle to the area's tourism industry and easy earnings from urbanization, despite the centuries of winemaking history. Wineries like Ottella have revived interest in the wines produced from this clayey soil that are now more than ever in demand by the market and were increasingly impressive during our tastings. The 2007 vintage witnessed a step change in the wines produced by the Montresor family, starting with the simplest Lugana, with its approachable aromas and a frankly drinkable palate. But the most interesting bottle is Le Creete. It's slow and stylish to yield up its aromas of first flowers and fruits, which then giving way to a still tart minerally sensations. The palate is nicely structured but also very drinkable and light thanks to the acidity typical of the grape. An honourable mention goes to the clear, dry Campo Sireso 2006, an original blend of merlot, cabernet and corvina.

● Amarone della Valpolicella Cl. Corte Vaona '04	▼▼ 6
● Amarone della Valpolicella Cl. Le Balze Ris. '03	▼▼ 8
● Valpolicella Cl. '06	▼▼ 3*
● Valpolicella Cl. Sup. I Cantoni '05	▼▼ 5
● Recioto della Valpolicella Cl. Le Novaje '05	▼ 5
● Valpolicella Cl. Sup. Ripasso '05	▼ 4
● Amarone della Valpolicella Cl. Le Balze '01	♀♀ 8
● Amarone della Valpolicella Cl. Le Balze '00	♀♀ 8
● Amarone della Valpolicella Cl. Le Balze '99	♀♀ 8
● Amarone della Valpolicella Cl. Le Balze '98	♀♀ 8

○ Lugana Le Creete '07	▼▼ 4*
○ Lugana '07	▼▼ 4*
○ Lugana Sup. Molceo '06	▼▼ 5
● Campo Sireso '06	▼▼ 5
● Rosso Ottella '07	▼ 4
● Campo Sireso '05	♀♀ 5
● Campo Sireso '04	♀♀ 5
● Campo Sireso '03	♀♀ 5
○ Lugana Le Creete '06	♀♀ 4
○ Lugana Le Creete '05	♀♀ 4
○ Prima Luce Passito '05	♀♀ 6
○ Prima Luce Passito '02	♀♀ 6
○ Prima Luce Passito '01	♀♀ 6

★ Leonildo Pieropan

VIA CAMUZZONI, 3
37038 SOAVE [VR]
TEL. 0456190171
www.pieropan.it

Piovene Porto Godi

FRAZ. TOARA
VIA VILLA, 14
36020 VILLAGA [VI]
TEL. 0444885142
www.piovene.com

ANNUAL PRODUCTION 400,000 bottles
HECTARES UNDER VINE 45
VITICULTURE METHOD Conventional

ANNUAL PRODUCTION 80,000 bottles
HECTARES UNDER VINE 32
VITICULTURE METHOD Conventional

Leonildo "Nino" Pieropan celebrated 40 harvests in the best possible way with a dizzying series of inimitable wines created with the invaluable help of his wife Teresita and sons Andrea and Dario. The fireworks display opens with Soave La Rocca 2006, which is more impressive than it has been for several years. Very subtle, despite the generous, full and complex body, a long period on the lees and shrewd use of oak have enhanced it with an extraordinary level of harmony to guarantee longevity. The Calvarino 2006 is even more enthralling with fresh hints of aromatic herbs, peaches and citrus fruit, strong minerality and varietal almonds making this a classic of its type and a classic Three Glasses. Soave Classico 2007 did extraordinarily well, coming increasingly closer to its big brothers with an exemplary exhibition of style and continuity. Hints of hawthorn on the floral nose usher in a tangy, salty palate. Turning to the sweet wines, the Recioto Le Colombare 2004 is very impressive while the return of the Passito della Rocca, a 2003 from mainly sauvignon with riesling italico, brought us a tropical wine with nicely melded sweetness.

Colli Berici is an area whose potential is largely untapped. Producer Tommaso Piovene believes and invests in the zone, as his track record. With winemaker Flavio Prà, he began to develop a selection and vineyard management project and continued with careful, restrained winemaking work in the cellar. Over time, he has succeeded not only in giving an identity and a specific role to the tocai rosso grape; he has also communicated the typical features of the area through international varieties like merlot and cabernet. The Cabernet Pozzare 2006 opens slowly and then bursts exuberantly into nicely harmonized and already almost complex aromas, followed by a silky, captivating palate. From the same vintage, the Merlot Fra i Broli is also very well made with distinctive inborn elegance, marked by aromatic herbs, good finesse and nice grip. The Polveriera Rosso 2007 is an approachable and enjoyable Bordeaux blend while the Pinot Bianco Polveriera is practically guaranteed to please, showing fruity, harmonious and satisfyingly drinkable. The Tai Rosso Riveselle, Sauvignon and Garganego are simpler but by no means ordinary.

O Soave Cl. Calvarino '06	♟♟♟	5
O Soave Cl. La Rocca '06	♟♟	6
O Passito della Rocca '03	♟♟	7
O Recioto di Soave Le Colombare '04	♟♟	6
O Soave Cl. '07	♟♟	4*
O Soave Cl. Calvarino '05	♟♟♟	5
O Soave Cl. Calvarino '04	♟♟♟	5
O Soave Cl. Calvarino '03	♟♟♟	5
O Soave Cl. Calvarino '02	♟♟♟	5
O Soave Cl. Sup. Calvarino '98	♟♟♟	5
O Soave Cl. La Rocca '02	♟♟♟	6
O Soave Cl. Sup. La Rocca '00	♟♟♟	6
O Soave Cl. Sup. La Rocca '99	♟♟♟	6
O Soave Cl. Sup. La Rocca '98	♟♟♟	6
O Soave Cl. Sup. La Rocca '96	♟♟♟	6
O Soave Cl. Sup. La Rocca '95	♟♟♟	6

● Colli Berici Cabernet Vign. Pozzare '06	♟♟	5
● Colli Berici Merlot Fra i Broli '06	♟♟	5
● Polveriera Rosso '07	♟♟	4*
O Colli Berici Pinot Bianco Polveriera '07	♟♟	4*
O Colli Berici Garganega Vign. Riveselle '07	♟	4
O Colli Berici Sauvignon Vign. Fostine '07	♟	4
● Colli Berici Tai Rosso Vign. Riveselle '07	♟	3
● Colli Berici Cabernet Vign. Pozzare '03	♟♟	5
● Colli Berici Tocai Rosso Thovara '04	♟♟	6
● Colli Berici Tocai Rosso Thovara '03	♟♟	6
● Colli Berici Merlot Fra i Broli '04	♟♟	6

Umberto Portinari

LOC. BROGNOLIGO
VIA SANTO STEFANO, 2
37032 MONTEFORTE D'ALPONE [VR]
TEL. 0456175087
portinarivini@libero.it

ANNUAL PRODUCTION	30,000 bottles
HECTARES UNDER VINE	4
VITICULTURE METHOD	Conventional

Today, Soave is enjoying a great deal of attention thanks to a handful of producers who have made this white Veronese product one of the top wines in Italy, even though most of the area is in the hands of co-operative wineries. The key to the wine is the garganega grape, which can be versatile and multifaceted, depending on how it is cultivated and interpreted. Umberto Portinari has always emphasized its huskier and more unpredictable side, pursuing grip and essential features rather than sophistication or opulence. You'll see what we mean when you taste Ronchetto 2007, a Soave with vibrant fruity aromas streaked through with the vegetal hints typical of the variety and a tangy, beautifully harmonious palate with plenty of texture. The Soave Albare 2006 originates from the flatlands and undergoes "doppia maturazione", cane cutting that makes it possible to harvest ripe grapes along with slightly dried bunches. The resulting wine has generous aromas and a very enjoyable palate. Finally, the charming, sunny Recioto di Soave Oro 2002 underwent long maturation before release.

Prà

VIA DELLA FONTANA, 31
37032 MONTEFORTE D'ALPONE [VR]
TEL. 0457612125
grazianopra@libero.it

ANNUAL PRODUCTION	220,000 bottles
HECTARES UNDER VINE	20
VITICULTURE METHOD	Conventional

From sophisticated Soave man to red winemaker in Valpolicella is a leap that would make many hearts race, but not Graziano Prà's. With his renowned doggedness, he will have no trouble taking a leading role in this new adventure. While we wait to taste the first products from the Morandina estate, we are pleased to acknowledge the decision to steer the estate towards healthier, sustainable farming. Chemicals will be banned from the vineyards and there will be as little intervention in the cellar as possible, in an ongoing quest for territory-linked wines. We tasted two great, territorial wines. Staforte 2006 delivers extremely ripe, rounded fruit that only hints at its considerable ageing potential, while the palate is beautifully structured and linear with good grip. In fact, it walked away with Three Glasses. Once again, we noted an impressive performance from the 2007 Monte Grande, a perfect blend of minerality and citrus sensations, refreshed by floral aromas and a clearly defined, elegant palate. The Classico is impeccable and complex, with a drinkable, dynamic, free and easy palate. The S. Antonio 2006 is full and textured.

O Soave Cl. Ronchetto '07		♀♀ 4*
O Recioto di Soave Oro '02		♀♀ 6
O Soave Albare Doppia Maturazione Ragionata '06		♀♀ 4*
O Soave Sup. V. Albare Doppia Maturazione Ragionata '97		♀♀♀ 4
O Soave Albare Doppia Maturazione Ragionata '05		♀♀ 4
O Soave Albare Doppia Maturazione Ragionata '04		♀♀ 4
O Soave Cl. Ronchetto '06		♀♀ 4
O Soave Cl. Ronchetto '05		♀♀ 4
O Soave Cl. Ronchetto '04		♀♀ 4

O Soave Cl. Staforte '06		♀♀♀ 5
O Soave Cl. Monte Grande '07		♀♀ 5
O Soave Cl. '07		♀♀ 4*
O Soave Cl. Colle S. Antonio '06		♀♀ 5
O Soave Cl. Monte Grande '06		♀♀♀ 5
O Soave Cl. Monte Grande '05		♀♀♀ 5
O Soave Cl. Monte Grande '04		♀♀♀ 5
O Soave Cl. Monte Grande '03		♀♀♀ 5
O Soave Cl. Monte Grande '02		♀♀♀ 5
O Soave Cl. Sup. Monte Grande '00		♀♀♀ 5
O Soave Cl. Monte Grande '01		♀♀ 5
O Soave Cl. Staforte '05		♀♀ 5
O Soave Cl. Staforte '04		♀♀ 4

★ Giuseppe Quintarelli

VIA CERÈ, 1
37024 NEGRAR [VR]
TEL. 0457500016
giuseppe.quintarelli@tin.it

Le Ragose

FRAZ. ARBIZZANO
VIA LE RAGOSE, 1
37020 NEGRAR [VR]
TEL. 0457513241
www.leragose.com

ANNUAL PRODUCTION	60,000 bottles
HECTARES UNDER VINE	12
VITICULTURE METHOD	Conventional

Every year, as the Guide deadline nears, our hearts beat harder as we drive up Via del Cerè in the Negrar valley, a fine growing area in the municipality of Valpolicella, to visit Bepi Quintarelli. Despite many harvests and the weight of the years, this old lion is still the same. He's a man who makes a difference. It's not every day that you can retaste a bottle of Recioto 1995, the Recioto par excellence, to round off a session. After the sumptuous '99 Valpolicella, the 2000 had its work cut out but Quintarelli astounded us yet again. It is fresh, dry, with fine-grained tannins and pervasive lightness, with a wonderful never-ending whirl of flowers, aromatic herbs and fruit. Next up was Alzero, made from part-dried cabernet grapes, which first appeared in the early 1980s. The 1998 has intense ruby red colour and is closed, robust and impenetrable, gradually revealing its aromas of violets, black cherries, plums, vanilla, hazelnut cream and coffee. A wine for collectors. And then the simpler wines, the robust, mouthwatering Bianco Secco 2007 and the Primo Fiore 2005, a thoroughly respectable second wine, if we can call it that.

ANNUAL PRODUCTION	150,000 bottles
HECTARES UNDER VINE	19
VITICULTURE METHOD	Conventional

Le Ragose's best 40th anniversary present is the respect for tradition guaranteed by Paolo and Marco Galli in every product, faithful to the vision they share with their parents. Beefy, over-concentrated wines are banned with dogged determination so that fruit and freshness can shine through. Even the simplest wines are made to evolve and last over time. Sometimes they are penalized for this at comparative tastings, partly because their release dates do not coincide with the Guide's schedule. On the other hand, it pays off at table, where the wines drink light and supple. The Amarone has always shown exemplary finesse, even in a hot year like 2003, which comes through in the alcohol on the palate, but the wine has a fruity, herbal nose and manages to find momentum and lightness in the finish. The Amarone Marta Galli, also 2003, is more modern in style, showing full-bodied but not without a pinch of elegance. The standard-label Valpolicella is pleasant and nicely structured and we enjoyed the texture and complexity of the Superiore Le Sassine 2004.

● Alzero Cabernet Franc '98	♟♟	8
● Valpolicella Cl. Sup. '00	♟♟	8
● Primo Fiore '05	♟♟	6
O Bianco Secco '07	♟♟	5
● Amarone della Valpolicella Cl. '98	♟♟♟	8
● Amarone della Valpolicella Cl. '97	♟♟♟	8
● Amarone della Valpolicella Cl. '86	♟♟♟	8
● Amarone della Valpolicella Cl. '84	♟♟♟	8
● Amarone della Valpolicella Cl. Ris. '83	♟♟♟	8
● Amarone della Valpolicella Cl. Sup. Monte Cà Paletta '93	♟♟♟	8
● Amarone della Valpolicella Cl. Sup. Ris. '85	♟♟♟	8
● Recioto della Valpolicella Cl. '95	♟♟♟	8
● Rosso del Bepi '96	♟♟♟	8
● Valpolicella Cl. Sup. '99	♟♟♟	8

● Amarone della Valpolicella Cl. '03	♟♟	7
● Amarone della Valpolicella Cl. Marta Galli '03	♟♟	8
● Valpolicella Cl. Sup. Le Sassine Ripasso '04	♟♟	4*
● Valpolicella Cl. '07	♟	4
● Amarone della Valpolicella Cl. '88	♟♟♟	8
● Amarone della Valpolicella Cl. '86	♟♟♟	8
● Amarone della Valpolicella '99	♟♟	8
● Amarone della Valpolicella '01	♟♟	8
● Amarone della Valpolicella Marta Galli '01	♟♟	8
● Valpolicella Cl. Sup. Le Sassine '03	♟♟	4
● Amarone della Valpolicella '98	♟♟	8

Roccolo Grassi

VIA SAN GIOVANNI DI DIO, 19
37030 MEZZANE DI SOTTO [VR]
TEL. 0458880089
roccolograssi@libero.it

ANNUAL PRODUCTION   38,000 bottles
HECTARES UNDER VINE   14
VITICULTURE METHOD   Conventional

In the mid 1990s, 20-year-old Marco Sartori felt a strong desire to transform his family's winery from a quantity-focused business into an estate aiming for much higher quality. With great intelligence and courage, his father Bruno gave him room to work on it, abandoning the results achieved over the years to set off on a new journey into the unknown. Bruno's vision paid off and today Roccolo Grassi is one of the most successful estates in Valpolicella. Marco and his sister Francesca have shown shrewdness and determination in their unswerving pursuit of quality in the vineyard and in the cellar. As a result, the wines presented this year were all of excellent, starting with the white Soave La Broia 2006. Despite having gone into bottle not long before, it proved exciting, showing taut on the palate with a dry finish already marked by the wood. The same applies to Amarone 2004 and Valpolicella 2005, both still too young but with great character and vitality. The blend of fruit, acidity and discreet hints of oak bode well for their future evolution.

Vigna Roda

LOC. CORTELÀ
VIA MONTE VERSA, 1569
35030 VÒ [PD]
TEL. 0499940228
www.vignaroda.com

ANNUAL PRODUCTION   40,000 bottles
HECTARES UNDER VINE   17
VITICULTURE METHOD   Conventional

Vigna Roda continues to grow without missing a beat. This small estate achieves success on the market and praise from the critics, increasing output cautiously and striving to make the best possible use of the grapes grown in its vineyards. Gianni Strazzacappa, the heart and soul of the winery, is developing even greater sensitivity to events in the vineyard, cellar and also in the market. He has realized that his leading wine, Scarlatto, deserves more tender loving care and, at the risk of displeasing his clients, it will only be released after an adequate ageing period. In the meantime, he presented us with a very impressive Fior d'Arancio Passito, fragrant with candied citrus and tropical fruit, and possessed of a juicy palate where acidity backs up the alluring sweetness. Also very good are the two reds, a Merlot and a Cabernet 2007, which tell you that Gianni is a producer who is more concerned about substance than presentation. The two wines deliver clear, fruity aromas, with solid structure and excellent ageing prospects. The Chardonnay Ca' Zamira and the Fior d'Arancio Spumante are both enjoyable.

● Amarone della Valpolicella Roccolo Grassi '04	⚲⚲ 8
● Valpolicella Sup. Roccolo Grassi '05	⚲⚲ 6
○ Soave Sup. La Broia '06	⚲⚲ 4*
● Amarone della Valpolicella Roccolo Grassi '99	⚲⚲⚲ 8
● Amarone della Valpolicella Roccolo Grassi '00	⚲⚲⚲ 8
● Valpolicella Sup. Roccolo Grassi '04	⚲⚲⚲ 6
● Amarone della Valpolicella Roccolo Grassi '03	⚲⚲ 8
● Amarone della Valpolicella Roccolo Grassi '01	⚲⚲ 8
● Valpolicella Sup. Roccolo Grassi '03	⚲⚲ 6

● Colli Euganei Cabernet '07	⚲⚲ 3*
● Colli Euganei Merlot '07	⚲⚲ 3*
○ Colli Euganei Fior d'Arancio Passito '05	⚲⚲ 5
○ Colli Euganei Chardonnay Ca' Zamira '07	⚲ 3
○ Colli Euganei Fior d'Arancio Spumante '07	⚲ 3
● Colli Euganei Rosso '07	⚲ 3
● Colli Euganei Rosso Scarlatto '05	⚲⚲ 4
● Colli Euganei Rosso Scarlatto '04	⚲⚲ 4
● Colli Euganei Rosso Scarlatto '03	⚲⚲ 4
○ Colli Euganei Fior d'Arancio Passito '04	⚲⚲ 5

Roeno

VIA MAMA, 5
37020 BRENTINO BELLUNO [VR]
TEL. 0457230110
www.cantinaroeno.com

ANNUAL PRODUCTION	80,000 bottles
HECTARES UNDER VINE	25
VITICULTURE METHOD	Conventional

The Fugatti brothers' increasingly impressive range is becoming a benchmark for Valdadige, a narrow DOC zone between Trentino to the north and Valpolicella-Bardolino to the south. The appealingly approachable standard-label single-variety wines are now flanked by more substantial reds, starting with the Enantio 2005, from the lambrusco a foglia frastagliata variety, which is yielding very interesting results in this area. The vibrant red berry aromas are reflected on the solidly constructed palate with its dry, almost austere profile. The Roeno 2004 is very enjoyable and anything but ordinary. This original blend of cabernet franc and marzemino delivers intense aromas of fruit and overripeness with delicious hints of flowers and spices and a lovely palate backed up by the silky, stylish tannins. Once again, the most impressive wine is Cristina 2005, a blend of late harvested trebbiano, sauvignon, pinot grigio and chardonnay. The citrus and floral aromas highlight a still rather sharp minerality that will come out over the years, as happened with previous vintages. There's nice handling of the sweetness on the palate and a dry finish.

Ruggeri & C.

VIA PRÀ FONTANA
31049 VALDOBBIADENE [TV]
TEL. 04239092
www.ruggeri.it

ANNUAL PRODUCTION	1,000,000 bottles
HECTARES UNDER VINE	14
VITICULTURE METHOD	Conventional

If we were in Champagne, the Ruggeri estate would be a "négociant manipulant". Like Ruggeri, these wineries do not exclusively process their own grapes but buy fruit in from growers. Ruggeri's strength is its profound knowledge of the local area. The winery has its own long-standing growers, all with hillside vineyards and most in the municipality of Valdobbiadene, the heart of prosecco country. This lasting relationship has created a symbiosis between winery and growers, to the extent that owner Paolo Bisol proudly invited us to visit the vineyards where he purchases his grapes. This careful selection of fruit pays off during vinification, as we can see in Vecchie Viti, a Brut made from vines about 100 years old scattered across the various growers' holdings. The clear apple and pear fruit aromas herald a dry, characterful, tangy and very lingering palate. Giustino B., on the other hand, is the epitome of finesse, and explodes with floral aromas on the nose before unveiling a silky, harmonious palate. The Extra Brut did very well. It's a dry, upfront Prosecco from Valdobbiadene grapes, although this does not comply with the DOC protocol.

O Cristina V. T. '05	▼▼ 6
● Rosso Roeno '04	▼▼ 5
● Valdadige Terra dei Forti Enantio '05	▼▼ 5
O Müller Thurgau Le Giarre '07	▼ 4
O Valdadige Bianco '07	▼ 4
O Valdadige Chardonnay Le Fratte '07	▼ 4
O Valdadige Pinot Grigio Tera Alta '07	▼ 4
O Valdadige Terra dei Forti Pinot Grigio '07	▼ 4
O Cristina V. T. '04	♈ 6
O Passito Cristina Roeno '03	♈ 5

O P. di Valdobbiadene Brut Vecchie Viti '07	▼▼ 5
O P. di Valdobbiadene Extra Dry Giustino B. '07	▼▼ 5
O Cartizze	▼▼ 5
O L'Extra Brut '07	▼▼ 4*
O P. di Valdobbiadene Brut Quartese	▼▼ 4*
O P. di Valdobbiadene Dry S. Stefano	▼▼ 4*
O P. di Valdobbiadene Extra Dry Giall'Oro	▼▼ 4*
O Pinot Grigio Vign. Cornuda '07	▼ 4
O P. di Valdobbiadene Brut Vecchie Viti '06	♈ 5
O P. di Valdobbiadene Extra Dry Giustino B. '06	♈ 5

Le Salette

VIA PIO BRUGNOLI, 11C
37022 FUMANE [VR]
TEL. 0457701027
www.lesalette.it

ANNUAL PRODUCTION 180,000 bottles
HECTARES UNDER VINE 35
VITICULTURE METHOD Conventional

This winery tucked away at Fumane is owned by Monica and Franco Scamperle. There are no imposing buildings or gilt stuccoes yet the wines inside are impressive as well as seductive. The estate's strengths lie elsewhere on the slopes and valleys of Valpolicella where the extensive vineyards yield top quality grapes. The rest is down to the expertise of the men in charge, and to time. This year, the selection of wines is more impressive than ever and quality is very high across the range. We'll begin with the Amarone Pergole Vece 2004, which brings out the very soul of the designation with dried fruit fragrances in a powerful yet dry, savoury dry wine. The companion Recioto is more exuberant and impetuous, revealing a light hand with the considerable sugar content. The exemplary Valpolicella I Progni 2005 emphasizes its peppery corvina grapes, adding generous flavour without compromising finesse or grip. Last up is a non-DOC but still deeply Veronese wine, Ca' Carnocchio 2005, made from part-dried classic local grapes with very successful results.

● Amarone della Valpolicella Cl. Pergole Vece '04	🍷🍷 8
● Ca' Carnocchio '05	🍷🍷 5
● Recioto della Valpolicella Cl. Pergole Vece '05	🍷🍷 6
● Valpolicella Cl. Sup. Ripasso I Progni '05	🍷🍷 4*
● Amarone della Valpolicella Cl. La Marega '04	🍷🍷 6
● Recioto della Valpolicella Cl. Le Traversagne '05	🍷 6
● Valpolicella Cl. '07	🍷 3
● Amarone della Valpolicella Cl. Pergole Vece '95	🍷🍷🍷 8
● Amarone della Valpolicella Cl. Pergole Vece '03	🍷🍷 8
● Recioto della Valpolicella Cl. Pergole Vece '04	🍷🍷 6

La Sansonina

LOC. SANSONINA
37019 PESCHIERA DEL GARDA [VR]
TEL. 0457551905
www.sansonina.it

ANNUAL PRODUCTION 13,000 bottles
HECTARES UNDER VINE 12
VITICULTURE METHOD Conventional

On this clayey soil on the southern bank of Lake Garda, trebbiano di Lugana – formerly turbiana – grape has been grown for centuries. It is still grown today, except where – sadly – villas and other accommodation structures have been built for the tourist industry. It might seem odd to find here a winery dedicated to the production of just one wine, and a Merlot at that, but La Sansonina is rapidly gaining supporters in the market and among critics. This is thanks to Carla Prospero, the feisty producer who took up this challenge and is now renovating the old farm buildings, after which the winery is named, next to the vineyard. Although La Sansonina has seen just seven harvests, it has achieved an enviably high standard of quality that communicates its links with the variety, and even more so, with the local area, through the power of the clay combining with the finesse contributed by the climate. The 2005 benefits from the coolness of the growing year which has streaked the nose with lovely flower and spice aromas that are nicely reflected on the savoury, harmonious palate.

● Sansonina '05	🍷🍷 7
● Sansonina '04	🍷🍷 7
● Sansonina '03	🍷🍷 7
● Sansonina '01	🍷🍷 7
● Sansonina '00	🍷🍷 7
● Sansonina '98	🍷🍷 7
● Sansonina '97	🍷🍷 7

Tenuta Sant'Antonio

FRAZ. SAN BRICCIO
VIA MONTI GARBI
37030 MEZZANE DI SOTTO [VR]
TEL. 0457650383
www.tenutasantantonio.it

ANNUAL PRODUCTION	378,000 bottles
HECTARES UNDER VINE	53
VITICULTURE METHOD	Conventional

The surprising thing about the Castagnedis is the way they combine high quality and great value for money across a broad range. Again this year, there was a good performance from the reds and improvements in the whites, especially the Monte Ceriani. This is a Soave made exclusively from garganega grapes grown in an old pergola-trained plot in the vineyard of the same name. The grapes are picked in two passes: some early, for freshness; and some later for greater structure. Vinification and ageing are in steel on the fine lees. The wine has clear fresh fruit and floral aromas followed by an elegant, moderately powerful palate that offers savouriness and lovely grip. On the red front, we liked the Valpolicella La Bandina 2005 for its minerality and the graceful handling of its considerable texture. The Amarone Campo dei Gigli 2004 shows its usual exuberant but supple personality, lifted by complex aromas. This combination won it Three authoritative Glasses. The Amarone Antonio Castagnedi 2005 is simpler but equally well made. Valpolicella Ripasso Monti Garbi 2006 is very sound.

Santa Margherita

VIA ITA MARZOTTO, 8
30025 FOSSALTA DI PORTOGRUARO [VE]
TEL. 0421246111
www.santamargherita.com

ANNUAL PRODUCTION	12,500,000 bottles
HECTARES UNDER VINE	23
VITICULTURE METHOD	Conventional

This large winery at Fossalta near Portogruaro has always presented a well-constructed selection of products whose strong suit is uncomplicated, current wines reflecting the features of the grape varieties used and sold at very attractive prices. As we all know, the estate's workhorse is Pinot Grigio, which has an outstanding image and market particularly in the United States. However, we preferred Luna dei Feldi, an original white blend of flavoursome chardonnay with fresh, aromatic gewürztraminer and the acid thrust of müller thurgau. The result is a subtly aromatic wine with a dry, mouthwatering palate. Turning to the reds, we especially liked the Malbech 2006, which slowly unfolds an array of aromatics based on red berries and delicate vegetal hints, followed by a beautifully tangy palate with sweet tannins. Only a step behind it is the Refosco, another variety of particular interest to this the winery, which has a fruit-forward nose and a gutsy palate. The other products are all well typed and approachable in style.

● Amarone della Valpolicella Campo dei Gigli '04	❢❢❢ 8
○ Soave Monte Ceriani '06	❢❢ 4*
● Valpolicella Sup. La Bandina '05	❢❢ 6
● Amarone della Valpolicella Sel. Antonio Castagnedi '05	❢❢ 7
● Valpolicella Sup. Ripasso Monti Garbi '06	❢❢ 4*
● Amarone della Valpolicella Campo dei Gigli '99	♈♈♈ 8
● Amarone della Valpolicella Campo dei Gigli '98	♈♈♈ 8
● Amarone della Valpolicella Campo dei Gigli '97	♈♈♈ 8
● Valpolicella Sup. La Bandina '01	♈♈♈ 6
○ Soave Monte Ceriani '05	♈♈♈ 4
● Amarone della Valpolicella Campo dei Gigli '03	♈♈ 8

○ Luna dei Feldi '07	❢❢ 4*
● Malbech '06	❢❢ 4*
● Refosco '06	❢ 4
● Versato '06	❢ 4
○ Cartizze	❢ 5
○ Lison-Pramaggiore Verduzzo Dolce Dulcedo '05	❢ 4
○ P. di Valdobbiadene Extra Dry	❢ 4
○ Valdadige Pinot Grigio '07	❢ 4
○ A. A. Pinot Grigio Impronta del Fondatore '07	4
○ Trentino Chardonnay '07	3
● Malbech '05	♈♈ 4
● Refosco '05	♈♈ 4

Santa Sofia

FRAZ. PEDEMONTE
VIA CA' DEDÉ, 61
37020 SAN PIETRO IN CARIANO [VR]
TEL. 0457701074
www.santasofia.com

ANNUAL PRODUCTION	550,000 bottles
HECTARES UNDER VINE	N.A.
VITICULTURE METHOD	Conventional

Over the years, the Begnoni family has accustomed us to a broad, balanced range of products including practically all the Veronese denomination wines in reasonably priced, high-quality versions. But this year, the range includes an outstanding and particularly well-made Amarone from the 2004 vintage, which impressed all our tasters. In recent years, this wine has shifted to a more modern style, with the more mature, dried-grape aromas giving way to sounder, juicier fruit. The sweetness is nicely controlled on the palate and the wine opens out with light, classy precision. Amarone Gioé 2003 is more traditional, emphasizing aromas of dried red berry fruit and aromatic herbs, which are nicely reprised on the warm, soft palate. One of the winery's battle horses in recent years is Merlot Corvina and again the 2006 version of this red combines the increasingly sought-after characteristics of fullness and simplicity. All the simpler wines have improved nicely, from the fragrant Custoza Montemagrin to the juicy Valpolicella Classico 2006 and the floral Lugana.

Santi

VIA UNGHERIA, 33
37031 ILLASI [VR]
TEL. 0456520077
www.carlosanti.it

ANNUAL PRODUCTION	2,000,000 bottles
HECTARES UNDER VINE	70
VITICULTURE METHOD	Conventional

In recent years, much has changed at the Gruppo Italiano Vini but if you are worried that attention might shift from wine to finance, don't. This very respectable selection is not only good but corresponds perfectly to type and to vintage. Credit goes to all the technical staff, headed by Cristian Scrinzi, who knows his way around the soil types and varieties. The most interesting wine is again Proemio, a 2005 Amarone with a modern profile that has subtlety despite fullness lent by the dried grapes and redolent of fresh flowers and wild berries. This wine is excellent now and can only improve with the right length of time in bottle. It's a great Amarone and a great Three Glass winner. The Solane is impressive as ever. A 2006 Valpolicella which projects its own identity rather than mimicking its big brother, it foregrounds sound aromas and grip. The simple but perfectly harmonious standard-label 2005 Amarone is very good, even considering its price and the number released. Lastly, an honourable mention for the Bardolino Ca' Bordenis 2007, which has a peppery, floral nose followed by a light, savoury palate.

Santa Sofia	
● Amarone della Valpolicella Cl. '04	♟♟ 7
● Amarone della Valpolicella Cl. Gioé '03	♟♟ 8
● Merlot Corvina '06	♟♟ 3*
● Valpolicella Sup. Ripasso '06	♟♟ 4
● Valpolicella Cl. '06	♟ 4
O Bianco di Custoza Montemagrin '07	♟ 3*
O Garda Pinot Grigio Le Calderare '07	♟ 3
O Lugana '07	♟ 3
O Recioto di Soave Cl. '06	♟ 5
O Soave Cl. Montefoscarino '07	♟ 3
⊙ Bardolino Chiaretto Cl. '07	♟ 3
O Soave Cl. Costalta '06	4
● Bardolino Cl. '07	3
● Amarone della Valpolicella Cl. '03	♟♟ 7
● Amarone della Valpolicella Cl. Gioé '00	♟♟ 8

Santi	
● Amarone della Valpolicella Proemio '05	♟♟♟ 7
● Valpolicella Cl. Sup. Solane Ripasso '06	♟♟ 4*
● Amarone della Valpolicella '05	♟♟ 6
● Bardolino Cl. Vigneto Ca' Bordenis '07	♟♟ 4
O Soave Cl. Monteforte '07	♟ 4
● Amarone della Valpolicella Proemio '03	♟♟♟ 7
● Amarone della Valpolicella Proemio '00	♟♟♟ 7
● Amarone della Valpolicella Proemio '04	♟♟ 7
● Valpolicella Cl. Sup. Solane Ripasso '05	♟♟ 4

Casa Vinicola Sartori

FRAZ. SANTA MARIA
VIA CASETTE, 2
37024 NEGRAR [VR]
TEL. 0456028011
www.sartorinet.com

ANNUAL PRODUCTION 15,000,000 bottles
HECTARES UNDER VINE 40
VITICULTURE METHOD Conventional

The Sartori family's involvement in the world of wine deepens with the passing years. As well as dedicating his time to the estate, which produces millions of bottles, Andrea is in charge of the Unione Italiano Vini. Luca was elected chairman of the protection consortium this year. But other commitments do not distract their attention from winemaking, where the partnership with Franco Bernabei is yielding increasingly impressive results. The Amarone Corte Bra 2003 illustrates this. Released after appropriate ageing, it offers a traditional swath of aromatics with raisined fruit mingling with spices and aromatic herbs that introduce a broad, mature palate. The younger Reius is simpler but very harmonious. Turning to the lighter wines, Bardolino Ca' Nova 2006 did very well indeed, presenting fruity, spicy and refreshingly drinkable. The Soave Vigneti di Sella 2007 gives remarkable on a nose that heralds a solidly constructed palate with good grip. From the dried-grape wines, we preferred the approachably sunny and sweet Recioto Rerum 2005 while the Marani 2006, a nicely rounded garganega-based white, came close to a second Glass.

● Amarone della Valpolicella Cl. Corte Brà '03	🍷🍷	8
● Amarone della Valpolicella Cl. Reius '04	🍷🍷	7
● Bardolino Cl. Ca' Nova '06	🍷🍷	3*
● Recioto della Valpolicella Cl. Rerum '05	🍷🍷	7
● Valpolicella Sup. Ripasso Regolo '04	🍷🍷	4
○ Soave Cl. Vign. di Sella '07	🍷🍷	4
○ Lugana La Musina '07	🍷	4
○ Marani '06	🍷	4
○ Recioto di Soave Vernus '05	🍷	6
● Bardolino Cl. '07	🍷	3
● Amarone della Valpolicella Le Vigne di Turano I Saltari '03	🍸🍸	8

★ Serafini & Vidotto

VIA CARRER, 8/12
31040 NERVESA DELLA BATTAGLIA [TV]
TEL. 0422773281
serafinievidotto@serafinievidotto.com

ANNUAL PRODUCTION 100,000 bottles
HECTARES UNDER VINE 21
VITICULTURE METHOD Natural

At a time when most Italian DOCs seek to boost their prestige by talking about "terroir" and "indigenous", the Montello zone actually embodies them. Paradoxically, the grapes in question are merlot and cabernet but they have been acclimatized to this strip of land in the province of Treviso for over a century and communicate the characteristics of the local area through distinctive aromatics lifted by above average acidity. The result is Rosso dell'Abazia, which has collected many awards from this Guide, and thanks to its fresh, swath of aromatics and firm, creamy body with sweet tannins and juicy acidity, it won yet another Three Glass prize. Its younger brother, Phigaia, follows in its footsteps as tradition demands, showing lighter and simpler but equally classy. And from the reds, we loved the superb performance of the Pinot Nero 2005, another authentic expression of the area. Vibrant wild berry and aromatic herb aromas usher in a hefty palate with good grip. The sauvignon-based Bianco 2007 also performed well, with subtle aromas and a tangy, drinkable palate, while our favourite fizz was the Prosecco with its vigorous flavour.

● Montello e Colli Asolani Il Rosso dell'Abazia '05	🍷🍷🍷	6
● Montello e Colli Asolani Phigaia '05	🍷🍷	5
● Pinot Nero '05	🍷🍷	7
○ Bollicine di Prosecco	🍷🍷	4*
○ Il Bianco '07	🍷🍷	4*
⊙ Bollicine Rosé	🍷	4
● Montello e Colli Asolani Il Rosso dell'Abazia '04	🍸🍸🍸	6
● Montello e Colli Asolani Il Rosso dell'Abazia '03	🍸🍸🍸	6
● Il Rosso dell'Abazia '02	🍸🍸🍸	7
● Il Rosso dell'Abazia '01	🍸🍸🍸	7
● Il Rosso dell'Abazia '00	🍸🍸🍸	7
● Il Rosso dell'Abazia '98	🍸🍸🍸	7
● Il Rosso dell'Abazia '97	🍸🍸🍸	7
● Il Rosso dell'Abazia '96	🍸🍸🍸	7
● Il Rosso dell'Abazia '95	🍸🍸🍸	7
● Il Rosso dell'Abazia '94	🍸🍸🍸	7

F.lli Speri

LOC. PEDEMONTE
VIA FONTANA, 14
37020 SAN PIETRO IN CARIANO [VR]
TEL. 0457701154
www.speri.com

ANNUAL PRODUCTION	350,000 bottles
HECTARES UNDER VINE	60
VITICULTURE METHOD	Conventional

There are still corners of rare beauty in Valpolicella, where vines, olives and cherry trees adorn the landscape. Monte Sant'Urbano is one such place, where hills meet plains and vines sprawl across the sinuous slopes. The Speri family's Amarone produced here has always been one of the most stylish. The 2004 version seems to hint at a more modern style than in the past, but without going too far. It delivers well-defined aromas of cherries and herbs and a rounded, powerful yet subtle palate that signs off with a thrillingly long-lingering finish that earned it Three Glasses. The Ripasso 2006 made a big impression. This authentic territory-dedicated wine refuses to play second fiddle to the Amarone but instead maintains a personality of its own: acidic, taut, complex and stylishly drinkable. The Valpolicella Sant'Urbano 2005 is promising but still very young and needs more time in glass, giving vibrant fruit and still alcoholic aromas that introduce a slender, supple and drinkable palate. The Recioto La Roggia 2005 is good while the standard-label Valpolicella is mouthwatering and nicely gutsy.

I Stefanini

VIA CROSARA, 21
37032 MONTEFORTE D'ALPONE [VR]
TEL. 0456175249
tessari.francesco@genie.it

ANNUAL PRODUCTION	40,000 bottles
HECTARES UNDER VINE	20
VITICULTURE METHOD	Conventional

Francesco Tessari is a genuine sort and his wines reflect this, which is probably why people like them. He makes three Soaves: Il Selese, from the vineyards on the alluvial plain at the floor of Val d'Alpone, Monte de Toni and Monte di Fice. The last two take their names from two vineyards on Monte Tenda at two different altitudes, Fice being higher while Toni is halfway up. Both are on volcanic soil but the composition is different: one type is reddish in colour, the other black. In running this family estate, Francesco does his best to enhance the excellent quality of these grapes and highlight their differences in terms of terroir. He achieves this end in part through very careful, non-invasive cellar procedures, giving the wines space to find full expression in the context of their growing year. The Selese 2007 is husky and mineral with mouthfilling structure while the extremely complex, subtle Fice 2006 is a hefty white with excellent personality and a supple, racy palate. We'll have to wait till next year for the Monte de Toni.

● Amarone della Valpolicella Cl. Vign. Monte Sant'Urbano '04	♟♟♟ 8
● Valpolicella Cl. Sup. Ripasso '06	♟♟ 5
● Valpolicella Cl. Sup. Sant'Urbano '05	♟♟ 5
● Recioto della Valpolicella Cl. La Roggia '05	♟♟ 7
● Valpolicella Cl. '07	♟ 4
● Amarone della Valpolicella Cl. Vign. Monte Sant'Urbano '01	♟♟♟ 8
● Amarone della Valpolicella Cl. Vign. Monte Sant'Urbano '00	♟♟♟ 8
● Amarone della Valpolicella Cl. Vign. Monte Sant'Urbano '97	♟♟♟ 8
● Amarone della Valpolicella Cl. Vign. Monte Sant'Urbano '95	♟♟♟ 8
● Amarone della Valpolicella Cl. Vign. Monte Sant'Urbano '90	♟♟♟ 6

○ Soave Cl. Sup. Monte di Fice '06	♟♟ 3*
○ Soave Il Selese '07	♟♟ 2*
○ Togo Rosso Passito '06	♟ 4
○ Soave Cl. Monte de Toni '06	♟♟ 3
○ Soave Il Selese '06	♟♟ 3
○ Soave Il Selese '05	♟♟ 3

Suavia

FRAZ. FITTÀ DI SOAVE
VIA CENTRO, 14
37038 SOAVE [VR]
TEL. 0457675089
www.suavia.it

ANNUAL PRODUCTION	100,000 bottles
HECTARES UNDER VINE	12
VITICULTURE METHOD	Conventional

Ten harvests on, with Meri and Valentina now permanently on the winery team, Suavia has become synonymous with Soave, as its name suggests. It is also emblematic of authenticity, thanks to the family's passion for their vineyards and the black basalt hills in which this small winery is unobtrusively set. Attention focuses first on the vineyard and then the cellar, which releases just four wines that have something to say about all the facets of garganega's character, in the Tessari family's interpretation. Let's start with the Soave Classico 2007. You won't find light, uncomplicated sensations for it delivers characterful aromatics and a savoury, gutsy palate. Next up is Monte Carbonare. While the name might suggest deep, sulphuric, minerally sensations from the lava that forms the vineyard's subsoil, the 2007 growing year has made it warmer and more buttery than past versions, without reducing pressure in the mouth, a performance that won it Three Glasses. The Rive 2006 is rounded and sunny with unusual finesse and a lingering, juicy palate, while the Recioto di Soave Acinatium 2005 has distinct florality and spiciness.

Tamellini

VIA TAMELLINI, 4
37038 SOAVE [VR]
TEL. 0457675328
piofrancesco.tamellini@tin.it

ANNUAL PRODUCTION	160,000 bottles
HECTARES UNDER VINE	17
VITICULTURE METHOD	Conventional

The Tamellinis were long-standing growers for the Cantina Sociale di Soave, before the turning point of 1998. They decided to bottle their own wines and go for quality in a DOC that was reclaiming a leading position in Italian wine. Gaetano and Piofrancesco's vineyards are split between Costeggiola, in the Classico zone, and San Vittore. The volcanic, chalky soil provides wonderful growing conditions. Meanwhile work on the cellar is nearing completion. It's a crucial ingredient in the recipe for good results, which have not been long in coming at what is now one of the best wineries round here. Proof came in our impressive retasting of the 2004, 2002 and 2001 vintages of Soave Le Bine de Costjola. The 2006, which we are assessing this year, is on dazzling form. The golden colour introduces florality and apple, peach and pineapple fruit followed by a sumptuous yet fresh and remarkably moreish palate, which earned it Three Glasses. The lustrous amber Recioto 2004 is even more generous, giving subtle, lusciously vibrant perceptions. The standard-label Soave is one of the best in its category, a dry, gutsy and beautifully harmonious wine.

O Soave Cl. Monte Carbonare '07	▼▼▼	4*
O Recioto di Soave Acinatium '05	▼▼	6
O Soave Cl. Le Rive '06	▼▼	5
O Soave Cl. '07	▼▼	4*
O Soave Cl. Le Rive '02	♀♀♀	5
O Soave Cl. Sup. Le Rive '00	♀♀♀	5
O Soave Cl. Sup. Le Rive '98	♀♀♀	5
O Soave Cl. Monte Carbonare '06	♀♀♀	4
O Soave Cl. Monte Carbonare '05	♀♀♀	4
O Soave Cl. Monte Carbonare '04	♀♀♀	4
O Soave Cl. Monte Carbonare '02	♀♀♀	4
O Recioto di Soave Acinatium '04	♀♀	6
O Recioto di Soave Acinatium '03	♀♀	6
O Soave Cl. Le Rive '05	♀♀	5

O Soave Cl. Le Bine de Costjola '06	▼▼▼	4*
O Recioto di Soave V. Marogne '04	▼▼	6
O Soave '07	▼▼	4*
O Soave Cl. Le Bine '04	♀♀♀	4
O Soave Cl. Le Bine de Costjola '05	♀♀♀	4
O Soave '06	♀♀	4
O Soave '05	♀♀	4
O Soave Cl. Le Bine '03	♀♀	5
O Soave Cl. Le Bine '02	♀♀	5
O Recioto di Soave V. Marogne '03	♀♀	6
O Recioto di Soave V. Marogne '02	♀♀	6
O Recioto di Soave V. Marogne '01	♀♀	5
O Recioto di Soave V. Marogne '00	♀♀	5

Giovanna Tantini

LOC. OLIOSI
VIA GOITO, 10
37014 CASTELNUOVO DEL GARDA [VR]
TEL. 0457575070
www.giovannatantini.it

ANNUAL PRODUCTION	20,000 bottles
HECTARES UNDER VINE	11.5
VITICULTURE METHOD	Conventional

The south of Lake Garda is one of the most interesting areas for Bardolino. This fresh red wine, made primarily from corvina and rondinella, mirrors the imposing labels produced with the same grapes just a few kilometres to the east in Valpolicella. Giovanna Tantini has forged ahead in her short career as a grower and today, with the help of Federico Curtaz in the vineyard and Attilio Pagli and Laura Zuddas in the cellar, she produces some of the most captivating wines in the DOC, wines that also have good ageing prospects. There are only three products but they are all good, starting with the fragrant, floral Chiaretto with its nicely tangy palate. Even more impressive is the Bardolino, which is also the estate's workhorse. Made from corvina and rondinella with a little merlot, it delivers delicious spice alongside red berries on the nose followed by a rounded palate that reflects the light, simple features of the type. Finally, Ettore 2006 is from corvina with small additions of cabernet and merlot, all part-dried, and proffers vibrant aromas of wild berries and mint prefacing the taut, mouthwateringly drinkable palate.

● Bardolino '07	♥♥	4*
● Ettore '06	♥♥	5
☉ Bardolino Chiaretto '07	♥	4
● Bardolino '06	♀♀	4
● Ettore '05	♀♀	7
● Ettore '03	♀♀	5

F.lli Tedeschi

LOC. PEDEMONTE
VIA G. VERDI, 4
37029 SAN PIETRO IN CARIANO [VR]
TEL. 0457701487
www.tedeschiwines.com

ANNUAL PRODUCTION	500,000 bottles
HECTARES UNDER VINE	35
VITICULTURE METHOD	Conventional

The Tedeschis have bought five hectares at Le Pontare, in Sant'Ambrogio, in the upper Classico zone, where the first harvest was last September, and another 30 hectares out of a total of 84 at the Tenuta Maternigo in Tregnago and Mezzane di Sotto. There's also news about the wines. Rosso La Fabriseria, now without its distinctive dash of cabernet, has entered the Valpolicella DOC with lots of fruit and good grip. The everyday Lucchine has good texture and a tidy palate while Capitel dei Nicalò has fragrant, ripe fruit aromas and a good, solid, gutsy palate in the winery style. Capitel San Rocco, which aged in Slavonian oak for two years, has a sweetly inviting character and a well-rounded, expressive palate. The Amarone Classico has a generous nose with hints of its corvina grapes supported by all the traditional varieties, and a sweet deep finish. The Amarone Monte Olmi 2004 comes from a single vineyard of two and a half hectares and aged in large barrels. It delivers pervasive sensations of Alpine herbs and red berries, followed by a very rounded, firm-bodied palate whose exuberance is held in check by acidity and extract.

● Amarone della Valpolicella Cl. Capitel Monte Olmi '04	♥♥	8
● Amarone della Valpolicella Cl. '04	♥♥	6
● Valpolicella Cl. Sup. Capitel dei Nicalò '06	♥♥	4*
● Valpolicella Cl. Sup. La Fabriseria '06	♥♥	6
● Valpolicella Sup. Capitel San Rocco Ripasso '06	♥♥	5
● Valpolicella Cl. Lucchine '07	♥	3
● Amarone della Valpolicella Cl. Capitel Monte Olmi '01	♀♀♀	8
● Amarone della Valpolicella Cl. Capitel Monte Olmi '99	♀♀♀	8
● Amarone della Valpolicella Cl. Capitel Monte Olmi '97	♀♀♀	8
● Amarone della Valpolicella Cl. Capitel Monte Olmi '95	♀♀♀	8

Viticoltori Tommasi

LOC. PEDEMONTE
VIA RONCHETTO, 2
37020 SAN PIETRO IN CARIANO [VR]
TEL. 0457701266
www.tommasiwine.it

ANNUAL PRODUCTION	900,000 bottles
HECTARES UNDER VINE	165
VITICULTURE METHOD	Conventional

If you look at the production of close to 1,000,000 bottles per year, Tommasi might appear to be a large bottler but this family estate has very extensive vineyards where it grows the grapes for its wines. The winery style for Valpolicella reds is very traditional, with prolonged drying and the use of large barrels endows the wines with a mature, intriguing profile. Some of the labels, though, are more modern in style like Crearo della Conca d'Oro 2006, an original blend of lightly dried corvina, oseleta and cabernet franc aged in small wood. The vibrant aromas of wild berries are streaked through with aromatic herbs and spices while on the generous palate the oseleta lends the right level of tannin and keeps the wine on its rigorous track. The 2004 Amarones are more mature and mouthfilling, with the Ca' Florian particularly enjoyable with its dried-grape aromas. The Valpolicella 2006 is coming along, like the full, powerful Ripasso, while the Rafael has approachable aromas and a very pleasant palate.

Trabucchi

LOC. MONTE TENDA
37031 ILLASI [VR]
TEL. 0457833233
www.trabucchivini.it

ANNUAL PRODUCTION	70,000 bottles
HECTARES UNDER VINE	25
VITICULTURE METHOD	Certified organic

Giuseppe and Raffaella Trabucchi's splendid estate, overlooking Val Tramigna a few steps away from the castle of Illasi, comprises more than 20 hectares of completely organic vineyards using pergola and vertical trellis training systems. The range of wines presented is faithful to the designation and reflects tradition and local area. Results are outstanding. In recent years, the wines have acquired a fuller, more structured style, losing a touch of finesse in favour of greater strength and weight on the palate. This is the style of the Amarone 2004, which delivers generous stewed red fruit sensations with aromatic herbs and spices. The palate is remarkably powerful but the wine is still rigorous and nicely harmonious, so it won Three well-textured Glasses. Valpolicella Terre del Cereolo is excellent, giving depth, blueberry and cyclamen aromas and plenty of texture and acidic grip on the savoury palate. The new Valpolicella Dandarin, again from 2004, is also sound with simpler aromas and palate. Finally, the Recioto 2005 is fruity and manages its exuberant sweetness very well.

Wine	Rating
● Crearo della Conca d'Oro '06	♥♥ 5
● Amarone della Valpolicella Cl. '04	♥♥ 7
● Amarone della Valpolicella Cl. Ca' Florian '04	♥♥ 7
● Valpolicella Cl. Sup. Ripasso '06	♥♥ 5
● Valpolicella Cl. Sup. Vign. Rafael '06	♥♥ 5
○ Lugana Vign. San Martino Il Sestante '07	♥ 4
● Amarone della Valpolicella Cl. Monte Masua Il Sestante '03	♥♥ 8
● Amarone della Valpolicella Cl. Monte Masua Il Sestante '01	♥♥ 8
● Crearo della Conca d'Oro '04	♥♥ 5
● Crearo della Conca d'Oro '05	♥♥ 5
● Valpolicella Cl. Sup. Vign. Rafael '05	♥♥ 5

Wine	Rating
● Amarone della Valpolicella '04	♥♥♥ 8
● Valpolicella Sup. Terre del Cereolo '04	♥♥ 6
● Recioto della Valpolicella '05	♥♥ 8
○ Recioto di Soave '05	♥♥ 7
● Valpolicella Sup. Dandarin '04	♥♥ 5
● Valpolicella Sup. Terre di S. Colombano '03	♥♥♥ 5
● Amarone della Valpolicella '03	♥♥ 8
● Amarone della Valpolicella '01	♥♥ 8
● Amarone della Valpolicella '00	♥♥ 7
● Amarone della Valpolicella '99	♥♥ 7
● Valpolicella Sup. Terre del Cereolo '03	♥♥ 6
● Valpolicella Sup. Terre di S. Colombano '04	♥♥ 7

Cantina Sociale della Valpantena

FRAZ. QUINTO
VIA COLONIA ORFANI DI GUERRA, 5B
37034 VERONA
TEL. 045550032
www.cantinavalpantena.it

ANNUAL PRODUCTION	7,000,000 bottles
HECTARES UNDER VINE	N.A.
VITICULTURE METHOD	Conventional

The features that have made the wines of Valpolicella great are often limits for many enthusiasts, like high alcohol content, residual sugar and the seemingly intrusive acidity inherent to traditional grape varieties. Luca Degani has become the craftsman of a tamer style and today the wines of Cantina della Valpantena are the epitome of approachability, if perhaps a little predictable, and dependably good value for money. Valpolicella Torre del Falasco 2006 delivers aromas that recall the Amarone without reaching the same muscular strength. It's fruity with a well-rounded palate. Its partner Ripasso, on the other hand, delivers a fainter bouquet that is slower to emerge and follows this with a dry, attractively harmonious palate. The uncomplicated Valpantena Ritocco 2006 is also dependably good and very enjoyable. Our favourite Amarone was the Torre del Falasco 2004 with aromatic herbs alongside the fruit and spices, whereas the 2005 is lighter and more fragrant. The simpler wines are also good: Corvina, Garganega and Lugana Torre del Falasco are all uncomplicated with approachable aromatics and palates.

Cantina Sociale Valpolicella

VIA CA' SALGARI, 2
37024 NEGRAR [VR]
TEL. 0456014300
www.cantinanegrar.it

ANNUAL PRODUCTION	7,500,000 bottles
HECTARES UNDER VINE	500
VITICULTURE METHOD	Conventional

The Negrar co-operative winery presents the products of its leading line, Domini Veneti, which has embraced a modern style. Aromas are clearly defined, body is powerful body and the tannic weave is close-knit. While these choices have yielded excellent results in recent vintages, this year has seen a further thrust in this direction, bringing the wines even more imposing concentration at the cost of lightness, elegance and grip. The 2004 version of the Valpolicella La Casetta, which has always been the winery's most representative product, is emblematic. Its inky-black hue heralds fruit-led aromas with hints of dried grapes that are picked up on the weighty, alcohol-rich palate. The Valpolicella Verjago 2005 delivers lovely red berries over upfront oaky sensations while the palate is dry and austere. The most arresting wine is the Recioto Vigneti di Moron 2005, with its almost joyfully intoxicating explosion of fruitiness and richly sweet but very drinkable palate. The Soave Ca' de Napa 2007 put on an excellent performance.

● Amarone della Valpolicella Torre del Falasco '04	▼▼ 7
● Recioto della Valpolicella Tesauro '05	▼▼ 6
● Recioto della Valpolicella Valpantena '06	▼▼ 6
● Valpantena Ritocco '06	▼▼ 4*
● Valpolicella Sup. Torre del Falasco '06	▼▼ 4*
● Amarone della Valpolicella '05	▼ 6
● Corvina Torre del Falasco '07	▼ 2
● Valpolicella Sup. Ripasso Torre del Falasco '06	▼ 4
○ Garganega Torre del Falasco '07	▼ 2
○ Lugana Torre del Falasco '07	▼ 4
○ Chardonnay Baroncino '07	3
● Valpolicella Sup. Torre del Falasco '05	♈♈ 4

● Recioto della Valpolicella Cl. Vign. di Moron Domini Veneti '05	▼▼ 6
● Recioto della Valpolicella Cl. Domini Veneti '06	▼▼ 5
● Valpolicella Cl. Sup. La Casetta di Ettore Righetti Domini Veneti '04	▼▼ 5
○ Soave Cl. Vign. di Ca' de Napa Domini Veneti '07	▼▼ 4
● Amarone della Valpolicella Cl. Domini Veneti '04	▼ 6
● Valpolicella Cl. Sup. Verjago Domini Veneti '05	▼ 5
● Valpolicella Cl. Sup. Vign. di Torbe Domini Veneti '05	▼ 4
● Recioto della Valpolicella Cl. Vigneti di Moron Domini Veneti '01	♈♈♈ 6
● Valpolicella Cl. Sup. Verjago Domini Veneti '04	♈♈ 5

Massimino Venturini

FRAZ. SAN FLORIANO
VIA SEMONTE, 20
37020 SAN PIETRO IN CARIANO [VR]
TEL. 0457701331
www.viniventurini.com

ANNUAL PRODUCTION	90,000 bottles
HECTARES UNDER VINE	12
VITICULTURE METHOD	Conventional

In the world of wine, there is no room for distraction. Wines and estates that fail to maintain constant quality, value or typicality will be left by the wayside. Brothers Daniele and Mirco Venturini, helmsmen of the family ship for years, know this and work constantly to improve their products. As they are every year, the two Amarones are on top form. Look past the oak, still rather prominent, and the Classico 2004 gives lovely fruit streaked with aromatic herbs and spices. It's a solid, dry and beautifully rigorous wine. The Campomasua 2003 delivers more dried grape aromas with hints of jam and bitter chocolate although the gutsy palate again avoids sugary softness. We are happy to announce a great leap forward by Semonte Alto 2004, a Valpolicella made with the ripasso technique that gives cherries and flowers on the nose and a generous yet supple and mouthwateringly drinkable palate. Just what you want in a Valpolicella. In the absence of Le Brugnine, we enjoyed a very good Recioto 2005, simpler and accessible in style, and the standard-label Valpolicella is as dependable as ever.

Agostino Vicentini

FRAZ. SAN ZENO
VIA C. BATTISTI, 62C
37030 COLOGNOLA AI COLLI [VR]
TEL. 0457650539
vicentiniagostino@libero.it

ANNUAL PRODUCTION	60,000 bottles
HECTARES UNDER VINE	14
VITICULTURE METHOD	Conventional

The fact that Teresa and Agostino Vicentini's winery is gaining recognition from market and critics is due to the determination with which they have pursued their objective of making a great Soave outside the Classico zone. Expertise and care are as undeniably important as the quality of the local soil, and this couple certainly do not underestimate these features. Production is split between Soaves and Valpolicellas made entirely from estate-grown grapes and organized into a well-balanced, good-quality range. The wine that most impressed our tasting panels was the Soave Il Casale 2007, which embodies all Agostino's skill at bringing out the husky qualities of the garganega grape. Apples, vegetality and flowers mingle with evolving mineral sensations that will open out with time. Excellent concentration and strength on the dry, very lingering palate enabled this wine to pick up its first Three Glass prize. Terre Lunghe is fresher and suppler on the palate while from the reds we recommend the well-made Bacco 2005, with its complex nose and mouthwatering palate.

● Amarone della Valpolicella Cl. '04	♟♟	6
● Amarone della Valpolicella Cl. Campomasua '03	♟♟	7
● Recioto della Valpolicella Cl. '05	♟♟	5
● Valpolicella Cl. Sup. Ripasso Semonte Alto '04	♟♟	4*
● Valpolicella Cl. '07	♟	3
● Recioto della Valpolicella Cl. Le Brugnine '97	♟♟♟	6
● Amarone della Valpolicella Cl. '03	♟♟	6
● Amarone della Valpolicella Cl. '01	♟♟	6
● Amarone della Valpolicella Cl. '00	♟♟	7
● Amarone della Valpolicella Cl. '99	♟♟	7
● Amarone della Valpolicella Cl. Campomasua '01	♟♟	7
● Amarone della Valpolicella Cl. Campomasua '00	♟♟	7

○ Soave Sup. Il Casale '07	♟♟♟	5
○ Soave Vign. Terre Lunghe '07	♟♟	3*
● Valpolicella Sup. Selezione Bacco '05	♟♟	5
● Valpolicella Vign. Boccascalucce '06	♟	3
○ Recioto di Soave '06	♟♟	6
○ Soave Sup. Il Casale '06	♟♟	5
○ Soave Vign. Terre Lunghe '06	♟♟	3
○ Soave Vign. Terre Lunghe '05	♟♟	3
○ Soave Vign. Terre Lunghe '04	♟♟	3

Vignale di Cecilia

LOC. FORNACI
VIA CROCI, 14
35030 BAONE [PD]
TEL. 042951420
www.vignaledicecilia.it

ANNUAL PRODUCTION   25,000 bottles
HECTARES UNDER VINE   8
VITICULTURE METHOD   Conventional

The immediate impression on visiting this winery is of a people-friendly environment. The estate's four hectares of vineyards surround the small, well cared-for winery like an amphitheatre, with the adjacent house forming a single unit. Most of the vine stock comprises red varieties, with the exception of moscato used for the production of the Folìa, a dried-grape wine. Recently, the winery has rented another four hectares a few kilometres away, where garganega and moscato are grown for use in the white Benavides. The volcanic soil has a strong effect on the character of the wines produced here. This year, the estate's most ambitious wine, Passacaglia, a red fermented and aged in oak, was not released so the standard was held high this year by the simpler Covolo 2006, based on merlot and cabernet aged mainly in concrete vats. Its elegant, very drinkable palate's dry, fresh progression consoled us in the absence of its elder brother. Also light and accessible is the 2007 Benavides, which gives subtle florality and a lovely, tangy palate.

Vignalta

FRAZ. LUVIGLIANO
VIA DEI VESCOVI, 5
35038 TORREGLIA [PD]
TEL. 0499933105
www.vignalta.it

ANNUAL PRODUCTION   250,000 bottles
HECTARES UNDER VINE   55
VITICULTURE METHOD   Conventional

For years, Vignalta has turned out consistently high quality. This time, we found a new wine, less of a response to market demands than an echo of the versatile Colli Euganei terroir. The wine is named Arquà, after the location near the winery where the vineyards stand on soil liberally sprinkled with white and red stones. The grapes, mainly merlot, are made into a very concentrated wine that is still sun-fresh, juicy and powerful, contrasting with Gemola, all elegance and grip. Arquà's debut in the 2004 version is magnificent and it impressed us with enough strength and texture to cross the Three Glasses threshold. Alpianae is also extraordinary. A dried-grape Fior d'Arancio benefiting from the excellent vintage of 2006, it delivers vibrant, complex aromas with perfectly blended sweetness and a beautifully tangy palate. The rest of the range is consistently high quality, starting with the high profile Rosso Riserva 2005, which was just a step away from our final tastings, the rounded, mouthwatering Agno Tinto 2006 and the fresh, rangy Sirio 2007. The Agno Casto and Pinot Bianco from 2007 are dependable, well-textured whites.

O Benavides '07	♙♙	4*
O Colli Euganei Folìa '06	♙♙	5
● Colli Euganei Rosso Covolo '06	♙♙	4*
● Colli Euganei Rosso Covolo '05	♙♙	4
● Colli Euganei Rosso Passacaglia '04	♙♙	5
● Colli Euganei Rosso Passacaglia '03	♙♙	5
● Colli Euganei Rosso Passacaglia '02	♙♙	5
● Colli Euganei Rosso Passacaglia '01	♙♙	5

● Colli Euganei Rosso Arquà '04	♙♙♙	6
O Colli Euganei Fior d'Arancio Passito Alpianae '06	♙♙	5
O Colli Euganei Pinot Bianco '07	♙♙	4*
O Colli Euganei Pinot Bianco Agno Casto '07	♙♙	5
O Sirio '07	♙♙	4*
● Agno Tinto '06	♙♙	6
● Colli Euganei Rosso Ris. '05	♙♙	4*
● Il Nero '06	♙♙	6
● Colli Euganei Rosso Venda '06	♙	4
O Colli Euganei Moscato '07	♙	4
● Colli Euganei Rosso Gemola '01	♙♙♙	6
● Colli Euganei Rosso Gemola '00	♙♙♙	6
● Colli Euganei Rosso Gemola '99	♙♙♙	6
● Colli Euganei Rosso Gemola '98	♙♙♙	6
● Colli Euganei Rosso Gemola '97	♙♙♙	7

Le Vigne di San Pietro

VIA S. PIETRO, 23
37066 SOMMACAMPAGNA [VR]
TEL. 045510016
www.levignedisanpietro.it

ANNUAL PRODUCTION	80,000 bottles
HECTARES UNDER VINE	20
VITICULTURE METHOD	Conventional

By now, we are used to Carlo Nerozzi's choices, driven by his ability to interpret his estate and its terroir. His partnership with Giovanni Boscaini is not restricted to expanding the vine stock in the highly favourable wine country of Valpolicella. It has also given him an opportunity to learn and growth in full respect of the winery's philosophy of making elegant, light, distinctive wines. The process has been helped along by Federico Giotto, a winemaker of outstanding sensitivity. The Solocorvina 2006 provides a glowing example of where corvina-based wines can go the Garda area, turning simplicity into a virtue. The Refolà 2004, a part-dried cabernet sauvignon, is powerful and mature yet also fresh and juicy. Its beautiful harmony and length earned Three Glasses. The very enjoyable Due Cuori Passito 2006 is from moscato giallo grapes. Intriguing and aromatic, it has supporting acidity to offset its sweetness nicely. The CorDeRosa 2007, a corvina-based rosé, is a paragon of relaxed personality while the standard-label Valpolicella and the Riesling Renano 2004 are both more than just good.

Vigneto Due Santi

V.LE ASIAGO, 174
36061 BASSANO DEL GRAPPA [VI]
TEL. 0424502074
vignetoduesanti@virgilio.it

ANNUAL PRODUCTION	100,000 bottles
HECTARES UNDER VINE	18
VITICULTURE METHOD	Conventional

The indefatigable, award-winning Zontas, Stefano and Adriano, have hit the bull's eye again with Torcolato, a golden, alluringly sun-kissed wine that gives honey, dates and figs with apricot jam. The classic products include another exciting performance from Cabernet Vigneto Due Santi, one of the best reds in Veneto. Thanks in part to the excellent 2006 harvest, this is a reserved wine that opens out almost reluctantly into elegant aromas of spring herbs, violets, ink, blackcurrants and chocolate. The palate is fresh and generously fruity with fine-grained tannins. The basic Cabernet reels off an outstanding showing that opens on red berry fruit, cherries and spices followed by good body with compact tannins. The Breganze Rosso, a monovarietal Merlot, reveals forest floor, mushrooms and flowers, followed by varietal aromas of blackberries and plums that lead into an enjoyably lingering finish. The whites battle it out as only they know how. Breganze Bianco is an appetizing, vibrant and full-bodied Tocai while Malvasia Campo di Fiori is delightfully aromatic. The Sauvignon has a noteworthy hint of delicate yellow plums. The Prosecco is fragrant.

● Refolà Cabernet Sauvignon '04	♟♟♟	7
● Solocorvina '06	♟♟	3*
○ Due Cuori Passito '06	♟♟	6
○ Riesling Renano '04	♟♟	4*
☉ CorDeRosa '07	♟♟	4*
● Valpolicella '07	♟♟	4*
○ Custoza '07	♟	4
○ Sud '95	♟♟♟	7
● I Balconi Rossi '04	♟♟	6
● I Balconi Rossi '03	♟♟	6
● Refolà Cabernet Sauvignon '03	♟♟	7
● Refolà Cabernet Sauvignon '01	♟♟	7
● Refolà Cabernet Sauvignon '00	♟♟	7
○ Sanpietro '04	♟♟	4

● Breganze Cabernet Vign. Due Santi '06	♟♟	5
● Breganze Cabernet '06	♟♟	4*
● Breganze Rosso '06	♟♟	4*
○ Breganze Bianco Rivana '07	♟♟	4*
○ Breganze Sauvignon Vign. Due Santi '07	♟♟	4*
○ Breganze Torcolato '04	♟♟	6
○ Malvasia Campo di Fiori '07	♟♟	4*
○ Prosecco Extra Dry	♟	4
● Breganze Cabernet Vign. Due Santi '05	♟♟♟	5
● Breganze Cabernet Vign. Due Santi '04	♟♟♟	5
● Breganze Cabernet Vign. Due Santi '03	♟♟♟	5
● Breganze Cabernet Vign. Due Santi '00	♟♟♟	5

Villa Bellini

LOC. CASTELROTTO DI NEGARINE
VIA DEI FRACCAROLI, 6
37020 SAN PIETRO IN CARIANO [VR]
TEL. 0457725630
www.villabellini.com

ANNUAL PRODUCTION	10,000 bottles
HECTARES UNDER VINE	3
VITICULTURE METHOD	Certified organic

Two distinctive and very different production styles are emerging in Valpolicella. On the one hand, some producers go for massive concentration and rich texture by reducing yields in the vineyard and adopting more or less lengthy drying inspired by a Bordeaux style. Others hew to a more scrupulous quest for lightness, aiming for greater finesse and respect for the typical features of the classic local grape varieties, with a nod to Burgundy. Cecilia Trucchi is without doubt one of the latter group, and credit goes to her for pursuing this route even when it was less widely acknowledged. This year's tasting of her two wines, Recioto and Valpolicella Il Taso, reveal them to be a significant step closer to the wine concept that Villa Bellini subscribes. The Recioto Uva Passa 2006 has nice mature colour and a subtle, deep yet elegant nose. The sugar is nicely balanced on the palate by a dry finish that suggests a further period of bottle ageing might be a useful step towards perfection. The elegant Taso 2005 is very drinkable and reveals a strong personality.

Villa Monteleone

FRAZ. GARGAGNAGO
VIA MONTELEONE, 12
37020 SANT'AMBROGIO DI VALPOLICELLA [VR]
TEL. 0457704974
www.villamonteleone.com

ANNUAL PRODUCTION	40,000 bottles
HECTARES UNDER VINE	7
VITICULTURE METHOD	Conventional

Despite having very few wineries, Sant'Ambrogio is one of the most interesting areas of Valpolicella, with the top producers competing for quality vineyards, not least because nearby Valdadige brings fresh air in from the north. This is the area where Lucia Duran runs her winery. Lucia is just the person to carry on the work of Professor Raimondi, who believed so strongly in Gargagnago and its slopes. The range is kept to a bare minimum, with no frills, based entirely on the classic Valpolicella types. The standard-label Valpolicella, Santa Lena, delivers fresh fruit and a relaxed, drinkable palate while the Valpolicella Superiore, Campo San Vito 2006, achieves considerable concentration and complexity without compromising its subtle profile, marked by the trademark acidity found in the traditional local grapes. The nose is complex, the palate dry. The Amarone 2004 has good texture, well-defined black berry and floral aromas and a tangy, beautifully light palate. Finally, Pal Sun 2005 is a fragrant Recioto with beautifully integrated sweetness. This is an exemplary range of products with few rivals in terms of continuity and tradition.

● Recioto della Valpolicella Cl. Uva Passa '06	▼▼ 7
● Valpolicella Cl. Sup. Il Taso '05	▼▼ 6
● Recioto della Valpolicella Cl. Uva Passa '04	♈♈ 7
● Valpolicella Cl. Sup. Il Taso '04	♈♈ 6
● Valpolicella Cl. Sup. Il Taso '03	♈♈ 5
● Valpolicella Cl. Sup. Il Taso '02	♈♈ 4
● Valpolicella Cl. Sup. Il Taso '01	♈♈ 4

● Amarone della Valpolicella Cl. '04	▼▼ 8
● Valpolicella Cl. Sup. Campo S. Vito Ripasso '06	▼▼ 5
● Recioto della Valpolicella Cl. Pal Sun '05	▼▼ 6
● Valpolicella Cl. Campo S. Lena '07	▼ 4
● Amarone della Valpolicella Cl. '03	♈♈ 8
● Amarone della Valpolicella Cl. '01	♈♈ 8
● Amarone della Valpolicella Cl. '00	♈♈ 8
● Amarone della Valpolicella Cl. '99	♈♈ 8
● Amarone della Valpolicella Cl. Campo S. Paolo '01	♈♈ 8
● Valpolicella Cl. Sup. Campo S. Vito '04	♈♈ 5

Villa Spinosa

LOC. JAGO
37024 NEGRAR [VR]
TEL. 0457500093
www.villaspinosa.it

ANNUAL PRODUCTION	35,000 bottles
HECTARES UNDER VINE	18
VITICULTURE METHOD	Conventional

Negrar is well-known for two different reasons. On the one hand is the well-deserved fame of its sumptuous Amarone and Recioto, and on the other the equally justified notoriety for the way this area has been built up. These brutal attacks on local agriculture have even coined a neologism, "negrarizzazione", for this kind of defacement of the landscape. As we follow the hill up towards Jago, it is almost a surprise to find a little unspoilt nature, where vineyards alternate with cherry trees and olive groves. Then we glimpse Villa Spinosa, the winery so passionately and expertly managed by Enrico Cascella. Only traditional Valpolicella wines are produced here with none of the more imaginative wines that flourish locally. Two Amarones were presented this year, both well-made and nicely balanced. The Guglielmi di Jago, released after an incredible ten years' ageing, is complex, profound and long-lingering. The Classico 2001 is broader and silkier with a sophisticated, very drinkable palate. Finally, Valpolicella Jago 2005 is floral and fruity, a rigorous wine with the austerity typical of wines from this area.

Vigneti Villabella

FRAZ. CALMASINO
LOC. CANOVA, 2
37011 BARDOLINO [VR]
TEL. 0457236448
www.vignetivillabella.com

ANNUAL PRODUCTION	500,000 bottles
HECTARES UNDER VINE	220
VITICULTURE METHOD	Certified organic

The Villabella estate covers the province of Verona with vineyards and wines of all types. It is a joint effort by two families, Cristoforetti and Delibori, who manage the business together. Purchase of the beautiful Villa Cordevigo in 2002 launched a project that led, after remodelling of the buildings, to Villa Cordevigo Rosso. This wine is made from corvina, cabernet sauvignon and merlot and delivers fruity aromas still marked by the oak, followed by excellent body and densely woven tannins on the palate. Making its debut this year is the 2006 Villa Cordevigo white, from garganega and sauvignon. Generous and warm on both nose and palate, it unveils very firm structure at the expense of some agility and grip. The range includes a large number of Garda wines, from the mouthwatering Bardolino Terre di Cavagion to the fragrant Ca' del Lago, by way of the pleasant Chiaretto Brut. From Valpolicella, the Amarone Classico 2004 was on good form and very pleasantly drinkable. Last but not least, Passito Fiordilej 2005 proffers delicious dried flowers, candied fruit and liquorice on the nose, with a sweet, alluring palate.

● Amarone della Valpolicella Cl. '01	♟♟ 7
● Amarone della Valpolicella Cl. Guglielmi di Jago '98	♟♟ 8
● Valpolicella Cl. Sup. Ripasso Jago '05	♟♟ 4*
● Amarone della Valpolicella Cl. '00	♟♟ 7
● Amarone della Valpolicella Cl. '99	♟♟ 7
● Amarone della Valpolicella Cl. '98	♟♟ 8
● Valpolicella Cl. Sup. Jago '03	♟♟ 5

○ Fiordilej '05	♟♟ 4*
○ Lugana Ca' del Lago '07	♟♟ 4*
○ Villa Cordevigo Bianco '06	♟♟ 5
● Villa Cordevigo Rosso '04	♟♟ 6
● Amarone della Valpolicella Cl. '04	♟ 6
⊙ Bardolino Chiaretto Cl. Pozzo dell'Amore '07	♟ 4
⊙ Bardolino Chiaretto Cl. Brut	♟ 4
● Bardolino Cl. Sup. Terre di Cavagion '06	♟ 4
● Bardolino Cl. V. Morlongo '07	♟ 4
● Montemazzano Rosso '05	♟ 4
● Valpolicella Cl. I Roccoli '07	♟ 4
● Valpolicella Cl. Sup. Ripasso '05	♟ 4
○ Bianco di Custoza Fiordaliso '07	♟ 3
○ Soave Cl. La Torretta '07	♟ 4
○ Pinot Grigio V. di Pesina '07	4

Viviani

LOC. MAZZANO
VIA MAZZANO, 8
37020 NEGRAR [VR]
TEL. 0457500286
www.cantinaviviani.com

ANNUAL PRODUCTION   70,000 bottles
HECTARES UNDER VINE   10
VITICULTURE METHOD   Conventional

Conversations with Claudio Viviani are always interesting, covering all aspects of wine and winemaking. Valpolicella's own Hamlet is a restless but confident manager of one of the most prestigious estates in the DOC, at 400 metres in the famous Mazzano vineyard in the upper Negrar valley. Claudio presented three wines this year, each better than the last, so let's begin with a spectacular Valpolicella Campo Morar from 2005, with aromas of violets that lead into herbs, leaves, vanilla and spice. The palate is dominated by juicy cherry fruit with plums, rhubarb and chocolate, sweet tannins and a long finish. Three fully deserved Glasses. The Amarone Casa dei Bepi 2003 is a wonderful response to such a tricky vintage year. First, it has a fresh, extremely drinkable palate but there are hints of tree bark, blackberries, walnutskin and cocoa powder as well as beautiful balance in the intense finish. The Recioto 2005 is overwhelming, showing purplish, velvety and mouthfilling as the countryside after a rainstorm. Profound and penetrating, it fills the palate with delicious cherry jam. This wine is delightful now and will be wonderful in 20 years.

Zenato

FRAZ. S. BENEDETTO DI LUGANA
VIA S. BENEDETTO, 8
37019 PESCHIERA DEL GARDA [VR]
TEL. 0457550300
www.zenato.it

ANNUAL PRODUCTION   1,200,000 bottles
HECTARES UNDER VINE   70
VITICULTURE METHOD   Conventional

Owner Sergio Zenato, a leading figure in the Verona winemaking, passed away recently. Everyone will miss him, starting with his family, although his children Alberto and Nadia have already shown they can carry on making full, modern wines. The Amarone 2003 named after Sergio is his legacy: well-developed, mature aromas and a sumptuously fresh, tangy palate provide a fine interpretation revealing Sergio's profound knowledge of Amarone. We dedicate the Three Glasses to the memory of a great wine man. The Amarone Classico 2004 is fresher and more modern, a fragrant bouquet giving wild berries, flowers, spices and aromatic herbs followed by a taut, gutsy palate. The Ripassa is also impressed. Recent versions of this wine have seemed a little too simple but the 2005 vintage all the pressure Valpolicella needs. Lugana is another family passion and we liked the thoroughbred Vigneto Massoni 2007, which is floral, tangy and mouthwatering. San Benedetto focuses on freshness on the supple palate while the Sergio Zenato 2006 is sumptuous. Although still a little exuberant, this wine is bound to improve with ageing.

Viviani	
● Valpolicella Cl. Sup. Campo Morar '05	▼▼▼ 6
● Amarone della Valpolicella Cl. Casa dei Bepi '03	▼▼ 8
● Recioto della Valpolicella Cl. '05	▼▼ 7
● Amarone della Valpolicella Cl. Casa dei Bepi '01	▼▼▼ 8
● Amarone della Valpolicella Cl. Casa dei Bepi '00	▼▼▼ 8
● Amarone della Valpolicella Cl. Casa dei Bepi '98	▼▼▼ 8
● Amarone della Valpolicella Cl. Casa dei Bepi '97	▼▼▼ 8
● Amarone della Valpolicella Cl. Tulipano Nero '97	▼▼▼ 8
● Valpolicella Cl. Sup. Campo Morar '01	▼▼▼ 6

Zenato	
● Amarone della Valpolicella Cl. Sergio Zenato '03	▼▼▼ 8
● Amarone della Valpolicella Cl. '04	▼▼ 7
● Valpolicella Cl. Sup. '05	▼▼ 4*
● Valpolicella Sup. Ripassa '05	▼▼ 5
○ Lugana S. Benedetto '07	▼▼ 4*
○ Lugana Sergio Zenato '06	▼▼ 5
○ Lugana Vign. Massoni Santa Cristina '07	▼▼ 4*
● Amarone della Valpolicella Cl. '97	▼▼▼ 6
● Amarone della Valpolicella Cl. Sergio Zenato '00	▼▼▼ 8
● Amarone della Valpolicella Cl. Sergio Zenato Ris. '98	▼▼▼ 8
● Amarone della Valpolicella Cl. Sergio Zenato '95	▼▼▼ 8
● Amarone della Valpolicella Cl. Sergio Zenato '01	▼▼ 8

F.lli Zeni

VIA COSTABELLA, 9
37011 BARDOLINO [VR]
TEL. 0457210022
www.zeni.it

Zymè

VIA CA' DEL PIPA, 1
37029 SAN PIETRO IN CARIANO [VR]
TEL. 0457701108
www.zyme.it

ANNUAL PRODUCTION	800,000 bottles
HECTARES UNDER VINE	25
VITICULTURE METHOD	Conventional

The winery owned by Elena, Fausto and Federica Zeni is situated at Bardolino, on the slopes framing the eastern side of the Garda basin. The winery produces a very wide range of wines from the province of Verona, catering for all needs. Let's start with the Valpolicellas, among which we particularly liked the simpler, fragrant 2005 Amarone. Aged in small oak barrels, it is more mature, weighty and juicy than the 2004. The interesting Recioto della Valpolicella 2006 came close to a second Glass. The Valpolicella Marogne 2006 is also well made, with a profound, layered nose and a rigorous palate with good grip. Moving towards the west, we find wines from the Lake DOC zones, starting with the Lugana Vigne Alte 2007, which is subtly aromatic with a nicely harmonious palate. The reds are enjoyable and well structured, blending traditional and Bordeaux grapes and fresh and part-dried fruit, as in the Costalago and the Corvar, both from 2006. The various Bardolinos and Custozas are all nicely accessible, as one would expect from lakeside wines.

ANNUAL PRODUCTION	20,000 bottles
HECTARES UNDER VINE	9
VITICULTURE METHOD	Conventional

Celestino Gaspari and Francesco Parisi purchased an old quarry, once used as a store, and turned it into a reception facility, where some of their wine is aged in oak and they also have a tasting room and shop. All this is located along the main road, a lovely restoration of some very interesting buildings. The 2002 growing year was not, of course, good enough for the leading wine, Harlequin, but a very good range of wines was presented nonetheless. The most representative in terms of numbers is the Oz 2005, an Oseleta that seems to have found its ideal habitat in the estate's vineyards and succeeded in achieving harmony and elegance, uncommon features for this wild variety, thanks to the care and sensitivity shown by the two partners. The Kairos 2005 is very impressive. Made from a blend of several varieties of partially dried grapes, it delivers fruity aromas followed by a full body and taut, drinkable palate. The Amarone 2001 made an excellent debut after substantial ageing. The nose, still rather closed, releases its aromas slowly but it performs better on the classy palate with its silky tannins.

● Amarone della Valpolicella Cl. '05	♟♟ 6
● Amarone della Valpolicella Cl. Barrique '04	♟♟ 7
● Valpolicella Sup. Ripasso Marogne '06	♟♟ 4*
O Garda Garganega Vigne Alte '07	♟ 3
O Lugana V. Alte '07	♟ 3
O Soave Cl. Marogne '06	♟ 4
☉ Bardolino Chiaretto Cl. Vigne Alte '07	♟ 3
● Amarone della Valpolicella Cl. Vigne Alte '05	♟ 7
● Corvar Rosso '06	♟ 5
● Costalago Rosso '06	♟ 5
● Recioto della Valpolicella Cl. '06	♟ 5
● Valpolicella Cl. '07	♟ 4
● Bardolino Cl. Sup. '07	4
O Bianco di Custoza Vigne Alte '07	3

● Amarone della Valpolicella Cl. '01	♟♟ 8
● Kairos '05	♟♟ 8
● Oseleta Oz '05	♟♟ 6
O Il Bianco From Black to White '07	♟♟ 4*
● Harlequin '01	♟♟ 8
● Kairos '04	♟♟ 8
● Kairos '03	♟♟ 8
● Oseleta Oz '04	♟♟ 6
● Oseleta Oz '03	♟♟ 6

OTHER WINERIES

Antolini

VIA PROGNOL, 22
37020 MARANO DI VALPOLICELLA [VR]
TEL. 0457755351
www.antolinivini.it

Antolini generally gives us good wines still firmly rooted in tradition. The vibrant, juicy Recioto di Valpolicella 2006 performed well, like the Ripasso with its pervasive aromas and nicely savoury palate. The Amarone Moròpio is enjoyably husky.

● Recioto della Valpolicella Cl. '06	♥♥ 5
● Amarone della Valpolicella Cl. Moròpio '05	♥ 6
● Valpolicella Cl. Sup. Ripasso '06	♥ 4

Astoria Vini

VIA CREVADA, 44
31020 REFRONTOLO [TV]
TEL. 04236699
www.astoria.it

Paola and Giorgio Polegato's lovely estate in the Treviso hills makes prosecco-based sparklers and some interesting still wines. The Croder 2005 is a red with aromas of berry fruit, cocoa powder and spice leading into a robust palate with nice depth. The Cartizze is also well made.

● Colli di Conegliano Croder Rosso '05	♥♥ 4*
○ Cartizze	♥ 5
○ P. di Valdobbiadene Extra Dry Millesimato '07	♥ 4

La Bertolà

VIA S. NICOLÒ, 84
36070 TRISSINO [VI]
TEL. 0445410780
www.tenutalabertola.it

Viticulture had been abandoned in the Agno valley, in the upper province of Vicenza, so credit to wineries like La Bertolà for rediscovering the area's agricultural roots. Only three wines emerged from the first productive year but all are sound. The Riesling 2007 has subtle, penetrating aromas.

○ Vicenza Riesling '07	♥♥ 4*
○ Pinot Grigio '07	♥ 4
○ Vicenza Chardonnay '07	♥ 4

Le Bertole

VIA EUROPA, 20
31049 VALDOBBIADENE [TV]
TEL. 0423975332
www.lebertole.com

Conegliano Valdobbiadene is the home of the prosecco grape. Try this cellar's sparklers: a dry, creamy Extra Dry and a sunny Cartizze, the noblest Prosecco of all, with apple and wisteria aromas and an extraordinarily creamy palate. You'll see why Valdobbiadene is always Valdobbiadene.

○ Cartizze	♥♥ 5
○ P. di Valdobbiadene Extra Dry	♥♥ 4
○ P. di Valdobbiadene Brut	♥ 4
○ P. di Valdobbiadene Dry	♥ 4

Bigai

FRAZ. LISON
VIA CADUTI PER LA PATRIA, 29
30026 PORTOGRUARO [VE]
TEL. 0421287090
www.amimanera.com

Toni Bigai has cut loose from his father's winery, where he still does some work, to found his own. We have now tasted and enjoyed his first wines. The four labels all show healthy husky features that reflect the terroir, variety and weather in the growing year, which in this case was 2007.

● A Mi Manera Rosso '07	♥♥ 4*
○ A Mi Manera Bianco '07	♥♥ 4*
○ Lison-Pramaggiore Lison '07	♥ 3
○ Terra di Bonifica Passito	♥ 5

Bonotto delle Tezze

FRAZ. TEZZE DI PIAVE
VIA DUCA D'AOSTA, 16
31020 VAZZOLA [TV]
TEL. 0438488323
www.bonottodelletezze.it

Following an indifferent spell, this long-established Piave DOC cellar is swiftly recouping plaudits from critics and public. The addition of consultant Marina Polencic to the winery team, and the determination of Antonio Bonotto, have yielded excellent results throughout the range of wines.

● Piave Merlot Spezza '06	♥♥ 4*
● Piave Cabernet Barabane '06	♥ 4
● Raboso Passito '06	♥ 6
○ Chardonnay Oseada '07	♥ 4

OTHER WINERIES

Borgoluce

LOC. MUSILE, 2
31058 SUSEGANA [TV]
TEL. 0438435287
www.borgoluce.it

Borgoluce, the new winery owned by Caterina, Giuliana and Maria Trinidad Di Collalto, has ambition. Three wines were presented, an Extra Dry with pervasive, subtle aromas, an even more captivating Brut with Alpine herbs and flowers preceding a dry, confident palate. The Millesimato 2007 is nice.

O Prosecco di Valdobbiadene Brut	🍷🍷 4
O Prosecco di Valdobbiadene Extra Dry	🍷🍷 4
O Prosecco di Valdobbiadene Extra Dry Millesimato '07	🍷 5

Buglioni

FRAZ. CORRUBIO
VIA CAMPAGNOLE, 55
37029 SAN PIETRO IN CARIANO [VR]
TEL. 0456760681
www.buglioni.it

The Buglioni family is very active around Verona. In recent years, they have set up a chain of eateries in the area alongside their wine production business. The wines are dependably good, starting with the sunny, mature Amarone 2004. Valpolicella Il Ruffiano 2006 is nicely light with good pressure.

● Amarone della Valpolicella Cl. L'Amarone '04	🍷🍷 7
● Valpolicella Cl. Sup. Il Ruffiano '06	🍷 4

Le Carline

VIA CARLINE, 24
30020 PRAMAGGIORE [VE]
TEL. 0421799741
www.lecarline.com

We are convinced that a less invasive approach to growing and careful vineyard management are the keys to discovering the essence of wine. Daniele Piccinin took this approach some time ago with very positive results. The verduzzo-based Dogale Passito is excellent and the Pinot Grigio 2007 is sound.

O Dogale Passito	🍷🍷 5
O Lison-Pramaggiore Pinot Grigio '07	🍷🍷 3*
● Rosso Carline '03	🍷 5

Casa Cecchin

VIA AGUGLIANA, 11
36054 MONTEBELLO VICENTINO [VI]
TEL. 0444649610
www.casececchin.it

Lessinia is a little-known designation but the soil types and personality of the main variety grown here, durella, will put it in the limelight sooner or later. Casa Cecchin has been working to this end for many years. The interesting Brut 2003 shows off durello's gutsy, fresh acidity.

O Lessini Durello Brut M. Cl. '03	🍷🍷 4*
O Gambellara Cl. '07	🍷 3
O Lessini Durello Sup. '07	🍷 3

Case Paolin

VIA MADONNA MERCEDE, 53
31040 VOLPAGO DEL MONTELLO [TV]
TEL. 0423871433
www.casepaolin.it

Adelino and Mirco Pozzobon are committed to producing wines on the family estate beneath the Montello hills. The interesting Rosso del Milio 2006 has beautiful finesse on the nose and a balanced, full-bodied palate. The San Carlo is more structured and less subtle while the Prosecco is dependably good.

● Rosso del Milio '06	🍷🍷 4*
● Montello e Colli Asolani Sup. San Carlo '05	🍷 5
O Prosecco Extra Dry	🍷 3

Colle Mattara

FRAZ. CARBONARA
VIA G. VERDI, 80
35030 ROVOLON [PD]
TEL. 049 5227094
colle.mattara@aziendeccellenza.it

Filippo Livian supervises all stages of production at his small Colli Euganei winery at Rovolon. The range of wines presented closely reflects the DOC zone and includes a couple of high-quality wines. Our favourite is the Rosso, a blend of merlot and ripe cabernet with generous fruit and spice.

O Colli Euganei Fior d'Arancio Passito '04	🍷🍷 5
● Colli Euganei Rosso '04	🍷🍷 5*
● Colli Euganei Merlot '06	🍷 3*

OTHER WINERIES

Contrà Soarda

LOC. CONTRÀ SOARDA, 26
36061 BASSANO DEL GRAPPA [VI]
TEL. 0424566785
www.contrasoarda.it

Mirco Gottardi's winery started out in 2000 and after investing in the vineyard and cellar, it is one of the most interesting newcomers in the area. The Torcolato is generous and tropical; the Terre di Lava vibrant and elegant. Vigna Correjo, a characterful Pinot Noir, is a sound wine.

● Breganze Rosso		
Terre di Lava Ris. '05	♟♟	5
O Breganze Torcolato '05	♟♟	5
● Vigna Correjo '05	♟♟	7

Corteforte

VIA OSAN, 45
37022 FUMANE [VR]
TEL. 0456839104
www.corteforte.com

Lawyer Carlo Maria Cerruti is the owner of this small winery situated right behind the Valpolicella Enoteca. The very interesting Valpolicella Bertarole 2005 is slow to deliver its aromas and has a rounded, soft palate. The Amarone 2001 shows off the same mouthfilling, approachable style.

● Amarone della Valpolicella Cl.		
Vign. di Osan '01	♟♟	8
● Valpolicella Cl. Sup. Ripassato		
Podere Bertarole '05	♟♟	5

La Costa di Romagnano

LOC. LA COSTA
37034 GREZZANA [VR]
TEL. 0458650111
www.agricosta.it

This winery's limited range of products focuses on characteristic Valpantena wines and has peaks of interest. The Amarone 2003 performs well, suffering slightly from excess oak but also showing rounded and balanced. The Valpolicella 2004 is made in the same style but a little less pretentious.

● Amarone della Valpolicella		
Vign. Calandra di Romagnano '03	♟♟	7
● Valpolicella Sup.		
Vign. Calandra di Romagnano '04	♟	5

De Faveri

FRAZ. BOSCO
VIA SARTORI, 21
31020 VIDOR [TV]
TEL. 0423987673
www.defaverispumanti.it

Lucio De Faveri is a skilled Prosecco Brut maker, as this year's tastings show. The Selezione Nera is fresh, fragrant with floral and citrus aromas, and light and tangy on the palate. The other Brut is equally good. The Cartizze impressed with its distinctively soft, harmonious palate.

O Cartizze	♟♟	5
O P. di Valdobbiadene Brut	♟♟	4
O P. di Valdobbiadene Brut Sel. Nera	♟♟	4
O P. di Valdobbiadene Extra Dry	♟	4

De Stefani

VIA CADORNA, 92
30020 FOSSALTA DI PIAVE [VE]
TEL. 042167502
www.de-stefani.it

The De Stefani family have released a new red, Stefen 1624, from part-dried marzemino grapes. In the absence of the two most interesting whites, Olmera and Vitalys, we liked the forthright Kreda 2006, from refosco grapes, while the Cabernet and Merlot are very well typed and fragrant.

● Stefen 1624 '03	♟♟	8
● Cabernet '06	♟	4
● Merlot '06	♟	4
● Refosco P. R. Kreda '06	♟	6

Fasoli

FRAZ. SAN ZENO
VIA C. BATTISTI, 49
37030 COLOGNOLA AI COLLI [VR]
TEL. 0457650741
www.fasoligino.com

The Fasoli brothers own a lovely winery at Colognola ai Colli, an area that produces both Soave and Valpolicella wines. Their passion for drying gives the wines – even the whites – a full-bodied, powerful style. The most interesting is the sumptuously sun-ripe Recioto San Zeno 2005.

● Merlot Calle '06	♟♟	6
O Recioto di Soave S. Zeno '05	♟♟	6
O Soave Borgoletto '07	♟	4
O Soave Pieve Vecchia '06	♟	5

OTHER WINERIES

Filippi

LOC. CASTELCERINO
VIA LIBERTÀ, 55
37038 SOAVE [VR]
TEL. 0457675005
www.cantinafilippi.it

At Castelcerino, the Filippis never stop experimenting with garganega-based wines. The Soave Monteseroni delivers apples, hazelnuts and pepper and a lively husky palate with a long finish. The Recioto di Soave Calprea is evolved with a strong personality and generous, beautifully handled sugar.

O Recioto di Soave Calprea '06	♔♔ 6
O Soave Colli Scaligeri Monteseroni '06	♔♔ 4*
O Recioto di Soave Calprea '05	♔♔ 6

Fraccaroli

FRAZ. SAN BENEDETTO
LOC. BERRA VECCHIA, 1
37019 PESCHIERA DEL GARDA [VR]
TEL. 0457550949
www.fraccarolivini.it

The Fraccaroli family presents an entire range of turbiana-based whites that caters for all tastes. The Superiore I Fraccaroli 2006 is very impressive, unveiling subtle florality and a dry, nicely lingering palate. The Pansere is unfussy and approachable while the Brut is enjoyable.

O Lugana Sup. I Fraccaroli '06	♔♔ 4*
O Lugana Brut	♔ 4
O Lugana Podere Bazzola '07	♔ 3
O Lugana Vign. Pansere '07	♔ 3

Marchesi Fumanelli

FRAZ. SAN FLORIANO
LOC. SQUARANO
37029 SAN PIETRO IN CARIANO [VR]
TEL. 0457704875
www.squarano.com

At San Pietro in Cariano there is a visible but easily overlooked hill just a few dozen metres high. On it stands the Marchesi Fumanelli winery, surrounded by vineyards that provide some of the grapes used for the estate's wines. The Amarone 2003 delivers a spicy nose with a rounded, powerful palate.

| ● Amarone della Valpolicella Ris. '03 | ♔♔ 8 |

La Giaretta

FRAZ. VALGATARA
VIA DEL PLATANO, 12
37020 MARANO DI VALPOLICELLA [VR]
TEL. 0457701791
www.cantinalagiaretta.com

Francesco Vaona's excellent range includes classic local wines in two lines, one more traditional and the other, I Quadretti, more modern in style. The Amarone I Quadretti 2001 is very impressive, with clear fruit aromas. We also liked the Valpolicella 2005 from the same line.

| ● Amarone della Valpolicella Cl. I Quadretti '01 | ♔♔ 8 |
| ● Valpolicella Cl. Sup. I Quadretti '05 | ♔♔ 5 |

Giuseppe Lonardi

VIA DELLE POSTE, 2
37020 MARANO DI VALPOLICELLA [VR]
TEL. 0457755154
www.lonardivini.it

Bepi Lonardi has given up his dual role as wine producer and restaurateur, opting for wine. The Ripasso is excellent with red berries, aromatic herbs and a juicy, lingering palate. The dynamic, pleasantly savoury Amarone is just slightly behind it. The Privilegia and Valpolicella are again both good.

● Amarone della Valpolicella Cl. '04	♔♔ 8
● Valpolicella Cl. Sup. Ripasso '06	♔♔ 6
● Privilegia Rosso '05	♔ 7
● Valpolicella Cl. '07	♔ 4

Monte dall'Ora

VIA MONTE DALL'ORA, 5
37029 SAN PIETRO IN CARIANO [VR]
TEL. 0457501305
www.zyme.it

Monte dall'Ora is one of those small wineries that sprang up in the late 1990s on the growing commercial success of Amarone. The 2004 Amarone has clearly defined, elegant aromas and a dry, nimble palate. The pleasant Ripasso Saustò 2004 is powerful yet supple.

● Amarone della Valpolicella Cl. '04	♔♔ 7
● Valpolicella Cl. Sup. Ripasso Saustò '04	♔♔ 5
● Valpolicella Cl. '07	♔ 4

OTHER WINERIES

Montecariano

via Valena, 3
37029 San Pietro in Cariano [VR]
tel. 0456838335
www.montecariano.it

Montecariano is taking small but constant steps towards quality. Puntara, a Cabernet Sauvignon from part-dried grapes, is on top form and delivers morello cherries and plums before its firm, gutsy palate. The rustic, assertive Amarone is excellent while the Ripasso has fruit alongside oak and acidity.

● Amarone della Valpolicella Cl. '04	🍷🍷 8
● Puntara Cabernet Sauvignon '04	🍷🍷 6
● Valpolicella Cl. Sup. Ripasso '04	🍷 5
● Puntara Cabernet Sauvignon '03	🍷🍷 5

Marco Mosconi

via Paradiso, 5
37031 Illasi [VR]
tel. 0457834000
www.marcomosconi.it

Marco Mosconi works in Illasi, which yields both Soave and Valpolicella wines. He only has five hectares but the results are interesting. Marco's excellent Soave Corte Paradiso 2007 has very subtle floral aromas while the Recioto di Soave 2004 is just behind with deep citrus and ripe Mediterranean sensations.

O Recioto di Soave '04	🍷🍷 6
O Soave Corte Paradiso '07	🍷🍷 4*

Nardello

via IV novembre, 56
37032 Monteforte d'Alpone [VR]
tel. 0457612116
www.nardellovini.it

In recent years, Daniele and Federica Nardello have boosted the quality of their wines. Their vineyards, in some excellent locations, are coming along nicely, as the performance of the Soave Turbian 2007 shows. The Recioto is also very good and you can always rely on Meridies.

O Recioto di Soave Suavissimus '05	🍷🍷 7
O Soave Cl. V. Turbian '07	🍷🍷 4*
O Soave Cl. Meridies '07	🍷 3

Walter Nardin

loc. Roncadelle
via Fontane, 5
31024 Ormelle [TV]
tel. 0422851622
www.vinwalternardin.it

Walter Nardin's winery operates in the Lison-Pramaggiore and Piave DOCs making simple, fairly priced wines. But Walter also hankers to offer something more, as he demonstrates with the effort he pours into La Zerbaia wines and, especially, Rosso della Ghiaia 2004.

● Rosso della Ghiaia '04	🍷🍷 5
O Manzoni Bianco La Zerbaia '06	🍷 5
● Piave Raboso La Zerbaia '04	🍷 5

Paladin

via Postumia, 12
30020 Annone Veneto [VE]
tel. 0422768167
www.paladin.it

For years, the large winery owned by the Paladin brothers in the Lison-Pramaggiore DOC has been turning out good wines. The results are there this year, too, in the Malbech Gli Aceri 2005 and the excellent performance of the Wine & Art 2004, a blend of malbech and refosco.

● Malbech Gli Aceri '05	🍷🍷 5
● Wine & Art Celiberti '04	🍷🍷 7
● Lison-Pramaggiore Cabernet '07	🍷 3
O Traminer '07	🍷 4

Albino Piona

fraz. Custoza
via Bellavista, 48
37060 Sommacampagna [VR]
tel. 045516055
www.albinopiona.it

The efforts of the Piona family are focused on promoting local wines, especially Custoza and also Bardolino. Both Custozas are excellent. The basic version is clear, fragrant and light while the generous Campo Del Selese 2006 is taut and juicy. The upfront Bardolino 2007 is fresh and drinkable.

O Bianco di Custoza '07	🍷🍷 3*
O Bianco di Custoza Sup. Campo del Selese '06	🍷🍷 3*
● Bardolino '07	🍷 3
⊙ Bardolino Chiaretto '07	🍷 3

OTHER WINERIES

Provolo
VIA SAN CASSIANO, 2
37030 MEZZANE DI SOTTO [VR]
TEL. 0458880106
www.viniprovolo.com

Provolo is becoming a specialist in Valpolicella, a complicated wine that hovers between lightness in the standard-label versions and heavier structure in the Amarone-like wines. The Campoturbian delivers nicely expressed fruit while the Gino is fresher, spicy and supple.

- ● Valpolicella Sup. Gino '05 — 🍷🍷 5
- ● Valpolicella Sup. Ripasso Campotorbian '04 — 🍷🍷 6
- ● Amarone della Valpolicella '04 — 🍷 7

Tenuta S. Anna
LOC. LONCON
VIA MONS. P. L. ZOVATTO, 71
30020 ANNONE VENETO [VE]
TEL. 0422864511
letenute@genagricola.it

The 2005 Podere 47, a Cabernet Sauvignon Riserva, delivers fruit aromas followed by a generous, nicely lingering palate with assertive extract. The quality of the other simpler, current wines comes through in their approachable appeal.

- ● Lison-Pramaggiore Cabernet Sauvignon Podere 47 Ris. '05 — 🍷🍷 5
- O Lison-Pramaggiore Tai Lison '07 — 🍷 4

Santa Eurosia
FRAZ. SAN PIETRO DI BARBOZZA
VIA DELLA CIMA, 8
31040 VALDOBBIADENE [TV]
TEL. 0423973236
www.santaeurosia.it

We have to say that since its debut in the Guide in the mid 1990s, Giuseppe Geronazzo's winery has made a substantial contribution to the image of Prosecco. Its trademark style of beautifully expressed aromas echoed by exemplary bottle fermentation translates into remarkably prestigious wines.

- O P. di Valdobbiadene Brut — 🍷🍷 4*
- O P. di Valdobbiadene Dry Mill. '07 — 🍷🍷 5
- O Cartizze — 🍷 6
- O P. di Valdobbiadene Extra Dry — 🍷 4

Tenuta Santa Maria alla Pieve
FRAZ. PIEVE
VIA CAVOUR, 34
37030 COLOGNOLA AI COLLI [VR]
TEL. 0456152087
www.tenutapieve.com

The renewal started in 1990 in the vineyards of Gaetano Bertani's estate has yielded fine quality wines. His sons Guglielmo and Giovanni have joined the team to very good effect. The Decima Aurea 2004 is a monovarietal Merlot from part-dried grapes. The Torre Pieve is a sound Chardonnay.

- ● Decima Aurea '04 — 🍷🍷 7
- O Torre Pieve '06 — 🍷🍷 6

Emilio Sartor
LOC. VENEGAZZÙ
VIA MONTE GRAPPA, 19
31040 VOLPAGO DEL MONTELLO [TV]
TEL. 0423620567
www.vinisartor.it

Brothers Paolo and Carlo Sartor use grapes from about 20 hectares in the Montello e Colli Asolani DOC zone to make mainly standard-label products in a style that highlights the wines' accessibility and appeal. The simple Merlot is excellent and the Prosecco Tranquillo is reliably good.

- ● Montello e Colli Asolani Merlot '07 — 🍷🍷 2*
- O Montello e Colli Asolani Prosecco Tranquillo '07 — 🍷 3

Cantina di Soave
V.LE VITTORIA, 100
37038 SOAVE [VR]
TEL. 0456139811
www.cantinasoave.it

The top line, Rocca Sveva, focuses on typical Veronese products, from Soave to Amarone and the wines of the Garda DOC zone. The Amarone is dependably good with red berries, spice and aromatic herbs on the nose. The Soave Castelcerino is tangy and harmonious in the mouth.

- ● Amarone della Valpolicella Rocca Sveva '04 — 🍷🍷 7
- O Soave Cl. Sup. Castelcerino Rocca Sveva '06 — 🍷🍷 4*

OTHER WINERIES

David Sterza

LOC. CASTERNA
VIA CASTERNA, 37
37022 FUMANE [VR]
TEL. 0457704201
sterzadavid@libero.it

Cousins David Sterza and Paolo Mascanzoni produce wines focusing on the classic Valpolicella types. Their interpretation gives a nod to modernity without abandoning tradition. The most impressive wine is the Valpolicella Ripasso, with generous overripe fruit and a dry, firm palate.

● Amarone della Valpolicella Cl. '04	ΨΨ	6*
● Valpolicella Cl. Sup. Ripasso '06	ΨΨ	4*
● Recioto della Valpolicella Cl. '05	Ψ	6
● Valpolicella Cl. Sup. Ripasso '05	ΨΨ	5

Sutto

VIA SAN LORENZETTO, 9
31040 SALGAREDA [TV]
TEL. 0422744063
www.sutto.it

The Sutto brothers' wines impress us more each year. There are many different labels, all good. The Merlot Riserva 2005 is outstanding, generous and sophisticated on the nose with a harmonious, weighty palate. The very interesting Manzoni Bianco has a floral nose and confident, linear palate.

● Piave Merlot Ris. '05	ΨΨ	5
○ Manzoni Bianco '07	ΨΨ	5
○ Dogma Bianco '06	Ψ	6
● Dogma Rosso '06	Ψ	5

Tanorè

FRAZ. SAN PIETRO DI BARBOZZA
VIA MONT DI CARTIZZE, 3
31040 VALDOBBIADENE [TV]
TEL. 0423975770
www.tanore.it

In Prosecco, the sensitivity of the producer and the techniques used are crucial but the fact remains that if the grapes aren't up to scratch, you won't see results. Every year, the Follador brothers manage to put together a range of truly good wines. The Extra Dry and the Cartizze are both excellent.

○ Cartizze	ΨΨ	5
○ P. di Valdobbiadene Extra Dry	ΨΨ	4
○ P. di Valdobbiadene Brut	Ψ	4
○ P. di Valdobbiadene Dry Millesimato '07	Ψ	4

Tessere

LOC. SANTA TERESINA
VIA BASSETTE, 51
30020 NOVENTA DI PIAVE [VE]
TEL. 0421320438
www.tessereonline.it

Strong-willed Manuela Bincoletto conceals a gutsy character beneath those discreet manners. Her hard work has now paid off and we are pleased to welcome her back to the Guide. The unusual, captivating Dimmi Chi Sono is a tocai-based dried-grape wine. The Raboso Barbarigo 2004 is interesting.

○ Dimmi Chi Sono Passito '06	ΨΨ	5
● Piave Raboso Barbarigo '04	ΨΨ	5
● Raboso Passito Rebecca '03	Ψ	4

La Tordera

VIA ALNÈ BOSCO, 23
31020 VIDOR [TV]
TEL. 0423985362
www.latordera.it

La Tordera is an unusual winery for the Prosecco area, where estates usually own little land and buy in grapes. But using the fruit from their own 50 hectares enables them to make a rigorous selection. The Cartizze has floral, apple-like aromas and the Dry Millesimato 2007 is very pleasant.

○ Cartizze	ΨΨ	5
○ P. di Valdobbiadene Dry Cru Millesimato '07	ΨΨ	4*
○ P. di Valdobbiadene Brut	Ψ	4

Luigi Valetti

LOC. CALMASINO DI BARDOLINO
VIA PRAGRANDE, 8
37010 BARDOLINO [VR]
TEL. 0457235075
www.valetti.it

The Valetti brothers' winery is one of the estates that strives determinedly to raise the image of Bardolino. This fragrant, savoury light wine is currently enjoying a good response from consumers. The Bardolino Superiore 2006 is excellent. The Bardolino Classico 2007 is simpler but enjoyable.

● Bardolino Cl. Sup. '06	ΨΨ	3*
● Bardolino Cl. '07	Ψ	2
● Valpolicella Cl. '07	Ψ	3
○ Bianco di Custoza '07	Ψ	2

OTHER WINERIES

La Vigna

VIA SELVA, 6 A
36054 MONTEBELLO VICENTINO [VI]
TEL. 04446488
azienda.lavigna@libero.it

The Gambellara DOC may not be very well known but the local volcanic soil and the garganega grape enable wineries to make some excellent whites. At this Zonin-group operation, the fragrant, juicy Gambellara Monte Bisolo is joined by a very good Vin Santo with beautifully expressed dried fruit.

O Vin Santo di Gambellara '01	♀♀ 6
O Gambellara Cl. Monte Bisolo '07	♀ 3

Villa Brunesca

VIA SERENISSIMA, 12
31040 GORGO AL MONTICANO [TV]
TEL. 0422800026
www.villabrunesca.it

About 70 per cent of the Mason family's 70-hectare estate is planted to vine. It's a benchmark winery in the Treviso area. Paola and Giorgio run the cellar and in recent years the products have stepped up a gear. The Cabernet Vigna Tilia 2006 is excellent with good body and nice acidity and tannin.

● Piave Cabernet V. Tilia '06	♀♀ 4
● Piave Cabernet '07	♀ 4
● Refosco P. R. V. Olinda '06	♀ 4
O Bacchico Passito '05	♀ 5

Villa Giona

LOC. CENGIA
VIA CENGIA, 8
37029 SAN PIETRO IN CARIANO [VR]
TEL. 0456855011
www.villagiona.it

Villa Giona hides its gems away in the enclosed vineyard at Cengia but if you climb a little higher up, there is a view of the park and the neat rows of merlot, cabernet sauvignon and syrah that go into just one wine. The 2005 is subtle and generous with a creamy palate.

● Villa Giona '05	♀♀ 7
● Villa Giona '04	♀♀ 7
● Villa Giona '03	♀♀ 7
● Villa Giona '01	♀♀ 7

Villa Sandi

VIA ERIZZO, 112
31035 CROCETTA DEL MONTELLO [TV]
TEL. 0423665033
www.villasandi.it

The Polegato family has worked on Montello for over 30 years. The most interesting wine is the dry, gutsy Corpore, from merlot and cabernet franc, which is between Bolgheri and Bordeaux in style. The Avitus 2007 is a fragrant, full-bodied Incrocio Manzoni. The other wines are all good.

O Avitus '07	♀♀ 5
● Corpore '05	♀♀ 6
● Marinali Rosso '06	♀ 5
O Cartizze	♀ 6

Pietro Zardini

VIA DON P. FANTONI, 3
37029 SAN PIETRO IN CARIANO [VR]
TEL. 0456800589
www.pietrozardini.it

Pietro Zardini's products are growing in quality, more than in numbers. Again the most impressive wine is the Amarone. The 2004 delivers very unusual citrus and fresh floral aromas mingling with red berry fruit. The Lugana came up with another excellent performance.

● Amarone della Valpolicella '04	♀♀ 7
O Lugana '07	♀♀ 4*
● Valpolicella Austero Ripasso Sup. '04	♀ 5

Zonin

VIA BORGOLECCO, 9
36053 GAMBELLARA [VI]
TEL. 0444640111
www.zonin.it

This Gambellara-based group has always made typical Vicenza wines and other Veneto types, like the selections from nearby Valpolicella. The Amarone is sound, fruity and dry. Gambellara Il Giangio is a straightforward wine that highlights the simpler, more amenable side of the garganega grape.

● Amarone della Valpolicella '05	♀♀ 6
O Gambellara Cl. Podere Il Giangio '07	♀ 3
● Valpolicella Sup. Ripasso '06	♀ 4

FRIULI VENEZIA GIULIA

The 2007 growing year, from which most of the wines reviewed here come, was noteworthy for its incredibly early onset. A mild winter and springtime with above average temperatures, particularly in April, encouraged flowering in the first ten days of May, some three or four weeks earlier than usual. Rain in May offset the lack of precipitation in the preceding period and then in June, sunshine and rain alternated nicely. Apart from a wet, refreshing second week, July's weather was mainly hot and sunny. The combination meant that harvesting of white varieties started in the first ten days of August, something that had never happened before in Friuli in living memory. There was much concern before the harvest but it has to be said that although the season was premature, the vine's vegetative cycle was undisturbed. Doubts disappeared when the first musts were analysed. Alcohol was lower than in 2006 and nicely balanced by acidity. Reds were looking even better. Picking took place in the second half of September in perfect weather. The first samples examined were very favourably received, the only reservations being over the product's youth, but the vintage's potential was obvious. Other reds, most of which come from the 2004 to 2006 vintages, are less exciting. Often, acidity and extract are too evident, with the result that only four won Three Glasses. Springtime forecasts predicted a good year for pinot and this time the biggest award winner was Pinot Bianco, a wine the market underrates but which experts consider one of the most elegant around. Six top awards. Close behind with just one prize fewer is Friulano, the successor to Tocai after a bureaucratic compromise that now permits the use of the name Tocai Friulano only in Italy. Abroad, it has to be called Friulano. The Sauvignons took a step back, although many came very close to top honours, and there was a new development in Malvasia. Two wines stood out, one traditional wine, the other vinified with skin contact. Malvasia, too, is a wine type that the market tends to shun, convinced that it must be sweet. But the malvasia istriana grown in Friuli has always been vinified dry. It's a faintly aromatic product with great structure. Nonetheless, most of the Glasses went to blends. For the first time, top prizes went to Sirch, which also picked up the Best Priced Wine award, Zuani from Patrizia Felluga, Zidarich and Federico Frumento's Casa Zuliani. Back in the front rank are Mauro Drius, Gianfranco Gallo' Vie di Romans, Marco Felluga's Russiz Superiore, Isidoro Polencic, Nicola Manferrari's Borgo del Tiglio and Livio Felluga.

Alberice

VIA BOSCO ROMAGNO, 4
33040 CORNO DI ROSAZZO [UD]
TEL. 0422765571
www.tenutealeandri.it

ANNUAL PRODUCTION	210,000 bottles
HECTARES UNDER VINE	25
VITICULTURE METHOD	Conventional

Alberice is part of the Aleandri group, comprising three estates in Veneto and Alberice in Friuli. Recently, the group has also been managing the historic winery at the abbey of Rosazzo in Friuli. Size, serious numbers, business skills and excellent technicians combine with a range of reliably good products that in the case of the 2007 Malvasia and Pinot Grigio are genuinely outstanding. Malvasia is thought to have come to Friuli from Greece in the Middle Ages courtesy of Venetian traders. It gives star anise, spring flowers, apples and pears as it unfolds confidently on the palate. Equally entrancing is the complex Pinot Grigio, whose freshness and minerality make it remarkably appealing on the palate. The two reds from 2006, the native Refosco and the Cabernet Franc, are convincing. The Refosco foregrounds spice and quinine while its elegant partner discloses warm notes of sour cherry jam and chocolate. The Friulano 2007 has a varietal palate and the Merlot 2006 unveils fresh fruity fragrances but stopped short of a second Glass.

○ COF Malvasia '07	▼▼	4*
○ COF Pinot Grigio '07	▼▼	4*
● COF Cabernet Franc '06	▼▼	4
● COF Refosco P. R. '06	▼▼	4
● COF Cabernet Sauvignon '06	▼	4
○ COF Chardonnay '07	▼	4
○ COF Friulano '07	▼	4
● COF Merlot '06	▼	4
● COF Rosso Tango '05	▼	5
○ COF Sauvignon '07	▼	4
● COF Schioppettino '06	▼	4
○ COF Malvasia '06	♀♀	4
○ COF Sauvignon '06	♀♀	4
● COF Cabernet Franc '05	♀♀	4
● COF Rosso Tango '03	♀♀	5

Tenuta di Angoris

LOC. ANGORIS, 7
34071 CORMONS [GO]
TEL. 048160923
www.angoris.com

ANNUAL PRODUCTION	800,000 bottles
HECTARES UNDER VINE	150
VITICULTURE METHOD	Conventional

Over a year ago, we noted how good wines from Tenuta di Angoris are here we are again praising the products from an increasingly confident cellar. In 1968, Luciano Locatelli took over expansion has increased the vine stock to 640 hectares, with 150 planted to vine. For the past few years, his daughter Claudia has been in charge. Extensive replanting and new training systems under the watchful eye of Marco Simonit ensure that the fruit reaches the cellar in superb condition. Wine technician Alessandro Del Zovo has top-level consultancy input before he single-handedly directs vinification. You can see the results below. Yet again, the top scorers are the hillside Friulano and Sauvignon, released under the Vôs da Vigne label. The complex, long-lingering Friulano has an almondy note on the back palate while the Sauvignon is also straight out of the textbook, its assertive aromas tempered by buttery texture and warm alcohol. Bianco Spìule, from a barrel-matured chardonnay-heavy blend with tocai and ribolla gialla, shows nice fruit despite oak-derived creaminess. Finally, the hillslope-grown Ribolla Gialla is a wonderful wine for fish.

○ COF Friulano Vôs da Vigne '07	▼▼	5
○ COF Sauvignon Vôs da Vigne '07	▼▼	5
○ COF Bianco Spìule '06	▼▼	5
○ COF Ribolla Gialla Vôs da Vigne '07	▼▼	4*
● COF Cabernet Sauvignon Vôs da Vigne '06	▼	4
○ COF Chardonnay Vôs da Vigne '07	▼	5
● COF Refosco P. R. Vôs da Vigne '06	▼	5
● COF Schioppettino Vôs da Vigne '06	▼	5
○ Friuli Isonzo Pinot Bianco Villa Angoris '07	▼	4
○ Friuli Isonzo Sauvignon Villa Angoris '07	▼	4
○ COF Sauvignon Vôs da Vigne '06	♀♀	4
○ Collio Tocai Friulano Vôs da Vigne '06	♀♀	4

Antonutti

FRAZ. COLLOREDO DI PRATO
VIA D'ANTONI, 21
33037 PASIAN DI PRATO [UD]
TEL. 0432662001
www.antonuttivini.it

ANNUAL PRODUCTION 600,000 bottles
HECTARES UNDER VINE 17
VITICULTURE METHOD Conventional

Adriana and Lino Antonutti with their children Nicola and Caterina run the cellar that grandfather Ignazio started in 1921, as the winery motto puts it, "together, with passion". New developments include makeovers for the labels and bottles as well as a new premium line, Vis Terrae. Over the past few years, the winery has maintained a consistently high standard of quality for the DOC Grave wines the vineyards yield. A fine example is Pinot Grigio, both the 2007 base version and the 2006 Vis Terrae selection. The former is true to type, proffering fresh minerality and williams pears whereas Vis Terrae, which contains a proportion of oak-fermented wine, stands out for its rich melon, apricot, yellow peach and banana-like fruit melding deliciously with vanilla from the wood. We also liked the Chardonnays. The 2007 is fresh, supple and stylish while the Vis Terrae 2006 is more substantial, with creamy perceptions over an attractive backdrop of citrus. Finally, we would also mention the spice and youthful alcohol of the 2006 Merlot.

○ Friuli Grave Chardonnay Vis Terrae '06	ŸŸ 4*
○ Friuli Grave Pinot Grigio '07	ŸŸ 4*
○ Friuli Grave Pinot Grigio Vis Terrae '06	ŸŸ 4*
○ Friuli Grave Chardonnay '07	Ÿ 4
● Friuli Grave Merlot '06	Ÿ 4
● Friuli Grave Pinot Nero '07	Ÿ 4
● Friuli Grave Cabernet '06	4
● Friuli Grave Refosco P. R. '05	4
○ Friuli Grave Sauvignon '07	4
○ Friuli Grave Traminer Aromatico Vis Terrae '06	4
○ Friuli Grave Pinot Grigio '06	ΥΥ 3*
○ Friuli Grave Sauvignon Blanc Poggio Alto '06	ΥΥ 4*

Ascevi - Luwa

LOC. UCLANZI, 24
34070 SAN FLORIANO DEL COLLIO [GO]
TEL. 0481884140
www.asceviluwa.it

ANNUAL PRODUCTION 200,000 bottles
HECTARES UNDER VINE 30
VITICULTURE METHOD Conventional

Ascevi - Luwa was set up in the 1970s by Mariano Pintar and today has about 30 family run hectares. Ascevi is the hill where the estate's largest vineyard stands 270 metres above sea level, at San Floriano del Collio. There are two distinct lines, Ascevi and Luwa, the latter deriving from initial letters of Mariano's children Luana and Walter. The cellar's strong suit has always been Sauvignon and, ironically enough, Sauvignon's minerality also comes through in the other wines. Sauvignon Ronco dei Sassi was the outstanding performer at our tastings. Absolutely varietal sage and bell peppers introduce the savoury, rich-textured palate. All our panellists enjoyed this wine at our tastings but the overall situation of the winery is reassuringly consistent. We are confident that the road Ascevi - Luwa has chosen is one that will lead to even better results.

○ Collio Sauvignon Ronco dei Sassi Ascevi '07	ŸŸ 5
○ Col Martin Luwa '07	Ÿ 5
○ Collio Pinot Grigio Ascevi '07	Ÿ 4
○ Collio Ribolla Gialla Ronco de Vigne Vecie '07	Ÿ 4
○ Friuli Isonzo Tocai Friulano Ascevi '07	Ÿ 4
○ Collio Chardonnay Luwa '07	4
○ Collio Sauvignon Ronco dei Sassi Ascevi '06	ΥΥ 5

Attems

FRAZ. LUCINICO
VIA GIULIO CESARE, 36A
34170 GORIZIA
TEL. 0481393619
www.attems.it

ANNUAL PRODUCTION	450,000 bottles
HECTARES UNDER VINE	52
VITICULTURE METHOD	Conventional

The Attems estate is at Lucinico, in the Collio Goriziano in eastern Friuli Venezia Giulia. Founded by the Attems family in the 14th century, the estate has since 2000 been allied with one of Italy's greatest wine dynasties, Marchesi de' Frescobaldi. Production focuses on whites from native and international grapes and it was a blend of great white varieties that impressed us most this year. It takes its name from the hill where sauvignon, pinot bianco and friulano vines are planted in the 60-20-20 proportions we find in the bottle. Cicinis 2006 is intense on the nose, where smokiness mingles with caramel and confectioner's cream. Although oakiness is apparent, the fruit aromas are nicely distinct and backed up by attractive freshness. We also like the very varietal Sauvignon. Evident notes of sage herald a savoury, long-lingering palate with delicious fruit. Finally, the 2006 Merlot is more than decent.

Bastianich

LOC. GAGLIANO
VIA DARNAZZACCO, 44/2
33043 PREMARIACCO [UD]
TEL. 0432700943
www.bastianich.com

ANNUAL PRODUCTION	200,000 bottles
HECTARES UNDER VINE	28
VITICULTURE METHOD	Conventional

Over the past two years, Bastianich has moved to new headquarters at Gagliano, which has caused one or two blips in the wines but now the quality that the estate quickly reached after it was set up is back again. Having grown to 28 hectares under vine, the estate that Giuseppe – aka Joe – Bastianich and his mother Lidia own is punching its full weight again. Originally from Istria, the Bastianiches were keen to put down roots again in Italy after a successful career in the US restaurant business. The winery is managed by Valter Scarbolo and Denis Lepore while the oenologists are Emilio Del Medico and Maurizio Castelli, a top-ranking consultant. Each year, the cellar releases around 200,000 bottles. The 2006 Vespa Bianco is back on form. A selection of chardonnay and sauvignon, with ten per cent picolit, it is beautifully balanced and creamy as each variety makes its own contribution to the whole. Merlot, refosco and cabernet go into the very well executed Vespa Rosso 2005 and there is a welcome newcomer to the range, the fresh, crisp Sauvignon "B".

O Collio Bianco Cicinis '06	♟♟	5
● Collio Merlot '06	♟♟	4
O Collio Sauvignon '07	♟♟	4
O Chardonnay '07	♟	4
O Collio Friulano '07	♟	4
O Collio Pinot Bianco '07	♟	4
O Collio Pinot Grigio '07	♟	4
O Pinot Grigio Cupra Ramato '07	♟	4
● Refosco P. R. '06	♟	4
O Ribolla Gialla '07	♟	4

O Vespa Bianco '06	♟♟	6
O COF Tocai Plus '06	♟♟	4
O Sauvignon "B" '07	♟♟	4
● Vespa Rosso '05	♟♟	6
O COF Friulano '07	♟	4
O Vespa Bianco '99	♟♟♟	5
O Vespa Bianco '04	♟♟♟	5
O Vespa Bianco '03	♟♟♟	5
O Vespa Bianco '01	♟♟♟	5
O Vespa Bianco '00	♟♟♟	5
O Vespa Bianco '05	♟♟	5
● Vespa Rosso '04	♟♟	6

Tenuta Beltrame

FRAZ. PRIVANO
LOC. ANTONINI, 4
33050 BAGNARIA ARSA [UD]
TEL. 0432923670
www.tenutabeltrame.it

ANNUAL PRODUCTION	100,000 bottles
HECTARES UNDER VINE	25
VITICULTURE METHOD	Conventional

The Beltrame family acquired this estate over 15 years ago. They restored the main residence and replanted all the vineyards, which are now coming into full production. Most of the credit must go to Cristian Beltrame, who is always keen to experiment gets ever-better wines from his vineyards with help from consultant oenologist Bepi Gollino, who has been working with the estate since 1991. Very low yields per hectare and shrewd use of small and large wood have created wonderfully textured wines like Chardonnay Pribus with its solid structure, ripe fruit fragrances and crusty bread with confectioner's cream flavours. The Pinot Grigio gives fruit and aromatic herbs introducing a savoury, ripe fruit-themed palate, the Friulano hints at apples, pears and figs on the nose followed by lingering almondiness in the mouth and the intense yet subtle fragrances of the Sauvignon precede a full-bodied, savoury palate with plenty of alcohol. Refosco is the top red with its concentrated spice and forest fruits flavours to soften the boisterous extract. Equally appealing is the well-structured Cabernet Franc, which tempts with a nose of ripe fruit.

Anna Berra

VIA RAMANDOLO, 29
33045 NIMIS [UD]
TEL. 0432790296
www.annaberra.it

ANNUAL PRODUCTION	25,000 bottles
HECTARES UNDER VINE	7
VITICULTURE METHOD	Conventional

Verduzzo friulano is one of the region's signature varieties. It performs best in the hills at Nimis, where it acquires extra-special sensations and flavours. A few years ago, the grape's qualities were acknowledged by the creation of the Ramandolo DOCG zone. Ramandolo was first documented in 1409, when Gregory XII was in Friuli to preside over the general council. "Ramandolo di Torlano" was served at a dinner given in his honour by the municipality of Cividale. Today, one of the finest Ramandolos can be found at the Anna Berra cellar. Producer Ivan Monai, with expertise beyond his years, turns out increasingly special interpretations with each new vintage. Ivan's 2004 Anno Domini selection is wonderfully stylish. Its golden amber accompanies candied citrus peel, caramel-covered figs, roasted hazelnuts and an intriguing note of talcum powder. The grape's trademark extract nicely balances its fruit and sweetness. But the Nimis hillslopes also yield an excellent Refosco. Ivan's 2005 Riserva is a little reminiscent of an Amarone for its liqueur cherry, milk chocolate and confectioner's cream aromas lifted by a discreet hint of violets.

O Friuli Aquileia Chardonnay Pribus '06	♥♥ 4
● Friuli Aquileia Refosco P. R. '06	♥♥ 4
● Friuli Aquileia Cabernet Franc '06	♥ 4
● Friuli Aquileia Cabernet Sauvignon Ris. '04	♥ 4
O Friuli Aquileia Chardonnay '07	♥ 4
O Friuli Aquileia Friulano '07	♥ 4
O Friuli Aquileia Sauvignon '07	♥ 4
O Pinot Grigio '07	♥ 4
● Tazzelenghe '04	♥ 4
● Friuli Aquileia Cabernet Franc '05	♥♥ 4
● Friuli Aquileia Merlot '05	♥♥ 4

O Ramandolo Anno Domini '04	♥♥ 6
● COF Refosco P. R. Ris. '05	♥ 5
O Ramandolo Anno Domini '03	♥♥ 6
O Ramandolo Anno Domini '02	♥♥ 6
O COF Picolit Ris. '03	♥♥ 6
O COF Picolit Ris. '02	♥♥ 6
● COF Refosco P. R. Ris. '03	♥♥ 5
O Ramandolo Anno Domini '01	♥♥ 4

Bidoli

FRAZ. ARCANO SUPERIORE
VIA FORNACE, 19
33030 RIVE D'ARCANO [UD]
TEL. 0432810796
www.bidolivini.com

ANNUAL PRODUCTION	1,200,000 bottles
HECTARES UNDER VINE	N.A.
VITICULTURE METHOD	Conventional

The 2007 growing year was a difficult one in Friuli. It started early because of a very warm, dry spring and some areas were hit by hail, which reduced average production considerably. That's why we were expecting a drop in quality from estates like siblings Margherita and Arrigo Bidoli's winery, which buys in fruit from selected growers and emphasizes good value for money. But instead we found further confirmation of Arrigo Bidoli's winemaking skills in his dual role as owner and oenologist. There is no denying the dependability of the classic Pinot Bianco Fornas, with its complex nose of spring flowers, almond, apples, minerality and citrus, or the subtle herbaceousness of the Merlot Briccolo 2006, or the elegantly refreshing, varietal Pinot Grigio and Sauvignon. These traditional Bidoli wines are joined by a very good 2006 Ramandolo with sensations of apple jam, candied citrus peel and sweet nougat, echoed on a sweet but never cloying palate.

La Boatina

VIA CORONA, 62
34071 CORMONS [GO]
TEL. 048160445
www.paliwines.com

ANNUAL PRODUCTION	300,000 bottles
HECTARES UNDER VINE	51
VITICULTURE METHOD	Conventional

Loretto Pali's winemaking activities are all under the umbrella of Pali Wines but he makes a clear distinction between products from his 51 hectares of flatland vines at Cormons and those from the hill country. This year, only Friuli Isonzo DOC wines have been released under the La Boatina label. And what wines they are! For years, we have been admiring superb wines from the area and new top-level products can only be a good thing. The secret could be that Loretto has called in Marco Simonit to manage the vine stock while flanking his trusted Domenico Lovat with consultant Gianni Menotti in the cellar. Best of the range is a textbook Pinot Bianco. Intensely yet stylishly aromatic, it mingles fruit and flowers in a complex bouquet. Equally intriguing is the Pinot Grigio, which has dried flowers, pears and peaches. The unctuous, full-bodied Chardonnay lingers on the palate while the Sauvignon has classic, but never excessive, tomato leaf lifted by elderflower and faint hints of lavender. The reds need more work but the Merlot picked up Two Glasses for its attractive concentration and freshness.

● Friuli Grave Merlot Briccolo '06	♀♀ 4
○ Friuli Grave Pinot Bianco Fornas '07	♀♀ 2*
○ Friuli Grave Pinot Grigio '07	♀♀ 3
○ Friuli Grave Sauvignon '07	♀♀ 3
○ Ramandolo '06	♀♀ 4
● COF Refosco P. R. Fornas dai Fradis '06	3
○ Friuli Grave Traminer Aromatico Fornas '07	3
● Friuli Grave Cabernet Briccolo '05	♀♀ 4
● Friuli Grave Merlot Briccolo '05	♀♀ 4

○ Friuli Isonzo Chardonnay '07	♀♀ 4
● Friuli Isonzo Merlot '06	♀♀ 4
○ Friuli Isonzo Pinot Bianco '07	♀♀ 4*
○ Friuli Isonzo Pinot Grigio '07	♀♀ 4
○ Friuli Isonzo Sauvignon '07	♀♀ 4
● Friuli Isonzo Cabernet Franc '07	♀ 4
● Friuli Isonzo Cabernet Sauvignon '06	♀ 4
○ Friuli Isonzo Tocai Friulano '07	♀ 4
○ Ribolla Gialla '07	♀ 4
● Collio Rosso Picol Maggiore '03	♀♀ 5
○ Friuli Isonzo Pinot Bianco '06	♀♀ 4*

Borgo Conventi

S.DA DELLA COLOMBARA, 13
24070 FARRA D'ISONZO [GO]
TEL. 0481888004
www.ruffino.it

ANNUAL PRODUCTION	350,000 bottles
HECTARES UNDER VINE	30
VITICULTURE METHOD	Conventional

Borgo Conventi, founded in 1975, probably owes its name to a donation by Conte Strassoldo, called "il Rizzardo", to the Dominican friar Basilio Pica. The friars are believed to have built a monastery, hence the name Borgo Conventi. Many years later, the winery, now owned by Tuscany's Ruffino, comprises 30 hectares in the Collio and Isonzo DOC zones. In the past few vintages, we have seen steady growth in quality, culminating this year in the admission to our Three Glass finals of the 2006 Bianco Colle Russian, a blend of chardonnay, malvasia and riesling. Distinct banana, confectioner's cream, pineapple and vanilla tempt the nose, giving way to subtle pipe tobacco. Entry on the palate is elegant, the initial vanilla being followed by white-fleshed fruits to end on warm tobacco that mirrors the nose. The complex, velvety Sauvignon Colle Blanchis also impresses, as does the Collio Friulano with its poised almond, dried figs and golden delicious apple sensations. There are three fine 2007s from the Isonzo DOC: a fresh, savoury chardonnay, a youthfully alcoholic Refosco with varietal green pepper and very rich, soft-textured Pinot Grigio.

Borgo del Tiglio

FRAZ. BRAZZANO
VIA SAN GIORGIO, 71
34070 CORMONS [GO]
TEL. 048162166

ANNUAL PRODUCTION	35,000 bottles
HECTARES UNDER VINE	8.5
VITICULTURE METHOD	Conventional

There is little left to say about Nicola Manferrari and his lovely winery, including his skills in the vineyard. It's relatively common knowledge that his wines are controversial at tastings, not so much for their fruit, which is always top class, as for their oak-derived milky and buttery sensations. The technique certainly ensures the wines will age unhurriedly but it can confuse sensory analysis if the vintage is too young. But this year, the tocai-based Ronco della Chiesa surprised us with its supremely skilful use of oak that lends complexity without upsetting the fresh concentration, structure or nose-palate consistency of this apple, acacia blossom and almond-themed wine. We were equally pleased by the dark-labelled Chardonnay Selezione and the Malvasia, a wine that Nicola has been working on for some time. But the dark-labelled Studio di Bianco, beige-labelled Bianco and the Tocai Friulano are in the usual Manferrari mould. Hefty structure and depth accompany perceptions of coffee and vanilla that have yet to be absorbed. Wines for the patient.

O Collio Bianco Colle Russian '06	♥♥	5
O Collio Friulano '07	♥♥	4
O Collio Sauvignon Colle Blanchis '07	♥♥	5
O Friuli Isonzo Chardonnay '07	♥♥	4
O Friuli Isonzo Pinot Grigio '07	♥♥	4
● Friuli Isonzo Refosco P. R. '07	♥♥	4
O Collio Chardonnay '07	♥	4
● Collio Merlot '05	♥	4
O Collio Pinot Grigio '07	♥	4
O Collio Ribolla Gialla '07	♥	4
O Collio Sauvignon '07	♥	5
O Friuli Isonzo Sauvignon '07	♥	4
O Friuli Isonzo Friulano '07		4
● Schioppettino '07		5
O Collio Chardonnay '06	♥♥	4
● Collio Merlot '04	♥♥	4
O Collio Sauvignon Colle Blanchis '06	♥♥	5

O Collio Bianco Ronco della Chiesa '06	♥♥♥	7
O Collio Chardonnay Sel. '06	♥♥	7
O Collio Malvasia '06	♥♥	7
O Collio Chardonnay '06	♥♥	6
O Collio Studio di Bianco '06	♥♥	7
O Collio Tocai Friulano '06	♥♥	6
O Collio Bianco '06	♥	6
O Collio Bianco Ronco della Chiesa '02	♥♥♥	7
O Collio Bianco Ronco della Chiesa '01	♥♥♥	7
O Collio Tocai Friulano Ronco della Chiesa '90	♥♥♥	6
O Collio Chardonnay '04	♥♥	6
O Collio Chardonnay Sel. '05	♥♥	7
O Collio Chardonnay Sel. '03	♥♥	7

Borgo delle Oche

VIA BORGO ALPI, 5
33098 VALVASONE [PN]
TEL. 0434899398
www.borgodelleoche.it

Borgo San Daniele

VIA SAN DANIELE, 16
34071 CORMONS [GO]
TEL. 048160552
www.borgosandaniele.it

ANNUAL PRODUCTION	25,000 bottles
HECTARES UNDER VINE	7
VITICULTURE METHOD	Conventional

ANNUAL PRODUCTION	60,000 bottles
HECTARES UNDER VINE	18
VITICULTURE METHOD	Conventional

The medieval settlement of Valvasone is well worth a visit for its bewitching, history-soaked atmosphere. Take the opportunity to visit to the tiny Borgo delle Oche cellar when you go. The neat, unassuming tasting area speaks volumes for the authenticity of Luisa Menini and Nicola Pittini's operation. It is the couple's sheer energy that in a few short years has taken Borgo delle Oche to the front ranks of quality and kept it there, which is even more difficult. Even after a challenging growing year, Luisa and Nicola managed to send their 2007 Pinot Grigio and Bianco Alba to our finals and the two big hitters are flanked by a raft of Glass-winning wines. Bianco Alba, a dried-grape Traminer, has become one of the cellar's leaders. Its sun-blessed notes of honey, apricots and candied orange peel usher in a palate that nicely sets sweetness off against freshness. The pervasive aromas of the Pinot Grigio hinge on fresh fruit, leading to an elegantly vibrant finale. Other stand-outs are the very varietal 2007 Traminer, the creamy tocai and verduzzo-based Bianco Lupi Terrae and the fruity 2006 Refosco with its distinct pepper and hay nuances.

Borgo San Daniele is on the road from Cormons to the small outlying district of Brazzano. The Mauri siblings are in charge, Alessandra looking after business while Mauro keeps things shipshape in the vineyard and cellar. It's always a pleasure to chat with Mauro, who is ever modest and hospitable, as well as being an expert oenologist with very clear ideas. Mauro likes his wines well evolved, which is why he only released three products, two of which date from before the last vintage: Arbis Ros 2005, Tocai Friulano 2006 and Pinot Grigio 2007. We still have vivid memories of the 2003 Gortmarin that won Three Glasses last year. Sadly, Mauro makes it only in exceptional growing years when the grapes ripen to perfection. After a few years when the Tocai Friulano focused on minerality, the 2006 vintage has opted for the all-round appeal that comes with slow maturation. It's a Tocai that was made for the cellar, brilliantly maintaining the freshness and allure that only a great wine can offer. The Pinot Grigio is simply magnificent.

O Bianco Alba '07	�	5
O Pinot Grigio '07	�	4*
O Bianco Lupi Terrae '06	�	4
● Refosco P. R. '06	�	4
O Traminer Aromatico '07	�	4
O Chardonnay '06	�	4
● Merlot '06	�	4
● Rosso Svual '05	�	5
O Bianco Alba '06	�	5
O Bianco Alba '05	�	5
O Traminer Aromatico '06	�	4
O Bianco Alba '04	�	5

O Friuli Isonzo Pinot Grigio '07	�	5
O Friuli Isonzo Tocai Friulano '06	�	5
● Arbis Ros '05	�	6
O Arbis Blanc '06	�	5
O Arbis Blanc '05	�	5
O Friuli Isonzo Arbis Blanc '02	�	5
O Friuli Isonzo Pinot Grigio '99	�	5
O Friuli Isonzo Pinot Grigio '04	�	5
O Friuli Isonzo Tocai Friulano '97	�	5
O Friuli Isonzo Tocai Friulano '03	�	5
● Gortmarin '03	�	6
● Arbis Ros '04	�	6
● Arbis Ros '03	�	5
O Friuli Isonzo Pinot Grigio '06	�	5
O Friuli Isonzo Tocai Friulano '05	�	5

Borgo Savaian

VIA SAVAIAN, 36
34071 CORMONS [GO]
TEL. 048160725
stefanobastiani@libero.it

ANNUAL PRODUCTION	40,000 bottles
HECTARES UNDER VINE	12
VITICULTURE METHOD	Conventional

Borgo Savaian has expanded its vine stock, which stretches across the Collio and Isonzo DOC zones, and the recently restored cellar is now up and running. Stefano Bastiani, backed by his father Mario and mother Marinella, focuses on quality as he hones the personal style of his wines. Underpinning that style are freshness, approachability and respect for variety, as well as a very welcome attention to value for money. Stefano's abilities were nicely showcased in the excellent 2007 wines he submitted for tasting. We all know it wasn't a great vintage in Friuli but Stefano was up to the challenge. His Friulano has toasty almond notes over warm fruit while we particularly liked the elegant freshness of the Pinot Grigio's palate. The Sauvignon brings off a pleasing contrast of elderflower-led green notes with nice peach-like fruit and the Traminer is a textbook example of the variety's aromatics. We should also point out the rich tropical fruit of the Chardonnay and the intense flavours of the robustly structured Cabernet Franc. Merlot Torlem is one to watch. When we were tasting, it was warm and muscular but had still to find a point of equilibrium.

Cav. Emiro Bortolusso

VIA OLTREGORGO, 10
33050 CARLINO [UD]
TEL. 043167596
www.bortolusso.it

ANNUAL PRODUCTION	120,000 bottles
HECTARES UNDER VINE	35
VITICULTURE METHOD	Conventional

On the edge of the Marano lagoon, brother and sister Sergio and Clara Bortolusso have inherited all the passion for the land and the tenacious energy, of their father, Cavalier Emiro Bortolusso. Some of the rows still stand beside the fishing pools that for the past few years have been used only to farm sea bass and gilthead bream for the family table but were fully operational until the end of the 1990s. The alternating fishing pools and rows of vines are a memorable sight. The Bortolusso vineyards and cellar are located in a part of Friuli Venezia Giulia where it is not easy to find premium-quality wines but Sergio and Clara show what can be done. We hope that sooner of later their winemaking neighbours will decide to follow their example. The Bortolusso range is interesting and three labels stand apart, earning Two Glasses each. The Malvasia very well typed, varietal and tangy, proffering lavender, violets and liquorice on nose and palate. In contrast, the Pinot Bianco is elegant and refreshing, foregrounding ripe fruit and confectioner's cream. The very long Sauvignon is nicely balanced and convincingly true to its variety.

○ Collio Chardonnay '07	♥♥	4
○ Collio Friulano '07	♥♥	4
○ Collio Pinot Grigio '07	♥♥	4
○ Collio Sauvignon '07	♥♥	4
● Friuli Isonzo Cabernet Franc '06	♥♥	4
○ Friuli Isonzo Traminer Aromatico '07	♥♥	4
● Collio Merlot '06	♥	4
● Collio Merlot Tolrem '05	♥	5
○ Collio Pinot Bianco '07	♥	4
○ Friuli Isonzo Verduzzo Friulano '06	♥	4
● Collio Merlot Tolrem '04	♥♥	5

○ Friuli Annia Malvasia '07	♥♥	3*
○ Friuli Annia Pinot Bianco '07	♥♥	3*
○ Friuli Annia Sauvignon '07	♥♥	3*
○ Friuli Annia Friulano '07	♥	3
● Friuli Annia Merlot '07	♥	3
○ Friuli Annia Pinot Grigio '07	♥	3
○ Friuli Annia Verduzzo Friulano '07	♥	4
○ Friuli Annia Pinot Bianco '06	♥♥	3
○ Friuli Annia Sauvignon '06	♥♥	3

Rosa Bosco

VIA ROMA, 5
33040 MOIMACCO [UD]
TEL. 0432722461
www.rosabosco.it

ANNUAL PRODUCTION   14,000 bottles
HECTARES UNDER VINE   N.A.
VITICULTURE METHOD   Conventional

This year, Rosa Bosco sent us her 2005 Merlot. Boscorosso stayed in small oak barrels for two years and will improve even further with more time in bottle. It reveals pleasing balsam and star anise that bode well for the future but we thought the bouquet was still a little green. But the palate has substantial texture and we reckon it will be drinking at its peak in a couple of years' time. Rosa's instantly recognizable Sauvignon Blanc did even better. Ripe peach, confectioner's cream and sponge cake tempt the nose and although there is plenty of fruit, it is slightly masked by the oak, a typical Rosa Bosco touch. In all likelihood, Rosa's long-awaited spumante will be released in early 2009. As we write these notes, she and her son Alessio Dorigo are carrying out the final tastings. Knowing Alessio's experience with classic method sparklers, we are confident the new product will interest connoisseurs. We look forward to talking about it at length next year.

Branko

LOC. ZEGLA, 20
34071 CORMONS [GO]
TEL. 0481639826

ANNUAL PRODUCTION   45,000 bottles
HECTARES UNDER VINE   7.5
VITICULTURE METHOD   Conventional

The 2007 growing year wasn't easy for anyone in Friuli but outstanding winemakers still released top-quality wines. Igor Erzetic, a benchmark for small producers at Cormons, is one such. He farms just over seven hectares planted at a density of 5,500 vines per hectare. His father Branko is there to help him while his mother Daniela welcomes visitors. The cellar is small but attractive and there is even a small wine archive where Igor keeps samples of past vintages. The delightful tasting room is at the entrance to the winery and from there you pass into the cellar proper with large barrels in which some of the wines are part-aged. The Pinot Grigio and Friulano are excellent, both combining alcohol, tanginess and rich texture with surprising elegance. In the Pinot Grigio's case, a wealth of fruit earned Three Glasses and confirmed the cellar as one of the finest interpreters of what is a far from easy grape. We were impressed by the smoky hints of the Sauvignon and the weight of the Chardonnay. Red 2006, from merlot and cabernet sauvignon, is better on the palate and will be at its peak in a couple of years' time.

O Sauvignon Blanc '07	♟♟	6
● Il Boscorosso '05	♟♟	7
O COF Sauvignon Blanc '02	♟♟♟	6
● COF Rosso Il Boscorosso '04	♟♟	7
● COF Rosso Il Boscorosso '01	♟♟	7
O COF Sauvignon Blanc '06	♟♟	6
O COF Sauvignon Blanc '05	♟♟	6
O COF Sauvignon Blanc '04	♟♟	6
O COF Sauvignon Blanc '03	♟♟	6
● COF Rosso Il Boscorosso '03	♟♟	7
● COF Rosso Il Boscorosso '02	♟♟	7

O Collio Pinot Grigio '07	♟♟♟	5
O Collio Friulano '07	♟♟	5
O Collio Chardonnay '07	♟♟	5
O Collio Sauvignon '07	♟♟	5
● Red '06	♟	5
O Collio Pinot Grigio '06	♟♟♟	5
O Collio Pinot Grigio '05	♟♟♟	5
O Collio Pinot Grigio '04	♟♟	5

Livio e Claudio Buiatti

VIA LIPPE, 25
33042 BUTTRIO [UD]
TEL. 0432674317
www.buiattivini.it

Valentino Butussi

VIA PRÀ DI CORTE, 1
33040 CORNO DI ROSAZZO [UD]
TEL. 0432759194
www.butussi.it

ANNUAL PRODUCTION	30,000 bottles
HECTARES UNDER VINE	8
VITICULTURE METHOD	Conventional

This small Buttrio-based cellar has taken a firm step forward in overall quality. We knew that Claudio and his wife Viviana put a lot of effort into their work, and that they are very enthusiastic, but the excellence of the 2007 Sauvignon and the 2005 Rosso Momon Ros provide ample evidence of the couple's technical maturity. It gives us even more pleasure when we remember that the quality leap comes from a small estate that releases its wines at attractive prices. The Sauvignon is emblematic in the elderflower, yellow peach and tomato aromas that are faithfully echoed on the delicious palate, which is satisfyingly long. Rosso Momon Ros is a Bordeaux blend that spends almost two years in wood of various kinds. We liked its stylish oak-derived nuances laced with quinine, dried citrus fruits and balsam. The very elegant palate proffers mellow tannins and an attractive hint of blackberry tart. Also good are the fresh, Sauvignon-like Friulano, the Merlot, which is better in the mouth than on the nose, and the Verduzzo Friulano, redolent of baked apples lifted by confectioner's cream and candied citrus peel.

ANNUAL PRODUCTION	95,000 bottles
HECTARES UNDER VINE	16
VITICULTURE METHOD	Natural

The expression "family business" is over-used but not in the case of the Butussi operation. Angelo and Pierina have four children. Filippo is the oenologist, Tobia looks after production with his father and Erika and Mattia are in charge of marketing and distribution. To round things off, Pierina organizes hospitality at both the winery and the elegant agriturismo facilities. The results achieved by the long list of wines are steadily improving, as we noted from the 2006 Picolit. Its Two full Glasses were well deserved. The baked apple, candied citrus peel, raisin and sponge cake aromas are picked up on the full-bodied, almost opulently unctuous palate. The best of the rest also deserve comment. The Ribolla Gialla is very varietal, the Pinot Grigio tangy and long. Tropical fruit, tomato and elderflower mark out the Sauvignon while the Cabernet Franc is very fruity. The chardonnay, friulano and pinot bianco Bianco di Corte is creamy and its partner, Rosso di Corte from refosco, merlot and cabernet sauvignon, leads with subtle perceptions of liqueur cherries. Finally, the 2006 Verduzzo Friulano has curious citrus-like overtones.

● COF Rosso Momon Ros Ris. '05	♥♥	5
○ COF Sauvignon '07	♥♥	4*
○ COF Friulano '07	♥♥	4
● COF Merlot '06	♥♥	4
○ COF Verduzzo Friulano '06	♥♥	4
○ COF Picolit '06	♥	6
○ COF Pinot Bianco '07	♥	4
○ COF Pinot Grigio '07	♥	4
● COF Refosco P. R. '06	♥	4
● COF Cabernet '06		4
● COF Rosso Momon Ros Ris. '05	♥♥	5
● COF Rosso Momon Ros Ris. '04	♥♥	5
○ COF Sauvignon '06	♥♥	4*
○ COF Tocai Friulano '06	♥♥	4*

○ COF Picolit '06	♥♥	7
○ COF Bianco di Corte '07	♥♥	4
● COF Cabernet Franc '07	♥♥	4
○ COF Friulano '07	♥♥	4
○ COF Pinot Grigio '07	♥♥	4
○ COF Ribolla Gialla '07	♥♥	4
● COF Rosso di Corte '06	♥♥	5
○ COF Sauvignon '07	♥♥	4
○ COF Verduzzo Friulano '06	♥♥	4
● COF Cabernet Sauvignon '06	♥	4
○ COF Chardonnay '07	♥	4
● COF Refosco P. R. '07	♥	4
○ Friuli Grave Pinot Bianco '07	♥	4
● COF Merlot '07		4
● COF Cabernet Franc '06	♥♥	4
● Friuli Grave Refosco P. R. '06	♥♥	4

Maurizio Buzzinelli

LOC. PRADIS, 20
34071 CORMONS [GO]
TEL. 048160902
www.buzzinelli.com

ANNUAL PRODUCTION	100,000 bottles
HECTARES UNDER VINE	24
VITICULTURE METHOD	Conventional

Maurizio Buzzinelli is still a young wine man but he is well able to turn out a fine range of bottles. He is not alone, though, for his father Gigi and mother Luisa help out, as does his wife Marzia. Together they manage the family's agriturismo accommodation, in a splendidly panoramic location on the hills of Pradis near Cormons, as well as collaborating on various tasks in the vineyard and cellar. A couple of years ago, the cellar was extended and can now comfortably handle the grapes from 16 hectares in the hills and eight on the flatlands. Most of the wines are vinified in steel, apart from a few selections labelled Ronc dal Luis, which age in wood of various sizes. This year, Maurizio took us by surprise with a marvellous Friulano whose crisp pear and apple fragrances are mirrored in the palate, which finishes on the almondy note that is characteristic of the variety. The other Buzzinelli whites are equally fruit forward while the red Frututis (it means "baby girls" in Friulian) pays the price of the difficult 2005 growing year with its over-assertive extract. Both the Ribolla Gialla and the Pinot Bianco came close to a second Glass.

Ca' Bolani

VIA CA' BOLANI, 2
33052 CERVIGNANO DEL FRIULI [UD]
TEL. 043132670
www.cabolani.it

ANNUAL PRODUCTION	2,500,000 bottles
HECTARES UNDER VINE	550
VITICULTURE METHOD	Conventional

Here's a bit of history. Tenuta Ca' Bolani was at the height of its fame in the 16th century, when the Bolani family owned it and it was part of the Venetian empire. Domenico Bolani, the family's most celebrated scion, commissioned Andrea Palladio to design the Bolani Arch, which stands at the entrance to Udine castle. But let's get back to the winery. Ca' Bolani is far and away the largest estate in Friuli Venezia Giulia. Its three separate holdings, Ca' Bolani, Molin di Ponte and Ca' Vescovo, sprawl over some 900 hectares, of which 550 are planted to vine. There are two lines, Ca' Bolani for the base wines while the selections are released as Gianni Zonin Vineyards. Opimio, named after a Roman consul who encouraged viticulture at Aquileia, is a blend of chardonnay and tocai friulano. It's intense, refreshing, substantial and nicely acidic. The 2007 Traminer Aromatic also won a second Glass for its varietal typicity, honey and lime blossom.

O Collio Friulano '07		▼▼ 4
O Collio Pinot Bianco '07		▼ 3
O Collio Pinot Grigio '07		▼ 4
O Collio Ribolla Gialla '07		▼ 3
● Collio Rosso Frututis		
Ronc dal Luis '05		5

O Friuli Aquileia		
Traminer Aromatico '07		▼▼ 4
O Opimio Gianni Zonin Vineyards '07		▼▼ 4
● Friuli Aquileia Merlot '06		▼ 4
O Friuli Aquileia Pinot Bianco '07		▼ 4
O Friuli Aquileia Pinot Grigio '07		▼ 4
● Friuli Aquileia Refosco P. R. '06		▼ 4
O Friuli Aquileia Sauvignon '07		▼ 4
O Friuli Aquileia Sauvignon		
Tamànis Gianni Zonin Vineyards '07		▼ 4
O Friuli Aquileia Tocai Friulano '07		▼ 4
● Refosco P. R. Alturio		
Gianni Zonin Vineyards '04		▼ 5
O Friuli Aquileia Chardonnay '06		▽▽ 4

Ca' Tullio & Sdricca di Manzano

VIA BELIGNA, 41
33051 AQUILEIA [UD]
TEL. 0431919700
www.catullio.it

ANNUAL PRODUCTION	450,000 bottles
HECTARES UNDER VINE	78
VITICULTURE METHOD	Conventional

Ca' Tullio farms about 80 hectares, half in Friuli Aquileia the rest in the Colli Orientali del Friuli. Annual output comes to almost half a million bottles. The winery is a few minutes' drive from Aquileia, one of northern Italy's most important archaeological sites. Paolo Calligaris has converted a former tobacco drying house into a roomy cellar with an attractive sales outlet and a generous hospitality space used mainly for banquets and receptions. Ca' Tullio's competent staff includes husband and wife oenologists Francesco Visintin and Roberta Bassi while Patrizia Sepulcri busies herself with visitor hospitality and public relations. The nearby sea, salty air and sandy soil make this the ideal place to grow aromatic varieties and the 2007 Traminer Aromatico is tangible proof. Lavender and lime blossom florality emerge clearly on the nose, which introduces a moderately intense palate. The 2006 Sdricca selection of Verduzzo Friulano, reviewed in error last year, is outstanding for its finesse and intensity. Two Glasses also went to the Pinot Grigio for its varietal profile, elegance and power. The rest of the range is more than just decent.

Paolo Caccese

LOC. PRADIS, 6
34071 CORMONS [GO]
TEL. 048161062
www.paolocaccese.com

ANNUAL PRODUCTION	35,000 bottles
HECTARES UNDER VINE	6
VITICULTURE METHOD	Conventional

No longer chairman of the Collio protection consortium, Paolo Caccese is back working on his estate full time. This likeable wine man preferred making wine to employing the law degree he earned in his youth. It wasn't a question of snobbery. He was simply in love with an occupation that offers great personal satisfaction, plenty of human contact and the opportunity to work with nature. The six hectares yield ten or more different wines. To those who say he makes too many products, Paolo replies that he has to produce all the classic Friulian types to keep his customers happy. Whatever the case, we enjoyed two excellent Pinots, an intense, richly fruity Pinot Grigio and a stylish Pinot Bianco with a fresh palate, good breadth and lovely length. We are always surprised at Paolo's Müller Thurgau, a variety that has almost disappeared from the region but which Caccese makes with creditable results. The Traminer Aromatico is one of the most varietal you will find.

○ COF Verduzzo Friulano Sdricca '06	🍷🍷 6
○ COF Pinot Grigio Sdricca '07	🍷🍷 4*
○ Friuli Aquileia Traminer Aromatico '07	🍷🍷 4*
○ COF Friulano Sdricca '07	🍷 4
○ COF Ribolla Gialla Sdricca '07	🍷 4
● Friuli Aquileia Refosco P. R. '07	🍷 4
● Friuli Aquileia Rosso Il Patriarca d'Aquileia '06	🍷 4
● Rosso L'Ardito Casaforte Sdricca '05	🍷 5
○ COF Verduzzo Friulano Sdricca '05	🍷🍷 6
○ Traminer Viola '06	🍷🍷 5

○ Collio Friulano '07	🍷🍷 4*
○ Collio Müller Thurgau '07	🍷🍷 4*
○ Collio Pinot Bianco '07	🍷🍷 4*
○ Collio Pinot Grigio '07	🍷🍷 4*
○ Collio Traminer Aromatico '07	🍷🍷 4*
○ Collio Malvasia '07	🍷 4
○ Collio Riesling '07	🍷 4
○ Collio Sauvignon '07	🍷 4
○ La Veronica	🍷 6
● Collio Cabernet Franc '06	4

Alfieri Cantarutti

via Ronchi, 9
33048 San Giovanni al Natisone [UD]
tel. 0432756317
www.cantaruttialfieri.it

ANNUAL PRODUCTION 130,000 bottles
HECTARES UNDER VINE 54
VITICULTURE METHOD Conventional

Often when a winery reaches Alfieri Cantarutti's level of quality, it tends to play safe by doing the same things in vineyard and cellar. But not Antonella Cantarutti. When she met Giacomo Mela, who was teaching an in-service training course for oenologists, she was inspired to try out special cooling techniques to make a wine that would faithfully mirror the territory, do full justice to the grape and possess an assertive, original personality. Thus was born the Terre di Rosazzo project involving three wines: Merlot, Sauvignon and Friulano. The first releases are very good and the 2006 Sauvignon is excellent for it went through to the Three Glass final. Intense, crisp aromas of tropical fruits and citrus are mirrored nicely on the sumptuously full, well-structured palate. The Friulano from the same line and vintage offers pleasing balsamic notes that emerge against a backdrop of ripe fruit. Its partner from the standard line is creamy with a pervasive palate. As it has been for years, Bianco Canto, from friulano, pinot bianco and sauvignon, gives attractive dried roses and acacia honey.

○ COF Sauvignon Terre di Rosazzo Scacco al Re '06	🍷🍷	5
○ COF Bianco Canto '07	🍷🍷	4*
○ COF Friulano '07	🍷🍷	4*
○ COF Friulano Terre di Rosazzo Scacco al Re '06	🍷🍷	6
● COF Merlot Terre di Rosazzo Scacco al Re '05	🍷	6
○ COF Ribolla Gialla '07		4
○ COF Bianco Canto '06	♈︎♈︎	4
○ COF Tocai Friulano The Spirit of Ghost '04	♈︎♈︎	8

Canus

via Gramogliano, 21
33040 Corno di Rosazzo [UD]
tel. 0432759427
www.canus.it

ANNUAL PRODUCTION 35,000 bottles
HECTARES UNDER VINE 12
VITICULTURE METHOD Conventional

Canus comes from the family's old nickname, Grisòn, which means grey-haired old man. Actually, the Rossettos' recently established cellar is anything but a stick-in-the-mud operation. Dario, an accomplished designer, looks after production while Lara manages sales and keeps an eye on the accounts. Winemaking is the domain of oenologist Renato Cozzarolo. Work on the cellar was completed recently and the results are exciting. Spaces are attractive and designed to make working easier. The detail, the objets d'art and the colourful walls of the barrel cellar tell you that nothing has been left to chance. Our tasters had no doubt about the best wine: Jasmine, from chardonnay, sauvignon and pinot grigio, which tempts the nostrils with elegant summer flower scents before revealing nice mouthfilling weight and a long-lingering finish. Both versions of Ribolla Gialla are highly successful. Ribuele Blancie has perhaps a touch more minerality but the classic version is refined, very drinkable and lingers on the back palate. The rest of the range is well made with only the Chardonnay failing to earn more than a mention.

○ COF Bianco Jasmine '07	🍷🍷	5
○ COF Ribolla Gialla '07	🍷🍷	4*
○ COF Ribolla Gialla Ribuele Blancie '07	🍷🍷	5
○ COF Friulano '07	🍷	4
● COF Refosco P. R. '04	🍷	5
○ COF Sauvignon '07	🍷	4
● Rosso Cûar Neri '04	🍷	4
○ COF Chardonnay '07		4
○ COF Tocai Friulano '06	♈︎♈︎	4
○ COF Bianco Jasmine '06	♈︎♈︎	4
○ COF Sauvignon '06	♈︎♈︎	4

Il Carpino

LOC. SOVENZA, 14A
34070 SAN FLORIANO DEL COLLIO [GO]
TEL. 0481884097
www.ilcarpino.com

ANNUAL PRODUCTION	70,000 bottles
HECTARES UNDER VINE	16
VITICULTURE METHOD	Conventional

Anna and Franco Sosol have come a long way since they started in 1987. Today, they are showing that the creation of two lines for their hillside whites and reds from Mossa was a good move. Il Carpino wines age in wood, much of it large, whereas the Vigna Ruc range sees only steel. Marco Simonit still looks after the vines but there are new developments. Manuel and Naike, the Sosol youngsters, have joined the team and there are plans to extend the cellar. Overall, the wines are genuinely impressive. The 2005 Malvasia has confectioner's cream, candied orange peel and apricots with great nose-palate consistency. The Chardonnay from the same vintage gives aniseed, pineapple and fresh apples and the Sauvignon, also 2005, has spice and bell pepper before ripe fruit emerges on the palate. Pears and apricot tart theme of Bianco Carpino, a blend of sauvignon, ribolla gialla and chardonnay that melds oak sensations seamlessly with confectioner's cream and tea while Ribolla Gialla Vigna Runc puts the emphasis on citrus-driven freshness, rounded off by a tangy, lingering finale.

Casa Zuliani

VIA GRADISCA, 23
34070 FARRA D'ISONZO [GO]
TEL. 0481888506
www.casazuliani.com

ANNUAL PRODUCTION	120,000 bottles
HECTARES UNDER VINE	21
VITICULTURE METHOD	Conventional

This year's good news is the marriage of Federico Frumento, owner of the winery that once belonged to his great-grandfather Zuliano Zuliani, to Benedetta. Sadly, only a few days later Federico's father Franco passed away. Federico has partially renewed his team. Giovanni Bigot is now managing the vineyards and wine technician Omar Caffar is backed up by consultant Gianni Menotti in the cellar. After a year of transition, and despite extension work on the winery, Casa Zuliani has now set out again in pursuit of the quality objectives that Federico identified from the day he started. The excellent Bordeaux blend 2004 Rosso Winter, named for the previous owners, picked up Three Glasses, a fantastic achievement that caps a very fine all-round performance. Rosso Winter has touches of spice and tar, broad, concentrated fruit and incredible length on the palate. The Friulano, from tocai friulano, is elegant on the nose and gratifyingly substantial in the mouth. It's a superb wine from a poor year for the variety. The Sauvignon was a tad low key but the Pinot Bianco is a stand-out, with just a shade too much acidity.

O Bianco Carpino '05	♀♀	5
O Collio Chardonnay '05	♀♀	5
O Collio Malvasia '05	♀♀	6
O Collio Ribolla Gialla V. Runc '07	♀♀	4
O Collio Sauvignon '05	♀♀	5
O Collio Chardonnay V. Runc '07	♀	4
O Collio Malvasia V. Runc '07	♀	4
O Collio Pinot Grigio V. Runc '07	♀	4
O Collio Ribolla Gialla '05	♀	5
● Rubrum '99	♀♀♀	8
O Bianco Carpino '04	♀♀	5
O Collio Malvasia '04	♀♀	6
● Rubrum '03	♀♀	8

● Winter Rosso '04	♀♀♀	6
O Collio Friulano '07	♀♀	4*
O Collio Chardonnay '07	♀♀	4
O Collio Pinot Bianco '07	♀♀	4
O Chardonnay Winter '06	♀	5
O Collio Malvasia '07	♀	4
O Collio Pinot Grigio '07	♀	4
O Friuli Isonzo Pinot Grigio '07	♀	4
● Winter Rosso '03	♀♀	5

Casella Lino

VIA ALBANA, 55
33040 PREPOTTO [UD]
TEL. 0432713429
info.casella@libero.it

ANNUAL PRODUCTION	16,000 bottles
HECTARES UNDER VINE	3.5
VITICULTURE METHOD	Conventional

Lino Casella is a 40-something oenologist with lots of experience in local wineries, especially at Albana di Prepotto. In 2006, he rented 3.5 hectares from the Rieppi family, much with vines planted more than 40 years earlier. It's no surprise, then, that Lino has turned out such a fine range in only two years. His father, Francesco, has always grown grapes and today is Lino's anchor in all things viticultural. The cellar is cramped with a series of concrete vats, temperature-controlled steel containers and pre-used wood. Lino also gave us the 2006 Friulano, which is superior to the Friulano 2007. The 2006 is well structured and alcohol-rich but many wine lovers will prefer the more drinkable and less alcoholic younger wine. The stylishly fresh, rich-textured and long-lingering Pinot Bianco is a key wine for this new yet old cellar: the Rieppis had been making wine for over a century. Finally, the 2006 Franconia was a surprise. Few others can do so much with this variety, which is getting hard to find in Friuli.

O COF Pinot Bianco '07	♥♥	4*
O COF Tocai Friulano '06	♥♥	4*
● Franconia '06	♥♥	4*
O COF Friulano '07	♥	4
● COF Merlot '06	♥	4
● COF Tazzelenghe '06	♥	5
O COF Ribolla Gialla '07		4
● COF Schioppettino '06		5

La Castellada

FRAZ. OSLAVIA, 1
34170 GORIZIA
TEL. 048133670

ANNUAL PRODUCTION	23,000 bottles
HECTARES UNDER VINE	9
VITICULTURE METHOD	Conventional

Last year, we noted that this relatively young cellar in the wine enclave of Oslavia is to all intents a benchmark thanks to the seriously good wines it has released in recent years. The batch presented for this edition of the Guide seemed to be marking time but we are certain they will soon be back on top form. Beefy extract from extended maceration of the must and slow maturation in wood and then glass are not accompanied by the freshness and fruit that would give the wine the presence on the palate that we have come to expect from Bensa. From this year's offerings, we particularly liked the Tocai Friulano, which reprises the superlative quality of last year's wine, and the Rosso, which has been harder hit by the growing year. The Bianco, Chardonnay and Ribolla are all good, although the Sauvignon struggles to keep up.

● Collio Rosso della Castellada '02	♥♥	8
O Collio Tocai Friulano '04	♥♥	6
O Collio Bianco della Castellada '04	♥	6
O Collio Chardonnay '04	♥	6
O Collio Ribolla Gialla '04	♥	6
O Collio Sauvignon '04		6
● Collio Rosso della Castellada '99	♥♥♥	8
O Collio Tocai Friulano '03	♥♥♥	6
O Collio Bianco della Castellada '03	♥♥	6
O Collio Bianco della Castellada '02	♥♥	6
O Collio Bianco della Castellada '01	♥♥	6
O Collio Tocai Friulano '00	♥♥	6
O Collio Tocai Friulano '02	♥♥	6

Castello di Rubbia

SAN MICHELE DEL CARSO GORNJI VRH, 40
34070 SAVOGNA D'ISONZO [GO]
TEL. 0481882681
www.castellodirubbia.it

ANNUAL PRODUCTION	40,000 bottles
HECTARES UNDER VINE	10
VITICULTURE METHOD	Natural

In the late 1990s, tenacious Natasa Cernic decided to give the family winery a makeover. The Cernic family also owns the castle, which is currently being restored but will become a top-level resort facility. The cellar, dug out of the rock, is eye-catching with its attractive cross vault ceiling and stone walls but what makes it unique is its link with history. Just behind the barrel cellar is a First World War gun track trench that will soon be a museum. A few hundred metres away is the stunning main vineyard. Unusually for Carso, it boasts fully ten hectares of beautifully looked after vines planted in a single plot at an amazing 89,000 vines per hectare. The cellar's most emblematic wine is Malvasia, a very varietal version with fragrances of lavender and spring flowers followed by breadth on the palate and incredible persistence. For the second year running, Castello di Rubbia's Malvasia went through to our finals, where it very nearly claimed a top prize. The steel-fermented Bianco della Bora and oak-vinified and matured Trubar, both vitovska-only, are the two other wines that had our tasters nodding in approval.

O Malvasia '07	♟♟	5
O Bianco della Bora '06	♟♟	5
O Trubar '06	♟♟	5
O Leonard '06	♟	5
● Terrano '06	♟	5
O Vitovska '07	♟	5
O Malvasia '06	♟♟	5

Castelvecchio

VIA CASTELNUOVO, 2
34078 SAGRADO [GO]
TEL. 048199742
www.castelvecchio.com

ANNUAL PRODUCTION	250,000 bottles
HECTARES UNDER VINE	40
VITICULTURE METHOD	Conventional

It's well worth visiting Castelvecchio to see how hard work can tame a harsh, dry landscape without devastating it. Ecology is respected here and indeed enhanced by the estate's management policies and the viticultural heritage that give Carso wines their tangy austerity and high fixed acidity. These taut, aromatic whites and slightly rough-edged reds are perfect accompaniments respectively for fish and grilled meat or smoked and unsmoked pork-based dishes. Castelvecchio has always been a producer reds, whether international – the best this year was the Cabernet Sauvignon – or native, such as refosco dal peduncolo rosso or terrano, which also makes up 70 per cent of the blend in Turmino. This time, though, it was a quintessentially territorial white that made the best impression: Malvasia Istriana, whose elegant aromatics introduce a fresh, minerally palate with peach and medlar-like sensations that linger delightfully. Another wine worth uncorking is the attractively refreshing Traminer Aromatico, very different from some of the better-known, more challenging Gewürztraminers.

O Carso Malvasia Istriana '07	♟♟	4*
● Carso Cabernet Sauvignon '05	♟♟	5
● Carso Refosco P. R. '05	♟	5
● Carso Terrano '06		4
● Carso Cabernet Franc '05		5
O Carso Traminer Aromatico '07		4
● Carso Turmino '05		4
● Carso Merlot '03	♟♟	6
● Sagrado Rosso '03	♟♟	6
O Carso Malvasia Istriana '06	♟♟	4

Marco Cecchini

LOC. CASALI DE LUCA
VIA COLOMBANI
33040 FAEDIS [UD]
TEL. 0432720563
www.cecchinimarco.com

ANNUAL PRODUCTION	40,000 bottles
HECTARES UNDER VINE	10
VITICULTURE METHOD	Conventional

One of Marco Cecchini's bulletins points out how atypical the 2007 growing year was. Picking started in mid August in high temperatures that are very unusual for Friuli. It was quite a challenge and Marco took it on with his partner, oenology graduate Sonia dell'Oste, agronomist Gibril Crespan and the Terra&Vino consultancy group. Marco still has about ten hectares under vine in an area with a long wine tradition, even though it has slightly lower temperatures than average. Native varieties predominate. Pinot grigio, merlot and cabernet have been grown in the region for more than a century and are thoroughly acclimatized. This year, it was the Pinot Grigio that stood out from the rest, earning Two full Glasses for its combination of intensity, texture, elegance and long-lingering finish. Verlit 2006, the Cecchini version of Verduzzo Friulano, is amber in the glass, sweet on the palate and redolent of toffee apple and dried figs. Tovè, a tocai friulano-heavy blend with a splash of verduzzo, is less successful than before and the Picolit is very sweet. Finally, the 2006 Refosco is still young but shaping up well.

Eugenio Collavini

LOC. GRAMOGLIANO
VIA DELLA RIBOLLA GIALLA, 2
33040 CORNO DI ROSAZZO [UD]
TEL. 0432753222
www.collavini.it

ANNUAL PRODUCTION	1,500,000 bottles
HECTARES UNDER VINE	173
VITICULTURE METHOD	Conventional

Manlio Collavini sticks to the objectives he set himself some years ago when the cracks first began to show in the wine industry. His more than 170 hectares, most of which is not estate-owned, give him a flexibility smaller producers are denied. Manlio opted to raise quality standards and move into the market segment where competition is based on wine's sensory profile, not its price tag. Walter Bergnach, the competent oenologist who organizes the cellar, shows just how good he is in challenging years like 2007. Collio Bianco Broy, from tocai, chardonnay and sauvignon, is as convincing as ever, combining rich fruit with total consistency of nose and palate, shrewdly used oak and exceptional elegance. An astonishingly good wine. It's a shame that the superb Pinot Grigio Black Label is heading for Canada. We hop Manlio will keep a few cases of this impressively luscious, long wine for Italy. The Sauvignon Blanc Fumât is very varietal and reveals the faint smokiness that is reflected in its Friulian name. Forresco, from native refosco and pignolo grapes, is a wine for the cellar but is drinking very well now.

O COF Verduzzo Friulano Verlit '06	▼▼ 5
O Pinot Grigio Vigneto Bellagioia '07	▼▼ 4*
O COF Bianco Tovè '07	▼ 4
O COF Picolit '06	▼ 6
● COF Refosco P. R. '06	▼ 4
● COF Rosso Careme '05	4

O Collio Bianco Broy '07	▼▼▼ 5
● COF Rosso Forresco '04	▼▼ 6
O Collio Pinot Grigio Black Label '07	▼▼ 4*
O Collio Sauvignon Blanc Fumât '07	▼▼ 4*
O COF Ribolla Gialla Turian '07	▼▼ 6
● COF Refosco P. R. Pucino '07	▼ 4
O Collio Bianco Broy '06	♈♈♈ 5
O Collio Bianco Broy '04	♈♈♈ 5
O Collio Bianco Broy '05	♈♈ 5
● COF Rosso Forresco '03	♈♈ 6
● COF Schioppettino Turian '03	♈♈ 6
● Collio Merlot del Pic '03	♈♈ 6
● Collio Merlot del Pic '01	♈♈ 6

Colle Duga

LOC. ZEGLA, 10
34071 CORMONS [GO]
TEL. 048161177

ANNUAL PRODUCTION	35,000 bottles
HECTARES UNDER VINE	8
VITICULTURE METHOD	Conventional

Damian and Monica Princic, who own
Colle Duga, are a well-matched couple
and confirm the truth in the saying that
wine mirrors the people who make it. Their
courteous, forthright consultant Giorgio
Bertossi makes his own contribution but
freely admits that the range is crafted by
Damian, who manages the vine stock with
his father Luciano and takes the decisions
in the cellar. The vines are at the winery,
only a few metres from the Slovene border,
which thankfully is now open. The cellar
is spartan but has enough space for
Damian to work with both steel and oak.
Again this year, the whites were fighting
it out for top spot and it was the Collio
Bianco that picked up Three Glasses for
the complexity, freshness, intensity and
structure imbued by sauvignon, tocai,
chardonnay and malvasia fruit. The single-
variety Friulano 2007 failed to hit last year's
heights but continues to build on past
progress. Many observers thought that this
would be Pinot Grigio's year and in fact its
rich fruit, warmth and length earned it Two
full Glasses. Finally, Damian's Chardonnay
and Sauvignon are as good as ever.

Colli di Poianis

VIA POIANIS, 34A
33040 PREPOTTO [UD]
TEL. 0432713185
www.collidipoianis.com

ANNUAL PRODUCTION	45,000 bottles
HECTARES UNDER VINE	11
VITICULTURE METHOD	Conventional

Just after the Second World War, farmer
Paolino Marinig encouraged his sons
Danilo and Gabriele to take become
respectively an accountant and a banker,
albeit with a degree in agronomy and
oenology. Gabriele's love of the land
prompted the two brothers to restructure
and expand the original family farm, which
now has 25 hectares, 11 under vine.
The old cellar is now a farmstay run by
Gabriele's wife Maura and a new facility
with up-to-date technology and plenty
of space has been built nearby. Gabriele
keeps a watchful eye on events, and
admits getting a lot useful advice from that
great wine man Nicola Manferrari, as well
as the oenologist Stefano Menotti. This
year, we tasted some very good wines
indeed, starting with Rosso Ronco della
Poiana 2006 from 95 per cent merlot with
a dash of cabernet franc. It's rich, complex
and the tannins are nicely tucked in. The
Schioppettino is themed around liqueur
morello cherries while the Sauvignon gives
pennyroyal and tomato leaf. Elegance is the
keynote of the Friulano.

○ Collio Bianco '07	¶¶¶	5
○ Collio Friulano '07	¶¶	4*
○ Collio Pinot Grigio '07	¶¶	5
○ Collio Chardonnay '07	¶¶	5
○ Collio Sauvignon '07	¶¶	5
● Collio Merlot '06	¶	5
○ Collio Friulano '06	¶¶¶	4
○ Collio Friulano '05	¶¶¶	4
○ Collio Bianco '06	¶¶	5
● Collio Merlot '05	¶¶	5

○ COF Friulano '07	¶¶	4*
● COF Rosso Ronco della Poiana '06	¶¶	5
○ COF Sauvignon Vigna Baik '07	¶¶	4*
● COF Schioppettino '07	¶¶	6
○ COF Chardonnay Vigna dei Zuccoli '07	¶	5
○ COF Ribolla Gialla '07	¶	4

Colmello di Grotta

LOC. VILLANOVA
VIA GORIZIA, 133
34070 FARRA D'ISONZO [GO]
TEL. 0481888445
www.colmello.it

ANNUAL PRODUCTION 100,000 bottles
HECTARES UNDER VINE 21
VITICULTURE METHOD Conventional

Francesca Bortolotto's lovely estate has vineyards in the Collio and Friuli Isonzo DOCs. Last year, the cellar offered us some very fine wines and this year, there were good bottles on show alongside others that were less successful. The Pinot Grigios are on a par. In both, the nose is attractive but there is little weight on the palate. The Chardonnays scored similarly with the Collio version hinting at unusual but appealing aromatics and the Isonzo wine showing fruitier, fresher and more upfront. The Sauvignons are rather better. Made with textbook precision, they are nicely elegant and lack only a touch more personality. We also enjoyed the fresh-tasting, moreish Ribolla and the two Cabernets. The Franc has stylish fruit, although it is a little dilute, whereas the Cabernet Sauvignon puts too much emphasis on softness. But the best in the range is the broom, honey and yellow plum Bianco Sanfilip, which expands gratifyingly on the palate to sign off with a nice aromatic finish. The Friuli Isonzo DOC Merlot is not up to the standard of the 2004.

O Collio Bianco Sanfilip '07	ΨΨ	5
O Collio Chardonnay '07	Ψ	4
O Collio Friulano '07	Ψ	4
O Collio Pinot Grigio '07	Ψ	4
O Collio Ribolla Gialla '07	Ψ	4
O Collio Sauvignon '07	Ψ	4
● Friuli Isonzo Cabernet Franc '07	Ψ	4
● Friuli Isonzo Cabernet Sauvignon '06	Ψ	4
O Friuli Isonzo Chardonnay '07	Ψ	4
O Friuli Isonzo Pinot Grigio '07	Ψ	4
O Friuli Isonzo Sauvignon '07	Ψ	4
● Friuli Isonzo Merlot '06		4
● Friuli Isonzo Merlot '04	ΥΥ	4

Gianpaolo Colutta

VIA ORSARIA, 32/A
33044 MANZANO [UD]
TEL. 0432510654
www.coluttagianpaolo.com

ANNUAL PRODUCTION 150,000 bottles
HECTARES UNDER VINE 30
VITICULTURE METHOD Conventional

In 1846, the Coluttas forebear Antonio invented a product known all over the region, the Amaro di Udine digestive cordial. The estate's history is equally rich. The family coat of arms, featured in the Colutta winery logo, includes the blue and white shield that belonged to Contessa Anna di Prampero, Elisabetta's mother. With this heritage behind them, Elisabetta and her father Gianpaolo Colutta release a range that embraces long-standing Friulian varieties and international grapes. In fact, two international wines, the 2007 Pinot Bianco and Pinot Grigio, were the highest scorers, along with the prince of Friulian varieties, Pignolo, from the 2003 harvest. The Pinot Bianco's pineapple-led tropical fruits give the bouquet a sun-ripeness that is fully reflected on the palate. The minerally Pinot Grigio is lifted by hints of balsam and the Pignolo, which spends a year in large wood, has none of the rough edges that some versions reveal. It is beautifully soft, with warm morello cherry sensations and tannins nicely tucked in. The other nine wines in the range include a pungently herbaceous Sauvignon, a varietal Pinot Nero and a warm Refosco.

● COF Pignolo '03	ΨΨ	8
O COF Pinot Bianco '07	ΨΨ	4
O COF Pinot Grigio '07	ΨΨ	4
● COF Pinot Nero '07	Ψ	5
● COF Refosco P. R. '06	Ψ	4
O COF Sauvignon '07	Ψ	4
O COF Ribolla Gialla '07		5
● COF Rosso Frassinolo '03	ΥΥ	6
● COF Schioppettino '06	ΥΥ	6

Giorgio Colutta

VIA ORSARIA, 32
33044 MANZANO [UD]
TEL. 0432740315
www.colutta.it

ANNUAL PRODUCTION	150,000 bottles
HECTARES UNDER VINE	26
VITICULTURE METHOD	Conventional

The amiable Giorgio Colutta has a degree in pharmacy. He's a man with an almost understated way about him, just like the never over-the-top wines that he obtains by meticulous vineyard management and traditional vinification methods. Antonio Maggio looks after the vineyards and the cellar is the domain of Clizia Zambiasi, a shy yet determined oenologist who moved to Friuli from Trentino. Over the years, the winery has expanded to its current 26 hectares and the recently renovated and expanded cellar has spaces for both wood and steel containers. The estate also features farmstay accommodation in the 18th-century mansion. This year, Giorgio's biggest hitter was the 2006 Schioppettino, which delivers everything it portended when we tasted it in the spring. If the extract had been a shade less assertive, it would have gone on to the finals. In line with the growing year, the Pinot Grigio has plenty of good points, including a generous medley of fruit on the tangy, lingering palate. Finally, the Chardonnay Selezione has good weight in the mouth and the oak has been gauged to perfection.

Paolino Comelli

LOC. CASE COLLOREDO, 8
33040 FAEDIS [UD]
TEL. 0432711226
www.comelli.it

ANNUAL PRODUCTION	50,000 bottles
HECTARES UNDER VINE	12.5
VITICULTURE METHOD	Conventional

The Comelli family – Pierluigi, his wife Daniela and their children Nicola and Filippo – continues to administer this tranquil estate in the cool hills at Faedis. About a dozen hectares of vines planted to modern patterns at medium density yield mainly white wines but the Comellis have plans to increase the proportion of reds. The arrival of competent wine technician Emilio Del Medico has given this very valid operation a further boost. This year, only whites were on offer as the reds were still maturing. As usual, the Friulano was the bottle that most impressed our panel. Varietal pennyroyal, crusty bread and dried flowers mingle on the nose with a hint of sauvignon that returns on the palate, where the wine opens out, reprising the aromas of the nose and rounding off with a long almondy note. The Sauvignon performs better in the mouth, where the oiliness is nicely complemented by green notes of bell pepper and rue. We would also mention the antique rose, almost coppery, hue of the Pinot Grigio Amplius and the freshness of the Esprimo White, a blend of friulano, pinot grigio and chardonnay.

○ COF Pinot Grigio '07	♟	4
● COF Schioppettino '06	♟	5
● COF Cabernet '06	♟	4
○ COF Chardonnay Sel. Giorgio Colutta '07	♟	5
○ COF Friulano '07	♟	4
● COF Merlot Sel. Giorgio Colutta '05	♟	6
○ COF Ribolla Gialla '07		5
● COF Rosso Selenard '04		5
○ COF Sauvignon '07		4

○ COF Friulano '07	♟♟	4*
○ COF Sauvignon '07	♟♟	4
○ COF Pinot Grigio Amplius '07	♟	4
○ Esprimo White '07	♟	3
○ COF Chardonnay '07		4
○ COF Tocai Friulano '06	♟♟	4
● COF Cabernet Sauvignon '05	♟♟	5
● COF Rosso Soffumbergo '04	♟♟	5

Conte Brandolini

LOC. VISTORTA
VIA VISTORTA, 82
33077 SACILE [PN]
TEL. 0434782490
www.vistorta.it

ANNUAL PRODUCTION   300,000 bottles
HECTARES UNDER VINE   36
VITICULTURE METHOD   Conventional

Brandino Brandolini has changed the name
and label of his winery, which until last
year was known as Villa Ronche. Quality
continues to improve as Marco Simonit
watches over the rows and Alec Ongaro,
the meticulous in-house wine technician,
directs operations in the cellar. Only the
best of the fruit from the 36 hectares under
vine finds its way into the roughly 300,000
bottles. This year, we were impressed
by the Sauvignon, which joined the
Chardonnay in bidding for a place in the
finals. The Sauvignon is given a few days'
low temperature skin contact and then
stays on the fine lees for several months
with no oak. Part of the Chardonnay is
made with microbullage and the rest under
reducing conditions. The resulting blend is
outstandingly well balanced and the wine
is richly complex. The unusual Treanni
blend of 2004, 2005 and 2006 refosco,
cabernet franc and merlot aged in different
containers is wonderfully drinkable and
a distinct improvement on the previous
edition. All Brandino's products shine for
their elegance and moderate alcohol.

Dario Coos

LOC. RAMANDOLO
VIA RAMANDOLO, 5
33045 NIMIS [UD]
TEL. 0432790320
www.dariocoos.it

ANNUAL PRODUCTION   45,000 bottles
HECTARES UNDER VINE   7
VITICULTURE METHOD   Conventional

The winery that Dario Coos set up in
1986 is owned today by a group of friends
who look after distribution while Dario
himself remains in charge of winemaking.
Dario is the fifth generation of his family
to grow grapes at Ramandolo, a territory
whose virtues he has always strenuously
championed. Despite the achievement of
DOCG status, much work remains to be
done, especially convincing the territory's
growers to improve the overall quality of the
product. In recent years, the Coos winery
has expanded its vine stock to seven
hectares and with it the range of wines, for
a total output of 45,000 bottles. The late-
harvest 2004 Ramandolo is as impressive
as ever and leaves a deliciously lingering
aftertaste of caramel. The Sauvignon is
absolutely varietal, hinting at tomato leaf
and sage. Finally, the steel-fermented
Ramandolo Il Longhino 2005 is sweet but
not excessively so, very long and entirely
convincing.

O Friuli Grave Chardonnay '07	♥♥ 3*
O Friuli Grave Sauvignon '07	♥♥ 4*
O Friuli Grave Friulano '07	♥♥ 4
O Friuli Grave Pinot Grigio '07	♥♥ 4
O Friuli Grave Traminer Aromatico '07	♥♥ 4
● Treanni Rosso	♥♥ 4

O Ramandolo V. T. '04	♥♥ 5*
O Ramandolo Il Longhino '05	♥♥ 5
O Sauvignon Blanc '07	♥♥ 4
O Ribolla Gialla '07	♥ 4
O Ramandolo Romandus '04	♥♥ 6
O Ramandolo Romandus '02	♥♥ 6
O Ramandolo Il Longhino '04	♥♥ 5
O Ramandolo Il Longhino '03	♥♥ 5

Conte D'Attimis-Maniago

VIA SOTTOMONTE, 21
33042 BUTTRIO [UD]
TEL. 0432674027
www.contedattimismaniago.it

ANNUAL PRODUCTION	400,000 bottles
HECTARES UNDER VINE	85
VITICULTURE METHOD	Conventional

This historic estate sprawls over 110 hectares, almost entirely planted to vine, in the hills at Buttrio. Owner Alberto D'AttimisManiago has focused production on the major native Friulian vine types. Recently, there has been considerable interest in native grapes but here the decision was taken long ago. No one could accuse the estate of bandwagon jumping. Now that wisdom has borne fruit and this year confirms the excellence of the rarely grown tazzelenghe, yet another pointer to the outstanding work done on the estate. Tazzelenghe 2004, sourced from a vineyard planted in 1990, is both creamy and spicy, giving distinct pepper, milk chocolate, blackberry tart and hay yet with none of the variety's trademark rough edges. There were excellent performances from the other traditional wines. The Malvasia gives petits fours and dried flowers, the Schioppettino has currants and cinnamon while the Ribolla Gialla is all flowers and freshness. But there is more to this winery than just native grapes. Witness the wonderful Chardonnay 2007, which opens on elegant balsam and minerality followed by outstandingly refined, sincere progress on the palate.

O COF Chardonnay '07	♟♟	5
● COF Tazzelenghe '04	♟♟	6
O COF Malvasia '07	♟♟	4
O COF Pinot Grigio '07	♟♟	4
O COF Ribolla Gialla '07	♟♟	4
● COF Schioppettino '06	♟♟	6
O COF Picolit '06	♟	8
O COF Sauvignon '07	♟	4
O Ribula Brut	♟	5
● COF Cabernet '06		4
O COF Malvasia '06	♟♟	4
● COF Tazzelenghe '03	♟♟	6

di Lenardo

FRAZ. ONTAGNANO
P.ZZA BATTISTI, 1
33050 GONARS [UD]
TEL. 0432928633
www.dilenardo.it

ANNUAL PRODUCTION	600,000 bottles
HECTARES UNDER VINE	45
VITICULTURE METHOD	Conventional

Max Di Lenardo is a man who keeps up with the times. He knows how to get the best from his cellar and also has great flair for marketing. This year sees the debut of Di Lenardo's first-ever spumante whose name – Sarà Brut (It'll Be Awful) – is a classic example of Max's penchant for wordplay in the names of his wines. Ronco Nolè is another good example. "No l'è" is Friulian for "not there". The name means there is no "ronco", or hillside vineyard, for this is a flatlands wine. Di Lenardo is always on the lookout for new markets and sells very well abroad, especially in the United States. The vineyards are in the Grave DOC zone, the vast alluvial plain between the hills and the coast that produces, particularly here at Ontagnano, wines that are more easy drinking than muscular. It was the 2007 Pinot Bianco that impressed our panel most with its attractive fresh fruit, persistence and elegance. We also liked the very varietal Sauvignon.

O Friuli Grave Sauvignon '07	♟♟	3*
O Pinot Bianco '07	♟♟	3*
O Chardonnay '07	♟	4
O Friuli Grave Chardonnay '07	♟	3
O Friuli Grave Friulano Toh! '07	♟	4
● Merlot Just Me '06	♟	5
O Pinot Grigio '07	♟	3
● Ronco Nolè Rosso '06	♟	4
O Verduzzo Pass the Cookies '07	♟	4
● Friuli Grave Cabernet '07		3
O Sarà Brut '06		5
● Merlot Just Me '05	♟♟	5
● Merlot Just Me '04	♟♟	5

Carlo Di Pradis

LOC. PRADIS, 22BIS
34071 CORMONS [GO]
TEL. 048162272
www.carlodipradis.it

ANNUAL PRODUCTION 80,000 bottles
HECTARES UNDER VINE 15
VITICULTURE METHOD Conventional

Brothers Boris and David Buzzinelli farm seven hectares of hillside vines and eight more in the flatlands, a common pattern at Cormons, where the Collio and Friuli Isonzo DOCs rub shoulders. Some of the hillside plot at Pradis has been turned over to the large, practical cellar, where the two brothers live. Carlo is their father's name and Boris and David have named their winery in recognition of his decision to take the quality route about 20 years ago. Isonzo DOC wines released under the Bordavi label, a conflation of Boris and David, make up the bulk of the 80,000 bottles released each year. The Buzzinellis also want to try their hand with skin contact and to make their 2006 Friulano Scusse – the name means "skin" in Friulian – they left the must fermenting on the skins for 17 days. After ageing in 1,500-litre barrels and bottling without filtration, the wine is full bodied, savoury and richly textured but lacking in elegance. We preferred the fresh-tasting, fruit-forward Friulano BorDavi from steel-fermented fruit. The whites picked up plenty of Glassware but the reds tended to struggle.

O Friuli Isonzo Friulano BorDavi '07	🍷🍷	4*
O Collio Friulano '07	🍷	4
O Collio Friulano Scusse '06	🍷	5
O Collio Pinot Grigio '07	🍷	4
O Collio Sauvignon '07	🍷	4
O Friuli Isonzo Chardonnay BorDavi '07	🍷	4
O Friuli Isonzo Pinot Grigio BorDavi '07	🍷	4
O Friuli Isonzo Sauvignon BorDavi '07	🍷	4
● Friuli Isonzo Merlot BorDavi '05		4
● Friuli Isonzo Cabernet Franc BorDavi '07		4

Giovanni Donda

VIA MANLIO ACIDINIO, 4
33051 AQUILEIA [UD]
TEL. 043191185
www.vinidonda.it

ANNUAL PRODUCTION 30,000 bottles
HECTARES UNDER VINE 6
VITICULTURE METHOD Conventional

Last year, Giovanni Donda's cellar gave us a range of goodish wines without the quality spikes that we have come to expect from this operation near Aquileia. That's why we excluded it from the last edition of the Guide. But now it is back in, thanks above all to a 2005 Refosco dal Peduncolo Rosso that has reached its peak of maturation, giving rich spice and intense, blueberry-led berry fruit. On reflection, perhaps more producers should let their wines mature in the cellar longer and resist the siren song of a market with a thirst for young, fresh wines. Giovanni's consultant oenologist is the competent Giorgio Bertossi. From the current whites, we enjoyed the Sauvignon's tomato leaf-like aromas that pervade nose and palate. The fresh acidity of the fine Pinot Grigio is slightly penalized by a hint of softness. Stylish hawthorn is the keynote of the very varietal Pinot Bianco. Finally, the 2006 Merlot lacks the harmony we associate with this variety but there again, it might just need a bit longer in glass.

● Friuli Aquileia Refosco P. R. '05	🍷🍷	4*
O Friuli Aquileia Sauvignon '07	🍷🍷	4*
O Friuli Aquileia Pinot Bianco '07	🍷	3
O Friuli Aquileia Pinot Grigio '07	🍷	4
● Friuli Aquileia Merlot '06		4

★ Girolamo Dorigo

LOC. VICINALE
VIA DEL POZZO, 5
33042 BUTTRIO [UD]
TEL. 0432674268
www.montsclapade.com

ANNUAL PRODUCTION	200,000 bottles
HECTARES UNDER VINE	40
VITICULTURE METHOD	Conventional

At last, renovation of Girolamo Dorigo's cellar is nearly over. Truth to tell, the surprisingly unsophisticated conditions in which this emblematic Buttrio winemaker worked often raised eyebrows. Evidently, the gritty commitment of son Alessio in the cellar and daughter Alessandra in public relations has convinced the venerable – well, he is 74 – Girolamo that the estate's future is worth investing in. As you might expect, building work, compounded by the 2007 vintage, has had repercussions on the wines, especially the reds, which were below the standards of previous vintages. We are talking about the standard wines, which are still good and excellent value for money. Sauvignon Ronc di Juri again brings up the issue of oak ageing. Today, the oak is too prominent but we know from experience that it will endow the wine with longevity. The 2005 Pignolo may be young but it is truly outstanding and the Montsclapade, another 2005, confirms its ranking as one of the region's best Bordeaux blends. Dorigo Brut, from chardonnay and pinot nero, is eminently reliable so we are keen to taste the blanc de noir next year. For now, it is still being fine-tuned.

Mauro Drius

VIA FILANDA, 100
34071 CORMONS [GO]
TEL. 048160998
drius.mauro@adriacom.it

ANNUAL PRODUCTION	70,000 bottles
HECTARES UNDER VINE	11.5
VITICULTURE METHOD	Conventional

Some wineries never let you down and the one that Mauro Drius and his father run at Cormons is among that number. What's your idea of a classic Tocai Friulano? Deep straw with greenish tinges; concentrated nose, not too broad and slightly closed at first before it unfolds fruits and florality, including acacia blossom and elderflowers; sustained thrust on a palate that mirrors the nose, warmth, substantial structure, plenty of flesh, good supporting acidity? In that case, Mauro's Isonzo DOC Friulano is the Three Glass wine for you. It's not the only stunner. The prizewinner is joined by a Collio DOC Friulano that is only a shade greener, a superbly drinkable Pinot Grigio that is another paragon of reliability, a Chardonnay that takes full advantage of a favourable year for the variety, a Malvasia with lingering apple-like aromatics, and the tocai, sauvignon and pinot bianco Bianco Vìgnis di Sìris 2006, whose warm, caressing mouthfeel signs off with lingering hazelnut, peach and fresh-baked bread. Also good are the aromatic herb and honey-fragranced Pinot Bianco and the nicely structured Sauvignon, which is a touch dilute on the back palate.

● COF Pignolo di Buttrio '05	♟♟ 8
● COF Rosso Montsclapade '05	♟♟ 7
○ COF Chardonnay '07	♟♟ 6
○ COF Pinot Grigio '07	♟♟ 4
○ COF Traminer '07	♟♟ 4
○ COF Verduzzo Friulano '06	♟♟ 5
○ Dorigo Brut	♟♟ 5
● COF Refosco P. R. '05	♟ 6
● COF Merlot '07	4
○ COF Sauvignon Vign. Ronc di Juri '07	6
● COF Pignolo di Buttrio '03	♟♟♟ 8
● COF Pignolo di Buttrio '02	♟♟♟ 8
● COF Pignolo di Buttrio '01	♟♟♟ 8
● COF Rosso Montsclapade '04	♟♟♟ 7
● COF Rosso Montsclapade '01	♟♟♟ 7

○ Friuli Isonzo Friulano '07	♟♟♟ 4*
○ Collio Friulano '07	♟♟ 4
○ Friuli Isonzo Bianco Vìgnis di Sìris '06	♟♟ 5
○ Friuli Isonzo Chardonnay '07	♟♟ 4
○ Friuli Isonzo Malvasia '07	♟♟ 4
○ Friuli Isonzo Pinot Grigio '07	♟♟ 4
○ Collio Sauvignon '07	♟ 4
○ Friuli Isonzo Pinot Bianco '07	♟ 4
○ Collio Tocai Friulano '05	♟♟♟ 4
○ Collio Tocai Friulano '02	♟♟♟ 4
○ Friuli Isonzo Bianco Vignis di Siris '02	♟♟♟ 4
○ Collio Sauvignon '06	♟♟ 4
○ Friuli Isonzo Pinot Grigio '06	♟♟ 4
○ Friuli Isonzo Tocai Friulano '06	♟♟ 4

Le Due Terre

VIA ROMA, 68B
33040 PREPOTTO [UD]
TEL. 0432713189

ANNUAL PRODUCTION	20,000 bottles
HECTARES UNDER VINE	5
VITICULTURE METHOD	Natural

Mention Flavio and Silvana Basilicata and you can't help thinking about the sacrifices they have made to build this lovely winery. Happily, their efforts have been rewarded by the results they have attained and continue to achieve. Flavio is a sensitive wine man, concerned about environmental issues. He uses only sulphur and copper in the rows. His scrupulous picking enables him to bring perfect grapes to the cellar, where they are crushed and the must racked into small wood. From that point on, human hands have little to do. Fermentation is started by native yeasts only and the whites stay in wood for 18 months while the reds remain there for up to 22. Over time, the wines settle on their own and there is no need for filtration. Bianco Sacrisassi is a controversial but indisputably great wine. In 2006, Flavio produced 3,300 bottles in the traditional style from a blend of tocai friulano and ribolla gialla. Ripe fruit and flowers veined with balsamic notes precede a rich palate that reveals the wine's brief skin contact. The Merlot and Rosso Sacrisassi from the same vintage are distinctly good.

Dario e Luciano Ermacora

FRAZ. IPPLIS
VIA SOLZAREDO, 9
33040 PREMARIACCO [UD]
TEL. 0432716250
www.ermacora.com

ANNUAL PRODUCTION	165,000 bottles
HECTARES UNDER VINE	25
VITICULTURE METHOD	Conventional

In his book "Elogio dell'invecchiamento" (In Praise of Ageing), Andrea Scanzi wrote, referring to this winery: "Ermacora's whites are clean, fresh, frank and free of embellishment". We agree. We have always commended Dario Ermacora's wines for their textbook respect for variety and their sincerity. That lack of embellishment certainly affected the wines in what was a far from easy growing year in Friuli. Nevertheless, expert wine man Dario still managed to turn out a very fine range. As ever, the Pinot Bianco stands out for the elegance of its yeast, flowers, almonds and juicy orange-like aromas as well as its tanginess on the palate. The elegant Pignolo gives interesting toastiness, robust but not aggressive extract and a vibrantly dynamic palate that has you reaching for a second glass. Also very successful are the exemplary, varietal Friulano with its crusty bread, almonds and apples, the very minerally yet rich-textured Pinot Grigio and the Picolit, which finds a superb balance of sweetness and stylish balsam in the mouth.

O COF Bianco Sacrisassi '06	♀♀	5
● COF Merlot '06	♀♀	5
● COF Rosso Sacrisassi '06	♀♀	5
● COF Pinot Nero '06	♀	5
O COF Bianco Sacrisassi '05	♀♀♀	5
● COF Merlot '03	♀♀♀	7
● COF Merlot '02	♀♀♀	7
● COF Merlot '00	♀♀♀	7
● COF Rosso Sacrisassi '98	♀♀♀	7
● COF Rosso Sacrisassi '97	♀♀♀	7
O COF Bianco Sacrisassi '04	♀♀	5
O COF Bianco Sacrisassi '03	♀♀	5
O COF Bianco Sacrisassi '02	♀♀	5
● COF Merlot '04	♀♀	7
● COF Rosso Sacrisassi '04	♀♀	7

● COF Pignolo '04	♀♀	6
O COF Friulano '07	♀♀	4
O COF Picolit '06	♀♀	7
O COF Pinot Bianco '07	♀♀	4
O COF Pinot Grigio '07	♀♀	4
● COF Refosco P. R. '06	♀	4
O COF Sauvignon '07	♀	4
O COF Verduzzo Friulano '07	♀	4
● COF Pignolo '00	♀♀♀	5
● COF Pignolo '03	♀♀	6
● COF Pignolo '02	♀♀	6
● COF Pignolo '01	♀♀	6
O COF Pinot Bianco '06	♀♀	4
O COF Pinot Bianco '05	♀♀	4

★ Livio Felluga

FRAZ. BRAZZANO
VIA RISORGIMENTO, 1
34071 CORMONS [GO]
TEL. 048160203
www.liviofelluga.it

ANNUAL PRODUCTION   **950,000 bottles**
HECTARES UNDER VINE   **155**
VITICULTURE METHOD   **Conventional**

Terre Alte is back. Following a year's absence because the Fellugas decided the 2005 growing year wasn't good enough, the thoroughbred raced straight to a Three Glass prize. We are very pleased. Terre Alte is one of Friuli's iconic wines, a superb example of the region's unique potential. Obtained from a blend of steel-fermented pinot bianco and sauvignon with barrique-fermented friulano, the 2006 edition gives rue, bell peppers, peach and crusty bread veined with a restrained hint of vanilla that holds it all together. Elegance and consistency with the nose are the features of the long, well-sustained palate. The other flagship, the refosco, merlot and pignolo Sossò, is equally fine with its warmth and sun-ripe notes of candied citrus peel, dried roses, mint and confectioner's cream. Complexity on the palate is highlighted by good extract and an intense fruit-rich finish. Illivio was created in 1998 by Maurizio, Andrea, Filippo and Elda Felluga for their father Livio's 85th birthday and this version finds a convincing balance of fruit and vanilla. The Sauvignon is very refreshing and not at all aggressive while the subtle Pinot Grigio offers tropical fruit and fresh-baked bread.

Marco Felluga

VIA GORIZIA, 121
34070 GRADISCA D'ISONZO [GO]
TEL. 048199164
www.marcofelluga.it

ANNUAL PRODUCTION   **600,000 bottles**
HECTARES UNDER VINE   **120**
VITICULTURE METHOD   **Conventional**

You have to admit that Marco Felluga knew what he was doing from the start. The modern oenology concept he has developed at his winery long ago led him to forge close relationships with universities and create a quality project that extended to all his properties. Now, Marco's son Roberto Felluga is determinedly carrying on that project at this major Collio estate. The work enabled the winery to put on a fine performance across the entire range, despite the poor growing year. The Ribolla Gialla is fresh and minerally, the Pinot Grigio fragrantly fruity. We liked the tobacco and boiled sweets notes of the Chardonnay and the invitingly varietal Moscato Rosa. Pinot Grigio Riserva Mongris is a stunning cornucopia of youthful peach, apricot, white damson, melon and pineapple fruit. Bianco Molamatta, from friulano, ribolla e pinot bianco, is fresh and redolent of oranges. Finally, there are two excellent reds. Refosco Ronco dei Moreri is spicy on the nose and velvety on the palate and the Bordeaux blend Carantan impresses with its rounded palate, smooth tannins and lingering coffee-like finish.

○ COF Rosazzo Bianco Terre Alte '06	♀♀♀	7
● COF Rosazzo Sossò Ris. '04	♀♀	7
○ COF Bianco Illivio '06	♀♀	5
○ COF Pinot Grigio '07	♀♀	5
○ COF Sauvignon '07	♀♀	5
○ COF Friulano '07	♀	5
○ Collio Bianco Rosenplatz '06	♀	5
○ Shàrjs '07	♀	4
● COF Refosco P. R. '99	♀♀♀	7
○ COF Rosazzo Bianco Terre Alte '04	♀♀♀	7
○ COF Rosazzo Bianco Terre Alte '02	♀♀♀	6
○ COF Rosazzo Bianco Terre Alte '01	♀♀♀	6
○ COF Rosazzo Bianco Terre Alte '99	♀♀♀	6
○ COF Rosazzo Bianco Terre Alte '97	♀♀♀	6
○ COF Rosazzo Bianco Terre Alte '96	♀♀♀	6
● COF Rosazzo Sossò Ris. '01	♀♀♀	7

○ Collio Bianco Molamatta '07	♀♀	5
● Collio Carantan '04	♀♀	6
○ Collio Chardonnay '07	♀♀	4*
○ Collio Pinot Grigio Mongris '07	♀♀	4*
○ Collio Pinot Grigio Mongris Ris. '05	♀♀	5
○ Collio Ribolla Gialla '07	♀♀	5
☉ Moscato Rosa '05	♀♀	5
● Refosco P. R. Ronco dei Moreri '06	♀♀	5
● Carantan '03	♀♀	6
● Sorripa S. Nicolò a Pisignano '03	♀♀	5
○ Collio Pinot Grigio Mongris '06	♀♀	4

Fiegl

FRAZ. OSLAVIA
LOC. LENZUOLO BIANCO, 1
34070 GORIZIA
TEL. 0481547103
www.fieglvini.com

ANNUAL PRODUCTION	130,000 bottles
HECTARES UNDER VINE	26
VITICULTURE METHOD	Conventional

The hills of Oslavia are the highest in the Collio DOC, which exposes them to the Adriatic breezes that bring wide temperature fluctuations and good ventilation. Add to this the finest vine-growing soil in the whole of Friuli Venezia Giulia and it is no surprise that Oslavia boasts a raft of outstanding wineries. At Fiegl, everyone knows his or her job. The three brothers Ales, Josko and Rado mesh perfectly as a team managing the cellar that their children help to run. Consistently high quality is a given at Fiegl for the winery has achieved an admirable level of dependability. Wines are sold under two lines, Leopold, for products released after more than a year's ageing, and the traditional, more approachably fresh wines. Two Fiegl bottles came close to Three Glasses. Both find enviable balance between intensity and elegance, showing all the Fiegls' signature savouriness. Malvasia impressed us most. In fact, it's one of the best we tasted this year. Cuvée Blanc Leopold, from pinot bianco, ribolla, friulano and sauvignon, is coming on marvellously and the sweet Meja, from part-dried traminer, also won us over.

Flaibani

CASALI COSTA, 7
33040 CIVIDALE DEL FRIULI [UD]
TEL. 0432730943
www.flaibani.it

ANNUAL PRODUCTION	20,000 bottles
HECTARES UNDER VINE	4
VITICULTURE METHOD	Conventional

Pino Flaibani is one of those Friulians whose career took him all over Italy before he returned to his native soil to devote himself to his life's passion, making wine. He was supported in this by his wife Dorina, who is the cellar's owner and works alongside her husband in the cellar and organizing hospitality. Their children Maurizio and Michele lend a hand in their spare moments and dependable daughter-in-law Bruna is in charge of distribution. Friends Giorgio Braida and Carlo Petrussi chip in with vineyard management and, for white winemaking in particular, the cellar calls on the Terra&Vino group. With about four hectares, and very low yields in the vineyard, annual output is below 20,000 units. But the reds are a revelation, especially the Cabernet Sauvignon Riserva 2005 and the standard 2006 version. It is not often that the variety reaches these heights in Friuli. Wonderfully exposed rows, juice run-off for the Riserva and Pino's passion are behind these superior results. Riviere Bianco, a single-variety Friulano, is very successful. Finally, the Schioppettino is very varietal.

O Collio Malvasia '07	♈♈	4*
O Collio Sauvignon '07	♈♈	4*
O Collio Cuvée Blanc Leopold '06	♈♈	5
● Collio Merlot Leopold '03	♈♈	5
O Meja '05	♈♈	6
O Collio Chardonnay '07	♈	4
O Collio Friulano '07	♈	4
O Collio Pinot Grigio '07	♈	4
O Collio Ribolla Gialla '07	♈	4
O Collio Pinot Grigio '01	♈♈♈	4
● Collio Merlot Leopold '02	♈♈	5
● Collio Merlot Leopold '01	♈♈	5

● COF Cabernet Sauvignon '06	♈♈	4*
● COF Cabernet Sauvignon Ris. '05	♈♈	4*
O Riviere Bianco '07	♈♈	4*
● COF Cabernet Franc '06	♈	4
● COF Schioppettino '06	♈	5
O Pinot Grigio '07	♈	4
● COF Merlot '07		4

Foffani

FRAZ. CLAUIANO
P.ZZA GIULIA, 13
33050 TRIVIGNANO UDINESE [UD]
TEL. 0432999584
www.foffani.it

ANNUAL PRODUCTION 80,000 bottles
HECTARES UNDER VINE 10
VITICULTURE METHOD Conventional

North-east of the star-shaped town of Palmanova lies the lovely village of Clauiano, where Foffani stands in the eye-catching main square. This long-established cellar has origins in the 16th century and documents show that it was making wine before 1789. Giovanni and Elisabetta Foffani have given the estate new energy by putting on social events at the cellar and by crafting territorial wines. The soil is alluvial and not very fertile and the meticulously cared for vineyards are densely planted, which enables the reds in particular to scale the heights of quality. Last year, we praised the excellent Merlot Riserva and this time we tasted a seriously good Sauvignon 2005, and remember that this is not a sauvignon area. The Foffani version has ripe fruit, bitter chocolate and bay leaf introducing a fairly warm, vigorous palate. Equally impressive is the Friulano, which flaunts varietal almonds and apples backed by marked minerality and good thrust on the palate. From the rest of the range, try varietal banana and pear drop Chardonnay or the confectioner's cream and fruit fragrances of the Rosso Ter Vinum, a blend of merlot, refosco cabernet franc.

● Friuli Aquileia Cabernet Sauvignon '05	♥♥ 4*
○ Friuli Aquileia Friulano Sup. '07	♥♥ 4*
● Friuli Aquileia Cabernet Franc '06	♥ 4
○ Friuli Aquileia Chardonnay Sup. '07	♥ 4
○ Friuli Aquileia Pinot Grigio Sup. '07	♥ 4
○ Friuli Aquileia Sauvignon Sup. '07	♥ 4
● Friuli Aquileia Rosso Ter Vinum '05	♥ 3
● Friuli Aquileia Merlot Ris. '03	♥♥ 6
○ Friuli Aquileia Pinot Grigio Sup. '06	♥♥ 4

Forchir

FRAZ. PROVESANO
VIA CIASUTIS, 1B
33095 SAN GIORGIO DELLA RICHINVELDA [PN]
TEL. 042796037
www.forchir.it

ANNUAL PRODUCTION 970,000 bottles
HECTARES UNDER VINE 226
VITICULTURE METHOD Conventional

On other occasions, we have highlighted Forchir's size, modern technology and knack of combining big numbers with good quality. This time, we are lauding peaks of excellence with wines like Campo dei Gelsi. Enzo Bianchini, the oenologist and owner – with Enzo Deana – of the property, has worked hard to recover the estate's old pinot bianco vines, imported in the late 19th century by the Conte di Colloredo, to whom Forchir belonged at the time. The elegant 2007 has subtle citrus and fresh-baked bread, unfolding softly on a palate that reveals decent structure and breadth to sign off with a fresh, citrus-like finale. Three other bottles from native varieties testify to Forchir's close ties with the territory. The Friulano Lusôr is refreshing and very well typed, the Refoscone – from a subvariety of refosco – offers prominent ripe cherry and bramble fruit, creaminess and assertive but smooth tannins and the Bianco Un Blanc ("un blanc" is the Friulian way of ordering a glass of white wine), a blend of friulano and ribolla, is minerally and redolent of flowers, with a nice fresh finish.

○ Friuli Grave Bianco Campo dei Gelsi '07	♥♥ 4*
○ Bianco Un Blanc '07	♥♥ 4
○ Friuli Grave Friulano Lusôr '07	♥♥ 4
● Refoscone '06	♥♥ 5
● Friuli Grave Refosco P. R. Arnacis '07	♥ 4
○ Friuli Grave Sauvignon L'Altro '07	♥ 4
○ Friuli Grave Traminer Aromatico Glere '07	♥ 4
○ Ribolla Gialla '07	♥ 4
● Friuli Grave Cabernet Franc Braidate '07	4
● Friuli Grave Merlot Mirie '07	4
● Friuli Grave Cabernet Franc Braidate '06	♥♥ 4
○ Friuli Grave Pinot Bianco Campo dei Gelsi '06	♥♥ 4

Adriano Gigante

VIA ROCCA BERNARDA, 3
33040 CORNO DI ROSAZZO [UD]
TEL. 0432755835
www.adrianogigante.it

ANNUAL PRODUCTION **60,000 bottles**
HECTARES UNDER VINE **13**
VITICULTURE METHOD **Conventional**

There is no disputing that 2007 was less than kind to friulano. Even Adriano, Giuliana and Ariedo Gigante's Friulano Vigneto Storico felt the effects. It's still an outstanding wine, with sun-ripe tropical fruit and gentler sensations of almonds and apple offsetting each other delightfully, but it didn't quite scale the heights to pick up a third Glass. Nonetheless, the cellar showed what it can do with an all-round team performance of admirable calibre. A glance at the table below will confirm that this winery farms the hills at Corno with serious, quality-oriented skills. The textbook Pinot Grigio is subtle, the Chardonnay invitingly fresh and the Sauvignon has a tempting weave of fruit veined with savoury minerality. The Ribolla Gialla, too, presents a seamlessly sustained medley of almond, apple, crusty bread, fresh citrus and spring flowers. But the Gigante can also do reds, as three wines amply demonstrate. The Merlot Riserva 2005 gives intense balsam over bramble jam, the Schioppettino 2006 is warm with a swath of spices and the Pignolo 2004 is a wine with all the extract it needs to age successfully in the cellar.

Gradis'ciutta

LOC. GIASBANA, 10
34070 SAN FLORIANO DEL COLLIO [GO]
TEL. 0481390237
robigradis@libero.it

ANNUAL PRODUCTION **60,000 bottles**
HECTARES UNDER VINE **17**
VITICULTURE METHOD **Conventional**

Robert's family has been making wine for at least three generations. In 1989, he enrolled to study oenology and the family expanded the vine stock, purchasing a splendid hillside to add to the various other Princic parcels in the area. Since bottling its first wines in 1997, the cellar has gone from strength to strength, negotiating major building work on new facilities in 2005. The vineyards around the Collio DOC are managed with a careful eye on soil types, aspects and vine suitability. Robert is keen to find an ideal white blend and promises news soon. Bianco del Tüzz, from chardonnay, tocai and malvasia matured in large wood, gives dried figs, ripe peaches and orange cream before the elegant palate offers intense tropical fruits. The Ribolla Gialla tempts the nose with subtle acacia blossom and wisteria, laced with rennet apple. Bianco Bratinis, from steel-fermented chardonnay, sauvignon and ribolla gialla, hints at hazelnut and regales the palate with ripe white-fleshed fruits. Rue, bell pepper and peach set the tone for the attractive Sauvignon while the almondy Friulano is elegant and the Pinot Grigio proffers ripe fruit and citrus.

O COF Chardonnay '07	♟♟ 4*
O COF Friulano Vign. Storico '07	♟♟ 5
O COF Pinot Grigio '07	♟♟ 4*
O COF Ribolla Gialla '07	♟♟ 4*
O COF Sauvignon '07	♟♟ 4*
O COF Bianco Barbe Blanc '07	♟♟ 4
● COF Merlot Ris. '05	♟♟ 6
● COF Pignolo '04	♟♟ 6
● COF Schioppettino '06	♟♟ 5
● COF Refosco P. R. '05	♟ 4
● COF Merlot '05	4
O COF Tocai Friulano Vign. Storico '06	♟♟♟ 5
O COF Tocai Friulano Vign. Storico '05	♟♟♟ 5
O COF Tocai Friulano Vign. Storico '03	♟♟♟ 5
O COF Tocai Friulano Storico '00	♟♟♟ 5
● COF Pignolo '03	♟♟ 6

O Collio Bianco del Tùzz '05	♟♟ 4*
O Collio Ribolla Gialla '07	♟♟ 4*
O Collio Bianco Bratinis '06	♟♟ 4*
O Collio Chardonnay '07	♟♟ 4
O Collio Friulano '07	♟♟ 4
O Collio Pinot Grigio '07	♟♟ 4
O Collio Sauvignon '07	♟♟ 4
● Collio Cabernet Franc '06	♟ 4
● Collio Cabernet Franc '05	♟♟ 4
O Collio Pinot Grigio '06	♟♟ 4
O Collio Ribolla Gialla '06	♟♟ 4
O Collio Chardonnay '06	♟♟ 4
O Collio Sauvignon '06	♟♟ 4
O Collio Tocai Friulano '06	♟♟ 4

★ Gravner

FRAZ. OSLAVIA
LOC. LENZUOLO BIANCO, 9
34070 GORIZIA
TEL. 048130882
www.gravner.it

ANNUAL PRODUCTION	39,000 bottles
HECTARES UNDER VINE	18
VITICULTURE METHOD	Natural

Fermentation in open-topped oak vats, protracted skin contact for whites as well as reds, no filtration or clarification of any kind and of course those amphorae. At first, people thought he was just eccentric but when those great wines emerged from his cellar, and judgement was reversed. He was a genius and had proved it. Yet again this year, Josko Gravner's two – amber – whites are superb and, as we do every summer, we were scratching our heads about which of the duo we preferred, Ribolla or Breg. The former's mint, sage, plums in alcohol and dried flowers caress the nose, to be picked up on the palate, where varietal acidity accompanies a symphony of sensations. Breg behaves almost like a red with its burnished copper hue and alcohol visible from the way it clings to the glass as it gives acacia blossom, candied orange peel, gunflint, sage and origano. Robustly structured yet fresh-tasting, it has length and gravitas from a tight-knit tannic weave that time will hone as the wine makes its long journey of evolution. This year's more subtly floral Ribolla is a peerless thoroughbred of a Three Glass champion.

Iole Grillo

FRAZ. ALBANA, 60
33040 PREPOTTO [UD]
TEL. 0432713201
www.vinigrillo.it

ANNUAL PRODUCTION	40,000 bottles
HECTARES UNDER VINE	8.5
VITICULTURE METHOD	Conventional

This winery, founded in the 1970s, is run by Iole Grillo's daughter, Anna Muzzolini, with Giuseppe Tosoratti. The obvious determination behind every decision is striking. Risks are taken, such as topgrafting friulano onto pinot grigio vines because, as Anna writes: "We believe in the vines of our own land. Let the rest of the world grow pinot grigio". That's why she abandoned the long-standing Santa Justina white blend to vinify ribolla gialla as a single-variety wine. In the pipeline are further plantings of native Friulian grapes over the next few years. For the time being, we can enjoy an international vine type that thrives here in Anna's Sauvignon 2007. Elegant minerality on the nose is accompanied by subtle peach, tomato leaf and elderflower. Structure, balance, elegance and length are all there on the palate. The Refosco 2006 is varietal, its gamey notes nicely tempered by sour cherry, before the well-structured palate reveals tannins that meld beautifully with fruit softness. The Bordeaux blend Rosso Guardafuoco del 2005 is spicy but the excellent nose of the Schioppettino 2006 is not followed up by a correspondingly intense palate.

○ Ribolla Anfora '04	♟♟♟	8
○ Breg Anfora '04	♟♟	8
○ Breg '99	♟♟♟	8
○ Breg '98	♟♟♟	8
○ Breg '00	♟♟♟	8
○ Breg Anfora '03	♟♟♟	8
○ Breg Anfora '02	♟♟♟	8
○ Ribolla Anfora '02	♟♟♟	8
○ Ribolla Anfora '01	♟♟♟	8
○ Ribolla Anfora '03	♟♟	8
● Rosso Gravner '02	♟♟	8
● Rosso Gravner '01	♟♟	8

○ COF Sauvignon '07	♟♟	4*
● COF Refosco P. R. '06	♟♟	4
● COF Cabernet Franc '07	♟	4
○ COF Friulano '07	♟	4
● COF Rosso Guardafuoco '05	♟	5
● COF Schioppettino '06	♟	5
● COF Merlot '03	♟♟	5
○ COF Sauvignon '06	♟♟	4
● COF Refosco P. R. '05	♟♟	4
● COF Rosso Guardafuoco '05	♟♟	5
● COF Rosso Guardafuoco '04	♟♟	5

Marcello e Marino Humar

LOC. VALERISCE, 2
34070 SAN FLORIANO DEL COLLIO [GO]
TEL. 0481884094
www.humar.it

ANNUAL PRODUCTION 100,000 bottles
HECTARES UNDER VINE 30
VITICULTURE METHOD Conventional

The Humar family has been working in the Collio since the early 20th century, at first with a mixed estate for grapes and fruit as well as livestock farming. In the early 1960s, they took the plunge and opted for viticulture alone, bottling their first wines. The Humars have always been a good team. Today, they can call on Loreta, who looks after external relations, Stefano and Dario with their respective wives, active in cellar and vineyard, and uncle Marino, who continues to provide excellent advice. The cellar makes great whites, which you can now enjoy in the recently restored tasting room. The Friulano stands out for elegance. Tea, rose petals and tropical fruits aromas are perfectly mirrored on the palate, where citrus and peach emerge. The varietal Ribolla Gialla combines flowers and confectioner's cream with a refreshing palate. Also convincing is the Chardonnay, its warm, broad caramel-themed nose followed by aniseed in the mouth. The Sauvignon is elegant, fresh and minerally but the acidity still tends to intrude. From what we understand, experiments with a white blend should lead to interesting developments in the near future.

O Collio Chardonnay '07	🍷🍷 4*
O Collio Friulano '07	🍷🍷 4*
O Collio Ribolla Gialla '07	🍷🍷 4*
O Collio Sauvignon '07	🍷 4
O Collio Pinot Grigio '06	ΥΥ 4
O Collio Ribolla Gialla '06	ΥΥ 4

Jacùss

FRAZ. MONTINA
V.LE KENNEDY, 35A
33040 TORREANO [UD]
TEL. 0432715147
www.jacuss.com

ANNUAL PRODUCTION 50,000 bottles
HECTARES UNDER VINE 10
VITICULTURE METHOD Conventional

This classic family winery was set up in 1990 and has expanded to ten hectares. Vineyard management is quality-focused, with short pruning and reduced yields per hectare. Sandro and Andrea Jacuzzi personally supervise production. Sincerely passionate about their work, the two are always ready to tell you about their wines and the cellar's history in the picturesque tasting room. For years, the estate has been promoting native varieties so Andrea and Sandro will be happy to see two leading Friulian grapes at the top of the score sheet with the 2005 Picolit and Refosco. The subtly stylish Picolit charms the taste buds with dried apricots and orange peel leading into an impressive fig and caramel-covered date finish. The Refosco is austere, giving damp saddle leather and dried mint followed by good thrust on the palate, which reveals enough extract to age well. As usual, the Pinot Bianco is fabulous, offering an object lesson in elegance with its fresh citrus and golden delicious apple. We loved its minerality and exemplary nose-palate consistency. Finally, the Friulano was held back by a well-typed but rather predictable progression on the palate.

O COF Picolit '05	🍷🍷 7
O COF Pinot Bianco '07	🍷🍷 4*
● COF Refosco P. R. '05	🍷🍷 4*
O COF Friulano '07	🍷 4
● COF Rosso Boborosso '04	🍷 5
O COF Sauvignon '07	🍷 4
● COF Schioppettino Fucs e Flamis '06	🍷 4
● COF Tazzelenghe '04	🍷 5
O COF Verduzzo Friulano '05	🍷 4
● COF Cabernet Sauvignon '05	4
O COF Picolit '04	ΥΥ 7
O COF Pinot Bianco '06	ΥΥ 4
O COF Tocai Friulano '06	ΥΥ 4

★ ★ Jermann

FRAZ. RUTTARS
LOC. TRUSSIO, 11
34070 DOLEGNA DEL COLLIO [GO]
TEL. 0481888080
www.jermann.it

ANNUAL PRODUCTION	750,000 bottles
HECTARES UNDER VINE	110
VITICULTURE METHOD	Conventional

Silvio Jermann is slowly handing over to his son Angelo. Attention to detail is the secret of Silvio's constant success and details are the things that catch your eye when you visit the superb new environment-friendly Jermann cellar. Silvio has painstakingly put together apparently unconnected colours, lights and objects. Symbols of the family history refer to the central European culture to which Silvio feels inseparably attached. A couple of years ago, the estate had 110 hectares under vine and released 750,000 bottles. The property has grown today but Silvio is reluctant to talk numbers. Jermann is firmly back in the region's front rank, starting with the superb unctuously rich Chardonnay known as Dreams, which unfolds confectioner's cream and citrus laced with yellow peaches and passion fruit. A short head behind is Vinnae, a wine that embraces Friulian, Slovene and Austrian winemaking in its tocai, ribolla and riesling blend. It comes in a screw-cap bottle. Then there's the ribolla, malvasia and picolit Capo Martino and the pignolo-based red, Pignacolusse. Vintage Tunina is not quite its usual self but nonetheless valid.

Kante

FRAZ. S. PELAGIO
LOC. PREPOTTO, 1A
34011 DUINO AURISINA [TS]
TEL. 040200255
kante.edi@libero.it

ANNUAL PRODUCTION	40,000 bottles
HECTARES UNDER VINE	13
VITICULTURE METHOD	Natural

Everyone remembers the marvellous wines Edi Kante gave us a few years ago. If you were talking about chardonnay, sauvignon or malvasia istriana, Kante was the baseline. Meticulously grown raw material, a strong territorial imprint, plenty of minerality with the fruit and almost salt-like savouriness with marked fixed acidity always beautifully offset by softness. Well, those classic wines are on their way back. There may be one or two hurdles left to negotiate but the 2005 Malvasia is a truly great wine and worthy of the variety from which it was obtained. Shrewd use of oak enhances the flowers, citrus and liquorice bouquet while the close-knit, fresh-tasting palate tangy, long and elegant. The Chardonnay is just as persuasive, whether in the brighter, fresh-fruit-and-minerality base version or the Selezione, which has complex buttery perceptions veined with flowers, dried fruits and vanilla. The rest of the range is also nice but the Vitovska and Sauvignon have considerable room for improvement. Finally, the Terrano has bags of character, which means it is a tad rough, and the Brut KK has yet to find a point of equilibrium.

O W.... Dreams... ...... '06	♥♥♥	7
O Capo Martino '06	♥♥	7
● Pignacolusse '05	♥♥	6
O Vinnae '07	♥♥	5
O Vintage Tunina '06	♥♥	8
● Blau&Blau '06	♥	5
O Chardonnay '07	♥	5
O Collio Picolit Vino Dolce della Casa '06	♥	7
O Müller Thurgau '07	♥	5
O Sauvignon '07	♥	5
O Capo Martino '05	♥♥♥	7
O Capo Martino '97	♥♥♥	7
O Vintage Tunina '01	♥♥♥	8
O Vintage Tunina '00	♥♥♥	7
O Vintage Tunina '99	♥♥♥	7
O Vintage Tunina '97	♥♥♥	6

O Carso Malvasia '05	♥♥♥	6
O Carso Chardonnay '05	♥♥	6
O Carso Chardonnay Sel. '00	♥♥	7
O Carso Sauvignon '05	♥	6
● Carso Terrano '04	♥	5
O Carso Vitovska '05	♥	6
O Brut KK		5
O Carso Sauvignon '92	♥♥♥	6
O Carso Sauvignon '91	♥♥♥	6
O Carso Chardonnay '04	♥♥	6
O Carso Chardonnay '03	♥♥	6
O Carso Chardonnay Sel. '99	♥♥	6
O Carso Sauvignon '04	♥♥	6

★ Edi Keber

LOC. ZEGLA, 17
34071 CORMONS [GO]
TEL. 048161184
edi.keber@virgilio.it

ANNUAL PRODUCTION	60,000 bottles
HECTARES UNDER VINE	10
VITICULTURE METHOD	Natural

Edi Keber is getting ready to cut his short list of wines even further, putting all his white-grape wines into a single product to be called Collio, without so much as a "Bianco". We know how determined Edi is so this may well be the last vintage in which we can enjoy his Tocai Friulano as a single-variety wine. It is a great pity. We still remember some of the comments at Three Glass finals when blind tasters purred with delight at this archetypal expression of the tocai friulano grape. Barely reduced on the nose, it opens on tobacco and elegant herbaceousness before the well-orchestrated palate expounds its endlessly long theme of liquorice and pear. Even though it is from the latest vintage, the merlot and cabernet franc Collio Rosso is outstandingly drinkable, revealing wonderfully complex fruit, well-sustained structure and great ageing potential. Collio Collio, from tocai and malvasia, has all the elegance of wines crafted by our hero and his son Kristjan, a young man who has the best qualities of both his parents, Edi and Silvana. The macerated and fermented Collio Collio Bianco 2004 released in magnums has lots of personality.

Renato Keber

LOC. ZEGLA, 15
34071 CORMONS [GO]
TEL. 048161196
renatokeber@libero.it

ANNUAL PRODUCTION	65,000 bottles
HECTARES UNDER VINE	15
VITICULTURE METHOD	Conventional

Renato Keber has regained his full profile in the Guide. There are no particular new developments in this family-run operation, where Renato looks after vineyards and cellar on his own while his wife Savina manages the farmstay and hospitality facilities. Keber farms a total of 15 hectares under vine, some of it terraced, and releases around 60-65,000 bottles each year. Since we haven't said much about Keber wines for some time, we'd like to mention a product that isn't in the table below but which we were able to taste on a visit to the cellar: Collio Merlot Grici 2001. Its intense nose reveals raspberries and ripe cherries lifted by a touch of lemon balm before the warm, rich-textured palate unfolds in elegance. If you can still find a bottle or two, do try it. Meanwhile, the top of this year's range is Bianco Beli Grici 2005, an intriguing blend of pinot bianco, ribolla gialla, sauvignon and tocai friulano. All the other wines are very well crafted.

○ Collio Tocai Friulano '07	▼▼▼	5
● Collio Rosso '07	▼▼	5
○ Collio Collio '07	▼▼	4*
○ Collio Collio Bianco '04	▼	5
○ Collio Bianco '04	♀♀♀	5
○ Collio Bianco '02	♀♀♀	4
○ Collio Tocai Friulano '99	♀♀♀	4
○ Collio Tocai Friulano '97	♀♀♀	4
○ Collio Tocai Friulano '95	♀♀♀	4
○ Collio Tocai Friulano '06	♀♀♀	5
○ Collio Tocai Friulano '05	♀♀♀	5
○ Collio Tocai Friulano '01	♀♀♀	4

○ Collio Bianco Beli Grici '05	▼▼	4*
○ Collio Pinot Grigio '06	▼▼	4*
○ Collio Ribolla Gialla Extreme '05	▼▼	5
○ Collio Sauvignon '06	▼▼	4
○ Collio Tocai Friulano '06	▼▼	4

Thomas Kitzmüller

FRAZ. BRAZZANO
VIA XXIV MAGGIO, 56
34070 CORMONS [GO]
TEL. 048160853
www.vinikitzmueller.com

ANNUAL PRODUCTION	23,000 bottles
HECTARES UNDER VINE	4
VITICULTURE METHOD	Conventional

Thomas Kitzmüller is a typical small Friulian producer who started up in 1987. With only four hectares yielding 23,000 bottles, he has a total of eight labels. Some of the vines are on hillslopes and the rest are on the flatlands so they fall into two distinct DOCs, Collio and Isonzo. There are two lines, a superior range and a line called Corte Marie after his daughter, who was born in 2004. Since this is the winery's 20th harvest, a small bottling with the old label dating from 1992 has been made of the Cabernet Franc Collio, usually released as a Corte Marie, with the words "20° Vendemmia". An 18th-century structure has been transformed in to a small cellar and the Mummelhaus, so called because a century ago Aunt Mummel used to live in it, now has farmstay accommodation with three rooms. The labels themselves are truly beautiful. The best of the wines are the varietal, seductively mineral Sauvignon with its precise follow-through on the palate, and the elegant, unexpectedly buttery Traminer Aromatico, which signs off with hints of citrus.

★ Lis Neris

VIA GAVINANA, 5
34070 SAN LORENZO ISONTINO [GO]
TEL. 048180105
www.lisneris.it

ANNUAL PRODUCTION	350,000 bottles
HECTARES UNDER VINE	54
VITICULTURE METHOD	Conventional

Everyone knows that Alvaro Pecoraro's vineyards yield distinctive wines and that he himself is articulate, understanding and an outstanding winemaker. Admirably, Lis Neris has time for the less fortunate through the foundation named after Alvaro's late daughter Francesca and equally commendably, the quality of the wines is utterly reliable. This year, the vote went to Sauvignon Picol, whose stunning minerality melds with sage and rue before the elegantly varietal sensations of the palate unfold against a backdrop of fresh fruit softness. Nor is there much left to say about Tal Lùc. Riesling hydrocarbons are nicely offset by sweet candied citrus peel in a refined, well-orchestrated whole. Pinot Grigio Gris is fatty and full but velvet-smooth. Chardonnay Jurosa is a balanced wine, fusing sweet notes of sugared almonds and tobacco with tarter citrus sensations. Enticing rose petals, confectioner's cream, bananas and apricots are the themes of Lis, a pinot grigio, chardonnay and sauvignon blend, whereas Fiore di Campo is invitingly sun-ripe. Lovers of aromatic wines will enjoy the traminer-heavy Confini with its distinct ginger and wild roses.

O Collio Sauvignon '07	♈♈ 4*
O Collio Traminer Aromatico '07	♈♈ 4*
● Cabernet Franc Corte Marie '07	♈ 3
● Collio Cabernet Franc 20° Vendemmia '07	♈ 4
O Collio Friulano '07	♈ 4
O Collio Ribolla Gialla '07	♈ 4
O Friuli Isonzo Tocai Friulano Corte Marie '07	♈ 3
O Collio Tocai Friulano '06	♈♈ 4
O Friuli Isonzo Tocai Friulano Corte Marie '06	♈♈ 3

O Sauvignon Picol '06	♈♈♈ 4*
O Chardonnay Jurosa '06	♈♈ 5
O Lis '06	♈♈ 6
O Pinot Grigio Gris '06	♈♈ 5
O Tal Lùc '06	♈♈ 8
O Confini '06	♈♈ 6
O Fiore di Campo '07	♈♈ 5
O Friuli Isonzo Chardonnay '07	♈ 4
O Friuli Isonzo Pinot Grigio '07	♈ 4
O Fiore di Campo '06	♈♈♈ 4
O Friuli Isonzo Chardonnay Jurosa '00	♈♈♈ 5
O Friuli Isonzo Pinot Grigio Gris '01	♈♈♈ 6
O Lis '03	♈♈♈ 6
O Pinot Grigio Gris '04	♈♈♈ 5
O Tal Lùc '02	♈♈♈ 7

Livon

Fraz. Dolegnano
via Montarezza, 33
33048 San Giovanni al Natisone [UD]
tel. 0432757173
www.livon.it

ANNUAL PRODUCTION	700,000 bottles
HECTARES UNDER VINE	105
VITICULTURE METHOD	Conventional

Valneo and Tonino Livon farm more than 100 hectares, most of it in the Collio. They have managed to turn round a situation that had lasted two years and the wines are now back on form, thanks to in-house oenologist Rinaldo Stocco. The estate has vineyards in excellent locations and is working on its flatlands plots – a further 110 hectares – whose wine is released under the Villa Chiopris brand. But for a touch of softness, Braide Alte, from chardonnay, sauvignon, picolit and moscato giallo, would have gone through to the finals. Tocai Friulano Ronc di Zorz scored just as highly for its varietal savouriness and hints of almonds and pears. The Ribolla Gialla from RoncAlto, a jewel of a south-facing vineyard purchased in 1997, is true to type, giving spring flowers, apples and pears that are reprised on a palate refreshed by perky acidity. We also liked Solarco, a stylish, fresh-tasting white from tocai, ribolla, sauvignon and pinot bianco. The elegantly sweet Verduzzo Casali Godia mingles perceptible notes from oak ageing with apricot and peach and the Merlot TiareMate 2006 offsets the acidity of its vintage with a fine array of red berry fruits.

Tenuta Luisa

Fraz. Corona
via Cormons, 19
34070 Mariano del Friuli [GO]
tel. 048169680
www.viniluisa.com

ANNUAL PRODUCTION	350,000 bottles
HECTARES UNDER VINE	65
VITICULTURE METHOD	Conventional

Sixty-five hectares in the – almost – subzone of Corona in the heart of the Isonzo DOC yield 350,000 bottles a year released in a base line and the Ferretti selections. These are the numbers but they don't tell you everything. Behind them are Michele and Davide, who have taken over from Eddi and Nella, to the founders' great satisfaction. Not for the first time, we preferred the standard range. The Sauvignon is delicious and true to type both in its tomato, rue and yellow plum aromas and its acid structure. The Chardonnay gives mango, apple and yeast introducing the satisfyingly clean progression on the palate. Next up is the Pinot Bianco, a delightful example of a vine type as noble as it is neglected. But the former Tocai, now Friulano, wasn't punching its weight, particularly in its aromatics, and the Pinot Grigio is more attractive on nose than palate. The stand-out red is the 2003 Refosco Ferretti. Textbook cherry accompanies quinine and spice, and only slightly over-assertive extract disturbs the palate.

O Braide Alte '06	♀♀	6
O Collio Bianco Solarco '07	♀♀	5
O COF Verduzzo Friulano Casali Godia '06	♀♀	5
O Collio Braide Grande '07	♀♀	5
● Collio Merlot TiareMate '06	♀♀	5
O Collio Ribolla Gialla RoncAlto '07	♀♀	5
O Collio Tocai Friulano Ronc di Zorz '07	♀♀	5
● COF Refosco P. R. Riul '06		5
O Collio Sauvignon Valbuins '07		5
● TiareBlù '06		5
O Braide Alte Grand Cru '98	♀♀♀	6
O Braide Alte Grand Cru '97	♀♀♀	6
O Braide Alte Grand Cru '96	♀♀♀	6
● COF Refosco P. R. Riul '02	♀♀♀	5

O Friuli Isonzo Chardonnay '07	♀♀	4
O Friuli Isonzo Pinot Bianco '07	♀♀	4
O Friuli Isonzo Sauvignon '07	♀♀	4
O Friuli Isonzo Friulano '07	♀	4
O Friuli Isonzo Pinot Grigio '07	♀	4
● Friuli Isonzo Refosco P. R. I Ferretti '03	♀	5
● Friuli Isonzo Merlot '06		4
● Friuli Isonzo Refosco P. R. '06		4
O Friuli Isonzo Tocai Friulano '03	♀♀♀	4
O Friuli Isonzo Pinot Bianco '06	♀♀	4
O Friuli Isonzo Sauvignon '06	♀♀	4
O Friuli Isonzo Pinot Grigio '06	♀♀	4

Magnàs

VIA CORONA, 47
34071 CORMONS [GO]
TEL. 048160991
www.magnas.it

ANNUAL PRODUCTION	25,000 bottles
HECTARES UNDER VINE	10
VITICULTURE METHOD	Conventional

The Visintins are not just winemakers. They are also hospitality professionals with several lovely farmstay rooms and food prepared by Luciano's cheerful wife Sonia. There is nothing more tempting than a glass of the cellar's white with a slice of fresh cheese, which Magnàs, as Luciano is known, makes on an almost daily basis. The wines have had their ups and downs but Luciano and his son Andrea produce some bankers. We have learned not to worry if, at our spring tastings when the wine has just gone into bottle, they fail to convince. Wait a few months and by the end of the summer, they will be firing on all four cylinders. In fact, for Sauvignon, you need to wait for the second year to appreciate its evolution to the full. The 2007 edition starts off on the right foot with varietal tomato leaf and sage, followed by generous minerality and citrus sensations on the palate. The Pinot Grigio has all the fruit richness that the best examples of the variety from the vintage offer. Steel fermentation and ageing allows the Chardonnay to flaunt its butteriness, yellow-fleshed fruit and minerality. The Friulano and Merlot are more than decent.

○ Friuli Isonzo Chardonnay '07	♥♥	4*
○ Friuli Isonzo Pinot Grigio '07	♥♥	4*
○ Friuli Isonzo Sauvignon '07	♥♥	4*
○ Friuli Isonzo Friulano '07	♥	4
● Friuli Isonzo Merlot '06	♥	5
● Friuli Isonzo Cabernet Franc '06		5
○ Friuli Isonzo Pinot Grigio '06	♀♀	4
○ Friuli Isonzo Sauvignon '06	♀♀	4
○ Friuli Isonzo Tocai Friulano '06	♀♀	4

Valerio Marinig

VIA BROLO, 41
33040 PREPOTTO [UD]
TEL. 0432713012
www.marinig.it

ANNUAL PRODUCTION	25,000 bottles
HECTARES UNDER VINE	8
VITICULTURE METHOD	Conventional

The estate has eight hectares in the valley of the Judrio, the river that further north separates Slovenia and Italy and in this area is the dividing line between the Collio and Colli Orientali DOC zones. The winery started when great-grandfather Luigi, an expert grower, bought the property in 1921, since when it has passed from father to son in the traditional manner, which can't always be taken for granted. Since then, more than 80 years have passed and the Marinig winery is now run by Valerio, a dynamic professional who looks after the vine stock and cellar. His wife Michela helps out with administration and organises sales. The Sauvignon is unmistakably varietal and enviably elegant. Distinct perceptions of tomato leaf and sage precede substantial fruit palate with plenty of thrust. We found the fresh-tasting, fragrant Pinot Bianco to be just as good. In conclusion, we would point out that Marinig wines are dependable and excellent value for money. Even the simplest wines are extremely well made.

○ COF Pinot Bianco '07	♥♥	4*
○ COF Sauvignon '07	♥♥	4*
● Biel Cûr Rosso	♥	4
● COF Cabernet Franc '06	♥	4
○ COF Chardonnay '07	♥	4
○ COF Friulano '07	♥	4
● COF Merlot '06	♥	4
● COF Refosco P. R. '06	♥	4
● COF Schioppettino '06	♥	4
○ COF Sauvignon '06	♀♀	4

Masut da Rive

VIA MANZONI, 82
34070 MARIANO DEL FRIULI [GO]
TEL. 048169200
www.masutdarive.com

ANNUAL PRODUCTION	100,000 bottles
HECTARES UNDER VINE	20
VITICULTURE METHOD	Conventional

Fabrizio and Marco Gallo are determined. Unswayed by fashion, which calls for easy drinking whites, they continue to believe in their territory and the more structured wines it favours. The Gallos are also reducing output of single-variety wines to create a blended white that will capture the winery's potential. And they also feel ready to release a Pinot Nero, a source of joy and torment in Friuli which is sure to give a good account of itself, since the Gallos' vines are on very suitable terrain. With all this going on, the Gallos were still able to present us with a good to excellent range, particularly the Pinot Bianco, Sauvignon and Refosco. The Pinot Bianco combines elegant spring flowers and golden delicious apple sensations with intense crusty bread and almonds. The rich, tangy palate of the Sauvignon has a rue-themed finish and the Refosco melds well-gauged balsam with cinnamon, white pepper and clove-like spice. The Friulano is fruit-forward, the Pinot Grigio has warmth and breadth whereas the Cabernet Sauvignon offers austere perceptions of oak and quinine. Finally, the Merlot signs off with intriguing forest fruits.

Davino Meroi

VIA STRETTA, 7B
33042 BUTTRIO [UD]
TEL. 0432674025
parco.meroi@virgilio.it

ANNUAL PRODUCTION	20,000 bottles
HECTARES UNDER VINE	12
VITICULTURE METHOD	Conventional

Entrepreneurial instinct and love of the land have prompted Paolo Meroi to increase his vine stock over the years. At the winery itself, Paolo runs an excellent restaurant that is noted for its absolutely delicious grilled meats. This year, the Meroi range of wines is well made but slightly below the standard Paolo had accustomed us to in recent years. The blip affected the reds in particular. Both the 2006 Ros di Buri and Nestri seemed to lack the elegance, complexity and concentration with which they usually regale us. Still, Ros di Buri is a good wine with raspberry and pennyroyal-like aromas that make it much fresher than in other vintages. We also very much like the Friulano, Pinot Grigio and Picolit. Unfortunately, we were unable to taste the flag-carrier Rosso Dominin because it hadn't yet gone into bottle when we called.

O Friuli Isonzo Pinot Bianco '07	♟♟ 4*
● Friuli Isonzo Refosco P. R. '06	♟♟ 4*
O Friuli Isonzo Sauvignon '07	♟♟ 4*
● Friuli Isonzo Cabernet Sauvignon '06	♟♟ 4
O Friuli Isonzo Friulano '04	♟♟ 4
● Friuli Isonzo Merlot '06	♟♟ 4
O Friuli Isonzo Pinot Grigio '07	♟♟ 4
● Friuli Isonzo Cabernet Franc '06	♟ 4
O Friuli Isonzo Chardonnay '07	♟ 4
● Friuli Isonzo Cabernet Sauvignon '05	♟♟ 4
● Friuli Isonzo Merlot '03	♟♟ 4
O Friuli Isonzo Pinot Bianco '06	♟♟ 4
● Friuli Isonzo Merlot '04	♟♟ 4
O Friuli Isonzo Sauvignon '06	♟♟ 4

O COF Friulano '07	♟♟ 6
O COF Picolit '06	♟♟ 7
O COF Pinot Grigio '07	♟♟ 6
● COF Rosso Ros di Buri '06	♟♟ 6
● COF Rosso Nestri '06	♟ 4
O COF Sauvignon '06	♟ 7
O COF Verduzzo Friulano '06	♟ 6
● COF Rosso Dominin '03	♟♟ 8
● COF Rosso Dominin '02	♟♟ 8
● COF Rosso Dominin '01	♟♟ 8
● COF Merlot Ros di Buri '05	♟♟ 6
O COF Tocai Friulano '06	♟♟ 6

★ Miani

VIA PERUZZI, 10
33042 BUTTRIO [UD]
TEL. 0432674327
aletulissi@libero.it

ANNUAL PRODUCTION 8,000 bottles
HECTARES UNDER VINE 16
VITICULTURE METHOD Natural

We have always admired Enzo Pontoni, a highly disciplined grower and inspired winemaker. This year's top award brings his total of Three Glass prizes to 15, an incredible number for a winery that releases fewer than 10,000 bottles a year, divided into types for each variety and each vineyard. Perhaps only Burgundy's top winemakers make such meticulously precise distinctions. That's why we are crowning a superb Pontoni wine, the 2004 Merlot Filip, of which only about 1,000 bottles leave the cellar. Its deep ruby red gives elegant, complex aromas themed around blueberries and tobacco before the refined yet full-bodied palate unveils all its fantastic length. Only a notch below it is Merlot Buri, also from 2004. It's a shade less complex but still a huge wine. Pontoni is a little less convincing as a "white man". His Tocai Buri 2006 is massively fleshy but still dominated by wood. It's an outstanding wine but not what you could call an easy drinker. Tocai Filip is close behind but the Sauvignon is less convincing.

● COF Merlot Filip '04	▼▼▼	8
● COF Merlot Buri '04	▼▼	8
○ COF Tocai Friulano Buri '06	▼▼	7
○ COF Tocai Friulano Filip '06	▼▼	7
○ COF Sauvignon'06	▼	7
● Calvari '02	▽▽▽	8
○ COF Bianco '97	▽▽▽	7
● COF Merlot '99	▽▽▽	8
● COF Merlot '98	▽▽▽	8
● COF Merlot '94	▽▽▽	6
● COF Merlot '02	▽▽▽	8
● COF Rosso '97	▽▽▽	8
● COF Rosso '96	▽▽▽	8
○ COF Sauvignon '96	▽▽▽	6
○ COF Tocai Friulano '99	▽▽▽	7
○ COF Tocai Friulano '00	▽▽▽	7

Moschioni

LOC. GAGLIANO
VIA DORIA, 30
33043 CIVIDALE DEL FRIULI [UD]
TEL. 0432730210
vinimoschioni@libero.it

ANNUAL PRODUCTION 33,000 bottles
HECTARES UNDER VINE 13
VITICULTURE METHOD Conventional

Michele Moschioni's decision to merge his 2005 schioppettino and pignolo with the merlot and cabernet sauvignon Celtico as Bisest was bound to upset his old-style wine man father, Davide. It had been a poorish growing year for some red varieties, and a rainy harvest, so Michele's decision is an impeccable example of honesty towards consumers. We should remember that Moschioni's 13 hectares are planted almost exclusively to red varieties and yields are no more than 40 quintals per hectare. Normally, the grapes undergo a short period of dehydration, or "drying" as Michele call it, in cases before crushing, fermentation with ambient yeasts and maturation in small and medium wood followed by bottling without filtration. The process leaves hints of raisining in the wine but this year, the final products are much cleaner, so to speak, than usual. Bisest is fantastic, its schioppettino, pignolo, merlot and cabernet blend leading with forest fruits tart and plums. Only a step behind are the spice-rich Refosco and the Reâl, which surprised us because Michele has tamed the tannins of the tazzelenghe that went into the blend with merlot and cabernet.

● COF Rosso Bisest '05	▼▼	6
● COF Refosco P. R. '05	▼▼	5
● COF Rosso Reâl '05	▼▼	6
● COF Rosso Celtico '04	▽▽▽	6
● COF Pignolo '04	▽▽	8
● COF Rosso Celtico '02	▽▽	6
● COF Rosso Celtico '01	▽▽	6
● COF Refosco P. R. '04	▽▽	5
● COF Rosso Reâl '04	▽▽	6

Mulino delle Tolle

FRAZ. SEVEGLIANO
VIA MULINO DELLE TOLLE, 15
33050 BAGNARIA ARSA [UD]
TEL. 0432928113
www.mulinodelletolle.it

ANNUAL PRODUCTION 100,000 bottles
HECTARES UNDER VINE 22
VITICULTURE METHOD Conventional

One of the most original cellars in Friuli is the new stainless steel facility belonging to cousins Giorgio and Eliseo Bertossi. Every detail has been carefully designed to ensure the best possible conditions for vinification. It's a pleasure to taste wines in the old Bertossi headquarters because Giorgio, an oenologist, is absolutely sincere about their virtues and their defects, noting any mistakes that were made during vinification or weak points in the vintage. As usual, the whites impressed us more but we were pleased to note among the reds a native Pignolo, which turned out to be one of the best of its type. Needless to say, there was no escaping the iron law that overall quality takes a dip when there's work going on in the cellar. Knowing the Bertossis, however, we are confident that standards will quickly get back to normal. Going back to that Pignolo, it is quintessentially varietal, and emblematic of the Friulian hill country, in its quinine and tobacco-laced spectrum of aromatics. The Bertossis' first shot at bottle-refermenting chardonnay has come off well, the dosage making the product particularly pleasing.

● Pignolo '06	▼▼	6
○ Chardonnay Brut	▼	4
○ Friuli Aquileia Bianco Palmade '07	▼	4
○ Friuli Aquileia Friulano '07	▼	4
○ Friuli Aquileia Malvasia '07	▼	3
○ Friuli Aquileia Sauvignon '07	▼	4
● Friuli Aquileia Refosco P. R. '07		4
○ Friuli Aquileia Malvasia '06	▽▽	3
○ Friuli Aquileia Bianco Palmade '06	▽▽	4
○ Friuli Aquileia Tocai Friulano '06	▽▽	3
● Friuli Aquileia Refosco P. R. '07	▽	4

Muzic

LOC. BIVIO, 4
34070 SAN FLORIANO DEL COLLIO [GO]
TEL. 0481884201
www.cantinamuzic.it

ANNUAL PRODUCTION 90,000 bottles
HECTARES UNDER VINE 15
VITICULTURE METHOD Conventional

Ivan – as he is known – and his wife Orietta continue the wine business that his parents embarked upon in the early 1960s. Again, they have obtained excellent results from the 15 estate-owned hectares under vine, whose fruit is vinified in the ancient but fairly recently restored 16th-century cellar. Three new hectares of white grape vines near the cellar have led to this year's release of Tocai Vigna Valeris from 40-year-old plantings. It's a fresh-tasting Friulano with a subtle crusty bread nose and an almondy flavour. Sauvignon Pàjze is a territorial wine. Ripe fruit and tomato are reprised on the palate, which adds minerality to bell pepper and peach freshness. But the top wine is the tocai, malvasia istriana and ribolla gialla Bianco Bric, whose name refers to the local residents. An elegant wine, it tempts with gunflint, apple and tobacco on the nose introducing mint and banana in the mouth. The cellar's other big hitter is Pinot Grigio, which brings together sugared almonds and citrus in an elegant, tangily intense palate. The spice-rich Cabernet Franc is redolent of blackberry tart and the intense Cabernet Sauvignon leads with fruit.

○ Collio Bianco Bric '07	▼▼	4*
● Collio Cabernet Sauvignon '06	▼▼	4*
○ Collio Pinot Grigio '07	▼▼	4*
● Friuli Isonzo Cabernet Franc '06	▼▼	4*
○ Collio Chardonnay '07	▼	4
○ Collio Ribolla Gialla '07	▼	4
○ Collio Sauvignon V. Pàjze '07	▼	4
○ Collio Tocai Friulano Vigna Valeris '07	▼	4
○ Collio Bianco Bric '06	▽▽	4
○ Collio Sauvignon V. Pàjze '06	▽▽	4

Parovel

LOC. CARESANA, 81
34018 SAN DORLIGO DELLA VALLE [TS]
TEL. 040227050
www.parovel.com

ANNUAL PRODUCTION 35,000 bottles
HECTARES UNDER VINE 15
VITICULTURE METHOD Conventional

The Parovel family has been making wine for generations. It was also one of the first to recover olive growing in the lower Trieste Carso area, and the first to acquire an olive press. Euro Parovel is in charge of the cellar, where competent oenologist Marco Pecchiari helps him out. The modern facility is rationally laid out with excellent visibility from one room to another. Euro's sister Elena looks after guests, guiding visitors through their tasting of Parovel products. At our preliminary tastings, we very much liked the Malvasia Istriana's violets, lavender, apples, herbaceousness, minerality and richness, qualities that were on show again at the Three Glass finals. Confirmation of the cellar's predilection for native grapes comes from the outstandingly fresh, vigorous Vitovska and a very decent Terrano, with the variety's trademark edgy spice. Also intriguing was the sweet, aroma-rich moscato giallo-based Spomin whose orange blossom nose ushers in a long palate of confectioner's cream with baked pears and apples. Matos Nonet, from malvasia, sauvignon and sémillon, is held back by over-assertive oak.

○ Carso Malvasia Istriana Vinja Barde '07	🍷🍷	4*
○ Carso Vitovska Vinja Barde '07	🍷🍷	4
○ Spomin '07	🍷🍷	4
● Terrano Vinja Barde '06	🍷	4
○ Matos Nonet Vinja Barde '06		5
● Refosco P. R. Vinja Barde '06		4

Pierpaolo Pecorari

VIA TOMMASEO, 36C
34070 SAN LORENZO ISONTINO [GO]
TEL. 0481808775
www.pierpaolopecorari.it

ANNUAL PRODUCTION 140,000 bottles
HECTARES UNDER VINE 30
VITICULTURE METHOD Certified organic

In the upper Isonzo flatlands between Cormons and Gradisca, nature has provided shallow, well-drained, stony soil with plenty of minerals, ideal for growing grapes. This is the setting for Pierpaolo Pecorari's 30 hectares, from which our hero obtains a wide range of products catering for an equally wide range of consumers. Output is organized essentially on the age of the vines used. The 140,000 units released each year come in three lines. Riserva wines bear the place name of their vineyard of provenance, the ones with older vine stock that will imbue the must with enough structure to mature successfully in small oak. Altis selections see only steel, where they undergo skin contact and mature on the lees. Classic wines from younger vines are identified by the name of their variety and are often fresh-tasting easy drinkers. A special mention this year goes to Sauvignon Altis for its varietal rue and apricot, refreshing acidity and cleanness and to the elegantly fruity Altis Pinot Bianco. We picked out the Sauvignon Kolaus from the 2006 wines but the Olivers seemed a tad dilute and the Baolar lacked a little balance.

○ Pinot Bianco Altis '06	🍷🍷	5
○ Sauvignon Altis '06	🍷🍷	5
● Merlot Baolar '06	🍷	6
○ Pinot Grigio '07	🍷	4
○ Pinot Grigio Olivers '06	🍷	6
○ Sauvignon Kolaus '06	🍷	6
○ Traminer '06	🍷	4
● Refosco P. R. '06		4
○ Malvasia '07		4
○ Sauvignon '07		4
○ Sauvignon Kolaus '05	🍷🍷 (prev. ed.)	6
○ Chardonnay Soris '05	🍷🍷 (prev. ed.)	6

Perusini

LOC. GRAMOGLIANO
VIA TORRIONE, 13
33040 CORNO DI ROSAZZO [UD]
TEL. 0432675018
www.perusini.com

ANNUAL PRODUCTION	50,000 bottles
HECTARES UNDER VINE	12
VITICULTURE METHOD	Conventional

Teresa Perusini and her husband Giacomo De Pace run a splendid estate of about 60 hectares, of which 12 or 13 are given over to viticulture. Dotted about the rest of the property are accommodations that it would be misleading to call farmstays, given the elegance of their interiors. The property also features a small restaurant, managed by non-estate staff. Vineyard management is the responsibility of the Preparatori d'Uva (Fruitmakers) group while Terra&Vino looks after the cellar. The winery facilities next to the estate's impressive mansion were modernized a few years ago and an unusual truncated cone tower was built in collaboration with the University of Venice. Slabs of stone from the Far East were used to clad it and the space at the base of the tower has become a barrel cellar. Overall, the Perusini range is good, with positive spikes in the Chardonnay and the Picolit. The latter is redolent of candied orange peel, confectioner's cream and vanilla before the very sweet, well-sustained palate signs off with distinct dried figs. The elegant Chardonnay's yeasty aromas are perked up by nicely gauged acidity.

Petrucco

VIA MORPURGO, 12
33042 BUTTRIO [UD]
TEL. 0432674387
www.vinipetrucco.it

ANNUAL PRODUCTION	100,000 bottles
HECTARES UNDER VINE	25
VITICULTURE METHOD	Conventional

A few years ago, engineer Paolo Petrucco and his wife Lina, were on the point of throwing in the winemaking towel, so disappointed were they the results achieved. They decided to go for broke and called in Marco Simonit to look after the vines, rethinking pruning methods to extract the very best from their fruit. The other crucial move was to flank cellarman Flavio Cabas with one of the finest consultants around, Gianni Menotti. In farming, results are never immediate. You have to wait and, if the growing years aren't disastrous, sooner or later they arrive. At Petrucco, native vines give Paolo most to cheer about. The vines for Pignolo Ronco del Balbo enjoy the best aspects and oblige with a spice-rich wine whose extract is handled beautifully. The Refosco is up there with it, showing lovely structure and excellent cellar potential. The Picolit is very sweet and signs off with an elegantly attractive hint of almond paste. Tar and spice come through on the Merlot, whose tannins are wonderfully smooth for a challenging vintage like 2006. Getting the vineyard into step with the cellar seems to be paying off.

O COF Chardonnay '07	♟♟ 4*
O COF Picolit '06	♟♟ 8
O Brut	♟ 4
● COF Cabernet Franc '06	♟ 5
● COF Merlot '06	♟ 5
O COF Pinot Grigio '07	♟ 4
O COF Ribolla Gialla '07	♟ 4
● COF Rosso del Postiglione '06	♟ 5
O COF Sauvignon '07	♟ 4
● COF Cabernet Sauvignon '06	5
O COF Pinot Grigio '06	♟♟ 4

● COF Merlot '06	♟♟ 4*
O COF Picolit '06	♟♟ 7
O COF Sauvignon '07	♟♟ 4*
● COF Pignolo Ronco del Balbo '04	♟♟ 6
● COF Refosco P. R. '06	♟♟ 4*
O COF Chardonnay '07	♟ 4
O COF Friulano '07	♟ 4
O COF Pinot Bianco '07	♟ 4
O COF Pinot Grigio '07	♟ 4
O COF Ribolla Gialla '07	4
O COF Picolit '05	♟♟ 7
● COF Pignolo Ronco del Balbo '03	♟♟ 6

Petrussa

VIA ALBANA, 49
33040 PREPOTTO [UD]
TEL. 0432713192
www.petrussa.it

ANNUAL PRODUCTION	60,000 bottles
HECTARES UNDER VINE	10
VITICULTURE METHOD	Conventional

To the relief of Paolo and Gianni Petrussa, the cellar extension is nearly complete. Work spaces have been radically redesigned and all the space-related problems that we mentioned in past Guides will be gone. Far-sighted decision-making by its owners is manoeuvring Petrussa into the front rank of winemaking in the Colli Orientali del Friuli. Further proof comes in the new policy of bottling Merlot and Cabernet in the autumn for release the following spring, with the aim of giving the market wines that are properly mature. This will entail financial sacrifices but is sure to bear fruit in the long run. The winery is committed to promoting its flag-carrying variety and made a substantial contribution to the creation of the Schioppettino di Prepotto subzone, which from the 2008 harvest will be mentioned on the labels of the 30 wineries that have opted to comply with the production protocol. The 2007 Friulano is very good, too, delivering ripe pear and apple that return harmoniously on the intense, rich palate. Two other fine wines are the tangily varietal Pinot Bianco and the Chardonnay, which is herbaceous on the nose and lingers on the palate.

Roberto Picéch

LOC. PRADIS, 11
34071 CORMONS [GO]
TEL. 048160347
www.picech.it

ANNUAL PRODUCTION	28,000 bottles
HECTARES UNDER VINE	7
VITICULTURE METHOD	Conventional

Recently, Roberto Picéch wrote: "I want my winery to grow, and it doesn't matter if I have to do it one step at a time. The main thing is that my dream of becoming a good wine man should one day come true". Well, it has. Roberto is one of Friulian wine's leading figures by virtue of the distinctive products that his skills have created. Roberto has focused on a limited range of wines, which speaks volumes for his foresight. Yet again, the results are excellent this year, even with a less than compliant vintage like 2007. We'll start with the sun-ripe Pinot Bianco, which offers citrus, melon and subtle balsam. The velvet-smooth progression on the palate is lifted by tea leaf nuances. Hay and pear aromatics make the Malvasia an intriguing wine. Also outstanding is the 2006 Bianco Jelka, dedicated to Roberto's mother. This blend of ribolla, tocai and malvasia ages for ten months in wood and reveals delicious perceptions of rose petals, golden delicious apples, apricots and pears before sweet spice comes through in the finale. What we liked about the Bordeaux blend Rosso 2006 was its mouth-pervading fruity softness.

O COF Chardonnay '06	♀♀	5
O COF Friulano '07	♀♀	4*
O COF Pinot Bianco '07	♀♀	4*
O COF Sauvignon '07	♀	4
● COF Schioppettino '05	♀	6
O Pensiero '05	♀	6
● COF Schioppettino '04	♀♀	6
O COF Sauvignon '06	♀♀	4
O COF Tocai Friulano '06	♀♀	4

O Collio Pinot Bianco '07	♀♀	5
O Collio Bianco Jelka '06	♀♀	5
O Collio Malvasia '07	♀♀	5
● Collio Rosso '06	♀♀	5
O Collio Friulano '07	♀	5
O Collio Bianco Jelka '99	♀♀♀	5
O Collio Bianco Jelka '05	♀♀	5
O Collio Bianco Jelka '04	♀♀	5
O Collio Bianco Jelka '03	♀♀	5
● Collio Rosso Ris. '01	♀♀	6

Tenuta Pinni

VIA SANT'OSVALDO, 3
33096 SAN MARTINO AL TAGLIAMENTO [PN]
TEL. 0434899464
www.tenutapinni.com

ANNUAL PRODUCTION 45,000 bottles
HECTARES UNDER VINE 13.8
VITICULTURE METHOD Conventional

This barely ten-year-old winery and its able owners, Francesco and Roberto Pinni, who busily look after all things related to production and marketing, has a youthful eagerness to constantly renew its winemaking techniques and range of products. The action takes place in a venerable villa, whose cellars date from 1687, where time seems, paradoxically, to stand still. The contrast of tradition and modernity has again produced an excellent range of wines. Top of the range is the highly distinctive Sauvignon with its complex aromas of rain-washed stone, bell pepper and pipe tobacco. Austere but caressing, the palate yields up its secrets reluctantly as it proceeds to a fine minerally finish with overtones of smokiness. The extremely varietal, and this year particularly intense, Friulano gives almonds and crusty bread. Proving Tenuta Pinni's versatility are two more than just decent 2006 reds. The Cabernet Sauvignon is very spicy and the elegant balsam of the Refosco melds with cinnamon and cloves. Finally, the original Sauvignon della Tenuta 2005 spent a year in small wood and is well worth keeping an eye on as it evolves.

Vigneti Pittaro

VIA UDINE, 67
33033 CODROIPO [UD]
TEL. 0432904726
www.vignetipittaro.com

ANNUAL PRODUCTION 500,000 bottles
HECTARES UNDER VINE 90
VITICULTURE METHOD Conventional

The Pittaro family is proud of its four centuries in wine and since Piero founded the current winery in the 1970s, the focus has been on territory-oriented quality. Oenologist Stefano Trinco in his role as winery manager oversees the traditional range of products while exploring new ways to get the best out of the fruit. This has led to experiments with classic method sparkling wines, the production of grapes from new crosses and some impressive dried-grape wines. The estate is just outside Codroipo, where modern facilities house the cellar, a museum of wine and a lovely collection of wine-related glass artefacts. Actually, younger wines are stoppered with glass closures. Outstanding in the very good range is Apicio, a stylishly intense dried-grape wine from sauvignon, chardonnay and Manzoni bianco redolent of apricots and caramel. Dried figs, confectioner's cream and cherry jam theme the Picolit while the Moscato Rosa offers balanced sweetness with wild roses and oranges. The fresh, fruit-led Chardonnay Mousqué is elegant, the Brut 2000 came close to a second Glass for its lingering complexity and the Manzoni is a medley of fresh fruit.

O Friuli Grave Sauvignon '07	▼▼	3*
● Cabernet Sauvignon '06	▼▼	3
O Friuli Grave Friulano '07	▼▼	3
● Friuli Grave Refosco P. R. '06	▼▼	3
O Chardonnay '07	▼	3
● Friuli Grave Rosso della Tenuta '04	▼	5
O Pinot Grigio '07	▼	3
O Sauvignon della Tenuta '05	▼	4
● Cabernet Franc '06		3
● Friuli Grave Rosso '02	▽▽	5
● Friuli Grave Rosso '00	▽▽	5
● Friuli Grave Rosso della Tenuta '03	▽▽	5
● Refosco P. R. '05	▽▽	4
O Friuli Grave Tocai Friulano '06	▽▽	4
O Ucelut '01	▽▽	5

O Apicio '06	▼▼	5
O COF Picolit Ronco Vieri '05	▼▼	7
O Friuli Grave Chardonnay Mousqué '07	▼▼	4
● Moscato Rosa Valzer in Rosa '07	▼▼	4
● COF Refosco Ronco Vieri '05	▼	4
O Friuli Grave Sauvignon '07	▼	4
O Manzoni '07	▼	4
O Pittaro Brut Et. Oro '00	▼	7
O Ramandolo Ronco Vieri '05	▼	5

Plozner

VIA DELLE PRESE, 19
33097 SPILIMBERGO [PN]
TEL. 04272902
www.plozner.it

ANNUAL PRODUCTION	500,000 bottles	
HECTARES UNDER VINE	60	
VITICULTURE METHOD	Conventional	

The march to quality of this long-established Grave winery continues apace. The good-value standard line of fresh-tasting, clean varietal wines flanks premium bottles where the winemaker's skills are on show on an intriguing list. Rounding off the range, and confirming the potential of the Plozner cellar, is a wine that came within an ace of Three Glasses, the Sauvignon Quattroperuno Uno that in recent years has performed consistently well. In 2007, this star outshone itself with intense rue, bell pepper and sage that are reprised harmoniously in the mouth, which sports an attractively well-sustained tang. There were high marks for Pinot Grigio Malpelo, too, a subtle product with tempting orange and talcum powder fragrances, and Bianco Moscabianca, a Tocai that combines rich texture with freshness. The standard label wines also put in fine showings. We liked the true-to-type Traminer, which unfolds clean and almost wispily light in its progression, the classic, pear and gunflint Pinot Grigio and the Plozner workhorse Sauvignon, with its very green notes of bell pepper and elderflowers, which shows fresh yet unassertive.

Damijan Podversic

VIA BRIGATA PAVIA, 61
34170 GORIZIA
TEL. 048178217
damijan.go@virgilio.it

ANNUAL PRODUCTION	24,000 bottles	
HECTARES UNDER VINE	10	
VITICULTURE METHOD	Natural	

Damijan is one of those people that you get on with straight away, not so much because of his characterful wines, which not everyone likes, as for the ideas that make him tick. He loves his land and its traditions, which he interprets with meticulous technique, he is modest and tenacious, he acknowledges other people's contributions and is unswerving in pursuit of his own plans. Most of the winemaking goes on in wood after prolonged skin contact, encouraging ambient yeasts to do their job without temperature control, clarification or filtration. These are wines that demand attention. On the surface, they all look similar but closer examination reveals the differences that are typical of variety and zone. This nature-friendly approach exposes Damijan to ups and downs in quality, and blips are the area where he needs to concentrate his attention. There were two great wines this time: the excellent Kaplja white from malvasia, tocai and chardonnay, which went through to the finals, and the merlot and cabernet sauvignon Rosso. It may be a bit lean and acerbic on the finish but it unveils a backdrop of delightful red berry fruit and black pepper spices.

O Sauvignon Quattroperuno Uno '07	♈♈	4*
O Bianco Moscabianca '07	♈♈	4
O Friuli Grave Pinot Grigio '07	♈♈	4
O Friuli Grave Sauvignon '07	♈♈	4
O Friuli Grave Traminer Aromatico '07	♈♈	4
O Pinot Grigio Malpelo '07	♈♈	4
O Friuli Grave Chardonnay '07	♈	3
O Friuli Grave Friulano '07	♈	3
● Friuli Grave Pinot Nero '06	♈	4
O Magreis Frizzante		3
O Sauvignon Quattroperuno Uno '06	♈♈	4
O Bianco Moscabianca '06	♈♈	4
● Merlot Peeecora Nera '05	♈♈	4

O Kaplja '05	♈♈	6
● Rosso Prelit '05	♈	6
O Kaplja '04	♈♈	6
O Kaplja '03	♈♈	6
● Rosso Prelit '04	♈♈	6
● Rosso Prelit '03	♈♈	6

Aldo Polencic

LOC. PLESSIVA, 13
34071 CORMONS [GO]
TEL. 048161027
aldopolencic@virgilio.it

Isidoro Polencic

LOC. PLESSIVA, 12
34071 CORMONS [GO]
TEL. 048160655
www.polencic.com

ANNUAL PRODUCTION	20,000 bottles
HECTARES UNDER VINE	7
VITICULTURE METHOD	Conventional

Yet again, Aldo Polencic gave us a mighty range of wines. There aren't many of them but standards are high and the Merlot is a genuinely fine wine that earned Two very full Glasses. It's no use looking for elegance in Aldo's wines – he gives all of them a taste of wood – so if you like intense, buttery wines with serious structure, head this way. In some of the wines, we detected the hand of Aldo's sister and expert oenologist Marinka, especially the Pinot Grigio, which flaunts stylish fragrances that are mirrored perfectly on the palate to conclude with a long, fruit-rich finale. The Merlot is intense and complex on the nose, with hints of austerity, and a backbone of young but extremely promising extract. Vanilla on the palate in particular marks out the Pinot Bianco as a wine that has spent time in large wood. Confectioner's cream and vanilla again prevail on the Tocai Friulano but it also has oodles of fruit, which will come through in the next few months.

ANNUAL PRODUCTION	120,000 bottles
HECTARES UNDER VINE	25
VITICULTURE METHOD	Conventional

This is a classic family operation. Head of the household Doro has the experience and his children, Michele, Alex and Elisabetta, are full of ideas about the future of the business. Michele Polencic writes: "Ours is a trade that demands commitment and passion. If you work among the rows, you have to deal with the vagaries of the seasons. You have to read nature's moods, adapt to them and be patient". Michele certainly seems to have learned his father's lesson. In 2007, he was one of the most successful interpreters of a challenging growing year and the wines are magnificent. The Pinot Bianco is a stunner, giving intense, fresh apples, herbaceousness, pear drops and newly baked bread. On the palate, it unfolds vibrantly in apple-like fruit and florality to a very stylish, tangy finish. Three Glasses and our sincere congratulations. Up there with the leader were the fragrantly fresh, flower-themed Ribolla Gialla, the fresh yet full-textured Pinot Grigio and the Sauvignon, which hints at sage and mint laced with perfectly gauged fruitiness.

● Collio Merlot Rosso degli Ulivi '06	♈♈ 6
○ Collio Pinot Bianco Bianco degli Ulivi '07	♈♈ 6
○ Collio Pinot Grigio '07	♈♈ 5
○ Collio Tocai Friulano Bianco degli Ulivi '07	♈♈ 6
○ Collio Tocai Friulano '00	♈♈♈ 4
○ Collio Tocai Friulano Bianco degli Ulivi '06	♈♈ 6
○ Collio Pinot Bianco degli Ulivi '06	♈♈ 6
○ Collio Pinot Grigio '06	♈♈ 5
○ Collio Tocai Friulano Unico '05	♈♈ 6

○ Collio Pinot Bianco '07	♈♈♈ 5
○ Collio Pinot Grigio '07	♈♈ 5
○ Collio Ribolla Gialla '07	♈♈ 4*
○ Collio Sauvignon '07	♈♈ 4*
○ Collio Bianco '07	♈♈ 4
○ Collio Chardonnay '07	♈♈ 4
○ Collio Friulano '07	♈♈ 4
○ Collio Pinot Grigio '98	♈♈♈ 4
○ Collio Tocai Friulano '04	♈♈♈ 4
○ Collio Pinot Bianco '06	♈♈ 4
○ Collio Pinot Grigio '06	♈♈ 4
○ Collio Tocai Friulano Fisc '06	♈♈ 5
● Oblin Ros '03	♈♈ 6
● Oblin Ros '01	♈♈ 6

Primosic

FRAZ. OSLAVIA
LOC. MADONNINA DI OSLAVIA, 3
34070 GORIZIA
TEL. 0481535153
www.primosic.com

ANNUAL PRODUCTION	200,000 bottles
HECTARES UNDER VINE	31
VITICULTURE METHOD	Conventional

We can report another positive vintage from the Primosic winery, led by Marko and Boris, the sons of the man who founded it in the early 1950s, Silvestro. He was the first to bottle in 1956 and the first to put the Collio DOC mark on his label in 1967. Today, the vine stock extends over 26 hectares in the hills and five on the Isonzo flatlands. Isonzo-sourced wines are released under the Palmade label, which is also used for products made with bought-in grapes. Again, two wines went through to the finals. Klin, from sauvignon, chardonnay, ribolla and tocai fruit grown in the vineyard of the same name, has a dash of picolit in the mix. Intriguingly complex grapefruit, melon and tropical fruit usher in an exciting palate. This edition of Ribolla Gialla Oslavia has slightly over-assertive oak-derived confectioner's cream and vanilla that tend to mask the generous fruit. The Bordeaux blend Metamorfosis is lifted by forest fruits and spiciness from its splash of refosco while the wealth of fruit in the Pinot Grigio holds up right through the refreshing finish.

Doro Princic

LOC. PRADIS, 5
34071 CORMONS [GO]
TEL. 048160723
doroprincic@virgilio.it

ANNUAL PRODUCTION	55,000 bottles
HECTARES UNDER VINE	10
VITICULTURE METHOD	Conventional

Last year, we were astonished to note that none of Sandro Princic's whites had scored less than 84 out of 100. Well, Sandro has done it again, picking up Three more Glasses for his signature Pinot Bianco, which finished a length or two in front of the excellent Friulano. We have often made it clear how much we like Sandro, his wife Grazia and their marvellous hospitality to anyone who drops in to see them. It simply isn't possible to order wine at the Princic household without first tasting a raft of the cellar's finest offerings, accompanied by the delicious nibbles and dishes that Grazia sets in front of you. Sandro's vine stock covers just over ten hectares and annual output is close to 55,000 units. But let's go back to that Pinot Bianco. Intense ripe fruit fragrances are echoed on the long-lingering palate, which manages to be refreshing and rich-textured at the same time. Pear comes through on the Friulano to mingle with almondiness in a warm rich structure of long-lasting tanginess. Last up is Grazia's favourite wine, Sauvignon, which has been scoring high over the past couple of years for its varietal character and cleanliness.

○ Collio Bianco Klin '04	🍷🍷 6
○ Collio Ribolla Gialla di Oslavia Ris. '06	🍷🍷 5
○ Collio Pinot Grigio Murno '07	🍷🍷 4*
● Collio Rosso Metamorfosis '03	🍷🍷 6
○ Collio Sauvignon Blanc Gmajne '07	🍷🍷 5
○ Collio Chardonnay Gmajne '06	🍷 5
○ Collio Friulano Belvedere '07	🍷 4
○ Collio Picolit '06	🍷 6
○ Collio Bianco Klin Ris. '03	🍷🍷 6
○ Collio Chardonnay Gmajne '05	🍷🍷 5
○ Collio Ribolla di Oslavia Ris. '05	🍷🍷 5
○ Collio Sauvignon Gmajne '05	🍷🍷 5
○ Collio Tocai Friulano Belvedere '06	🍷🍷 4
○ Collio Bianco Klin Ris. '01	🍷🍷 5

○ Collio Pinot Bianco '07	🍷🍷🍷 5
○ Collio Friulano '07	🍷🍷 5
○ Collio Sauvignon '07	🍷🍷 5
○ Collio Malvasia '07	🍷🍷 5
○ Collio Pinot Grigio '07	🍷🍷 5
○ Collio Pinot Bianco '05	🍷🍷🍷 5
○ Collio Pinot Bianco '04	🍷🍷🍷 5
○ Collio Pinot Bianco '02	🍷🍷🍷 5
○ Collio Pinot Bianco '95	🍷🍷🍷 5
○ Collio Tocai Friulano '06	🍷🍷🍷 5
○ Collio Tocai Friulano '93	🍷🍷🍷 5
○ Collio Malvasia '06	🍷🍷 5
○ Collio Sauvignon '06	🍷🍷 5
○ Collio Tocai Friulano '05	🍷🍷 5

Dario Raccaro

VIA SAN GIOVANNI, 87
34071 CORMONS [GO]
TEL. 048161425
az.agr.raccaro@alice.it

ANNUAL PRODUCTION	26,000 bottles
HECTARES UNDER VINE	4.5
VITICULTURE METHOD	Conventional

It doesn't take long to visit Dario Raccaro's small, unfussy cellar but the quality of his wines is inversely proportional to the size of the place where they were made. The results are mainly down to Dario's skills in the vineyard, where he often works with his son Paolo, a basketball player as indeed was Dario in his day. For the past few years, Raccaro has been leasing the legendary Vigna del Rolat plot, where the tocai vines were planted in the early 20th century and subsequent replantings have always been carried out using scions from the same vines. Acclimatized to perfection, it has been producing a wine that is universally praised. It's no surprise that Dario again won Three Glasses for this stunner with its concentrated citrus nose and palate bursting with substance, structure and minerality. Incredibly, Dario came close to repeating last year's White of the Year title for a product that had similar awards showered on it by leading wine publications. Nor are the Malvasia's high marks unexpected when the superb quality of both the merlot, cabernet sauvignon and franc Rosso and the 2006 Merlot confirm Dario's all-round winemaking skills.

O Collio Friulano Vigna del Rolat '07	♈♈♈	5
O Collio Malvasia '07	♈♈	5
● Collio Merlot '06	♈♈	6
● Friuli Isonzo Rosso '06	♈♈	5
O Collio Bianco '07	♈♈♈	5
O Collio Bianco '03	♈♈♈	5
O Collio Bianco '02	♈♈♈	5
O Collio Tocai Friulano '05	♈♈♈	5
O Collio Tocai Friulano '04	♈♈♈	5
O Collio Tocai Friulano '01	♈♈♈	5
O Collio Tocai Friulano '00	♈♈♈	5
O Collio Tocai Friulano Vigna del Rolat '06	♈♈♈	5

Teresa Raiz

VIA DELLA ROGGIA, 22
33040 POVOLETTO [UD]
TEL. 0432679556
www.teresaraiz.it

ANNUAL PRODUCTION	140,000 bottles
HECTARES UNDER VINE	20
VITICULTURE METHOD	Conventional

This winery bears the name of its founders grandmother, Teresa Raiz, who inspired the young Paolo Tosolini. The child of distillers, Paolo graduated in oenology from Conegliano. Today, the cellar vinifies estate-grown fruit alongside quantities of scrupulously controlled bought-in fruit. There are 20 hectares all told, 13 of which are at the cellar. The winery's large spaces are organized rationally and there is also an area for offices and hospitality looking onto the vineyards. The vine stock itself has been replanted under the direction of French consultant Pépinières Guillaume, who has increased the density to 5,000 vines per hectare to obtain more structured wines. Vinification and maturation is almost entirely in steel and the wines evolve slowly so they are not entirely ready until late summer. As ever, we enjoyed the intense fruit and refreshing palate of the Ribolla Gialla. Pinot Grigio accounts for almost half of the cellar's production, most of it going abroad. More concentrated on the nose than in the mouth, it came close to a second Glass, as did the Chardonnay and the Sovrej, from 80 per cent chardonnay with sauvignon and picolit.

O COF Ribolla Gialla '07	♈♈	4
O Chardonnay Le Marsure '07	♈	4
O COF Friulano '07	♈	4
O COF Pinot Grigio '07	♈	4
O Pinot Grigio Le Marsure '07	♈	4
O Sovrej '06	♈	5
O Sauvignon Le Marsure '07		4
O COF Ribolla Gialla '06	♈♈	4
O COF Tocai Friulano '06	♈♈	4

Rocca Bernarda

FRAZ. IPPLIS
VIA ROCCA BERNARDA, 27
33040 PREMARIACCO [UD]
TEL. 0432716914
www.roccabernarda.com

ANNUAL PRODUCTION 200,000 bottles
HECTARES UNDER VINE 55
VITICULTURE METHOD Conventional

Rocca Bernarda is an integral part of the history of Friulian wine. The fortified manor that dominates the estate was built in 1567 but the cellars were constructed a decade earlier and there is a plaque to testify to this. Following tortuous inheritance-related issues, the estate is now owned by the Sovereign Order of Malta, which has invested large sums in both vineyards and general restoration. In fact, the property is now a venue for cultural events. Estate manager Paolo Dolce and consultant oenologist Marco Monchiero should take credit for the quality of the wines and this time the Friulano came close to perfection. Intense fruitiness is beautifully offset by classic varietal almondiness. Rocca Bernarda is one of the historic homes of Picolit and this edition proffers candied citrus peel and sweetness that is wonderfully balanced by the tangy acidity in the finish. The onionskin-hued Pinot Grigio is stylish and richly textured, the Sauvignon has vibrant minerality and the Bianco Vineis, from friulano, chardonnay and sauvignon, is delightfully sun-ripe. Missing from the list is the flagship Merlot Centis, which is still ageing in the cellar.

O COF Friulano '07	ŶŶ	4*
O COF Bianco Vineis '07	ŶŶ	4*
O COF Picolit '06	ŶŶ	8
O COF Pinot Grigio Ramato della Rocca '06	ŶŶ	4*
O COF Sauvignon '07	ŶŶ	4*
O COF Chardonnay '07	Ŷ	4
● COF Refosco P. R. '07	Ŷ	4
O COF Ribolla Gialla '07	Ŷ	4
O COF Picolit '03	ŶŶŶ	8
O COF Picolit '98	ŶŶŶ	8
O COF Picolit '97	ŶŶŶ	8
● COF Merlot Centis '99	ŶŶŶ	5
● COF Merlot Centis '03	ŶŶ	5
● COF Merlot Centis '01	ŶŶ	6
O COF Picolit '06	ŶŶ	8

Paolo Rodaro

LOC. SPESSA
VIA CORMONS, 60
33040 CIVIDALE DEL FRIULI [UD]
TEL. 0432716066
paolorodaro@yahoo.it

ANNUAL PRODUCTION 250,000 bottles
HECTARES UNDER VINE 42
VITICULTURE METHOD Conventional

The oenological history of the Rodaro family began in the spring of 1846 but the step change occurred in the 1960s and 1970s when brothers Edo and Luigi turned the estate into one of the largest and most respected in eastern Friuli. Paolo Rodaro is outgoing, articulate and very likeable, one of the shakers and movers of the local wine scene. Some of the Rodaro labels bear the word Romain, a line that embraces Refosco, Schioppettino, Pignolo, Cabernet Franc and Merlot made with overripe grapes that continue to ripen in plastic cases for about a month before going into the crusher. At the Three Glass finals, Verduzzo Pra Zenâr gave a good account of itself. The intense nose of honey and lime blossom ushers in a full, richly textured palate that is appealing but never cloys. In fact, it's a perfect example of how a sweet wine can marry power and elegance.

O COF Verduzzo Friulano Pra Zenâr '06	ŶŶ	6
O COF Picolit '06	ŶŶ	7
● COF Schioppettino Romain '06	ŶŶ	6
O Ronc '06	ŶŶ	4
● COF Cabernet Franc Romain '05	Ŷ	6
● COF Merlot Romain '05	Ŷ	6
O COF Pinot Grigio '07	Ŷ	4
O COF Ribolla Gialla '07	Ŷ	4
● Refosco P. R. '05	Ŷ	4
● Refosco P. R. Romain '05	Ŷ	6
O Ronc '00	ŶŶŶ	5
O COF Sauvignon Bosc Romain '96	ŶŶŶ	5
● Refosco P. R. Romain '03	ŶŶŶ	6
O COF Picolit '05	ŶŶ	7
O COF Picolit '04	ŶŶ	7

Roncada

LOC. RONCADA, 5
34071 CORMONS [GO]
TEL. 048161394
roncada@hotmail.com

ANNUAL PRODUCTION	100,000 bottles
HECTARES UNDER VINE	24
VITICULTURE METHOD	Conventional

On a hillside between Cormons and Capriva is the villa and estate of Roncada, which began to grow grapes in 1920 and has been managed by the Mattioni family since 1956. Vineyards both mature and recently planted are all well aspected, enabling the cellar to release premium wines. The owners are planning to renovate the facilities, especially the cellar, to make sure that the full potential of the harvest goes into bottle. The wines are all well made but the Tocai Friulano stands out for its golden delicious apple, pear and spring flowers nose leading in to a fresh, satisfying palate. We liked the Chardonnay's wisteria, lime blossom and ripe white-fleshed fruit mingling with yeast and golden delicious apple on the palate. Our tasters also enjoyed the Sauvignon's appealing elderflower nose and delicious fruit on the palate. The other whites are all attractive. Best of the reds is the 2006 Merlot, whose blackberry and quinine bouquet precedes a palate that has still to mellow out. The Cabernet Franc has elegant fruit led by cherries and plums on the palate.

Il Roncat - Giovanni Dri

LOC. RAMANDOLO
VIA PESCIA, 7
33045 NIMIS [UD]
TEL. 0432790260
www.drironcat.com

ANNUAL PRODUCTION	50,000 bottles
HECTARES UNDER VINE	10
VITICULTURE METHOD	Conventional

Giovanni Dri can claim to be one of the Ramandolo DOCG's historic wine men. For many years, he was the area's best-known producer and the one that set the bar for his neighbours. A few years ago, Giovanni built a splendid cellar. Quite deliberately, he kept instrumentation to a minimum while specially designing the spaces to welcome visitors. Surrounded as it is by vines on the steep slopes at Ramandolo, this winery is definitely one to visit. Growing grapes in this area is a challenge as it is exposed to cold north-east winds and hail is a frequent problem. In fact, most of the vines are protected with special netting. The 2006 Picolit is a classic of the type, showing deliciously elegant on nose and palate. The honey and baked apple 2005 Ramandolo is more persuasive than its fresher, less substantial companion from 2007. Sweet wines are Dri's strong suit but the range does include reds, the best of which is Refosco Il Roncat 2006.

○ Collio Tocai Friulano '07	♟♟	4*
● Collio Cabernet Franc '06	♟	5
● Collio Merlot '06	♟	5
○ Collio Chardonnay '07	♟	4
○ Collio Pinot Bianco '07	♟	5
○ Collio Pinot Grigio '07	♟	4
○ Collio Ribolla Gialla '07	♟	5
○ Collio Sauvignon '07	♟	4
● Refosco P. R. '07	♟	5
○ Collio Pinot Bianco '06	♟♟	4
○ Collio Pinot Grigio '06	♟♟	4

○ COF Picolit Il Roncat '06	♟♟	8
○ Ramandolo Il Roncat '07	♟♟	6
○ Ramandolo Il Roncat '05	♟♟	6
● COF Cabernet '06	♟	4
● COF Merlot '06	♟	4
● COF Refosco Il Roncat '06	♟	5
● COF Pignolo Monte dei Carpini '06		6
○ COF Sauvignon Il Roncat '07		5

Ronchi di Manzano

VIA ORSARIA, 42
33044 MANZANO [UD]
TEL. 0432740718
www.ronchidimanzano.com

ANNUAL PRODUCTION	300,000 bottles
HECTARES UNDER VINE	55
VITICULTURE METHOD	Conventional

The Ronchi di Manzano winery was founded in 1969 but the Borghese family has owned it only since 1984. Roberta looks after things full time with passion for her territory and for winemaking, personally supervising all stages of production from vineyard to marketing. Of course, she doesn't do it on her own. Vineyard management is Raiko's job and the cellar is run by Boris the oenologist and technicians Aldo and Ivan. The 55 hectares are split across three large terraced vineyards called Ronc di Scossai, Ronc di Subule and Ronc di Rosazzo, all three on marly soil. Merlot Ronc di Subule is subtle, giving clear morello cherry and ripe cherries before the intense, warm palate unveils its well-gauged extract. We like the Sauvignon's sage and spring flowers nose while the full-bodied palate has ripe peach and citrus that meld beautifully in the lingering finish. There follows a long list of wines that earned more or less comparable marks. They are not particularly characterful but are very well made, which almost always means they are enjoyably fresh.

Ronco Blanchis

LOC. BLANCHIS, 70
34070 MOSSA [GO]
TEL. 0438492250
www.venegazzu.com

ANNUAL PRODUCTION	30,000 bottles
HECTARES UNDER VINE	10
VITICULTURE METHOD	Conventional

This historic estate's vines are wonderfully aspected on the Blanchis hillside in the Collio Goriziano. Two centuries ago, the noble Austrian Catterini De Herzerberg family owned the property, which was already noted for its wines. Subsequently, it was acquired by one of the king of Spain's ministers, who stuck to the quality-oriented approach. Today, the competent Gianfranco Palla continues to concentrate on the Collio Goriziano's true forte, white wines. The bizarre weather of the 2007 growing year prevented the range from hitting the heights of 2006, which enabled Ronco Blanchis to storm into the Guide, but we were happy to note that potential was still in evidence. We tasted four wines. The Friulano is strikingly varietal with its fresh crusty bread, almond milk, pears and spring flower picked up precisely on the palate, which signs off with lingering almonds. The Pinot Grigio is a little dumb at first but then opens into attractive hay, gunflint and pears that introduce a fresh-tasting, vigorous palate. Finally, we would also mention the citrus-fresh Chardonnay and minerally Sauvignon.

● COF Merlot Ronc di Subule '05	♀♀	5
○ COF Sauvignon '07	♀♀	4*
● COF Rosazzo Rosso Braûros '05	♀	4
● COF Cabernet Franc '06	♀	4
○ COF Chardonnay '07	♀	4
○ COF Rosazzo Bianco Ellègri '07	♀	4
○ COF Friulano '07	♀	4
● COF Merlot '06	♀	4
● COF Refosco P. R. '06	♀	4
○ COF Rosazzo Picolit '05	♀	6
● Le Zuccule Rosso '03	♀	5
○ COF Chardonnay '06	♀♀	4
● COF Merlot Ronc di Subule '05	♀♀	5
○ COF Rosazzo Bianco '06	♀♀	4

○ Collio Friulano '07	♀♀	4*
○ Collio Pinot Grigio '07	♀♀	4*
○ Collio Chardonnay '07	♀	4
○ Collio Sauvignon '07	♀	4
○ Collio Chardonnay '06	♀♀	4
○ Collio Pinot Grigio '06	♀♀	4
○ Collio Sauvignon '06	♀♀	4
○ Collio Tocai Friulano '06	♀♀	4

Ronco dei Tassi

LOC. MONTE, 38
34071 CORMONS [GO]
TEL. 048160155
www.roncodeitassi.it

ANNUAL PRODUCTION	76,000 bottles
HECTARES UNDER VINE	12
VITICULTURE METHOD	Conventional

There's always something going on at Ronco dei Tassi. Fabio Coser plans and invests with evident gusto. He must be very happy to know that the estate's future is in the safe hands of his two enterprising sons, Matteo and Enrico. But that doesn't stop Fabio continuing to enjoy his work, despite the many awards his cellar has collected. His latest investment is the recovery of a vineyard on Monte Quarin with very old – some were planted a century ago – native Friulian vines. For the time being, the Cosers can savour the eighth Three Glass prize for Bianco Fosarin. This much-admired blend of friulano, malvasia and pinot bianco is temptingly complex, showing wisteria and rose petal florality, peach juice and confectioner's cream. All this is marvellously fused together with Ronco dei Tassi's trademark elegance. Other great wines are the subtle tobacco and pennyroyal Friulano, the minerally, aroma-rich Sauvignon, the elegant Bordeaux blend Rosso Cjarandon, with its fruit softness and tannins well tucked in, and the complex, varietal Pinot Grigio.

★ Ronco del Gelso

VIA ISONZO, 117
34071 CORMONS [GO]
TEL. 048161310
www.roncodelgelso.com

ANNUAL PRODUCTION	150,000 bottles
HECTARES UNDER VINE	22
VITICULTURE METHOD	Conventional

This time round, Giorgio Badin didn't quite manage Three Glasses, despite presenting us with a range that lived up to the cellar's well-deserved reputation, and despite sending four wines to our final tastings. No one doubts Giorgio's outstanding winemaking ability. His products are elegant, clean, superbly drinkable and balanced yet true to their variety and terroir. Top of the range again are the wines that made Ronco del Gelso famous. We liked the yellow plum and lavender Malvasia – and to think that the vines are very young – as well as the excellent Pinot Bianco, a classic with moderate but never wobbly structure, plenty of ripe fruit and bracing acidity. The Friulano is as impressive as ever, albeit a tad more rustic than its predecessors, as was to be expected. Pinot Grigio Sot lis Rivis also performed magnificently by virtue of its remarkable persistence and a special mention goes to the Merlot, which came within an ace of going to the national finals. All the other wines on the very long list are quite excellent.

O Collio Bianco Fosarin '07	♟♟♟	4*
O Collio Friulano '07	♟♟	4*
O Collio Pinot Grigio '07	♟♟	4*
O Collio Sauvignon '07	♟♟	4*
● Collio Rosso Cjarandon '05	♟♟	5
O Collio Malvasia '07	♟♟	4
O Collio Picolit '06	♟♟	6
O Collio Bianco Fosarin '96	♟♟♟	4
O Collio Bianco Fosarin '06	♟♟♟	4
O Collio Bianco Fosarin '04	♟♟♟	4
O Collio Sauvignon '98	♟♟♟	4
O Collio Sauvignon '05	♟♟♟	4
● Collio Rosso Cjarandon '01	♟♟♟	5
● Collio Rosso Cjarandon '00	♟♟♟	5

O Friuli Isonzo Friulano '07	♟♟	4*
O Friuli Isonzo Malvasia '07	♟♟	4*
O Friuli Isonzo Pinot Bianco '07	♟♟	4*
O Friuli Isonzo Pinot Grigio Sot lis Rivis '07	♟♟	4*
O Friuli Isonzo Bianco Latimis '07	♟♟	4
● Friuli Isonzo Merlot '05	♟♟	5
O Friuli Isonzo Sauvignon '07	♟♟	4
● Friuli Isonzo Cabernet Franc '07	♟	4
O Friuli Isonzo Riesling '07	♟	4
O Friuli Isonzo Tocai Friulano '06	♟♟♟	4
O Friuli Isonzo Tocai Friulano '05	♟♟♟	4
O Friuli Isonzo Tocai Friulano '04	♟♟♟	4
O Friuli Isonzo Tocai Friulano '03	♟♟♟	4
O Friuli Isonzo Tocai Friulano '01	♟♟♟	4
O Friuli Isonzo Sauvignon '00	♟♟♟	4

Ronco del Gnemiz

VIA RONCHI, 5
33048 SAN GIOVANNI AL NATISONE [UD]
TEL. 0432756238
roncodelgnemiz@libero.it

ANNUAL PRODUCTION   38,000 bottles
HECTARES UNDER VINE   15
VITICULTURE METHOD   Conventional

This year, Ronco del Gnemiz released a stunning range of whites. Despite the 15 hectares under vine, very low yields prevent annual output from rising above 40,000 units. Serena can call on Andrea Pittana, a keen wine technician with a good knowledge of international winemaking, and the two work very happily together. If there are any arguments, Cristian Patat is on hand to contribute his skills, inherited from the legendary Raul, a great wine man from the 1980s and 1990s. Exports absorb 70 per cent of output, direct sales account for ten per cent and the remaining bottles are sold in Italy, half of them in Friuli. We were impressed by Bianco San Zuan. From friulano only, it is elegant and complex, recalling aromatic herbs. We preferred the standard Chardonnay to the Sol edition, which is a tad over-vanillaed. The former is a selection from old vineyards whereas the Sol comes from the best of the barriques. Bianco di Jacopo is a fallback wine, made this year from chardonnay and sauvignon. If only all second wines were as good as this.

Ronco delle Betulle

LOC. ROSAZZO
VIA ABATE COLONNA, 24
33044 MANZANO [UD]
TEL. 0432740547
www.roncodellebetulle.it

ANNUAL PRODUCTION   70,000 bottles
HECTARES UNDER VINE   14
VITICULTURE METHOD   Conventional

Situated near the abbey of Rosazzo, Ronco delle Betulle extends over 14 hectares on marl and clay soil, the celebrated "ponca", from which Ivana Adami obtains about 70,000 bottles each year. This is one of the female-led wineries that have earned a place at the top of the region's winemaking league table. Rosso Narciso 2004 is intriguing and again went forward to the Three Glass final. The nose reveals distinct ripe plums and cherries laced with balsam, suggesting at once that this is a seriously good wine. The palate mirrors the nose as it progresses intensely to a lingering finale. Ivana Adami has always looked on Narciso as her flag-carrier and we can only agree. A step behind is the 2006 Picolit. Intense marmalade and acacia blossom pervade the nose before the palate reveals satisfying complexity. Any risk of cloying or heaviness in the mouth is avoided by beautifully handled acidity.

O COF Bianco San Zuan '06	▼▼	5
O COF Chardonnay '07	▼▼	5
O COF Chardonnay Sol '06	▼▼	6
● COF Schioppettino '06	▼▼	7
O COF Bianco di Jacopo '07	▼	4
O COF Sauvignon '07	▼	5
O COF Sauvignon Sol '06	▼	6
● COF Merlot Sol '03	▼▼	7
● COF Rosso del Gnemiz '03	▼▼	7

● COF Rosazzo Rosso Narciso '04	▼▼	6
O COF Rosazzo Picolit '06	▼▼	6
O COF Sauvignon '07	▼▼	4
● COF Cabernet Franc '06	▼	5
O COF Friulano V. Bocois '07	▼	4
● COF Merlot '06	▼	5
O COF Pinot Grigio '07	▼	4
O COF Ribolla Gialla '07	▼	4
● Franconia '06	▼	5
● Narciso Rosso '03	▼▼▼	6
● COF Rosazzo Rosso Narciso '03	▼▼	6
● COF Rosazzo Rosso Narciso '01	▼▼	6
● COF Rosazzo Rosso Narciso '00	▼▼	6
O COF Tocai Friulano '06	▼▼	4

Roncùs

VIA MAZZINI, 26
34070 CAPRIVA DEL FRIULI [GO]
TEL. 0481809349
www.roncus.it

ANNUAL PRODUCTION	30,000 bottles
HECTARES UNDER VINE	12
VITICULTURE METHOD	Conventional

Marco Perco's wines do not pass unobserved. Highly individual, distinctively mineral and nuanced with balsam, they are destined to improve with cellar time. That is certainly the case with the leading Roncùs wine, Bianco Vecchie Vigne. From vineyards with an average age of more than 40 years, the wine has attracted the attention of Udine university, where agronomist Giovanni Colugnati and Professor Zironi are conducting studies on vine genetics and the microbiology of wine. Not for the first time, Vecchie Vigne, a white from malvasia, friulano and ribolla, put on a fine show. Its balsam and rosemary perceptions meld seamlessly with sweeter citrus tart and pipe tobacco. Balanced on the palate, which echoes the nose, it discloses a hint of minerality that continues through to the long-lingering palate. In the Tocai, we noted original warm notes of ripe fruits and petits fours. The Pinot Bianco performed admirably for the breadth and softness of its banana and peach sensations and for its varietal mentholated nuances. Finally, a round of applause for Marco's decision not to release his Val Di Miez blended red, which did not come up to expectations.

Russiz Superiore

VIA RUSSIZ, 7
34070 CAPRIVA DEL FRIULI [GO]
TEL. 048199164
www.marcofelluga.it

ANNUAL PRODUCTION	200,000 bottles
HECTARES UNDER VINE	60
VITICULTURE METHOD	Conventional

Russiz Superiore is the front room of Marco Felluga's oenological household. Here in the noble heart of the Collio, the Russiz Superiore crest is equally aristocratic, having once belonged to the prince of Torre e Tasso, one of the first lords of Friuli, who arrived in 1273 with the patriarch, Raimondo della Torre. In this historic setting, Roberto Felluga's abilities and the marl and sandstone soil produced a series of winners culminating in a superb Pinot Bianco that earned Three Glasses. The aromas of fresh apple, white-fleshed fruits and acacia blossom precede progression on a palate that plays freshness off against soft texture through to a lingering citrus finish. Bianco Col Disôre is on a par with the champion, bringing together structure, softness and nice minerality. The velvet sweetness of the Verduzzo is a given at Villa Russiz and the first release of Pinot Bianco Riserva is intriguing. After three years in large wood and one in glass, it has stylish damson, crusty bread and vanilla cream aromatics as well as delightful balance of oak and fruit. Finally, we enjoyed the rich spice of the Bordeaux blend Rosso Riserva degli Orzoni.

O Collio Bianco Vecchie Vigne '05	♟♟	6
O Collio Tocai Friulano '06	♟♟	5
O Pinot Bianco '06	♟♟	5
O Sauvignon '06	♟	5
O Roncùs Bianco Vecchie Vigne '01	♟♟♟	6
O Collio Bianco Vecchie Vigne '04	♟♟	6
O Collio Bianco Vecchie Vigne '03	♟♟	6
O Collio Bianco Vecchie Vigne '02	♟♟	6
O Sauvignon '05	♟♟	5

O Collio Pinot Bianco '07	♟♟♟	5
O Collio Bianco Col Disôre '06	♟♟	6
O Collio Pinot Bianco Ris. '04	♟♟	6
O Verduzzo '05	♟♟	5
O Collio Friulano '07	♟♟	5
● Collio Cabernet Franc '05	♟♟	5
● Collio Merlot '05	♟♟	5
O Collio Pinot Grigio '07	♟♟	5
● Collio Rosso Ris. degli Orzoni '04	♟♟	7
O Collio Sauvignon Ris. '04	♟♟	6
O Collio Sauvignon '07	♟	5
O Collio Bianco Russiz Disôre '01	♟♟♟	6
O Collio Bianco Russiz Disôre '00	♟♟♟	5
● Collio Rosso Ris. degli Orzoni '94	♟♟♟	7
● Collio Rosso Ris. degli Orzoni '93	♟♟♟	7
O Collio Sauvignon '05	♟♟♟	5
O Collio Sauvignon '04	♟♟♟	6

Russolo

VIA SAN ROCCO, 58A
33080 SAN QUIRINO [PN]
TEL. 0434919577
www.russolo.it

ANNUAL PRODUCTION	150,000 bottles
HECTARES UNDER VINE	16
VITICULTURE METHOD	Conventional

Russolo is an unusual operation for the Grave DOC releasing original wines and planting varieties untypical of the area, such as müller thurgau and malvasia istriana. In addition, it makes a complex blended white called Doi Raps, which regularly garners critical approval. But there are very good reds on the list, including Pinot Nero Grifo Nero and this year Casali Bearzi, a blend that leaves the cellar some nine years after the harvest. All this comes from the sun-blessed, unfertile Pordenone flatlands. Müller Thurgau Mussignaz confirmed that its quality, giving fresh notes of moss and ginger lifted by softer tones of white peaches and apricots. Doi Raps 2006, from pinot grigio, pinot bianco, sauvignon and other grapes, has stepped up a gear. Its sumptuous banana, dried apricot and golden delicious aromatics are tinged with balsam, all of which is faithfully echoed on a palate with a savoury note that rounds off the alluring finale. We liked Pinot Nero Grifo Nero 2005's wild cherry aromas and tempting balsamic notes. Casali Bearzi '99 is a blend of several native Friulian red varieties that impressed with its breadth and well-honed extract.

San Simone

LOC. RONDOVER
VIA PRATA, 30
33080 PORCIA [PN]
TEL. 0434578633
www.sansimone.it

ANNUAL PRODUCTION	900,000 bottles
HECTARES UNDER VINE	50
VITICULTURE METHOD	Conventional

Just as San Simone was savouring one of its finest results ever, the Brisotto family suffered a tragic bereavement when Liviana, the cellar's anchor, passed on. Her children Chiara, Anna and Antonio reacted well to their loss, following Liviana's example and showing that even in an indifferent growing year, they can get the best out of their vineyards. In the past, San Simone has impressed with its reds but this time it also gave us two excellent whites. The Pinot Grigio is very true to type, giving lingering fresh pears, and a fragrant, fruit-rich Sauvignon flaunts everything from yellow peaches to refreshing citrus before it signs off with classic tomato leaf and sage. In line with cellar tradition, three reds stood out from the rest. The Cabernet Sauvignon Nexus 2005 is a surprising product for this area, its camphor and quinine notes accompanying great structure, balance and a lingering finish. Merlot Evante 2006 takes its time to open but then tempts the nose with cherries in alcohol, blackberry tart and spice. Finally, the steel-only Cabernet Franc Sugano 2006 has varietal hay complemented by ripe blackberries and solid extract.

O Doi Raps '06	♟♟ 4*
O Müller Thurgau Mussignaz '07	♟♟ 4*
● Casali Bearzi '99	♟♟ 6
O Chardonnay '06	♟♟ 4
O Malvasia Istriana '07	♟♟ 4
● Pinot Nero Grifo Nero '05	♟♟ 5
O Sauvignon Ronco Calaj '07	♟♟ 4
● Borgo di Peuma '04	♟ 5
O Pinot Grigio Ronco Calaj '07	♟ 4
O Ribolla Gialla Santarosa '07	4
O Müller Thurgau Mussignaz '06	♟♟ 4
● Borgo di Peuma '03	♟♟ 5
● Cabernet Ris. '02	♟♟ 4
● Pinot Nero Grifo Nero '04	♟♟ 5
● Refosco P. R. Ris. '04	♟♟ 4

● Friuli Grave Cabernet Franc Sugano '06	♟♟ 4
● Friuli Grave Cabernet Sauvignon Nexus '05	♟♟ 4
● Friuli Grave Merlot Evante '06	♟♟ 6
O Friuli Grave Pinot Grigio '07	♟♟ 3*
O Friuli Grave Sauvignon '07	♟♟ 3*
O Friuli Grave Friulano '07	♟ 3
O Friuli Grave Chardonnay '07	3
● Friuli Grave Refosco P. R. Re Sugano '06	4
● Friuli Grave Cabernet Franc Sugano '05	♟♟ 4
● Friuli Grave Merlot Evante '04	♟♟ 6
● Friuli Grave Merlot Evante '03	♟♟ 6

Sant'Elena

VIA GASPARINI, 1
34072 GRADISCA D'ISONZO [GO]
TEL. 048192388
www.sant-elena.com

ANNUAL PRODUCTION	120,000 bottles
HECTARES UNDER VINE	30
VITICULTURE METHOD	Conventional

Despite his many commitments, Dominic Nocerino manages his farm with shrewd attention. At first, his range was perhaps a little too inclined towards an international style but in recent years, the production philosophy has expanded to include a number of native Friulian varieties. The surprise this time was Mil Rosis, a very exciting first release that accompanies the rather too familiar notes of chardonnay with the aromatic punch and citrus tang of traminer and riesling. Yet again, the reliable Pinot Grigio pleased the panel with spring flowers, apple and hay introducing a warm, mouthfilling palate. There's no denying that the Sauvignon is attractive, although over-assertive wild roses and tropical fruits cost it a point or two. Finally, the reds include a good Cabernet but the Merlot showed a tad less character. We should however point out that when we called at the cellar, the top of the range bottles were not available for tasting.

O Bianco Mil Rosis '06	♟♟	6
O Pinot Grigio '07	♟♟	5
● Cabernet Sauvignon '05	♟	5
O Sauvignon '07	♟	5
● Merlot '05		5
O Pinot Grigio '06	♟♟	5
O Pinot Grigio '07	♟♟	5
● Tato Rosso '04	♟♟	6
● Ròs di Rôl Merlot '03	♟♟	6

Scarbolo

FRAZ. LAUZACCO
V.LE GRADO, 4
33050 PAVIA DI UDINE [UD]
TEL. 0432675612
www.scarbolo.com

ANNUAL PRODUCTION	140,000 bottles
HECTARES UNDER VINE	25
VITICULTURE METHOD	Conventional

Since Valter Scarbolo started vinifying only estate-grown grapes, the reliability of his wines has been improving year by year. Not that Valter has given up his thousand and one other activities, from his successful high-quality trattoria or the management of a couple of other estates, one in Friuli and the other in Maremma, or his promotional trips to the United States, his main export market. The estate extends over 25 hectares and annual output is around 140,000 units. This year's news is a product that looks to be aimed at the American market: Pinot Grigio Ramato XL, sold in a transparent bottle to draw attention to its "ramato" (coppery) hue. The wine is a delicious easy drinker that has style, freshness and plenty of fruit. We awarded a couple of extra points to the more complex version vinified off the skins. But best of all, we think, is the prune-led Merlot Campo del Viotto 2004, with its unerring follow-though on the mouthfilling palate. Finally, the 2005 Merlot is well executed.

● Friuli Grave Merlot Campo del Viotto '04	♟♟	4*
● Friuli Grave Cabernet '06	♟	4
O Friuli Grave Chardonnay '07	♟	4
O Friuli Grave Friulano '07	♟	4
● Friuli Grave Merlot '05	♟	4
O Friuli Grave Pinot Grigio '07	♟	4
O Friuli Grave Pinot Grigio Ramato XL '07	♟	4
O Friuli Grave Sauvignon '07		4
O Friuli Grave Bianco del Viotto '04	♟♟	5
O Friuli Grave Sauvignon '06	♟♟	4
O Friuli Grave Tocai Friulano '06	♟♟	4

★ Schiopetto

VIA PALAZZO ARCIVESCOVILE, 1
34070 CAPRIVA DEL FRIULI [GO]
TEL. 048180332
www.schiopetto.it

La Sclusa

LOC. SPESSA
VIA STRADA DI S. ANNA, 7/2
33043 CIVIDALE DEL FRIULI [UD]
TEL. 0432716259
www.lasclusa.it

ANNUAL PRODUCTION	189,000 bottles
HECTARES UNDER VINE	30
VITICULTURE METHOD	Conventional

The Schiopetto winery is back on the track marked out by the great Mario, trail-blazer of modern Friulian winemaking. Mario's three children, Maria Angela, Carlo and Giorgio, keep the focus on quality, taking decisions that other Friulian estates all too often shun, such as cutting back the number of labels. There are only eight now. With vineyard consultancy from Marco Simonit and Donato Lanati in the cellar, the Schiopettos earned Three Glasses for Blanc des Rosis, an elegantly intense blend of tocai, pinot grigio, sauvignon, malvasia and ribolla with florality and lashings of fruit perfectly mirrored on the broad palate, which finishes long and fresh. But we were even more impressed by the fact that high scores are now equally common for the Schiopetto reds, once the cellar's Achilles' heel. Podere dei Blumeri Rosso, from merlot, cabernet sauvignon and refosco, marries complexity with intensity and elegance, offsetting its generous fruit with robust alcohol. A short head behind is the Bordeaux blend Rivarossa while the Pinot Grigio is a thing of beauty, embodying the qualities that underpin all Schiopetto wines: elegance and cleanness.

ANNUAL PRODUCTION	200,000 bottles
HECTARES UNDER VINE	35
VITICULTURE METHOD	Conventional

Brothers Germano, Maurizio and Luciano Zorzettig are the current stars of this lovely winery, established by their grandfather Tita, known as Tramuntin, in 1963. A few years later, Gino took over the operation and even today continues to help his three sons out, especially in the vineyards. In the meantime, the former main activity, livestock farming, has been abandoned for wine and the cellar has passed from the few bottles and many demijohns that used to be sold to loyal clients to today's 200,000 bottles, all from estate-grown fruit. There are 35 hectares under vine, most planted to white varieties. Germano is the wine technician, Maurizio looks after the vines and Luciano is cellarman. For the second year running, the Picolit went through to the Three Glass final. It's one of the cleanest, most varietal Picolits around with its sweetness, freshness and elegant baked apples and warm peach laced with dried figs and caramel. But the Refosco also picked up Two red Glasses for its fruit-rich complexity, varietal spice and tannins well tucked in. The Ribolla Gialla is richly textured and all the other bottles merited One very full Glass.

O Blanc des Rosis '07	♥♥♥	5
O Collio Pinot Grigio '07	♥♥	5
● Poderi dei Blumeri Rosso '05	♥♥	6
● Rivarossa '06	♥♥	5
O Collio Sauvignon '07	♥♥	5
O Mario Schiopetto Bianco '07	♥♥	6
O Collio Pinot Bianco '07	♥	5
O Collio Friulano '07		5
O Blanc des Rosis '06	♥♥♥	5
O Collio Pinot Bianco '00	♥♥♥	5
O Collio Pinot Bianco Amrità '97	♥♥♥	6
O Collio Pinot Bianco Amrità '96	♥♥♥	5
O Collio Sauvignon '97	♥♥♥	
O Collio Tocai Friulano '95	♥♥♥	5
O Collio Tocai Friulano '00	♥♥♥	5
O Mario Schiopetto Bianco '03	♥♥♥	6
O Mario Schiopetto Bianco '02	♥♥♥	6

O COF Picolit '06	♥♥	7
● COF Refosco P. R. '07	♥♥	4*
O COF Ribolla Gialla '07	♥♥	4
O COF Friulano '07	♥	4
O COF Pinot Grigio '07	♥	4
O COF Sauvignon '07	♥	4
O COF Picolit V. del Torrione '05	♥♥	7
O COF Pinot Grigio '06	♥♥	4
O COF Ribolla Gialla '06	♥♥	4

Roberto Scubla

FRAZ. IPPLIS
VIA ROCCA BERNARDA, 22
33040 PREMARIACCO [UD]
TEL. 0432716258
www.scubla.com

ANNUAL PRODUCTION	60,000 bottles	
HECTARES UNDER VINE	8.5	
VITICULTURE METHOD	Conventional	

Roberto Scubla decided to take up winemaking in 1991, when with reckless enthusiasm he handed in his notice at the bank and bought a few hectares in the hills at Rocca Bernarda and Ipplis. Roberto's passion for viticulture started when he was still a child who loved to visit his uncle's farm, where he dreamed of having a winery of his own. Today, he has eight and a half hectares planted to vine. Red and white varieties each account for about half of the stock, enabling Roberto to release a very wide range of products. Still not content, Roberto also makes two white blends and one red. The wines are quite outstanding but the Sauvignon stands a head above the others, its intense sage and bell pepper introducing good thrust and fruitiness in the mouth, thanks in part to the collaboration of Gianni Menotti. Also superb are the blends Bianco Speziale 2007 and the by now celebrated Pomèdes from 2006, from pinot bianco, friulano and riesling renano. Its intense, wide-ranging nose precedes a complex, long-lingering palate.

Renzo Sgubin

VIA FAET, 15
34071 CORMONS [GO]
TEL. 0481630297
renzo.sgubin@tiscali.it

ANNUAL PRODUCTION	30,000 bottles	
HECTARES UNDER VINE	12	
VITICULTURE METHOD	Conventional	

Having made over the cellar in 1999, Renzo Sgubin is carrying out further expansion and rationalization to deal with his wines' continuing success. Renzo is the son of former sharecropper Bruno Sgubin and brother of Sergio, an expert earth-moving operator. He has taken particular over laying out his 12 hectares of vineyards, which adjoin the winery buildings. This was the springboard for the quality leap that led to abandonment of demijohns and the decision to bottle under the winery label. Cleanness and character are the distinguishing features of wines from this producer, who is just over 40. The top of the range wine bears a mysterious sequence of numbers: 3, 4, 3. It's not a magic formula, though; it's the date of birth of Renzo's son Leonardo, born on 3 April 2003. The blend is a selection of friulano, chardonnay, malvasia and sauvignon grapes fermented and aged in small barrels for 45 months. Complex in character, it proffers aromas of flowers and fresh fruits. Apple is the theme of the remarkably fresh-tasting Chardonnay and the stylish Friulano is well worth its full Glass.

O COF Bianco Pomèdes '06	♈♈ 6
O COF Bianco Speziale '07	♈♈ 4*
O COF Sauvignon '07	♈♈ 4*
● COF Cabernet Sauvignon '06	♈♈ 5
O COF Friulano '07	♈♈ 4
O COF Pinot Bianco '07	♈♈ 4
● COF Rosso Scuro '05	♈♈ 5
O COF Verduzzo Friulano Cràtis '05	♈♈ 6
● COF Merlot '06	♈ 5
O COF Bianco Pomèdes '04	♈♈♈ 6
O COF Bianco Pomèdes '99	♈♈♈ 6
O COF Bianco Pomèdes '98	♈♈♈ 6
O COF Verduzzo Friulano Cràtis '06	♈♈♈ 6
O COF Verduzzo Friulano Graticcio '99	♈♈♈ 6
O COF Bianco Pomèdes '05	♈♈ 6

O 3, 4, 3	♈♈ 4*
O Friuli Isonzo Chardonnay '07	♈♈ 4*
O Friuli Isonzo Friulano '07	♈ 4
O Friuli Isonzo Pinot Grigio '07	♈ 4
O Friuli Isonzo Sauvignon '07	♈ 4
O Friuli Isonzo Pinot Grigio '06	♈♈ 4
O Friuli Isonzo Sauvignon '06	♈♈ 4
O Friuli Isonzo Tocai Friulano '06	♈♈ 4

Giordano Sirch

VIA FORNALIS, 277
33043 CIVIDALE DEL FRIULI [UD]
TEL. 0432709835
www.sirchwine.com

ANNUAL PRODUCTION	50,000 bottles
HECTARES UNDER VINE	11
VITICULTURE METHOD	Conventional

Luca Sirch is now a full-time grower and winemaker, having given up his day job to work the nine superb hectares owned by his father Giordano, who also has a couple of leased hectares. In the previous two Guides, we were cautious about this new cellar but this time our tasters had no hesitation in awarding a top prize to the Sirch Friulano 2007, the result of hard work in the vineyard. The man in charge is Pierpaolo, a vine expert who travels Italy to consult for other growers. Equally crucial is work in the cellar, where Luca is flanked by Alessio Dorigo, a proven expert winemaker despite his relative youth. The Friulano corresponds to the profile the variety acquires in the Prepotto area, where exceptional minerality combines with a broad swath of aromatics. There is also a stylish hint of greenness to enhance this superb wine. Friulano Mis Mas (the name means jumble in Friulian) scored very high marks for the unwavering thrust of the fruit in the mouth and all-round intensity of the aromatics. The lavender and violet-themed Malvasia is only a step behind the two stand-outs and the value for money asterisk award to the Friulano is well deserved.

Skerk

FRAZ. S. PELAGIO
LOC. PREPOTTO, 20
34011 DUINO AURISINA [TS]
TEL. 040200156
www.skerk.com

ANNUAL PRODUCTION	20,000 bottles
HECTARES UNDER VINE	6
VITICULTURE METHOD	Natural

Boris Skerk's compact winery is managed by his son, Sandi. Results have been improving of late and this year the Skerk Sauvignon went on to impress the panel at the Three Glass finals. Sandi is finding his own a way forward, experimenting all the time and gradually developing ideas. One is that his wines shouldn't be filtered. Until only a few years ago, tasters tended to turn up their noses at a hazy wine, in deference to an old-fashioned view of things, but appearance has become less important. Nowadays the focus is on the pleasure the wine gives on nose and palate. Before we discuss the wines, a word about the estate. The vines stand on six hectares of red Carso soil, overlooking the gulf of Trieste, and the cellar is spectacular, literally carved out of hard limestone, the smooth walls pockmarked with deep holes. That Sauvignon is broad and aroma-rich, introducing a medley of citrus and minerality on the richly textured palate with its lingering finish. The equally rich, varietal, macerated Malvasia has a minerality that only the Carso can imbue. The native Vitovska is made on the same lines.

O COF Friulano '07	♟♟♟	4*
O COF Friulano Mis Mas '07	♟	3*
O COF Pinot Grigio '07	♟♟	4
O Malvasia '07	♟♟	4
O COF Ribolla Gialla '07	♟	4
O COF Sauvignon '07	♟	4
O COF Pinot Grigio '06	♟♟	4
O COF Sauvignon '06	♟♟	4
O COF Ribolla Gialla '06	♟♟	4
O COF Tocai Friulano '06	♟♟	4

O Carso Sauvignon Non Filtrato '06	♟♟	5
O Carso Malvasia Non Filtrato '06	♟♟	5
O Carso Vitovska Non Filtrato '06	♟♟	5
● Carso Terrano Non Filtrato '06	♟	5
O Carso Malvasia Non Filtrato '05	♟♟	4
O Carso Sauvignon Non Filtrato '05	♟♟	4
O Carso Vitovska Non Filtrato '05	♟♟	4

Edi Skok

LOC. GIASBANA, 15
34070 SAN FLORIANO DEL COLLIO [GO]
TEL. 0481390280
www.skok.it

ANNUAL PRODUCTION	35,000 bottles
HECTARES UNDER VINE	11
VITICULTURE METHOD	Conventional

Meeting Edi Skok and his sister Orietta is a thrilling experience. We suggest you find out for yourselves. These two wonderful growers think wine is a living creature – and of course they're right – and treat every stage of production and tasting with the same heart-warming care. For the past 40 years or so, the Skoks have owned these vineyards and they know every nuance of the site climates. Quality is the priority and they apply that philosophy personally at every stage from vineyard management to winemaking. The Skoks have bottled their wines since 1991 and whites are the cellar's strong suit. This year, it was the Pinot Grigio that shone for its subtle wisteria and a fresh fruit palate that lingers satisfyingly. The utterly typical Tocai Friulano has refreshing fruit and almonds. We also liked the Chardonnay for its subtle white-fleshed fruit palate. Finally, the Merlot has decent intensity, well-balanced extract and appealing forest fruits tones.

Leonardo Specogna

VIA ROCCA BERNARDA, 4
33040 CORNO DI ROSAZZO [UD]
TEL. 0432755840
www.specogna.it

ANNUAL PRODUCTION	100,000 bottles
HECTARES UNDER VINE	19
VITICULTURE METHOD	Conventional

The story of Specogna is typical of many other Friulian wineries. Grandfather Leonardo, who recently passed away, came home from Switzerland in 1963, where like many other Friulians he had emigrated after the war. He invested his savings in a plot of land at Corno di Rosazzo. Gradually, his sons Gianni and Graziano joined him in the hills, contributing new techniques and making over the vineyards to keep the winery abreast of the times. Now it is the turn of Leonardo's grandchildren, Andrea and Christian, who have added a touch of creativity. This year, there are two stand-out wines: Merlot Oltre 2004 and the Sauvignon 2007. The Merlot is warm, rich and creamy, unveiling a delicious, leisurely ripe cherry and citrus finish. The Sauvignon finds a point of equilibrium between sweet yellow peach fruit and bell pepper and sage herbaceousness. The onionskin, fruit-forward Pinot Grigio is in the classic mould while the Friulano offers depth and pervasiveness. We also liked the Chardonnay's pineapple and tropical fruit. Finally, our congratulations on the Specogna Pignolo 2005 which, unlike some others, is soft with tannins well tucked in.

O Collio Pinot Grigio '07	♟♟ 4*
O Collio Chardonnay '07	♟ 4
● Collio Merlot '06	♟ 4
O Collio Sauvignon '07	♟ 4
O Collio Tocai Friulano Zabura '07	♟ 4
O Collio Bianco Pe Ar '05	♟♟ 5
O Collio Pinot Grigio '06	♟♟ 4
O Collio Pinot Grigio '05	♟♟ 4

● COF Merlot Oltre '04	♟♟ 6
O COF Sauvignon '07	♟♟ 4*
O COF Friulano '07	♟♟ 4
O COF Chardonnay '06	♟♟ 4
● COF Pignolo '05	♟♟ 5
O Pinot Grigio '07	♟♟ 4
● COF Cabernet '06	♟ 4
● COF Merlot '06	♟ 4
O COF Picolit '06	♟ 7
● COF Refosco P. R. '06	♟ 4
O COF Ribolla Gialla '07	♟ 4
O COF Verduzzo Friulano '07	♟ 4
● COF Cabernet Franc '07	4
● COF Merlot Oltre '03	♟♟ 6
O COF Tocai Friulano '06	♟♟ 4

Castello di Spessa

VIA SPESSA, 1
34070 CAPRIVA DEL FRIULI [GO]
TEL. 0481639914
www.paliwines.com

ANNUAL PRODUCTION	120,000 bottles
HECTARES UNDER VINE	32
VITICULTURE METHOD	Conventional

Castello di Spessa has 32 hectares in a splendid south-facing amphitheatre with its own fantastic site climate. Loretto Pali has invested heavily in the property, flanking his long-standing wine technician, Domenico Lovat, with consultants Gianni Menotti in the cellar and Marco Simonit among the rows. He also decided to weed out duplicate products to present consumers with single varieties associated with a historic figure from the castle's past. Built in the late 19th century, Castello di Spessa has a cellar dating from the 14th century and a bunker constructed between the wars for military purposes. Today, the environment is ideal for barrel maturing the wines. Yet again, we were bowled over at our tastings, particularly by the magnificently rich bouquet and infinitely long palate of Sauvignon Segrè. The 2005 Pinot Bianco di Santarosa has less wood than in the past and is extremely gratifying, as are the steel-matured Pinot Bianco, the Pinot Grigio, the Friulano and the Bordeaux blend Conte di Spessa 2003. Lagging just behind were the Ribolla Gialla, the Merlot Torriani 2004 and the Pinot Nero Casanova 2005. The last two need more bottle time.

Oscar Sturm

LOC. ZEGLA, 1
34071 CORMONS [GO]
TEL. 048160720
www.sturm.it

ANNUAL PRODUCTION	70,000 bottles
HECTARES UNDER VINE	10
VITICULTURE METHOD	Conventional

Once again, Oscar Sturm sent two wines to our finals, just missing out on top honours. But time is on his side for Oscar can rely on the talents of his younger son. Patrick has grown up – oenologically speaking – very quickly and has an expert's touch. His brother Denis, a degree from Milan's Bocconi university safely tucked away, lends a hand with everything from vineyard management to administration. Oscar himself has taken a back seat, leaving all the production decisions to his sons, including drastic bunch thinning, a process that is a stab to the heart of an old-style wine man like our hero. Andritz is the name of the village in Austria the family came from in the 19th century, moving to this area and adopting the Slovene language. Bianco Andritz, from pinot grigio and sauvignon, is redolent of baked apples while the palate has a doughy texture, great richness, freshness and complexity. There's a nice hint of apricot on the nose of the intense, elegantly long Pinot Grigio. A couple of marks behind is the Friulano, whose acidity is set off by abundant fruit. Finally the Sauvignon is elegant, intense and very varietal, as it always is here.

O Collio Friulano '07	♟♟	5
O Collio Pinot Bianco '07	♟♟	5
O Collio Pinot Bianco di Santarosa '05	♟♟	5
O Collio Pinot Grigio '07	♟♟	5
● Collio Rosso Conte di Spessa '03	♟♟	6
O Collio Sauvignon Segrè '07	♟♟	6
O Collio Ribolla Gialla '07	♟♟	5
● Collio Merlot Torriani '04	♟	6
● Collio Pinot Nero Casanova '05	♟	6
O Collio Pinot Bianco '06	♟♟♟	5
O Collio Sauvignon Segrè '03	♟♟♟	6
O Collio Sauvignon Segrè '02	♟♟♟	6
O Collio Sauvignon Segrè '06	♟♟	6
O Collio Sauvignon Segrè '05	♟♟	6
O Collio Sauvignon Segrè '04	♟♟	6

O Collio Bianco Andritz '07	♟♟	5
O Collio Pinot Grigio '07	♟♟	4*
O Collio Friulano '07	♟♟	4
O Collio Sauvignon '07	♟♟	4
O Chardonnay Andritz '07	♟	4
● Collio Rosso Andritz '04	♟	5
O Collio Sauvignon '06	♟♟♟	4
O Collio Sauvignon '05	♟♟	4
O Collio Sauvignon '04	♟♟	4
O Collio Bianco Andritz '06	♟♟	5

Subida di Monte

LOC. MONTE, 9
34071 CORMONS [GO]
TEL. 048161011
www.subidadimonte.it

ANNUAL PRODUCTION 60,000 bottles
HECTARES UNDER VINE 10
VITICULTURE METHOD Conventional

Brothers Cristian and Andrea Antonutti are beginning to harvest the first fruits of the radical makeover they have given the vine stock of their ten-hectare property in the heart of the Collio DOC. The stated aim is to make wines in full respect of nature and the territory and every move in vineyard and cellar focuses on that objective. Last year, the reds weren't at their best but this time the entire range put on a splendid performance. The 2006 Merlot is a fine wine with Friuli's trademark Merlot hay and plum aromas, a superbly seamless, warm palate and assertive but elegant extract. The Cabernet Franc is almost as good, revealing the variety's herbaceousness lifted by subtle violets. But Subida di Monte has always been famed for its whites and there are two great wines to carry on that tradition, the 2007 Pinot Grigio and Malavasia. The former gives rich fruit sensations of nectarine, williams pear and citrus with a grace note of tea whereas the Malvasia, a variety that is enjoying a comeback in Friuli, delighted the panel with pervasive, appealing aniseed, confectioner's cream and white chocolate.

● Collio Merlot '06	🍷🍷	4*
O Collio Pinot Grigio '07	🍷🍷	4*
O Collio Malvasia '07	🍷🍷	4*
O Collio Friulano '07	🍷	4
O Collio Sauvignon '07	🍷	4
O Valeas Vincas Bianco '06	🍷	4
● Collio Cabernet Franc '06	🍷	4
O Collio Pinot Grigio '06	YY	4
O Collio Sauvignon '06	YY	4
O Collio Tocai Friulano '06	YY	4
● Collio Rosso Poncaia '03	YY	5
● Collio Rosso Poncaia '00	YY	5

Matijaz Tercic

LOC. BUKUJE, 9
34070 SAN FLORIANO DEL COLLIO [GO]
TEL. 0481884193
tercic@tiscalinet.it

ANNUAL PRODUCTION 30,000 bottles
HECTARES UNDER VINE 11.5
VITICULTURE METHOD Conventional

We were unable to taste the entire range this year. Wines that on other occasions we have very much enjoyed, like the Pinot Grigio or the Vino degli Orti, were not ready when we called but we did enjoy a few other selections that confirmed our previous favourable impressions. Matijaz is getting better every year. This is confirmed by the Pinot Bianco, the most intriguing wine on the list. Like all the other wines, it completes malolactic fermentation and prolonged ageing on the lees. The alcohol is well gauged, as is the tartaric acidity, and the minerally, fruity aromatics reveal fresh-baked bread, white melon and vine blossom, among other perceptions. Planta, from chardonnay with a splash of pinot bianco, is a shade less elegant and harmonious but still very persuasive on the palate for its tropical nuances. The Ribolla has summer flowers, ripe fruit and a tangily fresh body with loads of elegance. Finally, the Merlot, which ages in small wood for 14 months, is fairly pale ruby with blackberry and tar aromas preceding an approachable, fruit-rich palate.

O Pinot Bianco '07	🍷🍷	4*
O Collio Bianco Planta '05	🍷🍷	5
O Collio Ribolla Gialla '07	🍷🍷	4
● Collio Merlot '05	🍷	5
● Collio Merlot Seme '03	YY	5
O Collio Pinot Bianco '06	YY	5
O Vino degli Orti '06	YY	5

Franco Terpin

LOC. VALERISCE, 6A
34070 SAN FLORIANO DEL COLLIO [GO]
TEL. 0481884215
francoterpin@virgilio.it

ANNUAL PRODUCTION	15,000 bottles
HECTARES UNDER VINE	10
VITICULTURE METHOD	Natural

Franco Terpin is one of a kind. He knows his own mind, respects the environment and cossets his vines, shunning weedkillers, insecticides, fertilizers or anti-botrytis products and cover cropping with spontaneous plants. In the cellar, he selects a tiny proportion of fruit from the best vines to prepare the ambient yeasts that are inoculated into the must. The wines then ferment in wood of various sizes. All new plantings or replantings are carried out with native friulano or ribolla gialla vines. The wines are special, too. Not easy to approach, they reluctantly unveil their worth which, in the case of Bianco Quinto Quarto and Pinot Grigio Sialis, is considerable. Bianco Quinto Quarto is a very special table wine from the 2001 harvest of pinot grigio, chardonnay, sauvignon and friulano. This is its first release. We liked the balsam that complements tempting apricot tart and banana. The Pinot Grigio Sialis 2005 has petits fours, peach tea and strawberry jam perceptions preceding a vibrant, dynamic palate. Finally, there is robust extract and warmth on the Rosso Stamas 2004 and the Ribolla Gialla offers mouthfilling creaminess.

○ Bianco Quinto Quarto	♟♟	5
○ Pinot Grigio Sialis '05	♟♟	6
○ Collio Ribolla Gialla '04	♟♟	5
● Collio Rosso Stamas '04	♟♟	5
○ Bianco Sialis '05	♟	6
○ Collio Bianco Stamas '05	♟	5
○ Collio Bianco '02	♟♟	5
○ Collio Bianco '01	♟♟	5
○ Collio Bianco Stamas '04	♟♟	5
○ Collio Bianco Stamas '03	♟♟	5
● Rosso Sialis '03	♟♟	6

Terre di Ger

FRAZ. FRATTINA
S.DA DELLA MEDUNA
33076 PRAVISDOMINI [PN]
TEL. 0434644452
www.terrediger.it

ANNUAL PRODUCTION	120,000 bottles
HECTARES UNDER VINE	48
VITICULTURE METHOD	Conventional

Terre di Ger, founded in 1986 on the Treviso side of the Pordenone flatlands, is no longer a surprise in a zone known years ago only as a source of bulk wine. Ger is an acronym of the names of the three Spinazzès, led by Gianni, and today Pierpaolo Sirch oversees the vineyards near the headquarters at Casa Pralongo and in the municipality of Chions. The production process is tried and tested, from planning the wines to plantings, vineyard management and winemaking, ageing in small wood included. What emerges is a range of premium-quality products in which single-variety wines stand out. Experiments with blends continue apace, which bodes well for the future. The Sauvignon is warm and salt-tinged, giving tomato leaf and peaches, then a fresh, lingering palate with hints of grapefruit, sage and ripe fruit. The Pinot Grigio also impresses with its intense apple and lingering rich fruit on the palate. The Chardonnay is fresh and complex, unveiling grapefruit and citrus that meld with apple, peach and bananas. The complex Cabernet Franc has a varietal note of herbaceousness and the more straightforward Merlot offers cherries and refreshing spiciness.

○ Sauvignon Blanc '07	♟♟	4*
● Friuli Grave Cabernet Franc '06	♟♟	4
○ Friuli Grave Chardonnay '07	♟♟	4
○ Friuli Grave Pinot Grigio '07	♟♟	4
● Friuli Grave Merlot '06	♟	4
○ Sauvignon Blanc '06	♟♟	3
○ Friuli Grave Chardonnay '06	♟♟	3
○ Friuli Grave Pinot Grigio '06	♟♟	3

Toblâr

LOC. RAMANDOLO, 17
33045 NIMIS [UD]
TEL. 0432755840
www.specogna.it

ANNUAL PRODUCTION	150,000 bottles
HECTARES UNDER VINE	N.A.
VITICULTURE METHOD	Conventional

Andrea and Cristian Specogna quite correctly call themselves "vinifiers in Ramandolo". They have chosen this prestigious Friulian DOCG for their small but very modern cellar, where they vinify bought-in grapes. Every year, it is eye-opening to compare the cellar's scores with the ages of its young owners. Knowing how to select the right batches of fruit from growers requires a skill that was once held in the highest esteem by Friulian grape farmers. To see how two youngsters unerringly select the best fruit is quite astonishing. This year, the 2004 Uve Rosse impressed with its intense chocolate and cherry tart bouquet reprised on the palate and lifted by assertive but nicely honed tannins. The almost rosé Pinot Grigio Gris 2007 is delicious and very successful, intriguing wild strawberries coming through in the aromatics. This edition of the Sauvignon is more elegant and velvety. We liked the breadth of its bouquet and its attractive fresh peach finale. And since we are here, there had to be a house Ramandolo. The 2006 edition is true to type on the nose but lacks a little weight on the palate, which held back its score.

★ Franco Toros

LOC. NOVALI, 12
34071 CORMONS [GO]
TEL. 048161327
www.vinitoros.com

ANNUAL PRODUCTION	70,000 bottles
HECTARES UNDER VINE	10
VITICULTURE METHOD	Conventional

We begin with a tribute to a great grape: pinot bianco. Scientists have argued over its rather uncertain origins. It is often confused with chardonnay and it has ceded territory to that variety. The area planted to pinot bianco continues to contract, even in regions like Friuli, arguably its second homeland. This is a shame because the variety can offer elegance, depth, superb structure and velvety warmth, with subtle, satisfyingly broad aromas of white-fleshed fruits, citrus, vanillaed almonds, hay and spring flowers. Obviously, it takes the right winemaker but when pinot bianco finds one, it proffers endless thrills. Try Franco Toros' version. His 2007 Pinot Bianco earned Three splendid Glasses. But our hero can handle other varieties. Franco's equally legendary Friulano opens slowly but then rolls out all its lingering persistence in the mouth. His Pinot Grigio is another winner, marrying new-cut grass and minerality with a rich-textured, balanced palate. We also loved Franco's Merlot, reminiscent of his wonderful 1997, albeit in a minor key, and the Sauvignon. Rounding off is the Chardonnay, which struggles a little to keep up with the others.

● Uve Rosse '04	♟♟	5
○ Pinot Grigio Gris '07	♟♟	4*
○ Sauvignon '07	♟♟	4*
○ Ramandolo '06	♟	4
○ Ribolla Gialla Vino Spumante	♟	4
○ Sauvignonas '05	♟♟	4
○ Sauvignonas '06	♟♟	4
○ Gris '06	♟♟	4
○ Ramandolo '04	♟♟	4

○ Collio Pinot Bianco '07	♟♟♟	5
● Collio Merlot '05	♟♟	5
○ Collio Pinot Grigio '07	♟♟	5
○ Collio Friulano '07	♟♟	5
○ Collio Sauvignon '07	♟♟	5
○ Collio Chardonnay '07	♟	5
● Collio Merlot Sel. '97	♟♟♟	6
○ Collio Pinot Bianco '05	♟♟♟	5
○ Collio Pinot Bianco '03	♟♟♟	5
○ Collio Pinot Bianco '01	♟♟♟	5
○ Collio Pinot Bianco '00	♟♟♟	5
○ Collio Tocai Friulano '06	♟♟♟	5
○ Collio Tocai Friulano '04	♟♟♟	5
○ Collio Tocai Friulano '03	♟♟♟	5
○ Collio Tocai Friulano '02	♟♟♟	5

La Tunella

FRAZ. IPPLIS
VIA DEL COLLIO, 14
33040 PREMARIACCO [UD]
TEL. 0432716030
www.latunella.it

ANNUAL PRODUCTION	450,000 bottles
HECTARES UNDER VINE	80
VITICULTURE METHOD	Conventional

We know how hard it is to win Three Glasses, and how much effort is required to repeat the feat, particularly when the winery is relatively new. Kudos, then, to brothers Massimo and Marco Zorzettig, co-owners with their mother Gabriella of La Tunella. It's a fair-sized property – 80 hectares or so – and production is growing in quantity and in quality. But credit must also go to long-serving wine technician Luigino Zamparo in the cellar while Marco looks after the vineyards and Massimo travels to promote the wines on international markets. The new cellar, at last able to accommodate all stages of production, has several spectacular features, such as the large room that houses the few small, and many large, barrels. BiancoSesto confirmed its status as one of Italy's finest whites. This blend of friulano and ribolla gialla ferments in large Slavonian oak before maturing in steel tanks that bring out the aromatics to the full. Fresh-tasting, elegant and lavishly fruity, it has come on apace since our first tastings and we think it will improve even further. Noans, a dried-grape sweet wine from riesling, traminer and sauvignon, is very intriguing.

Valchiarò

FRAZ. TOGLIANO
VIA DEI LAGHI, 4c
33040 TORREANO [UD]
TEL. 0432715502
www.valchiaro.it

ANNUAL PRODUCTION	40,000 bottles
HECTARES UNDER VINE	15
VITICULTURE METHOD	Conventional

The team of five friends who almost 20 years ago got together to make premium wine has seen some changes but the enthusiasm is still there, and is shared by consultant oenologist Gianni Menotti, now a fixture in the Valchiarò line-up. A couple of years ago, the winery left its original Laurini home and moved into new premises on Via dei Laghi, where it vinifies grapes grown in the cool neighbouring valleys by each of the owners. This year, we were again so impressed by the Verduzzo that we sent it through to the Three Glass finals. Figs, bananas and currants emerge on the nose to return on the palate with tropical fruits, apricots and hazelnuts. The almond-themed Friulano is minerally, broad and intense, the fresh, flowery Pinot Grigio gives distinct apple and the Sauvignon's subtle minerality goes through the tangy palate to an appealing golden delicious apple finale. Blackberry tart is echoed on the palate of the well-structured Merlot with its rich cherry-like flavours. Finally, the peppery spice of the Refosco flanks ripe, upfront tannins and soft lingering cherries and plums.

○ COF BiancoSesto '07	♙♙♙	5
○ COF Chardonnay '07	♙♙	4*
○ COF Pinot Grigio '07	♙♙	4*
● COF Rosso L'Arcione '04	♙♙	6
● COF Schioppettino Selènze '05	♙♙	5
○ Noans '06	♙♙	6
○ COF Friulano Selènze '07	♙♙	4*
● COF Refosco P. R. Selènze '06	♙	4
○ COF Sauvignon '07	♙	4
○ COF BiancoSesto '06	♡♡♡	4
○ COF Bianco Campo Marzio '05	♡♡	5
○ COF Picolit '05	♡♡	7

○ COF Verduzzo Friulano '06	♙♙	4*
● COF Refosco P. R. '04	♙♙	4
○ COF Tocai Friulano '07	♙♙	4
● COF Merlot Ris. '04	♙	4
○ COF Pinot Grigio '07	♙	4
○ COF Sauvignon '07	♙	4
○ COF Tocai Friulano Nexus '07	♙	4
○ COF Verduzzo Friulano '05	♡♡	4
○ COF Verduzzo Friulano '04	♡♡	4
○ COF Tocai Friulano Nexus '06	♡♡	4

Valpanera

VIA TRIESTE, 5A
33059 VILLA VICENTINA [UD]
TEL. 0431970395
www.valpanera.it

ANNUAL PRODUCTION	300,000 bottles
HECTARES UNDER VINE	50
VITICULTURE METHOD	Conventional

Valpanera is a modern winery on the flatlands south of Udine. The vines stand on clay and sand soil, a stone's throw from the Adriatic, and are Guyot-pruned. Vineyard management and winemaking are carried out in-house and the functional new cellar stands right in the middle of the property. All this careful organization has but one aim: to get the very best out of refosco, an ancient native Friulian grape. Owner Giampiero Del Vecchio and oenologist Luca Marcolini can look back on this year with satisfaction. The 2005 edition of their flag-carrier sits atop the winery's table next to the very fine Chardonnay Carato 2006, which gives stylish confectioner's cream and tobacco laced with yellow-fleshed fruits leading to a mineral finish. We thought the estate's top wine was Refosco Superiore 2005, which spends several months in small wood. Utterly varietal, it has generous hay, sweet spice, red berry fruit and coffee. What we liked about the excellent Chardonnay was its intense apricot and melon bouquet and the minerally finish to the palate.

★ Venica & Venica

LOC. CERÒ, 8
34070 DOLEGNA DEL COLLIO [GO]
TEL. 048161264
www.venica.it

ANNUAL PRODUCTION	260,000 bottles
HECTARES UNDER VINE	34
VITICULTURE METHOD	Conventional

Gianni and Giorgio Venica have expanded the estate founded in 1921 by their grandfather Daniele to 29 hectares, plus five leased. A few years ago, the cellar's working area was increased and much stainless steel technology brought in. The Venicas think Friulian wines are already solidly structured so oak might compromise the depth and fragrance of the aromas. The vine stock, supervised by Marco Simonit and Pierpaolo Sirch, yields superb fruit. In the cellar, Gianni's son Gianpaolo vies with his father and uncle in red winemaking in particular. Ornella Venica, a natural communicator and former president of the Consorzio Collio, organizes promotional activities. Each year, the cellar releases more than 260,000 bottles and this time, Sauvignon Ronco delle Mele is back on form. Varietal, and less aggressive than in the past, it gives signature yellow peach with citrus, freshness, minerality, a rich mouthfeel and plenty of length. Tre Vignis, from tocai, sauvignon and chardonnay, is stylish and generously fruity, as is the attractive Pinot Bianco. Finally, freshness and rich texture are the keynotes of the Friulano Ronco delle Cime.

○ Friuli Aquileia Chardonnay Carato '06	♥♥ 4
● Friuli Aquileia Refosco P. R. Sup. '05	♥♥ 4
● Friuli Aquileia Cabernet Sauvignon '07	♥ 3
○ Friuli Aquileia Chardonnay '07	♥ 4
● Friuli Aquileia Refosco P. R. '06	♥ 3
○ Friuli Aquileia Sauvignon '07	♥ 4
○ Friuli Aquileia Verduzzo Friulano '07	♥ 4
● Rosso di Valpanera '06	♥ 3
○ Bianco di Valpanera '07	3
● Friuli Aquileia Refosco P. R. Ris. '03	♥♥ 5
● Friuli Aquileia Rosso Alma '03	♥♥ 5

○ Collio Sauvignon Ronco delle Mele '07	♥♥♥ 6
○ Collio Bianco Tre Vignis '07	♥♥ 6
○ Collio Friulano Ronco delle Cime '07	♥♥ 5
○ Collio Pinot Bianco '07	♥♥ 5
○ Collio Chardonnay Ronco Bernizza '07	♥♥ 5
○ Collio Malvasia '07	♥♥ 5
○ Collio Pinot Grigio Jesera '07	♥♥ 5
○ Collio Ribolla Gialla L'Adelchi '07	♥♥ 5
○ Collio Sauvignon Ronco del Cerò '07	♥♥ 5
○ Collio Sauvignon Ronco delle Mele '05	♥♥♥ 6
○ Collio Tocai Friulano Ronco delle Cime '06	♥♥♥ 5
○ Collio Tocai Friulano Ronco delle Cime '02	♥♥♥ 6
○ Collio Tocai Friulano Ronco delle Cime '00	♥♥♥ 5

La Viarte

VIA NOVACUZZO, 51
33040 PREPOTTO [UD]
TEL. 0432759458
www.laviarte.it

ANNUAL PRODUCTION	100,000 bottles
HECTARES UNDER VINE	25
VITICULTURE METHOD	Conventional

A glance at the table below will tell you that Giulio Ceschin's estate is in fine fettle and shaping up for even greater things. The winery is in a lovely hilltop location, surrounded by terraced vineyards that enchant the eye and extend over more than 25 hectares. If you decide to call in on La Viarte, you'll find the Ceschins ready to welcome you and give you a taste of the Colli Orientali del Friuli. A passion for native varieties and the conviction that some of them could vie with the world's best led Giulio to chair the association of producers committed to promoting Schioppettino di Prepotto. From the 2008 vintage, wines from this variety made in compliance with the special production protocol can bear the designation of the officially recognized subzone, Schioppettino di Prepotto. Siùm 2005, a great sweet wine blended from verduzzo friulano and picolit, came within an ace of a third Glass for its aromas of fruit in syrup, dates, dried figs and marmalade, all of which are mirrored on the palate.

Alessandro Vicentini Orgnani

FRAZ. VALERIANO
VIA SOTTOPLOVIA, 4A
33094 PINZANO AL TAGLIAMENTO [PN]
TEL. 0432950107
www.vicentiniorgnani.com

ANNUAL PRODUCTION	80,000 bottles
HECTARES UNDER VINE	18
VITICULTURE METHOD	Conventional

In last year's profile for Alessandro Vicentini Orgnani's winery, we wrote: "We are hoping for even more, particularly from the reds for which in our opinion the territory is especially well suited". Well, Alessandro came up with an immediate response in his marvellous Merlot 2006, reminiscent of the equally great 2003 version, as well as a 2007 Cabernet Franc that is not bad at all. But the vineyards, all on hillsides well protected by the mountains from northerly winds and with vines now at the height of maturity, had been hinting at results like these. The Merlot is youthfully alcoholic yet complex with perceptions of quinine, milk chocolate and ripe berry fruit, picked up on a palate whose robust tannins meld nicely with fruit softness. The Cabernet Franc has the variety's characteristic herbaceousness offset by cream and coffee sensations on nose and palate. A modest growing year for whites in Friuli had an impact on the range, although all are very well made and typed.

○ Siùm '05	♀♀	6
○ COF Friulano '07	♀♀	4
○ COF Pinot Grigio '07	♀♀	4
● COF Refosco P. R. '05	♀♀	5
● COF Tazzelenghe '04	♀♀	6
○ COF Bianco Liende '06	♀	5
● COF Merlot '05	♀	5
○ COF Pinot Bianco '07	♀	4
● COF Schioppettino '05	♀	5
○ COF Ribolla Gialla '07		4
○ Siùm '04	♀♀	6
○ Siùm '03	♀♀	6
● COF Schioppettino '04	♀♀	5

● Merlot '06	♀♀	4*
● Cabernet Franc '07	♀	3
● Cabernet Sauvignon '06	♀	3
○ Friuli Grave Tocai Friulano '07		3
○ Pinot Grigio '07		3
○ Sauvignon '07		3
● Friuli Grave Merlot '03	♀♀	4
○ Ucelut '03	♀♀	7
○ Ucelut '01	♀♀	7
○ Friuli Grave Tocai Friulano '06	♀	3
○ Friuli Grave Tocai Friulano '05	♀	3

Gestioni Agricole Vidussi

VIA SPESSA, 18
34071 CAPRIVA DEL FRIULI [GO]
TEL. 048180072
www.vinimontresor.it

ANNUAL PRODUCTION	400,000 bottles
HECTARES UNDER VINE	32
VITICULTURE METHOD	Conventional

The Vidussi estate was leased by the Verona-based Montresor family in 2000. There are about 25 hectares under vine around the winery itself plus seven at Rocca Bernarda in Colli Orientali del Friuli. Both zones are superb for growing grapes thanks to prevalently Eocene marl-based soils, sometimes mixed with sandstone, and their east and south-facing plots. This year, wine technician Luigino De Giuseppe had to deal with a far from easy growing year and it shows in the marks we gave. The range is good but in the past we have generally awarded several second Glasses whereas this time, only the Malvasia made the grade. It's a very varietal wine with a lavender and dried flowers nose introducing a refreshing mineral and salt palate. Bianco Ronchi di Ravez has a complex nose of baked apples and sweet florality, nicely reprised on the palate, but lacks sufficient weight in the mouth for a higher mark. But the Pinot Bianco was well received by our panel. After all, Capriva is where it grows best in Friuli. Finally, the Pinot Grigio also earned One very full Glass.

★ Vie di Romans

LOC. VIE DI ROMANS, 1
34070 MARIANO DEL FRIULI [GO]
TEL. 048169600
www.viediromans.it

ANNUAL PRODUCTION	230,000 bottles
HECTARES UNDER VINE	44
VITICULTURE METHOD	Conventional

Terroir is a French term that refers to the complex interaction of soil and climate that makes a location oenologically unique. But terroir alone is not enough. Winemakers also have to interpret its many manifestations and from that point of view, Gianfranco Gallo is second to none. His readings are very personal, and on occasion controversial, but great maestros have always had to face critics. The fundamental thing is intellectual honesty. That is the only way you are ever going to get four wines into the final taste-offs. Top of the range is a fantastic Malvasia with tropical fruits, pears, rennet apples and wisteria blossom following through on the vibrant softness of a long-lingering, velvet-smooth palate. Chardonnay Vie di Romans is one of Friuli's finest and the Sauvignon Piere is once again subtle and stylish, with a hint of toastiness on the back palate. We also enjoyed Dolee, a warm, powerful and almost austere wine from tocai grapes with elegantly tidy sensations of sage and mulberries. Our only regret is that the rosé we were looking forward to wasn't offered.

O Collio Malvasia '07	♟♟ 4*
O Collio Bianco Ronchi di Ravéz '07	♟ 5
O Collio Chardonnay '07	♟ 4
O Collio Friulano '07	♟ 4
O Collio Pinot Bianco '07	♟ 4
O Collio Pinot Grigio '07	♟ 4
O Collio Traminer Aromatico '07	♟ 4
O Collio Ribolla Gialla '07	4
● Collio Rosso Podere di Spessa Are di Miute '06	5
● Schioppettino Ribolla Nera '07	4
O Collio Pinot Bianco '06	♟♟ 4
O Collio Malvasia '06	♟♟ 4
O Collio Sauvignon '06	♟♟ 4

O Friuli Isonzo Malvasia Istriana Dis Cumieris '06	♟♟♟ 5
O Friuli Isonzo Bianco Dolée '06	♟♟ 6
O Friuli Isonzo Chardonnay Vie di Romans '06	♟♟ 6
O Friuli Isonzo Sauvignon Piere '06	♟♟ 5
O Dut'Un '05	♟♟ 7
O Friuli Isonzo Bianco Flors di Uis '06	♟♟ 5
O Friuli Isonzo Chardonnay Ciampagnis Vieris '06	♟♟ 5
O Friuli Isonzo Sauvignon Vieris '06	♟♟ 6
O Friuli Isonzo Pinot Grigio Dessimis '06	♟ 5
⊙ Friuli Isonzo Ciantons Rosé '06	6
O Dut'Un '02	♟♟♟ 7
O Friuli Isonzo Sauvignon Piere '01	♟♟♟ 5
O Friuli Isonzo Sauvignon Vieris '04	♟♟♟ 6
O Friuli Isonzo Sauvignon Vieris '02	♟♟♟ 6

Vigna del Lauro

LOC. MONTE, 38
34071 CORMONS [GO]
TEL. 048160155
www.roncodeitassi.it

ANNUAL PRODUCTION	42,000 bottles
HECTARES UNDER VINE	6
VITICULTURE METHOD	Conventional

Fabio Coser and Eberhard Spangenberg continue to make a success of this operation by concentrating on precisely typed easy drinkers sold at value for money prices. The estate's vine stock has recently been increased by the addition of two hectares in the Isonzo DOC zone while Fabio supervises, with his customary professional skill, the properties of several growers who supply him with grapes. Given the characteristics of the range, the wines find a flourishing market in Italy but are also much sought-after abroad, where much of the annual production is directed. But then who could resist a wine like the 2007 Sauvignon? Complex nectarine, elderflower and apricot usher in a rounded, seamlessly well-sustained palate that echoes the nose delightfully. The Pinot Grigio is very much in the classic mould with its fresh apple and gunflint aromas. Despite a less than favourable vintage, the Friulano is excellent, giving lovely sun-ripe citrus that meld attractively with varietal almonds. The rest of the range includes a Ribolla Gialla that hints at herbs and spring flowers, a wisteria-themed Chardonnay and a fresh, youthfully alcoholic Cabernet Franc.

Vigna Petrussa

VIA ALBANA, 47
33040 PREPOTTO [UD]
TEL. 0432713021
www.vignapetrussa.it

ANNUAL PRODUCTION	30,000 bottles
HECTARES UNDER VINE	6.5
VITICULTURE METHOD	Conventional

Hilde Petrussa resigned as chair of the winemakers' committee in this town on the border with Slovenia when the Prepotto subzone for Schioppettino was officially recognized. Hilde returned to her native town with her husband Renato Mecchia, since when she has been putting all her energies into the winery. Her daughter Francesca is an architect who lives in London and it was she who designed the lovely cellar and its attractive hospitality and tasting room. Schioppettino made Hilde's way, in compliance with the new protocol, means two years in wood and at least six months in glass. Intense black cherry syrup and raspberry are echoed on the well-structured palate, which is rich-textured and long-lingering. Hilde's Picolit offers fruit and dried flowers before volatile acidity offsets the intense sweetness and the finish reveals persistent caramel. Cleanness is the keynote of the Sauvignon. But the Richenza blended white, from case-dried, barrique-fermented riesling, malvasia, verduzzo, tocai and picolit, has too much residual sugar.

O Collio Sauvignon '07	♟♟	4*
O Collio Friulano '07	♟♟	4
O Collio Pinot Grigio '07	♟♟	4
O Collio Ribolla Gialla '07	♟	4
● Friuli Isonzo Cabernet Franc '07	♟	4
O Friuli Isonzo Chardonnay '07	♟	4
● Friuli Isonzo Merlot '06		4
O Collio Sauvignon '99	♟♟♟	4
O Collio Ribolla Gialla '06	♟♟	4
O Collio Sauvignon '06	♟♟	4

● COF Schioppettino '05	♟♟	5
O COF Picolit '05	♟♟	6
O COF Sauvignon '07	♟	4
O COF Friulano '07		4
O Richenza '06		5
● COF Schioppettino '05	♟♟	5
O COF Picolit '04	♟♟	6
O COF Tocai Friulano '06	♟♟	4
O Richenza '05	♟♟	5

Vigna Traverso

via Ronchi, 73
33040 Prepotto [UD]
tel. 0422804807
www.vignatraverso.it

ANNUAL PRODUCTION 60,000 bottles
HECTARES UNDER VINE 45
VITICULTURE METHOD Conventional

It's been a busy year for Stefano Traverso, the Veneto-born wine man who runs this promising estate for the Traverso Molon winery. The old cellar has been completely demolished and most of the new facilities will be built into the hillside, creating conditions of constant temperature and humidity. The estate can call on Alessio Dorigo's consultancy, which is evident in the increasing overall elegance of the wines. In the early years, they were sometimes robust to the point of excess. Molon's winemaker Simone Casazza takes all the final decisions. Prepotto's signature red, Schioppettino, gives sour cherries in syrup and raspberries preceding hints of liquorice on a heftily structured palate whose extract is just a shade to boisterous. Merlot Sottocastello is still very much in the cellar's chewy, pulpy original style. We liked the citrus-rich fragrances of the Friulano, as well as the tight-knit, rich-textured savouriness of its very long palate. Finally, the Chardonnay has a mix of varietal pear drops and green apples.

○ COF Chardonnay '07	🍷🍷	4*
○ COF Friulano '07	🍷🍷	4*
● COF Merlot Sottocastello '05	🍷🍷	6
● COF Schioppettino '06	🍷🍷	5
● COF Cabernet Franc '06	🍷	4
● COF Refosco P. R. '06	🍷	4
○ COF Ribolla Gialla '07	🍷	4
○ COF Sauvignon '07	🍷	4
● COF Rosso Troj '06	🍷	4
○ COF Pinot Grigio '07		4
● COF Cabernet Franc '05	YY	4
● COF Rosso Sottocastello '04	YY	6
● COF Rosso Sottocastello '01	YY	6
● COF Merlot Sottocastello '04	YY	6
● COF Rosso Schioppettino '05	YY	5

Vignai da Duline

loc. Villanova del Judrio
via IV Novembre, 136
33048 San Giovanni al Natisone [UD]
tel. 0432758115
www.vignaidaduline.com

ANNUAL PRODUCTION 18,000 bottles
HECTARES UNDER VINE 7.5
VITICULTURE METHOD Certified organic

La Duline is where the oldest vines of this San Giovanni al Natisone estate grow on two hectares of land. It was from here that Federica Magrini and Lorenzo Mocchiutto started out on their winemaking career in 1997. At the heart of their efforts is a very practical respect for the environment, care at every step of production and the quest for territory-driven excellence. As a result, the wines are distinctively personal, which is probably what Lorenzo and Federica were looking for in the first place. On occasion, wines like this can stir up discussion but this year, there is no doubt. All the wines are great and the Refosco picked up Three Glasses for the second time in a row. A velvety bouquet blends balsam with warmer sensations of blackberry tart and milk chocolate, leaving an impression of finesse. Nicely tucked in tannins then meld attractively with the palate's fruit. We also loved the banana and petits fours of the Chardonnay, the fresh wisteria blossom and savoury finish of the malvasia and sauvignon Bianco Morus Alba and the distinct quinine and chocolate of the Rosso Viburnum, a blend of cabernet franc, carmenère and merlot.

● Refosco P. R. Morus Nigra '06	🍷🍷🍷	6
○ COF Bianco Morus Alba '06	🍷🍷	6
○ COF Chardonnay Ronco Pitotti '06	🍷🍷	5
● COF Rosso Viburnum '06	🍷🍷	5
○ COF Pinot Grigio Ronco Pitotti '07	🍷	5
○ Friuli Grave Friulano '07	🍷	5
● Refosco P. R. Morus Nigra '05	YYY	6
● Refosco P. R. Morus Nigra '04	YY	6
○ COF Pinot Grigio '06	YY	4
○ COF Chardonnay '05	YY	5
● COF Rosso Viburnum '05	YY	5
● COF Rosso Viburnum '04	YY	5

★ Le Vigne di Zamò

LOC. ROSAZZO
VIA ABATE CORRADO, 4
33044 MANZANO [UD]
TEL. 0432759693
www.levignedizamo.com

ANNUAL PRODUCTION 250,000 bottles
HECTARES UNDER VINE 67
VITICULTURE METHOD Conventional

We never doubted that Zamò would soon be back at the top when we tasted the 2006 edition of Tocai Friulano Vigne Cinquant'Anni last spring. Sure enough, it won Three Glasses. The nose's complex ripe fruit is mirrored on the warm palate with rich texture and a mixed fruits finale. This great wine comes from a cellar that this year celebrates 30 years of activity since Tullio Zamò set up Vigne dal Leòn. Now his sons Pierluigi and Silvano carry the torch. They have expanded the vine stock on the slopes of Rosazzo, recently purchasing the six hectares of Querciabella, and leasing flatlands vineyards to enhance the aromatics of Bianco Zamò, a peach, apricot and apple wine with freshness, breadth and attractive fragrances. It's only the cellar's base white but the Zamò brothers insist on premium quality. This year, the elegant pinot bianco, sauvignon and riesling Ronco di Corte is back and evolving well. Also promising are the Bordeaux blend Ronco dei Roseti 2003 and Ronco delle Acacie 2006, a white from chardonnay, tocai, pinot bianco and picolit. Note that the Zamòs do not release their top reds in less favourable vintages, like 2002 and 2005.

Vigne Fantin Noda'r

LOC. ORSARIA
VIA CASALI OTTELIO, 4
33170 PREMARIACCO [UD]
TEL. 043428735
www.fantinnodar.it

ANNUAL PRODUCTION 60,000 bottles
HECTARES UNDER VINE 22
VITICULTURE METHOD Conventional

The vineyards Attilio Pignat purchased in 1991 and partially replanted two years later contain four red grape varieties and eight white. In these hills stretching from Buttrio to Premariacco and Manzano you can find some of the finest wine country around here. Stefano Bortolussi is the estate manager at Fantin Noda'r – the name means "Notary Fantino" – while cellar operations are directed by oenologist Francesco Spitaleri, who knows these varieties well. This year, we observed a slight wobble in the quality of the range, with the exception of an excellent Picolit Auràtus. This amber-coloured, very sweet wine is reminiscent of dried figs, raisins, almonds, confectioner's cream and honey. The Friulano is true to its variety – sauvignonasse – giving peaches and tomato leaf, as well as its trademark almondiness, all hinting at its relative, sauvignon. Carato Bianco is an 85-15 mix of riesling and sauvignon. It ages in oak, which has left the nose with traces of coffee, and the palate is nicely orchestrated, apart from a touch too much alcohol on the finish.

○ COF Tocai Friulano V. Cinquant'Anni '06	♟♟♟	6
● COF Rosazzo Rosso Ronco dei Roseti '03	♟♟	6
○ COF Bianco Zamò '07	♟♟	4
○ COF Rosazzo Bianco Ronco delle Acacie '06	♟♟	6
○ Ronco di Corte '07	♟♟	5
○ COF Pinot Grigio '07	♟	5
○ COF Sauvignon '07	♟	5
○ COF Pinot Bianco Tullio Zamò '06		5
● COF Schioppettino '04		6
● COF Rosazzo Pignolo '01	♟♟♟	8
○ COF Tocai Friulano V. Cinquant'Anni '99	♟♟♟	5
○ COF Tocai Friulano V. Cinquant'Anni '00	♟♟♟	5

○ COF Picolit Auràtus '06	♟♟	5
○ COF Bianco Carato '06	♟	5
○ COF Friulano '07	♟	4
○ COF Pinot Grigio '07	♟	4
○ COF Ribolla Gialla '07	♟	4
○ COF Sauvignon '07	♟	4*
○ COF Verduzzo '06	♟	4
○ COF Chardonnay '07		4
● COF Refosco P. R. Auràtus '06		4
○ COF Sauvignon '06	♟♟	4
○ COF Tocai Friulano '06	♟♟	4

Villa De Puppi

VIA ROMA, 5
33040 MOIMACCO [UD]
TEL. 0432722461
www.depuppi.it

ANNUAL PRODUCTION	50,000 bottles
HECTARES UNDER VINE	30
VITICULTURE METHOD	Conventional

For over two centuries, Luigi De Puppi's family has owned this 30-hectare estate, but until 2004, the farm was followed with only half an eye. At that point, Luigi's son Valfredo, about to graduate from the Bocconi university, volunteered to look after things as his father's business commitments kept taking him away from Friuli. A couple of years later, Valfredo's sister Caterina eased up on her studies to devote more time to the estate, instead of just helping out at harvest time. The vine stock is managed with help from the Preparatori d'Uva (Fruitmakers) group while Marco Pecchiari, who also works with Terra&Vino, oversees the cellar. Our early tastings this year at Vinitaly had us looking forward to these wines and we weren't disappointed. Refosco Cate, obtained after two bunch selections, first in the field and then in the cellar, is oak fermented and shows complex and spicy with an intense bouquet. The tannins are reined in and the finish reprises the spices and berry fruit of the nose. Taj Blanc is a tocai friulano-only wine with a wealth of fruit aromas, including candied orange peel. Finally, the smoky Sauvignon leads with minerality.

Villa Frattina

FRAZ. GHIRANO
VIA PALAZZETTO, 68
33080 PRATA DI PORDENONE [PN]
TEL. 0434605911
www.villafrattina.it

ANNUAL PRODUCTION	450,000 bottles
HECTARES UNDER VINE	50
VITICULTURE METHOD	Conventional

The Averna beverages group seems to be in the process of selling off this lovely estate of 50 hectares. It sprawls over the provinces of Pordenone, where the cellars are located, Treviso and Venice. Still, quality hasn't been affected. In fact, it's getting better, as if it wanted to prove how much potential this territory has. Obviously, consultancy from the great oenologist, Donato Lanati, has underpinned the cellar's reliability. This time, the best wine is the confectioner's cream and fruit Pinot Grigio with its complex palate and long, broad finish. The nice follow-through of this wine is a characteristic of the entire Frattina range, as it is now called, the previous Villa Frattina label now being restricted to the Brut. Another fine wine is the Sauvignon. Its assertive, yet elegant, aromas range from tomato leaf to peach with marked minerality and outstanding persistence. We gave One full Glass to the concentrated but only moderately long Lison, the name now given to Tocai Friulano in this DOC zone, and a Glass to the Cabernet Sauvignon, which is better on the palate than the nose.

● Refosco P. R. Cate '06	♟♟	6
○ Taj Blanc '07	♟♟	3*
○ Sauvignon '07	♟♟	3*
○ Chardonnay '07	♟	3
○ Chardonnay Cate '06	♟	6
○ Pinot Grigio '07	♟	3
● Merlot '06	♟	3
● Refosco P. R. '06	♟	4
● Cabernet '06		3
○ Chardonnay '06	♟♟	3
○ Sauvignon '06	♟♟	3
○ Taj Blanc '06	♟♟	3

○ Lison-Pramaggiore Pinot Grigio '07	♟♟	4
○ Lison-Pramaggiore Sauvignon '07	♟♟	4
● Lison-Pramaggiore Cabernet Sauvignon '07	♟	4
○ Lison-Pramaggiore Lison '07	♟	4
○ Bianco di Gale '07		5
○ Lison-Pramaggiore Pinot Grigio '05	♟♟	4
○ Lison-Pramaggiore Tocai Italico '06	♟♟	3

Villa Martina

FRAZ. BRAZZANO
LOC. CÀ DELLE VALLADE, 3B
34071 CORMONS [GO]
TEL. 048160733
www.villamartina.it

ANNUAL PRODUCTION	90,000 bottles
HECTARES UNDER VINE	10
VITICULTURE METHOD	Conventional

This Collio winery is proof that youthful enthusiasm coupled with a sense of adventure can produce very fine results. Mario Sfiligoi's three daughters – Michela, Patrizia and Martina – have taken over this long-established cellar, each with her own specific tasks. During the 1980s, the operation had slid back a tad but the three women have boosted its fortunes in double quick time. Last year's low-key Guide profile is followed this year by a second excellent performance in a challenging growing year. We tasted four wines, all outstanding. The 2006 Merlot is remarkably good. Matured only in steel, it is gives blackberries and plum tart with hints of balsam, and the thrust on the palate is seamless, echoing the nose and leading to a pervasive finale. We would also point out the Sauvignon's pungent varietal rue and tomato leaf and the satisfying solidity of the Friulano, which flaunts the grape's signature almonds and pennyroyal. Also true to type is the Pinot Grigio, which unveils minerality, williams pears, almonds and apples before concluding with a lingering finish.

● Collio Merlot '06	🍷🍷	4*
○ Collio Friulano '07	🍷🍷	4
○ Collio Pinot Grigio '07	🍷🍷	4
○ Friuli Isonzo Sauvignon '07	🍷🍷	4
● Cabernet Franc '05	🍷🍷	4
○ Collio Pinot Grigio '06	🍷🍷	4
○ Collio Tocai Friulano '06	🍷🍷	4
● Friuli Isonzo Refosco P. R. '06	🍷🍷	4

★★ Villa Russiz

VIA RUSSIZ, 6
34070 CAPRIVA DEL FRIULI [GO]
TEL. 048180047
www.villarussiz.it

ANNUAL PRODUCTION	220,000 bottles
HECTARES UNDER VINE	35
VITICULTURE METHOD	Conventional

It's hard to sum up this winery, which we like for all sorts of reasons. First of all, it is publicly owned by a charity, the Istituto Adele Cerruti, chaired by accountant Silvano Stefanutti, who is as passionate about the enterprise as estate manager Gianni Menotti. One of the great names in Friulian wine, Gianni is totally committed to Villa Russiz and thanks to him the cellar has had many significant successes over past years. We have admired Gianni since he joined the winery as a new graduate in 1988 and quickly turned round production. This time, five wines were competing for our top prize, which went to the Pinot Bianco. Intense yet broad and elegant on the nose, it reprises the aromas on the fruity, seamless palate and long finish. Merlot Graf de La Tour, named after Count Théodore de La Tour en Voivre, deceased husband of the Austrian owner Elvine von Ritter Zahony, offers complex, tar-veined aromatics that usher in warm red fruits and supple tannins. Violets, lavender and liquorice are the Malvasia's keynotes while the Sauvignon de La Tour has classic varietal fragrances. The Pinot Grigio is rich-textured, minerally and long.

○ Collio Pinot Bianco '07	🍷🍷🍷	5
○ Collio Malvasia '07	🍷🍷	5
○ Collio Pinot Grigio '07	🍷🍷	5
○ Collio Sauvignon de La Tour '07	🍷🍷	6
● Collio Merlot Graf de La Tour '05	🍷🍷	7
○ Collio Chardonnay Gräfin de La Tour '06	🍷🍷	7
○ Collio Friulano '07	🍷🍷	5
○ Collio Sauvignon '07	🍷🍷	5
○ Collio Ribolla Gialla '07	🍷	5
○ Collio Riesling '07	🍷	5
● Collio Cabernet Sauvignon '06	🍷	5
● Collio Merlot '06	🍷	5
● Collio Merlot Graf de La Tour '99	🍷🍷🍷	7
● Collio Merlot Graf de La Tour '02	🍷🍷🍷	7
○ Collio Sauvignon de La Tour '05	🍷🍷🍷	6
○ Collio Tocai Friulano '04	🍷🍷🍷	5

Tenuta Villanova

LOC. VILLANOVA
VIA CONTESSA BERETTA, 29
34072 FARRA D'ISONZO [GO]
TEL. 0481889311
www.tenutavillanova.com

ANNUAL PRODUCTION	500,000 bottles
HECTARES UNDER VINE	130
VITICULTURE METHOD	Conventional

The 2007 growing year was not easy. The mild winter and warm spring brought on early flowering and were followed by a warm and then rainy summer, which forced estates to harvest early in fits and starts. Despite all this, our tastings at Tenuta Villanova confirmed the excellent impressions we have had from this cellar in recent times. The estate has about 105 hectares in the Isonzo DOC zone, which provide fruit for the Masi di Villanova line, and about 20 in the Collio, selected grapes from which make the Ronco Cucco selections. We liked two of the Isonzo bottles and three from the Collio. The Masi di Villanovas that caught our eye were the Chardonnay, which lacks a little breadth but is well balanced, and the Malvasia, which impressed with its delicately lingering apples, pears and yeast. From the Ronco Cucco selections we enjoyed the Sauvignon's distinct bell pepper and elderflowers, the Friulano's acacia blossom and apple leading into a soft, attractive palate and the aristocratically elegant Picolit. Finally, the Villanova Brut is also worth uncorking.

O Friuli Isonzo Malvasia Saccoline '07	🍷🍷	4
O Collio Friulano Ronco Cucco '07	🍷🍷	5
O Collio Picolit Ronco Cucco '06	🍷🍷	6
O Collio Sauvignon Ronco Cucco '07	🍷🍷	5
O Friuli Isonzo Chardonnay '07	🍷🍷	4
O Collio Friulano '07	🍷	4
O Collio Pinot Grigio '07	🍷	4
O Collio Ribolla Gialla '07	🍷	4
O Villanova Brut	🍷	5

Vinài dell'Abbàte

LOC. ROSAZZO
P. ZZA ABBAZIA, 15
33044 MANZANO [UD]
TEL. 0432759429
www.tenutealeandri.it

ANNUAL PRODUCTION	120,000 bottles
HECTARES UNDER VINE	12
VITICULTURE METHOD	Conventional

This long-established winery, managed by the Aleandri group, is going through a transitional phase. The estate is owned by the diocese of Udine and boasts a jewel of a cellar, build by monks in the 13th century to store wine and olive oil. The first documented evidence of wine here dates from 1341, when the area was part of the patriarchate. The Aleandri group has renovated all the facilities and from this year is working without its leading outside consultants. The Sauvignon reveals elegant tomato leaf, reprised in the mouth, but tends to fade on the back palate. The Picolit owes its gold hue to part-dried grapes and wood maturation. Attractive almond paste pervades the bouquet before the palate gives sweet dates and caramel. Elegance is the theme of all the wines. This year's concentrated Pinot Grigio is no exception and neither is the fresh-tasting Ribolla Gialla, which has perhaps too much acidity in the finish. Finally, the long, well-sustained Chardonnay is more impressive on palate than nose. All told, it was a decent performance but below the winery's usual standards.

O COF Picolit '04	🍷🍷	7
O COF Chardonnay '07	🍷	4
O COF Pinot Grigio '07	🍷	4
O COF Ribolla Gialla '07	🍷	5
O COF Sauvignon '07	🍷	5
O COF Tocai Friulano '07	🍷	4
O COF Sauvignon '06	🍷🍷	4
O COF Chardonnay '06	🍷🍷	4
O COF Picolit '03	🍷🍷	6

Andrea Visintini

VIA GRAMOGLIANO, 27
33040 CORNO DI ROSAZZO [UD]
TEL. 0432755813
www.vinivisintini.com

ANNUAL PRODUCTION	150,000 bottles
HECTARES UNDER VINE	28
VITICULTURE METHOD	Conventional

Andrea Visintini founded this winery in 1973. Andrea is no longer with us but before he passed on, he handed formal ownership to his children Oliviero and twins Cinzia and Palmira. It's not often you meet such open, friendly people. They are modest, too, in the sense that they present their superb wines without fanfares, as if excellence was normality. Equally reassuring are the modest prices, which have increased little over the years. It's no surprise that the 150,000 bottles fly off the shelves. If the Visintinis applied the logic used by so many other producers, who factor in all their costs, consumers would have to face stiffer price tags. Three years ago, our heroes opened a new cellar, which entailed significant additional expense because of an adjacent listed watchtower dating from 1560. Once again, Sauvignon is the outstanding wine, unveiling sage and tomato leaf, a rich palate and good minerality, closely followed by the fresh-tasting Pinot Bianco, which is lifted by a hint of liquorice. Other wines we liked are the Ribolla Gialla and the Bianco, blended from half friulano, one third picolit and the remainder pinot bianco.

Vistorta

VIA VISTORTA, 82
33077 SACILE [PN]
TEL. 043471135
www.vistorta.it

ANNUAL PRODUCTION	80,000 bottles
HECTARES UNDER VINE	38
VITICULTURE METHOD	Certified organic

Yet again this year, we awarded Three Glasses to Vistorta's superb Merlot, a wine that owner Brandino Brandolini wants to keep distinct from the other estate label, Conte Brandolini d'Adda. Production philosophy here takes an entirely different shape. The aim is to make a single label in significant numbers – almost 80,000 units – in order to achieve international visibility. Brandino started off with the vine stock, calling in Marco Simonit of the Preparatori d'Uva (Fruitmakers) group. He then flanked his trusted oenologist Alec Ongaro with friends George Pauli and Samuel Tinon, two master winemakers from Bordeaux and the latter the creator of some great Hungarian Tokajis. About 40 hectares are planted to merlot and only the very best wine from the best barriques goes into Vistorta. The 2006 edition is a triumph, showing remarkably elegant, despite robust extract that lends it youthfulness and ensures it will mature very successfully. Like many Bordeaux wines, Vistorta needs time to evolve and vertical tastings of the past decade confirm its outstanding cellar potential.

O COF Pinot Bianco '07	♟	3*
O COF Sauvignon '07	♟♟	4
O COF Bianco '07	♟	3
O COF Friulano '07	♟	3
● COF Merlot '06	♟	3
● COF Merlot Ris. Torion '05	♟	4
O COF Pinot Grigio '07	♟	3
O COF Ribolla Gialla '07	♟	3
O Collio Malvasia '07	♟	3
O COF Sauvignon '06	♟♟	4
O COF Bianco '06	♟♟	4
O COF Pinot Bianco '06	♟♟	4
O COF Tocai Friulano '06	♟♟	4
O Collio Malvasia '06	♟♟	4

● Friuli Grave Merlot Vistorta '06	♟♟♟	5
● Friuli Grave Merlot Vistorta '05	♟♟♟	5
● Friuli Grave Merlot Vistorta '04	♟♟♟	5
● Friuli Grave Merlot Vistorta '03	♟♟♟	5
● Friuli Grave Merlot Vistorta '02	♟♟	5
● Friuli Grave Merlot Vistorta '00	♟♟	5
● Friuli Grave Merlot Vistorta '99	♟♟	5
● Friuli Grave Merlot Vistorta '98	♟♟	5
● Friuli Grave Merlot Vistorta '97	♟♟	5

Vodopivec

VIA COLLUDROZZA, 4
34010 SGONICO [TS]
TEL. 040229181
www.vodopivec.it

ANNUAL PRODUCTION	8,000 bottles
HECTARES UNDER VINE	4.5
VITICULTURE METHOD	Natural

The Vodopivec brothers, Paolo and Valter, made some difficult decisions when they took over in 1994. Around here, you find vitovska and malvasia growing side by side on the red soil recovered from the Carso depressions known as "doline", but Paolo and Valter opted for just one great native white, vitovska. Vine density was raised to 10,000 plants per hectare and the bush-trained vines stand on rock in just 30 centimetres of soil. No chemicals are used apart from sulphur and copper as fungicides. Bunch thinning is carried out in late July, leaving a final yield of about half a kilogram per vine. The healthy bunches are picked and crushed. Some of the juice ferments with skin contact in 30-hectolitre Slavonian oak rounds, the rest is left for a few months in amphorae imported from Georgia set in the ground out of doors. A couple of years later, the wine goes into bottle unfiltered. The wood-only wine becomes Vitovska Classica, a concentrated, rich-textured wine with a vanillaed fragrance yet elegantly fresh-tasting, and only slightly astringent, in the mouth. Lavender and violet herbaceousness marks out the minerally, lingering amphora-matured Vitovska.

O Vitovska Classica '05	♟♟	8
O Vitovska '05	♟♟	8
O Vitovska '04	♟♟	7
O Vitovska Solo '04	♟♟	8

Volpe Pasini

FRAZ. TOGLIANO
VIA CIVIDALE, 16
33040 TORREANO [UD]
TEL. 0432715151
www.volpepasini.it

ANNUAL PRODUCTION	400,000 bottles
HECTARES UNDER VINE	52
VITICULTURE METHOD	Conventional

The Volpe Pasini winery looks to be in a transitional phase that could be the prelude to further growth. Much new vine stock has now come onstream, which means that the Calabrian-born owner, Emilio Rotolo, relies less on bought-in fruit or wine to bolster production. Volpe Pasini is moving to a new point of balance under the guiding hands of consultant Alessio Dorigo and agronomist Pierpaolo Sirch in the vineyards. Rotolo is looking to produce big numbers without compromising on quality. That's why a couple of years ago, he invested in equipment that enables him to carry out all the early stages of vinification in a carbon dioxide-only environment, in the total absence of oxygen. We know that there are at least two approaches here – hyperoxygenation and reduction – and that both can produce fantastic results. As in the case of Pinot Bianco Zuc di Volpe, for example, a Three Glass winner for its intensity, elegance and breadth of aromatics complemented by a fresh-tasting citrus-like palate that lingers impressively. The Sauvignon Zuc di Volpe is extremely varietal while the Friulano can offer attractive freshness after a difficult growing year.

O COF Pinot Bianco Zuc di Volpe '07	♟♟♟	5
O COF Sauvignon Zuc di Volpe '07	♟♟	5
O COF Friulano Zuc di Volpe '07	♟♟	5
O COF Chardonnay Zuc di Volpe '06	♟	5
O COF Friulano Volpe Pasini '07	♟	4
O COF Pinot Grigio Grivò '07	♟	4
O COF Pinot Grigio Zuc di Volpe '07	♟	5
O COF Ribolla Gialla Zuc di Volpe '07	♟	5
O COF Sauvignon Volpe Pasini '07	♟	4
O COF Pinot Grigio Ipso '06		6
● COF Merlot Focus Zuc di Volpe '99	♟♟♟	5
● COF Refosco P. R. Zuc di Volpe '01	♟♟♟	5
O COF Sauvignon Zuc di Volpe '05	♟♟♟	5
O COF Sauvignon Zuc di Volpe '04	♟♟♟	5
O COF Tocai Friulano Zuc di Volpe '06	♟♟♟	5

Francesco Vosca

FRAZ. BRAZZANO
VIA SOTTOMONTE, 19
34070 CORMONS [GO]
TEL. 048162135
voscafrancesco@libero.it

ANNUAL PRODUCTION	15,000 bottles
HECTARES UNDER VINE	6
VITICULTURE METHOD	Conventional

Francesco Vosca is confirming potential we spotted a couple of years ago. In fact, three of the wines earned a second Glass. The cellar is striding ahead and we are very pleased. The winery is at Brazzano near Cormons, traditionally an area of great Friulian winemakers. Francesco has one foot in the Collio and the other in Isonzo and with help from his family farms about six hectares, growing mainly white grapes. Generally, about 15,000 units are bottled each year but the figure varies depending on market demand. Vosca only bottles what he is sure he can sell. Pinot Grigio, Sauvignon and Friulano were that wines we liked best. All are remarkably full bodied and savoury, with just a hint of rusticity that brings to mind the wines of yesteryear. We were particularly impressed by the citrus and flowers of the Pinot Grigio, which is substantial and long-lasting in the mouth. The varietal Sauvignon offers decent minerality and fragrance as well as good pressure on the palate. To round off, the Friulano is the best of the range this year thanks to its intense, subtly nuanced aromas and a full, well-sustained palate with good softness and balance.

Zidarich

LOC. PREPOTTO, 23
34011 DUINO AURISINA [TS]
TEL. 040201223
www.zidarich.it

ANNUAL PRODUCTION	18,000 bottles
HECTARES UNDER VINE	6
VITICULTURE METHOD	Natural

Planting density of 7-10,000 vines per hectare, yields of 40-50 quintals per hectare, manual harvesting, fermentation and maceration on the skins in open vats without temperature control and maturation in medium and large wood. This sums up the approach of a producer who is convinced that wines made this way are the healthiest and most environmentally friendly you can obtain. But a good wine is also made up of attractive sensory perceptions, which are not always guaranteed. Benjamin Zidarich, however, has managed to square that particular circle. His magnificent Malvasia swept up our top prize this year. Pale gold, it gives citrus, sweet spice and aromatic herbs before a lingering, fresh-tasting palate with excellent nose-palate consistency and a tight-knit texture. Also excellent is Benjamin's Prulke, from vitovska, malvasia and sauvignon, which gives carob, apricot and sultana fragrances. The very drinkable Vitovska is tangy and dry, pears, damsons and sage peeking through in the elegant aromatics. Finally, the Terrano is a fine wine in its category. Lovers of the type will appreciate it.

○ Collio Friulano '07	▼▼ 4*
○ Collio Pinot Grigio '07	▼▼ 4*
○ Friuli Isonzo Sauvignon '07	▼▼ 4*
○ Collio Malvasia '07	▼ 4
○ Friuli Isonzo Chardonnay '07	▼ 4
○ Collio Malvasia '06	♀♀ 4
○ Collio Tocai Friulano '06	♀♀ 4

○ Carso Malvasia '06	▼▼▼ 6
○ Prulke '06	▼▼ 6
○ Carso Vitovska '06	▼▼ 6
● Carso Terrano '06	▼ 6
○ Prulke '04	♀♀ 6
○ Carso Malvasia '05	♀♀ 6
○ Carso Vitovska '05	♀♀ 6
○ Prulke '05	♀♀ 6

Zof

FRAZ. SANT'ANDRAT DEL JUDRIO
VIA GIOVANNI XXIII, 32A
33040 CORNO DI ROSAZZO [UD]
TEL. 0432759673
www.zof.it

ANNUAL PRODUCTION 90,000 bottles
HECTARES UNDER VINE 13
VITICULTURE METHOD Conventional

The Zof family began its adventures in wine in the mid 1980s. Alberto was the man who first got involved but a few vintages later, command passed to his son, Daniele, who at once improved the quality of the wines the cellar was making, most of which were sold at the family's agriturismo. With help from consultant oenologist Donato Lanati, the cellar has come on apace and now Daniele can call on fruit from nine estate-owned hectares and four that are rented to go into his fine range. Meanwhile, his parents look after the agriturismo facilities, which are very popular with Austrian and German visitors. But let's get on to wines. The delicate, mouthfilling Sauvignon has distinct aromatics that recall tropical fruits and pineapple in the mouth, with a nicely balanced finish. The Ribolla Gialla is not quite up to recent standards, its green apple fragrances carrying over on the palate where varietal acidity is very marked. We enjoyed the citrus, apple and leaf-themed Tocai with its acidulous, long-lingering palate. Overall, this is a good, varied range with bags of personality. There may not be any stand-outs but average quality is gratifying.

○ COF Sauvignon '07	🍷🍷	4
● COF Pignolo '04	🍷	6
○ COF Ribolla Gialla '07	🍷	4
○ COF Tocai Friulano '07	🍷	4
● Refosco P. R. '06	🍷	4
● COF Cabernet Franc '06		4
○ COF Ribolla Gialla '06	🥂🥂	4

Zuani

LOC. GIASBANA, 12
34070 SAN FLORIANO DEL COLLIO [GO]
TEL. 0481391432
www.zuanivini.it

ANNUAL PRODUCTION 40,000 bottles
HECTARES UNDER VINE 14
VITICULTURE METHOD Conventional

When we visited Patrizia Felluga newly made over cellar, we tasted the latest versions of her two wines. Immediately, we knew that the daughter of the great Marco Felluga had scored a bull's eye. Patrizia leaves nothing to chance and her tenacity is reminiscent of her father's. She has expanded her small property and now has 14 hectares, of which ten are in production. On her way, she has found a small traditional hostelry and is already planning to use it to promote her new vision, Collio Bianco. Working alongside her is her son Antonio, who is active in the cellar and in marketing while Patrizia's daughter Caterina finishes her university studies. Patrizia doesn't like to talk about consultants – she rightly maintains that wine is made in the vineyard – but the rapport with Donato Lanati is too important to ignore. These bottles, however, are very much Zuani wines. This small cellar-cum-club, with lights reflecting off a spherical mirror, has produced a genuinely great product in Vigne, a complex, fresh-tasting blend of tocai friulano, chardonnay, sauvignon and pinot grigio. The barrique-aged Zuani has a citrus and yellow peach theme.

○ Collio Bianco Zuani Vigne '07	🍷🍷🍷	5
○ Collio Bianco Zuani '06	🍷🍷	6
○ Collio Bianco Zuani '05	🥂🥂	6
○ Collio Bianco Zuani '04	🥂🥂	5
○ Collio Bianco Zuani '03	🥂🥂	5
○ Collio Bianco Zuani '02	🥂🥂	5
○ Collio Bianco Zuani '01	🥂🥂	5
○ Collio Bianco Zuani Vigne '06	🥂🥂	5
○ Collio Bianco Zuani Vigne '04	🥂🥂	5
○ Collio Bianco Zuani Vigne '03	🥂🥂	4

OTHER WINERIES

Tenuta di Blasig

VIA ROMA, 63
34077 RONCHI DEI LEGIONARI [GO]
TEL. 0481475480
www.tenutadiblasig.it

Sadly, the new cellar opened to Friuli's indifferent 2007 growing year. Still, no need to panic. Wines like the sweet dried-grape Le Lule from verduzzo, or the Bordeaux blend Rosso, or the Pinot Grigio, show that the substance is there.

○ Friuli Isonzo Pinot Grigio '07	♀	4
○ Le Lule '06	♀	5
● Rosso '03	♀	5

Blason

VIA ROMA, 32
34072 GRADISCA D'ISONZO [GO]
TEL. 048192414
www.vinidocisonzo.it

Reliability is the keynote here. The cellar seems to do better with monovarietals than blends, which need fine-tuning. As you would expect for 2007, there is a good Pinot Grigio with a classic onionskin hue and rich fruit on the nose.

○ Friuli Isonzo Pinot Grigio '07	♀♀	4*
○ Friuli Isonzo Friulano '07	♀	4
● Friuli Isonzo Merlot '07	♀	4
○ Friuli Isonzo Sauvignon Bruma '07	♀	3

Alfredo Bracco

FRAZ. BRAZZANO
VIA XXIV MAGGIO, 28
34070 CORMONS [GO]
TEL. 048160002
www.braccovini.it

Tenacious wine woman Elisabetta Bracco releases very few labels, including a standout Bianco Bracco from tocai, sauvignon and malvasia which regales the senses with fruit and flowers. There's an unusual hint of hydrocarbons on the long-lingering Friulano Ultimo.

○ Friuli Isonzo Bianco Bracco '07	♀♀	4*
○ Friuli Isonzo Friulano Ultimo '07	♀	4

Ca' Selva

S.DA DI SEQUALS, 11A
33090 SEQUALS [PN]
TEL. 0421274704
www.caselva.it

The Bergamo family organically farms 34 hectares in the Grave zone of Friuli in the shadow of the Carnic Alps. All the wines have a Friulian trade name that testifies to the family's attachment to the land. We would point out the Cabernet Franc, Pinot Grigio and Tocai, among others.

○ Cabernet Franc Neri di Lune '06	♀♀	3*
○ Friuli Grave Tocai Friulano Sclavòn '07	♀	3
○ Pinot Grigio Gardisàne '07	♀	3

Cadibon

VIA CASALI GALLO, 1
33040 CORNO DI ROSAZZO [UD]
TEL. 0432759316
www.cadibon.com

Luca and Francesca gave us a fine selection of wines. The Ribolla Gialla has intense apple, Bianco Ronco del Nonno, from cask-conditioned pinot bianco, friulano and sauvignon, has peach and apricot aromas and the Friulano Bontaj offers apple and almond. The Refosco nearly picked up a second Glass.

○ COF Ribolla Gialla '07	♀♀	4
○ COF Bianco Ronco del Nonno '07	♀	4
○ COF Friulano Bontaj '07	♀	4
● COF Refosco P. R. '07	♀	4

Castello di Buttrio

VIA MORPURGO, 9
33042 BUTTRIO [UD]
TEL. 0432673015
www.castellodibuttrio.it

Alessandra Felluga, daughter of the great Marco, is expanding her range of very valid wines without compromising on quality. We liked Bianco Mon Blanc, from tocai, ribolla and malvasia. Close behind were the Friulano and Chardonnay, both of which scored well.

○ COF Bianco Mon Blanc '07	♀♀	4*
○ COF Chardonnay '07	♀	5
○ COF Friulano '07	♀	5
○ COF Sauvignon '07	♀	5

OTHER WINERIES

Catemario

LOC. GRAMOGLIANO
VIA DEL BARBARESCO, 11
33040 CORNO DI ROSAZZO [UD]
TEL. 0432753222
catemario@catemariowines.it

Manlio Collavini set up this winery to recover the name of the cellar he purchased from Duca Catemario di Quadri when he moved to Corno di Rosazzo. The varietal Ribolla Gialla is all fruit and flowers while the Chardonnay is full bodied, intense and true to type. The Sauvignon and the Refosco scored One full Glass each.

O COF Ribolla Gialla '07	♟♟	5
O Collio Chardonnay '07	♟♟	4*
O Collio Sauvignon '07	♟	4
● Friuli Isonzo Refosco P. R. '07	♟	4

Cantina Produttori di Cormons

VIA VINO DELLA PACE, 31
34071 CORMONS [GO]
TEL. 048161798
www.cormons.com

Director Gigi Soini aims to present a range that is reliable in all departments, rather than favour a few flagship labels. We liked the Tocai Friulano, which nearly earned a second Glass, and the various interpretations of Pinot Grigio, including the blush Rosänder, all performed well.

O Collio Tocai Friulano '07	♟	3
O Collio Pinot Grigio '07	♟	4
O Collio Sauvignon '07	♟	4
O Friuli Isonzo Tocai Friulano '07	♟	4
O Friuli Isonzo Pinot Grigio Rosänder '07	♟	4

Do Ville

VIA MITRAGLIERI, 2
34077 RONCHI DEI LEGIONARI [GO]
TEL. 0481775561
www.doville.it

Again this year, the Bonoras gave us a raft of wines to taste in their Ars Vivendi and Do Ville lines. We were intrigued by the Do Ville Chardonnay, which gives distinct crusty bread fragrances preceding a rich, very intense palate with plenty of elegance.

O Chardonnay Do Ville '07	♟♟	4
O Friuli Isonzo Pinot Grigio Ars Vivendi '07	♟	3
O Sauvignon Do Ville '07	♟	4

Draga

LOC. SCEDINA, 8
34070 SAN FLORIANO DEL COLLIO [GO]
TEL. 0481884182
www.draga.it

Milan Miklus farms about ten hectares of vineyards and this year his wines are all good. The Malvasia has attractive ripe fruit, the upfront Pinot Grigio recalls white peaches and the Tocai Friulano reveals subtle hints of minerality. The lingering persistence of the Sauvignon complements its fleshy palate.

O Collio Malvasia '06	♟	4
O Collio Pinot Grigio '07	♟	4
O Collio Sauvignon '06	♟	4
O Collio Tocai Friulano '07	♟	4

Conti Formentini

VIA OSLAVIA, 5
34070 SAN FLORIANO DEL COLLIO [GO]
TEL. 0481884131
www.contiformentini.it

This ancient estate whose cellar is managed by oenologist Marco Del Piccolo is planning its future with help from Christian Scrinzi, who is in charge of wine policy for GIV. The Pinot Grigio is rich in fruit, the Friulano stands out for its subtle fragrances and varietal almonds while the Ribolla Gialla is attractive.

O Collio Pinot Grigio '07	♟	4
O Collio Ribolla Gialla '07	♟	4
O Collio Friulano '07	♟	4
O Collio Sauvignon '07		4

Albano Guerra

LOC. MONTINA
V.LE KENNEDY, 39A
33040 TORREANO [UD]
TEL. 0432715077

Since 1997, Dario has been looking after the family cellar and this year the results are good. We liked the intense nose and velvety flavour of the Friulano in particular. The Merlot is extremely fresh-tasting with cherries on nose and palate. The Cabernet Franc and Gritul earned mentions.

O COF Friulano '07	♟♟	4
● COF Merlot '06	♟♟	4
● COF Cabernet Franc '06		3
● COF Rosso Gritul Ris. '03		4

OTHER WINERIES

Albino Kurtin

Loc. Novali, 9
34071 Cormons [GO]
tel. 048160685

Albino Kurtin's winery is at Novali, an area of Cormons that is well suited to the production of white wines. This year, we liked Opera Prima, a blend of pinot bianco, ribolla gialla and chardonnay. The stylish nose leads with tropical fruits that are reprised in the mouth. We thought the Sauvignon was equally delicious.

O Collio Sauvignon '07	♥♥	4
O Opera Prima Bianco '07	♥♥	4
O Collio Chardonnay '07	♥	4
O Collio Malvasia '07	♥	4
● Diamante Nero '05	♥	4

Lupinc

Fraz. Prepotto 11b
34011 Duino Aurisina [TS]
tel. 040200848

The Lupinc operation farms four hectares under vine but that doesn't prevent it releasing quality wines by relying on the land, not technology. The stand-out is Stara Brajda, from vitovska, malvasia, glera and tocai whose rich fruit melds seamlessly with oak-derived confectioner's cream. The other native wines are nice.

O Stara Brajda '06	♥♥	4
O Carso Malvasia '06	♥	4
● Carso Terrano '05	♥	4
O Carso Vitovska '06	♥	4

Giulio Manzocco

via C. Battisti, 61
34071 Cormons [GO]
tel. 048160590
www.vinimanzocco.com

Dario Manzocco's winery continues on its self-appointed path. The Pinot Grigio 2007 is interesting, giving fairly intense pears that lead into a tangy, full-textured palate with drinkability-enhancing acidity. Again this year, the Pinot Bianco is good.

O Collio Pinot Grigio '07	♥♥	4*
O Collio Pinot Bianco '07	♥	4
O Collio Tocai Friulano '07	♥	4
O Friuli Isonzo Sauvignon '07	♥	4

Midolini

via delle Fornaci, 1
33044 Manzano [UD]
tel. 0432754555
www.midolini.com

Gloria Midolini, who has the assistance of oenologist Alessandro Sandrin, can count herself satisfied. The 35 hectares produce the Rosacroce range. Pinot Grigio has powerful fruit, the honey-themed Bianco is stylish and the Sauvignon is reminiscent of bell peppers. Ripe white-fleshed fruit comes through on the Chardonnay.

O COF Pinot Grigio Rosacroce '07	♥♥	5
O COF Bianco Rosacroce '07	♥	5
O COF Chardonnay Rosacroce '07	♥	5
O COF Sauvignon Rosacroce '07	♥	4

Flavio Pontoni

via Peruzzi, 8
33042 Buttrio [UD]
tel. 0432674352
www.pontoni.it

Flavio gave us a solid all-round range without peaks of excellence. His whites were more convincing with the Pinot Grigio emerging for its peach and ripe fruits nose. The Malvasia is intense on the nose and dryish in the mouth. Lastly, the very varietal Friulano offers dried fruit sensations.

O COF Friulano '07	♥	3
O COF Malvasia '07	♥	3
O COF Pinot Grigio '07	♥	4*
O COF Verduzzo Friulano '07	♥	4

Ronco dei Pini

via Ronchi, 94
33040 Prepotto [UD]
tel. 0432713239
www.roncodeipini.it

Giuseppe and Claudio Novello, owners of Ronco dei Pini, turn out about 120,000 bottles a year. This year, there were no second Glasses but we liked the sweet Verduzzo Riccovino, the stylish yellow apple and wisteria Chardonnay, the refined Pinot Bianco and a Friulano that is very slightly out of kilter.

O COF Friulano '07	♥	4
O COF Pinot Bianco '07	♥	4
O Collio Chardonnay '07	♥	4
O Verduzzo Friulano Riccovino '07	♥	6

OTHER WINERIES

Ronco di Zegla - Maurizio Princic

LOC. ZEGLA, 12
34071 CORMONS [GO]
TEL. 048161155
mauriziozegla@libero.it

Maurizio Princic took us by surprise by sending 2005 wines, some of which turned out to be extremely good. The Ribolla Gialla has six days' skin contact and then spends a year in five-hectolitre barrels. The steel-only Sauvignon opens slowly. Aerate it, as you would with any wine that is not young.

O Collio Ribolla Gialla '05	♥♥ 5
O Collio Sauvignon '05	♥♥ 5
O Collio Chardonnay '05	♥ 5
O Collio Tocai Friulano '05	♥ 5

Rubini

LOC. SPESSA
VIA CASE RUBINI, 1
33043 CIVIDALE DEL FRIULI [UD]
TEL. 0432716141
www.villarubini.eu

This property has immense potential, given its terroir, the aspects of the hills at Spessa and its history, which goes back to 1814. This year, we point out the very fresh, minerally Ribolla Gialla, the flowers and citrus of the Friulano and the iodine and spice of the Refosco.

O COF Friulano What's in a name '07	♥♥ 4*
O COF Ribolla Gialla '07	♥♥ 4*
● COF Refosco P. R. '06	♥ 4
● COF Schioppettino '06	♥ 4

Torre Rosazza

FRAZ. OLEIS
LOC. POGGIOBELLO, 12
33044 MANZANO [UD]
TEL. 0422864511
www.torrerosazza.com

Distribution and marketing are now in the hands of Mario Zuliani, whose career has taken him to major wineries in Friuli and Umbria, while the estate staff is unchanged under Luca Zuccarello and consultant Donato Lanati. Ribolla Gialla, Picolit, Sauvignon and Pinot Grigio are our favourites from a long list.

O COF Picolit '05	♥ 6
O COF Pinot Grigio '07	♥ 4
O COF Ribolla Gialla '07	♥ 4
O COF Sauvignon '07	♥ 4

Venturini Paolo

VIA ISONZO, 135
34071 CORMONS [GO]
TEL. 048160446
venturini@spin.it

Paolo Venturini farms 15 hectares, mainly on the hill at Pradis in the Collio DOC and the rest on the flatlands of Borc di Sot at Medea in the Isonzo DOC. Generally, the wines are mid quality but this time Paolo gave us an intense, elegant Pinot Bianco and a very varietal Malvasia.

O Collio Pinot Bianco '07	♥♥ 4*
O Collio Malvasia '07	♥ 4
O Collio Pinot Grigio '07	♥ 4
O Collio Ribolla Gialla '07	♥ 4

Villa Vitas

LOC. STRASSOLDO
VIA SAN MARCO, 5
33050 CERVIGNANO DEL FRIULI [UD]
TEL. 043193083
www.vitas.it

At a lovely 18th-century mansion in the heart of Friuli, Roberto Vitas continues the family's winemaking saga with Andrea Pittana in the vineyards and Francesco Spitaleri in the cellar. Noteworthy wines include the surprisingly fresh, apple-themed Ribolla, the stylish Sauvignon and the vibrant, fruity Refosco.

O Ribolla Gialla '07	♥♥ 4*
● Friuli Aquileia Refosco dal P. R. '06	♥ 4
O Friuli Aquileia Sauvignon Blanc '07	♥ 4

Franco Visintin

VIA ROMA, 37
34072 GRADISCA D'ISONZO [GO]
TEL. 048199974

A step back to the Other Wineries section is not always indicative of deterioration. It might mean that solid quality is not enough to deal with increasingly fierce competition. Franco's fine Pinot Grigio, Rosso Stàngja and Cabernet Sauvignon couldn't quite keep up with some of the emerging wineries.

● Friuli Isonzo Cabernet Sauvignon '06	♥ 4
O Friuli Isonzo Pinot Grigio '07	♥ 3*
● Stàngja Rosso '05	♥ 4

EMILIA ROMAGNA

This year, the region notched up its best-ever result with nine Three Glass wines. It's a clear sign of the excitement in Emilia Romagna, which can however be interpreted in numerous different ways. Following the historic Via Emilia, which crosses the entire region marking the boundary between the quality production of the hills and the mass cultivation of the plains, the first DOC zone you encounter is the Colli Piacentini, which reconfirms the extraordinary flair of malvasia di Candia, one of the area's favourite grapes, for the production of dessert wines. Negrese's new Malvasia Passito and La Stoppa's familiar Vigna della Stoppa are among the best wines in Italy of this kind, along with La Tosa's uniquely distinctive Cabernet Sauvignon Luna Selvatica. The stretch of the road running through Lambrusco country in the provinces of Parma, Reggio Emilia and Modena is shining brighter than ever. It is now home to a significant number of excellent wines produced by large and small estates that become more reliable with each year that passes. This is a very encouraging signal for a sector that has in the past paid heavily for its strategic mistakes and which is currently the subject of renewed interest throughout Italy. The Colli Bolognesi is the last stronghold of the Emilian grape varieties before entering the very different ampelographic panorama of Romagna. While Tenuta Bonzara's Cabernet Sauvignon Bonzarone has returned to Three Glass form this year, the zone appears to be experiencing a lull, as though lacking the courage to assert some of the qualities that the terroir is nonetheless capable of expressing. Romagna won an impressive four Three Glass awards for its most representative wine, Sangiovese, from different areas. San Patrignano's Avi and San Valentino's Terra di Covignano from Rimini are warmer and more Mediterranean, Calonga's Michelangiolo from Forlì is opulent and Casetto dei Mandorli's Vigna del Generale from the Predappio Alta hills is austere and complex. Those seeking faults in the production of Sangiovese di Romagna will be hard put to find any in the peaks of the region's production. Four Three Glass winners – five, if we count Marzieno by the Faenza-based Fattoria Zerbina, which has a dash of cabernet – may not be very many but they reflect the current state of the DOC zone in its upper reaches. The problem, if anything, lies in the results obtained by the everyday wines, those suitable for day-to-day drinking that cost no more than eight euros a bottle. This category is increasingly pervaded by heavy, over-muscular, alcoholic wines, with just the opposite characteristics to those sought by attentive consumers, who expect to find elegance, lightness and good acidity in a Sangiovese, and perhaps even finish the bottle without noticing it.

Baraccone

LOC. CA' DEI MORTI, 1
29028 PONTE DELL'OLIO [PC]
TEL. 0523877147
www.baraccone.it

ANNUAL PRODUCTION	22,000 bottles
HECTARES UNDER VINE	7.5
VITICULTURE METHOD	Conventional

Baraccone is the name of the place where the winery was founded about a century years ago – the current premises are located a few kilometres away – and where circuses and travelling fairs, known locally as "baracconi", used to stop. The winery's recent history commenced in 1995, when it started to bottle its production. Today, Andreana Burgazzi and consultant oenologist Stefano Testa run this little estate in Val Nure, one of the most interesting wine areas around Piacenza. Their competence is reflected in the limited list of wines and the brave decision not to release the flagship wine in lesser vintages. Indeed, Gutturnio Riserva Ronco Alto, whose '04 vintage had impressed us so much, was not produced in 2005. However, we did admire the rich, complex mouthfeel of Gutturnio Frizzante. It's a full, juicy, wine with considerable alcoholic strength, countered by decent acidic backbone that ensures a confident finish. Gutturnio Superiore Colombaia shows ripe and fruity on the nose and chewy in the mouth, with a caressing mid palate and good acidity and extract on the finish.

● C. P. Gutturnio Frizzante '07	¶¶	3*
● C. P. Gutturnio Sup. Colombaia '06	¶¶	4*
○ Zagaia Frizzante '07	¶	3
● C. P. Gutturnio Ronco Alto Ris. '04	¶¶	4
● C. P. Gutturnio Sup. Colombaia '05	¶¶	4

Conte Otto Barattieri di San Pietro

VIA DEI TIGLI, 100
29020 VIGOLZONE [PC]
TEL. 0523875111
ottobarattieri@libero.it

ANNUAL PRODUCTION	120,000 bottles
HECTARES UNDER VINE	37
VITICULTURE METHOD	Conventional

It's not easy to talk about Albarola Vin Santo without seeming repetitive. However, the surprise is that this year the '98 vintage only came close to winning Three Glasses. The exuberant nose of balsam and honey is followed by a palate as broad and creamy as ever, although it seems to be lacking a little of the complexity, depth and aromatic verve of the better vintages. Still, we are talking about one of the great Italian dessert wines, which remains a benchmark for fans of the category. Another of the estate's historic sweet wines is Il Faggio, made from dried grapes from an old bracchetto vineyard. The '05 vintage vaunts a dense, juicy palate, bursting with fruit, which is sweet but not cloying. Gutturnio Montesprello lacks compactness on the nose but followed up with a well-knit palate and a fine lingering finish. Turning to the semi-sparkling wines, our favourite reds were Gutturnio and Barbera while the fresh, supple Valnure and the forthright aromatic Malvasia stand out from the other whites.

○ C. P. Vin Santo Albarola Val di Nure '98	¶¶	8
● Il Faggio '05	¶¶	6
● C. P. Barbera Frizzante '07	¶	3
● C. P. Gutturnio Frizzante '07	¶	3
● C. P. Gutturnio Montesprello '04	¶	4
○ C. P. Valnure Frizzante '07	¶	3
○ C. P. Malvasia Frizzante '07	¶	3
○ C. P. Vin Santo Albarola Val di Nure '97	¶¶¶	6
○ C. P. Vin Santo Albarola Val di Nure '96	¶¶¶	6
○ C. P. Vin Santo Albarola Val di Nure '95	¶¶	6
● Il Faggio '03	¶¶	6

Francesco Bellei

VIA PER MODENA, 80
41030 BOMPORTO [MO]
TEL. 059812449
www.francescobellei.it

ANNUAL PRODUCTION	60,000 bottles
HECTARES UNDER VINE	5
VITICULTURE METHOD	Conventional

This long-standing winery was recently purchased by the Cavicchioli family of San Prospero, but remains firmly in the hands of skilled "maitre de cave" Christian Bellei as far as technical aspects are concerned. The cellar is a benchmark for classic method production – used for all its wines – in Emilia Romagna and beyond. The consistency of the various wines is impressive, even in the case of first releases, such as the Blanc de Noirs, which completes the estate's list and captivated us with its complex, mouthfilling style, offering notes of cheese, moss and mushrooms, although we sensed that it has the potential for further improvement. Rifermentazione Ancestrale, basically an undisgorged bottle-refermented Lambrusco di Sorbara, is very well calibrated, with crisp cherry notes and a soft but lingering finish. The disgorged Brut Rosso has a full nose of red fruit and a rich, well-constructed palate with a pleasant slightly bitter finish. Brut Extra Cuvée is as reliable and enjoyable as ever while the vintage Cuvée Speciale is much more complex, layered and creamy.

Stefano Berti

LOC. RAVALDINO IN MONTE
VIA LA SCAGNA, 18
47100 FORLÌ
TEL. 0543488074
www.stefanoberti.com

ANNUAL PRODUCTION	30,000 bottles
HECTARES UNDER VINE	8
VITICULTURE METHOD	Natural

Stefano Berti is one of many Romagna growers who are working on sangiovese in the clay soils of the first band of hills between Predappio and Forlì. After the magical 2001 edition, when Stefano took Three Glasses at his debut in the Guide, our hero hasn't been able to replicate the delicate balance of weight and elegance and his wines, while always convincing, are a touch meaty with a lot of alcohol and a slightly dry mouthfeel caused by the tannins. A lighter hand might achieve greater equilibrium while longer bottle ageing could tame the somewhat aggressive tannins. Consequently, we approve the decision to keep Calisto '06 in the cellar for another year and are curious to see whether it will improve it. In its place, we tasted an admirable Ravaldo, a wine that is always very consistent and probably requires less radical decisions on Stefano's part. It's austere, complex and, despite its bold tannins, has the character to express itself with depth and quality. The palate unfolds with a vein of acidity that makes it very dynamic, although it's held back by a tad too much alcohol.

O Brut Blanc de Noirs '04	♟♟	6
O Brut Cuvée Speciale '04	♟♟	6
O Brut Extra Cuvée	♟♟	5
● Brut Rosso Extra Cuvée '06	♟♟	4*
● Lambrusco Rifermentazione Ancestrale '07	♟♟	4*
⊙ Brut Rosé Extra Cuvée '02	♟	6
O Brut Cuvée Speciale '99	♟♟	5
O Brut Cuvée Speciale '97	♟♟	5
⊙ Brut Rosé Extra Cuvée '98	♟♟	6
● Brut Rosso Extra Cuvée '04	♟♟	4

● Sangiovese di Romagna Sup. Ravaldo '07	♟♟	4*
● Sangiovese di Romagna Sup. Bartimeo '07	♟	3
O Suppergiù Chardonnay '07		3
● Sangiovese di Romagna Sup. Calisto '01	♟♟♟	5
● Sangiovese di Romagna Sup. Calisto '04	♟♟	5
● Sangiovese di Romagna Sup. Calisto '05	♟♟	5
● Sangiovese di Romagna Sup. Ravaldo '06	♟♟	4*
● Sangiovese di Romagna Sup. Ravaldo '05	♟♟	4*

Raffaella Alessandra Bissoni

LOC. CASTICCIANO
VIA COLECCHIO, 280
47032 BERTINORO [FC]
TEL. 0543460382
www.vinibissoni.com

ANNUAL PRODUCTION	13,000 bottles
HECTARES UNDER VINE	4.5
VITICULTURE METHOD	Natural

Today respect for the land is a challenging road to go down. It sets the rhythms of nature against those of the market, and the need to get results against an approach that seeks to understand complexities and interpret them. However, Raffaella Bissoni accepts no compromises, striving for the point of equilibrium, free from artifice, where quality comes naturally. Although the results are not yet perfect, her work is sure to yield exceptional fruits sooner or later. Sangiovese Riserva has a rather tired nose. Fresher fruit could perhaps have enabled it find subtler, more elegant expression, particularly in the white peach notes typical of the terroir. The estate is certainly capable of achieving greater fragrance and the Bertinoro area, with its chalky soil and dry breezes off the nearby sea, has the potential for producing enchantingly full but still refreshing wines. The admirable current Sangiovese is taut and vibrant, with lively fruit and a flavoursome palate.

Tenuta Bonzara

VIA SAN CHIERLO, 37A
40050 MONTE SAN PIETRO [BO]
TEL. 0516768324
www.bonzara.it

ANNUAL PRODUCTION	70,000 bottles
HECTARES UNDER VINE	16
VITICULTURE METHOD	Conventional

The grapes grown in the San Chierlo vineyards benefit from the altitude, between 350 and 450 metres, and the ensuing temperature swings. University professor and owner of the estate Francesco Lambertini has been drawing on the expertise of great winemaker Lorenzo Landi and skilled cellarmaster Mario Carboni for many years. Tenuta Bonzara's bottles clearly reflect their deep knowledge of the soil and the vineyard, and their skilled interpretation of the terroir. We were bowled over by the two flagship wines: Merlot Rocca di Bonacciara and Cabernet Sauvignon Bonzarone. The former displays a nose of peach and pencil lead and a full, well-structured palate whose carefully calibrated hardness gives it elegance and finesse. The sound, clean Bonzarone has a generous, lingering palate flaunting nicely balanced softness and richness, without excessive alcohol or tannins, which earned it Three Glasses. Sauvignon Le Carrate is also very convincing, with aromas of sage and tomato and a fresh, well-crafted palate with hints of grapefruit, as is the slightly aromatic Pignoletto Vigna Antica, characterized by good acidity and juicy citrus sensations.

● Sangiovese di Romagna Sup. '07	♟♟	4*
● Sangiovese di Romagna Sup. Ris. '05	♟♟	4*
○ Albana di Romagna Passito '05	♟♟	4
○ Albana di Romagna Passito '04	♟♟	4
○ Albana di Romagna Passito '03	♟♟	4
● Sangiovese di Romagna Sup. Ris. '04	♟♟	4
● Sangiovese di Romagna Sup. Ris. '03	♟♟	4

● C. B. Cabernet Sauvignon Bonzarone '05	♟♟♟	5
● C. B. Merlot Rocca di Bonacciara '05	♟♟	5
● C. B. Cabernet Sauvignon Rosso del Borgo '06	♟♟	4*
○ C. B. Pignoletto Cl. Vigna Antica '07	♟♟	4*
○ C. B. Sauvignon Sup. Le Carrate '07	♟♟	4*
● C. B. Merlot Rosso del Poggio '06	♟	4
○ C. B. Pignoletto Frizzante '07	♟	3
○ Monte Severo '06		4
● C. B. Cabernet Sauvignon Bonzarone '97	♟♟♟	5
● C. B. Cabernet Sauvignon Bonzarone '96	♟♟♟	5
● C. B. Cabernet Sauvignon Bonzarone '04	♟♟	5

Tenuta Ca' Lunga

FRAZ. SELVA
VIA CA' LUNGA BUORE, 5
40026 IMOLA [BO]
TEL. 0542609257
www.calunga.net

ANNUAL PRODUCTION	100,000 bottles
HECTARES UNDER VINE	10.5
VITICULTURE METHOD	Conventional

This winery is clear proof of the satisfaction that can be reaped by working the Imola hillsides and exploiting their many resources. Until a few years ago, before the explosion of initiatives and dozens of interesting new estates, these hills were considered a secondary area for Romagna's wine production. It is due to the commitment and efforts of businessmen such as Paolo Cassetta that we now have proof that this was mere prejudice. The excellent results are often achieved using the area's native grape varieties, although there are of course exceptions. Elisir is the product of the recent but successful invasion of the hills by cabernet sauvignon. It offers elegant simplicity, accompanied by generous ripe fruit, which is further enhanced by sweet, silky tannins. The fresh, fruity, highly drinkable Mistero is a traditional Sangiovese Superiore, while Diadema is a white blended from chardonnay and sauvignon that shows perfect balance, astonishing freshness and an unexpected tang.

Calonga

LOC. CASTIGLIONE
VIA CASTEL LEONE, 8
47100 FORLÌ
TEL. 0543753044
www.calonga.it

ANNUAL PRODUCTION	30,000 bottles
HECTARES UNDER VINE	8
VITICULTURE METHOD	Conventional

Maurizio Baravelli's rare sensitivity allows him to tend his grapes with finesse in a consistently hands-on style, using complex procedures. This gives him the opportunity to bring out all the expression of his great terroir in his wines, which always faithfully reflect its distinctive character. Maurizio works alongside his wife Monica and their three children. The unique soil of their vineyards is composed of a layer of molasse sand that rises out of a bed of clay and gives these cellarable wines a magical balance of weight and elegance, accompanied by freshness. Michelangiolo, one of the best Sangiovese di Romagnas, is the product of this synergy between man and soil and took our Three Glass award for the third year running. The '05 version has successfully handled the challenge of a complicated vintage. While apparently lighter, the wine is still very deep, with attractive sound, full, velvety fruit and a generous yet fresh palate displaying a sumptuous tannic weave. Michelangiolo is a pure Sangiovese that demonstrates how, when treated sensitively, this grape is able to express the differences in soil and climate, faithfully conveying its terroir.

○ Colli d'Imola Bianco Sup. Diadema '07	♀♀ 4*
● Colli d'Imola Cabernet Sauvignon Elisir '07	♀♀ 4*
● Sangiovese di Romagna Sup. Mistero '06	♀♀ 4*
○ Colli d'Imola Bianco Euforia '07	♀ 3
● Colli d'Imola Sangiovese Incantesimo '07	♀ 3
● Colli d'Imola Cabernet Sauvignon Imperius Ris. '04	♀♀ 5
● Colli d'Imola Sangiovese Regale Ris. '04	♀♀ 5
● Colli d'Imola Sangiovese Incantesimo '06	♀♀ 3
● Sangiovese di Romagna Sup. Mistero '05	♀♀ 4

● Sangiovese di Romagna Sup. Michelangiolo Ris. '05	♀♀♀ 5
● Ordelaffo Sangiovese '06	♀♀ 3*
○ Albana di Romagna Zenaide '07	♀ 3
● Sangiovese di Romagna Sup. Michelangiolo Ris. '04	♀♀♀ 5
● Sangiovese di Romagna Sup. Michelangiolo Ris. '03	♀♀♀ 5
● Sangiovese di Romagna Sup. Michelangiolo Ris. '01	♀♀ 5
● Castellione Cabernet Sauvignon '03	♀♀ 6
● Castellione Cabernet Sauvignon '01	♀♀ 6
● Castellione Cabernet Sauvignon '00	♀♀ 6

Cardinali

POD. MONTEPASCOLO
29014 CASTELL'ARQUATO [PC]
TEL. 0523803502
www.cardinalidoc.it

ANNUAL PRODUCTION	30,000 bottles
HECTARES UNDER VINE	8
VITICULTURE METHOD	Conventional

Laura and Alberto Cardinali have been competently and judiciously running the family estate, founded by their parents in 1973, since 1996. Alberto handles the technical side and is quieter, while Laura, who deals with the business aspects, is more outgoing. Their different personalities complement each other in a serious, reliable enterprise that gives particular resonance to Gutturnio, which shows structured and complex on the Montepascolo hill. The estate was one of the first to believe in the potential of still Monterosso. This year's Solata, from mainly malvasia and sauvignon, is complex with a savoury mineral palate and a confident finish. Let's take a look at the Gutturnios now. We were most impressed by Nicchio, which has lively sweet fruit aromas with floral hints and a big, dynamic, juicy palate exhibiting good potency and pleasant contrasts. Riserva Torquato opens with notes of spice and more austere fruit, without excessive oak. Nicely full and rounded on the palate, its weight is kept in check by well-calibrated, balanced tannins, while the long finish reveals notes of balsam.

Carra di Casatico

LOC. CASATICO
VIA LA NAVE, 10B
43013 LANGHIRANO [PR]
TEL. 0521863510
www.carradicasatico.com

ANNUAL PRODUCTION	100,000 bottles
HECTARES UNDER VINE	17
VITICULTURE METHOD	Conventional

Our annual tastings merely confirm what Bonfiglio Carra already knows. Although he's a relative newcomer to wine production, he has gone about his work with dedication and is now able to make attractive versions of the traditional wines of the Parma hills. His secrets are fine grapes, appropriate cellar technology, scrupulous attention to cellar hygiene and, above all, the aim of making wines as simply and coherently as possible. Once again his efforts have been rewarded by the excellent performance of Acuto, which is undoubtedly the area's best sparkler from malvasia and shows well typed, full and elegant with a magnificent mousse. The fragrant classic method Cinque Torre, from chardonnay and pinot nero, is equally good, with fresh citrus notes on the long finish. Arcòl '05, from croatina, merlot and pinot nero, is supple and incisive. We also tried the richly fruity '04 vintage, available in magnums only, which is dignified and austere. The entire list of semi-sparkling wines is very well made and easy drinking, with the fragrant Malvasia, the citrus Malvasia & Moscato and the juicy Lambrusco Torcularia leading the pack.

● C. P. Gutturnio Cl. Nicchio '07	♆♆ 4*
● C. P. Gutturnio Cl. Torquato Ris. '05	♆♆ 5
○ C. P. Monterosso Val d'Arda Solata '07	♆♆ 4*
○ Cardinali Brut M. Cl. '04	♆ 5
● C. P. Gutturnio Cl. Nicchio '06	♆♆ 4*
● C. P. Gutturnio Cl. Nicchio '05	♆♆ 4*
● C. P. Gutturnio Cl. Torquato Ris. '04	♆♆ 5
● C. P. Gutturnio Cl. Torquato Ris. '03	♆♆ 5

● Arcòl '06	♆♆ 4
● Arcòl Magnum '04	♆♆ 6
○ Cinque Torri Brut M.Cl. '06	♆♆ 5
○ Colli di Parma Malvasia Acuto Extra Dry '07	♆♆ 4*
○ Brut Camerapicta '01	♆ 5
○ Colli di Parma Malvasia Frizzante '07	♆ 3
○ Colli di Parma Sauvignon Frizzante '07	♆ 3
○ Eden Passito '06	♆ 5
○ Malvasia & Moscato Frizzante Dolce '07	♆ 3
● Torcularia Rosso '07	♆ 3
● Arcòl '05	♆♆ 4
● Arcòl '04	♆♆ 4

Casetto dei Mandorli

LOC. PREDAPPIO ALTA
VIA UMBERTO I, 21
47010 PREDAPPIO [FC]
TEL. 0543922361
www.vini-nicolucci.it

ANNUAL PRODUCTION	100,000 bottles
HECTARES UNDER VINE	12
VITICULTURE METHOD	Conventional

The experience of three generations may be an extraordinary advantage, but each has to adapting production to contemporary wine tastes. In order to make wine classic, you have to create a fine balance that interprets the differences naturally and adapts the idiom without touching the content. Alessandro Nicolucci has achieved this feat, preserving the essence of an authentic, well-defined style of Sangiovese while stripping away the obsolete traditional aspects, namely its unnecessary hardness, imprecision and roughness. He has been assisted by a great terroir for the variety: Predappio Alta, long considered special in Romagna and already renowned for its closely planted bush vines and the quality of its wine in the 19th century. This year Riserva di Sangiovese Vigna del Generale won our top honour for the first time, consecrating the estate as a benchmark with a style that doesn't distort Sangiovese but instead interprets it instead with freshness, elegance and taut, complex minerality. The current Sangiovese Tre Rocche is also classy, displaying a clean, fresh nose with floral hints and notes of white peach, and a full, complex, supple palate.

Castelluccio

LOC. POGGIOLO
VIA TRAMONTO, 15
47015 MODIGLIANA [FC]
TEL. 0546942486
www.ronchidicastelluccio.it

ANNUAL PRODUCTION	90,000 bottles
HECTARES UNDER VINE	14
VITICULTURE METHOD	Conventional

This renowned estate, which managed to achieve a superlative interpretation of Veronelli's concept of vineyard selection – known locally as "Ronco" – in which the terroir dominates the wine, has chosen a new direction for its products. Stripped of their agile complexity, multi-layered aromas and slow, almost austere development on the palate, today's wines are a response to more international tastes, offering prominent toastiness, where the fruit struggles to emerge and achieve sufficient balance. Ronco delle Ginestre is the best of this year's wines. Notwithstanding its oaky nose, it has flesh and substance, a certain elegance and a dynamic palate with a finish dried by a slight over-abundance of extract. Le More 2007, the estate's simplest Sangiovese, performed very well, recovering Castelluccio's hallmark traits and expressing itself with great poise. Although a touch hard, its elegant palate displays an admirably harmonious balance of tannins and freshness. Ronco del Re 2006, from sauvignon blanc fermented in oak, has an elegant nose and a deep, creamy, very zesty palate, driven by freshness and a pleasant varietal note that dominates the finish.

● Sangiovese di Romagna V. del Generale Ris. '05	¶¶¶ 5
● Nero di Predappio '05	¶¶ 5
● Sangiovese di Romagna Sup. Tre Rocche '07	¶¶ 4*
● Sangiovese di Romagna Sup. I Mandorli '07	¶ 3
● Sangiovese di Romagna V. del Generale Ris. '04	♀♀ 5
● Sangiovese di Romagna V. del Generale Ris. '01	♀♀ 5
● Sangiovese di Romagna V. del Generale Ris. '00	♀♀ 5
● Nero di Predappio '04	♀♀ 5
● Nero di Predappio '03	♀♀ 5

○ Ronco del Re '06	¶¶ 6
● Ronco delle Ginestre '05	¶¶ 6
● Sangiovese di Romagna Le More '07	¶¶ 4*
○ Lunaria '07	¶ 4
● Massicone '05	¶ 5
● Ronco dei Ciliegi '05	¶ 5
● Massicone '01	♀♀♀ 6
● Ronco dei Ciliegi '02	♀♀♀ 5
● Ronco dei Ciliegi '00	♀♀♀ 5
● Ronco delle Ginestre '90	♀♀♀ 6
● Ronco delle Ginestre '04	♀♀ 6
● Massicone '04	♀♀ 6
● Ronco dei Ciliegi '04	♀♀ 5
○ Ronco del Re '05	♀♀ 6

Cavicchioli U. & Figli

VIA CANALETTO, 52
41030 SAN PROSPERO [MO]
TEL. 059812411
www.cavicchioli.it

ANNUAL PRODUCTION	18,000,000 bottles
HECTARES UNDER VINE	150
VITICULTURE METHOD	Conventional

The wines of this long-standing Emilia estate are increasingly convincing. Cavicchioli has always been a respected name in the Lambrusco world and the reputation is well deserved, although the estate's star had been waning slightly in recent years. Now, however, it has returned to its former splendour. Much of the credit for this revival goes to Sandro Cavicchioli, who runs his winery with increasing confidence. We'd like to congratulate him on the splendid performance of Vigna del Cristo, a Lambrusco di Sorbara that displays all the charms of its type. Pink in hue, with delicate notes of fruit and flowers on the nose, it is brilliant, taut, broad and caressing on the palate. We also congratulate Sandro for his splendid idea of producing a classic method sparkler from lambrusco sorbara grapes. Rosé del Cristo '04 is even more convincing than the first release, displaying a complex, supple style that is sharp but also firm and satisfying. We were also impressed by several of the wines of the Tre Medaglie range, sold at competitive prices in supermarkets.

Cantine Ceci

VIA PROVINCIALE, 99
43030 TORRILE [PR]
TEL. 0521810252
www.lambrusco.it

ANNUAL PRODUCTION	800,000 bottles
HECTARES UNDER VINE	20
VITICULTURE METHOD	Conventional

The seemingly contradictory concepts of consistency and a desire to astound sum up the developments of recent years at this large, and increasingly influential, winery in the area that stretches north of Parma to the Po. The estate's benchmark wine is Otello NerodiLambrusco, which confirms itself as one of the region's best Lambruscos. The nose is very sound and clean, bursting with blackberry, blueberry and cherry, while the soft, austere palate is long and convincing, although perhaps a touch too sweet on the finish. Equally high quality comes from the Extra Dry Tre di Terre Verdiane, a unique sparkler from malvasia, sauvignon and pinot nero fermented off the skins, which has a broad nose of fresh fruit and a soft, attractively nuanced palate. The latest successful fruits of the fertile, freewheeling mind of Alessandro Ceci, who seems to have enormous fun researching and inventing new wines, are Demi Sec 13, a very fruity and moderately sweet Fortana, and Extra Dry Rosé Otello '07, which is fresh and clean on the nose and well behaved on the palate. Brut Desdemona, from malvasia, is a little less convincing.

● Lambrusco di Sorbara V. del Cristo '07	▼▼ 4*
⊙ Rosé del Cristo Spumante '04	▼▼ 6
● Lambrusco di Sorbara Contessa Matilde '07	▼▼ 3*
● Lambrusco di Sorbara Tre Medaglie	▼▼ 3*
● Lambrusco Grasparossa di Castelvetro Amabile Tre Medaglie	▼▼ 3*
● Malbo Gentile	▼▼ 3*
○ Bianco della Contessa	▼ 3
● Lambrusco Grasparossa di Castelvetro Col Sassoso '07	▼ 4
● Lambrusco Grasparossa di Castelvetro Tre Medaglie	▼ 3
⊙ Rosé del Cristo Spumante '03	▼▼ 6

○ Extra Dry Tre di Terre Verdiane	▼▼ 4
● Lambrusco Terre Verdiane '07	▼▼ 3*
● Otello NerodiLambrusco '07	▼▼ 4
○ Colli di Parma Malvasia Frizzante Otello '07	▼ 4
● Colli di Parma Rosso Arturo's '06	▼ 4
● Demi Sec 13 Terre Verdiane	▼ 4
⊙ Extra Dry Rosé Otello '07	▼ 4
● Otello Lambrusco Et. Nera '07	▼ 3
○ Brut Desdemona '07	4

Celli

via Carducci, 5
47032 Bertinoro [FC]
tel. 0543445183
www.celli-vini.com

ANNUAL PRODUCTION 300,000 bottles
HECTARES UNDER VINE 29
VITICULTURE METHOD Conventional

After last year's hesitation, we are relieved to see quickly how this historic Bertinoro estate has recovered, with a decidedly convincing list of wines. Despite their youth, the owners Mauro Sirri and Roberto Casadei – whose families are locally known by the nicknames Bron and Rusèval – are heirs to a long winemaking tradition and have wasted no time getting back on the right track. Evidence of this can be seen in their distinctly unusual Albana di Romagna I Croppi, which boasts a dark gold hue, slightly rustic floral nose and a fresh, juicy palate with a touch of extract on the finish. In short, it perfectly combines the traditional traits of the grape with an attractive modern version of the wine. Bron & Rusèval Chardonnay '07 is outstanding. The usually assertive oak has given way to an elegant fresh fruit style and good presence on the palate, which is perked up by a pleasant citrus finish. However, the highest quality peak on the list was scaled by the sangiovese and cabernet Bron & Rusèval, which is perfectly balanced and extremely drinkable. It's neither big nor powerful but charms with its fragrant rich fruit and impeccable palate.

● Bron & Rusèval Sangiovese-Cabernet '06	🍷🍷	5
○ Albana di Romagna Secco I Croppi '07	🍷🍷	3*
○ Bron & Rusèval Chardonnay '07	🍷🍷	4*
○ Albana di Romagna Passito Solara '05	🍷	5
○ Romagna Albana Spumante La Talandina	🍷	3
○ Pagadebit di Romagna Campi di Fratta '07	🍷	3
● Sangiovese di Romagna Sup. Le Grillaie '07	🍷	3
● Sangiovese di Romagna Sup. Le Grillaie Ris. '05	🍷	3

Umberto Cesari

via Stanzano, 1120
40050 Castel San Pietro Terme [BO]
tel. 051941896
www.umbertocesari.it

ANNUAL PRODUCTION 2,000,000 bottles
HECTARES UNDER VINE 128
VITICULTURE METHOD Conventional

This estate is owned by Umberto Cesari, who has played a leading role in Romagna winemaking for over 40 years. Umberto is now preparing to hand over to his son Gianmaria, who is increasingly focused on non-domestic markets, particularly North America, and is investing much time and effort in this direction. The two Moma wines are strategic for this purpose, as they are modern with well-defined personality, like Umberto himself. Moma Bianco is a trebbiano and chardonnay blend with a carefully calibrated hint of sauvignon. It's soft, with enviable freshness and a fine zesty finish. Moma Rosso, from cabernet, sangiovese and merlot, is convincing, showing dense and juicy with perfect balance. Among the blends of sangiovese and international varieties, pride of place goes to Liano, which strolled into our finals with its velvety fruit and well-finished structure, which make for very pleasant drinking. Sangiovese Tauleto is very firm and dense, although the tannins are still hard, if juicy. Sangiovese Laurento, with concentrated fruit, a light palate and crisp acidity, and the even more typical Riserva, are both true to the Romagna tradition.

● Liano '05	🍷🍷	5
● Tauleto Sangiovese '04	🍷🍷	6
● Moma Rosso '06	🍷🍷	4*
● Sangiovese di Romagna Laurento Ris. '05	🍷🍷	4*
● Sangiovese di Romagna Ris. '05	🍷🍷	4*
○ Albana di Romagna Passito Colle del Re '04	🍷🍷	5
○ Moma Bianco '07	🍷🍷	4*
● Tauleto Sangiovese '01	♡♡	6
● Tauleto Sangiovese '00	♡♡	6
● Liano '02	♡♡	5
● Liano '03	♡♡	5

Chiarli 1860

VIA DANIELE MANIN, 15
41100 MODENA
TEL. 0593163311
www.chiarli.it

Floriano Cinti

FRAZ. SAN LORENZO
VIA GAMBERI, 48
40037 SASSO MARCONI [BO]
TEL. 0516751646
www.collibolognesi.com

ANNUAL PRODUCTION   24,000,000 bottles
HECTARES UNDER VINE   110
VITICULTURE METHOD   Conventional

ANNUAL PRODUCTION   95,000 bottles
HECTARES UNDER VINE   17.5
VITICULTURE METHOD   Natural

Combining annual production of millions of bottles with almost artisanal attention to the huge quantities of grapes grown on the various family estates is a distinctive feature of this historic Modena winery. The two-pronged strategy is the brain-child of Anselmo Chiarli, who has invested heavily in the new Castelvetro cellar that produces the top wines, which are more convincing than ever this year. Consequently, it comes as no surprise that Vecchia Modena Premium made it through to our finals. This elegant Lambrusco di Sorbara flaunts a nose of fresh flowers and red fruit, and a rich soft palate displaying the distinctive penetrating acidity of the grape. Nivola Lambrusco Scuro is back with impressive richness and fruit preceding an appealing full, juicy palate. Chiarli also produces an interesting range of sparklers, topped by Brut Rosé and Pignoletto Brut Modén. The former offers satisfying notes of cherry and currants on a simple but convincing profile, while the latter is good evidence of pignoletto's suitability for bottle fermentation, showing a floral nose and a soft, caressing palate that reprises aromatic herbs.

This year, the Cinti winery celebrates its 30th anniversary. In 1978, Floriano and a group of friends decided to buy an estate at Sasso Marconi, a few kilometres from Bologna. Their intention was to establish an agricultural co-operative active in several sectors: livestock, fruit and vegetable crops and vineyards. It was the latter that fired the enthusiasm of Floriano, perhaps because of a family tradition, for his father and uncles were growers. In 1992, he had the opportunity to continue the experience as a one-man business and over the following years his perseverance, energy, intelligence and investments allowed him to become one of the most interesting producers in the Colli Bolognesi. The estate-grown grapes are vinified in the cellar under the supervision of expert oenologist Giovanni Fraulini. Pignoletto Sassobacco is excellent as usual, showing concentrated, flavoursome and packed with juicy fruit and elegant mineral notes, while Pignoletto Frizzante is simply charming. Cabernet Sauvignon Sassobacco and Merlot Sassobacco are both convincing but the real surprise this year is a very fruity new Barbera, which is coherent and supple.

● Lambrusco di Sorbara Vecchia Modena Premium MH '07		▼▼ 4*
● Nivola Lambrusco Scuro		▼▼ 3*
● Lambrusco di Sorbara del Fondatore '06		▼▼ 4
● Lambrusco Grasparossa di Castelvetro Vign. Enrico Cialdini '07		▼▼ 4
○ Pignoletto Brut Modén		▼▼ 4
⊙ Rosé Brut		▼▼ 4
● Lambrusco Grasparossa di Castelvetro Podere Franchina		▼ 3
● Lambrusco Grasparossa di Castelvetro Pruno Nero		▼ 3
● Lambrusco Grasparossa di Castelvetro Villa Cialdini '07		▼ 4
○ Pignoletto Extra Dry Cletò		▼ 4
● Lambrusco di Sorbara Centenario '07		3

○ C. B. Pignoletto Cl. Sassobacco '07		▼▼ 4*
○ C. B. Chardonnay '07		▼▼ 3*
○ C. B. Pinot Bianco '07		▼▼ 3*
● C. B. Barbera '06		▼▼ 4
● C. B. Cabernet Sauvignon '06		▼▼ 4
● C. B. Cabernet Sauvignon Sassobacco '05		▼▼ 4
● C. B. Merlot Sassobacco '06		▼▼ 4
● C. B. Merlot '07		▼ 4
● Rubrum Cor Laetificans '06		▼ 6
○ C. B. Pignoletto Frizzante '07		▼ 3
○ C. B. Sauvignon '07		▼ 3
○ C. B. Pignoletto Cl. Sassobacco '06		♈♈ 4
● C. B. Merlot Sassobacco '05		♈♈ 4

Consorzio Produttori di Brisighella

FRAZ. FOGNANO
VIA CAMPIUME, 6
48010 BRISIGHELLA [RA]
TEL. 054680112
www.campiume.it

ANNUAL PRODUCTION	25,000 bottles
HECTARES UNDER VINE	17
VITICULTURE METHOD	Natural

This small co-operative winery is formed by three separate producers: Andrea Bragagni, who tends three hectares of vineyards close to Fognano; Paolo Babini of Vigne dei Boschi, who has a few hectares near Pontenono in Valle del Lamone; and Filippo Manetti of Vigne di San Lorenzo whose vineyards are situated in Campiume. The three are environmentally aware and decided to venture into organic production several years ago, respecting the qualities and flaws of the various vintages. They are among the few Romagna producers to have followed this path but are still grappling with various problems that diminish the potential of a process that is hard to manage but offers great opportunities. We reckon the trio could initiate a cycle, if they closed their phase of experimentation, on varieties as well as farming techniques. The most interesting wines are Paolo Babini's Albana Monteré, which develops extraordinary complexity starting from its maceration on the skins, Filippo Manetti's Fieni, which could possibly express even greater elegance, and Manetti's Campaglione, a dynamic, uncomplicatedly fragrant Sangiovese.

O Albana di Romagna Monteré '04	♼♼	4
● Campaglione Sangiovese '06	♼♼	4*
● Fieni '05	♼♼	6
● Borgo Stignani '05	♼	4
● Rosso per Te '05	♼	5
● Campiume '04	♼♼	5
● San Lorenzo '05	♼♼	5
● San Lorenzo '04	♼♼	5
● Settepievi '05	♼♼	5
● Settepievi '03	♼♼	5
O Rigogolo '05	♼	4

Leone Conti

LOC. SANTA LUCIA
VIA POZZO, 1
48018 FAENZA [RA]
TEL. 0546642149
www.leoneconti.it

ANNUAL PRODUCTION	70,000 bottles
HECTARES UNDER VINE	17
VITICULTURE METHOD	Conventional

Leone Conti's original approach to wine doesn't stop him being one of the rare producers who calmly accept the verdict of their terroir. His wines are never contrived and Conti seeks to interpret them with a light hand, capturing the magic moment of each individual situation. His production shows impressive consistency and year after year his wines are a benchmark for the whole of Romagna. The top performance came from an extraordinary dessert wine that combines incredible complexity with a fresh, stylish palate: Tu Chiamale se Vuoi Emozioni Lato B, from dried sauvignon blanc grapes. The nose shows complex and layered, with elegant notes of pear, candied peel, pineapple, spring flowers and fresh herbs. It is accompanied by an opulent palate with good acidity, which shifts the accent towards suppleness and freshness. Sangiovese Le Betulle is also excellent, showing fresh, well calibrated, complex and dynamic. Albana Progetto 1 is clean with a nicely developed palate, where the variety's tannins taper off elegantly and discreetly in the finish, where it reveals its dual personality as a white wine with the tannins of a red.

O Tu Chiamale se Vuoi Emozioni Lato B '06	♼	7
O Albana di Romagna Passito Nontiscordardime '06	♼♼	6
O Albana di Romagna Secco Progetto 1 '07	♼♼	4*
● Arcolaio '06	♼♼	5
● Sangiovese di Romagna Sup. Le Betulle '06	♼♼	4*
● Sangiovese di Romagna '07	♼	3
O Trebbiano di Romagna '07		3
O Albana di Romagna Secco Progetto 1 '06	♼♼	4
O Albana di Romagna Secco Progetto 2 '06	♼♼	4
O Vino da Uve Stramature Oro et Laboro	♼♼	5
● Arcolaio '04	♼♼	5
● Rossonero '06	♼♼	5

Corte Manzini

LOC. CÀ DI SOLA
VIA MODENA, 131/3
41014 CASTELVETRO DI MODENA [MO]
TEL. 059702658
www.cortemanzini.it

ANNUAL PRODUCTION	80,000 bottles
HECTARES UNDER VINE	10
VITICULTURE METHOD	Natural

The fact that this year none of the Manzini family's Lambruscos made it through to our finals as usual should not be seen as the end of the estate's spectacular rise but rather as the consequence of a summer that was not kind to anyone in Castelvetro in 2007. Obviously, this setback has had greater effects on small wineries like this one, although the family's great efforts have nonetheless allowed a series of impressive results. The style, characterized by clean fruit and an exceptionally fragrant palate, has not changed, although the wines lack a little of the fullness on the palate that formerly distinguished them. Acino is undoubtedly the most convincing Lambrusco Grasparossa, with attractive notes of cherry and pear on the nose and very soft, fruity flesh. Grasparossa Secco is even more fragrant and fruity, while the Amabile version is impressive and well balanced. Finally, Bolla Rossa is dense and austere, offering one of the best fusions of traditional-style Lambrusco with a more innovative modern approach.

Drei Donà Tenuta La Palazza

LOC. MASSA DI VECCHIAZZANO
VIA DEL TESORO, 23
47100 FORLÌ
TEL. 0543769371
www.dreidona.it

ANNUAL PRODUCTION	120,000 bottles
HECTARES UNDER VINE	30
VITICULTURE METHOD	Natural

Enrico Drei Donà has taken over the helm of this historic estate founded by his father Claudio in the days when courage and vision were needed to run a quality winery in Romagna. Over the years, the estate has maintained a consistent style of austere, deep wines and its Sangiovese proves that freshness and depth can also be features of powerful wines. The estate's awareness of quality is underscored by the older vintages of the leading wines on the list, which now features Pruno Riserva 10 Anni, a patiently aged barrique selection. On the nose it is still fresh with notes of balsam, whereas the palate is dense and creamy. However, the most impressive offering is Pruno 2005. Its attractively sound nose is austere and reflects its variety very faithfully, with the notes of white peach that have always been a feature of the wine when young. On the palate, it is firm, dignified, dynamic and gutsy, with plenty of extract and faint whiffs of oak. Tornese '06 also performed well, recovering its freshness and drive after several vintages somewhat below par. It's deep, dense and full flavoured, with good fruit and fragrance.

● Lambrusco Grasparossa di Castelvetro Amabile '07	♟♟ 3*
● Lambrusco Grasparossa di Castelvetro L'Acino '07	♟♟ 4*
● Lambrusco Grasparossa di Castelvetro '07	♟♟ 4*
● Lambrusco Grasparossa di Castelvetro Bolla Rossa '07	♟♟ 3*
⊙ Brut Rosé Bollicine '07	♟ 4
O Diamante Brut	♟ 4
⊙ Lambrusco Grasparossa di Castelvetro Fior di Lambrusco '07	♟ 3
O Dolce Incanto Malvasia '07	3

O Il Tornese Chardonnay '06	♟♟ 5
● Sangiovese di Romagna Sup. Pruno Ris. '05	♟♟ 5
● Magnificat Cabernet Sauvignon '05	♟♟ 5
● Sangiovese di Romagna Sup. Pruno 10 Anni Ris. '97	♟♟ 6
● Notturno Sangiovese '06	♟ 3
● Magnificat Cabernet Sauvignon '94	♟♟♟ 6
● Sangiovese di Romagna Sup. Pruno Ris. '01	♟♟♟ 5
● Sangiovese di Romagna Sup. Pruno Ris. '00	♟♟♟ 5
● Sangiovese di Romagna Sup. Pruno Ris. '04	♟♟ 5
● Graf Noir '01	♟♟ 8
● Graf Noir '00	♟♟ 8

Stefano Ferrucci

VIA CASOLANA, 3045/2
48014 CASTEL BOLOGNESE [RA]
TEL. 0546651068
www.stefanoferrucci.it

ANNUAL PRODUCTION	95,000 bottles
HECTARES UNDER VINE	16
VITICULTURE METHOD	Conventional

Ilaria Ferrucci, who took over the running of the family estate following the premature death of her father a couple of years ago, is dedicatedly carrying on the projects that he had envisaged for the estate. Although she continues her father's approach, without any revolutionary changes, her different eyes and new sensibilities have reshaped the style and identity of the estate's wines. Slight drying of the grapes – a technique experimented by Stefano and never abandoned – remains one of the hallmarks of Domus Caia, a fresh, nicely focused Sangiovese Riserva with beautifully intact aromas of morello cherry and a very pleasant palate of impressive balance and finesse. The two current Sangioveses are up to snuff. Centurione offers rich fruit and a refreshing, velvety, supple palate while the fruity Auriga is simpler and lighter. Albana Passito Domus Aurea '06 is as good as ever, its moderate sweetness balanced by just the right amount of acidity, which lengthens the attractive apricot jam finish.

●	Sangiovese di Romagna Sup. Domus Caia Ris. '05	♛♛ 6
○	Albana di Romagna Passito Domus Aurea '06	♛♛ 6
●	Sangiovese di Romagna Sup. Centurione '07	♛♛ 4*
●	Sangiovese di Romagna Auriga '07	♛ 3
○	Colli di Faenza Bianco Chiaro della Serra '07	♛ 3
○	Trebbiano di Romagna Mattinale '07	♛ 2
●	Sangiovese di Romagna Domus Caia Ris. '01	♛♛ 6
●	Sangiovese di Romagna Sup. Domus Caia Ris. '02	♛♛ 6
●	Sangiovese di Romagna Sup. Domus Caia Ris. '03	♛♛ 6
●	Sangiovese di Romagna Sup. Domus Caia Ris. '04	♛♛ 6

Paolo Francesconi

LOC. SARNA
VIA TULIERO, 154
48018 FAENZA [RA]
TEL. 054643213
pfrancesconi@racine.ra.it

ANNUAL PRODUCTION	15,000 bottles
HECTARES UNDER VINE	14
VITICULTURE METHOD	Certified organic

Paolo Francesconi has decided to produce his wines as naturally as possible, adopting organic farming methods and chemical-free vinification. It is a laborious path, which requires patience and years of experience, but in Paolo's case there is a further complication in the clay soil that intensifies structure and tannins, making it difficult to stick to the philosophy. Production has not yet reached the level of quality at which Paolo is aiming and while most of the wines display undoubted qualities, they still suffer from a few style wobbles. But we should remember that purchasers of these wines are buying into a production philosophy, and in this respect Paolo is extremely reliable. Impavido, a monovarietal Merlot, has always been one of the estate's best wines, with attractively austere fruit and a full palate. It's perhaps a little heavy on the tannins but follows through nicely. Sangiovese Riserva Le Iadi is also interesting, with plenty of body but a slightly mouth-drying finish. The current Sangiovese Limbecca is as reliable as ever, with lots of character, prominent tannins and a dynamically lean, close-knit palate.

●	Impavido Merlot '06	♛♛ 5
●	Sangiovese di Romagna Sup. Le Iadi Ris. '06	♛♛ 5
●	Sangiovese di Romagna Sup. Limbecca '07	♛♛ 4*
○	Albana di Romagna Passito Idillio '06	♛ 5
●	Colli di Faenza Rosso Miniato '06	♛ 4
●	D'Incanto Passito '07	♛ 5
●	Symposium Merlot '07	♛ 4
●	Impavido Merlot '04	♛♛ 5
●	Impavido Merlot '05	♛♛ 5
●	Sangiovese di Romagna Sup. Le Iadi Ris. '04	♛♛ 5
●	Sangiovese di Romagna Sup. Le Iadi Ris. '05	♛♛ 5
●	Sangiovese di Romagna Sup. Limbecca '06	♛♛ 4

Maria Letizia Gaggioli

VIA RAIBOLINI DETTO IL FRANCIA, 55
40069 ZOLA PREDOSA [BO]
TEL. 051753489
www.gaggiolivini.it

ANNUAL PRODUCTION	160,000 bottles
HECTARES UNDER VINE	24
VITICULTURE METHOD	Conventional

Again this year, the joint efforts of Maria Letizia Gaggioli, who owns the estate with her father Carlo, and expert oenologist Giovanni Fraulini have proved highly effective. The wines continue to be very pleasant, exceptionally well crafted and good value for money. The estate's lovely, carefully tended vineyards are located in the Colli Bolognesi, at an altitude between 150 and 300 metres above sea level. Although production is perhaps a little too diversified, with 15 different wines, the ones we tasted were all more than satisfactory. Good results were achieved by the whites, although the reds were perhaps a little under par. Two well-deserved Glasses went to Pignoletto Superiore for its full fruity nose of attractive pear perceptions that are echoed on the well-calibrated, juicy palate, and to Barbera Frizzante, characterized by fresh, fragrant fruit and appealing supporting acidity. We also liked Pignoletto Frizzante, with a creamy mousse and citrus finish, and the very fresh Pinot Bianco Crilò, which has sound fruit and distinct tanginess.

Gallegati

VIA ISONZO, 4
48018 FAENZA [RA]
TEL. 0546621149
www.aziendaagricolagallegati.it

ANNUAL PRODUCTION	15,000 bottles
HECTARES UNDER VINE	6
VITICULTURE METHOD	Natural

The Gallegati brothers' well-established estate makes authentic Sangiovese that shows the way for others growing the variety on the clay soils of the first band of hills around Faenza. For Cesare and Antonio, along with many others who farm on clay, the challenge for the future will be to balance the alcohol and powerful extract of the wines without losing finesse. This will be difficult but exciting and will set the standards for quality over the coming years in Romagna. Sangiovese Corallo Nero has a difficult nose, which is rather closed and a tad unfocused. But the palate is fresh and supported by an attractive swath of acidity through to a long finish, albeit with a slightly dry mouthfeel caused by rough, clenched tannins. Corallo Blu, a blend of equal amounts of cabernet sauvignon and merlot plus ten per cent sangiovese, has an austere, fruit-rich nose and a deep palate with plenty of texture and rigid, rather excessive tannins. It still has excellent substance, though. Albana Passito Regina di Cuori is impressive, packed with aromas of dried figs, apricots and dates, and unveils a convincingly fat palate.

● C. B. Barbera Frizzante '07	♟♟ 3*
○ C. B. Pignoletto Sup. '07	♟♟ 3*
○ C. B. Pignoletto Frizzante '07	♟ 3
○ C. B. Pinot Bianco Crilò '07	♟ 3
○ C. B. Sauvignon Sup. '07	♟ 3
● Bagazzana Rosso '07	♟ 4
○ Brut Carlèt	3
● C. B. Cabernet Sauvignon Il Francia Rosso Ris. '03	♟♟ 4
● C. B. Cabernet Sauvignon Il Francia Rosso Ris. '04	♟♟ 4

○ Albana di Romagna Passito Regina di Cuori '04	♟♟ 5
● Colli di Faenza Rosso Corallo Blu Ris. '05	♟♟ 5
● Sangiovese di Romagna Sup. Corallo Nero Ris. '05	♟♟ 5
○ Albana di Romagna Passito Regina di Cuori '03	♟♟ 5
● Sangiovese di Romagna Sup. Corallo Nero Ris. '04	♟♟ 5

Gradizzolo

VIA INVERNATA, 2
40050 MONTEVEGLIO [BO]
TEL. 051830265
www.gradizzolo.it

ANNUAL PRODUCTION	30,000 bottles
HECTARES UNDER VINE	5
VITICULTURE METHOD	Conventional

Until now, Antonio Ognibene has been known as one of the leading connoisseurs and producers of Barbera in the entire Colli Bolognesi. Although he maintains that status, he has recently widened his outlook with the addition of negrettino, an old grape variety that has almost disappeared from the area. He planted it in his vineyards a few years ago and has just bottled for the first time. The estate's interpretation of this wine is in keeping with the style that distinguishes its other products: dynamic extract, a quest for weight and confident use of oak for ageing. This Negrettino seems to have withstood the impact of the wood, revealing attractive fruity pulp that is still a slightly masked by the sweet vanilla notes. On the palate it is slightly lightweight but has mellow, close-knit tannins. Our pick of the Barberas was Bricco dell'Invernata, whose attractive clean-cut aromas of red fruit are echoed on the palate, which finishes a touch dry. Garò, on the other hand, shows clenched tannins and a hard palate that quashes the fruit, although its potential may emerge with further ageing.

Isola

FRAZ. MONGIORGIO
VIA G. BERNARDI, 3
40050 MONTE SAN PIETRO [BO]
TEL. 0516768428
isola1898@interfree.it

ANNUAL PRODUCTION	60,000 bottles
HECTARES UNDER VINE	12.5
VITICULTURE METHOD	Natural

The Franceschinis, who run this estate, appear to live a tranquil farming life, marked by the rhythms of the seasons and with little that is new going on. But beneath the enviably peaceful surface lurks insatiable curiosity and the wish to experiment that inspires both young Gianluca and his father Marco. Careful not to lose the heritage of country lore they have acquired over the years, the pair are also receptive to new methods for natural vineyard management and sustainability. Their wine list also displays several new features, including the debut of a first-rate monovarietal Merlot, with full fruit and a stylish palate. Cabernet Monte Gorgii is as good as ever, giving attractive chewy fruit that's perfectly ripe and crisp, and a velvety, weighty, very Mediterranean palate. While Chardonnay Monte Gorgii '07 is expected to require longer ageing than usual, Brut Essè Spumante, from pignoletto, is ready to drink and very good. Produced with the assistance of Maurizio Vallona, this elegant, juicy wine has you reaching for the corkscrew.

● C. B. Barbera Bricco dell'Invernata '06	▼▼ 3*
● Naigar Tén Negrettino '06	▼▼ 4
● C. B. Barbera Garò Ris. '05	▼ 4
● Rovo Nero Cabernet '06	▼ 4
○ Pignoletto Spumante Pign'Oro	▼ 3
● C. B. Barbera Bricco dell'Invernata '04	▼▼ 3
● C. B. Barbera Bricco dell'Invernata '03	▼▼ 3
● C. B. Barbera Garò Ris. '04	▼▼ 4
● C. B. Barbera Garò Ris. '03	▼▼ 4
● C. B. Merlot Calastrino '03	▼▼ 4
● Calastrino Merlot '05	▼▼ 4

● C. B. Cabernet Sauvignon Monte Gorgii '06	▼▼ 4
● C. B. Merlot '07	▼▼ 3*
○ Essè Brut Spumante '07	▼▼ 4
○ C. B. Chardonnay '07	▼ 3
○ C. B. Pignoletto Frizzante '07	▼ 3
○ C. B. Pignoletto Sup. '07	▼ 3
● C. B. Cabernet Sauvignon '07	▼ 3
● C. B. Barbera Monte Gorgii '05	▼▼ 3
● C. B. Cabernet Sauvignon Monte Gorgii '05	▼▼ 4
● C. B. Cabernet Sauvignon Monte Gorgii '04	▼▼ 4

Luretta

LOC. CASTELLO DI MOMELIANO
29010 GAZZOLA [PC]
TEL. 0523971070
www.luretta.com

ANNUAL PRODUCTION	250,000 bottles
HECTARES UNDER VINE	43
VITICULTURE METHOD	Certified organic

Over the years, this estate has often shaken the conventions of the quiet Piacenza winemaking scene, tracing alternative paths with wines of varying success but always with the clear intention of offering a less banal interpretation of the terroir. The aromatic Malvasia Boccadirosa displays its usual captivating style, with a fruity nose and soft texture sustained by good acidity. Le Rane, a sweet Malvasia, has aromas of apples and pears, honey and hints of balsam, combined with moderately deep structure. Sauvignon Cardass is this year's surprise and strolled into our finals. It comes from a selection of grapes from a vineyard with calcareous-marl soil, giving a nose of concentrated varietal aromas, underscored by an elegant, racy palate with great tanginess and length. I Nani e Le Ballerine is a sharper, simpler Sauvignon, offering less substance and a lighter palate. The estate presented two versions of its Pantera, from barbera, bonarda and cabernet. The fruity, supple '06 has pleasantly clear fruit and drinkability while the Riserva '03 has a ripe, rounded palate with a long, well-coordinated finish.

Gaetano Lusenti

LOC. CASE PICCIONI, 57
29010 ZIANO PIACENTINO [PC]
TEL. 0523868479
www.lusentivini.it

ANNUAL PRODUCTION	100,000 bottles
HECTARES UNDER VINE	17
VITICULTURE METHOD	Conventional

Lodovica Lusenti and her husband Giuseppe Ferri are great believers in the potential of this corner of Val Tidone. They farm their 17 hectares of vineyards following the philosophy on which the estate was founded in 1960 by Lodovica's father, Gaetano. They have deep respect for the land and they vinify their grapes without invasive cellar techniques. The resulting wines display a strong personality, pervaded with the vigour and power of the prevalently clay soil. Gutturnio Frizzante is as reliable as ever and the '07 vintage is one of the best of its kind. Exceptionally drinkable, it draws on alluringly taut fruit that develops a seamlessly stylish, supple progression. Our favourite still red is Vigna Martin, from barbera, croatina and merlot, which is the product of a good vintage. Although approachable, it shows considerable depth and a full, assertive palate with good structure and appealing roundness. Malvasia Bianca Regina combines succulent fruit with more complex spicy notes and aromatic herbs, enhanced by maceration on the skins. The palate is big and weighty, shot through with a pleasant bitterish sensation.

○ C. P. Malvasia Boccadirosa '07	🍷🍷 4*
○ C.P. Sauvignon Cardass '07	🍷🍷 5
○ C. P. Brut On Attend les Invités Ris. Speciale	🍷🍷 5
○ C. P. Malvasia Dolce Le Rane '05	🍷🍷 6
● Come La Pantera e I Lupi nella Sera Ris. '03	🍷🍷 5
○ C. P. Sauvignon I Nani e Le Ballerine '07	🍷 4
● Come La Pantera e I Lupi nella Sera '06	🍷 5
● C. P. Cabernet Sauvignon Corbeau '00	🍷🍷🍷 6
● C. P. Cabernet Sauvignon Corbeau '04	🍸🍸 7
☉ C. P. Brut Rosé On Attend les Invités '02	🍸🍸 5
○ C. P. Malvasia Boccadirosa '06	🍸🍸 4

○ C. P. Malvasia V. T. Bianca Regina '06	🍷🍷 4*
● C. P. Gutturnio Frizzante '07	🍷🍷 3*
● Vigna Martin '07	🍷🍷 4*
● C. P. Cabernet Sauvignon Villante '05	🍷 4
● C. P. Gutturnio Sup. Cresta al Sole '06	🍷 4
○ C. P. Malvasia Passito Il Piriolo '06	🍷 5
○ C. P. Pinot Grigio Fiocco di Rose '07	🍷 4
○ C. P. Malvasia V. T. Bianca Regina '05	🍸🍸 4
● C. P. Cabernet Sauvignon Villante '04	🍸🍸 4
● C. P. Gutturnio Sup. Cresta al Sole '04	🍸🍸 4

Giovanna Madonia

LOC. VILLA MADONIA
VIA DE' CAPPUCCINI, 130
47032 BERTINORO [FC]
TEL. 0543444361
www.giovannamadonia.it

ANNUAL PRODUCTION 45,000 bottles
HECTARES UNDER VINE 12
VITICULTURE METHOD Conventional

Small is Beautiful is a collection of essays that topped the bestseller lists in the 1970s. It focuses on a concept that fits this little Romagna estate and its charming owner to a T, for its limited dimensions allow it to pursue and attain perfection. We like to think that here, among the Bertinoro hills, the work of Giovanna and her trusted assistants, oenologist Attilio Pagli and agronomist Remigio Bordini, represents a sort of revenge of the small over the big. The duel is an unequal one. Small producers run risks, bend with the changes in the weather and the seasons, toil, struggle and sometimes lose, before they can release a wine that bowls you over like Ombroso 2005, an authentically great Sangiovese di Romagna. We were enchanted by its elegant, seductive nose but it's on the palate that the wine reveals its juicy stuffing, long soft balance, velvet-smooth tannins and a succession of complex sensations of spice, vanilla, cocoa powder and liquorice. This admirable performance deservedly earned it a place in our finals. Fermavento, on the other hand, appeared a little under par, albeit refreshing and easy drinking.

● Sangiovese di Romagna Sup. Ombroso Ris. '05	▼▼	5
○ Albana di Romagna Passito Chimera '05	▼	5
● Sangiovese di Romagna Sup. Fermavento '06	▼	4
● Tenentino		3
● Sangiovese di Romagna Sup. Ombroso Ris. '01	▽▽▽	5
● Sangiovese di Romagna Sup. Ombroso Ris. '00	▽▽	5
● Sangiovese di Romagna Sup. Ombroso Ris. '04	▽▽	5
● Sangiovese di Romagna Sup. Fermavento '05	▽▽	4
● Sterpigno Merlot '03	▽▽	6

La Mancina

FRAZ. MONTEBUDELLO
VIA MOTTA, 8
40050 MONTEVEGLIO [BO]
TEL. 051832691
www.lamancina.it

ANNUAL PRODUCTION 120,000 bottles
HECTARES UNDER VINE 31
VITICULTURE METHOD Conventional

We approve the decision of Francesca Zanetti – the enthusiastic young owner of this estate, which is one of the largest in the Colli Bolognesi – to concentrate on pignoletto in view of the winery's future goals. Similarly, we agree with her that the potential of the area's most typical and deep-rooted variety has as so far been little explored and that much remains to be done. We encourage her to continue, backed by the technical expertise of oenologist Giandomenico Negro. In the meantime, we were intrigued by the decision to postpone the release of the estate's top Pignoletto, Terre di Montebudello, by a year, thus giving it further complexity, savouriness and balance. We liked the idea of flanking this wine with Pinolieto, a fresher, fruitier vintage Pignoletto at its first release this year. Despite the efforts lavished on the whites, the quality of the reds has remained high, commencing with Barbera Il Foriere, which displays attractive notes of cherry and a very fruity, juicy, balanced palate. Merlot Lanciotto is refreshing and approachable.

● C. B. Barbera Il Foriere '07	▼▼	3*
● C. B. Merlot Lanciotto '07	▼▼	3*
○ C. B. Pignoletto Terre di Montebudello '06	▼▼	3*
○ C. B. Pignoletto Frizzante '07	▼	3
○ C. B. Pignoletto Pinolieto '07	▼	3
⊙ Chiosa Rosato Frizzante '07	▼	3
● C. B. Barbera Il Foriere '06	▽▽	3
● C. B. Merlot Lanciotto '06	▽▽	3
● C. B. Cabernet Sauvignon Comandante della Guardia '04	▽▽	4
● C. B. Cabernet Sauvignon Comandante della Guardia '03	▽▽	4

Ermete Medici & Figli

LOC. GAIDA
VIA NEWTON, 13A
42040 REGGIO EMILIA
TEL. 0522942135
www.medici.it

ANNUAL PRODUCTION 800,000 bottles
HECTARES UNDER VINE 60
VITICULTURE METHOD Conventional

The Medici family's estate best embodies the rising star of Lambrusco at the moment. The secrets of its success are plain to see: hard work in the vineyards, which even look different from the surrounding ones; Giorgio and Valter Medici's unfailing propensity for improvement and their meticulous care to every single stage in the cellar; and the enthusiasm of their respective sons Alberto and Pierluigi, who proudly accompany their Lambrusco all over the world. This year, the usual contest between the estate's two flagship wines for our top accolade was practically a draw, with both entering the finals. Concerto is truly excellent, showing more elegant and perfectly calibrated than ever. It throws a precise nose with flawless fruit, showcasing blackberries and blueberries, and a fragrantly rewarding palate that makes it very drinkable. Assolo is more mouthfilling and has fuller body, while preserving beautifully fresh fruit on the nose and lively softness on the palate. The floral, flavoursome, slightly rustic Libesco and the soft, down-to-earth I Quercioli are almost as good.

● Reggiano Assolo '07	🍷🍷	3*
● Reggiano Lambrusco Secco Concerto '07	🍷🍷	3*
● Reggiano Lambrusco Secco I Quercioli '07	🍷🍷	3
● Reggiano Lambrusco Secco Libesco '07	🍷🍷	3
⊙ Brut Rosé M. Cl. Unique '06	🍷🍷	4
○ Colli di Scandiano e di Canossa Malvasia Daphne '07	🍷	3
● Antica Osteria Lambrusco	🍷	2
● Reggiano Lambrusco Secco '07	🍷	2
● Colli di Scandiano e di Canossa Grasparossa Bocciolo '07		3

Monte delle Vigne

LOC. OZZANO TARO
VIA MONTICELLO, 13
43046 COLLECCHIO [PR]
TEL. 0521309704
www.montedellevigne.it

ANNUAL PRODUCTION 250,000 bottles
HECTARES UNDER VINE 45
VITICULTURE METHOD Conventional

The dream that Andrea has been cultivating on the splendid hills of Ozzano Taro for many years is starting to come true. It has cost him many sacrifices and thankless work with no immediate rewards, other than the knowledge of doing things well and the hope that time will prove him right. Andrea's only tangible assets were the vineyards, which have now reached productive maturity and were joined a couple of years ago by an efficient new winery. Today they are also flanked by a list of high-quality wines, three of which made it into our finals. The estate's historic flagship wine Nabucco, a blend of 70 per cent barbera and 30 per cent merlot, has an elegant, austere style, flowing over the palate with confidence and seamless progression, offering exemplary full, sound fruit. Malvasia Callas impressed us with its full, perfectly calibrated nose, which is reprised on the appealingly soft, pervasively lingering palate. Finally, we were pleasantly surprised by the firm, juicy Lambrusco's crisp fruit and gratifying drinkability. But this is just the beginning for this winery. We are sure that it will give us even more satisfaction in the future.

○ Callas Malvasia '07	🍷🍷	5
● Lambrusco '07	🍷🍷	3*
● Nabucco '06	🍷🍷	5
● Colli di Parma Rosso '06	🍷🍷	4*
○ Brut Blanc de Blancs	🍷	4
⊙ Rubina Brut Rosé '06	🍷	4
○ Colli di Parma Malvasia Frizzante '07		3
○ Colli di Parma Sauvignon Frizzante '07		3
○ Callas Malvasia '06	YY	5
● Nabucco '05	YY	5
● Nabucco '04	YY	5

Francesco Montesissa

FRAZ. REZZANO
LOC. BUFFALORA, 91
29013 CARPANETO PIACENTINO [PC]
TEL. 0523850123
www.vinimontesissa.it

ANNUAL PRODUCTION 280,000 bottles
HECTARES UNDER VINE 37.72
VITICULTURE METHOD Conventional

The Monesissa family have been making wine for five generations and although production was originally destined almost exclusively for their eatery in Piacenza, the wines' range and distribution are now considerably wider. Today's estate is the result of the work of the recently deceased Francesco Montesissa and is now skilfully run by his children and grandchildren, including the young Nicola, a skilled agronomist who also handles public relations. A range of interesting still wines has recently joined the winery's many semi-sparkling wines. We were impressed by the two versions of still Gutturnio, which have made the estate one of the most interesting in the Piacenza area. Gutturnio Classico Superiore has a close-focused, elegant, fruity nose and a balanced, well-sustained palate with good depth. The lingering finish ends on slightly balsamic notes. Gutturnio Riserva Bosco del Sole Cuccon has fruity aromas softened by well-calibrated oak on the nose before the full, juicy palate develops confidently. Al Ladar is a rich, concentrated Bonarda, in which the variety's characteristic exuberance is underscored by a slightly astringent finish.

● C. P. Gutturnio Cl. Sup. '06	🍷🍷	3*
● C. P. Gutturnio Bosco del Sole Cuccon Ris. '05	🍷🍷	5
O Gocce di Frutto Moscato '07	🍷🍷	4
O C. P. Malvasia Passito Ronco della Santa '05	🍷	6
● C. P. Bonarda Al Ladar '06	🍷	5
● C. P. Gutturnio Frizzante Sel. Ronco Stagnino '07	🍷	3

Fattoria Monticino Rosso

VIA MONTECATONE, 7
40026 IMOLA [BO]
TEL. 054240577
www.fattoriadelmonticinorosso.it

ANNUAL PRODUCTION 65,000 bottles
HECTARES UNDER VINE 16
VITICULTURE METHOD Conventional

Fattoria Monticino Rosso is one of the most northerly Romagna wineries, situated in an area with a unique climate that Mussolini chose as the site for an important sanatorium in the 1930s. The estate is run by the Zeoli brothers with the aid of consultant oenologist Giancarlo Soverchia. Together they are steadfastly experimenting with a fermentation process in which the wines remain on the fine lees for an extended period. The aim is to achieve a complexity that is not currently completely expressed, even though these wines have many admirers in Romagna. The best of the estate's recent reds is Cabernet Sauvignon Pradello with chewy notes of ripe morello cherry and a soft, velvety palate. Sangiovese Superiore is also very convincing, with slightly tired fruit but excellent richness of flavour. But the most interesting wine on the list is still Albana Codronchio, a highly complex dry wine made from overripe grapes with a note of botrytis on the complex nose of dried herbs and flowers, and an elegant, long, full-flavoured palate.

O Albana di Romagna Secco Codronchio '06	🍷🍷	4
● Colli d'Imola Cabernet Sauvignon Pradello Ris. '04	🍷🍷	4
● Sangiovese di Romagna Sup. '06	🍷🍷	3*
O Albana di Romagna Secco '07	🍷	3
O Malvasia Passito '04	🍷	5
O Albana di Romagna Secco Codronchio '04	🍷🍷	4
O Albana di Romagna Secco Codronchio '05	🍷🍷	4
O Malvasia Passito '03	🍷🍷	5

Poderi Morini

LOC. ORIOLO DEI FICHI
VIA GESUITA
48018 FAENZA [RA]
TEL. 0546634257
info@poderimorini.com

ANNUAL PRODUCTION	100,000 bottles
HECTARES UNDER VINE	40
VITICULTURE METHOD	Conventional

This 40-hectare estate in the Faenza hills is one of the places where Alessandro Morini's restless spirit has been most active. Although a newcomer to the world of wine, he is seriously committed to quality. With the excellent assistance of Luciano Lusa in the vineyard and Stefano Ragazzini in the cellar, Alessandro is investing energy in research and production. Indeed, the preference for quality over quantity in the vineyards and the use of advanced technology in the cellar continue to improve the contents of the artistically labelled bottles, although results are still a long way from the potential suggested by the estate's resources. As several important wines were not ready in time for our tastings, it fell to Sangiovese Riserva Nonno Rico to defend the winery's reputation but its sturdy confident fruit clashes fiercely with the powerful oak that partially dries its meatiness and freshness. The delightful Savignone '06, from centesimino, known locally as sâvignon rosso, has a pleasantly sweet nose and palate, with prominent notes of violet and candied peel.

Il Negrese

LOC. IL NEGRESE
29010 ZIANO PIACENTINO [PC]
TEL. 0523864804

ANNUAL PRODUCTION	30,000 bottles
HECTARES UNDER VINE	8
VITICULTURE METHOD	Natural

Matteo Braga is the heart of this estate, which continues to polish its profile year after year and is now one of the benchmark wineries of the Colli Piacentini. Il Negrese has eight hectares under vine, planted to the main traditional varieties of the area – barbera, croatina, malvasia and ortrugo – in various sites around Ziano, under the Montepo hill. Matteo's philosophy is based on precision in the vineyard, followed by limited, essential intervention in the cellar to produce wines that are always redolent of their terroir. Gutturnio Frizzante is among the best in its category, thanks to rich, fresh, juicy fruit that supports a weighty structure. The powerful, dynamic still Gutturnio is also very interesting, showing firmness and good drive on the palate. Following brief maceration on the skins, Malvasia '07 is forthright and true to type. Malvasia Passito took our Three Glasses for the first time this year. The grapes are dried in the sun and the wine they yield discloses a seductive nose of dried figs, apricots and peaches. On the palate, balance and flesh are exemplary, with nicely gauged continuity that makes this a highly drinkable proposition.

● Sangiovese di Romagna Sup. Nonno Rico Ris. '04	▽▽ 5
● Savignone '06	▽▽ 4*
● Nadèl '04	▽ 5
● Sangiovese di Romagna Sup. Beccafico '07	▽ 3
○ Albana di Romagna Secco Sette Note '07	3
○ Albana di Romagna Passito Cuore Matto Ris. '04	▽▽ 5
● Nadèl '01	▽▽ 5
● Rubacuori da Uve Stramature '04	▽▽ 5
● Traicolli '03	▽▽ 5
● Sangiovese di Romagna Sup. Nonno Rico Ris. '03	▽▽ 5

○ C. P. Malvasia Passito '06	▽▽▽ 5
● C. P. Gutturnio '07	▽▽ 3*
● C. P. Gutturnio Frizzante '07	▽ 3
○ C. P. Malvasia '07	▽ 3
○ C. P. Malvasia Passito '05	▽▽ 5

Perinelli

LOC. I PERINELLI
29028 PONTE DELL'OLIO [PC]
TEL. 0523877185
www.perinelli.it

ANNUAL PRODUCTION **60,000 bottles**
HECTARES UNDER VINE **17**
VITICULTURE METHOD **Conventional**

Around 20 years ago, the Sguazzi family purchased this estate named after the village in Val Nure. Today, it is run by young Giorgia Sguazzi, the granddaughter of its founder Rino. High-density planting, with up to 8,000 vines per hectare, carried out in the early 1990s has resulted in reliable wines of consistent quality over the years, although a genuine pinnacle has yet to be reached. Malvasia Torre della Ghiacciaia displays an alluring citrus nose, followed by a well-structured palate whose alcoholic warmth is attenuated by decent acidity. Turning to the reds, Costa dei Salina is the most interesting of the current Gutturnios, with a stylish racy personality and great suppleness that make it highly drinkable. The more ambitious Vigna Vecchia is a blend of pinot nero, cabernet sauvignon and barbera, which opens with a spicy nose and powers through to a slightly balsamic finish on the palate. Finally, we were impressed by Anno Cinque, a late-harvest dessert wine made from dried malvasia, sémillon and viognier grapes, which has nicely balanced structure and moderate complexity.

Poderi dal Nespoli

LOC. NESPOLI
VILLA ROSSI, 50
47012 CIVITELLA DI ROMAGNA [FC]
TEL. 0543989637
www.poderidalnespoli.com

ANNUAL PRODUCTION **300,000 bottles**
HECTARES UNDER VINE **41**
VITICULTURE METHOD **Conventional**

Montaigne said that ambition is not a vice of little people and the Ravaioli family are anything but little. Similarly, their ambition cannot really be called a vice. It's more the corollary of a strong determination to emerge in the wine world, which so often is made up of ordinariness and unprepossessing wineries. But the Ravaiolis and their faithful oenologist Giuseppe Caviola are fired by a desire to astound. Prugneto, a fantastic current Sangiovese is one of the best in the region. It both astounds and surprises but does so with its simplicity and authenticity. The elegant, delicate nose hides what is revealed on the full, juicy, satisfying palate, brimming with sweetness and lingering notes. Il Nespoli – now a Sangiovese Riserva – is distinguished by greater weight and extraordinary balance, giving elegant softness and alluring notes of spice and ripe red fruit. The white Da Maggio, from chardonnay, is rich and refreshing, showing soft sweetness and attractive drinkability.

O Anno Cinque '05	♥♥	4
O C. P. Malvasia Torre della Ghiacciaia '07	♥♥	4*
● C. P. Gutturnio Costa dei Salina '07	♥♥	4*
● Vigna Vecchia '06	♥♥	4
● C. P. Gutturnio Vivace '07	♥	4
O C. P. Ortrugo Vivace '07	♥	3
O Anno Quattro '04	♀♀	4
● C. P. Gutturnio Costa dei Salina '06	♀♀	4
● Vigna Vecchia '04	♀♀	4
● Vigna Vecchia '03	♀♀	4

● Sangiovese di Romagna Prugneto '07	♥♥	4*
O Da Maggio Chardonnay '07	♥♥	3*
● Sangiovese di Romagna Sup. Il Nespoli Ris. '05	♥♥	5
● Sangiovese di Romagna Sup. Santodeno '07	♥	3
● Borgo dei Guidi '04	♀♀	6
● Borgo dei Guidi '03	♀♀	6
● Borgo dei Guidi '01	♀♀	6
● Borgo dei Guidi '00	♀♀	6
● Il Nespoli Sangiovese '04	♀♀	5
● Il Nespoli Sangiovese '03	♀♀	5
● Sangiovese di Romagna Prugneto '06	♀♀	4

Il Poggiarello

LOC. SCRIVELLANO DI STATTO
29020 TRAVO [PC]
TEL. 0523957241
www.ilpoggiarellovini.it

ANNUAL PRODUCTION	100,000 bottles
HECTARES UNDER VINE	18
VITICULTURE METHOD	Conventional

Poggiarella is a reliable winery. Quality is consistent with each vintage and the well-crafted low-key wines are made with an eye on price. Barbera 'L Piston is unbeatable in this respect. Available only in magnums, known locally as "bottiglioni", it boasts lashings of fruit, a dynamic, juicy palate and a lingering finish. Among the Gutturnios, Perticato Valandrea is still rather unfocused on the nose but reveals a juicy palate with perceptible but not overpowering tannins. La Barbona Riserva is even more convincing, with an attractive hue and aromas, and a soft palate with just the right amount of body supported by discreet extract. Cabernet Sauvignon Perticato Il Novarei shows purplish with fresh, slightly grassy aromas and a long, supple palate, and Pinot Nero Perticato Le Giastre vaunts simple, supple fruit and a soft, juicy palate. Malvasia Perticato Beatrice Quadri offers its usual well-calibrated typicity, with florality and pleasantly bitter notes, while Sauvignon Perticato I Quadri has a fresh, stylish palate veined with mineral sensations.

Podere Riosto

VIA DI RIOSTO, 12
40065 PIANORO [BO]
TEL. 051777109
www.podereriosto.it

ANNUAL PRODUCTION	80,000 bottles
HECTARES UNDER VINE	15.8
VITICULTURE METHOD	Conventional

The Gallettis have accustomed us to several new entries in their already extensive wine list every year. This testifies to the passion for experimentation on the estate, which only has only been concentrating its efforts on quality production for a few years. Barbera Vigna della Valle, possibly the best of its kind that we tasted in the Colli Bolognese this year, was the wine that impressed us most, easily winning Two Glasses. The slightly alcoholic palate does not mask the excellent fresh, juicy fruit that gives the wine suppleness, fragrance and great drinkability. This year's attractive new arrivals are the refreshing, easy drinking Doraluce, a nicely varietal Sauvignon that is not too obvious but lingers, perked up by subtle tanginess, and Gaudio, a perfect Bordeaux blend with well-gauged sound fresh fruit, a supple palate and an alluringly soft finish. The two versions of Pignoletto are also improving, although we expect further progress in this direction in the future.

● C. P. Barbera 'L Pistòn '07		▼▼ 4*
● C. P. Cabernet Sauvignon Perticato Il Novarei '06		▼▼ 5
● C. P. Gutturnio La Barbona Ris. '06		▼▼ 5
● C. P. Gutturnio Perticato Valandrea '07		▼▼ 4*
○ C. P. Malvasia Perticato Beatrice Quadri '07		▼ 4
● C. P. Pinot Nero Perticato Le Giastre '07		▼ 5
○ C. P. Sauvignon Perticato I Quadri '07		▼ 4
○ C. P. Ortrugo Frizzante '07		▼ 3
● C. P. Gutturnio La Barbona Ris. '05	▼▼ 5	
● C. P. Gutturnio La Barbona Ris. '04	▼▼ 5	
● C. P. Cabernet Sauvignon Perticato Il Novarei '05	▼▼ 5	
● C. P. Cabernet Sauvignon Perticato Il Novarei '04	▼▼ 5	

● C. B. Barbera V. della Valle '06		▼▼ 4*
○ C. B. Sauvignon Doraluce '07		▼▼ 4*
● Gaudio '05		▼▼ 4
● C. B. Cabernet Sauvignon V. Bel Poggio '06		▼ 4
○ C. B. Pignoletto Frizzante V. della Torre '07		▼ 3
○ C. B. Pignoletto Sup. V. della Torre '07		▼ 3
● C. B. Cabernet Sauvignon Grifone '04	▼▼ 5	

San Patrignano

VIA SAN PATRIGNANO, 53
47853 CORIANO [RN]
TEL. 0541362362
www.sanpatrignano.org

ANNUAL PRODUCTION	500,000 bottles
HECTARES UNDER VINE	110
VITICULTURE METHOD	Conventional

San Patrignano's 110 hectares of vineyards are reaching maturity and the progress in quality is proof of the potential in the Rimini hills. The cellar is also more focused and aimed at increasingly elegant, complex wines with greater depth and freshness. The ability to look ahead, knowing that there is always room for improvement, is key to this estate and the practical translation of a way of thinking that stimulates all the community's guests and then becomes a way of life. Avi is one of the most impressive interpretations of Sangiovese in all Romagna and deservedly took Three Glasses. The cool vintage has brought out great elegance and the wines display crisp fruit with smooth sumptuous tannins that carry the long finish. Montepirolo '05 is austere, close focused and vibrant, gaining depth on the palate by eschewing excessive weight and reconfirming the area's great vocation for Bordeaux varieties. Noi, from sangiovese with cabernet and merlot, is firm and austere while Aulente bianco, from chardonnay with 20 per cent sauvignon, is fresh and juicy with citrus notes. The monovarietal Sauvignon Vie is tangy and true to type.

San Valentino

FRAZ. SAN MARTINO IN VENTI
VIA TOMASETTA, 13
47900 RIMINI
TEL. 0541752231
www.vinisanvalentino.com

ANNUAL PRODUCTION	140,000 bottles
HECTARES UNDER VINE	28
VITICULTURE METHOD	Conventional

Roberto Mascarin's estate was a pioneers of quality in the Colli di Rimini. Its wines have always been exciting with plenty of elegance, appeal and structure. After picking up our top accolade for three years running, Sangiovese Terre di Covignano missed out in one edition of the Guide. It was sound enough but the quest for maximum concentration was accompanied by a few minor flaws due chiefly to its lack of finesse. This year, however, the wine has recovered its usual allure. Despite rich flesh and extract, it shows elegance and personality. Released after adequate maturation, it's rich and full of character but has kept all of its finesse. The nose shows ripe, almost estery fruit and the dynamic fragrant palate develops into a juicy finish with smooth tannins. This wonderful interpretation earned the '05 vintage Three resounding Glasses. We were also impressed by the spicy, mouth-caressing Scabi, a current Sangiovese in an alluringly warm, ripe style with plenty of pulp. Luna Nuova, from cabernet sauvignon with small amounts of merlot and cabernet franc, also performed well, showing a faint hint of raisining and thoroughly extracted grapes.

● Sangiovese di Romagna Sup. Avi Ris. '05	♟♟♟ 6
● Colli di Rimini Cabernet Montepirolo '05	♟♟ 6
● Colli di Rimini Rosso Noi '06	♟♟ 5
○ Aulente Bianco '07	♟♟ 4*
○ Vie '07	♟♟ 5
● Aulente Rosso '07	♟ 4
● Colli di Rimini Cabernet Montepirolo '01	♟♟♟ 6
● Colli di Rimini Cabernet Montepirolo '04	♟♟♟ 6
● Colli di Rimini Rosso Noi '04	♟♟♟ 6
● Sangiovese di Romagna Sup. Avi Ris. '99	♟♟♟ 6
● Sangiovese di Romagna Sup. Avi Ris. '00	♟♟♟ 6
● Sangiovese di Romagna Sup. Avi Ris. '01	♟♟♟ 6

● Sangiovese di Romagna Sup. Terra di Covignano Ris. '05	♟♟♟ 6
● Luna Nuova '05	♟♟ 6
● Sangiovese di Romagna Sup. Scabi '07	♟♟ 4*
● Sangiovese di Romagna Sup. Terra di Covignano Ris. '03	♟♟♟ 5
● Sangiovese di Romagna Sup. Terra di Covignano Ris. '02	♟♟♟ 5
● Sangiovese di Romagna Sup. Terra di Covignano Ris. '01	♟♟♟ 5
● Luna Nuova '04	♟♟ 6
● Luna Nuova '03	♟♟ 6
● Montepulciano '04	♟♟ 8
● Eclissi di Sole '05	♟♟ 5

Santarosa

FRAZ. SAN MARTINO IN CASOLA
VIA SAN MARTINO, 82
40050 MONTE SAN PIETRO [BO]
TEL. 051969203
www.santarosavini.com

ANNUAL PRODUCTION	30,000 bottles
HECTARES UNDER VINE	10
VITICULTURE METHOD	Conventional

Apart from the native barbera grape, the red varieties traditionally cultivated in the Colli Bolognesi are cabernet sauvignon and merlot. It has long been debated which is more suited to the area but increasingly, the answer is merlot. This seems to be confirmed by the playful contest that Giovanna della Valentina's two leading wines indulge in every year. Again this year, Merlot Giòtondo and Cabernet Sauvignon Giòrosso fought it out on our tasting table and the duel was won by Giòtondo. We sent it to our finals for the power of its elegant, highly varietal aromas, well-calibrated fruit and perfect austerity, which gives compactness and finesse. Giòrosso is harder and more structured with slightly excessive alcoholic warmth but it does have a fine, elegant tannic weave. Santarosa Rosso, an equal blend of merlot and cabernet, suggests that a combination of the two varieties is the most convincing recipe of all, bearing in mid that this second wine also has a low price tag. It shows intensely fruity on the nose and very supple on the palate, with an attractive, satisfyingly soft finish. Pignoletto is full flavoured, zesty and packed with fruit.

● C. B. Merlot Giòtondo '06	♀♀	5
● C. B. Cabernet Sauvignon		
Giòrosso '06	♀♀	5
○ Pignoletto '07	♀♀	4*
● Santarosa Rosso '07	♀♀	3*
● C. B. Merlot Giòtondo '00	♀♀♀	4
● C. B. Merlot Giòtondo '04	♀♀	4
● C. B. Merlot Giòtondo '05	♀♀	5
● C. B. Cabernet Sauvignon		
Giòrosso '03	♀♀	4
● C. B. Cabernet Sauvignon		
Giòrosso '04	♀♀	4
● C. B. Cabernet Sauvignon		
Giòrosso '05	♀♀	5

Tenuta Santini

FRAZ. PASSANO
VIA CAMPO, 33
47853 CORIANO [RN]
TEL. 0541656527
www.tenutasantini.com

ANNUAL PRODUCTION	30,000 bottles
HECTARES UNDER VINE	22
VITICULTURE METHOD	Conventional

Tenuta Santini's vineyards are at Passano di Coriano, less than ten kilometres from the coast in a landscape of wheat and sunflowers constantly swept by a sea breeze that cools hot days and makes cold ones more bearable. We have repeatedly stressed the exceptional suitability of the Rimini hills for Bordeaux varieties, which develop freshness and depth in this special terroir that invites comparison with Bolgheri. It is no coincidence that in normal growing years, the estate's most convincing wine has always been Battareo, from cabernet sauvignon and merlot. However, the '06 vintage of this wine is still ageing in bottle ageing. Sangiovese Riserva Cornelianum took a well-deserved Two Glasses. While its nose is penalized by rather sweet oak, alcohol masking the fruit and expression that is less than clean, its attractively nuanced palate makes amends with attractive freshness and close-knit tannins. Beato Enrico brilliantly interprets the allure of Sangiovese from these hills, giving an approachable, meaty nose with a juicy note reminiscent of the fragrant flesh of freshly cut fruit. The palate shows confident development and a smooth finish.

● Sangiovese di Romagna Sup.		
Beato Enrico '07	♀♀	4*
● Sangiovese di Romagna Sup.		
Cornelianum Ris. '05	♀♀	5
● Battarreo '04	♀♀	4
● Sangiovese di Romagna Sup.		
Cornelianum Ris. '03	♀♀	5
● Battarreo '05	♀♀	4
● Sangiovese di Romagna Sup.		
Beato Enrico '06	♀♀	4
● Sangiovese di Romagna Sup.		
Cornelianum Ris. '04	♀♀	5

Spalletti Colonna di Paliano

LOC. CASTELLO DI RIBANO
VIA SOGLIANO, 104
47039 SAVIGNANO SUL RUBICONE [FC]
TEL. 0541945111
www.spalletticolonnadipaliano.com

ANNUAL PRODUCTION	500,000 bottles
HECTARES UNDER VINE	75
VITICULTURE METHOD	Conventional

Change is in the air at this long-standing estate, onto whose ancient roots new stock has recently been grafted. Regular readers will be familiar with the winery's desire to innovate and ensure quality, along with the way it intends to do this. Consequently, a limited slowdown in the laborious process of change gives no real cause for concern. Last year's consistent quality has been replaced by a relative lack of continuity, characterized by peaks of excellence and other less successful results. It's not a problem for the estate's management and winemaker Leonardo Conti, who must be given credit for his commitment to the quest for the excellence this illustrious winery deserves. Good performances came from Monaco di Ribano, a juicy, chewy Cabernet that is extraordinarily soft and caressing on the palate with notes of ripe cherry, attractive alcohol and body given by sweet tannins. The result is an incredibly elegant wine. Sabinio is made from the same grapes but shows greater freshness, making it easier drinking. Villa Rasponi repeats the successes of the family's great Sangiovese wines, displaying a soft, delicate palate with a lingering finish.

La Stoppa

LOC. ANCARANO
29029 RIVERGARO [PC]
TEL. 0523958159
www.lastoppa.it

ANNUAL PRODUCTION	160,000 bottles
HECTARES UNDER VINE	32
VITICULTURE METHOD	Natural

La Stoppa's wines are complicated. They accurately reflect the long years of hard work put in by the estate's owner Elena Pantaleoni and oenologist Giulio Armani in the quest for the purest expression of their splendid terroir. This objective is driven by philosophy, ecology, culture and sustainability, and it is necessary to bear all these aspects in mind when tasting the wines, as do the estate's many fans. As these wines, particularly the reds, faithfully express their terroir, we have decided not to describe them in the usual manner, partly because they all share marked notes of reduction that open up after several minutes – or sometimes hours – to reveal their attractive essence and character. We leave you with the pleasure of enjoying them as you think best, allowing sufficient time to monitor their development in the glass. We will comment only on Vigna del Volta, a Malvasia made from sun-dried grapes that is a benchmark for the entire Piacenza area and beyond. Three Glasses went to this captivating, perfectly calibrated dessert wine, a model of elegance and finesse with a slightly tannic finish.

● Monaco di Ribano Cabernet '05	￼	5
● Sabinio Cabernet '06	￼	4*
● Sangiovese di Romagna Sup. Villa Rasponi Ris. '05	￼	4*
○ Albana di Romagna Duchessa di Montemar '07	￼	3
○ Albana di Romagna Passito Maolù '06	￼	5
○ Pagadebit di Romagna Ribano Bianco '07	￼	3
○ Principessa Ghika '07	￼	4
● Sangiovese di Romagna Sup. Principe di Ribano '07	￼	4
● Sangiovese di Romagna Sup. Rocca di Ribano '05	￼	4
● Gianello Merlot '05	￼	4
● Sangiovese di Romagna Sup. Villa Rasponi Ris. '04	￼	5

○ C. P. Malvasia Passito V. del Volta '06	￼	6
○ Buca delle Canne '06	￼	7
● Barbera della Stoppa '05	￼	5
● I Padri '05	￼	5
● Macchiona '04	￼	5
● Stoppa '04	￼	5
● C. P. Gutturnio Frizzante '07	￼	3
○ C. P. Malvasia Passito V. del Volta '97	￼	6
○ C. P. Malvasia Passito V. del Volta '03	￼	6
○ C. P. Malvasia Passito V. del Volta '04	￼	6
○ Ageno '04	￼	5
○ Ageno '05	￼	5
● I Padri '04	￼	5
● Macchiona '03	￼	5

Tenuta La Viola

VIA COLOMBARONE, 888
47032 BERTINORO [FC]
TEL. 0543445496
www.tenutalaviola.it

ANNUAL PRODUCTION	30,000 bottles
HECTARES UNDER VINE	5
VITICULTURE METHOD	Certified organic

Bertinoro is a rich, generous land and a prime wine area. In recent years, the general change in climate, along with the trend to lower vineyard yields, has meant that the area, one of the best in Romagna, has been producing potent wines that are difficult to tame, particularly in terms of alcohol content. Consequently, our compliments go to the Gabellini family – Stefano and particularly his mother Lidia, who personally tends the vineyards – and oenologist Franco Calini for having been able to hold back this abundance and produce a truly exceptional wine. We're referring to Pethra Honorii, a thoroughbred Sangiovese, which has a fresh, intense nose with clear floral and peach aromas, followed by a sumptuous elegant palate that reveals masterly balance and a refined full-flavoured encore of fresh fruit. It deservedly won a place in our finals. Its only flaw lies in the limited number of bottles produced, just 6,000. The estate's second Sangiovese, Il Colombarone, is also well balanced. It shows concentrated notes of peach and red fruit on the nose and austere and slightly alcoholic on the palate, which is nonetheless fresh, juicy and crisp.

Tizzano

VIA MARESCALCHI, 13
40033 CASALECCHIO DI RENO [BO]
TEL. 051571208
visconti@tizzano.191.it

ANNUAL PRODUCTION	140,000 bottles
HECTARES UNDER VINE	35
VITICULTURE METHOD	Conventional

Again this year, Luca Visconti's estate presented wines that reflect his care in vineyard and cellar. As usual, Gabriele Forni's contribution has proven itself fundamental. Tizzano's long-standing manager, Gabriele is a great expert on farming, of which he has detailed knowledge, and he also boasts an enviably impressive store of ancient country lore. He combines this store of knowledge with lively curiosity about new technologies and scientific discoveries, which means he can turn out a range of consistently good wines that never fail to live up to market expectations from his 35 hectares under vine in one of the most picturesque settings in the Colli Bolognese. We awarded Two Glasses to his Cabernet Sauvignon Riserva '03, which displays a slightly vegetal entry on a nose that then opens out into austere Bordeaux-style varietal hints and notes of spice that take you into a palate that is soft, caressing and fruity. The clean, well-structured Merlot '06 also picked up Two Glasses for its attractive, well-calibrated ripe fruit, as did Pignoletto Spumante, characterized by alluring fruitiness, a fresh entry and a soft finish.

● Sangiovese di Romagna Sup. Pethra Honorii Ris. '05	♛ 5
● Sangiovese di Romagna Sup. Il Colombarone '06	♛♛ 4*
● Sangiovese di Romagna Sup. Oddone '07	♛ 3
● Particella 25 '05	♙♙ 6
● Sangiovese di Romagna Sup. Petra Honorii Ris. '04	♙♙ 5
● Sangiovese di Romagna Sup. La Badia Ris. '03	♙♙ 5
● Sangiovese di Romagna Sup. La Badia Ris. '01	♙♙ 4
● Sangiovese di Romagna Sup. Il Colombarone '05	♙♙ 4
● Sangiovese di Romagna Sup. Il Colombarone '04	♙♙ 4

● C. B. Cabernet Sauvignon Ris. '03	♛♛ 5
● C. B. Merlot '06	♛♛ 4*
○ C. B. Pignoletto Spumante Brut	♛♛ 4*
● C. B. Cabernet Sauvignon '06	♛ 4
○ C. B. Pignoletto Frizzante '07	♛ 3
○ C. B. Pignoletto Sup. '07	♛ 3
○ C. B. Riesling Italico '07	♛ 3
○ C. B. Sauvignon '07	3
● C. B. Cabernet Sauvignon '05	♙♙ 4
● C. B. Cabernet Sauvignon Ris. '01	♙♙ 5
● C. B. Merlot '05	♙♙ 4
● C. B. Merlot '04	♙♙ 4

Torre Fornello

LOC. FORNELLO
29010 ZIANO PIACENTINO [PC]
TEL. 0523861001
www.torrefornello.it

ANNUAL PRODUCTION	450,000 bottles
HECTARES UNDER VINE	61
VITICULTURE METHOD	Conventional

In 2008, Torre Fornello celebrated the tenth anniversary of its first harvest. The winery is currently in a period of renewal and transition, and at the same time reshaping its identity. The new path that Enrico Sgorbati has chosen to follow with the guidance of consultant oenologist Nico Danesi should lead to more dynamic, expressive wines with less invasive use of oak and prove capable of a more forthright interpretation of the terroir. While we await disgorgement of the more ambitious sparklers, we singled out the supple, well-crafted Olubra Extra Dry, from marsanne and malvasia. Ortrugo Frizzante won Two Glasses with an alluring nose displaying exemplary soundness and pleasantly deep, balanced palate. Our pick of the whites is Pratobianco, from malvasia, sauvignon and chardonnay, whose aromatic breadth is followed by a long, juicily assertive palate. Having undergone brief skin contact, Malvasia Donna Luigia has an expressive varietal nose bursting with floral hints, spirited development and a bitterish finish. From the reds, we liked Diacono Gerardo 1028, a Gutturnio Riserva with an austere spicy profile.

La Tosa

LOC. LA TOSA
29020 VIGOLZONE [PC]
TEL. 0523870727
www.latosa.it

ANNUAL PRODUCTION	120,000 bottles
HECTARES UNDER VINE	13
VITICULTURE METHOD	Natural

Colli Piacentini manages to bring out the best in malvasia di Candia and much of the credit should go to La Tosa. Sorriso di Cielo was the first chapter of a new story that has yet to be concluded. We don't know whether Stefano Pizzamiglio has managed to square the circle, but the '07 vintage of this wine is truly excellent, with flawless fruit and cleanliness, and a soft, fat palate supported by good, refreshing acidity that prolongs the finish. Other finalists were the estate's varietal, fresh, full-bodied Sauvignon, which has a dynamic, lingering finish, and a great vintage of Cabernet Sauvignon Luna Selvatica, with warm, juicy aromas and a deep, rounded, close-knit palate, to which we awarded Three Glasses. The terrific Valnure Riodeltordo, from malvasia, ortrugo and trebbiano, is the estate's newest wine. It's approachable and well-balanced, with a zesty tang on the finish. L'Ora Felice, from part-dried malvasia grapes, has a very balanced, dynamic palate with a long finish and lots of freshness. Gutturnio has impressive structure, warmth and depth while Vignamorello combines full body with vigour nicely marked by soft tannins.

● C. P. Gutturnio Diacono Gerardo 1028 Ris. '05	♈♈ 5
○ C. P. Ortrugo Frizzante '07	♈♈ 3*
○ Olubra Extra Dry M. Cl. '06	♈♈ 4*
○ Pratobianco '07	♈♈ 4*
○ C. P. Malvasia Donna Luigia '07	♈ 4
○ C. P. Sauvignon Cà del Rio '07	♈ 4
● C. P. Bonarda Latitudo 45 '05	♈ 5
● C. P. Gutturnio Sup. Sinsäl '06	♈ 4
● C. P. Gutturnio Sup. Sinsäl '05	♈♈ 4*

● C. P. Cabernet Sauvignon Luna Selvatica '06	♈♈♈ 6
○ C. P. Malvasia Sorriso di Cielo '07	♈♈ 4*
○ C. P. Sauvignon '07	♈♈ 4*
● C. P. Gutturnio '07	♈♈ 4*
● C. P. Gutturnio Vignamorello '07	♈♈ 5
○ C. P. Malvasia Passito L'Ora Felice '07	♈♈ 5
○ C. P. Valnure Riodeltordo '07	♈♈ 3*
○ C. P. Valnure Frizzante '07	♈ 3
● C. P. Cabernet Sauvignon Luna Selvatica '97	♈♈♈ 5
● C. P. Cabernet Sauvignon Luna Selvatica '04	♈♈♈ 6
● C. P. Cabernet Sauvignon Luna Selvatica '05	♈♈ 6
● C. P. Gutturnio Vignamorello '05	♈♈ 5
● C. P. Gutturnio Vignamorello '06	♈♈ 5

Tre Monti

LOC. BERGULLO
VIA LOLA, 3
40026 IMOLA [BO]
TEL. 0542657116
www.tremonti.it

ANNUAL PRODUCTION 180,000 bottles
HECTARES UNDER VINE 55
VITICULTURE METHOD Conventional

This historic Imola estate is in transition, with David and Vittorio, the young sons of founder Sergio Navacchia, are gradually assuming control. Year after year, Vittorio in particular, who is responsible for work in the vineyards and cellar, is building his knowledge and exploring the estate's potential. This year, we noticed a slight reshuffle in the pecking order and there is a newcomer called Thea. This blend of various white grapes has an impressively full-flavoured palate with freshness and a very long, zesty finish with nice lingering notes of pineapple. Chardonnay Ciardo is always a safe bet, particularly now that greater attention to the oak used in ageing allows it to express its fruit softly and fully, with almost tropical notes. From the reds, we preferred Sangiovese Petrignone to Thea, although the latter is very good. Petrignone has a soft, juicy style with impressive freshness on the nose and palate. It's attractively nuanced with light tannins and great suppleness. Thea is more structured and compact, and consequently still rather stiff and alcoholic, which tends to mask the softness and succulence of the fruit.

○ Colli d'Imola Bianco Thea Bianco '06	🍷🍷	5
● Sangiovese di Romagna Sup. Petrignone Ris. '05	🍷🍷	4*
○ Colli d'Imola Chardonnay Ciardo '07	🍷🍷	4
● Sangiovese di Romagna Sup. Thea Ris. '06	🍷🍷	5
● Colli d'Imola Rosso Boldo '06	🍷	5
● Sangiovese di Romagna Sup. Campo di Mezzo '07	🍷	3
○ Albana di Romagna Passito Casa Lola '06	🍷	5
○ Albana di Romagna Secco V. Rocca '07	🍷	4
○ Trebbiano di Romagna V. Rio '07		4
● Sangiovese di Romagna Sup. Thea Ris. '05	(🍷🍷)	5
● Sangiovese di Romagna Sup. Petrignone Ris. '04	(🍷🍷)	4

Trerè

LOC. MONTICORALLI
VIA CASALE, 19
48018 FAENZA [RA]
TEL. 054647034
www.trere.com

ANNUAL PRODUCTION 200,000 bottles
HECTARES UNDER VINE 35
VITICULTURE METHOD Conventional

Morena Trerè is an all-round businesswoman, who added now-thriving farmstay and restaurant facilities to her winemaking activities several years ago. Morena has a well-defined strategy that is almost a production philosophy: preserving local traditions in all aspects of her business, from tableware to the wines that are served with it. Of course, over the years some changes have taken place in growing techniques, particularly planting patterns and yields per hectare, but the estate has steadfastly stuck with indigenous grape varieties. This brings us to the real challenge, which sometimes looks more of a pipe dream: the preservation of typicity. It's no coincidence that the estate's top products are precisely those in which Romagna is most lacking, namely young Sangioveses. The highly drinkable Vigna del Monte is fresh with impressive ripe, chewy fruit, elegance and balance. Sperone, which contains a small amount of merlot, is slightly richer and more concentrated. Finally, the unpretentious Trebbiano Vigna dei Pini deserves a mention for its notes of fresh fruit and attractive tangy finish.

○ Albana di Romagna Secco '07	🍷🍷	3*
○ Trebbiano di Romagna V. dei Pini '07	🍷🍷	2*
● Sangiovese di Romagna Sup. Sperone '07	🍷🍷	3*
● Sangiovese di Romagna V. del Monte '07	🍷🍷	2*
○ Albana di Romagna Passito '05	🍷	5
○ Colli di Faenza Bianco Rebianco '07	🍷	3
● Sangiovese di Romagna Amarcord d'un Ross Ris. '06	🍷	4
● Colli di Faenza Rosso Montecorallo Ris. '05	(🍷🍷)	4*
● Sangiovese di Romagna Amarcord d'un Ross Ris. '05	(🍷🍷)	4*
● Sangiovese di Romagna Amarcord d'un Ross Ris. '04	(🍷🍷)	4

Uccellaia

LOC. ALBAROLA DI VIGOLZONE
29028 VIGOLZONE [PC]
TEL. 0523870298
www.vinipiacentini.net

ANNUAL PRODUCTION	20,000 bottles
HECTARES UNDER VINE	7
VITICULTURE METHOD	Natural

Chicca and Lali Nicoletti's estate has proved itself one of the most interesting around Piacenza. Its few hectares of vineyards are set among the woods of the Val Nure, on the edge of the Val Trebbiola. This area is one of the subzones of the Colli Piacentini with the greatest potential and offers ideal conditions for quality wine production. For evidence, look no further than the estate's recent output, which is pleasant, well crafted and consistently interesting. The winery has an unusual list for the DOC zone, featuring only still reds and a rosé. Its star is Gutturnium '07, which confirms the fine performance of the previous vintage with strikingly clean fruit and a deep palate that melds softness with suppleness. Bauscia dell'Uccellaia is a firm, dynamic Merlot with an elegant juicy nose, full body and supple, rounded palate. The current Cerasuolo is uncomplicated and pleasant.

Tenuta Valli

LOC. RAVALDINO IN MONTE
VIA DELLE CAMINATE, 38
47100 FORLÌ
TEL. 054524393
www.tenutavalli.it

ANNUAL PRODUCTION	120,000 bottles
HECTARES UNDER VINE	33
VITICULTURE METHOD	Conventional

To an outsider, everything at Tenuta Valle might appear to be proceeding as normal but the impression is contradicted by several decidedly interesting new features. To start with, the labels of the entire range have been very attractively restyled. Then there's the new arrival Trio, a blend of Longanesi, sangiovese and cabernet sauvignon, which impressed us with the firm, austere character that it reveals before progressing over the palate with firm fruitiness and caressing softness. Finally, there's the fine-tuning of Capomaggio, a trebbiano selection from old vines. It's vinified without oak but undergoes prolonged ageing prior to bottling. The '06 vintage is very convincing, showing nice complexity and density, and a rich, full palate. Here's proof that you can make an interesting wine even from this much underrated variety without having to resort to extravagant techniques. Sangiovese Riserva della Beccaccia shows good depth and a lively palate with a slightly estery finish, while Borgo Rosso, a supple, fruity Cabernet Sauvignon, appeared a bit under par.

● Bauscia dell'Uccellaia Merlot '06	♟♟ 5
● C. P. Gutturnio Gutturnium '07	♟♟ 4*
☉ Cerasuolo dell'Uccellaia '07	4
● C. P. Gutturnio Gutturnium '06	♟♟ 4
● Rosso dell'Uccellaia '04	♟♟ 5
● Merlot '05	♟♟ 5

○ Trebbiano di Romagna Capomaggio Sel. Vecchie Vigne '06	♟♟ 4*
● Trio '06	♟♟ 5
● Sangiovese di Romagna Sup. Riserva della Beccaccia Ris. '06	♟♟ 4*
● Borgo Rosso Cabernet Sauvignon '06	♟ 4
● Sangiovese di Romagna Sup. Palazzetto '07	♟ 3
● Sangiovese di Romagna Sup. Tibano '07	♟ 3
○ Albana di Romagna Secco Vinchi '07	♟ 3
○ Trebbiano di Romagna Battilana '07	3
● Borgo Rosso Cabernet Sauvignon '05	♟♟ 5
● Sangiovese di Romagna Sup. Riserva della Beccaccia Ris. '04	♟♟ 4

Vallona

FRAZ. FAGNANO
VIA SANT'ANDREA, 203
40050 CASTELLO DI SERRAVALLE [BO]
TEL. 0516703333
fattorie.vallona@serravallewifi.net

ANNUAL PRODUCTION	90,000 bottles
HECTARES UNDER VINE	29
VITICULTURE METHOD	Conventional

Although the estate's top three wines – Cabernet Diggioanni, Merlot Affederico and the white Permartina – were missing from our tastings to allow them time to age further, the other wines turned in a thoroughly decent performance. This proves that Maurizio Vallona lavishes painstaking care not only on his finest wines but across the range, ensuring his admirers get quality in their bottle. Scrupulous vineyard management is lavished on the entire estate and it is the soil, aspect and seasonal trends that give the grapes their different characteristics and determine their ultimate destiny. While the still wines are impeccable – particularly Pignoletto, with its citrus nose and complex palate, and the austere varietal vintage Cabernet – Maurizio also has a flair for sparklers. Cà Novina is an appealingly creamy metodo classico sparkler, with tasty complex notes of apple and hazelnut. We were even more impressed by the second release of Essè Brut, largely pignoletto vinified in collaboration with the Isola winery. It's elegant, juicy and fragrant. Uncork it now and you won't stop at one glass.

Villa Bagnolo

LOC. BAGNOLO
VIA BAGNOLO, 160
47011 CASTROCARO TERME [FC]
TEL. 0543769047
www.villabagnolo.it

ANNUAL PRODUCTION	80,000 bottles
HECTARES UNDER VINE	15
VITICULTURE METHOD	Conventional

Vito Ballarati is from Lombardy but he fell in love with the Castrocaro hills long ago. Having thrown himself into a complex project when he had already achieved security in life, he can now admire the sea in the distance from a little valley that funnels the gustiest salty breezes, making the Adriatic seem much nearer than it actually is. And as he gazes, he can rest assured that his hunch was right and that the instinct that brought him here was no less sound than his rational mind. The wines are the product of clay soils, which give lots of power and structure, and the work of skilled oenologist Franco Calini, who tempers this trait to achieve freshness and elegance. Sangiovese Bagnolo displays rather prominent oak on the nose but we found velvety fruit and close-knit tannins on the palate, although fresh, better-calibrated sweetness would have lent the wine more personality. Sorgara expresses itself more fully on the palate than on the nose, showing stylish, supple and full-bodied with plenty of flesh and a dry, dynamic finish. Alloro, a 50-25-25 blend of sangiovese, cabernet sauvignon and cabernet franc, boasts ripe fruit and velvety depth.

O Cà Novina Brut M. Cl. '05	▼▼ 5
● C. B. Cabernet Sauvignon '07	▼▼ 4*
O C. B. Pignoletto '07	▼▼ 4*
O Essè Brut Spumante	▼▼ 4*
O Pignoletto Vivace '07	▼▼ 3*
O Primedizione Cuvée 2008 '07	▼▼ 4
O C. B. Sauvignon '07	▼ 4
● C. B. Cabernet Sauvignon Sel. '99	▼▼▼ 5
● C. B. Cabernet Sauvignon Sel. '97	▼▼▼ 5
● C. B. Merlot Affederico '01	▼▼▼ 5
● Diggioanni Cabernet Sauvignon '04	▼▼▼ 5
● Diggioanni Cabernet Sauvignon '05	▼▼ 5
● Affederico Merlot '05	▼▼ 5
● Affederico Merlot '04	▼▼ 5

● Alloro '06	▼▼ 5
● Sangiovese di Romagna Sup. Bagnolo Ris. '06	▼▼ 5
● Sangiovese di Romagna Sup. Sorgara '06	▼▼ 4*
● Sangiovese di Romagna Sup. Sassetto '07	3
● Sangiovese di Romagna Sup. Sassetto '06	▼▼ 3

Villa di Corlo

LOC. BAGGIOVARA
S.DA CAVEZZO, 200
41100 MODENA
TEL. 059510736
www.villadicorlo.com

ANNUAL PRODUCTION	95,000 bottles
HECTARES UNDER VINE	32
VITICULTURE METHOD	Certified organic

The winery that keeps the enthusiastic Maria Antonia Munari Giacobazzi busy on a day-to-day basis has two aspects and two different locations. Many of the organically farmed vineyards are situated on the high hills of Reggio Emilia and are planted to Bordeaux varieties. Like a Médoc château, the estate produces two wines, both made from cabernet sauvignon, cabernet franc and merlot. Giaco enchanted us with its refined nose and smooth palate laden with fresh fruit, which makes it a very pleasant easy-drinking wine, while Gelsomoro has slightly riper fruit, with pronounced notes of stewed morello cherries, and is a touch less supple on the palate but equally fresh and concentrated. As for the Lambruscos produced at Baggiovara, just outside Modena where the plain starts to give way to the first hills, the current results are good but there is even more potential to be exploited. Rosso Estella, from grasparossa with 40 per cent lambrusco salamino, is very fresh, fragrant and fruity, while Corleto, a monovarietal Grasparossa, is a full-bodied wine with strong notes of ripe cherries.

● Gelsomoro di Viano '06	▼▼	4*
● Giaco di Viano '06	▼▼	4*
● Corleto Lambrusco '07	▼	3
● Rosso Estella Lambrusco '07	▼	3
● Lambrusco di Sorbara '07		3
● Lambrusco Grasparossa di Castelvetro '07		3
● Giaco di Viano '05	▼▼	4

Villa Liverzano

VIA VALLONI, 47
48013 BRISIGHELLA [RA]
TEL. 054680461
www.liverzano.it

ANNUAL PRODUCTION	9,000 bottles
HECTARES UNDER VINE	3
VITICULTURE METHOD	Conventional

Marco Montanari left Tuscany to make wine in Romagna and, considering the surprising results achieved several years on, we suspect that he did so to find somewhere without such a strong tradition. He was probably looking for absolute freedom and the opportunity to produce original wines without having to conform to a long-established territorial style. The estate's special sand and chalk soils are Marco's other route to freedom, for they allow him to emphasize structure without detracting from the great elegance that they confer on the wine. Don, the quintessential outsider, proclaims its diversity with a double label. Uncork it to find extremely concentrated, chewy fruit marked by hot, peppery spiciness that stimulates and invigorates. The palate is deep, dense and velvety, with ripe, creamy, caressing tannins, and the finish is very fresh and poised, with lingering fruit. Rebello is its more retiring brother with a less exuberant personality. The '06 vintage has a dense, fruity tone. Although the general structure is slightly too sweet in both fruit and oak, the palate shows good structure and quality.

● Don '06	▼▼	6
● Rebello '06	▼▼	6
● Don '05	▼▼	6
● Don '04	▼▼	6
● Rebello '05	▼▼	6
● Rebello '04	▼▼	6
● Rebello '03	▼▼	5

Villa Papiano

VIA IBOLA, 24
47015 MODIGLIANA [FC]
TEL. 0546941790
www.villapapiano.it

ANNUAL PRODUCTION	25,000 bottles
HECTARES UNDER VINE	10
VITICULTURE METHOD	Conventional

It was no easy feat to replicate last year's performance, when this small, recently established winery in one of the most beautiful, unspoiled areas of Romagna won our Three Glass trophy. We know for sure that Maria Rosa and Francesco Bordini, who run the estate with a cluster of young partners, are continuing their fine work of raising the quality of the winery without bothering about awards, concentrating on doing things well and allowing nature to take its time. Although very young, Francesco has considerable experience in both the vineyard and the winery, which augurs well for interesting wines full of personality now and in the future. While Papiano di Papiano didn't reach last year's heights, perhaps because of a slight ruggedness, it still displays fine structure and a clear aromatic profile. Sangiovese I Probi di Papiano is pleasantly acid, intensely fruity and extremely drinkable whereas the simpler Le Papesse di Papiano has an intriguing fresh floral note and a fragrant palate, dried somewhat by its substantial alcohol. The sweet Tregenda, from botrytized albana grapes, proffers original elegant notes of candied citron and mandarin.

★ Fattoria Zerbina

FRAZ. MARZENO
VIA VICCHIO, 11
48018 FAENZA [RA]
TEL. 054640022
www.zerbina.com

ANNUAL PRODUCTION	220,000 bottles
HECTARES UNDER VINE	33
VITICULTURE METHOD	Conventional

It's not easy to find new ways to describe what Cristina Geminiani has been doing with unflagging enthusiasm at Fattoria Zerbina for years. One suspects that if her estate were in a more prestigious winegrowing area – neighbouring Tuscany, for example – her efforts would have achieved much greater visibility. But Cristina is not only proud of her Romagna identity: she constantly seeks to promote the area and its producers in Italy and the world. Her wines maintain the high profile that has distinguished them for years, commencing with the splendid new edition of Scacco Matto. This sumptuous, incredibly full-flavoured wine is perfectly balanced by good acidity and an exceptionally stylish mineral vein, which prolongs the elegant sensation of candied citrus fruit on the palate. The fabulous Marzieno is as handsome, elegant and austere as ever, fully deserving its Three Glasses. Finally, there's the exceptional Albana Passito AR Riserva '05, which only a lucky few will be able to taste – the production run is just 300 half bottles – which is a quintessential dessert wine and a once-in-a-lifetime experience.

● Papiano di Papiano '05	▼▼ 5
● Sangiovese di Romagna I Probi di Papiano Ris. '05	▼▼ 4*
● Sangiovese di Romagna Le Papesse di Papiano '06	▼▼ 4*
○ Tregenda '05	▼▼ 5
○ Le Tresche di Papiano '07	▼ 4
● Papiano di Papiano '04	♈♈♈ 5
● Papiano di Papiano '02	♈♈ 6
● Papiano di Papiano '01	♈♈ 6
● Sangiovese di Romagna Le Papesse di Papiano '05	♈♈ 4
● Sangiovese di Romagna I Probi di Papiano Ris. '04	♈♈ 4
● Sangiovese di Romagna I Probi di Papiano Ris. '03	♈♈ 4

● Marzieno '04	▼▼▼ 6
○ Albana di Romagna Passito Scacco Matto '06	▼▼ 7
● Sangiovese di Romagna Sup. Ceregio '07	▼▼ 3*
○ Albana di Romagna Passito Arrocco '06	▼▼ 6
○ Tergeno '06	▼▼ 5
○ Trebbiano di Romagna Dalbiere '07	▼ 3
● Marzieno '03	♈♈♈ 6
● Marzieno '01	♈♈♈ 6
● Marzieno '00	♈♈♈ 6
● Marzieno '99	♈♈♈ 6
● Marzieno '98	♈♈♈ 6
● Sangiovese di Romagna Sup. Pietramora Ris. '04	♈♈♈ 6
● Sangiovese di Romagna Sup. Pietramora Ris. '03	♈♈♈ 7

OTHER WINERIES

Aldrovandi

VIA MARZATORE, 36
40050 MONTEVEGLIO [BO]
TEL. 0516810296

Since the '03, the first release Alto Vanto has always reached our finals, showing how well Federico Aldrovandi works. There are only 3,000 bottles of this incredibly classy Merlot but it flaunts perfectly ripe chewy fruit and shows austere and velvety on the sound, full-bodied palate.

● C. B. Merlot Alto Vanto '06	♛♛	5
● C. B. Merlot Alto Vanto '05	♛♛	5
● C. B. Merlot Alto Vanto '04	♛♛	5

Tenuta Amalia

FRAZ. DIEGARO
VIA EMILIA PONENTE, 2619
47023 CESENA
TEL. 0547347037
www.tenutaamalia.com

Tenuta Amalia presented two good Sangioveses in different styles. Case Rosse is soft and modern, with full, velvety fruit, whereas Riserva Pergami is austere with more structure, hefty alcohol and dazzling acidity on the finish.

● Sangiovese di Romagna Sup. Pergami Ris. '04	♛♛	4*
● Sangiovese di Romagna Sup. Le Case Rosse '06	♛♛	4*

Ancarani

VIA SAN BIAGIO ANTICO, 14
48018 FAENZA [RA]
TEL. 0546642162
www.viniancarani.it

Claudio Ancarani presented three great wines. The well-typed, tangy Santa Lusa is an old-style Albana with nice freshness and elegance. Sâvignon Rosso gives varietal roses and geraniums and a fragrant, chewy palate while the sweet Uvappesa offers a wealth of fruit and spice before the balsam-veined finish.

○ Albana di Romagna Santa Lusa '06	♛♛	4*
● Sâvignon Rosso '06	♛♛	4*
● Uvappesa Vino da Uve Stramature	♛♛	5

Luigi Bassi

VIA VALTIERA, 14
40012 CALDERARA DI RENO [BO]
TEL. 051722233
www.bassiviniaziendaagricola.com

This estate has progressed steadily to earn itself a place in the Guide. The Pinot Bianco has tasty fruit and a soft, tangy palate and the Barbera offers sweet ripe cherry on the nose and a fresh-tasting palate. Pignoletto Frizzante displays a well-calibrated, juicy, zesty palate with full, lingering fruit.

● Barbera '06	♛♛	4
○ Pinot Bianco '07	♛♛	3*
○ Reno Pignoletto Frizzante '07	♛♛	3*

La Berta

VIA BERTA, 13
48013 BRISIGHELLA [RA]
TEL. 054684998
azienda@laberta.it

The two Sangioveses produced by Constantino Giovannini are highly convincing. Solano has chewy fruit and pronounced florality ushering in a pleasing palate, despite the slightly dry finish. Riserva Olmatello flaunts a firmer, more austere style with ripe morello cherry-led fruit and a supple palate.

● Sangiovese di Romagna Sup. Olmatello Ris. '06	♛♛	5
● Sangiovese di Romagna Sup. Solano '07	♛♛	4*

Cà de' Medici

LOC. CADÈ
VIA DELLA STAZIONE, 32
42040 REGGIO EMILIA
TEL. 0522942141
www.cademedici.it

As usual, the most interesting wine produced by Marica Medici's estate is Terra Calda, a solid blend of lambrusco Maestri, lambrusco salamino and ancellotta, which presents dark hued with a dense mousse and a convincingly austere palate. The light San Giacomo Maggiore is limpid with good fresh acidity.

● Terra Calda Frizzante	♛♛	3*
● Reggiano Lambrusco Chiaro San Giacomo Maggiore	♛	2

OTHER WINERIES

Fattoria Camerone

LOC. BIANCANIGO
VIA BIANCANIGO, 1485
48014 CASTEL BOLOGNESE [RA]
TEL. 054650434
www.fattoriacamerone.it

In the absence of their two flagship wines – Sangiovese Millennium and Sangiovese Rosso del Camerone – the Marabini family presented Marafò, a very fresh, consistent current Sangiovese with almost candied fruit. Azdora, an old-style Albana Secco, is well crafted with lots of fruit and a lip-smacking finish.

O Albana di Romagna Secco Azdora '07	▼ 3
● Sangiovese di Romagna Sup. Marafò '07	▼ 3
● Sangiovese di Romagna Sup. Millennium Ris. '03	♈♈ 4

Campodelsole

VIA CELLAIMO, 850
47032 BERTINORO [FC]
TEL. 0543444562
www.campodelsole.it

The estate presented three good Sangioveses. Vertice has a nose of American grapes and peach leading to a soft palate with well-honed extract and a sweetish finish. Durano is simple, fruity and decent on the palate while the richly extracted San Maglorio gives toastiness and a faintly bitter finish.

● Sangiovese di Romagna Sup. Vertice Ris. '05	♈♈ 6
● Sangiovese di Romagna Durano '07	▼ 3
● Sangiovese di Romagna Sup. San Maglorio '07	▼ 3

Castelli del Duca

VIA MORETTA, 58
29011 BORGONOVO VAL TIDONE [PC]
TEL. 0523862168
www.castellidelduca.it

This joint venture between the Medici family of Reggio Emilia and Cantina Valtidone gave us two good Gutturnios in different styles. Sigillum Riserva is firm on the palate while the easy-drinking Augusto is soft and fruity, with pleasant freshness, moderate body and a stylish palate.

● C. P. Gutturnio Cl. Augusto '06	♈♈ 3*
● C. P. Gutturnio Sigillum Ris. '04	♈♈ 5
● C. P. Barbera Ranuccio '06	▼ 2

La Collina

VIA PAGLIA, 19
48013 BRISIGHELLA [RA]
TEL. 054683110
www.lacollina-vinicola.com

The small estate owned by Swiss grower Andre Eggli, returns to the Guide with two vintages of its only wine. Cupola '04 has an attractive style and good development with enough acidity to support the firm, well-integrated tannins. The austere, dignified '05 probably requires a bit more time in bottle.

● Colli di Faenza Sangiovese Cupola '04	♈♈ 5
● Colli di Faenza Sangiovese Cupola '05	♈♈ 5

Corte d'Aibo

VIA MARZATORE, 15
40050 MONTEVEGLIO [BO]
TEL. 051832583
www.cortedaibo.it

In the absence of Cabernet Sauvignon Orfeo '05, which is still ageing in the cellar, it fell to Merlot Roncovecchio to keep the estate's flag flying. We like the very ripe fruit and structure on the palate but there's perhaps a tad too much alcohol. The current Bianco is convincing and uncomplicated.

● C. B. Merlot Roncovecchio '06	♈♈ 4*
O Bianco '07	▼ 3
● C. B. Cabernet Sauvignon Orfeo Ris. '04	♈♈ 6

Costa Archi

LOC. SERRA
VIA RINFOSCO, 1690
48014 CASTEL BOLOGNESE [RA]
TEL. 3384818346

Gabriele Succi, the estate's youthful owner, is rather generous when it comes to oak maturation and his full-bodied Il Beneficio is heavily marked by sweetness that dries the palate. The young, soft, fruity Assiolo is more convincing.

● Sangiovese di Romagna Sup. Assiolo '07	♈♈ 3*
● Sangiovese di Romagna Sup. Il Beneficio '06	▼ 4

OTHER WINERIES

Fondo Cà Vecja

LOC. PONTICELLI
VIA MONTANARA, 204
40020 IMOLA [BO]
TEL. 0542665194
www.fondocavecja.it

Gian Paolo and Simone Padovani's entire range is very good and there are two excellent reds. The Cabernet Sauvignon is exceptionally firm and incisive on the palate while Vigna delle Poiane has more fruit and a rounded, well-finished palate, attractive freshness and excellent texture.

● Colli d'Imola Cabernet Sauvignon Ris. '05	🍷🍷 4*
● Colli d'Imola Sangiovese V. delle Poiane Ris. '05	🍷🍷 4*

Lamoretti

LOC. CASATICO
S.DA DELLA NAVE, 6
43013 LANGHIRANO [PR]
TEL. 0521863590
www.lamorettivini.com

This long-established estate's Malvasia Frizzante is always a safe bet and this year it did better than ever. It may not be over-complex but it is well crafted with good acidity and great aromatics. The red that impressed us most was Serbato, a muscular blend of barbera and cabernet.

○ Colli di Parma Malvasia Frizzante '07	🍷🍷 3*
○ Moscato Dolce '07	🍷 3
● Serbato '06	🍷 4

Lini 1910

VIA VECCHIA CANOLO, 7
42015 CORREGGIO [RE]
TEL. 0522690162
www.vinilini.it

The Lini family's long experience in the production of metodo classico sparklers and Lambruscos is confirmed by the release of convincing new products. Despite its age, the Brut Rosso '04 displays fresh aromas of cherry and morello cherry and a fragrantly ripe, well-structured palate.

● In Correggio Brut Rosso M. Cl. '04	🍷🍷 5
☉ In Correggio Lambrusco Rosato '07	🍷 3
● In Correggio Lambrusco Scuro '07	🍷 3

Daniele Longanesi

VIA BONCELLINO, 114
48012 BAGNACAVALLO [RA]
TEL. 054560289
www.longanesiburson.com

Daniele Longanesi, the grandson of the discoverer of the local Longanesi grape, has proved himself a skilled interpreter of the variety. Bursôn Etichetta Nera, from part-dried grapes, has a full fruity nose and a rich, nuanced palate with firm but well-rounded tannins. Etichetta Blu is simpler and fresher.

● Bursôn Etichetta Nera '03	🍷🍷 4
● Anemo Passito	🍷 4
● Bursôn Etichetta Blu '06	🍷 3

Enrico Loschi

FRAZ. BACEDASCO ALTO
VIA RIVA, 10
29010 CASTELL'ARQUATO [PC]
TEL. 0523895560
www.loschivini.it

Enrico Loschi's Malvasia Passito is very attractive, showing jammy notes on the nose and a nicely unctuous palate, with good acidity to support the marked sweetness. Terre di Guccio has a heady nose, with notes of lavender, flowers and icing sugar preceding a dry, rather simple palate with a faintly bitter finish.

○ C. P. Malvasia Passito L'Arte Contadina '03	🍷🍷 6
○ C. P. Monterosso Val d'Arda Terre di Guccio '07	🍷 4
● C. P. Gutturnio Frizzante Le Rivette '07	🍷 3

Manara

FRAZ. VICOMARINO
29010 ZIANO PIACENTINO [PC]
TEL. 0523860209
manara@netline.it

The Manara family's estate put on an excellent performance. The very sound list is topped by two Gutturnios. The Superiore shows austere and dignified on both the nose and the palate, where it deepens with mellow tannins, while the easy-drinking, fragrant Frizzante is juicy and has lots of fruit.

● C. P. Gutturnio Frizzante '07	🍷🍷 3*
● C. P. Gutturnio Sup. '05	🍷🍷 4*
● Ferraia Ris. '04	🍷🍷 5

OTHER WINERIES

Massina

VIA MASSINA, 1
29010 VERNASCA [PC]
TEL. 0523895384
www.vitivinicolamassina.it

It may have been the very warm growing year but we found this version of Paolo Loschi's Vin Santo less convincing than in the past. While it is still a great dessert wine, it lacks its previous rich complexity. The opulent palate gives attractive lingering sensations of dried fruits and walnutskin.

○ C. P. Vin Santo di Vigoleno '03	♥♥	6

Mattarelli

VIA MARCONI, 35
44049 VIGARANO MAINARDA [FE]
TEL. 053243123
www.mattarelli-vini.it

RosaxEmy, a rosé sparkler, is the latest new wine crafted by Emanuele Mattarelli, the enthusiastic, dynamic owner of the Ferrara estate. Pleasant and easy drinking, it has a soft, satisfying finish. Fortana Frizzante is as reliable as ever, proffering cherry aromas and good acidity.

● Bosco Eliceo Fortana Frizzante '07	♥	3
⊙ Spumante RosaxEmy	♥	3
○ Bosco Eliceo Sauvignon '07		3

Il Monticino

VIA PREDOSA, 72
40069 ZOLA PREDOSA [BO]
TEL. 051755260
www.ilmonticino.it

Following its great debut in last year's Guide, Il Monticino has again done well, presenting a great Barbera Frizzante that bursts with morello cherry on the nose and pleasant fragrant aromas on the palate. The Merlot shows somewhat overripe fruit but a stylish palate while the Pignoletto is fresh and uncomplicated.

● Barbera Frizzante '06	♥♥	4*
● C. B. Merlot '06	♥	4
○ C. B. Pignoletto '07	♥	4

Moro - Rinaldini

FRAZ. CALERNO
VIA ANDREA RIVASI, 27
42049 SANT'ILARIO D'ENZA [RE]
TEL. 0522679190
www.rinaldinivini.it

Paola Rinaldini presented a fine version of his sparkling Pjcol Ross, from the almost extinct lambrusco variety of the same name. Its ripe fruit nose contrasts with a highly original fresh palate. The spicy, caressing Moro del Moro, from dried pjcol ross and ancellotta, is firm, characterful and alcoholic.

● Moro del Moro '04	♥♥	5
● Pjcol Ross Brut	♥	4
● Colli di Scandiano e di Canossa Cabernet Sauvignon Ris. '05	♥	4

Orsi - San Vito

FRAZ. OLIVETO
VIA MONTE RODANO, 8
40050 MONTEVEGLIO [BO]
TEL. 051964521
www.vignetosanvito.it

This historic estate returns to the Guide under the leadership of dynamic owner Federico Orsi. Its Cabernet Sauvignon is outstanding, with juicy, velvet-smooth fruit, excellent softness and fine structure. Pignoletto Superiore has an attractively crisp, stylish palate, good fruit and a dazzling tangy finish.

● C. B. Cabernet Sauvignon Monte Rodano '06	♥♥	4*
○ C. B. Pignoletto Sup. Monte Rodano '07	♥♥	3*

Fattoria Paradiso

LOC. CAPOCOLLE
VIA PALMEGGIANA, 285
47032 BERTINORO [FC]
TEL. 0543445044
www.fattoriaparadiso.com

Graziella Pezzi is back at the helm of the estate her father Mario founded and, knowing her character, we're sure she'll soon achieve good results. For now, we can enjoy the attractive, highly drinkable Barbarossa, which offers slightly aromatic floral notes. The easy-drinking Bellablu shows fresh and fruity.

● Barbarossa '06	♥♥	5
● Bella Blu '06	♥	4
○ Gradisca '07	♥	4
● Mito '05	♥♥	6

OTHER WINERIES

Tenuta Pennita

LOC. TERRA DEL SOLE
VIA PIANELLO, 34
47011 CASTROCARO TERME [FC]
TEL. 0543767451
www.lapennita.it

Gianluca Tumidei Edmeo knows his wines need plenty of time to express themselves so he has kept the flagship Edmeo '05 in the cellar for further ageing. In its place, he gave us a fine Sangiovese Riserva, which shows nice fruity sweetness on the palate and a crisp finish. Superiore La Pennita is very even.

● Sangiovese di Romagna Ris. '05	♟♟ 4
● Sangiovese di Romagna Sup. La Pennita '06	♟ 4

Tenuta Poggio Pollino

VIA MONTE MELDOLA, 2T
40026 IMOLA [BO]
TEL. 0522942135
www.agriturismotenutapoggiopollino.it

Tenuta Poggio Pollino is jointly owned by the Manzi and Medici families. Campo Rosso is a Sangiovese Riserva with a nose of ripe, chewy fruit and a well-structured palate with a slightly dry finish. The highly drinkable Vigna di Cambro has a much simpler and more straightforward style.

● Sangiovese di Romagna Campo Rosso Ris. '05	♟♟ 4*
● Sangiovese di Romagna Sup. V. di Cambro '07	♟ 3

Rontana

VIA RONTANA, 50
48013 BRISIGHELLA [RA]
TEL. 030736094
www.rontana.it

Rontana is owned by the Ricci Curbastro family, best known for their Franciacorta estate. This winery produces just three reds, of which our favourite is Colle Torre Monte, a sangiovese, cabernet and merlot blend with full, perfectly ripe fruit. Sangiovese '06 is simpler and more restrained.

● Colli di Faenza Rosso Colle Torre Monte Ris. '03	♟♟ 5
● Colli di Faenza Sangiovese '06	♟ 3

Tenimenti San Martino in Monte

VIA SAN MARTINO IN MONTE
47015 MODIGLIANA [FC]
TEL. 3292984507

Once again, we were impressed by the two reds. Vigna alle Querce, from merlot, syrah and cabernet franc, has excellent structure and concentrated after-aromas of fresh fruit. Sangiovese Vigna 1922 is initially a little closed but opens out to reveal fruit and spice, followed by an elegant, well-sustained palate.

● Sangiovese di Romagna Vigna 1922 '05	♟♟ 7
● Vigna alle Querce '05	♟♟ 5

Gaetano Solenghi

LOC. BATTIBÒ DI CORANO, 160
29011 BORGONOVO VAL TIDONE [PC]
TEL. 0523860352
www.solenghigaetano.it

Gaetano Solenghi produces rich, gutsy wines, like the only example that we had the chance to taste this time. Danza del Sole, from naturally dried malvasia grapes, is one of the finest of its kind with complex ripe aromatics and a long, full, dynamic palate.

○ Danza del Sole '04	♟♟ 5

Terre della Pieve

FRAZ. DIEGARO
VIA EMILIA PONENTE, 2412
47023 CESENA
TEL. 0547611535
www.terredellepieve.com

This estate's two wines produced surprising results at our tastings. A Virgilio has sound, well-calibrated fruit and is a little tannic on the palate, but nonetheless muscular with good continuity and a soft finish. The more prestigious Nobis, however, is stiff and alcoholic with an over-abundance of edgy tannins.

● Sangiovese di Romagna Sup. A Virgilio '06	♟♟ 3*
● Sangiovese di Romagna Sup. Nobis Ris. '05	♟ 4

OTHER WINERIES

Tenuta La Torretta

LOC. TORRETTA, 1
29010 NIBBIANO VAL TIDONE [PC]
TEL. 0523997008

Franco Carlappi's winery presented us with two very interesting reds. I Salari, a vintage blend of bonarda, cabernet and merlot, has vigour, a soft, fruity palate and moderate body. The Cabernet Sauvignon is also fruity, with slightly firmer structure but an equally stylish, assertive palate.

● C. P. Cabernet Sauvignon '05	♟♟	4
● I Salari '07	♟♟	4*
● C. P. Gutturnio Cl. '07	♟	3

Cantina Valtidone

VIA MORETTA, 58
29011 BORGONOVO VAL TIDONE [PC]
TEL. 0523862168
www.cantinavaltidone.it

Brut Perlage, available only in magnums, is as usual one of the region's best sparklers, showing fragrant, zesty and flavoursome. The highly drinkable Gutturnio Julius offers attractively refreshing fruit in the mouth and firm, well-calibrated structure. Ortrugo Frizzante is full and fragrant.

○ Brut Perlage	♟♟	5
● C. P. Gutturnio Cl. Julius '06	♟♟	4*
○ C. P. Ortrugo Frizzante Armonia '07	♟	3

Vigneto delle Terre Rosse

VIA PREDOSA, 83
40069 ZOLA PREDOSA [BO]
TEL. 051755845
www.terrerosse.com

The Vallania family presented three fine whites that confirmed the estate's long tradition. We were particularly impressed by the tropical fruit of the Chardonnay Speciale Cuvée, which has a light yet deep palate with velvet-soft fruit. The Malvasia has well-balanced sweetness and fragrant notes of candied peel.

○ C. B. Chardonnay Cuvée Speciale '05	♟♟	5
○ Malvasia Adriana Vallania '07	♟♟	4
○ Riesling Italico Malagò V. T. '05	♟	5

Torricella

VIA SAMOGGIA, 534G
40060 SAVIGNO [BO]
TEL. 0516708552

Alessandro Bartolini confirmed last year's good results. We particularly liked Barbera Amelio, which gives generous chewy fruit and a firm, rounded palate. Cabernet Narciso is complex and nicely balanced in the mouth with a soft, crisp finish whereas Merlot Lanselmo shows pleasantly spicy but a tad lightweight.

● C. B. Barbera Amelio '07	♟♟	4
● C. B. Cabernet Sauvignon Narciso '06	♟♟	4
● C. B. Merlot Lanselmo '06	♟	4

Podere Vecciano

VIA VECCIANO, 23
47852 CORIANO [RN]
TEL. 0541658388
www.poderevecciano.it

Davide Bigucci is one of the few Rimini producers to make a single-variety Rebola and the results impress. VignalaGinestra is refreshing and tangy, with slightly terpenic aromas, but it certainly convinces. Sangiovese D'Enio shows firm and lean, with rather ripe fruit but good acidity.

○ Colli di Rimini Rebola VignalaGinestra '07	♟♟	4*
● Sangiovese di Romagna Sup. D'Enio Ris. '06	♟♟	5

Villa Trentola

LOC. CAPOCOLLE DI BERTINORO
VIA MOLINO BRATTI, 1305
47032 BERTINORO [FC]
TEL. 0543741389
www.villatrentola.it

This year, the Prugnoli sisters presented just one wine, having decided to leave their finest offerings in the cellar for further ageing. Il Prugnolo is an excellent Sangiovese for everyday drinking, with full, nicely ripe fruit and a subtle palate supported by refreshing acidity.

● Sangiovese di Romagna Sup. Il Prugnolo di Villa Trentola '06	♟♟	4*
● Sangiovese di Romagna Sup. Il Moro di Villa Trentola '05	♟♟	5

This time, Tuscany's haul of Three Glass prizes fell to just 49. The vintages presented in the various winemaking zones were challenging, especially so in the case of Brunello di Montalcino with the '03. It was a torrid growing season, to put it mildly, and the sangiovese failed to ripen properly. Tannins in particular were acerbic and mouth-drying, a characteristic that all the wines share to some degree and which are more obvious in bottles from the warmer areas. The upshot was that only one 2003 Brunello di Montalcino, from Biondi Santi, took our top award, thanks to old vines and a more traditional winemaking technique, which reined in the extract. Elsewhere in the region, from coast to hinterland, it was the 2005 vintage that featured most often. This, too, was a complicated growing year when quality had its ups and downs. But although the year was fraught, that doesn't mean the wines aren't worth uncorking. The ones that stood out show similarities, despite coming from different areas. They are elegant, acidity-led wines that may not have muscle but will, we think, be exceptionally long-lived. Time will tell. It would be impossible, as well as tedious, to list them all so here are one or two we think are emblematic. From the coast, there is a magisterially sophisticated Bolgheri Sassicaia. Further north, Nambrot from Tenuta di Ghizzano and Colline Lucchesi Tenuta di Valgiano from the estate of the same name show a more linear, austere side. Some of the Chianti Classico Riservas were much praised, including Capraia from Tenuta di Capraia, Ruffino's Riserva Ducale Oro and Rancia from Felsina. By the way, we would also point out that Felsina, the much-respected winery at Castelnuovo Berardenga, was nominated our Winery of the Year. Twenty-four Three Glass prizes over the Guide's history bear witness, if any were needed, to what Felsina stands for in terms of absolute quality and consistency. Nor is it a surprise that Fontalloro and a fine array of single-variety Sangioveses triumphed. Also honoured were Flaccianello della Pieve, I Sodi di San Niccolò, Cepparello and a Tignanello that is not quite sangiovese-only but very nearly. Among all the '05s were one or two advance releases of 2006, a year that looks to be more even in quality and rather more exciting. A standard-label Chianti Classico from Badia a Coltibuono took Three Glasses, as did the usual suspects, Galatrona and Blu from Brancaia. There were also newcomers to Three Glass honours in Kepos from Ampeleia and Pugnitello from San Felice. But these are only a few of the winners. For the others, you will have to leaf through the Guide.

Abbadia Ardenga

FRAZ. TORRENIERI
VIA ROMANA, 139
53028 MONTALCINO [SI]
TEL. 0577834150
www.abbadiardengapoggio.it

ANNUAL PRODUCTION	35,000 bottles
HECTARES UNDER VINE	10
VITICULTURE METHOD	Conventional

This winery in the north of the Montalcino area is brilliantly managed by Mario Ciacci, who presented a splendid range of wines. Quality is constantly improving, especially where Brunello di Montalcino is concerned. There are two versions this year, both highly successful. The '03 Brunello di Montalcino is very traditional in its garnet-flecked ruby hue and on the nose, where florality and tobacco come through. The deliciously drinkable palate is nicely balanced. Nicely resolved tannins are apparent, especially in the finish. It's a wine that will appeal to lovers of elegance. Brunello di Montalcino Vigna Piaggia '03 is slightly different. A fruit-forward bouquet foregrounds plums and cherry jam. In the mouth, it is rather gutsier, youthful but nicely gauged tannins playing their part, and the finish is intriguing. Don't forget to try the good '06 Rosso di Montalcino. Its broad swath of aromatics accompanies the cellar's trademark drinkability. Last but not least, prices across the range are very competitive.

● Brunello di Montalcino '03	♥♥	6
● Brunello di Montalcino Vigna Piaggia '03	♥♥	6
● Rosso di Montalcino '06	♥	4
● Brunello di Montalcino '01	♥♥	6
● Brunello di Montalcino '00	♥♥	6

Agricola Alberese

FRAZ. ALBERESE
LOC. SPERGOLAIA
58010 GROSSETO [GR]
TEL. 0564407180
www.alberese.com

ANNUAL PRODUCTION	100,000 bottles
HECTARES UNDER VINE	53
VITICULTURE METHOD	Certified organic

Agricola Alberese is managed directly by the Tuscan regional authority, an almost unique example of public engagement in agriculture. The estate lies within the Maremma regional park. A recent makeover did much for the grape growing and winemaking sectors and the range of wines we received this year was encouragingly good. The stand-outs were Morellino di Scansano Pellegrone '06 and Morellino di Scansano Serrata dei Cavalleggeri '07. Pellegrone has a smoke-veined nose that fuses lavish fruit and convincing structure with a tangy, nicely contrasted flavour. Warm, upfront fragrances grace the Serrata dei Cavalleggeri, a delightfully moreish bottle with a juicy succession of tasty sensations on the palate. The Morellino di Scansano Barbicato '05 is equally well gauged with its liqueur fruits and pencil lead aromatics, although the palate is held back a little by over-generous oak. Morellino Poggio del Collegio '07 did well, showing full flavoured if a tad fuzzy on the nose. Finally, the Vermentino Castelmarino '07 is enjoyable.

● Morellino di Scansano Pellegrone '06	♥♥	4*
● Morellino di Scansano Serrata dei Cavalleggeri '07	♥♥	4*
● Morellino di Scansano Barbicato '05	♥	6
● Morellino di Scansano Poggio del Collegio '07	♥	4
○ Vermentino Castelmarino '07	♥	4
● Morellino di Scansano '05	♥♥	4
● Morellino di Scansano Barbicato '04	♥♥	4

Agricoltori del Chianti Geografico

LOC. MULINACCIO, 10
53013 GAIOLE IN CHIANTI [SI]
TEL. 0577749489
www.chiantigeografico.it

ANNUAL PRODUCTION	1,600,000 bottles
HECTARES UNDER VINE	580
VITICULTURE METHOD	Conventional

What a historic result for the Agricoltori del Chianti Geografico! It's the first time a Tuscan co-operative has earned Three Glasses. Kudos to the Chianti Classico Montegiachi Riserva '05, which had been performing magnificently in recent vintages and this year went one better with subtle, wide-ranging aromatics and excellent structure in a palate that remains elegant and stylish. Director Carlo Salvadori must be very happy with this reward for all his hard work motivating winery workers and all the member growers hard at work in vineyard and cellar. As ever, the sangiovese and cabernet sauvignon '05 Ferraiolo is attractive, giving herbaceousness and black berry fruit in a complex, lingering palate. This was also the first year of production for the new Montalcino wines and the debut was positive for both the Rosso '06 and the '03 Brunello, two wines whose hallmark is territory focus. The rest of the range did well, the attractively easy-drinking Chianti Classicos attracting compliments.

Fattoria dell'Aiola

LOC. VAGLIAGLI
53010 CASTELNUOVO BERARDENGA [SI]
TEL. 0577322615
www.aiola.net

ANNUAL PRODUCTION	200,000 bottles
HECTARES UNDER VINE	36
VITICULTURE METHOD	Conventional

Quality stays gratifyingly high at Maria Grazia Malagodi's winery, where Chianti Classico is the leading product. You could justifiably call the estate historic, since the family purchased it in the 1930s and then opted to focus on premium-quality wines. The two Supertuscans were missing this year but the other wines stepped into the breach left by the absence of Rosso del Senatore, named after Maria Grazia's father, who was a senator, and Logaiolo. We found Cancello Rosso '05 the most convincing. It's a rich ruby red Chianti Classico Riserva with elegant aromatics that meld minerality and gamey notes with well-defined hints of jam. Rounded and full-bodied on the palate, it flaunts nicely tucked in tannins and a convincing, rising finish. The extract of the other Chiantis is a little more aggressive. Finally, we would point out that the estate also has farmstay facilities and makes a range of other products, including brandy distilled from its own wines and a large selection of honeys.

● Chianti Cl. Montegiachi Ris. '05	▼▼▼ 5
● Brunello di Montalcino Castello Tricerchi '03	▼▼ 8
● Ferraiolo '05	▼▼ 6
● Rosso di Montalcino Castello Tricerchi '06	▼▼ 5
O Campo Vernino '07	▼ 4
● Chianti Cl. '06	▼ 4
● Chianti Cl. Contessa di Radda '06	▼ 4
● Chianti dei Colli Senesi Torri Ris. '05	▼ 4
● Morellino di Scansano Le Preselle '07	▼ 4
O Vernaccia di S. Gimignano Pietravalle '07	▼ 4
● Chianti Cl. Contessa di Radda '05	♀♀ 4
● Chianti Cl. Montegiachi Ris. '04	♀♀ 5
● Ferraiolo '04	♀♀ 6
● Pulleraia '05	♀♀ 6
● Pulleraia '03	♀♀ 5
● Pulleraia '01	♀♀ 6

● Chianti Cl. Cancello Rosso Ris. '05	▼▼ 7
● Chianti Cl. '06	▼ 4
● Chianti Cl. Ris. '05	▼ 5
● Chianti Cl. Cancello Rosso Ris. '00	♀♀ 7
● Chianti Cl. Cancello Rosso Ris. '99	♀♀ 7
● Logaiolo '03	♀♀ 4
● Rosso del Senatore '04	♀♀ 6
● Rosso del Senatore '03	♀♀ 6
● Rosso del Senatore '01	♀♀ 6

Podere l'Aione

LOC. AIONE, 12
56040 MONTECATINI VAL DI CECINA [PI]
TEL. 058830339
stefano-baldacci@libero.it

ANNUAL PRODUCTION	25,000 bottles
HECTARES UNDER VINE	6
VITICULTURE METHOD	Conventional

Another fine performance from Podere L'Aione earned the winery a full profile, which we are sure it will keep in future. This is a great result for a cellar set up in 1992, when owners Robert Walti and Doris Portner recovered an old vineyard after restructuring the estate building. The vineyard, Aione, makes a wine of the same name from previously neglected vines about 80 years old. The purchase of a new vineyard in 1998 led to two new wines, Salve and Etico. There is a common thread linking all the cellar's products: careful bunch selection in the vineyard to produce clean, impressively structured wines in a modern, but not over-adventurous, style. This time, it was the wines from the younger vineyards that went forward to the national finals. The merlot-heavy Etico '05 is characterful, giving grassy notes on the nose followed by a densely textured body with amazing acidity. The sangiovese-only '05 Salve has rich texture and outstanding thrust on the palate. Once it has lost a little of its youthful impetuousness, we think it will age very well indeed. The '05 Aione, distributed only abroad, is held back by slightly over-assertive extract.

● Etico '05	▼▼	6
● Salve '05	▼▼	6
● Aione '05	▼	6
● Aione '03	♥♥	6
● Aione '01	♥♥	6
● Etico '04	♥♥	6
● Salve '03	♥♥	6

Castello d'Albola

LOC. PIAN D'ALBOLA, 31
53017 RADDA IN CHIANTI [SI]
TEL. 0577738019
www.albola.it

ANNUAL PRODUCTION	800,000 bottles
HECTARES UNDER VINE	157
VITICULTURE METHOD	Conventional

It's been a transitional year for the Zonin family's Chianti estate. Chianti Classico Riserva '04 sailed through to our finals but the Supertuscan Acciaiolo '05, from sangiovese and cabernet sauvignon, was less convincing. It lacks a little balance in the mouth, where the tannins protrude, and is not the wine we have been used to drinking in the past. Still, we were happy to note that this winery manages to make very attractive wines in serious numbers while continuing its effort to give more personality to each label, especially the bottles that are most characteristic of their territory of provenance. One wine that does this well is the Riserva '04, thanks to fresh aromas of Mediterranean shrubland and menthol introducing a vibrantly fresh, juicy palate that signs off with a lingering note of attractive aromatic herbs. The wines from Maremma are decently drinkable, and a special mention must go to the Monteregio di Massa Marittima Sassabruna '06.

● Chianti Cl. Ris. '04	▼▼	5
● Acciaiolo '05	▼	7
○ Calasole '07	▼	4
○ Chardonnay '07	▼	4
● Chianti Cl. Le Ellere '05	▼	5
● Le Focaie '07	▼	4
● Monteregio di Massa Marittima Sassabruna '06	▼	4
○ Vin Santo del Chianti Cl. '00	▼	7
● Acciaiolo '04	♥♥♥	7
● Acciaiolo '01	♥♥♥	7
● Acciaiolo '95	♥♥♥	6

★★ Castello di Ama

FRAZ. LECCHI IN CHIANTI
LOC. AMA
53013 GAIOLE IN CHIANTI [SI]
TEL. 0577746031
www.castellodiama.com

ANNUAL PRODUCTION	350,000 bottles
HECTARES UNDER VINE	95
VITICULTURE METHOD	Conventional

It might not have been a great growing year in Chianti Classico, especially on the higher ground where the Ama vineyards are situated, but Chianti Classico Castello di Ama '05 still swept up Three Glasses. It's an iconic wine that in this incarnation reveals only a slightly more emphatic hint of the merlot in the blend, especially on the nose, where the variety's sometimes warm, evolved nuances come through clearly. As usual, good acidity braces the palate, adding a tautness that extends the finish. Forward notes turned out to be a theme of the entire range, for example in the normally fantastic Chianti Classico Bellavista – this time we tasted the '04 – and the Apparita Merlot, again from '04. The Rosato '07 and Chardonnay al Poggio '07 are very fine examples of their respective genres and we look forward to the Chianti Classico '06, of which we enjoyed a very promising advance tasting.

Fattoria Ambra

VIA LOMBARDA, 85
59015 CARMIGNANO [PO]
TEL. 3358282552
www.fattoriaambra.it

ANNUAL PRODUCTION	80,000 bottles
HECTARES UNDER VINE	19
VITICULTURE METHOD	Conventional

Fattoria di Ambra always regales us with a range of wines that manage to combine premium quality with territory focus. The Carmignano Elzana Riserva '05 is fantastic, earning a spot in our finals by virtue of its red fruits, spice and coffee aromas and a palate with rich extract, attractively taut acidity and an assertive, gutsy finale. We were also delighted with the '05 Carmignano Le Vigne Alte di Montalbiolo Riserva's juicy mouthfeel, soft, delicate tannic weave and attractive persistence. Carmignano Vigna Santa Cristina in Pilli '06 is one of the anchors of the range. Its juicy, fruit-led deliciously textured palate reveals polished, well tucked in tannins and signs off with a deep, limpid finish. The Carmignano Vigna di Montefortini '06 offers youthful alcohol and a whistle-clean palate. Flavour and balance characterize the Rosato while Barco Reale is attractively clean, giving red berry fruit and fairly lightweight structure. Both are '07s.

● Chianti Cl. Castello di Ama '05	▼▼▼	6
● Chianti Cl. Bellavista '04	▼▼	8
○ Al Poggio Chardonnay '07	▼	5
● l'Apparita Merlot '04	▼	8
⊙ Rosato '07	▼	4
● Chianti Cl. Bellavista '01	♟♟♟	8
● Chianti Cl. Bellavista '99	♟♟♟	8
● Chianti Cl. Bellavista '95	♟♟♟	6
● Chianti Cl. Castello di Ama '03	♟♟♟	6
● Chianti Cl. Castello di Ama '01	♟♟♟	6
● Chianti Cl. Castello di Ama '00	♟♟♟	6
● Chianti Cl. Castello di Ama '99	♟♟♟	5
● Chianti Cl. La Casuccia '01	♟♟♟	8
● Chianti Cl. La Casuccia '97	♟♟♟	8
● l'Apparita Merlot '01	♟♟♟	8
● l'Apparita Merlot '00	♟♟♟	8

● Carmignano Elzana Ris. '05	▼▼	5
● Carmignano Le Vigne Alte di Montalbiolo Ris. '05	▼▼	5
● Barco Reale '07	▼	3
● Carmignano V. di Montefortini '06	▼	4
● Carmignano V. S. Cristina in Pilli '06	▼	4
⊙ Rosato di Carmignano Vin Ruspo '07	▼	3
● Carmignano Elzana Ris. '04	♟♟	5
● Carmignano Elzana Ris. '01	♟♟	5
● Carmignano Le Vigne Alte di Montalbiolo Ris. '04	♟♟	5
● Carmignano Le Vigne Alte di Montalbiolo Ris. '00	♟♟	5
● Carmignano V. S. Cristina in Pilli '05	♟♟	4
● Carmignano V. S. Cristina in Pilli '03	♟♟	4
● Carmignano V. S. Cristina in Pilli '01	♟♟	4
○ Vin Santo di Carmignano '00	♟♟	6
○ Vin Santo di Carmignano '99	♟♟	6

Ampeleia

LOC. MELETA
58036 ROCCASTRADA [GR]
TEL. 0564567155
www.ampeleia.it

ANNUAL PRODUCTION	100,000 bottles
HECTARES UNDER VINE	50
VITICULTURE METHOD	Conventional

The Ampeleia story began in 2002 with the purchase of the former Fattoria di Meleta, which in the 1980s had been one of the benchmarks of the at that time unfashionable Maremma winemaking scene. The moving spirits behind this enterprise, which is much more than a humdrum winemaking operation, are three friends, Elisabetta Foradori, Thomas Widmann and Giovanni Podini. Their backgrounds and origins are varied, Elisabetta being a grower while the other two are businessmen, but a deep passion for wine unites them. Their uncompromising efforts are focused firmly on the future as they search for an innovative, personal style that can interpret the territory. Crowning those efforts now is their first Three Glass award for Kepos '06, a blend of five Mediterranean varieties: grenache, mourvèdre, marselan, carignano and alicante. This highly original wine has complex aromas that unfold to reveal oriental spices, flowers and Mediterranean shrubland. Approachable yet far from banal, it maintains pressure on the palate before taking its leave with a savoury, fresh-tasting finish.

★★ Marchesi Antinori

P.ZZA DEGLI ANTINORI, 3
50123 FIRENZE
TEL. 05523595
www.antinori.it

ANNUAL PRODUCTION	20,000,000 bottles
HECTARES UNDER VINE	1400
VITICULTURE METHOD	Conventional

Our astonishment last year at Tignanello, which won another Three Glass prize after an 11-year gap, is repeated this year. Last time, it was the wine's return to top honours after ten lean years outshining serial Three Glass winner Solaia, but this time it was Tignanello's extraordinary stylistic perfection, something that couldn't be taken for granted in the 2005 growing year. From sangiovese with 15 per cent cabernet sauvignon and cabernet franc, the initially hesitant, reduced nose unfolds into a complex weave of red fruits, freshness, saddle leather and damp earth. The very taut palate is dominated by acidity and incredibly long. All in all, it's a wonderfully exciting wine that stands comparison with some past vintages. Solaia '05, from cabernet sauvignon with a dash of franc, is not quite up to its usual standard, perhaps because of the cool growing year. Black berry fruit, balsam and rain-soaked earth herald a palate whose assertive tannins prevent the wine from unfolding to the full. The highly drinkable Chianti Classico Peppoli '06 is great value for money but the entire range is utterly reliable.

● Kepos '06	♟♟♟ 6
● Ampeleia '05	♟♟ 6
● Ampeleia '04	♟♟ 6

● Tignanello '05	♟♟♟ 8
● Chianti Cl. Pèppoli '06	♟♟ 4
● Solaia '05	♟♟
● Chianti Cl. Tenute del Marchese Ris. '04	♟ 6
● Santa Cristina '07	♟ 4
● Santa Cristina Merlot delle Maestrelle '07	♟ 3
○ Vin Santo del Chianti Cl. '04	♟ 6
● Solaia '01	♟♟♟ 8
● Solaia '00	♟♟♟ 8
● Solaia '99	♟♟♟ 8
● Solaia '98	♟♟♟ 8
● Solaia '97	♟♟♟ 8
● Solaia '96	♟♟♟ 6
● Tignanello '04	♟♟♟ 8

Argentiera

LOC. DONORATICO
VIA AURELIA, 410
57024 CASTAGNETO CARDUCCI [LI]
TEL. 0565773176
www.argentiera.eu

ANNUAL PRODUCTION 400,000 bottles
HECTARES UNDER VINE 60
VITICULTURE METHOD Conventional

This Castagneto Carducci-based joint
venture by brothers Corrado and Marcello
Fratini with Piero Antinori confirmed
that it is working well. The estate's vines
extend from hillsides to seaside, from
Castiglioncello to Baratti. Despite a
less than thrilling growing year, the '05
Bolgheri Superiore Argentiera lived up to
expectations and earned Three Glasses.
From equal parts of cabernet sauvignon
and merlot with 20 per cent cabernet
franc, it is a wine with a fresh green nose of
baked peppers. The deliciously caressing
mouthfeel is tautened by the distinct acidity
delivered by the vintage. Bell peppers
return on the long, juicy back palate. Villa
Donoratico '05, from 65 per cent cabernet
sauvignon, 25 per cent merlot and ten per
cent franc, is everything you would expect
from a second wine. Fresh and appealing
with well-defined berry fruit, it is held back
only by slight pungency on the back palate.
Finally, the lean, fresh Poggi ai Ginepri '06
from half cabernet sauvignon with equal
parts of syrah and merlot, is a nice easy
drinker.

★ Avignonesi

FRAZ. VALIANO DI MONTEPULCIANO
VIA COLONICA, 1
53040 MONTEPULCIANO [SI]
TEL. 0578724304
www.avignonesi.it

ANNUAL PRODUCTION 700,000 bottles
HECTARES UNDER VINE 119
VITICULTURE METHOD Conventional

Avignonesi may now have a new majority
shareholder with a Belgian passport but
the Valiano-based winery is still a major
force in Montepulciano and synonymous
with Vino Nobile, and especially Vin Santo.
The celebrated sweet wine has a long
tradition at Montepulciano and Avignonesi
always produces memorable versions.
Fittingly, the extraordinarily sophisticated
Vin Santo '96 won Three Glasses for
its intense, classic dried fruit and honey
fragrances, preceding a vibrant, creamy-
textured palate whose marked acidity
contrasts with the sweetness to lend the
wine awesome depth. The Occhio di
Pernice '96 is intriguing. Emblematic of
its genre, it gives pervasive aromas and
impressively dense texture. The stand-
outs in a good range of reds were the rich,
juicy and surprisingly affordable Cortona
Desiderio '06, from merlot and cabernet
sauvignon, and the Rosso Avignonesi '06,
from sangiovese, cabernet sauvignon and
merlot, which unveils great complexity
on the nose. All the other wines are up to
snuff.

● Bolgheri Sup. Argentiera '05	♟♟♟	8
● Bolgheri Villa Donoratico '05	♟♟	5
● Bolgheri Poggio ai Ginepri '06	♟	4
● Bolgheri Sup. Argentiera '04	♟♟♟	8
● Bolgheri Sup. Argentiera '03	♟♟	8
● Bolgheri Villa Donoratico '04	♟♟	5

○ Vin Santo '96	♟♟♟	8
● Vin Santo Occhio di Pernice '96	♟♟	8
● Cortona Desiderio '06	♟♟	7
● Rosso Avignonesi '06	♟♟	4*
● 50 & 50 Avignonesi e Capannelle '04	♟	8
○ Cortona Il Marzocco '06	♟	6
○ Cortona Sauvignon Blanc '07	♟	4
● Nobile di Montepulciano '05	♟	5
● Rosso di Montepulciano '07	♟	4
● 50 & 50 Avignonesi e Capannelle '99	♟♟♟	8
○ Vin Santo '95	♟♟♟	8
○ Vin Santo '93	♟♟♟	8
● Vin Santo Occhio di Pernice '93	♟♟♟	8
○ Vin Santo Occhio di Pernice '90	♟♟♟	8
○ Vin Santo Occhio di Pernice '89	♟♟♟	8

Badia a Coltibuono

LOC. BADIA A COLTIBUONO
53013 GAIOLE IN CHIANTI [SI]
TEL. 0577746110
www.coltibuono.com

ANNUAL PRODUCTION	1,100,000 bottles
HECTARES UNDER VINE	72
VITICULTURE METHOD	Certified organic

Last year, we mentioned the new direction taken by this Gaiola-based winery, managed by the tenacious Emanuela Stucchi Prinetti. Confirmation came this year, crowned by the exploit of the Chianti Classico '06, which was the best bottle from Coltibuono and won Three Glasses. It was an excellent performance that had the panel nodding in approval as tasters savoured the invitingly fresh aromas and intriguing fruit ushering in a thoroughly enjoyable palate whose key feature is equilibrium. This is a highly drinkable, everyday wine. Also impressive is the Riserva '05, its structure only slightly penalized by an indifferent growing year, while the lovely all-sangiovese Siangioveto '04 has gained in body and softness on the palate. Vin Santo fans will enjoy the '02 release, which is firmly back on the rails of tradition and combines creaminess with sweetness. All in all, this was a good showing from the Coltibuono list, which offers attractive value for money.

Badia di Morrona

VIA DEL CHIANTI, 6
56030 TERRICCIOLA [PI]
TEL. 0587656013
www.badiadimorrona.it

ANNUAL PRODUCTION	200,000 bottles
HECTARES UNDER VINE	85
VITICULTURE METHOD	Conventional

We were keen to see how Badia wines would perform this year. The Badia in question is Badia di Morrona, a lovely property near Pisa that in recent years has had its ups and downs in terms of production. But this time, the results were highly gratifying and, taken with last year's, suggest that we can look forward to reliable quality from a winery that is very important for the territory. The reds amazed our tasters with their whistle-clean fragrances and attractive palates. Emblematic of this across-the-range quality is Chianti I Sodi del Paretaio '07, a sincere, wonderfully drinkable wine with exceptional breadth on the nose. N'Antia '05, a 60-30-10 blend of cabernet sauvignon, merlot and cabernet franc is still austere but gives plenty of bright acidity and attractive fruit. We think it will age very well indeed. Also outstanding is the syrah and sangiovese Taneto '06 with its spice-veined nose and long, juicy palate. The whites are all well made but without any quality peaks.

● Chianti Cl. '06	♟♟♟ 5*
● Chianti Cl. Ris. '05	♟♟ 6
● Sangioveto '04	♟♟ 7
○ Vin Santo del Chianti Cl. '02	♟♟ 6
● Chianti Cetamura '06	♟ 4
● Chianti Cl. R. S. '07	♟ 4
● Chianti Cl. Ris. '04	♟♟♟ 6
● Sangioveto '95	♟♟♟ 6
● Sangioveto '01	♟♟ 7

● Chianti I Sodi del Paretaio '07	♟♟ 3*
● N'Antia '05	♟♟ 5
● Taneto '06	♟♟ 4*
○ Felciaio '07	♟ 3
○ La Suvera '07	♟ 4
● N'Antia '04	♟♟ 5
● N'Antia '01	♟♟ 6
● Vigna Alta '04	♟♟ 6
● Vigna Alta '01	♟♟ 6
● Vigna Alta '99	♟♟ 6
○ Vin Santo '03	♟♟ 6

Fattoria di Bagnolo

LOC. BAGNOLO-CANTAGALLO
VIA IMPRUNETANA PER TAVARNUZZE, 48
50023 IMPRUNETA [FI]
TEL. 0552313403
www.bartolinibaldelli.it

ANNUAL PRODUCTION	27,000 bottles
HECTARES UNDER VINE	10
VITICULTURE METHOD	Conventional

We recorded another excellent result for the winery owned by Marco Bartolini Baldelli, a man who has made farming his raison d'être and who scrupulously manages his properties scattered across Tuscany. A tireless promoter of his wines around the world, Marco is a firm believer in the potential of his territory. He already has a well established reputation for his premium extra virgin olive oil and today is also making a name for wine. Sangiovese is the main variety and the basis for the fruit that goes into all his labels, although cabernet sauvignon and colorino are also on hand for the Capro Rosso Supertuscan. The management programme developed with oenologist Lorenzo Landi has a solid foundation and has produced consistent results. All the wines are on a par for quality so plans for the future could hinge on creating a portfolio of better defined profiles. For now, we appreciated the fresh, fragrant Chianti Colli Fiorentini '06, the austere, muscular Riserva '05 and the soft, flavoursome Capro Rosso '05.

★ Castello Banfi

LOC. SANT'ANGELO SCALO
CASTELLO DI POGGIO ALLE MURA
53024 MONTALCINO [SI]
TEL. 0577840111
www.castellobanfi.com

ANNUAL PRODUCTION	13,500,000 bottles
HECTARES UNDER VINE	850
VITICULTURE METHOD	Conventional

This large Montalcino operation managed by Enrico Viglierchio is always reliable and has done much to spread the gospel of Montalcino around the world. The list is long and all the wines are good. It was a challenging growing year for Brunello di Montalcino, a DOCG zone that was particularly hard hit by the extreme weather of 2003 but there are highly gratifying results from the Sant'Antimo designation. Sant'Antimo Cum Laude '05, from 30 per cent each of cabernet sauvignon and merlot, 25 per cent sangiovese and 15 per cent syrah is inky dark and weaves wonderful cedar and pencil lead with its trademark currants and blackberries. The tannins are slightly clenched on the attractively savoury palate but the finish is long-lingering and complex. Also very good is the cabernet sauvignon-only Sant'Antimo Tavernelle '05, which has a fresh, grassy nose and a juicily long, relaxed palate. Other bottles to watch out for are the intense golden Moscadello di Montalcino Florus '06, with its swath of aromatics on the nose, the merlot-only Sant'Antimo Mandrielle '05, which gives supple extract, and the spicy, syrah-based Sant'Antimo Colvecchio '05.

● Capro Rosso '05	♀♀ 6
● Chianti Colli Fiorentini '06	♀♀ 4*
● Chianti Colli Fiorentini Ris. '05	♀♀ 5
● Capro Rosso '04	♀♀ 5
● Capro Rosso '03	♀♀ 5
● Capro Rosso '02	♀♀ 5
● Chianti Colli Fiorentini '05	♀♀ 3*
● Chianti Colli Fiorentini '04	♀♀ 3*
● Chianti Colli Fiorentini Ris. '04	♀♀ 5
● Chianti Colli Fiorentini Ris. '03	♀♀ 5
● Chianti dei Colli Fiorentini Ris. '01	♀♀ 5

● Sant'Antimo Cum Laude '05	♀♀ 4
● Sant'Antimo Tavernelle '05	♀♀ 5
● Brunello di Montalcino Poggio alle Mura '03	♀♀ 8
O Moscadello di Montalcino Florus '06	♀♀ 5
● Sant'Antimo Colvecchio '05	♀♀ 5
● Sant'Antimo Mandrielle '05	♀♀ 5
● Brunello di Montalcino '03	♀ 7
● Centine '07	♀ 3
● Colle Pino '07	♀ 2
● Rosso di Montalcino '06	♀ 4
O Sant'Antimo Fontanelle '07	♀ 4
● Sant'Antimo Summus '05	♀ 7
● Brunello di Montalcino Poggio alle Mura '99	♀♀♀ 8
● Brunello di Montalcino Poggio alle Mura '98	♀♀♀ 8

Riccardo Baracchi

LOC. CAMUCIA
VIA CEGLIOLO, 21
52042 CORTONA [AR]
TEL. 0575612679
www.baracchiwinery.com

ANNUAL PRODUCTION 45,000 bottles
HECTARES UNDER VINE 22
VITICULTURE METHOD Conventional

Little has changed at Riccardo Baracchi's winery, one of the most consistently reliable in the Cortona area. This means that the wines are once again excellent, beautifully made in the modern style, reasonably approachable and instinctively likeable. A genuine thoroughbred might be missing from the stable but we reckon that in a cellar as new as this, there is plenty of reason to be happy about the results achieved so far. The most ambitious bottle on the list is Ardito '05, a blend of syrah and cabernet. It's a beefy wine all right, its compact profile revealing hints of pencil lead and printer's ink under the dark berry fruit. Thick, pulpy with a lovely tannic weave, it fills the palate with its breadth and weight, unfolding a little slowly but with attractive depth. We thought the better of the two '06 Cortona Smeriglios was the warmly ripe, spice-rich Merlot, which has a lovely follow-through on the fruit-rich, well-balanced palate '06. The Sangiovese is fresher and more nuanced in its aromatics and unfolds attractively only to close fairly stiffly, with assertive alcohol.

Fattoria dei Barbi

LOC. PODERNOVI, 170
53024 MONTALCINO [SI]
TEL. 0577841111
www.fattoriadeibarbi.it

ANNUAL PRODUCTION 800,000 bottles
HECTARES UNDER VINE 90
VITICULTURE METHOD Conventional

This historic operation is a Brunello di Montalcino landmark, having played a crucial role in promoting the wine by being the first cellar to release it at prices the ordinary wine drinker could afford. Even today, the cellar is proud of its moderate price tags. Moreover, Stefano Cinelli has at last put the finishing touches to the helpful museum that introduces visitors to the history of Brunello and to Montalcino's social fabric. We liked the wines presented, both from Montalcino and from Maremma. Our favourite was Brunello di Montalcino Vigna del Fiore '03. Its classic ruby red introduces layered aromatics on the twin themes of cola nuts, quinine and vanilla with classic but riper than usual fruit. That's down to the growing year but the flavour is elegant, as the cellar's style dictates. Acidity and extract are nicely balanced, giving thrust and drinkability, while supporting an attractively long finale. The very appealing '07 Sole selection was the best of the Morellino di Scansano wines, showing more fragrant than its fellows.

● Ardito '05	♟♟	7
● Cortona Smeriglio Merlot '06	♟♟	5
○ Astore '07	♟	4
● Cortona Smeriglio Sangiovese '06	♟	5
● Ardito '04	♟♟	6
● Ardito '03	♟♟	6
● Ardito '02	♟♟	6
● Cortona Smeriglio Merlot '05	♟♟	5
● Cortona Smeriglio Sangiovese '05	♟♟	5

● Brunello di Montalcino V. del Fiore '03	♟♟	8
● Morellino di Scansano Sole '07	♟♟	5
● Brunello di Montalcino '03	♟	6
● Morellino di Scansano '06	♟	4
● Brunello di Montalcino '01	♟♟	6
● Brunello di Montalcino '00	♟♟	6
● Brunello di Montalcino Ris. '01	♟♟	8
● Brunello di Montalcino Ris. '00	♟♟	8
● Brunello di Montalcino Ris. '99	♟♟	8
● Brunello di Montalcino Ris. '97	♟♟	8
● Brunello di Montalcino V. del Fiore '01	♟♟	7

★ Barone Ricasoli

LOC. CASTELLO DI BROLIO
53013 GAIOLE IN CHIANTI [SI]
TEL. 05777301
www.ricasoli.it

Fattoria di Basciano

V.LE DUCA DELLA VITTORIA, 159
50068 RUFINA [FI]
TEL. 0558397034
www.renzomasibasciano.it

ANNUAL PRODUCTION	2,000,000 bottles
HECTARES UNDER VINE	250
VITICULTURE METHOD	Conventional

ANNUAL PRODUCTION	200,000 bottles
HECTARES UNDER VINE	35
VITICULTURE METHOD	Conventional

Francesco Ricasoli's operation put on a three-star performance sending three wines to the finals and winning Three Glasses for Casalferro '05, a sangiovese and merlot mix that has picked up the baton from last year's winner, Chianti Castello di Brolio. Nevertheless, it is the overall average standard of the range that bespeaks the solidity of the winemaking project set up in the 1990s and today in full swing. The best places to replant the vine stock were selected from the estate's 1,200 hectares and a zoning study was carried out with Florence-based Institute for Soil Study and Conservation while clonal selection is under way in collaboration with Florence University and the Experimental Viticultural Institute at Arezzo. The star wine has a fine range of aromatics including intense black berry fruit and spices, a solid palate, good depth and balance, and an enjoyably savoury finish. The pulpy Castello di Brolio '05 also did well, showing powerful if perhaps a tad taut, whereas the Riserva Rocca Guicciarda '05 is more relaxed, its extract melding nicely with the other components and ending appropriately long.

It's always a pleasure to write about the Masi family's wines. Every year, the line-up of labels has impressive peaks. After all these years of positive reviews, though, we believe it is time to take the plunge and create even more quality-focused selections, something that the owner's son Paolo, who doubles as agronomist and oenologist, must certainly be mulling over. The business has been operating since 1930 but it was in the 1980s that it began to devote more attention to farming while continuing its distribution activities. Erta e China is a banker and the '06 vintage expresses all its allure to the full. The sangiovese and cabernet sauvignon blend tempts the nose with spice and fruit before the palate wins you over with its perfectly gauged texture. Il Corto '06, from sangiovese with a dash of cabernet, is austere and flavoursome. I Pini '06, from syrah, cabernet sauvignon and merlot, breaks away from oak-derived aromatics to flaunt fruitier fragrances and a nimbly supple palate. Finally, a special mention goes to the Vin Santo Rufina '02, with its pervasively appealing raft of aromatics.

● Casalferro '05	♈♈♈	8
● Chianti Cl. Castello di Brolio '05	♈♈	8
● Chianti Cl. Rocca Guicciarda Ris. '05	♈♈	6
● Chianti Cl. Brolio '06	♈♈	6
O Torricella '07	♈	6
● Casalferro '03	♈♈♈	6
● Casalferro '99	♈♈♈	6
● Casalferro '98	♈♈♈	6
● Casalferro '97	♈♈♈	6
● Chianti Cl. Castello di Brolio '04	♈♈♈	8
● Chianti Cl. Castello di Brolio '03	♈♈♈	7
● Chianti Cl. Castello di Brolio '01	♈♈♈	7

● Erta e China '06	♈♈	3*
● I Pini '06	♈♈	5
● Il Corto '06	♈♈	5
O Vin Santo Rufina '02	♈♈	4
● Chianti Ris. '05	♈	3
● Chianti Rufina '06	♈	3
● Chianti Rufina Ris. '05	♈	5
● Chianti Rufina Ris. '03	♈♈	5
● Il Corto '05	♈♈	5
O Vin Santo Rufina '01	♈♈	4

Podere Le Berne

LOC. CERVOGNANO
VIA POGGIO GOLO, 7
53040 MONTEPULCIANO [SI]
TEL. 0578767328
www.leberne.it

ANNUAL PRODUCTION	25,000 bottles
HECTARES UNDER VINE	6
VITICULTURE METHOD	Conventional

Nowadays, Andrea Natalini's wines are some of the most interesting in Montepulciano. Andrea takes no shortcuts and uses no technical wizardry, relying on superb fruit and carefully gauged wood for ageing. In consequence, his wines are paragons of poise, balance and drinkability. Add to this a generous dose of personality, and prices that are not over-ambitious, and you have a fine range. The wines are reliable all through the list and again this year we gave them excellent scores. Nobile di Montepulciano Riserva '04 is still very young, as you can tell from its austere bouquet that foregrounds mixed flowers with earthy notes and incense. The tannic weave is solid, sometimes almost too much so, but the acid backbone is equally vigorous. We thought the Nobile di Montepulciano '05 was spot on from its fresh flowers bouquet to its bright tasty palate, which is perhaps a little thin. The enjoyable but not terribly supple Rosso di Montepulciano '07 is a little weighed down by its structure.

Tenuta di Bibbiano

VIA BIBBIANO, 76
53011 CASTELLINA IN CHIANTI [SI]
TEL. 0577743065
www.tenutadibibbiano.com

ANNUAL PRODUCTION	70,000 bottles
HECTARES UNDER VINE	23
VITICULTURE METHOD	Conventional

After a few up and down years, the Morrocchesi family's operation is back with a full profile. We applaud a fine performance from a winery with a great tradition that had faded a little but is now shining again. This is all down to patient, skilled work dedicated to recovering the potential of an estate that has the soil and climate to make great wine. The range is all Chianti Classico, in tribute to the area, and the wines are released as vineyard selections make the most of the various parcels, on the lines of French crus. Standards are uniformly high, with the Riserva Vigna del Capannino '05 impressing for its balsam and menthol fragrances, tight-knit but unforced tannic weave and refreshing acidity. Simple as it is, the Chianti Classico '06 manages to be very convincing on nose and palate, unfolding without effort in the mouth. The most austere of the wines is Chianti Classico Montornello '06, its restrained aromatics hinting at tobacco and saddle leather. The crunchy tannins are more assertive but meld nicely with the alcohol to sign off in a satisfying finale.

● Nobile di Montepulciano '05	♟♟ 4*
● Nobile di Montepulciano Ris. '04	♟♟ 6
● Rosso di Montepulciano '07	♟ 4
● Nobile di Montepulciano '04	♟♟ 4
● Nobile di Montepulciano '03	♟♟ 4
● Nobile di Montepulciano Ris. '03	♟♟ 6
● Nobile di Montepulciano Ris. '01	♟♟ 6
● Nobile di Montepulciano Ris. '00	♟♟ 6

● Chianti Cl. '06	♟♟ 4*
● Chianti Cl. Montornello '06	♟♟ 4*
● Chianti Cl. V. del Capannino Ris. '05	♟♟ 5
● Chianti Cl. V. del Capannino Ris. '04	♟♟ 5

Bindella

FRAZ. ACQUAVIVA
VIA DELLE TRE BERTE, 10A
53040 MONTEPULCIANO [SI]
TEL. 0578767777
www.bindella.it

ANNUAL PRODUCTION	120,000 bottles
HECTARES UNDER VINE	30
VITICULTURE METHOD	Conventional

Bindella wines are sometimes austere to the point of severity. Often, it is hard to read them while they are still young. Obviously, wines as characterful as these are made to go the distance and we find the same determined personality even in the products at the bottom of the range. Once again, the most representative of the style is Nobile di Montepulciano I Quadri, which went through to our finals in the '05 edition, as it has before. Fragrances that are clear but still finding definition precede a lovely palate with good progression and an exceptionally long finish. Toastiness holds back the fruit aromatics of the Nobile Riserva '04 but it is pleasingly taut in the mouth, where bright acidity and attractive savouriness lend the finish attractive momentum. Flowers dominate the nose of the Nobile di Montepulciano '05, which has attractive balance and depth. Rosso di Montepulciano Fosso Lupaio '07 is flavoursome and has decent depth whereas the fragrant, very sweet Vin Santo Dolce Sinfonia '04 is a tad dilute.

Biondi Santi Spa

VIA DEI PIERI, 1
53024 MONTALCINO [SI]
TEL. 0577947121
www.biondisanti.it

ANNUAL PRODUCTION	280,000 bottles
HECTARES UNDER VINE	65
VITICULTURE METHOD	Conventional

We have included all the wines distributed by Biondi Santi in one profile so you will find Il Greppo products here with those of Pierluigi Tagliabue's Villa Poggio Salvi. Best of the bunch is the Brunello di Montalcino '03 from Il Greppo, which was also the only one to win Three Glasses. Our tastings revealed that the best wines from this vintage were from old vine, which evidently stood up better to the drought. This medium intense ruby champion shades into garnet and proffers a very traditional nose of medicinal herbs with saddle leather and sweet tobacco. Perky acidity, which nicely offsets the alcohol, makes it surprisingly fresh. Outstandingly fine-grained tannins allow the palate to progress smoothly to an excitingly long finish. The Poggio Salvi wines didn't reach quite the same heights. The Brunello di Montalcino '03 is held back by slightly unruly extract that tends to dry the palate. The sangiovese-based Tosco '06 is intriguing for its intense cherry-led fruit and elegantly impressive progression in the mouth. Finally, the Rosso di Montalcinos from both cellars are well made, the '06 from Poggio Salvi and Il Greppo's '05.

● Nobile di Montepulciano I Quadri '05	ŶŶ 5
● Nobile di Montepulciano '05	ŶŶ 6
● Nobile di Montepulciano Ris. '04	ŶŶ 6
● Rosso di Montepulciano Fosso Lupaio '07	Ŷ 4
○ Vin Santo Dolce Sinfonia '04	Ŷ 6
● Nobile di Montepulciano '03	ŶŶ 5
● Nobile di Montepulciano I Quadri '04	ŶŶ 5
● Nobile di Montepulciano I Quadri '03	ŶŶ 5
● Nobile di Montepulciano I Quadri '01	ŶŶ 5
● Nobile di Montepulciano I Quadri '00	ŶŶ 5
● Vallocaia '04	ŶŶ 6
● Vallocaia '03	ŶŶ 6
● Vallocaia '98	ŶŶ 6
○ Vin Santo Dolce Sinfonia '99	ŶŶ 6
○ Vin Santo Dolce Sinfonia '96	ŶŶ 6

● Brunello di Montalcino '03	ŶŶŶ 8
● Il Tosco '06	ŶŶ 4*
● Rosso di Montalcino '05	ŶŶ 6
● Rosso di Montalcino Poggio Salvi '06	ŶŶ 5
● Brunello di Montalcino Poggio Salvi '03	Ŷ 7
○ Vermentino '07	Ŷ 4
● Brunello di Montalcino '01	ŶŶŶ 8
● Brunello di Montalcino '83	ŶŶŶ 6
● Brunello di Montalcino Ris. '01	ŶŶŶ 8
● Brunello di Montalcino Ris. '99	ŶŶŶ 8
● Brunello di Montalcino Ris. '95	ŶŶŶ 6
● Brunello di Montalcino '00	ŶŶ 8
● Brunello di Montalcino '99	ŶŶ 8

Il Borghetto

LOC. MONTEFIRIDOLFI
VIA COLLINA SANT'ANGELO, 21
50026 SAN CASCIANO IN VAL DI PESA [FI]
TEL. 0558244491
www.borghetto.org

ANNUAL PRODUCTION	16,000 bottles
HECTARES UNDER VINE	6
VITICULTURE METHOD	Conventional

Looking back on the results from this likeable cellar, we note the steady, year-on-year progress that denotes a seriously well-planned project. Indeed, this time round, the Chianti Classico Bilaccio '05 went through to the national finals. The breath-takingly production zone enables growers to obtain good results from other varieties apart from the local favourite, sangiovese. That finalist is a lustrous ruby wine with a very expressive nose mingling fruitiness with faint nuances of tobacco and tiny grace notes of minerality. The palate is warm and balanced, thanks to the seamless melding of extract and alcohol before the finish ends with good momentum. The other wine presented this year is called Collina 21 '05, an odd name that is in fact the winery's postal address. In the bottle is a blend of sangiovese, cabernet sauvignon and merlot that tempts the nose with spices over berry fruit, following up with dynamic progression on the palate and good length.

Borgo Scopeto

LOC. VAGLIAGLI
53010 CASTELNUOVO BERARDENGA [SI]
TEL. 0577322729
www.borgoscopeto.com

ANNUAL PRODUCTION	225,000 bottles
HECTARES UNDER VINE	70
VITICULTURE METHOD	Conventional

Borgo Scopeto continues to produce switchback performances. The estate belongs to the portfolio of properties owned by Elisabetta Gnudi Angelini, which also includes Tenuta Carpazo and Altesino at Montalcino, as well as La Doga at Magliano in Maremma. It was the wines from La Doga that obtained the highest scored, even though the potential of the Chianti estate is much greater. The wines that on paper should have been at the top of the scoresheet were the ones that struggled, like athletes who arrive at the big race a little out of condition. Borgonero '04, a Supertuscan blended from sangiovese, syrah and cabernet sauvignon, is rough and untidy on the palate, although its nose is very appealing. We preferred the Chianti Classico '06's fresh bouquet and attractively complex palate. The stand-out from Maremma was the '07 Vermentino with its swath of penetrating aromas, full, juicy palate and nice sea salt-tinged finish. The '07 Rosato is enjoyable and the Morellino '07 is an easy drinker.

● Chianti Cl. Bilaccio '05	♥♥ 4*
● Collina 21 '05	♥♥ 4*
● Chianti Cl. Ris. '04	♥♥ 7
● Collina 21 '03	♥♥ 5

○ Vermentino Doga delle Clavule '07	♥♥ 4*
● Borgonero '04	♥ 6
● Chianti Cl. '06	♥ 4
● Morellino di Scansano Doga delle Clavule '07	♥ 4
⊙ Rosé Doga delle Clavule '07	♥ 4
● Chianti Cl. '03	♥♥ 4
● Chianti Cl. Ris. '98	♥♥ 4*
○ Vin Santo del Chianti Cl. '01	♥♥ 6

Il Borro

FRAZ. SAN GIUSTINO VALDARNO
LOC. IL BORRO, 1
52020 LORO CIUFFENNA [AR]
TEL. 0559772921
www.ilborro.it

ANNUAL PRODUCTION	150,000 bottles
HECTARES UNDER VINE	40
VITICULTURE METHOD	Conventional

Il Borro is best known for its wines nowadays but is in fact a full-blown rural settlement with medieval homes used now as a venue for various arts events. The Ferragamo has made major investments in the site since purchasing it from its previous owner, Duca Amedeo d'Aosta. The initial period is now over and reliable quality standards have been identified. The house style is modern, measured and technically competent, privileging softness, pervasiveness and intensity of both colour and extract. All those characteristics are embodied to the full in Il Borro, from merlot, cabernet, syrah and petit verdot. As usual, the '06 is a profusion of ripe fruit and spices, combined with rich, sweet tannins and a hint of wood that holds the palate back, making progression a tad stiffish. Sangiovese Polissena '06 is better on the nose, where fruit, earth and hints of pepper come through, than on the alcohol-led palate. Finally, the ripe, juicy syrah and sangiovese Pina di Nova '06 is savoury and unfolds nicely.

Poderi Boscarelli

FRAZ. CERVOGNANO
VIA DI MONTENERO, 28
53045 MONTEPULCIANO [SI]
TEL. 0578767277
www.poderiboscarelli.com

ANNUAL PRODUCTION	80,000 bottles
HECTARES UNDER VINE	13.5
VITICULTURE METHOD	Conventional

The wines from the De Ferrari family winery may well be the most authentic expression of Montepulciano's territory. It's not that the wines are all that approachable: they have their own style are built to last. Again this year, the range earned plenty of Stemware but the less than excellent growing year meant that the Cervognano-based operation revealed the occasional wobble. The Nobile Nocio dei Boscarelli '05 sailed through to the finals with its earthy, floral aromas lifted by an unusually prominent hint of spice from the small wood. The palate, too, which has all its customary brio and thrust, is rather soft and signs off with a distinctly oak-tinged finish. The Nobile di Montepulciano Riserva '04 has good fruit on the nose, enhanced by minerality, and a vibrantly fleshy palate with a slightly mouth-drying finish. The '05 Nobile is very youthful has restrained aromas and plenty of flavour. Boscarelli dei Boscarelli '05 is an interesting blend of sangiovese, merlot and carmenère that shows sweet and intense. And to round off, the Rosso di Montepulciano Prugnolo '06 and De Ferrari '07 from sangiovese and merlot have nice appeal.

● Il Borro '06	♈♈ 7
● Pian di Nova '06	♈♈ 4*
● Polissena '06	♈♈ 6
● Il Borro '05	♈♈ 7
● Il Borro '04	♈♈ 7
● Il Borro '03	♈♈ 7
● Il Borro '02	♈♈ 8
● Il Borro '01	♈♈ 8
● Il Borro '00	♈♈ 8
● Il Borro '99	♈♈ 8
● Pian di Nova '05	♈♈ 4
● Polissena '05	♈♈ 6

● Nobile di Montepulciano Nocio dei Boscarelli '05	♈ 7
● Boscarelli dei Boscarelli '05	♈♈ 8
● Nobile di Montepulciano '05	♈♈ 6
● Nobile di Montepulciano Ris. '04	♈♈ 6
● De Ferrari '07	♈ 4
● Rosso di Montepulciano Prugnolo '06	♈ 4
● Nobile di Montepulciano Nocio dei Boscarelli '04	♈♈♈ 7
● Nobile di Montepulciano Nocio dei Boscarelli '03	♈♈♈ 7
● Nobile di Montepulciano Nocio dei Boscarelli '01	♈♈♈ 7
● Nobile di Montepulciano V. del Nocio '00	♈♈ 7
● Nobile di Montepulciano V. del Nocio '99	♈♈ 7
● Nobile di Montepulciano V. del Nocio '97	♈♈ 5

Castello di Bossi

LOC. BOSSI IN CHIANTI
53019 CASTELNUOVO BERARDENGA [SI]
TEL. 0577359330
www.castellodibossi.it

ANNUAL PRODUCTION	600,000 bottles
HECTARES UNDER VINE	124
VITICULTURE METHOD	Conventional

It's been a year of major developments for Marco and Maurizio Bacci's operation. The cellar's first sweet wine went straight into our finals and the first Brunello released at Montalcino is described in a separate profile. We could add that things are going swimmingly in Maremma, too. The Morellino di Scansano Tempo '07 went through to our finals thanks in particular to its vibrant aromatics and the '07 Vermentino Vento is one of the best versions ever. Nevertheless, Castelnuovo Berardenga remains the hub of activities, although this year we were less enamoured of Girolamo '05, a single-variety Merlot with strong territorial links, which has plenty of structure but is hampered by its tannins. Vin San Laurentino '99 from trebbiano and malvasia is intriguing. Produced with the traditional Vin Santo technique, with the bunches dried on nets, it matures at length in small oak barrels. When it emerges, the wine is luscious with aromas ranging from citrus to spices and a sweet, creamy palate that signs off with a lingering finale.

Tenuta Bossi

LOC. BOSSI
VIA DELLO STRACCHINO, 32
50065 PONTASSIEVE [FI]
TEL. 0558317830
www.gondi.com

ANNUAL PRODUCTION	30,000 bottles
HECTARES UNDER VINE	18.6
VITICULTURE METHOD	Conventional

The Gondi family confirmed their winery's progress this year. Starting last year from solid foundations, they came back with equally fine products this time. It's all a very long way from the extract-heavy bottles of some earlier vintages. The plan prepared in collaboration with oenologist Fabrizio Moltard is being scrupulously implemented and results are coming through in the quality of the products. Designation-bearing wines performed well. Chianti Rufina San Giuliano '06 has intense colour followed by balsam and menthol aromas that meld with black berry fruits and then a warm, mouthfilling body with mellow tannins and a savoury finish. Even better is the Riserva '05 Pian dei Sorbi whose complex range of aromas features hints of tobacco and saddle leather, blackberry jam and classic spices like cinnamon and cloves. The juicy, upfront entry on the palate gives way to crunchy tannins and an enjoyably long finish. Less expressive, though, is Mazzaferrata '05, from cabernet sauvignon, has massive body that has yet to unfold but offers attractive fragrances led by aromatic herbs.

● Morellino di Scansano Tempo Terra di Talamo '07	♀♀ 4
○ Vin San Laurentino '99	♀♀ 8
● Girolamo '05	♀♀ 8
○ Vento Vermentino '07	♀♀ 4
● Chianti Cl. '06	♀ 5
☉ Piano...Piano '07	♀ 4
● Corbaia '03	♀♀♀ 7
● Corbaia '99	♀♀♀ 8
● Corbaia '01	♀♀ 7
● Corbaia '00	♀♀ 7
● Girolamo '04	♀♀ 7
● Girolamo '03	♀♀ 7

● Chianti Rufina Pian dei Sorbi Ris. '05	♀♀ 4*
● Chianti Rufina San Giuliano '06	♀♀ 4*
● Mazzaferrata '05	♀ 5
● Chianti Rufina San Giuliano '04	♀♀ 3
○ Vin Santo del Chianti Rufina Ris. '02	♀♀ 5

★ Brancaia

LOC. POPPI, 42
53017 RADDA IN CHIANTI [SI]
TEL. 0577742007
www.brancaia.com

ANNUAL PRODUCTION	400,000 bottles
HECTARES UNDER VINE	26 + 20
VITICULTURE METHOD	Conventional

The Widmer family's winery deservedly picks up a Star for its tenth Three Glass prize, awarded to Il Blu '06, a blend of sangiovese and merlot with a splash of cabernet sauvignon. It is the estate's most representative bottle and the one that has embodied the house style for the wine-loving public with its invariably crisp fragrances ranging from forest fruits to spice and a palate that progresses effortlessly along on alcohol that melds beautifully with the extract. It signs off with a very long finale, lifted by an intriguing note of torrefaction. Wines from Maremma get better by the year, as we noted from the Ilatraia '06, a cabernet sauvignon-heavy blend with sangiovese and petit verdot. The 2006 growing year also smiled on the Chianti Classico, which is firm and juicy while the only wine that was not quite up to speed was Tre '06, a sangiovese-based wine with cabernet sauvignon. It's well made but the nose is faint and the body slender.

La Casa di Bricciano

LOC. LA CASA DI BRICCIANO, 43
53013 GAIOLE IN CHIANTI [SI]
TEL. 0577 749297

ANNUAL PRODUCTION	N.A.
HECTARES UNDER VINE	4
VITICULTURE METHOD	Conventional

We welcome the Guide debut of this small Gaiola-based winery run by owner-manager Peter O'Kelly. The four hectares are planted to sangiovese, merlot and cabernet sauvignon. Consultancy input comes from a long-standing professional: Vittorio Fiore. The wines presented impressed us with their power and structure, especially in Il Ritrovo '05, the cabernet sauvignon and merlot Supertuscan, whereas the Chianti Classico '05 has its strong suit in finesse. Its understated bouquet foregrounds aromatic herbs mingling with fruit before the effortless palate unveils its bright acidity, silky extract and rising finish. The IGT wine has a strikingly wide, pervasive nose of forest fruits and spiciness. The broad front palate introduces plenty of texture, good depth and a long-lingering finish with a vibrant aftertaste.

● Brancaia Il Blu '06	♥♥♥	7
● Chianti Cl. '06	♥♥	6
● Ilatraia '06	♥♥	7
● Brancaia Tre '06	♥	5
● Brancaia '99	♥♥♥	8
● Brancaia '98	♥♥♥	6
● Brancaia Il Blu '05	♥♥♥	7
● Brancaia Il Blu '04	♥♥♥	7
● Brancaia Il Blu '03	♥♥♥	7
● Brancaia Il Blu '01	♥♥♥	7
● Brancaia Il Blu '00	♥♥♥	7

● Chianti Cl. Ris. '05	♥♥	5
● Il Ritrovo '05	♥♥	6

Brunelli - Le Chiuse di Sotto

LOC. PODERNOVONE
53024 MONTALCINO [SI]
TEL. 0577849337
www.giannibrunelli.it

ANNUAL PRODUCTION	35,000 bottles
HECTARES UNDER VINE	6.3
VITICULTURE METHOD	Conventional

First of all, we would like to wish Gianni Brunelli the best of luck with a complicated situation. We are sure the world-famous exuberance of his character will carry him though to a positive outcome. His winery is split between two estates, the former the original property at Le Chiuse on the northern slope of Montalcino while the more recent holding, Poderovone, is on the southern side of the same location. The best wine this year, in fact a Three Glass winner, is Amor Costante '05, an 80-20 sangiovese and merlot blend. Crisp morello cherry and black berry-led fruit graces the elegant nose, to be followed by an equally elegant palate hinging on savouriness that sustains the impressive but never excessive structure. The tannins are perfectly ripe, fine-grained and beautifully poised. The DOCG wines were a tad less convincing. The '03 Brunello di Montalcino is a little too dried by its oak and the fresh, pleasing Rosso di Montalcino '06 is let down by a shortish finish.

Wine	Rating
● Amor Costante '05	♟♟♟ 6
● Brunello di Montalcino '03	♟ 7
● Rosso di Montalcino '06	♟ 5
● Amor Costante '03	♟♟ 6
● Brunello di Montalcino '01	♟♟ 7
● Brunello di Montalcino '00	♟♟ 7
● Brunello di Montalcino '99	♟♟ 8
● Brunello di Montalcino Ris. '01	♟♟ 8

Bruni

FRAZ. FONTEBLANDA
LOC. LA MARTA, 6
58010 ORBETELLO [GR]
TEL. 0564885445
www.aziendabruni.it

ANNUAL PRODUCTION	400,000 bottles
HECTARES UNDER VINE	36
VITICULTURE METHOD	Conventional

The Bruni winery, run by brothers Marco and Moreno, generally turns out well crafted and very drinkable wines with distinctive personality that now and again suffers from over-extraction or a heavy hand with the oak. As soon as it manages to avoid these stylistic blips, this Fonteblanda cellar will be right at the front of Maremma winemaking, as this year's results confirm. The Morellino Marteto '07 is a fine, fresh-tasting product redolent of black berry fruit and spice that flow across the palate into a deliciously sweet finish. Jammy red fruits and balsam are the keynotes of the Morellino di Scansano Laire Riserva '05, followed by a deep, soft and nicely relaxed mouthfeel. Breezy aromas and tangy flavour distinguish the vermentino and viognier-based Plinio '07 while the sangiovese, syrah and cabernet sauvignon Moresco '05 gives balsam on the nose, only to present slightly clenched in the mouth, where oak-derived toastiness predominates. Perlaia '07 is an interesting product, also from vermentino and viogner, some of it harvested late.

Wine	Rating
● Morellino di Scansano Laire Ris. '05	♟♟ 5
● Morellino di Scansano Marteto '07	♟♟ 4*
○ Plinio '07	♟♟ 4*
● Moresco '05	♟ 4
○ Vermentino Perlaia '07	♟ 4
● Morellino di Scansano Laire '04	♟♟ 5
● Morellino di Scansano Laire '03	♟♟ 5
● Morellino di Scansano Marteto '04	♟♟ 4
○ Vermentino Perlaia '06	♟♟ 4

Fattoria del Buonamico

LOC. CERCATOIA
VIA PROVINCIALE DI MONTECARLO, 43
55015 MONTECARLO [LU]
TEL. 058322038
www.buonamico.it

ANNUAL PRODUCTION	120,000 bottles
HECTARES UNDER VINE	21
VITICULTURE METHOD	Conventional

There is important news from Fattoria del Buonamico. The property has been purchased by well-known Lucca-based business people Dino and Eugenia Fontana. The two have always been passionately interested in farming and are looking to promote the wines and territory of Montecarlo. Work on vineyard expansion has started and the first decisions have been taken by the new, high-profile winemaking staff, oenologist Alberto Antonini and agronomist Stefano Dini. Amidst all this change, several things have remained unchanged, fortunately. Estate manager Vasco Grassi continues after 40 years at the helm and the range is as good as ever. This year, Cercatoja '05 went through to the finals. Its ruby hue ushers in violets, ripe berry fruit and spice before the palate reveals the freshness of the vintage while maintaining admirable finesse and persistence. The cellar's two base wines, the eminently cellarable Montecarlo Rosso '07 and the fragrant new Villa Lombardi '07 are both excellent. Finally, the youthful syrah-only Il Fortino '06 is still a little boisterous.

Ca' Marcanda

LOC. SANTA TERESA, 272
57022 CASTAGNETO CARDUCCI [LI]
TEL. 0173635158
info@gajawines.com

ANNUAL PRODUCTION	390,000 bottles
HECTARES UNDER VINE	100
VITICULTURE METHOD	Conventional

The wines that Angelo Gaja makes at Castagneto Carducci are impeccable. Some of the 100 hectares under vine are at the cellar, where they make a wonderful setting for its lovely architecture, and the rest is nearby. Currently, 400,000 bottles a year are released but the aim is to raise this to 500,000 in the next few years. The stand-out wine is Bolgheri Camarcanda '05, from half merlot with cabernet sauvignon and a little cabernet franc. Clear notes of fresh and jammy blackberries and raspberries meld with balsam and liquorice leading into a tight-knit, well-defined palate with good breadth and assertive extract. Also impressive is Magari '06, from half merlot with equal parts of cabernet sauvignon and franc, which offers distinct herbaceous notes and fresh notes of baked peppers laced with aromatic herbs. Delicious acidity lends thrust to the palate, which signs off with a long, juicy finish. Promis '06 is from 55 per cent merlot with 35 per cent syrah and the rest sangiovese. It's a less complex wine but still very appealing. Black berry fruit and grassiness give way to a well-balanced palate that just needs to rein its tannins in.

● Cercatoja Rosso '05	♟♟	5
● Montecarlo Rosso '07	♟♟	3*
● Villa Lombardi '07	♟♟	4
● Il Fortino Syrah '06	♟	6
○ Montecarlo Bianco '07	♟	3
○ Vasario '04	♟	5
● Cercatoja Rosso '04	♟♟	5
● Cercatoja Rosso '99	♟♟	6
● Cercatoja Rosso '95	♟♟	6
● Il Fortino Syrah '98	♟♟	7
● Montecarlo Rosso '01	♟♟	4*

● Bolgheri Camarcanda '05	♟♟	8
● Magari '06	♟♟	8
● Promis '06	♟♟	8
● Bolgheri Camarcanda '01	♟♟♟	8
● Magari '03	♟♟♟	7
● Bolgheri Camarcanda '04	♟♟	8
● Magari '05	♟♟	8
● Magari '04	♟♟	8

Tenuta Le Calcinaie

LOC. SANTA LUCIA, 36
53037 SAN GIMIGNANO [SI]
TEL. 0577943007
www.tenutalecalcinaie.it

La Calonica

FRAZ. VALIANO DI MONTEPULCIANO
VIA DELLA STELLA, 27
53040 MONTEPULCIANO [SI]
TEL. 0578724119
www.lacalonica.com

ANNUAL PRODUCTION   60,000 bottles
HECTARES UNDER VINE 10
VITICULTURE METHOD   Certified organic

ANNUAL PRODUCTION   180,000 bottles
HECTARES UNDER VINE 40
VITICULTURE METHOD   Conventional

Over the years, Simone Santini has built up
a solid reputation around San Gimignano
thanks to his clear vision of how he wants
his wines, which unfortunately scored
lower than they might have because they
went into bottle just before our tastings.
In consequence, they seemed to lack
a little complexity, which is a shame,
especially for the flag-carrying wines like
Vernaccia di San Gimignano Vigna ai Sassi.
Nonetheless, the '06 went through to our
finals. There's no denying it's a very fine
wine with a characterful nose ranging from
fruit to aromatic herbs and gunflint. Good
pulp on the well-sustained, fresh-tasting
palate takes you through to an attractively
long finish with an almondy aftertaste.
The Vernaccia '07 is a wine to bank on, its
overwhelmingly fresh nose recalling sage,
spring flowers and tropical fruits. Acidity
braces the lively palate as it progresses
confidently and very drinkably indeed.
Missing from the line-up were the Chianti
dei Colli Senesi and Teodoro, which had
yet to go into bottle when we called.

La Calonica has regained its full profile
in the best possible manner: by winning
Three Glasses. It's the first time for this
Valiano-based winery, on the border of the
Montepulciano and Cortona designation.
In fact, the highly competent Ferdinando
Cattanei is president of the Cortona DOC.
The wine that earned our applause was
the '04 Nobile di Montepulciano Riserva.
You can tell it's special from the first
sniff of the glass. Elegant, whistle-clean
fruit is enhanced by toasty notes and
understated spice. Harmonious and well
orchestrated in the mouth, it unveils solid
yet polished tannins, attractively vibrant
acidity and a lovely rising finish. The
very good Nobile di Montepulciano '05
has a wealth of fruit followed by distinct
sweetness on the palate and a touch
too much oak. The fresh-tasting, relaxed
Cortona Sangiovese '06 is aroma-rich,
lean and very flavoursome whereas the
'07 Rosso di Montepulciano is upfront and
approachable. Finally, the '99 Vin Santo
is compact and vibrant in the mouth,
although a touch closed on the nose.

O Vernaccia di S. Gimignano V. ai Sassi '06	♟♟ 4
O Vernaccia di S. Gimignano '07	♟♟ 4*
● Teodoro '99	♟♟ 5
O Vernaccia di S. Gimignano '06	♟♟ 4*
O Vernaccia di S. Gimignano '05	♟♟ 3
O Vernaccia di S. Gimignano '04	♟♟ 3
O Vernaccia di S. Gimignano V. ai Sassi '05	♟♟ 4
O Vernaccia di S. Gimignano V. ai Sassi '04	♟♟ 4
O Vernaccia di S. Gimignano V. ai Sassi '03	♟♟ 4
O Vernaccia di S. Gimignano V. ai Sassi '02	♟♟ 4

● Nobile di Montepulciano Ris. '04	♟♟♟ 6
● Cortona Sangiovese '06	♟♟ 4*
● Nobile di Montepulciano '05	♟♟ 5
● Rosso di Montepulciano '07	♟ 4
O Vin Santo di Montepulciano '99	♟ 6
● Cortona Girifalco '05	♟♟ 6
● Cortona Girifalco '04	♟♟ 6
● Nobile di Montepulciano '04	♟♟ 5
● Nobile di Montepulciano '03	♟♟ 5

Campo alla Sughera

LOC. CACCIA AL PIANO, 280
57020 BOLGHERI [LI]
TEL. 0565766936
www.campoallasughera.com

ANNUAL PRODUCTION	90,000 bottles
HECTARES UNDER VINE	16.25
VITICULTURE METHOD	Conventional

Baldwin Knauf's winery has been active for more than a decade. Almost all the vine stock is around Bolgheri, where the classic local varieties are grown, and again quality was as reliable as ever. The wines presented this year faithfully reflected their respective growing years. Like most '05s, the Bolgheri Superiore Arnione, from cabernet sauvignon, cabernet franc, merlot and petit verdot, lacks a pinch of complexity and structure. This means that oak tends to get the upper hand on nose and palate, at least while the wine is young, masking the aromas and extract. But good underlying acidity bodes well for positive evolution in the future. The Bolgheri Rosso Adeo '06, from cabernet sauvignon and merlot, is more approachable and has all the concentration and structure of its growing year. Pervasive ripe fruit on the nose is echoed on the full-bodied palate, which signs off with a fruit flourish. Finally, the house white, Arioso '07 from sauvignon with a touch of viognier, is always delightful with its well-defined tomato leaf and sage preceding a fresh, supple palate.

● Bolgheri Rosso Adeo '06	🍷🍷	5
● Bolgheri Superiore Arnione '05	🍷🍷	7
○ Arioso '07	🍷	4
○ Arioso '07	🍷🍷	4
● Arnione '02	🍷🍷	6
● Arnione '01	🍷🍷	7
● Bolgheri Superiore Arnione '04	🍷🍷	7
● Bolgheri Superiore Arnione '03	🍷🍷	7

Canalicchio di Sopra

LOC. CASACCIA, 73
53024 MONTALCINO [SI]
TEL. 0577848316
www.canalicchiodisopra.com

ANNUAL PRODUCTION	40,000 bottles
HECTARES UNDER VINE	15
VITICULTURE METHOD	Conventional

For years, this cellar has been the flag-carrier of the Canalicchi subzone, a historic hillslope vineyard on the road to Buonconvento, and it confirmed its high standards again this time. The structure of the soil changes here, losing much of its clay for pebbles and stones. The Ripaccioli family has been growing grapes here for a very long time and the wines always convey a unique character that in recent years, since the new generations started calling the shots, has come across in a cleaner style and greater rigour. We liked the Rosso di Montalcino '06, one of the best of its category. Morello cherry and blackberries on the nose are lifted by aromatic herbs usher in a rich palate braced by nice acidity and tannins well tucked in. The '03 Brunello di Montalcino is a tad edgy on nose and palate, where the tannins are particularly tetchy, drying the wine on the back palate. More time in glass will sort that out.

● Rosso di Montalcino '06	🍷🍷	5
● Brunello di Montalcino '03	🍷	7
● Brunello di Montalcino Ris. '01	🍷🍷🍷	8
● Brunello di Montalcino '01	🍷🍷	6
● Brunello di Montalcino '00	🍷🍷	6
● Brunello di Montalcino '99	🍷🍷	8
● Brunello di Montalcino Ris. '99	🍷🍷	7
● Brunello di Montalcino Ris. '97	🍷🍷	8

Tenuta Cantagallo

VIA VALICARDA, 35
50056 CAPRAIA E LIMITE [FI]
TEL. 0571910078
www.enricopierazzuoli.com

ANNUAL PRODUCTION   126,000 bottles
HECTARES UNDER VINE 29.5
VITICULTURE METHOD   Conventional

We've admired Tenuta Cantagallo for some time for the steady way it has worked on quality, consolidating its results each year with intriguing wines and a very honest pricing policy. Again this year, we tasted a seamlessly good range of wines, all technically very well made. The cellar's best wine was once more the Carmignano Le Farnete Riserva, whose '05 version went through to our finals. An elegant spectrum of aromatics pervades the nostrils and the palate layers fruit over tasty, tight-knit tannins that progress deliciously with plenty of depth of flavour. Depth is also a keynote of the Carmignano '05, which has just the right touch of acidity to brighten the finish. The Chianti Montalbano Riserva '05 proffers its customary profusion of dark berry fruit aromas and a soft, relaxed mouthfeel while the Chianti Montalbano '07 gives supple fruit on nose and palate but the sangiovese-only Gioveto '05 is still a little stiff on the palate. Finally, the Vin Santo del Chianti Montalbano Millarium '03 is intense but a tad dilute.

Capanne Ricci

FRAZ. SANT'ANGELO IN COLLE
LOC. CASELLO
53024 MONTALCINO [SI]
TEL. 0564902063
www.tenimentiricci.it

ANNUAL PRODUCTION   40,000 bottles
HECTARES UNDER VINE 12
VITICULTURE METHOD   Conventional

This long-established winery has come on in leaps and bounds in a very short time, thanks in large part to the skills of Ferruccio Ricci, who has always believed in his terrain. Over the years, the wines' style has also gained in elegance now that wood is being used more shrewdly. The '03 Brunello di Montalcino '03 is proof positive that the cellar is on the right track. In fact, it went through to our finals and was one of the best in its class. A ruby hue introduces blackberry and morello cherry fruit and toasty notes that meld seamlessly. There's plenty of fine-grained extract on the palate, which never threatens to hamper the thrust of the rich progression, well sustained by acid backbone. It signs off with a very deep and satisfyingly intense finale. The '06 Rosso di Montalcino is almost Brunello-like with its saddle leather and tobacco notes lifting the fruitiness. The tannins are slightly over the top, although they have plenty of support from the alcohol.

● Carmignano Le Farnete Ris. '05	♟♟	6
● Carmignano Le Farnete '05	♟♟	4*
● Chianti Montalbano Ris. '05	♟♟	4*
● Barco Reale '07	♟	4
● Chianti Montalbano '07	♟	3
● Gioveto '05	♟	5
○ Vin Santo del Chianti Montalbano Millarium '03	♟	6
● Carmignano Le Farnete Ris. '97	♟♟♟	5
● Carmignano Le Farnete Ris. '04	♟♟	6
● Carmignano Le Farnete Ris. '03	♟♟	7
● Carmignano Le Farnete Ris. '01	♟♟	7
● Chianti Montalbano '04	♟♟	3*
● Chianti Montalbano Ris. '04	♟♟	4
● Gioveto '03	♟♟	5
○ Vin Santo del Chianti Millarium '01	♟♟	6

● Brunello di Montalcino '03	♟♟	7
● Rosso di Montalcino '06	♟♟	5
● Brunello di Montalcino '02	♟♟	6
● Brunello di Montalcino '99	♟♟	7

Capannelle

VIA CAPANNELLE, 13
53013 GAIOLE IN CHIANTI [SI]
TEL. 057774511
www.capannelle.com

ANNUAL PRODUCTION **60,000 bottles**
HECTARES UNDER VINE **16**
VITICULTURE METHOD **Conventional**

James B. Sherwood's Capannelle winery is back with a full profile and an excellent score for the '04 edition of its flag-carrier, Solare, which went through to our finals. We were certain that the cellar's potential would be fulfilled this year and the results speak for themselves. Capannelle has been operating for more than three decades, when founder Raffele Rossetti purchased a 17th-century farmhouse in the Chianti countryside. Major restructuring transformed the entire operation. Capannelle was also one of the first wineries to concentrate on image, dreaming up its silver and gold labels. All the wines are good. That finalist has a delicate, complex spectrum of mineral and fruit aromatics, a juicy, savoury palate with nice texture and carefully gauged tannins leading to a lingering finish and after-aroma. The spicy, aromatic '06 Chardonnay is intriguing, showing tautness in the mouth and a nice rising finish. Finally, the attractive 50&50 '04 is produced in collaboration with Avignonesi. The Chianti Classico Riserva '04 is well typed.

● Solare '04	🍷🍷	8
● 50 & 50 Avignonesi e Capannelle '04	🍷🍷	8
O Chardonnay '06	🍷🍷	7
● Chianti Cl. Ris. '04	🍷	6
● 50 & 50 Avignonesi e Capannelle '99	ΥΥΥ	8
● 50 & 50 Avignonesi e Capannelle '97	ΥΥΥ	8
● 50 & 50 Avignonesi e Capannelle '03	ΥΥ	8
● 50 & 50 Avignonesi e Capannelle '01	ΥΥ	8
● 50 & 50 Avignonesi e Capannelle '00	ΥΥ	8
● 50 & 50 Avignonesi e Capannelle '98	ΥΥ	8
● Solare '00	ΥΥ	8
● Solare '99	ΥΥ	8
● Solare '98	ΥΥ	8

Tenuta Caparzo

LOC. CAPARZO
S.P. DEL BRUNELLO
53024 MONTALCINO [SI]
TEL. 0577848390
www.caparzo.it

ANNUAL PRODUCTION **455,000 bottles**
HECTARES UNDER VINE **80**
VITICULTURE METHOD **Conventional**

The Caparzo winery's lovely headquarters is worth a visit just to admire the wonderful prospect it offers. Radical change effected by the strong-willed owner, Elisabetta Gnudi, is beginning to bear fruit. Younger non-DOCG wines achieved very good results, especially the Rosso '07 blend of cabernet sauvignon, sangiovese, merlot, syrah and colorino. It's a delightful wine released at a very affordable price. Fruity, fresh and intense on the nose, it tempts with blackberries, cherries and blueberries in alcohol. The attractively rich palate unveils nicely resolved tannins and good acidity that make it irresistibly moreish. The Brunello di Montalcino '03, sourced from old vines in the northern part of the estate, also scored well. Its medium intense ruby introduces faint oak and spices over red fruits that lend a sensation of freshness. The acidity on the palate is remarkably restrained and takes you through to an attractively relaxed finish, supported by the well-honed tannins. Finally, the Rosso di Montalcino '06, the sangoivese and cabernet sauvignon Sant'Antimo Ca' del Pazzo '04 and Sangiovese '07 are all well made.

● Brunello di Montalcino '03	🍷🍷	7
● Rosso Caparzo '07	🍷🍷	4*
● Caparzo Sangiovese '07	🍷	4
● Rosso di Montalcino '06	🍷	5
● Sant'Antimo Ca' del Pazzo '04	🍷	6
● Brunello di Montalcino '00	ΥΥ	7
● Brunello di Montalcino La Casa '00	ΥΥ	8
● Brunello di Montalcino La Casa '99	ΥΥ	8
● Brunello di Montalcino La Casa '97	ΥΥ	7
● Brunello di Montalcino Ris. '01	ΥΥ	8
● Brunello di Montalcino Ris. '99	ΥΥ	8

Tenuta di Capezzana

LOC. SEANO
VIA CAPEZZANA, 100
59015 CARMIGNANO [PO]
TEL. 0558706005
www.capezzana.it

ANNUAL PRODUCTION	600,000 bottles
HECTARES UNDER VINE	106
VITICULTURE METHOD	Conventional

This year Capezzana sent three wines to our finals, the Vin Santo di Carmignano, an excellent Trebbiano and the quite magnificent Carmignano Villa di Capezzana, which duly picked up Three Glasses. In fact, the award winner is the Contini Bonacossi family's most representative wine. The '05 edition is a fantastic product that reaffirms its status as the entire designation's flag-carrier. Breadth and complexity on the nose unveil spice that melds seamlessly with generous, full-bodied fruit then the palate offers remarkable structure that progresses determinedly and deliciously through to fruit-like sensations on the finish. The '05 Trebbiano is a wine built for the cellar and will need ageing to enable it to evolve its minerality to the full. Complexity on the nose thanks to a successful marriage of oak and fruit precedes a full, soft palate sustained by assertive acidity and rounded off by an intriguing, lingering finale. The Vin Santo di Carmignano Riserva '02 finds a nice equilibrium and its sweetness never cloys. Also nice is the ripe-nosed '04 Ghiaie della Furba with its broad finish while the '06 Barco Reale is attractive.

Capoverso

LOC. BADELLE
VIA DI GRACCIANO NEL CORSO, 85
53045 MONTEPULCIANO [SI]
TEL. 0578757921
www.vinicapoverso.com

ANNUAL PRODUCTION	32,000 bottles
HECTARES UNDER VINE	14.5
VITICULTURE METHOD	Conventional

Adriana Avignonesi's cellar made a flattering Guide debut by presenting us with a nicely assorted range of well-chosen wine types that seem already to have found a very solid stylistic framework. The wines are technically impeccable and oak is used sparingly for maturation but they also have a very natural feel and a decent dose of personality. The merlot-only Cartiglio '05 is broad and elegant on the nose, where lashings of fruit lifted by tobacco and earth hold it up well. Tight-knit tannins in the mouth provide a nice contrast and good thrust. Less substantial but very well judged is the Nobile di Montepulciano '05, which offers herbaceousness and savoury, attractively taut extract. Rosso di Montepulciano '06 is a minor masterpiece of drinkability, perhaps one of the best around, showing full, fresh and flavoursome. But there are one or two uncertain notes on the nose of the sangoivese, syrah and canaiolo Rosso Toscano Capoverso '05. It's better in the mouth, where vigorous, well-sustained acidity restores it to full vitality.

● Carmignano Villa di Capezzana '05	♛♛♛	5
○ Trebbiano '05	♛♛	5
○ Vin Santo di Carmignano Ris. '02	♛♛	6
● Ghiaie della Furba '04	♛♛	6
● Barco Reale '06	♛	4
● Carmignano Villa di Capezzana '99	♛♛♛	6
● Ghiaie della Furba '01	♛♛♛	6
● Ghiaie della Furba '98	♛♛♛	5
● Carmignano Villa di Capezzana '04	♛♛	5
● Carmignano Villa di Trefiano '04	♛♛	6
● Carmignano Villa di Trefiano '00	♛♛	6
● Ghiaie della Furba '03	♛♛	6
● Ghiaie della Furba '99	♛♛	6
○ Trebbiano '04	♛♛	5
○ Trebbiano '03	♛♛	6
○ Vin Santo di Carmignano Ris. '01	♛♛	6

● Cartiglio '05	♛♛	7
● Nobile di Montepulciano '05	♛♛	5
● Rosso di Montepulciano '06	♛♛	4*
● Capoverso '05	♛	5

Podere La Cappella

FRAZ. SAN DONATO IN POGGIO
S.DA CERBAIA, 10
50020 TAVARNELLE VAL DI PESA [FI]
TEL. 0558072727
www.poderelacappella.it

ANNUAL PRODUCTION	20,000 bottles
HECTARES UNDER VINE	10
VITICULTURE METHOD	Conventional

The Rossini family likes to keep us on our toes by presenting us with different labels each year as part of a laudable cellar policy that aims gradually to extend maturation times for all the wines. It was 1979 when Bruno Rossini first fell in love with Tuscany and purchased the farm where he started to grow apples and pears as well as the existing crops of grapes and olives. But it was only in 1995 that winemaking got off the ground as the first products went into bottle and Bruno's daughter Natascia came on board. The winery started to expand and make a name for itself. Organic farming was the norm here before it became a fashion, proving that the Rossinis have a firm commitment to the environment. The Chianti Classico '06 did well with its crisp aromas of cherries and forest fruits, lean but lively body, good backbone and tasty savouriness. Idilio fills the mouth. It's a much sweeter Vin Santo than usual with a creamy, velvet-smooth texture, pervasive aromas and very long-lingering persistence. The merlot-only Cantico '04 was less impressive, lacking elegance although it does have plenty of structure.

Podere Il Carnasciale

LOC. PODERE IL CARNASCIALE
52020 BUCINE [AR]
TEL. 0559911142

ANNUAL PRODUCTION	2,500 bottles
HECTARES UNDER VINE	2
VITICULTURE METHOD	Conventional

As the new vine stock comes onstream, the overall quantity of Caberlot available in the market is increasing. Currently, it stands at around 2,500 magnums. That doesn't mean it's any easier to get hold of but lovers and admirers of this unique wine will be happy to hear the news. Not least because the increased output doesn't appear to have jeopardized quality. After the splendid '04, owner Bettina Rogosky and oenologist Peter Schilling had high hopes for the '05, which they believed would be even better. We won't take sides but we can confirm that Caberlot '05 is a fantastic wine that effortlessly picked up Three Glasses. As usual, the spectrum of aromatics is highly distinctive and very broad, revealing grassiness, oriental spices, white pepper and coffee against a backdrop of sweet, ripe and very well-defined dark berry fruit. Structure in the mouth is full bodied yet balanced with vibrant acidity as well as unhurried elegance, depth and superbly burnished tannins.

O Vin Santo del Chianti Cl. Idilio	♟♟	7
● Chianti Cl. '06	♟♟	4*
● Cantico '04	♟	8
● Cantico '03	♟♟	8
● Cantico '01	♟♟	8
● Corbezzolo '01	♟♟	7
● Corbezzolo '00	♟♟	7

● Caberlot '05	♟♟♟	8
● Caberlot '04	♟♟♟	8
● Caberlot '00	♟♟♟	8
● Caberlot '03	♟♟	8
● Caberlot '02	♟♟	8
● Caberlot '01	♟♟	8
● Caberlot '99	♟♟	8
● Caberlot '98	♟♟	6
● Caberlot '97	♟♟	6
● Caberlot '96	♟♟	6

Fattoria Carpineta Fontalpino

FRAZ. MONTAPERTI
LOC. CARPINETA
53019 CASTELNUOVO BERARDENGA [SI]
TEL. 0577369219
www.carpinetafontalpino.it

ANNUAL PRODUCTION	70,000 bottles
HECTARES UNDER VINE	17
VITICULTURE METHOD	Natural

Yet again, Gioia and Filippo Cresti's cellar sent two wines to our national finals. There's nothing new in that. The winery, based at Montaperti where Siena and Florence fought a celebrated battle in the 13th century, has accustomed us to results like this, establishing itself in the front rank of winemaking in the province of Siena. But if we look closer, there is a new development this year. This is the first time we have tasted Chianti Classico Fontalpino and the '06 edition put on a splendid debut performance. Its aromas are still very concentrated but the palate has plenty of flesh and attractive acidity that enables it to finish with a flourish. Now on to those finalists. Dofana '06, from sangiovese and petit verdot, is again outstandingly fresh on the nose, which overlays grassy notes on a basso continuo of spice, and in the mouth, where close-knit extract is offset by assertively bright acidity. The cabernet sauvignon, merlot and sangiovese Do Ut Des '06 sings to a different tune, showing impressive power and concentration. Finally, the Chianti Colli Senesi '06 is uncomplicated and approachable.

Casa alle Vacche

FRAZ. PANCOLE
LOC. LUCIGNANO, 73A
53037 SAN GIMIGNANO [SI]
TEL. 0577955103
www.casaallevacche.it

ANNUAL PRODUCTION	120,000 bottles
HECTARES UNDER VINE	21.5
VITICULTURE METHOD	Conventional

The Ciappis lived up to their reputation as skilled San Gimignano viticulturists with a convincing range of wines. Best of the bunch was the Vernaccia di San Gimignano I Macchioni '07, which came within an ace of the finals. Its expressively elegant nose, full, nicely contrasted flavour and good progression lead to a crunchy fruit finish that offers a grace note of almonds. Equally impressive is the Vernaccia di San Gimignano Riserva Crocus '06, which marries a well-defined nose of attractively oak-laced ripe fruit with a juicy, fresh-tasting palate that offers complexity and good length. The Vernaccia di San Gimignano '07 also impressed with its bright, full-bodied palate and varietal almondy finish. Aglieno, from sangiovese and merlot, is as dependable as ever. The '06 gives tempting fruit on the nose and a soft, well-sustained palate with a polished, close-knit tannic weave. The balanced, attractively savoury Chianti dei Colli Senesi Cinabro Riserva '05 is very nice, the Chianti dei Colli Senesi '07 is lean, fresh-tasting and fruit-forward while the San Gimignano Rosso Acantho was missing from the line-up.

● Do Ut Des '06	♟♟	6
● Dofana '06	♟♟	8
● Chianti Cl. Fontalpino '06	♟♟	4*
● Chianti Colli Senesi '06	♟	4
● Do Ut Des '05	♟♟	6
● Do Ut Des '04	♟♟	6
● Do Ut Des '03	♟♟	6
● Do Ut Des '02	♟♟	6
● Do Ut Des '01	♟♟	6
● Do Ut Des '00	♟♟	6
● Do Ut Des '99	♟♟	6
● Do Ut Des '98	♟♟	6
● Do Ut Des '97	♟♟	6
● Dofana '04	♟♟	8

● Aglieno '06	♟♟	4*
● Chianti Colli Senesi Cinabro Ris. '05	♟♟	4*
○ Vernaccia di S. Gimignano '07	♟♟	2*
○ Vernaccia di S. Gimignano Crocus Ris. '06	♟♟	4*
○ Vernaccia di S. Gimignano I Macchioni '07	♟♟	4*
● Chianti Colli Senesi '07	♟	2
● Aglieno '05	♟♟	4
● Aglieno '04	♟♟	4
● Chianti Colli Senesi Cinabro Ris. '02	♟♟	4
● S. Gimignano Rosso Acantho '04	♟♟	4
● S. Gimignano Rosso Acantho '01	♟♟	6
○ Vernaccia di S. Gimignano Crocus '01	♟♟	4
○ Vernaccia di S. Gimignano Crocus Ris. '05	♟♟	4
○ Vernaccia di S. Gimignano I Macchioni '06	♟♟	3*

Casa Emma

LOC. CORTINE
S.P. DI CASTELLINA IN CHIANTI, 3
50021 BARBERINO VAL D'ELSA [FI]
TEL. 0558072239
www.casaemma.com

ANNUAL PRODUCTION	85,000 bottles
HECTARES UNDER VINE	21
VITICULTURE METHOD	Conventional

Fiorella Lepri Bucalossi's winery of is up to full strength and confirms last year's good results, once more sending the Chianti Classico Riserva into our finals. The '05 shows a fine ruby hue, accompanying aromas ranging from animal skins to saddle leather and fruit, with interesting notes of spice. It develops well on the palate with well-integrated tannins taking you through to an appetizing finish with a medley of jammy fruit. The Soloìo '05, a single-variety Merlot, is also sound and satisfies the palate with its attractive liveliness. The Chianti Classico '06 is interesting as an expression of the special terroir at Barberino Val d'Elsa. For wine tourists who keen to see Tuscan cellars, we should mention that the estate organizes a guided tour not only of the production facilities but also of its botanical park, which covers five hectares around the main building.

★ Casanova di Neri

POD. FIESOLE
53024 MONTALCINO [SI]
TEL. 0577834455
www.casanovadineri.com

ANNUAL PRODUCTION	225,000 bottles
HECTARES UNDER VINE	55
VITICULTURE METHOD	Conventional

Giacomo Neri is back with his Brunello di Montalcino after skipping the 2002 vintage, which he didn't consider up to scratch. The new company premises at Cetine, where the offices and winery are situated, are working at full steam. The cellar, which is entirely below ground level, has some very interesting technical solutions while upstairs the terrace offers a breathtaking view. We cannot stress strongly enough the overall high quality of the wines presented, with a pair of convincing '03 Brunello di Montalcinos, the standard and the Tenuta Nuova selection, in addition to the Rosso di Montalcino '06. Of course, this year there's another treat that won the winery a Three Glass award: the '05 Pietradonice. This monovarietal Cabernet Sauvignon has a dark aubergine colour and a complex nose, with light vegetable notes, candied citrus, blackcurrant and an attractive hint of pencil lead, melding with the more evident toast and spice notes of oak. The palate has great impact, revealing dense, still clenched tannins and a broad finish that echoes the nose. This is a wine with a great future ahead of it.

● Chianti Cl. Ris. '05	♟♟	6
● Chianti Cl. '06	♟♟	4*
● Soloìo '05	♟♟	7
● Soloìo '94	♟♟♟	5
● Chianti Cl. Ris. '04	♟♟	6
● Chianti Cl. Ris. '03	♟♟	6
● Chianti Cl. Ris. '00	♟♟	6
● Chianti Cl. Ris. '99	♟♟	6
● Chianti Cl. Ris. '97	♟♟	4
● Soloìo '04	♟♟	7
● Soloìo '03	♟♟	7
● Soloìo '01	♟♟	8
● Soloìo '00	♟♟	6

● Pietradonice '05	♟♟♟	8
● Brunello di Montalcino '03	♟♟	7
● Brunello di Montalcino Tenuta Nuova '03	♟♟	8
● Rosso di Montalcino '06	♟♟	5
● Brunello di Montalcino '00	♟♟♟	6
● Brunello di Montalcino Cerretalto '01	♟♟♟	8
● Brunello di Montalcino Cerretalto '99	♟♟♟	8
● Brunello di Montalcino Tenuta Nuova '01	♟♟♟	7
● Brunello di Montalcino Tenuta Nuova '99	♟♟♟	7
● Brunello di Montalcino Tenuta Nuova '97	♟♟♟	7
● Sant'Antimo Pietradonice '01	♟♟♟	8
● Sant'Antimo Pietradonice '00	♟♟♟	8

★ Castellare di Castellina

LOC. CASTELLARE
53011 CASTELLINA IN CHIANTI [SI]
TEL. 0577742903
www.castellare.it

ANNUAL PRODUCTION	180,000 bottles
HECTARES UNDER VINE	24
VITICULTURE METHOD	Conventional

Three Glasses were a foregone conclusion for I Sodi di San Niccolò in a vintage like '04. It's another success for the publisher Paolo Panerai and Alessandro Cellai, who every day devotes his impeccable professionalism to the winery he so scrupulously manages. Back to I Sodi, from predominantly sangiovese topped up with malvasia, which has a bouquet where ripe red berry fruits meet violets and juniper. The young tannins are close-knit and solid while perfectly calibrated acidity underpins the whole without intruding. This year, we again preferred the standard version of the two Chianti Classico Riserva '05s, which we found more intact and fresher both on the nose and palate than the Vigna il Poggiale selection. We were also impressed by Coniale '04, a monovarietal Cabernet Sauvignon with a brooding, intriguing nose, whose main qualities are drinkability and excellent expansion. The merlot-only Poggio ai Merli '06 gives black cherry-dominated aromatics with vegetal nuances, although this year it lacks that touch of extra complexity. The Chianti Classico '06 is well made and moreish.

La Castellina

LOC. FERROZZOLA, 1
53011 CASTELLINA IN CHIANTI [SI]
TEL. 0577740454
www.lacastellina.it

ANNUAL PRODUCTION	175,000 bottles
HECTARES UNDER VINE	39
VITICULTURE METHOD	Conventional

Monica Targioni and Tommaso Bojola's operation is back in the Guide, after an absence of some years. The wines vary but on the whole show interesting characteristics. The estate has a long history, and dates back to the Middle Ages, when it belonged to the Squarcialupi family, to whom the owners have dedicated a wine. In fact, Palazzo Squarcialupi, in the centre of this town in Chianti, is where the ageing cellars are situated. It is also interesting to visit the Enoteca Antiquaria, one of the most comprehensive collections of historic local bottles from wineries operating over the last century, some of which no longer exist. We were extremely impressed with the '05 Chianti Classico Riserva, which gives fruity tones, faint notes of tobacco and leather and a firm body with perfectly integrated fine-grained tannins, the whole being livened up by bright acidity that takes you through to a long, rising finish. The Vin Santo Occhio di Pernice '03 is intriguing, with its spectrum of aromatics ranging from dried fruit to citrus zest. On the palate it is creamy, sweet, and incredibly long.

● I Sodi di San Niccolò '04	♟♟♟ 8
● Chianti Cl. Ris. '05	♟♟ 5
● Chianti Cl. V. il Poggiale Ris. '05	♟♟ 6
● Coniale '04	♟♟ 7
● Chianti Cl. '06	♟ 4
● Poggio ai Merli '06	♟ 8
● Chianti Cl. V. il Poggiale Ris. '01	♟♟♟ 6
● Chianti Cl. V. il Poggiale Ris. '00	♟♟♟ 6
● I Sodi di San Niccolò '03	♟♟♟ 8
● I Sodi di San Niccolò '02	♟♟♟ 8
● I Sodi di San Niccolò '01	♟♟♟ 8
● I Sodi di San Niccolò '98	♟♟♟ 8
● I Sodi di San Niccolò '97	♟♟♟ 8

● Chianti Cl. Squarcialupi Ris. '05	♟♟ 5
○ Vin Santo del Chianti Cl. Occhio di Pernice '03	♟♟ 6
○ Vin Santo del Chianti Classico '02	♟ 5

Castelvecchio

LOC. SAN PANCRAZIO
VIA CERTALDESE, 30
50026 SAN CASCIANO IN VAL DI PESA [FI]
TEL. 0558248032
www.castelvecchio.it

ANNUAL PRODUCTION 100,000 bottles
HECTARES UNDER VINE 27
VITICULTURE METHOD Conventional

This full-length profile for the winery of the Rocchi family is well-deserved. The Rocchis manage to maintain a very evident enthusiasm, and are unswervingly committed to further improvement, despite having already achieved more than respectable results and in fact, every year the wines presented acquire greater stylistic definition, while remaining anchored to the territory, both in style and the varieties used to make them. The best was Il Brecciolino '05, a blend dominated by sangiovese with small quantities of petit verdot and merlot, which showed a broad aromatic spectrum ranging through spices, black berry fruits and balsamic notes. On the palate, the tannins unfurl beautifully in the powerful body to a fresh-tasting, convincing finale. The two versions of Chianti dei Colli Fiorentini also performed well, both the '06 vintage, which was incredibly drinkable, relaxed and succulent, and the Riserva Vigna La Quercia '05, with its smooth tannins and intriguing tanginess. The San Lorenzo '07, from a 50-50 blend of malvasia and trebbiano, is simpler but well made.

Tenuta Castiglioni

FRAZ. MONTAGNANA VAL DI PESA
VIA MONTEGUFONI, 35
50020 MONTESPERTOLI [FI]
TEL. 0571671387
www.frescobaldi.it

ANNUAL PRODUCTION 1,000,000 bottles
HECTARES UNDER VINE 148
VITICULTURE METHOD Conventional

Tenuta Castiglioni proves that quality and quantity need not be mutually exclusive, and has been demonstrating the fact for many years now. This fine estate owned by the Frescobaldi family is situated on the hills overlooking the town of Montespertoli where the Tenuta Castiglioni cellars turn out excellent wines that are quite impeccably made. In some cases, they are also available at extremely competitive prices. Giramonte '06, from sangiovese and merlot, confirms its status as a high-profile product. The aromas of dark berry fruit alternate with elegant spiced and balsamic nuances, bringing out the best of the complex, elegantly textured palate with its compact tannins and good length. Tenuta di Castiglioni '06, a blend of cabernet sauvignon and sangiovese, is also good. The rich aromas on the nose alternate fresh sensations of black berry fruits with toastiness, ushering in a weighty palate with smooth tannins and a tasty yet restrained finale. The easy-drinking Chianti '07 is well balanced. We also liked the rosé, Saltagrilli '07.

● Chianti Colli Fiorentini Il Castelvecchio '06	♥♥ 4*
● Chianti Colli Fiorentini V. La Quercia Ris. '05	♥♥ 5
● Il Brecciolino '05	♥♥ 6
○ San Lorenzo '07	♥ 3
● Chianti Colli Fiorentini V. La Quercia '03	♥♥ 4
● Il Brecciolino '04	♥♥ 6
● Il Brecciolino '03	♥♥ 6
● Il Brecciolino '02	♥♥ 6
● Numero Otto '06	♥♥ 5

● Giramonte '06	♥♥ 8
● Tenuta di Castiglioni '06	♥♥ 5
● Chianti '07	♥ 3*
☉ Saltagrilli '07	♥ 4
● Giramonte '00	♥♥♥ 8
● Cabernet Sauvignon '05	♥♥ 5
● Cabernet Sauvignon '04	♥♥ 5
● Cabernet Sauvignon '03	♥♥ 5
● Cabernet Sauvignon '01	♥♥ 5
● Giramonte '05	♥♥ 8
● Giramonte '04	♥♥ 8
● Giramonte '03	♥♥ 8
● Giramonte '02	♥♥ 8
● Giramonte '01	♥♥ 8

Famiglia Cecchi

LOC. CASINA DEI PONTI, 56
53011 CASTELLINA IN CHIANTI [SI]
TEL. 057754311
www.cecchi.net

ANNUAL PRODUCTION	7,200,000 bottles
HECTARES UNDER VINE	292
VITICULTURE METHOD	Conventional

When a benchmark winery has been operating for well over a century, it must be on the right track. Cesare and Andrea Cecchi look confidently to the future and one of the most important decisions taken this year was to get rid of all the Supertuscans from the winery's portfolio and concentrate entirely on designation-compliant wines. This is not an easy choice when you are releasing over 7,000,000 bottles of wine a year so credit to the owners for taking the plunge and choosing to focus on the personality of the individual labels. The best proof of their success came from the Maremma wines, with the Morellino di Scansano Riserva '05 offering fine aromatic intensity, a full, well-balanced body and good length. The cellar's Chianti Classico is well executed and a special mention goes to the Riserva di Famiglia '05, with its mineral nose and appealing, flavour-rich palate. Nor should we forget the premium Villa Cerna wines. We were extremely impressed by the Chianti Classico Riserva '05 with its breadth of aromas and succulence on the palate, where close-woven tannins lead into a tasty finish. We also liked Chianti Classico '06.

Cennatoio Intervineas

VIA DI SAN LEOLINO, 35
50020 PANZANO [FI]
TEL. 0558963230
www.cennatoio.it

ANNUAL PRODUCTION	100,000 bottles
HECTARES UNDER VINE	17
VITICULTURE METHOD	Conventional

The Alessi family is back in the Guide with an overall result they will satisfy them. Despite the small size of the winery, they produce a large range of wines, with some blends doubling up. Potential is undoubtedly high. The technical staff has always been under the guidance of David Picci, who deals with the agronomy side of things, and Gabriella Tani, who is in charge of winemaking. The best wine turned out to be the Etrusco '04, a monovarietal sangiovese with an austere nose revealing strong overtones of leather and tobacco, combined with well-developed fruit. The palate progresses confidently, with fresh acidity coming to the fore and a satisfyingly long finish. Arcibaldo '04, a blend of cabernet sauvignon and sangiovese grosso, was also attractive, with a seductively sweet bouquet of forest fruits and vanilla. Full-bodied and creamy on entry, the palate is well rounded, leading into a finish with an appealing after-aroma. The other wines are well executed, from the two versions of Chianti Classico, the '06 and the Riserva '04, to Mammolo '04, a single-variety Merlot.

● Chianti Cl. Villa Cerna Ris. '05	♼♼	5
● Morellino di Scansano Ris. '05	♼♼	5
● Chianti Cl. '06	♼	5
● Chianti Cl. Messer Piero di Teuzzo '06	♼	5
● Chianti Cl. Riserva di Famiglia '05	♼	6
● Chianti Cl. Villa Cerna '06	♼	5
● Morellino di Scansano '07	♼	3
○ Vernaccia di S. Gimignano Castello di Montauto '07	♼	4
● Chianti Cl. Riserva di Famiglia '02	♼♼	5
● Chianti Cl. Riserva di Famiglia '01	♼♼	6
● Chianti Cl. Villa Cerna Ris. '04	♼♼	5
● Spargolo '04	♼♼	7
● Vigneto La Gavina '01	♼♼	6

● Arcibaldo '04	♼♼	7
● Etrusco '04	♼♼	6
● Chianti Cl. '06	♼	5
● Chianti Cl. O'Leandro Ris. '04	♼	5
● Mammolo '04	♼	6
● Arcibaldo '99	♼♼	7
● Chianti Cl. Ris. '01	♼♼	5
● Chianti Cl. Ris. '00	♼♼	5
● Etrusco '03	♼♼	6
● Etrusco '01	♼♼	6
● Etrusco '00	♼♼	6
● Rosso Fiorentino '03	♼♼	8
● Rosso Fiorentino '01	♼♼	6

Centolani

LOC. FRIGGIALI
S.DA MAREMMANA
53024 MONTALCINO [SI]
TEL. 0577849454
www.tenutafriggialiepietranera.it

ANNUAL PRODUCTION	250,000 bottles
HECTARES UNDER VINE	43
VITICULTURE METHOD	Conventional

This beautiful family winery is led by the flamboyant Olga Peluso, and has two separate estates: Friggiali, situated in the west Montalcino, and Pietranera, in an area of volcanic soil near Castello della Velona. The two zones are very different in terms of climate and terroir, and yield wines with a highly distinctive style that the '03 harvest made even more evident. The effects of the growing year's high temperatures were evident in the Brunello di Montalcino Pietranera, with its somewhat overripe bouquet clearly showing notes of plum jam and liquorice. The tannins are stiffish and the palate is not exactly easy drinking. We preferred the Brunello di Friggiali, from a cooler area, which has morello cherry and blackberry fruit over intense sensations of balsamic herbs, followed by a harmonious palate. Tannins are in evidence but softening, and never threaten to cramp drinkability. Of the two Rosso di Montalcino '06s, we preferred Pietranera, which has more density and better development thanks to richer raw material and riper extract. Brunello di Montalcino Donna Olga '03, from Olga's own winery, is also first-rate.

La Cerbaiola

P.ZZA CAVOUR, 19
53024 MONTALCINO [SI]
TEL. 0577848499

ANNUAL PRODUCTION	15,000 bottles
HECTARES UNDER VINE	4
VITICULTURE METHOD	Conventional

Giulio Salvioni is a positive volcano of enthusiasm and when he talks about Brunello, he becomes even more impassioned, unafraid to show his love of the territory and the wine he produces there. The winery has grown over the years and now has four hectares planted to Brunello. The entire vinification process takes place in small premises near the vineyard so as to minimize transport times and the vines are managed by Giulio's son, Davide. Unfortunately, only one wine was presented this year, Brunello di Montalcino '03, while the Rosso di Montalcino was not produced in 2006 because Giulio considered the year so good that he dedicated his entire production to Brunello. The '03 is decidedly interesting and reflects a new winery style. Deep ruby in colour, it gives a classic fruity, slightly spicy bouquet with intense notes of cherry. Texture on the palate is close-knit, underpinned by tannins that somewhat tighten up the finish. Given the vintage, one of the most difficult in recent years, this is a good result.

● Brunello di Montalcino Donna Olga '03	▲▲ 7
● Brunello di Montalcino Tenuta Friggiali '03	▲▲ 6
● Brunello di Montalcino Pietranera '03	▲ 7
● Rosso di Montalcino Pietranera '06	▲ 4
● Rosso di Montalcino Tenuta Friggiali '06	▲ 4
● Brunello di Montalcino Tenuta Friggiali Ris. '99	▼▼▼ 8
● Brunello di Montalcino Pietranera '02	▼▼ 7
● Brunello di Montalcino Pietranera '01	▼▼ 7
● Brunello di Montalcino Pietranera '99	▼▼ 7
● Brunello di Montalcino Tenuta Friggiali '01	▼▼ 6
● Brunello di Montalcino Tenuta Friggiali '00	▼▼ 6
● Brunello di Montalcino Tenuta Friggiali Ris. '01	▼▼ 7

● Brunello di Montalcino '03	▲▲ 8
● Brunello di Montalcino '00	▼▼▼ 8
● Brunello di Montalcino '99	▼▼▼ 8
● Brunello di Montalcino '97	▼▼▼ 8
● Brunello di Montalcino '90	▼▼▼ 8
● Brunello di Montalcino '01	▼▼ 8
● Brunello di Montalcino '98	▼▼ 8
● Brunello di Montalcino '95	▼▼ 8
● Brunello di Montalcino '93	▼▼ 8
● Brunello di Montalcino '91	▼▼ 8

Cerbaiona

LOC. CERBAIONA
53024 MONTALCINO [SI]
TEL. 0577848660

ANNUAL PRODUCTION **15,000 bottles**
HECTARES UNDER VINE **3.2**
VITICULTURE METHOD **Conventional**

Diego Molinari has two nicknames in Montalcino: the first is Commander, a tribute to his past as a pilot, and the second, earned in winemaking, is Maestro. Surrounded by his wife Nora's cats, holding his trademark cigarette, he moves around the barrels and pool at Cerbaiona, sorting out the problems presented by the harvest. He even managed to find a solution for the 2003 vintage, which was anything but straightforward, and his deep ruby Brunello di Montalcino manages to display a similar style to its predecessors. On the nose it shows its dual spirit – on one hand slightly more developed, with notes of autumn leaves and brambles, and on the other with well-integrated fruit that lends a subtle sensation of complexity. This personal interpretation of the vintage is also evident on the palate, where powerful alcohol is tempered by unexpected acidity, making this a smooth, attractive drink. The tannins are well structured but will require further bottle ageing. We liked the Cerbaiona '05, from sangiovese, which was extremely tidy albeit somewhat predictable.

Fattoria del Cerro

FRAZ. ACQUAVIVA
VIA GRAZIANELLA, 5
53040 MONTEPULCIANO [SI]
TEL. 0578767722
www.saiagricola.it

ANNUAL PRODUCTION **800,000 bottles**
HECTARES UNDER VINE **170**
VITICULTURE METHOD **Conventional**

Fattoria del Cerro, owned by the Saiagricola group, is one of the solidest businesses in Montepulciano not only because of its longevity, with almost 30 years of operation under its belt, but also for quality. The wines are always reliable and well executed. A further strength is a policy of fair pricing to ensure that enthusiasts will come back. The wine that stood out, as is always reassuringly the case, was Nobile Antica Chiusina, which reached our finals. This is a wine whose style has been perfected over the years and which today stands out for its well-gauged extract and a judicious use of new oak. The '05 version possesses a concentrated aromatic profile, exuding clear-cut yet lush fruitiness. On the palate, the wine is fresh, succulent and full bodied, with a taut finish tending towards tanginess. The Nobile di Montepulciano Riserva '04 shows solid structure, although the progression of flavours on the palate is still somewhat clenched. The sauvignon-only Corte d'Oro Vendemmia Tardiva '06 offers caressing aromas and fresh, racy taste. The other wines are well made.

● Brunello di Montalcino '03	♟♟	8
● Cerbaiona '05	♟	6
● Brunello di Montalcino '01	♟♟♟	8
● Brunello di Montalcino '99	♟♟♟	8
● Brunello di Montalcino '97	♟♟♟	8
● Brunello di Montalcino '02	♟♟	8
● Brunello di Montalcino '00	♟♟	8
● Brunello di Montalcino '98	♟♟	8

● Nobile di Montepulciano Vign. Antica Chiusina '05	♟♟	7
○ Corte d'Oro V.T. '06	♟♟	6
● Nobile di Montepulciano Ris. '04	♟♟	5
○ Braviolo '07	♟	2
● Chianti dei Colli Senesi '07	♟	3
● Nobile di Montepulciano '05	♟	5
○ Poggio a Tramontana '07	♟	4
● Rosso di Montepulciano '07	♟	4
● Nobile di Montepulciano Vign. Antica Chiusina '00	♟♟♟	7
● Nobile di Montepulciano Vign. Antica Chiusina '99	♟♟♟	7
● Nobile di Montepulciano Ris. '01	♟♟	5
● Nobile di Montepulciano Vign. Antica Chiusina '04	♟♟	7
● Nobile di Montepulciano Vign. Antica Chiusina '01	♟♟	7

Vincenzo Cesani

FRAZ. PANCOLE
VIA PIAZZETTA, 82D
53037 SAN GIMIGNANO [SI]
TEL. 0577955084
www.agriturismo-cesani.com

ANNUAL PRODUCTION 100,000 bottles
HECTARES UNDER VINE 19
VITICULTURE METHOD Conventional

In recent years, some of the most characterful, territory-focused wines around here have come from this family winery led by the highly experienced Vincenzo Cesani. The fact that the subzone of Pancole is so well-suited for both red grapes and vernaccia is demonstrated by the splendid results achieved by the San Gimignano Cellori and by the two Vernaccias, the basic version and the Sanice selection. Cellori '04, which went through to the final tastings, is a fine wine with a well-textured, fruit-forward palate underpinned by solid acidity that offers a well-coordinated taste profile and good length. The Vernaccia di San Gimignano Sanice '06 is making good progress and gives ripe fruit and florality, fine acidic verve, good length and a varietal aftertaste. The Vernaccia di San Gimignano '07 has attractive aromas and is fresh and vigorous, with a fluid, enjoyable palate. Chianti dei Colli Senesi '07 is spot-on and a well-structured easy drinker. It's also great value for money. The Luenzo '05, a blend of sangiovese and colorino, is nicely textured and fruity but not really its usual self, with somewhat over-assertive tannins.

Ciacci Piccolomini D'Aragona

FRAZ. CASTELNUOVO DELL'ABATE
LOC. MOLINELLO
53024 MONTALCINO [SI]
TEL. 0577835616
www.ciaccipiccolomini.com

ANNUAL PRODUCTION 200,000 bottles
HECTARES UNDER VINE 40
VITICULTURE METHOD Conventional

Paolo Bianchini, who owns this historic winery in Castelnuovo together with his sister Lucia, continues to introduce innovations and to extend the vineyards to satisfy the growing demand for Brunello. The newest vineyards provided a new Brunello di Montalcino which debuts with the '03 vintage and is presented alongside the well-established version from the vineyard at Pianrosso, in the Sesta area. The winery also has an outpost at Montecucco, which this year has provided an extremely well-made Sangiovese '06 that we found attractive, juicy and highly drinkable. The star, however, remains the Brunello Vigna di Pianrosso. Although less explosive than usual on the nose, after brief aeration it shows warm, jammy aromatics, notably slightly balsamic hints of medicinal herbs and saddle leather. The palate is convincing, and not diluted by alcohol, but still presents over-assertive tannins that will require further bottle ageing in order to unbend. The finish is powerful and lingers. The other Brunello is simpler, although more elegant and immediate. The Rosso di Montalcino '06, meanwhile, is a little overripe with mouth-drying extract.

● San Gimignano Rosso Cellori '04	¶¶ 5
● Chianti Colli Senesi '07	¶¶ 3*
○ Vernaccia di S. Gimignano '07	¶¶ 3*
○ Vernaccia di S. Gimignano Sanice '06	¶¶ 4*
● Luenzo '05	¶ 5
● Luenzo '99	¶¶¶ 5
● Luenzo '97	¶¶¶ 5
● Chianti Colli Senesi '05	¶¶ 3*
● Luenzo '04	¶¶ 5
● Luenzo '01	¶¶ 6
● Luenzo '00	¶¶ 6
● San Gimignano Rosso Cellori '03	¶¶ 6
● San Gimignano Rosso Cellori '02	¶¶ 6
○ Vernaccia di S. Gimignano Sanice '05	¶¶ 4
○ Vernaccia di S. Gimignano Sanice '04	¶¶ 4

● Brunello di Montalcino V. di Pianrosso '03	¶¶ 7
● Montecucco Sangiovese '06	¶¶ 5
● Brunello di Montalcino '03	¶ 6
● Rosso di Montalcino '06	¶ 5
● Brunello di Montalcino V. di Pianrosso '98	¶¶¶ 7
● Brunello di Montalcino V. di Pianrosso Ris. '01	¶¶¶ 8
● Brunello di Montalcino V. di Pianrosso Ris. '99	¶¶¶ 8
● Brunello di Montalcino V. di Pianrosso '01	¶¶ 8
● Brunello di Montalcino V. di Pianrosso '00	¶¶ 7
● Brunello di Montalcino V. di Pianrosso '99	¶¶ 7

Cima

FRAZ. ROMAGNANO
VIA DEL FAGIANO, 1
54100 MASSA
TEL. 0585831617
www.aziendagricolacima.it

ANNUAL PRODUCTION	110,000 bottles
HECTARES UNDER VINE	30
VITICULTURE METHOD	Conventional

What a fantastic decline we have seen in the products from the Cima winery! We hope you will forgive the paradox but it's the best way to sum up the winemaking story of this estate in a beautiful strip of land between Tuscany and Liguria. Over recent years, we have appreciated the turnaround as Aurelio Cima's wines have shifted from a powerful, concentrated, and in our opinion pretentious, style towards less clichéd, more territorial products. The winery's step back to step forward became evident at this year's tastings. Success here is driven by native varieties, presented as straightforward single-variety bottles. The prime example is Massaretta '06, a full-flavoured harmonious red that reveals great extractive finesse and excellent drinkability. We also very much enjoyed Vermentino Nero, from an unusual variety with lots of potential. The 2006 Cima is a wine built around aromas of dark berry fruit and Mediterranean scrub, which develops on the palate by virtue of its juiciness and acidic backbone. Cima is also one of the best interpreters of the Candia DOC, releasing a full-flavoured, and incredibly well-orchestrated, wine.

Fattoria di Cinciano

LOC. CINCIANO, 2
53036 POGGIBONSI [SI]
TEL. 0577936588
www.cinciano.it

ANNUAL PRODUCTION	70,000 bottles
HECTARES UNDER VINE	25
VITICULTURE METHOD	Conventional

There was an impressive debut for the Garrè family winery, which makes its entry in the Guide with a full profile. The origins of the property date back to the Middle Ages, and its position, bang on the border between the provinces of Florence and Siena, made it for long periods of time a bone of contention between the two cities. Originally an aristocratic residence, it was then converted into a convent before once more becoming a stately home. Now renovated, it is at the centre of a small settlement entirely made up of tourist accommodation. We were most convinced by the designation wines, starting with the Riserva '05, with mature but well-balanced notes of fruit and tobacco that are rounded off by subtle balsamic hints. It reveals a well-balanced, flavoursome palate and a juicy finish. We found the Chianti Classico '06 more immediate and drinkable, with forthright violet scents on the nose mingling with cherry and nutmeg. The palate has a remarkably soft mouthfeel. Although richly textured, the Pietraforte '06, a blend of sangiovese and merlot, has stiffish tannins.

O Candia dei Colli Apuani Vign. Candia Alto '07		ⵏⵏ 5
● Gamo '06		ⵏⵏ 8
● Massaretta '06		ⵏⵏ 6
● Romalbo '06		ⵏⵏ 6
● Vermentino Nero '06		ⵏⵏ 6
● Anchigi '06		ⵏ 5
O Candia dei Colli Apuani '07		ⵏ 4
● Montervo '06		ⵏ 6
O Vermentino '07		ⵏ 4
● Montervo '01		ⵝⵝ 6
● Romalbo '01		ⵝⵝ 6
● Romalbo '00		ⵝⵝ 6

● Chianti Cl. '06		ⵏⵏ 4*
● Chianti Cl. Ris. '05		ⵏⵏ 5
● Pietraforte '06		ⵏ 5

Le Cinciole

VIA CASE SPARSE, 83
50020 PANZANO [FI]
TEL. 055852636
www.lecinciole.it

ANNUAL PRODUCTION	45,000 bottles
HECTARES UNDER VINE	24
VITICULTURE METHOD	Certified organic

Wines from Luca Orsini and Valeria Viganò are always a safe bet since the range is very respectable overall, in particular those based on sangiovese. Even if they didn't bag a Three Glass award, our friends came very close this year with their Chianti Classico Riserva Petresco '04, which again went to the finals. Thirty hectares of the estate are planted with vineyards and olive groves, and managed to organic farming methods in line with a project which lays great importance on respect for the territory. Moving on to the wines, the Petresco has an intense mineral nose, underpinned by spicy notes of nutmeg and set off by lively fruity notes of blackberries and plums. The structure is solid, with well distributed tannins, refreshing acidity, good length and an aftertaste of fresh herbs. The Camalaione '05 is well executed, even though it did not scale the heights of last year's offering. This blend of cabernet sauvignon, merlot and syrah has a well-developed complex nose, a juicy, caressing body with good softness and a finish only slightly held back by tannins. The Chianti Classico '06 is well executed and enjoyable.

● Chianti Cl. Petresco Ris. '04	♟♟	6
● Camalaione '05	♟♟	8
● Chianti Cl. '06	♟	5
● Camalaione '04	♟♟♟	8
● Chianti Cl. Petresco Ris. '01	♟♟♟	6

Tenuta La Cipressaia

VIA ROMITA, 38
50025 MONTESPERTOLI [FI]
TEL. 0571670868
www.tenutalacipressaia.it

ANNUAL PRODUCTION	100,000 bottles
HECTARES UNDER VINE	22
VITICULTURE METHOD	Conventional

After many years with a short profile, this year the Alvino family winery earned a full-length profile. Located near Florence, the main villa was built in the 18th century by the aristocratic Florentine Della Gherardesca family. The construction of the winery dates back to 1901, when it was hewn from the rock where there once stood a small Etruscan town known as Ripa. As well as making wine, the family also runs a farmstay. The varieties used are those of tradition, such as sangiovese, canaiolo and white varieties such as trebbiano and malvasia, which are used for Vin Santo. We were most impressed by Borgoricco '06, a sangiovese-only bottle that gives ripe notes of blackberry jam with and hints of flowers, violets in particular. On the palate, there is body and structure, with a refreshing acidic vein and a fine, full-flavoured finish. The Chianti Colli Fiorentini also performed well, its intense aromas of cherry and strawberry fusing with lightly spiced hints of vanilla. Supple and well-balanced on the palate, it signs off with a moderately long but satisfyingly intense finish. The rest of the wines are agreeable.

● Borgoricco '06	♟♟	5
● Chianti Colli Fiorentini '06	♟♟	3
● Chianti '07	♟	3
● Chianti Magolo '07	♟	3
○ Vino Santo del Chianti '04	♟	4
● Borgoricco '04	♟♟	5
● Borgoricco '00	♟♟	4

★ Tenuta Col d'Orcia

LOC. SANT'ANGELO IN COLLE
53020 MONTALCINO [SI]
TEL. 057780891
www.coldorcia.it

Col di Bacche

S.DA DI CUPI
58010 MAGLIANO IN TOSCANA [GR]
TEL. 0577738526
www.coldibacche.com

ANNUAL PRODUCTION	800,000 bottles
HECTARES UNDER VINE	142
VITICULTURE METHOD	Conventional

ANNUAL PRODUCTION	65,000 bottles
HECTARES UNDER VINE	11
VITICULTURE METHOD	Conventional

It was a year of transition for this solid Montalcino winery. The leading wines were missing. Brunello di Montalcino Poggio al Vento, one of the symbols of the DOCG zone, was not produced in 2002 and was replaced by a weakish Riserva, and Olmaia, the winery's Cabernet Sauvignon, was not ready in time for our tastings. Another two products did keep the flag flying high. One is Nearco, a blend of 50 per cent merlot, 30 per cent cabernet sauvignon and syrah, whose '04 vintage is extremely convincing, and the other is the attractively priced Rosso di Montalcino '06, probably the best the winery has ever produced. The Nearco shows ruby with hints of aubergine purple, and an intense, persistent bouquet hinging on blackberry, blackcurrant and raspberry-like fruit. The attack is attractive preceding sustained sweetness and a mouthfilling progression with close-knit tannins and good acidity that underpins the weighty extract. The finish is complex and lingering with citrus and chocolate notes. The Rosso di Montalcino '06 put on a textbook performance, giving fragrant cherry on the nose and a complex, very drinkable palate with lingering length.

Once again, this winery at Magliano in Toscana consolidated its strong position in Maremma wine, presenting a range of products that are quite simply some of the best in the area in their respective types. Skilfully, Alberto Carnasciali has managed to impart impeccable character and a deliberately sober style to his faultlessly made wines, without forcing the vinification process. It was no surprise that two of his wines made it through to the finals. The Morellino di Scansano Rovente '06 has an aromatic profile of extreme clarity, dominated by fruit and spices. This very well-calibrated wine shows its strength in the mouth, which progresses confidently if perhaps without as much complexity as we would have liked. Stylistically similar is the Cupinero '06, from merlot grapes with a dash of cabernet sauvignon, which shows full, ripe aromas and a palate of excellent density, nicely offset by fine acidity, leaving an impression of lively roundness. We were surprised by the attractiveness and balance of the aromatic, fresh and delightfully tasty Morellino '07.

● Sant'Antimo Nearco '04	ΨΨ	6
● Rosso di Montalcino '06	ΨΨ	4*
● Brunello di Montalcino '03	Ψ	6
● Brunello di Montalcino Ris. '02	Ψ	8
○ Sant'Antimo Pinot Grigio '07	Ψ	4
● Brunello di Montalcino Poggio al Vento Ris. '99	ΨΨΨ	8
● Brunello di Montalcino Poggio al Vento Ris. '97	ΨΨΨ	8
● Brunello di Montalcino Poggio al Vento Ris. '95	ΨΨΨ	8
● Olmaia '01	ΨΨΨ	7
● Brunello di Montalcino '01	ΨΨ	6
● Brunello di Montalcino '00	ΨΨ	6
● Brunello di Montalcino '97	ΨΨ	5*

● Cupinero '06	ΨΨ	6
● Morellino di Scansano Rovente '06	ΨΨ	5
● Morellino di Scansano '07	ΨΨ	4*
● Morellino di Scansano Rovente '05	ΨΨΨ	5
● Cupinero '05	ΨΨ	6
● Cupinero '04	ΨΨ	6
● Cupinero '03	ΨΨ	6
● Cupinero '02	ΨΨ	6
● Cupinero '01	ΨΨ	5
● Morellino di Scansano '06	ΨΨ	4
● Morellino di Scansano '05	ΨΨ	4
● Morellino di Scansano '04	ΨΨ	4
● Morellino di Scansano '03	ΨΨ	4
● Morellino di Scansano Rovente '04	ΨΨ	5
● Morellino di Scansano Rovente '03	ΨΨ	5

Colle Bereto

LOC. COLLE BERETO
53017 RADDA IN CHIANTI [SI]
TEL. 0554299330
www.collebereto.com

ANNUAL PRODUCTION	50,000 bottles
HECTARES UNDER VINE	15
VITICULTURE METHOD	Conventional

The Pinzauti family is back with a full-length profile, thanks to their two Supertuscans and an excellent edition of their Chianti Classico. The village has ancient origins, dating back to the 11th century, and still conserves its period atmosphere. Originally bought as a country residence by the Pinzautis, over the years, grape growing and winemaking became an increasingly important adjunct to the family's main activity. This year, our finals were graced by Il Cenno '06, a single-variety Pinot Nero with an elegant, understated style and light structure, fresh aromas of violets and blackcurrants lifted by spiciness. Although somewhat insubstantial, the wine has an inviting finish. We also liked the Tocco '06, from merlot with a small percentage of sangiovese, which avoids excessive concentration and flaunts a wide aromatic spectrum that puts the accent on fruitiness. Attractively firm and juicy on the palate, it moves on to an appealing, long-lingering finish. Last up is the first-rate Chianti Classico '06, which has an inviting floral nose, well-balanced structure and satisfying drinkability.

Colle Massari

LOC. POGGI DEL SASSO
58044 CINIGIANO [GR]
TEL. 0564990496
www.collemassari.it

ANNUAL PRODUCTION	250,000 bottles
HECTARES UNDER VINE	69
VITICULTURE METHOD	Certified organic

Claudio Tipa, president of the Montecucco DOC growers' association, will be doubly satisfied with this year's successes. His winery earned Three Glasses, bringing the Montecucco DOC zone its first award. It is difficult to imagine Colle Massari not being involved in the future of this DOC zone, which is both a business project aimed at commercial success and a concrete plan to boost the territory as a whole. The Three Glasses were awarded to the Montecucco Sangiovese Lombrone Riserva '04, a wine with real character that unveils seductive scents of flowers, earthiness and tobacco, and a palate with vibrant, dynamic flavour with good contrast. The Montecucco Rosso Colle Massari Riserva '05 also got through to the finals. It's an aromatically fresh, intense wine with a full-flavoured, gutsy palate. We found the Montecucco Rosso Rigoleto '06 and the Montecucco Vermentino Le Melacce '07 to be highly drinkable, the former full-bodied and complex, the latter fresh and tasty. The Montecucco Vermentino Irisse '06 is fuller bodied but somewhat less dynamic. The Grottolo '07 is a fragrant rosé from sangiovese, ciliegiolo and montepulciano grapes.

● Il Cenno '06	YY 6
● Chianti Cl. '06	YY 4*
● Il Tocco '06	YY 6
● Chianti Cl. Ris. '04	YY 5
● Il Cenno '03	YY 5

● Montecucco Sangiovese Lombrone Ris. '04	YYY 7
● Montecucco Rosso Colle Massari Ris. '05	YY 5
● Montecucco Rosso Rigoleto '06	YY 4*
O Montecucco Vermentino Le Melacce '07	YY 4*
⊙ Grottolo '07	Y 4
O Montecucco Vermentino Irisse '06	Y 5
● Montecucco Rosso Colle Massari Ris. '04	YY 6
● Montecucco Rosso Colle Massari Ris. '03	YY 6

Collelungo

LOC. COLLELUNGO
53011 CASTELLINA IN CHIANTI [SI]
TEL. 0577740489
www.collelungo.com

ANNUAL PRODUCTION	30,000 bottles
HECTARES UNDER VINE	20
VITICULTURE METHOD	Conventional

The performance of the wines presented by the Cattelan family was a little below par. There was no Riserva or Vin Santo, but it is also true that the Campo Cerchi selection of Chianti Classico Riserva, from the '04 vintage, did not hit the expected heights because of both a lack of cleanness on the nose, which nevertheless displayed fresh menthol notes, and to particularly rigid tannins, which failed to unfold entirely. The Merlot '06 is clearly better, showing uncomplicated but intense on the nose of upfront red berry fruit and enjoyable on the mouthfilling palate. The Chianti Classico '06 is basically well made. The overall impression, however, is that the wines we tasted had great potential that for various reasons they have failed to capitalize to the full in recent years. We confidently await better results in the future.

● Merlot '06		♈♈ 5
● Chianti Cl. '06		♈ 4
● Chianti Cl. Campo Cerchi Ris. '04		♈ 6
● Chianti Cl. Campo Cerchi Ris. '01		♈♈ 7
● Chianti Cl. Campo Cerchi Ris. '00		♈♈ 8
● Chianti Cl. Ris. '04		♈♈ 5
● Chianti Cl. Ris. '03		♈♈ 5
● Chianti Cl. Ris. '01		♈♈ 6

Collemattoni

LOC. SANT'ANGELO IN COLLE
POD. COLLEMATTONI, 100
53020 MONTALCINO [SI]
TEL. 0577844127
www.collemattoni.it

ANNUAL PRODUCTION	35,000 bottles
HECTARES UNDER VINE	6.7
VITICULTURE METHOD	Conventional

You should not be fooled by Marcello Bucci apparent simplicity. Whether in the vineyard or in the winery, he pays meticulous attention to the smallest details, which to some other might seem insignificant. The estate is near Sant'Angelo in Colle, in the southern part of Montalcino, which is usually also the warmest. This accounts for the difficulties experienced by the Brunello di Montalcino '03, which on the nose is reluctant to unfold on the more classic notes of saddle leather, tobacco and spice. This rigidity is reflected on the palate, where the acidity and especially the tannins have yet to unfold and slightly cut the finish short. The Rosso di Montalcino '06, one of the best from the growing year, was interesting with its forthright nose of blackberry, cherry and mulberry meshing well with elegantly spicy undertones. The palate is rich, well-rounded and juicy, with mellow tannins of rare finesse, braced by stylishly restrained acidity. The finish is impressive, without affecting the wine's great drinkability. We also enjoyed the Adone '07, which is also available at a very attractive price.

● Rosso di Montalcino '06		♈♈ 4*
● Adone '07		♈ 3
● Brunello di Montalcino '03		♈ 7
● Brunello di Montalcino '01		♈♈♈ 6
● Brunello di Montalcino Fontelontano Ris. '01		♈♈♈ 7
● Brunello di Montalcino Fontelontano Ris. '99		♈♈ 7

Tenuta di Collosorbo

FRAZ. CASTELNUOVO DELL'ABATE
LOC. VILLA A SESTA, 25
53024 MONTALCINO [SI]
TEL. 0577835534
www.collosorbo.com

ANNUAL PRODUCTION	90,000 bottles
HECTARES UNDER VINE	27
VITICULTURE METHOD	Natural

Tenuta di Collosorbo, which was established in 1994 following the division of a previous winery, is located in a marvellous setting in the heart of Sesta, one of the most sought-after parts of Montalcino. Around 27 hectares are planted to vine, 11 of them for Brunello. New to the winery is Paolo Caciorgna, who works alongside the owner, Giovanna Ciacci. Results are positive and the wines have shown significant progress, especially in terms of style, since that the quality of the raw materials has never been in doubt. The Brunello di Montalcino '03 is well made, and shows how this territory, with its deep layer of clay, enables the oldest vineyards to cope better with drought. The nose is beautiful, with tones of white-fleshed fruit, blackberry and wild cherry, rounded off with faint balsamic hints. The palate is dense thanks to excellent raw material and the smooth, mature tannins. Well-judged acidity is evident yet never unruly, and powers a broad, harmonious finish of impressive length. The Rosso di Montalcino '06 has a lightly floral bouquet but is still excessively tannic.

● Brunello di Montalcino '03	🍷🍷	7
● Rosso di Montalcino '06	🍷	5
● Sant'Antimo '06	🍷	5
● Brunello di Montalcino '00	🍷🍷	6
● Brunello di Montalcino Ris. '01	🍷🍷	8
● Brunello di Montalcino Ris. '98	🍷🍷	8

Il Colombaio di Cencio

LOC. CORNIA
53013 GAIOLE IN CHIANTI [SI]
TEL. 0577747178
colombaiodicencio@tin.it

ANNUAL PRODUCTION	100,000 bottles
HECTARES UNDER VINE	25
VITICULTURE METHOD	Conventional

We admired the good performance from the winery of Werner Wilhelm, the German businessman who chose this site in the Chianti Classico region as his refuge after a career in insurance in Munich. Every year, the results are excellent, even when they don't quite reach the highest levels. What is important, however, is to consider the reliably high quality achieved in only a few years. Wine production here only dates back to the mid 1990s and it is nice to see that one of the wines, Il Futuro, has already become a benchmark Supertuscan. Made from cabernet sauvignon, merlot and a small percentage of sangiovese, the '05 vintage gives a nose with tones of jam lifted by balsamic hints and marked florality. The body is firm yet smooth, revealing forthright freshness and mouthfilling extractive weight before it signs of with a fresh, tasty finish. For the first time, the '03 Guglielmo is presented in a magnum version. It's a merlot-only offering with sweet tones on the nose and a warm, full-bodied palate, rounded off by good length. The other products are interesting and enjoyable.

● Chianti Cl. I Massi Ris. '05	🍷🍷	6
● Guglielmo '03	🍷🍷	8
● Il Futuro '05	🍷🍷	7
● Monticello '05	🍷🍷	4*
● Chianti Cl. '05	🍷	5
● Chianti Cl. I Massi Ris. '03	🍷🍷🍷	6
● Il Futuro '99	🍷🍷🍷	7
● Il Futuro '97	🍷🍷🍷	7
● Il Futuro '95	🍷🍷🍷	7
● Chianti Cl. I Massi '04	🍷🍷	5
● Chianti Cl. I Massi Ris. '04	🍷🍷	6
● Il Futuro '04	🍷🍷	7

Il Colombaio di Santa Chiara

LOC. SAN DONATO, 1
53037 SAN GIMIGNANO [SI]
TEL. 0577942004
www.colombaiosantachiara.it

ANNUAL PRODUCTION	47,000 bottles
HECTARES UNDER VINE	7
VITICULTURE METHOD	Conventional

The work of the Logi brothers, who have only been in wine for a few years, continues to progress with extremely well-made products. They can also count on the advice of their father Mario, and every year bring out reliable wines that live up to their fans' expectations. A good example is the San Gimignano Rosso Colombaio '05, one of the best of its type, which throws a spicy, cherry-themed nose and offers satisfyingly full body on the palate, with well-balanced tannins. The Priore '06, from a blend of sangiovese and canaiolo, is equally impressive, combining elegant fruit aromas with a powerful palate that echoes the nose, crisp tannins and a fruity finish. The Vernaccia di San Gimignano Selvabianca '07 is a highly attractive steel-fermented wine that opens with florality on the nose and follows up with a soft fleshy palate, where the acidity falls of slightly on the finish. The Vernaccia di San Gimignano Albereta '07 is also noteworthy, smooth and full-bodied, but with a touch too much oakiness. The Vin Santo di San Gimignano Di Mario '03 is well-executed, unctuous, spirited and satisfyingly long.

Fattoria Le Corti

LOC. LE CORTI
VIA SAN PIERO DI SOTTO, 1
50026 SAN CASCIANO IN VAL DI PESA [FI]
TEL. 055829301
www.principecorsini.com

ANNUAL PRODUCTION	230,000 bottles
HECTARES UNDER VINE	50
VITICULTURE METHOD	Conventional

Maybe he didn't expect his Chianti Classico Cortevecchia Riserva '05 to be given Three Glasses, but we are sure that Duccio Corsini is satisfied with the result, seeing that he hadn't managed to win the award for a few years. Last year, we were already beginning to see constant regular improvements over the whole of the range, and this year brought confirmation, seeing that the Chianti Classico Don Tommaso '05 also managed to reach our finals. The decision to focus on designation wines clearly reaped its rewards. The top wine has a wide aromatic spectrum, showing fruit and floral overtones, hints of tobacco and mixed spice, vibrant structure, crisp, well-integrated tannins and a nicely thrusting finish. The other finalist displayed some limitations in terms of bouquet but had plenty of energy and weight in the body. Among the wines from the Maremma, we particularly liked the Marsiliana '05, a blend of sangiovese, cabernet sauvignon and merlot, with seductively sweet, appealing aromas, and a weighty, velvety body completed by a satisfying, albeit shortish, finish.

● Il Priore '06	▼▼ 4
● S. Gimignano Rosso Colombaio '05	▼▼ 5
○ S. Gimignano Vin Santo Di Mario '03	▼ 6
○ Vernaccia di S. Gimignano Albereta '07	▼ 4
○ Vernaccia di San Gimignano Selvabianca '07	▼ 4
● Il Priore '04	▼▼ 4
● S. Gimignano Rosso Colombaio '04	▼▼ 5
○ Vernaccia di S. Gimignano Albereta '06	▼▼ 4
○ Vernaccia di S. Gimignano Albereta '05	▼▼ 4
○ Vernaccia di San Gimignano Selvabianca '06	▼▼ 3*
○ Vernaccia di San Gimignano Selvabianca '05	▼▼ 3*

● Chianti Cl. Cortevecchia Ris. '05	▼▼▼ 5
● Chianti Cl. Don Tommaso '05	▼▼ 6
● Marsiliana '05	▼▼ 6
● Birillo '07	▼ 4
● Chianti Cl. '06	▼ 4
● Chianti Cl. Don Tommaso '99	▼▼▼ 5
● Chianti Cl. Don Tommaso '04	▼▼ 6
● Marsiliana '04	▼▼ 6

Fattoria Corzano e Paterno

FRAZ. SAN PRANCAZIO
VIA PATERNO, 8
50020 SAN CASCIANO IN VAL DI PESA [FI]
TEL. 0558248179
www.corzanoepaterno.it·

ANNUAL PRODUCTION	75,000 bottles
HECTARES UNDER VINE	16
VITICULTURE METHOD	Conventional

This year, saw the second Three Glass award for Alioscia Goldschmidt, who won his first accolade for the '97 vintage of Il Corzano. Now the '05 has repeated that success. This is a wine that offers great power, expressing individual character as well as its territory. This blend of sangiovese, cabernet sauvignon and merlot seduces on the nose with its intriguing, complex aromas of red and black berry fruit, aromatic herbs, balsamic hints and a light spiciness. It is elegant on the palate, with tannins already well integrated into the structure and excellent acidity, ensuring a long, pleasant finish with after-aromas that echo the nose. The Chianti I Tre Borri Riserva '04 is not at all bad, with floral, earthy and mineral aromas. It shows well-balanced tannins and acidic sinew on the palate, which signs off with a long, tasty finish. The '05 vintage of the same wine is a little less convincing, somewhat intractable and characterized by over-assertive, edgy tannins. We also liked a couple of other reliable performers: the firm, fruity Chianti Terre di Corzano '06, and the attractive Corzanello '07, from chardonnay, sémillon and trebbiano.

● Il Corzano '05	♟♟♟	6
● Chianti I Tre Borri Ris. '04	♟♟	6
● Chianti I Tre Borri Ris. '05	♟	6
● Chianti Terre di Corzano '06	♟	4
O Il Corzanello '07	♟	4
● Il Corzano '97	♟♟♟	5
● Chianti I Tre Borri Ris. '03	♟♟	6
● Chianti Terre di Corzano '03	♟♟	4
● Il Corzano '04	♟♟	6
● Il Corzano '03	♟♟	6
● Il Corzano '02	♟♟	5
O Passito di Corzano '98	♟♟	7
O Passito di Corzano '97	♟♟	7
O Passito di Corzano '96	♟♟	7
O Passito di Corzano '95	♟♟	6

Cupano

LOC. CAMIGLIANO
PODERE CENTINE, 31
53024 MONTALCINO [SI]
TEL. 0577816055
www.cupano.it

ANNUAL PRODUCTION	13,000 bottles
HECTARES UNDER VINE	3.12
VITICULTURE METHOD	Certified organic

The south-west, Maremma side of Montalcino, near Camigliano, is the hottest part of the zone. On a hillside overlooking the river Ombrone, Ornella Tondini and Lionel Cousin have established Cupano, an organic winery. French influence led them to use barriques for ageing their wines from the very beginning, a choice that initially caused excessive oakiness, although this tendency is now much less evident. Proof of this is in the Rosso di Montalcino '05, which also benefits from a year's delay in its release, a move that seems to have reaped rewards. Intensely fruity, with hints of black berry fruit and fruit preserve, it is extremely clean, with caressing undertones of vanilla and clove-led spices. On the palate it is weighty, yet never cloying, thanks to perfectly judged acidity and tannins, which offset the softer notes. Progression is intense, well-balanced and fragrant, and leads into a vibrant finish. We were less convinced by the Brunello di Montalcino '03, with its intensely floral nose showing notes of sweet tobacco and toffee. The attack is good but the wine tends to be held back by the tannins, which are still edgy.

● Rosso di Montalcino '05	♟♟	6
● Brunello di Montalcino '03	♟	8
● Sant'Antimo Ombrone '05	♟	7
● Brunello di Montalcino '02	♟♟	8

Tenimenti Luigi D'Alessandro

VIA DI MANZANO, 15
52042 CORTONA [AR]
TEL. 0575618667
www.tenimentidalessandro.it

ANNUAL PRODUCTION 150,000 bottles
HECTARES UNDER VINE 50
VITICULTURE METHOD Conventional

Tenimenti D'Alessandro is a winery to which the Cortona area should be very grateful. After all, it has promoted syrah, a variety that has found a perfect growing environment here, giving the territory a decisive boost in terms of overall image in consequence. Having said that, we are disappointed to see a slight downturn in what over recent years has been a champion in its category, Cortona Il Bosco, whose '05 vintage is not in the same league as those presented by the winery in recent years. Most likely, this is due to the growing year, which was very cool and wet, and so less suited to the characteristics of the variety, which lacks the fullness and harmonious fruit richness that usually distinguish it. On the other hand, however, its younger sibling, Cortona Syrah '06, did very well indeed. In fact, it may never have been so good. Generous and clean, with dark berry fruits and fresh, spicy, floral and balsamic notes, it reveals a lean but succulent, moreish palate with plenty length and complexity.

● Cortona Il Bosco '05	🍷🍷	7
● Cortona Syrah '06	🍷🍷	4
● Cortona Il Bosco '04	YYY	7
● Cortona Il Bosco '03	YYY	7
● Cortona Il Bosco '01	YYY	7
● Podere Il Bosco '97	YYY	5
● Podere Il Bosco '95	YYY	5
● Podere Il Bosco '99	YY	6
● Podere Il Bosco '98	YY	5

Maria Caterina Dei

VIA DI MARTIENA, 35
53045 MONTEPULCIANO [SI]
TEL. 0578716878
www.cantinedei.com

ANNUAL PRODUCTION 200,000 bottles
HECTARES UNDER VINE 55
VITICULTURE METHOD Conventional

This is the first time that the Maria Caterina Dei winery has won Three Glasses. It was bound to happen sooner or later. This is a cellar that has always pursued absolute excellence and since its debut with the '99 vintage, the Nobile Riserva Bossona had always stood out for its great expressive finesse. Produced with grapes from an excellent subzone of Montepulciano, Bossona, the '04 version of this wine has great elegance and character, avoiding the trap of banal softness. The nose has breadth, roundness and complexity. Although young, and like all the wines produced at Villa Martiena, made for the cellar, the palate is already assertive, taut and deep. Equally successful, albeit showing less personality, is the Sancta Catharina '06, a blend of sangiovese, cabernet sauvignon, syrah and petit verdot. Its aromas are concentrated and on the palate the excellent density is only prevented from giving of its best by a touch too much oak. The fresh, approachably, tasty Rosso di Montepulciano '07 is first-rate. Finally, the Nobile di Montepulciano '05 is aromatic and nicely linear.

● Nobile di Montepulciano Bossona Ris. '04	🍷🍷🍷	6
● Rosso di Montepulciano '07	🍷🍷	4
● Sancta Catharina '06	🍷🍷	6
● Nobile di Montepulciano '05	🍷	5
● Nobile di Montepulciano '01	YY	5
● Nobile di Montepulciano '99	YY	5
● Nobile di Montepulciano Bossona Ris. '03	YY	6
● Nobile di Montepulciano Bossona Ris. '01	YY	6
● Nobile di Montepulciano Bossona Ris. '99	YY	6
● Sancta Catharina '04	YY	6
● Sancta Catharina '03	YY	6
● Sancta Catharina '01	YY	6
● Sancta Catharina '00	YY	6

Fattoria di Dievole

VIA DIEVOLE, 6
53010 CASTELNUOVO BERARDENGA [SI]
TEL. 0577322613
www.dievole.it

ANNUAL PRODUCTION	550,000 bottles
HECTARES UNDER VINE	89
VITICULTURE METHOD	Conventional

The Schwenn family winery is interesting for a number of reasons. It was one of the first to promote organized winery visits, organizing tastings and theme dinners. It was also one of the first to make an effort to manage the image of its wines, both in terms of labels and of marketing in general, attaching great importance to the people who work in the vineyards and the winery itself, and promoting their active involvement in the business. Lastly, Schwenns managed to give the business a decisive turnaround two years ago, rethinking management and once more committing themselves to the production of fine wine. The results were not long in coming. The bottles presented for our tastings are only those from the top of the range, the Oro line. We liked Broccato '05, a blend of sangiovese, merlot and petit verdot, giving attractive vegetal aromas that herald a firm, taut body and a long, tasty finish. The very drinkable Chianti Classico La Vendemmia '06 is also first-rate, proffering subtle cherry and blueberry ushering in a well-orchestrated, supple structure. The other wines are simpler and display still evident tannins.

Donatella Cinelli Colombini

LOC. CASATO PRIME DONNE
53024 MONTALCINO [SI]
TEL. 0577849421
www.cinellicolombini.it

ANNUAL PRODUCTION	180,000 bottles
HECTARES UNDER VINE	37
VITICULTURE METHOD	Conventional

Donatella Cinelli Colombini is an important part of Montalcino and the social life of Siena. In the space of only a few years, this many-talented woman with impressive managerial skills has made her winery one of the most important in Montalcino, thanks to the quality of her excellent, top-quality wines. As often happens, we preferred the Brunello di Montalcino '03 to Prime Donne, the selection whose final blend is decided by a tasting panel made up solely of women. The nose is classic in approach, signs of the hot growing year coming through in notes of saddle leather and tobacco, rounded off by varietal notes of morello cherry. It progresses nicely across the palate, revealing surprising acidity given the vintage. The extract is softened by a vein of alcohol while the finish has a faint hint of smokiness. Prime Donne is a more modern wine with evident spiciness on the nose, together with medicinal herbs, opening onto a palate well-sustained by tannins. The first-rate Rosso di Montalcino '06 is modern in style, giving herbaceousness on both the nose and palate, and perfect tannic structure.

● Broccato '05	♟♟ 6
● Chianti Cl. La Vendemmia '06	♟♟ 5
● Chianti Cl. '05	♟ 4
● Chianti Cl. Novecento Ris. '05	♟ 6
● Broccato '01	♟♟ 5
● Chianti Cl. Dieulele Ris. '01	♟♟ 5

● Brunello di Montalcino '03	♟♟ 6
● Brunello di Montalcino Prime Donne '03	♟♟ 7
● Il Drago e le Sette Colombe '05	♟♟ 5
● Orcia Cenerentola '05	♟♟ 6
● Rosso di Montalcino '06	♟♟ 5
● Leone Rosso '06	♟ 4
● Brunello di Montalcino Prime Donne '01	♟♟♟ 7
● Brunello di Montalcino '00	♟♟ 6
● Brunello di Montalcino Ris. '01	♟♟ 7
● Brunello di Montalcino Ris. '00	♟♟ 7

I Fabbri

LOC. LAMOLE
VIA CASOLE, 52
50022 GREVE IN CHIANTI [FI]
TEL. 3394122622
www.agricolaifabbri.it

ANNUAL PRODUCTION	30,000 bottles
HECTARES UNDER VINE	9
VITICULTURE METHOD	Conventional

There's a return to a full profile for Susanna and Maddalena Grassi, two enthusiastic growers from Lamole, a small village ten kilometres from Greve in Chianti. Their wines are very elegant, never too heavy and all are distinguished by their obvious finesse. Susanna has come over from Ferrara, where she lives, to take over with her sister the reins of a winery that was originally a place used mainly for summer holidays. Rising to the challenge, they managed to restart production, and were soon achieving high levels of quality. The next step was the introduction of organic viticulture methods. The pair only produce two wines, both Chianti Classicos, which differ only in the selection of grapes used to vinify them. Both performed well.
The Chianti Classico '06 shows evident minerality on the nose, together with minty overtones and bluberry-like berry fruit. On the palate, it is fresh, approachable and discreet, its well-honed tannins preceding an appetizing finish. Terre di Lamole '06 foregrounds florality and fruit before unveiling a soft, well-balanced structure and an agreeable finish that signs off with spiciness.

Fanti - San Filippo

FRAZ. CASTELNUOVO DELL'ABATE
POD. PALAZZO
53020 MONTALCINO [SI]
TEL. 0577835795
balfanti@tin.it

ANNUAL PRODUCTION	150,000 bottles
HECTARES UNDER VINE	50
VITICULTURE METHOD	Conventional

Now that he is back working exclusively for the winery, Filippo Fanti can enjoy his new premises, which are finally finished. He has an attractive, efficient facility that blends into its hillside surroundings and commands a view over the majestic abbey of Sant'Antimo. Filippo has a very large stock of large and small barrels while the fermentation vats are the result of in-house experiments. The wines we tasted performed outstandingly, with the Brunello di Montalcino '03 proving to be one of the vintage's best. The new style has now clearly taken hold, all to the benefit of the Brunello, partly thanks to the vicinity to the cooler zone of Castelnuovo dell'Abate. The nose gives intense fruit with evident but discreet oak, paving the way for a palate of real character, whose development is underpinned by good raw material and smooth tannins that do not stand in the way of the finale. Sant'Antimo '06, the winery's laboratory for research into new varieties and clones, is also interesting. Finally, the tannins in the Rosso di Montalcino '06 are a touch over-assertive.

● Chianti Cl. '06	▼▼ 4*
● Chianti Cl. Terra di Lamole '06	▼▼ 4*
● Chianti Cl. Ris. '03	♈ 5
● Chianti Cl. Ris. '01	♈ 5
● Chianti Cl. Terra di Lamole '03	♈ 4

● Brunello di Montalcino '03	▼▼ 7
● Sant'Antimo Rosso '06	▼▼ 4
● Rosso di Montalcino '06	▼ 5
● Brunello di Montalcino '00	♈♈♈ 7
● Brunello di Montalcino '97	♈♈♈ 7
● Brunello di Montalcino Ris. '95	♈♈♈ 7
● Brunello di Montalcino '01	♈♈ 7
● Brunello di Montalcino '99	♈♈ 7
● Brunello di Montalcino '98	♈♈ 7

Fassati

FRAZ. GRACCIANO
VIA DI GRACCIANELLO, 3A
53040 MONTEPULCIANO [SI]
TEL. 0578708708
www.fazibattaglia.com

ANNUAL PRODUCTION	800,000 bottles
HECTARES UNDER VINE	80
VITICULTURE METHOD	Conventional

Fassati, the Montepulciano winery owned by Fazi Battaglia, was recently bought out by the Sparaco Giannotti family. The wines are fundamentally reliable. The stand-out, partly thanks to a particularly good growing season, is the Nobile Riserva Salarco '04, with its fresh, complex spectrum of aromatics and a nicely textured palate, albeit partially compromised by oakiness from barrel ageing. Nobile di Montepulciano Pasiteo '05 has a coherent aromatic profile, and a touch of dryness on the finish, and Nobile Gersemi '05, proffers a concentrated nose exuding attractive morello cherry but progression on the palate is somewhat held back by a tad too much oak. Both are rather stiff. We were impressed by the wines from the Molto Greto delle Fate winery in Maremma. The Morellino di Scansano '07 shows well-defined, generously ripe aromas, following this on the palate with verve and regaling an intensely fruity finish. The Vermentino '07 is fresh and discreet on the nose while the palate shows vibrant flavour good progression. The Rosso di Montepulciano Selciaia '07 and the Rosato Spigo '07, from sangiovese, are well made.

★★ Fattoria di Felsina

VIA DEL CHIANTI, 101
53019 CASTELNUOVO BERARDENGA [SI]
TEL. 0577355117
www.felsina.it

ANNUAL PRODUCTION	350,000 bottles
HECTARES UNDER VINE	62
VITICULTURE METHOD	Conventional

The 2005 vintage was not an easy one for Tuscany or sangiovese but Felsina took home two Three Glass awards, and topped them off with the Winery of the Year award. To be honest, this is no surprise. The vine stock is situated at Castelnuovo Berardenga, in the south of the zone, which tends to suffer more in hot years. Add to this the magic touch of people who know sangiovese inside out and obtained the very best from the vintage, highlighting its trademark elegance. The Chianti Classico Rancia Riserva is nothing short of spectacular, offering an attractive nose of firm, ripe red berry fruit, with notes of forest fruits, violets and rain-drenched earth. The palate is utterly captivating, elegant and long, with perfectly ripe tannins and lovely acidity. Quite simply a masterpiece. Fontalloro is equally superb, from 100 per cent sangiovese, and flaunts a spicy, balsamic nose leading into a palate whose are tannins more forthright but very well behaved. Two wines of this calibre and a history of successes, in addition to our esteem, explain why Felsina is our Winery of the Year. The other wines are extremely good.

● Morellino di Scansano Greto delle Fate '07	🍷🍷	4*
● Nobile di Montepulciano Salarco Ris. '04	🍷🍷	6
○ Vermentino Greto delle Fate '07	🍷🍷	4*
● Nobile di Montepulciano Gersemi '05	🍷	6
● Nobile di Montepulciano Pasiteo '05	🍷	5
● Rosso di Montepulciano Selciaia '07	🍷	4
⊙ Spigo '07	🍷	4
● Nobile di Montepulciano Gersemi '03	🍷🍷	6
● Nobile di Montepulciano Gersemi '01	🍷🍷	6
● Nobile di Montepulciano Gersemi '00	🍷🍷	6
● Nobile di Montepulciano Pasiteo '04	🍷🍷	5
● Nobile di Montepulciano Pasiteo '03	🍷🍷	5
● Nobile di Montepulciano Salarco Ris. '03	🍷🍷	6
● Nobile di Montepulciano Salarco Ris. '01	🍷🍷	6

● Chianti Cl. Rancia Ris. '05	🍷🍷🍷	6
● Fontalloro '05	🍷🍷🍷	7
● Chianti Cl. '06	🍷🍷	5
● Chianti Cl. Ris. '05	🍷🍷	5
○ I Sistri '06	🍷🍷	5
● Maestro Raro '04	🍷🍷	6
○ Pepestrino '07	🍷	3
● Chianti Cl. Rancia Ris. '04	🍷🍷🍷	6
● Chianti Cl. Rancia Ris. '03	🍷🍷🍷	6
● Fontalloro '01	🍷🍷🍷	6
● Fontalloro '99	🍷🍷🍷	6
● Fontalloro '98	🍷🍷🍷	6
● Fontalloro '97	🍷🍷🍷	6
● Fontalloro '95	🍷🍷🍷	6
● Fontalloro '93	🍷🍷🍷	6
● Maestro Raro '01	🍷🍷🍷	6

Le Filigare

LOC. LE FILIGARE
VIA SICELLE, 35
50020 BARBERINO VAL D'ELSA [FI]
TEL. 0558072796
www.lefiligare.it

ANNUAL PRODUCTION   40,000 bottles
HECTARES UNDER VINE   N.A.
VITICULTURE METHOD   Conventional

The results of Carlo Burchi's winery were positive but did not really live up to the potential. Carlo runs the estate with passion, together with his son Alessandro, who is responsible for the business side of things. The wines are clearly reliable but we would like to see more daring and allure. Earlier vintages in particular lack a certain definition on the nose while in the other cases it is the roughness of the tannins that holds back development on the palate. The best wines comply with designation protocols, such as the impenetrably dark Chianti Classico Riserva '05 Maria Vittoria, which shows a broad aromatic spectrum dominated by spicy notes of cloves and vanilla before it reveals its warmth, pervasiveness and satisfyingly length. The Chianti Classico Lorenzo '06 is more drinkable and consistent, offering floral notes and good intensity. Supertuscan Podere Le Rocce '05, from sangiovese and cabernet sauvignon, has difficulty shrugging off animal sensations on the nose and shows a weighty, dense palate. The merlot-heavy Pietro '03 fails to achieve a balance between the weight of the body and robust tannins.

★ Tenute Ambrogio e Giovanni Folonari

LOC. PASSO DEI PECORAI
VIA DI NOZZOLE, 12
50022 GREVE IN CHIANTI [FI]
TEL. 055859811
www.tenutefolonari.com

ANNUAL PRODUCTION   150,000 bottles
HECTARES UNDER VINE   60
VITICULTURE METHOD   Conventional

This year, Cabreo Il Borgo '06 won Three Glasses. Ambrogio and Giovanni Folonari managed to take home top honours despite having to do without the '05 Pareto. They decided not to produce it in a below-par growing year and concentrated on the blend of sangiovese and cabernet sauvignon. Already on the nose, this wine offers a complex, intense bouquet, with notes of red berry fruit, strawberry jam and delicate oak. The palate is taut and close-knit, still perhaps a shade too tannic but ideal for the cellar. The single-variety Chardonnay, Cabreo La Pietra '06, is as ever full flavoured and intriguing. We were also very impressed by the products from the winery's many Tuscan outposts. The Brunello di Montalcino '03 is close-knit and intense, held back only by slightly edgy tannins. The spicy, mouthfilling Bolgheri Rosso '06 della Campo al Mare is also very good. Thanks to an extremely good growing season, Nobile di Montepulciano Riserva '04 also convinces, giving sumptuous fruit well integrated with the oaky notes of barrel maturation. In the mouth, the wine is firm and progresses confidently. The Nobile '05 is subtle and delicately aromatic.

● Chianti Cl. Lorenzo '06	♥♥	5
● Chianti Cl. Maria Vittoria Ris. '05	♥♥	6
● Pietro '03	♥	8
● Podere Le Rocce '05	♥	7
● Podere Le Rocce '00	♥♥♥	7
● Chianti Cl. Maria Vittoria Ris. '04	♥♥	6
● Podere Le Rocce '01	♥♥	7

● Cabreo Il Borgo '06	♥♥♥	6
● Bolgheri Campo al Mare '06	♥♥	5
● Brunello di Montalcino La Fuga '03	♥♥	7
O Cabreo La Pietra '06	♥♥	6
● Nobile di Montepulciano Torcalvano Ris. '04	♥♥	6
● Nobile di Montepulciano Torcalvano '05	♥	4
● Il Pareto '04	♥♥♥	8
● Il Pareto '01	♥♥♥	8
● Il Pareto '00	♥♥♥	8
● Il Pareto '98	♥♥♥	7
● Il Pareto '97	♥♥♥	7
● Cabreo Il Borgo '04	♥♥	6
● Cabreo Il Borgo '03	♥♥	6
● Cabreo Il Borgo '01	♥♥	6

Fontaleoni

LOC. SANTA MARIA, 39A
53037 SAN GIMIGNANO [SI]
TEL. 0577950193
www.fontaleoni.com

ANNUAL PRODUCTION	100,000 bottles
HECTARES UNDER VINE	23.5
VITICULTURE METHOD	Conventional

Fontaleoni is back in the headlines. This small winery at Santa Maria has recovered its knack of bringing out the potential of its territory. The professional commitment of Franco Troiani over the years is demonstrated by the series of top-quality products presented. Vernaccia Vigna Casanuova '07 is well executed and shows appealing fruit and florality and a forthright, succulently tasty palate, braced by attractive acidity, and a satisfyingly long finish. The Vernaccia Notte di Luna '07, which undergoes brief skin contact, also displayed character. The nose has scents of summer flowers and ripe fruit, leading to a dense yet racy palate that takes its leave with a full-flavoured finish. The Vernaccia '07 is well made and has a fruity nose introducing a well-balanced, rounded palate. We also liked the fruity, invigorating, well-balanced Chianti dei Colli Senesi '07 and, to a slightly lesser degree, the firm, tannin-rich Chianti dei Colli Senesi Sciroc Riserva '05, and the easy-drinking, good value Chianti Tramonto '07. The Merlot '06 and the San Gimignano La Cerreta '04 just about pass muster.

★★ Castello di Fonterutoli

LOC. FONTERUTOLI
VIA OTTONE III DI SASSONIA, 5
53011 CASTELLINA IN CHIANTI [SI]
TEL. 057773571
www.fonterutoli.it

ANNUAL PRODUCTION	710,000 bottles
HECTARES UNDER VINE	117
VITICULTURE METHOD	Conventional

The Mazzei family winery never misses a beat. If the Chianti Classico wins top honours one year then the next it's the turn of Siepi. This year, it's the '05 vintage of the Supertuscan that took home the Three Glass award. We were particularly impressed by this version of the blend of equal quantities of merlot and sangiovese. Fresh and inviting on the nose, it unfolds an aromatic spectrum ranging from balsamic notes to vanilla and cinnamon, with upfront berry fruit. But it is on the palate that it really comes into its own, with dense structure and an almost creamily soft mouthfeel, thanks to very finely woven tannins. On the finish, it is still lively with a complex after-aroma. Castello di Fonterutoli '05, the winery's flagship Chianti Classico, is still too young and tannin-heavy to aspire to a top award, although it made it through to the final tastings. The enjoyable Chianti Classico '06 has a rounded, well-developed body. Finally, Poggio alla Badiola '06, a blend of sangiovese topped up with merlot, offers uncomplicated easy drinking.

● Chianti Colli Senesi '06	♟♟ 4*
○ Vernaccia di S. Gimignano Notte di Luna '07	♟♟ 3*
○ Vernaccia di S. Gimignano V. Casanuova '07	♟♟ 4*
● Chianti Colli Senesi Sciroc Ris. '05	♟ 4
● Chianti Tramonto '07	♟ 3
● Merlot '06	♟ 4
● S. Gimignano Rosso La Cerreta '04	♟ 5
○ Vernaccia di S. Gimignano '07	♟ 4
● Chianti Tramonto '06	♟♟ 3*
○ Vernaccia di S. Gimignano '06	♟♟ 4*
○ Vernaccia di S. Gimignano Notte di Luna '06	♟♟ 3*
○ Vernaccia di S. Gimignano V. Casanuova '06	♟♟ 4*

● Siepi '05	♟♟♟ 8
● Chianti Cl. Castello di Fonterutoli '05	♟♟ 7
● Chianti Cl. '06	♟ 5
● Poggio alla Badiola '06	♟ 4
● Siepi '03	♟♟♟ 8
● Siepi '01	♟♟♟ 8
● Siepi '00	♟♟♟ 8
● Siepi '99	♟♟♟ 8
● Siepi '98	♟♟♟ 8
● Siepi '97	♟♟♟ 8
● Siepi '96	♟♟♟ 8
● Siepi '95	♟♟♟ 8
● Siepi '94	♟♟♟ 8
● Siepi '93	♟♟♟ 8

★ Tenuta Fontodi

FRAZ. GREVE IN CHIANTI
VIA SAN LEOLINO, 89
50020 PANZANO [FI]
TEL. 055852005
www.fontodi.com

ANNUAL PRODUCTION	300,000 bottles
HECTARES UNDER VINE	70
VITICULTURE METHOD	Conventional

Flaccianello della Pieve '05 has brought Three Glasses back to Fontodi. This is one of those vintages that is unlikely to be remembered in Tuscany for uniform quality. Having said that, those who managed to produce good wines produced excellent ones, which look set to age long and well. This is certainly the case with Flaccianello, a single-variety Sangiovese, which right from the nose shows well-developed, complex notes of ripe red berry fruit, leather, autumn leaves and Mediterranean scrub. On the palate, the tannins are sure-footed, close-knit and luscious. As we expect from this wine, the acidity is lip-smackingly forthright. Fontodi also cheered us up with a fine version of Chianti Classico Vigna del Sorbo Riserva '04, which is only penalized by some reduction on uncorking, which tends to affect nose and palate. All it requires is a little patience and normality is restored as the wine breathes in the glass. Tobacco, sweet spices, a certain animal sensation, morello cherry usher in a well-sustained palate that is tightened slightly on the finish by boisterous extract. Pinot Nero Case Via '06 is as appealing as ever.

Fornacina

POD. FORNACINA, 153
53024 MONTALCINO [SI]
TEL. 0577848464
www.cantinafornacina.it

ANNUAL PRODUCTION	25,000 bottles
HECTARES UNDER VINE	5
VITICULTURE METHOD	Certified organic

This small winery at Cerbaie, in the east of Montalcino, did outstandingly well this year. The estate is a strictly family-run business, inspired by the ideas of Simone Biliorsi, whose vision of winemaking is closely tied up with the heritage that has made Brunello di Montalcino famous the world over. It is this production philosophy that lies behind his Brunello '03, one of the best from this vintage. Despite the sweltering heat of the growing season, the nose offers clear notes of varietal morello cherry, here tending towards jamminess and nicely complemented by riper notes of tobacco. The judicious use of oak never compromises aromas or extract, which are extremely well gauged. Alcohol is prominent on the palate, without being overpowering, as it is offset by good acidity and well-balanced tannins. The finish has breadth and beautifully echoes the nose. This is a classic wine from a challenging year and deservedly made it into the final tastings. Rosso di Montalcino '06 is a somewhat pedestrian offering but offers pleasant, easy drinking hinging on a well-defined ripe cherry nose.

● Flaccianello della Pieve '05	♟♟♟	7
● Chianti Cl. V. del Sorbo Ris. '04	♟♟	7
● Pinot Nero Case Via '06	♟	7
● Chianti Cl. V. del Sorbo Ris. '01	♟♟♟	7
● Chianti Cl. V. del Sorbo Ris. '94	♟♟♟	7
● Chianti Cl. V. del Sorbo Ris. '90	♟♟♟	7
● Flaccianello della Pieve '03	♟♟♟	7
● Flaccianello della Pieve '01	♟♟♟	7
● Flaccianello della Pieve '00	♟♟♟	7
● Flaccianello della Pieve '97	♟♟♟	7
● Flaccianello della Pieve '91	♟♟♟	7
● Flaccianello della Pieve '90	♟♟♟	7
● Flaccianello della Pieve '85	♟♟♟	6

● Brunello di Montalcino '03	♟♟	6
● Rosso di Montalcino '06	♟	4
● Brunello di Montalcino '01	♟♟	7
● Brunello di Montalcino Ris. '01	♟♟	7

Podere Forte

LOC. PETRUCCI, 13
53023 CASTIGLIONE D'ORCIA [SI]
TEL. 05778885100
www.podereforte.it

ANNUAL PRODUCTION	10,000 bottles
HECTARES UNDER VINE	12
VITICULTURE METHOD	Natural

Pasquale Forte's winery is back with a full-length profile, after earning a reputation as one of the benchmark operations for viticultural innovation not only in its local area, the Orcia DOC, but throughout Tuscany. It's all down to uncompromising standards in a project that started out less than ten years ago and focuses unswervingly on excellence. The wine that symbolizes this pursuit is once again Guardiavigna, whose '05 vintage deservedly reached our finals. Obtained from a blend of sangiovese, cabernet sauvignon, merlot and petit verdot, this wine has deep, multi-layered aromas and verve on the palate, accompanied by an extremely long finish, occasionally disturbed by a touch too much oak. The Orcia Petrucci '05 is not up to the same standard. Don't get us wrong. This is a good wine but it just seems to lack the touch of character and personality that we expect to find in a sangiovese-only product. Orcia Petruccino '06, a blend of sangiovese and cabernet sauvignon, is a real treat, providing fresh, approachable easy drinking.

Podere La Fortuna

LOC. LA FORTUNA, 83
53024 MONTALCINO [SI]
TEL. 0577848308
www.tenutalafortuna.it

ANNUAL PRODUCTION	60,000 bottles
HECTARES UNDER VINE	13
VITICULTURE METHOD	Conventional

Gioberto Zannoni's enthusiasm is contagious. Having just finished extensive renovation of the winery, which now has spacious premises and a rational layout, Gioberto has decided to take a short holiday. To plant new vineyards! Helped by his son Angelo, especially in the more technological aspects of the business, our friend continues to produce excellent Brunellos and they just seem to get better and better. The product of a difficult year, Brunello di Montalcino '03 was convincing enough to get through to the national finals. This deep ruby wine shows a satisfyingly complex nose, revealing hints of autumn leaves and well-defined jammy red berry fruit. The palate is complex and shows excellent length, braced by acidity and tannins, which are already being absorbed by the ripe substance of the fruit. The oak is evident in the spicy notes, but remains understated and unobtrusive, highlighting the aromatic spectrum. We liked the Rosso di Montalcino '06 a great deal for its fragrant nose and good structure, set off by a well-rounded, mellow finish.

● Orcia Guardiavigna '05	🍷🍷 8
● Orcia Petruccino '06	🍷🍷 6
● Orcia Petrucci '05	🍷 8
● Orcia Guardiavigna '01	🍷🍷🍷 8
● Orcia Guardiavigna '04	🍷🍷 8
● Orcia Guardiavigna '03	🍷🍷 8
● Orcia Guardiavigna '02	🍷🍷 8
● Orcia Petrucci '02	🍷🍷 8
● Orcia Petrucci '01	🍷🍷 8
● Orcia Petruccino '05	🍷🍷 5

● Brunello di Montalcino '03	🍷🍷 7
● Rosso di Montalcino '06	🍷🍷 5
● Sant'Antimo La Fortuna '05	🍷 6
● Brunello di Montalcino '01	🍷🍷🍷 7
● Brunello di Montalcino '00	🍷🍷 6
● Brunello di Montalcino Ris. '01	🍷🍷 7
● Brunello di Montalcino Ris. '99	🍷🍷 7
● Brunello di Montalcino Ris. '97	🍷🍷 7

Frascole

LOC. FRASCOLE, 27A
50062 DICOMANO [FI]
TEL. 0558386340
www.frascole.it

ANNUAL PRODUCTION	55,000 bottles
HECTARES UNDER VINE	15
VITICULTURE METHOD	Certified organic

If we could lay bets every year on Frascole's Potessimo Vin Santo making the finals, we would already be rich, considering the consistently high results that this unique product achieves. The '99 vintage is true to form. Its well-defined amber colour frames a bouquet infused with broad, varied aromas, from dates to dried apricots, not to mention ripe figs and aromatic herbs. The wine seems literally to spread over the palate, thanks to its incredibly soft texture, which lacks only a touch of freshness to be more enjoyable. The rest of the wines continue to be held back by a certain flabbiness, the result of tannins that have yet to mellow. The fault was particularly evident in the Riserva '05, which on the other hand has a fresh inviting nose, with deep mineral notes. The Chianti Rufina '06 is more direct on the nose, showing black berry fruits such as blueberry and plum. Its finest quality is the acidic counterpoint that offsets the wine's potent alcohol.

Eredi Fuligni

VIA SALONI, 33
53024 MONTALCINO [SI]
TEL. 0577848039
brunellofuligni@virgilio.it

ANNUAL PRODUCTION	50,000 bottles
HECTARES UNDER VINE	12
VITICULTURE METHOD	Conventional

Visiting this winery is like taking a trip back in time to days when no one was in a hurry and the pace of life was more leisurely. The welcome is friendly and you can sense a real taste for culture and the good things in life. These are the sensations you experience when talking to Maria Fuligni and above all, when you are discussing the finer technical aspects of winemaking with Roberto Guerrini, a man of many talents. Lately, some of their stylistic choices seem to have fallen wide of the mark, with oak not always handled to best effect. The Brunello di Montalcino '03, without doubt partly because of the growing season, seemed very much in thrall to its oak, especially on the palate, where the tannins are hard and decidedly clenched. The nose was better, with aromas of peach and generous floral notes rounded off by toasty hints of coffee and caramel. Rosso di Montalcino Ginestreto '06 is much more interesting, with cherry and morello cherry, notes of blackberry, and an elegant hint of spice paving the way for a taut, well-orchestrated palate, bolstered by appealing tannins and good acidity.

O Vin Santo del Chianti Rufina '99	♟♟	8
● Chianti Rufina '06	♟♟	4*
● Chianti Rufina Ris. '05	♟	5
● Chianti Rufina Ris. '03	♟♟	5
O Vin Santo del Chianti Rufina '96	♟♟	8
O Vin Santo del Chianti Rufina '95	♟♟	8

● Rosso di Montalcino Ginestreto '06	♟♟	5
● Brunello di Montalcino '03	♟	7
● Brunello di Montalcino Ris. '01	♟♟♟	8
● Brunello di Montalcino Ris. '97	♟♟♟	8
● Brunello di Montalcino '01	♟♟	7
● Brunello di Montalcino '99	♟♟	7
● Brunello di Montalcino Ris. '99	♟♟	8

Castello di Gabbiano

FRAZ. MERCATALE VAL DI PESA
VIA GABBIANO, 22
50024 SAN CASCIANO IN VAL DI PESA [FI]
TEL. 055821053
www.castellogabbiano.it

ANNUAL PRODUCTION	270,000 bottles
HECTARES UNDER VINE	127
VITICULTURE METHOD	Conventional

The winery's two oenologists evident work well together, to judge by the aptly named Alleanza. Produced by Giancarlo Roman, who oversees production at Castello di Gabbiano, and Ed Sbragia, consultant for the American parent company Beringer Blass, the '05 vintage of this merlot-heavy blend, with a splash of sangiovese and cabernet sauvignon, again reached our finals. Deep ruby in colour, it gives herbaceousness, hints of eucalyptus and morello cherry and redcurrant-led red berry fruits on the nose. The palate develops smoothly, showing good flavour with well-integrated wood and the finish is fresh and well-balanced. We were also impressed by Bellezza '05, a monovarietal Sangiovese, which owes its name – literally "beauty" – to the pleasure that can be had from growing a variety like sangiovese in Tuscany. In short, it is a genuine declaration of love for the territory. Notes of tobacco and leather dominate the nose, which is nicely rounded off by spicy hints of vanilla and cloves. The palate unfolds with suppleness, leading to a measured but tasty finish. The Chianti Classico Riserva '05 passes muster.

Gattavecchi

LOC. SANTA MARIA
VIA DI COLLAZZI, 74
53045 MONTEPULCIANO [SI]
TEL. 0578757110
www.gattavecchi.it

ANNUAL PRODUCTION	280,000 bottles
HECTARES UNDER VINE	40
VITICULTURE METHOD	Conventional

Again this year, Luca Gattavecchi confirmed the improving quality of his wines. Once and for all, he has put behind him indecisions of style or form, which were evident in previous years, and the range of products released by this long-established Montepulciano winery has acquired stability. We preferred the Gattavecchi wines to those from the Poggio alla Sala estate, as they were more drinkable and characterful, even though the winery hierarchy puts them the other way round. Nobile di Montepulciano '05 is spot-on, with well-defined, fresh aromas, and a taut, juicily full-flavoured palate. We liked the Nobile Riserva dei Padri Serviti '04, with subtly fruity aromas and a spirited follow-through on the palate showing good contrast. The wines from Poggio alla Sala have a somewhat more docile style and less individuality. Nobile di Montepulciano Riserva '04 is approachable and appealing, and revealing an aromatic profile focusing on sweet fruit perfectly echoed on the palate. The Nobile di Montepulciano '05 is sweet, subtle and very supple but could perhaps do with a little more stuffing. We also enjoyed the '07 Chianti dei Colli Senesi.

● Alleanza '05	🍷🍷 6
● Bellezza '05	🍷🍷 6
● Chianti Cl. Ris. '05	🍷 5
● Alleanza '04	🍷🍷 6
● Alleanza '01	🍷🍷 7
● Bellezza '04	🍷🍷 6
● Bellezza '01	🍷🍷 7
● Chianti Cl. Ris. '04	🍷🍷 5
● Chianti Cl. Ris. '01	🍷🍷 5

● Nobile di Montepulciano '05	🍷🍷 5
● Nobile di Montepulciano Ris. dei Padri Serviti '04	🍷🍷 5
● Chianti Colli Senesi '07	🍷 4
● Nobile di Montepulciano Poggio alla Sala '05	🍷 5
● Nobile di Montepulciano Poggio alla Sala Ris. '04	🍷 5
● Nobile di Montepulciano '04	🍷🍷 5
● Nobile di Montepulciano Poggio alla Sala '04	🍷🍷 5
● Nobile di Montepulciano Poggio alla Sala Ris. '03	🍷🍷 5
● Nobile di Montepulciano Riserva dei Padri Serviti '03	🍷🍷 5

La Gerla

LOC. CANALICCHIO
POD. COLOMBAIO, 5
53024 MONTALCINO [SI]
TEL. 0577848599
www.lagerla.it

ANNUAL PRODUCTION	70,000 bottles
HECTARES UNDER VINE	11.5
VITICULTURE METHOD	Conventional

A technical hitch kept La Gerla's profile out of last year's Guide, which is why the grid below also includes our assessments of last year's wines. The winery presented two Brunello di Montalcino '03s, a standard version and a vineyard selection. We preferred the former, with its deep ruby colour and rich complex nose showing notes of morello cherry and cherry, and somewhat intrusive sensations of quinine. On the palate, it is constricted by oversized tannins that prevent the wine from unbending, especially on the finish, which is edgy and clenched. With further bottle ageing, things will no doubt improve. The Brunello di Montalcino Vigna gli Angeli, also from the '03 vintage, has a rather heavy nose with ripe aromas of red berry fruit overshadowed by toasty oak. On the palate, it is rich and intense but also here weighed down by the boisterous tannins. The monovarietal Sangiovese, Birba '05, was a success, gaining pleasant drinkability and pleasant vegetal notes on the nose from the cool growing season.

Tenuta di Ghizzano

FRAZ. GHIZZANO
VIA DELLA CHIESA, 4
56030 PECCIOLI [PI]
TEL. 0587630096
www.tenutadighizzano.com

ANNUAL PRODUCTION	70,000 bottles
HECTARES UNDER VINE	20
VITICULTURE METHOD	Certified organic

A year in the cellar was just what the Nambrot '05 needed and it arrived at our tastings in fine form. This is a Three Glass wine and no mistake, in the wake of what almost seems to have become a habit for the princely Ghizzano estate and its princess, Ginevra Venerosi Pesciolini. The wine, a merlot-heavy blend topped up with cabernet sauvignon, cabernet franc and petit verdot, opens on the nose with notes of slightly jammy black berry fruits, blackberry and blackcurrant. On the palate, it shows nicely taut, with good acidity underpinning incisive tannins that will further soften over time. The finish is toothsome and displays a fine fruity aftertaste. The Veneroso '05 struck us as still a touch youthful but and we're sure that some bottle ageing will bring out its best. As it is, the fruit is somewhat overpowered by wood on the nose and assertive tannins on the palate. We really liked the juicy Ghizzano '07, which provides undemanding easy drinking with its red berry fruits on the nose and good acidity on the palate.

● Brunello di Montalcino V. gli Angeli '01	▼▼ 7
● Brunello di Montalcino '03	▼▼ 6
● Birba '05	▼ 6
● Brunello di Montalcino V. gli Angeli '03	▼ 7
● Brunello di Montalcino '02	♀♀ 6
● Brunello di Montalcino '01	♀♀ 6
● Brunello di Montalcino '00	♀♀ 6
● Brunello di Montalcino Gli Angeli Ris. '99	♀♀ 8

● Nambrot '05	▼▼▼ 7
● il Ghizzano '07	▼▼ 4
● Veneroso '05	▼▼ 6
● Nambrot '04	♀♀♀ 7
● Nambrot '03	♀♀♀ 7
● Nambrot '01	♀♀♀ 8
● Nambrot '00	♀♀♀ 8
● Veneroso '04	♀♀♀ 6
● Veneroso '01	♀♀♀ 6

I Giusti e Zanza

VIA DEI PUNTONI, 9
56043 FAUGLIA [PI]
TEL. 058544354
www.igiustiezanza.it

ANNUAL PRODUCTION	84,000 bottles
HECTARES UNDER VINE	17
VITICULTURE METHOD	Conventional

It's always a pleasure to talk to Paolo Giusti. His opinions, almost always voiced in a calm whisper, are never tendentious and whether you agree with them or not, they are a wonderful blend of intellectual knowledge and country wisdom. His approach to wine is relaxed. He has no need to seek approval for he is well aware of the quality of his products. His wines are just like him. Made using modern farming methods, they preserve a sense of place and ancestral knowledge, which emerge in the firm colour, concentrated fruit and soft tannins. These are the secret weapons of wines like PerBruno '06, from syrah grown in a vineyard planted at 10,000 vines per hectare and aged in 300-litre barrels for a year. It has a graceful pepper spice and a surprisingly dynamic palate, and waltzed into our finals. We were also impressed by the Belcore '06, from sangiovese and merlot, which gives violets and plums over a finely-woven palate. Dulcamara '05 confirms its prestige and focuses on its strengths of fruitiness and an approachable palate. We also liked the basic wines, the Nemorinos Rosso and Bianco, both from 2007.

Podere Grattamacco

LOC. LUNGAGNANO
57022 CASTAGNETO CARDUCCI [LI]
TEL. 0565765069
www.collemassari.it

ANNUAL PRODUCTION	80,000 bottles
HECTARES UNDER VINE	30
VITICULTURE METHOD	Certified organic

In Bolgheri area, Claudio Tipa's Grattamacco is a very safe bet. Depending on the vintage, the wine's character changes, showing greater fleshiness and intensity last year, while the finer '05 played on sensations of freshness and elegance. Either way, it's still Grattamacco. Situated on the hillside overlooking the sea, between Castagneto Carducci and Bolgheri, the winery has 30 hectares, much of which is on top of the hill. The Bolgheri Rosso Superiore presents a classic local blend of cabernet sauvignon and some merlot, topped up with a splash of sangiovese to provide a sensation of leanness and juiciness. The other Bolgheri Superiore, the Alberello '05, is also very good, despite being just a touch disturbed by the wood when we tasted it. It just needs time. The Bolgheri Rosso '06, which has a better vintage on its side, is firm and full-bodied with an attractive mulberry-themed aftertaste.

● PerBruno '06	♟♟ 5
● Belcore '06	♟♟ 4
● Dulcamara '05	♟♟ 6
○ Nemorino Bianco '07	♟ 4
● Nemorino Rosso '07	♟ 4
● Belcore '01	♟♟ 4
● Belcore '00	♟♟ 4
● Belcore '99	♟♟ 4*
● Belcore '98	♟♟ 4
● Dulcamara '01	♟♟ 6
● Dulcamara '00	♟♟ 6
● Dulcamara '99	♟♟ 6
● Dulcamara '98	♟♟ 6
● PerBruno '05	♟♟ 5
● PerBruno '04	♟♟ 5
● PerBruno '03	♟♟ 5

● Bolgheri Rosso Sup. Grattamacco '05	♟♟♟ 8
● Bolgheri Rosso '06	♟♟ 5
● Bolgheri Sup. L'Alberello '05	♟♟ 7
● Bolgheri Rosso Sup. Grattamacco '04	♟♟♟ 8
● Bolgheri Rosso Sup. Grattamacco '03	♟♟♟ 8
● Bolgheri Rosso Sup. Grattamacco '01	♟♟♟ 8
● Bolgheri Rosso Sup. Grattamacco '99	♟♟♟ 8

Castelli del Grevepesa

FRAZ. MERCATALE IN VAL DI PESA
VIA GREVIGIANA, 34
50024 SAN CASCIANO IN VAL DI PESA [FI]
TEL. 055821911
www.castellidelgrevepesa.it

ANNUAL PRODUCTION	5,800,000 bottles
HECTARES UNDER VINE	1000
VITICULTURE METHOD	Conventional

We inspected a wide range of wines from the largest co-operative in Chianti Classico, achieving a good overall result, but without those peaks of excellence that you would expect from a producer with over 1,000 hectares under vine. Important work has been done, above all to release good wines at competitive prices, but more could be done to produce top-quality products. The territorial distinction between the various types of Chianti Classico, however, shows that the management is interested in giving each wine its own personality while the Typical Geographical Indication wines, produced using international varieties, are now showing greater individuality. The best this year were the Chianti Classico Clemente VII '06, with a broad nose of flowers and cherry, which has soft tannins and a well-balanced finish, and Chianti Classico Panzano '06, with aromas ranging from blackberry to autumn leaves, and powerful, dynamic structure. We enjoyed Syrah '06, whose bouquet of roses and black cherries pave the way for a mouthfilling body, with well-integrated tannins and a rounded finish.

Grignano

FRAZ. GRIGNANO
VIA DI GRIGNANO, 22
50065 PONTASSIEVE [FI]
TEL. 0558398490
www.fattoriadigrignano.com

ANNUAL PRODUCTION	150,000 bottles
HECTARES UNDER VINE	49
VITICULTURE METHOD	Natural

The Inghirami family winery did well, continuing to show its commitment to quality and turning out highly respectable results. The setting is delightful, with small villages and farmhouses scattered over the estate creating an environment which has all the charm of a bygone age. The designation wines are a constant source of satisfaction, starting with the mint and mineral-lace Chianti Rufina '06 soon frees itself of its tannic grip, unfolding and caressing the palate. The Riserva '05, which shows a more austere aromatic profile, progresses nicely, alternating softer and firmer notes, with a rich, well-balanced and intriguingly long palate. The deep amber Vin Santo '01 opens on the nose to candied peel, caramel and almonds. The palate is soft, creamy, sweet and lingering, and rounds off with a delicate apricot after-aroma.

● Chianti Cl. Clemente VII '06	♥♥ 4*
● Chianti Cl. Panzano '06	♥♥ 4*
● Syrah '06	♥♥ 5
● Chianti Cl. Castelgreve '06	♥ 4
● Chianti Cl. Clemente VII Ris. '05	♥ 5
● Chianti Cl. Lamole '06	♥ 4
● Gualdo al Luco '04	♥ 6
● Merlot Aprile '07	♥ 3
○ Vermentino di Maremma '07	♥ 4
● Coltifredi '01	♥♥ 6

● Chianti Rufina '06	♥♥ 3*
● Chianti Rufina Ris. '05	♥♥ 4*
○ Vin Santo del Chianti Capsula Oro '01	♥♥ 5
● Pietramaggio Rosso '07	♥ 2
● Chianti Rufina Ris. '04	♥♥ 4
● Salicaria '04	♥♥ 6
● Salicaria '03	♥♥ 6

Tenuta Guado al Tasso

LOC. BELVEDERE, 140
57020 BOLGHERI [LI]
TEL. 0565749735
www.antinori.it

ANNUAL PRODUCTION	700,000 bottles
HECTARES UNDER VINE	300
VITICULTURE METHOD	Conventional

Guado al Tasso, a beautiful winery owned by the Antinori family, is situated in Bolgheri's famous amphitheatre. On this gentle slope hemmed in by the sea on one side and the hills on the other, the warm, wind-caressed site climate brings forth wines that are both Mediterranean and aristocratic. The Tenuta's gem is Bolgheri Superiore Guado al Tasso, from a blend of cabernet sauvignon, merlot and syrah. The 2005, not one of Tuscany's best vintages, shows intense on the nose of herbaceousness and black berry notes, lifted by faint hints of oak. The palate is full and firm, with good acidity, and only held back by the tannins, especially on the finish. A little time in the bottle will help it unwind. As usual, we enjoyed the Bolgheri Rosato Scalabrone '07, which has brilliant colour and an inviting, berry fruit-themed nose that leads on to an attractive juicy palate with a clean finish. The Bolgheri Vermentino '07 is a delicious easy drinker. Bolgheri Bruciato '06 didn't quite live up to expectations, revealing a slightly imperfect nose and intrusive tannins on the palate.

Gualdo del Re

LOC. NOTRI, 77
57028 SUVERETO [LI]
TEL. 0565829888
www.gualdodelre.it

ANNUAL PRODUCTION	100,000 bottles
HECTARES UNDER VINE	20
VITICULTURE METHOD	Conventional

It was another up-and-down year for Nico Rossi's winery. To be honest, we thought that Gualdo del Re was at last set to consolidate the leading role it had worked for over the years. We are particularly dubious about the cellar's flagship wines, such as Rennero and Federico Primo, both from the good '06 growing season. We found them significantly weighed down by what seem excessive tannins, deriving from injudicious use of oak. The rest of the wines are pleasant enough and some are available at rather tempting prices. We particularly liked the Aleatico Amansio '07, with aromas of ripe cherry, leading to a full-bodied, vibrantly dynamic palate that echoes the nose deliciously and closes with a long finish. We liked the Val di Cornia Rosso Eliseo '07, with its floral, headily alcoholic nose and well-proportioned palate. Val di Cornia Bianco Eliseo '07 is also well-made, with citrus notes on the nose and a bright, full-flavoured palate. The moreish, varietal Vermentino Valentina '07 also performed well. We look forward to a return to top form for this is a winery with fantastic potential.

● Bolgheri Rosso Sup. Guado al Tasso '05	♈♈ 8
☉ Bolgheri Rosato Scalabrone '07	♈ 4
● Bolgheri Rosso Bruciato '06	♈ 5
○ Bolgheri Vermentino '07	♈ 4
● Bolgheri Rosso Sup. Guado al Tasso '01	♈♈♈ 8
● Bolgheri Rosso Sup. Guado al Tasso '90	♈♈♈ 8
● Bolgheri Rosso Sup. Guado al Tasso '04	♈♈ 8
● Bolgheri Rosso Sup. Guado al Tasso '03	♈♈ 8

● Val di Cornia Aleatico Amansio '07	♈♈ 6
● Federico Primo '06	♈ 6
○ Val di Cornia Bianco Eliseo '07	♈ 4
● Val di Cornia Rosso Eliseo '07	♈ 4
● Val di Cornia Rosso l'Rennero '06	♈ 7
○ Val di Cornia Vermentino Valentina '07	♈ 4
● Federico Primo '05	♈♈ 6
● Federico Primo '04	♈♈ 6

Guicciardini Strozzi
Fattoria Cusona
Loc. Cusona, 5
53037 San Gimignano [SI]
tel. 0577950028
www.guicciardinistrozzi.it

ANNUAL PRODUCTION	650,000 bottles	
HECTARES UNDER VINE	70	
VITICULTURE METHOD	Conventional	

Renovation work on the various vineyards and winemaking facilities belonging to Principe Guicciardini Strozzi, from the headquarters at Fattoria di Cusona to the wineries in the Bolgheri area and Maremma, is nearing completion, which bodes well for future production. The highly drinkable Bolgheri Ocra '06 is well executed, showing a fresh nose of aromatic herbs and red berry fruit ushering in a sweet, succulent palate. The Maremma provided an attractively aromatic and juicy '06 version of Morellino di Scansano Poggio Moreto whereas Morellino Titolato '07 is somewhat simpler. The best of the bunch from Fattoria di Cusona is the single-variety Sangiovese, Sodole '05, which shows ripe fruit on the nose and a streamlined palate. It wasn't a great year for the cabernet and merlot Millanni, because the '05 is untogether on a palate that is held back by extract. We enjoyed the Vernaccia Riserva '06 and the vermentino Arabesque '07, as well as the Vernaccia di San Gimignano Titolato Strozzi '07.

★ Isole e Olena
Loc. Isole, 1
50021 Barberino Val d'Elsa [FI]
tel. 0558072763
www.isoleolena.it

ANNUAL PRODUCTION	220,000 bottles	
HECTARES UNDER VINE	50	
VITICULTURE METHOD	Conventional	

After missing only one year, Paolo De Marchi is back with another Three Glass wine, thanks to the excellent performance of his monovarietal Sangiovese, Cepparello '05, one of the symbols of the Chianti renaissance after the difficult times of the 1970s. Perhaps it is Paolo's Piedmontese origins which led him to focus on single-variety wines, saving the traditional formula of blending solely for his Chianti Classico. Far from wanting to be a modernist, focusing on the potential of each individual variety, native or international, he has discovered unexpected potential in a territory already known for its ability to give remarkable staying power to sangiovese. The wine is a well-defined ruby colour and flaunts an aromatic spectrum that ranges across sensations of violet-like violets to cherries, beautifully underpinned by fine spices and aromatic herbs. The soft, supple palate reveals a refreshing vein of acidity an appealing, flavour-rich finish. We liked the other wines, in particular the Vin Santo '00, with citrus notes and a long, sweet mouthfeel that caresses the palate.

● Bolgheri Ocra '06	♥♥ 4*
● Morellino di Scansano Poggio Moreto '06	♥♥ 5
● Sodole '05	♥♥ 6
○ Arabesque '07	♥ 4
● Millanni '05	♥ 7
● Morellino di Scansano Titolato '07	♥ 4
○ Vernaccia di S. Gimignano Ris. '06	♥ 4
○ Vernaccia di S. Gimignano Titolato Strozzi '07	♥ 4
● Millanni '99	♥♥♥ 7
● Bolgheri Vignarè '04	♥♥ 7
● Millanni '04	♥♥ 7
● Millanni '00	♥♥ 7
● Sodole '04	♥♥ 6
○ Vernaccia di S. Gimignano Cusona 1933 '06	♥♥ 5

● Cepparello '05	♥♥♥ 8
○ Chardonnay Collezione De Marchi '06	♥♥ 7
○ Vin Santo del Chianti Classico '00	♥♥ 8
● Chianti Cl. '06	♥ 5
● Cepparello '03	♥♥♥ 8
● Cepparello '01	♥♥♥ 7
● Cepparello '00	♥♥♥ 7
● Cepparello '99	♥♥♥ 6
● Cepparello '98	♥♥♥ 6
● Cepparello '97	♥♥♥ 5
● Syrah '99	♥♥♥ 7

Lanciola

LOC. POZZOLATICO
VIA IMPRUNETANA, 210
50023 IMPRUNETA [FI]
TEL. 055208324
www.lanciola.it

ANNUAL PRODUCTION	250,000 bottles
HECTARES UNDER VINE	50
VITICULTURE METHOD	Conventional

We report a good overall result for the Guarneri family, who achieved excellent scores with the wines presented. They are obviously on the right track, producing designation wines that perform well for we were not so enthusiastic about some of their previous experiments with pinot nero and chardonnay, which gave uneven results. The winery has two vineyards, one in Impruneta, where there are 40 hectares under vine and 40 planted to olive trees, and the other in Chianti Classico, where the ten hectares are planted with varieties such as colorino and canaiolo, alongside sangiovese and some international grapes like syrah. We enjoyed the Riserva '04 Le Masse di Greve, with its rich, sumptuous nose heralding a caressingly soft, well-rounded body and a nicely developed finish. The Vin Santo '03 flaunts an enchanting nose with notes of nuts and dried fruit, followed by a creamy, rich palate with an attractive aftertaste of vanilla. The Chianti Colli Fiorentini '06 is worth investigating for its attractive fresh aromas and invitingly lean, smooth body paving the way to an enjoyable, lingering finish.

Castello La Leccia

LOC. LA LECCIA
53011 CASTELLINA IN CHIANTI [SI]
TEL. 0577743148
www.castellolaleccia.com

ANNUAL PRODUCTION	30,000 bottles
HECTARES UNDER VINE	18
VITICULTURE METHOD	Conventional

At last, Francesco Daddi's winery is back with a full profile after a result that shows the improvement in the wines from the hard work over recent years, with focus on detail in the vineyard and during vinification. The castle has historic origins dating back to the 11th century while the first mentions of wine production are from the 1500s. In 2001, renovation work began on the houses in the village to provide accommodation for the estate's agriturismo activities. Only two wines are produced, as a result of a deliberate choice to give priority to the terroir, with the Bruciagna vineyard selection used for production of the Riserva. This year, the '05 version reached our finals, where it performed well. On the nose, it shows fresh minty aromas with sensations of pencil lead and leather, nicely meshed with the cherry fruit. Entry on the palate is broad and juicy and the richly textured rising finish. We also liked the Chianti Classico '06, with its intense aromas of blackcurrant and blackberry preceding the alluring, well-defined body.

● Chianti Cl. Le Masse di Greve Ris. '04	¶¶	5
● Chianti Colli Fiorentini '06	¶¶	3*
○ Vin Santo del Chianti '03	¶¶	6
● Chianti Cl. Le Masse di Greve Ris. '02	¶¶	5
● Terricci '01	¶¶	6
○ Vin Santo del Chianti '02	¶¶	6

● Chianti Cl. Bruciagna Ris. '05	¶¶	5
● Chianti Cl. '06	¶¶	4*
● Chianti Cl. Bruciagna Ris. '01	¶¶¶	6

Cantine Leonardo da Vinci

VIA PROVINCIALE MERCATALE, 291
50059 VINCI [FI]
TEL. 0571902444
www.cantineleonardo.it

ANNUAL PRODUCTION	4,000,000 bottles
HECTARES UNDER VINE	660
VITICULTURE METHOD	Conventional

Cantine Leonardo is now a veritable institution in Chianti Fiorentino territory. It releases a wide range of wines for all bands of the market, with consistently reliable average quality, especially when you consider their prices. This year, we tasted no fewer than 23 different wines. There's not enough space here to describe them all but we would like to stress that the wines share a similar stylistic approach, as well as an average level of quality. The ones we found most convincing were the fragrant, fruity Chianti Leonardo '07 and Chianti Da Vinci '07 and the well-balanced, tasty new Trebbiano '07. The Chardonnay Ser Piero '07 is refreshing and we also liked the Brunello di Montalcino Da Vinci '03, the Rosso di Montalcino Leonardo '06 and the Morellino di Scansano '07. Sangiovese Poggio del Sasso '07 and Vin Santo Tegrino '03 are well executed and they are flanked by a first-rate Brunello di Montalcino '03 and Rosso di Montalcino '06 from the Cantina di Montalcino winery. The rest of the wines are good.

Tenuta di Lilliano

LOC. LILLIANO, 8
53011 CASTELLINA IN CHIANTI [SI]
TEL. 0577743070
www.lilliano.com

ANNUAL PRODUCTION	250,000 bottles
HECTARES UNDER VINE	50
VITICULTURE METHOD	Conventional

You reap what you sow, as the old saying goes. The ever-improving results of the Ruspoli family's winery bode well for coming years for growth in quality has been consistent over recent years. Credit should go to their commitment to promoting a territory which has always been looked on as ideal for wine production. Since it is situated in a borderland, it was destroyed and rebuilt on many occasions until the 19th century, whose architectural style survives today and past owners include the hospital of Santa Maria Nuova in Florence. The present ownership, which has always considered winemaking as fundamental part of the estate's activity, took over in 1920. The wines are extremely good, particularly the Chianti Classico '06, which offers traditional aromas of cherry and violet, a solid tannic base well integrated with the alcohol, and a tasty, appetizing finish. We also liked the Riserva '05, with its fine, complex swath of aromatics and a robust, well-balanced palate, as well as the Anagallis '05, a blend of sangiovese, colorino and merlot that serves up an elegant spectrum of aromatics in a distinctly drinkable glass.

● Brunello di Montalcino Da Vinci '03	♥♥	7
● Chianti Da Vinci '07	♥♥	3
● Chianti Leonardo '07	♥♥	3
● Rosso di Montalcino Cantina di Montalcino '06	♥♥	4
O Ser Piero '07	♥♥	3
O Trebbiano Leonardo '07	♥♥	3*
● Brunello di Montalcino Cantina di Montalcino '03	♥	6
● Morellino di Scansano '07	♥	3
● Poggio del Sasso '07	♥	3
● Rosso di Montalcino Leonardo '06	♥	4
O Vin Santo Tegrino d'Anchiano '03	♥	5

● Chianti Cl. '06	♥♥	4*
● Anagallis '05	♥♥	6
● Chianti Cl. Ris. '05	♥♥	5
● Anagallis '04	♀♀	6
● Chianti Cl. Ris. '04	♀♀	5

Lisini

LOC. SANT'ANGELO IN COLLE
53020 MONTALCINO [SI]
TEL. 0577844040
www.lisini.com

ANNUAL PRODUCTION	100,000 bottles
HECTARES UNDER VINE	19
VITICULTURE METHOD	Conventional

This historic Montalcino winery has the good fortune to own vineyards in one of the DOCG zones best areas, to the south, and produces consistently excellent wines. Even in a sweltering year such as 2003, Lisini managed to turn out a Brunello di Montalcino with no sign of overripeness. This result is above all down to the cellar's ability to make the most of the raw materials from the vineyards during vinification. The Brunello di Montalcino '03 flaunts a well-rounded nose with notes of coffee and quinine in addition to characteristic red and black berry fruit, with blackberry to the fore. The entry on the palate is confident and followed by good development limited only by slightly boisterous tannins, which constrict the finish. It is in any case one of the vintage's best bottles. The Rosso di Montalcino '06 is also well up to the winery's solid standards. Somewhat youthful on the nose with hints of damson and fresh cherry, it follows through feistily on the palate with finely woven, elegant tannins and pleasant acidity. The San Biagio '06 is a fragrant pleaser.

Livernano

LOC. LIVERNANO, 67A
53017 RADDA IN CHIANTI [SI]
TEL. 0577738353
www.livernano.it

ANNUAL PRODUCTION	50,000 bottles
HECTARES UNDER VINE	12.5
VITICULTURE METHOD	Natural

Robert Cuillo's winery is clearly not a flash in the pan. This US-born Broadway producer has staged one of his best shows in Chianti Classico, which brings home top honours every year. This time it's the turn of Livernano '05, a Supertuscan that has become a local benchmark. Three Glasses went to this cabernet sauvignon and merlot based red with a splash of sangiovese for its attractively elegant, well-rounded nose with hints of autumn leaves, ripe fruit, camphor and undertones of cinnamon, followed by a rich, well-defined palate of overwhelming sensuality, rounded off by a satisfyingly alluring finish. The two Chianti Classico Riservas did well, although their styles are different. Livernano is topped up with merlot while the Riserva from the Casalvento estate has cabernet sauvignon. Both flaunt crisp aromas, good entry on the palate and an attractive finish. This excellent standard of quality was confirmed by Anima '06, a complex white from traminer aromatico, viogner, sauvignon and chardonnay, whose style is anything but international. The Janus '05, based on cabernet sauvignon, is well made and drinkable.

● Brunello di Montalcino '03	▼▼	7
● Rosso di Montalcino '06	▼▼	5
● San Biagio '06	▼	4
● Brunello di Montalcino Ugolaia '01	▼▼▼	8
● Brunello di Montalcino Ugolaia '00	▼▼▼	8
● Brunello di Montalcino '01	▼▼	7
● Brunello di Montalcino '00	▼▼	7
● Brunello di Montalcino Ugolaia '98	▼▼	8
● Brunello di Montalcino Ugolaia '97	▼	8

● Livernano '05	▼▼▼	7
○ Anima '06	▼▼	6
● Chianti Cl. Casalvento Ris. '05	▼▼	5
● Chianti Cl. Ris. '05	▼▼	5
● Janus '05	▼	8
● Chianti Cl. Ris. '04	▼▼▼	5
● Livernano '03	▼▼▼	8
● Livernano '99	▼▼▼	8
● Livernano '98	▼▼▼	8
● Livernano '97	▼▼▼	8

Tenuta della Luia

VIA TRENTO, 32
50052 CERTALDO [FI]
TEL. 0571 667330
www.tenutadellaluia.it

ANNUAL PRODUCTION	30,000 bottles
HECTARES UNDER VINE	60
VITICULTURE METHOD	Conventional

Tenuta della Luia gave us a first taste of its potential in the last edition of the Guide and this year its wines confirmed their promise. This family-run winery in Tuscany, situated on the hills overlooking Certaldo, has been owned by the Gori family since the 1960s. Under the expert guidance of the talented Fabrizio Moltard, new vineyards have been planted and the wines can now be relied on for their quality. The Luia '05, a blend of merlot, colorino and cabernet, made it through to the final tastings. On the nose, it exudes intriguing aromas of black berry fruit, bramble and hints of balsam leading into a soft, compact and powerful palate. With just a touch more personality, this wine would be quite a thoroughbred. The Luia Syrah '06 is not far behind, with its attractive, varietal aromatic profile and deep, rich palate. The Chianti Poggiolaia Riserva '05, with well-behaved tannins, comfortably passed muster.

Lunadoro

FRAZ. VALIANO DI MONTEPULCIANO
LOC. TERRAROSSA PAGLIERETO
53040 MONTEPULCIANO [SI]
TEL. 0578748154
www.lunadoro.com

ANNUAL PRODUCTION	45,000 bottles
HECTARES UNDER VINE	12
VITICULTURE METHOD	Conventional

The Lunadoro winery seems to be firmly on course for top honours. It was established just over six years ago but has clearly its sights set on becoming a big name in Montepulciano winemaking. The wines presented by Dario Cappelli and Gigliola Cardinali achieved the same flattering results as they did in last year's Guide, confirming promisingly consistent quality. This means we again welcomed to the finals Quercione '05, a Nobile di Montepulciano selection that manages to combine winemaking technique with a natural style and character. A touch too much oak overshadows the lush fruit and attractive flinty notes that characterize the aromas, although wood is more judiciously dosed on the palate where the wine is lively, well balanced, juicy and savoury. The Nobile di Montepulciano '05 is simpler, focusing on fruit sweetness both on the coherent, well-defined nose and on the palate, where its subtle structure unfolds with suppleness. The Rosso di Montepulciano '06 is much simpler but enjoyable and Pagliareto '07, from trebbiano and malvasia grapes, is almost salty.

● Luia '05	♟♟ 6
● Luia Syrah '06	♟♟ 6
● Chianti Poggiolaia Ris. '05	♟ 4
● Luia '04	♟♟ 6

● Nobile di Montepulciano Quercione '05	♟♟ 5
● Nobile di Montepulciano '05	♟♟ 5
○ Pagliareto '07	♟ 3
● Rosso di Montepulciano '06	♟ 4
● Nobile di Montepulciano '04	♟♟ 5
● Nobile di Montepulciano Quercione '04	♟♟ 5

★ Le Macchiole

VIA BOLGHERESE, 189A
57020 BOLGHERI [LI]
TEL. 0565766092
www.lemacchiole.it

Machiavelli

LOC. SANT'ANDREA IN PERCUSSINA
50026 SAN CASCIANO IN VAL DI PESA [FI]
TEL. 055828471
www.giv.it

ANNUAL PRODUCTION	100,000 bottles
HECTARES UNDER VINE	22
VITICULTURE METHOD	Conventional

ANNUAL PRODUCTION	180,000 bottles
HECTARES UNDER VINE	26.57
VITICULTURE METHOD	Conventional

Another year has passed without Three Glasses for Cinzia Campolmi. The style of her latest vintages is profoundly different from that of the past, especially regarding the use of wood for the wines have a common thread in their rather overwhelming oakiness. This is obviously a matter of taste for we know that many enthusiasts love the wines of Le Macchiole, as do many critics. The wine that convinced us most this year was the cabernet franc-only Paleo Rosso '05 with its nose of marked herbaceousness and evident oak. The palate is compact and concentrated, with persistent tannins that constrict the finish. Notes of lusciously ripe, jammy fruit characterize Messorio '05, a single-variety Merlot. Here, too, and more evidently, the uninvited guest is that intrusive extract, with the result that not even the good acidity enables the finish to unbend. Scrio '05, from syrah, shows attractive spice on the nose and hints of torrefaction from the wood. On the palate, spicy sensations return but again oak-derived tannins dominate. Not even the Bolgheri Rosso '06, with its nice underlying acidic tautness, manages to shrug them off.

Continuing on the crest of a wave is one of the leading brands in the Italiano Vini Group, situated just down the road from the Chianti Classico consortium offices. The winery's owes its distinctive name to the fact that Sant'Andrea in Percussina was where Nicolò Machiavelli was sent into exile in 1513. Moving on to the wines, this year saw a great result for the Chianti Classico Riserva Vigna di Fontalle '05, which was back in the national finals. This wine is the quintessence of the territory and, appropriately, the vineyard it comes from is opposite the consortium. The impressive spectrum of aromatics ranges from jam to complex hints of tobacco and leather, with hints of rain-drenched earth, before the palate unveils powerful structure, subtly laced with incisive tannins that lead into a long, succulent finish braced by perfect acidity. We loved the Chianti Classico Solatìo del Tani '06, which is more modern in style. It shows sumptuous ripe red berry fruit, with hints of aromatic herbs, paving the way for a juicy, fresh-tasting palate perked up by very appealing acidity and topped off with good length. A delight to drink.

● Paleo Rosso '05	❦❦ 8
● Messorio '05	❦❦ 8
● Scrio '05	❦❦ 8
● Bolgheri Rosso '06	❦ 5
● Bolgheri Rosso Sup. Paleo '97	❦❦❦ 8
● Bolgheri Rosso Sup. Paleo '96	❦❦❦ 8
● Bolgheri Rosso Sup. Paleo '95	❦❦❦ 8
● Messorio '01	❦❦❦ 8
● Messorio '99	❦❦❦ 8
● Messorio '98	❦❦❦ 8
● Messorio '97	❦❦❦ 8
● Paleo Rosso '03	❦❦❦ 8
● Paleo Rosso '01	❦❦❦ 8
● Scrio '01	❦❦❦ 8

● Chianti Cl. V. di Fontalle Ris. '05	❦❦ 6
● Chianti Cl. Solatìo del Tani '06	❦❦ 5
● Chianti Cl. V. di Fontalle Ris. '97	❦❦❦ 5
● Chianti Cl. V. di Fontalle Ris. '95	❦❦❦ 5
● Chianti Cl. Solatìo del Tani '05	❦❦ 6
● Chianti Cl. V. di Fontalle Ris. '04	❦❦ 6
● Chianti Cl. V. di Fontalle Ris. '03	❦❦ 7
● Chianti Cl. V. di Fontalle Ris. '01	❦❦ 5
● Chianti Cl. V. di Fontalle Ris. '00	❦❦ 5

La Madonnina - Triacca

LOC. STRADA IN CHIANTI
VIA PALAIA, 39
50027 GREVE IN CHIANTI [FI]
TEL. 055858003
www.triacca.com

ANNUAL PRODUCTION	600,000 bottles
HECTARES UNDER VINE	100
VITICULTURE METHOD	Conventional

The Triacca winery likes to alternate things. After astounding us last year with a performance that saw one of their Tuscan properties awarded Three Glasses for the first time, this time the wines were well executed but nothing exceptional. There will be time to make up over the coming year. The Triacca family history is interesting. Originally from Switzerland, they moved to Italy over 100 years ago to produce wine in Tuscany and Valtellina while keeping their administrative offices in Switzerland. This has above all allowed them to develop their foreign market, especially for wines from Chianti. The best of the bunch is the Chianti Classico Riserva '05, with a complex aromatic spectrum dominated by leather, tobacco and animal skins underpinned by hints of blackberry jam. On the palate it is juicy, with tight-knight tannins and fresh, lively acidity, rounded off by an attractive, rising finish. The two '06 Chianti Classicos, La Palaia and Bello Stento, provide pleasurable drinking.

Fattoria di Magliano

LOC. STERPETI, 10
58051 MAGLIANO IN TOSCANA [GR]
TEL. 0564593040
www.fattoriadimagliano.it

ANNUAL PRODUCTION	200,000 bottles
HECTARES UNDER VINE	47
VITICULTURE METHOD	Conventional

Agostino Lenci's winery releases richly fruity wines with impressive extract and good support from barrique oak. The products are crafted with great technical skill and despite their hefty structure can be extremely drinkable. It is thanks to precisely this quality, so naturally expressed, that the Morellino di Scansano Heba '07 made the finals. We found beautifully fresh fruit on the nose that usher in a vibrantly energetic palate and a lingering fruit finale. The Poggio Bestiale '06, a 50-50 blend of cabernet sauvignon and merlot, also got through to the finals, charming us with its depth and impressively well-rounded, succulent palate. The monovarietal Syrah, Perenzo '06, was spot-on, offering a nice alternation of balsamic notes and ripe fruit tones on the nose, elegantly echoed on the palate, where the wine is full and taut. Sinarra '07, the winery's new product, is a pleasant, fresh-tasting easy drinker. This Sangiovese with a splash of petit verdot offers clean, approachable aromas and a full-flavoured palate with an almost piquant finish. We enjoyed the Pagliatura '07, from vermentino grapes.

● Chianti Cl. Ris. '05	♈♈ 4*
● Chianti Cl. Bello Stento '06	♈ 4
● Chianti Cl. V. La Palaia '06	♈ 5
● Chianti Cl. Ris. '04	♈♈♈ 4
● Chianti Cl. Bello Stento '03	♈♈ 4

● Morellino di Scansano Heba '07	♈♈ 4*
● Poggio Bestiale '06	♈♈ 6
● Perenzo '06	♈♈ 7
● Sinarra '07	♈♈ 4*
○ Pagliatura '07	♈ 4
● Morellino di Scansano Heba '03	♈♈ 4
● Morellino di Scansano Heba '02	♈♈ 4
○ Pagliatura '06	♈♈ 4
○ Pagliatura '04	♈♈ 4
● Perenzo '04	♈♈ 6
● Perenzo '03	♈♈ 7
● Poggio Bestiale '05	♈♈ 6
● Poggio Bestiale '02	♈♈ 6
● Poggio Bestiale '01	♈♈ 6

Malenchini

LOC. GRASSINA
VIA LILLIANO E MEOLI, 82
50015 BAGNO A RIPOLI [FI]
TEL. 055642602
www.malenchini.it

ANNUAL PRODUCTION	90,000 bottles
HECTARES UNDER VINE	17
VITICULTURE METHOD	Conventional

We gave a full profile this time to the winery owned by the Malenchini family for almost two centuries. Now, Diletta is at the helm, coordinating all the work in the vineyard and olive groves. Great attention is focused on safeguarding the territory, to the point where integrated farming methods are employed to ensure respect for the environment. Of the wines presented, we were most convinced by the Bruzzico '05, a cabernet sauvignon-rich blend topped up with sangiovese, which presents a well-structured aromatic profile ranging from fruitiness to spice, with some tertiary aromas such as tobacco. On the palate, it is rich, tasty and bursting with firm, well-distributed tannins that lead to an enjoyably long finish. The toothsome, more approachable Chianti Colli Fiorentini '06 is also fresh and inviting. Finally, the Vin Santo del Chianti Colli Fiorentini '00 is undemanding but sweet and enjoyable.

La Mannella

LOC. LA MANNELLA, 322
53024 MONTALCINO [SI]
TEL. 0577848268
http://www.lamannella.it

ANNUAL PRODUCTION	30,000 bottles
HECTARES UNDER VINE	8
VITICULTURE METHOD	Conventional

Marco Cortonesi's La Mannella has earned a full profile this year. The winery started operations in 1990 and after substantial improvements in quality over the years, this time presented an extremely interesting range of wines. From the eight hectares planted to brunello, some in the north and some in the south-east of the DOCG zone, La Mannella gave us two Brunello di Montalcinos with marked differences. The Brunello '03 is a classic version, both in terms of its vinification in steel vats and maturation, in 30 and 40-hectolitre barrels. The Poggiarelli selection, in contrast, is vinified in wood and matures in large and small wood before going into bottle. This year, we preferred the classic version, with its well-rounded nose of fruity notes and florality followed by a rich palate. The tannins are well tucked in, especially if we bear in mind the growing season. The Rosso di Montalcino '06 is extremely well executed, with a fragrant nose of fresh, intense fruit aromas leading into a substantial body supported by good acidity.

● Bruzzico '05	♟♟ 5
● Chianti Colli Fiorentini '06	♟♟ 4
○ Vin Santo del Chianti Colli Fiorentini '00	♟ 5
● Bruzzico '04	♟♟ 5
● Bruzzico '03	♟♟ 5
● Bruzzico '02	♟♟ 4
● Bruzzico '01	♟♟ 4

● Brunello di Montalcino '03	♟♟ 6
● Rosso di Montalcino '06	♟♟ 4*
● Brunello di Montalcino I Poggiarelli '03	♟ 7
● Brunello di Montalcino '02	♟♟ 6
● Rosso di Montalcino '02	♟♟ 4*

Mantellassi

LOC. BANDITACCIA, 26
58051 MAGLIANO IN TOSCANA [GR]
TEL. 0564592037
www.fatt-mantellassi.it

ANNUAL PRODUCTION	550,000 bottles
HECTARES UNDER VINE	60
VITICULTURE METHOD	Conventional

The wines produced by Aleardo and Giuseppe Mantellassi at their historic winery in Magliano in Toscana always have character. This cellar has become a benchmark for anyone who wants to fully understand the soul of the Morellino denomination, in its various incarnations. The wine that best reflects this winemaking tradition is the Morellino di Scansano Le Sentinelle Riserva '05, with its smoky aromatics and floral notes, offset by a certain earthiness. The palate displays well-orchestrated development, driven by incisive acidic verve only slightly weighed down on the finish by some unabsorbed oakiness. Querciolaia '05, a monovarietal Alicante, has plenty to say for itself but shows less character, although the nose is well focused and the fresh palate has lots of flavour. Both the Morellino Mentore '07 and the Morellino San Giuseppe '07 are approachable and a joy to drink. The former is toothsome but extremely simple while the latter shows intensely mature aromas and better development on the palate, although the finish is a touch mouth-drying. We enjoyed Scalandrino '07 and Lucumone '07, both from vermentino grapes.

La Marcellina

VIA CASE SPARSE, 74
50020 PANZANO [FI]
TEL. 055852126
www.lamarcellina.it

ANNUAL PRODUCTION	70,000 bottles
HECTARES UNDER VINE	13
VITICULTURE METHOD	Conventional

The wines from the cellar owned by the Castellacci family failed to match last year's performance, which is a shame because the vineyards have potential. We are sure that this is just a temporary setback on the road to quality on which the management set out last year with such determination. Chianti Classico, in various versions, is still the main wine, which seems only natural considering that the terroir is rightly considered the natural cradle of sangiovese. Chianti Classico Sassocupo '06 is most impressive, with its compelling ruby colour and spicy tones on the nose accompanied by ripe cherry fruit. On the palate it displays well-balanced weight and structure, leading to a highly satisfying finish. The other wines show a certain lack of balance in their individual components but display and overall fullness. A few adjustments are required, and more care with the first-rate raw material.

● Morellino di Scansano Le Sentinelle Ris. '05	♟♟ 5
● Querciolaia '05	♟♟ 5
○ Lucumone '07	♟ 3
● Morellino di Scansano Mentore '07	♟ 4
● Morellino di Scansano San Giuseppe '07	♟ 4
○ Vermentino Scalandrino '07	♟ 4
● Morellino di Scansano Le Sentinelle Ris. '04	♟♟ 5
● Morellino di Scansano Le Sentinelle Ris. '03	♟♟ 5
● Morellino di Scansano Le Sentinelle Ris. '01	♟♟ 5
● Morellino di Scansano San Giuseppe '06	♟♟ 4
● Querciolaia '04	♟♟ 5
● Querciolaia '03	♟♟ 5

● Chianti Cl. Sassocupo '06	♟♟ 4*
● Chianti Cl. Comignole '06	♟ 5
● Chianti Cl. Sassocupo Ris. '05	♟ 5
● Ser Marcello '06	♟ 5
○ Vin Santo del Chianti L'Oro del Cavaliere '98	♟ 6
● Chianti Cl. Comignole '04	♟♟ 5
● Chianti Cl. Sassocupo '01	♟♟ 5

★ Marchesi de' Frescobaldi

VIA SANTO SPIRITO, 11
50125 FIRENZE
TEL. 05527141
www.frescobaldi.it

ANNUAL PRODUCTION	9,000,000 bottles
HECTARES UNDER VINE	1200
VITICULTURE METHOD	Conventional

The main Frescobaldi winery in Chianti Classico is back on form with Mormoreto '05, which won Three Glasses. There are various innovations in the ageing and blends. For example, Chianti Rufina Montesodi was not presented. Now a Riserva, it is maturing for an extra year. Mormoreto itself now has a more rounded palate, with more merlot in the blend with respect to the cabernet sauvignon and cabernet franc. It offers rich aromas, the vanilla and cinnamon melding with balsamic notes and well-defined fruit. Entry on the palate is pervasive, generous, full-bodied and succulent, with discreet, well-integrated tannins leading to a finish of great intensity and power. The exceptional Chianti Rufina Riserva Nipozzano, of which 1,000,000 units go into bottle, is one of the best wines in the range. Others worth mentioning include Pomino Il Benefizio, which is minerally on the nose and savoury in the mouth, and the seductive Vendemmia Tardiva '06 with its rich, creamy palate. The Castelgiocondo winery in Montalcino sent us a Brunello di Montalcino '03, with rather stiff tannins and the Luce '05 from the winery of the same name has nice acidity.

● Mormoreto '05	▼▼▼	7
○ Castello di Pomino Vin Santo '03	▼▼	6
● Chianti Rufina Nipozzano Ris. '05	▼▼	4*
● Luce '05	▼▼	8
○ Pomino Il Benefizio '06	▼▼	6
○ Pomino V.T. '06	▼▼	5
○ Albizzia '07	▼	3
● Brunello di Montalcino Castelgiocondo '03	▼	7
○ Pomino Bianco '07	▼	4
◉ Rosa di Corte '07	▼	3
● Chianti Rufina Montesodi '01	♀♀♀	7
● Chianti Rufina Montesodi '99	♀♀♀	7
● Chianti Rufina Montesodi '97	♀♀♀	7
● Mormoreto '01	♀♀♀	7
● Mormoreto '97	♀♀♀	6

Renzo Marinai

VIA CASE SPARSE, 6
50020 GREVE IN CHIANTI [FI]
TEL. 0558560237
www.renzomarinai.it

ANNUAL PRODUCTION	30,000 bottles
HECTARES UNDER VINE	5.5
VITICULTURE METHOD	Certified organic

With the tireless energy of a marathon runner, Renzo Marinai again managed to get his Riserva di Chianti Classico into the finals, showing that ideas can grow feet, as an old Tuscan saying goes. His driving force is his love for nature and things of beauty, and the pursuit of absolute quality. This is the philosophy behind his uncompromising approach, and explains why Renzo manages to achieve excellence in everything he does. He looks after his olive oil as if it were his own child and the way he grows Cappelli wheat is an example for other local farmers to follow. Moving on to the wines, Renzo's finalist has a complex spectrum of aromatics in which notes of gunflint and forest fruits are prominent, accompanied by hints of rain drenched earth. The body is vibrant, with well-distributed tannins and a fresh, lively, long-lingering finish. The current version of the Chianti Classico is also good, with intense aromas and a juicy, refreshingly vibrant palate.

● Chianti Cl. Ris. '05	▼▼	5
● Chianti Cl. '06	▼▼	4*
● Chianti Cl. Ris. '04	♀♀	5

★ La Massa

VIA CASE SPARSE, 9
50020 PANZANO [FI]
TEL. 055852722
info@fattorialamassa.com

Massanera

FRAZ. CHIESANUOVA
VIA FALTIGNANO, 76
50020 SAN CASCIANO IN VAL DI PESA [FI]
TEL. 0558242222
www.massanera.com

ANNUAL PRODUCTION   110,000 bottles
HECTARES UNDER VINE 25
VITICULTURE METHOD   Conventional

ANNUAL PRODUCTION   35,000 bottles
HECTARES UNDER VINE 7
VITICULTURE METHOD   Conventional

If Giampaolo Motta had his way, we wouldn't be writing this profile. He didn't send any samples to Italian guides or publications, although he did give them to non-domestic reviewers, above all the Americans. In his view, our sin is not having gone to visit his winery or talked to him recently. As if Robert Parker or the editor of Wine Spectator were frequent visitors. And as if the ten Three Glass awards since 1998 didn't hint that perhaps we know his winery pretty well already, including the jagged rock on the drive that tore a whole in the sump of one of our tasters' cars a few years back. In any case, we invested a few euros in two bottles of La Massa 2006, which we bought from the Bomprezzi wine shop in Rome. The bottles were on sale and freedom of the press means we can write what we think. The wine, which is a blend of mainly sangiovese and merlot, was as always extremely good and made it through to our finals. On the nose, it gives tobacco and violets, tight-knit, faintly dusty tannins and excellent body. It lacks a touch of complexity but there again it is a second wine. Next year, we'll invest in a bottle of Giorgio Primo 2006.

Carlo Cattaneo's winery repeated last year's results, although with different wines. The estate seems to be bursting with new enthusiasm, after making a name for itself in the 1970s when it began to bottle higher-quality wines and then in the mid 1980s when it started breeding the local cinta senese pigs. Now that the agriturismo side of the business is up and running, we can quite happily say that quality is to be found everywhere in this winery in San Casciano. This year, the Chianti Classico '06 distinguished itself for its complex fruit nose and prominent notes of violet and iris followed by a lean yet intriguingly spirited, juicily enjoyable palate. We also liked Per Me '05, a 50-50 blend of sangiovese and merlot, which showed a less evolved nose but a supple and lean, well-distributed body with a well-proportioned finish. The '05 version of the single-variety Sangiovese, Prelato di Massanera, was less of a success, with over-assertive tannins that make for difficult drinking.

● La Massa '06	♟♟	6
● Chianti Cl. Giorgio Primo '01	♟♟♟	8
● Chianti Cl. Giorgio Primo '00	♟♟♟	7
● Chianti Cl. Giorgio Primo '99	♟♟♟	7
● Chianti Cl. Giorgio Primo '98	♟♟♟	7
● Chianti Cl. Giorgio Primo '97	♟♟♟	7
● Chianti Cl. Giorgio Primo '96	♟♟♟	7
● Chianti Cl. Giorgio Primo '95	♟♟♟	7
● Chianti Cl. Giorgio Primo '94	♟♟♟	7
● Chianti Cl. Giorgio Primo '93	♟♟♟	7
● Giorgio Primo '03	♟♟♟	8
● La Massa '01	♟♟♟	5

● Chianti Cl. '06	♟♟	4*
● Per Me '05	♟♟	5
● Prelato di Massanera '05	♟	6
● Per Me '04	♟♟	5
● Prelato di Massanera '04	♟♟	6
● Prelato di Massanera '03	♟♟	6

Mastrojanni

FRAZ. CASTELNUOVO DELL'ABATE
POD. LORETO SAN PIO
53024 MONTALCINO [SI]
TEL. 0577835681
www.mastrojanni.com

ANNUAL PRODUCTION	80,000 bottles
HECTARES UNDER VINE	24
VITICULTURE METHOD	Conventional

We are sad to tell you that the Mastrojanni family has decided to sell its winery, which for so many years has played a leading role in the area of Montalcino, indeed becoming something of a standard bearer. We hope that the new owners will follow the path mapped out in over 30 years of activity. The technical staff have been kept on, in a promising sign of continuity, with Andrea Machetti at the helm and the renowned Maurizio Castelli as consultant oenologist. For this edition of the Guide, the best wine turned out to be San Pio '05, a blend of 80 per cent cabernet sauvignon topped up with sangiovese. Intense on the nose, with notes of blueberries, blackcurrants and blackberries, it is livened up by a faint, intriguing vegetal note that fuses perfectly with the spiciness of the oak. The tannins are slightly aggressive but decently tucked in, considering the imposing structure. The finish is well rounded and persistent. The Brunello di Montalcino '03 was less successful, stiffened by its tannins, and requires further bottle ageing. On the nose there are displays warm notes of jammy fruit, medicinal herbs and tobacco.

Castello di Meleto

LOC. MELETO
53013 GAIOLE IN CHIANTI [SI]
TEL. 0577749217
www.castellomeleto.it

ANNUAL PRODUCTION	480,000 bottles
HECTARES UNDER VINE	120
VITICULTURE METHOD	Conventional

There have been various changes at Castello di Meleto, starting with the top job, which is now held by Roberto Stucchi Prinetti, an expert on the territory and its wines. The results of this year's tastings are not exactly exceptional but the entry into the finals of the Chianti Classico '06 Pieve di Spaltenna would suggest that the work done over recent years, especially replantings in the vineyard, is producing interesting results. The wine that made the taste-offs showed an intriguing nose, with faintly toasty notes, concentrated forest fruit and attractive balsamic hints. On the palate, it won us over with its sweetness combined with soft structure and a subdued finish. The rest of the wines still need to find balance, such as the Fiore '05, a blend of sangiovese and merlot that is rendered edgy by assertive tannins. The simpler wines are well made and flow nicely across the palate.

● San Pio '05	▼▼	5
● Brunello di Montalcino '03	▼	7
● Brunello di Montalcino '97	▼▼▼	7
● Brunello di Montalcino '90	▼▼▼	7
● Brunello di Montalcino Schiena d'Asino '93	▼▼▼	7
● Brunello di Montalcino Schiena d'Asino '90	▼▼▼	7
● Brunello di Montalcino '01	▽▽	7
● Brunello di Montalcino '00	▽▽	7
● Brunello di Montalcino V. Schiena d'Asino '01	▽▽	8
● Brunello di Montalcino V. Schiena d'Asino '99	▽▽	8

● Chianti Cl. Pieve di Spaltenna '06	▼▼	4*
● Chianti Cl. '06	▼	5
● Chianti Cl. Ris. '05	▼	6
● Fiore '05	▼	6
● Rosso Toscano '06	▼	3
● Sangiovese Merlot Pieve di Spaltenna '06	▼	3
● Chianti Cl. Ris. '03	▼▼▼	5
● Chianti Cl. Pieve di Spaltenna '04	▽▽	4
● Chianti Cl. Pieve di Spaltenna '02	▽▽	4
● Rainero '04	▽▽	7
● Rainero '03	▽▽	7

Melini

LOC. GAGGIANO
53036 POGGIBONSI [SI]
TEL. 0577998511
www.cantinemelini.it

ANNUAL PRODUCTION	5,000,000 bottles
HECTARES UNDER VINE	145
VITICULTURE METHOD	Conventional

The Melini winery, which was set up at Pontassieve in the late 19th century, owes its name to the dynasty which led it to success in the early 20th century when, thanks to young Laborel's idea of using glass flasks, the wine began to be win admirers all over the world. The estate is currently owned by the Italiano Vini Group. Despite a somewhat difficult vintage, especially for the beautiful Selvanella vineyard situated at an altitude which makes ripening more difficult in cooler years, the Chianti Classico La Selvanella Riserva '05 retains its character and impetus. In fact, it sailed into the finals and only failed to take home top honours because of the limitations of its vintage. The nose shows well-defined aromas of strawberry and redcurrant, with hints of minerals, leather and cocoa powder. On the palate, it is supple, elegant, and above all taut, thanks to forthright acidity. The tannins are still spiky but will soften with time. We liked both the Chianti San Lorenzo and the Chianti Classico Garanaio '06.

Le Miccine

S.S. TRAVERSA CHIANTIGIANA
53013 GAIOLE IN CHIANTI [SI]
TEL. 0577749526
www.lemiccine.com

ANNUAL PRODUCTION	18,000 bottles
HECTARES UNDER VINE	6.22
VITICULTURE METHOD	Conventional

They evidently like playing hide and seek at the winery of Clifford and Donna Meneghetti Weaver, seeing that they present wines for our tastings with a certain irregularity. This year the wines were convincing, although we have never really had any doubts about the production potential, not least because the staff is excellent, with Vittorio Fiore in charge of winemaking and Remigio Bordini in the vineyard. After 12 years of hard work, the wines are beginning to give good results. Let's start with the latest arrival, La Principessa '06, a sangiovese-based Supertuscan with appealing mineral notes on the nose, accompanied by hints of pencil lead and leather, which lead into a smooth, harmonious and well-balanced body with silky tannins and a satisfyingly long finish. We were also impressed by the Chianti Classico '06, which offers restrained aromas of violet, blackberry and hints of spice, with well-judged acidity underpinning a firm body and good development on the palate into an impressive finale. The other wines are generally well made but could do with greater aromatic clarity.

● Chianti Cl. La Selvanella Ris. '05	♥♥	6
● Chianti Cl. Granaio '06	♥	4
● Chianti San Lorenzo '07	♥	4
○ Vernaccia di S. Gimignano Le Grillaie '07	♥	4
● Chianti Cl. La Selvanella Ris. '03	♥♥♥	5
● Chianti Cl. La Selvanella Ris. '01	♥♥♥	5
● Chianti Cl. La Selvanella Ris. '00	♥♥♥	5
● Chianti Cl. La Selvanella Ris. '04	♥♥	7

● Chianti Cl. '06	♥♥	4*
● La Pricipessa '06	♥♥	6
● Chianti Cl. '05	♥	4
● Chianti Cl. Don Alberto Ris. '04	♥	5
● Chianti Cl. Don Alberto Ris. '02	♥♥	5
○ Vin Santo del Chianti Cl. La Gloria '00	♥♥	6

Il Molino di Grace

LOC. IL VOLANO LUCARELLI
50022 PANZANO [FI]
TEL. 0558561010
www.ilmolinodigrace.com

ANNUAL PRODUCTION 270,000 bottles
HECTARES UNDER VINE 45
VITICULTURE METHOD Conventional

The owner of this winery, Frank Grace, seems to be running some kind of relay race, since in the space of only a few years he has produced several different Three Glass wines. This time it was again the turn of Chianti Classico Riserva Il Margone '05, a selection of the best sangiovese grapes, to pick up the baton. Rounded and complex on the nose, it offers aromas ranging from fine clove and vanilla spice to sensations of blueberry and blackcurrant, with faint wafts of aromatic herbs. On the palate, it is complex, generous and incisive, with an attractive aftertaste and a lingering finish. The rest of the wines keep up the overall standard, despite not achieving the heights of excellence we had become accustomed to. This is also true of Gratius '06, a monovarietal Sangiovese vineyard selection, which showed less clarity on the nose and seemed a little tired on the palate, which has little of interest to offer. Things will undoubtedly improve in 2009, when the winery will also be celebrating its tenth birthday!

Castello di Monastero

LOC. MONASTERO D'OMBRONE, 19
53019 CASTELNUOVO BERARDENGA [SI]
TEL. 0577355789
www.castellodimonastero.com

ANNUAL PRODUCTION 250,000 bottles
HECTARES UNDER VINE 62
VITICULTURE METHOD Conventional

After a year's absence, the Guide welcomes back the winery of Lionello Marchesi, an entrepreneur who loves every aspect of viticulture, so much so that he has dedicated the last 30 years of his life to it. He started in Chianti Classico, where he bought an 11th-century monastery and created a fine winery, also providing tourist accommodation in a series of fine apartments, this year joined by a luxury country resort. Marchesi has made other purchases in Tuscany, in Montalcino and the Maremma, but his centre in Chianti is the most important. Alongside the Chianti Classico '05, which has a pleasing aromatic spectrum and intriguing weight, the best scores were earned by two whites, the Vin Santo '02 and the Chardonnay '06. The former has inebriating aromas of almond-like nuts and dried fruit, including figs and dates. On the palate, it is generous, unctuous and creamy, with a lingering finish. The Chardonnay is a more straightforward wine, showing flowers and fruit on the nose and then a supple, spirited structure leading to a satisfyingly long, savoury finish. The rest of the wines are well executed.

● Chianti Cl. Il Margone Ris. '05	♟♟♟	7
● Chianti Cl. '06	♟	5
● Chianti Cl. Ris. '05	♟	6
● Gratius '06	♟	7
● Le Falcole '06	♟	7
● Chianti Cl. Il Margone Ris. '04	♟♟♟	7
● Chianti Cl. Ris. '01	♟♟♟	5
● Gratius '04	♟♟♟	7
● Gratius '00	♟♟♟	7

O Chardonnay '06	♟♟	4*
● Chianti Cl. '05	♟♟	4*
O Vin Santo del Chianti Lunanuova '02	♟♟	7
● Chianti Cl. Ris. '04	♟	6
● Sangiovese '05	♟	3
● Infinito '03	♟♟	7
O Vin Santo del Chianti Lunanuova '99	♟♟	7

Castello di Monsanto

FRAZ. MONSANTO
VIA MONSANTO, 8
50021 BARBERINO VAL D'ELSA [FI]
TEL. 0558059000
www.castellodimonsanto.it

ANNUAL PRODUCTION	400,000 bottles
HECTARES UNDER VINE	72
VITICULTURE METHOD	Conventional

This year saw an improvement on last year's performance by the winery set up in 1962 by Fabrizio Bianchi, whose daughter Laura now also works with him. We feel that the results could improve further, knowing just how much attention is given to detail in the vineyard and at the winery. The wines are designed for long ageing and improve over time. The keynote is an elegant style, where priority is given to finesse rather than power. We were impressed by the Chardonnay Fabrizio Bianchi '06, whose unusual vegetal aromas are accompanied by notes of moss and distinct mineral hints. The palate is particularly savoury and juicy, revealing good length. The Riserva Il Poggio '04 di Chianti Classico confirmed its class, as you would expect from one of the first officially recognized vineyard selections in Chianti Classico. Fresh on the nose, with almost minty tones, cherry fruit and some cinnamon spice, it has good acidity on the palate, with well-proportioned tannins and satisfying weight. We liked the other products. They are perhaps a little clenched by their tannins on the palate but finish well.

Fattoria di Montecchio

FRAZ. SAN DONATO IN POGGIO
VIA MONTECCHIO, 4
50020 TAVARNELLE VAL DI PESA [FI]
TEL. 0558072235
www.fattoriamontecchio.it

ANNUAL PRODUCTION	113,000 bottles
HECTARES UNDER VINE	33
VITICULTURE METHOD	Conventional

After last year's return to the Guide by this winery with a long tradition in Chianti comes proof this year that it was not just a flash in the pan. The wines not only maintain their high standards but have actually improved. We were particularly pleased to see this pursuit of excellence, with more clearly defined aromas and greater overall balance beginning to show. Once again, the best wine turned out to be Pietracupa, a blend of sangiovese and cabernet sauvignon, whose '05 version shows aromatic notes themed to moss and tobacco that open into pepper and cinnamon spice. Entry on the palate is warm and harmonious, with a good balance of extract and alcohol. We noted significant improvement in La Papessa, a monovarietal Merlot, whose '05 vintage was smoother on the palate and nicely dense, refreshed by a prominent acid backbone. We loved the two characterful versions of Chianti Classico: the more austere and complex Riserva '05, and the smoother, fruity '05.

● Chianti Cl. Il Poggio Ris. '04	♟♟	7
○ Fabrizio Bianchi Chardonnay '06	♟♟	5
● Chianti Cl. '06	♟	5
● Chianti Cl. Ris. '05	♟	7
● Nemo '01	♟♟♟	7
● Chianti Cl. Ris. '01	♟♟	5
● Nemo '04	♟♟	7
● Nemo '00	♟♟	7

● Chianti Cl. '05	♟♟	4*
● Chianti Cl. Ris. '05	♟♟	5
● La Papessa '05	♟♟	6
● Pietracupa '05	♟♟	6
● Pietracupa '04	♟♟	6

Fattoria Montellori

VIA PISTOIESE, 5
50054 FUCECCHIO [FI]
TEL. 0571260641
www.fattoriamontellori.it

ANNUAL PRODUCTION	300,000 bottles
HECTARES UNDER VINE	40
VITICULTURE METHOD	Conventional

In the world of wine, tradition carries great weight, and Fattoria Montellori boasts a leading role as a champion of traditional winemaking in the province of Florence. The winery maintains a high standard of quality in its wines, as exemplified by Syrah Tuttosole '05, which made the national finals showing excellent complexity on the nose, characterized by hints of dark berry fruit over a background of spice and balsam. On the palate, it is full bodied and well balanced, showing tight-knit, already well-integrated tannins. We also enjoyed the Salamartano '05, from cabernet sauvignon and merlot, which offers an intense, well-orchestrated nose with vegetal aromas nicely rounded off by notes of spice. This is a powerful, well-rounded wine, with firm tannins and a long finish. We had no complaints about the Chianti Fattoria Le Caselle '07, which is fleshy, fruity and invigorating. The drinkable Mandorlo '07 is well balanced. The rest of the wines are well up to scratch, as always. It is also worth remembering that the consultant oenologist is Luca D'Attoma.

Montenidoli

LOC. MONTENIDOLI
53037 SAN GIMIGNANO [SI]
TEL. 0577941565
www.montenidoli.com

ANNUAL PRODUCTION	120,000 bottles
HECTARES UNDER VINE	25
VITICULTURE METHOD	Conventional

Elisabetta Fagiuoli has a golden rule: never betray the spirit of the land and respect its language. Faithful to this creed, year after year Elisabetta has become a champion of the difficult vernaccia variety, exploiting its potential in three different versions with a convincing style, all perfect examples of their type. Two of them made it to the finals: the excellent Vernaccia di San Gimignano Carato '04, elegant and intriguing on the nose, showing well-calibrated concentration that never holds back the suppleness of the long, expressive palate; and the sumptuous Vernaccia di San Gimignano Tradizionale '06, with its well-defined, lingering aftertaste. We also liked the Vernaccia di San Gimignano Fiore '06, which has a fine aromatic profile, prominent acid backbone and a full-flavoured, persistent finish. We greatly enjoyed Vin Brusco '05, from malvasia and trebbiano, a fine country white that weaves its seduction with silky body and good balance, offering racy, refreshing drinkability. Lastly, we were impressed by the Chianti dei Colli Senesi Il Garrulo '05, and the Chianti dei Colli Senesi '05, from sangiovese and canaiolo.

● Tuttosole '05	♈♈	6
● Chianti Fattoria Le Caselle '07	♈♈	3*
● Salamartano '05	♈♈	6
● Chianti '07	♈	3
○ Mandorlo '07	♈	3
○ Montellori Brut '04	♈	5
● Moro '06	♈	4
● Chianti Fattoria Le Caselle '06	♈♈	3*
● Dicatum '04	♈♈	6
● Dicatum '03	♈♈	5
● Dicatum '01	♈♈	6
○ Montellori Brut '01	♈♈	5
● Salamartano '04	♈♈	6
● Salamartano '03	♈♈	6
● Salamartano '01	♈♈	6

○ Vernaccia di S. Gimignano Carato '04	♈♈	6
○ Vernaccia di S. Gimignano Tradizionale '06	♈♈	4*
○ Vernaccia di S. Gimignano Fiore '06	♈♈	4
○ Vin Brusco '05	♈♈	4
● Chianti Colli Senesi '05	♈	4
● Chianti Colli Senesi Il Garrulo '05	♈	4
○ Vernaccia di S. Gimignano Carato '02	♈♈♈	6
○ Il Templare '03	♈♈	4
○ Il Templare '99	♈♈	4
● Sono Montenidoli '01	♈♈	5
○ Vernaccia di S. Gimignano Carato '03	♈♈	6
○ Vernaccia di S. Gimignano Carato '01	♈♈	5
○ Vernaccia di S. Gimignano Fiore '05	♈♈	4

★ Montevertine

LOC. MONTEVERTINE
53017 RADDA IN CHIANTI [SI]
TEL. 0577738009
www.montevertine.it

ANNUAL PRODUCTION	75,000 bottles
HECTARES UNDER VINE	15
VITICULTURE METHOD	Conventional

No Pergole Torte this year from the Manetti family winery, impeccably run by Martino, son of founder Sergio, in Radda in Chianti. The '05 was not considered a good enough vintage to produce this iconic wine. Unfortunately, there were no Three Glasses either, since Montevertine, also from '05, tripped at the final hurdle. Its personality and delicate yet vibrant character are all there but it failed to find the complexity that has made it a great wine in other years. The aromas are redolent of small berry fruit, flowers, Parma violets and rhubarb jam while on the palate, the wine retains its classic grace, delicate balance, and mouthwatering acidity. It just lacks a touch of presence, above all on the finish. The Pian del Ciampolo '06 is extremely well executed and has on its side a vintage with greater structure, from which this, the cellar's third wine, also benefits. The nose is well orchestrated, giving notes of flowers, strawberry and wild herbs that lead in to a fresh-flavoured and satisfyingly long palate. We can't wait for the release of the '06 wines, as we are sure they will be magnificent.

Moris Farms

LOC. CURA NUOVA
FATTORIA POGGETTI
58024 MASSA MARITTIMA [GR]
TEL. 0566918010
www.morisfarms.it

ANNUAL PRODUCTION	450,000 bottles
HECTARES UNDER VINE	70
VITICULTURE METHOD	Conventional

The winery run by Adolfo Parentini and his son Giulio is one of the most important in the Maremma. Without making a fuss, this Massa Marittima producer has always released wines of excellent quality, rightfully earning a reputation as one of the most reliable growers not just in Tuscany but anywhere. This explains why two of Adolfo's wines reached the finals, the Avvoltore '06, which earned Three Glasses, and the Morellino di Scansano Riserva '05. The former, a blend of sangiovese, cabernet sauvignon and syrah, shows clean-cut, ripe aromas and close-woven tannins, a touch too much toastiness, but great acidity that lends verve and dynamism. The Riserva proffers well-defined notes of ripe morello cherry on the nose leading to an appealing, lively palate. We also loved the new Scalabreto, a dried-grape dessert wine from sangiovese grapes, offering subtle aromas and a sweet palate with attractive contrast. The aromas of Morellino '07 seem muzzy but are offset for by fresh, feisty drinkability. We liked the Monteregio di Massa Marittima '06, which has slightly masked aromas but a tasty palate. The Vermentino '07 is simple and coherent.

● Montevertine '05	▼▼	6
● Pian del Ciampolo '06	▼▼	4*
● Le Pergole Torte '04	▼▼▼	8
● Le Pergole Torte '03	▼▼▼	8
● Le Pergole Torte '01	▼▼▼	8
● Le Pergole Torte '99	▼▼▼	8
● Le Pergole Torte '92	▼▼▼	8
● Le Pergole Torte '90	▼▼▼	8
● Le Pergole Torte '88	▼▼▼	8
● Le Pergole Torte '86	▼▼▼	8
● Le Pergole Torte '83	▼▼▼	8
● Montevertine '04	▼▼▼	6
● Montevertine '01	▼▼▼	6

● Avvoltore '06	▼▼▼	6
● Morellino di Scansano Ris. '05	▼▼	5
● Scalabreto '06	▼▼	5
● Monteregio di Massa Marittima Rosso '06	▼	4
● Morellino di Scansano '07	▼	4
○ Vermentino '07	▼	4
● Avvoltore '04	▼▼▼	6
● Avvoltore '01	▼▼▼	6
● Avvoltore '00	▼▼▼	6
● Avvoltore '99	▼▼▼	6
● Avvoltore '03	▼▼	6
● Avvoltore '98	▼▼	5
● Avvoltore '97	▼▼	5
● Avvoltore '95	▼▼	6
● Morellino di Scansano Ris. '01	▼▼	5
● Morellino di Scansano Ris. '00	▼▼	5
● Morellino di Scansano Ris. '99	▼▼	5

La Mormoraia

LOC. SANT'ANDREA, 15
53037 SAN GIMIGNANO [SI]
TEL. 0577940096
www.mormoraia.it

ANNUAL PRODUCTION **170,000 bottles**
HECTARES UNDER VINE **27**
VITICULTURE METHOD **Conventional**

Yet again, the wines from this beautiful winery, whose vineyards offer breathtaking views of San Gimignano, were quite superb. Pino and Franca Passoni, two Milanese with a passion for Tuscany, presented a range of superlative wines, whose high points were the red Mytilus '05 and Vernaccia Riserva '06. The former, from sangiovese, merlot and syrah grapes, cut a fine figure at the finals where it won friends with its attractive nose of cedar, black berry fruits and tobacco laced with iodine. On the palate, it is firm, with fresh, fleshy fruit and smooth tannins. Also in our finals was – not for the first time – the smooth, firmly structured Vernaccia Riserva '06, with its elegant, oaky tones. All it needs is a little more freshness. While the Vernaccia '07 struck us as undemanding, if crisp and enjoyable, the Ostrea Grigia '06, a blend of vernaccia and sauvignon, is richer and more complex, showing great freshness, subtle vegetality and a savoury, lingering palate. We loved the other reds. Chianti Colli Senesi '07 is one of the year's best, the San Gimignano Merlot '06 is soft and mouthfilling, and the meaty Sangiovese Neitea '06 has personality.

Niccolai - Palagetto

VIA MONTEOLIVETO, 46
53037 SAN GIMIGNANO [SI]
TEL. 0577943090
www.tenuteniccolai.it

ANNUAL PRODUCTION **350,000 bottles**
HECTARES UNDER VINE **100**
VITICULTURE METHOD **Conventional**

Palagetto is back with a worthy performance, not only achieving a good overall result but sending one of its wines to the finals. This is what we had been expecting from a winery whose great potential we had noted over the years. We particularly enjoyed the San Gimignano Syrah Uno di Quattro '05, with its intriguing aromatic profile of pepper and dark berry fruit, which shows dense and tight-knit on a palate bolstered by well-gauged tannins that thrust into a characterful finish. The Vernaccia di San Gimignano Riserva '05 also performed superbly, its intense nose showing spice well integrated with the flowers and fruit. The full-bodied, complex palate signs off with a lingering aftertaste. The Niccolò '07, from chardonnay, vermentino and sauvignon, has more body and a more balanced style than past editions. The Vernaccia Vigna Santa Chiara '07 is reliably good and presents good structure, lacking only a touch of freshness. We were also impressed with the mature, full-bodied San Gimignano Sottobosco '04, the tannic Chianti dei Colli Senesi '06 and the fresh Vernaccia '07.

● Mitylus '05	♟♟ 6
○ Vernaccia di S. Gimignano Ris. '06	♟♟ 5
● Chianti Colli Senesi '07	♟♟ 4*
● Neitea '06	♟♟ 5
○ Ostrea Grigia '06	♟♟ 4*
● San Gimignano Merlot '06	♟♟ 5
○ Vernaccia di S. Gimignano '07	♟ 4
○ Vernaccia di S. Gimignano Passoni '07	♟ 4
● Mitylus '01	♟♟ 6
● Neitea '05	♟♟ 5
○ Vernaccia di S. Gimignano Ris. '05	♟♟ 5*
○ Vernaccia di S. Gimignano Ris. '04	♟♟ 4

● San Gimignano Syrah Uno di Quattro '05	♟♟ 7
● Brunello di Montalcino La Bellarina '03	♟♟ 7
○ l'Niccolò '07	♟♟ 4
○ Vernaccia di S. Gimignano Ris. '05	♟♟ 4
● Chianti Colli Senesi '06	♟ 3
● Rosso di Montalcino '06	♟ 5
● San Gimignano Sottobosco '04	♟ 5
○ Vernaccia di S. Gimignano '07	♟ 3
○ Vernaccia di S. Gimignano V. Santa Chiara '07	♟ 4
○ l'Niccolò '05	♟♟ 5
● San Gimignano Sottobosco '03	♟♟ 5
● San Gimignano Uno di Quattro '03	♟♟ 8
○ Vernaccia di S. Gimignano Ris. '04	♟♟ 4
○ Vernaccia di S. Gimignano Ris. '02	♟♟ 4
○ Vernaccia di S. Gimignano V. Santa Chiara '06	♟♟ 4*
○ Vernaccia di S. Gimignano V. Santa Chiara '05	♟♟ 4

Fattoria Nittardi

LOC. NITTARDI
53011 CASTELLINA IN CHIANTI [SI]
TEL. 0577740269
www.chianticlassico.com

ANNUAL PRODUCTION	90,000 bottles
HECTARES UNDER VINE	27
VITICULTURE METHOD	Conventional

Once again, the wines of the Femfert Canali family impressed. Every year, they manage to produce excellent quality, consolidating an image that has been created in over a quarter of a century, seeing that they purchased the estate, whose past owners include Michelangelo, back in 1982. Over the years, the couple have worked in various fields – he as a publisher in Frankfurt, she as a historian of Venetian art – and they threw themselves into this completely new adventure with great enthusiasm, renovating farmhouses, replanting vineyards and building the new winery in 1994. Subsequently, they purchased their estate in Maremma. This year, we were only presented with Chianti Classico wines. The Riserva '05, fine ruby red in colour, impresses on the nose with its spicy aromas, alternating these with notes of ripe fruit and hints of chocolate. Entry on the palate is pervasive and mouthfilling, with perfectly orchestrated tannins. The finish is interesting and satisfyingly long. We also liked the drinkable Chianti Classico '06, with its penetrating, fresh aromas and warm, appealing palate.

★ Tenuta dell'Ornellaia

FRAZ. BOLGHERI
VIA BOLGHERESE, 191
57022 CASTAGNETO CARDUCCI [LI]
TEL. 056571811
www.ornellaia.it

ANNUAL PRODUCTION	730,000 bottles
HECTARES UNDER VINE	97
VITICULTURE METHOD	Conventional

The vintage was not one that allows every top wine to take home Three Glasses, which is what happened last year with the '04. But then again, this is Ornellaia, and even in the face of a difficult year, this is a winery that gives results. Top honours went to the Bolgheri Superiore Ornellaia '05, from 60 per cent cabernet sauvignon, topped up with merlot, cabernet franc and petit verdot. The nose of ripe fruit, with estery notes, hints of tobacco and hay, is followed up by close-knit structure on a palate whose tannins are still a shade over-assertive. This is a young wine that will continue to improve with age. The monovarietal Merlot, Masseto '05, failed to live up to expectations, with the wood masking the fruit both on the nose and on the palate. Above all, the tannins are mouth-drying. Obviously a wine like this, from a distinctly difficult vintage, will take a long time to unfold. The Bolgheri Rosso Serre Nuove and the Le Volte, both from the '06 vintage, are leaner and less pretentious but still show an over-lavish hand with the oak.

● Chianti Cl. Casanuova di Nittardi '06	♟♟ 5
● Chianti Cl. Ris. '05	♟♟ 7
● Chianti Cl. Ris. '98	♟♟♟ 7
● Chianti Cl. Casanuova di Nittardi '04	♟♟ 5
● Chianti Cl. Ris. '04	♟♟ 7
● Nectar Dei '05	♟♟ 7

● Bolgheri Sup. Ornellaia '05	♟♟♟ 8
● Masseto '05	♟♟ 8
● Bolgheri Rosso Serre Nuove '06	♟ 7
● Le Volte '06	♟ 4
● Bolgheri Sup. Ornellaia '04	♟♟♟ 8
● Bolgheri Sup. Ornellaia '02	♟♟♟ 8
● Bolgheri Sup. Ornellaia '01	♟♟♟ 8
● Bolgheri Sup. Ornellaia '99	♟♟♟ 8
● Masseto '04	♟♟♟ 8
● Masseto '01	♟♟♟ 8
● Masseto '00	♟♟♟ 8
● Masseto '99	♟♟♟ 8
● Masseto '98	♟♟♟ 8

Siro Pacenti

LOC. PELAGRILLI, 1
53024 MONTALCINO [SI]
TEL. 0577848662
pacentisiro@libero.it

ANNUAL PRODUCTION	80,000 bottles
HECTARES UNDER VINE	20
VITICULTURE METHOD	Conventional

Giancarlo Pacenti is one of the people who know most about the evolution of Brunello since the 1990s. We could justly call him an innovator of Brunello di Montalcino, especially regarding the use of barriques for vinification. He has always been concerned with understanding the interaction of terroir, grape and winemaking techniques. This has resulted in wines of considerable personality which have enjoyed success the world over. Every last detail has been studied, such as the decision to use vats to reduce to a minimum the impact of tannins from grape pips during vinification. The Brunello di Montalcino '03 displays a well-orchestrated, complex nose, even if the wood is still too evident and tends to smother the fruit. On the palate, the tannins are still are extremely tight-knit, and hamper progression, cutting short the finish with mouth-drying sensations. It's only a matter of time, since there is good background acidity here. This is a wine that demands patience. The same holds true for the Rosso di Montalcino '06, which is clenched by its tannins.

Podere Paganico

FRAZ. TORRENIERI
VIA EX CASSIA, 54
53028 MONTALCINO [SI]
TEL. 0577834606
www.poderepaganico.it

ANNUAL PRODUCTION	N.A.
HECTARES UNDER VINE	N.A.
VITICULTURE METHOD	Conventional

This small winery at Torrenieri has already proved the quality of its wines in recent editions, and this year, thanks to the excellent quality of the products presented, earns a full-length profile in the Guide. With only a few hectares in the DOCG zone, they managed to offer us an appealing Brunello di Montalcino that beautifully embodies the vintage and the terroir. On the nose, it shows complexity, with intense black cherry-led fruit nicely underpinned by light cinnamon and vanilla spice. The palate has not been affected by the hot growing year and flaunts well-honed tannins that are not overly mouth-drying, and give the wine a smoothness and drinkability that are hard to find in an '03. The wine also reflects the characteristics of the Torrenieri area, and is particularly elegant. The Rosso di Montalcino '05 clearly benefited from an extra year in the cellars and has emerged with a complex nose dominated by fruit while on the palate the acidity is offset by good alcohol.

● Brunello di Montalcino '03	♟♟	8
● Rosso di Montalcino '06	♟	6
● Brunello di Montalcino '97	♟♟♟	8
● Brunello di Montalcino '96	♟♟♟	8
● Brunello di Montalcino '95	♟♟♟	8
● Brunello di Montalcino '01	♟♟	8
● Brunello di Montalcino '00	♟♟	8
● Brunello di Montalcino '99	♟♟	8
● Brunello di Montalcino '98	♟♟	8

● Brunello di Montalcino '03	♟♟	7
● Rosso di Montalcino '05	♟♟	5
● Rosso di Montalcino '02	♟♟	4*

Il Palagione

VIA PER CASTEL SAN GIMIGNANO, 36
53037 SAN GIMIGNANO [SI]
TEL. 0577953134
www.ilpalagione.com

ANNUAL PRODUCTION	40,000 bottles
HECTARES UNDER VINE	10
VITICULTURE METHOD	Conventional

Il Palagione has won back the full profile its deserves. In recent years, results have been chequered partly because we tasted just after bottling and partly because of below-par vintages. This year, however, Giorgio Comotti's wines seem to have recovered their previous definition and character. On the nose, the Vernaccia Ori Riserva '05 presents intense fruit aromas and notes of ripe almond. Entry on the mouth is soft and fleshy, livened up by good acidic backbone that leads into a flavourful, almond-laced, persistent finish. The Vernaccia Hydra '07 foregrounds subtle hints of aromatic herbs and flint before the palate reveals the balance that is its strong suit as fruit and good acidity join forces to ensure suppleness and enjoyable easy drinking. The red Antajr '05, from sangiovese, merlot and cabernet sauvignon, has fine fruit and herb aromas, accompanied by a suggestion of oakiness. On the palate, it shows a coherent structure with attractive tannins and a pleasing, if somewhat short, finish. We liked the white Enif '07, from trebbiano and malvasia grapes, which has character, and the mature, savoury Chianti Colli Senesi Draco Riserva '05.

La Palazzetta

FRAZ. CASTELNUOVO DELL'ABATE
VIA BORGO DI SOTTO
53020 MONTALCINO [SI]
TEL. 0577835631
www.palazzettafanti.com

ANNUAL PRODUCTION	39,000 bottles
HECTARES UNDER VINE	12.8
VITICULTURE METHOD	Conventional

Flavio Fanti is always forthright and his sometimes vitriolic pronouncements often turn out to be close to the truth, which is why we like him. In his winery at Castelnuovo dell'Abate, Flavio and his wife produce wines that are just like him: a little rough, but extremely genuine and always expressive of the vintage. These are wines to be listened to and understood; often, they need to be waited for. The Brunello di Montalcino '03 is outstanding and helps us to understand what Flavio means when he says: "Summer 2003 should have been spent in the vineyard, not on the beach". It is mid ruby in colour and on the nose, in addition to the typical cherry in various guises, but always ripe, there comes through a touch of tobacco, accompanied by great definition and general crispness. Impressive on the palate, it gives evident alcohol that melds nicely with the upfront tannins. The extract may seem slightly edgy but it doesn't prevent the wine from unfolding into a long finish that signs off with a flourish of mellow tannins. The attractively rich Rosso di Montalcino '06 also performed well.

● Antajr '05	♟♟	6
O Vernaccia di S. Gimignano Hydra '07	♟♟	3*
O Vernaccia di S. Gimignano Ori Ris. '05	♟♟	5
● Chianti Colli Senesi Draco Ris. '05	♟	4
O Enif '07	♟	3
O Vernaccia di S. Gimignano Hydra '06	♟♟	3*
O Vernaccia di S. Gimignano Ori Ris. '04	♟♟	5

● Brunello di Montalcino '03	♟♟	7
● Rosso di Montalcino '06	♟♟	5
● Brunello di Montalcino Ris. '97	♟♟♟	8
● Brunello di Montalcino '01	♟♟	6
● Brunello di Montalcino '00	♟♟	6
● Brunello di Montalcino '99	♟♟	6
● Brunello di Montalcino Ris. '99	♟♟	7

Il Palazzone

LOC. DUE PORTE, 245
53024 MONTALCINO [SI]
TEL. 0577846142
www.ilpalazzone.com

ANNUAL PRODUCTION   **20,000 bottles**
HECTARES UNDER VINE   **3.8**
VITICULTURE METHOD   **Conventional**

The quality of these wines has improved considerably over the years, and specifically since Richard Parson bought the estate. The winery's principal, and by no means trifling, attribute is the ability to get the best out of every growing year without thereby creating standardized products that are all and always the same. For example, although 2003 was a complicated vintage with very dry, hot weather, Il Palazzone succeeded in producing a very pleasant Brunello di Montalcino that still reflects the features of the growing year in its aromas and polyphenolic ripeness. The colour is a nice ruby red with garnet hues while the nose needs a while to release its captivating balsamic hints and aromas of toasted almonds, plum jam, tobacco, leather and medicinal herbs. The palate is not bad despite very upfront alcohol and the gritty tannins typical of the year are softened in the very nicely assembled finish. The IGT wines were not yet bottled at the time of our tasting.

Castello della Paneretta

LOC. MONSANTO
S.DA DELLA PANERETTA, 35
50021 BARBERINO VAL D'ELSA [FI]
TEL. 0558059003
stefano.paneretta@tin.it

ANNUAL PRODUCTION   **120,000 bottles**
HECTARES UNDER VINE   **22.5**
VITICULTURE METHOD   **Conventional**

Fewer wines were presented by Castello di Paneretta than usual this year but the results are good enough to guarantee a full profile. The local area has always been very highly suited to wine – witness the 400-year-old castle – and its hallmark feature is ageing potential. These wines cannot really be described as accessible or immediately appealing since they need time to express themselves, hence the decision to prolong the ageing period for the Terrine '04. This blend of sangiovese and canaiolo has striking minerally, black berry fruit aromas and a powerful structure with firm tannins and plenty of freshness to make it beautifully drinkable. The Riserva Torre a Destra '05 delivers its aromas reluctantly, opening out at last into a varied array of prevalently fruity sensations. The palate is tangy and nicely lingering. The Chianti Classico '06 has a fresher nose than some of the others, with hints of aromatic herbs, but the length of the palate is held back by stiff tannins.

● Brunello di Montalcino '03	♟♟	7
● Brunello di Montalcino '01	♟♟♟	7
● Brunello di Montalcino Ris. '01	♟♟♟	7
● Brunello di Montalcino Ris. '99	♟♟♟	7
● Brunello di Montalcino '00	♟♟	7
● Brunello di Montalcino '99	♟♟	7
● Brunello di Montalcino Ris. '97	♟♟	8

● Chianti Cl. Torre a Destra Ris. '05	♟♟	5
● Terrine '04	♟♟	6
● Chianti Cl. '06	♟	4
● Chianti Cl. Torre a Destra Ris. '04	♟♟	5
● Terrine '03	♟♟	6
○ Vin Santo del Chianti Cl. '01	♟♟	6

Giovanni Panizzi

FRAZ. SANTA MARGHERITA
LOC. RACCIANO, 34
53037 SAN GIMIGNANO [SI]
TEL. 0577941576
www.panizzi.it

ANNUAL PRODUCTION	200,000 bottles
HECTARES UNDER VINE	30
VITICULTURE METHOD	Conventional

If we were to confer an honour on Giovanni Pannizzi, ambassador of Vernaccia would fit like a glove, given the expertise and authority with which he runs his winery and chairs the Consorzio della Vernaccia. Despite his achievements, he still has one preoccupation: that the potential of this terror has not yet achieved full expression. He thinks further work is needed. This year, the Vernaccia Riserva is absent from the range but there is a new label, Evoè 2006, a Vernaccia fermented and aged in wood. We didn't think this first version was a success but the vibrant Vernaccia di San Gimignano Vigna Santa Margherita '07 did well with shrewd use of wood. The oaky aromas are nicely blended with the fruit and the palate is flavoursome and dynamic with a crescendo finish. The Vernaccia di San Gimignano '07 is as dependable as ever, showing fresh, balanced and dynamic. The reds are also doing well, starting with the nicely structured Chianti dei Colli Senesi Vertunno Riserva '05, the juicy San Gimignano Rubente '05 and the compact San Gimignano Folgòre '03. The Ceraso '07 is extremely drinkable.

Il Paradiso

LOC. STRADA, 21A
53037 SAN GIMIGNANO [SI]
TEL. 0577941500
www.telematicaitalia.it/ilparadiso

ANNUAL PRODUCTION	150,000 bottles
HECTARES UNDER VINE	27.84
VITICULTURE METHOD	Conventional

It was an up-and-down performance this time from Poderi del Paradiso, although this has no impact on the esteem the winery's professionalism has earned over the years. In a break with tradition, none of the wines presented from the full range reached the final tastings. The most impressive were the Vernaccia Biscondola '06 and Sauvignon Saublà '07. The former shows good character, with a nicely coordinated, well-balanced and lightly minerally palate while the Sauvignon has a pleasantly varietal nose and an invigorating, fairly lingering, medium-bodied palate. The reds are below par, probably because '05 was less than favourable in many parts of Tuscany. The Merlot A Filippo '05 has tantalizing aromas and a nicely weighty palate though the finish is lacks depth. Mangiafoco '05, a monovarietal Cabernet Sauvignon, is warm, powerful and well structured but the finish is shortish. The Saxa Calida '05, made from cabernet sauvignon and merlot, is soft and well-rounded but stiff tannins prevent it from opening out further. Paterno II '04 is sweet and weighty with a stiff finish. The Chianti Colli Senesi '06 and Vernaccia '07 are as good as ever.

O Vernaccia di San Gimignano V. Santa Margherita '07	▼▼ 4*
● Ceraso '07	▼▼ 4*
● Chianti Colli Senesi Vertunno Ris. '05	▼▼ 4*
● S. Gimignano Rubente '05	▼▼ 6
● S. Gimignano Rosso Folgòre '03	▼ 6
O Vernaccia di S. Gimignano '07	▼ 4
O Vernaccia di S. Gimignano Ris. '98	▼▼▼ 6
O Bianco di Gianni '04	▼▼ 4
● S. Gimignano Rosso Folgòre '01	▼▼ 6
● S. Gimignano Rubente '04	▼▼ 6
O Vernaccia di S. Gimignano '06	▼▼ 4
O Vernaccia di S. Gimignano Ris. '03	▼▼ 6
O Vernaccia di S. Gimignano Ris. '02	▼▼ 5
O Vernaccia di San Gimignano V. Santa Margherita '06	▼▼ 4

● A Filippo '05	▼▼ 5
● Chianti Colli Senesi '06	▼▼ 2*
O Saublà '07	▼▼ 4
O Vernaccia di S. Gimignano Biscondola '06	▼▼ 4
● Mangiafoco '05	▼ 6
● Paterno II '04	▼ 6
● Saxa Calida '05	▼ 7
● Silicum '05	▼ 5
O Vernaccia di S. Gimignano '07	▼ 2
● A Filippo '02	▼▼▼ 5
● Saxa Calida '00	▼▼▼ 6
● Saxa Calida '99	▼▼▼ 5
● Mangiafoco '04	▼▼ 6
● Paterno II '99	▼▼ 6
● Saxa Calida '04	▼▼ 7
O Vernaccia di S. Gimignano Biscondola '05	▼▼ 4

Petra

LOC. SAN LORENZO ALTO, 131
57028 SUVERETO [LI]
TEL. 0565845308
www.petrawine.it

ANNUAL PRODUCTION   **250,000 bottles**
HECTARES UNDER VINE   **98**
VITICULTURE METHOD   **Conventional**

This estate, owned by the Moretti group and one of the leading wineries in the Suvereto area, put on a very satisfactory performance. The leading wine, Petra, was missing because '05 was not considered up to scratch but the Quercegobbe '05, a monovarietal Merlot, kept the flag flying and reached the finals. Terroir seems to be part of this wine's DNA. The nose is closed at first but opens out into grassy aromas blending with earth, leather and even gamy sensations. The very impressive palate is soft with well-controlled weight, smooth flavoursome tannins and a lingering finish. The Val di Cornia Ebo '05 has ripe fruit aromas and light vegetal hints, a fairly weighty palate and fluid, dynamic complexity right up to the pleasantly savoury finish. Zingari '06, a blend of sangiovese, merlot, syrah and petit verdot, has a nice fresh nose and enjoyable palate. The new arrival, L'Angelo di San Lorenzo, has an unusual, viscous mouthfeel. This sweet wine is a blend from three different years: '97, '99 and '00.

● Quercegobbe '05	▲▲	7
● Val di Cornia Ebo '05	▲▲	4
○ L'Angelo di San Lorenzo	▲	8
● Zingari '06	▲	4
● Petra Rosso '04	▲▲▲	8
● Petra Rosso '03	▲▲	8
● Petra Rosso '98	▲▲	6
● Petra Rosso '97	▲▲	5

Villa Petriolo

VIA DI PETRIOLO, 7
50050 CERRETO GUIDI [FI]
TEL. 057155284
www.villapetriolo.com

ANNUAL PRODUCTION   **55,500 bottles**
HECTARES UNDER VINE   **14**
VITICULTURE METHOD   **Conventional**

Silvia Maestrelli, who owns Villa Petriolo, has made her intentions clear from the beginning. She wants to make wines that can hold their own, and not just locally. The tastings provided us with a portrait of a winery on the way up so it is no surprise that another new wine has come along. L'Imbrunire '07, a monovarietal Canaiolo is a beautifully made wine with a delightful aroma, delicate structure and such a compelling flavour that you risk finishing the bottle without realizing it. The Chianti Rosae Mnemosis '07 is again a good wine, showing youthful and already full of character with fruity, floral and earthy aromas and exemplary complexity and balance on the palate, which finishes long and pleasantly fruity. The sangiovese, merlot and cabernet Golpaia '06 is making progress. Red berry aromas wrapped in spice precede the mouthwatering entry with nicely tucked in, flavoursome tannins and a good lingering finish. The Chianti '07 is freshly drinkable, as usual.

● Chianti Rosae Mnemosis '07	▲▲	5
● Golpaja '06	▲▲	5
● Chianti Villa Petriolo '07	▲	4
● L'Imbrunire '07	▲	5
● Chianti Rosae Mnemosis '06	▲▲	5
● Golpaja '05	▲▲	5
● Golpaja '04	▲▲	5
● Golpaja '03	▲▲	5
● Golpaja '01	▲▲	5
● Golpaja '00	▲▲	4
● Golpaja '99	▲▲	4
○ Vin Santo del Chianti '00	▲▲	5
○ Vin Santo del Chianti '98	▲▲	5

Fattoria di Petroio

LOC. QUERCEGROSSA
VIA DI MOCENNI, 7
53019 CASTELNUOVO BERARDENGA [SI]
TEL. 0577328045
www.fattoriapetroio.it

ANNUAL PRODUCTION	60,000 bottles
HECTARES UNDER VINE	12.8
VITICULTURE METHOD	Conventional

This very well-orchestrated performance doesn't quite fully express the potential of a winery that has in the past picked up Three Glasses. On the other hand, the Lenzis have always lavished loving care on this farm in one of the most favourable areas of Chianti Classico, showing they can produce richly characterful wines. We believe the next appointment with our highest accolade has simply been postponed. Let's start our look at the wines with the well-typed Chianti Classico Riserva '05, which presents an intense ruby red with a broad spectrum of aromas ranging from cherries to cinnamon against well-judged hints of tobacco. The dynamic entry on the palate ushers in firm body, fine-grained tannins and a juicy, relaxed finish. The Chianti Classico '06 is well made with fresh aromas on the nose and a supple body refreshed by bright acidity.

Fattoria Petrolo

FRAZ. MERCATALE VALDARNO
LOC. GALATRONA
VIA PETROLO, 30
52021 BUCINE [AR]
TEL. 0559911322
www.petrolo.it

ANNUAL PRODUCTION	55,000 bottles
HECTARES UNDER VINE	31
VITICULTURE METHOD	Conventional

Three Glasses for the Galatrona probably doesn't surprise anyone anymore but we imagine the Sanjust family will still be very pleased as they continue to reap the fruits of years of work focused on absolute, uncompromising quality. The '06 version of this monovarietal Merlot, which has found its ideal environment in the hills between Valdarno and Chianti, confirms the features that have made it one of the most famous and sought-after wines in Tuscany: very generous fruit, uncommon complexity and well-developed aromas with spicy, balsamic and floral hints. The winemaking style is measured, above all in the use of small oak barrels. The palate shows very good dense extract with generous fruit pulp and close-knit, clearly defined extract free of excessive weight or over-accessible softness, manages to maintain fresh acidity and a savoury minerality that closely reflects its terroir of origin. The Torrione '06, a Sangiovese in a modern style, is also excellent with sweet, dark, ripe fruit and a nicely complex palate that discloses confident tannin.

● Chianti Cl. Ris. '05	♈♈ 5
● Chianti Cl. '06	♈ 4
● Chianti Cl. Ris. '97	♈♈♈ 5
● Chianti Cl. Ris. '04	♈♈ 5
● Chianti Cl. Ris. '03	♈♈ 5
● Chianti Cl. Ris. '01	♈♈ 5
● Chianti Cl. Ris. '00	♈♈ 5
● Chianti Cl. Ris. '99	♈♈ 6

● Galatrona '06	♈♈♈ 8
● Torrione '06	♈♈ 5
● Galatrona '05	♈♈♈ 8
● Galatrona '04	♈♈♈ 7
● Galatrona '01	♈♈♈ 8
● Galatrona '00	♈♈♈ 8
● Galatrona '99	♈♈♈ 7
● Galatrona '98	♈♈♈ 7
● Galatrona '97	♈♈♈ 7
● Galatrona '03	♈♈ 8
● Galatrona '02	♈♈ 8

Piaggia

LOC. POGGETTO
VIA CEGOLI, 47
59016 POGGIO A CAIANO [PO]
TEL. 0558705401
aziendapiaggia@virgilio.it

ANNUAL PRODUCTION	65,000 bottles
HECTARES UNDER VINE	15
VITICULTURE METHOD	Conventional

Mauro Vannucci's winery confirms its status as one of the most solid and reliable in the Carmignano area, turning out products of unquestionably high quality. Despite the vintage, which was difficult to handle, the Carmignano Riserva '05 made it to the final tastings in a less concentrated and austere style than recent past versions. Nice, fresh, healthy fruit aromas on the nose precede well-adjusted structure with sustained, lingering development. The Carmignano Sasso '06 is initially reticent on the nose but opens out into ripe fruit and spices. The wine performs better on the weighty palate, where well-rounded fruit and close-knit, nicely formulated tannins lead to a long, fruity finish. The Poggio de' Colli put on an interesting performance with pleasantly grassy sensations on the nose and a soft palate, slightly ruffled by the very close-knit tannins which will smooth down with time.

Piancornello

LOC. PIANCORNELLO
53024 MONTALCINO [SI]
TEL. 0577844105
piancorello@libero.it

ANNUAL PRODUCTION	50,000 bottles
HECTARES UNDER VINE	10
VITICULTURE METHOD	Conventional

Claudio Monaci is a pleasant, calm person: a doctor who has been involved in the world of Brunello for years. He releases very characterful, very territory-dedicated wines from the deepest south-east corner of Montalcino. For the first time this year, there are two Brunello di Montalcinos: the classic '03 vintage and the Piancornello selection from the same year. Continual fermentation tests are carried out in the pursuit of greater expression of the terroir. Both wines are very interesting. The Brunello '03 delivers enviably fresh aromas with blackberry and cherry jam enhanced by hints of aromatic herbs. It's fresh on the palate too with mature, smooth tannins, a sign of good vineyard management in a complicated summer like 2003, and the finish is well developed and mouthfilling. The Piancornello selection shows more influence from the oak, more complex spice and tannins that need to be fully absorbed by a bit of bottle ageing. The wine has huge structure and unquestionably good potential. The Rosso di Montalcino '06 is enjoyable and juicy with just slightly piquant tannin.

● Carmignano Ris. '05	▼▼	6
● Carmignano Sasso '06	▼▼	5
● Poggio de' Colli '06	▼	7
● Carmignano Ris. '99	▼▼▼	6
● Carmignano Ris. '98	▼▼▼	6
● Carmignano Ris. '97	▼▼▼	5
● Il Sasso '01	▼▼▼	5
● Carmignano Ris. '03	▼▼	6
● Carmignano Ris. '02	▼▼	6
● Carmignano Ris. '01	▼▼	6
● Carmignano Ris. '00	▼▼	6
● Il Sasso '03	▼▼	5
● Il Sasso '00	▼▼	5
● Poggio de' Colli '05	▼▼	7
● Poggio de' Colli '04	▼▼	8

● Brunello di Montalcino '03	▼▼	7
● Brunello di Montalcino Piancornello '03	▼▼	7
● Rosso di Montalcino '06	▼	4
● Brunello di Montalcino '99	▼▼▼	7
● Brunello di Montalcino '01	▼▼	7
● Brunello di Montalcino '00	▼▼	7

Piazzano

VIA DI PIAZZANO, 5
50053 EMPOLI [FI]
TEL. 0571994032
www.fattoriadipiazzano.it

ANNUAL PRODUCTION	60,000 bottles
HECTARES UNDER VINE	34
VITICULTURE METHOD	Conventional

The Bettarini brothers have been
frenetically busy. They've reorganized
the cellar, made over the vineyards and
implemented new production strategies
to improve the range. After all this work,
our tastings highlighted the fact that each
of the wines has its own, successfully
expressed features, although we expect
even more ambitious results in the future
from a go-ahead winery like this. This year,
the Sangiovese '06 proffers well-rounded,
varied aromas of spices and red berries.
It performs better on the palate, though,
with good structure and a nice profound
acidic edge. The Syrah '06 is good,
giving inky colour and vibrant aromas of
pepper and red berries on the nose before
the enjoyably textured, well-developed
palate shows good finesse and close-
knit but smooth tannins pushing ahead
to a piquant, lingering finish. The Merlot
'06 is ruffled by excessive oak and the
palate is flavoursome but stiff and lacking
in harmony. The Chianti and Chianti Rio
Camerata, both from '07, are enjoyable
while the Ventoso '07, a blend of 70 per
cent sangiovese, 20 per cent canaiolo
and the rest malvasia and trebbiano, is
approachable and uncomplicated.

Il Pinino

LOC. PODERE PININO, 327
53024 MONTALCINO [SI]
TEL. 0577849381
www.pinino.com

ANNUAL PRODUCTION	95,000 bottles
HECTARES UNDER VINE	13
VITICULTURE METHOD	Conventional

Max Hernandez, the only Spanish producer
of Brunello di Montalcino, is gaining
confidence. His love for this wine has
led him to make huge investments in the
estate which is now equipped with its own,
albeit quite small, cellar. Perhaps it was
the lack of storage space that determined
the – in our view, premature – release of
the Rosso di Montalcino Clandestino '06,
which improves tangibly after a year in
bottle. In the cellar are mainly 30-hectolitre
barrels as well as a multitude of barriques
for the aforementioned Rosso. Max only
bottles DOCG wines from his 13 hectares.
The Rosso di Montalcino '06 is very well
typed and one of the best from that year,
giving vibrant, well-defined aromas of
blackberries, morello cherries and flowers,
and a well-rounded palate supported by
lovely acidity for an enjoyable development.
The tannin is sweet and well modulated
and the finish reflects the nose nicely. The
Clandestino selection is flawed, as we said,
by its youth, with slightly clenched tannin
and a nose dominated by peach fruit and
hints of eucalyptus. We'll just have to wait.
The Brunello di Montalcino '03 also has
rather mouth-drying extract.

● Piazzano Sangiovese '06	▼▼	5
● Piazzano Syrah '06	▼▼	5
● Chianti '07	▼	3
● Chianti Rio Camerata '07	▼	4
● Merlot '06	▼	5
● Ventoso '07	▼	3
● Chianti Rio Camerata Ris. '04	♀♀	5
● Piazzano Sangiovese '05	♀♀	5
● Piazzano Sangiovese '04	♀♀	6
● Piazzano Syrah '05	♀♀	5
● Piazzano Syrah '04	♀♀	5

● Rosso di Montalcino '06	▼▼	4
● Brunello di Montalcino '03	▼	6
● Rosso di Montalcino Clandestino '06	▼	5
● Brunello di Montalcino '02	♀♀	7
● Brunello di Montalcino '01	♀♀	7

La Poderina

FRAZ. CASTELNUOVO DELL'ABATE
LOC. PODERINA
53020 MONTALCINO [SI]
TEL. 0577835737
www.saiagricola.it

ANNUAL PRODUCTION	100,000 bottles
HECTARES UNDER VINE	23
VITICULTURE METHOD	Conventional

Last year, we did not publish La Poderina's profile because of a technical hitch. The table below therefore includes the scores obtained by the wines tasted last time. The Moscadello di Montalcino is on top form as ever, and the '06 version confirms it as a local benchmark for this type. Intense straw yellow in colour, it unveils spring flowers and peach and apricot fruit on the nose, and an excellent flavour with beautifully balanced sweetness and acidity for a captivating, never cloying palate. The nose is reflected nicely in the buttery, mouthfilling finish. The Brunello di Montalcino Poggio Banale '01 is also very good, offering an intense ruby red colour and a complex nose with good balance of red berry fruit and spicier, oak-derived sensations. The palate shows good personality thanks to the tannins which fuse beautifully with the texture, culminating in a lingering, well-rounded finish. The Rosso di Montalcino '06 is also impressive, its fruity nose giving classic cherries up front and an extremely appealing palate thanks to good mellow tannins. The Brunello di Montalcino '03 is well made and confidently balanced.

Poggerino

LOC. POGGERINO
53017 RADDA IN CHIANTI [SI]
TEL. 0577738958
www.poggerino.com

ANNUAL PRODUCTION	60,000 bottles
HECTARES UNDER VINE	10
VITICULTURE METHOD	Conventional

Once again, one of the Lanza family's wines made the final tastings, a clear sign that Piero's maniacal care in the vineyard and cellar always yields satisfying results. A successful division of labour has created a team that functions well and brings out the best in each aspect of business. Piero works in the vineyard and cellar while his sister looks after guests in the holiday accommodation. This year, the Chianti Classico Bugialla Riserva '04 made the final tastings with its vibrant fruity aromas, hints of aromatic herbs and pencil lead, and a broad, solid entry on the plate with subtle tannins spreading into a nice, juicy, well-developed finish. There was a good result also for Primamateria '04, a blend of sangiovese and merlot in variable quantities according to the year. The nose is sweet and appealing with hints of chocolate, aromatic tobacco and cinnamon and the nicely rounded palate, supported by considerable acidity, leads into a fruity finish. The Chianti Classico '05 is well typed and nicely structured.

○ Moscadello di Montalcino V. T. '06	▼▼	6
● Brunello di Montalcino '03	▼▼	7
● Rosso di Montalcino '06	▼▼	5
● Brunello di Montalcino '01	♙♙	7
● Brunello di Montalcino '00	♙♙	7
● Brunello di Montalcino Poggio Banale '01	♙♙	8
○ Moscadello di Montalcino V. T. '05	♙♙	6
● Rosso di Montalcino '05	♙♙	5

● Chianti Cl. Bugialla Ris. '04	▼▼	6
● Primamateria '04	▼▼	6
● Chianti Cl. '05	▼	4
● Primamateria '01	♙♙♙	6
● Chianti Cl. '04	♙♙	4
● Chianti Cl. Bugialla Ris. '99	♙♙	6

Poggio al Tesoro

LOC. FELCIAINO
VIA BOLGHERESE, 189B
57020 BOLGHERI [LI]
TEL. 0565765245
info@poggioaltesoro.it

ANNUAL PRODUCTION 80,000 bottles
HECTARES UNDER VINE 40
VITICULTURE METHOD Conventional

After a few appearances in the Other Wineries section of the Guide, it's a full profile at last for this winery, which is the result of a partnership between the Allegrini family, producers of great wines in Valpolicella, and American wine distributor Leonardo Lo Cascio. This conquest comes thanks to a very high-quality range of wines, demonstrating that the gears are turning in the right direction, and from a winery like this we can only expect success. The two leading wines from '05, Dedicato a Walter and Sondraia, are both very impressive. The former, a monovarietal Cabernet Franc, has mainly black berry fruit on the nose with unobtrusive oaky hints, and a mouthfilling, densely textured palate that still has to open out fully but shows unquestionable potential. The oaky aromas are still prominent in the Sondraia, a blend of mainly cabernet sauvignon with merlot and cabernet franc, but the palate is markedly and enjoyably characterful. The Bolgheri Bianco Solosole '07 is very good, showing juicy, lingering and crisp with a subtle, floral nose. The Mediterra '06 has rather mouth-drying, intrusive tannin.

O Bolgheri Bianco Solosole '07	TT	5
● Dedicato a Walter '05	TT	6
● Sondraia '05	TT	6
● Mediterra '06	T	5
● Dedicato a Walter '04	YY	6
● Sondraia '04	YY	6
● Sondraia '03	YY	6

Poggio Antico

LOC. POGGIO ANTICO
53024 MONTALCINO [SI]
TEL. 0577848044
www.poggioantico.com

ANNUAL PRODUCTION 120,000 bottles
HECTARES UNDER VINE 32.50
VITICULTURE METHOD Natural

This is a beautiful winery, starting from the long cypress-lined avenue that guides visitors from the main Grosseto road to the heart of the estate. The cellars are all underground and heat-controlled, creating an ideal environment for storing the wines as they age. Paola Gloder, who hails from Milan, is at the helm. Both the Brunello di Montalcinos from '03 were presented: the Altero, aged in 500 and 750 litre oak barrels, and the vintage version which prefers traditional 30 to 50-hectolitre barrels. This year, the Altero gave the more distinctive performance, thanks to better defined aromas of ripe cherries and currants while the well-balanced flavour reduces the tannin to the right level. Madre, from the cool growing year of 2005, is also good. From sangiovese with a small percentage of cabernet sauvignon, it has deep, bright ruby red colour and blackberries and blueberries on the nose. The tannin holding back the finish needs time to be absorbed.

● Brunello di Montalcino Altero '03	TT	7
● Madre '05	TT	6
● Brunello di Montalcino '03	T	7
● Rosso di Montalcino '06	T	5
● Brunello di Montalcino Altero '99	YYY	7
● Brunello di Montalcino Ris. '01	YYY	8
● Brunello di Montalcino '01	YY	7
● Brunello di Montalcino '00	YY	7
● Brunello di Montalcino '99	YY	7
● Brunello di Montalcino Altero '01	YY	7
● Brunello di Montalcino Ris. '00	YY	7
● Brunello di Montalcino Ris. '99	YY	7

Poggio Argentiera

S.DA BANDITELLA DELL'ALBERESE, 2
58010 GROSSETO
TEL. 0564405099
www.poggioargentiera.com

ANNUAL PRODUCTION	200,000 bottles
HECTARES UNDER VINE	30
VITICULTURE METHOD	Conventional

Giampaolo Paglia's well-stocked range of wines represents one of the best and most continuous examples of quality in Maremma winemaking. These are vibrant, enjoyably well-made wines which are unlikely to leave enthusiasts, and the many admirers of this Banditella dell'Alberese winery, unmoved. As regularly happens, the Morellino di Scansano Capotosta '06 stands out confidently with beautiful ripe fruit aromas and a juicy, profound palate with a strong contrast enhanced by confident tangy sensations in the finish. The Finisterre '06, made from alicante and syrah, is very young. Its aromas are still concentrated and show particularly marked balsamic sensations. The dense, weighty palate unfolds with nice dynamic energy to a flavoursome, almost piquant finish. Distinctive warm, vibrant fruit is delivered on the nose of the Morellino di Scansano Bellamarsilia '07, while the flavour is sweet, rounded and supple. The Maremmante '07, made from syrah and alicante, is very drinkable. The '07 whites Fonte_40, from chardonnay and fiano, and the ansonica and vermentino Guazza, are uncomplicated and approachable.

Poggio Bonelli

LOC. POGGIO BONELLI
53019 CASTELNUOVO BERARDENGA [SI]
TEL. 0577355382
www.poggiobonelli.it

ANNUAL PRODUCTION	230,000 bottles
HECTARES UNDER VINE	85
VITICULTURE METHOD	Natural

This estate, owned by the Monte dei Paschi di Siena bank, hit the target again, this time with the Poggiassai '06. A Supertuscan, based on sangiovese and cabernet sauvignon, it earned Three Glasses thanks to a varied array of vibrant aromas of cinnamon and cloves blended with cherries and blackberries in the background; well-balanced body, tannins nicely fused with the other components, and a long, enthralling finish. These wines are becoming increasingly land-rooted and leaving behind that distinctive international style of the early production years. The Chianti Classico Riserva '05 confirms its quality with ripe fruit jam counterpointed by tertiary aromas of animal skins and tobacco. The palate is flavoursome with firm tannins, and nicely dynamic especially in the finish. Only the Tramonto d'Oca '05, a blend of sangiovese and merlot, fell short of our expectations as it is too slender and simple. The other wines are all flavoursome and enjoyable.

● Morellino di Scansano Capatosta '06	♔♔ 6
● Finisterre '06	♔♔ 7
● Maremmante '07	♔♔ 4*
● Morellino di Scansano Bellamarsilia '07	♔♔ 4*
O Fonte_40 '07	♔ 4
O Guazza '07	♔ 3
● Morellino di Scansano Capatosta '00	♔♔♔ 6*
● Finisterre '05	♔♔ 7
● Finisterre '03	♔♔ 7
● Finisterre '02	♔♔ 7
● Finisterre '01	♔♔ 7
● Morellino di Scansano Capatosta '05	♔♔ 6
● Morellino di Scansano Capatosta '04	♔♔ 6
● Morellino di Scansano Capatosta '03	♔♔ 6
● Morellino di Scansano Capatosta '02	♔♔ 6
● Morellino di Scansano Capatosta '01	♔♔ 6

● Poggiassai '06	♔♔♔ 6
● Chianti Cl. Ris. '05	♔♔ 6
● Chianti Villa Chigi Saracini '07	♔ 3
● Tramonto d'Oca '05	♔ 6
● Chianti Cl. Ris. '01	♔♔ 6
● Poggiassai '05	♔♔ 6
● Tramonto d'Oca '04	♔♔ 6
● Tramonto d'Oca '03	♔♔ 6

Poggio di Sotto

FRAZ. CASTELNUOVO DELL'ABATE
LOC. POGGIO DI SOTTO
53024 MONTALCINO [SI]
TEL. 0577835502
www.poggiodisotto.com

ANNUAL PRODUCTION	40,000 bottles
HECTARES UNDER VINE	12
VITICULTURE METHOD	Certified organic

You couldn't call Piero Palmucci easy to get on with but he is dedicated to his winery and, above all, Brunello di Montalcino. Piero's clear ideas on terroir, and determination to respect the vintage years as they are, entail difficult decisions and deserve the respect of the wine sector. In the Castelnuovo dell'Abate area, the 2003 vintage, already troublesome because of very high temperatures, was rendered even more tricky by the lack of rain. Palmucci was forced to reduce production drastically in order to maintain high quality in the wines. The Brunello di Montalcino '03 is in effect a good wine in the true winery style: ruby red colour, not excessively dense; candied orange peel, tobacco and medicinal herbs on the nose; and a heady, nicely concentrated flavour with slightly harsh tannin hemming in on the finish. The Rosso di Montalcino '05 is also very well-made, and from a completely different vintage year, when Piero managed to keep up an interesting vein of fruit with hints of cherries and tobacco and a sprinkling of spice. The attractive flavour is very moreish thanks to up-front acidity that also guarantees ageing potential.

Poggio Molina

LOC. POGGIO MOLINA
52021 BUCINE [AR]
TEL. 0559789402
www.poggiomolina.it

ANNUAL PRODUCTION	60,000 bottles
HECTARES UNDER VINE	16
VITICULTURE METHOD	Conventional

Not only did Poggio Molina substantiate the good performances achieved in recent years, it came close to hitting the jackpot with its leading wine, Le Caldie, which made it into the national finals. This is a very satisfying result for Claudio and Alba Bossini, who only started making wine, something they do with enthusiasm, a few years ago. The impressive Le Caldie '05 is a blend of merlot, cabernet and sangiovese in a modern style with dark, compressed aromas, fruit marmalade featuring alongside fresher balsamic hints. The palate has fine quality, close-knit tannins and a nicely modulated, mouthfilling progression. Tasty echoes of fruit on the palate lead to a finish stiffened by slightly bitterish sensations. Lo Scopaio '05, made from sangiovese, cabernet franc and merlot, is very similar in quality and style, showing warm, ripe and chocolate-like on the nose with floral, spicy hints to lighten the impact before the soft, vibrant palate reveals its savouriness and depth.

● Brunello di Montalcino '03	▼▼ 8
● Rosso di Montalcino '05	▼▼ 7
● Brunello di Montalcino '99	▼▼▼ 8
● Brunello di Montalcino Ris. '99	▼▼▼ 8
● Brunello di Montalcino Ris. '95	▼▼▼ 8
● Brunello di Montalcino '01	▼▼ 8
● Brunello di Montalcino '00	▼▼ 8

● Le Caldie '05	▼▼ 6
● Lo Scopaio '05	▼▼ 5
● Vinobono '06	▼ 4
● Le Caldie '04	▼▼ 6
● Le Caldie '03	▼▼ 6
● Le Caldie '02	▼▼ 6
● Le Caldie '01	▼▼ 6

Podere Poggio Scalette

LOC. RUFFOLI
VIA BARBIANO, 7
50022 GREVE IN CHIANTI [FI]
TEL. 0558546108
www.poggioscalette.it

ANNUAL PRODUCTION   35,000 bottles
HECTARES UNDER VINE   15
VITICULTURE METHOD   Natural

It's getting harder to find new adjectives to describe the Fiore family's work on their estate at Greve. The wines are of a high standard every year, and faithfully reflect the local area. Our Three Glasses went to the Carbonaione '05 as the natural consequence of good work in the vineyard and in the cellar. Vittorio's enthusiasm drives him to carry out his work in the cellar with scrupulous care while his son Jurij engages in a constant, meticulous pursuit of perfection in the vineyards. This combination of father and son, potentially highly explosive on paper, actually yields positive results. The prizewinning wine foregrounds elegance, with well-controlled aromas balancing fruit, spices and minerally hints on the nose, and a fresh, appetizing, nicely balanced palate culminating in a nicely open finish with well-judged weight. Piantonaia '05 is a very interesting monovarietal Merlot that reflects the terroir much more than the grape variety. As a result, the extract is much more prominent than we might have expected. There's pencil lead on the nose and the well-judged palate has good acidity.

Il Poggiolo

LOC. POGGIOLO, 259
53024 MONTALCINO [SI]
TEL. 0577848412
www.ilpoggiolomontalcino.com

ANNUAL PRODUCTION   40,000 bottles
HECTARES UNDER VINE   7
VITICULTURE METHOD   Conventional

As usual, there were plenty of wines on show at this long-established Montalcino estate, each one distinct and different from the last. It gives an insight into why the fiery Rudy Cosimi produces three Brunellos and two Rosso di Montalcinos. Very impressive among the new arrivals is the Rosso di Montalcino Quello Buono, which is as good as its name – "the good stuff" – suggests and is the best of its type this year. Intense ruby red in colour, it delivers generous, clean, vibrant aromas of typical sour cherry and blackberries enhanced with stylish spicy cinnamon and vanilla. The compelling velvety palate winks at Brunello with sweet, mellow tannin and nice acidity supporting the finish in a modern, elegant style. Of the '03 Brunello di Montalcinos, the Beato selection stood out for improved resolution of acidity and tannin on the palate, although the nose is less impressive than previous years. The herbs and leather are already there but the fruit component struggles to find full expression. The other selection, Terra Rossa, opens out nicely although the finish is slightly clenched. The standard version has rather evolved aromas.

● Il Carbonaione '05	♟♟♟ 7
● Piantonaia '05	♟♟ 8
● Il Carbonaione '03	♟♟♟ 8
● Il Carbonaione '00	♟♟♟ 8
● Il Carbonaione '98	♟♟♟ 8
● Il Carbonaione '96	♟♟♟ 8
● Piantonaia '04	♟♟ 8
● Piantonaia '03	♟♟ 8

● Brunello di Montalcino Beato '03	♟♟ 8
● Rosso di Montalcino Quello Buono '06	♟♟ 4
● Brunello di Montalcino '03	♟ 7
● Brunello di Montalcino Terra Rossa '03	♟ 7
● Rosso di Montalcino '06	♟ 5
● Brunello di Montalcino Terra Rossa '01	♟♟♟ 7
● Brunello di Montalcino Beato '01	♟♟ 8
● Brunello di Montalcino Poggiolo '01	♟♟ 7
● Brunello di Montalcino Poggiolo Ris. '97	♟♟ 8
● Brunello di Montalcino Terra Rossa '97	♟♟ 7

Tenuta Il Poggione

FRAZ. SANT'ANGELO IN COLLE
LOC. MONTEANO
53024 MONTALCINO [SI]
TEL. 0577844029
www.tenutailpoggione.it

ANNUAL PRODUCTION	500,000 bottles
HECTARES UNDER VINE	118
VITICULTURE METHOD	Conventional

We welcome the very good performance from this classic Montalcino winery, owned by the Franceschi family and impeccably managed by Fabrizio Bindocci, who has dedicated a large part of his life to the estate. The beautiful new buildings with adjacent oil press have helped raise quality, thanks above all to improved storage facilities. The Brunello di Montalcino '03 is excellent and shows no ill effects from that very hot year. This is due to the age of some of the older vineyards which suffered less from the drought, and these very vineyards gave birth to one of the best Brunellos of that torrid year. It is classic in style, as always at Il Poggione, with intense ruby red colour and a broad, clean nose delivering fruity morello and black cherries with light floral hints. The palate is remarkably fresh thanks to good acidity and mature, mellow tannins that enable the wine to spread elegantly over the palate into a beautifully lingering, generous finish. The Il Poggione '06 is a nicely put together blend of 70 per cent sangiovese and merlot available at an interesting price. The Rosso di Montalcino '06 has rather excessively mouth-drying tannin.

Fattoria Poggiopiano

VIA DI PISIGNANO, 28/30
50026 SAN CASCIANO IN VAL DI PESA [FI]
TEL. 0558229629
www.fattoriapoggiopiano.it

ANNUAL PRODUCTION	100,000 bottles
HECTARES UNDER VINE	9
VITICULTURE METHOD	Conventional

Once again Rosso di Sera, a blend of sangiovese and colorino, made it to the finals in the 2006 version, so no surprises there. But there is something new in the form of the Bartoli family's newest wine, Chianti Classico La Tradizione '05, whose name gives away the theory behind the project. The finalist shows nice bright ruby red with vegetal and floral aromas on the nose alongside minerally and fresh fruit hints. Tight-knit tannins on the palate accompany solid body and nicely dynamic flavour. The new wine delivers old-style aromas with hints of cherries and plums laced with a touch of oak. The palate is broad, mouthwatering and appetizing, thanks to sound acidity. The other wines are all nicely put together, fresh and enjoyable. It is worth noting that the estate's other products include, alongside the classic extra virgin olive oil, grappa and poultry with the black Valdarno hen, the breed that appears on the Consorzio del Chianti Classico logo.

● Brunello di Montalcino '03	♟♟	7
● Il Poggione '06	♟♟	4*
● Rosso di Montalcino '06	♟	4
● Brunello di Montalcino Ris. '97	♟♟♟	8
● Brunello di Montalcino '02	♟♟	6
● Brunello di Montalcino '99	♟♟	6
● Brunello di Montalcino '97	♟♟	6

● Rosso di Sera '06	♟	7
● Chianti Cl. La Tradizione '05	♟♟	5
● Chianti Cl. '06	♟	4
● M'ama non m'ama '07	♟	4
● Rosso di Sera '04	♟♟♟	7
● Rosso di Sera '03	♟♟♟	7
● Rosso di Sera '99	♟♟♟	6
● Rosso di Sera '98	♟♟♟	6
● Rosso di Sera '97	♟♟♟	5

★★ Poliziano

LOC. MONTEPULCIANO STAZIONE
VIA FONTAGO, 1
53045 MONTEPULCIANO [SI]
TEL. 0578738171
www.carlettipoliziano.com

ANNUAL PRODUCTION	600,000 bottles
HECTARES UNDER VINE	140
VITICULTURE METHOD	Conventional

Three Glasses arrived for Poliziano this year with their usual implacable regularity. Hardly a surprise, given the unanimous approval of this estate by consumers in Italy and beyond, for its disarmingly consistent quality which never seems to suffer from dips, hiccups or poorly interpreted vintage years. But this umpteenth award will undoubtedly have a different flavour for Federico Carletti as it brings the total of Three Glasses to 20, which means two Stars and entry into the elite of Italian winemaking. Top of the class as usual is the Nobile di Montepulciano Asinone '05 but average quality throughout the range is striking. Le Stanze '06, a blend of cabernet sauvignon and merlot, and Mandrone di Lhosa '06, from cabernet sauvignon, alicante, petit verdot and carignano, also made it through to the finals. The Vin Santo di Montepulciano '95 is delicious, though the winery hasn't produced this type of wine since the early 1990s. The Nobile '05 and Cortona Merlot In Violas '06 are both impressive while the Rosso di Montepulciano and the Morellino di Scansano, both '07, are reliably good.

Castello di Poppiano

FRAZ. POPPIANO
VIA DI FEZZANA, 45
50025 MONTESPERTOLI [FI]
TEL. 05582315
www.conteguicciardini.it

ANNUAL PRODUCTION	600,000 bottles
HECTARES UNDER VINE	130
VITICULTURE METHOD	Conventional

The variety of wines presented for tasting by Count Ferdinando Guicciardini is really remarkable. Credit for the excellent overall performance also goes to the Maremma estate, purchased long before the local boom, which today produces very good quality wines. One of the cellar's secrets is the shared capacity of Ferdinando and his wife Titti, who supervises the various production phases, to keep all their colleagues involved. The Maremma selections and wines are very impressive, showing a distinctive minerally sensation alongside rich, concentrated and pleasant vibrant fruit. The Castello products, in contrast, are all excellent value for money although the traditional wines were in subdued form. The Syrah '06 stands out for its spicy, captivating nose and nice weighty palate with a fresh vein of acidity. The Toscoforte '06, made mainly from sangiovese, is very enjoyable and well made with fresh, appetizing aromas and a rounded, mouthwatering flavour.

● Nobile di Montepulciano Asinone '05	♥♥♥ 7
● Le Stanze '06	♥♥ 8
● Mandrone di Lohsa '06	♥♥ 6
● Cortona Merlot In Violas '06	♥♥ 6
● Nobile di Montepulciano '05	♥♥ 5
○ Vin Santo di Montepulciano '95	♥♥ 7
● Morellino di Scansano '07	♥ 4
● Rosso di Montepulciano '07	♥ 4
● Le Stanze '00	♥♥♥ 7
● Nobile di Montepulciano Asinone '04	♥♥♥ 7
● Nobile di Montepulciano Asinone '03	♥♥♥ 7
● Nobile di Montepulciano Asinone '01	♥♥♥ 7
● Nobile di Montepulciano Asinone '00	♥♥♥ 7
● Nobile di Montepulciano Asinone '99	♥♥♥ 6
● Nobile di Montepulciano Asinone '98	♥♥♥ 6
● Nobile di Montepulciano Asinone '97	♥♥♥ 6

● Colpetroso Massi di Mandorlaia '05	♥♥ 5
● Morellino di Scansano Massi di Mandorlaia '06	♥♥ 4*
● Morellino di Scansano Massi di Mandorlaia Ris. '04	♥♥ 5
● Syrah '06	♥♥ 5
● Toscoforte '06	♥♥ 4*
● Chianti Colli Fiorentini Il Cortile '06	♥ 4
● Chianti Colli Fiorentini Ris. '05	♥ 5
● Morellino di Scansano Massi di Mandorlaia '07	♥ 4
⊙ Rosato di Poppiano '07	♥ 3
● Syrah '05	♥♥ 4
● Tricorno '00	♥♥ 6

Fattoria di Presciano

LOC. PIEVE A PRESCIANO
VIA GIOVANNI XXIII, 2
52020 PERGINE VALDARNO [AR]
TEL. 0575897160
www.fattoriadipresciano.it

ANNUAL PRODUCTION	100,000 bottles
HECTARES UNDER VINE	24
VITICULTURE METHOD	Conventional

As usual, Fattoria di Presciano presented a multitude of wines, mostly focusing on the recently created Pietraviva DOC, of which Pasquale Cometti is a loyal supporter. The variety of different expressions reflects the winery's ongoing work to promote and recover local native varieties. The range is consistently good throughout, without particular peaks, showing reliable, well-typed technique and style. At out tastings, the wines that emerged above the rest were the classic IGTs like the I Greti '04, a dark, shadowy sangiovese rich in character and personality and earthy huskiness. The Rosso Veleno Marina Mouritch '05, from sangiovese with merlot and ciliegiolo, is less precise and more ruffled than previous versions, the nose veiled with sweet vanilla sensations from the oak. From the Pietraviva wines, we liked the pleasantly fresh and aromatic Bianco '07, made from chardonnay, sauvignon and malvasia, and preferred the more characterful and tangy Canaiolo '06 to the Ciliegiolo '06. The floral, sweet-yet-not-sweet Primadonna '06 is an interesting blend of late-harvested malvasia, moscato and traminer.

★ Fattoria Le Pupille

LOC. PIAGGE DEL MAIANO
58040 GROSSETO [GR]
TEL. 0564409518
www.elisabettageppetti.com

ANNUAL PRODUCTION	450,000 bottles
HECTARES UNDER VINE	66
VITICULTURE METHOD	Conventional

We must remember that Fattoria Le Pupille was the first winery to reveal to enthusiasts all the potential of the Morellino hills back when they were generally considered to be wild and desolate. Today, Elisabetta Geppetti still works with the same commitment and passion she has always shown and the impeccable quality of the wines is her most reliable witness. The Three Glasses arrived punctually for Saffredi '05, a sophisticated blend of cabernet sauvignon, merlot and alicante that delivers spice, aromatic herbs and flowers on the nose, with fluffy, velvety tannins on a soft, powerful palate with good breadth. Also very good is the Solalto '06, a late-harvested blend of traminer, sauvignon and sémillon with candied fruit aromas and nicely contrasting flavour. The extremely elegant Morellino Poggio Valente delivers mature, vibrant aromas and sweet tannin on the palate with a fresh, deep finish. The winery's new Pelofino '06, made from sangiovese, syrah, cabernet franc and cabernet sauvignon, is a deliciously flavoursome little masterpiece. The Morellino '07 and Poggio Argentato 07, made from traminer and sauvignon, are both reliable.

● I Greti '04	▼	6
● Chianti Ris. '04	▼	5
○ Pietraviva Bianco '07	▼	4
● Pietraviva Canaiolo '06	▼	5
● Pietraviva Ciliegiolo '06	▼	5
○ Primadonna Vign. di Marina Mouritch '06	▼	5
● Rosso Veleno Vign. di Marina Mouritch '05	▼	6
● I Greti '03	▼▼	6
● Priscus '03	▼▼	5
● Priscus '01	▼▼	5
● Rosso Veleno Vign. di Marina Mouritch '04	▼▼	6
● Rosso Veleno Vign. di Marina Mouritch '03	▼▼	6
● Rosso Veleno Vign. di Marina Mouritch '01	▼▼	6

● Saffredi '05	▼▼▼	8
● Morellino di Scansano Poggio Valente '06	▼▼	6
● Pelofino '06	▼▼	4*
○ Solalto '06	▼▼	5
● Morellino di Scansano '07	▼	4
○ Poggio Argentato '07	▼	4
● Morellino di Scansano Poggio Valente '04	▼▼▼	6
● Morellino di Scansano Poggio Valente '99	▼▼▼	6
● Morellino di Scansano Poggio Valente '98	▼▼▼	6
● Saffredi '04	▼▼▼	8
● Saffredi '03	▼▼▼	8
● Saffredi '02	▼▼▼	8
● Saffredi '01	▼▼▼	8
● Saffredi '00	▼▼▼	8

La Querce

VIA IMPRUNETANA PER TAVARNUZZE, 41
50023 IMPRUNETA [FI]
TEL. 0552011380
www.laquerce.com

ANNUAL PRODUCTION   22,000 bottles
HECTARES UNDER VINE 8
VITICULTURE METHOD   Conventional

Nothing changes at Massimo Marchi's winery. This is positive. Like actors who deliver repeat the same performance every evening without becoming tired or bored, the wines from this Impruneta estate have repeated identical results in our tastings for several years. Le Querce, well known since the 1970s, has survived a period in which its wine activities went onto the back burner, but since 2000 much has changed. The vineyards have been totally replanted and there are developments in the cellar, with the purchase of new machinery and old barrels replaced by barriques and tonneaux. This has led to a general increase in quality, with products that are much more modern in style but very much able to reflect the features of the terroir in the glass. The '06 La Querce, from sangiovese and colorino, made the final once again, with spice and wild berries on its generous, concentrated nose and a firm, nicely broad palate with well-measured acidity and a sweet, lingering finish. The two Chiantis are both pleasant and well made while the Colli Fiorentini La Torretta '06 has fuller body.

Castello di Querceto

LOC. QUERCETO
VIA A. FRANÇOIS, 2
50020 GREVE IN CHIANTI [FI]
TEL. 05585921
www.castellodiquerceto.it

ANNUAL PRODUCTION   600,000 bottles
HECTARES UNDER VINE 60
VITICULTURE METHOD   Conventional

Let's start by immediately correcting what we wrote last year. The Sole di Alessandro, a monovarietal Cabernet Sauvignon reviewed in the previous edition of the Guide, was the '03 version. The '04 was presented for this year's tastings, with perfectly respectable results since it made it to the finals, where it kept the Chianti Classico Riserva '05 company. This characterful wine has oaky aromas on the nose and beautifully defined body with a good tannic texture and a lingering, tangy finish. In fact, all the products made a good impression. The Cignale '04 made from cabernet sauvignon with a dash of merlot has fresh aromas and a powerful structure. The La Corte '05, an excellent example of a territory-dedicated monovarietal Sangiovese, has a subtle, stylish nose with a slender, well-balanced body. The Chianti Classico Il Picchio Riserva '05 has a mouthfilling, satisfying palate supported by delicious acidity. The Chianti Classico '06 is well typed while the Querciolaia '04, a classic Chianti blend of sangiovese and cabernet, suffers a little from roughish tannins.

● La Querce '06	♥♥ 5
● Chianti Colli Fiorentini La Torretta '06	♥♥ 4*
● Chianti Sorrettole '07	♥ 3
● La Querce '05	♀♀ 5
● La Querce '04	♀♀ 5

● Chianti Cl. Ris. '05	♥♥ 5
● Il Sole di Alessandro '04	♥♥ 8
● Chianti Cl. Il Picchio Ris. '05	♥♥ 6
● Cignale '05	♥♥ 8
● La Corte '04	♥♥ 7
● Chianti Cl. '06	♥ 4
● Querciolaia '04	♥ 7
● Chianti Cl. Il Picchio Ris. '03	♀♀ 6
● Chianti Cl. Ris. '04	♀♀ 5
● Chianti Cl. Ris. '03	♀♀ 5
● Chianti Cl. Ris. '01	♀♀ 5
● Cignale '03	♀♀ 7
● Il Sole di Alessandro '01	♀♀ 8
● Querciolaia '01	♀♀ 7

Querceto di Castellina

LOC. QUERCETO, 9
53011 CASTELLINA IN CHIANTI [SI]
TEL. 0577733590
www.querceto.com

ANNUAL PRODUCTION	35,000 bottles
HECTARES UNDER VINE	11
VITICULTURE METHOD	Conventional

A different year, a different result for the Di Battista family winery. Through to the finals went the Podalirio '06, a blend of sangiovese and merlot, named after a butterfly and a figure from Greek mythology famous for his powers of healing. Aided by winemaker Gioia Cresti, Jacopo's work continues at full throttle with some very sound performances. The finalist delivers very respectable complex aromas of wild berries, vanilla and an emphatic oaky sensation, followed by a soft entry on the palate, which opens out well with well-judged weight, nicely even tannic texture and a crescendo finish. The Chianti Classico L'Aura '06 is simpler but based on the same style, with fruitier aromas and an enjoyably slender body. The winery also has holiday accommodation and holds cookery courses, which include a basic food and wine matching course.

● Podalirio '06	♟	6
● Chianti Cl. L'Aura '06	♟	4
● Podalirio '01	♟♟♟	6
● Chianti Cl. L'Aura '03	♟♟	4

Quercia al Poggio

FRAZ. MONSANTO
S.DA QUERCIA AL POGGIO, 4
50021 BARBERINO VAL D'ELSA [FI]
TEL. 0558075278
www.quercialpoggio.com

ANNUAL PRODUCTION	20,000 bottles
HECTARES UNDER VINE	15
VITICULTURE METHOD	Natural

This Barberino Val d'Elsa winery never ceases to amaze us, offering products with strong personality that beautifully represent an area that is well on the way to realizing its huge potential. There is a very good selection of fine wineries here in one of the smallest municipal areas of Chianti Classico, highlighting the area's excellent weather and soil types. Visitors to the estate have a chance to understand how life in the countryside used to work. There was once a perfectly self-sufficient village of 60 houses belonging to country workers where the holiday centre is located today. The most impressive wine is the Chianti Classico Riserva '04, which delivers aromas of pencil lead, aromatic herbs and blueberry and currant berry fruit. The palate is balanced with a good backbone of acidity that harmonizes well with the alcohol through to a nice mouthwatering finish. The Chianti Classico '05 is also very good, giving more classic aromas of violets, cherries and some minty hints. Supple entry on the palate and well-measured tannins take you into a nice appetizing finish.

● Chianti Cl. Ris. '04	♟♟	5
● Chianti Cl. '05	♟	4
● Chianti Cl. Ris. '01	♟♟	5

★ Querciabella

VIA BARBIANO, 17
50022 GREVE IN CHIANTI [FI]
TEL. 05585927777
www.querciabella.com

ANNUAL PRODUCTION	200,000 bottles
HECTARES UNDER VINE	76.5
VITICULTURE METHOD	Natural

Every year, Querciabella gets closer to Chianti Classico. This doesn't mean that the cellar no longer intends to release its flagships, Camartina – the '05 won Three Glasses again this year – or Batàr. Rather, it means that in terms of both quality and quantity, Chianti Classico is becoming the focus of attention and the change is perceptible. The use of higher percentages of sangiovese creates a nose in which the cherry and violets aromas are joined by delicious hints of damp earth and aromatic herbs while acid backbone on the palate allows the wine to open out nicely into a long fresh finish. Camartina, from 60 per cent cabernet sauvignon with sangiovese, is impeccable even in a complicated year like '05, with ripe fruit and vegetal, minerally hints on the nose and a healthy, dynamic and characterful palate. The very long finish is not the slightest bit affected by the close-knit, silky extract. The Batàr '06, from chardonnay and pinot bianco in equal quantities, has a clearly defined style in which oak plays a fundamental role. Finally, the new Mongrana '05 from the Maremma also features, even though for now it is only distributed abroad.

Castello di Radda

LOC. IL BECCO
53017 RADDA IN CHIANTI [SI]
TEL. 030652382
www.castellodiradda.it

ANNUAL PRODUCTION	100,000 bottles
HECTARES UNDER VINE	50
VITICULTURE METHOD	Conventional

This Chianti winery owned by the Beretta family makes its debut in the Guide although it has been active in winemaking for many years in both Franciacorta, with the Sparviere estate, and Abruzzo, with the Orlando Contucci Ponno property. The wines presented made a very good impression, so much so that the Chianti Classico '05 made it through to our finals. The Tuscan project began in 2003 with the purchase of this estate and replanting of the 45 hectares of vineyards. Subsequent work included the construction of the cellar building and accommodation for tourists. That finalist has varied aromas ranging from florality to marked fruitiness while the palate is nicely measured with broad tannic texture and appetizing acidity in a weighty body. The rising finish is very flavoursome. The Riserva '04 was good, too, delivering hints of pencil lead and leather with hints of Mediterranean scrubland and a sound entry on the lively, flavoursome and attractively deep palate. The Chianti Classico '04 is simpler and more linear.

● Camartina '05	▼▼▼	8
● Chianti Cl. '06	▼▼	5
○ Batàr '06	▼▼	7
● Mongrana '05	▼	4
● Camartina '04	▼▼▼	8
● Camartina '03	▼▼▼	8
● Camartina '01	▼▼▼	8
● Camartina '00	▼▼▼	8
● Camartina '99	▼▼▼	8
● Camartina '97	▼▼▼	8
● Camartina '95	▼▼▼	8
● Camartina '94	▼▼▼	8
● Camartina '90	▼▼▼	8
● Camartina '88	▼▼▼	8

● Chianti Cl. Poggio Selvale '05	▼▼	4*
● Chianti Cl. Poggio Selvale Ris. '04	▼▼	5
● Chianti Cl. Poggio Selvale '04	▼	4

★ Castello dei Rampolla

VIA CASE SPARSE, 22
50020 PANZANO [FI]
TEL. 055852001
castellodeirampolla.cast@tin.it

ANNUAL PRODUCTION	**90,000 bottles**
HECTARES UNDER VINE	**42**
VITICULTURE METHOD	**Natural**

Thinking about the wines produced by the Di Napoli family brings to mind the mathematical rule that says reversing the order of the factors does not change the product. Three Glasses always turn up here, for one wine or another. This year was the turn of the Sammarco '05 made from cabernet sauvignon with a small percentage of sangiovese and merlot. Its strong, confident purple ushers in an alluring, violet-led nose, concentrated fruit aromas of redcurrants and blueberries, and subtle spicy hints. The palate is generous and impresses with velvety tannins and a nice fresh sensation on the long, mouthwatering finish. The D'Alceo '05, a blend of cabernet sauvignon and petit verdot, is also very good indeed with striking aromas of bell peppers, cherries and black pepper on the nose and an elegant, powerful palate, free of excess, and a complex aftertaste in the finish. The Chianti Classico '05 is also very good, with enjoyable aromas and a clean satisfying palate. An excellent performance overall with enviably reliable production.

Rasa - La Serena

PODERE RASA I, 133
53024 MONTALCINO [SI]
TEL. 0577848659
la_serena@virgilio.it

ANNUAL PRODUCTION	**23,500 bottles**
HECTARES UNDER VINE	**8.50**
VITICULTURE METHOD	**Conventional**

Andrea Mantengoli has always worked in wine. He has come a long way since he wandered through the vineyards with his father or among the barrels of a leading Montalcino producer. His winery, La Serena, has earned a full profile this year thanks to the mature, unvarying quality and style throughout the range. The new winery, designed by Andrea's architect brother Marcello, has improved his working conditions with adequate spaces and better management of post-bottling storage temperatures. Again this year, the Brunello di Montalcino made it through to the national finals. This great result was obtained with the '03 version whose classic, quite concentrated ruby red leads into vibrant, broad, classic aromas that never yield to excessive warmth. Yellow peaches meld with morello cherries as faint hints of tobacco punctuate the sweet vein of fruit. The palate shows very elegant flavour thanks to soft tannins and pleasant acidity supporting its well-rounded structure, which opens into a fragrant, well-developed finish. The Rosso di Montalcino '06 is excellent, giving fresh hints of red berries and an impressive palate.

● Sammarco '05	♟♟♟ 8
● d'Alceo '05	♟♟ 8
● Chianti Cl. '05	♟♟ 5
● d'Alceo '04	♟♟♟ 8
● d'Alceo '03	♟♟♟ 8
● d'Alceo '01	♟♟♟ 8
● d'Alceo '00	♟♟♟ 8
● La Vigna di Alceo '99	♟♟♟ 8
● La Vigna di Alceo '98	♟♟♟ 8
● La Vigna di Alceo '97	♟♟♟ 8

● Brunello di Montalcino '03	♟♟ 7
● Rosso di Montalcino '06	♟♟ 4
● Brunello di Montalcino Gemini '01	♟♟ 8

La Rasina

LOC. RASINA, 132
53024 MONTALCINO [SI]
TEL. 0577848536
www.larasina.it

ANNUAL PRODUCTION	35,000 bottles
HECTARES UNDER VINE	8.5
VITICULTURE METHOD	Conventional

After skipping the 2002 edition of his Brunello because the vintage was not judged up to scratch, Marco Mantengoli, the skilled owner of this small estate planted to over eight hectares of brunello, again presented his full range of wines. There are two Brunello di Montalcinos and Divasco stands out for the use of barriques and tonneaux in ageing. This year, we preferred it despite its still assertive oakiness. The colour is a nice intense ruby red and the sweet spicy aromas from the wood are joined by distinctive yellow peaches enhancing the classic hints of red berry fruit. The palate is well structured despite youthful and still very marked tannin. This is nice and sweet, though, and should therefore soften with bottle age. The Brunello di Montalcino '03 is less successful. Its nose is more classic, with hints of medicinal herbs, leather and pipe tobacco, but the palate is less structured than its stablemate's, although the tannin is better balanced. These two different styles will satisfy different tastes. There's a tad too much extract on the Rosso di Montalcino '06.

Renieri

S.DA CONSORZIALE DELL'ASSO
53024 MONTALCINO [SI]
TEL. 0577359330
www.renierimontalcino.com

ANNUAL PRODUCTION	189,000 bottles
HECTARES UNDER VINE	35
VITICULTURE METHOD	Conventional

Renieri is situated in the eastern part of Montalcino between Torrenieri and the red-earthed ravines facing Monte Amiata. Marco Bacci's Brunello di Montalcino project began back in 1997 when he planted the vineyard following a careful study of the land to identify clones and the right rootstocks for sangiovese and the other varieties. The estate covers a total of 100 hectares, ten of which are planted to Montalcino DOCG vineyards and 20 or so at Sant'Antimo. The first vintage of Brunello di Montalcino to be produced was the 2003 and considering the fact that it was anything but a simple year, the wine made a good debut. Medicinal herbs and tobacco on the nose are subsequently joined by floral notes. The palate is a little stiff, because of excessive tannin, and the finish is mouth-drying. The monovarietal syrah Regina '05 is better, offering currants and blueberries alongside spiciness on the nose, which fuse well with the toasty hints from the oak.

● Brunello di Montalcino Il Divasco '03	▼▼	8
● Brunello di Montalcino '03	▼	7
● Rosso di Montalcino '06	▼	5
● Brunello di Montalcino '01	♀♀♀	7
● Brunello di Montalcino '00	♀♀♀	6
● Brunello di Montalcino Il Divasco '01	♀♀♀	7
● Brunello di Montalcino '98	♀♀	7

● Regina di Renieri '05	▼▼	7
● Brunello di Montalcino '03	▼	8
● Re di Renieri '04	♀♀	6
● Re di Renieri '03	♀♀	6
● Regina di Renieri '03	♀♀	6

Riecine

LOC. RIECINE
53013 GAIOLE IN CHIANTI [SI]
TEL. 0577749098
www.riecine.com

ANNUAL PRODUCTION	45,000 bottles
HECTARES UNDER VINE	11
VITICULTURE METHOD	Certified organic

Gary Baumann's winery didn't manage to win Three Glasses this year but it wasn't easy without the leading wine, a single-variety Sangiovese called La Gioia which has brought the owner a great deal of satisfaction in recent years. It wasn't produced in this vintage. We have a correction regarding last year's review: the Chianti Classico described was the basic 2004 while the Riserva is the one we tasted this year. Anyway, it's a good result that demonstrates the consistently positive results yielded by the scrupulous work of Sean O'Callaghan, oenologist, agronomist and supervisor of all stages of production. We were particularly impressed by the Chianti Classico Riserva '04, which has plum and cherry fruit standing out among the subtle fruit aromas. The palate is extremely, indeed surprisingly, racy, and generously tangy with refreshing acidity and a crescendo finish. The Chianti Classico '05 is also good, with gamy, tobacco and leather aromas and a mouthwatering, dynamic palate. The Rosé '07 is enjoyably drinkable.

Rietine

LOC. RIETINE, 27
53013 GAIOLE IN CHIANTI [SI]
TEL. 0577731110
www.rietine.com

ANNUAL PRODUCTION	60,000 bottles
HECTARES UNDER VINE	13
VITICULTURE METHOD	Conventional

The winery owned by Mario and Galina Gafuri-Lazarides is no a flash in the pan. Last year, it won Three Glasses and this year the Chianti Classico Riserva '05 made it to the finals, a good result which reveals how the couple combine their shared enthusiasm for the winemaking business. The decision to adopt organic growing methods in the vineyard further demonstrates the love for the land that prompted them to move to the Chianti Classico area. The finalist shows a lovely purple with hints of blueberries and raspberries on a subtle elegant nose alongside Mediterranean scrubland and herbs, followed by a firm, substantial body with spiky tannins, noticeable but nicely integrated acidity and a pleasantly lingering finish. The Tiziano '04, a blend of cabernet sauvignon and merlot, is less interesting, although it is unusual since lambrusco was originally supposed to be part of the blend. This year, we found it less rounded than usual although the aromas are interesting. The Chianti Classico '06 is good and well made.

● Chianti Cl. '05		♟♟ 5
● Chianti Cl. Ris. '04		♟♟ 6
⊙ Rosé '07		♟ 4
● Chianti Cl. Ris. '99		♟♟♟ 8
● La Gioia '04		♟♟♟ 7
● La Gioia '01		♟♟♟ 7
● La Gioia '98		♟♟♟ 8
● La Gioia '95		♟♟♟ 8
● La Gioia '00		♟♟ 8
● La Gioia '99		♟♟ 8

● Chianti Cl. Ris. '05		♟♟ 5
● Chianti Cl. '06		♟ 4
● Tiziano '04		♟ 5
● Chianti Cl. Ris. '04		♟♟♟ 5

Rigoloccio

VIA PROVINCIALE, 82
58023 GAVORRANO [GR]
TEL. 056645464
www.rigoloccio.it

ANNUAL PRODUCTION   60,000 bottles
HECTARES UNDER VINE   9.5
VITICULTURE METHOD   Conventional

At our tasting, the wines produced by the Abati and Puggelli family all seemed to be beautifully made and the winery deserves a full profile. What's more, the products from this Gavorrano winery are all keenly priced, which is another strongpoint in times like these. The Cabernet Alicante '06 is intriguing, with a lovely fresh nose where clearly defined fruity aromas blend harmoniously with hints of spice and light smoky sensations. The wine flows easily across the juicy, firm-textured palate, showing nicely dynamic with very good contrast. Also nice, but with less personality, is the Merlot '06. Attractive grassy sensations enhance the fragrant nose and a close-knit, well-coordinated though still very young palate, and mouth-drying sensations in the finish. The Chardonnay Fiano '07 is absolutely delicious, unveiling refreshing aromas of flowers and apple and pear fruit on the nose, and an interesting tangy note on the palate. The Rosato '07, made from cabernet sauvignon, is very drinkable.

Rocca delle Macìe

LOC. MACÌE, 45
53011 CASTELLINA IN CHIANTI [SI]
TEL. 05777321
www.roccadellemacie.com

ANNUAL PRODUCTION   4,500,000 bottles
HECTARES UNDER VINE   200
VITICULTURE METHOD   Conventional

Sergio Zingarelli's Chianti Classico winery, Rocca delle Macìe, performed well this year. There were lots of wines and average scores were high, especially in the leading wines. Roccato '05 reached the finals, with tertiary and already mature aromas on the nose and a compact, rounded palate that still shows a little stiffness due to assertive tannins. The Chianti Classico Fizzano Riserva '05 is juicy, vibrant and lingering if a little lean-edged in the finish, while the nose delivers ripe red berries, especially strawberries, and damp earth. The Chianti Classico Tenuta Sant'Alfonso '06 also impressed, perfectly reflecting the characteristics of the growing year with an alcohol-rich nose of bottled fruit liqueur and a rounded, mouthfilling, intense palate with a heady finish. The Chianti Classico '06 is pleasant and fresh, with red berries on the nose and a juicy taut palate, while the Chianti Classico Riserva '05 is a little weary both on the nose, with aromas of tomato preserve, and the palate, where the tannin is over-extracted. The Vermentino Occhio a Vento '07 and the Morellino di Scansano Campomaccione '07, both from Maremma, are good.

● Cabernet Alicante '06	♈♈	4*
○ Chardonnay Fiano '07	♈♈	4*
● Merlot '06	♈♈	4*
⊙ Rosato '07	♈	4
○ Chardonnay Fiano '06	♈♈	4
● Il Sorvegliante '05	♈♈	5

● Roccato '05	♈♈	7
● Chianti Cl. '06	♈♈	4
● Chianti Cl. Fizzano Ris. '05	♈♈	6
● Chianti Cl. Tenuta S. Alfonso '06	♈♈	5
○ Vermentino Occhio a Vento '07	♈♈	4
● Chianti Cl. Ris. '05	♈	5
● Morellino di Scansano Campomaccione '07	♈	4
● Roccato '00	♈♈♈	7
● Roccato '99	♈♈♈	7

Rocca di Castagnoli

LOC. CASTAGNOLI
53013 GAIOLE IN CHIANTI [SI]
TEL. 0577731004
www.roccadicastagnoli.com

ANNUAL PRODUCTION	300,000 bottles
HECTARES UNDER VINE	132
VITICULTURE METHOD	Conventional

And after last year's success, the second Three Glass prize for a DOCG wine was not long in coming for Calogero Calì's winery, this time for a Riserva di Chianti Classico. Last year, it was Poggio ai Frati di Rocca di Castagnoli while this year it is the turn of the Tenuta di Capraia Chianti Classico, again a Riserva. This fresh and less structured '05 version has benefited from a good year for the Capraia area in Castellina in Chianti, which has endowed it with a confident, clearly defined nose of ripe red berries, leather and dry leaves and a rounded, generous palate with impressively impeccable extract. The Chianti Classico Poggio ai Frati Riserva '05 is also very good, with more bite than the previous wine from acidity that is always very tangible in the Rocca di Castagnoli area. A nice version of the Stielle '05, from 70 per cent sangiovese with cabernet sauvignon, has fresh fruit and vegetal hints on the nose and a long, mouthwatering, really broad palate. All the other wines are good.

Rocca di Frassinello

LOC. GIUNCARICO
58040 GAVORRANO [GR]
TEL. 056688400
www.roccadifrassinello.it

ANNUAL PRODUCTION	180,000 bottles
HECTARES UNDER VINE	70
VITICULTURE METHOD	Conventional

French group Lafite-Rothschild and Chianti-based Castellare di Castellina combine forces in a Maremma winemaking project, Rocca di Frassinello, which reprised last year's incredible results. Three Glasses went once again to the '06 Rocca di Frassinello, which looks confidently set on its way to join the finest examples of winemaking in Tuscany and beyond. The elegant aromas are veined with lush fruit that blends harmoniously with the spice from the well-judged use of oak during maturation. Density, volume and depth are the distinguishing features of the juicy palate with its long, intense finish. The other wines are also laudably good. Le Sughere di Frassinello '06 has an equally stylish but fresher and more approachable nose, and a mouthwatering, weighty, nicely drinkable palate. The Poggio alla Guardia '06, aged in stainless steel and concrete vats, is deliciously drinkable with spicy aromas and a flavoursome palate. These three wines are made from a blend of sangiovese, cabernet sauvignon and merlot in varying percentages.

● Chianti Cl. Tenuta di Capraia Ris. '05	▼▼▼	5
● Chianti Cl. Poggio ai Frati Ris. '05	▼▼	5
● Buriano '04	▼▼	7
● Chianti Cl. '06	▼▼	4
● Stielle '05	▼▼	7
● Le Pratola '06	▼	6
○ Molino delle Balze '06	▼	5
○ Vin Santo del Chianti Cl. '00	▼	8
● Chianti Cl. Poggio ai Frati Ris. '04	♟♟♟	5
● Stielle '00	♟♟♟	8
● Chianti Cl. Tenuta di Capraia Ris. '04	♟♟	5
● Stielle '04	♟♟	5
● Stielle '01	♟♟	8

● Rocca di Frassinello '06	▼▼▼	6
● Le Sughere di Frassinello '06	▼▼	5
● Poggio alla Guardia '06	▼▼	4*
● Rocca di Frassinello '05	♟♟♟	7
● Le Sughere di Frassinello '05	♟♟	6
● Le Sughere di Frassinello '04	♟♟	6
● Poggio alla Guardia '05	♟♟	5
● Poggio alla Guardia '04	♟♟	5
● Rocca di Frassinello '04	♟♟	7

Rocca di Montegrossi

FRAZ. MONTI IN CHIANTI
53010 GAIOLE IN CHIANTI [SI]
TEL. 0577747977

ANNUAL PRODUCTION	80,000 bottles
HECTARES UNDER VINE	18
VITICULTURE METHOD	Conventional

It wasn't such a good year for Montegrossi. The estate star, Vin Santo'01, is the only wine to do really well. Marco Ricasoli Firidolfi was one of the first to believe that this traditional product could become an example of a great Italian dessert wine. But the care lavished on the Vin Santo should really be extended the red wines. While it's true that the Riserva Vigneto San Marcellino is absent since it was not produced in 2005, the Supertuscan Geremia '05, from cabernet sauvignon and merlot, was no more than good. All the right components for producing excellent wines are there, especially the ability to highlight the most distinctive features of the terroir. Perhaps tannin could be expressed with more definition to achieve greater depth and balance. The Vin Santo has very vibrant aromas ranging from dried fruit to honey, citrus fruit and sweet spice. Velvety, weighty and creamy on the palate, it signs off with a very leisurely finale. Geremia '05 has gunflint, sage and moss on the nose and a well-defined body that is just slightly lean in the finish. The Chianti Classico '06 is deliciously drinkable.

Castello Romitorio

LOC. ROMITORIO, 279
53024 MONTALCINO [SI]
TEL. 0577897220
www.castelloromitorio.com

ANNUAL PRODUCTION	150,000 bottles
HECTARES UNDER VINE	25
VITICULTURE METHOD	Conventional

After a rather dim period which coincided with refurbishment of the cellar, the winery owned by Sandro Chia, maestro of Transavanguardia art, makes an authoritative return to the Guide. The austere and beautiful castle gave us an interesting Brunello di Montalcino '03, which sailed through to the final tastings, missing the highest accolade by a hair's breadth. Something has changed in this winery's style, as is already obvious from the colour of the wine, an intense ruby, pigeon-blood red, and the clear, vibrant aromas ranging from red berries to spicy vanilla with cloves and medicinal herbs. A good sweet, confident entry on the palate follows through well thanks to beautiful, smooth-honed tannins that are nicely supported by acidity. There is a pleasant reprise of the aromas in the surprisingly long finish. The wines from Scansano also did well, and the Morellino Ghiaccio Forte '07 was more than usually impressive with its well-defined, vibrant nose and fragrant flavour.

○ Vin Santo del Chianti Cl. '01	¶¶ 8
● Geremia '05	¶¶ 6
● Chianti Cl. '06	¶ 4
● Chianti Cl. Vign. S. Marcellino Ris. '99	¶¶¶ 5
● Chianti Cl. Vign. S. Marcellino Ris. '04	¶¶ 6
● Geremia '03	¶¶ 6
● Geremia '99	¶¶ 6
○ Vin Santo del Chianti Cl. '00	¶¶ 8
○ Vin Santo del Chianti Cl. '98	¶¶ 8
○ Vin Santo del Chianti Cl. '97	¶¶ 8

● Brunello di Montalcino '03	¶¶ 8
● Morellino di Scansano Ghiaccio Forte '07	¶¶ 6
● Morellino di Scansano '07	¶ 4
● Brunello di Montalcino Ris. '97	¶¶¶ 8
● Brunello di Montalcino '02	¶¶ 8
● Brunello di Montalcino '99	¶¶ 8

★ Tenimenti Ruffino

P.LE RUFFINO, 1
50065 PONTASSIEVE [FI]
TEL. 0556499717
www.ruffino.it

Russo

LOC. PODERE LA METOCCHINA
VIA FORNI, 71
57028 SUVERETO [LI]
TEL. 0565845105
www.vinirusso.it

ANNUAL PRODUCTION	14,500,000 bottles
HECTARES UNDER VINE	600
VITICULTURE METHOD	Conventional

ANNUAL PRODUCTION	70,000 bottles
HECTARES UNDER VINE	14
VITICULTURE METHOD	Conventional

Another Three Glasses went to this Pontassieve winery's classic Chianti Classico Riserva Ducale Oro '04. This textbook, traditional version offers ripe, austere aromas on the nose, particularly jam and tobacco, before opening softly on the palate with subtle, fine-grained tannins, refreshing acidity and a lingering finish. The rest of the Folonari family's range is good with a special mention for the basic wines, which have improved markedly. Modus, from sangiovese, cabernet sauvignon and merlot, is as enjoyable as ever. The '05 version has toasty aromas with hints of chocolate, a rounded, well-balanced body and a pleasant finish. The colorino-based Romitorio di Santedame '05 is more austere with pencil lead and ink on the nose and a palate clenched by tannin. The other bottles are very enjoyable. The Chianti Classicos from Tenuta Santedame are fruity and nicely drinkable while the whites have well-defined aromas and nice acidic backbone. There's more good news from Montalcino. The '03 Brunello from Greppone Mazzi has a broad nose and very taut palate thanks to juicy acidity that adds length.

Russo is one of the most interesting wineries in the Suvereto area. Owned by the Russo brothers, it regularly presents a range of very good wines. For the past several years, though, the flagship Barbicone and Sassobucato have shown blips that may be due to complicated vintage years in Val di Cornia. The '06 version of the Sassobucato, made from merlot and cabernet in equal quantities, was wrongly reviewed last year but is the most impressive in this year's range. The well-gauged aromas deliver vegetal sensations with earthy and balsamic hints, reprised on the weighty, broad, balanced palate with its slightly oaky but lingering finish. The Val di Cornia Ceppitaio '07 is solid and enjoyable, offering impressive aromas and an enjoyably mouthwatering palate. The fresh-tasting Vermentino Pietrasca '07 has fruit-led aromatics and a supple palate. The monovarietal Cabernet, Val di Cornia La Mandria del Pari '04, makes its debut with still rather stiff tannins. Val di Cornia Barbicone '06 is still maturing.

● Chianti Cl. Ris. Ducale Oro '04	TTT	6
● Brunello di Montalcino Greppone Mazzi '03	TT	7
● Modus '05	TT	6
● Romitorio di Santedame '05	TT	7
● Chianti Cl. Santedame '06	T	4
● Chianti Cl. Santedame Ris. '05	T	5
O La Solatia Chardonnay '07	T	5
O La Solatia Pinot Grigio '07	T	3
O Libaio '07	T	3
● Chianti Cl. Ris. Ducale Oro '01	YYY	6
● Chianti Cl. Ris. Ducale Oro '00	YYY	6
● Modus '04	YYY	6
● Romitorio di Santedame '00	YYY	8
● Romitorio di Santedame '99	YYY	7

● Sassobucato '06	YY	6
● Pietrasca '07	Y	3
● Val di Cornia La Mandria del Pari '04	Y	8
● Val di Cornia Rosso Ceppitaio '07	Y	4
● Val di Cornia Rosso Barbicone '00	YYY	5*
● Barbicone '05	YY	5
● Barbicone '04	YY	5
● Sassobucato '04	YY	5
● Sassobucato '03	YY	5
● Sassobucato '02	YY	6
● Sassobucato '01	YY	5
● Sassobucato '00	YY	6
● Val di Cornia Rosso Barbicone '01	YY	5
● Val di Cornia Rosso Ceppitaio '04	YY	4

La Sala

LOC. PONTEROTTO
VIA SORRIPA, 34
50026 SAN CASCIANO IN VAL DI PESA [FI]
TEL. 055828111
www.lasala.it

ANNUAL PRODUCTION　**85,000 bottles**
HECTARES UNDER VINE　**21**
VITICULTURE METHOD　**Conventional**

Laura Baronti's winery is back with a full profile after a thoroughly decent overall result. We have never doubted the area's potential and this year's results prove us right. The historical origins date back to the 11th century and the land was later owned by the Medici. Viticulture subsequently played a significant role in the area. The unusual feature of La Sala is that it is entirely run by women. Even the consultant winemaker is female, Gabriella Tani. The Riserva di Chianti Classico '05 scored well thanks to an array of subtle, varied aromas, particularly black berries and a hint of tobacco. Solid and firm on the palate, it has nice acid backbone to liven up the well-structured body and a generous, tangy finish. The Campo all'Albero '05, from mainly cabernet sauvignon with some sangiovese, is equally interesting, with fresh aromatic herbs on the nose alongside floral and vegetal sensations. The nicely mouthfilling palate opens broad and deep, and is sustained by subtle tannins through to an intriguing finish.

Salcheto

LOC. SANT'ALBINO
VIA DI VILLA BIANCA, 15
53045 MONTEPULCIANO [SI]
TEL. 0578799031
www.salcheto.it

ANNUAL PRODUCTION　**130,000 bottles**
HECTARES UNDER VINE　**33**
VITICULTURE METHOD　**Conventional**

The wines presented by Michele Manelli this year were very well gauged, revealing respectably put-together aromas and flavour. The Nobile di Montepulciano Salco Evoluzione '03 is in some ways an extreme wine after prolonged ageing in wood. It's an excellent interpretation of the tricky 2003 vintage, when Salcheto's altitude played in its favour: some of the vineyards are as high as 500 metres. The resulting wine delivers broad, mature aromas with healthy fruit sensations that are fully reflected on the palate, despite burred, mouth-drying tannins and quite assertive oak. The Nobile di Montepulciano '05 is also very good. While it doesn't show outstanding personality, it is skilfully made without pointless elaboration. The clean aromas alternate impressively between fruit and coffee with tobacco. The palate is juicy and well balanced, finding plenty of support from the oak used for ageing. The Rosso di Montepulciano and the Chianti dei Colli Senesi, both '07, are very reliable.

● Campo all'Albero '05	🍷🍷 6
● Chianti Cl. Ris. '05	🍷🍷 6
● Chianti Cl. '06	🍷 4
O Vin Santo del Chianti Cl. '01	🍷 6
● Campo all'Albero '01	🍷🍷 6
● Chianti Cl. Ris. '03	🍷🍷 6
O Vin Santo del Chianti Cl. '98	🍷🍷 5

● Nobile di Montepulciano '05	🍷🍷 5
● Nobile di Montepulciano Salco Evoluzione '03	🍷🍷 7
● Chianti Colli Senesi '07	🍷 4
● Rosso di Montepulciano '07	🍷 4
● Nobile di Montepulciano '97	🍷🍷🍷 5
● Nobile di Montepulciano Salco Evoluzione '01	🍷🍷🍷 7
● Nobile di Montepulciano '04	🍷🍷 5
● Nobile di Montepulciano '03	🍷🍷 5
● Nobile di Montepulciano '02	🍷🍷 5
● Nobile di Montepulciano Salco '01	🍷🍷 6
● Nobile di Montepulciano Salco '00	🍷🍷 6
● Nobile di Montepulciano Salco '99	🍷🍷 6
● Nobile di Montepulciano Salco Evoluzione '99	🍷🍷 7

Salustri

FRAZ. POGGI DEL SASSO
LOC. LA CAVA
58040 CINIGIANO [GR]
TEL. 0564990529
www.salustri.it

ANNUAL PRODUCTION **80,000 bottles**
HECTARES UNDER VINE **12**
VITICULTURE METHOD **Conventional**

Leonardo and Marco Salustri, who are not prone to run after the latest winemaking fad, produce wines from impeccable fruit: wines that are serious and authentic in style, and which display quite distinctive personalities. While the recent past has not witnessed flawless reliability from Salustri, which has shown a somewhat unsteady hand with the oak, this year's performances reveal that they are getting closer to their ultimate goal. Both Montecucco Sangiovese Santa Marta '05 and Montecucco Sangiovese Grotte Rosse '05, each outstanding for equilibrium and finesse, went through to the national finals. Santa Marta, apart from a momentary closure due to its youth, introduces bright, crisp fruit, followed by a solid profile and a nicely sinewy progression with admirable energy. Grotte Rosse is a bit more austere but with superb aromatic definition on the nose. It then opens very wide, vibrant and smooth, with just a small rough patch from an extra note of oak. Narà '07 is a fragrantly savoury Vermentino, enjoyable now.

Castello di San Donato in Perano

LOC. SAN DONATO IN PERANO
53013 GAIOLE IN CHIANTI [SI]
TEL. 0577744121
www.castellosandonato.it

ANNUAL PRODUCTION **100,000 bottles**
HECTARES UNDER VINE **75**
VITICULTURE METHOD **Conventional**

This year's Guide raises Castello di San Donato to a full profile, in recognition of fine work over these past few years. Mario Tribuzio, assisted by winemaking consultant Maurizio Alongi, directs the operation, which owns some 360 hectares, much of it woodland, in addition to vineyards and olive groves. A classy agriturismo facility offers separate farm buildings converted into lodgings. Chianti Classico Riserva '05, which went to the national taste-offs, put on a top-notch performance. It lays out an inviting array of fragrances such as cinnamon and clove that nicely lift compact, self-confident fruit on the nose, followed by terrific volume in the mouth and a finish that drives very long, with crunchy tannins and vibrant acidity along the way. Equally fine are the two Chianti Classico versions. They may show a little less power but are nevertheless admirable, with supple, agile palates and appealing, straightforward aromas. The remaining wines get the thumbs up for their clean, enjoyable aromatics.

● Montecucco Grotte Rosse '05	♟♟	6
● Montecucco Santa Marta '05	♟♟	5
○ Narà '07	♟	4
● Montecucco Grotte Rosse '04	♟♟	6
● Montecucco Grotte Rosse '02	♟♟	6
● Montecucco Marleo '04	♟♟	4

● Chianti Cl. Ris. '05	♟♟	6
● Chianti Cl. '06	♟♟	4*
● Chianti Cl. '05	♟♟	4*
○ Il Dolce del Castello	♟	6
○ Bianco di Castello di San Donato '07	♟	5
● Merlot '05	♟	7

San Fabiano Calcinaia

LOC. CELLOLE
53011 CASTELLINA IN CHIANTI [SI]
TEL. 0577979232
www.sanfabianocalcinaia.com

San Felice

LOC. SAN FELICE
53019 CASTELNUOVO BERARDENGA [SI]
TEL. 05773991
www.agricolasanfelice.it

ANNUAL PRODUCTION	160,000 bottles
HECTARES UNDER VINE	42
VITICULTURE METHOD	Conventional

We might consider this a transitional year for Guido Serio's winery, which didn't put the ball quite as far as we have come to expect. Even a new wine, Cabernet Sauvignon '06, didn't provide the extra push. All of the bottlings betray excessive power, which compromises the overall balance necessary for a pleasurable experience. The chardonnay-based Cerviolo Bianco '06 is certainly on a high level, with a lovely minerally edge that enlivens the varietal aromas, and rich, savoury flavours in the mouth. The newly arrived Cabernet Sauvignon releases a nice packet of aromas and develops leisurely and velvety in the mouth, but with structure perhaps a little on the slender side. The remaining wines are powerful, sometimes to the point of excessive. That is true of Cerviolo '05, a blend of sangiovese, merlot and cabernet sauvignon with rough, drying tannins, and of Casa Boschino '06, with the same varieties but from younger vineyards. The two Chianti Classico versions lack their usual grace perhaps, in the case of the Riserva, because of a less than wonderful vintage. We look forward with great anticipation to next year's offerings.

ANNUAL PRODUCTION	1,000,000 bottles
HECTARES UNDER VINE	210
VITICULTURE METHOD	Conventional

San Felice steps up to the podium again to receive Three Glasses and does so, unusually, with Pugnitello '06, made exclusively from the grape of the same name. Leonardo Bellaccini, in charge of production, has achieved his goal. Before anyone else, he believed in the potential of this ancient and practically extinct variety. Fabrizio Nencioni, marketing director, and Alessandro Marchionne, general manager since 2007, share in the credit for this outstanding accomplishment. Returning to the Pugnitello, we found alluring impressions of fruit and spice on the nose and wonderfully lush, vigorous tannins in the mouth. Vigorello '04, a partnership of cabernet sauvignon, merlot and sangiovese, turned in its customary fine performance, as did Chianti Classico Poggio Rosso Riserva '04. Both are rich, though they still show their youth, particularly with tannins that still need to unfurl. Chianti Classico Il Grigio Riserva '05 is the offspring of a challenging year, and its tannins dominate the close, where it needs a bit more heft. Chianti Classico '06 is impressive, reflecting its usual tight, extract-rich style.

● Cabernet Sauvignon '06	▼▼	5
○ Cerviolo Bianco '06	▼▼	5
● Casa Boschino '06	▼	4
● Cerviolo Rosso '05	▼	7
● Chianti Cl. '06	▼	4
● Chianti Cl. Cellole Ris. '05	▼	6
● Cerviolo Rosso '00	▼▼▼	7
● Cerviolo Rosso '99	▼▼▼	6
● Cerviolo Rosso '98	▼▼▼	6
● Cerviolo Rosso '97	▼▼▼	6
● Cerviolo Rosso '96	▼▼▼	6
● Chianti Cl. Cellole Ris. '00	▼▼▼	6
● Chianti Cl. Cellole Ris. '04	▼▼	6
● Chianti Cl. Cellole Ris. '03	▼▼	6

● Pugnitello '06	▼▼▼	7
● Brunello di Montalcino Campogiovanni '03	▼▼	6
● Chianti Cl. Poggio Rosso Ris. '04	▼▼	6
● Vigorello '04	▼▼	7
● Chianti Cl. '06	▼	4
● Chianti Cl. Il Grigio Ris. '05	▼	5
● Chianti Cl. Poggio Rosso Ris. '03	▼▼▼	6
● Chianti Cl. Poggio Rosso Ris. '00	▼▼▼	6
● Chianti Cl. Poggio Rosso Ris. '95	▼▼▼	5
● Chianti Cl. Poggio Rosso Ris. '90	▼▼▼	6
● Vigorello '97	▼▼▼	5
● Vigorello '88	▼▼▼	5
● Chianti Cl. Poggio Rosso Ris. '01	▼▼	6
● Chianti Cl. Poggio Rosso Ris. '99	▼▼	6

San Giorgio

FRAZ. CASTELNUOVO DELL'ABATE
LOC. SAN GIORGIO
53020 MONTALCINO [SI]
TEL. 0272094585
www.tenutasangiorgio.it

ANNUAL PRODUCTION	42,000 bottles
HECTARES UNDER VINE	10
VITICULTURE METHOD	Conventional

Guido Folonari's operation in Montalcino made an outstanding debut in the Guide. Giorgio possesses some ten hectares of vineyards in the area between Sesta and Castelnuovo dell'Abate. After a couple of less than stellar vintages, Brunello di Montalcino struts in its '03 edition. The wine is all about balance, with smooth, spicy nuances of French oak melding into sangiovese's classic wild cherry and evolved notes of tobacco leaf. The palate is captivating with supple tannins and measured acidity contributing to a feeling of compactness while avoiding any muscularity. In short, this is an elegant, balanced and terroir-reflective offering. Cacciacone '05, on the other hand, is at the modern end of the style spectrum. This cask-aged blend of syrah and cabernet sauvignon ranges in appearance from purple to aubergine then parades a rich panoply of fruit, with blueberry, redcurrant, and citron nicely enriched by hints of clove and pink pepper. The palate enters decisively into a fine progression, with an impressive duet of tannins and alcohol. Rosso di Montalcino '06 is uncomplicated and tasty.

San Giusto a Rentennano

FRAZ. MONTI IN CHIANTI
LOC. SAN GIUSTO, 20
53013 GAIOLE IN CHIANTI [SI]
TEL. 0577747121
www.fattoriasangiusto.it

ANNUAL PRODUCTION	85,000 bottles
HECTARES UNDER VINE	29
VITICULTURE METHOD	Certified organic

The Martini di Cigala brothers earned high marks, if not as exalted as last year's. But we were unable to taste Percarlo, one of the two thoroughbreds, the other being Vino San Giusto, the sweet wine that opened people's eyes to the stylistic possibilities of Vin Santo-style grapes. San Giusto a Rentennano was the first Cistercian monastery to build its own fortress defining the boundary between Florence and Siena in the 13th century. Respect for the land is obvious here, not least for having adopted organic viticulture. As to the wines themselves, Chianti Classico Riserva Le Baroncole '05 emerged on top. An appealing integration of evolved impressions of tobacco leaf and leather into rich cherry preserves makes for a most effective beginning while the palate shows powerful, nervy development, with tannins nicely in place, concluding long and leisurely. La Ricolma '05 is as interesting as ever. Made exclusively from merlot, it is not conventionally varietal, for there is complex minerality with sturdy structure, while the palate is succulent enough if slow to develop. The finale is incisive but promises well. Chianti Classico '06 is fine.

● Brunello di Montalcino '03	▼▼ 7
● Cacciacone '05	▼▼ 6
● Rosso di Montalcino '06	▼ 5
● Brunello di Montalcino Ugolforte '01	♀♀ 7

● Chianti Cl. Le Baroncole Ris. '05	▼▼ 6
● La Ricolma '05	▼▼ 8
● Chianti Cl. '06	▼ 5
● Percarlo '99	♀♀♀ 8
● Percarlo '97	♀♀♀ 8
● Percarlo '95	♀♀♀ 8
● Chianti Cl. Le Baroncole Ris. '02	♀♀ 6
● La Ricolma '04	♀♀ 7

★ Tenuta San Guido

LOC. CAPANNE, 27
57020 BOLGHERI [LI]
TEL. 0565762003
www.sassicaia.com

San Luciano

LOC. SAN LUCIANO, 90
52048 MONTE SAN SAVINO [AR]
TEL. 0575848518
www.sanlucianovini.it

ANNUAL PRODUCTION	495,000 bottles
HECTARES UNDER VINE	90
VITICULTURE METHOD	Conventional

ANNUAL PRODUCTION	350,000 bottles
HECTARES UNDER VINE	63
VITICULTURE METHOD	Conventional

The fact that Sassicaia '05 is an extraordinary wine will surprise no one. It is every year, in one way or another. However, considering the overall release of 2005 vintages, the result was far from certain. Our tastings of the wines from Bolgheri revealed that high quality was not widespread, particularly when compared to '04. That does not hold true, though, for Bolgheri Sassicaia, since it shows refined, elegant and spacious, with tannins that are fine-grained and indeed velvety. The nervy vein of acidity is such as to make this wine well nigh immortal. The '04 version may have bewitched some into considering the '05 a lesser offering but we beg to differ, since we believe that in 20 years or so the '05, utterly unscathed by time, will still be at its stellar peak. The '06 Guidalberto is also a fine edition. As the cellar's second wine, it is made from fleshier materials. Merlot, cabernet sauvignon and touch of sangiovese provide a rich nose of dark fruit and nuances of pungent balsam. Firm structure completes a wine that shows its usual tasty drinkability. Le Difese '06 displays just a tad too much oak.

San Luciano, managed with exemplary dedication by the Ziantoni family, normally succeeds in drawing out the best from each vintage and from a growing area that is not historically counted in the top ranks. The wines are reliable, sound, well executed and affordable. D'Ovidio is their standard-bearer, largely sangiovese and montepulciano, with some merlot and cabernet. The '05 is an outstanding version, with a deep, dark nose revealing an array of ink, liquorice, carob and a hint of gunflint backgrounding fine fruit. A powerful, tannic palate with emphatic alcohol needs more time to integrate its wealth. Impressive as well is Boschi Salviati '06, from sangiovese, montepulciano and cabernet, layering blackberry, dried plum and aromatic herbs over sweet, dark-toned fruit, then building a medium-structured, vibrant palate that concludes a bit stiffish. The sangiovese and montepulciano Colle Carpito gave its usual fine performance, the '06 showing sapid and earthy, with a character worthier than its role as a second label. The two '07 whites are reliable and soundly made. Luna di Monte is the crisper, while Resico is more richly flavoured.

● Bolgheri Sassicaia '05	♟♟♟ 8
● Guidalberto '06	♟♟ 7
● Le Difese '06	♟♟ 5
● Bolgheri Sassicaia '04	♟♟♟ 8
● Bolgheri Sassicaia '03	♟♟♟ 8
● Bolgheri Sassicaia '02	♟♟♟ 8
● Bolgheri Sassicaia '01	♟♟♟ 8
● Bolgheri Sassicaia '00	♟♟♟ 8
● Bolgheri Sassicaia '99	♟♟♟ 8
● Bolgheri Sassicaia '98	♟♟♟ 8
● Bolgheri Sassicaia '97	♟♟♟ 8
● Bolgheri Sassicaia '96	♟♟♟ 8
● Bolgheri Sassicaia '95	♟♟♟ 8
● Sassicaia '93	♟♟♟ 6
● Sassicaia '92	♟♟♟ 8
● Sassicaia '90	♟♟♟ 8
● Sassicaia '88	♟♟♟ 8
● Sassicaia '85	♟♟♟ 8

● Boschi Salviati '06	♟♟ 4*
● D'Ovidio '05	♟♟ 6
● Colle Carpito '06	♟ 4
○ Resico '07	♟ 3
○ Valdichiana Luna di Monte '07	♟ 3
● Boschi Salviati '05	♟♟ 4*
● D'Ovidio '04	♟♟ 6
● D'Ovidio '03	♟♟ 6
● D'Ovidio '01	♟♟ 6
● D'Ovidio '00	♟♟ 7
● D'Ovidio '99	♟♟ 5
● D'Ovidio '98	♟♟ 5

San Michele a Torri

VIA SAN MICHELE, 36
50020 SCANDICCI [FI]
TEL. 055769111
www.fattoriasanmichele.it

ANNUAL PRODUCTION	230,000 bottles
HECTARES UNDER VINE	50
VITICULTURE METHOD	Certified organic

After years spent among the Other Wineries, Paolo Nocentini's San Michele a Torri returns to the big time. The winery is located near Florence, with a small parcel of six hectares in Chianti Classico. Its origins, and its first buildings, go back to the Middle Ages, but the chapel and the neo-Gothic well are from the 18th century, and winemaking got off the ground around 1800. The structure was restored first in 1822 and then completely rebuilt after the Second World War. Our tastings this year were particularly impressive, beginning with the Supertuscan Murtas, whose name honours the cellarman who has worked with the family forever. A blend of sangiovese, cabernet sauvignon and colorino, it releases peremptory wild berry, spices and chocolate, and the palate is rich and sturdy, with an admirable fabric of tannins and scrumptious flavours. Plaudits for Vin Santo, which offers the traditional dried figs and almonds, then develops an enviable creaminess and velvet texture in the mouth. Chianti Colli Fiorentini Riserva '05 impresses with its considerable volume and well-delineated nose. The remaining wines are pleasures to drink.

San Polo

LOC. PODERE SAN POLO DI PODERNOVI, 161
53024 MONTALCINO [SI]
TEL. 0577835101
www.poggiosanpolo.com

ANNUAL PRODUCTION	70,000 bottles
HECTARES UNDER VINE	15
VITICULTURE METHOD	Conventional

After passing through several hands, Poggio San Polo is now owned by Marilisa Allegrini, a long-time figure in the wine world. The cellar is in a gorgeous position, on the north flank of the Montalcino hill, looking towards Val d'Orcia, and Allegrini can take advantage of the restructurings carried out by previous owners in both vineyards and cellar, particularly its contingent of barrels. We are sure that her valuable experience will fuel the rapid ascent of San Polo in its territory. Brunello di Montalcino '03 is a stand-out, obtained from an extremely painstaking selection of wine lots in the cellar, which left it free of those hot notes that are the hallmark of the 2003 vintage. The nose proffers emphatic fruit lifted with smooth vanilla and clove, and the considerable extractive weight on the palate is nicely offset by vibrant acidity and fine-grained tannins. Kudos to the winemaking staff. We recommend too Mezzopane '05, with white peach and a hint of menthol. A set of noticeable tannins stiffens the palate somewhat at this point but time will cure that.

● Chianti Colli Fiorentini S. Giovanni Novantasette Ris. '05	♟♟ 5
○ Colli dell'Etruria Centrale Vin Santo '03	♟♟ 7
● Murtas '05	♟♟ 6
● Chianti Cl. La Gabbiola '06	♟ 4
● Chianti Cl. La Gabbiola Ris. '05	♟ 5
● Chianti Colli Fiorentini '06	♟ 3
● Murtas '03	♟♟ 6
● Murtas '02	♟♟ 6
● Murtas '01	♟♟ 6

● Brunello di Montalcino '03	♟♟ 7
● Mezzopane '05	♟♟ 6
● Rosso di Montalcino '05	♟ 5
● Rubio '06	♟ 4
● Brunello di Montalcino '99	♟♟ 7
● Mezzopane '00	♟♟ 6

Castello di San Sano

FRAZ. SAN SANO
LOC. PALAZZINO
53013 GAIOLE IN CHIANTI [SI]
TEL. 0577746056
www.castellosansano.com

ANNUAL PRODUCTION   200,000 bottles
HECTARES UNDER VINE 87
VITICULTURE METHOD   Conventional

Owned by Calogero Calì, also the proprietor of Tenuta di Capraia and Rocca di Castagnoli, Castello di San Sano offered our tasters a fine group of bottlings, even of the 2005 vintage, which proved not one of the best in Chianti Classico. Such results just go to confirm the quality level of the huge investments made here in both the vineyards and the winemaking cellar. Chianti Classico Guarnellotto Riserva '05 provided the best performance, releasing deep draughts of dark wild berry fruit, moist earth and mineral essences. The palate offers a structure in which dense-packed tannins are well inserted, nervy acidity and a flavoursome finale. The Supertuscan Borro al Fumo '05, a partnership of sangiovese and cabernet sauvignon, is deeply fragrant on the nose, but its tannins still show a tad clenched. Chianti Classico '06 is truly classic, showing succulent, bright and vibrant in the mouth, while Chianti Vigneto della Rana '07 is a delicious quaffer.

Tenuta San Vito

VIA SAN VITO, 59
50056 MONTELUPO FIORENTINO [FI]
TEL. 057151411
www.san-vito.com

ANNUAL PRODUCTION   170,000 bottles
HECTARES UNDER VINE 34
VITICULTURE METHOD   Certified organic

The Drighi family earns a full profile for the Guide debut of Tenuta San Vito, which they acquired in 1960. This was one of the first Tuscan agricultural operations to identify itself with organic farming, motivated by a respect for the earth and the local environment. That same respect is visible in the restructuring of the venerable farm buildings, which are now an agriturismo. The winemaking is overseen by Attilio Pagli, in collaboration with Marinka Polencic. We felt that the all-merlot Colle dei Mandorli '06 was the most impressive in the line-up. A tasty base of blackberry jelly foregrounds rich spice essences, followed by a vigorous attack, then juicy succulence and alluring complexity on the palate, through to a dynamic finish. We also liked Madiere '06, made of sangiovese, merlot and cabernet sauvignon. It sports a variegated medley of impressions, mostly tending to the herbaceous, and benefits from an agile, dynamic structure. The remaining wines are all easy-drinking and display clean-edged aromatics: Chianti Colli Fiorentini Darno '07, the all-Chardonnay Amantiglio '07, and the richly aromatic Chianti '07.

● Chianti Cl. Guarnellotto Ris. '05	♟♟ 5
● Chianti Cl. '06	♟♟ 4*
● Borro al Fumo '05	♟ 6
● Chianti Vign. della Rana '07	♟ 3
● Borro al Fumo '04	♟♟ 6
● Chianti Cl. Guarnellotto Ris. '04	♟♟ 5

● Colle dei Mandorli '06	♟♟ 6
● Madiere '06	♟♟ 5
○ Amantiglio '07	♟ 4
● Chianti '07	♟ 3
● Chianti Colli Fiorentini Darno '07	♟ 4
● Colle dei Mandorli '05	♟♟ 6
● Colle dei Mandorli '04	♟♟ 6
● Madiere '05	♟♟ 5
● Madiere '04	♟♟ 5

Podere Sapaio

LOC. LO SCOPAIO, 212
57022 CASTAGNETO CARDUCCI [LI]
TEL. 0565765187
www.sapaio.com

ANNUAL PRODUCTION	75,000 bottles
HECTARES UNDER VINE	25
VITICULTURE METHOD	Conventional

A full profile goes to Podere Sapaio, Massimo Piccin's cellar at Castagneto Carducci. Some of the 25 hectares of vineyards are with the winery there, the remainder at Bibbiena. Piccin, moved by a sincere passion for his wines, focuses here on achieving high-quality results, with meticulous attention to detail.
The vineyards are planted to cabernet sauvignon, cabernet franc and merlot, plus a few lesser-known varieties and the fruit goes into the two winery labels, Bolgheri Superiore Sapaio and Bolgheri Volpolo. The '05 edition of the former was so impressive it went to the national taste-offs. First to emerge is rich red and dark wild berry fruit, nicely ripe, flanked by pungent spice and black pepper. The palate is taut and fragrant, supported by a bright, crisp acidity and dense-packed tannins, and concluding with a spice-infused finale of great length. Bolgheri Volpolo splendidly performs its role as Podere Sapaio's second label, since it makes up for a lack of complexity and breadth with wonderful approachability and savouriness, where it has no rival.

● Bolgheri Sapaio Sup. '05	♟♟	7
● Bolgheri Volpolo '06	♟♟	5
● Bolgheri Sapaio Sup. '04	♟♟	7

Sassotondo

PIAN DI CONATI, 52
58010 SOVANA [GR]
TEL. 0564614218
www.sassotondo.it

ANNUAL PRODUCTION	50,000 bottles
HECTARES UNDER VINE	12
VITICULTURE METHOD	Certified organic

If every grape variety were to select its own patron saint, ciliegiolo would without doubt choose Saint Laurence, since San Lorenzo is the iconic wine of Sassotondo, the operation of Edoardo Ventimiglia and his wife Carla Benini. Without San Lorenzo, ciliegiolo, a variety with ancient roots, would not have regained, at least in some parts of Tuscany, the dignity and reputation it currently enjoys. This year, too, San Lorenzo went to the national finals, on the strength of its by now customary high quality and personal characteristics. The aromatic component in the '05 edition privileges wild berry fruit, spice and a refreshing vein of black pepper while the palate shows lush and juicy, and lengthy on the finish, with just a touch of oak left to absorb. Ciliegiolo '07 shines as well, if at a slightly lower wattage. Less complex than San Lorenzo and matured only in steel, it offers truly superb pleasure in the glass. It's a wine as perfumed and fresh as it is vibrant and savoury. Sovana Rosso Superiore '06 is well crafted. If the nose is a tad closed, it shows fine body and progression. Bianco di Pitigliano '07 is tasty.

● San Lorenzo '05	♟♟	7
● Ciliegiolo '07	♟♟	3*
○ Bianco di Pitigliano '07	♟	4
● Sovana Rosso Sup. '06	♟	4
● San Lorenzo '04	♟♟	6
● San Lorenzo '03	♟♟	6
● San Lorenzo '02	♟♟	6
● San Lorenzo '01	♟♟	6
● San Lorenzo '00	♟♟	6
● San Lorenzo '99	♟♟	5
● San Lorenzo '98	♟♟	5
● San Lorenzo '97	♟♟	4
● Sassotondo Rosso '98	♟♟	3
● Sovana Rosso Sup. Franze '03	♟♟	5
● Sovana Rosso Sup. Franze '00	♟♟	5
● Sovana Rosso Sup. Franze '99	♟♟	4

Michele Satta

LOC. CASONE UGOLINO, 23
57022 CASTAGNETO CARDUCCI [LI]
TEL. 0565773041
www.michelesatta.com

ANNUAL PRODUCTION	160,000 bottles
HECTARES UNDER VINE	28
VITICULTURE METHOD	Conventional

Michele Satta surprised us this year since his most impressive wines were whites. For a Bolgheri-based operation that has historically focused on reds, this is a departure. Cask ageing, however, has had some negative results. Bolgheri Superiore I Castagni '05 shows emphatic oak influence on the nose that carries over to the palate in tannins that are very drying and even powdery. It's a real shame, since the wine displays lovely acidity and great texture but it has little chance, at least in its youth, of revealing its qualities. More approachable and enjoyable is Bolgheri Rosso '06, with crisp, fresh herbaceousness and a supple, lithe body. Bolgheri Piastraia '05, after slight hesitation on the nose, lays out a spacious, succulent palate, slowed down a bit at the end by bitterish tannin. Diambra '06, largely sangiovese with some colorino, malvasia and ciliegiolo, shows a similar style and ends a tad short. But Bolgheri Bianco '07 is splendid, offering florality, savoury flavours and a long conclusion, as is the very lengthy and tautly wound Costa di Giulia '07. Giovin Re '07 is tropical and complex, if somewhat abbreviated.

Savignola Paolina

VIA PETRIOLO, 58
50022 GREVE IN CHIANTI [FI]
TEL. 0558546036
www.savignolapaolina.it

ANNUAL PRODUCTION	35,000 bottles
HECTARES UNDER VINE	7
VITICULTURE METHOD	Conventional

Small is beautiful would come to mind when you consider how much is accomplished at this tiny operation in Chianti Classico. The history is lovely too, since the name Savignola pays homage to an ancient Etruscan settlement, but a town arose only in the 17th century. Paolina, a member of the Fabbri family that still owns the operation, laid the foundations for the emergence of the area in the period between the two world wars. Granddaughter Ludovica and her husband Antonio modernized the complex, creating a small, precious jewel of a winery. Chianti Classico Riserva '05 is again their most impressive wine. Very refined, ethereal essences emerge on the nose, nicely offset by wild dark berry fruit, and the palate too is slender and subtle, also showing fresh and inviting. It's not very broad but has a self-confident finish. The sangiovese-merlot Supertuscan, Granaio '06, also scored well. A traditional duet of subtle spice and toasty oak on the nose is followed by an appealing, rounded palate and impressive weight, with a nice broad, full finale. Chianti Classico '06 is good and ambitious.

O Bolgheri Bianco '07	♟♟	4
● Bolgheri Rosso '06	♟♟	6
● Bolgheri Rosso Sup. I Castagni '05	♟♟	8
O Costa di Giulia '07	♟♟	5
● Bolgheri Rosso Diambra '06	♟	4
● Bolgheri Rosso Piastraia '05	♟	7
● Diambra Rosso '06	♟	4
O Giovin Re '07	♟	6
● Bolgheri Rosso Piastraia '02	♟♟♟	7
● Bolgheri Rosso Piastraia '01	♟♟♟	7
● Bolgheri Rosso Piastraia '00	♟♟	7
● Bolgheri Rosso Sup. I Castagni '04	♟♟	8
● Bolgheri Rosso Sup. I Castagni '03	♟♟	8
● Bolgheri Rosso Sup. I Castagni '01	♟♟	8

● Chianti Cl. Ris. '05	♟♟	5
● Granaio '06	♟♟	5
● Chianti Cl. '06	♟	4
● Chianti Cl. Ris. '04	♟♟	5
● Granaio '01	♟♟	6

Scopetani

VIA FIORENTINA, 33
50068 RUFINA [FI]
TEL. 0558397032
www.scopetani.it

ANNUAL PRODUCTION	1,000,000 bottles
HECTARES UNDER VINE	13
VITICULTURE METHOD	Conventional

The Scopetani brothers emerge from some years spent in the limbo of the Other Wineries section and gain a full profile. This is a prominent cellar in the Rufina area. The family were bottlers for a long time but then began producing wines from their own vineyards. Giulio Gerardo Scopetani founded the business in 1930, and Graziano Scopetani and his sister Gisella continue it today. The wines we tasted all came from Villa Masseto, the property where all of the winemaking takes place. We liked Chianti Rufina 813 Riserva '05 best. Modern in style and quite likeable, it opens with toastiness, wild berries and smooth spice, then builds a spacious, solid, appealing palate that is very rich and succulent, ending with a lovely burst of energy. All of the other wines are well made, similar in style, and enjoyable.

La Selva

FRAZ. SAN DONATO - ALBINIA
LOC. LA SELVA
58010 ORBETELLO [GR]
TEL. 0564885799
www.laselva-bio.eu

ANNUAL PRODUCTION	200,000 bottles
HECTARES UNDER VINE	31
VITICULTURE METHOD	Certified organic

For the second year in a row, Karl Egger's winery actually sent two wines to the final taste-offs, confirmation that La Selva is one of the most impressive producers in the fecund Maremma wine scene. His two Morellinos, made in the cellar in Magliano, signal impressive consistency in quality. Morellino di Scansano Colli dell'Uccellina '06 presents gorgeous definition and decent complexity on the nose, where delicate spice infuses lush fruit and slaty minerality. The palate is spacious, succulent and well sculpted. Morellino di Scansano '07 shows in the same general register, perhaps a little less complex, but bright and supple in the mouth. Prima Causa '06, a blend of cabernet sauvignon and merlot, is quite alluring, with ripe fragrances and robust, dense tannins. Ciliegiolo '06 is vivacious and full flavoured while the sangiovese Rosso La Selva '07 is sturdily built. Scents of lime blossom and hints of toasted almond nicely enliven Vermentino '07, which shows self-confident and rich in the mouth. Bianco Toscana '07, from vermentino and ansonica, is quite simple.

● Chianti Rufina 813 Ris. '05	♥♥	4*
● Chianti Rufina Stellario Ris. '05	♥	4
● Chianti Rufina V. Macereto Ris. '05	♥	4
● Nemus '05	♥	4

● Morellino di Scansano '07	♥♥	4*
● Morellino di Scansano Colli dell'Uccellina '06	♥♥	4*
● Ciliegiolo '06	♥♥	5
● Prima Causa '06	♥♥	6
O Bianco Toscana '07	♥	3
● Rosso La Selva '07	♥	4
● Ciliegiolo '05	♥♥	5
● Morellino di Scansano '05	♥♥	3
● Prima Causa '05	♥♥	6
● Prima Causa '04	♥♥	6
● Prima Causa '01	♥♥	5
O Vermentino La Selva '05	♥♥	3
O Vermentino La Selva '04	♥♥	3

Fattoria Selvapiana

LOC. SELVAPIANA, 43
50068 RUFINA [FI]
TEL. 0558369848
www.selvapiana.it

ANNUAL PRODUCTION	220,000 bottles
HECTARES UNDER VINE	59.7
VITICULTURE METHOD	Conventional

Federico Giuntini Antinori has poured incredible energy into Fattoria Selvapiana in recent years. After restructuring the cellar, he finished converting the vineyards to organic methods, thus putting into final form his programme of achieving complete naturalness for his wines. Respect for his grapes and for their terroir will mean, of course, that he will not have the same characteristics each year. But 2004 certainly did him proud, since the superb character of Chianti Rufina Vigneto Bucerchiale again sent it to the final national tasting round. It releases an intriguing mosaic of evolved impressions, such as tanned leather, tobacco leaf and raw leather, along with rich fruit preserves. A sturdy palate showcases pulpy fruit, well tucked-in tannins and a vibrant vein of acidity, then finishes with a dynamic flourish. All in all, it's a lip-smacking wine. Pomino Fattoria di Petrognano returns this year in the '06 edition. It's a real treat, since the wine is made only in the best vintages. Its strong suit is its crisp, refreshing appeal, as well as a bright suite of fruit and floral aromas. Chianti Rufina '06 is well made and tasty.

Serraiola

FRAZ. FRASSINE
LOC. SERRAIOLA
58025 MONTEROTONDO MARITTIMO [GR]
TEL. 0566910026
www.serraiola.it

ANNUAL PRODUCTION	60,000 bottles
HECTARES UNDER VINE	10
VITICULTURE METHOD	Conventional

Fiorella Lenzi's winery is one of the longest-producing in Monteregio di Massa Marittima denomination, and recent years have seen Serraiola's production reach very high quality levels. The wines are well crafted and a pleasure in the glass but they could display a bit more personality. Shiraz '06 competed in the national finals, thanks to a solidly varietal nose and a palate that shows depth and balance but retains a pleasing freshness. Campo di Montecristo '06 is a superb blend of merlot, sangiovese and syrah but it does show slightly excessive toast on both nose and palate. Monteregio Lentisco '06 and Monteregio Cervone '07 are sound and enjoyable. The first is notably succulent but with a note of dryness on the finish. The second is less complex and still on the way to complete wholeness. Monteregio Bianco Violina '07 is well made, through quite straightforward, as is Vermentino '07, both of them displaying an emphatic mineral edge and interesting counterpoint through the palate.

● Chianti Rufina Bucerchiale '04	♥♥ 6
● Pomino Fattoria di Petrognano '06	♥♥ 4*
● Chianti Rufina '06	♥ 4
● Chianti Rufina Bucerchiale Ris. '03	♀♀ 6
● La Fornace '00	♀♀ 7

● Shiraz '06	♥♥ 5
● Campo Montecristo '06	♥♥ 6
○ Monteregio di Massa Marittima Bianco Violina '07	♥ 4
● Monteregio di Massa Marittima Cervone '07	♥ 4
● Monteregio di Massa Marittima Rosso Lentisco '06	♥ 4
○ Vermentino '07	♥ 4
● Campo Montecristo '05	♀♀ 6
● Campo Montecristo '04	♀♀ 6
● Campo Montecristo '01	♀♀ 6
● Monteregio di Massa Marittima Rosso Lentisco '05	♀♀ 5
● Shiraz '05	♀♀ 5
● Shiraz '04	♀♀ 5

Sesti - Castello di Argiano

FRAZ. SANT'ANGELO IN COLLE
LOC. CASTELLO DI ARGIANO
53024 MONTALCINO [SI]
TEL. 0577843921
giuseppesesti@sesti.net

ANNUAL PRODUCTION	62,000 bottles
HECTARES UNDER VINE	8.5
VITICULTURE METHOD	Conventional

From their 13th-century tower, once the southern boundary of the republic of Siena, Giuseppe and Elisa Sesti turn out terrific quality wines. Their many – perhaps too many – bottlings are always admirable, made with respect for lunar cycles and sourced from vines that see only a bare minimum of any kind of treatments. We couldn't taste Brunello di Montalcino Phenomena since it wasn't made in the poor year of 2002. From the wines tasted, we liked many of those based on '06 sangiovese, which promises to be a fine year. Rosso di Montalcino '06 is outstanding, with a nose where classic tobacco leaf and leather predominate over a fruit base, and a palate whose firm structure is well supported by elegant, relaxed tannins. Its acidity is noticeable but measured and drives the progression into a long-lingering finale. The all-sangiovese Grangiovese '06 is terrific, richly redolent of aromatic herbs and with a seductive finish. We recommend Sauvignon '07 for its brightly varietal herbaceous and balsamic nose and fabulous palate. It's simply Montalcino's best white wine. The tannins on the still unrelaxed Brunello di Montalcino '03 are keeping it taut.

Setriolo

LOC. SETRIOLO, 61
53011 CASTELLINA IN CHIANTI [SI]
TEL. 0577743079

ANNUAL PRODUCTION	10,000 bottles
HECTARES UNDER VINE	3.5
VITICULTURE METHOD	Conventional

The Soderi family follows their debut in last year's Guide with a terrific performance that merits a long profile as well as with Chianti Classico '06 that went to the national finals. Passion and dedication are the ingredients that propelled them into a vineyard project that has roots in the past. Its symbol could be the single olive tree right in the middle of the vineyard, which survived the 1985 freeze, its message that if one has firm resolve one can begin again from any disaster. Setriolo's few hectares are planted to sangiovese and merlot, with a generous plot dedicated to olive trees as well, since the Soderis produce a highly-respected olive oil, and there's an agriturismo too. All of this testifies to a lifelong contact with nature which they welcome all the year through. We were impressed with the inviting nose of Chianti Classico '06, with its sour cherry and subtle spice, as well as its extreme drinkability and delicate fabric of velvety tannins. Memores '06 is an equal partnership of merlot and sangiovese; its nose is sound, but incisive tannins throw off the balance somewhat.

● Grangiovese '06	▼▼	5
● Rosso di Montalcino '06	▼▼	6
O Sauvignon '07	▼▼	4
● Brunello di Montalcino '03	▼	7
● Sant'Antimo Terra di Siena '04	▼	6
● Brunello di Montalcino Phenomena Ris. '01	♈♈♈	8
● Brunello di Montalcino '01	♈♈	7
● Brunello di Montalcino Phenomena Ris. '00	♈♈	8
● Brunello di Montalcino Phenomena Ris. '99	♈♈	8

● Chianti Classico '06	▼▼	4*
● Memores '06	▼	5
● Memores '05	♈♈	5

Tenuta Sette Ponti

LOC. VIGNA DI PALLINO
52029 CASTIGLION FIBOCCHI [AR]
TEL. 055477857
www.tenutasetteponti.it

ANNUAL PRODUCTION	230,000 bottles
HECTARES UNDER VINE	50
VITICULTURE METHOD	Conventional

Tenuta Setteponti fielded a reduced team this year. There was no Chianti Vigna di Pallino '07, which hadn't been bottled when we tasted, and above all no superstar Oreno '06, which needs more ageing. We'll be tasting it for the next edition of the Guide. Still, Crognolo was present to uphold the team honour and the '06 edition did so magnificently. Largely sangiovese with a dollop of merlot, it's modern in bent but judiciously so. The aromas are mostly dark fruit but nicely relieved by blossoms and balsam that freshen the nose and expand its wings a bit. The palate is quite appealing, with good depth and breadth, dense tannins, and generous aromas and flavours. Poggio al Lupo, the winery's Maremma property, releases a wine of the same name in the '06 version. Primarily cabernet sauvignon with some alicante and petit verdot, it faithfully reflects its provenance. It opens with ripe, dark fruit, Mediterranean scrub and emphatic notes of oak. The attack is huge and incisive tannins will need time to smoothen out. Morellino '07 is well measured, a dark, rich, dense version, yet fresh and fully flavoured.

Solaria - Cencioni

POD. CAPANNA, 102
53024 MONTALCINO [SI]
TEL. 0577849426
www.solariacencioni.com

ANNUAL PRODUCTION	30,000 bottles
HECTARES UNDER VINE	8.5
VITICULTURE METHOD	Conventional

Patrizia Cencioni is a true wine woman and we have always liked her wines. You might well see her in the vineyard as she does the winter pruning or drives the tractor, or in the cellar doing a racking, always with the same dedication and care. This year was quite unusual in that none of her wines went to the national finals, where she has participated ever since the Brunello '95. The culprit was Brunello di Montalcino '03, from a truly challenging growing year. After a few moments of oxygen, it opens to a nose of medium intensity, but nicely complex, showing medicinal herbs, tobacco leaf and spices that metamorphose the underlying fruit. It enters impetuously on the palate, even if stiffish tannins somewhat slow the progression, more so than in previous vintages. The finish is nicely aromatic, and the absence of bitter notes augurs a positive development of the tannins over time. Rosso di Montalcino '06 is brightly delicious, with clean, well-delineated fragrances of cherry.

● Crognolo '06	▼▼ 5
● Morellino di Scansano Poggio al Lupo '07	▼▼ 4
● Poggio al Lupo '06	▼▼ 6
● Oreno '05	▼▼▼ 8
● Oreno '00	▼▼▼ 6
● Crognolo '05	▼▼ 5
● Oreno '04	▼▼ 8
● Oreno '03	▼▼ 7
● Oreno '01	▼▼ 6
● Oreno '99	▼▼ 6
● Poggio al Lupo '05	▼▼ 6
● Poggio al Lupo '03	▼▼ 6
● Poggio al Lupo '01	▼▼ 6

● Brunello di Montalcino '03	▼▼ 7
● Rosso di Montalcino '06	▼ 5
● Brunello di Montalcino '97	▼▼▼ 7
● Brunello di Montalcino '01	▼▼ 7
● Brunello di Montalcino '00	▼▼ 6
● Brunello di Montalcino '99	▼▼ 7
● Brunello di Montalcino '98	▼▼ 8

Le Sorgenti

LOC. VALLINA
VIA DI DOCCIOLA, 8
50012 BAGNO A RIPOLI [FI]
TEL. 055696004
www.fattoria-lesorgenti.com

ANNUAL PRODUCTION	40,000 bottles
HECTARES UNDER VINE	17
VITICULTURE METHOD	Conventional

The Ferrari family fielded an excellent set of wines. All impressed our tasters, confirming that the new direction taken by Filippo and his father Gabriele is now yielding the desired fruit. They have covered a lot of ground: painstaking attention in the vineyard and cellar, determination to keep up-to-date, watching other producers to learn about and adopt new practices. All of these ingredients have allowed Le Sorgenti to grow in a disciplined, judicious manner. Scirus '05, the flagship wine, doesn't lack much for that final push to the laurels. An equal partnership of cabernet sauvignon and merlot, the nose proffers dark, rich spice and ethereal menthol while the palate shows good volume, compelling juicy pulp and succulent aromas on the finish. We admired the performance from the all-sangiovese Gaiacci '06, in which minerally impressions predominate on the nose and bright, sapid flavours infuse the palate. Sghiras '06, a delicious blend of chardonnay and sauvignon, ably blends citrus and pungent herbs on the nose and refreshing acidity complements a sturdy structure. Chianti Colli Fiorentini Respiro '06 is notable for its great value.

Spadaio e Piecorto

VIA SAN SILVESTRO, 1
50021 BARBERINO VAL D'ELSA [FI]
TEL. 0558072915
spadaiopiecorto@tiscali.it

ANNUAL PRODUCTION	60,000 bottles
HECTARES UNDER VINE	14
VITICULTURE METHOD	Conventional

The fine overall quality of the Stefanelli family's wines brings them back to a full profile. In the border area between Florence and Siena, Spadaio e Piecorto is a small 12th-century hamlet built near a Roman road. In addition to producing wine and olive oil, the Stefanellis run an agriturismo in the municipality of Poggibonsi. We liked Pietra Rossa '05 best from the range presented. Although a Bordeaux blend of cabernet sauvignon and merlot, it shows little of the international, reflecting rather impressions typical of a terroir whose style is becoming quite versatile and impressive. After crisp, refreshing sensations of forest floor and pungent herbs, the wine builds body that is sturdy yet rounded and smooth, with barely noticeable tannins, then concludes masterfully long and spacious. We also very much liked Chianti Classico Piecorto '06. Made from a selection of the finest estate-grown grapes, it shows superb fruit on the nose and a supple palate, gratifying the senses instantly. Chianti Classico '06 is pleasurable and well balanced.

● Chianti Colli Fiorentini Respiro '06	▼▼	4*
● Gaiaccia '06	▼▼	5
● Scirus '05	▼▼	6
○ Sghiras '06	▼▼	5
● Gaiaccia '05	♈♈	4
● Gaiaccia '04	♈♈	4
● Scirus '04	♈♈	6
● Scirus '01	♈♈	6
● Scirus '00	♈♈	6
● Scirus '99	♈♈	5

● Chianti Cl. Piecorto '06	▼▼	4*
● Pietra Rossa '05	▼▼	4*
● Chianti Cl. '06	▼	4
● Pietra Rossa '04	♈♈	4

Talenti

FRAZ. SANT'ANGELO IN COLLE
LOC. PIAN DI CONTE
53020 MONTALCINO [SI]
TEL. 0577844064
www.talentimontalcino.it

ANNUAL PRODUCTION	80,000 bottles
HECTARES UNDER VINE	21
VITICULTURE METHOD	Conventional

We felt slight disappointment at the showing by the wines from the attractive Talenti winery. But the seasons are not at our beck and call, a fact Riccardo Talenti, one of Montalcino's most careful, unassuming growers, can testify is not only true but at times inconvenient. As it was in 2003, one of the hottest in memory. That vintage's Brunello di Montalcino shows ripe fruit on the nose that struggles to express its qualities but is held down by a heavy dose of oak and its concomitant vanilla and toastiness. The tannins are incisive on the palate and the finish fairly rigid, although decently rich. More time in the bottle will of course help the various elements to meld together better and the tannins to polymerize and soften. Rosso di Montalcino, on the other hand, benefited from the excellent 2006, and it's a charmer. Cherry and bramble, lively acidity, and a juicy, lengthy progression make it fresh and delicious all the way through. The sangiovese-heavy Pian di Conte '06 is very nice, ending long and dynamic.

● Pian di Conte '06	▼▼ 6
● Rosso di Montalcino '06	▼▼ 4
● Brunello di Montalcino '03	▼ 7
● Brunello di Montalcino Ris. '99	♔♔♔ 7
● Brunello di Montalcino Ris. Vigna del Paretaio '01	♔♔♔ 7
● Brunello di Montalcino '01	♔♔ 6
● Brunello di Montalcino '00	♔♔ 6

Tenimenti Angelini

LOC. VAL DI CAVA
53024 MONTALCINO [SI]
TEL. 057780411
www.tenimentiangelini.it

ANNUAL PRODUCTION	890,000 bottles
HECTARES UNDER VINE	173
VITICULTURE METHOD	Conventional

Tenimenti Angelini has completed its overall restructuring of both vineyards and winemaking facility, and is now looking for the fruits of such an ambitious undertaking. But vineyards respond slowly and more time must pass before the bright results take shape. Meantime, the two wines presented this year certainly showed fine mettle, with Brunello di Montalcino '03 being particularly impressive. A garnet-edged ruby, it opens first to rich notes of roasted coffee beans and caramel, which then yield to juicy white-fleshed fruit. Self-confident acidity and tannin, particularly the latter, predominate on the palate, which is medium-bodied, and without the excessive alcohol all too frequent in this vintage. We liked Rosso di Montalcino '06, although it is on the straightforward side. It opens to yellow peach with subtle spice, then offers a succulent, attractive palate with a vibrant vein of acidity and well-crafted, subdued tannins. Nobile di Montepulciano La Villa '04, produced at Tre Rose in Montepulciano, is lovely, as is Chianti Classico '06, from San Leonino, in the Chianti Classico zone.

● Brunello di Montalcino '03	▼▼ 7
● Chianti Cl. San Leonino '06	▼ 4
● Nobile di Montepulciano La Villa '04	▼ 6
● Rosso di Montalcino '06	▼ 5
● Brunello di Montalcino V. del Lago '95	♔♔♔ 8
● Brunello di Montalcino V. del Lago '93	♔♔♔ 8
● Brunello di Montalcino V. Spuntali '95	♔♔♔ 8
● Brunello di Montalcino V. Spuntali '93	♔♔♔ 8
● Brunello di Montalcino '01	♔♔ 6
● Brunello di Montalcino V. del Lago '99	♔♔ 8
● Brunello di Montalcino Vigna Spuntali '97	♔♔ 8

Terrabianca

LOC. SAN FEDELE A PATERNO
53017 RADDA IN CHIANTI [SI]
TEL. 057754029
www.terrabianca.com

ANNUAL PRODUCTION	360,000 bottles
HECTARES UNDER VINE	52
VITICULTURE METHOD	Conventional

Roberto Guidener's wines continue to be good, hence the full profile. But just as teachers may suspect that certain students could do a lot better, we feel that only a part of Terrabianca's potential is being realized. On the one hand they have plethora of bottlings, which has to complicate work in vineyard and cellar, and on the other, the search for the right style, which at the moment is gradually shifting away from the international and towards greater terroir focus. Thus there are reasons to believe that performances may improve. This year the wine that impressed us the most was Chianti Classico Croce Riserva '05, with its traditional-style nose of tobacco leaf, fresh leather and wild red berry fruit, followed by a fine-textured palate and a compelling finale. Pian del Cipresso '05 too, all sangiovese, receives an enthusiastic nod. Here, a fresher nose features pungent underbrush-like notes and dark berry fruit, lively energy and bright, pulpy fruit on a palate that develops quite lengthy. The remaining wines are sound, including a monovarietal Merlot, Il Tesoro '05, and Campaccio '05, a blend of sangiovese and cabernet sauvignon.

Terralsole

VILLA COLLINA D'ORO
53024 MONTALCINO [SI]
TEL. 0577835678
www.terralsole.com

ANNUAL PRODUCTION	45,000 bottles
HECTARES UNDER VINE	12
VITICULTURE METHOD	Conventional

Terralsole's growth is maintaining momentum, offering every year well-executed wines with a modern slant, but not excessively so, so that terroir succeeds in leaving its mark. The cellar is situated atop a beautiful rise from which you look right down into the Val d'Orcia while the barrel room boasts large casks of every style and dimension, with a preference for tonneaux and capacities around 700 litres. Barriques are utilized largely for non-denomination wines. This year, Pasticcio '06 struck us, so much so that it competed in the national finals. A classic Bordeaux blend, it starts off with a fetching aubergine hue, followed by blueberry, redcurrant and other wild berry fruit that then yield to pencil lead and elegant hints of spice. You savour the spacious volume in the mouth and fine acidity drives an impressive, delicious progression, concluding with a finale that is expansive and aromatic. Brunello di Montalcino '03 is well up to snuff. A few moments of oxygen in the glass bring out rich fruity essences and it shows nice balance on the palate, thanks to tannins that are already supple and relaxed.

● Chianti Cl. Croce Ris. '05	♟♟	6
● Piano del Cipresso '05	♟♟	5
● Campaccio '05	♟	6
● Chianti Cl. Scassino '06	♟	5
● Il Tesoro '05	♟	6
● Campaccio '00	♟♟	5
● Ceppate '01	♟♟	7

● Pasticcio '06	♟♟	5
● Brunello di Montalcino '03	♟♟	8
● Rosso di Montalcino '06	♟♟	6
● Solista '06	♟♟	4

Terre Vitate
Tenute Bruna Baroncini

via Fontallera, 21
53045 Montepulciano [SI]
tel. 0577 940600
www.terrevitate.com

ANNUAL PRODUCTION 250,000 bottles
HECTARES UNDER VINE 55
VITICULTURE METHOD Conventional

Once an offshoot of the San Gimignano cellar, Terre Vitate is now Bruna Baroncini's operation, with four properties in Tuscany's most prestigious growing areas, Montepulciano, Montalcino, the Maremma and Chianti Classico. Her most recent acquisition, Casuccio Tarletti, at Castelnuovo Berardenga, is not fully operational yet but we tasted wines from the other estates, made with the assistance of Nicola Berti and Andrea Mazzoni. The fine Morellino Rinaldone dell'Osa '07 comes from Quercia Rossa, in Tuscany's Magliano, as does Morellino di Scansano Campo della Paura '06. Fleshy and well built, it boasts alluring scents of dried plum and spices. Nobile di Montepulciano Pietra Nera Riserva '04 is masterful, showing incisive fruit on nose and palate, plus an elegant tannic weave and fine harmony. Rosso di Montepulciano Lupaio '07 is ready and refreshing. The fruit on Brunello '03, from Poggio Il Castellare in Montalcino, is smooth, with no overripeness, soft textured and nicely complex. We liked Rosso di Montalcino '06, with its tasty balsam and firm structure, as well as Passo del Capriolo '06, an appealing blend of sangiovese and merlot.

● Brunello di Montalcino '03	🍷🍷	6
● Morellino di Scansano Campo della Paura '06	🍷🍷	4*
● Nobile di Montepulciano Pietra Nera Ris. '04	🍷🍷	6
● Rosso di Montalcino '06	🍷🍷	5
● Morellino di Scansano Rinaldone dell'Osa '07	🍷	4
● Passo del Capriolo '06	🍷	4
● Rosso di Montepulciano Lupaio '07	🍷	3

★ Castello del Terriccio

via Bagnoli, 16
56040 Castellina Marittima [PI]
tel. 050699709
www.terriccio.it

ANNUAL PRODUCTION 320,000 bottles
HECTARES UNDER VINE 62
VITICULTURE METHOD Conventional

Once again, laurels go to Castello del Terriccio. Again we stood, glasses still in midair, enraptured by these peerless wines that weave, in their innermost sensory depths, the salty spray of the Tyrrhenian and the minerally tang of their reddish "terriccio" soil. Praise again to the management skills of Gian Annibale Medelana Ferri and to his winemaking staff. Lupicaia '05, an assemblage of cabernet sauvignon, merlot and petit verdot, seems to soar, like a red kite over the clouds, beyond the challenges of a difficult year, expressing itself with jaw-dropping energy, warmth and noble texture. A balsamic, earthy, herbaceous nose announces a palate of tremendous power and verve. Castello del Terriccio '05 "only" went through to the finals, thanks to black pepper spice and rich pungent balsam tones, plus a full-volume body still showing a sign or two of adolescence. Tassinaia '05 gives delicious aromatic freshness and impressive depth, although that difficult vintage has left its mark, presumably on the sangiovese component. All of the rest of the wines we tasted were as superb as ever.

● Lupicaia '05	🍷🍷🍷	8
● Castello del Terriccio '05	🍷🍷	8
O Rondinaia '07	🍷🍷	5
● Tassinaia '05	🍷🍷	7
● Castello del Terriccio '04	YYY	8
● Castello del Terriccio '00	YYY	8
● Lupicaia '04	YYY	8
● Lupicaia '01	YYY	8
● Lupicaia '00	YYY	8
● Lupicaia '99	YYY	8
● Lupicaia '98	YYY	8
● Tassinaia '01	YY	6
● Tassinaia '00	YY	6

Teruzzi & Puthod

LOC. CASALE, 19
53037 SAN GIMIGNANO [SI]
TEL. 0577940143
www.teruzzieputhod.it

Testamatta

VIA DI VINCIGLIATA, 19
50014 FIESOLE [FI]
TEL. 055597289
www.bibigraetz.com

ANNUAL PRODUCTION	1.200.000 bottles
HECTARES UNDER VINE	73
VITICULTURE METHOD	Conventional

ANNUAL PRODUCTION	N.A.
HECTARES UNDER VINE	50
VITICULTURE METHOD	Conventional

Teruzzi & Puthod, now part of the Campari group, shrugs off the plateau of last year with a battery of very fine performers. The new management was not only able to quickly assemble a capable winemaking team but also to carry out a thorough reorganization of the vineyards. Terre di Tufi '07 was sent immediately to our national finals, for its elegant, ethereal notes of spring flowers, pear and wild herbs, as well as for its lengthy, energy-laden palate and broad, dense finish. Vernaccia di San Gimignano '07, produced in 450,000 bottles, is spot on, showing an eloquent nose and an incisive but even-handed palate that concludes with a hint of tasty mineral. Impressive, too, is San Gimignano Vigna Rondolino '07, which starts with citrus and floral notes then unleashes a steady, nervy progression that is utterly appealing. The same goes for Peperino '06, a sangiovese-merlot blend with fine tannic texture and a tasty conclusion. Vermentino '07 is aromatic and pleasurable.

Full marks for the wines of Bibi Graetz, and in particular for Testamatta '06, which went to the national final round. A monovarietal Sangiovese, it seems to take firm steps every year towards greater overall harmony. A lively ruby precedes a luscious, ultra-fruity nose mingling with abundant spice. The palate boasts a magisterial duet of tannins and alcohol plus an endless finale. Bibi deserves particular credit for believing in the potential of an undervalued growing area, for bringing it prestige, and for making clear to the world its fine qualities. Not content with this first discovery, he then ventured onto the Isola del Giglio, and contributed to relaunching the local ansonica grape, whose fine characteristics had been neglected for a long time. The result was a new path for the white wines of Tuscany. Bugia '06 simply confirms the value of ansonica. It is perhaps one of the best versions Graetz has made, apart from the surfeit of oak in this edition. High marks too for Soffocone '06 and Grilli '06, both relying on sangiovese with amounts of colorino and canaiolo. Elegant and classy, they flaunt delicious drinkability as their strong point.

O Terre di Tufi '07	▼▼ 5
O Vernaccia di S. Gimignano '07	▼▼ 4
O Vernaccia di S. Gimignano V. Rondolino '07	▼▼ 4
● Peperino '06	▼ 5
O Vermentino '07	▼ 4
● Peperino '05	♀♀ 4
O Vernaccia di S. Gimignano V. Rondolino '06	♀♀ 4

● Testamatta '06	▼▼ 8
O Bugia '06	▼▼ 7
● Grilli del Testamatta '06	▼▼ 6
● Soffocone di Vincigliata '06	▼▼ 6
O Bugia '04	♀♀ 7
● Colore '05	♀♀ 8
● Testamatta '05	♀♀ 8
● Testamatta '04	♀♀ 8

Tolaini

S. P. 9 DI PIEVASCIATA, 28
53019 CASTELNUOVO BERARDENGA [SI]
TEL. 0577356972
www.tolaini.it

ANNUAL PRODUCTION 200,000 bottles
HECTARES UNDER VINE 50
VITICULTURE METHOD Conventional

While the performances did not quite replicate those of last year, Pier Luigi Tolaini presented three wines with interesting and distinctive personalities that express, each in a different way, the challenging 2005 growing year. But nothing will tamp down the contagious enthusiasm of Tolaini, the driving force of the operation. Picconero, a partnership of merlot, cabernet sauvignon and petit verdot, was this year's stand-out. The nose compels with balsamic and herbaceous impressions, plus some notes of black pepper. It couldn't be more succulent and pulpy in the mouth, with tannins well in view, impressive expansion, and a lengthy finale. Tolaini's second label has been rechristened Valdisanti but the makeup remains the same: cabernet franc and cabernet sauvignon plus some merlot. Cinnamon and clove compose the nose, with some hints of toasty oak and chocolate. It enters supple on the palate and expands to considerable volume for a very tasty offering overall. Al Passo, from sangiovese and merlot, is simpler and shows a rough spot here and there.

Torraccia di Presura

LOC. STRADA IN CHIANTI
VIA DELLA MONTAGNOLA, 130
50027 GREVE IN CHIANTI [FI]
TEL. 0558588656
www.torracciadipresura.it

ANNUAL PRODUCTION 190,000 bottles
HECTARES UNDER VINE 31
VITICULTURE METHOD Conventional

After we noticed with regret somewhat lacklustre results for Torraccia di Presura's wines in last year's line-up, the Osti family responded with a sterling performance this year, even sending one wine, Supertuscan Lucciolaio '04, to the national taste-offs. Made primarily of sangiovese, with some cabernet sauvignon, a blend that is now a classic, it spreads generous nuances of tanned leather and chocolate over a base of blueberry and raspberry. Dense, spacious and multi-layered in the mouth, it exhibits well-balanced tannins and lush impressions of spice on the finish. The other IGT, Arcante '04, from merlot, cabernet and sangiovese, is a wine with impressive character. Vegetal notes and attractive oak are followed by very solid weight and good balance in the mouth, and it concludes crisp and succulent. The best of the Chianti Classico versions, we thought, was Riserva '05. It exudes personality, releasing interesting mineral, Mediterranean scrub and wild berries before offering a deep texture full of pulpy fruit.

● Picconero '05	▼▼ 8
● Valdisanti '05	▼▼ 6
● Al Passo '05	▼ 5
● Al Passo '04	♈ 5
● Al Passo '03	♈ 5
● Due Santi '03	♈ 6
● Due Santi '02	♈ 5
● Picconero '04	♈ 8
● Valdisanti '04	♈ 6

● Lucciolaio '04	▼▼ 6
● Arcante '04	▼▼ 6
● Chianti Cl. Il Tarocco Ris. '05	▼▼ 5
● Chianti Cl. '05	▼ 5
● Chianti Cl. Il Tarocco '06	▼ 4
● Chianti Cl. Il Tarocco Ris. '03	♈ 5
● Lucciolaio '00	♈ 6

Fattoria Torre a Cona

LOC. SAN DONATO IN COLLINA
50010 RIGNANO SULL'ARNO [FI]
TEL. 055699000
www.villatorreacona.com

ANNUAL PRODUCTION	30,000 bottles
HECTARES UNDER VINE	14
VITICULTURE METHOD	Conventional

The Rossi di Montelera family has held onto its profile in the Guide. The news item is that an ancient granary on this striking property has been converted for use as a space for wine tastings and other social and promotional activities. Meanwhile, the restructuring of the cellar, scheduled for completion in summer 2009, proceeds apace, as does the replanting of some blocks in the vineyard. All of this work amply shows the family's ever-increasing commitment to the estate. As to the wines tasted, we saw stylistic coherence and plenty of character. According to the vintage charts, 2005 was only a so-so year but Terre di Cino '05 emerged far superior to that tepid rating. A monovarietal Sangiovese, it unleashes attractive notes of crisp red berry fruit, strawberry, wild herbs and blossoms, maintaining the elegance on a palate that shows the influence of vivacious acidity at every stage. Chianti Colli Fiorentini '06 is appealing, fruit-filled and tasty. Vin Santo del Chianti Merlaia '03 is fabulous, inviting on both nose and palate. Dates, citrus zest and dried apricot pave the way for alluring sweetness and refreshing supporting acidity.

● Terre di Cino '05	▼▼ 4
○ Vin Santo del Chianti Merlaia '03	▼▼ 5
● Chianti Colli Fiorentini '06	▼ 2
● Terre di Cino '04	♀♀ 4
○ Vin Santo del Chianti Merlaia '01	♀♀ 5

Travignoli

VIA TRAVIGNOLI, 78
50060 PELAGO [FI]
TEL. 0558361098
www.travignoli.com

ANNUAL PRODUCTION	250,000 bottles
HECTARES UNDER VINE	70
VITICULTURE METHOD	Conventional

This year brings good showing from Giovanni Busi, president of the Consorzio del Chianti Rufina, who has recently been giving a good, healthy shake to the denomination. The farming estate has existed since the 12th century and the ancestors of the present owners took over in the late 18th century, providing a boost to the local wine sector. Travignoli's main focus has always been on Chianti Rufina and on improving the local vineyards. Proof is this year's most impressive wine, Vin Santo '00, which proffers bewitching, sweet scents of candied fruit, a lush, velvety smoothness and a compelling finish. Equally gorgeous is Riserva '05, which opens crisp and pungent, conveying ripe red berry fruit and gamey nuances. In the mouth, it shows complex and nicely proportioned, and while the finish is not of the longest, it is appealing and intriguing. Less impressive are the Supertuscans. Calice del Conte '05, a merlot and cabernet blend, and Tegolaia '05, from cabernet sauvignon and sangiovese, are both fairly unyielding. Chianti Rufina '06 is supple and enjoyable right now while Gavignano '07 is a clean, pleasurable Chardonnay.

● Chianti Rufina Ris. '05	▼▼ 5
○ Vin Santo Chianti Rufina '00	▼▼ 5
● Calice del Conte '05	▼ 6
● Chianti Rufina '06	▼ 3
○ Gavignano '07	▼ 3
● Tegolaia '05	▼ 5
● Chianti Rufina Ris. '04	♀♀ 5
● Chianti Rufina Ris. '03	♀♀ 5
● Chianti Rufina Ris. '01	♀♀ 4
● Chianti Rufina Ris. '00	♀♀ 4

Castello del Trebbio

VIA SANTA BRIGIDA, 9
50060 PONTASSIEVE [FI]
TEL. 0558304900
www.vinoturismo.it

ANNUAL PRODUCTION	340,000 bottles
HECTARES UNDER VINE	52
VITICULTURE METHOD	Conventional

The wines proposed by Anna Baj-Macario and Stefano Casadei can in no way be considered commonplace. You can argue about them and even criticize them, as we have done in the past, but there's no doubt these are wines with personality. There's no mistaking the hand of Casadei, an expert agronomist who loves to make wines even from the least known areas in Sardinia or to carry out challenging experimentation near Suvereto. But his vineyard work finds fertile results right here and his winemaking practices are calculated to bring out the best from the fruit. However you define his style, it could never be mistaken for anything near to the international. Casadei's Chianti Rufina Lastricato Riserva '04 impresses with intense hues, alluring aromatics that include tobacco leaf and smooth spice, complex and multi-faceted structure with firm, juicy tannins, and a finish with lots of length and interest. Both Supertuscans showed well. Pazzesco '04 is a sturdy but engaging blend of syrah, merlot and sangiovese, Bianco della Congiura '07 a crisp, assertive partnering of riesling, pinot and sauvignon. Chianti '07 is very tasty.

Tenuta di Trinoro

VIA VAL D'ORCIA, 15
53047 SARTEANO [SI]
TEL. 0578267110
www.trinoro.it

ANNUAL PRODUCTION	90,000 bottles
HECTARES UNDER VINE	29
VITICULTURE METHOD	Conventional

Andrea Franchetti's wine adventure is still unique in the world of Italian wine. His project was launched in the early 1990s but it began to compel wide respect only some ten years later, when the terroir he had selected for his rather bold experiment, which many considered improbable, actually began to produce the complexity he had sought. The wines are all made from grapes harvested late, between the end of October and early November. They all exhibit high-quality characteristics, even if reds of such profound depth require significant time to develop all of their potential. This is certainly the case with Tenuta di Trinoro '06, a medley of cabernet sauvignon, cabernet franc, merlot and petit verdot. It opens to emphatic aromas, then develops an interplay between silk-smooth, sweet fruit and a vein of high-energy acidity through to lush finish. It does seem a bit one-dimensional, however. Le Cupole '06 is made from the same blend, but from Tenuta di Trinoro's youngest vineyards. It is more mature and approachable, boasting a rich, intense nose and significant suppleness in the mouth.

○ Bianco della Congiura '07	▼▼	5
● Chianti Rufina Lastricato Ris. '04	▼▼	5
● Pazzesco '04	▼▼	6
● Chianti '07	▼	2
● Chianti Rufina Lastricato Ris. '03	♀♀	5
● Pazzesco '03	♀♀	6
● Pazzesco '99	♀♀	6
● Pazzesco '97	♀♀	4
● Rosso della Congiura '03	♀♀	7

● Tenuta di Trinoro '06	▼▼	8
● Le Cupole di Trinoro '06	▼▼	6
● Tenuta di Trinoro '04	♀♀♀	8
● Tenuta di Trinoro '03	♀♀♀	8
● Le Cupole di Trinoro '04	♀♀	6
● Le Cupole di Trinoro '03	♀♀	6
● Le Cupole di Trinoro '02	♀♀	6
● Tenuta di Trinoro '05	♀♀	8
● Tenuta di Trinoro '01	♀♀	8

★ Tua Rita

LOC. NOTRI, 81
57028 SUVERETO [LI]
TEL. 0565829237
www.tuarita.it

Uccelliera

FRAZ. CASTELNUOVO DELL'ABATE
POD. UCCELLIERA, 45
53020 MONTALCINO [SI]
TEL. 05778305729
www.uccelliera-montalcino.it

ANNUAL PRODUCTION	8,000 bottles
HECTARES UNDER VINE	25
VITICULTURE METHOD	Conventional

ANNUAL PRODUCTION	43,000 bottles
HECTARES UNDER VINE	6
VITICULTURE METHOD	Conventional

It had to be a blip. For Tua Rita to go without Three Glasses even one year was already unusual. Any longer than that would have been science fiction. Redigaffi '06, the jewel in Tua Rita's crown, is back at the top, and almost effortlessly. Exclusively merlot, it exploits all the fine qualities of its vintage. There's delicacy and intensity at the same time on the nose, with a melange of dark berry fruit, blackberry and blueberry, plus moist earth and pungent herbs. The palate is extremely dense but focused, thanks to acidity of Platonic perfection, and quite savoury, reflecting its terroir of Notri. Syrah '06 too is superb, showing self-confident, even assertive, spice and then a palate that is tannic yet mouthfilling, with a succulent, steady, seamless finale. On the same level is the cabernet sauvignon and merlot Giusto di Nostri '06. We liked the pungent vegetal nose, with its notes of baked peppers, its volume on the palate, and then the sheer dynamic energy of its development. Rosso di Notri '07 exhibits the expected balance and fine character, while the two Perlato del Bosco versions, Rosso '06 and Bianco '07 are ready and delicious.

This is the tenth year that Andrea Cortonesi has been producing Brunello di Montalcino, and a lot of changes have occurred at Uccelliera since his debut. The number of vines has increased and he now has a true winemaking cellar, a contrast with his first years when barrels were stacked in rooms of his home. Well-merited success has come to him over the decade, thanks to his unassuming modesty and to his abilities as a grower. The masterful Brunello di Montalcino '03 embodies the winery's style perfectly. A deep, all-but-opaque ruby presages an expressive aromatic amalgam on the nose. Lush, violet-led florality is flanked by lychee, white peach and morello cherry with just the lightest touch of toasty oak. The tannins are already nicely supple, allowing the palate to show crisp, yet supple and expansive. The finish is impressively aromatic. Rapace '05, a mix of sangiovese and cabernet, also scored high marks for its generous spice and wild berry fruit. There's plenty of rich flavour on the palate, with zippy acidity as an appealing foil to velvety tannins.

● Redigaffi '06	♟♟♟	8
● Giusto di Nostri '06	♟♟	8
● Syrah '06	♟♟	8
● Rosso dei Notri '07	♟♟	6
○ Perlato del Bosco Bianco '07	♟	4
● Perlato del Bosco Rosso '06	♟	6
● Redigaffi '04	♟♟♟	8
● Redigaffi '03	♟♟♟	8
● Redigaffi '02	♟♟♟	8
● Redigaffi '01	♟♟♟	8
● Redigaffi '00	♟♟♟	8
● Redigaffi '99	♟♟♟	8
● Redigaffi '98	♟♟♟	8
● Redigaffi '96	♟♟♟	8
● Syrah '05	♟♟	8
● Syrah '04	♟♟	8

● Brunello di Montalcino '03	♟♟	7
● Rapace '05	♟♟	6
● Rosso di Montalcino '06	♟	5
● Brunello di Montalcino Ris. '97	♟♟♟	8
● Brunello di Montalcino '02	♟♟	7
● Brunello di Montalcino '01	♟♟	7
● Brunello di Montalcino '00	♟♟	7
● Brunello di Montalcino '99	♟♟	7
● Brunello di Montalcino Ris. '01	♟♟	8
● Brunello di Montalcino Ris. '99	♟♟	8

Uggiano

LOC. SAN VINCENZO A TORRI
VIA EMPOLESE
50018 SCANDICCI [FI]
TEL. 055769087
www.uggiano.it

ANNUAL PRODUCTION	900,000 bottles
HECTARES UNDER VINE	100
VITICULTURE METHOD	Conventional

Uggiano, located in the castle at Montespertoli, not far from Florence, has been absent from these pages for quite a while, not because it ceased to exist, but simply because the performances of its wines in our tastings had slipped below par. This cellar produces and bottles a wide array of wines, their common characteristic being the staff's commitment to keeping their alcohols moderate. Chianti Classico Falco dè Neri '05 turned in good results, exhibiting an intense ruby, classic red berry fruit and floral impressions, plus a palate that is crisp, lively and flavourful. We liked Petraia '05, too. It's from largely merlot, with pungent spice and herbaceous notes nicely lifting rich preserves and chocolate. Judicious density in the mouth, toothsome flavours, and the rising, generous finish complete a very good offering. Chianti Colli Fiorentini '06 and Falco dè Neri '07 are appealing and delicious quaffers.

F.lli Vagnoni

LOC. PANCOLE, 82
53037 SAN GIMIGNANO [SI]
TEL. 0577955077
www.fratellivagnoni.com

ANNUAL PRODUCTION	120,000 bottles
HECTARES UNDER VINE	20
VITICULTURE METHOD	Conventional

The high quality of Vagnoni wines owes much to the brothers' deep understanding of their terroir and vineyards in the Pancole subzone. The parabola of their growth has been remarkably even, with no real loss of rhythm, since they have succeeded, better than other producers, in harnessing innovation without in any way lessening their respect for traditions. We were delighted this year with the Vernaccia di San Gimignano Mocali Riserva '06, so much so that we sent it on to the national finals. Clean-edged fruit and citrus, with just a whiff of toasty oak are quite attractive, as is the crisp, fresh savouriness in the mouth and on the lengthy finish. At the same time, the palate shows tremendous volume. Vernaccia Vigna Fontabuccio '07 has depth of colour and fruit, largely tropical, and supple development, while Vernaccia '07, vibrant and refreshing, serves up tasty peach and pear. Not quite up to those levels are I Sodi Lunghi '05, from sangiovese colorino, and San Gimignano Rosso San Biagio '05, but Il Pancolino '07, a rosé, Vin Brusco '07 and Chianti dei Colli Senesi '06 are all delightful.

● Chianti Classico Falco de' Neri '05	▼▼ 4*
● Petraia Merlot '05	▼▼ 6
● Chianti Colli Fiorentini La Casa di Dante Alighieri '06	▼ 3
O Falco de' Neri Chardonnay '07	▼ 4

O Vernaccia di S. Gimignano Mocali Ris. '06	▼▼ 5
● Chianti Colli Senesi '06	▼ 3
● I Sodi Lunghi '05	▼ 4
⊙ Il Pancolino '07	▼ 3
● San Gimignano Rosso San Biagio '05	▼ 4
O Vernaccia di S. Gimignano '07	▼ 2
O Vernaccia di S. Gimignano V. Fontabuccio '07	▼ 4
O Vin Brusco '07	▼ 2
● I Sodi Lunghi '04	▼▼ 4
O Vernaccia di S. Gimignano Mocali Ris. '05	▼▼ 5
O Vernaccia di S. Gimignano Mocali Ris. '04	▼▼ 4
O Vernaccia di S. Gimignano V. Fontabuccio '06	▼▼ 4*
O Vernaccia di S. Gimignano V. Fontabuccio '04	▼▼ 3

Tenuta Valdipiatta

VIA DELLA CIARLIANA, 25A
53040 MONTEPULCIANO [SI]
TEL. 0578757930
www.valdipiatta.it

ANNUAL PRODUCTION	120,000 bottles
HECTARES UNDER VINE	30
VITICULTURE METHOD	Conventional

Year after year, Miriam Caporali turns out wines at Tenuta Valdipiatta that flaunt originality expressed in their essential elegance and equilibrium. The wines are delectable for their aromatic delineation and finely chiselled structure but each one is distinct. The standard-bearer of this style is Nobile Vigna d'Alfiero, which in its '05 edition went to our final taste-offs. That elegance is personified here by a very particular earthiness that infuses a rich charge of fruit, as well as by the vibrant yet delicately poised balance of fresh acidity and hearty tannic expression, not to mention the well-sculpted, dynamic palate itself. Nobile di Montepulciano '05 has nicely gauged oak influence, along with aromas that are plush yet quick off the mark, and a palate that is subtle but with good contrasts. The merlot component in Trincerone '06 benefited from a year's ageing, and the wine, a partnership of merlot, cabernet sauvignon and petit verdot, is quite impressive, its delicately scented fruit finding completion in a savoury, energy-driven palate. Nibbiano '07 is a nice straightforward blend of grechetto, trebbiano and malvasia.

Tenuta di Valgiano

FRAZ. VALGIANO
VIA DI VALGIANO, 7
55018 LUCCA
TEL. 0583402271
www.tenutadivalgiano.it

ANNUAL PRODUCTION	70,000 bottles
HECTARES UNDER VINE	25
VITICULTURE METHOD	Natural

Tenuta di Valgiano continues to be culturally committed. Making wines with intriguing personalities is now the natural outcome of an ethical approach to agriculture that bestows dignity on those who have always worked the land. In a Tuscany increasingly invaded by entrepreneurial types who see agriculture only in terms of investment and profit, it is a pleasure to reward this kind of stubborn devotion. So our Three Glasses go to a great Tenuta di Valgiano '05, a blend of sangiovese, syrah and merlot that is a magisterial interpretation of the 2005 vintage. Vegetal and balsamic influences interleave spice-laden fruit on a nose that still shows lean and austere. The palate has too high a charge of acidity to suggest allure. We prize the elegance of its sculpted character, the rising, almost piercing thrust that releases the spark to inflame the palate into a conflagration of driving, almost endless tactile impressions. We also liked Palistorti Rosso '06, mostly sangiovese but with merlot and syrah, with emphatic fruit and finesse in the mouth. Palistorti Bianco '07 debuts to good marks, thanks to refined blossoms and a savoury, dynamic palate.

● Nobile di Montepulciano V. d'Alfiero '05	♊	7
● Nobile di Montepulciano '05	♊♊	5
● Trincerone '06	♊♊	6
○ Nibbiano '07	♊	3
● Nobile di Montepulciano V. d'Alfiero '99	♊♊♊	6
● Nobile di Montepulciano '04	♊♊	5
● Nobile di Montepulciano '99	♊♊	5
● Nobile di Montepulciano '98	♊♊	5
● Nobile di Montepulciano '97	♊♊	5
● Nobile di Montepulciano Ris. '97	♊♊	5
● Nobile di Montepulciano Ris. '95	♊♊	5
● Nobile di Montepulciano V. d'Alfiero '04	♊♊	7
● Nobile di Montepulciano V. d'Alfiero '01	♊♊	6
● Trincerone '97	♊♊	5

● Colline Lucchesi Tenuta di Valgiano '05	♊♊♊	7
○ Colline Lucchesi Palistorti Bianco '07	♊♊	
● Colline Lucchesi Palistorti Rosso '06	♊♊	5
● Colline Lucchesi Tenuta di Valgiano '04	♊♊♊	7
● Colline Lucchesi Tenuta di Valgiano '03	♊♊♊	7
● Colline Lucchesi Tenuta di Valgiano '01	♊♊♊	8
● Colline Lucchesi Tenuta di Valgiano '00	♊♊	8
● Colline Lucchesi Tenuta di Valgiano '99	♊♊	8

Vecchie Terre di Montefili

VIA SAN CRESCI, 45
50022 PANZANO [FI]
TEL. 055853739
www.vecchieterredimontefili.com

ANNUAL PRODUCTION	40,000 bottles
HECTARES UNDER VINE	13.5
VITICULTURE METHOD	Conventional

Tasting performances such as the one this year would be good news to many a winery, but the Acuti family has long been accustomed to better. These results could be considered perhaps as a transitional year, since 2005 was not one of the best vintages, and also because the wines from Vecchie Terre di Montefili just seem to lack the distinctive touch that usually renders them so recognizable. The best player on the team is Supertuscan Bruno di Rocca '05. A Cabernet Sauvignon, it parades a lovely herbaceousness, plus wild berry and minerally essences. The structure is quite imposing, and slow to power up, but after few moments it becomes fluent, concluding with a very tasty and lengthy finale. We liked Anfiteatro '05 as well, exclusively from sangiovese, offering up an elegant florality appealingly twinned with dark wild fruit. It achieves good balance and the palate is lithe, becoming a little light in mid-mouth, but recovering fully on the finish. Chianti Classico '05 disappoints with a somewhat muddled nose, but there is pulpy fruit and weight in the mouth.

Castello di Vicchiomaggio

LOC. LE BOLLE
VIA VICCHIOMAGGIO, 4
50022 GREVE IN CHIANTI [FI]
TEL. 055854079
www.vicchiomaggio.it

ANNUAL PRODUCTION	300,000 bottles
HECTARES UNDER VINE	33
VITICULTURE METHOD	Conventional

John Matta fell just shy of Three Glasses but sent a fine pair of wines to the national taste-offs. Matta consistently turns out labels with grand character, understandably so given his near-maniacal work in the vineyards and painstaking attention among the tanks. What we find fascinating about Castello di Vicchiomaggio is that each wine tasted embodies very different characteristics. Once again, we loved the all-merlot FSM '05. It delivers a lush medley of fragrances that range from notes of raspberry, strawberry and ripe cherry to spicier nuances, such as nutmeg and clove. Entry on the palate is equally dense and impressive, followed by delicious acidity and an attractive, lingering finish. Ripa delle More '05 gave an impeccable performance as well. This monovarietal Sangiovese shows nicely typical ripe fruit on the nose, then glides into a ductile palate with well-placed tannins, and finishes savoury and full. The remaining wines are less impressive, among them Riserva La Prima, showing a tad overripe, and the standard Chianti Classico San Jacopo, which is fresh and juicy.

● Anfiteatro '05	▼▼	8
● Bruno di Rocca '05	▼▼	7
● Chianti Cl. '05	▼	5
● Anfiteatro '03	▼▼▼	8
● Anfiteatro '94	▼▼▼	8
● Anfiteatro '04	▼▼	8
● Anfiteatro '01	▼▼	8

● FSM '05	▼▼	8
● Ripa delle More '05	▼▼	8
● Chianti Cl. La Prima Ris. '05	▼	7
● Chianti Cl. San Jacopo '06	▼	5
● FSM '04	▼▼▼	8
● Ripa delle More '97	▼▼▼	6
● Chianti Cl. Agostino Petri Ris. '04	▼▼	6
● Ripa delle More '04	▼▼	7
● Ripa delle More '01	▼▼	7

Villa Cafaggio

VIA SAN MARTINO A CECIONE, 5
50020 PANZANO [FI]
TEL. 0558549094
www.villacafaggio.it

ANNUAL PRODUCTION	400,000 bottles
HECTARES UNDER VINE	40
VITICULTURE METHOD	Conventional

There is no let-up to Villa Cafaggio's relentless ascent to higher quality. A part of the Trentino-based Lavis group, it has recently acquired new contiguous vineyards as part of an ambitious project to produce a world-class red right in the cradle of the sangiovese grape, as many believe the area of Panzano in fact to be. The results thus far may not be all that one expects, but the potential is undeniably there. The two Supertuscans provided the best showings. The largely sangiovese San Martino '04 delivers a complex aromatic array that privileges emphatic bramble jelly and spice, followed by a well-delineated palate that is not too broad but shows perfect depth. Cortaccio '04 exhibits its cabernet sauvignon in menthol and balsam nuances nicely set off by punchy green pepper. A fine balance of subtle tannins and alcohol supports a lean, taut palate that concludes lengthy and very toothsome. The two Chianti Classicos are stiffer and down a few rungs from where they should be.

Villa Calcinaia

FRAZ. GRETI
VIA CITILLE, 84
50022 GREVE IN CHIANTI [FI]
TEL. 055854008
www.villacalcinaia.it

ANNUAL PRODUCTION	100,000 bottles
HECTARES UNDER VINE	30
VITICULTURE METHOD	Natural

The Chianti Classico-focused Capponi family turned in a textbook performance. They have owned Villa Calcinaia for generations: the property deed dates back to May 23, 1524. The Conti Capponi have always placed great importance on agriculture in general and on viticulture in particular, amply illustrated by documents that show the family producing and dealing in wine and oil in earlier centuries. Sebastiano Capponi is the family member who currently oversees everything in the vineyard and cellar. The wine we preferred was again their Chianti Classico Riserva '05, which proffers a crisp, fresh bouquet where pungent herbs and Mediterranean scrub emerge over nuances of dried plum and other fruit. The palate shows savoury, pulpy fruit, with an intriguing contrast between smoothness and firmness, finally gaining a succulent, spacious finish. Chianti Classico '06 suffers from excessively rough tannins, and Casarsa '05 can't seem to spread out the imposing extractive mass of its merlot fruit.

● Cortaccio '04	♥♥	8
● San Martino '04	♥♥	8
● Chianti Cl. '06	♥	5
● Chianti Cl. Ris. '05	♥	6
● Chianti Cl. Ris. '03	♥♥♥	6
● Cortaccio '01	♥♥♥	8
● Cortaccio '97	♥♥♥	6
● San Martino '00	♥♥♥	8
● San Martino '99	♥♥♥	7
● San Martino '98	♥♥♥	6
● San Martino '97	♥♥♥	5

● Chianti Cl. Ris. '05	♥♥	6
● Casarsa '05	♥	6
● Chianti Cl. '06	♥	5
● Chianti Cl. Ris. '04	♥♥	6
● Chianti Cl. Ris. '03	♥♥	6

Villa Pillo

VIA VOLTERRANA, 24
50050 GAMBASSI TERME [FI]
TEL. 0571680212
www.villapillo.com

ANNUAL PRODUCTION	200,000 bottles
HECTARES UNDER VINE	40
VITICULTURE METHOD	Conventional

We are always impressed at our annual tasting of the wines from Villa Pillo. They are all monovarietals, invariably well designed, incredibly reliable, wines that this year though seem to show a tiny bit less of their usual distinctiveness. Beginning with the solid Merlot Sant'Adele '06, we were impressed by the beautiful dance between spice and dark fruit on the nose, as we were with the masterful balance in the mouth, where dense tannins integrate well into the alcohol component. It finishes with an energy-laden flourish. Syrah '06 is a top-notch version, with luscious spice and faithful varietal typicity from start to finish, and a dense, even-handed palate that is quite fresh. Vivaldaia '06 is a monovarietal Cabernet Franc with an expressive nose of dark wild berry and balsam, a solid palate with steady energy and a refreshing, leisurely finale. Borgoforte '06 is as good as always, like the Vin Santo '99, which shows vibrant richness on the palate and a tempting sea-salt edge on the nose.

Villa Trasqua

LOC. TRASQUA
53011 CASTELLINA IN CHIANTI [SI]
TEL. 0577743075
www.villatrasqua.it

ANNUAL PRODUCTION	250,000 bottles
HECTARES UNDER VINE	54
VITICULTURE METHOD	Conventional

Villa Trasqua returns to the Guide this year with a good, fat profile. From its origins as a mixed-crop sharecropping operation, Villa Trasqua turned to viticulture and winemaking in the 1960s. After their first harvest in 1968, they expanded prudently, increasing the area under vine and then restructuring the old farm buildings into an agriturismo. In 1998, the estate started replanting the vineyards, and a new cellar was completed in 2005. At our tastings, we were most impressed by Trasgaia '05, a blend of equal parts of sangiovese and cabernet sauvignon. Attractively nuanced notes of menthol, balsam and wild berries emerge elegantly on the nose, followed by a solid entry in the mouth that expands to considerable width to conclude with nice length. High marks go to Chianti Classico Riserva '05 as well, for its clean-edged, austere bouquet, opening initially to raw and tanned leather then revealing riper fruit preserves. It shows a sturdy body, a dense weave of well tucked-in tannins, and a tasty, savoury finale. The other wines are pleasurable enough.

● Borgoforte '06	♈♈	4*
● Merlot Sant'Adele '06	♈♈	6
● Syrah '06	♈♈	6
○ Vin Santo del Chianti '99	♈♈	7
● Vivaldaia '06	♈♈	6
● Syrah '97	♈♈♈	5
● Borgoforte '05	♈♈	4
● Merlot Sant'Adele '05	♈♈	6
● Merlot Sant'Adele '04	♈♈	6
● Syrah '05	♈♈	6
● Syrah '03	♈♈	6
● Syrah '99	♈♈	5
● Vivaldaia '05	♈♈	6

● Chianti Cl. Ris. '05	♈♈	4*
● Trasgaia '05	♈♈	6
● Chianti Cl. '06	♈	4
⊙ Rosato '07	♈	4

Villa Vignamaggio

VIA DI PETRIOLO, 5
50022 GREVE IN CHIANTI [FI]
TEL. 055854661
www.vignamaggio.com

ANNUAL PRODUCTION	240,000 bottles
HECTARES UNDER VINE	48
VITICULTURE METHOD	Conventional

Unlike Paganini, Giovanni Nunziante does encores. This is the second year running he has taken the Three Glasses palm for his Vignamaggio, this time in the 2005 edition. It's still one hundred per cent cabernet franc, of course, a variety that has found exquisite expression in this corner of Chianti. This extraordinary growing area has produced a wine you could quite easily take for a Bordeaux, with its elegant, refined nose that privileges fresh green pepper and aromatic herbs, and a solid yet supple body sculpted by perfectly integrated tannins and measured but vibrant acidity. Villa Vignamaggio has more than met the terroir challenge, seeing that few believed that cabernet franc could find a comfortable home around here. Vin Santo del Chianti Classico '03 is also excellent. It gives sweet honey and dried figs and dates, then a velvety palate, creamy and dense, crowned with a finish that is the quintessence of pleasure. All of the remaining wines are sound if straightforward, with the standard version Chianti Classicos showing enjoyable and tasty.

Vistarenni

LOC. VISTARENNI
53013 GAIOLE IN CHIANTI [SI]
TEL. 0577738186
www.vistarenni.com

ANNUAL PRODUCTION	67,000 bottles
HECTARES UNDER VINE	77
VITICULTURE METHOD	Conventional

We devote a single profile to the two Tuscan operations of the Santa Margherita group. Villa Vistarenni is located in the municipality of Gaiole, and the Pile e Lamole farm is at Greve, in a very unusual terroir. The Gaiole property comprises a little more than 30 hectares of vineyard, plus olive groves and wooded areas, while the Lamole vineyards cover more than 47 hectares, which is quite a lot considering that the area is very heavily parcelled, and the fields intensively terraced. The group also has a new winery in Maremma, Sassoregale. We felt that the best performance this year came from Vistarenni. Chianti Classico Riserva '05 exhibits rich mouthfeel, a seductive bouquet and a richly-flavoured finish while Chianti Classico '06 fascinates with an emphatic, incisive nose and an appealing, tasty finale. Pile e Lamole's offerings are well executed, if perhaps slender in structure, and with bouquets that are well-delineated but lack energy. Vigneto Campolungo is the best of the various Chianti Classico versions, revealing fine texture and good pulpy fruit.

● Vignamaggio '05	▼▼▼ 8
○ Vin Santo del Chianti Cl. '03	▼▼ 6
● Chianti Cl. '06	▼ 5
● Chianti Cl. Terre di Prenzano '06	▼ 4
● Chianti Cl. Monna Lisa Ris. '99	♈♈♈ 6
● Vignamaggio '04	♈♈♈ 7
● Vignamaggio '01	♈♈♈ 7
● Vignamaggio '00	♈♈♈ 7
● Obsession '01	♈♈ 7
● Obsession '00	♈♈ 7
● Obsession '99	♈♈ 7
○ Vin Santo del Chianti Cl. '01	♈♈ 6
○ Vin Santo del Chianti Cl. '99	♈♈ 6
○ Vin Santo del Chianti Cl. '98	♈♈ 6

● Chianti Cl. '06	▼▼ 4*
● Chianti Cl. Ris. '05	▼▼ 4*
● Chianti Cl. Campolungo Ris. '04	▼ 5
● Chianti Cl. Lamole di Lamole '06	▼ 4
● Chianti Cl. Lamole di Lamole Etichetta Blu '06	▼ 4
● Chianti Cl. Lamole di Lamole Ris. '05	▼ 5
● Chianti Cl. Campolungo Ris. '99	♈♈ 5
● Chianti Cl. Lamole di Lamole '03	♈♈ 4*
○ Vin Santo del Chianti Cl. '00	♈♈ 6

Tenuta Vitereta

VIA CASA NUOVA, 108
52020 LATERINA [AR]
TEL. 057589058
www.tenutavitereta.com

ANNUAL PRODUCTION   **80,000 bottles**
HECTARES UNDER VINE   **45**
VITICULTURE METHOD   **Natural**

This seems to be a transitional year for
Tenuta Vitereta, a cellar in the Arezzo area
that has aroused a good bit of interest in
the last few years with wines that display
a modern bent. But following standard
canons in the cellar has not deprived their
wines of a touch of originality. The star,
Cabernet Villa Bernetti, was not presented,
so the second Cabernet, Capitoni '06, was
the one we tasted, with excellent results.
It boasts ripe red berry and just the right
level of toast, then outstanding depth and
weight in the mouth, nervy acidity and
incisive tannins that need more time to
smoothen out. We were impressed by the
debut of Vin Santo '03. It's traditionally
styled, sweet, lush, rich and nicely
lingering, but production quantities are not
known. Completing the battery are two
whites. Donna Aurora '06 is a quite crisp
Chardonnay lifted by well-gauged oak,
as were the previous editions. Trebbiano
'06, half of it made from semi-dried
grapes, shows dense and powerful, in an
uncommon style.

Viticcio

VIA SAN CRESCI, 12A
50022 GREVE IN CHIANTI [FI]
TEL. 055854210
www.fattoriaviticcio.com

ANNUAL PRODUCTION   **200,000 bottles**
HECTARES UNDER VINE   **35**
VITICULTURE METHOD   **Conventional**

This year, Alessandro Landini's wines
scored precisely the same as last year's.
We consider that a clear sign of continuity,
and at a high level of quality to boot.
Landini's father purchased the farm when
everyone else was leaving Chianti during
the economic boom years. Today, the
vineyards have been upgraded and a
refurbished cellar boasts new winemaking
equipment. Landini also directs I Greppi
at Bolgheri on the Tuscan coast. The
stand-out wine this year was Chianti
Classico Riserva '05. Pungent balsam
and chocolate make a terrific pair on the
nose, and firm-fleshed fruit spreads out
beautifully over the palate and on into
the tasty finale. High marks also went to
the sangiovese-only Prunaio '05 for its
attractive delicacy and the finesse of its
red berry aromas, followed by an elegant
entry into the mouth and a gorgeous, long-
lasting conclusion. Chianti Classico '06
sports a compelling nose and a palate that
is firmly textured and finely balanced. The
remaining wines show fairly stiff, including
Riserva Beatrice '05 and the largely
cabernet sauvignon Monile '05. Bolgheri
produced a spot-on Bolgheri Superiore
Greppicaia '05, its first release.

● Capitoni '06	♈♈	5
○ Vin Santo '03	♈♈	8
○ Donna Aurora '06	♈	5
○ Trebbiano di Toscana '06	♈	5
● Capitoni '05	♈♈	4*
● Villa Bernetti '04	♈♈	5
● Villa Bernetti '03	♈♈	5
● Villa Bernetti '01	♈♈	5

● Chianti Cl. '06	♈♈	4*
● Chianti Cl. Ris. '05	♈♈	5
● Greppicaia I Greppi '05	♈♈	6
● Prunaio '05	♈♈	7
● Chianti Cl. Beatrice Ris. '05	♈	6
● Monile '05	♈	7
● Prunaio '99	♈♈♈	7
● Chianti Cl. Beatrice Ris. '00	♈♈	6
● Prunaio '01	♈♈	8

Castello di Volognano

DI VOLOGNANO, 12
50067 RIGNANO SULL'ARNO [FI]
TEL. 0558303125
www.volognano.it

ANNUAL PRODUCTION   N.A.
HECTARES UNDER VINE N.A.
VITICULTURE METHOD   Conventional

Castello di Volognano debuts in the Guide with a full profile. Located in the Colli Fiorentini denomination, it's a historic operation whose first buildings go back to the 11th century, and which over the years has given hospitality to a long string of influential figures. Ezio Pecchioli acquired the property in the 1960s, and immediately converted the promiscuously planted vineyards over to the modern, specialized style. Volognano currently has more than 200 hectares, which include olive trees and wooded areas. At the tastings, we were most impressed by Baccante '05, a pairing of sangiovese and merlot that offers an effective contrast between impressions of smooth spice and wild red berry fruit. The palate has good breadth and a smooth mouthfeel, the tannins are spacious and rich, bright flavours continue through into the finish. Donna Patrizia '07, a blend of trebbiano and malvasia, surprised us with the well-delineated complexity of its aromas, followed by a firm palate, a refreshing, tangy acidity and a dynamic conclusion. Chianti Colli Fiorentini '05 is uncomplicated but enjoyable.

● Baccante '05	♈♈	5
○ Donna Patrizia '07	♈♈	4
● Chianti Colli Fiorentini '05	♈	4

Castello di Volpaia

LOC. VOLPAIA
P.ZZA DELLA CISTERNA, 1
53017 RADDA IN CHIANTI [SI]
TEL. 0577738066
www.volpaia.com

ANNUAL PRODUCTION   250,000 bottles
HECTARES UNDER VINE 46
VITICULTURE METHOD   Certified organic

Three Glasses eluded the grasp of Giovannella Stianti this year, even though her Chianti Classico Riserva '05 did well in the final round. The Volpaia area lies at an elevation at the limit for quality viticulture, and the 2005 growing year complicated the situation. The characteristics of the terroir here largely determine the sensory qualities of the local wines. Stianti's finalist showed remarkable clarity on the nose, with balsam and spice in fine evidence, then exemplary structure. The tannins exert themselves somewhat over the other components, though not excessively so, and the finish is very savoury. Bianco di Volpaia '07 is fresh and alluring, both for its emphatic fruit and for a vein of mouthwatering acidity, a perfect example of a terroir-driven wine. The rest of the range gave fine performances. One piece of news is the debut of Morello di Prile, a wine from Prelius, a Maremma-based winery directed by Federica Mascheroni, daughter of Stianti and her husband Carlo. A partnering of cabernet sauvignon, cabernet franc and merlot, it is a successful marriage between the Mediterranean qualities of that area and Volpaia's elegance.

● Chianti Cl. Ris. '05	♈♈	6
○ Bianco '07	♈♈	4*
● Morello di Prile Prelius '07	♈♈	4*
● Balifico '05	♈	7
● Chianti Cl. '06	♈	5
● Chianti Cl. Coltassala Ris. '05	♈	7
○ Vin Santo del Chianti Cl. '01	♈	6
● Balifico '00	♈♈♈	7
● Chianti Cl. Coltassala Ris. '04	♈♈♈	7
● Chianti Cl. Coltassala Ris. '01	♈♈♈	7
○ Vin Santo del Chianti Cl. '98	♈♈	6

OTHER WINERIES

Acquabona

LOC. ACQUABONA
57037 PORTOFERRAIO [LI]
TEL. 0565933013
www.acquabonaelba.it

Wines from Acquabona performed well overall this year. We felt the most convincing was the Elba Aleatico '05, which is full, sweet and round without being cloying. The other wines, the juicy Elba Rosso '06 and tangy, fresh-drinking Ansonica dell'Elba '07, are pleasant.

● Aleatico dell'Elba '05	🍷🍷	6
○ Ansonica dell'Elba '07	🍷	4
● Elba Rosso '06	🍷	4

Podere Allocco

LOC. SEANO
CAPEZZANA, 19
59015 CARMIGNANO [PO]
TEL. 0558705259
podereallocco@texfee.it

Podere Allocco only began bottling in 2000 and this year submitted a double vintage of Carmignano, the '06 and '05, both interesting. The '06 is more mature with an invigorating palate. The nose of the '05 is not very expressive but the palate is juicy and zesty. The chardonnay Bacano '07 is fragrant.

○ Bacano '07	🍷	4
● Carmignano '06	🍷	5
● Carmignano '05	🍷	5

Altura

LOC. MULINACCIO
58012 GIGLIO [GR]
TEL. 0564806106

Francesco Carfagna produces a charming wine from ansonica on the rough but generous Isola del Giglio. Ansonico '07 has sunny, complex aromas. The dense, mineral, long palate evokes sensations near those of a red wine. As the label says: "drink whenever you feel like it".

○ Ansonico dell'Isola del Giglio '07	🍷🍷	5
○ Ansonico dell'Isola del Giglio '06	🍷🍷	5

Armilla

VIA TAVERNELLE, 6
53024 MONTALCINO [SI]
TEL. 0577816012
www.armillawine.com

This small estate at Tavernelle did well again. The '03 Brunello is especially agreeable. Its intense, clean nose has distinct tobacco, leather and fruit. The complex palate is long, relaxed and drinkable, the finish showing temptingly expansive. The Rosso '06 is also well executed.

● Brunello di Montalcino '03	🍷🍷	7
● Rosso di Montalcino '06	🍷🍷	4
● Brunello di Montalcino '99	🍷🍷	7

Artimino

FRAZ. ARTIMINO
V.LE PAPA GIOVANNI XXIII, 1
59015 CARMIGNANO [PO]
TEL. 0558751423
www.artimino.com

Vin Santo di Carmignano '04 gives dried figs and cakes, and then a dense, fresh palate. The well-crafted Carmignano Villa Medicea Riserva '05 is structured and fluid. Carmignano Villa Artimino '06 is vegetal on the nose with a dynamic, flavourful palate. The Carmignano Vigna Grumarello Riserva '04 is mature.

○ Vin Santo di Varmignano Villa Artimino '04	🍷🍷	5
● Carmignano V. Grumarello Ris. '04	🍷	5
● Carmignano Villa Artimino '06	🍷	4
● Carmignano Villa Medicea Ris. '05	🍷	5

Fattoria di Bacchereto

LOC. BACCHERETO
VIA FONTEMORANA, 179
59015 CARMIGNANO [PO]
TEL. 0558717191
fattoriadibacchereto@libero.it

Fattoria di Bacchereto debuts with well-made wines from one of the most interesting areas around Carmignano. Carmignano Terre a Mano '05 shows an inviting profile on the nose and good balance on the palate. The interesting Sassocarlo '05, from trebbiano and malvasia, has ripe aromas and a juicy palate.

● Carmignano Terre a Mano '05	🍷🍷	5
○ Sassocarlo '05	🍷	5

OTHER WINERIES

Tenuta di Bagnolo

FRAZ. BAGNOLO
VIA MONTALESE, 156
50045 MONTEMURLO [PO]
TEL. 0574652439
www.pancrazi.it

Tenuta di Bagnolo was slightly under par this year. Pinot Nero Vigna Baragazza '06 is good with fruit aromas and a palate with decent pulp, acid backbone and a dry finish. Villa di Bagnolo '06 is small and supple in the mouth. Casaglia '05 from colorino is not that invigorating. The Rosato '07 is very drinkable.

● Pinot Nero V. Baragazza '06	❦❦	8
● Casaglia '05	❦	6
● Pinot Nero Villa di Bagnolo '06	❦	7
☉ Pinot Nero Villa di Bagnolo Rosato '07	❦	4

I Balzini

LOC. PASTINE, 19
50021 BARBERINO VAL D'ELSA [FI]
TEL. 0558075503
www.ibalzini.it

Major reds from Balzini showed less brilliant than usual. We liked the juicy White Label '04, from sangiovese and cabernet, with nice acid agility and a lingering finish. The merlot and cabernet Black Label '04 is a bit evolved and the palate is not that lively. The new Green Label '06 is easy drinking.

● I Balzini White Label '04	❦❦	5
● I Balzini Black Label '04	❦	6
● I Balzini Green Label '06	❦	4

Mattia Barzaghi

LOC. SAN DONATO, 13
53037 SAN GIMIGNANO [SI]
TEL. 0577941501
www.mattiabarzaghi-wines.com

After learning from his friend Giovanni Pannizi, Mattia Barzaghi debuts with his own wines. The fragrant Vernaccia Zeta '07 is intense with good development on the palate. The sangiovese Sorriso '07 is very drinkable. Chianti Zingaro '07 is gutsy and fruity. The Vernaccia Impronta '07 is taut and balanced.

○ Vernaccia di S. Gimignano Zeta '07	❦❦	5
● Chianti Colli Senesi Zingaro '07	❦	4
● Sorriso '07	❦	3*
○ Vernaccia di S. Gimignano Impronta '07	❦	4

Tenuta Belguardo

LOC. MONTEBOTTIGLI - VIII ZONA
58100 GROSSETO
TEL. 057773571
www.belguardo.it

The sangiovese and alicante Serrata di Belguardo '06 is juicy and moreish. Cabernet sauvignon and franc go into the complex Tenuta di Belguardo '05, which is weighed down by oak. Morellino Bronzone '06 is spicy and juicy but not very characterful. The Rosé '07 from sangiovese and syrah is nice.

● Serrata di Belguardo '06	❦❦	5
● Morellino di Scansano Bronzone '06	❦	6
☉ Rosé Belguardo '07	❦	5
● Tenuta Belguardo '05	❦	8

Bellafonte

VIA VITTORIO VENETO, 70
50050 GAMBASSI TERME [FI]
TEL. 0571638342
marradigdf@libero.it

Bellafonte makes a good debut. The sound Marrado, from sangiovese, merlot and other minor varieties, was presented in '06 and '05 versions. The former is more successful thanks to better definition and a dynamic profile on the nose. The same vintages of Capei, from a similar blend, are simpler and more immediate.

● Il Marrado '06	❦❦	5
● Il Marrado '05	❦❦	5
● Il Capei '06	❦	4
● Il Capei '05	❦	4

Soc. Agr. Belpoggio

FRAZ. CASTELNUOVO DELL'ABATE
LOC. BELLARIA
53020 MONTALCINO [SI]
TEL. 0423982147
www.belpoggio.it

This small operation in Castelnuovo dell'Abate submitted a lovely Brunello di Montalcino '03 that almost won our highest award. The rich nose ranges from wild cherry to bramble with a hint of medicinal herbs and tobacco in the background. Its remarkable development shows dense but already mellow tannins.

● Brunello di Montalcino '03	❦❦	7
● Di Paolo Rosso '07	❦	4
● Rosso di Montalcino '06	❦	5

OTHER WINERIES

Bindi Sergardi

LOC. POGGIOLO
FATTORIA I COLLI, 2
53035 MONTERIGGIONI [SI]
TEL. 0577309107
www.bindisergardi.it

Nicolò Casini is revamping the family farm and the wines are interesting. There was no high point but the two versions of Chianti Classico put up a good show. The Riserva '05 is better, with intriguing aromas and well-layered structure. The Chianti Classico '06 is enjoyably drinkable.

● Chianti Cl. Ris. '05	♀♀	5
● Chianti Cl. '06	♀	4
● Chianti Cl. Ris. '04	♀♀	5

Castello di Bolgheri

LOC. BOLGHERI
57020 CASTAGNETO CARDUCCI [LI]
TEL. 055213084
www.castellodibolgheri.eu

Castello di Bolgheri is in the Guide this time but it has been doing well for a couple of years now. We liked both the Bolgheri Superiore '05, with its ripe nose and juicy palate, and Bolgheri Varvàra '06, with torrefaction on the nose and a mouthfilling palate, slightly held back by tannins in the finish.

● Bolgheri Sup. '05	♀♀	8
● Bolgheri Varvàra '06	♀♀	5

Tenuta Bonomonte

VIA SAN FILIPPO, 27
50021 BARBERINO VAL D'ELSA [FI]
TEL. 0558079131
www.bonomonte.com

The Formichi estate confirms last year's results with well-defined wines, especially on the nose. From only sangiovese, the good Camp'albracco '06 is fresh and aromatic with a soft, silky palate. Campodoro '07, from trebbiano and malvasia, is pleasant and Chianti Classico '06 is juicy.

● Camp'albracco '06	♀♀	5
O Campodoro '07	♀	4
● Chianti Cl. '06	♀	4

Borgo Casignano

LOC. CASIGNANO, 212
52020 CAVRIGLIA [AR]
TEL. 055 967090

This organically managed estate in the hills near Cavriglia returns to the Guide. From the wines tasted, Poggione '05 is an especially centred blend of sangiovese, merlot and cabernet. Delicately floral, fruity and spicy, it has a juicy, well-balanced texture and pleasant freshness.

● Poggione '05	♀♀	5
● Chianti '05	♀	4
● Solatio '05	♀	4

Borgo Salcetino

LOC. LUCARELLI
53017 RADDA IN CHIANTI [SI]
TEL. 0577733541
www.livon.it

Vintages may change but our opinion of the Livon estate in Chianti never varies. In almost a photocopy of last year's entry, the wines are characterized by a lack of balance on the palate. The best is the '06 Rossole, a sangiovese-merlot blend with soft structure and good length in the finish.

● Rossole '06	♀♀	4
● Chianti Cl. '06	♀	4
● Chianti Cl. Lucarello Ris. '05	♀	5

Botrona

FRAZ. PUNTONE
LOC BOTRONA, 41
58020 SCARLINO [GR]
TEL. 0566866129
www.agriturismobotrona.com

Davide and Simone Ceccarelli made a nice debut in the Guide. Vedetta '06, from cabernet sauvignon, has a fresh, slightly grassy, nose and a gutsy palate with good complexity. The simple Monteregio di Massa Marittima Rosso '07 has fragrant drinkability, well-centred aromas and a contrasting palate.

● Vedetta '06	♀♀	5
● Monteregio di Massa Marittima Rosso '07	♀	4

OTHER WINERIES

Fattoria La Braccesca

LOC. CORTONA
VIA STELLA DI VALIANO, 10
53045 MONTEPULCIANO [SI]
TEL. 0578724252
www.antinori.it

The syrah-based Cortona Bramasole '05
is quite good, with focused fresh aromas,
marked by rich pepper-led spice. The
palate is sweet, solid and juicy with a deep,
fruity finish. The Nobile '05 is still very
concentrated. Oak from ageing blocks the
aromas and development on the palate.

● Cortona Bramasole '05	�� 6
● Nobile di Montepulciano '05	� 5
● Cortona Bramasole '01	♔♔ 6

Buccia Nera

LOC. CAMPRIANO, 10
52100 AREZZO
TEL. 0575361040
www.buccianera.it

In the hills near the city of Arezzo,
Buccianera makes wines with a sober,
traditional design. Outstanding among
these, and great value for money, is the
sangiovese with ciliegiolo Camprianese,
which shows savoury and lean, expanding
nicely with a clean, fruit, flowers and spice
profile on the nose.

● Il Camprianese '06	♔♔ 2*
● Chianti '07	♔ 4
● Amadio '04	♔♔ 5
● Il Camprianese '05	♔♔ 3*

Bulichella

LOC. BULICHELLA, 131
57028 SUVERETO [LI]
TEL. 0565829892
www.bulichella.it

Bulichella wines are nice but lack a pinch
of personality. Val di Cornia Tuscanio '05
convinced us most, with red berries on the
nose and an invigorating, if quite simple,
palate. The concentrated Val di Cornia
Coldipietrerosse '05 has a stiff finish.
Rubino '07 has an intriguing nose and soft,
measured palate.

● Val di Cornia Rosso Tuscanio '05	♔♔ 6
● Val di Cornia Col di Pietre Rosse '05	♔ 7
● Val di Cornia Rosso Rubino '07	♔ 4

Castello di Cacchiano

FRAZ. MONTI IN CHIANTI
LOC. CACCHIANO
53010 GAIOLE IN CHIANTI [SI]
TEL. 0577747018
cacchiano@chianticlassico.com

This year, the standard-bearer Vin Santo
was missing. Other wines remain in a
well-typed limbo without achieving precise
stylistic definition. However, the Chianti
Classico '05 stands out for its menthol and
mineral tones on the nose and fluid body,
well sustained by acidity.

● Chianti Cl. '05	♔♔ 5
● Castello di Cacchiano Rosso '05	♔ 4
● Chianti Cl. Ris. '04	♔ 5

Caccia al Piano 1868

VIA BOLGHERESE, 279
57022 CASTAGNETO CARDUCCI [LI]
TEL. 056557022
www.berlucchi.it

The Bolgheri branch of Guido Berlucchi on
20 hectares at Castagneto Carducci did
nicely. The convincing Bordeaux blend, Levia
Gravia '04, has a broad black berry nose
with balsamic hints. The solid, fragrant palate
shows nice upfront tannins while the simpler
Ruit Hora '06 is still pleasant.

● Bolgheri Levia Gravia '04	♔♔ 8
● Bolgheri Ruit Hora '06	♔ 6

Camigliano

LOC. CAMIGLIANO
VIA D'INGRESSO, 2
53024 MONTALCINO [SI]
TEL. 0577816061
www.camigliano.it

The Ghezzis have had to face two growing
seasons that were challenging, especially
for Camigliano in the southern part of the
area. The Brunello di Montalcino '03 and
Rosso '06 show mature notes on the nose
with hints of plum preserves, and a dense,
warm, round palate that lacks a little acidity.

● Brunello di Montalcino '03	♔♔ 6
● Rosso di Montalcino '06	♔ 4

OTHER WINERIES

Camperchi

LOC. LA CORNIA
VIA DEL BURRONE, 38
52040 CIVITELLA IN VAL DI CHIANA [AR]
TEL. 0575440281
www.camperchi.com

The project by the Italo-Argentine Cartellone family to restore the Camperchi estate in Val di Chiana is taking shape. New wines have been crafted with input from consultant oenologist Roberto Cipresso. Outstanding among them is the dark, ripely mouthfilling Merlot '06, which is nicely balanced.

● Merlot '06	♀♀	7
● Anno 0 '06	♀	6
● Sangiovese '06	♀	7

Campriano

LOC. CAMPRIANO
53016 MURLO [SI]
TEL. 0577814232
www.campriano.it

The Vin Santo from Ranuccio Neri's estate is authentic, giving confident smoky aromas of nuts and dates, and delicious, well-contrasted complexity on the palate. The Colli Senesi Riserva '04 has outstanding personality, with still-edgy tannins, while the sangiovese-canaiolo Rosato '07 is pleasant.

○ Vin Santo del Chianti '01	♀♀	6
⊙ Campriano Rosato '07	♀	3
● Chianti Colli Senesi Ris. '04	♀	4

Candialle

VIA SAN LEOLINO, 71
50020 PANZANO [FI]
TEL. 055852201
www.candialle.com

This small estate, managed by a Finnish-German couple, makes well-crafted wines. The nice Ciclope '06, from merlot and sangiovese with a dash of syrah, has elegant aromas over a dynamic, invigorating body that finishes juicy. The inviting, well-gauged Chianti Classico '06 lacks some power.

● Ciclope '06	♀♀	5
● Chianti Cl. '06	♀	5
● Ciclope '04	♀♀	5

Canneto

VIA DEI CANNETI, 14
53045 MONTEPULCIANO [SI]
TEL. 0578757737
www.canneto.com

Filippone '05, from sangiovese and merlot, is the outstanding wines from the estate managed by Ottorino De Angelis, showing elegance, clear aromas and dynamic flavour. Well-made wines include the solid, immediate Nobile '05 and juicy Nobile Riserva '04, which wavers a little on the nose.

● Filippone '05	♀♀	6
● Nobile di Montepulciano '05	♀	5
● Nobile di Montepulciano Ris. '04	♀	5

Canonica a Cerreto

LOC. CANONICA A CERRETO
53019 CASTELNUOVO BERARDENGA [SI]
TEL. 0577363261
www.canonicacerreto.it

The 2005 vintage was the best for the Lorenzi family's wines. Standing out for its marked tannicity is the Chianti Classico Riserva '05, with menthol tones and a powerful body that needs to unwind. The agreeable Sandiavolo '05 is from sangiovese, merlot and cabernet.

● Chianti Cl. Ris. '05	♀♀	5
● Sandiavolo '05	♀	5
● Sandiavolo '04	♀♀	5

Caparsa

CASE SPARSE CAPARSA, 47
53017 RADDA IN CHIANTI [SI]
TEL. 0577738174
www.caparsa.it

This year, Paolo Cianferoni's correct, pleasant wines lack those elements of clarity and depth that made them so enjoyable a few years ago. The best is Chianti Classico Caparsino '05, with mineral tones and complex structure, and the Riserva '05 Doccio a Matteo, with a richer spectrum of aromatics.

● Chianti Cl. Caparsino '05	♀♀	5
● Chianti Cl. Doccio a Matteo Ris. '05	♀	6
● Chianti Cl. Doccio a Matteo Ris. '00	♀♀♀	6

OTHER WINERIES

Fattoria il Capitano

VIA SAN MARTINO A QUONA, 2B
50065 PONTASSIEVE [FI]
TEL. 0558315600

This new Rufina estate enters the Guide with traditional wines. For now, the best is the Vin Santo '98. The varietal nose has touches of almond and hazelnut-like nuts and fig-themed dried fruit. The palate is dense, broad and caressing. The two well-made Chianti Rufinas have a supple drinkability.

O Vin Santo Colli dell'Etruria Centrale '98	ŸŸ 5
● Chianti Rufina '05	Ÿ 4
● Chianti Rufina '04	Ÿ 4

Carobbio

VIA SAN MARTINO IN CECIONE, 26
50020 PANZANO [FI]
TEL. 0558560133
info@carobbiowine.com

One of Panzano's most famous estates is changing tack. With the vineyards leased, we do not yet know if the label will survive. For now, the good Riserva '05 fuses aromas and balanced structure. The two Supertuscans, Leone di Carobbio and Pietraforte, both '04, aren't quite as successful.

● Chianti Cl. Ris. '05	ŸŸ 5
● Leone di Carobbio '04	Ÿ 6
● Pietraforte del Carobbio '04	Ÿ 6

Casa Dei

LOC. SAN ROCCO
57028 SUVERETO [LI]
TEL. 0558300800
info@tenutacasadei.it

The Casa Dei estate is back. Filare 41 '06, from petit verdot, gives spice, fruit and a full-textured but rather lethargic palate. Filare 18 '06, from cabernet franc, has a black berry nose with vegetal hints and an invigorating palate. The decent Armonia '07 is from sangiovese, syrah and alicante.

● Armonia '06	Ÿ 4
● Filare 18 '06	Ÿ 6
● Filare 41 '06	Ÿ 6

Casali in Val di Chio

VIA SANTA CRISTINA, 16
52043 CASTIGLION FIORENTINO [AR]
TEL. 0575650179
www.casaliinvaldichio.com

This small agriturismo estate at Castiglion Fiorentino makes a delicious Merlot Merigge '05 with a graceful profile of chewy, almost pinot nero-like red berry fruits, wild berries and forest floor, reflected on the savoury palate with its sweet tannins and plenty of appeal, despite moderate depth.

● Merigge '05	ŸŸ 4*
● Poventa '05	Ÿ 4

Fattoria Casaloste

VIA MONTAGLIARI, 32
50020 PANZANO [FI]
TEL. 055852725
www.casaloste.com

While awaiting the new vintage of Don Vincenzo, the Riserva dedicated to the owner's father, we tasted the standard Riserva with complex, layered aromas and a stiffish body with still prominent extract. The standard label Chianti Classico is more relaxed with fresh aromas and a vigorous palate.

● Chianti Cl. '06	ŸŸ 5
● Chianti Cl. Ris. '05	Ÿ 6
● Chianti Cl. Don Vincenzo Ris. '01	ŸŸŸ 7

Fattoria Le Casalte

FRAZ. SANT'ALBINO
VIA DEL TERMINE, 2
53045 MONTEPULCIANO [SI]
TEL. 0578798246
lecasalte@libero.it

While her flagship Nobile Quercetonda is maturing for a further year, Chiara Barioffi gave us a fragrant, juicy Rosso Toscano from sangiovese and canaiolo, which is also amazingly well priced. The Rosso di Montepulciano '06 is pleasant and the Nobile '05 is a bit rustic, especially on the nose.

● Rosso Toscano '06	ŸŸ 2*
● Nobile di Montepulciano '05	Ÿ 5
● Rosso di Montepulciano '06	Ÿ 4

OTHER WINERIES

Podere Casina

FRAZ. ISTIA D'OMBRONE
PIAGGE DEL MAIANO
58040 GROSSETO
TEL. 0564408210
www.poderecasina.com

Wines from Rahel Kimmich and Marcello Pirisi's estate did well again. The Morellino '07 offers clear fruity aromas and lovely fresh-tasting, relaxed drinkability. The sangiovese Aione '06 is spicy on the nose and well layered on the palate, where the oak is at times a bit too upfront.

● Aione '06	♟♟	6
● Morellino di Scansano '07	♟♟	4*
● Aione '05	♟♟	5
● Morellino di Scansano '06	♟♟	4*

Podere Il Castagno

LOC. IL CASTAGNO
52040 CORTONA [AR]
TEL. 063223541
fabdio@tin.it

Fabrizio Dionisio, a Rome-based lawyer with a passion for Cortona wines, shows he has achieved reliably high quality with his Syrah. The '06 is attractive, showing dark, ripe and spicy on the nose. There's a nice follow-through on the savoury, succulently rich palate with its warm alcohol.

● Cortona Syrah '06	♟♟	5
● Cortona Syrah '05	♟♟	5
● Cortona Syrah '04	♟♟	5
● Cortona Syrah '03	♟♟	5

Castagnoli

LOC. CASTAGNOLI
53011 CASTELLINA IN CHIANTI [SI]
TEL. 0577740446
castagnoli@valdelsa.net

Hans Joachim Dobbelin's estate was less successful than usual. Best of the labels submitted is the Chianti Classico '06 with complex black berry and tobacco aromatics and a racy, fresh-tasting palate. The Supertuscan Hortulus '05 is less defined on the nose than on the palate.

● Chianti Cl. '06	♟♟	5
● Hortulus '05	♟	7

Fattoria Castellina

VIA PALANDRI, 27
50050 CAPRAIA E LIMITE [FI]
TEL. 057157631
www.fattoriacastellina.com

This small, organic operation located on the slopes of Montalbano debuted well. The convincing Syrah Geos '06 has a spicy nose with fruit preserves and a substantial, vibrant palate with well-gauged tannins and nice depth. The sangiovese Terra e Cielo '06 is fluid and savoury.

● Geos '06	♟♟	6
● Terra e Cielo '06	♟	6

Giovanni Chiappini

LOC. LE PRESELLE
POD. FELCIAINO, 189B
57020 BOLGHERI [LI]
TEL. 0565749665
www.giovannichiappini.it

Giovanni Chiappini turns out very convincing wines. Sadly, the numbers released are small. From the Lienà line, we particularly liked the Cabernet Sauvignon and Cabernet Franc, both '05 and both with an intact nose and juicy, nicely acidic palate. The Ferruggini '06 is a bit tertiary and evanescent.

● Lienà Cabernet Franc '05	♟♟	8
● Lienà Cabernet Sauvignon '05	♟♟	8
● Ferruggini '06	♟	4
● Lienà Cabernet Sauvignon '04	♟♟	8

La Ciarliana

FRAZ. GRACCIANO
VIA CIARLIANA, 31
53040 MONTEPULCIANO [SI]
TEL. 0578758423
www.laciarliana.it

Luigi Frangiosa makes good wines. The Nobile Vigna Scianello '05 has concentrated, intense aromatics that anticipate a broad, well-profiled palate, weighed down somewhat by the oak. The Rosso di Montepulciano '06 is deliciously flavourful. The Nobile '05 remains a bit clenched.

● Nobile di Montepulciano V. Scianello '05	♟♟	6
● Rosso di Montepulciano '06	♟♟	4*
● Nobile di Montepulciano '05	♟	5

OTHER WINERIES

Cigliano

VIA CIGLIANO, 17
50026 SAN CASCIANO IN VAL DI PESA [FI]
TEL. 055820033
www.villadelcigliano.it

It's the first Guide appearance for the estate owned by Eleonora Antinori's descendants. We were most convinced by the Supertuscan Suganella '06 from sangiovese, merlot and cabernet sauvignon, with spicy tones on the nose and a soft, invitingly acidic palate. The Nettuno '05 Cabernet Sauvignon is more rigid.

● Suganella '06	♥♥	5
● Chianti Cl. '06	♥	4
● Nettuno '05	♥	6

I Cipressi

LOC. GRACCIANO DI MONTEPULCIANO
VIA DELLA CIARLIANA, 4A
53040 MONTEPULCIANO [SI]
TEL. 0578717454
icipressi@virgilio.it

Hubert Ciacci has only been making Brunello for a short while but results are good. His '03 has a fruity nose with notes of morello cherry and spice. The palate is nice and broad thanks to restrained, mellow tannins and well-balanced acidity that supports the wine through to the long, appealing finish.

● Brunello di Montalcino '03	♥♥	7
● Rosso di Montalcino '06	♥	5

La Cipriana

LOC. CAMPASTRELLO 176B
57022 CASTAGNETO CARDUCCI [LI]
TEL. 0565775568
www.lacipriana.it

Products from the Fabianis' estate are always decent. This year, first place goes to the Bolgheri Rosso Superiore San Martino '05 thanks to a broad, complex nose with ripe fruit accompanying spicy notes, and an intense, juicy, expansive palate. The Bolgheri Scopaio '05 shows upfront tannins.

● Bolgheri Rosso Sup. San Martino '05	♥♥	6
● Bolgheri Rosso Scopaio '05	♥	5
● Bolgheri Rosso Sup. San Martino '04	♥♥	6
● Bolgheri Rosso Sup. San Martino '03	♥♥	6

Fattoria Colle Verde

FRAZ. MATRAIA
LOC. CASTELLO
55010 LUCCA
TEL. 0583402310
www.colleverde.it

Fattoria Colle Verde wines were below par. An unfavourable growing year meant they weren't up to recent standards. The best wine is the Brania delle Ghiandaie '05, which has a well-defined red berry nose and a palate that may not be complex but is eminently drinkability.

● Colline Lucchesi Rosso Brania delle Ghiandaie '05	♥♥	5
O Brania del Cancello '06	♥	5
● Colline Lucchesi Rosso Brania delle Ghiandaie '04	♥♥	5

Collelceto

LOC. CAMIGLIANO
POD. LA PISANA
53024 MONTALCINO [SI]
TEL. 0577816606
www.collelceto.it

Elia Palazzesi makes characterful wines in the southwest of Montalcino. His good Brunello '03 has an oaky nose with vanilla and coffee notes and slightly exuberant toast. The palate is better, rich and elegant with an intense finish. The Rosso '06 is pleasant but slightly drying in the finish.

● Brunello di Montalcino '03	♥♥	6
● Rosso di Montalcino '06	♥	4

Colognole

LOC. COLOGNOLE
VIA DEL PALAGIO, 15
50068 RUFINA [FI]
TEL. 0558319870
www.colognole.it

The Trivelli Spalletti estate presented only one, excellently made wine this year, fulfilling recent promises of improvement. The bouquet gives lovely menthol aromas with upfront minerality. As it takes its leave, the caressing palate gives fresh sensations in support of the alcohol.

● Chianti Rufina '06	♥♥	4*
● Chianti Rufina '01	♥♥	3
● Chianti Rufina Ris. del Don '04	♥♥	5

OTHER WINERIES

Villa la Colombaia

LOC. BAGNOLO
VIA IMPRUNETANA PER TAVARNUZZE, 50
50023 IMPRUNETA [FI]
TEL. 0552025041
www.villabagnolo.it

This Beltrami estate makes an excellent debut in the Guide. After dedicating themselves for some time to growing olives, they have moved to making wine with the same passion and convincing results. The Chianti Colli Fiorentini '06 and monovarietal Sangiovese Terre del Cotto '06 are both very good.

● Chianti Colli Fiorentini Terre delle Fornaci '06	♟♟ 4*
● Terre del Cotto '06	♟♟ 5

Podere Concori

LOC. FIATTONE
PROVINCIALE, 1
55027 GALLICANO [LU]
TEL. 0583766039
www.podereconcori.com

Gabriele Da Prato returns to the Guide with a sumptuous Melograno Rosso '06. The wine is a product of natural farming methods informed by long winemaking experience. The result is among the best bottles from Lucca this year for its complexity on the nose and length on the palate.

● Melograno Rosso '06	♟♟ 5
● Melograno Rosso '04	♟♟ 5

Il Conventino

VIA DELLA CIARLIANA, 25B
53040 MONTEPULCIANO [SI]
TEL. 0578715371
www.ilconventino.it

Elegance trumps power in this Nobile Riserva '04, with its austere aromatics and complexity on the measured, subtle palate, blocked only by a touch of over-exuberant oak. Uncertainty on the nose penalizes the Nobile '05, which is better on the palate where the wine is dynamic and contrasting.

● Nobile di Montepulciano Ris. '04	♟♟ 6
● Nobile di Montepulciano '05	♟ 5
● Nobile di Montepulciano Ris. '03	♟♟ 6
● Nobile di Montepulciano Ris. '01	♟♟ 6

Corte Pavone

LOC. CORTE PAVONE
53024 MONTALCINO [SI]
TEL. 0577848110
www.loacker.net

We combine here the Alto Adige-based Loackers' two estates in Tuscany. Brillando '06 is from Tenuta Val di Falco in Maremma. The clean, intense nose shows currants, blueberries and blackberries before the acidity-braced palate reveals elegant extract. The warm Brunello '03 is less centred with evolved tones.

● Brillando Val di Falco '06	♟♟ 4*
● Brunello di Montalcino '03	♟ 8

F.lli Dal Cero

LOC. MONTECCHIO DI CORTONA
S.S. 403
52042 CORTONA [AR]
TEL. 0457460110
www.vinidalcero.com

The Dal Cero property is split into two estates, one near Cortona and the other in Roncà, Verona. The Tuscan estate produces soft, modern-style wines of grace and proportion. One of these is the round Sangiovese Selverello '06, which leads with rich, ripe fruit and good freshness.

● Selverello '06	♟♟ 3*
O Podere Bianchino '07	♟ 3
● Preziosaterra '06	♟ 4

Tenuta degli Dei

VIA SAN LEOLINO, 56
50020 PANZANO [FI]
TEL. 055852593
www.deglidei.com

This year, Tommaso Cavalli gave us a fine wine. From a blend of merlot, cabernet franc and sauvignon with dashes of alicante, petit verdot and bouschet, it has a broad nose of aromatic herbs, balsamic notes and delicate fruit. The broad, deep palate has a good tannic weave and long finish.

● Cavalli Selection '05	♟♟ 6

OTHER WINERIES

Tenuta Di Sesta

FRAZ. CASTELNUOVO DELL'ABATE
LOC. SESTA
53020 MONTALCINO [SI]
TEL. 0577835612
www.tenutadisesta.it

This estate near Sesta is makes reliably good wines. Rosso '06 received the best scores. The broad nose has precise notes of blackberry, cherry and light spice. The well-balanced palate shows already smooth tannins and good supporting acidity before the long finish reprises the nose.

● Rosso di Montalcino '06	🍷🍷 4*
● Brunello di Montalcino '03	🍷 6
● Poggio d'Arna '06	🍷 4

Diadema

VIA IMPRUNETANA PER TAVERNUZZE, 21
50022 IMPRUNETA [FI]
TEL. 0552311330
www.diadema-wine.com

Diadema gave us two excellent wines, released under the estate name. Diadema Rosso '06, from sangiovese, merlot and cabernet sauvignon, is succulent, juicy, complex and long. Diadema Bianco '07, a blend of chardonnay, sauvignon blanc and viognier, is fragrant, dense, invigorating and long.

O Diadema Bianco '07	🍷🍷 8
● Diadema Rosso '06	🍷🍷 8

Donna Olimpia 1898

LOC. MIGLIARINI, 142
57020 BOLGHERI [LI]
TEL. 0272094585
www.donnaolimpia1898.it

Wines from Donna Olimpia 1898 are quite convincing. With a fresh nose showing hints of bell pepper, the Bolgheri '05 is tannic with good acidity. On a par for quality is Tageto '06, which has a more coherent aromatic profile and palate, with alcohol upfront. The Bolgheri Bianco Obizzo '07 is juicy and fresh.

● Bolgheri '05	🍷🍷 5
● Tageto '06	🍷🍷 6
O Bolgheri Bianco Obizzo '07	🍷 5

Due Mani

LOC. ORTACAVOLI
56046 RIPARBELLA [PI]
TEL. 0583975048
www.duemani.eu

Luca D'Attoma has a dual role as oenologist and owner at the Duemani estate and presents three wines. Suisassi '05, a Syrah with outstanding personality and thrust, and Duemani '05, a Cabernet Franc with great finesse on the palate, are particularly convincing. Altrovino '06 is pleasant.

● Duemani '05	🍷🍷 5
● Suisassi '05	🍷🍷 5
● Altrovino '06	🍷 5

Cantine Faralli

LOC. FASCIANO, 4
52040 CORTONA [AR]
TEL. 0575613128
www.cantinefaralli.com

The Faralli estate, a small, family-run operation at Cortona, submitted only the new Cortona Merlot '05, which proved interesting. Powerful, warm and caressing, but also a bit marked by oak, it shows a very Mediterranean profile with sweet fruit, grilled bell peppers, lavender and capers.

● Cortona Merlot '05	🍷🍷 6
● Il Sorbo '04	🍷🍷 5

Farnetella

S.DA SIENA-BETTOLLE, KM 37
53048 SINALUNGA [SI]
TEL. 0577355117
www.felsina.it

Managed by the Felsina staff, Farnetella had a less successful vintage, partly because the showcase Poggio Granoni was missing. The good Sauvignon '06 shows inviting vegetality and nice fullness. The slightly rigid Lucilla '06 is a blend of sangiovese and cabernet. Nero di Nubi '04 is light-bodied.

O Sauvignon '06	🍷🍷 4
● Lucilla '06	🍷 4
● Nero di Nubi '04	🍷 5
● Poggio Granoni '99	🍷🍷🍷 8

OTHER WINERIES

Fattoi

LOC. SANTA RESTITUTA
POD. CAPANNA, 101
53024 MONTALCINO [SI]
TEL. 0577848613
www.fattoi.it

This historic estate makes characterful classic wines like the Brunello '03, with a white peach and not too ripe briary fruit nose that lifts nice, sweet tobacco. This wine has good concentration with still young tannins supporting alcoholic sweetness. This wine will improve with ageing.

● Brunello di Montalcino '03	♥♥	6
● Rosso di Montalcino '06	♥	4

Fertuna

LOC. GRILLI
VIA AURELIA VECCHIA KM 205
58040 GAVORRANO [GR]
TEL. 056688138
www.fertuna.it

Recently sold by Ezio Rivella to wine distributors Gruppo Meregalli, this Maremma estate makes impeccable wines. The sangiovese, cabernet sauvignon and merlot Lodai '06 is dense and flavourful. The fresh, light Plato '05, from sangiovese and cabernet sauvignon, has slightly muted aromatics.

● Lodai '06	♥♥	5
● Plato '05	♥	5
● Lodai '05	♥♥	5
● Messiio '05	♥♥	6

La Festeggiata

LOC. SAN LEOLINO, 33
50022 PANZANO [FI]
TEL. 055852316
alisonhilary@yahoo.com

This new estate for the Guide is located at Panzano. It is actually quite difficult to make bad wine there and proof comes with the rich, complex La Festeggiata '04, with its good definition and caressing mouthfeel, and the Chianti Classico Riserva '04, which foregrounds finesse.

● La Festeggiata '04	♥♥	5
● Chianti Cl. Ris. '04	♥	5

Fattoria di Fiano

LOC. FIANO
VIA FIRENZE, 11
50050 CERTALDO [FI]
TEL. 0571669048
www.fattoriadifiano.it

Ugo Bing's Fianesco '06, from sangiovese with equal amounts colorino, merlot and syrah, is the stand-out, giving sweet spice and fruit before the soft, fluid palate shows good texture with tannins that stiffen on the finish. The two Colli Fiorentini Chiantis, a standard label and Riserva '05, are interesting.

● Fianesco '06	♥♥	6
● Chianti Colli Fiorentini '05	♥	4
● Chianti Colli Fiorentini Ris. '05	♥	5

Ficomontanino

LOC. FICOMONTANINO
53043 CHIUSI [SI]
TEL. 0578821180
www.agricolaficomontanino.it

The '05 Lucumone, perhaps the most successful version, is of the most interesting monovarietal Cabernet Sauvignons from Tuscany. The aromas are fresh, spicy and almost piquant. Juicy, taut and subtle on the palate, it is lacking just a bit more complexity. The Chianti dei Colli Senesi Tutulus '06 is well made.

● Lucumone '05	♥♥	6
● Chianti Colli Senesi Tutulus '06	♥	5
● Lucumone '04	♥♥	6
● Lucumone '03	♥♥	6

Fattoria Le Fonti

LOC. LE FONTI
50020 PANZANO [FI]
TEL. 055852194
www.fattorialefonti.it

Results from the Schmitt-Vitali estate were less brilliant than usual. Fontissimo '04, a blend of sangiovese and cabernet sauvignon, mingles fresh eucalyptus with red berries over a long, solid palate. The other wines are well typed, though not that characterful, and Rosato '07 is fragrant and appetizing.

● Fontissimo '04	♥♥	6
● Chianti Cl. '06	♥	4
● Chianti Cl. Ris. '05	♥	5
☉ Sangiovese Rosato '07	♥	3

OTHER WINERIES

Le Fonti

LOC. SAN GIORGIO
53036 POGGIBONSI [SI]
TEL. 0577935690
www.fattoria-lefonti.it

Wines from the Imbenis have more territory focus but tend to be muzzy on the nose. The convincing Chianti Classico '06 has good tannic weight, and freshness from the well-balanced acidity, rounded off by a rising finish. The rest of the range is very drinkable.

● Chianti Cl. '06	♟♟	4*
● Chianti Cl. Ris. '05	♟	6
● Sangiovese '06	♟	3
● Vito Arturo '05	♟	6

Tenuta di Frassineto

S.DA VICINALE DEL DUCA, 14
52100 AREZZO
TEL. 0575367033
www.tenutadifrassineto.com

An interesting newcomer to the Arezzo area in the heart of Val di Chiana, Tenuta di Frassineto debuts with a well-made white. A blend of mostly vermentino with traminer and sémillon, Rancoli '07 is very clean with tropical fruit and flowers supported by good freshness.

O Rancoli '07	♟♟	4*

Gagliole

LOC. GAGLIOLE, 42
53011 CASTELLINA IN CHIANTI [SI]
TEL. 0577740369
www.gagliole.com

Thomas and Monika Bar's estate was below par. From sangiovese and cabernet sauvignon, Gagliole '06 is not bad thanks to a fruity, minerally nose laced with spice and a juicy, savoury palate with a lovely, long finish. The less centred Chianti Classico Rubiolo '06 has clear aromas but a rough, insubstantial palate.

● Gagliole Rosso '06	♟♟	7
● Chianti Cl. Rubiolo '06	♟	4
● Gagliole Rosso '04	♟♟	6

Rosa Gasser Bagnoli

FRAZ. DONORATICO
LOC. GREPPI CUPI, 212
57024 CASTAGNETO CARDUCCI [LI]
TEL. 0565775272
greppi.cupi@libero.it

Rosa Gasser Bagnoli's estate is back with a nice performance from the Bolgheri Superiore '05. The nose offers clear red, ripe berries with hints of Mediterranean scrub. Its juicy, deep palate lacks concentration but is elegant and long, with only slightly acidulous tannins in the finish.

● Bolgheri Sup. '05	♟♟	7

Giannoni Fabbri

LOC. SAN MARCO IN VILLA, 2
52044 CORTONA [AR]
TEL. 3475883939
www.giannonifabbri.it

The Giannoni Fabbri estate in Cortona is a name to keep in mind for aficionados of Vin Santo. The '02 version is excellent with lovely Mediterranean dried figs, dates and capers followed by a caressingly sweet, rich palate with good length and contrasting fresh acidity.

O Cortona Vin Santo '02	♟♟	6
● Cortona Amato '07	♟	4
● Cortona Cabernet '04	♟♟	4

Azienda Agricola Godiolo

VIA DELL'ACQUAPUZZOLA, 13
53045 MONTEPULCIANO [SI]
TEL. 0578757251
www.godiolo.it

The convincing Nobile '05 from Franco Fiorini's estate has sustained, fresh aromas. The palate is vital, well crafted and harmonious with a savoury note that amplifies character, drinkability and verve in the finish. The simple yet well-constructed Rosso '05 shows floral aromas and an approachable palate.

● Nobile di Montepulciano '05	♟♟	5
● Rosso di Montepulciano '05	♟	4
● Nobile di Montepulciano '03	♟♟	5
● Nobile di Montepulciano Ris. '03	♟♟	6

OTHER WINERIES

Tenuta di Gracciano della Seta

FRAZ. GRACCIANO
VIA UMBRIA, 59
53045 MONTEPULCIANO [SI]
TEL. 0578708340
g.rigoli@agriconsulting.it

The Della Seta family's estate has returned to the Guide after a couple of years' absence. The Nobile Riserva '04 has great personality, floral aromas alternating with savoury, gutsy earthy hints and good density on the palate. The Nobile '05 is a bit dilute with high alcohol. Rosso '06 is fresh and enjoyable.

● Nobile di Montepulciano Ris. '04	▼▼ 5
● Nobile di Montepulciano '05	▼ 4
● Rosso di Montepulciano '06	▼ 4

Granducato

VIA BORGACCIO, 19
53036 POGGIBONSI [SI]
TEL. 0577936057
www.capsi.it

The co-operative Granducato winery returns to the guide. The best wine this year was the Chianti Classico San Piero Riserva '05. Its pleasant aromatics are characterized by fruit and spice and the well-gauged extract leads to a long, flavourful finish. The other wines are very decent.

● Chianti San Piero Ris. '05	▼▼ 5
● Chianti Cl. '06	▼ 4
● Chianti Cl. Ris. '05	▼ 5
● Chianti San Piero '05	▼ 5

Gruppo Vini Selezionati

VIA VALCANORO, 32
50021 BARBERINO VAL D'ELSA [FI]
TEL. 0558078834
www.viniselezionati.com

This is a Guide debut for a group owning large holdings in Maremma, Chianti Classico and Val di Cornia, as well as managing a farm in Montalcino. We felt the best product was Chianti Classico Roccamena '06, which has a traditional style on the nose and a solid, vibrant body. The other wines are pleasant.

● Chianti Cl. Roccamena '06	▼▼ 4
● Poggio ai Lecci '07	▼ 4
● Poggio ai Lecci '06	▼ 4
● Tenuta Il Casone Malacreta '06	▼ 5

Icario

VIA DELLE PIETROSE, 2
53045 MONTEPULCIANO [SI]
TEL. 0578758845
www.icario.it

Nobile Vitaroccia '05 has a broad, well-profiled bouquet and gutsy, dense palate with acid verve and nice energy. The complexity in the mouth of the Nobile '05 is held back by too much oak and toastiness also weighs down the aromas. The fresh, light Nysa '07 is from pinot grigio and gewürztraminer.

● Nobile di Montepulciano Vitaroccia '05	▼▼ 6
● Nobile di Montepulciano '05	▼ 5
○ Nysa '07	▼ 6

Incontri

LOC. FOSSONI, 38
57028 SUVERETO [LI]
TEL. 0565829401
www.incontriwine.it

Incontri wines have ups and downs. The good Val di Cornia Martellino Bianco '07 has lovely apple and pear aromas, zest and a caressing, continuous flavour. Val di Cornia Vermentino Ildobrandino '07 shows fruity pulp, tanginess and a decent finish. The small Merlò degli Incontri '05 is supple and appealing.

○ Val di Cornia Martellino Bianco '07	▼▼ 3*
● Val di Cornia Suvereto Merlò degli Incontri '05	▼ 6
○ Val di Cornia Vermentino Ildobrandino '07	▼ 4

Innocenti

FRAZ. TORRENIERI
LOC. CITILLE DI SOTTO, 45
53028 MONTALCINO [SI]
TEL. 0577834227
www.innocentivini.com

Here at Torrenieri, quality is improving. After oxygenating, the Brunello '03 opens on slightly smoky medicinal herbs, tobacco and leather. It's very moreish, with mellow tannins and rather surprising supporting acidity, given the vintage. The well-typed Rosso '06 is fragrant on the nose.

● Brunello di Montalcino '03	▼▼ 7
● Rosso di Montalcino '06	▼ 4
● Vignalsole '05	▼ 5

OTHER WINERIES

La Cura

LOC. CURA NUOVA, 12
58024 MASSA MARITTIMA [GR]
TEL. 0566918094
www.cantinalacura.it

The Merlot La Cura is still the most successful wine from the talented Enrico Corsi's estate. Again, refined aromas and a well-measured palate distinguish the '06, making it one of the best in its type, at least from Maremma. The rest of the range shows reliable quality.

● La Cura Merlot '06	♥♥ 5
● Monteregio di Massa Marittima Rosso Breccerosse '07	♥ 4
○ Trinus '07	♥ 4

Fattoria La Striscia

VIA DEI CAPPUCCINI, 3
52100 AREZZO
TEL. 057526740
fattorialastrisc@hotmail.com

This Arezzo estate owned by Conti Occhini makes slightly edgy wines with character. The Chianti Bernardino '07 has a muddled nose but lots of rich, juicy fruit. Occhini '06, from sangiovese with merlot and cabernet, is robust and structured, showing warm, soft and caressing, with more breadth than depth.

● Occhini '06	♥♥ 4*
● Chianti Berardino '07	♥ 3
● Occhini '05	♥♥ 4

Lavacchio

VIA DI MONTEFIESOLE, 55
50065 PONTASSIEVE [FI]
TEL. 0558317472
www.fattorialavacchio.com

Only two labels were submitted to our tastings this year. We were particularly convinced by the Pachar '06, a blend of viognier, chardonnay and sauvignon distinguished by its mineral and citrus notes on the nose and rich, zesty flavour. The Chianti Rufina Cedro '06 is well made and nicely drinkable.

○ Pachar '06	♥♥ 4*
● Chianti Rufina Cedro '06	♥ 4

Az. Agr. Lazzaretti

POD. CANCHI, 84
53024 MONTALCINO [SI]
TEL. 0577848475
www.vinilazzaretti.it

The '03 Brunello di Montalcino from this small estate in the north-east of the zone is very good. Its broad nose has red berries and light floral, spicy sensations. The rich, harmonious palate is already balanced, boasts a lingering finish and has tannins nicely tucked in.

● Brunello di Montalcino '03	♥♥ 7

Villa Le Prata

LOC. LE PRATA, 261
53024 MONTALCINO [SI]
TEL. 0577848325
www.villaleprata.com

Benedetta Losappio is passionate about his estate and these results show it. The Brunello '03 is good, although spicy shades of vanilla and cloves tend to compromise the fruit on the otherwise intense nose. The tannin-rich palate has good vitality with poised acidity that makes for pleasant drinking.

● Brunello di Montalcino '03	♥♥ 7

Il Lebbio

LOC. SAN BENEDETTO, 11C
53037 SAN GIMIGNANO [SI]
TEL. 0577944725
www.illebbio.it

The best wine from Lebbio is the Vernaccia Tropìe '07, confirming uneven production. Elegant lime blossom mingles with tropical fruit before the structured, confident palate shows attractive acidity and a full-favoured finish. The Cicogio '07 is still young and I Grottoni '07 has nice freshness of fruit.

○ Vernaccia di S. Gimignano Tropìe '07	♥♥ 4*
● Cicogio '07	♥ 4
● I Grottoni '07	♥ 4
○ Malvasia '07	♥ 3

OTHER WINERIES

Fattoria Lornano

LOC. LORNANO, 11
53035 MONTERIGGIONI [SI]
TEL. 0577309059
www.fattorialornano.it

We were not fully convinced by wines from the Taddei estate, which have muzzy aromas and a general lack of balance. The only good bottle is Commendator Enrico '05, a blend of sangiovese and merlot with a soft, delicate flavour. The Chianti Classicos are only well made.

● Commendator Enrico '05	♟♟	5
● Chianti Cl. '06	♟	4
● Chianti Cl. Le Bandite '05	♟	4

Luiano

LOC. MERCATALE VAL DI PESA
VIA DI LUIANO, 32
50024 SAN CASCIANO IN VAL DI PESA [FI]
TEL. 0558211039
www.luiano.it

The Palombo estate stays in the Guide although last year's results had us hoping for significant improvement. The most convincing wine this year is Sangiò '06, from a base of sangiovese and merlot, with round, elegant aromas and a soft palate, although it fades a bit on the finish.

● Sangiò '06	♟♟	4
● Chianti Cl. '06	♟	4
● Chianti Cl. Ris. '05	♟	4

Az. Agr. Macea

LOC. MACEA, 1
55023 BORGO A MOZZANO [LU]
TEL. 3394777149
macea@freemail.it

Macea lies between the Apuan Alps and the Apennines. The Barsanti children carry on their father's labour of love and struggle with vineyards where mechanization is near impossible. The wines are vibrant. Campo Caturesi '06 has an impressive crystalline simplicity and easy drinking.

● Campo Caturesi '06	♟♟	4
● Pinot Nero '05	♟	4

La Magia

LOC. LA MAGIA
53024 MONTALCINO [SI]
TEL. 0577835667
fattorialamagia@tiscali.it

This lovely estate looking onto the church of Sant'Antimo makes reliable wines. The interesting Rosso '06 presents an intense ruby and lavish fruit on the nose. The palate is rich but never cloys, thanks to good acidity. The Brunello '03 shows faintly evolved sensations and a satisfying, gutsy palate.

● Rosso di Montalcino '06	♟♟	5
● Brunello di Montalcino '03	♟	8

Marchesato degli Aleramici

FRAZ. CAMIGLIANO
POD. IL GALAMPIO
53024 MONTALCINO [SI]
TEL. 0577816056
www.marchesatodeglialeramici.it

This estate makes increasingly good wines after major investment in the cellar and more focused choices in the vineyard. The good Brunello '03 reveals floral, yellow peach and light oaky sensations on the nose. The palate is relaxed thanks to already smooth tannins and alcohol that is not excessive.

● Brunello di Montalcino '03	♟♟	7

Podere La Marronaia

POD. LA MARRONAIA, 14
53037 SAN GIMIGNANO [SI]
TEL. 0577907265
www.marronaia.com

The organic Podere La Marronaia debuts with well-made wines. The good, sangiovese-only Intenso della Marronaia '07 has a fruity nose and nice acid attack with soft tannins and a consistent finish. San Gimignano Rosso Quattrorsi '06 is dense and flavourful. The Vernaccia '07 and Visila '07 selection are decent.

● Intenso della Marronaia '07	♟♟	4
● San Gimignano Rosso Quattrorsi '06	♟	5
○ Vernaccia di S. Gimignano '07	♟	3*
○ Vernaccia di S. Gimignano Visila '07	♟	4

OTHER WINERIES

Il Marroneto

LOC. MADONNA DELLE GRAZIE, 307
53024 MONTALCINO [SI]
TEL. 0577849382
www.ilmarroneto.it

Il Marroneto is high on the western slope of Montalcino. The good Brunello '03 has an ethery nose with yellow peach and cherry notes. The elegant palate is offset by excellent acidity and the finish gives good length and depth. The selection Madonna delle Grazie '03 is juicy but a bit small.

● Brunello di Montalcino '03	🍷🍷 7
● Brunello di Montalcino Madonna delle Grazie '03	🍷 8

Cosimo Maria Masini

VIA POGGIO AL PINO, 16
56028 SAN MINIATO [PI]
TEL. 0571465032
www.cosimomariamasini.it

The young, biodynamic Cosimo Maria Masini estate is a surprisingly vibrant operation on the Tuscan coast. As well as the complex, characterful Annick '07 white from chardonnay and sauvignon, we also liked the red Nicole '06, a wonderfully appealing, moreish monovarietal Sangiovese.

O Annick '07	🍷🍷 4*
● Nicole '06	🍷🍷 4*
O Annick '06	YY 4

Micheletti

LOC. MARCACCIO, 58
57022 CASTAGNETO CARDUCCI [LI]
TEL. 0565763516
agricolamicheletti@interfree.it

The Micheletti estate is back in the Guide after a great showing by the Bolgheri '06. Lovely intense currant and blackberry fruit melds with balsam and leather. Concentration and clenched tannins are supported by good acidity on a palate that should improve with bottle age.

● Bolgheri '06	🍷🍷 4

Mocali

LOC. MOCALI
53024 MONTALCINO [SI]
TEL. 0577849485
azmocali@tiscali.it

Tiziano Ciacci gave us two Brunello di Montalcinos and we preferred the standard label to Vigna delle Raunate, both '03s. The former's muzzy nose allows white cherry, peach and blackberry to emerge. On the palate, the alcohol is not excessive but the finish is held back by rigid tannins.

● Brunello di Montalcino '03	🍷🍷 7
● Brunello di Montalcino V. delle Raunate '03	🍷 8
● I Piaggioni '06	🍷 4
● Rosso di Montalcino '06	🍷 5

Podere Monastero

LOC. MONASTERO
53011 CASTELLINA IN CHIANTI [SI]
TEL. 0577740436
alessandrocellai@virgilio.it

Alessandro Cellai has given form to his project. He makes two wines: La Pineta, a monovarietal Pinot Nero, and Campanaio, a 50-50 blend of cabernet sauvignon and merlot. Both are from '06. Alluring and distinctly well styled, they are currently penalized only by coming from recently planted vineyards.

● Campanaio '06	🍷🍷 6
● La Pineta '06	🍷🍷 6

Montecalvi

VIA CITILLE, 85
50022 GREVE IN CHIANTI [FI]
TEL. 0558544665
www.montecalvi.com

This has been another unexciting year for wines from the Bolli-O'Byrne couple, who struggle to recover the lustre of the past. The best is Montecalvi Vielle Vigne '06, from a base of mostly cabernet sauvignon and sangiovese, with clear notes of fruit and a body held back by rough tannins.

● Montecalvi V. V. '06	🍷🍷 7
● Chianti Cl. '06	🍷 5
● San Piero '06	🍷 6

OTHER WINERIES

Fattoria di Montemaggio

LOC. MONTEMAGGIO
53017 RADDA IN CHIANTI [SI]
TEL. 0577738323
www.montemaggio.com

Torre di Montemaggio '06 is a sound single-variety Merlot with fresh, balsamic tones on the nose and pleasant wild berry touches. The solid, rich palate finishes long with a pleasing after-aroma. The good Chianti Classico '06 offers fruit, flowers, refreshing acidity and plenty of flavour.

● Chianti Cl. '06	🍷🍷	4*
● Torre di Montemaggio '06	🍷🍷	5
● Chianti Cl. Ris. '04	🍷	5
● Torre di Montemaggio '04	🍷🍷	5

Castello di Montepò

LOC. PANCOLE
CASTELLO DI MONTEPÒ
58054 SCANSANO [GR]
TEL. 0564580231

Jacopo Biondi Santi's Maremma estate did well. The Morellino di Scansano '06 is quite good with fresh, well-sustained aromas and a full-flavoured, very juicy palate. The well-executed Sassoalloro '05, a monovarietal Sangiovese, shows energetic tannins but a slightly mouth-drying finish.

● Morellino di Scansano '06	🍷🍷	5
● Sassoalloro '05	🍷	5
● Montepaone '00	🍷🍷	6
● Sassoalloro '03	🍷🍷	5

Monteraponi

LOC. MONTERAPONI
53017 RADDA IN CHIANTI [SI]
TEL. 055352601
www.monteraponi.it

Last year's results weren't repeated at this estate owned by Michele Braganti, an enthusiastic young winemaker from Radda. His wines show character and personality but need just a bit more balance. The stand-out is Riserva Il Campitello '05, which finishes a touch light.

● Chianti Cl. '06	🍷	5
● Chianti Cl. Il Campitello Ris. '05	🍷	6

Castello di Monteriggioni

VIA DEL CASTELLO, 24
53035 MONTERIGGIONI [SI]
TEL. 0577304081
www.fattoriacastellodimonteriggioni.com

Luisa Maria Gozzi's estate debuts in the Guide. We liked this traditional cellar's selection, which mixes jam with leather and tobacco aromatics. The solid, structured palate has poised tannins, fresh acidity and a savoury finish. The Chianti Classico '06 is simpler.

● Chianti Cl. Luisa Maria Gozzi '05	🍷🍷	5
● Chianti Cl. '06	🍷	4

Montesalario

LOC. MONTESALARIO, 27
58040 CASTEL DEL PIANO [GR]
TEL. 0564954173
montesalario@interfree.it

Mario Pasqui has still to achieve consistent quality. Yet his wines do show genuineness and character, as proved by a delicious, floral Montecucco Sangiovese '06, with a savoury, energy-filled palate. Riserva '05 shows some evolution in its aromas, and Montecucco Rosso '06 is delightful.

● Montecucco Sangiovese '06	🍷🍷	5
● Montecucco '06	🍷	4
● Montecucco Sangiovese Ris. '05	🍷	5
● Montecucco Sangiovese Ris. '00	🍷🍷	5

Giacomo Mori

FRAZ. PALAZZONE
P.ZZA SANDRO PERTINI, 8
53040 SAN CASCIANO DEI BAGNI [SI]
TEL. 0578227005
giacomo.mori@libero.it

Although from a difficult year, Giacomo Mori's Vin Santo stands out with lovely amber followed by clean aromas and a weighty, bracing palate. Chianti Castelrotto Riserva '05 yields a rich, dense bouquet and is just a bit stiff in the mouth. Chianti '06 is uncomplicated but supple.

○ Vin Santo del Chianti '02	🍷🍷	6
● Chianti '06	🍷	4
● Chianti Castelrotto Ris. '05	🍷	6

OTHER WINERIES

Tenute Silvio Nardi

LOC. CASALE DEL BOSCO
53024 MONTALCINO [SI]
TEL. 0577808269
www.tenutenardi.com

There were only average performances for the current vintages but we were impressed by the quality of Silvio Nardi's Brunello '03. A classic nose presents subtle but intriguing evolved notes of leather and sweet tobacco and the assertive extract does nothing to hinder very supple progression.

● Brunello di Montalcino '03	♔	7

No, vo' li'

VIA DI FONTECORNINO, 9
53045 MONTEPULCIANO [SI]
TEL. 3470804401
www.no-vo-li.it

Cavernano '06, from sangiovese, cabernet sauvignon, merlot and syrah, has clean-edged aromas and a palate whose acidic grip sets off velvety fruit, ensuring refreshing suppleness. Fontecornino '06, from sangiovese, merlot, petit verdot and syrah, is husky on the nose and straightforward in the mouth.

● Cavernano '06	♔	6
● Fontecornino '06	♔	4
● La Scudiscia '05	♔♔	7
● Tavernaia '05	♔♔	8

Podere Il Palazzino

FRAZ. MONTI IN CHIANTI
POD. IL PALAZZINO
53013 GAIOLE IN CHIANTI [SI]
TEL. 0577747008
www.podereilpalazzino.it

Very little remains of the Il Palazzino's past elegance. The wines we tasted lacked cleanness and definition on both nose and palate, and tannins were often obstreperous. The sangiovese Casina Girasole '06 is uncomplicated but fresh and clean. We await a return to past quality.

● Bertinga '05	♔	6
● Casina Girasole '06	♔	3
● Chianti Cl. Argenina '06	♔	4
● Chianti Cl. Grosso Sanese '05	♔	6
● Chianti Cl. La Pieve '05	♔	5

Palazzo

LOC. PALAZZO, 144
53024 MONTALCINO [SI]
TEL. 0577848479
www.aziendapalazzo.it

Both of Palazzo's denomination wines earned high marks. Rosso '06 offers a fragrant mix of dense red berry, blackberry and morello cherry nicely shot through with spice. Magisterial tannins contribute to its broad, supple finish. But oak leaves too much of a mark on Brunello '03.

● Rosso di Montalcino '06	♔♔	5
● Brunello di Montalcino '03	♔	7

Panzanello

VIA CASE SPARSE, 86
50022 PANZANO [FI]
TEL. 055852470
www.panzanello.it

The Sommaruga family's wines were below par this year. The younger wines did better, a case in point being Chianti Classico '06 and the all-sangiovese Le Piazzole '07. But Chianti Classico Riserva '05 and Il Manuzio '04, also all sangiovese, showed good weight but the palates were unsettled and rough.

● Chianti Cl. Panzanello '06	♔♔	4
● Chianti Cl. Panzanello Ris. '05	♔	6
● Il Manuzio '04	♔	7
● Le Piazzole '07	♔	3

Tenuta La Parrina

S.DA VICINALE DELLA PARRINA
58010 ALBINIA [GR]
TEL. 0564862636
www.parrina.it

Franca Spinola's wines are on the way up and we're expecting a stand-out soon. The all-merlot Radaia '06 was impressive, as was Parrina Rosso Riserva '06, mostly sangiovese with some cabernet and merlot. Both Muraccio '06 and Bianco '07 are enjoyable.

● Parrina Rosso Ris. '06	♔♔	5
● Radaia '06	♔♔	7
○ Parrina Bianco '07	♔	3
● Parrina Rosso Muraccio '06	♔	4

OTHER WINERIES

Pasolini Dall'Onda

P.ZZA MAZZINI, 10
50021 BARBERINO VAL D'ELSA [FI]
TEL. 0558075019
www.pasolinidallonda.com

In the last few years, Pasolini dall'Onda has returned good quality and now needs only to maintain it. Chianti Classico '05 is most impressive, showing fresh and straightforward on the nose, tasty in the mouth, with rich, succulent texture and a dynamic finish that just keeps expanding.

● Chianti Cl. Sicelle '05	♙♙ 4*

Pian del Pino

LOC. CAMPOGIALLI 164
52048 TERRANUOVA BRACCIOLINI [AR]
TEL. 055977048
www.piandelpino.com

This Arezzo estate, which adopts natural viticulture, repeated its fine performance of last year. In particular, the new Chianti Pianalti '06 beautifully represents both typicity and its terroir. It lays out clean-edged berry, blossoms and earth, then opens a crisp, pulpy palate brimming with flavour.

● Chianti Pianalti '06	♙♙ 4*
● Pian del Pino '06	♙ 4
● Jubilus '05	♙♙ 4

Piccini

LOC. PIAZZOLE
53011 CASTELLINA IN CHIANTI [SI]
TEL. 057754011
www.tenutepiccini.it

Tenute Piccini is one of Chianti Classico's largest cellars, with over 250 hectares of vines. Two wines brought them into the Guide. High marks went to Brunello di Montalcino Villa Al Cortile '03 with its generous nose and powerful structure. Chianti Classico Riserva '05 is lithe and pleasurable.

● Brunello di Montalcino Villa al Cortile '03	♙♙ 6
● Chianti Cl. Ris. '05	♙♙ 4*
○ Sangiovese Sel. Rosa '07	♙ 2

Pietrafitta

LOC. CORTENNANO, 54
53037 SAN GIMIGNANO [SI]
TEL. 0577943200
www.pietrafitta.com

This long-standing operation is back with fine performances. Vernaccia Vigna La Costa Riserva '06 is again the star with aromatic harmony of oak and fruit, and an expansive palate supported by sprightly acidity. Vernaccia Borghetto '07 is smooth and savoury. Vernaccia '07 is fresh and delightful.

○ Vernaccia di S. Gimignano V. La Costa Ris. '06	♙♙ 5
○ Vernaccia di S. Gimignano '07	♙ 4
○ Vernaccia di S. Gimignano V. Borghetto '07	♙ 4

La Pieve

LOC. LA PIEVE
VIA SANTO STEFANO
50050 MONTAIONE [FI]
TEL. 0571697764
simonetognetti@virgilio.it

La Pieve has been organic for some time and we note growth in the number and quality of the wines. The new syrah Il Gobbo Nero '06 is very good with a well-defined nose, then juicy fruit and complexity, and a long finish. Chianti '07 is supple and tasty, and Chianti Fortebraccio '06 is soundly made.

● Chianti '07	♙♙ 3*
● Il Gobbo Nero '06	♙♙ 5
● Chianti Fortebraccio '06	♙ 3*
● Rosso del Pievano '05	♙♙ 4

Podere Brizio

LOC. PODERE BRIZIO, 67
53024 MONTALCINO [SI]
TEL. 0577846004
www.poderebrizio.it

After Roberto Bellini's splendid results last year, it's back to a short profile this time. We bend with the seasons, and not vice versa, so 2001 brought Three Glasses last year to Riserva but the torrid 2003 growing year was less fortunate. Bellini's Brunello lacks the requisite balance.

● Rosso di Montalcino '06	♙♙ 4
● Brunello di Montalcino '03	♙ 7
● Brunello di Montalcino Ris. '01	♙♙♙ 8

OTHER WINERIES

Podere Ciona

LOC. MONTEGROSSI
53013 GAIOLE IN CHIANTI [SI]
TEL. 0577749127
www.podereciona.com

Franco Gatteschi entered the Guide last year but this year has a short profile. Supertuscan Le Diaccie '05, largely merlot, impressed us with the finesse of its lovely spice and ripe fruit nose, and with its graceful, vibrant palate and dynamic finish, both well balanced. Riserva '05 is more coarse.

● Le Diaccie '05	❦❦ 6
● Chianti Cl. Ris. '05	❦ 5

Podere Fortuna

VIA SAN GIUSTO A FORTUNA, 7
50037 SAN PIERO A SIEVE [FI]
TEL. 0558487214
www.poderefortuna.com

Podere Fortuna debuts in the Guide. Its vineyards, planted in 2001 to pinot nero, are in the Mugello hills, where they enjoy outstanding exposures and temperature ranges. Fortuni '05 flaunts exemplary, clean-edged aromas and balanced finesse on the palate. Coldaia '05 is equally fine.

● Pinot Nero Fortuni '05	❦❦ 6
● Pinot Nero Coldaia '05	❦❦ 6

Tenuta Podernovo

LOC. TERRICCIOLA
VIA PODERNUOVO, 13
56030 PISA
TEL. 0587655173
www.tenutapodernovo.it

It's no news that the Lunelli brothers produce fine results. The sangiovese and merlot Teuto '05 presents well-delineated liqueur fruit then a rich, lingering palate. Aliotto '06 shows self-confident and tasty, with red berry fruit and Mediterranean scrub, plus a palate with smoothed-down tannins.

● Aliotto '06	❦❦ 4
● Teuto '05	❦❦ 5
● Aliotto '05	❦❦ 4
● Teuto '03	❦❦ 5

Poggio al Sole

LOC. BADIA A PASSIGNANO
S.DA RIGNANA, 2
50028 TAVARNELLE VAL DI PESA [FI]
TEL. 0558071850
www.poggioalsole.com

This year, there's only a short profile for Giovanni Davaz's winery. The aromas lack cleanness and powerful structures militate against decent suppleness. Syrah '06 is the most approachable, showing spicy but stiff on the palate, while the cabernet and merlot Seraselva '04 is a bit over-extracted.

● Syrah '06	❦❦ 7
● Chianti Cl. '06	❦ 5
● Chianti Cl. Casasilia '05	❦ 7
● Seraselva '04	❦ 6

Poggio Amorelli

LOC. POGGIO AMORELLI
53011 CASTELLINA IN CHIANTI [SI]
TEL. 0571668733
poggioamorelli@libero.it

Marco Mazzarrini's wines don't impress any more, despite the potential on show in the past. They lack personality, and are often compromised by excessive oak, as in Oracolo '06, a largely sangiovese Supertuscan. The two Chianti Classicos, '06 and Riserva '05, are too slight and enervated.

● Chianti Cl. '06	❦ 4
● Chianti Cl. Ris. '05	❦ 5
● Oracolo '06	❦ 6

Poggio Capponi

LOC. SAN DONATO A LIVIZZANO
VIA MONTELUPO, 184
50025 MONTESPERTOLI [FI]
TEL. 0571671914
www.poggiocapponi.it

The star Tinorso '06 scored high again. This merlot-syrah blend has nicely delineated aromatics and a vibrant attack, then dense-packed tannins and an endless finale. Chianti '07 exhibits fine fruit, mouthfeel and balance, while Chianti Petriccio '06 is simpler, and Chardonnay Sovente '07 listless.

● Chianti Poggio Capponi '07	❦❦ 3*
● Tinorso '06	❦❦ 5
● Chianti Montespertoli Petriccio '06	❦ 4
O Sovente '07	❦ 4

OTHER WINERIES

Poggio Foco

LOC. POGGIO FUOCO
58014 MANCIANO [GR]
TEL. 0564620537
www.poggiofoco.com

Sesà is again the leader among the Kovarich family's wines. It's a blend of cabernet sauvignon and merlot, and the '05 edition releases clean aromas, then builds a vigorous palate showing elegant complexity, capped by an impressively lengthy finale laden with fine, sweet fruit.

● Sesà '05	♙♙	6
● Sesà '04	♙♙	6
● Sesà '03	♙♙	6
● Sesà '02	♙♙	6

Poggio Torselli

VIA SCOPETI, 10
50026 SAN CASCIANO IN VAL DI PESA [FI]
TEL. 0558290241
www.poggiotorselli.it

Poggio Torselli's offerings are less interesting than usual. There's a certain hardness that may be due to fruit that was not quite ripe. We did like the chardonnay Monna Aldola '07, which shows nicely citrussy and floral. Despite rather slender structure, it's vibrant and fresh in the mouth.

○ Monna Aldola '07	♙♙	4*
● Chianti Cl. '05	♙	4
● Chianti Cl. Ris. '05	♙	5
● Raniero '05	♙	4

Tenuta Poggio Verrano

S.DA PROVINCIALE 9, KM 4
58051 MAGLIANO IN TOSCANA [GR]
TEL. 0564589943
www.poggioverrano.it

Francesco Bolla is still maturing Dròmos '06, so he offered us a new wine, Dròmos L'Altro, a sangiovese. The '06 edition is characterized by well-crafted, lavish aromas and an impressive, well-proportioned body as a vein of lively acidity propels taut progression.

● Dròmos L'Altro '06	♙♙	8
● Dròmos '05	♙♙	8
● Dròmos '04	♙♙	8
● Dròmos '03	♙♙	8

Poggiopaoli

LOC. POMONTE
VIA LE RAGNAIE, 64
58054 SCANSANO [GR]
TEL. 0564599408
poggiopaoli@infinito.it

Paolo Fiorani and Paola Emanuelli put out wines of terrific character, particularly the reds. A rich, multi-layered nose adorns Capel Rosso '06, from sangiovese, ciliegiolo and merlot, and it continues taut, dynamic and succulent. Morellino Lorenzolo '07 is still a tad closed but delicious.

● Capel Rosso '06	♙♙	5
● Morellino di Scansano Lorenzolo '07	♙	4
● Morellino di Scansano Lorenzolo '06	♙♙	4
● Morellino di Scansano Pomonte '06	♙♙	4

Il Pozzo

VIA PIAVE, 1
50068 RUFINA [FI]
TEL. 0558399102
gianfranco.caselli@tin.it

The Bellini family has accustomed us to outstanding consistency. Their wines are deliciously drinkable and excellent value for money. The Riserva is usually the better of their two Chianti Rufinas. The '05 unfolds a generous bouquet, the palate is sturdy and refreshing, and the finish lingering.

● Chianti Rufina Ris. '05	♙♙	4*
● Chianti Rufina '06	♙	3

Provveditore

LOC. SALAIOLO
POD. PROVVEDITORE, 174
58054 SCANSANO [GR]
TEL. 0564599237
www.provveditore.it

Alessandro Bargagli's cellar is reassuringly reliable. Morellino Primo Riserva '04 is taut and tasty, with dense texture. Morellino '06 shows fine weight but a tad too much oak tends to slow it down. The nose on Morellino Sassato '07 seems slightly blurred and the palate is not very complex.

● Morellino di Scansano Primo Ris. '04	♙♙	5
● Morellino di Scansano '06	♙	4
● Morellino di Scansano Sassato '07	♙	3
● Morellino di Scansano Primo Ris. '03	♙♙	5

OTHER WINERIES

Rampa di Fugnano

LOC. FUGNANO, 55
53037 SAN GIMIGNANO [SI]
TEL. 0577941655
www.rampadifugnano.it

Rampa di Fugnano has yet to return to elegance. Vi Ogni è '07 is quite nice with a refreshing palate and citrus-laced finish. Merlot Gisèle '06 offers generous tannins but a stumpy finish while Vernaccia Alata '07 has good typicity on the nose and decent balance. Vernaccia Privato '07 lacks energy.

O Vi Ogni è '07	⚱⚱ 4*
● Gisèle '06	⚱ 6
O Vernaccia di S. Gimignano Alata '07	⚱ 4
O Vernaccia di S. Gimignano Privato '07	⚱ 4

La Regola

VIA A. GRAMSCI, 1
56046 RIPARBELLA [PI]
TEL. 0586698145
www.laregola.com

The Nuti brothers should be pleased with the style and quality their wines have achieved. Among the reds, Beloro '04 delivers a wealth of fruit, refined tannic weave and nervy acidity. Steccaia '07 is as always an impressive white, showing refreshing, full-flavoured and harmonious.

O Montescudaio Bianco Steccaia '07	⚱⚱ 4
● Montescudaio Rosso Beloro '04	⚱⚱ 6
● Montescudaio Rosso La Regola '05	⚱ 6
● Montescudaio Rosso Ligustro '07	⚱ 4

Il Rio

VIA DI PADULE, 131
50039 VICCHIO [FI]
TEL. 0558407904

Il Rio encores last year's fine performance. The star Ventisei is still maturing but Annita '07 does the business. This chardonnay and pinot nero blend shows fine weight and grip, plus flowing progression. Terosè '07, a toothsome rosé from pinot nero, is absolutely textbook.

O Annita '07	⚱⚱ 4
☉ Terosè '07	⚱ 4
● Ventisei '05	⚱⚱ 5

Fattoria La Ripa

FRAZ. SAN DONATO IN POGGIO
S.P. PER CASTELLINA IN CHIANTI, 27
50021 BARBERINO VAL D'ELSA [FI]
TEL. 0558072948
www.laripa.it

Fattoria La Ripa's performance this year was quite uncharacteristic. The only wine presented that impressed us was Chianti Classico Riserva '04. The nose presents spice-lifted fruit preserves and hints of tobacco leaf, while the palate shows fine volume and length.

● Chianti Cl. Ris. '04	⚱⚱ 5
● Chianti Cl. Ris. '01	⚱⚱ 5
● Chianti Cl. Ris. '00	⚱⚱ 6

Massimo Romeo

FRAZ. GRACCIANO
LOC. NOTTOLA, S.S. 326, 25
53040 MONTEPULCIANO [SI]
TEL. 0578708599
www.massimoromeo.it

Nobile Riserva dei Mandorli '04 yields lovely floral notes and subtle vanilla, then good pulpy fruit in the mouth and measured acidity that supports a finish that is just a tad rough. Lean, crisp aromatics and a steady, even development on the palate mark Nobile '05.

● Nobile di Montepulciano Ris. dei Mandorli '04	⚱⚱ 5
● Nobile di Montepulciano '05	⚱ 5
● Nobile di Montepulciano Lipitiresco '04	⚱⚱ 5

Italo Rubicini

LOC. SAN BENEDETTO, 17c
53037 SAN GIMIGNANO [SI]
TEL. 0577944816
www.rubicini.com

Rubicini is justly back in the Guide. Vernaccia '07 gives bright florality, balance in the middle and a tasty finale. Apple and blossoms infuse Vernaccia Eterea '07. The development is fluid but not exciting. San Gimignano Rosso '05 opens slowly to fruit and greens that continue in the mouth.

O Vernaccia di S. Gimignano '07	⚱⚱ 3
● San Gimignano Rosso Pepe Nero '05	⚱ 4
O Vernaccia di S. Gimignano Eterea '07	⚱ 3

OTHER WINERIES

Podere Salicutti

POD. SALICUTTI, 174
53024 MONTALCINO [SI]
TEL. 0577847003
www.poderesalicutti.it

Francesco Leanza continues to offer quite distinctive wines. Brunello '03 pours out spice, medicinal herbs and sweet tobacco but smoky oak nuances slightly dominate the course of its fruit. The weight is impressive in the mouth, even if stiffened somewhat by still-impetuous tannins.

● Brunello di Montalcino Piaggione '03	▼ 8
● Rosso di Montalcino '06	▼ 5

Fattoria San Fabiano Borghini Baldovinetti

LOC. SAN FABIANO, 33
52100 AREZZO
TEL. 057524566
www.fattoriasanfabiano.it

Nobile Poggio Uliveto, from Montepulciano, has lately been the strong suit of San Fabiano. The '05 shows refreshing, crisp fruit, a palate that is tangy, rich and expansive, and a tannin-laced finish. Armaiolo '05, a 50-50 blend of sangiovese and cabernet, is rich and well constructed.

● Armaiolo '05	▼▼ 5
● Nobile di Montepulciano Poggio Uliveto '05	▼▼ 5
● Chianti '07	▼ 2
○ Vin Santo Cannicci '01	▼ 6

Tenuta San Jacopo

LOC. CASTIGLIONCELLI, 151
52022 CAVRIGLIA [AR]
TEL. 055966003
info@tenutasanjacopo.it

This young operation makes wine skilfully. Orma del Diavolo '05, from merlot, cabernet and sangiovese, is sturdy and modern. Chianti Poggio ai Grilli '05 is spot on, pale in colour but richly flavoured, floral and uncommonly delicious.

● Chianti Cl. Poggio ai Grilli '05	▼▼ 4*
● Orma del Diavolo '05	▼▼ 4*
● Chianti Classico Poggio ai Grilli Ris. '05	▼ 4
○ Quarto di Luna '06	▼ 4

Fattoria San Donato

LOC. SAN DONATO, 6
53037 SAN GIMIGNANO [SI]
TEL. 0577941616
www.sandonato.it

San Donato's wines performed well. Chianti Fiamma '06 flaunts a palate that is vibrant, balanced and appealing while Chianti Fede Riserva '05 is fragrant, tasty and multi-layered, with generous fruit on the finish. Vin Santo '03 is enviably classic and Vernaccia Benedetta Riserva '05 is savoury.

● Chianti Colli Senesi Fede Ris. '05	▼▼ 4*
● Chianti Colli Senesi Fiamma '06	▼▼ 4*
○ Vin Santo '03	▼▼ 4*
○ Vernaccia di S. Gimignano Benedetta Ris. '05	▼ 4

San Filippo

LOC. SAN FILIPPO, 134
53024 MONTALCINO [SI]
TEL. 0577847176
www.sanfilippomontalcino.com

Brunello di Montalcino '03, from rigorously selected fruit, impresses. Bright black berries and morello cherry meld into espresso bean. The tannins are still a tad rough but the acidity is right, the finish complex, and the palate delicious. Sant'Antimo Staffato '06, largely sangiovese, is tasty.

● Brunello di Montalcino '03	▼▼ 7
● Sant'Antimo Staffato '06	▼ 4
● Brunello di Montalcino Le Coste Ris. '01	♀♀ 7

Fattoria San Pancrazio

LOC. SAN PANCRAZIO
VIA CERTALDESE, 63/65
50026 SAN CASCIANO IN VAL DI PESA [FI]
TEL. 0558248046
www.fattoriasanpancrazio.com

Valentina Masti and Simone Priami debut in the Guide. We liked the '05 Merlot, with its fine menthol and mineral on the nose and robust, broad palate that flaunts a juicy, rich finish. The other wine, Chianti Classico '06, is interesting and very savoury, if not terribly complex.

● Merlot '05	▼▼ 6
● Chianti Cl. '06	▼ 4

OTHER WINERIES

Sant'Agnese

LOC. CAMPO ALLE FAVE, 1
57025 PIOMBINO [LI]
TEL. 0565277069
giglipa@hotmail.com

Sant'Agnese is back in the Guide with well-crafted, affordable wines. The cabernet sauvignon-merlot Spirto '04 is the most successful, with concentration, rich fruit and toasty oak. Val di Cornia Rubido '06 has acidic verve and a tannin-edged finish. Vermentino Kalendemaia and Lilium are sound and tasty.

O Kalendamaia '07	♀	4
O Lilium '07	♀	2
● Spirto '06	♀	6
● Val di Cornia Rubido '06	♀	3

Fattoria Sant'Agnese

LOC. SANT'AGNESE, 7
53011 CASTELLINA IN CHIANTI [SI]
TEL. 0577 740983
www.fattoriasantagnese.it

The Milanesi family debuts in our Guide with just two wines, both of which we liked. We preferred the traditional-styled Riserva '05, which displays good character and structure. Chianti Classico '06 is also refreshing and tasty.

● Chianti Cl. Ris. '05	♀♀	5
● Chianti Cl. Abete di Sant'Agnese '06	♀	4

Fattoria Sant'Appiano

LOC. SANT'APPIANO, 11
50021 BARBERINO VAL D'ELSA [FI]
TEL. 0558075541
www.santappiano.it

Good performances bring Sant'Appiano back into the Guide. Monteloro '05, from sangiovese with colorino, is emphatic, energy-laden and well proportioned. The smooth-textured Chianti Superiore Cottaccio '05 has abundant fruit while Vin Santo Divinum '99 shows how delicious tradition can be.

● Chianti Sup. Cottaccio '05	♀♀	4*
● Monteloro '05	♀♀	4
O Vin Santo Divinum '99	♀♀	5

Fattoria Santa Vittoria

LOC. POZZO
VIA PIANA, 43
52042 FOIANO DELLA CHIANA [AR]
TEL. 0575661807
www.fattoriasantavittoria.com

The '06 Poggio al Tempio was right on the mark for Santa Vittoria. A blend of sangiovese, pugnitello and foglia tonda, it's a bit harsh at the outset but it offers good depth, zesty tannins and lively terroir expression. The sangiovese-cabernet Scannagallo '05 is crisp and gutsy.

● Poggio del Tempio '05	♀♀	4*
● Scannagallo '05	♀	4
O Vin Santo '03	♀	6

Scopone

LOC. PODERE SCOPONE, 180
53024 MONTALCINO [SI]
TEL. 050939058
www.winescopone.com

This all-female cellar showed great results. Brunello '03 is admirable, with hints of pungent blue-green mould lifting bright-edged fruit. The appealingly elegant tannins make for a relaxed palate and a dense finale. Rosso '06 is attractive, with clean, straightforward fruit.

● Brunello di Montalcino '03	♀♀	8
● Rosso di Montalcino '06	♀	6

Podere Sesta di Sopra

LOC. CASTELNUOVO DELL'ABATE
53020 MONTALCINO [SI]
TEL. 0577835698
www.sestadisopra.it

Owner Enrica Bandirola can be justly proud of her handiwork. Brunello '03 gives red berries, ripe cherry and sensations of blossoms, peach and apricot. Emphatic acidity supports rich structure, concluding with great finesse and plenty of length.

● Brunello di Montalcino '03	♀♀	8
● Rosso di Montalcino '06	♀	5

OTHER WINERIES

Sonnino

VIA VOLTERRANA NORD, 6A
50025 MONTESPERTOLI [FI]
TEL. 0571609198
www.castellosonnino.it

The '05 edition of Lo Schiavone is superb. Compelling aromas precede a palate with just the right depth, fine-grained tannins and a fine, broad finish. The medium-bodied Leone Rosso '07, from syrah, sangiovese, canaiolo and ancellota, shows crisp and fruity while Chianti Montespertoli '06 is very well made.

● Leone Rosso '07	♟♟ 3*
● Lo Schiavone '05	♟♟ 6
● Chianti Montespertoli Castello di Sonnino '06	♟ 3

Casale dello Sparviero

LOC. CASALE, 93
53011 CASTELLINA IN CHIANTI [SI]
TEL. 0577743062
campoperi@libero.it

The wines here continue to be well made but can't seem to rise any higher, although the potential is there. New developments include Chianti Classico Vigna Paranza '04. It's evolved and multi-layered on the nose but the tannins bring slight hesitation on the palate. Rosso '07 vaunts bright acidity.

● Chianti Cl. Vigna Paranza '04	♟♟ 5
● Chianti Cl. '06	♟ 4
● Chianti Cl. Ris. '05	♟ 5
● Rosso dello Sparviero '07	♟ 4

Tenuta di Sticciano

VIA DI STICCIANO, 207
50052 CERTALDO [FI]
TEL. 0571669191
www.tenutadisticciano.it

This vigorous operation is turning out wines of quality. We were impressed by Sysame '05, an equal blend of sangiovese, merlot and syrah, for its firm body, fine balance and length. The sangiovese and cabernet Cantastorie '05 builds a superb attack and structure. The two Chiantis are very solid.

● Cantastorie '05	♟♟ 5
● Sysame '05	♟♟ 4*
● Chianti Casa La Fornace '07	♟ 3*
● Chianti della Villa Ris. '05	♟ 4

Streda in Belvedere

VIA DI STREDA, 46
50059 VINCI [FI]
TEL. 0571729195
www.streda.it

Streda gave us clean, modern wines that brought it back to the Guide. Syrah '06 stands out for varietal character, depth, smooth texture and its spice-laced finale. Toiano Merlot '07 shows fresh, velvety and well-fruited. Chardonnay '07 is fat and full; Casanova '07 well executed and fruity.

● Syrah '06	♟♟ 6
● Casanova '07	♟ 4
O Chardonnay '07	♟ 4
● Toiano Merlot '07	♟ 4

Fattoria della Talosa

VIA PIETROSE, 15
53045 MONTEPULCIANO [SI]
TEL. 0578758277
www.vinodocg.it

The Jacorossi family made an impressive Guide debut. Nobile Riserva '04 releases luscious aromas and compelling complexity in the mouth, with plenty of pulpy fruit. Nobile '05 pleases with its clean fragrances and tasty palate, but has a slightly burred finish. Rosso '05 is nicely executed.

● Nobile di Montepulciano Ris. '04	♟♟ 5
● Nobile di Montepulciano '05	♟ 4
● Rosso di Montepulciano '05	♟ 4

Terre del Marchesato

LOC. SANT'UBERTO, 164
57020 BOLGHERI [LI]
TEL. 0565749752
www.fattoriaterredelmarchesato.it

Overall, the wines here are fine, particularly Tarabuso '05. Almost all cabernet sauvignon, it offers lovely spice and tannins in evidence. Marchesato Syrah '05 is good, showing succulent and fruited with dark berries. We liked the two Emilio Primo versions, Rosso '06, and the vermentino Bianco '07.

● Syrah del Marchesato '05	♟♟ 8
● Tarabuso '05	♟♟ 6
● Emilio Primo '06	♟ 4
O Emilio Primo Bianco '07	♟ 6

OTHER WINERIES

Terreno

LOC. GRETI
VIA CITILLE, 4
50022 GREVE IN CHIANTI [FI]
TEL. 055854001
www.terreno.se

The Ruhne family did well with their Chianti Classico '06. Cherry, strawberry and floral impressions enrich sound fruit on the nose, then it is delicate, delicious and approachable on the palate, with a thrilling, savoury finale. The heavier, more firmly structured Riserva '05 is fine as well.

● Chianti Cl. '06	♟♟	4*
● Chianti Cl. Ris. '05	♟♟	5

Podere Torcilacqua

LOC. BADIA A PASSIGNANO
S.DA DI GREVE, 8
50028 TAVARNELLE VAL DI PESA [FI]
TEL. 0558071598
www.agriturismotorcilacqua.it

Mauro Bianchi's modest cellar, near the celebrated abbey at Passignano, makes its debut. We liked the merlot Supertuscan Kai Zen '06, flaunting mineral and balsam, a vibrant, multi-layered palate and plenty of flavour and length at the end. Mauro's Chianti Classico '06 is more straightforward.

● Kai Zen '06	♟♟	6
● Chianti Cl. '06	♟	4

Castello di Tornano

LOC. TORNANO
53013 GAIOLE IN CHIANTI [SI]
TEL. 0577746067
www.castelloditornano.it

Chianti Classico is the Selvolini family strong suit. Riserva '04 is a stand-out, showing typical on the nose, with evolved fruit, preserves, and subtle animal skins, followed by chewy tannins, nice acidity and a luscious finale. Graal '04, a 50-50 blend of sangiovese and merlot, shows smoother and rounded.

● Chianti Cl. Ris. '04	♟♟	6
● Graal '04	♟♟	5
O Vin Santo '02	♟	6

La Torraccia

LOC. TORRACCIA
53024 MONTALCINO [SI]
TEL. 0577848156
www.latorracciamontalcino.com

Excellent performances are the order of the day, particularly the Brunello '03, which seems to shrug off the torrid growing year. It unveils lovely blackberry and ripe cherry, even cherry preserves, before acidity, tannins and alcohol elegantly merge to craft an elegant, relaxed and expansive palate.

● Brunello di Montalcino '03	♟♟	7
● Rosso di Montalcino '06	♟	5

Torre

LOC. VICO D'ELSA
P.ZZA TORRIGIANI, 15
50021 BARBERINO VAL D'ELSA [FI]
TEL. 0558073001
www.marchesitorrigiani.it

Torre continues to make outstanding wines. Guidaccio '06, from sangiovese with some merlot and cabernet, weaves rich, seductive aromatics followed by taut progression and appealing complexity. The succulent sangiovese, colorino, canaiolo and merlot Torre di Ciardo '06 has glossy tannins.

● Guidaccio '06	♟♟	5
● Torre di Ciardo '06	♟♟	4
● Guidaccio '04	♟♟	5
● Torre di Ciardo '04	♟♟	4

Fattoria La Traiana

LOC. TRAIANA, 16
52028 TERRANUOVA BRACCIOLINI [AR]
TEL. 0559179004
fatt.latraiana@libero.it

Fattoria La Traiana steadily turns out clean, well-measured wines. This year, the bottles came from their Sassorlando estate in Suvereto. The Cabernet Terra di Sasso '05 impressed on its debut, as did the Cabernet Pian del Pazzo '04.

● Pian del Pazzo '04	♟♟	6
● Terra di Sasso Sassorlando '05	♟♟	5
● Campo Arsiccio '04	♟	6
● Chianti Sup. '06	♟	4

OTHER WINERIES

Fattoria Tregole

LOC. TREGOLE, 86
53011 CASTELLINA IN CHIANTI [SI]
TEL. 0577740991
www.fattoria-tregole.com

Fattoria Tregole's vineyard makeover
has yielded fine results. The '05 Chianti
Classico intrigues with minerality, crisp
spice, and vibrant, abundant fruit. The
palate is succulent and appealing, the finale
enchanting. Also good is Fanero '05, from
sangiovese with some merlot and cabernet
sauvignon.

● Chianti Cl. '05	♥♥ 4*
● Fanero '05	♥♥ 5

Dell'Uccellina

LOC. ALBERESE
S.DA SPERGOLAIA
58010 GROSSETO
TEL. 0564418731
www.uccellina.com

The Pratesi family, long established on the
Maremma wine scene, recently started
to bottle. Morellino Spergolaia '06 is spot
on, and Rosso di Rendola '07 and Rosa
di Rendola '07, both from sangiovese and
merlot, are delicious. The same goes for
the vermentino and sauvignon Bianco di
Rendola '07.

● Morellino di Scansano Spergolaia '06	♥♥ 4*
○ Bianco di Redola '07	♥ 3
⊙ Rosa di Redola '07	♥ 3
● Rosso di Redola '07	♥ 3

Varramista

LOC. VARRAMISTA
VIA RICAVO
56020 MONTOPOLI IN VAL D'ARNO [PI]
TEL. 057144711
www.varramista.it

Varramista is back in the spotlight with a
fine line-up. The aromatic, sangiovese,
merlot and syrah Frasca '05 shines,
offering a rounded, splendid palate.
Ottopioppi '05, a dense sangiovese and
grenache blend, is beautifully proportioned
and represents delicious drinkability.

● Frasca '05	♥♥ 5
● Ottopioppi '05	♥♥ 4
● Varramista '00	♥♥♥ 7

I Veroni

VIA TIFARITI, 5
50065 PONTASSIEVE [FI]
TEL. 0558368886
www.iveroni.it

Veroni this year is back to a short profile,
a shame after last year's performances.
But the balance is simply not there in the
structure and the wines display evident
edginess, although the aromatics are
sound. Chianti Rufina '06 stands out for its
freshness and appeal.

● Chianti Rufina '06	♥♥ 4*
● Chianti Rufina Ris. '05	♥ 5
● Terre del Pelacane '06	♥ 4
○ Vin Santo del Chianti Rufina '00	♥ 6

Cantina Cooperativa Vignaioli del Morellino di Scansano

LOC. SARAGIOLO
58054 SCANSANO [GR]
TEL. 0564507288
www.cantinadelmorellino.it

Morellino di Scansano Roggiano '07 is fine,
showing elegant fragrances and smooth,
steady progression. Morellino Vin del
Fattore '07 seems a tad rustic with a rich
enough nose but some overly stiff tannins
in the mouth. Morellino Sicomoro '05 is
too forward on the nose but the palate is
savoury.

● Morellino di Scansano Roggiano '07	♥♥ 4*
● Morellino di Scansano Sicomoro '05	♥ 5
● Morellino di Scansano Vin del Fattore '07	♥ 4

Vignavecchia

VIA SDRUCCIOLO DI PIAZZA, 7
53017 RADDA IN CHIANTI [SI]
TEL. 0577738090
www.vignavecchia.com

Performances from the Beccari family
scaled no heights. The wines are too
rigid on the palate, mostly unbalanced,
and none too clean on the nose. The all-
chardonnay Titanum '07 was the best, with
crisp citrus and blossoms on the nose, and
good enough flavours in the mouth.

● Chianti Cl. '06	♥ 4
● Chianti Cl. Ris. '04	♥ 5
○ Titanum '07	♥ 5

OTHER WINERIES

Villa a Sesta

LOC. VILLA A SESTA
P.ZZA DEL POPOLO,1
53019 CASTELNUOVO BERARDENGA [SI]
TEL. 0577359014
www.villasesta.com

Only one of the Tattoni family's wines impressed us this year. The Supertuscan Vas '06, from sangiovese, merlot and colorino, releases appealing cinnamon, clove, wild red berries and vanilla, followed by a rounded palate and an intriguing, compelling finish.

● Vas '06	🍷🍷 5
● Vas '03	🍷🍷 5

Villa Corliano

VIA DI CORLIANO, 4
50055 LASTRA A SIGNA [FI]
TEL. 0558734542
www.villacorliano.com

This is a first entry for the Pancani family, thanks to enviable quality wines. The best is the Ghirigoro '06, from cabernet sauvignon with some sangiovese and a recently rediscovered variety, foglia tonda. Chianti Colli Fiorentini Briccole '06 and Vin Santo Delicato '01 are both pleasurable.

● Ghirigoro '06	🍷🍷 4*
● Chianti Colli Fiorentini Briccole '06	🍷 4
○ Colli dell'Etruria Centrale Vin Santo Dedicato '01	🍷 6

Villa La Selva

LOC. MONTEBENICHI
52021 BUCINE [AR]
TEL. 055998203
www.villalaselva.it

Villa la Selva has tip-toed back into the Guide. The traditional stars failed to match past editions except for Sangiovese Felciaia '05, which is savoury, succulent and expansive. Cabernet Selvamaggio '05 is a tad insipid and slightly evolved while Vin Santo Vigna del Papa '03 is lean and measured.

● Felciaia '05	🍷🍷 5
● Selvamaggio '05	🍷 5
○ Vin Santo del Chianti Vigna del Papa '03	🍷 5

Villa Mangiacane

VIA FALTIGNANO, 4
50026 SAN CASCIANO IN VAL DI PESA [FI]
TEL. 0558290123
www.mangiacane.it

It wasn't a great year for these modern, international-style wines that focus on power. There were below-par performances form wines that seemed unbalanced and over-muscular. The tasty, unfussy Chianti Classico '06 is the most enjoyable, showing crisp, fresh fruit.

● Aleah '05	🍷 6
● Chianti Cl. '06	🍷 4
☉ Shamiso '06	🍷 4

Villa Sant'Anna

FRAZ. ABBADIA DI MONTEPULCIANO
53045 MONTEPULCIANO [SI]
TEL. 0578708017
www.villasantanna.it

Nobile Poldo '05, the Frabroni family's iconic wine, is impressively put together. Its aromas are rich and compelling, while the palate exhibits considerable extractive weight, accompanied by oak that at times slows the progression. Rosso '06 is perfect; the Nobile '05 a bit stiff.

● Nobile di Montepulciano Poldo '05	🍷🍷 6
● Nobile di Montepulciano '05	🍷 5
● Rosso di Montepulciano '06	🍷 4

Tenuta Vitanza

FRAZ. TORRENIERI - POD. BELVEDERE, 145
S.P. 71 DI COSONA KM 2,050
53024 MONTALCINO [SI]
TEL. 0577832882
www.tenutavitanza.it

We enjoyed an outstanding Brunello '03 from Vitanza this year that flaunts dense cherry, morello, blackberry and toasty oak. The palate couldn't be richer, thanks to a glossy tannic weave and acidity that holds everything nicely together.

● Brunello di Montalcino '03	🍷🍷 7

MARCHE

Verdicchio is increasingly receiving its due as one of Italy's great white wines. The number of Three Glass awards this year for wines made from this variety – nine, the highest ever – attests its pre-eminence. Quite apart from the fine performances, interpretations of the grape are coming into better focus, even though different specific expressions abound and levels of success vary. We very much like what we might call the rawer versions from fruit picked at the cusp of ripeness and fermented in steel. Such traditional-style Verdicchios release hallmark floral and mineral notes, plus a palate that flaunts youthful grip and superb richness of flavour. Following this logic, we paid tribute to Garofoli's Podium 2006 Verdicchio dei Castelli di Jesi along with Vallerosa Bonci's San Michele 2006, Tenuta di Tavignano's Misco Riserva 2005, as well as two magnificent examples of Verdicchio di Matelica that we felt typified the denomination, Mirum 2006 from La Monacesca, and the 2007 version made by Collestefano. But we appreciate the cask-aged style as well, when it is done judiciously, and we are perfectly aware that this production strategy yields some fine wines. Proof is the ease with which wines such as San Sisto 2005 from Fazi Battaglia, Plenio 2005 from Umani Ronchi, Villa Bucci 2006 of Bucci and Stefano Antonucci 2006 of Santa Barbara came away with our top award. At the same time, we should not forget the good number of offerings from the 2007 vintage, not a harvest to reckon among the recent best but certainly one that yielded up a multitude of good, fine-quaffing Verdicchios with reasonable price tags. Good performances, though, were not limited to the Marche's noblest white since a growing number of reds receive high marks as well. Heading the team this year was the region's other great grape, montepulciano, which carries the imprint of its many, diverse terroirs. It's smooth and juicy in Piantate Lunghe's Conero Rossini, more dense and multi-layered in Regina del Bosco from Fattoria Dezi and austere yet sinewy in Maria Pia Castelli's Erasmo Castelli. Add a tot of cabernet and merlot to the montepulciano, and you have the vibrant, edgy Barricadiero from Aurora. Add some sangiovese and you have Rosso Piceno Superiore Roggio from Filare di Velenosi, the only wine to keep the colours flying of the most important denomination in the southern Marche and on precisely the 40th anniversary of the launching of the great regional DOC, Rosso Piceno. San Savino's Fedus, on the other hand, pays homage to sangiovese, an oft-neglected variety but one that is the backbone of many Marche operations, and which of course in years past brought in significant revenue from sales in bulk to other regions.

Aurora

LOC. SANTA MARIA IN CARRO
C.DA CIAFONE, 98
63035 OFFIDA [AP]
TEL. 0736810007
www.viniaurora.it

ANNUAL PRODUCTION	45,000 bottles
HECTARES UNDER VINE	9
VITICULTURE METHOD	Certified biodynamic

Barricadiero rises again. Not on the barricades, mind you, as its combative name might suggest, but in the ranks of Italy's best wines. It has stood at the top for four seasons running, faltering only last year when the weak 2005 vintage was in play. Competing on its own terms, Barricadiero has its customary austere nose of blackberry, liquorice, emphatic spice and even more pungent impressions. The energy in the mouth seems pure and utterly instinctive, helped by impressive integration of succulent tannins with crunchy but supple fruit. Aurora, a local organic pioneer and with a philosophy that respects the environment, is widely imitated locally. As well it should be, judging from results such as Rosso Piceno Superiore and Offida Pecorino Fiobbo. The former is along the lines of Barricadiero but perhaps somewhat more agile, and less massively structured or complex. The Rosso is multi-faceted and boasts creative tensions and rich contrasts through to its decisive, assertively savoury finish. The standard Rosso Piceno is less clearly delineated, its nose somewhat blurred initially, but it there's brawny fruit and dense, supple tannins.

Belisario

VIA ARISTIDE MERLONI, 12
62024 MATELICA [MC]
TEL. 0737787247
www.belisario.it

ANNUAL PRODUCTION	820,000 bottles
HECTARES UNDER VINE	300
VITICULTURE METHOD	Conventional

Belisario is the name of the Cantina Sociale di Cerreto d'Esi e Matelica. It's also shorthand for "reliability", "typicity" and "value for money", above all in Verdicchio di Matelica. This consistent quality is particularly true of bottlings such as Vigneti del Cerro. Boasting a limpid florality, it develops a dynamic palate where crisp acidity and lean minerality predominate, giving the wine an elegant yet vital profile. Vigneti Belisario, from organically grown fruit, has much the same nose but with an even more incisive palate. The reasonably priced Terre di Valbona is lighter but still offers snappy drinking. From the many other wines, we singled out a new label, Meridia. The first vintage, 2006, is a nice gold, showing more breadth than depth but with tasty fruit throughout. We conclude the lengthy series with Cambrugiano. Smooth enough, it is off its usual standard. You can sense the unfavourable vintage in its advanced evolution and transgressive oak. Among the reds, we liked a new one, Aeno, a medium-bodied blend of equal parts sangiovese and merlot. Fresh greens and spice on the nose are matched by good thrust in the mouth.

● Barricadiero '06	♟♟♟	5
○ Offida Pecorino Fiobbo '06	♟♟	4*
● Rosso Piceno '07	♟♟	3*
● Rosso Piceno Sup. '06	♟♟	4
○ Falerio dei Colli Ascolani '07	♟	2
● Barricadiero '04	♟♟♟	5
● Barricadiero '03	♟♟♟	5
● Barricadiero '02	♟♟♟	5
● Barricadiero '01	♟♟♟	5
● Barricadiero '05	♟♟	5
○ Offida Pecorino Fiobbo '04	♟♟	4
● Barricadiero '00	♟♟	5
○ Offida Pecorino Fiobbo '05	♟♟	4
● Rosso Piceno Sup. '05	♟♟	4

○ Verdicchio di Matelica Vign. del Cerro '07	♟♟	3*
● Aeno '07	♟♟	4
○ Verdicchio di Matelica Cambrugiano Ris. '05	♟♟	4
○ Verdicchio di Matelica Meridia '06	♟♟	4
○ Verdicchio di Matelica Terre di Valbona '07	♟♟	2*
○ Verdicchio di Matelica Vign. Belisario '07	♟♟	4
● Colli Maceratesi Rosso Coll'Amato '07	♟	3
● Colli Maceratesi Rosso San Leopardo Ris. '05	♟	4
☉ Rosasenzaspine '07	♟	2
○ Verdicchio di Matelica Cambrugiano Ris. '02	♟♟♟	4
○ Verdicchio di Matelica Cambrugiano Ris. '04	♟♟	4

Boccadigabbia

LOC. FONTESPINA
C.DA CASTELLETTA, 56
62012 CIVITANOVA MARCHE [MC]
TEL. 073370728
www.boccadigabbia.com

ANNUAL PRODUCTION	150,000 bottles
HECTARES UNDER VINE	25
VITICULTURE METHOD	Conventional

Elvio Alessandri's operation has won a solid reputation for its versions of the classic French varieties, cabernet sauvignon, merlot, chardonnay, as well as pinot grigio and pinot nero. The intrinsic quality of these wines has often been enriched by a hint of atavistic throwback to their origins in Napoleonic influence over the Marche. But for some time now, the sheen of Boccadigabbia has dimmed. True, attention today has shifted more to native varieties, but the wines here just seem to lack their old definition. The cabernet sauvignon Akronte, for example, usually flaunts ripe fruit, but always alongside exceptional texture and balance. This 2004 version, however, shows both excessive ripeness and some immature greenness while the palate, which is muscular enough, suffers from clenched tannins. Pix Merlot performs better. Rich and glossy smooth, its only defect is an invasive note of oak that blunts the fruit. Rosso Piceno impresses with fine weight and depth, although the finish is slightly drying, as does Saltapicchio, a lean, edgy blend of sangiovese and merlot with aggressive notes of ripe red berry fruit.

Bucci

FRAZ. PONGELLI
VIA CONA, 30
60010 OSTRA VETERE [AN]
TEL. 071964179
www.villabucci.com

ANNUAL PRODUCTION	120,000 bottles
HECTARES UNDER VINE	26
VITICULTURE METHOD	Natural

There's a moment of suspense when you pull the cork of a bottle of Villa Bucci. Will the miracle be repeated? Will we be assured of finding that same style, that elegant sapidity, that proverbial refinement married to enthralling savouriness and never-ending length that have always marked this celebrated Italian white wine? History tells us that, no, we will never be disappointed and the story, incredibly, continues. A profound bow, then, yet again for the latest edition of that masterpiece crafted by Ampelio Bucci, a man of deep culture, but one who also demonstrates wisdom, grace, and cleverness in directing colleagues such as Giorgio Grai, master blender, agronomist Gabriele Tanfani, and venerable cellarmaster Bruno Lorenzini, with young Stefano Vici in training. Villa Bucci 2006 is just as we expected, with perhaps an added degree of succulence to the fruit and an even livelier sapidity. The standard Verdicchio receives its usual high marks as well, of course, showing measured and subtle like Villa Bucci, but with less depth and a tad warmer alcohol. Rosso Piceno Tenuta Pongelli is crisp, straightforward, stylish and distinctive.

● Akronte Cabernet Sauvignon '04	♟♟	8
● Pix Merlot '04	♟♟	7
● Rosso Piceno Boccadigabbia '06	♟♟	4*
● Saltapicchio Sangiovese-Merlot '05	♟♟	5
○ Colli Maceratesi Ribona Le Grane '07	♟	4
○ Klepsydra '02	♟	6
○ Garbì Bianco '07		3
● Akronte '98	♟♟♟	7
● Akronte '97	♟♟♟	7
● Akronte '95	♟♟♟	7
● Akronte '94	♟♟♟	7
● Akronte '93	♟♟♟	7
● Akronte '03	♟♟	8
● Akronte '01	♟♟	7
● Pix Merlot '03	♟♟	7
● Pix Merlot '01	♟♟	7
● Girone Pinot Nero '04	♟♟	6
○ Montalperti Chardonnay '04	♟♟	5

○ Verdicchio dei Castelli di Jesi Cl. Villa Bucci Ris. '06	♟♟♟	7
○ Verdicchio dei Castelli di Jesi Cl. Sup. '07	♟♟	4*
● Rosso Piceno Tenuta Pongelli '06	♟♟	4
○ Verdicchio dei Castelli di Jesi Cl. Villa Bucci Ris. '05	♟♟♟	6
○ Verdicchio dei Castelli di Jesi Cl. Villa Bucci Ris. '04	♟♟♟	6
○ Verdicchio dei Castelli di Jesi Cl. Villa Bucci Ris. '03	♟♟♟	6
○ Verdicchio dei Castelli di Jesi Cl. Villa Bucci Ris. '01	♟♟♟	6
○ Verdicchio dei Castelli di Jesi Cl. Villa Bucci Ris. '00	♟♟♟	6
○ Verdicchio dei Castelli di Jesi Cl. Villa Bucci Ris. '99	♟♟♟	6
○ Verdicchio dei Castelli di Jesi Cl. Villa Bucci Ris. '98	♟♟♟	6

Le Caniette

C.DA CANALI, 23
63038 RIPATRANSONE [AP]
TEL. 07359200
www.lecaniette.it

ANNUAL PRODUCTION	60,000 bottles
HECTARES UNDER VINE	16
VITICULTURE METHOD	Natural

We admire producers who decline to follow the market but make wines they like, teaching their customers to appreciate them, too, whatever the media say. The Vagnoni brothers have never hidden their determination to follow their own path. Their wines are loved or shunned precisely for their extravagance and for straddling no middle line. The brightest example is Offida Pecorino Iosonogaia non sono Lucrezia. Fermented and aged over one year in cask, it appears a luminous gold with a panoply of fragrances, opening with toasty notes then building a close-knit, alcohol-warm palate that makes no attempt to be approachable. It will be at its best in a few years, when the oak has receded. Tastings of past vintages reveal a wine whose capability for evolution is always impressive. The same is true, only more so, for Nero di Vite, with an evolved, alcohol-rich palate of enormous dimensions that almost groans under its extractive weight, concluding with generous toast and oak. Vino Santo Sibilla Chimica has measured oxidation, showing concentrated and vibrant, while the refreshing Passerina Lucrezia seems almost lightweight in such company.

La Canosa

C.DA SAN PIETRO, 6
63030 ROTELLA [AP]
TEL. 0736374556
www.lacanosaagricola.it

ANNUAL PRODUCTION	80,000 bottles
HECTARES UNDER VINE	25
VITICULTURE METHOD	Conventional

Riccardo Reina, head of the Illva Saronno group, made a promising debut last year. He poured capital and equipment into La Canosa but such investments will ensure quality only if they are focused on a well-founded project. In this case, reassurance has come quickly. Agronomist Marco Cavalieri and Simone Fedeli, who directs winemaking with the assistance of consultant Roberto Cipresso, have made wines of fine character, grace and equilibrium. Nummaria 2006 releases plenty of succulent fruit, ranging from blackcurrant and blueberry to cassis and morello cherry. The palate is juicy and fluid, nicely charged with silky tannins and a slight spiciness needing a bit more integration. Signator is also compelling, opening with bright fruit and flowers followed by a well-balanced but spirited palate and complex finish, making an inviting wine. Nullius, a brand-new all sangiovese offering full of crisp, vivacious fruit, made quite an impressive debut. Its depth is all you could expect but it needs time to smooth out still aggressive tannins. Among the whites, the passerina-based Servator 2007 has stylish floral delicacy, fine depth and delicious minerality.

O Offida Pecorino Iosonogaia non sono Lucrezia '06	♀♀ 5
O Offida Passerina Vino Santo Sibilla Chimica '04	♀♀ 5
● Rosso Piceno Nero di Vite '04	♀♀ 7
O Offida Passerina Lucrezia '07	♀ 4
● Rosso Piceno Morellone '03	♀♀ 5
● Rosso Piceno Nero di Vite '01	♀♀ 7
O Offida Pecorino Iosonogaia non sono Lucrezia '05	♀♀ 5
● Rosso Piceno Nero di Vite '03	♀♀ 7
● Rosso Piceno Nero di Vite '02	♀♀ 7
● Rosso Piceno Nero di Vite '00	♀♀ 7

● Nullius '05	♀♀ 5
● Rosso Piceno Signator '06	♀♀ 3*
● Rosso Piceno Sup. Nummaria '06	♀♀ 4
O Servator '07	♀♀ 3*
● Rosso Piceno Sup. Nummaria '05	♀♀ 4
O Servator '06	♀♀ 2

Carminucci

VIA SAN LEONARDO, 39
63013 GROTTAMMARE [AP]
TEL. 0735735869
www.carminucci.com

ANNUAL PRODUCTION	200,000 bottles
HECTARES UNDER VINE	46
VITICULTURE METHOD	Conventional

Giovanni Carminucci, like so many Piceno producers, is focusing his efforts on passerina and pecorino. He gets high marks not only for his results but also for his imaginative riffs on the names of the varieties. Pecorino's evocation of the Italian word for sheep prompted the "bleating" of Belato. But it's the scrumptious fruit of white peach that graces nose and mouth, with a smooth palate of considerable volume. The "chaste" Passerina Casta is more audacious, as is its execution with ripe pear that segues into a tasty palate almost electrified by tangy acidity. The remainder of the line-up is reliably good. Falerio Naumachos, as usual one of the best interpretations of this category, is characterized by delicate aromatics on the nose, and crisp citrus in the mouth, while Litora displays multi-faceted minerality. From the reds, we very much liked Rosso Piceno Superiore Naumachos with its highly polished tannins, savoury flavours and all-around approachability. Paccaosso incorporates as much phenolic extraction and body as you could want but it does need some time to balance its massive components.

Casalfarneto

VIA FARNETO, 16
60030 SERRA DE' CONTI [AN]
TEL. 0731889001
www.casalfarneto.it

ANNUAL PRODUCTION	480,000 bottles
HECTARES UNDER VINE	43
VITICULTURE METHOD	Conventional

Casalfarneto is a historic high-quality Verdicchio producer that has belonged to the large Togni family group for a few years now. New investments went into vineyard replantings and a handsome new winemaking facility. Manager Danilo Solustri, assisted by talented oenologist Roberto Potentini, has used these assets well, keeping up quality as well as increasing production. The only red presented for tasting this year was a newly introduced Lacrima, which was soundly enough made although not particularly varietal. We focused on the Verdicchios, which are always reliable and present a spectrum of characteristics that admirably suit them to different tastes. We liked Grancasale best. It opens to delicious nuances of toasty oak and cakes that soon yield to luscious apple and peach, married to lovely florality. The attack is slow and stately but quickly picks up the pace propelled by vibrant acidity, showcasing crisp citrus. Fontevecchia is very straightforward, a model of correctness, and exhibits satisfactory body, savouriness and a luscious, smooth conclusion. The youthful Solustro is uncomplicated and reasonably even.

O Falerio dei Colli Ascolani Naumachos '07	🍷🍷 3*
O Litora '04	🍷🍷 5
O Offida Passerina Casta '07	🍷🍷 3*
O Offida Pecorino Belato '07	🍷🍷 4
● Paccaosso '05	🍷🍷 8
● Rosso Piceno Sup. Naumachos '05	🍷🍷 4*
O Falerio dei Colli Ascolani Grotte sul Mare '07	🍷 2
⊙ Rosato Grotte sul Mare '07	🍷 2
● Rosso Piceno Grotte sul Mare '07	🍷 3
● Paccaosso '04	🍷🍷 8
● Paccaosso '03	🍷🍷 8
● Paccaosso '02	🍷🍷 7
● Paccaosso '01	🍷🍷 7
● Rosso Piceno Sup. Naumachos '04	🍷🍷 4
O Chardonnay Naumachos '06	🍷🍷 4

O Verdicchio dei Castelli di Jesi Cl. Grancasale Ris. '06	🍷🍷 4
O Verdicchio dei Castelli di Jesi Cl. Sup. Fontevecchia '07	🍷🍷 3*
● Lacrima di Morro d'Alba Rosae '07	🍷 4
O Verdicchio dei Castelli di Jesi Cl. Solustro '07	🍷 3
● Rosso Piceno Pitulum '05	🍷🍷 4
● Rosso Piceno Pitulum '04	🍷🍷 4
O Verdicchio dei Castelli di Jesi Cl. Grancasale Ris. '05	🍷🍷 4
O Verdicchio dei Castelli di Jesi Cl. Sup. Fontevecchia '06	🍷🍷 3

Maria Pia Castelli

C.DA S. ISIDORO, 22
63015 MONTE URANO [AP]
TEL. 0734841774
www.mariapiacastelli.it

ANNUAL PRODUCTION   20,000 bottles
HECTARES UNDER VINE 8
VITICULTURE METHOD   Natural

The Three Glasses for Erasmo Castelli are the realization of a much-cherished dream for Maria Pia Castelli and her husband Enrico Bartoletti. Years ago, they gave up their respective professions to grow grapes full time on the fine properties given them by Maria Pia's father Erasmo. With their passion for wine, they had accumulated a wealth of knowledge over years of visiting Italy's finest producers, to which they then added all the precious experience that a conscientious farmer absorbs day by day in the fields. The award also signals the variety of expressions that the montepulciano grape can achieve in the various areas of the Marche, in this case in the Fermo area. Erasmo Castelli needs a few moments open up but the superb, complex mouth snaps to attention immediately with admirable verve and backbone, showing wonderful depth and concentration. Stella Flora, a blend of pecorino, passerina, trebbiano and malvasia fermented on the skins, reveals some notes of oak awaiting integration. But it is still a terrific example of its style, displaying refreshing aromas of citrus and apricot, then gorgeous flavours in the mouth and a magisterial finish.

Cantine di Castignano

C.DA SAN VENANZO, 31
63032 CASTIGNANO [AP]
TEL. 0736822216
www.cantinedicastignano.com

ANNUAL PRODUCTION   350,000 bottles
HECTARES UNDER VINE 520
VITICULTURE METHOD   Conventional

Cantine di Castignano, a growers' co-operative, focused marketing on its regional territory some time ago, acquiring a compact distribution network of mostly local outlets. It's not surprising that 65 per cent of its 350,000-bottle production stays in the Marche. The wines are good bargains, at times outstanding, and they are styled modern and clean. We didn't find the one wine whose complexity might stand out from the rest but this seems not to bother the winery. They have other arrows in their quality quiver. The sharpest is Pecorino Montemisio, and not solely for its vibrant acidity, admirably integrated into the wine's structure, but also for the ease with which it layers the palate with vivid citrus and pineapple. Only a neck behind is Offida Gran Maestro, a big, full partnering of montepulciano, cabernet and merlot, boasting succulent, juicy fruit but also a streak of worrisome oak that weighs on the nose and dries the finish. Offida Passerina 2007 is a delicious, easy quaffer, its balance bolstered by acidity. Finally, we liked the two Destrieros, Falerio and Rosso Piceno Superiore, for their approachability and lean, crisp palates.

● Erasmo Castelli '06	▼▼▼ 6
○ Stella Flora '06	▼▼ 4*
● Orano Sangiovese '07	▼ 4
☉ Sant'Isidoro '07	3
● Erasmo Castelli '05	♀♀ 6
● Erasmo Castelli '04	♀♀ 6
● Erasmo Castelli '03	♀♀ 6
● Erasmo Castelli '02	♀♀ 6
● Orano '06	♀♀ 4
○ Stella Flora '05	♀♀ 4
○ Stella Flora '04	♀♀ 4

○ Falerio dei Colli Ascolani Destriero '07	▼▼ 3*
○ Gramelot '06	▼▼ 4
○ Offida Passerina '07	▼▼ 3*
○ Offida Pecorino Montemisio '07	▼▼ 3*
● Offida Rosso Gran Maestro '04	▼▼ 5
● Rosso Piceno '07	▼▼ 2*
● Rosso Piceno Sup. Destriero '06	▼▼ 3*
● Templaria '06	▼▼ 4
● Sangiovese '06	▼ 3
○ Falerio dei Colli Ascolani '07	2
○ Gramelot '05	♀♀ 3
○ Offida Pecorino Montemisio '06	♀♀ 3
● Offida Rosso Gran Maestro '03	♀♀ 4
● Offida Rosso Gran Maestro '02	♀♀ 4
● Templaria '05	♀♀ 3

Ciù Ciù

LOC. SANTA MARIA IN CARRO
C.DA CIAFONE, 106
63035 OFFIDA [AP]
TEL. 0736810001
www.ciuciu.com

ANNUAL PRODUCTION	430,000 bottles
HECTARES UNDER VINE	98
VITICULTURE METHOD	Natural

The brothers Bartolomei have made their winery into one of the most reliable in the Piceno area and turned in another fine performance. Two of Ciù Ciù's bottlings stand out, Pecorino Le Merlettaie and Rosso Piceno Superiore Gotico, both of which competed in our national finals. The first displays lovely florality and a silky mouthfeel, plus zesty acidity, mineral impressions and elegant citrus notes that compose a well-proportioned offering overall. Gotico is very well balanced, its fruit is fleshier on the nose and creamier on the palate than Le Merlettaie. The energy-filled development is quick off the blocks but it runs into stiff tannins that still need to mellow. Sound, crisp, varietal fruit, particularly wild strawberry and raspberry, permeates the all-sangiovese Saggio and its initially sluggish attack quickens into a lean, fluid palate. The attractively priced San Carro, an unusual blend of barbera, sangiovese and merlot, is quite impressive, showing ripe fruit on the nose and a dynamic, crisply lean palate. The all-montepulciano Oppidum preserves its customary ultra-firm, austere style, with granite-stiff tannins and full, rich alcohol.

Cocci Grifoni

LOC. SAN SAVINO
C.DA MESSIERI, 12
63038 RIPATRANSONE [AP]
TEL. 073590143
www.tenutacoccigrifoni.it

ANNUAL PRODUCTION	360,000 bottles
HECTARES UNDER VINE	50
VITICULTURE METHOD	Conventional

Pecorino has become quite fashionable of late all, not simply for its intriguing name but also because of the admirable results it can yield. Much of the credit for this goes to Guido Cocci Grifoni, who sought out the grape some 20 years ago in the Arquata valley and transplanted it into his own vineyards at Offida. He generously shared the vines with other growers and pecorino is now widespread throughout the Ascoli Piceno area. In addition to its personal and historical interest, then, Pecorino Colle Vecchio still remains a benchmark for its category and deservedly went into the finals. It's traditional in style, giving scents of flowers and white peaches while perky acidity carries through to a velvet-smooth finish. We also liked Falerio San Basso's crisp, zippy flavours that contribute to a supple agility on the palate. Some reds are still slumbering in the cellar so we'll have to wait to try the latest vintages of Cocci Grifone's Offida Rosso Il Grifone and Rosso Piceno Superiore Vigna Messieri. We consoled ourselves with the youthful Rosso Piceno Superiore Le Torri, giving high marks to its subtle fruit aromas and silky, refined palate.

○ Offida Pecorino Le Merlettaie '07	♟♟	4*
● Rosso Piceno Sup. Gotico '06	♟♟	4*
● Saggio Sangiovese '06	♟♟	5
● Oppidum '04	♟♟	5
● San Carro '07	♟♟	4*
○ Evoè Passerina '07	♟	3
○ Falerio dei Colli Ascolani Oris '07	♟	3
● Rosso Piceno Bacchus '07	♟	3
○ Offida Pecorino Le Merlettaie '06	♟♟	4
● Offida Rosso Esperanto '04	♟♟	5
● Oppidum '03	♟♟	5
● Oppidum '02	♟♟	5
● Oppidum '01	♟♟	5
● Rosso Piceno Sup. Gotico '05	♟♟	4
● Saggio Sangiovese '04	♟♟	4
● Rosso Piceno Sup. Orum '05	♟♟	4
● Saggio Sangiovese '05	♟♟	5

○ Offida Pecorino Podere Colle Vecchio '07	♟♟	4*
○ Falerio dei Colli Ascolani Vign. San Basso '07	♟♟	3*
● Rosso Piceno Sup. Le Torri '05	♟♟	3*
○ Offida Passerina Gaudio Magno Brut '07	♟	4
○ Offida Pecorino Podere Colle Vecchio '05	♟♟	4
● Rosso Piceno Sup. V. Messieri '02	♟♟	4
○ Offida Pecorino Podere Colle Vecchio '06	♟♟	4
● Offida Rosso Il Grifone '02	♟♟	5
● Rosso Piceno Sup. Le Torri '04	♟♟	3
● Rosso Piceno Sup. Le Torri '03	♟♟	3
● Rosso Piceno Sup. V. Messieri '03	♟♟	4

Collestefano

LOC. COLLE STEFANO, 3
62022 CASTELRAIMONDO [MC]
TEL. 0737640439
www.collestefano.com

ANNUAL PRODUCTION	60,000 bottles
HECTARES UNDER VINE	10
VITICULTURE METHOD	Certified biodynamic

Fabio and Silvia Marchionni reprised last year's coup, winning another Three Glasses for their Verdicchio di Matelica. This is no surprise when you see the painstaking attention they give to their vines, and you expect top results from Fabio, whose winemaking talent belies his youth. Collestefano is superb, proffering clean-edged, beguiling scents of both fresh and dried flowers, then a stylish palate, showing subtle, delicate citrus that drives through almost endlessly. One thing we did notice, however, was that this year's version is different in style from previous vintages. What is missing perhaps is the firm, almost piercing acidity that previous versions exhibited, sometimes to the point of imbalance. The long-organic vineyards in Castelraimondo produce a high acidity naturally and Fabio adds none in the winery, given his aversion to vinification adjuvants. His philosophy is to let the wine make itself as far as possible. This approach of course leaves him at the mercy of the vagaries of the growing season and the wines can swing widely in style. Impressively, the Marchionnis steadily put out superlative Verdicchios.

O Verdicchio di Matelica Collestefano '07	▼▼▼	4*
O Verdicchio di Matelica Collestefano '06	♈♈♈	4
O Verdicchio di Matelica Collestefano '05	♈♈	4
O Verdicchio di Matelica Collestefano '04	♈♈	4
O Verdicchio di Matelica Collestefano '03	♈♈	4
O Verdicchio di Matelica Collestefano '02	♈♈	4
O Verdicchio di Matelica Collestefano '01	♈♈	4

La Cantina dei Colli Ripani

VIA TOSCIANO, 28
63038 RIPATRANSONE [AP]
TEL. 07359505
www.colliripani.it

ANNUAL PRODUCTION	600,000 bottles
HECTARES UNDER VINE	1100
VITICULTURE METHOD	Conventional

The recent election of Emilio Malavolta as president of this outstanding co-operative has brought no change to its quality-first philosophy. Comforting proof is that Colli Ripani's two star wines, Offida Rosso Leo Ripanus and Khorakhanè, were not presented for tasting since they need more time in bottle. That means that the team is missing its big hitters but the other players upheld the honour of the Pharus line. In particular, using value for money as the yardstick, Falerio Brezzolino, Offida Pecorino Rugaro and Rosso Piceno Superiore Castellano are big hitters, too. The first pair are standard versions, and both whites are distinctively varietal, each in its own way, with the expected floral scents, and that characteristic, finely crafted structure marked by freshness and dense, ripe flavour. These days, Falerios tend to betray the emphatic aromatics contributed by the international varieties but Brezzolino has an increasingly rare elegance. Castellano has intriguing straw, morello cherry and balsam matched by a full-bodied palate with somewhat burrish but nonetheless effective tannins.

O Falerio dei Colli Ascolani Brezzolino '07	♈♈	3*
O Offida Pecorino Rugaro '07	♈♈	4
● Rosso Piceno Rupenero '07	♈♈	2*
● Rosso Piceno Sup. Castellano '05	♈♈	4
O Leukon Chardonnay '05	♈	4
⊙ Melograno '07	♈	1
O Offida Passerina Ninfa Ripana '07	♈	2
O Offida Passerina Passito Anima Mundi '04	♈	5
● Offida Rosso Leo Ripanus '03	♈♈	4
● Offida Rosso Leo Ripanus '02	♈♈	4
● Khorakhanè '03	♈♈	6
● Khorakhanè '02	♈♈	6

Colonnara

VIA MANDRIOLE, 6
60034 CUPRAMONTANA [AN]
TEL. 0731780273
www.colonnara.it

ANNUAL PRODUCTION	1,200,000 bottles
HECTARES UNDER VINE	180
VITICULTURE METHOD	Conventional

Carlo Pigini has again taken over the reins of this major co-operative, giving it new life and direction. Most of his career has been spent here and he has the talented Agostino Pisani for the vineyards and Daniela Sorana for communications. The positive shift is most obvious in Cuprese, once more a star-category Verdicchio. Traditional in style, it displays elegance and a graceful palate that has plenty of character, length and definition. The classic method Ubaldo Rosi rises to the occasion as usual, proffering florality and camomile before the full, refreshing palate. Tùfico, already showing some maturity, offers great weight and crisp tanginess. Turning to the reds, Tornamagno, a blend of montepulciano and sangiovese, finally won high marks. A touch of black pepper spices up well-crafted fruit on the nose and a rich, tempting palate shows nice evolution. Colonnara has made an intelligent move by dedicating a line of wines to all the principal Marche denominations, including Bianchello del Metauro, Lacrima di Morro d'Alba and the impressive, almond-laced Pecorino, with its refined minerality and smooth length.

Il Conte

VIA COLLE NAVICCHIO, 28
63033 MONTEPRANDONE [AP]
TEL. 073562593
www.ilcontevini.it

ANNUAL PRODUCTION	130,000 bottles
HECTARES UNDER VINE	25
VITICULTURE METHOD	Conventional

Under Emmanuel De Angelis, Il Conte has unabashedly followed the international style for its wines, crafting them along clean, modern lines. If any doubts ever arose, they were put to rest by the wines' lack of any significant territoriality. Our latest tastings simply confirmed this direction, as well as the winery's deepening interest in native grapes. Take the excellent versions of pecorino and passerina. Mown grass and an appreciable savouriness characterize Passerina Cavaceppo while the expressive Pecorino Navicchio flaunts generous, ripe fruit and impressive fullness, marked by warm alcohol and considerable extraction. Proving that passerina is now a fixture in its repertoire, Il Conte also makes a fine passito version, Estro del Mastro, with nicely measured sweetness and notes of tasty candied lemon. Zipolo, from 60 per cent montepulciano plus equal parts sangiovese and merlot, carries the flag for the reds. On the nose, expansive fruit is matched by emphatic toastiness and a vein of pungent greens before the energy-laden attack introduces a dense, supple tannic weave. The supple, inviting fruit in Conte Rosso also deserves attention.

○ Verdicchio dei Castelli di Jesi Cl. Sup. Cuprese '07	♈♈ 4*
○ Brut Riserva Ubaldo Rosi M. Cl. '02	♈♈ 5
○ Offida Pecorino '07	♈♈ 4
● Tornamagno '03	♈♈ 4
○ Verdicchio dei Castelli di Jesi Cl. Sup. Tùfico '05	♈♈ 4
○ Bianchello del Metauro '07	♈ 3
○ Colonnara Brut Charmat	♈ 3
○ Colonnara Class Dolce	♈ 3
● Lacrima di Morro d'Alba '07	♈ 4
● Rosso Piceno Lyricus '07	♈ 3
○ Verdicchio dei Castelli di Jesi Cl. Lyricus '07	♈ 3
○ Verdicchio dei Castelli di Jesi Cl. Sup. Cuprese '06	♈♈ 4
○ Verdicchio dei Castelli di Jesi Cl. Sup. Cuprese '05	♈♈ 4

○ Cavaceppo Passerina '07	♈♈ 4
○ Offida Passerina Passito L'Estro del Mastro '06	♈♈ 5
○ Offida Pecorino Navicchio '07	♈♈ 4
● Rosso Piceno Conte Rosso '07	♈♈ 3*
● Zipolo '05	♈♈ 6
○ Falerio dei Colli Ascolani Aurato '07	♈ 3
● Rosso Piceno Sup. Marinus '06	♈ 4
○ Offida Pecorino Spumante Emmanuel Maria '07	4
○ Navicchio '04	♈♈ 4
● Rosso Piceno Sup. Marinus '04	♈♈ 4
● Zipolo '04	♈♈ 6
● Zipolo '03	♈♈ 6

Conti di Buscareto

FRAZ. PIANELLO
VIA S. GREGORIO, 66
60010 OSTRA [AN]
TEL. 0717913180
www.contidibuscareto.com

ANNUAL PRODUCTION 130,000 bottles
HECTARES UNDER VINE 70
VITICULTURE METHOD Conventional

Computer-industry figures Enrico Giacomelli and Claudio Gabellini have focused the attention of their young operation on Lacrima di Morro d'Alba, sourcing fruit exclusively from estate vineyards planted in various locations. This year's Lacrimas may be down a step from the heights of past vintages but they display sound quality across the line, and some are quite impressive. Compagnia della Rosa shows off rounded, plump fruit and a creamy, silk-smooth mouthfeel while the nervy acidity and harder edges of Nicolò di Buscareto tamp down the fruit a bit but give the wine fine thrust. The standard Lacrima lacks the complexity of its siblings but is dynamic, with varietal florality and expressive tannins. Two Glasses here, too, all the more impressive for a grape less than malleable. Conti di Buscareto also has space in its vineyards for Verdicchio. We liked the fruit and snappy palate of the basic bottling, which is drinking well even now. We'll see Ammazzaconte next year, since it needs some more ageing. We retasted the 2006 edition, and enjoyed the more stylish aromatics it has developed, so we think the 2007 will be worth the wait.

Coroncino

C.DA CORONCINO, 7
60039 STAFFOLO [AN]
TEL. 0731779494
coroncino@libero.it

ANNUAL PRODUCTION 45,000 bottles
HECTARES UNDER VINE 9.5
VITICULTURE METHOD Conventional

Lucio Canestrari has spent years studying the Staffolo area, working tirelessly in his vineyards and cellar. He has succeeded in creating wines that reflect his elected terroir. The wines are powerful and austere but not over the top. Lucio has been able to craft complex, well-gauged expressions of an over-opulent land that wants to stuff its wines with fruit and alcohol. Gaiospino is exemplary. The expansive florality that opens the nose is quickly charged with ripe, almost tropical, fruit and the alluringly flavoursome palate snaps open immediately, with toasty oak perfectly layered into juicy, succulent fruit. It deservedly went to the finals. Coroncino no longer excites wonder. We're used to the volume, firm body and rich intensity that make it a benchmark. Il Bacco, though, is amazing. This standard-version Verdicchio imposes itself with fine weight and volume but also exhibits agile suppleness plus a bouquet infused with fresh blossoms and well-ripened fruit. Irresistible. Crackling rich fruit opens Ganzerello, an uncomplicated but zippy red that Canestrari releases every now and then for fans.

● Lacrima di Morro d'Alba '07	♥♥	4
● Lacrima di Morro d'Alba Compagnia della Rosa '05	♥♥	5
● Lacrima di Morro d'Alba Nicolò di Buscareto '05	♥♥	6
○ Verdicchio dei Castelli di Jesi '07	♥♥	3*
● Crimà '07	♥	3
⊙ Rosa '07	♥	3
● Lacrima di Morro d'Alba Compagnia della Rosa '04	♥♥	5
● Lacrima di Morro d'Alba Nicolò di Buscareto '04	♥♥	6
○ Verdicchio dei Castelli di Jesi Ammazzaconte '06	♥♥	4
○ Verdicchio dei Castelli di Jesi Passito '04	♥♥	5

○ Verdicchio dei Castelli di Jesi Cl. Sup. Gaiospino '06	♥♥	5
○ Verdicchio dei Castelli di Jesi Cl. Sup. Coroncino '06	♥♥	4
○ Verdicchio dei Castelli di Jesi Cl. Sup. Il Bacco '07	♥♥	3*
● Ganzerello	♥	4
○ Verdicchio dei Castelli di Jesi Cl. Sup. Gaiospino '97	♥♥♥	5
○ Verdicchio dei Castelli di Jesi Cl. Sup. Gaiospino '03	♥♥♥	5
○ Verdicchio dei Castelli di Jesi Cl. Sup. Gaiospino '05	♥♥	5
○ Verdicchio dei Castelli di Jesi Cl. Sup. Gaiospino '04	♥♥	5
○ Verdicchio dei Castelli di Jesi Cl. Sup. Coroncino '05	♥♥	4

Costadoro

VIA MONTE AQUILINO, 2
63039 SAN BENEDETTO DEL TRONTO [AP]
TEL. 073581781
www.vinicostadoro.com

ANNUAL PRODUCTION	1,500,000 bottles
HECTARES UNDER VINE	87
VITICULTURE METHOD	Conventional

The Brancadoro family owns vineyards scattered throughout Ascoli Piceno, from the Adriatic coast almost up to San Benedetto del Tronto and nearby Acquaviva, and then quite inland as high up as Offida and Ripatransone. Sourcing grapes from various terroirs and with different characteristics allows them to produce wines in a wide gamut of styles. This philosophy is on gorgeous display in the two Rosso Piceno Superiore versions we tasted. Il Cardinale projects an austere persona whose poles are stiff tannicity and sturdy alcohol that bolster an expansive, fruit-filled palate. Our preference, as usual, is for La Rocca, a red that is at once vibrantly crisp and very supple. Its juicy, fresh fruit makes it an absolutely scrumptious quaffer. Giuseppe Costantini Brancadoro, who has long directed Costadoro, expanded the vine stock by introducing the native pecorino, as well as merlot and cabernet sauvignon. The last of these partners with larger amounts of montepulciano to make up Diciottoquarantotto, an Offida Rosso with delicious spices notes and an impressively full body.

Tenuta De Angelis

VIA SAN FRANCESCO, 10
63030 CASTEL DI LAMA [AP]
TEL. 073687429
www.tenutadeangelis.it

ANNUAL PRODUCTION	500,000 bottles
HECTARES UNDER VINE	50
VITICULTURE METHOD	Conventional

Quinto Fausti never ceases to amaze, turning out both superlative red wines as well as bottlings that represent fine value at modest price tags. His considerable experience is key, of course, but so are his numerous vineyards which enable him to select fruit, his quick intelligence and his foresight. Again, Anghelos emerges as one of the finest wines in the Piceno area. Made of montepulciano with some cabernet sauvignon, it pleases right from the start with a medley of pungent balsam and scrub interleaved with bright fruit, then opens to magisterial volume in the mouth, with an ultra-refined weave of aristocratic tannins. Rosso Piceno Oro stirs the same emotions, with fleshy fruit aplenty on nose and palate, followed by a complex, dynamic development and a mouthfeel as smooth as you could wish. Rosso Piceno Superiore is a slight step down, showing pungent aromas and a silky, full-fruited palate. Rosso Piceno is a consumer's dream, leaner and simpler, but delicious and a pleasure to drink. Among the whites, we liked the fresh greens and crunchy almond of Offida Pecorino, as well as its acidic grip and appealing sapidity.

● Offida Rosso Diciottoquarantotto '03	▼▼ 5
● Rosso Piceno Sup. Il Cardinale '05	▼▼ 4
● Rosso Piceno Sup. La Rocca '06	▼▼ 3*
○ Falerio dei Colli Ascolani Le Ginestre '07	▼ 3
○ Offida Pecorino Danù '07	▼ 5
☉ Rosè '07	4
● Il Crinale Merlot '02	▼▼ 5
● Offida Rosso Diciottoquarantotto '02	▼▼ 4
● Offida Rosso Diciottoquarantotto '01	▼▼ 5
● Rosso Piceno Sup. La Rocca '05	▼▼ 3
● Rosso Piceno Sup. La Rocca '04	▼▼ 3
● Rosso Piceno Sup. La Rocca '03	▼▼ 3

● Anghelos '06	▼▼ 5
● Rosso Piceno Sup. Oro '06	▼▼ 4*
○ Offida Pecorino '07	▼▼ 3*
● Rosso Piceno '07	▼▼ 2*
● Rosso Piceno Sup. '06	▼▼ 3*
○ Falerio dei Colli Ascolani '07	▼ 2
● Anghelos '99	▼▼▼ 5
● Anghelos '01	▼▼▼ 5
● Anghelos '05	▼▼ 5
● Anghelos '04	▼▼ 5
● Anghelos '03	▼▼ 5
● Anghelos '02	▼▼ 5
● Anghelos '00	▼▼ 5
● Rosso Piceno Sup. Oro '05	▼▼ 4
● Rosso Piceno Sup. Oro '04	▼▼ 4
● Rosso Piceno Sup. Oro '03	▼▼ 4

Fattoria Dezi

VIA FONTE MAGGIO, 14
63029 SERVIGLIANO [AP]
TEL. 0734710090
fattoriadezi@hotmail.com

ANNUAL PRODUCTION	50,000 bottles
HECTARES UNDER VINE	15
VITICULTURE METHOD	Natural

Stefano Dezi's contagious laughter and extroverted style complement the more subdued manner of his brother Davide. These two very different brothers are intriguingly mirrored by their sibling wines Regina del Bosco and Solo. The first, all montepulciano, opens with a rich amalgam of smooth spice and then showcases a palate of dense, fleshy fruit caressed into glossy perfection by the supplest of tannins. Solo is all cabernet, stunning with its ultra-focused, almost chewy fruit on the nose and sinewy grip on the palate. Both wines work in synergy with the other, each a widely acclaimed ambassador for the painstaking efforts that have gone into their creation, with Davide labouring in the vineyards and Stefano in the cellar. This year's superb version of Regina del Bosco won Three Glasses while Solo is "only" first-rate. Dezio rounds out the reds, its energy-charged fruit giving the palate supple fluidity and aromatic distinctiveness. The Dezi whites are likewise fine efforts. The verdicchio and malvasia Solagne features vibrant aromatic fruitiness.

La Distesa

VIA ROMITA, 28
60034 CUPRAMONTANA [AN]
TEL. 0731781230
www.ladistesa.it

ANNUAL PRODUCTION	10,000 bottles
HECTARES UNDER VINE	3
VITICULTURE METHOD	Natural

Corrado Dottori has a rigorous, nature-centred philosophy. His core practices include strictly organic farming, ambient yeasts and minimal intervention winemaking. This comes out in his wines, which may be a tad rough-edged, with the odd slight defect, but are imaginative and appreciated by those who seeking novel sensations. The most simple, if we say that about any La Distesa wine, is Terre Silvate. The sweetish floral notes are a bit sharp perhaps, and lack complexity, but the palate has fine sinew and acidity, which works with the savoury finish to keep in check the residual sugar. Nur, produced from overripe trebbiano dorato, malvasia and verdicchio grapes, ferments on the skins and matures in barriques, hence its amber-flecked hue and nose of bitterish herbs, tangerine skin and hazelnut. It enters decisively in the mouth, building considerable alcohol and strong contrasts, then concludes long with marked influence of the fermented skins. Finally, Bianco 99 is a solera-method blend of trebbiano and verdicchio. Sweet but not cloying, it gives tasty almond paste and dried fruits and nuts while the palate, a tad oxidative, is sound enough.

● Regina del Bosco '05	♟♟♟	7
● Dezio Vign. Beccaccia '06	♟♟	5
● Solo Sangiovese '06	♟♟	7
○ Le Solagne '07	♟♟	4
○ Le Solagne V. T. '07	♟	4
● Regina del Bosco '03	♟♟♟	6
● Solo Sangiovese '05	♟♟♟	7
● Solo Sangiovese '01	♟♟♟	6
● Solo Sangiovese '00	♟♟♟	6
● Regina del Bosco '02	♟♟	6
● Regina del Bosco '01	♟♟	6
● Solo Sangiovese '03	♟♟	7
● Solo Sangiovese '02	♟♟	6
● Dezio Vign. Beccaccia '05	♟♟	5

○ Bianco 99	♟♟	6
○ Nur '06	♟♟	4
○ Verdicchio dei Castelli di Jesi Cl. Sup. Terre Silvate '07	♟♟	4
○ Verdicchio dei Castelli di Jesi Cl. Sup. Terre Silvate '06	♟♟	3
○ Verdicchio dei Castelli di Jesi Cl. Sup. Terre Silvate '05	♟♟	3
○ Verdicchio dei Castelli di Jesi Cl. Sup. Gli Eremi Ris. '05	♟♟	4
○ Verdicchio dei Castelli di Jesi Cl. Sup. Gli Eremi Ris. '04	♟♟	4

Fausti

c.da Castelletta, 15
63023 Fermo [AP]
tel. 0734620492
faustini@lycos.it

ANNUAL PRODUCTION	65,000 bottles
HECTARES UNDER VINE	11
VITICULTURE METHOD	Natural

Cristina Fausti and Domenico D'Angelo continue their capable management of this modest operation just outside Fermo. Domenico has always displayed creative energy, first in applying decades of viticultural experience with other wineries to his own careful tending of the estate vineyards, and second in keeping a weather eye on the demands of the market. We have often mentioned his passion for syrah. Perdomenico displays it to the full, the syrah so ripe it seems almost candied, juicy and succulent, filling the huge palate, then finishing racier at the end. Vespro, Fausti's standard-bearer, marries syrah to montepulciano. This 2006 version boasts sound, pulpy fruit and then smooth, densely woven tannins supporting firm structure, and stylish mouthfeel. Overall, a fine, distinctive offering. We very much liked the final red, Rosso Piceno Fausto, for its stand-out fruit and for the dynamic fluidity of its progression. The cellar has also now debuted a Pecorino. Traditional in style, it seemed a tad overripe in the fruit but it concludes nicely bitterish.

Fazi Battaglia

via Roma, 117
60032 Castelplanio [AN]
tel. 073181591
www.fazibattaglia.it

ANNUAL PRODUCTION	3,000,000 bottles
HECTARES UNDER VINE	300
VITICULTURE METHOD	Conventional

Dino Porfiri has been in charge of winemaking here for 30 years so we can't talk about a sea change. Continuity does not imply immobility, however, and new wines emerging from Fazi Battaglia are proof of that. Ekeos appears in red and white versions and we like the white better. It's youthful in style, slightly fizzy and easy to like. A big surprise awaited us with San Sisto 2005. It has thrown the oak overboard and become a magnificently varietal Verdicchio both on the nose as well as on the savoury, sophisticated palate. The oak is restricted to a strictly supporting role in the progression and to a subtle note of vanilla cakes. In so doing, it picked up Three Glasses for the first time. The other wines turned in equally fine performances. Conero Passo del Lupo 2005 glories in pungent Mediterranean scrub and delicious fruit on the finale. Arkezia is as reliable as one expects, loaded with fruit that has a slight, seductive sweetness and complemented by a creamy texture. Moie represents the continuing winery classics, here in an uncomplicated but masterful Verdicchio version. Massaccio 2006 still needs additional time in the cellar.

● Vespro '06	♟♟ 5
● Perdomenico Syrah '06	♟♟ 5
● Rosso Piceno Fausto '07	♟♟ 3*
○ Offida Pecorino Ale '07	♟ 3
● Vespro '05	♟♟♟ 5
● Vespro '03	♟♟♟ 5
● Vespro '04	♟♟ 5
● Vespro '02	♟♟ 4
● Vespro '01	♟♟ 4
● Perdomenico Syrah '05	♟♟ 5
● Rosso Piceno Fausto '06	♟♟ 3

○ Verdicchio dei Castelli di Jesi Cl. San Sisto Ris. '05	♟♟♟ 5
○ Arkezia Muffo di S. Sisto '05	♟♟ 6
○ Verdicchio dei Castelli di Jesi Cl. Sup. Ekeos '07	♟♟ 4*
○ Verdicchio dei Castelli di Jesi Cl. Sup. Le Moie '07	♟♟ 4*
● Conero Passo del Lupo Ris. '05	♟♟ 5
● Rosso Conero Ekeos '07	♟ 4
○ Verdicchio dei Castelli di Jesi Cl. Titulus '07	♟ 4
○ Verdicchio dei Castelli di Jesi Cl. Sup. Massaccio '03	♟♟♟ 4
○ Verdicchio dei Castelli di Jesi Cl. Sup. Massaccio '01	♟♟♟ 4
○ Verdicchio dei Castelli di Jesi Cl. Sup. Massaccio '05	♟♟ 5

Fiorini

VIA GIARDINO CAMPIOLI, 5
61040 BARCHI [PU]
TEL. 072197151
www.fioriniwines.it

ANNUAL PRODUCTION	200,000 bottles
HECTARES UNDER VINE	42
VITICULTURE METHOD	Conventional

Winemaker Carla Fiorini directs this reliable operation, ably assisted by Roberto Potentini. The winery's performance is ample proof that she has admirable professional competence and also a restless, fertile curiosity that compels her to search for just the right styles for her wines. Tenuta Campioli still stands out as Fiorini's most impressive white. Alluringly good and silky in the mouth, it also puts out gorgeous notes of pear and blossoms. Vigna Sant'Ilario may be less complex but its generous fruit and gloriously full-flavoured finale make it a very attractive bottling. Among the reds, Sangiovese Sirio is impressive for its austere character and steady progression. When we tasted Bartis, a montepulciano with 30 per cent cabernet sauvignon, it was still showing the effects of the cask but we are sure that a bit more time in the bottle will smooth its edges and allow its considerable fruit to shine through. We were pleased to see the debut of an Extra Dry-styled sparkler, Perle. Made largely from bianchello, filled out with some white-fermented sangiovese, it shows a smooth, velvety texture and lovely notes of fruit.

★ Gioacchino Garofoli

P.LE G. GAROFOLI, 1
60022 CASTELFIDARDO [AN]
TEL. 0717820162
www.garofolivini.it

ANNUAL PRODUCTION	2,000,000 bottles
HECTARES UNDER VINE	50
VITICULTURE METHOD	Conventional

Both Carlo Garofoli and Verdicchio have followed the same trajectory, with Garofoli always putting out magisterial versions of each style of the variety. All of them are distinctive for their grace, character and longevity. Now he and his daughter Beatrice, who assists with winemaking, provided more proof of this, winning Three Glasses for their Podium. Absolutely flawless throughout, is displays aromatic depth, with florality and fruit in an elegant duet with almond and aniseed. An expansive, ultra-delicious palate shows equal style and a lengthy, savoury finish. Serra Fiorese exhibits admirable proportion, with a rich interweaving of fruit, honey and toast and an appealingly complex, tasty finish edged with menthol. Glossy fruit marks Macrina, plus well-integrated, tangy minerality. On the red side, Grosso Agontano open leans and tight but the succulent palate is nicely aromatic and shows fine-grained tannins and a bright energy. Kòmaros is a tasty, crisply fragrant rosé. Finally, we found both sparklers impressive. Metodo Classico is savoury with lots of depth while the newly introduced montepulciano rosé promises well.

○ Bianchello del Metauro Tenuta Campioli '07	♥♥ 3*
○ Bianchello del Metauro V. Sant'Ilario '07	♥♥ 2*
● Colli Pesaresi Rosso Bartis '06	♥♥ 4
● Colli Pesaresi Sangiovese Sirio '07	♥ 3
○ Perle Extra Dry	♥ 3
○ Bianchello del Metauro Tenuta Campioli '06	♀♀ 3
● Colli Pesaresi Rosso Bartis '04	♀♀ 4

○ Verdicchio dei Castelli di Jesi Cl. Sup. Podium '06	♥♥♥ 5*
● Conero Grosso Agontano Ris. '05	♥♥ 5
○ Verdicchio dei Castelli di Jesi Cl. Serra Fiorese Ris. '05	♥♥ 5
○ Brut Riserva M. Cl. '04	♥♥ 5
○ Verdicchio dei Castelli di Jesi Cl. Sup. Macrina '07	♥♥ 3*
⊙ Brut Rosa M. Cl. '06	♥♥ 5
○ Brut Charmat '06	♥ 3
○ Dorato Moscato Passito '06	♥ 4
⊙ Kòmaros '07	♥ 3
● Rosso Conero Piancarda '05	♥ 4
● Rosso Conero Grosso Agontano Ris. '01	♀♀♀ 5
○ Verdicchio dei Castelli di Jesi Cl. Sup. Podium '04	♀♀♀ 4

Piergiovanni Giusti

LOC. MONTIGNANO
VIA CASTELLARO, 97
60019 SENIGALLIA [AN]
TEL. 071918031
www.lacrimagiusti.it

ANNUAL PRODUCTION   42,000 bottles
HECTARES UNDER VINE   12.5
VITICULTURE METHOD   Conventional

No news may or may not be good news
at the Giusti winery. In fact, we were
expecting a new development. No, not a
launch of white wines, nor even an opening
to varieties other than lacrima. We were
looking for the release of a dried-grape
wine. It had been previously announced
but the debut has been put off for now.
The standard Lacrima shifts this year from
the classical floral register to impressions
of fruit. The palate is as huge as usual, with
perhaps a slight tannic edge, but it is still
an eminently enjoyable wine. Rubbjano
once again won the competition between
the two Lacrima cru selections and went
to our national finals. We were convinced
by its dense-packed bouquet of dried
rose petals. The palate open steeply
to massive extraction and volume but
everything remains nicely under control,
and it concludes impressively long. Luigino,
sourced from old vines, displays a slight
overripeness, followed by a palate similar
to that of Rubbjano but a tad more austere,
which tends to stiffen the finale too much.
Rose di Settembre, a lacrima-based rosé,
is its usual refreshing, supple self, once
again with an ultra-floral bouquet.

Esther Hauser

C.DA CORONCINO, 1A
60039 STAFFOLO [AN]
TEL. 0731770203
esther.hauser@virgilio.it

ANNUAL PRODUCTION   6,000 bottles
HECTARES UNDER VINE   1
VITICULTURE METHOD   Conventional

Esther Hauser won admiration for
her courageous move from her
native Switzerland to her hectare
of montepulciano in Staffolo. She
determinedly confronted the challenges
of the small grower, and for some years
now has steered her production in the right
direction, so much so that once again both
of her two splendid wines competed in the
finals for our Three Glasses. Cupo differs
from Ceppo, which could be regarded as
Hauser's second wine, only in the selection
of fruit and in the characteristics of the final
wine. Ceppo is bursting with just the right
amount of generous fruit, and shows pulpy
and perfectly ripe, before its impressive
concentration in the mouth does nothing to
impede a fluid, supple progression. Cupo,
in contrast, betrays more austerity and
more complex layering. Of the two, it will
require longer cellaring to achieve its full
potential and when it reaches that point, its
qualities will be hard to match. At present,
we are fortunate to enjoy Cupo's rich
earthy tones and a sturdy tannic structure
that nevertheless allows full scope to the
creamy goodness of its fruit.

● Lacrima di Morro d'Alba Rubbjano '06	♥♥ 4*
● Lacrima di Morro d'Alba '07	♥♥ 4
● Lacrima di Morro d'Alba Luigino '06	♥♥ 5
☉ Le Rose di Settembre '07	♥ 3
● Lacrima di Morro d'Alba Rubbjano '05	♀♀ 4
● Lacrima di Morro d'Alba Rubbjano '04	♀♀ 4
● Lacrima di Morro d'Alba Luigino '05	♀♀ 5
● Lacrima di Morro d'Alba Luigino '04	♀♀ 5

● Il Ceppo '06	♥♥ 5
● Il Cupo '06	♥♥ 6
● Il Cupo '05	♀♀ 6
● Il Cupo '04	♀♀ 6
● Il Cupo '03	♀♀ 6
● Il Ceppo '05	♀♀ 5
● Il Ceppo '04	♀♀ 5

Fattoria Laila

VIA S. FILIPPO SUL CESANO, 27
61040 MONDAVIO [PU]
TEL. 0721979353
www.fattorialaila.it

ANNUAL PRODUCTION	100,000 bottles
HECTARES UNDER VINE	40
VITICULTURE METHOD	Conventional

Producer Andrea Crocenzi makes one superb wine and a whole series of very impressive and reliable bottlings. He also releases them at very reasonable prices, more than justifying his determination to use only native varieties. He's a past master at managing his 40 hectares of vineyards, sited in the Verdicchio Classico zone and quite a long way from the cellar, which is just over the border of the province of Pesaro. Andrea's wines seem to improve every year, thanks in part the shrewd assistance of oenologist Lorenzo Landi. Rosso Piceno Lailum is their finest wine, which in this vintage offers rich impressions of black liquorice and pungent earth. It shows agile and vibrant on the palate, quite a different animal from the dense, rounded fruit that we have come to expect. Intense florality on the nose and a complex, silky palate allow Eklektikos to stand out among the Verdicchios. The standard versions of Piceno and Conero are well matched. The taut energy and impressions of wild cherry of the Piceno are a nice foil to the rich scents of dried plum preserves pervading the Conero.

Conte Leopardi Dittajuti

VIA MARINA II, 24
60026 NUMANA [AN]
TEL. 0717390116
www.conteleopardi.com

ANNUAL PRODUCTION	220,000 bottles
HECTARES UNDER VINE	52
VITICULTURE METHOD	Conventional

Piervittorio Leopardi Dittajuti has sun-blessed vineyards on limestone marl at the foot of Mount Conero and Adriatic breezes to ripen his grapes to perfection, infusing aromas, structure and flavours. The vineyard near Coppo di Sirolo, amid green-clad hills that seem to leap into the sea, produces two fascinating Sauvignon Blancs, Calcare and Bianco del Coppo. The first lays out a severe, uncompromising bouquet of mineral and fresh greens but relaxes on a palate that expands and deepens, finding nice balance. Well-rounded fruit marks the second, and crispness makes for immediate approachability. The area of Svarchi at Numana yields the montepulciano-based offerings, the best of which is Pigmento 2005. After initial hesitation, it releases good fruit and sweet spice, then reveals significant power in the mouth with somewhat rough tannins that make the finish a tad stiffish. Vigneti del Coppo 2006 gains appeal from its wild cherry on the nose and from supple development and youthful, exuberant tannins. Casirano offers pulpy fruit, effective progression and measured tannins, while the young Rosso Conero Fructus is fruity enough but a bit hot.

● Rosso Piceno Lailum '05		▼▼ 5
○ Verdicchio dei Castelli di Jesi Cl		
Sup. Eklektikos '07		▼▼ 4*
● Rosso Conero Fattoria Laila '07		▼ 4
● Rosso Piceno Fattoria Laila '07		▼ 3
○ Verdicchio dei Castelli di Jesi Cl.		
Sup. Fattoria Laila '07		▼ 3
● Lailum '02		▼▼ 5
● Lailum '01		▼▼ 5
● Rosso Piceno Lailum '04		▼▼ 5
● Rosso Piceno Lailum '03		▼▼ 5
○ Verdicchio dei Castelli di Jesi Cl.		
Lailum Ris. '04		▼▼ 4
○ Verdicchio dei Castelli di Jesi Cl.		
Lailum Ris. '05		▼▼ 4

○ Bianco del Coppo Sauvignon '07		▼▼ 3*
○ Calcare Sauvignon '07		▼▼ 4
● Conero Pigmento Ris. '05		▼▼ 6
● Rosso Conero		
Vigneti del Coppo '06		▼▼ 5
● Rosso Conero Casirano '06		▼ 5
● Rosso Conero Fructus '07		▼ 4
○ Brut Villa Marina		▼ 4
○ Verdicchio dei Castelli di Jesi Cl.		
Castelverde '07		▼ 4
● Conero Pigmento Ris. '04		▼▼ 6
● Rosso Conero Casirano '05		▼▼ 5
● Rosso Conero Pigmento '03		▼▼ 5
● Rosso Conero		
Vigneti del Coppo '05		▼▼ 5

Roberto Lucarelli

LOC. RIPALTA
VIA PIANA, 20
61030 CARTOCETO [PU]
TEL. 0721893019
www.laripe.com

ANNUAL PRODUCTION	90,000 bottles
HECTARES UNDER VINE	18
VITICULTURE METHOD	Conventional

Roberto Lucarelli's winery is perhaps the best producer in the Pesaro hills. If some past vintages left us perplexed, things have been going well over the last two years or so. Lucarelli is a hard-working producer who has winemaking assistance from Aroldo Belelli. It all means that the current direction is positive and results will improve in the future. In the meantime, there are two magisterial versions of Bianchello del Metauro to enjoy, each showing intriguing stylistic differences. Rocho presents huge extractive power, even on the nose, laden with lush white peach and other ripe fruit, but its nervy acidity keeps everything in impeccable equilibrium. Accessibility is the key to La Ripe. Elegant pineapple and other fruit laced with pungent spice segue into a succulent, fluid and savoury palate. The two Sangioveses reflect different interpretations. La Ripe communicates exquisite smoothness throughout, opening impressively wide to rounded, sweet fruit and developing a palate of alluring sapidity. Goccione tends in the same direction, with the densest of fruit, but with tight-woven tannins and more emphatic alcoholic weight.

O Bianchello del Metauro La Ripe '07	▼▼	2*
O Bianchello del Metauro Rocho '07	▼▼	3*
● Colli Pesaresi Sangiovese Goccione '06	▼▼	5
● Colli Pesaresi Sangiovese La Ripe '06	▼▼	3*
O Bianchello del Metauro La Ripe '06	♀♀	2
O Bianchello del Metauro Rocho '06	♀♀	3

Stefano Mancinelli

VIA ROMA, 62
60030 MORRO D'ALBA [AN]
TEL. 073163021
www.mancinelli-wine.com

ANNUAL PRODUCTION	150,000 bottles
HECTARES UNDER VINE	25
VITICULTURE METHOD	Conventional

The local custom of enjoying Lacrima in the months after harvest has held it back since it is often seen as a simple wine for immediate consumption. But Stefano Mancinelli, convinced that lacrima could make a more ambitious wine, has striven to develop its complexity and structure. The fact that Superiore 2006 went to our Three Glass finals represents a triumph for Stefano and oenologist Roberto Potentini. The nose proposes elegant, pulpy fruit with good varietal character while the mouth is full and balanced, with tannins well tucked in. There's energetic progression that drives a lengthy finish. Sensazioni di Frutto is the standard Lacrima. It's flawless, fragrant and delicious while well-ripened fruit and a rounded palate mark Terre dei Goti, a 2003 Lacrima. The 2005 passito Re Sole impresses with its mix of bottled cherries, black pepper and chocolate over a sweet, leisurely development. A superb Verdicchio S. Maria del Fiore proves that Mancinelli is far from a one-variety operation. Crisp, tangy fruit and mouthwatering acidity follow a bouquet of blossoms, citrus and aniseed and put this Verdicchio among the best of its class.

● Lacrima di Morro d'Alba Sup. '06	▼▼	4*
O Verdicchio dei Castelli di Jesi Cl. Sup. S. Maria del Fiore '07	▼	3*
● Lacrima di Morro d'Alba Passito Re Sole '05	▼	5
● Lacrima di Morro d'Alba Sensazioni di Frutto '07	▼▼	4
● Terre dei Goti	▼▼	6
O Verdicchio dei Castelli di Jesi Passito Stell '06	▼▼	5
O Verdicchio dei Castelli di Jesi Cl. '07	▼	2
● Lacrima di Morro d'Alba S. Maria del Fiore '06	♀♀	4
● Lacrima di Morro d'Alba Sup. '05	♀♀	4
● Rubrum '03	♀♀	3
● Terre dei Goti '01	♀♀	6

Fattoria Mancini

S.DA DEI COLLI, 35
61100 PESARO [PU]
TEL. 072151828
www.fattoriamancini.com

Marchetti

FRAZ. PINOCCHIO
VIA DI PONTELUNGO, 166
60131 ANCONA [AN]
TEL. 071897386
www.marchettiwines.it

ANNUAL PRODUCTION	75,000 bottles
HECTARES UNDER VINE	31
VITICULTURE METHOD	Conventional

ANNUAL PRODUCTION	60,000 bottles
HECTARES UNDER VINE	18
VITICULTURE METHOD	Conventional

The magnificent vineyards of Luigi Mancini's winery, located in the San Bartolo nature park in the hills behind Pesaro, face right out over the Adriatic. This hard-working grower dedicates his efforts mainly to pinot nero and albanella. The Burgundian native is an unusual variety to find here while albanella has always been grown only in this spot. Most of Mancini's production reflects his efforts to translate into wine the distinctive characteristics of these varieties and of this terroir. He produces a Sangiovese as well, which is a bit slow to wake, but then impresses with its crisp, sound fruit in perfect harmony with a finely crafted palate and measured acidity. The Pinot Nero opens to clean varietal definition, offering wonderfully ripe red berry fruit. If the palate is a little short, it betrays good agility and savoury flavours. Roncaglia, made from albanella with some white-fermented pinot nero, might be a length behind previous performances but impresses nonetheless. Good fruit and a hint of fresh greens make up an attractive nose, and nervy, electric acidity energizes the succulent palate.

Maurizio Marchetti's line-up is superb. He makes a distinctive, affordable team of wines. The Marchetti family's long experience with growing has given Maurizio the opportunity to learn one of the key lessons in agriculture: all things reach perfection in their own time. Year after year, with expert technical help from Lorenzo Landi, our hero has found precisely the right stylistic register for the four wines he produces, each spot on in its particular category. His most impressive bottling is Villa Bonomi, a powerfully built Conero that has benefited from later than usual release. The nose flaunts dense, fleshy, perfectly ripe fruit, and a huge charge of tannins is well distributed and doesn't impede the palate's supple, fluid progression. We were impressed by Rosso Conero. It opens surprisingly crisp on the nose and then spreads out a wide swath of crunchy fruit in the mouth. Among the Verdicchios, Tenuta del Cavaliere has appreciable weight, good alcohol and tons of juicy succulence. The standard version, nicely smooth, tends more to citrus but exhibits a similarly savoury thrust.

● Colli Pesaresi Focara Pinot Nero '06	¶¶ 5
● Colli Pesaresi Sangiovese '06	¶¶ 4*
○ Colli Pesaresi Roncaglia '07	¶¶ 4*
● Blu '00	♈♈ 6
● Blu '01	♈♈ 6
● Colli Pesaresi Focara Pinot Nero Impero Ris. '01	♈♈ 6
● Colli Pesaresi Focara Pinot Nero Impero '05	♈♈ 6
● Colli Pesaresi Focara Pinot Nero Impero '04	♈♈ 6
● Colli Pesaresi Focara Pinot Nero Impero '03	♈♈ 6
● Colli Pesaresi Sangiovese '05	♈♈ 4

● Conero Villa Bonomi Ris. '05	¶¶ 6
● Rosso Conero '06	¶¶ 4*
○ Verdicchio dei Castelli di Jesi Cl. '07	¶¶ 3*
○ Verdicchio dei Castelli di Jesi Cl. Sup. Tenuta del Cavaliere '07	¶¶ 4*
● Rosso Conero Villa Bonomi Ris. '02	¶¶¶ 5
● Rosso Conero Villa Bonomi Ris. '04	♈♈ 5
● Rosso Conero Villa Bonomi Ris. '03	♈♈ 5
● Rosso Conero Villa Bonomi Ris. '01	♈♈ 5
● Rosso Conero '05	♈♈ 4
○ Verdicchio dei Castelli di Jesi Cl. Sup. Tenuta del Cavaliere '06	♈♈ 4

Marotti Campi

VIA S. AMICO, 14
60030 MORRO D'ALBA [AN]
TEL. 0731618027
www.marotticampi.it

ANNUAL PRODUCTION	170,000 bottles
HECTARES UNDER VINE	56
VITICULTURE METHOD	Conventional

The Marotti Campi family boasts one of the largest plantings of lacrima and their devotion to the variety has won them high marks in recent years. That is especially true this year since their Lacrima Superiore Orgiolo entered the national taste-offs. It is a rich, juicy example, exuding alluring scents of raspberry and wild strawberry. The progression is textbook perfect and the finale thrilling. Rùbico gives us a more straightforward, and more slender, interpretation of lacrima, but still nicely varietal. Young Lorenzo Marotti Campi and oenologist Roberto Potentini also deserve kudos for their fine work with verdicchio, of which they produce three versions. Each is different from its partners but they all show high craftsmanship and are real bargains for the price. The most impressive, with a velvety, seductive mouthfeel, is Salmariano, which stands out for its evolved character, marked by impressions of tropical fruit. The equally smooth Luzano is less full and concludes with crisp fruit, whereas Albiano shows a classic straightforwardness that translates into superlative drinking pleasure.

La Monacesca

C.DA MONACESCA
62024 MATELICA [MC]
TEL. 0733812602
www.monacesca.it

ANNUAL PRODUCTION	170,000 bottles
HECTARES UNDER VINE	27
VITICULTURE METHOD	Conventional

We reckoned last year that Mirum 2006 would be superb but we had no idea that it would turn out this sumptuous. It gives the classic aromas of great Verdicchios, following fresh flowers with by ripe fruits, then scrub, rosemary, wild fennel and aniseed. Complex, juicy and savoury in the mouth, it displays almost endless progression while the texture is dense yet surprisingly light and smooth. This utterly delicious Merum is one of the best ever, easily meriting Three Glasses. Kudos goes to Aldo Cifola not only for this wine but also for the reliability that he has built up for this admirable winery. The Merum is a thoroughbred but hardly less so is the other Verdicchio di Matelica, the so-called standard version, although that term seems inappropriate. The nose pours out the tastiest of fruit, while the well proportioned palate is fat and savoury. We were mightily intrigued by Ecclesia, a distinctive, refined Chardonnay. Pale in hue, it features stylish notes of pear and white peach on the nose then follows with intense minerality that makes for unsurpassed drinking pleasure. We suggest a slogan: terroir through chardonnay.

● Lacrima di Morro d'Alba Sup. Orgiolo '06	♈♈ 4*
○ Verdicchio dei Castelli di Jesi Cl. Albiano '07	♈♈ 2*
○ Verdicchio dei Castelli di Jesi Cl. Salmariano Ris. '05	♈♈ 4
○ Verdicchio dei Castelli di Jesi Cl. Sup. Luzano '07	♈♈ 3*
● Lacrima di Morro d'Alba Rùbico '07	♈ 4
● Xyris Mosto Parzialmente Fermentato '07	♈ 4
○ Verdicchio dei Castelli di Jesi Cl. Salmariano Ris. '03	♈♈ 4
● Donderè '05	♈♈ 5
● Donderè '04	♈♈ 5
● Lacrima di Morro d'Alba Orgiolo '05	♈♈ 4

○ Verdicchio di Matelica Mirum Ris. '06	♈♈♈ 5
○ Ecclesia Chardonnay '07	♈♈ 4*
○ Verdicchio di Matelica La Monacesca '07	♈♈ 4*
● Camerte '05	♈ 5
● Duerosso '05	♈ 4
● Camerte '99	♈♈♈ 5
○ Mirum '94	♈♈♈ 5
○ Mirus '91	♈♈♈ 5
○ Verdicchio di Matelica Mirum Ris. '04	♈♈♈ 5
○ Verdicchio di Matelica Mirum Ris. '02	♈♈♈ 5
○ Verdicchio di Matelica La Monacesca '06	♈♈ 4
○ Verdicchio di Matelica La Monacesca '05	♈♈ 4

Monte Schiavo

FRAZ. MONTESCHIAVO
VIA VIVAIO
60030 MAIOLATI SPONTINI [AN]
TEL. 0731700385
www.monteschiavo.it

ANNUAL PRODUCTION 1,800,000 bottles
HECTARES UNDER VINE 115
VITICULTURE METHOD Conventional

Gianluigi Calzetta runs the Pietralisi family cellar with winemaking consultancy from Pierluigi Lorenzetti. We again tasted a range of impressive bottlings, wines that will please both demanding tasters as well as those looking for aromas and approachability. We'll start with the reds. Rosso Conero Adeodato 2005 gave a superlative performance with smooth spice married to succulent, dense fruit. Good energy and dense-packed tannins ensure overall elegance and appeal. Aromas of sweet fruit characterize Piceno Superiore Sassaiolo 2006, plus crisp acidity and lush flavours. Rosso Conero Conti Cortesi lays out a fine palate but fruit and spice lack integration on the nose. Lacrima di Morro d'Alba is youthful, heady and fragrant. On the Verdicchio side, Riserva Le Giuncare 2006 flaunts luscious pineapple, honey and peach, then a round, measured palate nicely lifted by tangy minerality. Pallio di S. Floriano is as fine as expected, thanks to initial lovely florality and to acidity and slate-like minerality that bolster firm structure. Nativo 2006, on the other hand, displays a palate that is well-rounded but seems a tad flabby despite decent sapidity.

Montecappone

VIA COLLE OLIVO, 2
60035 JESI [AN]
TEL. 0731205761
www.montecappone.com

ANNUAL PRODUCTION 120,000 bottles
HECTARES UNDER VINE 70
VITICULTURE METHOD Conventional

Business offers the opportunity to link your name to high quality. The Mirizzi family strives to do just that with their Montecappone. Although they have yet to win Three Glasses, the entire line offers solid quality and good varietal definition. The whites earn particularly high marks, thanks to Tabano, Utopia and Montesecco. The first, an Esino Bianco, is rounded and fruity, with the verdicchio grape furnishing savouriness and body, while a tot of sauvignon adds richness to the bouquet. Utopia is more ambitious. Here verdicchio's stay in casks is noticeable but never hampers the palate's crisp citrus impressions or its steady progression. In Verdicchio Montesecco, which seems to be more tempting with each vintage, nervy acidity enlivens dried fruit and nuts. The Mirizzi ably draw out the qualities inherent in their monovarietal Sauvignon and Chardonnay, respectively La Breccia and Colle Onorato. Both display alluring, cleanly delineated varietal bouquets and palates that are both expansive and invigorating. Tabano, a contemporary Montepulciano with crackling fruit, leads the reds. The botrytized Rèsio offers gorgeous candied fruit.

● Rosso Conero Adeodato '05	▼▼	6
● Lacrima di Morro d'Alba '07	▼▼	3*
● Rosso Piceno Sup. Sassaiolo '06	▼▼	4
○ Verdicchio dei Castelli di Jesi Cl. Le Giuncare Ris. '06	▼▼	4
○ Verdicchio dei Castelli di Jesi Cl. Sup. Nativo '06	▼▼	4
○ Verdicchio dei Castelli di Jesi Cl. Sup. Pallio di S. Floriano '07	▼▼	4
○ Verdicchio dei Castelli di Jesi Cl. Coste del Molino '07	▼	3
○ Verdicchio dei Castelli di Jesi Cl. Ruviano '07	▼	3
● Rosso Conero Conti Cortesi '06	▼	4
● Rosso Conero Adeodato '00	▼▼▼	6
● Esino Pieralisi For Friends '04	▼▼	6
● Esio '04	▼▼	5

○ Esino Bianco Tabano '07	▼▼	5
○ Verdicchio dei Castelli di Jesi Cl. Utopia Ris. '06	▼▼	5
○ Colle Onorato Chardonnay '07	▼▼	4
○ La Breccia Sauvignon '07	▼▼	4
○ Verdicchio dei Castelli di Jesi Cl. Sup. Colle Paradiso '07	▼▼	3*
○ Verdicchio dei Castelli di Jesi Cl. Sup. Montesecco '07	▼▼	4
○ Verdicchio dei Castelli di Jesi Rèsio Passito '06	▼▼	6
● Esino Rosso Tabano '06	▼▼	5
● Rosso Piceno Montesecco '07	▼▼	4
○ Verdicchio dei Castelli di Jesi Cl. Sup. Montesecco '06	▼▼	4
○ Verdicchio dei Castelli di Jesi Cl. Utopia Ris. '04	▼▼	5

Alessandro Moroder

LOC. MONTACUTO
VIA MONTACUTO, 121
60029 ANCONA
TEL. 071898232
www.moroder-vini.it

ANNUAL PRODUCTION	140,000 bottles
HECTARES UNDER VINE	32
VITICULTURE METHOD	Natural

Serenella and Alessandro Moroder's winery continues to be one of the most impressive montepulciano producers in the Conero area. Their vineyards, planted on powerful clay-limestone soils near Montacuto di Ancona, just back from the steep cliffs of Promontorio, receive the moderating influence of sea breezes and yield wines of superb depth. Conero Riserva Dorico 2004, just a whisker away from Three Glasses, opens stiffish but then presents nice dark berry fruit, morello cherry and toasty oak, with the alcohol just a shade warm. The palate shows fine power and extractive weight, plus an interplay between elegant fruit and subtle tannins while the finish is expansive and graceful. Rosso Conero 2006 was not yet ready for tasting but we liked the more economical Aiòn. Pungent rosemary nicely lifts raspberry and morello cherry, followed by judicious extract. Rosa di Montacuto, well rounded on the palate, is redolent of cyclamen, rose petals and strawberries. BianConero, made from moscato and white-fermented alicante, offers its customary citrus and blossoms, along with stylish effervescence on the palate.

Oasi degli Angeli

C.DA SANT'EGIDIO, 50
63012 CUPRA MARITTIMA [AP]
TEL. 0735778569
www.kurni.it

ANNUAL PRODUCTION	5,000 bottles
HECTARES UNDER VINE	7
VITICULTURE METHOD	Natural

Marco Casolanetti and his wife Eleonora have created an oasis at Cupra Marittima, with a farmstay and highly respected restaurant, but Marco's passion is his land and wine. Over the past 20 years, Casolanetti has made a solid name for himself, thanks to his character and to his philosophy as a grower. Year after year, that philosophy produces a great, absolutely unique wine that sets our tasters debating fiercely. Kurni is an icon of winemaking in Marche and beyond. At past tastings, it amazed, perplexed and utterly seduced us. Those were the years in which winemaking in Italy was searching for its own road, and Casolanetti was able to interpret a particular moment, which saw immensely powerful wines that shunned finesse and were so ultra-extracted that you almost had to chew them. This style of wine is no longer as esteemed as it was in the past and we gave Kurni 2006 a high, but not the highest, score. We must confess that the 2006 is more complex and multi-layered than the previous edition, and that Kurni ages effortlessly, a fact that many tastings of older vintages have put beyond doubt.

● Conero Dorico Ris. '04	♟♟	6
● Rosso Conero Aiòn '06	♟♟	3*
○ BianConero Filtrato Dolce '07	♟	4
☉ Rosa di Montacuto '07	♟	3
● Rosso Conero Dorico '93	♟♟♟	5
● Rosso Conero Dorico '90	♟♟♟	5
● Rosso Conero Dorico '88	♟♟♟	5
● Rosso Conero Dorico Ris. '03	♟♟	6
● Rosso Conero Dorico Ris. '01	♟♟	6
● Rosso Conero Dorico '00	♟♟	5
● Ankon '03	♟♟	6
● Ankon '00	♟♟	6
● Rosso Conero '05	♟♟	4

● Kurni '06	♟♟	8
● Kurni '98	♟♟♟	8
● Kurni '97	♟♟♟	8
● Kurni '04	♟♟♟	8
● Kurni '03	♟♟♟	8
● Kurni '02	♟♟♟	8
● Kurni '01	♟♟♟	8
● Kurni '00	♟♟♟	8
● Kurni '05	♟♟	8
● Kurni '99	♟♟	8
● Kupra '05	♟♟	8

Piantate Lunghe

FRAZ. CANDIA
VIA PIANTATE LUNGHE, 91
60131 ANCONA
TEL. 07136464
www.piantatelunghe.it

ANNUAL PRODUCTION 30,000 bottles
HECTARES UNDER VINE 12.5
VITICULTURE METHOD Conventional

When Roberto and Guido Mazzoni met Amedeo Giustini, it led to the launch of Piantate Lunghe. With a few hectares of montepulciano and sangiovese near Angeli di Ancona, and the vineyard expertise of Federico Curtaz and Aroldo Bellelli with Paolo Caciorgna in the cellar, the goal was to produce wines with character that would reflect the Conero terroir. Results were positive from the start. The wines have not stopped improving, acquiring ever more character. At once austere and fragrant, they are always powerful but never unctuous. Conero Riserva Rossini 2005 had these precedents to rely on, and deservedly won our Three Glasses. An intense, rich wine from first to last, showing aromas of black pepper, tobacco leaf and pencil lead interwoven into smooth, lively fruit. Excellent volume and energy mark the palate, along with well-distributed tannins and admirable balance, and it closes with finesse and length. Rosso Conero 2006 scored well for subtle oak and emphatic thyme and mint over crisp, vibrant cherry, and for its rounded expansiveness in the mouth, where lively tannins, tangy acidity and full flavours bring suppleness and a sustained finale.

● Conero Rossini Ris. '05	ꝩꝩꝩ	6
● Rosso Conero '06	ꝩꝩ	4*
● Conero Ris. '04	ꝨꝨ	6
● Rosso Conero '05	ꝨꝨ	4

Pievalta

VIA MONTESCHIAVO, 18
60030 MAIOLATI SPONTINI [AN]
TEL. 0309848311
www.baronepizzini.it

ANNUAL PRODUCTION 53,000 bottles
HECTARES UNDER VINE 27
VITICULTURE METHOD Certified biodynamic

If the difficult 2005 growing year affected everyone, then imagine its impact on a grower who farms organically and cultivates a single variety, verdicchio, and that fairly recently. But Alessandro Fenino, a Lombard winemaker entrusted by Barone Pizzini with their Iesi project, was up to the challenge. His Riserva San Paolo is splendid. Slightly overripe grapes bring us pungent thyme and wild herbs lightly scented with honey and mature fruit that infuse the palate. Fine weight in the mouth marries with well-integrated acidity and alcohol. The 2006 vintage was less difficult. Dominè is all warmth and smoothness, releasing ripe apple and almond, followed by a palate of judicious but graceful dimensions, fine alcohol and the savoury flavours you expect from the variety. Curina is a meditation wine that is sweet but not cloying. After smooth balsam and crisp menthol, warm but subdued alcohol takes over, yielding to a salty tang that acts as an intriguing foil and creates a superlative equilibrium on the palate. The standard Verdicchio offers well-ripened fruit then a rounded, sweetish palate ending on a pleasant almondy note.

○ Verdicchio dei Castelli di Jesi Cl. San Paolo Ris. '05	ꝩꝩ	5
○ Verdicchio dei Castelli di Jesi Cl. Sup. Dominè '06	ꝩꝩ	4*
○ Verdicchio dei Castelli di Jesi Passito Curina '06	ꝩꝩ	5
○ Verdicchio dei Castelli di Jesi Cl. Sup. Pievalta '07	ꝩ	3
○ Verdicchio dei Castelli di Jesi Cl. San Paolo Ris. '04	ꝨꝨ	4
○ Verdicchio dei Castelli di Jesi Cl. Sup. Dominè '04	ꝨꝨ	4
○ Verdicchio dei Castelli di Jesi Cl. Sup. Pievalta '06	ꝨꝨ	3
○ Verdicchio dei Castelli di Jesi Passito Curina '04	ꝨꝨ	5

Il Pollenza

VIA CASONE, 4
62029 TOLENTINO [MC]
TEL. 0733961989
www.ilpollenza.it

ANNUAL PRODUCTION	80,000 bottles
HECTARES UNDER VINE	50
VITICULTURE METHOD	Conventional

The new development at Aldo Brachetti Peretti is that Tuscan Carlo Ferrini took over winemaking in early 2008. Otherwise they continue with same high quality across their line. The winery aces are Pius IX Mastai and Il Pollenza. The first, from botrytized sauvignon grapes, sports rich, penetrating scents of dried figs, orange preserves, dates and medicinal syrup on both nose and palate, plus an expansive sweetness in the mouth and a tasty vein of acidity. Il Pollenza is a mosaic of cabernet sauvignon, cabernet franc and merlot. A slight herbaceous tone lends elegance to the nose while silky texture and fine delineation on the palate conjure up an artist's fine brush strokes and create the kind of surpassing elegance typical of the finest bottles from Bordeaux. Both of the remaining reds, each outstanding, are single-variety wines. The cabernet sauvignon Cosmino offers an evolved herbaceousness followed by notable volume in the mouth, smooth-textured fruit and energetic acidity. Merlot confers on Porpora intriguing notes of dried nuts but overall this is huge, almost excessive, wine with a well-rounded finale.

Saladini Pilastri

VIA SALADINI, 5
63030 SPINETOLI [AP]
TEL. 0736899534
www.saladinipilastri.it

ANNUAL PRODUCTION	800,000 bottles
HECTARES UNDER VINE	160
VITICULTURE METHOD	Certified biodynamic

This long-established producer's winemaker is Pasqualino Gabrielli, with Alberto Antonini consulting. Quality is consistent over the entire range of its 2006 Rosso Picenos, each with its own personality. In Parnaso, largely sangiovese, flowers alternate with blackberry and raspberry while the nicely expressed palate exhibits fine flavours. Equal parts of sangiovese and montepulciano go into Piediprato, which presents rich, almost candied, fruit and a well-delineated, weighty palate edged in bitter almond. Montepulciano makes up 70 per cent of the two Superiores, with the remainder sangiovese. Montetinello shows delicate and light, both in appearance and taste, with a velvety finale that is tangy and crisp. Monteprandone, with great elegance and finesse, turned in the most impressive performance. Rich fruit is lifted by a clean vein of balsam and the palate is juicy and dynamic. The whites were just as good. Thanks to its rich, tangy citrus palate, Falerio Palazzi is still one of the finest in the denomination. Pregio del Conte Bianco, a new 50-50 blend of falanghina and fiano, impressed us with its finesse and energetic progression.

● Il Pollenza '04	♟♟ 8
○ Pius IX Mastai '06	♟♟ 6
● Cosmino '04	♟♟ 5
● Porpora '05	♟♟ 4*
○ Briano '07	♟ 4
● Cosmino '03	♟♟ 5
● Il Pollenza '03	♟♟ 8
● Il Pollenza '02	♟♟ 7
● Il Pollenza '01	♟♟ 7
● Porpora '04	♟♟ 4
○ Pius IX Mastai '03	♟♟ 6
○ Pius IX Mastai '05	♟♟ 6
○ Pius IX Mastai '04	♟♟ 6

○ Falerio dei Colli Ascolani V. Palazzi '07	♟♟ 3*
○ Pregio del Conte Bianco '07	♟♟ 4*
● Pregio del Conte '06	♟♟ 5
● Rosso Piceno Parnaso '06	♟♟ 4*
● Rosso Piceno Piediprato '06	♟♟ 4*
● Rosso Piceno Sup. V. Monteprandone '06	♟♟ 5
● Rosso Piceno Sup. V. Montetinello '06	♟♟ 4*
○ Falerio dei Colli Ascolani '07	♟ 3
○ Offida Pecorino '07	♟ 4
● Rosso Piceno Sup. V. Monteprandone '00	♟♟♟ 4
● Rosso Piceno Sup. V. Monteprandone '04	♟♟ 5
● Pregio del Conte '04	♟♟ 5

San Filippo

LOC. BORGO MIRIAM
C.DA CIAFONE, 17A
63035 OFFIDA [AP]
TEL. 0736889828
www.vinisanfilippo.it

ANNUAL PRODUCTION   20,000 bottles
HECTARES UNDER VINE   28
VITICULTURE METHOD   Certified biodynamic

You have to wonder what gave respected vineyard designers and brothers Lino and Fabrizio Stracci the idea of building a wine cellar from scratch. But watching the entire family working together at picking time like a colony of ants, and worrying over the harvest and the fermentations, you realize that wine is an essential part of their life and that the path they are treading is the only one possible. Their wines bear out that conclusion. In Lupo del Ciafone 2005, a 70-30 blend of montepulciano and cabernet sauvignon, we notice some burred tannins on the finish. They betray its difficult growing year, when the unfavourable conditions presented a greater challenge to organic farming. But the palate is huge and sapid, with toasty oak well tucked into its massive fruit and a lovely aromatic vein of green pepper. The measured Offida Pecorino offers wild herbs, almond and subtle aniseed on a sturdy palate, which appreciable energy pushes through impressively to a rich, toothsome finale. San Filippo's standard version wines are perfect quaffers, such as the smooth Falerio and the fragrant, dynamic merlot-based Rubino Ventoso.

San Francesco

VIA FONTEMERCATO, 9
63030 ACQUAVIVA PICENA [AP]
TEL. 0735764416
www.vinicherri.it

ANNUAL PRODUCTION   100,000 bottles
HECTARES UNDER VINE   20
VITICULTURE METHOD   Conventional

The best news from Marche comes from Acquaviva Picena, a modest village in the vine-covered landscape inland from San Benedetto del Tronto, where the Cherri family has produced wine for three generations. Our tastings this year revealed such leaps in quality that it was hard to pick their finest bottling. We'll begin with Passerina Radiosa, about the best of the many Marche passerinas we tried this year. We liked its richly citrus nose, its voluminous palate and bright, flavourful conclusion. The other whites are equally good. Pecorino Altissimo is clean-edged, fragrant and approachable. The Oriente version of Falerio offers juicy impressions of blossoms and grapefruit while Creato, equally fruity, builds more volume and progression. The reds are modern in style and well crafted, their tannins nicely subdued. Laudi is a Rosso Piceno Superiore with great heft and concentration, giving peppery balsam over red fruit. The more youthful Notturno is a slightly more emphatic version, brimming with personality. Finally, there is a surprising, all-montepulciano rosé, Cedrone, a terrific mix of a good red's body with the aromatic crispness of a white.

● Offida Rosso Lupo del Ciafone '05	▼▼ 5
○ Offida Pecorino '07	▼▼ 4
○ Falerio dei Colli Ascolani '07	▼ 3
● Rubino Ventoso Merlot '07	▼ 3
○ Offida Passerina '07	3
● Lupo del Ciafone '04	♈♈ 5
● Lupo del Ciafone '03	♈♈ 5
○ Offida Pecorino '06	♈♈ 4
○ Offida Pecorino '05	♈♈ 4

⊙ Cedrone '07	▼▼ 4*
○ Falerio dei Colli Ascolani Creato '07	▼▼ 4*
○ Offida Passerina Radiosa '07	▼▼ 4*
○ Offida Pecorino Altissimo '07	▼▼ 4*
● Rosso Piceno Sup. Laudi '03	▼▼ 5
● Rosso Piceno Sup. Notturno '06	▼▼ 4*
○ Falerio dei Colli Ascolani Oriente '07	▼ 3
○ Pecorino Brut	▼ 4
● Rosso Piceno Canto '07	▼ 3

San Giovanni

C.DA CIAFONE, 41
63035 OFFIDA [AP]
TEL. 0736889032
www.vinisangiovanni.it

ANNUAL PRODUCTION   90,000 bottles
HECTARES UNDER VINE   30
VITICULTURE METHOD   Natural

Gianni Di Lorenzo began by rationalizing the San Giovanni line, ending up with three reds, three whites and a sweet wine, and by giving a more modern look to his labels. He has now taken the final step in his renovation, entrusting winemaking to Enzo Pica and Giovanni Basso. The quality of the wines, though, has not changed; they are still top-notch. True, the whites differ with respect to past editions but the culprit here is the 2007 growing season, which did no favours to aromatic compounds. The winery flagship remains Pecorino Kiara. While the nose is restrained, it opens to a huge palate, beautifully proportioned and with the tangiest of finales. Among the reds, we gave high marks to Offida Rosso Zeii for elegant complexity on the nose and a juicy, superbly fluid development in now way hindered by a weave of dense tannins and a solid charge of fruit. Rosso Piceno Superiore Leo Guelfus exhibits crisper, more self-assured fruit but with slightly more alcohol than desirable on the finish. Passerina Passito also went through to our national finals. It is a sumptuous, glycerine-rich gem of great seductive power and impeccable balance.

Poderi San Lazzaro

C.DA SAN LAZZARO, 65/67
63035 OFFIDA [AP]
TEL. 0736889189
www.poderisanlazzaro.it

ANNUAL PRODUCTION   50,000 bottles
HECTARES UNDER VINE   15
VITICULTURE METHOD   Natural

Nowadays, to stand out from the crowd making good, or even technically superb, wines is not enough. No, the wine must exemplify an interpretation of a particular point of origin, and that terroir must be clear in the wine. That is precisely what Paolo Capriotti and Pino Ottavi do. Their much-acclaimed Grifola is a monovarietal montepulciano whose expansive palate effortlessly showcases all of that grape's meaty fruit, with dynamic progression and dense tannic structure that are free of viticultural acrobatics, over-extraction or abuse of oak. Along the same lines is Podere 72, is a Rosso Piceno Superiore from old vineyards. It's an equal blend of sangiovese and montepulciano and the former makes its influence felt in florality and in acidity that, far from overwhelming, softens the wine's impact without in any way slowing its juicy development. The standard-label all-sangiovese Polesio shows ultra-fragrant. Pistillo is the only white, a quite intriguing Pecorino, with overtones from its stay in oak and hints of citrus zest from a brief maceration on the skins. Large both in alcohol and volume, it concludes with a beguiling hint of mineral salt.

O Offida Passerina Passito '04	▼▼	5
● Offida Rosso Zeii '04	▼▼	5
O Offida Pecorino Kiara '07	▼▼	4*
● Rosso Piceno Sup. Leo Guelfus '05	▼▼	4*
O Falerio dei Colli Ascolani Leo Guelfus '07	▼	3
O Offida Passerina Marta '07	▼	3
O Offida Pecorino Kiara '06	♀♀	4
● Offida Rosso Zeii '03	♀♀	5
● Offida Rosso Zeii '02	♀♀	5
● Offida Rosso Zeii '01	♀♀	5
● Rosso Piceno Sup. Leo Guelfus '04	♀♀	4
● Rosso Piceno Sup. Axeé '04	♀♀	5
● Rosso Piceno Sup. Axeé '03	♀♀	5

● Grifola '06	▼▼	5
● Rosso Piceno Sup. Podere 72 '06	▼▼	4*
O Offida Pecorino Pistillo '07	▼▼	4*
● Polesio Sangiovese '07	▼	2
● Grifola '05	♀♀	5
● Grifola '04	♀♀	5
● Podere 72 '04	♀♀	4
● Rosso Piceno Sup. Podere 72 '05	♀♀	4

Fattoria San Lorenzo

VIA SAN LORENZO, 6
60036 MONTECAROTTO [AN]
TEL. 073189656
az-crognaletti@libero.it

ANNUAL PRODUCTION	100,000 bottles
HECTARES UNDER VINE	36
VITICULTURE METHOD	Natural

What a clever move by Natalino Crognaletti. A full ten years after harvest, he pulls out of his cellar a Verdicchio from 1997. Left to mature all that time in steel, it is a fabulous wine, boasting pungent, evolved impressions of undergrowth and medicinal herbs that flow out in ordered profusion. On the palate, it is still perfectly sound and supple, with alluring depth. And the cellar has more surprises, he tells us. But those who prize Crognaletti's wines have long understood that they require time, evolving more slowly than others. That is a small price to pay to a grower who manages his vines in an uncompromisingly natural manner, allowing time and not artificial adjuvants to round out imperfections and craft the wines. That discourse does not change even for the more straightforward Verdicchio Vigna Di Gino. Its performance is already impressive, with fine fruit on the nose and a hedonistic sapidity, but it too will improve around the edges. Vigna delle Oche enjoys smooth contours and rounded fruit, without compromising its elegance or minerality while the cru Riserva shows analogous characteristics, but with more maturity and fluidity.

San Savino - Poderi Capecci

LOC. SAN SAVINO
VIA SANTA MARIA IN CARRO, 13
63038 RIPATRANSONE [AP]
TEL. 073590107
www.sansavino.com

ANNUAL PRODUCTION	120,000 bottles
HECTARES UNDER VINE	32
VITICULTURE METHOD	Natural

Simone Capecci has managed to translate the traditional into the contemporary. That he has done so without betraying nature is obvious in his wines, which eloquently speak of the sun-filled vineyards of the Contrada Ciafone, one Piceno's finest crus. Crafting your own stylistic register requires time, sensitivity and a willingness to face challenges and make sacrifices, to spend most of your time in the vine rows and among the barrels. The results are there to see. Fedus won our top honour, Three Glasses. A monovarietal Sangiovese, it flaunts stunningly beautiful fruit both on nose and mouth, a palate that is deep but vibrant and ductile, and an ever-expanding finish. Picus, super-savoury and velvet textured, is on a par but doesn't quite achieve the same overall harmony. Ver Sacrum, a monovarietal Montepulciano vinified in steel, exemplifies Capecci's hallmark roundness, its forceful grip tamped down just a whisker by an exuberant alcohol. The whites are no less fine. Ciprea is a superb Pecorino with clean-cut aromatics, vibrant acidity and a masterfully stylish palate. Tufilla, a fragrant, tasty Passerina, made its debut.

○ Il San Lorenzo '97	♥♥ 7
○ Verdicchio dei Castelli di Jesi Cl. Sup. Vigna delle Oche '06	♥♥ 4*
○ Verdicchio dei Castelli di Jesi Cl. Vigna delle Oche Ris. '05	♥♥ 5
○ Verdicchio dei Castelli di Jesi Cl. Vigna di Gino '07	♥♥ 3*
● Rosso Conero '05	♥ 4
● Rosso Piceno Vigna Burello '05	♥ 4
● Vigna Paradiso '04	♥ 4
○ Verdicchio dei Castelli di Jesi Cl. Vigna delle Oche Ris. '01	♥♥♥ 5
○ Verdicchio dei Castelli di Jesi Cl. Vigna delle Oche Ris. '04	♥♥ 5
○ Verdicchio dei Castelli di Jesi Cl. Vigna delle Oche Ris. '03	♥♥ 5
○ Verdicchio dei Castelli di Jesi Cl. Sup. Vigna delle Oche '05	♥♥ 4

● Fedus Sangiovese '06	♥♥♥ 5
● Rosso Piceno Sup. Picus '06	♥♥ 4*
○ Offida Pecorino Ciprea '07	♥♥ 4*
○ Offida Passerina Tufilla '07	♥♥ 3*
● Ver Sacrum '06	♥♥ 4
● Rosso Piceno Collemura '07	♥ 3
● Moggio Sangiovese '98	♥♥♥ 6
● Quinta Regio '01	♥♥♥ 6
● Quinta Regio '00	♥♥♥ 6
● Quinta Regio '03	♥♥ 6
● Quinta Regio '02	♥♥ 6
● Fedus Sangiovese '05	♥♥ 5
● Fedus Sangiovese '03	♥♥ 6
● Rosso Piceno Sup. Picus '05	♥♥ 4
● Ver Sacrum '05	♥♥ 4
● Ver Sacrum '03	♥♥ 6
○ Offida Pecorino Ciprea '06	♥♥ 4

Santa Barbara

B.GO MAZZINI, 35
60010 BARBARA [AN]
TEL. 0719674249
www.vinisantabarbara.it

ANNUAL PRODUCTION	650,000 bottles
HECTARES UNDER VINE	40
VITICULTURE METHOD	Conventional

Stefano Antonucci produces wines of very high quality. The bottles we tasted had personality and gorgeous fruit, particularly the Verdicchios. Le Vaglie repeated last year's fine performance, showing classy almond and citrus, vibrant fruit and excellent balance. Creamy impressions of vanilla and ripe fruit open Riserva Stefano Antonucci, which then has terrific minerality that set of an impressive, rounded palate. This superb version echoed the performance of Le Vaglie 2006 and brought Antonucci Three more Glasses. We liked Pignocco and Nidastore, both easy-drinking consumer bargains. The first has good varietal qualities, body and balance while the second boasts crisp, bright citrus and florality. From the reds, Pathos, a medley of merlot, cabernet and syrah, scored high. A vein of pungent greens girders smooth fruit and alluring succulence on the palate is nicely enriched by vigorous, well-calibrated tannins. The montepulciano shines through in Il Maschio da Monte, with youthful tannins and hints of black cherry, cassis and morello. Stefano Antonucci Rosso offers crackling fruit on the palate but loses some energy along the way.

Santa Cassella

C.DA SANTA CASSELLA, 7
62018 POTENZA PICENA [MC]
TEL. 0733671507
www.santacassella.it

ANNUAL PRODUCTION	70,000 bottles
HECTARES UNDER VINE	32
VITICULTURE METHOD	Conventional

Santa Cassella again lived up to its role as one of the Marche's top producers. Production still rests on a virtuoso medley of native grapes, which have been cultivated for centuries here, and of more recent international plantings in the 1970s. It is chardonnay, with some help from sauvignon that shapes the cask-aged Donna Eleonora. Opening with stylish, ripe notes of peach and banana, lifted by a touch of well-integrated toast, it then lays out juicy, sweet fruit in the mouth, concluding with an impressively lengthy finale. Donna Angela is both more straightforward and aromatic. Here malvasia takes the place of sauvignon, bringing its hallmark herbaceousness, while vinification in steel accentuates the palate's varietal expression and crisp intensity. Among the reds, the montepulciano and sangiovese Cardinal Bonaccorso is first rate, perhaps austere but with magisterial, rich fruit all the way through. Conte Leopoldo Cabernet Sauvignon is much the same, but with a bit more emphasis on extract. We concluded with Rosso Piceno, which has lively, fleshy fruit and steady, fluid progression.

O Verdicchio dei Castelli di Jesi Cl. Stefano Antonucci Ris. '06	♔♔♔ 4*
O Verdicchio dei Castelli di Jesi Cl. Le Vaglie '07	♔♔ 4*
O Verdicchio dei Castelli di Jesi Nidastore '07	♔♔ 3*
O Verdicchio dei Castelli di Jesi Pignocco '07	♔♔ 3*
● Pathos '06	♔♔ 7
● Rosso Piceno Il Maschio da Monte '06	♔♔ 6
● Stefano Antonucci Rosso '06	♔♔ 4
● Rosso Piceno '07	♔ 4
● Vigna San Bartolo '06	♔ 4
● Rosso Piceno Il Maschio da Monte '04	♔♔♔ 5
O Verdicchio dei Castelli di Jesi Cl. Le Vaglie '06	♔♔♔ 4

● Colli Maceratesi Rosso Cardinal Bonaccorso Ris. '05	♔♔ 4*
● Conte Leopoldo Cabernet Sauvignon '06	♔♔ 4*
O Donna Angela '07	♔♔ 4*
O Donna Eleonora '07	♔♔ 4*
O Colli Maceratesi Bianco '07	♔ 3
● Rosso Piceno '06	♔ 3
● Conte Leopoldo '03	♔♔ 4
● Colli Maceratesi Rosso Cardinal Bonaccorso Ris. '03	♔♔ 4
● Colli Maceratesi Rosso Cardinal Bonaccorso Ris. '02	♔♔ 4
● Conte Leopoldo '05	♔♔ 4
● Conte Leopoldo '04	♔♔ 4
O Donna Eleonora '06	♔♔ 4

Sartarelli

VIA COSTE DEL MOLINO, 24
60030 POGGIO SAN MARCELLO [AN]
TEL. 073189732
www.sartarelli.it

ANNUAL PRODUCTION	290,000 bottles
HECTARES UNDER VINE	60
VITICULTURE METHOD	Conventional

Sartarelli is a star performer in wine shops focusing on Italy's best whites and it owes is spot on the shelves to Balciana. Although the wine's production numbers have been going up, its artisanal quality is unchanged, indubitably helped by Sartarelli's stubborn focus on producing only Verdicchio. The line is pyramid-shaped. Classico provides the foundation, in both fact and style, for it displays hallmark acacia blossom and almond, with a decisive yet supple palate. Higher up, and more ambitious, is Tralivio. A more rigorous selection of grapes and an extra year's ageing bring very refined aromas but there is still the classic touch of dried nuts, while a firm structure bolsters pulpy, smooth fruit that goes on and on. Ultra-ripe fruit is the key to its sibling, Balciana, which gives rich scents of honey, wild herbs and tropical fruit. Generous, juicy flavours in the mouth and a glycerine-rich mouthfeel continue their allure right to the end of a long-lingering finish. In this panoply of fine performers there is room for a lovely newcomer. Sartarelli's alluring Passito releases clean-edged scents of candied fruit and well-gauged sweetness.

Sparapani - Frati Bianchi

VIA BARCHIO, 12
60034 CUPRAMONTANA [AN]
TEL. 0731781216
www.fratibianchi.it

ANNUAL PRODUCTION	35,000 bottles
HECTARES UNDER VINE	12
VITICULTURE METHOD	Conventional

In compiling this annual Guide, we treasure the opportunity of discovering new producers and introducing readers to wines that they can then find in shops and restaurants, or even at the wineries themselves. It's also important to check that these new wineries continue to improve the performances of their wines, as is the case with Sparapani. We have noticed for several years now improvement in the wines and we admire the family's single-mindedness in their work in vineyard and cellar. After their exploit of last year, when Verdicchio Il Priore won Three Glasses, we hoped for a performance of the same calibre, which is in fact what happened. The 2007 Il Priore, although from a lesser vintage than the 2006, nonetheless easily went through to the national taste-offs. This stellar wine has a huge bouquet of crisp, well-ripened fruit, showing big and fat on the palate but sporting nice acidity that keeps everything well calibrated. Salerna, the Sparapani second-tier Verdicchio, tends to softer tones and is tasty and approachable now.

O Verdicchio dei Castelli di Jesi Cl. Sup. Balciana '06	🍷🍷 6
O Verdicchio dei Castelli di Jesi Cl. Sup. Tralivio '06	🍷🍷 4*
O Verdicchio dei Castelli di Jesi Cl. '07	🍷🍷 3*
O Verdicchio dei Castelli di Jesi Passito '06	🍷🍷 5
O Verdicchio dei Castelli di Jesi Cl. Sup. Balciana '04	🍷🍷🍷 6
O Verdicchio dei Castelli di Jesi Cl. Sup. Contrada Balciana '98	🍷🍷🍷 6
O Verdicchio dei Castelli di Jesi Cl. Sup. Contrada Balciana '97	🍷🍷🍷 6
O Verdicchio dei Castelli di Jesi Cl. Sup. Tralivio '05	🍷🍷 4
O Verdicchio dei Castelli di Jesi Cl. Sup. Tralivio '04	🍷🍷 4

O Verdicchio dei Castelli di Jesi Cl. Sup. Il Priore '07	🍷🍷 4*
O Verdicchio dei Castelli di Jesi Cl. Salerna '07	🍷🍷 3*
O Verdicchio dei Castelli di Jesi Cl. Sup. Il Priore '06	🍷🍷🍷 4
O Verdicchio dei Castelli di Jesi Cl. Sup. Il Priore '05	🍷🍷 4
O Verdicchio dei Castelli di Jesi Cl. Salerna '06	🍷🍷 3

Spinsanti

VIA FONTE INFERNO, 11
60021 CAMERANO [AN]
TEL. 071731797
catiaspinsanti@alice.it

ANNUAL PRODUCTION	30,000 bottles
HECTARES UNDER VINE	7.5
VITICULTURE METHOD	Natural

Catia Spinsanti and Andrea Gaggiotti did well to keep Rosso Conero Camars in the cellar maturing in cement vats for another year. It shows superlative balance, its fruit still lovely, sound and refreshing, and its palate supple and vibrant, with perhaps just a tad too much alcohol on the finale. It was right to postpone its release. But that's very much their style. They pay painstaking attention to all of the seemingly small details, in the vineyards and cellar, which often make a difference in terms of a wine's quality. The best confirmation of that modus operandi is furnished by Sassòne. An all-montepulciano sourced from old vines, without the DOCG Conero designation, it displays the same stiff, austere style that has always characterized it, with a noble depth of red berry and delicate spices on the nose and a profoundly dense, almost piercing palate. Unbending tannicity marks the standard-label Rosso Conero Adino as well but it is softened by crisp, pulpy fruit that infuses the wine from first to last and makes it the delicious masterpiece that it is.

Silvano Strologo

VIA OSIMANA, 89
60021 CAMERANO [AN]
TEL. 071731104
www.vinorossoconero.com

ANNUAL PRODUCTION	60,000 bottles
HECTARES UNDER VINE	15
VITICULTURE METHOD	Conventional

Silvano Strologo is a producer with picture-postcard vineyards that yield splendid fruit, which his winemaking transforms into wines that privilege structure and power over crisp fruit and accessibility. Not all share his opinion about this being the best register for montepulciano grown in the Conero area, since, all things considered, they seem somewhat heavy and complicated. On the other hand, Strologo holds to his convictions and maintains his style, and his many dyed-in-the-wool fans seem to appreciate his perseverance. Decebalo presents dense and deep, releasing dark notes of spice, baked herbs and liquorice before developing smooth and supple in the mouth, all the while freshened by a zippy vein of acidity and concluding with well-ripened fruit. Their new Caesar, partly matured in barrique, offers emphatic dried plum, sturdy structure and warm alcohol but we preferred the more traditional, straightforward Julius, a masterful steel-vinified montepulciano. It leads with a heady blend of pungent balsam, greens and underbrush, then plays off acidity and tannins, concluding with rich impressions of liqueur fruit.

● Sassòne '06	🍷🍷	6
● Rosso Conero Adino '07	🍷🍷	3*
● Rosso Conero Camars '06	🍷🍷	4*
● Sassòne '05	🍷🍷	6
● Sassòne '04	🍷🍷	5
● Sassòne '03	🍷🍷	5
● Sassòne '02	🍷🍷	5
● Sassòne '01	🍷🍷	5
● Sassòne '00	🍷🍷	5
● Rosso Conero Adino '06	🍷🍷	3
● Rosso Conero Adino '05	🍷🍷	3
● Rosso Conero Camars '05	🍷🍷	4
● Rosso Conero Camars '04	🍷🍷	4

● Conero Decebalo Ris. '05	🍷🍷	6
● Rosso Conero Julius '07	🍷🍷	4*
● Rosso Conero Caesar '07	🍷🍷	4*
⊙ Rosa Rosae '07		3
● Rosso Conero Traiano '00	🍷🍷🍷	5
● Rosso Conero Traiano '05	🍷🍷	5
● Rosso Conero Traiano '04	🍷🍷	5
● Rosso Conero Traiano '03	🍷🍷	5
● Rosso Conero Traiano '02	🍷🍷	5
● Rosso Conero Traiano '01	🍷🍷	5
● Conero Decebalo Ris. '04	🍷🍷	6
● Rosso Conero Decebalo Ris. '02	🍷🍷	5
● Rosso Conero Julius '06	🍷🍷	4

Tenuta di Tavignano

LOC. TAVIGNANO
62011 CINGOLI [MC]
TEL. 0733617303
www.tenutaditavignano.it

ANNUAL PRODUCTION   120,000 bottles
HECTARES UNDER VINE 30
VITICULTURE METHOD   Conventional

A photograph would communicate better than words the beauty in which Stefano Aymerich's vineyards are set. The hillslope location receives the Adriatic breezes as well as cool winds coming down from the Apennine mountains, represented here by the stocky mass of Mount San Vicino. As if to confirm its special status, Tavignano released, even in the difficult 2005 vintage, its Misco Riserva in a version that picked up our top award, Three Glasses. It manages to embody that straightforward, varietal style of Verdicchio that privileges rich, succulent fruit and marries tactile richness in the mouth to a delicate aromatic medley of blossoms, citrus and dried nuts. Hardly less superb is Misco 2007, from another poor year. But it too displays hallmark varietal white-fleshed fruit on the nose and a lengthy, savoury finale. The remaining Verdicchio bottlings display clean florality and fruit impressions, refreshing crispness and tasty approachability. We thought the Tavignano was best. But all these whites should not overshadow the reds, and Libenter 2005 is a big, generous Rosso Piceno with massive fruit.

Fattoria Le Terrazze

VIA MUSONE, 4
60026 NUMANA [AN]
TEL. 0717390352
www.fattorialeterrazze.it

ANNUAL PRODUCTION   90,000 bottles
HECTARES UNDER VINE 21
VITICULTURE METHOD   Conventional

The list of wines tasted this year reveals no Three Glass symbol. Bear in mind, though, that we were unable to taste two of Fattoria Le Terrazze's star wines, Vision of J and Planet Waves, and that the wines we did taste were from a less than stellar vintage, 2005. Nonetheless, Chaos and Sassi Neri both received high marks. We preferred the latter, a thoroughbred of a Montepulciano crafted in a style that is austere and far from facile. The nose requires time to unfold but the palate is dynamic enough, multi-layered and complex, although stiff at times and a bit clenched towards the end. Chaos, half montepulciano plus equal amounts of syrah and merlot, did not quite equal past performances. Elegant scents of balsam and black pepper suffer from an intrusive vegetal note, while the palate is admirably vibrant but somewhat hobbled at the moment by a heavy hand with the oak. Further ageing will be useful. The standard-label Rosso Conero is its usual fine self, with tasty morello preceding an agile palate that shows emphatic tannin. The only white, Chardonnay Le Cave, expresses delicate dried flowers and develops a fresh, flavoursome palate.

O Verdicchio dei Castelli di Jesi Cl. Misco Ris. '05	ŦŦŦ 5
O Verdicchio dei Castelli di Jesi Cl. Sup. Misco '07	ŦŦ 4*
● Rosso Piceno Libenter '05	ŦŦ 4*
● Rosso Piceno Castel Rosino '07	Ŧ 3
● Rosso Piceno Tavignano '06	Ŧ 4
O Verdicchio dei Castelli di Jesi Cl. Sup. Tavignano '07	Ŧ 4
O Verdicchio dei Castelli di Jesi Cl. Vigna Verde '07	3
O Verdicchio dei Castelli di Jesi Cl. Sup. Misco '06	♈♈♈ 4
O Verdicchio dei Castelli di Jesi Cl. Sup. Misco '05	♈♈ 4
O Verdicchio dei Castelli di Jesi Cl. Misco Ris. '04	♈♈ 5

● Chaos '05	ŦŦ 7
● Conero Sassi Neri Ris. '05	ŦŦ 6
● Rosso Conero '06	ŦŦ 4*
O Le Cave Chardonnay '07	Ŧ 4
● Chaos '04	♈♈♈ 7
● Chaos '01	♈♈♈ 7
● Chaos '97	♈♈♈ 7
● Conero Sassi Neri Ris. '04	♈♈♈ 6
● Rosso Conero Sassi Neri '02	♈♈♈ 6
● Rosso Conero Sassi Neri '99	♈♈♈ 6
● Rosso Conero Sassi Neri '98	♈♈♈ 6
● Rosso Conero Visions of J '01	♈♈♈ 8
● Rosso Conero Visions of J '97	♈♈♈ 8
● Conero Visions of J Ris. '04	♈♈ 8
● Planet Waves '03	♈♈ 7
● Planet Waves '04	♈♈ 6

Terre Cortesi Moncaro

VIA PIANDOLE, 7A
60036 MONTECAROTTO [AN]
TEL. 073189245
www.moncaro.com

ANNUAL PRODUCTION	7,500,000 bottles
HECTARES UNDER VINE	1618
VITICULTURE METHOD	Conventional

The high quality consistently achieved by this large co-operative continue to impress at all price levels. Two Conero Riservas stood out. Vigneti del Parco displays dense, concentrated weight that follows dark notes of black cherry, blackberry and cassis. The rather alcoholic Nerone gives fully ripe, exquisitely fragrant fruit then weaves a velvety fabric of fleshy tannins. Two other wines are just a rung down. Cimerio, after smooth red berry on the nose, offers a palate that is powerful but in check, and stiffish tannins. Montescuro's aromatic fruit runs to ripe, fleshy black cherry, and it offers succulent elegance in the mouth, with slightly drying alcohol on the finish. Vigna Novali emerges easily from the Verdicchios, sporting a nose that is nicely varietal but a bit evolved and a dynamic, savoury mouth. Fresh pineapple, white peach and subtle spice characterize Le Vele, which flaunts a palate with hard-to-beat freshness and drinkability. Passito Tordiruta's botrytized fruit embellishes the expansive complexity of its nose and it boasts a fat palate with nice acidity that lifts the sweetness and drives a superb, appealing progression.

Umani Ronchi

VIA ADRIATICA, 12
60027 OSIMO [AN]
TEL. 0717108019
www.umanironchi.com

ANNUAL PRODUCTION	4,000,000 bottles
HECTARES UNDER VINE	230
VITICULTURE METHOD	Conventional

The Bernetti family's operation is a beacon in Marche. Some of their wines are virtual guarantees of quality. Pelago, for instance, has never been so fine, with rich raspberry creating a crisp succulence that glides through to a lengthy conclusion. Cùmaro Riserva 2005 is another fine version of montepulciano but perhaps not quite as personal as in the past. Again, there were Three Glasses for Plenio, whose 2005 version gives a voluminous, creamy-textured palate with magisterially calibrated oak that does nothing to hinder the savouriness. With the 2006 edition, Le Busche changes to a less impressive international register, tending towards tropicality on the nose, with a fat mouthfeel showing subtle oak and new, supple energy. Casal di Serra shows less assertive in 2007, attractive in its crisp fruit and almond, and with a palate of fine depth and weight but a tad too warm. Maximo 2005 is a sweet dried-grape Sauvignon but well this side of cloying. This brilliant line of wines is superbly executed, convincing evidence of a well thought-out philosophy. The latest, Pecorino Vellodoro, made in Abruzzo, is a worthy addition.

● Conero Nerone Ris. '05	♟♟	5
● Conero Vigneti del Parco Ris. '05	♟♟	5
○ Verdicchio dei Castelli di Jesi Cl. Vigna Novali Ris. '04	♟♟	4*
○ Verdicchio dei Castelli di Jesi Passito Tordiruta '05	♟♟	7
● Conero Cimerio Ris. '05	♟♟	4
● Conero Montescuro Ris. '05	♟♟	4
○ Offida Pecorino Ofithe '07	♟♟	4
● Rosso Piceno Sup. Campo delle Mura '05	♟♟	5
○ Verdicchio dei Castelli di Jesi Cl. Le Vele '07	♟♟	3*
○ Verdicchio dei Castelli di Jesi Cl. Sup. Verde Ca' Ruptae '07	♟♟	4
● Barocco '05	♟	4
○ Verdicchio dei Castelli di Jesi Cl. Vigna Novali Ris. '03	♟♟	4

○ Verdicchio dei Castelli di Jesi Cl. Plenio Ris. '05	♟♟♟	5
● Conero Cùmaro Ris. '05	♟♟	5
● Pelago '05	♟♟	6
● Rosso Conero S. Lorenzo '06	♟♟	4
○ Le Busche '06	♟♟	5
○ Maximo '05	♟♟	5
○ Vellodoro Pecorino '07	♟♟	4
○ Verdicchio dei Castelli di Jesi Cl. Sup. Casal di Serra '07	♟♟	4
● Rosso Conero Serrano '07	♟	3
○ Verdicchio dei Castelli di Jesi Cl. Sup. Villa Bianchi '07	♟	3
○ Verdicchio dei Castelli di Jesi Cl. Plenio Ris. '04	♟♟♟	5
○ Verdicchio dei Castelli di Jesi Cl. Plenio Ris. '03	♟♟♟	5
● Pelago '04	♟♟	6

Vallerosa Bonci

VIA TORRE, 13
60034 CUPRAMONTANA [AN]
TEL. 0731789129
www.vallerosa-bonci.com

ANNUAL PRODUCTION 250,000 bottles
HECTARES UNDER VINE 35
VITICULTURE METHOD Conventional

For 30 years, Beppe Bonci has been working with Verdicchio, hewing to tradition but also experimenting with new practices and dedicating patient efforts, with the University of Milan, to identifying superior verdicchio clones. Beppe knows this grape like few others and he produces it in a wide range of styles. At each new vintage, he releases wines of superb quality. Two wines this year competed in the final taste-offs and San Michele brought home Three Glasses. Splendidly varietal, it is archetypal of Verdicchios coming from the right bank of the Esino river. Its classy floral aromatics inform a masterfully crafted palate, simply a model of suppleness, which displays a stunning minerality. Le Case is no less fine but in a different style, fatter but no less fluid, restrained but flavourful, and with a bouquet brimming with expansive fresh flowers, camomile and aniseed. Just a hair behind is Pietrone, which perhaps needed a bit more cellar time. The nose is somewhat tight but shows fine depth and flavour. Passito Rojano is well balanced and soundly made while Brut Metodo Classico displays appealing maturity and crisp acidity.

Valturio

LOC. CALTRAVAGLIO
61033 MACERATA FELTRIA [PU]
TEL. 0722728049
www.valturio.com

ANNUAL PRODUCTION 12,000 bottles
HECTARES UNDER VINE 9
VITICULTURE METHOD Conventional

In the heart of Montefeltro, Adriano Galli and his wife Isabella have developed a beacon for the entire territory. The soils here at 450 metres' elevation are loose and nutrient-poor, unsuited to the previous farming system that demanded only quantity, but they are promising for high-quality grapes. Galli, a man of deep culture and wine knowledge, reckoned this land could again produce wines of elegance. In 2002, the couple bought and planted a few hectares that had not seen vines for a century and restructured a historic building into a wine production and ageing cellar. Now their dream has finally come true, with the entrance into full production of those first plantings, vines trained to the traditional bush style at densities up to 10,000 vines per hectare. Their all-sangiovese Valturio, which we are convinced will enjoy a very long life, was a worthy competitor at our final round of tastings. Elegant overall, it shows complex, angular and nicely mineral. There were also good marks for Solco, an interesting product of the rebo grape. It gives varietal spice and pungency, developing loads of character.

○ Verdicchio dei Castelli di Jesi Cl. Sup. S. Michele '06	♛♛♛ 5
○ Verdicchio dei Castelli di Jesi Cl. Sup. Le Case '06	♛♛ 5
○ Bonci Brut M. Cl. '04	♛♛ 5
○ Verdicchio dei Castelli di Jesi Cl. Pietrone Ris. '06	♛♛ 5
○ Verdicchio dei Castelli di Jesi Passito Rojano '06	♛♛ 5
○ Bonci Brut	♛ 4
○ Verdicchio dei Castelli di Jesi Cl. Viatorre '07	♛ 3
○ Verdicchio dei Castelli di Jesi Cl. Pietrone Ris. '04	♛♛♛ 5
○ Verdicchio dei Castelli di Jesi Cl. Sup. Le Case '04	♛♛♛ 4
○ Verdicchio dei Castelli di Jesi Cl. Sup. S. Michele '00	♛♛♛ 4

● Valturio '06	♛♛ 5
● Solco '06	♛♛ 6

Velenosi

LOC. MONTICELLI
VIA DEI BIANCOSPINI, 11
63100 ASCOLI PICENO
TEL. 0736341218
www.velenosivini.com

ANNUAL PRODUCTION	1,300,000 bottles
HECTARES UNDER VINE	105
VITICULTURE METHOD	Conventional

Velenosi is an all-female operation. That was not a decision by Attilio Pagli, consultant winemaker of the first water, but stems from the character of Angela Velenosi. The winery owes its success to never making a wrong move, thanks to Angela's feminine sensitivity, rendered even more concrete by Katia Gabrielli's bravura in the cellar. Their line is broad and masterfully executed, down to the two new versions of Lacrima di Morro d'Alba. All display a common stylistic thread that makes the wines here both varietal and house-distinctive. Three Glasses again went to Roggio del Filare for its customary measured elegance while Ludi fell short by a hair's breadth. From montepulciano with help from Bordeaux varieties, it bursts with energy-laden, crunchy fruit. Velenosi makes one of Italy's best rosé sparklers, The Rose. Not far behind in performance are the generous, rich Brut, and Pecorino Villa Angela, which in its second year of production has acquired lovely crispness and varietal fidelity. Brecciarolo, an everyday quaffer, has never been so tasty. Praise is superfluous when buoyant sales underline the fine success of this ever-busy winery.

Vignamato

VIA BATTINEBBIA, 4
60038 SAN PAOLO DI JESI [AN]
TEL. 0731779197
www.vignamato.com

ANNUAL PRODUCTION	55,000 bottles
HECTARES UNDER VINE	16
VITICULTURE METHOD	Conventional

Maurizio Ceci has put in place an ideal system for running Vignamatto. He and his eldest son work the vine rows while his wife Serenella, helped by their younger offspring, attend to the cellar operations. And all of this is carried out with common sense and sensitivity, those small-farmer virtues that are becoming increasingly rare. It is all the more disappointing then that their Verdicchio Riserva Ambrosia fell just shy of receiving our Three Glasses. It opens to lavish, optimally ripe fruit, then develops succulent force on the palate, plus a nice interleaving of tannin and pulpy fruit, finally concluding with a compelling finish that is mineral-edged and citrussy. Verdicchio Versiano performed impressively too, offering a delicate bouquet in which scents of blossoms and mint quickly appear, then a very expressive palate that builds with constrained but steady energy to considerable volume. The less expensive Verdicchio Valle delle Lame is its usual fine self, showing linear but polished and fully laden with crisp, luscious fruit. The intriguing Rosso Piceno Campalliano is also fruit-driven, expanding onto a rounded, stylish palate.

Wine	Rating
● Rosso Piceno Sup. Roggio del Filare '05	♟♟♟ 6
● Offida Rosso Ludi '05	♟♟ 6
⊙ The Rose Brut Rosé '05	♟♟ 6
○ Falerio dei Colli Ascolani V. Solaria '07	♟ 3*
○ Offida Pecorino Villa Angela '07	♟♟ 4
○ Rêve Chardonnay '06	♟♟ 5
○ Velenosi Brut M. Cl.	♟♟ 5
● Lacrima di Morro d'Alba '07	♟♟ 3*
● Lacrima di Morro d'Alba Sup. '07	♟♟ 4
● Rosso Piceno Sup. Brecciarolo '05	♟♟ 3*
○ Verdicchio dei Castelli di Jesi Cl. '07	♟ 4
○ Villa Angela Chardonnay '07	♟ 4
● Rosso Piceno Sup. Roggio del Filare '04	♟♟♟ 6
● Rosso Piceno Sup. Roggio del Filare '03	♟♟♟ 6

Wine	Rating
○ Verdicchio dei Castelli di Jesi Cl. Ambrosia Ris. '05	♟ 4
○ Verdicchio dei Castelli di Jesi Cl. Sup. Versiano '07	♟♟ 4*
○ Verdicchio dei Castelli di Jesi Cl. Valle delle Lame '07	♟♟ 3*
● Rosso Piceno Campalliano '05	♟♟ 4
● Esino Rosso Rosolaccio '06	♟ 3
○ Verdicchio dei Castelli di Jesi Passito Antares '06	♟ 5
● Rosso Piceno Campalliano '04	♟♟ 4
○ Verdicchio dei Castelli di Jesi Cl. Sup. Versiano '06	♟♟ 4
○ Verdicchio dei Castelli di Jesi Cl. Sup. Versiano '05	♟♟ 4
○ Verdicchio dei Castelli di Jesi Cl. Valle delle Lame '06	♟♟ 3

Villa Pigna

C.DA CIAFONE, 63
63035 OFFIDA [AP]
TEL. 073687525
www.villapigna.com

Zaccagnini

VIA SALMÀGINA, 9/10
60039 STAFFOLO [AN]
TEL. 0731779892
www.zaccagnini.it

ANNUAL PRODUCTION	600,000 bottles
HECTARES UNDER VINE	100
VITICULTURE METHOD	Conventional

The winery founded by Agostino Rozzi offers four particularly impressive wines. Cabernasco 2005, half montepulciano and the balance a mix of cabernet sauvignon and merlot, went to the national taste-offs. It has a beguiling nose of raspberry, blueberry and other fruit caressed by subtle herbaceousness, and a well-fruited, generous palate, although the finish is a tad tight. The all-montepulciano Rozzano 2006 shows an intriguing bouquet of very well-delineated blueberry preserves. The palate is dense and self-assured, but the tannins tend to tamp down somewhat its pulpy fruit. Passerina Majia 2007 displays impressive varietal character, its ripe fruit bringing forth rich impressions of honey and citrus zest plus a subtle touch of botrytis. The palate, though, is very crisp and vibrant. Pecorino Rugiasco is less complex but displays a velvety texture, lovely notes of citrus and almond and lengthy progression. So we have four pieces of evidence to show that the restructuring of the winery carried out in recent years by Annamaria Rozzi, Costantino's daughter, was successful. Villa Pigna takes its place among the most reliable producers in the Piceno area.

ANNUAL PRODUCTION	200,000 bottles
HECTARES UNDER VINE	25
VITICULTURE METHOD	Conventional

Rosella Zaccagnini manages this family winery, where top-notch consultant Alberto Musatti assists in the cellar. We recently noticed a slight drop-off in wine quality but this year's Verdicchios are great. The house style is solidly in the local tradition, focusing on straightforward interpretations of the variety from fruit grown in the hills on the right bank of the Esino river. Maestro di Staffolo is emblematic. An appealing, clean-edged varietal mix of blossoms and mineral essences leaps from the glass and the crisp, clean palate continues that headlong energy into a savoury finale. Salmàgina is similar but subtler. The nose displays enrapturing florality while the palate shows graceful restraint. The more reasonably priced Il Castello is in the old style, drinking deliciously and driving well. Cesolano is a classy dried-grape Verdicchio. A lovely gold and pungent on the nose, it shows a measured palate with just a nice balance of acidity and sweetness. Finally, Vigna Vescovi is mainly cabernet sauvignon, with some montepulciano and pinot nero. The nose highlights good fruit ripeness and the palate is rounded and supple.

● Offida Rosso Cabernasco '05	豆豆	5
● Rozzano '06	豆豆	5
○ Offida Passerina Majia '07	豆豆	4*
○ Offida Pecorino Rugiasco '07	豆豆	4*
○ Falerio dei Colli Ascolani Pliniano '07	豆	3
● Rosso Piceno Eliano '07	豆	3
● Rosso Piceno Sup. Vergaio '06	豆	4
● Rozzano '03	豆豆豆	5
● Rozzano '05	豆豆	5
● Rozzano '04	豆豆	5
● Offida Rosso Cabernasco '04	豆豆	5
● Offida Rosso Cabernasco '03	豆豆	5

○ Verdicchio dei Castelli di Jesi Cl. Maestro di Staffolo Ris. '05	豆豆	5
○ Cesolano '01	豆豆	5
○ Verdicchio dei Castelli di Jesi Cl. Sup. Salmàgina '07	豆豆	4*
○ Brut	豆	4
○ Verdicchio dei Castelli di Jesi Cl. Il Castello '07	豆	3
● Vigna Vescovi '04	豆	5
○ Verdicchio dei Castelli di Jesi Cl. Sup. Pier delle Vigne '04	豆豆	4
○ Verdicchio dei Castelli di Jesi Cl. Sup. Salmàgina '05	豆豆	4
● Vigna Vescovi '03	豆豆	5

OTHER WINERIES

Accadia

FRAZ. CASTELLARO
VIA AMMORTO, 19
60048 SERRA SAN QUIRICO [AN]
TEL. 0731859007
az.accadia@tiscali.it

Angelo Accadia's Verdicchios are as good as ever, both mountain grown, but with different characters. Consono is expressive, with vibrant acidity that softens into a smooth finale, while Conscio's intense citrus aromas continue onto a succulent palate, closing with refined savouriness.

O Verdicchio dei Castelli di Jesi Cl.		
Consono '07	🍷🍷	3*
O Verdicchio dei Castelli di Jesi Cl.		
Sup. Conscio '07	🍷🍷	4

Maria Letizia Allevi

VIA ORAZI, 58
63030 CASTORANO [AP]
TEL. 073687646
www.vinimida.it

Allevi and husband Roberto Corradetti direct this winery with its three hectares under vines. Both wines are excellent. The montepulciano-only Mida Rosso is emphatic, sturdy and warmly alcoholic. Mida Bianco is a Trebbiano fermented on the skins.

O Mida Bianco '06	🍷🍷	4*
● Mida Rosso '05	🍷🍷	4*

Mario & Giorgio Brunori

V.LE DELLA VITTORIA, 103
60035 JESI [AN]
TEL. 0731207213
www.brunori.it

We can always rely on the Verdicchios from Carlo Brunori and son Giorgio. San Nicolò is great and eminently varietal, showing rich, ripe fruit and a lengthy, flawless development. Le Gemme displays less volume but expresses itself very well indeed.

O Verdicchio dei Castelli di Jesi Cl.		
Le Gemme '07	🍷🍷	3*
O Verdicchio dei Castelli di Jesi Cl.		
Sup. San Nicolò '07	🍷🍷	4

Irene Cameli

C.DA GAICO, 19
63030 CASTORANO [AP]
TEL. 073687435
info@vinorossomarche.it

Giovanni Allevi tends little more than four hectares, almost all planted to sangiovese and montepulciano. Dolce Vite, sangiovese only, releases balsam and spice then builds an elegant, full-flavoured palate. Carpe Diem is a rosé with lip-smacking, tangy acidity to enliven its fine fruit.

☉ Carpe Diem '07	🍷🍷	3*
● Dolce Vite Sangiovese '05	🍷🍷	4
● Ozio '04	🍷	4
O Offida Passerina Milia '07	🍷	3

Capinera

VIA CROCETTE, 12
62010 MORROVALLE [MC]
TEL. 0733222444
www.capinera.com

The Capinera brothers excel at marrying sangiovese and cabernet in their fine reds. Equal parts of both go into Beato Masseo, a distinctive, self-confident wine with generous fruit on the nose and alcohol on the palate. Giacopetto, largely sangiovese, is crisp, approachable and tasty.

● Colli Maceratesi Rosso		
Beato Masseo Ris. '05	🍷🍷	5
● Colli Maceratesi Rosso		
Giacopetto '06	🍷🍷	3*

Enrico Ceci

VIA SANTA MARIA D'ARCO, 7
60038 SAN PAOLO DI JESI [AN]
TEL. 0731779033
www.verdicchiomarche.it/ceci

Enrico Ceci's Verdicchios have always been very traditional and austere. This straightforward Santa Maria d'Arco stands out for its commendable elegance and tasty acidity. The Rosso Piceno of the same name is dry and evolved, with sound fruit and a lively palate.

● Rosso Piceno		
Santa Maria d'Arco '06	🍷🍷	4*
O Verdicchio dei Castelli di Jesi Cl.		
Sup. Santa Maria d'Arco '07	🍷🍷	4*

OTHER WINERIES

Cantina Cològnola

LOC. COLÒGNOLA
62011 CINGOLI [MC]
TEL. 0733616438
www.agrarialombardi.it

From Antonietta Lombardi's whites, we preferred the Esino Bianco to the Verdicchio. Condotto, half verdicchio with some trebbiano and malvasia, offers blossoms and straw then a succulent, vibrant palate that drives to a lengthy, smooth finish. Passito Cingulum is refined and long-lingering.

O Esino Bianco Condotto '07	🍷🍷 3*
O Verdicchio dei Castelli di Jesi Passito Cingulum '06	🍷🍷 5
O Verdicchio dei Castelli Cl. di Jesi Ghiffa '07	🍷 4

Degli Azzoni Avogadro Carradori

C.SO CARRADORI, 13
62010 MONTEFANO [MC]
TEL. 0733850002
www.degliazzoni.it

This winery's stars are the montepulciano Passatempo and Rosso Cantalupo, half merlot with montepulciano and cabernet. The first opens with smooth, sweet oak then offers a first-rate palate while the second gives fine, fleshy fruit. Bianco di Cantalupo, verdicchio with a bit of sauvignon, is well made.

O Bianco di Cantalupo '07	🍷🍷 3*
● Passatempo '06	🍷🍷 5
● Rosso Cantalupo '06	🍷🍷 3*
O Beldiletto Brut '07	🍷 4

Fiorano

C.DA FIORANO, 19
63030 COSSIGNANO [AP]
TEL. 073598446
www.agrifiorano.it

Paolo Beretta left Milan to make wine in Marche. His Terre di Giobbe 2006 is still resting in the cellar but Pecorino Donna Orgilla is wonderful. Intense draughts of crisp citrus precede an expansive, full-flavoured palate. The standard-label Sangiovese, Fiorano, is straightforward and well fruited.

O Donna Orgilla Pecorino '07	🍷🍷 4*
● Fiorano Sangiovese '07	🍷 3
● Rosso Piceno Sup. Terre di Giobbe '05	🍷🍷 4

Cantine Fontezoppa

C.DA SAN DOMENICO, 24
62012 CIVITANOVA MARCHE [MC]
TEL. 0733790504
www.cantinefontezoppa.it

From Piero Luzi's many bottlings, we were most impressed by the all-cabernet sauvignon Carapetto. Austere and firm, it has fine acidic grip and an aromatic palate. Just as fine is the new Marche Rosso, from sangiovese and cabernet, which shows even progression and terrific, crisp fruit.

● Carapetto '06	🍷🍷 5
● Marche Rosso '06	🍷🍷 2*
● Colli Maceratesi Rosso Vardò '07	🍷 4
O Verdicchio di Matelica '07	🍷 4

Lanari

FRAZ. VARANO
VIA POZZO, 142
60029 ANCONA
TEL. 0712861343
cantinalanari@libero.it

Luca Lanari is a dedicated, careful producer but we noticed a slight quality dip in his reds. Conero Aretè releases notes of smooth, ripe fruit but the palate shows tight and tannic. Fibbio is a tad coarse on the nose and very stiff tannins tend to dry the mouth.

● Conero Aretè Ris. '06	🍷🍷 6
● Conero Fibbio Ris. '06	🍷🍷 6
● Rosso Conero '07	🍷 4
● Rosso Conero D'Inclite Terre '06	🍷 5

Luciano Landi

VIA GAVIGLIANO, 16
60030 BELVEDERE OSTRENSE [AN]
TEL. 073162353
www.aziendalandi.it

Luciano Landi's Passito di Lacrima is outstanding. Opaque to the eye, it releases wild cherry and forest berry fruit while the palate is velvet smooth and alluring. Gavigliano gives thick, creamy fruit with a nice edge to it, but its vibrant drinkability comes up against a stiffish finale.

● Lacrima di Morro d'Alba Passito '06	🍷🍷 6
● Lacrima di Morro d'Alba Sup. Gavigliano '06	🍷🍷 4*
● Lacrima di Morro d'Alba '07	🍷 3

OTHER WINERIES

Malacari

VIA ENRICO MALACARI, 6
60020 OFFAGNA [AN]
TEL. 0717207606
malacari@tin.it

Alessandro Starabba's character is reflected in his sound, reliable wines. His Rosso Conero unveils thrusting, succulent progression while Grigiano serves up rich, ripe morello cherry on the nose and builds a powerful, austere palate whose massive tannins do nothing to impede excellent development.

● Conero Grigiano Ris. '04	♥♥	5
● Rosso Conero '06	♥♥	4*
● Rosso Conero '05	♥♥	4

Clara Marcelli

VIA FONTE VECCHIA, 9
63030 CASTORANO [AP]
TEL. 073687289
info@claramarcelli.it

Emanuele and Daniele Colletta, Clara Marcelli's children, ably manage this organic operation. Their K'un is fabulous, with rich, multi-layered notes of red berry fruit and underbrush, a palate that is broad and delicious, and dense-packed tannins. Pecorino Irata boasts well-ripened aromatics.

● K'un '06	♥♥	4*
○ Offida Pecorino Irata '07	♥♥	4*
● Corbù '07	♥	3

Maurizio Marconi

VIA MELANO, 25
60030 SAN MARCELLO [AN]
TEL. 0731267223
www.cantinemarconi.it

Maurizio Marconi is back in the Guide with three top-notch wines. His Verdicchio Etichetta Nera shows admirable fruit, energetic progression and an intensely flavoured finish. Classico is less complex but just as fruit-filled while Lacrima Superiore is rich, polished and impressively varietal.

● Lacrima di Morro d'Alba Sup. Etichetta Nera '06	♥♥	4*
○ Verdicchio dei Castelli di Jesi Cl. '07	♥♥	3*
○ Verdicchio dei Castelli di Jesi Cl. Sup Etichetta Nera '06	♥♥	4*

Claudio Morelli

V.LE ROMAGNA, 47B
61032 FANO [PU]
TEL. 0721823352
www.claudiomorelli.it

We liked two of the three Bianchellos that Morelli releases. San Cesareo presents a duet of fruit and almost herbal fresh greens before its rich-flavoured, forward-driving palate. Borgo Torre releases richer, riper fruit and follows with more volume and roundedness, as well as crisp drinkability.

○ Bianchello del Metauro Borgo Torre '07	♥♥	4*
○ Bianchello del Metauro S. Cesareo '07	♥♥	3*

Pantaleone

VIA COLONNATA ALTA, 118
63100 ASCOLI PICENO
TEL. 3478757476
pantaloni@hotmail.it

Federica and Francesca Pantaloni's production is modest but their quality is high. We liked Io Boccascena, a montepulciano and cabernet blend with generous, pulpy fruit and a power-filled palate with glossy tannins. Equally good marks go to Sipario, a partnering of sangiovese and cabernet.

● Io Boccascena '06	♥♥	4
● Sipario '06	♥♥	3*
● Atto I '07	♥	3
○ Chicca '07	♥	2

Poggio Montali

VIA FONTE ESTATE, 6
60030 MONTE ROBERTO [AN]
TEL. 0731702825
www.poggiomontali.it

Carla Panicucci gave Conero Poggio al Cerro considerable cellaring. It is now integrated and just right, showing ripe fragrant fruit and a crisp, heady palate. Cerqueto, an equal blend of montepulciano and sangiovese, is more straightforward, quite supple and offers expansive, well-nuanced fruit.

● Cerqueto '06	♥♥	5
● Conero Poggio al Cerro Ris. '04	♥♥	5
○ Verdicchio dei Castelli di Jesi Cl. Sup. '07	♥	4

OTHER WINERIES

Pontemagno

VIA BORGO SANTA MARIA
60038 SAN PAOLO DI JESI [AN]
TEL. 0731703214
www.piersantivini.com

Quota 311 is a scrumptious Verdicchio, with fragrances of delicious citrus and pineapple, and a fresh, vibrant palate. Very ripe grapes yielded a Bachero with sweet fruit on the nose and fatness in the mouth while it ends on a note of tangy acidity. Conero Il Rubjo is impressively spicy and balsamic.

● Conero Il Rubjo Ris. '04	♟♟ 4
○ Verdicchio dei Castelli di Jesi Cl. Quota 311 '07	♟♟ 2*
○ Verdicchio dei Castelli di Jesi Cl. Sup. Bachero '07	♟♟ 3*

Rio Maggio

C.DA VALLONE, 41
63014 MONTEGRANARO [AP]
TEL. 0734889587
www.riomaggio.it

The marks for Rio Maggio are not quite as high as usual but its principal wines are fine performers. The nose on Rosso Piceno Granarijs shows pungent spice and the mouth is lean and complex. Falerio Telusiano has appreciable verve and rich flavours, as well as a finish laden with tangy citrus.

○ Falerio dei Colli Ascolani Telusiano '07	♟♟ 4*
● Rosso Piceno Granarijs '06	♟♟ 5
○ Colle Monteverde Sauvignon '07	♟ 4

Sabbionare

VIA SABBIONARE, 10
60036 MONTECAROTTO [AN]
TEL. 0731889004
sabbionare@libero.it

Donatella Paoloni's Verdicchios just get better all the time. Sabbionare went to the national finals for its blossoms and citrus, dynamic palate, succulent, smooth fruit and lively acidity that keeps everything in balance. I Pratelli is full fruited, particularly on the crisp, refreshing palate.

○ Verdicchio dei Castelli di Jesi Cl. Sup. Sabbionare '07	♟♟ 4*
○ Verdicchio dei Castelli di Jesi Cl. I Pratelli '07	♟♟ 3*

Saputi

C.DA FIASTRA, 2
62020 COLMURANO [MC]
TEL. 0733508137
www.saputi.it

Alvaro Saputi introduces the nicely fragrant, richly flavoured Verdicchio Giuvì but Castru Vecchiu remains its classic self. From the maceratino, or ribona, grape, it is broad but measured, silky and delicious on the palate, with fine acidity. Rosso Piceno Monte Nereto has fruit and volume.

○ Colli Maceratesi Ribona Castru Vecchiu '07	♟♟ 3*
○ Verdicchio dei Castelli di Jesi Cl. Giuvì '07	♟♟ 3*
● Rosso Piceno Monte Nereto '06	♟ 3

Fattoria Serra San Martino

VIA SAN MARTINO, 1
60030 SERRA DE' CONTI [AN]
TEL. 0731878025
www.serrasanmartino.com

Kirsten and Thomas Weydemann's young cellar makes three excellent wines from their three hectares. Merlot Costa dei Zoppi is complex and evolved while Il Roccuccio, from montepulciano, merlot and syrah, shows spicy and deep on the palate. The sagrantino Lo Sconosciuto has ripe fruit and impressive density.

● Costa dei Zoppi Merlot '05	♟♟ 5
● Il Roccuccio '05	♟♟ 4*
● Lo Sconosciuto '05	♟♟ 6

Tenuta dell'Ugolino

LOC. MACINE
VIA COPPARONI, 32
60031 CASTELPLANIO [AN]
TEL. 360487114
www.tenutaugolino.it

Year after year, Andrea Petrini's skills as a grower are improving, as are his Verdicchios. Vigneto del Balluccio boasts a stunning palate, subtle yet chewy and utterly delicious. Classico offers lovely white peach and appreciably sharp acidity that gives it considerable seductive power.

○ Verdicchio dei Castelli di Jesi Cl. Sup. Vigneto del Balluccio '07	♟♟ 4*
○ Verdicchio dei Castelli di Jesi Cl. '07	♟♟ 3*

UMBRIA

The history of Umbrian wine, at least in the most modern sense of the term, has largely been written over the last 20 years. Of course, prior to this there was Lungarotti and the invention of an extraordinary territory – Torgiano – but this was a one-off entrepreneurial initiative. It is no surprise that the wines have been credited with putting the region on the world wine map. Then there was Orvieto but its noble past was scarcely reflected in the post-war period. Sagrantino is similar, in that its name based mainly on sweet wines, and it was not until the 1990s and the inspired genius of Caprai that the wine world sat up and took notice. In short, it is only recently that Umbria has become the region we know today with a growing number of estates and varieties, plenty of media and institutional attention and no less than 11 DOCs with two DOCGs. As in other revolutions, the early turbulent, heady days have been followed by a period of calm and reflection. Across the region's entire wine map, wines are seeking sharper definition and clearer hierarchies, as well as distinctive stylistic, territorial and estate identities. Now is not the right time to hazard absolute judgements or to stamp a variety or a zone with a specific label. Unrealized potential, a radical change of direction; you never know what's around the corner. Just look at Montefalco and Sagrantino, which to our minds still haven't found a length. The promise is enormous but further study may be needed to bring out the full potential of territory and variety, so no hasty generalizations. The most urgent issue is the rather slack regulations that allow the sale of wines when they are still undeveloped, difficult to understand and nowhere near expressing any kind of balance. We shall see. Great wines destined to become even greater include Marco Caprai's 25 Anni '05, an inimitable landmark, Còlpetrone's new Gold '04 selection, confirmation from Perticaia's '05, and Francesco Antano's cru, Colle Allodole '05, which takes home its first trophy after years of hard work. Entering the hallowed Three Glass circle for the first time is Barberani's Villa Monticelli Rosso '04 from the Orvieto hills overlooking Lake Corbara. But there are plenty of others. Alongside the usual immense performance from the '06 Cervaro della Sala, the Torgiano Rubesco Riserva Vigna Monticchio is a pinnacle of territorial expression and, thanks to the fine 2004 growing year, offers fans an edition full of thrilling appeal. It's the same story for wines like the Cotarellas' Montiano '06, the latest in a long line of must-try bottles that is actually obtained from the estate's vineyards in the neighbouring region of Lazio, near Montefiascone.

Adanti

LOC. ARQUATA
06031 BEVAGNA [PG]
TEL. 0742360295
www.cantineadanti.com

ANNUAL PRODUCTION	150,000 bottles
HECTARES UNDER VINE	30
VITICULTURE METHOD	Conventional

There is a lot of Sagrantino history in the house and vineyards belonging to the Adanti family. The story has taken shape over time, from the first rows of vines planted in the early 1970s to the 30 hectares of what today is recognized as one of the landmark brands in the zone. In recent years, renovation has given the cellar new momentum and there is a new arrival in consultant oenologist Maurizio Castelli. He brings solid support to the skilled, passionate Daniele Palini, son of Alvaro, a real character who knows all there is to know about the estate and the entire territory. This year's wines include two fascinating versions of Sagrantino that earned a place on our final tasting tables. The dry wine, from the substantially typical '04 growing year, displays its customary energy derived from minerally notes, depth and relaxed structure, although it is a little more evolved than expected. The '05 Passito is an absolute thoroughbred, perhaps the best of its category. It is flavoursome and perfectly balanced, full of dried fruit and elegant spice aromas. The Montefalco Rosso '06 also put on a fine performance.

Antonelli - San Marco

LOC. SAN MARCO, 60
06036 MONTEFALCO [PG]
TEL. 0742379158
www.antonellisanmarco.it

ANNUAL PRODUCTION	300,000 bottles
HECTARES UNDER VINE	45
VITICULTURE METHOD	Conventional

Filippo Antonelli is a mild, thoughtful man who likes to make a thorough, honest analysis of every situation. He's a bit like his wines, which low key rather than in your face, opening out slowly to reveal an elegant, refined style that can be difficult to grasp but is always deeply fascinating. In our opinion this is the best route for an old estate that aims to develop and improve without sacrificing any of its true character. This year sees a newcomer in the form of the wine that was also the one that most impressed us: Montefalco Sagrantino Pannone, a selection vinified separately for the first time, which promises to be one of the future's great classics. It is slightly penalized by the growing year, 2003, which leaves it roughish and lacking in harmony. As for the other wines on offer, Montefalco Rosso Riserva '05 is elegant and flavoursome. This year's Sagrantino is good but fails to achieve the standards of last year's edition, and the Passito is also nice. The flowery Montefalco Rosso '06 is extremely drinkable and the new Trebbiano Spoletino '07, a white, and the Grechetto, also '07, are excellent.

● Montefalco Sagrantino Arquata '04	♛♛ 6
● Montefalco Sagrantino Passito Arquata '05	♛♛ 7
● Montefalco Rosso Arquata '06	♛♛ 4*
○ Colli Martani Grechetto '07	♛ 3
● Montefalco Sagrantino Arquata '02	♛♛ 6
● Montefalco Sagrantino Arquata '01	♛♛ 6
● Montefalco Sagrantino Passito '99	♛♛ 7
● Montefalco Sagrantino Passito '01	♛♛ 6
● Montefalco Sagrantino Passito Arquata '04	♛♛ 7

● Montefalco Rosso Ris. '05	♛♛ 5
● Montefalco Sagrantino Pannone '03	♛♛ 7
○ Colli Martani Grechetto '07	♛♛ 3*
● Montefalco Rosso '06	♛♛ 4*
● Montefalco Sagrantino '05	♛♛ 6
● Montefalco Sagrantino Passito '05	♛♛ 6
○ Trebbiano Spoletino '07	♛♛ 4*
● Baiocco '06	♛ 3
● Montefalco Sagrantino '04	♛♛ 6
● Montefalco Rosso Ris. '04	♛♛ 5
● Montefalco Sagrantino '99	♛♛ 6
● Montefalco Sagrantino '01	♛♛ 7

Barberani - Vallesanta

LOC. CERRETO
05023 BASCHI [TR]
TEL. 0763341820
www.barberani.it

ANNUAL PRODUCTION	350,000 bottles
HECTARES UNDER VINE	55
VITICULTURE METHOD	Conventional

Some producers do an excellent job while maintaining a low profile, working hard and improving a step at a time. They are well aware that wine does not appreciate peaks, troughs or extreme procedures. There is a longer, more arduous road and it can be dispiriting if it means remaining out of the spotlight. But ultimately this way is the most rewarding if it leads to success. Metaphors aside, Barberani in Orvieto, a splendid estate founded in 1962 in the hills around Lake Corbara, is one of the most solid in Orvieto, and this year won its first Three Glass trophy. The wine is a fabulous Villa Monticelli Rosso '04, obtained from 50 per cent sangiovese with equal parts of merlot and cabernet offering black cherry and sweet spice aromas with the odd intriguing hint of balsam. The palate is complex and layered yet also enjoyably relaxed, intensely vibrant and fruity. And more can we say about Calcaia? One of the best Orvieto Muffatos on the market, it gives saffron-like aromas and brings to mind Sauternes. The rest of the range did well, with the Orvieto Classico Superiore Pomaio '05, matured in large barrels, deserving a special mention.

Bigi

LOC. PONTE GIULIO
05018 ORVIETO [TR]
TEL. 0763315888
www.cantinebigi.it

ANNUAL PRODUCTION	4,300,000 bottles
HECTARES UNDER VINE	196
VITICULTURE METHOD	Conventional

The Gruppo Italiano Vini estate in Orvieto continues to impress by virtue of its efforts to improve winemaking practices both in the zone and on the property itself, where reliability is a watchword. The wines are balanced and very often have equally balanced prices. For example, the Grechetto Strozza Volpe '07, is a white that fascinates from the outset with its magnolia-led flowery aromas and pear and banana fruit. The palate nicely fuses acid backbone and considerable richness of flavour, well supported by a full body with superb structure and long-lingering continuity in the finish. The Sartiano '06, a red, is up to its usual standards. Obtained from a blend of sangiovese, merlot and pinot nero, it offers youthful but fairly intense aromas ranging from cherry to clear balsamic notes, and a well-made palate that is a little behind with its maturation curve. The Orvieto Classico Torricella '07 is simple yet pleasing but the hot growing year has exacted a price in terms of elegance.

● Lago di Corbara Rosso Villa Monticelli '04	♈♈♈ 5
○ Orvieto Cl. Sup. Calcaia '05	♈♈ 6
○ Grechetto '07	♈♈ 4*
● Lago di Corbara Foresco '06	♈♈ 4*
○ Orvieto Cl. Sup. Castagnolo '07	♈♈ 4*
○ Orvieto Cl. Sup. Pomaio Villa Monticelli '05	♈♈ 5
○ Orvieto Cl. '07	♈ 4
● Lago di Corbara Rosso Villa Monticelli '01	♉♉ 5
○ Orvieto Cl. Sup. Calcaia '04	♉♉ 6
○ Orvieto Cl. Sup. Calcaia '03	♉♉ 6
○ Orvieto Cl. Sup. Calcaia '97	♉♉ 5
○ Orvieto Cl. Sup. Calcaia '00	♉♉ 6

● Sartiano '06	♈♈ 5
○ Strozza Volpe Grechetto '07	♈♈ 3*
○ Orvieto Cl. Vigneto Torricella '07	♈ 4
● Sartiano '05	♉♉ 4
● Tamante '06	♉♉ 3
● Tamante '05	♉♉ 3*

★ Arnaldo Caprai

LOC. TORRE
06036 MONTEFALCO [PG]
TEL. 0742378802
www.arnaldocaprai.it

ANNUAL PRODUCTION	750,000 bottles
HECTARES UNDER VINE	136
VITICULTURE METHOD	Conventional

Anyone who expects a wine to perform at its peak immediately, or applies to one type parameters that belong to another, will run the risk of getting things wrong. If the wine in question is a Sagrantino, the risk is even higher and with Marco Caprai's 25 Anni it becomes a certainty. This wine is so rich and complex as to be almost unapproachable, at least until it has had a few months in bottle. But as the years pass, it reveals all its power and energy, eventually reaching heady heights of elegance. Those who have had the great good fortune to taste a '93, a '95 or a '98 will know exactly what we are talking about. The '05 version is a monumental wine that needs only time. It's another of tomorrow's great classics from this territory. By contrast, the Collepiano '05 is excellent and already enjoyable, giving wild berry and sweet spice aromas. We also applaud the return after a long absence of the Montefalco Rosso Riserva '05. The other wines on offer are all very good. At least for those who, like us, would expect a Caprai wine to behave like a Caprai.

Cardeto

FRAZ. SFERRACAVALLO
LOC. CARDETO
05018 ORVIETO [TR]
TEL. 0763341286
www.cardeto.com

ANNUAL PRODUCTION	3,000,000 bottles
HECTARES UNDER VINE	880
VITICULTURE METHOD	Conventional

If you consider that some of the vine stock dates back to the 1950s, and that today there are over 800 hectares distributed among its many member growers, you immediately understand that this is one of the most important wine operations in Orvieto. But these numbers are only a small part of the picture and do not do full justice to a winery that is also significant in terms of quality and value for money. Turning to the labels on offer, Nero della Greca '06 is a pure Sangiovese aged for 12 months in barrique. It's an impressive wine, if a tad extreme in the ripeness of its fruit and its concentration. The nose offers aromatics from bramble to mulberry blossom to balsamic sensations while the palate is very compact and shows good tannic texture. We preferred the Arciato '06, an elegant, citrussy Bordeaux blend with traces of minerality that lift the palate. Rupestro '07 is also rather good, it's a merlot-sangiovese mix with grassy, fruity notes in lovely synergy. On the white front, Grechetto '07, Orvieto Classico Pierleone '07 and Orvieto Classico Superiore Febeo '07 all made a good impression.

● Montefalco Sagrantino 25 Anni '05	▼▼▼ 8
● Montefalco Rosso Ris. '05	▼▼ 7
● Montefalco Sagrantino Collepiano '05	▼▼ 7
○ Anima Umbra Bianco '07	▼▼ 4*
○ Colli Martani Grechetto Grecante '07	▼▼ 4*
● Montefalco Rosso '06	▼▼ 5
● Montefalco Sagrantino Passito '05	▼▼ 8
● Anima Umbra Rosso '06	▼ 4
● Montefalco Sagrantino 25 Anni '99	♛♛♛ 8
● Montefalco Sagrantino 25 Anni '98	♛♛♛ 8
● Montefalco Sagrantino 25 Anni '97	♛♛♛ 8
● Montefalco Sagrantino 25 Anni '96	♛♛♛ 8
● Montefalco Sagrantino 25 Anni '95	♛♛♛ 8
● Montefalco Sagrantino 25 Anni '04	♛♛♛ 8
● Montefalco Sagrantino Collepiano '02	♛♛♛ 7

● Arciato '06	▼▼ 5
○ Grechetto '07	▼▼ 3*
● Nero della Greca '06	▼▼ 5
○ Orvieto Cl. Pierleone '07	▼▼ 3*
○ Orvieto Cl. Sup. Febeo '07	▼▼ 4*
● Rupestro '07	▼▼ 3*
● Alborato '07	▼ 3
○ Colbadia '07	▼ 4
● Nero della Greca '04	♛♛ 4*
● Nero della Greca '01	♛♛ 5
● Arciato '04	♛♛ 4
● Nero della Greca '05	♛♛ 5

Carini

FRAZ. COLLE UMBERTO
S.DA DEL TEGOLARO
06070 PERUGIA
TEL. 0755829102
www.agrariacarini.it

ANNUAL PRODUCTION	40,000 bottles
HECTARES UNDER VINE	10
VITICULTURE METHOD	Conventional

This little gem of an estate at Colle Umberto has made quite a name for itself over the last few years and stands comparison with the best in the region. Enjoying the cool temperatures of Mount Tezio and the Mediterranean climate of Lake Trasimeno, it has earned its place among the top Umbrian estates. All credit to those who believed in this project and worked so hard each day to help it reach the levels it has achieved today. This year brings us a chardonnay, pinot bianco and grechetto-based Poggio Canneto '07 that has never been so good. The Òscano '07 also lived up to all expectations. It's a best buy obtained from local sangiovese and is very pleasing indeed. But it was the Tegolaro '06 that turned out to be the star turn at our tastings. Although an international wine from merlot, cabernet and a little sangiovese, it is a bona fide Umbrian product with a personal style that shows elegant and complex rather than muscular. It's as good a red as you'll find in central Italy. Rich notes of wild berries and tar announce a creamy palate with gorgeous tannic texture and a lingering finish.

La Carraia

LOC. TORDIMONTE, 56
05018 ORVIETO [TR]
TEL. 0763304013
www.lacarraia.it

ANNUAL PRODUCTION	550,000 bottles
HECTARES UNDER VINE	119
VITICULTURE METHOD	Conventional

Founded in 1988 at Tordimonte by the Gialletti and Cotarella families of outstanding growers and oenologists, La Carraia has over the years demonstrated consistent quality and an ability to reinvent itself. It is no coincidence that the wines feature in the upper echelons of our score sheet, winning – or coming very close to – our highest awards. Although this year's line-up is missing its heavyweight, we enjoyed the rest of the labels offered by the estate. The Fobiano '06, a Bordeaux blend based predominantly on merlot, went all the way to our finals: dark, dense, perhaps a tad overly concentrated, its nose opens on notes of black cherry and coffee and although consistent on the palate, it is still in search of its true identity. We applauded the usual fine performance from Giro di Vite '06, a varietal Montepulciano, and Tizzonero '06 from sangiovese and montepulciano, which gives rich pepper and spice on the nose and a flavoursome palate. The Orvieto Classico Poggio Calvelli '07 is still one of the best in its class and Le Basque '07, the new white from equal parts of grechetto and viognier, put on a good show.

● Tegolaro '06	�	6
● Òscano '07	♟♟	4*
○ Poggio Canneto '07	♟♟	4*
● Tegolaro '05	♟♟	6
● Tegolaro '04	♟♟	6
● Tegolaro '02	♟♟	6
● Tegolaro '01	♟♟	6

● Fobiano '06	♟♟	5
● Giro di Vite '06	♟♟	5
○ Le Basque '07	♟♟	4*
○ Orvieto Cl. Poggio Calvelli '07	♟♟	3*
● Tizzonero '06	♟♟	4*
○ Orvieto Cl. '07	♟	2
● Sangiovese '07	♟	3
● Fobiano '99	♟♟♟	6
● Fobiano '98	♟♟♟	5
● Fobiano '03	♟♟♟	5
● Fobiano '04	♟♟	5
● Giro di Vite '04	♟♟	5
● Tizzonero '04	♟♟	4

Fattoria Colle Allodole

LOC. COLLE ALLODOLE
06031 BEVAGNA [PG]
TEL. 0742361897

ANNUAL PRODUCTION	30,000 bottles
HECTARES UNDER VINE	10
VITICULTURE METHOD	Conventional

Having been a tenant farmer on various Umbrian estates for many years, Milziade Antano in 1969 decided to buy some plots around Bevagna, where he planted vines and raised livestock. This was the start of what was and still is one of Sagrantino's symbolic figures, the founder of a cellar that today more than ever is one of the most characteristic in the entire DOCG. Much of the credit goes to Milziade's son, Francesco, a true wine man who has stepped neatly into his father's shoes to continue bringing out the full potential of this jewel of an estate. It hasn't all been plain sailing of course but the odd hiccup has only added to the estate's artisanal status, a claim very few can make these days. But when everything is running smoothly, the Fattoria's wines have very few rivals. The '05 Montefalco Sagrantino Colle delle Allodole selection has stunning energy and power, as well as austerity and extraordinary elegance. This unique, timeless red takes home Three Glasses. Thrilling as it is today, we can only wonder what delights it has in store for us in future.

Cantina dei Colli Amerini

LOC. FORNOLE
ZONA INDUSTRIALE
05022 AMELIA [TR]
TEL. 0744989721
www.colliamerini.it

ANNUAL PRODUCTION	1,000,000 bottles
HECTARES UNDER VINE	400
VITICULTURE METHOD	Conventional

Last year's tastings left us in some doubt about the general direction in which this co-operative cellar was going, to the point that we spoke about early days and wondered whether the group ought to consider changing strategy. Much of this had to do with the important role that Colli Amerini plays in the territory, safeguarding quality and promoting the local varieties. We are happy to note that the process of renewal is beginning to bear fruit. In particular, the reds presented to our panel this year are back on form. We start our notes with Carbio '06, the cellar's standard bearer obtained from a blend of merlot, cabernet, sangiovese, ciliegiolo and montepulciano, which is warm and Mediterranean. Ameroe '07 is based on merlot, ciliegiolo and montepulciano whereas Olmeto '07 is an elegant, spicy Merlot whose only defect is its rather overripe fruit. We liked the crunchy, flavoursome and very drinkable '07 edition of the Ciliegiolo. Narni 30 Anni '06 is more complex and deep, mingling fresh, ripe cherry aromas with more delicate flowery sensations. Of the whites on offer, the Grechetto '07 is good and the Malvasia Rocca Nerina '07 aromatic.

● Montefalco Sagrantino Colle delle Allodole '05	￥￥￥	7
● Montefalco Rosso Ris. '05	￥￥	6
● Montefalco Rosso '06	￥￥	5
● Montefalco Sagrantino '05	￥￥	6
● Montefalco Sagrantino Passito '05	￥￥	5
● Montefalco Sagrantino '04	￥￥	6
● Montefalco Sagrantino Colle delle Allodole '04	￥￥	7
● Montefalco Rosso Ris. '04	￥￥	6
● Montefalco Sagrantino '98	￥￥	5
● Montefalco Sagrantino '02	￥￥	6
● Montefalco Sagrantino Colle delle Allodole '98	￥￥	6

● C. Amerini Ameroe '07	￥￥	2*
● C. Amerini Rosso Sup. Carbio '06	￥￥	5
● Ciliegiolo di Narni '07	￥￥	4*
● Ciliegiolo di Narni 30 Anni '06	￥￥	6
● Olmeto '07	￥￥	4*
○ Grechetto Il Vignolo '07	￥	2
○ Rocca Nerina '07	￥	4
● C. Amerini Rosso Sup. Carbio '04	￥￥	5
● C. Amerini Rosso Sup. Carbio '99	￥￥	5
● C. Amerini Rosso Sup. Carbio '01	￥￥	5

★ Còlpetrone

LOC. MARCELLANO
VIA PONTE LA MANDRIA, 8/1
06035 GUALDO CATTANEO [PG]
TEL. 057899827
www.colpetrone.it

ANNUAL PRODUCTION	132,000 bottles
HECTARES UNDER VINE	63
VITICULTURE METHOD	Conventional

Còlpetrone, a leading Saigricola group estate in Umbria, continues to forge confidently ahead, achieving excellence in the region and proving that it has got to firm grips with a territory and a variety that are fascinating yet extremely difficult: Montefalco and sagrantino. Indeed, rather than sitting on the laurels of their previous results, the team led by managing director Guido Sodano is heading in new, creative directions. Metaphors aside, this year we were presented with an intriguing new wine that won Three Glasses and raised the Sagrantino quality bar. Gold '04 is a selection of rare, vibrant elegance that has indubitably benefited from a year longer in the bottle than some of its nearest rivals. We believe it heralds a new chapter for the type. Compact yet enjoyable, it displays depth and aromatic complexity rather than excesses of concentration, standing out for its tannic texture and unbelievably long length. The elegant, spicy Sagrantino '05 is as good as ever, as is the Passito '05 with its rich notes of wild berry fruit. Last but not least, the Montefalco Rosso '06 is excellent.

Castello di Corbara

LOC. CORBARA, 7
05018 ORVIETO [TR]
TEL. 0763304035
www.castellodicorbara.it

ANNUAL PRODUCTION	200,000 bottles
HECTARES UNDER VINE	100
VITICULTURE METHOD	Certified organic

Castello di Corbara doesn't have to invent a claim to history. It has an entry in the land register dating back to the 13th century and a long list of aristocratic families who lived here. In contrast, the Corbara wine project was conceived in 1997 under the auspices of a group of entrepreneurs who provided major investment to protect and enhance the local varieties, plant new vineyards, build a cellar and bring in consultant oenologist Franco Bernabei and his son, Marco. The results are very gratifying, particularly for the reds, and show that this estate has mastered the zone's new designated areas. The wines on offer include a show-stopping Calistri '05 from sangiovese offering faintly oaky notes mingled with a generous, fluent, fruity vein on the nose, and a fleshy palate with nice freshness and lovely tannins. The Lago di Corbara Cabernet Sauvignon '06 keeps its grassy notes in check and swathes them in a warm, fluid palate of satisfying length. Podere Il Caio Rosso '07 from sangiovese, cabernet and merlot is crisp and pleasant, but we found the Merlot De Coronis '05 a little tired.

● Montefalco Sagrantino Gold '04	▼▼▼ 8
● Montefalco Sagrantino '05	▼▼ 6
● Montefalco Rosso '06	▼▼ 4
● Montefalco Sagrantino Passito '05	▼▼ 6
● Montefalco Sagrantino '99	♈♈♈ 6
● Montefalco Sagrantino '98	♈♈♈ 5
● Montefalco Sagrantino '97	♈♈♈ 5
● Montefalco Sagrantino '96	♈♈♈ 4
● Montefalco Sagrantino '04	♈♈♈ 6
● Montefalco Sagrantino '01	♈♈♈ 6

● Calistri '05	▼▼ 5
● Lago di Corbara Cabernet Sauvignon '06	▼▼ 5
● Lago di Corbara Rosso '06	▼▼ 5
● Podere Il Caio Rosso '07	▼▼ 4*
● Lago di Corbara De Coronis '05	▼ 5
O Orvieto Cl. Sup. Podere Il Caio '07	▼ 3
● Lago di Corbara De Coronis '03	♈♈ 5
● Calistri '04	♈♈ 5
● Calistri '03	♈♈ 5
● Lago di Corbara Cabernet Sauvignon '04	♈♈ 5

Duca della Corgna

VIA ROMA, 236
06061 CASTIGLIONE DEL LAGO [PG]
TEL. 0759652493
www.ducadellacorgna.it

ANNUAL PRODUCTION 280,000 bottles
HECTARES UNDER VINE 55
VITICULTURE METHOD Conventional

Cantina del Trasimeno is a co-operative winery and the Duca della Corgna brand is its top line. It was launched several years ago, with selected fruit from some member growers, and offers an impressive range of wines at very competitive prices. This is the result of a major project to upgrade the vine stock that saw the planting of new vineyards, modernization of the vat cellar and a new maturation cellar at the historic premises in Città della Pieve. This year's wines impressed us. The Corniolo '05 from sangiovese, gamay del Trasimeno and cabernet sauvignon swept into our finals with a stunning performance that sets tobacco and minty aromas against a backdrop of ripe red fruit before the no-nonsense body fuses well with the rich boisé sensations. Divina Villa Etichetta Bianca '07 is also fabulous, showing dynamic but not forced with a pleasant, elegant raspberry palate. The Baccio del Rosso '07 from sangiovese and gamay is extraordinary value. This standard, bay leaf-themed wine is often a stand-out. Baccio del Bianco '07 from trebbiano, grechetto and malvasia is also spot on, as are the two Grechettos, Nuricante '07 and Ascanio '07.

● C. del Trasimeno Rosso Corniolo '05	🍷🍷	5
○ C. del Trasimeno Baccio del Bianco '07	🍷🍷	3*
● C. del Trasimeno Baccio del Rosso '07	🍷🍷	3*
● C. del Trasimeno Gamay Divina Villa Et. Bianca '07	🍷🍷	4*
○ C. del Trasimeno Grechetto Nuricante '07	🍷🍷	4*
○ Ascanio '07	🍷	3
● C. del Trasimeno Rosso Corniolo '03	🍷🍷 (white)	4
● C. del Trasimeno Gamay Divina Villa Et. Nera '05	🍷🍷 (white)	4
● C. del Trasimeno Rosso Corniolo '04	🍷🍷 (white)	4

★ Falesco

LOC. SAN PIETRO
05020 MONTECCHIO [TR]
TEL. 07449556
www.falesco.it

ANNUAL PRODUCTION 2,900,000 bottles
HECTARES UNDER VINE 370
VITICULTURE METHOD Conventional

Founded in 1979 at Montefiascone, the Cotarellas' estate has grown exponentially over the years. The most recent transformation is the beautiful new cellar at Montecchio which puts Falesco at the forefront of trans-regional winemaking, located as it is on the border of Umbria and Lazio. Added to this are the skills and experience of a family with few rivals in the Italian wine world. Once again, it is the magnificent Montiano '06 that wins our Three Glass prize. Complex notes of red berry fruit, elegant and crisp, melt into oak sensations. The solid, perfectly balanced structure is buttressed by remarkable freshness and tannins of refined elegance that linger on through notes of fruit and restrained vanilla and spice toastiness. The Marciliano '06 from cabernet sauvignon and franc is another fine wine, its only defect a slight excess of ripe fruit. A special mention goes to Ferentano '06, a white from a local variety, roscetto, which will win you over with its depth, harmony and elegance. The rest of the range is very good, from the Vitiano Rosso '07 with its fresh, tangy sour cherry aromas to the two fresh, aromatic, minerally Est Est Ests.

● Montiano '06	🍷🍷🍷	6
○ Ferentano '06	🍷🍷	4*
● Marciliano '06	🍷🍷	6
○ Est Est Est di Montefiascone Falesco '07	🍷🍷	2*
○ Est Est Est di Montefiascone Poggio dei Gelsi '07	🍷🍷	3*
● Pomele '07	🍷🍷	5
● Tellus '07	🍷🍷	4*
● Vitiano '07	🍷🍷	3*
○ Passirò '06	🍷	5
⊙ Vitiano Rosato '07	🍷	2
● Montiano '99	🍷🍷🍷 (white)	6
● Montiano '05	🍷🍷🍷 (white)	6
● Montiano '01	🍷🍷🍷 (white)	6
● Montiano '00	🍷🍷🍷 (white)	6

Goretti

LOC. PILA
S.DA DEL PINO, 4
06132 PERUGIA
TEL. 075607316
www.vinigoretti.com

ANNUAL PRODUCTION	400,000 bottles
HECTARES UNDER VINE	60
VITICULTURE METHOD	Conventional

This is not one of the long list of estates that have sprung up over the last few years. The Goretti family cellar is long-established with ancient farming traditions and a thriving business based on the production and sale of wine. However, revolution is afoot here too. The estate's most beautiful properties are being renovated, Sara, daughter of one of the owners, has taken over and the winemaking side is now run by the team of Vittorio Fiore and Barbara Tamburini. Today's bottles are the result of all these changes and indicate a renewed, more modern style. The estate's flagship wine, Arringatore '05 from sangiovese, merlot and ciliegiolo, is a delightfully complex red whose balsam and toast notes are flanked by gorgeous black berry fruit on the nose, with depth and structure on the palate. From the whites, we preferred the superb Grechetto '07 to Il Moggio '07, from the same variety but barrique-fermented, which is takes toastiness too far. Le Mura Saracene, at Montefalco, brings us a well-made Sagrantino '04 but it the oak is slightly too prominent and the finish is a tad bitterish.

Lamborghini

LOC. SODERI, 1
06064 PANICALE [PG]
TEL. 0758350029
www.lamborghinionline.it

ANNUAL PRODUCTION	132,000 bottles
HECTARES UNDER VINE	32
VITICULTURE METHOD	Conventional

Bright and bubbly Patrizia Lamborghini is one of the young producers who have given the world of Italian wine a new burst of energy. Working in Bologna and Panicale, where her estate's vineyards and cellar are located, she has launched a winning brand on the market with wines that open a major new chapter in the renaissance of Umbrian winemaking. Foremost among these is Campoleone, a merlot and sangiovese blend that in the '06 edition reached our Three Glass finals. Its fruit-forward aromas are intense yet fresh and blend marvellously well with the nuances of spice and vanilla. The palate is solid but supple, showing still very young with lively tannins. The estate's second wine is Trescone '06 from sangiovese, ciliegiolo and merlot. Better than ever this year, it weds sensations of bell pepper and morello cherry on the nose with energy and freshness on the palate, all in a well-defined style that is anything but banal. Riccardo Cotarella contributes his invaluable support as consultant oenologist.

● Colli Perugini Rosso L'Arringatore '05	♟♟ 5
○ Colli Perugini Grechetto '07	♟♟ 3*
● Montefalco Sagrantino Le Mure Saracene '04	♟♟ 6
○ Il Moggio '07	♟ 4
● Colli Perugini Rosso L'Arringatore '04	♟♟ 5
● Colli Perugini Rosso L'Arringatore '03	♟♟ 5
● Colli Perugini Rosso L'Arringatore '01	♟♟ 5
● Colli Perugini Rosso L'Arringatore '00	♟♟ 5

● Campoleone '06	♟♟ 6
● Trescone '06	♟♟ 4*
● Campoleone '99	♟♟♟ 6
● Campoleone '04	♟♟♟ 7
● Campoleone '00	♟♟♟ 6
● Campoleone '05	♟♟ 6
● Campoleone '02	♟♟ 6

Lungarotti

VIA MARIO ANGELONI, 16
06089 TORGIANO [PG]
TEL. 075988661
www.lungarotti.it

ANNUAL PRODUCTION	2,900,000 bottles
HECTARES UNDER VINE	310
VITICULTURE METHOD	Conventional

The enthusiasm with which their makers and admirers talk about them leaves no doubt. Not only are Lungarotti wines back on form, they have reacquired the timeless allure that has earned this Torgiano estate a place among the most prestigious winemaking houses in Italy and indeed the world. The allure derives from born of history, tradition, territory and, most of all, thrilling bottles of very influential wines. This is an estate that continues to reinvent itself. Lungarotti triumphed this year with yet another sumptuous vintage of Rubesco Vigna Monticchio Riserva. The '04 version of this selection, obtained as always from sangiovese and canaiolo, already flaunts a texture of super-fine elegance and vibrant minerality, with complex aromas that only time will reveal in all their power and depth. This absolute champion lives up to its heritage. Flanking it is a long list of superb labels, including a San Giorgio '04 that weds fruit with spicy notes of pepper and rhubarb, and a white Torre di Giano Vigna Il Pino Riserva '06 of enormous potential that we continue to prefer to the excellent but more predictable Chardonnay Aurente.

Madonna Alta

LOC. PIETRAVIA
VIA LUDOVICO ARIOSTO
06036 MONTEFALCO [PG]
TEL. 0742378568
www.madonnalta.it

ANNUAL PRODUCTION	130,000 bottles
HECTARES UNDER VINE	18
VITICULTURE METHOD	Conventional

Originally from Naples, the Ferraro family started buying plots in 1992 and today the estate embraces no less than 50 hectares of vineyards and olive groves, a new cellar and an established commercial wine operation in the Montefalco area. But it was those early acquisitions next to the 16th-century church of Madonna Alta that inspired the estate's name, marked the Ferraros' arrival and sealed their links with this new territory. Today, Madonna Alta is a solid estate that has carved out a place for itself on the local scene. The Sagrantino '05 is modern in style and reveals immense power and intensity, unveiling aromas that run the gamut from briary fruit to chocolate with intense balsamic sensations. Our only criticism is a slight bitterish note in the finish. The aromatic, flavoursome Grechetto dei Colli Martani '07 also showed very well, combining notes of peachy fruit with hints of sage and medicinal herbs. To our minds the Montefalco Rosso '06 fails to reach the same heights and is rather overwhelmed and dried by the oak.

● Torgiano Rosso Vigna Monticchio Ris. '04	▼▼▼ 6
● San Giorgio '04	▼▼ 6
○ Torgiano Bianco Torre di Giano V. il Pino Ris. '06	▼▼ 4*
○ Aurente '06	▼▼ 5
● Montefalco Sagrantino '05	▼▼ 5
○ Torgiano Bianco Torre di Giano '07	▼▼ 3*
● Torgiano Rosso Rubesco '05	▼▼ 4*
● Montefalco Rosso '06	▼ 4
● Torgiano Rosso Vigna Monticchio Ris. '88	♀♀♀ 5
● Torgiano Rosso Vigna Monticchio Ris. '03	♀♀♀ 6
● Torgiano Rosso Vigna Monticchio Ris. '01	♀♀♀ 7

○ Colli Martani Grechetto '07	▼▼ 4*
● Montefalco Sagrantino '05	▼▼ 6
● Montefalco Rosso '06	▼ 5
● Falconero Rosso '06	♀♀ 3
● Montefalco Rosso '04	♀♀ 4
● Montefalco Sagrantino '04	♀♀ 6
● Montefalco Sagrantino '02	♀♀ 6
● Montefalco Sagrantino Passito '04	♀♀ 6
● Montefalco Sagrantino Passito '03	♀♀ 6

Castello di Magione

VIA DEI CAVALIERI DI MALTA, 31
06063 MAGIONE [PG]
TEL. 075843547
www.castellodimagione.it

ANNUAL PRODUCTION	90,000 bottles
HECTARES UNDER VINE	30
VITICULTURE METHOD	Conventional

Like Beaune in Burgundy, Umbria also has its own hospice. The castle at Magione was built by the knights of Malta as a refuge for pilgrims on their way to Rome or Jerusalem. And again like its illustrious French cousin, the castle has links with the wine world, housing as it does a beautiful winery comprising a vat cellar, areas for oak maturation barrels and a bottle cellar. And the results are rather good. Castello di Magione's emblematic variety is grechetto, the subject of a major research and improvement project. Monterone is a selection obtained from a plot of clay and sand, fossil-rich soil. Although it fails to achieve the standards of the most favourable growing years, the '07 has elegant aromas of white peach and sage, and a flavoursome, quite dynamic palate. The other Grechetto '07 isn't bad either, offering simpler notes of apple and citrus fruit. From the reds, we found the '07 Carpaneto, from 45 per cent sangiovese, 25 per cent each merlot and cabernet with a little gamay, very nice and the first vintage of Pinot Nero Vino dei Cavalieri, the '06, is enjoyable, fragrant and faintly estery.

Martinelli

LOC. VOC. SASSO
VIA MADONNA DELLA NEVE, 1
06031 BEVAGNA [PG]
TEL. 0742362124
www.cantinemartinelli.com

ANNUAL PRODUCTION	155,000 bottles
HECTARES UNDER VINE	20
VITICULTURE METHOD	Conventional

We may have been slowish in granting the Martinelli estate its rightful space until last year when two very interesting Sagrantinos arrived on our tasting table, signalling a certain maturity in the estate and its style. However, we did want to see further proof that the progress we noted was significant and lasting. And here we have it. We are delighted to pay Martinelli its due for the 20 or so hectares planted to sagrantino in 1999, a brand new cellar a stone's throw from delightful Bevagna, two young entrepreneurs and the collaboration of Riccardo Cotarella. On the wine front, Sagrantino Soranna '05 impressed us so much that it shot straight into our finals. This selection is a limited run and bowled us over with its expressive compactness, its intensely fruity aromas mingling with notes of balsam and spice, and its robust yet very tangy, deep palate. The rather good Sagrantino '05 is similar in approach, if not as full. A step behind come the Montefalco Rosso '06, the Cimardone '07 from sangiovese, sagrantino and merlot, and the white Gaite '07 from chardonnay, pinot bianco and grechetto.

○ C. del Trasimeno Grechetto Monterone '07	♍♍ 3*
○ Grechetto '07	♍♍ 2*
● C. del Trasimeno Rosso Carpaneto '07	♍ 4
● Vino dei Cavalieri '06	♍ 4
○ C. del Trasimeno Grechetto Monterone '05	♍♍ 3*
○ C. del Trasimeno Grechetto Monterone '04	♍♍ 3*
○ C. del Trasimeno Grechetto Monterone '06	♍♍ 3*
● C. del Trasimeno Rosso Morcinaia '04	♍♍ 5

● Montefalco Sagrantino Sel. Soranna '05	♍♍ 7
● Montefalco Sagrantino '05	♍♍ 5
● Cimardone '07	♍ 4
○ Gaite '07	♍ 4
● Montefalco Rosso '06	♍ 4
● Montefalco Sagrantino '04	♍♍ 5
● Montefalco Sagrantino '03	♍♍ 6
● Montefalco Sagrantino Sel. Soranna '04	♍♍ 7
● Montefalco Sagrantino Sel. Soranna '03	♍♍ 7

Cantina Monrubio

FRAZ. MONTERUBIAGLIO
LOC. LE PRESE, 22
05010 CASTEL VISCARDO [TR]
TEL. 0763626064
www.monrubio.com

ANNUAL PRODUCTION	900,000 bottles
HECTARES UNDER VINE	700
VITICULTURE METHOD	Conventional

The history of Monrubio goes back a long way, yet it manages to remain on top of its game thanks to the men and women who have worked here the professionals who established, and continue to guarantee, its tangible added value. To take an example, one of the most famous oenologists in the world, Riccardo Cotarella, cut his teeth here and continues an amicable collaboration with this estate, founded in 1980. Monrubio's wines benefit from this pedigree, as well as some hefty technical investments. Palaia is the best estate red, an almost equal blend of cabernet, merlot and pinot nero that in the '06 edition flaunts harmonious florality and black cherry fruit that are nicely complemented by a chewy, yet fairly supple, palate and smooth tannins. The incredibly good value Monrubio Rosso '07 is obtained from merlot, sangiovese, ciliegiolo and montepulciano. Mature and balsamic on the nose, it has a taut, layered palate of elegantly grassy notes that imbue it with freshness and a touch of complexity. Of the whites, we found the Orvieto Classico Superiore Soana '07 to be excellent. This vibrant, dynamic wine has become a benchmark for the zone.

La Palazzola

LOC. VASCIGLIANO
05039 STRONCONE [TR]
TEL. 0744609091
info@lapalazzola.it

ANNUAL PRODUCTION	150,000 bottles
HECTARES UNDER VINE	36
VITICULTURE METHOD	Conventional

Vascigliano, Stroncone, Terni, Umbria. Although this territory has long been linked to wine – since ancient times, in fact – credit for the oenological fame it enjoys today goes exclusively to a real character, the eccentric, brilliant and sometimes cantankerous Stefano Grilli. His estate is a perennial work in progress with new flavours, new experiments, new wines and new grapes to assess. It's a kaleidoscope that comes into focus only if you look carefully and concentrate hard. We'll start our tasting notes with the red. Rubino '05 is from a blend of cabernet sauvignon and franc, merlot, petit verdot and montepulciano. Complex aromas range from black berry fruit to spices to hints of tobacco and smokiness. Complex and compact on the palate, it still manages to offer great drinkability and dynamic depth. The Merlot '05 isn't bad either, if a tad overwhelmed by toasty sensations, and neither is the Syrah Le Petrare '06, although it still needs to find its feet. Moving on to the spumantes, the '03 Riesling is fabulous, displaying stunning intensity, energy, acid backbone and gorgeous hints of green citrus fruit.

● Monrubio '07	♥♥	3*
○ Orvieto Cl. Sup. Soana '07	♥♥	3*
● Palaia '06	♥♥	4
○ Orvieto Cl. Salceto '07	♥	2
● Monrubio '06	♥♥	3*
○ Orvieto Cl. Sup. Soana '06	♥♥	3
● Palaia '05	♥♥	5
● Palaia '04	♥♥	5
● Palaia '03	♥♥	5

○ Gran Cuvée Brut '05	♥♥	5
● Le Petrare '06	♥♥	4*
○ Merlot '05	♥♥	5
○ Riesling Brut M. Cl. '03	♥♥	5
● Rubino '05	♥♥	5
● Vin Santo Bacca Rossa '05	♥♥	5
● Merlot '97	♥♥♥	5
○ V. T. da Uve Muffate '04	♥♥	4
○ Gran Cuvée Brut '01	♥♥	5
● Merlot '04	♥♥	5
○ Riesling Brut M. Cl. '01	♥♥	5
● Rubino '04	♥♥	5
● Syrah '05	♥♥	4
○ Vin Santo '01	♥♥	5
○ Vin Santo '00	♥♥	5

Palazzone

LOC. ROCCA RIPESENA, 68
05018 ORVIETO [TR]
TEL. 0763344921
www.palazzone.com

ANNUAL PRODUCTION	100,000 bottles
HECTARES UNDER VINE	24
VITICULTURE METHOD	Conventional

If a territory with the extraordinary tradition and potential of Orvieto continues to fascinate despite recent vicissitudes, we must thank passionate wine men like Giovanni Dubini. Giovanni resides in one of the most wine-friendly zones in the area, at least as far as a particular type of white wine is concerned, and he dedicates himself to producing truly fascinating, distinctive wines. Those who have had the great good fortune and pleasure to taste a vertical his past vintages will attest to this. It's a "vin de garde", as the French would say, to be tasted from a long-term perspective and harder to pin down definitively in the short term. No matter. The Orvieto Classico Superiore Campo del Guardiano '07 is a classic blend of procanico, grechetto, verdello, drupeggio and malvasia. This white is full of surprises. Elegant, if as yet not entirely defined, it shows unusual aromatic complexity ranging from florality to balsamic hints of rosemary to iodine nuances, all set in an overall framework of immense flavour and pressure. The Terre Vineate '07 and the Muffa Nobilis '06 are also very good.

F.lli Pardi

VIA GIOVANNI PASCOLI, 7/9
06036 MONTEFALCO [PG]
TEL. 0742379023
www.cantinapardi.it

ANNUAL PRODUCTION	38,000 bottles
HECTARES UNDER VINE	11
VITICULTURE METHOD	Conventional

This is the heart of Montefalco, not just because the estate practically touches the town walls but mainly because the Pardi family has long been an important part of the socio-economic fabric of "Umbria's balcony", as the town is known. Fabric was in fact the Pardis' business before they branched out into wine, picking up where they left off in the early 1900s. The estate's grapes come from 11 hectares of its own vineyards at Casale, Lesinano and Pietrauta. The splendid Montefalco Sagrantino '05 is an already enjoyable, laid-back wine that alternates sensations of citrus fruit and quinine with notes of red berry fruit and citron leaf. It is also very fresh on the palate, which shows depth, mineral sensations and fully developed – yet restrained for the variety – tannins. The Montefalco Rosso '06 is more or less its equal and opens decisively on notes of red berry fruit and faint herbaceousness, accompanied by nuances of saddle leather and damsons. The Pinot Nero is a wine that means business and confirmed our positive impressions of the estate's overall standard and style.

O Orvieto Cl. Campo del Guardiano '07	🍷 5
O Grechetto '07	🍷 4*
O Muffa Nobilis '06	🍷 6
O Orvieto Cl. Sup. Terre Vineate '07	🍷 4*
● Rubbio '07	🍷 4*
O L'Ultima Spiaggia '07	🍷 5
● Armaleo '98	🍷🍷🍷 6
● Armaleo '97	🍷🍷🍷 6
● Armaleo '95	🍷🍷🍷 6
● Armaleo '00	🍷🍷🍷 6
O Orvieto Cl. Campo del Guardiano '04	🍷🍷 5
O Muffa Nobilis '05	🍷🍷 6
O Orvieto Cl. Campo del Guardiano '03	🍷🍷 5
O Orvieto Cl. Sup. Terre Vineate '06	🍷🍷 4

● Montefalco Rosso '06	🍷🍷 4*
● Montefalco Sagrantino '05	🍷🍷 6
● Montefalco Sagrantino Passito '05	🍷 6
● Montefalco Sagrantino '04	🍷🍷 6
● Montefalco Rosso '05	🍷🍷 4
● Montefalco Sagrantino '03	🍷🍷 6
● Montefalco Sagrantino Passito '03	🍷🍷 6

Perticaia

VIA E. CATTANEO, 39
06035 GUALDO CATTANEO [PG]
TEL. 0742920328
www.perticaia.it

ANNUAL PRODUCTION	90,000 bottles
HECTARES UNDER VINE	15
VITICULTURE METHOD	Conventional

This is elegance. It could be the land, the vineyards or the zone's site climate, next door to the small town of Casale di Montefalco, or it could be the experience amassed by a real character of the Italian wine world, Guido Guardigli, Perticaia's owner. There again, it could be the model cellar, perfect to the last detail, or the invaluable collaboration of Emiliano Falsini, a young oenologist with a real flair for Sagrantino. Or it could be a combination of all of these, as well as a million other factors that all come to bear on the complex and fascinating process that creates a great wine. The fact is that the territory has yielded another top estate and one of the most intriguing versions of Sagrantino. The '05 growing year has produced a wine that alternates very complex nuances of forest fruits with earthiness and refined spices. The palate unfolds confident and tangy, showing breadth, unrivalled depth and perfect tannins. This is a Sagrantino with balance and refinement, stamped by its territory of origin and also by a truly distinctive style.

● Montefalco Sagrantino '05	ŦŦŦ	6
● Montefalco Rosso '06	ŦŦ	4*
○ Trebbiano Spoletino '07	ŦŦ	4*
● Umbria Rosso '07	Ŧ	3
● Montefalco Sagrantino '04	ŲŲŲ	6
● Montefalco Sagrantino '03	ŲŲ	6
● Montefalco Sagrantino '01	ŲŲ	6
● Montefalco Sagrantino '00	ŲŲ	6

Pucciarella

LOC. VILLA DI MAGIONE
06063 MAGIONE [PG]
TEL. 0758409147
www.pucciarella.it

ANNUAL PRODUCTION	130,000 bottles
HECTARES UNDER VINE	50
VITICULTURE METHOD	Conventional

Let's be honest. Although this cellar, today owned by the Cariplo bank pension fund, has been up and running for some time now, it is only in recent years that its wines have achieved real recognition. New investments and the arrival of highly skilled technicians are the strategies that have done the trick. But to get back to the subject, this year's top offering is the sumptuous Colli del Trasimeno Vin Santo Eletto '04. Obtained from equal parts of malvasia and trebbiano part-raisined on traditional drying racks, it has an intense copper hue and wonderfully rich, layered aromas that range from chestnut honey to dried fruit via spicy sensations of ancient oak, then veer off, almost as if the wine is refreshing itself in the glass, to reveal hints of rosemary and iodine. Merlot Empireo '06 is another magnificent wine that offers smoky sensations, unusual energy and aromatic nuances. The Berlingero '06 from sangiovese, cabernet and gamay is not quite so impressive since its aromas are not as fresh as usual but the white Agnolo '07 is very good.

○ C. del Trasimeno Bianco Agnolo '07	ŦŦ	4*
○ C. del Trasimeno Vin Santo Eletto '04	ŦŦ	4*
● Empireo '06	ŦŦ	4*
● C. del Trasimeno Rosso Berlingero '06	Ŧ	4
○ C. del Trasimeno Vin Santo Eletto '01	ŲŲ	4*
● Empireo '05	ŲŲ	4*

Castello delle Regine

LOC. LE REGINE
VIA DI CASTELLUCCIO
05022 AMELIA [TR]
TEL. 0744702005
www.castellodelleregine.com

ANNUAL PRODUCTION 350,000 bottles
HECTARES UNDER VINE 87
VITICULTURE METHOD Conventional

This estate sprawls over more than 400 hectares in the municipalities of Narni and Amelia, a stone's throw from the San Liberato exit on the E45 motorway. Here, in this little earthly paradise of woodlands, olive groves, a Chianina cattle farm and even a superb restaurant, the Nodaris have established an estate that is firmly focused on the land. In a relatively short time, they have created a winery with a considerable reputation. This year's range had no real stand-out, with the Merlot '06 getting no further than the final rounds. Make no mistake about it, it's still a fine wine but its aromas are rather too sweet and its tannins not quite as smooth as usual. The Sangiovese Selezione del Fondatore '03 tells a similar tale. However, the range of wines on offer did display its customary authoritativeness and quality was very high overall. We were particularly impressed by Princeps '05 from cabernet with some merlot and sangiovese, which opens crisp and powerful on the nose to reveal notes of black berry fruit followed by a compact, very gutsy palate.

● Merlot '06	🍷🍷	7
● Sangiovese Sel. del Fondatore '03	🍷🍷	6
● Princeps '05	🍷🍷	6
○ Bianco delle Regine '07	🍷	4
⊙ Rose delle Regine '07	🍷	4
● Merlot '05	YYY	7
● Merlot '04	YYY	7
● Merlot '03	YYY	7
● Merlot '02	YYY	6
● Merlot '01	YYY	7
● Merlot '00	YY	7
● Princeps '04	YY	6

Rocca di Fabbri

LOC. FABBRI
06036 MONTEFALCO [PG]
TEL. 0742399379
www.roccadifabbri.com

ANNUAL PRODUCTION 230,000 bottles
HECTARES UNDER VINE 64.5
VITICULTURE METHOD Conventional

To our minds, Rocca di Fabbri is one of the most important estates in the Montefalco area. It has a fascination all of its own, deriving from its history and, above all, from the clear direction its production has taken. Established by antiquarian Pietro Vitali, it is run today by his daughters Roberta and Simona, and for the last ten years or so has enjoyed the support of the excellent Giorgio Marone in the role of consultant oenologist. The wines are alluring and unique, their only defect being a tendency to slightly muzzy aromatics. At least such was the case when we came to taste them. The Sagrantino '05, for example, has rather a muddled nose as yet while the palate derives remarkable energy derived from its flavour, freshness and fine-grained, elegant tannins. This is a very drinkable thoroughbred, indeed we would go so far as to say it is relaxed compared to many others from the designation. Among the other wines were a rugged, taut, fleshy Montefalco Rosso '06 and an equally interesting Sagrantino Passito '05.

● Montefalco Rosso '06	🍷🍷	5
● Montefalco Sagrantino '05	🍷🍷	7
● Montefalco Sagrantino Passito '05	🍷🍷	6
○ Chardonnay '07	🍷	3
● Montefalco Sagrantino '03	YY	7
● Montefalco Sagrantino '02	YY	7
● Faroaldo '04	YY	6
● Montefalco Sagrantino '04	YY	7
● Montefalco Sagrantino '01	YY	7
● Montefalco Sagrantino Passito '04	YY	6

Ruggeri

via Montepennino, 5
06036 Montefalco [PG]
tel. 0742379294

ANNUAL PRODUCTION 20,000 bottles
HECTARES UNDER VINE 5
VITICULTURE METHOD Conventional

Giuliano Ruggeri is a wine man from the traditional Montefalco mould. He planted his first vines in 1974 yet his estate is one of the smallest in the area. Giuliano has just over five hectares and in the hills of Montepennino, set in some truly stunning countryside. It's also home to his new cellar with its tasting room, vinification, bottling and cellaring areas and, most importantly, the traditional big barrels that bespeak a very specific wine philosophy. It's a philosophy we approve, having tasted the wines. The cream of the crop is the Sagrantino '05, one of the best on the market thanks to its heady nose of delightful black and red berry fruit enveloped by sensations of tobacco and dried flowers, followed by a caressing, chewy palate with plenty of flavour and depth. The Montefalco Rosso '06 is excellent, as is the Sagrantino Passito '05, a concentrated, dark wine displaying hints of jam, coffee and chocolate.

● Montefalco Sagrantino '05	🍷🍷	6
● Montefalco Rosso '06	🍷🍷	4*
● Montefalco Sagrantino Passito '05	🍷🍷	6
● Montefalco Sagrantino '04	🍷🍷 (white)	6
● Montefalco Sagrantino '03	🍷🍷 (white)	6

★ Castello della Sala

loc. Sala
05016 Ficulle [TR]
tel. 076386051
www.antinori.it

ANNUAL PRODUCTION 600,000 bottles
HECTARES UNDER VINE 160
VITICULTURE METHOD Conventional

Castello della Sala, one of Antinori's most beautiful estates, was acquired in the 1940s to complement the family's properties in an area that produces fine whites. It stands on a chalkstone promontory in the Umbrian Apennines at an altitude of more than 500 metres, halfway between the River Paglia and Mount Nibbio. This is a stunning, wine-friendly zone that combined with the tenacity of the owners and the skill of the professionals who work here – notably Renzo Cotarella – to give Umbria and Italy an extraordinary white. This extremely long-lived wine, Cervaro della Sala, more than holds its own against its peers around the world and in fact the '06 edition won another Three Glass award. It is perhaps a shade less vibrant than the previous two versions yet it still fascinates right from its intense gold and green-flecked straw and envelops the nose with aromas of wild flowers, medicinal herbs, tropical fruit and a supremely elegant but never intrusive oak note. This flavoursome, very complex wine is generous, deep, seemingly never-ending on the palate. Flanking it are other thoroughbreds worthy of the estate's fame.

○ Cervaro della Sala '06	🍷🍷🍷	7
○ Bramito del Cervo '07	🍷🍷	4*
○ Muffato della Sala '06	🍷🍷	6
○ Orvieto Cl. Sup. San Giovanni della Sala '07	🍷🍷	4*
○ Conte della Vipera '06	🍷	5
○ Cervaro della Sala '97	🍷🍷🍷 (white)	6
○ Cervaro della Sala '96	🍷🍷🍷 (white)	6
○ Cervaro della Sala '95	🍷🍷🍷 (white)	6
○ Cervaro della Sala '94	🍷🍷🍷 (white)	6
○ Cervaro della Sala '93	🍷🍷🍷 (white)	6
○ Cervaro della Sala '90	🍷🍷🍷 (white)	6
○ Cervaro della Sala '05	🍷🍷🍷 (white)	7
○ Cervaro della Sala '04	🍷🍷🍷 (white)	7
○ Cervaro della Sala '03	🍷🍷🍷 (white)	6
○ Cervaro della Sala '02	🍷🍷🍷 (white)	6
○ Cervaro della Sala '01	🍷🍷🍷 (white)	6
○ Cervaro della Sala '00	🍷🍷🍷 (white)	6

Scacciadiavoli

LOC. CANTINONE, 31
06036 MONTEFALCO [PG]
TEL. 0742371210
scacciadiavoli@tin.it

ANNUAL PRODUCTION	200,000 bottles
HECTARES UNDER VINE	32
VITICULTURE METHOD	Conventional

Only 32 of the 130 hectares are planted to vine, output is about 250,000 bottles a year and the cellar is one of the most beautiful in Italy. This rare example of agricultural and industrial archaeology was built in the mid-1800s to French plans by Principe Ugo Boncompagni and has recently been restored. It was a revolutionary concept in its time, particularly here, and comprises four floors, one of which is underground and earned it the name of Cantinone (Big Cellar). Welcome to Scacciadiavoli, a jewel of an estate bought and then developed by Amilcare Pambuffetti and his family. In recent years, it has made a huge leap in quality. The Sagrantino '05 is a remarkable wine, if perhaps less exciting than its predecessor, but it has quite a distinctive style. The concentrated nose melds notes of black berry fruit with nuances of chocolate and vanilla while the palate is refined and soft, with good balance and lovely tannins. It stumbles a bit in the finish, which is a bit simple and alcoholic. The Sagrantino Passito '05 is in the same league but the Montefalco Rosso '06 overdoes the toasty notes.

Sportoletti

LOC. CAPITAN LORETO
VIA LOMBARDIA, 1
06038 SPELLO [PG]
TEL. 0742651461
www.sportoletti.com

ANNUAL PRODUCTION	230,000 bottles
HECTARES UNDER VINE	30
VITICULTURE METHOD	Conventional

Villa Fidelia is one of Umbria's most delightful spots, set in an absolutely stunning Italianate garden. It lends its name to the flagship wine of the Sportoletti estate, which is nearby at the foot of a hill not far from the small towns of Spello and Assisi. Derived from a blend of merlot, cabernet sauvignon and cabernet franc, this red is much acclaimed worldwide and has received countless plaudits from many an international wine guru. The '06 offers a balsamic nose on which oak is still a little too present but nevertheless hints at wonderfully ripe, fleshy fruit and elegant, soft tannins. This is an impeccably made wine with perfect definition that may well have some surprises in store for us. We'll see. In contrast, the Assisi Rosso '07 from sangiovese, merlot and cabernet thrills instantly, displaying intense aromas ranging from forest fruits to wild herbs and the odd faint spicy sensation. Villa Fidelia Bianco '06 from grechetto and chardonnay is another excellent wine, if a tad too generous with toastiness, and as ever the Grechetto '07 is a winner.

● Montefalco Sagrantino '05	♟♟	6
● Montefalco Sagrantino Passito '05	♟♟	6
● Montefalco Rosso '06	♟	4
● Montefalco Sagrantino '04	♟♟	6
● Montefalco Sagrantino '03	♟♟	6
● Montefalco Sagrantino '01	♟♟	6
● Montefalco Sagrantino '00	♟♟	6

● Villa Fidelia Rosso '06	♟♟	6
○ Assisi Grechetto '07	♟♟	3*
● Assisi Rosso '07	♟♟	4*
○ Villa Fidelia Bianco '06	♟♟	4*
● Villa Fidelia Rosso '98	♟♟♟	6
● Villa Fidelia Rosso '99	♟♟	6
● Villa Fidelia Rosso '05	♟♟	6
● Villa Fidelia Rosso '04	♟♟	6
● Villa Fidelia Rosso '03	♟♟	6
● Villa Fidelia Rosso '00	♟♟	7
● Villa Fidelia Rosso '02	♟♟	6
● Villa Fidelia Rosso '01	♟♟	7

Tabarrini

FRAZ. TURRITA
06036 MONTEFALCO [PG]
TEL. 0742379351
www.tabarrini.com

ANNUAL PRODUCTION	70,000 bottles
HECTARES UNDER VINE	11
VITICULTURE METHOD	Conventional

It is said that wines often resemble their producers. Never was this truer than in the case of Giampaolo Tabarrini and his bottles. Generosity, sincerity, obsession with detail, passionate enthusiasm and a way of balancing exuberance and excess are all traits embodied by Giampaolo and reflected in the wines he makes. Giampaolo's are complex, personal products that may even appear awkward because of the wealth of traits they feature. There are two Sagrantinos this year and the number may increase with further selections. Both are splendid, if very rich and still in the settling down phase. Colle alle Macchie '03 is better defined but it comes from a very hot growing year while Colle Grimaldesco '05 is spicy and full of black berry fruit. But the cream of the Turritas' crop this year is the trebbiano spoletino-only white Adarmando '06, which came within a whisker of Three Glasses for its vibrancy and extraordinary complexity. It offers the perfect aromatic wedding of tropical fruit, mango and kiwi with refreshing green sensations of lime and citrus. What, we wonder, will future versions be like if they are just a shade less ripe?

Terre de La Custodia

LOC. PALOMBARA
06035 GUALDO CATTANEO [PG]
TEL. 0742929595
www.terredelacustodia.it

ANNUAL PRODUCTION	750,000 bottles
HECTARES UNDER VINE	82
VITICULTURE METHOD	Conventional

Terre de La Custodia is a new but already influential estate that the Farchioni have dedicated to the producing of wine. On the borders of the municipalities of Gualdo Cattaneo and Montefalco, it boasts 82 hectares of vineyards and releases an extraordinary 750,000 bottles. This large volume includes an impressive number of labels and, most of all, quality overall is very good indeed. The Sagrantino Exubera '05 is very dense and extract-rich, indeed so concentrated that it is still difficult to understand with its big tannic texture. The Sagrantino '05 is a more relaxed wine with an elegant nose and well-made palate, even if extract is a force to be reckoned with here, too. The enjoyable Passito Melanto '04 has aromas of jam and curry. Among the whites on offer, there is a superb Grechetto '07, which is more successful than the rather pretentious and not very varietal Plentis '06. Finally, Collezione '06 from sangiovese, merlot and a dash of sagrantino is a simple yet pleasing wine.

○ Adarmando '06	▼▼ 4*
● Montefalco Sagrantino Colle alle Macchie '03	▼▼ 8
● Montefalco Sagrantino Colle Grimaldesco '05	▼▼ 6
⊙ Bocca di Rosa '07	▼▼ 4*
● Montefalco Rosso Colle Grimaldesco '06	▼▼ 5
● Il Padrone delle Vigne '07	▼ 4
● Montefalco Sagrantino Colle Grimaldesco Passito '05	▼ 7
● Montefalco Sagrantino Colle Grimaldesco '01	▼▼▼ 6
● Montefalco Sagrantino Colle Grimaldesco '04	▼▼ 6
● Montefalco Sagrantino Colle Grimaldesco '02	▼▼ 6
○ Adarmando '05	▼▼ 4*

○ Colli Martani Grechetto '07	▼▼ 4*
● Montefalco Sagrantino '05	▼▼ 6
● Montefalco Sagrantino Exubera '05	▼▼ 8
● Montefalco Sagrantino Passito Melanto '04	▼▼ 7
● Collezione '06	▼ 4
○ Colli Martani Grechetto Plentis '06	▼ 5
● Montefalco Sagrantino Exubera '04	▼▼ 7
● Montefalco Sagrantino Exubera '03	▼▼ 7

Todini

FRAZ. ROSCETO
VIA COLLINA, 29
06059 TODI [PG]
TEL. 075887122
www.cantinafrancotodini.com

ANNUAL PRODUCTION	200,000 bottles
HECTARES UNDER VINE	70
VITICULTURE METHOD	Conventional

The Todini family estate has impressed us enormously with its growth in recent years. Now that the new cellar is complete, we have great expectations of this beautiful 300-hectare property nestling among the hills of Collevalenza, a short distance from the charming town of Todi. This year's line-up was missing the Nero della Cervara. The estate's trusty warhorse was not deemed ready by the estate cellar technicians and will remain in bottle for a few more months to complete maturation. It's a wise decision that bears witness to the seriousness and expertise of winemaking in these parts. The top picks of our tasting panel include the Grechetto di Todi Bianco del Cavaliere '07, which is on fighting form. It bowled us over with its complex, lively range of aromas and stands out for its coherent acidity and wonderful body. The Rubro '06, predominantly from sangiovese, also showed well, focusing on dark notes running from chocolate to blackberry to currant. The Grechetto Eteria '07 and the Tiaso '07, a red obtained from sangiovese, cabernet sauvignon and merlot, are simple but pleasing.

Tudernum

PIAN DI PORTO, 146
06059 TODI [PG]
TEL. 0758989403
www.tudernum.it

ANNUAL PRODUCTION	1,000,000 bottles
HECTARES UNDER VINE	350
VITICULTURE METHOD	Conventional

Around 350 members work a patchwork of tiny plots in the Martani hills, coordinated by a president with his finger on the pulse who has turned around this estate. Tudernum seemed stuck with a range of hard-to-distinguish, rather unattractive products but investment and a carefully constructed team of in-house and consulting oenologists have brought about the step change in quality. These are the simple yet fundamental secrets of success of a co-operative that should be held up as an example of how to make very decent, often very good wines at extremely reasonable prices. Our choice this year is the Merlot '07 with a concentrated, complex with aromas of ripe cherry and blackcurrant shot through with spicy echoes of nutmeg and cinnamon. These are followed by a chewy, creamy palate and a fabulously velvety finish. A notch below, but still very well-made, are the Sagrantino '05 and the Rojano '05, a red obtained from sangiovese, merlot and sagrantino that recalls some Malbecs from Argentina. The varietal Sangiovese '07 and Cabernet '07 are excellent. From this year's whites, we preferred the Colle Nobile '07 to the basic Grechetto '07.

O Colli Martani Grechetto di Todi Bianco del Cavaliere '07	♀♀ 4*
● Colli Martani Sangiovese Rubro '06	♀♀ 5
O Eteria '07	♀ 3
● Tiaso '07	♀ 4
● Nero della Cervara '05	♀♀ 6
● Nero della Cervara '04	♀♀ 6
● Nero della Cervara '03	♀♀ 6

● Merlot '07	♀♀ 3*
● Cabernet Sauvignon '07	♀♀ 3*
O Colli Martani Grechetto di Todi Colle Nobile '07	♀♀ 4*
● Colli Martani Sangiovese '07	♀♀ 2*
● Montefalco Sagrantino Tudernum '05	♀♀ 6
● Rojano '05	♀♀ 4*
O Colli Martani Grechetto di Todi '07	♀ 2
● Merlot '05	♀♀ 3*
● Montefalco Sagrantino Tudernum '04	♀♀ 6
● Montefalco Sagrantino Tudernum '01	♀♀ 5

Tenuta Le Velette

FRAZ. CANALE DI ORVIETO
LOC. LE VELETTE, 23
05019 ORVIETO [TR]
TEL. 076329090
www.levelette.it

ANNUAL PRODUCTION   400,000 bottles
HECTARES UNDER VINE   109
VITICULTURE METHOD   Conventional

Perhaps the most wonderful thing about wine is that it is a living, unpredictable product that refuses to conform to any rigid pattern. This may be why, having triumphed in the extremely challenging growing year of '03, Le Velette's Calanco is rather disappointing in '04, a vintage when it should have excelled. This wouldn't be the first time either, if we look back on the performance of the estate's other flagship wine, Gaudio. That was the state of play when we tasted but this is not to say that things might not change in future. The fact is that this Sangiovese-Cabernet from Orvieto seems to have lost some body and fruit ripeness in the '04 version. It gives nicely elegant aromas but has slightly excessive toastiness and the palate is far from perfect in its acidity and vegetal sensations. We shall see. Moving on, we tasted a splendid Gaudio '05, a refined, silky Merlot with distinctive characteristics. The rest of the range was also on top form, and we were particularly impressed by the juicy Sangiovese Accordo '05, the vibrant Orvieto Classico Superiore Lunato '07, and the highly unusual barrique-conditioned Grechetto, Sole Uve '07.

Villa Mongalli

LOC. CAPPUCCINI
06031 BEVAGNA [PG]
TEL. 3485110506
www.villamongalli.com

ANNUAL PRODUCTION   70,000 bottles
HECTARES UNDER VINE   15
VITICULTURE METHOD   Conventional

The iron will of the owners, major investments, vineyards in the most beautiful parts of Sagrantino, a position on the spectacular hills between Bevagna and Montefalco, and expert consultants and collaborators. These few but fundamental features explain why Villa Mongalli was on such fine form this year. This new estate is one of the most interesting in the area. Admittedly, it's early days yet. Wine needs time, patience and adjustments, at least when it comes to products as serious as these. That said, the wines we sampled were very good indeed. The Sagrantino Della Cima '04 made it all the way to our finals. This selection has wonderful nuances of black berry fruit, with brambles and blackcurrants to the fore, swathed in Eastern spices and oaky notes that, to be honest, still tend to overwhelm. The Sagrantino Pozzo del Curato '05 shows warm and embracing from aromas that find a perfect balance of morello cherry fruit and intensely spicy aromas led by nutmeg, cinnamon and cloves. We also liked the Montefalco Rosso Le Grazie '06 and Col Cimino '06 from sagrantino, cabernet and merlot.

● Gaudio '05	♟♟ 5
● Accordo '05	♟♟ 4*
● Calanco '04	♟♟ 5
○ Orvieto Cl. Berganorio '07	♟♟ 3*
○ Orvieto Cl. Sup. Lunato '07	♟♟ 4*
● Rosso Orvietano Rosso di Spicca '07	♟♟ 3*
○ Sole Uve '07	♟♟ 4*
● Calanco '95	♟♟♟ 5
● Calanco '03	♟♟♟ 5
● Gaudio '03	♟♟♟ 5
● Calanco '01	♟♟ 5
● Gaudio '04	♟♟ 5
● Gaudio '01	♟♟ 5
● Accordo '04	♟♟ 4
● Rosso Orvietano Rosso di Spicca '06	♟♟ 3*
○ Traluce '07	♟♟ 4

● Montefalco Sagrantino Della Cima '04	♟♟ 7
● Col Cimino '06	♟♟ 4*
● Montefalco Rosso Le Grazie '06	♟♟ 4*
● Montefalco Sagrantino Pozzo del Curato '05	♟♟ 5
● Umbria Rosso '07	♟ 3

OTHER WINERIES

Cantina Altarocca

LOC. ROCCA RIPESENA, 62
05019 ORVIETO [TR]
TEL. 0763344210
www.cantinaaltarocca.com

The Altarocca estate on the chalk spur of Rocca Ripesena is part of the farming activities of the Ceprini family. The wines are excellent. The whites, especially the Albaco '07 from chardonnay, grechetto and procanico, are intriguing while Merlot Rosso d'Altarocca '06 is the best red.

○ Albaco '07	🍷🍷	4*
○ Arcosesto '07	🍷🍷	3*
● Rosso d'Altarocca '06	🍷🍷	7
● Librato '07	🍷	4

Tenuta Alzatura

LOC. FRATTA - ALZATURA, 108
06036 MONTEFALCO [PG]
TEL. 0742399435
www.tenuta-alzatura.it

The Cecchis' second estate in Umbria continues to grow. Proof comes in the fine Sagrantino Uno di Otto '05, a wine with a modern slant that combines notes of ripe fruit with oaky sensations, and a Montefalco Rosso '06 that is satisfying and concentrated, if a tad pretentious and overly tannic.

● Montefalco Rosso '06	🍷🍷	4
● Montefalco Sagrantino Uno di Otto '05	🍷🍷	6

Argillae

LOC. POMARRO, 45
05010 ALLERONA [TR]
TEL. 0763624604
www.argillae.it

This brand new estate lies in a hilly zone between Allerona and Ficulle, north-west of Orvieto. The white wines we tasted made quite an impression. Chardonnay-Grechetto Panata '07 is superb, as is the Grechetto '07. The Orvieto '07 isn't bad, either.

○ Grechetto '07	🍷🍷	4*
○ Panata '07	🍷🍷	4*
○ Orvieto '07	🍷	3

Benincasa

VIA CAPRO, 23
06031 BEVAGNA [PG]
TEL. 0742361307
www.aziendabenincasa.com

We enjoyed the classic duo from one of the first estates to start growing sagrantino here. Despite its rather estery nose, the '05 version of the Sagrantino is embracing and has a warm fruity vein, while the Rosso '06 is once again flavoursome and deep.

● Montefalco Rosso '06	🍷🍷	4*
● Montefalco Sagrantino '05	🍷🍷	6

Brogal Vini

LOC. BASTIA UMBRA
VIA DEGLI OLMI, 9
06083 PERUGIA
TEL. 0758001501
www.brogalvini.com

It was an excellent year for Antigniano wines, a range that includes a lot of very good labels. Two of the best are the Sagrantino Guado alle Chiavi '05 and, above all, Montefalco Rosso Riserva Re Migrante '05, a very elegant wine that shows concentrated and balanced, with aromas of wild cherry and spices.

● Montefalco Rosso Re Migrante Ris. '05	🍷🍷	6
● Montefalco Sagrantino Guado alle Chiavi Antigniano '05	🍷🍷	7
● Torgiano Rosso Antigniano '05	🍷🍷	4*
● Torgiano Rosso Santa Caterina Ris. '04	🍷🍷	6

Flavio Busti

FRAZ. SANT'ELENA
06052 MARSCIANO [PG]
TEL. 075879458
www.cantinebusti.it

Flavio Busti grows his vines in a magnificent part of the hills between Perugia and Marsciano. Once again, we liked the Grechetto '07, an intense, complex wine that is also balanced and very drinkable. The varietal and anything but banal Merlot '05 is also excellent.

○ Grechetto '07	🍷🍷	3*
● Merlot '05	🍷🍷	4*

OTHER WINERIES

Tenuta Castelbuono

LOC. BEVAGNA
VOC. FOSSATO, 54
06031 PERUGIA
TEL. 0742362060
www.ferrarispumante.it

The Castelbuono estate belonging to the Lunelli family did well. The Sagrantino '04 and the Montefalco Rosso '06 are good, if muzzy on the nose at first, but they develop well on the palate showing balance, sweet fruit and a long finish.

● Montefalco Rosso '06	♥♥	4*
● Montefalco Sagrantino '04	♥♥	6

Cesarini Sartori - Signae

LOC. PURGATORIO TORRI
VIA SANTA MARIA
06035 GUALDO CATTANEO [PG]
TEL. 074299590
www.rossobastardo.it

This new estate belonging to husband and wife Fiorella Sartori and Luciano Cesarini presented two splendid versions of Sagrantino '05 and Rosso di Montefalco '05. Both spend a short period in barrique and a longer time in large barrels. The resulting wines are relaxed, flavoursome, very concentrated and full.

● Montefalco Rosso '05	♥♥	4*
● Montefalco Sagrantino '05	♥♥	5
● Montefalco Sagrantino Passito '05	♥	6
● Rossobastardo '05	♥	4

Chiorri

LOC. SANT'ENEA
VIA TODI, 100
06132 PERUGIA
TEL. 075607141
www.chiorri.it

The last year or two have seen the Chiorri estate wines find their groove and a new confidence, despite a still rather rustic style. In short, all of the wines seem to have taken a step forward in the quality stakes and scores are consequently higher.

● Colli Perugini Saliato '06	♥♥	4*
O Grechetto '07	♥♥	3*
● Merlot Sel. Antonio Chiorri '06	♥♥	5
● Colli Perugini Rosso '06	♥	3

Tenuta Corini

VOC. CASINO, 53
05010 MONTEGABBIONE [TR]
TEL. 0763837535
www.tenutacorini.it

This lovely estate near Montegabbione was acquired by the Corini family when they returned to Italy after years in Switzerland. This time, though, Frabusco, from montepulciano, sangiovese and merlot, Camerti, a rather unpredictable Pinot Nero, and the Sauvignon Casteldifiori were below par.

O Casteldifiori '07	♥	4
● Frabusco '06	♥	6
● Pinot Nero Camerti '06	♥	6

Custodi

LOC. CANALE
V.LE VENERE
05010 ORVIETO [TR]
TEL. 076329053
www.cantinacustodi.com

There was a good display from the Custodi family estate in the Canale hills at Orvieto, which is particularly strong in the classic local designations. Both the Orvieto Classico Belloro '07 and the flower and balsam Orvieto Classico Superiore Vendemmia Tardiva Pertusa '07 are excellent.

O Orvieto Cl. Belloro '07	♥♥	2*
O Orvieto Cl. Sup. Pertusa V. T. '07	♥♥	5
● Piancoleto '07	♥	3

Cantina La Spina

FRAZ. SPINA
VIA EMILIO ALESSANDRINI, 1
06050 MARSCIANO [PG]
TEL. 0758738120
www.cantinalaspina.it

Moreno Peccia continues to make wine meticulously at Spina. Rosso Spina '06 from montepulciano, merlot and gamay is still they linchpin, flanked by the merlot-based Merlato '07 and, one step below, Polimante '06 from 70 per cent merlot with gamay, which is however getting better.

● Merlato '07	♥♥	4*
● Rosso Spina '06	♥♥	5
● Polimante '06	♥	5

OTHER WINERIES

Cantine Novelli

LOC. PERDELLE
VIA MOLINO CAPALDINI
06036 MONTEFALCO [PG]
TEL. 0744803301
www.cantinanovelli.it

Based on a major project from the Novelli family, this new Umbria estate has clear potential. The wines still leave something to be desired, though. Sagrantino di Montefalco '05 is modern and balsamic, Rosso '06 is too oaky but the Trebbiano Spoletino '07 is coming on nicely.

● Montefalco Sagrantino '05	🍷🍷	6
○ Trebbiano Spoletino '07	🍷🍷	4*
○ Bianco Cube '07	🍷	3
● Montefalco Rosso '06	🍷	4

Peppucci

LOC. SANT'ANTIMO
FRAZ. PETRORO, 4
06059 TODI [PG]
TEL. 0758947253
www.cantinapeppucci.com

This new entry to the Guide belongs to the Peppucci family. Situated on a splendid hill overlooking Todi, it has a range of very decent wines. Alter Ego '05, an almost pure Sagrantino, is warm and embracing, Sangiovese Petroro 4 '06 is supple and deep while Grechetto Montorsolo '07 is not bad.

● Alter Ego '05	🍷🍷	5
● Petroro 4 '06	🍷🍷	4*
○ Montorsolo '07	🍷	4

Poggio Bertaio

FRAZ. CASAMAGGIORE
VIA FRATTAVECCHIA, 29
06061 CASTIGLIONE DEL LAGO [PG]
TEL. 075956921
poggiobertaio@libero.it

The Ciufoli brothers manage their vineyards and cellars with scrupulous care. Crovello '05, a Bordeaux blend, did well, showing great power with its weave of wild berry fruits and spices. Sangiovese Stucchio '05 is simpler and enjoyable.

● Crovello '05	🍷🍷	7
● Stucchio '05	🍷	4

Tenuta Poggio del Lupo

VOC. BUZZAGHETTO, 100
05011 ALLERONA [TR]
TEL. 0763628350
www.tenutapoggiodellupo.it

Poggio del Lupo is a model estate that, this year at least, gave rather a mixed performance. We preferred the spicy, fresh-tasting, flavoursome Lupiano '07 from 40 per cent each merlot and cabernet with ciliegiolo to the shaky, over-ambitious Montepulciano Silentis '06. The Orvieto Novilunio '07 is enjoyable.

● Rosso Orvietano Lupiano '07	🍷🍷	3*
● Rosso Silentis '06	🍷	5
○ Orvieto Novilunio '07	🍷	3

Rio Grande

LOC. MONTECCHIE
05028 PENNA IN TEVERINA [TR]
TEL. 0666416440
www.aziendaagricolariogrande.com

Two excellent wines see the Pastore family's Rio Grande estate back in the Guide. Rosso Casa Pastore '05 is a classic Bordeaux blend that beautifully marries fruit and oak-derived aromas. Campo Antico '07 is a rich, full, deep mix of chardonnay and grechetto.

○ Campo Antico '07	🍷🍷	3*
● Casa Pastore Rosso '05	🍷🍷	5

Tenuta di Salviano

LOC. CIVITELLA DEL LAGO
VOC. SALVIANO, 44
05020 BASCHI [TR]
TEL. 0744950459

The 70 hectares of vines on the slopes around Lake Corbara are just part of this property, which has few rivals in Umbria. Our vote this year goes to two extremely good '07 Orvieto Classico Superiores, the citrussy, chewy dry version and the soft Vendemmia Tardiva.

○ Orvieto Cl. Sup. '07	🍷🍷	4*
○ Orvieto Cl. Sup. V. T. '07	🍷🍷	4*
● Lago di Corbara Solideo '05	🍷	4
● Lago di Corbara Turlò '06	🍷	4

OTHER WINERIES

Spoletoducale

LOC. PETROGNANO, 54
06049 SPOLETO [PG]
TEL. 074356224
www.spoletoducale.it

Spoletoducale, aka the Petrognano co-operative, offered us a fine range of wines to taste this year. The Sagrantino Casale Triocco '05 is excellent, giving never intrusive jammy sensations in perfect harmony with spiciness and a palate of personality. It's the best from recent vintages.

● Montefalco Sagrantino Casale Triocco '05	¶¶ 6
○ Trebbiano Spoletino '07	¶ 2
○ Trebbiano Spoletino Kio '07	¶ 2

Terre de' Trinci

VIA FIAMENGA, 57
06034 FOLIGNO [PG]
TEL. 0742320165
www.terredetrinci.com

In terms of numbers, this is the most important co-operative in the region and its president is also head of the Montefalco wine protection consortium. This year's showing by Sagrantino Ugolino '05 was exceptional. It's very elegant and melds oak and fruit seamlessly.

● Montefalco Sagrantino Ugolino '05	¶¶ 7
○ Luna '07	¶ 4
● Montefalco Sagrantino '05	¶ 6

Tordimaro

LOC. TORDIMONTE, 37
05019 ORVIETO [TR]
TEL. 0763304227
www.tordimaro.com

It was a bit of a mixed year for the wines from Tordimaro, an estate that had accustomed us to much better things. It was saved by Rosso Orvietano Cabernet '05 with its ripe nose and nice density on the palate, and the Orvieto Classico '07, which to be honest is a little lightweight and acidulous.

○ Orvieto Cl. '07	¶ 2
● Rosso Orvietano Cabernet '05	¶ 4

Tenuta Vitalonga

LOC. MONTIANO
05016 FICULLE [TR]
TEL. 0763836722
www.vitalonga.it

What a performance from the Vitalonga estate belonging to the Maravalle family. Terra di Confine '06, a montepulciano and merlot blend, exceeded all expectations and vies with the best for its extraordinarily intense nose and very complex palate. The Elcione '06, a Bordeaux blend, is good.

● Terra di Confine '06	¶¶ 5
● Elcione '06	¶¶ 4*

LAZIO

It is no easy task to talk about the results of Lazio's winemakers. One reason is the small step back in terms of Three Glasses awards, down to a hardly brilliant "one of each" but on the other hand we note improvements in the region's average standard of production, as we have pointed out for the past two or three years. In fact, the region as a whole seems to be increasingly geared to quality, particularly on some of the larger estates and the co-operative wineries of the Castelli Romani area, such as Fontana Candida whose Frascati Luna Mater '07 has reached the finals, or on a lesser scale the very favourable results of Gotto d'Oro and the reappearance in the guide of Fontana di Papa. Even so, there are some differences of approach in this drive for quality in Lazio's three main growing areas. Production in the Castelli, with the honourable exceptions mentioned above, gives an impression of inactivity. In the dynamic viticultural panorama of wine in the rest of Italy, this amounts to taking a step backwards, particularly after a growing year like 2006, which brought hope for renaissance in wine-friendly territory brimming with potential that has never been fully exploited. On the other hand, elsewhere in the region, we were pleased to note steps forward. From the Latina area, as many as four wineries went through to our finals and in the Viterbo area, where overall advances in winemaking forced us into making some difficult choices about which wineries to include in the Guide, there has been an increase in the number of wineries. In the province of Frosinone, the award of DOCG status to Cesanese del Piglio has been a great spur to improvement in quality, triggering an increase in the number of Frosinone wineries included in the Guide and nurturing hope that this improvement is more than a flash in the pan. Who knows, it may translate into a first Three Glass award for a Cesanese. Summing up then, the results are positive but not outstanding, especially if, as many producers maintain, Lazio wants to compete with the best wine-producing areas in Italy for top awards. Which brings us back to those Three Glass wines. As we said at the start of this introduction, there are two winners and neither of them could be called a surprise. Grechetto Latour a Civitella '06, the only Lazio white ever to win this prize, ironically for a region perceived as a producer of whites, and Montiano '06, the red with the fullest trophy cupboard in Lazio but also the one that is most difficult to consider as being truly from Lazio, in view of the parent winery's move to Umbria.

Marco Carpineti

LOC. CAPO LE MOLE
S.P. VELLETRI-ANZIO, KM 14,300
04010 CORI [LT]
TEL. 069679860
www.marcocarpineti.it

ANNUAL PRODUCTION	100,000 bottles
HECTARES UNDER VINE	41
VITICULTURE METHOD	Certified organic

Marco Carpineti's wines continue to impress. In the absence of the estate's flag-carrier, Dithyrambus, Moro '07 came out on top. It's one of the best whites of the region and went through to the finals again this year, thanks to almost opulent richness that still manages to be elegant and well-balanced. The innovation here of fermenting one third of the must in new small barrels with subsequent malolactic fermentation promise further sensory subtleties. Joining it are the Collesanti '07, which shows off the aromatics and savouriness of the arciprete grapes to perfection while Cori Bianco Capolemole '07, though well made, is not up to 2006's brilliant standards. You can't say that about Tufaliccio '07, from montepulciano and a little cesanese, which combines immediacy and early drinkability with lovely richness on nose and palate. We thought the new rosé, Os Rosae, which has all the ripeness of nero buono in its almost 15 per cent alcohol, was tantalizing but in need of further refinement and the Ludum '06 is offered in a very successful version, a stylish passito made from arciprete grapes.

O Moro '07	▼▼	4*
O Collesanti '07	▼▼	3*
O Ludum '06	▼▼	5
● Rosso Tufaliccio '07	▼▼	3*
O Cori Bianco Capolemole '07	▼	3
● Cori Rosso Capolemole '06	▼	4
⊙ Os Rosae '07	▼	4
O Cori Bianco Capolemole '06	♀♀	4*
● Dithyrambus '03	♀♀	6
● Dithyrambus '01	♀♀	5
O Moro '06	♀♀	4*
O Moro '05	♀♀	4*
● Rosso Tufaliccio '06	♀♀	4

Casale del Giglio

LOC. LE FERRIERE
S.DA CISTERNA-NETTUNO KM 13
04100 LATINA
TEL. 0692902530
www.casaledelgiglio.it

ANNUAL PRODUCTION	1,200,000 bottles
HECTARES UNDER VINE	125
VITICULTURE METHOD	Conventional

Antonio Santarelli and oenologist Paolo Tiefenthaler have managed to combine quality and quantity with a range of a dozen or so labels. Top of the list is Mater Matuta '05, a classy Bordeaux blend in a sumptuous version that skilfully balances fruit and wood with red berry fruits on the nose and broad, elegant palate. The monovarietals are equally good drinking, in terms of both fruit and structure, although Petit Verdot '05 is a partial exception in that its tannins are presently somewhat aggressive. The Bordeaux blend Madreselva '05 suffers from a somewhat mouth-drying palate but makes up for this with a long and complex finish. We were impressed by the range of whites, from Antinoo '06, a chardonnay and viognier blend almost surpassed by an exceptionally good Chardonnay '07, Satrico '07, again offering excellent value for money, and Petit Manseng '07, which has come through an experimental period and now has attractively well-defined character. Both Aphrodisium '07, a refreshing sweet wine that doesn't cloy, and the delightful rosé Albiola '07 rank among the region's best in their categories.

● Mater Matuta '05	▼▼	7
⊙ Albiola '07	▼▼	3*
O Antinoo '06	▼▼	4
O Aphrodisium V. T. '07	▼▼	6
● Cabernet Sauvignon '05	▼▼	5
O Chardonnay '07	▼▼	4*
● Merlot '06	▼▼	4*
O Petit Manseng '07	▼▼	4*
O Satrico '07	▼▼	3*
● Shiraz '06	▼▼	4*
● Madreselva '05	▼	5
● Petit Verdot '06	▼	4
O Sauvignon '07	▼	4
● Mater Matuta '04	♀♀	6
● Mater Matuta '03	♀♀	6
● Mater Matuta '01	♀♀	6

Castel de Paolis

VIA VAL DE PAOLIS
00046 GROTTAFERRATA [RM]
TEL. 069413648
www.casteldepaolis.it

ANNUAL PRODUCTION	90,000 bottles
HECTARES UNDER VINE	14
VITICULTURE METHOD	Certified organic

This long-established estate is currently celebrating full conversion to organic farming and production focuses on typicity and terroir of provenance. This year, the spotlight is again on Quattro Mori '05, in which a syrah base is fuses harmoniously with merlot, cabernet sauvignon and petit verdot to excellent effect, with profound aromas of red berries, remarkable structure and pleasing length. Our positive notes chiefly concern the classic sweet wines of the estate, especially Muffa Nobile '07, from sémillon and a little sauvignon, which is rounded, elegant and well able to carry the ripeness of the white fruit to unusual levels of complexity, while Rosathea '07, a single-variety Moscato Rosa, gratifying the palate with pleasing florality and aromatic tones of great elegance. All the other labels confirm the distinctive personality which has always been the hallmark of this grower. It is also worth noting the powerful personality of Donna Adriana '07, the clear typicity of Frascati Superiore '07 and the appeal of the two Campo Vecchios, dedicated to a small, long-established local vineyard.

Cantina Agricola Cincinnato

VIA CORI-CISTERNA KM 2
04010 CORI [LT]
TEL. 069679380
www.cantinacincinnato.it

ANNUAL PRODUCTION	300,000 bottles
HECTARES UNDER VINE	400
VITICULTURE METHOD	Certified organic

We thought we had comprehensively praised the Cantina Cincinnato in our notes last year when we wrote about the skill and hard work of the president, Nazareno Milita, oenologist Carlo Morettini and all the members. Yet here we are reporting some great new achievements, in particular Bellone '06, which deservedly reached our finals and is the finest interpretation to date of this often underrated variety. We particularly liked its nose-palate coherence, elegance and lovely length. Cori Bianco Illirio '07 is equally good, a textbook example of how a wine can be both drinkable and complex, and also offers superb value for money. The beginnings look good for a new winery line in Castore '07 and Pollùce '06, from monovarietal bellone and nero buono grapes respectively, while the Arcatura '06 made a good debut. It's a Cesanese that hits you with aromatics ranging from cherries to rhubarb and a nicely balanced palate. Lovely big tertiary and leather notes come through in the Nero Buono '05. Worth keeping an eye on but also needing refinement are the two bellone-based experiments, the Cincinnato Brut sparkler and the sweet Solina '05.

O Muffa Nobile '07	▼▼	6
● Quattro Mori '05	▼▼	6
O Campo Vecchio Bianco '07	▼	4
● Campo Vecchio Rosso '06	▼	4
O Donna Adriana '07	▼	5
O Frascati Sup. '07	▼	4
● Rosathea '07	▼	5
O Muffa Nobile '05	♈	6
● Quattro Mori '01	♈	6
● Quattro Mori '03	♈	6

O Bellone '06	▼▼	4*
● Arcatura '06	▼▼	4*
O Cori Bianco Illirio '07	▼▼	3*
● Nero Buono '05	▼▼	4*
O Brut Cincinnato Spumante	▼	2*
O Castore '07	▼	2*
● Cori Rosso Raverosse '05	▼	3
● Pollùce '06	▼	2*
O Solina V. T. '05	▼	5
● Cori Rosso Raverosse '04	♈	3*
● Nero Buono '04	♈	4
● Rosso dei Dioscuri '05	♈	2*

Antonello Coletti Conti

VIA VITTORIO EMANUELE, 116
03012 ANAGNI [FR]
TEL. 0775728610
www.coletticonti.it

ANNUAL PRODUCTION	20,000 bottles
HECTARES UNDER VINE	20
VITICULTURE METHOD	Conventional

With two great finalists, this cellar confirms a status that may yet improve further. In an area of cesanese and passerina, we prefer to start with the least typical wine, Arcadia '07, a monovarietal Incrocio Manzoni that apparently has little in common with Frosinone. It's a strongly territorial wine in which the riesling component comes through in all its fascinating minerality and tanginess yet freshness keeps the alcohol in check. This is not a wine of half measures: you either love it or hate it. We also look forward to seeing how it stands up to prolonged cellar ageing. Its partner, the Cesanese del Piglio Romanico '06 is still in the early stages of development. It brings out big tannins after a bouquet in which great tertiary aromas of spices and saddle leather begin to emerge. We think is that longer bottle ageing could give it the finishing touch. We felt the same about the Cesanese del Piglio Hernicus '07, which is too young just now but already able to offer a complex bouquet of currants, wild berries and vanilla followed by a well-structured palate that will soon find a balance of oak against fruit, and extract with alcohol.

Colle Picchioni - Paola Di Mauro

LOC. FRATTOCCHIE
VIA COLLE PICCHIONE, 46
00040 MARINO [RM]
TEL. 0693546329
www.collepicchioni.it

ANNUAL PRODUCTION	120,000 bottles
HECTARES UNDER VINE	13
VITICULTURE METHOD	Conventional

Shunning unnecessary fuss and working with the customary application, the Di Mauro family runs an exemplary wine estate whose approach was laid down by the outstanding Paola. From her secluded winery, today looked after by her son Armando, she crafted and distributed wines of quality and prestige, with Vassallo being both the symbol and an eminent example. Although the 2006 has retained the unique character of the wine, it lacks something of the usual flamboyance. But there was success nonetheless for the two most important house whites both reached our finals. It is good to find such an exquisite interpretation of Le Vignole '06 with such richness and wonderful intensity, not to mention a finish that could further improve over time. A model of elegance and typicity, Marino Donna Paola '07 offers a personality of rare eloquence with fragrant notes of wild flowers and medlar blossom preceding a broad palate with an unwavering finish. Coste Rotonde '07 is more substantial and traditional, with forthright flavours and a refreshing follow-through while the red Perlaia '07 still has its trademark tannic weave set off by generous, lingering fruit.

O Arcadia '07	▼▼	4
● Cesanese del Piglio Romanico '06	▼▼	6
● Cesanese del Piglio Hernicus '07	▼▼	4
● Cesanese del Piglio Hernicus '06	▽▽	4*
● Cesanese del Piglio Hernicus '05	▽▽	4
O Arcadia '05	▽▽	4
● Cesanese del Piglio Romanico '05	▽▽	6

O Le Vignole '06	▼▼	4*
O Marino Donna Paola '07	▼▼	4*
● Il Vassallo '06	▼▼	6
O Marino Coste Rotonde '07	▼	3
● Perlaia '07	▼	4
● Il Vassallo '05	▽▽▽	6
● Vigna del Vassallo '01	▽▽▽	6
● Vigna del Vassallo '00	▽▽▽	6
● Vigna del Vassallo '04	▽▽	6
● Vigna del Vassallo '03	▽▽	6
● Vigna del Vassallo '02	▽▽	6
● Vigna del Vassallo '99	▽▽	5*
● Vigna del Vassallo '98	▽▽	5

Colletonno

LOC. COLLETONNO
03012 ANAGNI [FR]
TEL. 0775769271
www.colletonno.it

ANNUAL PRODUCTION	30,000 bottles
HECTARES UNDER VINE	20
VITICULTURE METHOD	Conventional

Some years ago the Di Cosimo family identified a high-quality grape zone on their large farm of about 200 hectares to assess its suitability for local vines, and wine, or for international varieties. They didn't have to wait long for the results and from last year's short profile the estate has moved straight up to a large one. And from the wines we tasted, it is no easy task to choose the best from the range. This is because the average level is well above good, as the two cesanese-based wines in particular show. The younger wine, Cesanese del Piglio Colle Ticchio '07, has a nose of red fruits, attractive approachability and a palate where the prominent tannins are mitigated by softness and structure. The other, the Cesanese del Piglio San Magno '06, has a lovely broad spectrum of aromatics ranging from forest fruits to faint rhubarb and that follow through onto an equally complex palate. The Colle Sape Corte dei Papi '07 is completely out of the ordinary. A blend of malvasia, chardonnay and trebbiano, it gives spring flowers, cedar and pennyroyal, leading to a consistent, refreshingly zesty palate.

Paolo e Noemia D'Amico

FRAZ. VAIANO
LOC. PALOMBARO
01024 CASTIGLIONE IN TEVERINA [VT]
TEL. 0761948034
www.paoloenoemiadamico.it

ANNUAL PRODUCTION	110,000 bottles
HECTARES UNDER VINE	25
VITICULTURE METHOD	Conventional

This lovely winery set in the upper reaches of the Tiber valley, jutting out over the steeply eroded ravines, is so stunningly beautiful that it was becoming known more for these nonetheless attractive features than for the actual quality of its wines. Things have changed in the last few years, though, and with a vengeance. As we predicted last year, D'Amico's production has grown in both quality and stylistic definition and sent two single-variety Chardonnays to our finals as a result. The oak-aged version, Falesia '06, is the best ever, giving balsam, citrus and spring flowers before the discreetly oaked palate presents rich, taut and clean, with florality and faintly aromatic perceptions. The current Calanchi di Vaiano, aged only in stainless steel, is one of the best, proffering a complex nose that follows scents of almond, apricot and rue with hints of apricot and rue. The firm palate follows through nicely, with minerals and citrus, ending long and refreshing. The other wines are good and a special mention goes to Seiano Rosso '07, a skilful, fruit-forward blend of merlot and sangiovese.

● Cesanese del Piglio Colle Ticchio '07	▼▼	4*
● Cesanese del Piglio San Magno '06	▼▼	4*
○ Colle Sape Corte dei Papi '07	▼▼	3*
● Cesanese del Piglio Colle Ticchio '05	♡♡	4*
○ Colle Sape Corte dei Papi '06	♡♡	3*

○ Calanchi di Vaiano '07	▼▼	4*
○ Falesia '06	▼▼	5
● Seiano Rosso '07	▼▼	4*
○ Orvieto Noe '07	▼	4
○ Seiano Bianco '07	▼	4
● Villa Tirrena '05	▼	5
○ Calanchi di Vaiano '06	♡♡	4*
○ Calanchi di Vaiano '05	♡♡	4*
○ Falesia '05	♡♡	5
○ Falesia '04	♡♡	5

Fontana Candida

VIA FONTANA CANDIDA, 11
00040 MONTE PORZIO CATONE [RM]
TEL. 069401881
www.fontanacandida.it

ANNUAL PRODUCTION   6,000,000 bottles
HECTARES UNDER VINE   97
VITICULTURE METHOD   Conventional

For the first time, a Frascati joined our finalists with the debut '07 edition of Luna Mater, a just reward for the entire DOC zone. Sourced from vines more than 50 years old, and with three months' bottle age in the ancient estate caves, it brims with character and class, combining fruit and intense aromatics through to a long, complex finish. This famous Gruppo Italiano Vini winery in the Castelli Romani has stepped up a gear, a fact that is confirmed by other good whites. The traditional Frascati Superiore Santa Teresa '07 offers lovely white-fleshed apple in a fine combination of structure, length and style. The utterly varietal, very solid Malvasia '07 shows impressive power and delightful freshness. A more traditional bottle, the clean-tasting, drinkable Frascati Terre dei Grifi '07 is reliable and convincing. As we wait for further news from the reds, we can only applaud the efforts of Francesco Bardi and Mauro Merz in mapping and selecting the vineyards of Fontana Candida's 220 growers.

Marcella Giuliani

LOC. VICO
VIA ANTICOLANA KM 5
03012 ANAGNI [FR]
TEL. 0644235908
www.aziendaagricolamarcellagiuliani.it

ANNUAL PRODUCTION   30,000 bottles
HECTARES UNDER VINE   10.5
VITICULTURE METHOD   Conventional

Marcella Giuliani's Dives has sometimes prompted discussion about how international Cesanese has become and we fear that DOCG status for Cesanese del Piglio could start it up again. We consider Dives to be one of the finest examples of wine from this grape so we would encourage Marcella and oenologist Riccardo Cotarella to carry on regardless. In fact, we thought that the '06 Cesanese del Piglio Dives was one of the best we had ever tasted and a most worthy finalist. Its wonderfully balanced nose is intense without being intrusive, giving nice red berries over a balsamic undertone that lead into a long, rounded palate that echoes the nose. Graffio '07, a blend of petit verdot and cabernet sauvignon aged in once-used barrels, shows good concentration but is still a little tart and needs more time to find its balance. Finally, the Alagna Bianco '07, made from passerina grapes, has a somewhat one-dimensional flower-themed nose followed by a nice clean palate that is refreshing and quite zesty.

O Frascati Sup. Luna Mater '07	▼▼	6
O Frascati Sup. Santa Teresa '07	▼▼	5
O Malvasia '07	▼▼	5
O Frascati Sup. Terre dei Grifi '07	▼	3
O Frascati Sup. Santa Teresa '06	♈♈	5
● Kron '04	♈♈	6

● Cesanese del Piglio Dives '06	▼▼	5
O Alagna Bianco '07	▼	3
● Il Graffio '07	▼	4
● Cesanese del Piglio Dives '04	♈♈	5
● Cesanese del Piglio Dives '05	♈♈	5
● Il Graffio '06	♈♈	4

Sergio Mottura

LOC. POGGIO DELLA COSTA, 1
01020 CIVITELLA D'AGLIANO [VT]
TEL. 0761914533
www.motturasergio.it

ANNUAL PRODUCTION	95,000 bottles
HECTARES UNDER VINE	37
VITICULTURE METHOD	Certified organic

Motturas' passion for viticulture is common knowledge. Organic farming, low yields per plant, attention to detail in the cellar and respect for typicity and territory are the rules that have made this operation a benchmark for the entire region and beyond. So the '06 Latour a Civitella '06 picked up its customary Three Glasses. The fruity aromas, from peach through damson to apricot, and curry-led oriental spices, follow through onto a full-bodied, elegantly refined palate that reveals complexity and tension, with a long finish that reprises the nose. It's one of the best whites in Italy. The steel-aged Poggio della Costa '07 is a worthy little brother to the Latour, showing flavoursome and zesty at the same time. Both are built for the long haul and will be at their best in a few years' time. The Orvieto Vigna Tragugnano '07 is well handled, with notes of apple and pear and a lovely almondy finish. Nenfro '05, a blend of 60 per cent merlot with montepulciano, is supple, with floral and red berry notes. The rest of the range is good, although we expected more from Mottura Brut and the Muffo.

L'Olivella

VIA DI COLLE PISANO, 5
00044 FRASCATI [RM]
TEL. 069424527
www.racemo.it

ANNUAL PRODUCTION	96,000 bottles
HECTARES UNDER VINE	12
VITICULTURE METHOD	Certified organic

If we were betting people, we would put money on this delightful winery without a second's hesitation. This is the home of some very carefully made wines that reflect an area particularly well-suited to wine and with some potential yet to be expressed. Often the varieties are ancient varieties and the interpretations are very well typed and utterly characteristic. That description could sum up Tre Grome '07. A blend of local grape types, it is balanced and elegant in its florality and white-fleshed fruit tones, with a dry, savoury, robust palate and a long, dynamic finish. In contrast, Maggiore '05 has all the generosity of cesanese, putting the emphasis on morello cherry and a spicy weave on the dry, full palate rounded off by a nice long finish. Racemo Rosso '05 is also good, showing character and substance, with a tasty, mouth-filling palate, while the 40/60 '06 is an intriguingly harmonious blend of syrah and cesanese. Two whites complete the range: Bombino '07, with its slightly citrussy aromas and minerality; and the clean-tasting, broad Frascati Superiore Racemo '07, offering classic structure and expression.

O Grechetto Latour a Civitella '06	♟♟♟ 5*
O Grechetto Poggio della Costa '07	♟♟ 4*
● Nenfro '05	♟♟ 5
O Orvieto Cl. V. Tragugnano '07	♟♟ 4*
● Civitella Rosso '07	♟ 4
● Magone '06	♟ 5
O Mottura Brut '04	♟ 6
O Muffo '06	♟ 6
O Orvieto '07	♟ 4
O Grechetto Latour a Civitella '05	♟♟♟ 5*
O Grechetto Latour a Civitella '04	♟♟♟ 5*
O Grechetto Latour a Civitella '01	♟♟♟ 4
O Grechetto Poggio della Costa '06	♟♟ 4*
O Grechetto Poggio della Costa '05	♟♟ 4

● Maggiore '05	♟♟ 5
O Tre Grome '07	♟♟ 5
● 40/60 '06	♟ 4
O Bombino '07	♟ 4
O Frascati Sup. Racemo '07	♟ 4
● Racemo Rosso '05	♟ 5
● Racemo Rosso '04	♟♟ 5

Principe Pallavicini

VIA CASILINA KM 25,500
00043 COLONNA [RM]
TEL. 069438816
www.vinipallavicini.com

ANNUAL PRODUCTION	450,000 bottles
HECTARES UNDER VINE	80
VITICULTURE METHOD	Conventional

This important estate is forging ahead with a development project closely linked to the quality and character of the territory under vine. In addition to the Castelli Romani vineyards, other estate properties closer to the coast are increasingly supplying grapes. This means different soils and different characters, which is a useful way to distinguish the stamp of the many wines present in the estate's range, which has various new developments this year. The 1670 '06 is one, a blend based on malvasia puntinata with elegant aromatic expressions, good structure, length and balanced. The stylish, full-bodied Moroello '05 has unusual breadth and depth. The 2007 version of the now famous Stillato is excellent, combining complexity and fullness in delightful harmony. An interesting Syrah '07 and the varietal Frascati Superiore Poggio Verde '07, which again shows its generosity in its fruit, are both decent. There was a good debut for the cabernet-based Casa Romana '06, which impresses with its full, lingering flavour. Finally, the slightly too ripe dark berry jam-like notes of the Amarasco '06 are in no hurry to depart.

O 1670 '06	♀♀ 5
● Moroello '05	♀♀ 6
O Stillato '07	♀♀ 5
● Amarasco '06	♀ 5
● Casa Romana '06	♀ 6
O Frascati Sup. Poggio Verde '07	♀ 4
● La Cavata '05	♀ 4
● Soleggio '05	♀ 4
● Syrah '07	♀ 4
● Moroello '04	♀♀ 6
● Moroello '03	♀♀ 6
O Stillato '05	♀♀ 5

Pietra Pinta

S.P. PASTINE KM 20,300
04010 CORI [LT]
TEL. 069678001
www.pietrapinta.it

ANNUAL PRODUCTION	250,000 bottles
HECTARES UNDER VINE	115
VITICULTURE METHOD	Certified organic

The Ferrettis don't stand still. From farmstay accommodation to their olive oil-based cosmetics, their estate is a hive of industry where the wines are getting their due attention again. This shows in the recent collaboration with oenologist Lorenzo Costantini and experimentation with new vines, which has led to new wines in the pipeline, such as those from monovarietal procanico and malvasia puntinata. As if to emphasise this new initiative, all the wines presented are from the 2007 vintage The Merlot and Shiraz '07 stand out, mutually complementing one another, the first soft and succulent while the second is still nicely tannic. Both the Petit Verdot '07 and the new Nero Buono '07 are less developed and seem to need more time to find their balance. Costa Vecchia '07 already seems more evolved, especially on the nose with notes of jam and oak. The two whites are well thought out and expertly made. The Chardonnay '07 did very well with its fine nose of spring flowers and palate with bags of personality while the Falanghina '07 has nice floral and fruity notes.

O Chardonnay '07	♀♀ 4*
● Merlot '07	♀♀ 4*
● Shiraz '07	♀♀ 4*
● Costa Vecchia '07	♀ 4
O Falanghina '07	♀ 4
● Nero Buono '07	♀ 4
● Petit Verdot '07	♀ 4
● Petit Verdot '05	♀♀ 4

Poggio Le Volpi

VIA COLLE PISANO, 27
00040 MONTE PORZIO CATONE [RM]
TEL. 069426980
www.poggiolevolpi.it

ANNUAL PRODUCTION	224,000 bottles
HECTARES UNDER VINE	30
VITICULTURE METHOD	Conventional

Our notes are all positive regarding the reliability this estate has achieved in just a few years, putting it head and shoulders above the competition in the region. The cellar makes wines of distinct character that have hordes of faithful fans, delighted at this new style in the area. Novel experiments with fermentation methods and careful field selections continue under the watchful eye of Riccardo Cotarella. As ever, the '06 Baccarossa is good. The elegance and depth of its nero buono di Cori grapes charm through to the complex, lingering finish. The two whites are excellent. Frascati Superiore Epos '07, with its virtually explosive aromas, suggests aromatic herbs melding into tropical fruit and then has plenty of flavour through to a lingering almondy finish. Donnaluce '07 is a blend of 60 per cent malvasia puntinata, 30 per cent greco and chardonnay with apricot and peach notes, delicate toasty sensations and ripe tones that introduce body, length, fullness and wonderful complexity in the mouth. Finally, the sweet Odôs '06 is appealing, showing complexity and pervasiveness with its ripe scents of dried fruits.

Sant'Andrea

LOC. BORGO VODICE
VIA RENIBBIO, 1720
04010 TERRACINA [LT]
TEL. 0773755028
www.cantinasantandrea.it

ANNUAL PRODUCTION	200,000 bottles
HECTARES UNDER VINE	70
VITICULTURE METHOD	Conventional

By a happy coincidence that will have delighted Gabriele and Andrea Pandolfo, the first year of the DOC for Moscato di Terracina, 2007, coincided with a fantastic harvest, which in turn led to the greatest Oppidum of all time. This marvel leapt into the finals with its varietal cleanliness, delightful aromatics, savoury, intense palate and long, clean finish. The same sensations can be found in the dry spumante version of Oppidum and indeed in the two versions of Moscato di Terracina Amabile Templum'07, which are simpler but pleasant, both the still and the spumante. The standard-bearer for the Circeo DOC is the Sogno '05. Fruit and oak on the one hand and alcohol and extract on the other combine in a highly successful balance. We continue to believe in Circeo Dune, and in the idea of marrying malvasia and small wood, even if we found the '06 version at the tasting less balanced than in previous years. The rest of the range is very clean and well managed. Don't miss Capitolium '06, whose aromatic intensity is as controlled and deftly handled as ever.

● Baccarossa '06	♟♟ 5
○ Donnaluce '07	♟♟ 4*
○ Frascati Sup. Epos '07	♟♟ 4*
○ Passito Odôs '06	♟♟ 5
● Baccarossa '05	♟♟ 6
● Baccarossa '04	♟♟ 6
○ Donnaluce '06	♟♟ 5
○ Donnaluce '05	♟♟ 5
○ Frascati Sup. Epos '06	♟♟ 5

○ Moscato di Terracina Secco Oppidum '07	♟♟ 3*
● Circeo Rosso Il Sogno '05	♟♟ 4*
○ Moscato di Terracina Passito Capitolium '06	♟♟ 4*
○ Moscato di Terracina Secco Oppidum Spumante '07	♟♟ 3*
○ Circeo Bianco Dune '06	♟ 4
○ Circeo Bianco Riflessi '07	♟ 2*
◉ Circeo Rosato Riflessi '07	♟ 2*
● Circeo Rosso Preludio alla Notte '06	♟ 3
● Circeo Rosso Riflessi '07	♟ 2*
○ Moscato di Terracina Amabile Templum '07	♟ 3
○ Moscato di Terracina Amabile Templum Spumante '07	♟ 3
○ Circeo Bianco Dune '03	♟♟ 4*
○ Circeo Bianco Dune '05	♟♟ 4

Sant'Isidoro

LOC. PORTACCIA
01016 TARQUINIA [VT]
TEL. 0766869716
www.santisidoro.net

ANNUAL PRODUCTION	120,000 bottles
HECTARES UNDER VINE	57
VITICULTURE METHOD	Conventional

The Palombo family flies the flag for viticulture on the upper Lazio coast, the glorious continuation of the Tuscan Maremma which has not yet managed to achieve serious standards of quality. Even though it did not reach our finals this year, Soremidio is sound. Made from montepulciano only aged in small barrels, the 2006 has hints of cinnamon and pepper spice on the nose, with saddle leather and red berries, while the palate is fruity, beautifully long and refreshing. On the downside, the structure is not quite firm enough to make the leap in quality we are expecting for this product. Also offered this year, and on the same level, is the Corithus '07, a blend of 50 per cent sangiovese, 30 per cent montepulciano and merlot. It has good body and vigour, with scents of flowers and dark berry fruits, for a very nice, well-made wine. The Terzolo '07 is a moreish blend of cabernet sauvignon with ten per cent merlot that has refreshing notes of Mediterranean scrubland. Finally, Forca di Palma '07, from chardonnay with 30 per cent trebbiano toscano, sets too much store by sweetness on the nose and in the mouth.

Giovanni Terenzi

LOC. LA FORMA
VIA FORESE, 13
03010 SERRONE [FR]
TEL. 0775594286
www.viniterenzi.com

ANNUAL PRODUCTION	80,000 bottles
HECTARES UNDER VINE	12
VITICULTURE METHOD	Conventional

It is always nice to find room for family estates that respect the environment in general and the territory in particular. This is an excellent example. The wines offered were the best ever in the history of the estate so we have a fine long list of tasting notes and to round things off, a Cesanese del Piglio Velobra '06 that went through to our finals. The wine's balance and elegance on nose and palate are impressive without detracting from typicity or overdoing the structure or alcoholic warmth. The new Cesanese DOCG is starting out well. Its worthy representatives are Vajoscuro '05 and Colle Forma '06. The former has an appealing nose of roses and forest fruits and a well-rounded palate without too much extract while Colle Forma nicely marries fruit and oak-derived balsam leading into a lingering, well-balanced finish. If that were not enough, the versatility of the variety can also be seen in Rosato Villa Santa '07, one of the cleanest, most agreeable rosés in the region. Passerina Villa Santa '07 completes the range, giving acerbic citrus and green apple notes followed by a tidier, decently complex palate.

● Corithus '07	♟♟	4*
● Soremidio '06	♟♟	5
O Forca di Palma '07	♟	3
● Terzolo '07	♟	3
● Soremidio '05	♟♟	6
● Soremidio '04	♟♟	5
● Soremidio '01	♟♟	5

● Cesanese del Piglio Velobra '06	♟♟	4*
● Cesanese del Piglio Colle Forma '06	♟♟	5
● Cesanese del Piglio Vajoscuro '05	♟♟	5
⊙ Rosato Villa Santa '07	♟♟	3*
O Passerina Villa Santa '07	♟	4
● Cesanese del Piglio Colle Forma '05	♟♟	5
● Cesanese del Piglio Velobra '04	♟♟	3*

Trappolini

via del Rivellino, 65
01024 Castiglione in Teverina [VT]
tel. 0761948381
www.trappolini.com

ANNUAL PRODUCTION 150,000 bottles
HECTARES UNDER VINE 25
VITICULTURE METHOD Conventional

For several years, the Trappolini family's estate has been one of the benchmarks for Viterbo winemakers, both in terms of quality of and for their interest in promoting the upper Tiber valley. In contrast to most of the estates in the area, the flagship wine is a red, Paterno, a single-variety Sangiovese that reached our finals this year. The 2006 has scents of cherry, tobacco and sweet spices, laced with hints of bay leaf-led Mediterranean scrubland. The palate is echoes the nose, with good fruit, plums and damsons showing rich and well balanced, with aromatic herbs reprised on the finish. All in all, not bad for a wine made for the first time from young vines - the old vineyard was no longer productive and was grubbed up. The Brecceto '07 is also good. From a 50-50 blend of grechetto and chardonnay, although the grechetto clearly predominates, it has fine structure and fragrance. Cenereto '07, made from sangiovese and montepulciano, is tangy, juicy and pleasantly drinkable. Lastly, Est Est Est, one of the best of its designation, is citrussy, lightly aromatic and attractively long-lingering.

● Paterno '06	🍷🍷 4*
O Brecceto '07	🍷🍷 4*
● Cenereto '07	🍷🍷 3*
O Est Est Est di Montefiascone '07	🍷🍷 2*
● Idea '07	🍷 4
O Orvieto '07	🍷 3
O Sartei '07	🍷 2*
● Paterno '05	🍷🍷 4
● Paterno '04	🍷🍷 4
● Paterno '03	🍷🍷 4*

Villa Gianna

loc. B.go San Donato
s.da Maremmana
04010 Sabaudia [LT]
tel. 0773250034
www.villagianna.it

ANNUAL PRODUCTION 830,000 bottles
HECTARES UNDER VINE 50
VITICULTURE METHOD Conventional

Gianluca Giannini will be happy that his winery has a full profile, having worked hard to reach this goal. For some years, there have been some quite refined bottles emerging from this estate, prompting reappraisal of an often underrated area. The new Circeo Bianco Innato '07 is one example, offsetting high alcohol content with refreshing tanginess and aromatics. The Sauvignon Vigna del Borgo '07 is one of the best whites of the year from the Pontine flatlands, rich in the varietal aromas of tomato leaf, summer flowers and tropical fruits and clean in its follow-through on the palate. From the reds, the Cabernet Sauvignon Vigna del Borgo '06 shows its class in the complexity of the nose, which gives red berry fruits and red pepper, as well as tobacco and liquorice, and its velvety, well-balanced palate. As they did last year, the straightforwardness and immediacy of the Rudèstro '06 seemed more convincing than the ambitious complexity of Barriano '05, whose wood struggles to find a balance with the fruit. The other Circeo DOC wines are well styled, in particular the Circeo Rosso '07 with its lovely notes of forest fruits.

O Circeo Bianco Innato '07	🍷🍷 4*
● Rudèstro '06	🍷🍷 3*
● Vigne del Borgo Cabernet Sauvignon '06	🍷🍷 4
O Vigne del Borgo Sauvignon '07	🍷🍷 4*
● Barriano '05	🍷 4
O Bianco di Caprolace Chardonnay '07	🍷 3
O Brut Villa Gianna	🍷 3
● Circeo Bianco '07	🍷 2*
● Circeo Rosso '07	🍷 2*
O Vigne del Borgo Chardonnay '07	🍷 3
● Vigne del Borgo Cabernet Sauvignon '05	🍷🍷 4

OTHER WINERIES

Camponeschi

VIA PIASTRARELLE, 14
00040 LANUVIO [RM]
TEL. 069374390
www.collilanuvini.it

The wines from this family-run cellar are consistently good, with the Carato Rosso '05 standing out this year for its intense fruit and harmonious finish. The typical Colli Lanuvini Superiore '07, still nicely fragrant, and the zesty Sauvignon '07 also pass muster.

● Carato Rosso '05	♟ 5
○ Colli Lanuvini Sup. '07	♟ 2
○ Sauvignon '07	♟ 3

Casale Cento Corvi

VIA AURELIA KM 45,500
00052 CERVETERI [RM]
TEL. 069903902
www.casalecentocorvi.com

This interesting winery at Cerveteri maintains its high standard with Giacché '06, from the grape of the same name, which is spicy with dark berry preserve notes and varietal character. The whites on offer are decent: the flavoursome Kottabos '07 and the more intense Kantharos '07.

● Giacché '06	♟♟ 7
○ Kantharos Bianco '07	♟ 4
○ Kottabos Bianco '07	♟ 4

Casale della Ioria

P.ZZA REGINA MARGHERITA, 1
03010 ACUTO [FR]
TEL. 0775744282
www.casaledellaioria.com

Curiously, the absence of the Cesaneses makes the quality of Paolo Perinelli's two outsiders stand out. Passerina Colle Bianco '07 has breadth and a splendid follow-through in the mouth while Olivella '07 makes an interesting debut. Kudos to Paolo for rediscovering this indigenous grape variety.

○ Colle Bianco '07	♟♟ 3*
● L'Olivella '07	♟♟ 4

Casale Marchese

VIA DI VERMICINO, 68
00044 FRASCATI [RM]
TEL. 069408932
www.casalemarchese.it

We record a step back by this fine and admirably hospitable winery. The Clemens '07 is excellent, its bouquet elegant and invigorating as it embraces the palate while the Frascati Superiore '07 is refreshing, subtle and quaffable. Rosso '07 is full-bodied and generous.

○ Clemens '07	♟♟ 4*
○ Frascati Sup. '07	♟ 3
● Rosso di Casale Marchese '07	♟ 4

Casale Mattia

LOC. COLLE MATTIA
VIA MONTE MELLONE, 19
00040 MONTECOMPATRI [RM]
TEL. 069426249
www.casalemattia.it

This is one of the best areas for Frascati and Roberto Rotelli is a passionate supporter of viticulture in Castelli Romani. Merlot Terre Laviche '07 is stylish, well balanced and agreeably spicy. We would also mention the characterful Frascati Superiore Linea Storica '07's and the velvety Cannellino '07.

● Merlot Terre Laviche '07	♟♟ 4*
○ Frascati Cannellino '07	♟ 4
○ Frascati Sup. Linea Storica '07	♟ 4

Cavalieri

VIA MONTECAGNOLO, 16
00045 GENZANO DI ROMA [RM]
TEL. 069375807
www.cavalieri.it

Fabrizio Cavalieri has been trying hard to put some oomph back into the Colli Lanuvini. No surprise, then, that his refined, fragrant 2007 is the star of the year. Rutilo '05 is soundly made, Infiorata '07 is fruity with a lovely finish and the Teresa '07 is more subtle and spirited.

○ Colli Lanuvini Sup. '07	♟♟ 2*
○ Infiorata '07	♟ 3
● Rutilo '05	♟ 5
○ Teresa '07	♟ 3

OTHER WINERIES

Cantina Cerquetta

VIA DI FONTANA CANDIDA, 20
00040 MONTE PORZIO CATONE [RM]
TEL. 069424147
www.cantinacerquetta.it

The Ciuffa family runs one of the most important estates in Frascati very shrewdly. In fact, the Antico Cenacolo '07 is one of the best wines in the designation, showing generous, convincing and wonderfully varietal. Also worthy of note are the lovely Montecompatri '07 and the soft Cannellino '06.

O Frascati Sup. Antico Cenacolo '07	♟♟	4*
O Frascati Cannellino '06	♟	4
O Montecompatri Colonna Sup. '07	♟	2

Cantina Cerveteri

VIA AURELIA KM 42,700
00052 CERVETERI [RM]
TEL. 06994441
www.cantinacerveteri.it

Sheer numbers seem to be holding back the potential of this much-admired estate. This year, the red Viniae Grande '05 stands out, combining good fruit with stylish, spicy maturity. The white version is somewhat less convincing while the Malvasia Novae '07 excels for freshness and structure.

O Cerveteri Bianco Viniae Grande '07	♟	4
● Cerveteri Rosso Viniae Grande '05	♟	4
O Novae '07	♟	3

Colacicchi

VIA ROMAGNANO, 2
03012 ANAGNI [FR]
TEL. 064469661
info@trimani.com

It was a low-key year for Colacicchi. Torre Ercolana '05, a blend of cesanese, cabernet sauvignon and merlot, is good with spice, dark berry fruit and toasty notes echoed on the supple palate. Tobacco-veined Schiaffo '07, from the same grapes, is pleasant and the two Romagnanos are well styled.

● Torre Ercolana '05	♟♟	7
O Romagnano Bianco '07	♟	5
● Romagnano Rosso '06	♟	5
● Schiaffo '07	♟	5

Colle di Maggio

VIA PASSO DEI CORESI, 25
00049 VELLETRI [RM]
TEL. 0696453072
www.colledimaggio.com

This is still the most interesting estate in Velletri, even if nowadays it seems to concentrate on its farmstay and eatery. Among the wines on offer we find an excellent Tulino Rosso '06, showing spicy and deep with its rich, fruity tone. The fragrant Tulino Chardonnay '07 and the two dependable Porticatos are also good.

● Tulino Rosso '06	♟♟	4*
O Porticato Bianco '07	♟	4
● Porticato Rosso '06	♟	4
O Tulino Chardonnay '07	♟	4

Federici

VIA SANTA APOLLARIA VECCHIA, 30
00039 ZAGAROLO [RM]
TEL. 0695461022
www.vinifederici.com

The output of quality wines in Zagarolo is growing, thanks to the reliability of this small producer. Le Ripe Bianco '07 is particularly good, with clean, generous aromas and lingering, fresh-tasting fruit. The varietal Zagarolo Superiore '07 is satisfyingly dry and well structured.

O Le Ripe Bianco '07	♟♟	3*
O Zagarolo Sup. '07	♟	2*

La Ferriera

LOC. ROSAMISCO
03042 ATINA [FR]
TEL. 0776610413
www.laferriera.it

This young winery is reviving an ancient tradition with interesting results. Atina Cabernet Forgiato '06 is outstanding, with a good balance of oak and fruit, while the cabernet, syrah and petit verdot Ferrato '07 is already drinking well with its cherry aromas and soft tannins.

● Atina Cabernet Forgiato '06	♟♟	5
● Ferrato '07	♟	4

OTHER WINERIES

Fontana di Papa

VIA NETTUNENSE, KM 10,800
00040 ARICCIA [RM]
TEL. 06934781
www.fontanadipapa.com

This historic Castelli Romani winery is back in the spotlight, thanks to a sound wide-ranging list that reveals a serious commitment to wine production. The noteworthy Castelli Romani Calathus '06 is one of the most interesting reds in the territory. The other wines are all well made.

● Castelli Romani Calathus '06	¶¶ 3*
○ Colli Albani Sup.	
Vign. Poggio del Cardinale '07	¶ 3
○ Malvasia "U" '07	¶ 2

Giangirolami

LOC. BORGO MONTELLO
VIA DEL CAVALIERE, 1414
04100 LATINA
TEL. 3358394890
www.donatogiangirolami.it

There was a good debut from Domenico Giangirolami's organic winery. The new Sauvignon Regius '07 has aromatic freshness and pleasant tanginess while Syrah Prodigo '06 nicely blends succulent fruit and discreet wood. The Peschio '05, a blend of cabernet, merlot and syrah, is more evolved with tertiary aromas.

○ Sauvignon Regius '07	¶¶ 3*
● Syrah Prodigo '06	¶¶ 3*
● Peschio '05	¶ 3

Gotto d'Oro

LOC. FRATTOCCHIE
VIA DEL DIVINO AMORE, 115
00040 MARINO [RM]
TEL. 0693022211
www.gottodoro.it

This estate has shown improvement across the board. The Merlot '06 is lovely, with remarkable structure and balance, and so too is Mithra '06, an elegant, pervasive blend of sangiovese, merlot and syrah. The excellent Sol '06 and the classic Marino Superiore '07 both impressed.

● Merlot del Lazio '06	¶¶ 3*
● Mitreo Mithra '06	¶¶ 3*
○ Marino Sup. '07	¶ 3
○ Mitreo Sol '06	¶ 3

Antica Cantina Leonardi

VIA DEL PINO, 12
01027 MONTEFIASCONE [VT]
TEL. 0761826028
www.cantinaleonardi.it

This historic Montefiascone estate is back in the Guide after a year off, thanks to a good all-round showing and especially to Pensiero '07, a grechetto with tropical fruits-laced aromas that are still redolent of wood echoed on a palate with plenty of body and a refreshing finish.

○ Pensiero '07	¶¶ 3*
● Don Carlo '05	¶ 4
○ Est Est Est di Montefiascone	
Poggio del Cardinale '07	¶ 3

Mazziotti

LOC. MELONA BONVINO
VIA CASSIA, KM 110
01023 BOLSENA [VT]
TEL. 0644291377
www.mazziottiwines.com

Valeria Mazziotti's winery did well again, especially her flag-carrier, Canuleio '07. From chardonnay, sauvignon and malvasia, it tempts with wafts of tropical fruit that precede good body on the palate. The Est Est Est '07 is also nice, with a nose of flowers and sage-like herbaceousness and a clean, refreshing palate.

○ Canuleio '07	¶¶ 4*
○ Est Est Est di Montefiascone '07	¶ 3
● Volgente Rosso '06	¶ 5

Isabella Mottura

LOC. RIO CHIARO, 1
01020 CIVITELLA D'AGLIANO [VT]
TEL. 3357077931
www.isabellamottura.com

We include this winery after a sound performance that lacked last year's brilliance. The 50-50 sangiovese and cabernet sauvignon Siren '07 is good, showing spicy, fresh-tasting and appealing, as is the fruit-led merlot-only Akemi '07. The Amadis '06, a monovarietal violone, is somewhat disappointing.

● Akemi '07	¶ 4
● Amadis '06	¶ 6
● Siren '07	¶ 3

OTHER WINERIES

Cantine Palombo

LOC. PONTE MELFA
C.SO MUNANZIO PLANCO
03042 ATINA [FR]
TEL. 0776610200
www.vinipalombo.it

With Duca Cantelmi missing, we were reviewed a modest range. Rosso delle Chiaie '07, from 80 per cent merlot, makes great drinking and Atina Cabernet '06 is more firmly structured. The Bianco delle Chiaie '07's malvasia puntinata is pleasantly aromatic and Somigliò '07's tangy freshness is lovely.

● Atina Cabernet '06	♟	4
○ Bianco delle Chiaie '07	♟	3
● Rosso delle Chiaie '07	♟	3
○ Somigliò '07	♟	4

I Pampini

LOC. ACCIARELLA
S.DA FOGLINO, 1126
04010 LATINA
TEL. 0773643144
www.ipampini.it

Enzo and Carmen Oliveto's commitment is producing increasingly good wines. Currently, reds prevail. Merlot is intelligently handled in the steel-only Coboldo '05 and in the Kubizzo '05, aged in small barrels. The Cabernet Sauvignon '05 is good as is the clean, varietal Bellone '07 from the whites.

● Coboldo '05	♟♟	3*
○ Bellone '07	♟	3
● Cabernet Sauvignon '05	♟	4
● Kubizzo '05	♟	4

La Pazzaglia

S.DA DI BAGNOREGIO, 4
01024 CASTIGLIONE IN TEVERINA [VT]
TEL. 0761947114
www.tenutalapazzaglia.com

It was a fine debut for the Verdecchia family's winery, which has come on apace. Poggio Triale '07, from grechetto, and Montijone '07, from merlot, are both very attractive, both from very low yields per plant and ruthless selection in the cellar. The other wines are better than agreeable.

● Montijone '07	♟♟	5
○ Poggio Triale '07	♟♟	5
● Aurelius '07	♟	4
○ Il Corno '07	♟	3

Tenuta Le Quinte

VIA DELLE MARMORELLE, 71
00040 MONTECOMPATRI [RM]
TEL. 069438756

The Papi family kept up its usual fine standard. The best from the cellar this year is the Malvasia Orchidea '07, a convincing, flavoursome wine with a wealth of varietal aromas. The Grechetto Canestraro '07 is beautifully refreshing and the better known Virtù Romane '07 is ready for the corkscrew.

○ Malvasia Orchidea '07	♟♟	3*
○ Grechetto Canestraro '07	♟	3
○ Montecompatri Colonna Sup. Virtù Romane '07	♟	3

Tenuta Ronci di Nepi

LOC. VALLE RONCI
01036 NEPI [VT]
TEL. 0761555125
www.roncidinepi.com

The Improta family's beautiful estate is back in the Guide, thanks to its two most important wines. Vigna Manti '06, a monovarietal Chardonnay, has citrus peel and spice with a complex palate reflecting the nose. The elegant, well-balanced Veste Porpora '05 is a blend of sangiovese and cabernet.

● Veste Porpora '05	♟♟	4*
○ Vigna Manti '06	♟♟	5
○ Oro di Nepi '07	♟	4

Cantine San Marco

LOC. VERMICINO
VIA DI MOLA CAVONA, 26/28
00044 FRASCATI [RM]
TEL. 069409403
www.sanmarcofrascati.it

Whoever said big numbers couldn't do justice to varietal character or terroir hasn't tried this historic Frascati estate's vast range. The Soloshiraz '06 is excellent, showing nicely structured and deep, and close behind are the nice Frascati Superiore Meraco '06 and a caressing, ripe Meraco Rosso '04.

● Soloshiraz '06	♟♟	4*
○ Frascati Sup. Meraco '06	♟	4
● Meraco Rosso '04	♟	4

OTHER WINERIES

Tenuta Santa Lucia

LOC. SANTA LUCIA
02047 POGGIO MIRTETO [RI]
TEL. 076524616
www.tenutasantalucia.com

Otio '06, an equal blend of montepulciano, cabernet sauvignon and merlot, is attractively well balanced, with lovely notes of dark fruit and liquorice. Morrone Riserva '04 is also fine, a Syrah with good flesh, and also good is Elodia '06, a supple, flower-led blend of malvasia, falanghina and sauvignon.

● Otio '06	♈♈ 5
○ Elodia '06	♈ 5
● Morrone Ris. '04	♈ 6

Terra delle Ginestre

VIA FORNELLO, 94
04020 SPIGNO SATURNIA [LT]
TEL. 0771700297
www.terradelleginestre.it

The star of Giulio Marrone and oenologist Maurizio De Simone's winery is moscato di Terracina in the fine barrique-aged Stellaria '07, the simpler Invito '07 and Promessa '06, a sweet wine with poise. Bellone aged in chestnut wood goes into Lentisco '07, which needs more time in bottle.

○ Stellaria '07	♈♈ 4*
○ Invito '07	♈ 3
○ Lentisco '07	♈ 4
○ Promessa Passito Dolce '06	♈ 4

Castello Torre in Pietra

VIA DI TORRIMPIETRA, 247
00050 FIUMICINO [RM]
TEL. 0661697070
www.castelloditorreinpietra.it

This striking, welcoming winery on the coast is worth a visit for its own merits but the Tarquinia wines are also intriguing, showing sound, characteristic expression in both types. Terre di Breccia Rosso '06 is a good Merlot with plenty of flavour and an appealing personality.

○ Tarquinia Bianco '07	♈ 2*
● Tarquinia Rosso '07	♈ 2*
● Terre di Breccia Rosso '06	♈ 4

Villa Simone

VIA FRASCATI COLONNA, 29
00040 MONTE PORZIO CATONE [RM]
TEL. 069449717
www.pierocostantini.it

It wasn't an especially brilliant year for Piero Costantini. No other big hitters joined the usual good-quality Ferro e Seta '05, made from cesanese and sangiovese grapes. Both Frascati Superiores are nice. Villa dei Preti '07 is more fragrant and deeper while the Villa Simone makes lovely drinking.

● Ferro e Seta '05	♈♈ 6
○ Frascati Sup. Villa dei Preti '07	♈ 4
○ Frascati Sup. Villa Simone '07	♈ 3

Cantine Volpetti

VIA NETTUNENSE, 21
00040 ARICCIA [RM]
TEL. 069342000
www.cantinevolpetti.it

This winery has gradually learnt how to find its place in the Guide, adding together several interesting bottles with a territorial bias. In the Elegie Romane range, the stand-out wine is Colli Albani '07, a soft, palate-pervading white, followed by the '07 Frascati. Chardonnay Le Piantate '07 is also good.

○ Chardonnay Le Piantate '07	♈ 3
○ Colli Albani Elegie Romane '07	♈ 3
○ Frascati Sup. Elegie Romane '07	♈ 3
● Shiraz Le Piantate '06	♈ 3

Conte Zandotti

VIA VIGNE COLLE MATTIA, 8
00132 ROMA
TEL. 0620609000
www.cantinecontezandotti.it

Leone Massimo Zandotti's range alternates traditional wines and innovative bottles. For now, the best results come from the former. The excellent, spice-laced La Petrosa '04 has a vibrant palate, the Rumon '07 is wonderfully varietal and the Frascati is fine.

● La Petrosa '04	♈♈ 5
○ Frascati Sup. '07	♈ 4
○ Malvasia del Lazio Rumon '07	♈ 4

ABRUZZO

The most significant event on the Abruzzo wine scene this year was some very bad news. Gianni Masciarelli died on 31 July 2008, aged just 52, depriving the region's winemaking sector without its key, charismatic figure, and just two years after the death of Edoardo Valentini. Abruzzo has lost the driving force behind the recent success of its wines worldwide. Now it's all up to their successors, Francesco Paolo Valentini and Gianni Masciarelli's widow, Marina Cvetic, as well as all those producers who believed, and still believe strongly, that Abruzzo's wines can play a leading role in Italy and abroad. For this is genuine wine country, often set midway between the sea and the mountains, and the vineyards boast the outstanding montepulciano grape. Abruzzo's wine production comprises a line-up of players ranging from small wineries to enormous co-operatives, but there are also quite a few medium-size operations. Let's not forget that Abruzzo is Italy's fifth biggest producer. That said, we might point out that in the 2009 edition of Wine of Italy, 12 Abruzzo wines picked up Three Glasses, the biggest haul so far. Gianni and Marina Masciarelli's wines are always at the top of the list and this time two impressive 2005 versions of Montepulciano d'Abruzzo, Villa Gemma and Marina Cvetic, won honours but we thought the whole range was on top form. There was a debut appearance for a Montepulciano d'Abruzzo Cerasuolo: Francesco Paolo Valentini's sensual, elegant 2007 rosé, in tandem with his 2005 Trebbiano d'Abruzzo, which was subtle and aristocratic. Luigi Cataldi Madonna sent us a 2006 Pecorino, with a tropical fruits nose and impressive entry, alongside his best-ever Montepulciano d'Abruzzo Malandrino, the 2006. Emidio Pepe shot back with a mature 1998 Montepulciano d'Abruzzo, aged for a decade to embody a pure expression of the region's rural traditions. Of the young bloods, Federica Morricone, won praise for her top-notch Montepulciano d'Abruzzo Villa Medoro 2006, as did Leonardo Pizzolo for his Montepulciano d'Abruzzo Valle Reale 2006, but we should also mention La Valentina's Sabatino Di Properzio, who produced a fine Montepulciano d'Abruzzo Bellovedere 2005. Our round-up closes with Dino Illuminati's timeless Montepulciano d'Abruzzo Colline Teramane Zanna Riserva 2005, and a welcome back to Abruzzo's front rank for Giannicola Di Carlo, whose Agriverde offered an opulent 2003 Montepulciano d'Abruzzo Solarea.

Agriverde

LOC. CALDARI
VIA STORTINI, 32A
66020 ORTONA [CH]
TEL. 0859032101
www.agriverde.it

ANNUAL PRODUCTION	700,000 bottles
HECTARES UNDER VINE	N.A.
VITICULTURE METHOD	Certified organic

We like Agriverde: lovely seaside vineyards on the slopes at Ortona; a winery inspired by bioarchitecture; a stylish contemporary hotel; focus on organic farming and wine therapy; and Giannicola Di Carlo's drive. It all makes for original, wholesome wines that are sometimes over the top but always interesting. This year, there was a fine selection and Three Glasses went to the promising '03 Solarea, a mature Montepulciano with a full, evolved nose and succulent, extract-rich palate. It's a heavyweight but progression is compact and fresh. Almost as good is the aristocratic Montepulciano d'Abruzzo Plateo '03, a fine, full-bodied red, hindered only by the torrid heat of that vintage. Apart from these two gems, we liked the whole range: the delicious, undemanding Natum organic line is admirable; the spirited Riseis '06 is a well-typed, agreeably rustic Montepulciano; the fragrant '07 Pecorino is slim-bodied, with the pleasing acidity typical of this grape and body and backbone that emerge on the palate. Lastly, the Montepulciano d'Abruzzo Cerasuolo Solàrea '07 shows the potential of this rosé, with pervasive aromas and healthy structure.

F.lli Barba

LOC. SCERNE DI PINETO
S.DA ROTABILE PER CASOLI
64020 PINETO [TE]
TEL. 0859461020
www.fratellibarba.it

ANNUAL PRODUCTION	300,000 bottles
HECTARES UNDER VINE	68
VITICULTURE METHOD	Conventional

Year after year, with the patience that is so typical of farming, the Barba family has expanded its presence in the Abruzzo wine sector while never biting off more than it could chew. All it needs now is a thoroughbred, a flagship label, and we suspect that won't be long in coming. The two wines we tasted in the finals were fairly convincing. The Montepulciano d'Abruzzo Vignafranca '05 has close-woven, varietal aromas with black cherry notes to the fore, preceding rich pulp on the juicy, velvet-textured palate. This year's revelation is Trebbiano d'Abruzzo '05, a traditional wine fermented in big oak. We found it to be a down-to-earth country item, perhaps a tad husky but very persuasive, and it just missed a top award. The Colle Morino line fulfils its purpose with well-typed, well-made wines that are good value for money. The last wine we sampled was the Trebbiano d'Abruzzo Vignafranca '06, a modern white that came across a little woody but it's early days yet.

● Montepulciano d'Abruzzo Solàrea '03	♟♟♟	5
● Montepulciano d'Abruzzo Plateo '03	♟♟	7
○ Chardonnay Riseis di Recastro '07	♟♟	4*
● Montepulciano d'Abruzzo Natum '07	♟♟	4*
● Montepulciano d'Abruzzo Riseis di Recastro '06	♟♟	4*
○ Pecorino Riseis di Recastro '07	♟♟	4*
⊙ Montepulciano d'Abruzzo Cerasuolo Solàrea '07	♟	4
● Montepulciano d'Abruzzo Piane di Maggio '07	♟	3
● Montepulciano d'Abruzzo Plateo '98	♟♟♟	6
● Montepulciano d'Abruzzo Plateo '01	♟♟♟	7
● Montepulciano d'Abruzzo Plateo '00	♟♟♟	7
● Montepulciano d'Abruzzo Plateo '97	♟♟	6

● Montepulciano d'Abruzzo Vignafranca '05	♟♟	4*
○ Trebbiano d'Abruzzo '05	♟♟	5
● Montepulciano d'Abruzzo Colle Morino '07	♟♟	2*
○ Trebbiano d'Abruzzo Colle Morino '07	♟♟	2*
○ Trebbiano d'Abruzzo Vignafranca '06	♟♟	4*
● Montepulciano d'Abruzzo Colle Morino '06	♟	2
● Montepulciano d'Abruzzo Vignafranca '04	♟♟	4
● Montepulciano d'Abruzzo Vignafranca '03	♟♟	4*

Barone Cornacchia

C.DA TORRI, 20
64010 TORANO NUOVO [TE]
TEL. 0861887412
www.baronecornacchia.it

ANNUAL PRODUCTION	300,000 bottles
HECTARES UNDER VINE	42
VITICULTURE METHOD	Certified organic

This well-established Torano Nuovo winery continues to make progress. It's one of the oldest, most traditional in the Colline Teramane district and is slowly but surely renewing its operation. All the labels we tried this year were good with only a big hitter missing from the line-up. The new Vigna Le Coste '05 is a fragrant Montepulciano with refined black cherry aromas and a well-defined, flavoursome palate. The basic Montepulciano '06 red has crisp, ripe fruit on the nose with a tempting hint of new oak in the background. We enjoyed the sturdy structure and fluid, savoury progression in the mouth. The very drinkable Trebbiano '07 had distinct, varietal aromas and a fresh, even flavour. Montepulciano d'Abruzzo Colline Teramane Vizzarro is promising, with balsamic and mild oak on the nose and some forward notes echoed on the palate. The Montepulciano d'Abruzzo Poggio Varano '05 is underpinned by richness of flavour but is let down by some slightly green, gritty tannins. At the end of the day, the most interesting wines were actually the traditional ones, which seem to work better for this Abruzzo winery.

● Montepulciano d'Abruzzo '06	♥♥	3*
● Montepulciano d'Abruzzo V. Le Coste '05	♥♥	4*
○ Trebbiano d'Abruzzo '07	♥♥	3*
● Montepulciano d'Abruzzo Colline Teramane Vizzarro '04	♥	5
● Montepulciano d'Abruzzo Poggio Varano '05	♥	4
● Montepulciano d'Abruzzo Poggio Varano '04	♥♥	4

Nestore Bosco

C.DA CASALI, 147
65010 NOCCIANO [PE]
TEL. 085847345
www.nestorebosco.com

ANNUAL PRODUCTION	550,000 bottles
HECTARES UNDER VINE	80
VITICULTURE METHOD	Certified organic

Nestore Bosco was up to scratch so we're happy to give it back a full profile, not just for its track record but especially for the quality we tasted this year. The cellar has always had something of a split personality: an old-school spirit that makes rustic wines and a forward-looking soul that tends to more aspirational products, with trendy labels and exotic names. We were won over by the Don Bosco '04, a Montepulciano d'Abruzzo with a historic name that aged in large oak. It has a traditional feel with a well-typed, balsamic nose and a spirited, savoury palate. The latest arrival is the '03 110, a healthy, varietal Montepulciano with a convincingly rustic nose and intense progression. The well-defined Pecorino '07 is true to type although the aromas are rather blurred. We weren't so impressed by the ambitious Montepulciano d'Abruzzo Pan '04, which declares its modernity on the label but whose credible body falters under too much oak and a tart finish. The Montepulciano d'Abruzzo Eclipse '06 was only a tad better while Chardonnay Pan and Trebbiano d'Abruzzo Eclipse, both 2007, are just average.

● Montepulciano d'Abruzzo 110 '03	♥♥	7
● Montepulciano d'Abruzzo Don Bosco '04	♥♥	5
○ Chardonnay Pan '07	♥	4
● Montepulciano d'Abruzzo Eclipse '06	♥	3
● Montepulciano d'Abruzzo Pan '04	♥	5
○ Pecorino '07	♥	4
○ Trebbiano d'Abruzzo Eclipse '07	♥	2
● Montepulciano d'Abruzzo Don Bosco '03	♥♥	5

Luigi Cataldi Madonna

LOC. PIANO
67025 OFENA [AQ]
TEL. 0862954252
cataldimadonna@virgilio.it

ANNUAL PRODUCTION	260,000 bottles
HECTARES UNDER VINE	27.5
VITICULTURE METHOD	Conventional

There's no stopping the "Professor" and his excellent winery at Ofena, in the Gran Sasso foothills, where the nights are frosty but the days are sunny and sultry. Luigi's wines are very individual, and over the years we've come to expect stunning results, so it's no surprise that we had another winning twosome. The Montepulciano d'Abruzzo Malandrino '06 relies on bright charm with well-defined fruit on the nose and a juicy, fragrant palate. We're sure the Pecorino will develop into one of Italy's truly great whites. This version has its citrussy grapefruit and minerality as well as cool terpenic nuances. There's some sturdy structure with sedate oak underpinning that leads to a long-lingering finish. Montepulciano d'Abruzzo Tonì '05 is still very young and undeveloped, showing some slightly rustic notes on the nose and assertive tannins in the mouth. Montepulciano d'Abruzzo Cerasuolo Piè delle Vigne '06 is simply one of Italy's best rosés. Nor should we forget the winery's commendable basic range, which is always right on target with its solid traditional range of well-typed, fragrant, value-for-money wines.

Centorame

LOC. CASOLI DI ATRI
VIA DELLE FORNACI, 15
64030 ATRI [TE]
TEL. 0858709115
www.centorame.it

ANNUAL PRODUCTION	75,000 bottles
HECTARES UNDER VINE	8
VITICULTURE METHOD	Conventional

This Atri winery, run with enthusiasm by Lamberto Vannucci, is a byword for quality and characteristic, well-made wines. We took to these products from the word go and we're fond of their fidelity to varietal and terroir character, the skilled use of oak in ageing and the substantial extract. The promising Montepulciano d'Abruzzo Colline Teramane Castellum Vetus '06 has typical, fruit-rich aromas and just the right amount of oak. We found it to be juicy and compact on the palate but its youth tends to crop the tannins. A more clear-cut varietal Montepulciano is the juicy San Michele '06, whose savoury, tannin-rich palate closes nicely on a note of roasted coffee beans. From the whites, we liked the concentrated, mouthfilling Trebbiano d'Abruzzo Castellum Vetus '06, with its good varietal integrity. The other Trebbiano, a San Michele '07, is straightforward and consistent on the nose, with supporting savouriness on the palate. An apt close to our tasting was the '07 Tuapina, a cool, uncomplicated sauvignon and pecorino blend that is eminently persuasive.

● Montepulciano d'Abruzzo Malandrino '06	▼▼▼	5
○ Pecorino '06	▼▼▼	6
⊙ Montepulciano d'Abruzzo Cerasuolo Piè delle Vigne '06	▼▼	5
● Montepulciano d'Abruzzo Tonì '05	▼▼	6
● Montepulciano d'Abruzzo '06	▼▼	4*
⊙ Montepulciano d'Abruzzo Cerasuolo '07	▼▼	3*
○ Trebbiano d'Abruzzo '07	▼▼	3*
● Montepulciano d'Abruzzo Malandrino '04	♟♟♟	5*
● Montepulciano d'Abruzzo Malandrino '03	♟♟♟	5
● Montepulciano d'Abruzzo Tonì '04	♟♟♟	6
● Montepulciano d'Abruzzo Tonì '03	♟♟♟	6
○ Pecorino '05	♟♟♟	6

● Montepulciano d'Abruzzo Colline Teramane Castellum Vetus '06	▼▼	5
● Montepulciano d'Abruzzo San Michele '06	▼▼	3*
○ Trebbiano d'Abruzzo Castellum Vetus '06	▼▼	4*
○ Trebbiano d'Abruzzo San Michele '07	▼	3
○ Tuapina '07	▼	4
● Montepulciano d'Abruzzo Colline Teramane Castellum Vetus '05	♟♟	5
● Montepulciano d'Abruzzo Colline Teramane Castellum Vetus '04	♟♟	5
● Montepulciano d'Abruzzo San Michele '05	♟♟	3*
● Montepulciano d'Abruzzo San Michele '04	♟♟	3*

Cerulli Irelli Spinozzi

LOC. CASALE 26
S.S. 150 DEL VOMANO KM 17,600
64020 CANZANO [TE]
TEL. 086157193
www.cerullispinozzi.it

ANNUAL PRODUCTION	130,000 bottles
HECTARES UNDER VINE	60
VITICULTURE METHOD	Certified organic

Last year, Cerulli Irelli Spinozzi made an encouraging debut and the winery is living up to it with a good range of labels that impressed us at our tasting. This Canzano-based operation is managed by the dedicated Enrico Cerulli Irelli, who produces promising, well-made contemporary wines. His Montepulciano d'Abruzzo Colline Teramane Torre Migliori Riserva '04 earned a place at the national finals because of its commendable sensory profile of well-defined, elegant aromas and a full palate of close-woven tannins and top-notch structure, taking you through to a long-lingering finish. The straightforward, heady Montepulciano '06 may not be too well-defined on the nose but its almost salty acidity gives plenty of support. We preferred the Pecorino Cortalto '07, whose well-typed unfussy aromas and zesty spirited progression sign off a long, almond-tinged finish. The Trebbiano d'Abruzzo '07 is precisely as it should be: a very drinkable white with no pretensions and a brisk, clean nose.

● Montepulciano d'Abruzzo Colline Teramane Torre Migliori Ris. '04	🍷🍷	5
○ Pecorino Cortalto '07	🍷🍷	3*
● Montepulciano d'Abruzzo '06	🍷	4
○ Trebbiano d'Abruzzo '07	🍷	3

Chiarieri

C.DA GRANARO, 18
65019 PIANELLA [PE]
TEL. 085971365
www.chiarieri.it

ANNUAL PRODUCTION	180,000 bottles
HECTARES UNDER VINE	35
VITICULTURE METHOD	Conventional

For years, the Chiarieri family has focused on managing this Pianella winery in the Colline Pescaresi district. Giovanni and Ciriaco Chiarieri, respectively father and son, make traditional wines in an uncomplicated country style. We found this year's contenders to be a bit more convincing and complex. The unfussy Granaro '07 is a typically full Montepulciano, with a compact hint of textbook black cherry on the nose followed by a well-defined, mature palate. The new Montepulciano d'Abruzzo Invidia '07 is a gutsy, go-getting red with sleek, well-typed aromas introducing a savoury palate that follows through well. We enjoyed the Trebbiano d'Abruzzo Granaro '07's clean, distinct aromas and a pleasantly bright tangy palate. The Trebbiano d'Abruzzo Invidia '07 is slightly heavier and we noticed a tad too much wood. There's obviously a lot of effort being made to streamline and enhance the wines, which will hopefully pay off in future vintages.

● Montepulciano d'Abruzzo Granaro '07	🍷🍷	3*
○ Trebbiano d'Abruzzo Granaro '07	🍷🍷	3*
● Montepulciano d'Abruzzo Invidia '07	🍷	3
○ Trebbiano d'Abruzzo Invidia '07	🍷	3
● Montepulciano d'Abruzzo Granaro '06	🍷🍷	3*
● Montepulciano d'Abruzzo Hannibal '03	🍷🍷	5
● Montepulciano d'Abruzzo Hannibal '02	🍷🍷	5

Col del Mondo

c.da Campotino, 35c
65010 Collecorvino [PE]
tel. 0858207831
www.coldelmondo.com

ANNUAL PRODUCTION 40,000 bottles
HECTARES UNDER VINE 9
VITICULTURE METHOD Conventional

We applaud a good performance at this year's tasting for this Pescara winery, an offshoot of the long-standing Tenuta del Priore estate at Collecorvino. Col del Mondo offered us a very commendable selection. The Montepulciano d'Abruzzo '05 deservedly reached the finals thanks to its modern, elegant aromas lifted by a seductive note of liquorice. The well-defined, concentrated body is dazzling, its acidic underpinning tinged with sea salt. This is a young red that is bound to improve with age. The Kerrias '04 Montepulciano has mature, pervasive aromas and a robust, succulent palate with a pleasant acidity-tinged close that enhances drinkability. The very moreish Sunnae '06 is an upfront, varietal Montepulciano d'Abruzzo that throws a fragrant, varietal nose. Exuberant alcohol on the nose of the Trebbiano d'Abruzzo Sunnae '07 tend to overshadow the graceful toasty aromas.

● Montepulciano d'Abruzzo '05 ▼▼ 4*
● Montepulciano d'Abruzzo Kerrias '04 ▼▼ 5
● Montepulciano d'Abruzzo Sunnae '06 ▼▼ 3*
O Kerrias '07 ▼ 4
O Trebbiano d'Abruzzo Sunnae '07 ▼ 3
● Montepulciano d'Abruzzo '04 ▽▽ 4*
● Montepulciano d'Abruzzo '03 ▽▽ 4
● Montepulciano d'Abruzzo Kerrias '03 ▽▽ 5
● Montepulciano d'Abruzzo Sunnae '04 ▽▽ 3*

Collefrisio

loc. Piane di Maggio
66030 Frisa [CH]
tel. 0859039074
www.collefrisio.it

ANNUAL PRODUCTION 205,000 bottles
HECTARES UNDER VINE 35
VITICULTURE METHOD Certified organic

Last year, we welcomed this newcomer to the Abruzzo wine scene with a short profile and the quality of the products this year persuaded us to upgrade it to a full entry. These ambitious wines are sourced from hillside vineyards on the coast at Ortona and Giuliano Teatino, real wine country. We'll begin with the winery's basic Zero line, including a well-made, affordable Montepulciano d'Abruzzo '06 whose sound aromas precede a palate underpinned by close-knit but unobtrusive extract and zesty, intense progression. The Trebbiano d'Abruzzo '07 has a distinctly fruit-rich nose introducing a palate with surprising backbone and body for a wine of this level. This year, the go-getting Uno line is more successful than in the past. The Montepulciano d'Abruzzo '05 is a forceful, richly extracted red with varietal nuances. The Trebbiano d'Abruzzo '07 has striking structure, despite liberal use of oak that disturbs the nose. The Pecorino '07 is simply one of the best we tasted this year, giving varietal notes on the nose and a fresh, full-flavoured palate. The last bottle we uncorked was a satisfying Montepulciano d'Abruzzo Cerasuolo '07.

⊙ Montepulciano d'Abruzzo Cerasuolo '07 ▼▼ 4*
● Montepulciano d'Abruzzo Uno '05 ▼▼ 4*
● Montepulciano d'Abruzzo Zero '06 ▼▼ 4*
O Pecorino '07 ▼▼ 4*
O Trebbiano d'Abruzzo Uno '07 ▼▼ 4*
O Trebbiano d'Abruzzo Zero '07 ▼ 3
● Montepulciano d'Abruzzo Zero '05 ▽▽ 3*

Contesa

C.DA CAPARRONE, 4
65010 COLLECORVINO [PE]
TEL. 0858205078
www.contesa.it

ANNUAL PRODUCTION	200,000 bottles
HECTARES UNDER VINE	39
VITICULTURE METHOD	Conventional

Rocco Pasetti is a colourful character. He's always in the front line promoting Abruzzo's wines but he never loses track of his own business, located on the Collecorvino hills. This year, the estate offered us six very persuasive labels. The stirring Montepulciano d'Abruzzo '05 has compact, pervasive aromas themed to notes of black cherry and cocoa powder. The mouthfeel is impressive and the close-knit tannins herald a balanced finish. The new Nerone '04 is a mature, varietal Montepulciano with a surprisingly fresh progression, given the vintage. The famous Vigna Corvino '06 is a less complex red with savoury progression. We were a little disappointed by the Trebbiano d'Abruzzo Vigna Corvino '07, which is very modern, with inadequately layered fermentation aromas. But we were very taken with the Pecorino '07, a feisty white with hints of tropical fruit and an inspired almondy finish. The white Chardonnay '07 has good minerality and a palate enhanced by skilled use of oak.

O Chardonnay '07	♟♟	4*
● Montepulciano d'Abruzzo '05	♟♟	5
● Montepulciano d'Abruzzo Nerone '04	♟♟	5
O Pecorino '07	♟♟	4*
● Montepulciano d'Abruzzo V. Corvino '06	♟	3
O Trebbiano d'Abruzzo V. Corvino '07	♟	3
● Montepulciano d'Abruzzo '03	♟♟	5
O Pecorino '06	♟♟	4

De Angelis Corvi

C.DA PIGNOTTO
64010 CONTROGUERRA [TE]
TEL. 086189475
www.deangeliscorvi.it

ANNUAL PRODUCTION	30,000 bottles
HECTARES UNDER VINE	9
VITICULTURE METHOD	Certified organic

Corrado De Angelis Corvi's winery has ceased to be a revelation and is here to stay. The attractive organic vineyards on the Abruzzo-Marche border are managed with loving care, producing some typical fragrant and very genuine wines with total respect for tradition. The ambitious Elèvito '05, Montepulciano d'Abruzzo Colline Teramane has a mature varietal nose but it's still a young wine and we noted boisterous tannins that still have to be tamed. The winery's basic yet surprising Montepulciano '06 had no trouble getting to the finals after we enjoyed the rich, juicy mouthfeel of this vigorous, velvety red which flaunts a compact, dense body. The Montepulciano d'Abruzzo Fonte Raviliano '06 has intense fruit aromas and a savoury palate, which is still a little held back but will find the right balance with age. The Montepulciano d'Abruzzo Cerasuolo '07 is one of the best in the region, its husky, appealing palate standing out from the crowd before the finish signs off with a classic almondy note. The Trebbiano d'Abruzzo Fonte Raviliano '07 is less successful, its nose being a little blurred and the palate lacking complexity.

● Montepulciano d'Abruzzo '06	♟♟	4*
● Montepulciano d'Abruzzo Colline Teramane Elèvito '05	♟♟	6
⊙ Montepulciano d'Abruzzo Cerasuolo '07	♟♟	4*
● Montepulciano d'Abruzzo Fonte Raviliano '06	♟♟	4*
O Trebbiano d'Abruzzo Fonte Raviliano '07	♟	3
● Montepulciano d'Abruzzo '05	♟♟	4*

Cantina Frentana

VIA PERAZZA, 32
66020 ROCCA SAN GIOVANNI [CH]
TEL. 087260152
www.cantinafrentana.it

ANNUAL PRODUCTION	430,000 bottles
HECTARES UNDER VINE	N.A.
VITICULTURE METHOD	Conventional

This year's results confirmed the obvious. Cantina Frentana is one of the Abruzzo co-operative wineries to keep an eye on. Traditional viticulture is applied to make serious wines offering excellent value for money. The vigorous Panarda '05 Montepulciano is solid, focused and very well-balanced. The aromas are true to type and mature on the nose, the palate is juicy and well-extracted and the rich mouthfeel is velvety. Rubesto '06 is a Montepulciano with intense black cherry and new oak. We were struck by the seriously textured mouthfeel, thanks to well-handled raw material. The uncomplicated Terre Valse '07 Montepulciano d'Abruzzo is a cost-friendly red that we found to be well typed and fragrant, with appealing even, fruit-forward aromas and a smooth, full palate that lingers. From the whites, we liked the promise of the Donna Greta '06 Chardonnay, with its subtle floral notes on the nose and zesty, enticingly fresh flavour. We thought the Cococciola Costa del Mulino '07 was a bright, uncomplicated version of this white, which comes from the local grape of the same name. The nose reveals intriguing citrus and the palate is cool and tangy.

● Montepulciano d'Abruzzo Panarda '05	♟♟	5*
○ Donna Greta '06	♟♟	5
● Montepulciano d'Abruzzo Rubesto '06	♟♟	4*
● Montepulciano d'Abruzzo Terre Valse '07	♟♟	2*
○ Costa del Mulino '07	♟	3
● Montepulciano d'Abruzzo Frentano '07	♟	2

Gentile

VIA DEL GIARDINO, 7
67025 OFENA [AQ]
TEL. 0862956618
www.gentilevini.it

ANNUAL PRODUCTION	90,000 bottles
HECTARES UNDER VINE	12
VITICULTURE METHOD	Conventional

Last year, we had some doubts about the Gentile winery but it's back with a full profile this years, thanks to a positive performance from its typical husky Montepulciano d'Abruzzo Zeus '05, which we sent on to our finals. This red with sound well-typed aromas has always been Gentile's trump card. Its appealingly subtle nose is typically fruity for a district like Ofena, where the Montepulcianos are less challenging than those from the coast. The Montepulciano d'Abruzzo Zefiro '04 is a very acceptable varietal version of the grape. The lively palate boasts fruit-rich flesh and is very savoury. The Montepulciano d'Abruzzo Cerasuolo Narciso '07 is a rich, extractive rosé with a nice hint of rusticity, supported by just the right amount of acidity. Not quite so successful is the Montepulciano d'Abruzzo Orfeo '07, which feeling the effects of a difficult vintage.

● Montepulciano d'Abruzzo Zeus '05	♟♟	6
⊙ Montepulciano d'Abruzzo Cerasuolo Narciso '07	♟♟	3*
● Montepulciano d'Abruzzo Zefiro '04	♟♟	4
● Montepulciano d'Abruzzo Orfeo '07	♟	3
○ Trebbiano d'Abruzzo Adone '07	♟	3

Dino Illuminati

C.DA SAN BIAGIO, 18
64010 CONTROGUERRA [TE]
TEL. 0861808008
www.illuminativini.it

ANNUAL PRODUCTION	1,200,000 bottles
HECTARES UNDER VINE	120
VITICULTURE METHOD	Conventional

Dino Illuminati is a character and the younger generations here are all smiles and charm. It's an effective business combination for this long-established Controguerra winery making many fine territory-focused wines. Illuminati wines come from Colline Teramane, one of the finest areas for native Abruzzo vines. Zanna '05 Montepulciano d'Abruzzo Colline Teramane is a great red with traditional true-to-type aromas and a fruity, layered progression – It strolled to Three Glasses again this year – but we liked the entire range. The enticing Illuminati Brut, a trebbiano, passerina and verdicchio blend, is a fresh, citrussy sparkler. The pleasantly rustic Controguerra Ciafré '06 is a subtle white with varietal aromas from trebbiano and passerina grapes. Controguerra Daniele '05 is an ambitious white a little overshadowed by new oak. Ilico '06, a varietal new Montepulciano that holds together well, its dense, powerful palate slightly veiled by new oak. Riparosso '07 is a fragrant, uncomplicated Montepulciano with sound traditional aromas and fresh, crunchy fruit. The Montepulciano d'Abruzzo Cerasuolo '07 is a fragrant, drinkable rosé.

★ Masciarelli

VIA GAMBERALE, 1
66010 SAN MARTINO
SULLA MARRUCINA [CH]
TEL. 087185241
www.masciarelli.it

ANNUAL PRODUCTION	1,200,000 bottles
HECTARES UNDER VINE	195
VITICULTURE METHOD	Conventional

This is a sombre profile for one simple reason: on 31 July 2008, the great winemaker Gianni Masciarelli died unexpectedly, aged only 52. Italian wine lost one of its most competent, intelligent figures. His wife, Marina Cvetic, lost her life partner; Miriam, Chiara Ludovica and little Riccardo, lost an adoring father. And we all lost a dear friend. But life at the winery must go on. Marina will continue the business with her customary skill and we're sure future wines bearing the Masciarelli label will be, as Gianni used to say, "at the very top level". It seems almost meaningless to describe this year's wines under the circumstances but it's our job and it has to be done. We gave two wines Three Glasses: the majestic Montepulciano d'Abruzzo Villa Gemma '05 and the Montepulciano d'Abruzzo Marina Cvetic '05, making a total of 19 overall and a step from a second Star. Then there is a series of unbeatable wines that we've included in the table, such as the excellent Chardonnay Marina Cvetic '06, an admirable Cerasuolo Villa Gemma '07 and a very good Trebbiano Castello di Semivicoli '06.

● Montepulciano d'Abruzzo Colline Teramane Zanna Ris. '05	♟♟♟ 6
○ Controguerra Bianco Ciafré '06	♟♟ 4*
○ Controguerra Bianco Daniele '05	♟♟ 5
○ Illuminati Brut M. Cl.	♟♟ 5
● Montepulciano d'Abruzzo Ilico '06	♟♟ 4*
● Montepulciano d'Abruzzo Riparosso '07	♟♟ 3*
⊙ Montepulciano d'Abruzzo Cerasuolo Campirosa '07	♟ 3
● Montepulciano d'Abruzzo Colline Teramane Pieluni Ris. '01	♟♟♟ 7
● Montepulciano d'Abruzzo Colline Teramane Pieluni Ris. '00	♟♟♟ 7
● Montepulciano d'Abruzzo Colline Teramane Zanna Ris. '03	♟♟♟ 6
● Montepulciano d'Abruzzo Colline Teramane Zanna Ris. '01	♟♟♟ 5

● Montepulciano d'Abruzzo Marina Cvetic '05	♟♟♟ 5
● Montepulciano d'Abruzzo Villa Gemma '05	♟♟♟ 8
○ Chardonnay Marina Cvetic '06	♟♟ 6
⊙ Montepulciano d'Abruzzo Cerasuolo Villa Gemma '07	♟♟ 4*
○ Trebbiano d'Abruzzo Castello di Semivicoli '06	♟♟ 6
● Montepulciano d'Abruzzo '06	♟♟ 3*
○ Trebbiano d'Abruzzo '07	♟♟ 2*
○ Trebbiano d'Abruzzo Marina Cvetic '06	♟♟ 6
● Montepulciano d'Abruzzo Villa Gemma '04	♟♟♟ 8
● Montepulciano d'Abruzzo Villa Gemma '03	♟♟♟ 8
● Montepulciano d'Abruzzo Villa Gemma '01	♟♟♟ 8
○ Trebbiano d'Abruzzo Castello di Semivicoli '05	♟♟♟ 6

Camillo Montori

LOC. PIANE TRONTO, 82
64010 CONTROGUERRA [TE]
TEL. 0861809900
www.montorivini.it

ANNUAL PRODUCTION	600,000 bottles
HECTARES UNDER VINE	50
VITICULTURE METHOD	Conventional

We're happy to give this winery its full profile back. All five wines tasted this year scored well, as you would expect one of the main movers in the creation of the Colline Teramane DOCG. The Montepulciano d'Abruzzo Fonte Cupa '05 is a sound red with a crisp fruit nose that's a shade too estery and alcoholic. The palate is savoury, indeed almost salty, with close-knit but not aggressive tannins. We enjoyed the Pecorino, a workhorse from this winery, which was one of the first to focus on this now-fashionable grape. The 2007 version is a fresh-tasting white with a nose and a silky enticing palate whose excellent acidity underpins the structure. The ambitious Montepulciano d'Abruzzo Colline Teramane '04, with impressive structure and texture, reveals a hint of oxidization on the nose and fruit that is verging on overripe on the palate. The uncomplicated Montepulciano d'Abruzzo '06 is well-made and pleasant, with husky aromas and lean, varietal progression. Lastly, the savoury Trebbiano d'Abruzzo Fonte Cupa '07 is a traditional interpretation of the grape, with a touch of reduction on the nose and good structure in the mouth.

● Montepulciano d'Abruzzo '06	▼▼ 3*
● Montepulciano d'Abruzzo Colline Teramane Fonte Cupa '05	▼▼ 6
○ Pecorino '07	▼▼ 4*
○ Trebbiano d'Abruzzo Fonte Cupa '07	▼▼ 4*
● Montepulciano d'Abruzzo Colline Teramane '04	▼ 4

Bruno Nicodemi

C.DA VENIGLIO
64024 NOTARESCO [TE]
TEL. 085895493
www.nicodemi.com

ANNUAL PRODUCTION	200,000 bottles
HECTARES UNDER VINE	30
VITICULTURE METHOD	Conventional

This Notaresco winery was one of the first to work towards quality and modernity in Abruzzo, thanks to the zeal of Alessandro and Elena Nicodemi, the stars of leading Colline Teramane DOCG operation. This year, they just missed out on Three Glasses but overall performance improved for all the wines we tasted. The Montepulciano d'Abruzzo Colline Teramane Neromoro Riserva '04 with mature, balsamic aromas, reveals an impressively succulent mouthfeel, closing on a lovely liquorice note. The fragrant red Montepulciano d'Abruzzo '06 is true to type, with well-defined, fruit-driven aromas. We were favourably surprised by the dense structure, although the tannins are still slightly clenched. We found the Notàri line Trebbiano d'Abruzzo '07 to have improved this year, showing elegant varietal aromas and a tangy palate with good, fresh acidity supporting the progression. Trebbiano d'Abruzzo '07 is an unexpectedly stylish and ambitious white for its category. The Montepulciano d'Abruzzo Colline Tramane Notàri '05 is less balanced and despite its interesting texture, still hasn't quite got the mix right.

● Montepulciano d'Abruzzo Colline Teramane Neromoro Ris. '04	▼▼ 6
● Montepulciano d'Abruzzo '06	▼▼ 4*
○ Trebbiano d'Abruzzo '07	▼▼ 3*
○ Trebbiano d'Abruzzo Notàri '07	▼▼ 4
● Montepulciano d'Abruzzo Colline Teramane Notàri '05	▼ 5
● Montepulciano d'Abruzzo Colline Teramane Neromoro Ris. '03	▼▼▼ 6
● Montepulciano d'Abruzzo Colline Teramane Neromoro Ris. '02	▼▼ 5
● Montepulciano d'Abruzzo Colline Teramane Ris. '00	▼▼ 5
● Montepulciano d'Abruzzo '05	▼▼ 4*
○ Trebbiano d'Abruzzo '06	▼▼ 3*

Emidio Pepe

VIA CHIESI, 10
64010 TORANO NUOVO [TE]
TEL. 0861856493
www.emidiopepe.com

ANNUAL PRODUCTION	80,000 bottles
HECTARES UNDER VINE	16
VITICULTURE METHOD	Certified organic

We gave Three Glasses to Emidio Pepe's 1998 Montepulciano d'Abruzzo. That's right, the 1998. Because this traditional winery is quite capable of releasing an extraordinary red ten years after a harvest. The first hint comes from the colour, with garnet notes that are slightly paler than usual for a Montepulciano. The subtle, delicate Burgundy-style aromas have hints of wild strawberries and forest fruits, and the elegantly persuasive palate is very subtle. Part of Emidio Pepe's secret is that he adheres to biodynamic viticulture and only uses cement tanks for vinification, leaving the wine on fine lees for years. Thanks to this approach, three more wines were a hair's breadth from the podium: Trebbiano d'Abruzzo '06, which is brisker and cleaner than in the past, with attractive citrussy aromas and an elegant, true-to-type palate; Trebbiano d'Abruzzo '03, an outstandingly complex white that foregrounds refined florality; and the intense Montepulciano d'Abruzzo '05, a big, enjoyably husky wine, with some good mineral notes on the nose and a forceful fruity palate. The Montepulciano d'Abruzzo Cerasuolo '07 is a succulent varietal rosé.

● Montepulciano d'Abruzzo '98	♟♟♟	8
● Montepulciano d'Abruzzo '05	♟♟	6
○ Trebbiano d'Abruzzo '06	♟♟	6
○ Trebbiano d'Abruzzo '03	♟♟	6
⊙ Montepulciano d'Abruzzo Cerasuolo '07	♟♟	5
● Montepulciano d'Abruzzo '04	♟♟	5
● Montepulciano d'Abruzzo '03	♟♟	5
○ Trebbiano d'Abruzzo '01	♟♟	6

La Quercia

C.DA COLLE CROCE
64020 MORRO D'ORO [TE]
TEL. 0858959110
www.vinilaquercia.it

ANNUAL PRODUCTION	100,000 bottles
HECTARES UNDER VINE	12.5
VITICULTURE METHOD	Conventional

We've been keeping an eye on this recent Colline Teramane winery because we're impressed by the uncomplicated elegance of its well-typed wines. This year, La Quercia sent perhaps too many labels for only 13 hectares under vine. The Montepulciano d'Abruzzo '05 Primamadre had no trouble getting into the finals with its refined balsamic aromas and very rich, juicy palate, rounded off by a savoury finish. Good acidity will help it to age. The very drinkable Peladi '07 is a typically aromatic Montepulciano with a well-balanced velvety palate. The husky red Montepulciano d'Abruzzo '06 has a fragrant, varietal nose. We were taken off guard by Montonico '07, from the premium Santapupa line. It's a white with pleasing edginess, refined hints of honey and spirited progression in the mouth. Montepulciano d'Abruzzo Cerasuolo Primamadre '07 is simply one of the best in its category. We were less thrilled by the long list of Trebbianos, which are well made but undistinguished, and so do not feature in this Guide.

● Montepulciano d'Abruzzo Primamadre '05	♟♟	4*
● Montepulciano d'Abruzzo '06	♟♟	4*
⊙ Montepulciano d'Abruzzo Cerasuolo Primamadre '07	♟♟	4*
● Montepulciano d'Abruzzo Peladi '07	♟♟	2*
○ Santapupa Montonico '07	♟♟	4*
● Montepulciano d'Abruzzo Colline Teramane Primamadre '04	♟♟	5

San Lorenzo

c.da Plavignano, 2
64035 Castilenti [TE]
tel. 0861999325
www.sanlorenzovini.com

ANNUAL PRODUCTION N.A.
HECTARES UNDER VINE 150
VITICULTURE METHOD Conventional

San Lorenzo is a large, successful Colline Teramane winery with 150 hectares on the border of the provinces of Pescara and Teramo. Its enthusiastic young managers are scions of the Galasso family, a local wine dynasty. They presented several labels, from ambitious Montepulciano d'Abruzzos to wines made with non-native grapes. Escol '05 is a Montepulciano d'Abruzzo Colline Teramane Riserva with an elegantly complex nose and a powerful palate that is almost too concentrated. Oinos '05 is another Montepulciano Colline Teramane, with rounded, varietal aromas and distinct ripe. Sadly, the finish tends to a slightly bitterish aftertaste. We enjoyed the heady rustic Montepulciano d'Abruzzo Antares '07, an uncomplicated red with sound, well-typed fragrances and a fresh-tasting, succulent palate. The white Chioma di Berenice '07 is a persuasively unpretentious Chardonnay and Pecorino '07 is crisp and cool, with a tangy palate and good body.

○ Chardonnay Chioma di Berenice '07	🍷🍷 4*
● Montepulciano d'Abruzzo Antares '05	🍷🍷 3*
● Montepulciano d'Abruzzo Colline Teramane Escol Ris. '05	🍷🍷 5
● Montepulciano d'Abruzzo Colline Teramane Oinos '05	🍷🍷 5
○ Pecorino '07	🍷🍷 3*
● Montepulciano d'Abruzzo Antares '04	🍷🍷 3*
● Montepulciano d'Abruzzo Colline Teramane Escol Ris. '04	🍷🍷 5
● Montepulciano d'Abruzzo Colline Teramane Escol Ris. '03	🍷🍷 5
● Montepulciano d'Abruzzo Colline Teramane Escol Ris. '02	🍷🍷 5

Strappelli

loc. Torri
via Torri, 15
64010 Torano Nuovo [TE]
tel. 0861887402
www.cantinastrappelli.it

ANNUAL PRODUCTION 60,000 bottles
HECTARES UNDER VINE 10
VITICULTURE METHOD Natural

Strappelli is back. Last year, there were only two wines, both whites, but this year we're on track again. We're very fond of the products from this Torano winery in Colline Teramane territory. The wines are traditional and typical, made in a genuine farmer's style from grapes grown at Villa Torri. Alas, they haven't yet managed a champion to establish their absolute credentials but it's just a matter of time. Celibe 2004, a Montepulciano d'Abruzzo Colline Teramane Riserva, is an ambitiously powerful red with good pervasive, varietal aromas. The palate has plenty of power and well-handled raw material, revealing a full-bodied savoury progression. The Montepulciano d'Abruzzo 2005 is deceptively simple. A fruit-driven, varietal nose leads into a palate of richness and balance that closes with an appealing liquorice-like note. The fragrant Montepulciano d'Abruzzo Cerasuolo 2007 is well rounded, agreeably velvety and succulence. From the whites, we tried Trebbiano d'Abruzzo 2007, which gives toasty varietal nuances and a bright tangy palate. The two interesting 2007 Pecorinos are very drinkable. Both are fragrant and clean but perhaps a little too simple.

● Montepulciano d'Abruzzo '05	🍷🍷 4*
⊙ Montepulciano d'Abruzzo Cerasuolo '07	🍷🍷 4*
● Montepulciano d'Abruzzo Colline Teramane Celibe Ris. '04	🍷🍷 6
○ Trebbiano d'Abruzzo '07	🍷🍷 3*
○ Pecorino Nubile V. T. '07	🍷 5
○ Pecorino Soprano '07	🍷 4
● Montepulciano d'Abruzzo Colline Teramane Celibe Ris. '03	🍷🍷 6
● Montepulciano d'Abruzzo '04	🍷🍷 4*
○ Trebbiano d'Abruzzo '06	🍷🍷 3*

Terra d'Aligi

LOC. PIAZZANO
VIA PIANA LA FARA, 90
66041 ATESSA [CH]
TEL. 0872897916
www.terradaligi.it

ANNUAL PRODUCTION   550,000 bottles
HECTARES UNDER VINE   60
VITICULTURE METHOD   Conventional

The Colline Frentane area is challenging
and the Terra d'Aligi winery works hard
to produce enjoyable wines that are well
made and often rather ambitious, like
the Tolos '05, a powerful, persuasive
Montepulciano d'Abruzzo that strolled
into the finals. It gives intense spice-
led varietal aromas and a firm-textured,
concentrated body that does not hold
back the well-executed savoury palate.
The second house Montepulciano, Tatone,
which means grandfather in the Abruzzo
dialect, is also very good. The 2005 has
mature, fruity aromas and a pure succulent
palate but is slightly heavy on the alcohol.
The Montepulciano '06 is precisely as it
should be: a pleasant, drinkable red with
good varietal character. As always, the
well-typed Montepulciano Cerasuolo '07 is
very tasty with velvet texture. This year, the
vintage has given it some extra body. The
Trebbiano d'Abruzzo '07 is uncomplicated
and very drinkable.

Tiberio

C.DA LA VOTA
65020 CUGNOLI [PE]
TEL. 0858576744
www.tiberio.it

ANNUAL PRODUCTION   50,000 bottles
HECTARES UNDER VINE   27
VITICULTURE METHOD   Conventional

The passion of Cristiana Tiberio, the feisty
young owner and oenologist of this inland
Colli Pescaresi winery, has assured its
success. Again this year, we thought the
wines we tasted were well worth uncorking
and an interesting expression of the
terrain. They are contemporary wines,
clean and well defined but not lacking in
varietal character. Most were whites this
year, in what we acknowledge to be the
winery's emerging style. The Pecorino
'07 has varietal aromas of tropical and
citrus fruit followed by a palate with lots of
well-managed structure and good acidity
supporting the progression. The enjoyable
Trebbiano d'Abruzzo '07 is a clean white
with good texture and refreshing tanginess.
The promising 50-50 sauvignon and
chardonnay blend, Althea Bianco '06, is
a fragrant, modern white with intrusive
notes of new oak and banana. The only
red presented was the Montepulciano
d'Abruzzo Althea '06, which has intense
aromas of fruit and vanilla leading into a
mouthfilling, succulent palate.

● Montepulciano d'Abruzzo Tolos '05	▼▼ 6
⊙ Montepulciano d'Abruzzo Cerasuolo Terra d'Aligi '07	▼▼ 3*
● Montepulciano d'Abruzzo Tatone '05	▼▼ 4*
● Montepulciano d'Abruzzo '06	▼ 3
○ Trebbiano d'Abruzzo '07	▼ 3
● Montepulciano d'Abruzzo '04	♈♈ 3*
● Montepulciano d'Abruzzo Tatone '04	♈♈ 4
● Montepulciano d'Abruzzo Tolos '04	♈♈ 6
● Montepulciano d'Abruzzo Tolos '03	♈♈ 5
● Montepulciano d'Abruzzo Tolos '02	♈♈ 4

● Montepulciano d'Abruzzo Althea '06	▼▼ 5
○ Pecorino '07	▼▼ 4*
○ Trebbiano d'Abruzzo '07	▼▼ 4*
○ Althea '06	▼ 4
● Montepulciano d'Abruzzo '06	♈♈ 3*
● Montepulciano d'Abruzzo Althea '05	♈♈ 5
○ Trebbiano d'Abruzzo '06	♈♈ 3*

Cantina Tollo

VIA GARIBALDI, 68
66010 TOLLO [CH]
TEL. 087196251
www.cantinatollo.it

ANNUAL PRODUCTION	12,500,000 bottles
HECTARES UNDER VINE	3500
VITICULTURE METHOD	Conventional

Cantina Tollo is a juggernaut on the Abruzzo wine scene and every year confirms its leadership in the vibrant regional co-operative sector. The grapes the Cantina collects grapes from its thousands of growers ensure the significant success of the cellar's wines. This year, we tasted ten labels and no less than three made it to the national finals. One very focused wine is the Montepulciano d'Abruzzo Cagiòlo '05, with seamless varietal aromas and a complex palate with close-knit texture although the palate is a tad cropped because of its youth. Montepulciano d'Abruzzo Aldiano '06 has subtle, fruit-led varietal notes and a savoury palate that echoes the nose. The surprise is Colle Secco Rubino '05, a big numbers, big value wine with an intense black cherry nose and a flavoursome palate. One favourite from the whites is the ambitious Trebbiano Menir '06, an old-fashioned white fragrant with tropical fruit. The palate is surprisingly juicy, despite the cavalier use of new oak. Lastly, the Chardonnay Cretico '06 has a stylish nose, extract-rich palate and well-handled structure. All the other wines are above average.

Torre dei Beati

C.DA POGGIORAGONE, 56
65014 LORETO APRUTINO [PE]
TEL. 3333832344
www.torredeibeati.it

ANNUAL PRODUCTION	60,000 bottles
HECTARES UNDER VINE	19
VITICULTURE METHOD	Certified organic

Adriana Galasso and Fausto Albanesi are partners in life and business who own this reliable Loreto Aprutino winery. They run a lovely organic estate, producing wines that are characterful yet true to type, the tangible outcome of the enthusiasm that drives all their plans. This year, we missed Cocciapazza Montepulciano d'Abruzzo, which is the star of the range. The cellar's standard flag was thus defended by just three wines. The Montepulciano '06 was not as focused as usual, let down by some overripe nuances and slightly heavy on the palate for a wine of this range. Mazzamurello '05 sets out to be an imposing Montepulciano and gives wild cherry and vanilla followed by excellent structure on the palate with the close-knit tannins of extreme youth. In just a few years, Rosa-ae Montepulciano d'Abruzzo Cerasuolo has established itself as one of the best in the region. The '07 has a stylish, fruit-driven nose, set off by a persuasive, velvety palate and, thanks to the growing year, unexpected structure.

● Montepulciano d'Abruzzo Aldiano '06	♊♊ 4*
● Montepulciano d'Abruzzo Cagiòlo '05	♊♊ 5
● Montepulciano d'Abruzzo Colle Secco Rubino '05	♊♊ 4*
○ Chardonnay Cretico '06	♊♊ 5
● Montepulciano d'Abruzzo Colle Secco '05	♊♊ 4*
○ Trebbiano d'Abruzzo Menir '06	♊♊ 5*
⊙ Montepulciano d'Abruzzo Cerasuolo Hedòs '07	♊ 4
○ Pecorino '07	♊ 4
○ Trebbiano d'Abruzzo Aldiano '07	♊ 4
○ Trebbiano d'Abruzzo Colle Secco '07	♊ 3
● Montepulciano d'Abruzzo Cagiòlo '04	♊♊ 5
● Montepulciano d'Abruzzo Aldiano '05	♊♊ 4*
○ Trebbiano d'Abruzzo Aldiano '06	♊♊ 4*

⊙ Montepulciano d'Abruzzo Cerasuolo Rosa-ae '07	♊♊ 3*
● Montepulciano d'Abruzzo Mazzamurello '05	♊♊ 5
● Montepulciano d'Abruzzo '06	♊ 4
● Montepulciano d'Abruzzo Cocciapazza '04	♊♊ 5
● Montepulciano d'Abruzzo Cocciapazza '03	♊♊ 5
● Montepulciano d'Abruzzo Mazzamurello '04	♊♊ 5
● Montepulciano d'Abruzzo '05	♊♊ 4*
● Montepulciano d'Abruzzo '04	♊♊ 4*
⊙ Montepulciano d'Abruzzo Cerasuolo Rosa-ae '06	♊♊ 3*

La Valentina

VIA TORRETTA, 52
65010 SPOLTORE [PE]
TEL. 0854478158
www.fattorialavalentina.it

ANNUAL PRODUCTION 330,000 bottles
HECTARES UNDER VINE 40
VITICULTURE METHOD Conventional

It's taken a good many years of unremitting hard work, including the construction of a modern new winery, to achieve this well-earned result for its energetic owners, Sabatino Di Properzio and family. We gave the 2005 Bellovedere, a great Mediterranean red, its first Three Glasses. This is a Montepulciano with bags of character and pervasive black cherry and cocoa whose impressive, but not heavy, structure shows rich but not cloying. We also liked the Montepulciano d'Abruzzo Binomio '05, a joint venture with Stefano Inama, the well-known winemaker from Soave in Veneto. In this, the most balanced version so far, we perceived stylish toast and black cherry preceding a palate with substantial varietal texture that is still seeking a point of equilibrium for its alcohol and extract, but this will come with time. The winery's basic labels are well made and pleasant. From splendid vineyards in a superb territory, they include the lustrous Montepulciano d'Abruzzo Cerasuolo '07, with its fine charred oak aromas, the Pecorino '07, which offers tropical fruit and good body, the Trebbiano d'Abruzzo '07 and the Montepulciano d'Abruzzo '06.

★★ Valentini

VIA DEL BAIO, 2
65014 LORETO APRUTINO [PE]
TEL. 0858291138

ANNUAL PRODUCTION 40,000 bottles
HECTARES UNDER VINE 64
VITICULTURE METHOD Conventional

It's only been two years since Edoardo Valentini died and his son talented, rigorous Francesco Paolo is showing us that he is a worthy successor. He presented only two wines this year but both hit the Three Glass bull's eye. Not only was it a first for his Montepulciano d'Abruzzo Cerasuolo, it was also the first time the Guide has given top marks to a rosé. The 2006 version is a quite deep antique rose colour, with aromas that are reluctant at first but develop black cherry, strawberry and toast nuances after aerating for a few minutes in the glass. The palate is forthright, powerful and perfectly underpinned by refreshing acidity. The Trebbiano d'Abruzzo '05 was also very good. It may not be the best ever but it's still up there with Italy's best whites. The nose opens with hints of yeast and yellow plum before the close-textured palate, well supported by acidity, reveals and the usual hint of prickle that makes it so unique. This wine is aristocratic and rustic in equal measure but above all it's a genuine wine from genuine wine territory.

● Montepulciano d'Abruzzo Bellovedere '05	▼▼▼	7
● Montepulciano d'Abruzzo Binomio '05	▼▼	6
☉ Montepulciano d'Abruzzo Cerasuolo '07	▼▼	3*
○ Bianco Pecorino Colline Pescaresi '07	▼	4
● Montepulciano d'Abruzzo '06	▼	3
○ Trebbiano d'Abruzzo '07	▼	3
● Montepulciano d'Abruzzo Bellovedere '01	♈♈	7
● Montepulciano d'Abruzzo Bellovedere '00	♈♈	7

☉ Montepulciano d'Abruzzo Cerasuolo '06	▼▼▼	7
○ Trebbiano d'Abruzzo '05	▼▼▼	7
● Montepulciano d'Abruzzo '97	♈♈♈	7
● Montepulciano d'Abruzzo '95	♈♈♈	6
● Montepulciano d'Abruzzo '92	♈♈♈	6
● Montepulciano d'Abruzzo '90	♈♈♈	6
● Montepulciano d'Abruzzo '88	♈♈♈	6
● Montepulciano d'Abruzzo '02	♈♈♈	8
● Montepulciano d'Abruzzo '01	♈♈♈	8
● Montepulciano d'Abruzzo '00	♈♈♈	8
○ Trebbiano d'Abruzzo '99	♈♈♈	8
○ Trebbiano d'Abruzzo '96	♈♈♈	5
○ Trebbiano d'Abruzzo '95	♈♈♈	5
○ Trebbiano d'Abruzzo '04	♈♈♈	7
○ Trebbiano d'Abruzzo '02	♈♈♈	7
○ Trebbiano d'Abruzzo '01	♈♈♈	6
○ Trebbiano d'Abruzzo '00	♈♈♈	6

Valle Reale

LOC. SAN CALISTO
65026 POPOLI [PE]
TEL. 0859871039
www.vallereale.it

ANNUAL PRODUCTION   577,000 bottles
HECTARES UNDER VINE   60
VITICULTURE METHOD   Conventional

We didn't taste the selection that made this winery famous as owner Leonardo Pizzolo courageously decided not to present his famous Montepulciano d'Abruzzo San Calisto. He's going to wait until next time to give the wine time to mature further, which is the way to go with star products. The worthy stand-in was the best version so far of Montepulciano '06 Valle Reale, a stylish red with sound fruit-driven aromas, sourced from the Popoli vineyards which have always yielded wines that are more elegant than powerful. This trait was evident at our tasting, where we enjoyed the succulent body and incisive, acidic progression that makes the palate so taut and appealing. We were also very happy with the Trebbiano d'Abruzzo '07, an interesting white from the economical Vigne Nuove line. The well-defined aromas are nuanced with peaches and yellow plums leading into a rounded, succulent palate. This year, Montepulciano d'Abruzzo Vigne Nuove '07 seems to lack focus, with a little too much alcohol, which we suspect is the result of a difficult harvest. The Montepulciano d'Abruzzo Cerasuolo '07 was delicious, as always, and typical of this rosé wine type.

Valori

VIA TORQUATO AL SALINELLO, 8
64027 SANT'OMERO [TE]
TEL. 086188461
vinivalori@tin.it

ANNUAL PRODUCTION   30,000 bottles
HECTARES UNDER VINE   16
VITICULTURE METHOD   Conventional

This successful Controguerra winery is in the habit of presenting well-typed classic wines every year. There are three interesting, very successful labels, as befits tradition. Gianni Masciarelli's masterly touch is evident in these stylish, uncomplicated wines and we have no doubt that his technique will live on after his untimely death in the summer. The Vigna Sant'Angelo '06 is a Montepulciano with elegant varietal and charred oak aromas, introducing sweet succulent pulp and compact progression on the palate. The less complicated Montepulciano d'Abruzzo '07 is varietal and fragrant, with intense aromas and clean fruit. It closes with a mouth-drying tannin note but is nonetheless a grand red, produced in serious numbers and easy on the pocket. The Trebbiano d'Abruzzo '07 is true to type, showing clean and crisp with agreeable varietal aromas and nimble, lightweight progression.

● Montepulciano d'Abruzzo Valle Reale '06	♀♀♀	4*
☉ Montepulciano d'Abruzzo Cerasuolo Vigne Nuove '07	♀♀	3*
○ Trebbiano d'Abruzzo Vigne Nuove '07	♀♀	3*
● Montepulciano d'Abruzzo Vigne Nuove '07	♀	2
● Montepulciano d'Abruzzo San Calisto '05	♀♀♀	6
● Montepulciano d'Abruzzo San Calisto '04	♀♀♀	6
☉ Montepulciano d'Abruzzo Cerasuolo Vigne Nuove '06	♀♀	2*
● Montepulciano d'Abruzzo Valle Reale '05	♀♀	4
● Montepulciano d'Abruzzo Valle Reale '04	♀♀	4
● Montepulciano d'Abruzzo Vigne Nuove '06	♀♀	2*

● Montepulciano d'Abruzzo V. S. Angelo '06	♀♀	5
● Montepulciano d'Abruzzo '07	♀♀	3*
○ Trebbiano d'Abruzzo '07	♀	3
● Montepulciano d'Abruzzo Vigna S. Angelo '03	♀♀♀	5
● Montepulciano d'Abruzzo Vigna S. Angelo '05	♀♀	5
● Montepulciano d'Abruzzo Vigna S. Angelo '04	♀♀	5
● Montepulciano d'Abruzzo '06	♀♀	3*
● Montepulciano d'Abruzzo '05	♀♀	3*

Villa Medoro

FRAZ. FONTANELLE
64030 ATRI [TE]
TEL. 0858708142
www.villamedoro.it

ANNUAL PRODUCTION	300,000 bottles
HECTARES UNDER VINE	N.A.
VITICULTURE METHOD	Conventional

Villa Medoro doesn't rest on its laurels. This lovely Fontanelle d'Atri winery has quickly reached the top of the competitive Colline Teramane district. Credit to the owner, Federica Morricone, her efficient winemaking team and the great, scrupulously tended vineyards. We were again impressed this year by the wines we tasted, despite the absence of the flagship Montepulciano d'Abruzzo Colline Teramane Adrano, whose 2006 version is being aged for another year. Surprisingly, Three Glasses went to the '06 Montepulciano, a stunning red with intense varietal fruit and an assertive palate skilfully forged by rich, powerful raw material. A big wine at a small price. The more aristocratic Montepulciano d'Abruzzo Rosso del Duca '06 strolled into the finals thanks to its typically rich aromas and a progression that is almost too richly extracted and tight-knit. The Trebbiano d'Abruzzo '07 is a tempting white with remarkable body and complex notes of honey on the nose. The trebbiano and falanghina Chimera '07 is a clean, drinkable white blend and the Montepulciano d'Abruzzo Cerasuolo '07 has distinctive fragrances and lots of sheer drinkability.

Ciccio Zaccagnini

C.DA POZZO
65020 BOLOGNANO [PE]
TEL. 0858880195
www.cantinazaccagnini.it

ANNUAL PRODUCTION	800,000 bottles
HECTARES UNDER VINE	128
VITICULTURE METHOD	Conventional

Zaccagnini is an icon of Abruzzo quality and quantity, working from the excellent Bolognano estate at the foot of Mount Majella to produce interesting and often exciting wines that are always very focused. As usual, the prestigious San Clemente '06, a Montepulciano d'Abruzzo, had no problems getting into the finals, thanks to its succulent body and pleasant, varietal palate, despite slightly intrusive new oak. We were very taken with the Montepulciano Tralcetto '06, which is released in substantial numbers. Agreeable and well-typed, it releases marvellously distinct, close-woven aromas leading into a fresh, succulent palate. The Castello di Salle '05 is a modern Montepulciano with intense aromas of ripe red berries. The palate impressed us with its power and juicy succulence. A little too much new oak veils the Chronichon '05 Montepulciano d'Abruzzo, and the fruit is a little too ripe, but there is good support from the tight-knit tannins. As expected, the best whites were the Trebbiano d'Abruzzo San Clemente and the zesty Chardonnay San Clemente, both 2007s and both slightly held back by a heavy hand with the new oak.

● Montepulciano d'Abruzzo '06	▼▼▼	3*
● Montepulciano d'Abruzzo Rosso del Duca '06	▼▼	4*
○ Chimera Bianco '07	▼▼	4*
⊙ Montepulciano d'Abruzzo Cerasuolo '07	▼▼	3*
○ Trebbiano d'Abruzzo '07	▼▼	3*
● Montepulciano d'Abruzzo Colline Teramane Adrano '05	♉♉♉	6
● Montepulciano d'Abruzzo Colline Teramane Adrano '04	♉♉♉	6
● Montepulciano d'Abruzzo Colline Teramane Adrano '03	♉♉♉	6
● Montepulciano d'Abruzzo Rosso del Duca '05	♉♉	4*
● Montepulciano d'Abruzzo Rosso del Duca '04	♉♉	4*
● Montepulciano d'Abruzzo '05	♉♉	3*
○ Trebbiano d'Abruzzo '06	♉♉	3*

● Montepulciano d'Abruzzo S. Clemente '06	▼▼	6
○ Chardonnay S. Clemente '07	▼▼	5
● Montepulciano d'Abruzzo Castello di Salle '05	▼▼	4*
● Montepulciano d'Abruzzo Chronicon '05	▼▼	4*
● Montepulciano d'Abruzzo Tralcetto '06	▼▼	3*
○ Trebbiano d'Abruzzo S. Clemente '07	▼▼	5
● Montepulciano d'Abruzzo S. Clemente '05	♉♉	6
○ Chardonnay S. Clemente '06	♉♉	5
● Montepulciano d'Abruzzo Castello di Salle '04	♉♉	4
● Montepulciano d'Abruzzo Chronicon '04	♉♉	4
● Montepulciano d'Abruzzo Cuvée dell'Abate '05	♉♉	3*
● Montepulciano d'Abruzzo Tralcetto '05	♉♉	3*

OTHER WINERIES

Tenute Barone di Valforte

C.DA PIOMBA
64029 SILVI MARINA [TE]
TEL. 0859353432
www.baronedivalforte.it

This new winery that has potential although the wines we tasted lack focus and are made in a commercial style. The chardonnay and trebbiano Colle Sale '06 is pleasant and has good structure. The Montepulciano Colline Teramane Colle Sale '05 has a fruit-driven nose and is very savoury in the mouth.

- ○ Colle Sale Bianco '06 — 🍷🍷 4*
- ● Montepulciano d'Abruzzo Colline Teramane Colle Sale '05 — 🍷 4

Giuseppe Ciavolich

LOC. QUATTRO STRADE
C.DA CERRETO, 18
66010 MIGLIANICO [CH]
TEL. 0871958797
www.ciavolich.com

This traditional winery has been producing well-styled wines for over a century. Divus '06 is a Montepulciano with refined, fruity aromas, a fragrant, varietal palate and fresh appealing progression. Ancilla '07 is a crisp, intense Montepulciano with unusual rustic fragrances.

- ● Montepulciano d'Abruzzo Ancilla '07 — 🍷🍷 4*
- ● Montepulciano d'Abruzzo Divus '06 — 🍷🍷 5

Citra

C.DA CUCULLO
66026 ORTONA [CH]
TEL. 0859031342
www.citra.it

We've chosen just two of the many wines presented by this famous large co-operative. The best of the bunch were its Sistina '06 Montepulciano, with well-defined fruit fragrances, a well-rounded, lingering palate and a slightly tart finish, and Laus Vitae '03, a firm-bodied red with intense, evolved aromas.

- ● Montepulciano d'Abruzzo Sistina '06 — 🍷🍷 4*
- ● Montepulciano d'Abruzzo Laus Vitae '03 — 🍷 6

Tenuta I Fauri

S.DA CORTA, 9
66100 CHIETI
TEL. 0871332627
www.tenutaifauri.it

This fine winery performed well with its Ottobre Rosso '07, a fragrant Montepulciano with a hint of overripeness and a silky, nicely acid palate. The Santa Cecilia '05 is another varietal, fruit-led Montepulciano with a smooth, crisp palate.

- ● Montepulciano d'Abruzzo Ottobre Rosso '07 — 🍷🍷 4*
- ● Montepulciano d'Abruzzo Santa Cecilia '05 — 🍷🍷 5

Filomusi Guelfi

VIA F. FILOMUSI GUELFI, 11
65028 TOCCO DA CASAURIA [PE]
TEL. 085986908
elleffegi@tiscali.it

This is a beautiful, long-established winery. The '04 version of the historic Montepulciano Fonte Dei is evolved and alcoholic. Scuderie del Cielo '07 is a chardonnay, cococciola and malvasia toscana blend with husky aromas and an intense palate. The '07 Cerasuolo, as always, is one of the best in Abruzzo.

- ○ Le Scuderie del Cielo '07 — 🍷🍷 4*
- ⊙ Montepulciano d'Abruzzo Cerasuolo '07 — 🍷🍷 4*
- ● Montepulciano d'Abruzzo Fonte Dei '04 — 🍷 6

Lepore

C.DA CIVITA, 29
64010 COLONNELLA [TE]
TEL. 086170860
www.vinilepore.it

This important Colline Teramane winery is struggling to recover the ranking it and its lovely Colonnella vineyards deserve. The Tramonto '07 is a well-typed, contemporary Montepulciano. Cerasuolo '07 is a seriously good, concentrated wine with enticing hints of almond.

- ⊙ Montepulciano d'Abruzzo Cerasuolo '07 — 🍷🍷 4*
- ● Montepulciano d'Abruzzo Tramonto '07 — 🍷 3

OTHER WINERIES

Lidia e Amato

C.DA SAN BIAGIO
64010 CONTROGUERRA [TE]
TEL. 0861817041
www.lidiaeamatoviticoltori.com

This new Controguerra winery sent us some strikingly fragrant, rustic wines. Riccardo '05 is a well-typed Montepulciano Colline Teramane with a distinct, velvety flavour. Forty '07, another Montepulciano, is a coherent varietal red with fragrantly enjoyable progression and serious, well-handled raw material.

- Montepulciano d'Abruzzo
  Colline Teramane Riccardo '05 ‍🍷🍷 4*
- Montepulciano d'Abruzzo Forty '07 🍷🍷 3*

Cantina Sociale Miglianico

VIA SAN GIACOMO, 40
66010 MIGLIANICO [CH]
TEL. 087195831
www.cantinamiglianico.it

The Murelle '06 is a well-typed, fruit-forward Montepulciano with an enticingly husky varietal nose preceding a juicy, mouthfilling palate. Another Montepulciano d'Abruzzo, Montupoli '05, is elegant and modern, with good structure and texture.

- Montepulciano d'Abruzzo
  Montupoli '05 🍷🍷 3*
- Montepulciano d'Abruzzo Murelle '06 🍷🍷 3*

Antonio e Elio Monti

VIA PIGNOTTO, 62
64010 CONTROGUERRA [TE]
TEL. 086189042
www.vinimonti.it

It was only a middling year for this well-established Controguerra winery. We tasted only two wines and they were not up to previous standards. The red Controguerra Rio Moro Riserva '06 is again modern and intense with a sweet mouthfilling palate and the concentrated, typical Voluptas '07 is clenched and bitterish on the finish.

- Controguerra Rosso
  Rio Moro Ris. '06 🍷🍷 5
- Montepulciano d'Abruzzo
  Voluptas '07 🍷 3

Montipagano

C.DA CASAL THAULERO
64026 ROSETO DEGLI ABRUZZI [TE]
TEL. 0717201210
www.montipagano.com

This Teramo winery is an offshoot of Umani Ronchi, the famous Marche cellar. We tasted just two wines: a Costamorro '05 Montepulciano, with hints of new oak and structure nicely balanced by acidity, and the very drinkable Trebbiano '07, which is characteristically pleasant and uncomplicated.

- Montepulciano d'Abruzzo
  Colline Teramane Costamorro '05 🍷🍷 5
- O Trebbiano d'Abruzzo '07 🍷 4

Orlandi Contucci Ponno

LOC. PIANA DEGLI ULIVI, 1
64026 ROSETO DEGLI ABRUZZI [TE]
TEL. 0858944049
www.orlandicontucci.com

This well-known Roseto winery wasn't quite so surefooted as usual. Colline Teramane Riserva '05 Montepulciano has stylish, varietal aromas and a balanced palate. Roccesco '07 is an enticingly refined Chardonnay. Montepulciano Podere La Regia Specula '06 isn't bad.

- Montepulciano d'Abruzzo
  Colline Teramane Ris. '05 🍷🍷 6
- O Roccesco '07 🍷🍷 4*
- Montepulciano d'Abruzzo Colline Teramane
  Podere La Regia Specula '06 🍷 4

Franco Pasetti

C.DA PRETARO
VIA SAN PAOLO, 21
66023 FRANCAVILLA AL MARE [CH]
TEL. 08561875
www.pasettivini.it

It wasn't a great year for this Francavilla al Mare winery that is treading water somewhat, although we're certain it is a positive contribution to the Abruzzo scene. We tasted two wines: an elegantly modern Montepulciano Fattoria Pasetti 2006 and a feisty, aroma-rich Montepulciano Tenuta Testarossa 2004 red.

- Montepulciano d'Abruzzo
  Fattoria Pasetti '06 🍷🍷 4*
- Montepulciano d'Abruzzo
  Tenuta di Testarossa '04 🍷🍷 5

OTHER WINERIES

Pietrantonj

VIA SAN SEBASTIANO, 38
67030 VITTORITO [AQ]
TEL. 0864727102
www.vinipietrantonj.it

This mountain winery makes wines with a typically traditional feel and marked acidity. The Cerano '05 is a well-typed, mature Montepulciano with boisterous tannins. Trebbiano '07 has enticing tropical aromas and great structure.

● Montepulciano d'Abruzzo Cerano '05	♟♟ 3*
○ Trebbiano d'Abruzzo Cerano '07	♟ 4

Roxan

C.DA TRATTURO, 1
65020 ROSCIANO [PE]
TEL. 0858505767
www.roxan.it

There was a good Guide debut from this long-standing co-operative. Galelle '05 is a Montepulciano with subtle aromas and a pleasant palate. Campo Sacro '04 is a Montepulciano with a fruit-driven nose and a persuasive savoury palate. We also liked the Chardonnay Acanto and the Pecorino Corale, both 2007s.

○ Acanto '07	♟♟ 4*
● Montepulciano d'Abruzzo Campo Sacro '04	♟♟ 5
● Montepulciano d'Abruzzo Galelle '05	♟♟ 3*
○ Corale '07	♟ 4

Cantine Talamonti

C.DA PALAZZO
65014 LORETO APRUTINO [PE]
TEL. 0858289039
www.cantinetalamonti.it

This Loreto winery has long been a promise on the Abruzzo wine scene. Modà '07 is a Montepulciano with refined aromas and a dense, well-balanced palate. Aternum '06 is an oak-aged Trebbiano with well-managed structure. We liked the Cerasuolo '07.

☉ Montepulciano d'Abruzzo Cerasuolo '07	♟♟ 3*
● Montepulciano d'Abruzzo Modà '07	♟♟ 3*
○ Trebbiano d'Abruzzo Aternum '06	♟♟ 4*

Tenimenti del Grifone

VIA ISTONIA, 81
66054 VASTO [CH]
TEL. 3358390720
www.vinimastrangelo.com

This winery sent us a good range of traditional wines, including a fine Trebbiano '07 with varietal fruit on the nose. The Riserva del Vicario '03 is a varietal Montepulciano with evolved aromas and a firm palate, bolstered by sturdy body and acidity. The Pecorino Nunthius '07 isn't bad.

○ Trebbiano d'Abruzzo Tenuta del Grifone '07	♟♟ 4*
● Montepulciano d'Abruzzo La Riserva del Vicario '03	♟ 5
○ Nunthius '07	♟ 4

Valle Martello

C.DA VALLE MARTELLO, 10
66010 VILLAMAGNA [CH]
TEL. 0871300330
katmasci@vallemartello.net

The Masci family put passion into their farm, making well-typed easy drinkers like Brado '07, a fragrant, uncomplicated Montepulciano with excellent texture. We liked the drinkable, unfussy white Cococciola Brado '07. The Montepulciano '07 is straightforward but likeable and good value for money.

● Montepulciano d'Abruzzo Brado '07	♟♟ 4*
○ Brado '07	♟ 4
● Montepulciano d'Abruzzo '07	♟ 3*

Villa Bizzarri

LOC. VILLA BIZZARRI
64010 TORANO NUOVO [TE]
TEL. 0861856933
www.villabizzarri.com

This Torano Nuova winery, a branch of Monte Schiavo in the Marche, is proving an interesting operation. The Colle Creta '04 has sombre, minerally aromas with a fragrant, varietal palate. Girone dei Folli '04 is a full-bodied, mature Montepulciano that could do with a little more bite.

● Montepulciano d'Abruzzo Colle Creta '04	♟♟ 4*
● Montepulciano d'Abruzzo Girone dei Folli '04	♟ 3

MOLISE

Many Italians would be hard put to place Molise on a map but this small central-southern region is rapidly shaping up as one of the jewels of Italy's food and wine scene. Molise has superb extra virgin olive oil as well as wonderful cold meats and cheeses, such as ventricina and scamorza di Boiano. Then there are the wines. Actually, there aren't very many wineries, and even fewer top-drawer ones, but the overall picture is promising as new names join established stars. The beacon of Molise winemaking continues to be the Di Majo Norante estate at Campomarino, where Alessio Di Majo is in charge. Again this year, Alessio's Molise Rosso Don Luigi, this time in the '06 Riserva edition, picked up Three Glasses to affirm its status as Molise's top wine. Two other bottles from the same cellar went through to our finals, Molise Aglianico Contado Riserva '05 and Molise Moscato Apianae '06, making up a trio of eminent wines. This was quite a feather in the Di Majo Norante cap but also a sign that a little commitment and experience can produce outstanding wines in these parts. Other cellars are also achieving prominence. We would like to point out the excellent showing by Masseria Flocco, a relative newcomer that could quickly become one of the benchmark labels in central and southern Italy, if not the entire peninsula. Borgo di Colloredo and Cipressi are two more exciting cellars. Equally interesting is the return of an elsewhere near-forgotten native variety that has been the focus of attention in Molise for decades and perhaps centuries, tintilia. This colour-heavy grape yields wines that may be a tad rustic, and even rugged when young, but are brilliantly territorial as few other varieties can be. Uncork a bottle of Cipressi's Macchiarossa '06 to be convinced. Another feature of the region is that you find varieties normally planted in Puglia, Campania and Basilicata, as well as other grapes usually associated with Abruzzo and Marche. Whites like falanghina, greco and trebbiano flank reds such as aglianico and montepulciano, either as single-variety wines or blends, confirming that Molise, like Tolkein's Middle Earth, is a land of passage. Different traditions meet, giving rise to highly original wines in an oenological melting pot that reveals a vast range of possibilities and new developments. But in Molise, there is no recourse to alchemy, esoteric incantation, improbable vine types or invasive vinification techniques.

Borgo di Colloredo

LOC. NUOVA CLITERNIA
86042 CAMPOMARINO [CB]
TEL. 087557453
www.borgodicolloredo.com

ANNUAL PRODUCTION	300,000 bottles
HECTARES UNDER VINE	60
VITICULTURE METHOD	Conventional

The '07 Greco from Borgo di Colloredo is the real deal. Here is object proof that this essentially Campanian variety can perform very well indeed around Campomarino, near the Molise coast. It's a white with varietal aromas of almonds, tropical fruit and crusty bread followed by a confidently full, slightly rustic palate with a long, convincing finale, held back only by faint aftertaste of bitterness. The full-bodied, tannin-heavy Aglianico '05 also did well, revealing none of the accommodating softness so many southern wines tend to have. The two montepulciano and aglianico-based Biferno Gironias were decent, as was the Rosso, an '03 and understandably evolved on the nose, while the rosé was very fresh and drinkable. Molise Falanghina '07 was punching below its weight. In the past, we have enjoyed the citrus-like nose of this white but this edition seemed a little less expressive and a touch more mature than usual.

Cipressi

C.DA MONTAGNA
86030 SAN FELICE DEL MOLISE [CB]
TEL. 0874874535
www.cantinecipressi.it

ANNUAL PRODUCTION	50,000 bottles
HECTARES UNDER VINE	16
VITICULTURE METHOD	Certified organic

Cipressi is Molise's leading winery for Tintilia, a deep-coloured, full-bodied red from the grape of the same name. Molise Tintilia Macchiarossa '06 lives up to expectations. The very intense purplish ruby red ushers in sour cherry and spice, followed by a tannic palate with lots of power and a slightly rustic feel. In other words, it's a fine Tintilia. But the Cipressi range is much wider, going far beyond this admittedly fundamental variety for the region. Molise Aglianico Elkon '06 is every bit as good. Spice and balsam on the nose take you into an assertive, tannic palate with plenty of body, just as you would expect from a red like this. In contrast, Molise Rosso Mekan '06 is a single-variety wine from montepulciano grapes. Ripe fruit and vanilla come through, lifted by briary fruit and sour cherry notes. The new wood still has to be absorbed but the outlook is good. On the other hand, the montepulciano-only Molise Rosso Rumen '06 is only so-so. The nose enfolds but it's a little too soft and lacks oomph. Closing the list is the Venas Rosato '07, again from montepulciano. It's upfront, fresh-tasting, appealing and eminently drinkable.

● Aglianico '05		▼▼ 4*
○ Greco '07		▼▼ 3*
⊙ Biferno Rosato Gironia '07		▼ 4
● Biferno Rosso Gironia '03		▼ 4
○ Molise Falanghina '07		▼ 4

● Molise Aglianico Elkon '06		▼▼ 4*
● Molise Rosso Mekan '06		▼▼ 4*
● Molise Tintilia Macchiarossa '06		▼▼ 5
● Molise Rosso Rumen '06		▼ 4
⊙ Venas Rosato '07		▼ 3
● Molise Tintilia Macchiarossa '05		▼▼ 6

Di Majo Norante

FRAZ. NUOVA CLITERNIA
C.DA RAMITELLI, 4
86042 CAMPOMARINO [CB]
TEL. 087557208
www.dimajonorante.com

ANNUAL PRODUCTION	800,000 bottles
HECTARES UNDER VINE	85
VITICULTURE METHOD	Certified organic

We applauded a superb performance by
the wines from Di Majo Norante, still the
benchmark winery in Molise. Credit must
go to the serious management style of
Alessio Di Majo, who has steered this ship
of state for years. Three Glasses went to
Molise Rosso Don Luigi Riserva '06, from
montepulciano with a splash of aglianico.
This solid, powerful red has pervasive
fragrances redolent of sour cherries in
alcohol and a richly intense palate with
a long, warm finish. Equally good is the
moscato reale-based Moscato Apianae
'06 with its crisp aromatic fragrances and
sweet but never cloying, full palate. We
think it's one of Italy's finest sweet whites.
Also good, and very affordable, is the
characterful Molise Aglianico Contado '05,
a red with faint smokiness and a palate well
supported by boisterous but not aggressive
extract. The base wines on the list are also
worth uncorking. Molise Greco '07 is nice
but even better is Molise Falanghina Ramì
'07, a deliciously fruity easy drinker. Biferno
Rosso Ramitello '05 and Molì Rosso '07
are only decent. Both are unpretentious
aglianico and montepulciano-based wines
with a slightly bitterish back palate.

● Molise Don Luigi Ris. '06	▼▼▼	6
● Molise Aglianico Contado '05	▼▼	4*
○ Molise Apianae '06	▼▼	5
○ Molise Falanghina Ramì Bianco '07	▼▼	3*
○ Molise Greco '07	▼▼	4*
● Biferno Rosso Ramitello '05	▼	4
● Molì Rosso '07	▼	3
● Molise Aglianico Contado '99	♀♀♀	4*
● Molise Aglianico Contado '03	♀♀♀	4*
● Molise Don Luigi '99	♀♀♀	5
● Molise Don Luigi '05	♀♀♀	6
● Molise Aglianico Contado '04	♀♀	4*
● Molise Don Luigi '04	♀♀	6

Masserie Flocco

C.DA DIFENSOLA
86045 PORTOCANNONE [CB]
TEL. 0875590032
www.masserieflocco.com

ANNUAL PRODUCTION	300,000 bottles
HECTARES UNDER VINE	110
VITICULTURE METHOD	Conventional

The wines of Masseria Flocco at
Portocannone, in the province of
Campobasso, are coming on. The range
is solid and some of the bottles are
impressive. In fact, one or two nearly
made it to our finals. We thought the best
of the bunch was Molise Rosso Podere
di Sot '07, a single-variety Montepulciano.
It's just a little young, so the aromas are
very penetrating, ethery and fruity while
the palate is full, tannic and still a little
boisterous. Nevertheless, this is a wine
with excellent prospects. Attractively fruity,
easy drinking and charitably priced are
three qualities of the excellent Falanghina
'07, another of the cellar's workhorses.
The Chardonnay Podere del Canneto
'07 is good, if a little predictable with
its fermentation aromas, firm body and
absence of rough edges. The other
reds are decent, the montepulciano and
aglianico Biferno Sangue di Buoi '07
showing a little more interesting than the
two wines from international varieties,
the Merlot Podere dei Castelli and the
Cabernet Sauvignon, both from '07. Neither
fills any obvious need.

○ Falanghina '07	▼▼	3*
● Molise Rosso Podere di Sot '07	▼▼	4*
○ Podere del Canneto '07	▼▼	4*
● Biferno Sangue di Buoi '07	▼	5
● Cabernet Sauvignon '07	▼	3
● Podere dei Castelli '07	▼	4

OTHER WINERIES

Azienda Agricola Cianfagna

C.DA BOSCO PAMPINI, 3
86030 ACQUAVIVA COLLECROCE [CB]
TEL. 0875970253
www.cianfagna.com

There are two decently made Tintilias, with Pietrafitta showing better. It's an '05 and has more complexity and structure. The other is a DOC Molise wine, but younger and less exciting. Cianfagna takes its place in the small circle of specialists who make this lovely native red.

● Pietrafitta '05	🍷🍷 5
● Molise Sator '06	🍷 5

D'Uva

C.DA RICUPO, 13
86035 LARINO [CB]
TEL. 0874822320
www.cantineduva.com

This year, the D'Uva cellar presented very few wines. We thought the most interesting was the upfront Molise Trebbiano Kantharos '07. Keres, from trebbiano, is more complex but also more evolved.

O Keres '07	🍷 3
O Molise Trebbiano Kantharos '07	🍷 4

I.A.C. - Catabbo

C.DA PETRIERA
86046 SAN MARTINO IN PENSILIS [CB]
TEL. 0875604945
www.catabbo.it

Decent wines well made. The dark, assertively flavoured Molise Tintilia Riserva '04 is nice. Petriera Rosso '07, from montepulciano, is not bad but still a bit young. Finally Falanghina Xaatuis '07 and Petriera Bianco '07, from chardonnay and trebbiano, are attractively fresh.

● Molise Tintilia Ris. '04	🍷🍷 6
O Molise Falanghina Xaatuis '07	🍷 4
O Petriera Bianco '07	🍷 2
● Petriera Rosso '07	🍷 2

Salvatore

C.DA VIGNE
86049 URURI [CB]
TEL. 0874830656
www.cantinesalvatore.it

Cantina Salvatore at Ururi, in the province of Campobasso, gave us two very well-made reds. Molise Rosso Biberius '06 from montepulciano is a caressing wine with robust alcohol. Tintilia Rutilia '06 is slightly overripe on the nose but has good body and a lingering finale.

● Molise Rosso Biberius '06	🍷 4
● Rutilia '06	🍷 4

CAMPANIA

It is evident that development on the Campanian wine scene is verging on the explosive. But the record 16 Three Glasses this year, and the many wines that reached the finals, goes only part of the way to explaining the process. And while the boom is not totally unexpected, its real essence is concentrated in what you don't see on these pages: the nearly 1,000 wines tasted; the roughly 200 estates submitting wines; and the numerous wines that achieved Two Glasses without gaining a listing. Such numbers obviously make our work more complex but also more exciting, opening the field to new debate about new versus old, long-standing locals versus newcomers and huge producers versus boutique wineries. If proof were needed, just take a look at the Three Glass wines, never before so varied in their origins, styles and production philosophies. The province of Avellino once more takes the lion's share of the awards, good vintages for the wines from its three DOCG zones helping them shine. The prizewinners include three Taurasis, all very different but all from the classic year of 2004: there's Contrade's beautifully elegant example, Molettieri's monumental Cinque Querce and the renowned Mastroberardino's modern yet uncompromising Naturalis Historia. This last winery is the only one to gain a second Three Glass prize, for Novaserra, a stunning exemplar of the 2007 vintage. Alongside it are Pietracupa's Greco di Tufo and Feudi di San Gregorio's Cutizzi. There was even greater jockeying for position among the top 2007 Fiano di Avellinos but the first two past the post were marvellous wines that express the Lapio terroir to perfection: Colli di Lapio and a new entry, Rocca del Principe, the Guide's Up-and-Coming Winery of the Year. Leading the offerings from the much-discussed 2006 vintage is the iconic Fiano di Avellino Vigna della Congregazione from Villa Diamante. But while great wines from Irpinia may not be a surprise, we should not overlook the stunning results from the province of Caserta, produced by the many-sided souls of its subzones. Villa Matilde is back in great form with its '04 Falerno del Massico Camarato from vineyards in Cellole, and the extinct volcano of Roccamonfina yielded yet another Terra di Lavoro of Three Glass standard, the '06. Gladius '06 reflects the potential of the Galluccio district and brings Adolfo Spada his first Three Glass wine. Also in the spotlight is the Colline Caiatine as Terre del Principe joins the front rank with Pallagrello Nero Ambruco '06. Meanwhile, the strengths of Sannio are focused on Taburno Aglianico Bue Apis, the '04 vintage being the best ever. And once more it is Montevetrano, the '06, and the '07 Fiorduva that raise the province of Salerno to the heights, the latter the linchpin of the Costa d'Amalfi where a crop of new, staunchly determined talents is hard at work.

Aminea

VIA SANTA LUCIA
83040 CASTELVETERE SUL CALORE [AV]
TEL. 082765787
www.aminea.com

ANNUAL PRODUCTION	500,000 bottles
HECTARES UNDER VINE	22
VITICULTURE METHOD	Conventional

We don't suppose Michele Fede and his partners, who turn out significant quantities of wine in a part of Irpinia where production is fragmentary, will be content with a performance that is merely good. The solidity of the range is undeniable but what we crave is that extra burst of character and identity that could lift the winery onto a higher plane. Nevertheless, there is no lack of attack or assertion in Greco di Tufo '07, which shines right from first sight of its gleaming pale straw hue. The nose is anything but the standard fruit monologue. There are cereal-like sensations and shots of chlorophyll before full, earthy flavours grow through the mouth to a finish redolent of bitter herbs. Fiano di Avellino '07 is distinctly too sweet but Taurasi Baiardo '03 shows well, especially considering the vintage. It avoids the pitfall of too much alcohol and extract, and has good balance throughout, although the finish lacks complexity and the tannins are slightly dusty. Quindici '06, a dried-grape wine from fiano, is less emphatic than we remember from previous vintages, too much dried fruit and honey throwing it off balance.

Antonio Caggiano

C.DA SALA
83030 TAURASI [AV]
TEL. 082774723
www.cantinecaggiano.it

ANNUAL PRODUCTION	150,000 bottles
HECTARES UNDER VINE	20
VITICULTURE METHOD	Conventional

They call Antonio Caggiano "The Fox", and not without reason because his success over the years has derived from his carefully planned approach. He was partly behind his friend, Professor Luigi Moio's, ventures in Irpinia and Caggiano's efforts led to the creation of one of Taurasi's first crus, the now famed Vigna Macchia dei Goti. One of the first modern-style Irpinian reds, it remains the emblem of Taurasi village. The '05 will be ready next year but in the meantime we set our tastebuds to work on its aglianico-based fellows. First came an impressive Salae Domini '06, nicely shaped by mineral, elegantly vegetal tones. The fruit seems a touch withdrawn but there is substance, zip and flavour right through the mouth. We also enjoyed the less intense but racy and well put-together Taurì, again '06, penalized only by slightly green tannins. The '07 whites, though, compare slightly unfavourably with last year's '06s. Indeed, Fiano di Avellino Béchar and Greco di Tufo Devon gained just One Glass, being outpaced by a successful version of the fiano and greco blend Fiagre, which is better than we've seen for many a year.

O Greco di Tufo '07	♟♟	4*
● Taurasi Baiardo '03	♟♟	5
O Fiano di Avellino '07	♟	4
O Quindici '06	♟	6
O Fiano di Avellino '06	♟♟	4*
O Greco di Tufo '06	♟♟	4*
● Taurasi Baiardo '02	♟♟	5

O Fiagre '07	♟♟	4*
● Irpinia Salae Domini '06	♟♟	6
● Taurì '06	♟♟	4*
O Fiano di Avellino Béchar '07	♟	5
O Greco di Tufo Devon '07	♟	5
● Taurasi V. Macchia dei Goti '99	♟♟♟	7
● Taurasi V. Macchia dei Goti '04	♟♟♟	6
● Taurasi V. Macchia dei Goti '98	♟♟	7
● Taurasi V. Macchia dei Goti '03	♟♟	6
● Taurasi V. Macchia dei Goti '01	♟♟	7
● Taurasi V. Macchia dei Goti '00	♟♟	7
O Fiano di Avellino Béchar '06	♟♟	4*
● Taurì '05	♟♟	4*

Viticoltori del Casavecchia

VIA MADONNA DELLE GRAZIE, 28
81040 PONTELATONE [CE]
TEL. 0823659198
www.viticoltoridelcasavecchia.it

ANNUAL PRODUCTION	50,000 bottles
HECTARES UNDER VINE	20
VITICULTURE METHOD	Conventional

The growers forming this co-operative know how to handle the local casavecchia variety, and how! Their enterprise started quietly enough but has grown, step by step, to the point where they can now claim a full entry in our Guide. It's unlikely to be a one-off, given the authority with which Vigna Prea '05 swung into the finals, despite the year being anything but easy for the grape. This is an ambitious wine that hangs on balance and firm structure, resisting all temptation towards over-extraction, and is cohesive in its slight gaminess and spicy shots of cinnamon and pepper. Corte Rosa '06 is almost as good, with a touch less substance being compensated by a wealth of personality. The pencil lead and blackberry notes are clearer, the tannic weave is softer, the acid backbone more distinct. The fruit-forward Erta dei Ciliegi '07, from casavecchia and pallagrello, seems the natural result of conjuring up the ideal attributes for a wine of gentleness and drinkability. The rosé Sfizio Rosa '07, from casavecchia and pallagrello, and Futo '06, from sun-dried casavecchia, are also most successful.

Colli di Castelfranci

C.DA BRAUDIANO
83040 CASTELFRANCI [AV]
TEL. 082772392
www.collidicastelfranci.com

ANNUAL PRODUCTION	160,000 bottles
HECTARES UNDER VINE	20
VITICULTURE METHOD	Conventional

Once more Luciano Gregorio and Gerardo Colucci can be proud of their wines, a high-quality range that has already elevated the brothers-in-law to sit with the great and the good, and which this year is topped by Fiano di Avellino Pendino. In most years, this an exuberant, flavoursome wine, one of the cheeriest examples of the denomination, but this year's '07 is lifted by an extra burst of freshness and dynamism, which comes through right from the nose, all white flowers and greenery, elderflower and sage. It easily earned Two Glasses, as did the other whites, the straight-down-the-line Greco di Tufo Grotte '07 and the '07 Irpinia Fiano Paladino, for several years now one of the region's best late-harvest wines. The '07 release of Crote, a rosé from aglianico, also sees great improvement. It now has an eclectic character that marries the juicy fragrance on the nose of golden delicious apples and peaches with a palate of weight and incisiveness throughout. Irpinia Campi Taurasini Candriano '06 and Taurasi Gagliardo '03 are fairly good but they come from one of the zone's top aglianico selections so it is legitimate to expect better.

● Vigna Prea '05	⚥⚥ 5
● Corte Rosa '06	⚥⚥ 4*
O Erta dei Ciliegi '07	⚥⚥ 3*
O Futo '06	⚥ 5
O Pallagrello Bianco '07	⚥ 3*
☉ Sfizio Rosa '07	⚥ 3*
● Erta dei Ciliegi '06	⚥⚥ 3*

O Fiano di Avellino Pendino '07	⚥⚥ 4*
O Greco di Tufo Grotte '07	⚥⚥ 4*
☉ Irpinia Aglianico Rosato Crote '07	⚥⚥ 4*
O Irpinia Paladino V. T. '07	⚥⚥ 4*
● Irpinia Campi Taurasini Candriano '06	⚥ 4
● Taurasi Gagliardo '03	⚥ 6
O Fiano di Avellino Pendino '06	⚥⚥ 4
O Fiano di Avellino Pendino '05	⚥⚥ 4*
O Fiano di Avellino Pendino '04	⚥⚥ 4
☉ Irpinia Aglianico Rosato Crote '07	⚥⚥ 4*
O Paladino V.T. '06	⚥⚥ 4
O Paladino V.T. '05	⚥⚥ 5

Colli di Lapio

VIA ARIANIELLO, 47
83030 LAPIO [AV]
TEL. 0825982184
collidilapio@libero.it

Contrade di Taurasi

VIA MUNICIPIO, 39
83030 TAURASI [AV]
TEL. 0815442457
www.contradeditaurasi.it

ANNUAL PRODUCTION	50,000 bottles
HECTARES UNDER VINE	6
VITICULTURE METHOD	Conventional

ANNUAL PRODUCTION	20,000 bottles
HECTARES UNDER VINE	5
VITICULTURE METHOD	Conventional

Blue signs along the road that rises from Chiusano to the small zone of Arianiello indicate "Colli di Lapio" but visitors to these parts always seem to end up asking where they can find Clelia Romano's Fiano. Her name is a guarantee that you will have a wine of provenance in the truest sense of the term, one that brings definition to the distinctive traits of each vintage like few others while retaining a strong aromatic identity that is irrefutably that of Lapio. The '07 is in that sense emblematic. Its open, lively, pervasive grapefruit-and-melon character expresses the more generous character of the vintage compared with the leaner, more difficult '06. More incisive, more penetrating touches of fresh herbs and iodine bring a more Nordic profile. The palate starts gently, becoming tauter and almost salty mid way through, before gaining a finish of rare vigour and beauty. It is without doubt one of Italy's top whites and not only won Three Glasses but threatens to overshadow both one of the best Taurasi Vigna Andrea's ever, the '04, and an impressive Irpinia Campi Taurasini Donna Chiara '06.

The evolution of a wine zone with high quality potential should surely be measured by the number of estates on the verge of excellence. But that unadorned figure can mask other signs of progress, ones that may embrace more aesthetic factors and probably have a deeper, more long-lasting impact. Take, for example, Irpinia where the number of estates is certainly increasing, as is the average quality of the wines, but where development is additionally, indeed primarily, due to estates like Enza Lonardo's and wines like her Taurasi, a product that, quite apart from its intrinsic value, brings a completely modern look to the interplay of old and new. The '04 is centred on the most elegant aspects of aglianico. Tertiary aromas impact the nose, which has broad, spicy, tropical wafts, and touches of citrus and florality. The palate is guided by pronounced acidity that lends verve, enhances its flavour and leads to a firm and very long finish. The wine won Three Glasses without any debate and we are sure that those patient enough to let it mature will enjoy something even greater.

O Fiano di Avellino '07	♟♟♟	5
● Taurasi Vigna Andrea '04	♟♟	6
● Campi Taurasini Irpinia Donna Chiara '06	♟♟	5
O Fiano di Avellino '05	♟♟♟	5
O Fiano di Avellino '04	♟♟♟	5
O Fiano di Avellino '03	♟♟	5
● Taurasi Vigna Andrea '03	♟♟	6
● Taurasi Vigna Andrea '01	♟♟	6
● Campi Taurasini Irpinia Donna Chiara '06	♟♟	5
O Fiano di Avellino '97	♟♟	5
O Fiano di Avellino '96	♟♟	5
O Fiano di Avellino '02	♟♟	5
O Fiano di Avellino '01	♟♟	5
O Fiano di Avellino '00	♟♟	5*

● Taurasi '04	♟♟♟	7
● Aglianico '06	♟	4
O Greco Musc' '06	♟	5
● Taurasi '03	♟♟	6
● Taurasi '00	♟♟	6
● Taurasi Ris. '01	♟♟	7
● Taurasi '99	♟♟	7
● Taurasi '01	♟♟	6

Marisa Cuomo

G. B. Lama, 16/18
84010 Furore [SA]
tel. 089830348
www.granfuror.it

ANNUAL PRODUCTION	97,000 bottles
HECTARES UNDER VINE	14.5
VITICULTURE METHOD	Natural

Perhaps the secret is in the name, which evokes symbols and scenery that are hard to convey by other means. The wine is Fiorduva but the name behind it is Costa d'Amalfi, a corner of paradise whose inhabitants have now discovered the territory's fabulous proclivity for wine production, and are clustering around Cuomo, its leading producer, as they seek a way forward. It is Marisa Cuomo and Andrea Ferraioli's vineyard and cellar work, and their blend of ripoli, fenile and ginestra, which reveals what can be achieved in a wine made where land meets sea. The '07 creates deep emotions on this level, evoking mimosa, chlorophyll and iodine. The palate is crisp and full of flavour, with notable weight but even more notable drinkability. It's a wine that gains in stature year by year, sublimating any overt sensations of dried grapes and the use of small oak in a profile of rare elegance and luminosity. And it is not on its own for it leads an impressive range of clean, deep and harmonious wines. The Riservas, the firm, compact Furore Rosso Riserva '04 and the greener but irresistibly lively Ravello Rosso Riserva '05 are its closest disciples.

D'Ambra Vini d'Ischia

fraz. Panza
via Mario D'Ambra, 16
80075 Forio [NA]
tel. 081907210
www.dambravini.com

ANNUAL PRODUCTION	500,000 bottles
HECTARES UNDER VINE	18
VITICULTURE METHOD	Conventional

Calling a 100-plus-year-old winery "new" might seem risible but what Andrea D'Ambra has been doing over the last few years has far more to do with the future than the past. There are his experiments with vines from the Aegean sea, his purchases around Calitto, and the second line he created primarily to develop new stylistic pathways. But the most significant developments have been with the most classic wines. Tenuta Frassitelli, a biancolella cru grown on the slopes of Monte Epomeo, triumphed last year and this year's '07 nearly matches it. The individuality of its aromatic profile, its notes of fennel and fresh almond interwoven with wafts of iodine, is truly exciting. Crisp and mouthwatering, it is also subtle and delicate from beginning to end. Just a touch more flesh and it would really take flight. There is no lack of flesh, though, on the '07 Ischia Forastera Euposia. This has never been so good. Mediterranean herbs and pepper make a decisive stamp on the powerful nose and the palate is close-knit and assertive with a just a hint of bitterness on the finish. The '07 Ischia Biancolella also reflects the good year for the winery.

○ Costa d'Amalfi Fiorduva '07	♛♛♛ 7
● Costa d'Amalfi Rosso Furore Ris. '04	♛♛ 7
● Costa d'Amalfi Rosso Ravello Ris. '05	♛♛ 6
○ Costa d'Amalfi Bianco Furore '07	♛♛ 5
● Costa d'Amalfi Rosso Furore '07	♛♛ 5
● Costa d'Amalfi Rosso Furore Ris. '05	♛♛ 7
○ Costa d'Amalfi Bianco Ravello '07	♛ 5
☉ Costa d'Amalfi Rosato '07	♛ 5
○ Costa d'Amalfi Fiorduva '06	♟♟♟ 7
○ Costa d'Amalfi Fiorduva '05	♟♟♟ 7
○ Costa d'Amalfi Fiorduva '04	♟♟♟ 7
● Costa d'Amalfi Rosso Furore Ris. '03	♟♟ 7
● Costa d'Amalfi Rosso Furore Ris. '02	♟♟ 7
○ Costa d'Amalfi Fiorduva '03	♟♟ 7
○ Costa d'Amalfi Fiorduva '01	♟♟ 7
● Costa d'Amalfi Rosso Furore Ris. '01	♟♟ 7

○ Ischia Biancolella Tenuta Frassitelli '07	♛♛ 5
○ Ischia Forastera Euposia '07	♛♛ 5
○ Ischia Biancolella '07	♛♛ 4*
○ Ischia Biancolella Calitto '07	♛ 4
○ Ischia Biancolella Tenuta Frassitelli '90	♟♟♟ 4
○ Ischia Bianco Kyme '05	♟♟ 5
○ Ischia Biancolella Tenuta Frassitelli '06	♟♟ 5
○ Ischia Biancolella Tenuta Frassitelli '01	♟♟ 5
○ Ischia Bianco Kyme '04	♟♟ 5
○ Ischia Bianco Kyme '02	♟♟ 5
○ Ischia Biancolella Tenuta Frassitelli '05	♟♟ 5
○ Ischia Biancolella Tenuta Frassitelli '04	♟♟ 5
○ Ischia Forastera Euposia '05	♟♟ 4

D'Antiche Terre - Vega

c.da Lo Piano - s.s. 7 bis
83030 Manocalzati [AV]
tel. 0825675358
www.danticheterre.it

ANNUAL PRODUCTION 390,000 bottles
HECTARES UNDER VINE 40
VITICULTURE METHOD Conventional

There wasn't the fillip of a wine in the finals this year for Gaetano Ciccarella, one of the great little veterans of Irpinian winemaking with almost 20 years experience under his belt. Even so, the performance of his wines across the board was admirable, keeping his estate in its high-ranking, authoritative position. The three leading wines, all very fine examples of the three Irpinia DOCGs, easily gained Two Glasses apiece. The '07 Fiano di Avellino may be a touch less impressive than the fabulous '06 but the '07 Greco di Tufo gained on last year's score with a full, decisive palate counterbalancing rather developed fruit and strongly incisive acidity. Even better, though, especially considering the vintage, is the '03 Taurasi, with its focus on warm, dark fruitiness enlivened by lightly smoky touches and deepened by sensations of tobacco. The palate is firm and pervasive from its first impact, and has plentiful backbone and tannic weave, making for a highly pleasing wine despite a lightly bitter finish. Irpinia Aglianico Rosato Ebe '07 made an excellent debut and the '07 Irpinia Coda di Volpe is as good as ever.

O Fiano di Avellino '07	🍷🍷	4*
O Greco di Tufo '07	🍷🍷	4*
● Taurasi '03	🍷🍷	6
⊙ Irpinia Aglianico Rosato Ebe '07	🍷	3
O Irpinia Coda di Volpe '07	🍷	3
O Fiano di Avellino '06	ŸŸ	4*
O Greco di Tufo '03	ŸŸ	4*
● Taurasi '00	ŸŸ	5

Viticoltori De Conciliis

loc. Querce
84060 Prignano Cilento [SA]
tel. 0974831090
www.viticoltorideconciliis.it

ANNUAL PRODUCTION 150,000 bottles
HECTARES UNDER VINE 28
VITICULTURE METHOD Conventional

If Bruno De Conciliis didn't exist, you'd have to invent him, a man who in private enjoys the obscure sensations of wines from the north while publicly releasing a range that hase more than a hint of affinity with the New World. He's like a sort of modern samurai, having gathered round him a group of young growers and winemakers whose spirit is closer to anarchy than single-mindedness. Every year, understanding and contextualising his wines is a challenge. Bruno has embraced the character of the Cilento territory in full over the years, excesses included. As a result, his wines are always clearly recognizable for their warmth, substance, fruity richness and impact. So much so that it would take nothing for them to go over the top. But this isn't the case with the two '07 Donnaluna wines, the Aglianico and the Fiano, both particularly commendable for their dynamism and length. Had there been a touch more complexity, we'd have been even more pleased but Bruno seems to have this in hand. A cask sample of Naima '05 leaves the issue open and nor was Nero available for tasting. That will have to be for next time.

● Donnaluna Aglianico '07	🍷🍷	4*
O Donnaluna Fiano '07	🍷🍷	4*
O Perella '06	🍷	6
● Naima '01	ŸŸŸ	6
● Naima '99	ŸŸ	6
● Naima '04	ŸŸ	7
● Naima '03	ŸŸ	7
● Naima '02	ŸŸ	7
● Naima '00	ŸŸ	6

Di Meo

C.DA COCCOVONI, 1
83050 SALZA IRPINA [AV]
TEL. 0825981419
www.dimeo.it

ANNUAL PRODUCTION	500,000 bottles
HECTARES UNDER VINE	50
VITICULTURE METHOD	Conventional

The winery is one of the larger and longer-standing in the province and its wines are always of substance though not yet, we feel, at a definitive stance. The three Di Meo siblings, Roberto, Erminia and Generoso, continue to work with huge commitment and their wines can – no, will – become truly excellent if they can get everything to come together. With the Taurasi Riserva, Don Generoso and the Fiano Alessandra selection still in ageing, a smaller range was submitted. We couldn't have asked more from it, especially since it allowed the Coda di Volpe to rise to the fore, and not for the first time. The '07 is extremely typical in its aromas of pear and fennel, and its notably dense palate. The '07 Greco di Tufo is also good. Although a touch fermentative on the nose, it is incisive and multi-faceted on the palate. Fiano di Avellino '07 has a very open, lychees and mango nose preceding a more linear palate and slightly cutting finish. The '06 Isso again makes for a great everyday drinker. It's not huge, and also somewhat linear, but delightfully juicy.

Di Prisco

C.DA ROTOLE, 27
83040 FONTANAROSA [AV]
TEL. 0825475738
www.cantinadiprisco.it

ANNUAL PRODUCTION	100,000 bottles
HECTARES UNDER VINE	10
VITICULTURE METHOD	Conventional

Have you ever come across one of those garrulous producers who, whether at a fair or in his cellar, practically takes you hostage, giving you chapter and verse on why he makes such good wines? Now just imagine the complete opposite and you'll have the character of grower Pasqualino Di Prisco. His work is all silence, consistency and lots of patience. His whites are always some of the last to appear on the market and his Taurasis are invariably some of the most elegant from the denomination. In summer 2004, the cool, stable weather conditions looked ideal for this stylistic approach and so it has proved. The Taurasi is a very bright pale ruby. The nose isn't classic but there are fresh aromas of rose and orange peel and more complex hints of rain-soaked earth and pine needles. The beautifully measured palate works along similar lines with good follow-through and zippy acidity, only slightly austere tannins holding it back. A touch more flesh and Three Glasses would have come Pasqualino's way. Irpinia Aglianico '04 is less complex but hangs together well. Greco di Tufo '06 has impressive warmth, fullness and grip.

O Coda di Volpe '07	♥♥ 4*
O Greco di Tufo '07	♥♥ 4*
O Fiano di Avellino '07	♥ 4
● Isso '06	♥ 4
O Fiano di Avellino Alessandra '03	♥♥ 5
O Fiano di Avellino Alessandra '04	♥♥ 5
● Taurasi Ris. '98	♥♥ 6
● Taurasi Ris. '97	♥♥ 6
● Taurasi Ris. '01	♥♥ 6
● Taurasi Ris. '00	♥♥ 6

● Taurasi '04	♥♥ 6
O Greco di Tufo '06	♥♥ 4*
O Coda di Volpe '07	♥ 3
● Irpinia Aglianico '04	♥ 4
O Greco di Tufo '03	♥♥ 4*
O Greco di Tufo Pietrarosa '05	♥♥ 4*
O Greco di Tufo Pietrarosa '04	♥♥ 4
● Taurasi '03	♥♥ 6
● Taurasi '01	♥♥ 6

I Favati

P.ZZA DI DONATO
83020 CESINALI [AV]
TEL. 0825666898
www.cantineifavati.it

★★ Feudi di San Gregorio

LOC. CERZA GROSSA
83050 SORBO SERPICO [AV]
TEL. 0825986611
www.feudi.it

ANNUAL PRODUCTION	50,000 bottles
HECTARES UNDER VINE	10
VITICULTURE METHOD	Conventional

Brothers Piersabino and Giancarlo Favati run this estate with Giancarlo's wife, the doughty Rosanna Petrozziello, and young consultant Vincenzo Mercurio, who joined a couple of years ago. This year's wines again stand out for their special sense of proportion and elegance. This is exemplified by Taurasi Terzo Tratto '04 with its vibrant nose of berry fruits, fresh almond and liquorice and its harmonious well-melded palate, which is given length by firm but supple tannins. Things become more complex with Fiano di Avellino '07, which is made in two styles that to some extent mirror each other. The classic Pietramara shines for its incisive, penetrating nose and well-paced palate. Pietramara Etichetta Bianca is on a different wavelength. Grapeskin sensations initially override the more vigorous, mineral and balsamic aromas while the palate is broad but still quite rigid and even aggressive, creating the impression that it's still very young, maybe too young. It gained Two red Glasses but we wouldn't be surprised if, in time, this very unusual Fiano became worthy of the ultimate accolade. The robust Greco di Tufo Terrantica '07 is well typed.

ANNUAL PRODUCTION	3,900,000 bottles
HECTARES UNDER VINE	320
VITICULTURE METHOD	Conventional

The sun is bright over Feudi di San Gregorio, even more so now that it has gained a second Star for having accumulated 20 Three Glass awards. This has been achieved in little over a decade and Feudi di San Gregorio is the first Campanian winery to gain such an honour. The wine that tipped it over the threshold was Greco di Tufo Cutizzi, a bottle of class and substance that, with time, is changing face, becoming lighter while gaining a more precise sense of provenance. The '07 revels in a beautiful mix of exuberance and composure. Fruity aromas of peach, pineapple and citron combine with sage and aniseed-like sensations. The enticing palate is composed without losing the sometimes wild energy typical of the variety. Fiano di Avellino Pietracalda '07 is more restrained but has great promise. Serpico '06, tasted from cask, is still very backwards. A new sparkling wine Dubl, made in conjunction with Anselme Selosse, made an excellent impression although the Greco Brut upstaged it. The rosé, from aglianico, also stands up well. Nevertheless it is the quality of the range as a whole that has made the estate pivotal for southern Italian wine.

○ Fiano di Avellino Pietramara Et. Bianca '07	♟♟ 4*
● Taurasi Terzo Tratto '04	♟♟ 5
○ Fiano di Avellino Pietramara '07	♟♟ 4*
○ Greco di Tufo Terrantica '07	♟♟ 4*
● Irpinia Campi Taurasini Cretarossa '06	♟♟ 4*
○ Fiano di Avellino Pietramara '06	♟♟ 4
○ Fiano di Avellino '04	♟♟ 4*
○ Fiano di Avellino Pietramara '05	♟♟ 4
○ Greco di Tufo Terrantica '06	♟♟ 4
● Taurasi Terzo Tratto '03	♟♟ 5

○ Greco di Tufo Cutizzi '07	♟♟♟ 4*
○ Campanaro '07	♟♟ 5
○ Fiano di Avellino Pietracalda '07	♟♟ 4*
○ Albente '07	♟♟ 3*
○ Dubl Greco Brut '04	♟♟ 6
○ Fiano di Avellino '07	♟♟ 4*
○ Greco di Tufo '07	♟♟ 4*
● Pàtrimo '05	♟♟ 8
● Rubrato '06	♟♟ 4*
○ Sannio Falanghina '07	♟♟ 4*
○ Sannio Falanghina Serrocielo '07	♟♟ 4
○ Dubl Falanghina Brut '05	♟ 5
⊙ Dubl Rosato Brut '05	♟ 6
⊙ Irpinia Ros'Aura '07	♟ 3
○ Greco di Tufo Cutizzi '06	♟♟♟ 4*
● Irpinia Serpico '05	♟♟♟ 8

Galardi

FRAZ. SAN CARLO
S.P. SESSA-MIGNANO
81030 SESSA AURUNCA [CE]
TEL. 0823708900
www.terradilavoro.com

ANNUAL PRODUCTION	25,000 bottles
HECTARES UNDER VINE	10
VITICULTURE METHOD	Certified organic

It's one thing to talk about making a unique, inimitable wine that can faithfully express the character of its provenance and happily stand the test of time and quite another to make it. For many, it's their long-term objective and for others it's an instinctive urge. And there aren't many wines that can respond to this sort of almost genetic imperative and reliably steal scenes. Those that can are usually controversial soloists rather than team players; gutsy, capricious and anything but perfect, like great leaders who divide opinion but always take centre stage. And that is exactly the character that Terra di Lavoro has had from its earliest releases. It's a wine of mythical proportions in southern Italy. Its beguiling slip from perfection is the anything but subtle smokiness that has made it unique and which is again prominent in the '06. Tar, charcoal, grilled meat: the nose brooks no curbs on an almost wild power that seems locked in battle with its incredibly clean black berry fruit and spiciness. The same elements faithfully reappear on the very young, earthy, explosively assertive palate.

Cantina Giardino

VIA PETRARA, 21B
83031 ARIANO IRPINO [AV]
TEL. 0825873084
www.cantinagiardino.com

ANNUAL PRODUCTION	13,000 bottles
HECTARES UNDER VINE	4
VITICULTURE METHOD	Natural

In a sector that all too often yields to the temptation of making wines to fit preordained categories, Antonio and Daniela De Gruttola's small estate is often presented as the only one in the area to give its wines free stylistic rein. It may be more significant, though, to note that the couple consistently make wines that are good. These are products in traditional Irpinian style, even if sometimes taken to the extreme, and it's not so much that they're different from the general run for the sake of it; more that there's a deeper search for proportion and balance, especially in the use of oak. This is typified by the development of Nude. The quality of the '04 bears comparison with the region's best, its earthy, spicy vigour showing multi-faceted and satisfying, tipped off perfection only by a slight ethery pungency. Aglianico Drogone '05 is slimmer, yet more extrovert and just as incisive. Aglianico Le Fole '06 is more docile and the winery's most comforting wine. T'Ara Rà '06, made from 100 per cent greco, skin-macerated and oak-aged, is a wine of substance with a clear varietal slant and one that will certainly provoke a reaction.

● Terra di Lavoro '06	▼▼▼	8
● Terra di Lavoro '99	♀♀♀	7
● Terra di Lavoro '05	♀♀♀	8
● Terra di Lavoro '04	♀♀♀	8
● Terra di Lavoro '03	♀♀♀	7
● Terra di Lavoro '02	♀♀♀	7
● Terra di Lavoro '01	♀♀	7
● Terra di Lavoro '00	♀♀	7
● Terra di Lavoro '98	♀♀	7
● Terra di Lavoro '97	♀♀	7

● Nude '04	♀♀	7
● Drogone '05	♀♀	6
○ T'Ara Rà '06	♀♀	6
● Le Fole '06	♀	4
● Drogone '04	♀♀	6

Cantine Grotta del Sole

VIA SPINELLI, 2
80010 QUARTO [NA]
TEL. 0818762566
www.grottadelsole.it

ANNUAL PRODUCTION 850,000 bottles
HECTARES UNDER VINE 35
VITICULTURE METHOD Conventional

It doesn't take much to explain why the Martusciello family has become an indispensable element of the Campanian wine scene. A glance at their wide range and the impressive number of Glasses they've amassed is enough to realize the extent to which their winery is a bastion of the region. Significantly, they have worked to bring esteem to many erstwhile "minor" denominations, from Gragnano and Lettere della Penisola Sorrentina to Asprinio d'Aversa, Vesuvio Lacryma Christi, and Falanghina and Piedirosso dei Campi Flegrei. But even more significantly, Martusciello wines are always on the button, be they the easy drinking ones aimed at satisfying purse as much as palate, or those with loftier aspirations. This year, we again enjoyed the zest and definition of the asprinio-based sparklers, both the cuve close and classic method ones, while the restraint and complexity of Greco di Tufo Quarto di Luna '06 and Campi Flegrei Falanghina Coste di Cuma '06 impressed us further. However, it would appear that the neoclassical Quarto di Sole '05, made solely from aglianico grown in Castelfranci, is still searching for a more complete stylistic identity.

● Aglianico '07	🍷🍷	4*
○ Asprinio d'Aversa Brut	🍷🍷	4*
○ Asprinio d'Aversa Extra Brut M. Cl.	🍷🍷	5
○ Campi Flegrei Falanghina Coste di Cuma '06	🍷🍷	5
○ Fiano di Avellino '07	🍷🍷	4*
○ Greco di Tufo Quarto di Luna '06	🍷🍷	5
● Quarto di Sole '05	🍷🍷	5
○ Campi Flegrei Falanghina '07	🍷	4
● Campi Flegrei Piedirosso '07	🍷	4
● Campi Flegrei Piedirosso Montegauro Ris. '05	🍷	5
○ Coda di Volpe '07	🍷	3
○ Greco di Tufo '07	🍷	4
● Penisola Sorrentina Gragnano '07	🍷	4
● Penisola Sorrentina Lettere '07	🍷	4
○ Vesuvio Lacryma Christi Bianco '07	🍷	4
○ Vesuvio Lacryma Christi Dolce	🍷	4

La Guardiense

LOC. SANTA LUCIA, 104-105
82034 GUARDIA SANFRAMONDI [BN]
TEL. 0824864034
www.janare.it

ANNUAL PRODUCTION 4,000,000 bottles
HECTARES UNDER VINE N.A.
VITICULTURE METHOD Conventional

Part of the fun of preparing a Guide like this is that, as well as being intrigued by all the new things we get to taste, we also come across wines we thought we knew well but which suddenly gain a new dimension. Guardiense is a case in point. For years, we found the wines from this co-operative to be decent, even quite good sometimes, but they never really excited us. Then last year, we found ourselves tasting an impeccable range and this time the performance has been repeated. Such an achievement might have simply been chance, were it not for the high standard of the base-level wines. These have precision and substance and in addition they are brilliantly priced. For example, there is the firm, strongly perfumed Sannio Fiano Selezione '07; the more serious Sannio Greco '07, full of vigour and citrus aromas; and the eclectic Guardiolo Rosso Riserva '06, one of the region's best choices for value for money drinking. Guardiolo Aglianico Cantari Riserva '06 is more ambitious and has more power; the fruity, delicately acidulous Guardiolo Falanghina Selezione '07 is also successful.

● Guardiolo Aglianico Cantari Ris. '06	🍷🍷	5
● Guardiolo Rosso Ris. '06	🍷🍷	3*
○ Sannio Fiano Sel. '07	🍷🍷	3*
○ Sannio Greco Sel. '07	🍷🍷	3*
● Guardiolo Aglianico Lucchero '07	🍷	4
● Guardiolo Aglianico Sel. '07	🍷	3
○ Guardiolo Falanghina Sel. '07	🍷	3
● Guardiolo Aglianico Sel. '06	🍷🍷 (white)	3*
● Guardiolo Aglianico Lucchero '05	🍷🍷 (white)	4*
● Guardiolo Rosso Ris. '04	🍷🍷 (white)	3*

Luigi Maffini

FRAZ. SAN MARCO
LOC. CENITO
84048 CASTELLABATE [SA]
TEL. 0974966345
www.maffini-vini.com

★ Mastroberardino

VIA MANFREDI, 75/81
83042 ATRIPALDA [AV]
TEL. 0825614111
www.mastroberardino.com

ANNUAL PRODUCTION	100,000 bottles
HECTARES UNDER VINE	14
VITICULTURE METHOD	Conventional

ANNUAL PRODUCTION	2,400,000 bottles
HECTARES UNDER VINE	350
VITICULTURE METHOD	Conventional

Overall Maffini's wines put on an outstanding show and Three Glasses were just a whisper away. But does that level of proximity mean celebrations or commiserations? We have a feeling that Luigi Maffini would go for the latter, but not us. That's firstly because his top wine, Cenito, wasn't tasted, the '06 benefiting from longer pre-release ageing than usual, and then because the standard of the base-level wines is indicative of a continuing quality rise. Klèos '06, a blend of aglianico, piedirosso and barbera, is a refined mix of fruity aromas and more complex nuances of scrubland and red earth, sublimated in a stylish, well-melded palate of uncommon balance. Kràtos has long been one of the best wines from fiano made outside of the classic Irpinia heartland and the '07 is no exception. Succulent and multi-faceted, it alternates edginess and softness, showing lots of flavour and length. The wine that caused Luigi's regret, if that's the right word, is Pietraincatenata '06, a barrique-aged Fiano with a smoky nose of almond and mango. It fell short simply through a touch too much warmth and bitterness on its finish.

One new star, one retaining its twinkle and one fixed in the galaxy. That's the sparkle for Campania's oldest winery. The new star is Taurasi Naturalis Historia, gaining its first Three Glasses for the '04, a glory of force and fruit. It's decidedly modern in style, and the least Mastroberardinoesque of the group, but with its great cleanliness and beautifully judged tannicity, it should age very well. The twinkle retainer is Greco di Tufo Novaserra, the '07 once more on the region's Three Glass list. Serious and fascinating, its main allure is its subtle mineral character, a facet that is even more laudable given the overripeness that characterized the vintage. The fixture, though, is the entire, reliable, broad range with Taurasi Radici Riserva '03 soaring through the finals, as did Fiano di Avellino Radici '07, which needed nothing more than a touch of flesh in mid palate to join the stars. The '06 Aglianico is, as usual, one of the best examples of the variety to be found while an impressive '06 brings into ever-sharper focus the Fiano di Avellino More Maiorum. Everything else is somewhere between fair and excellent.

O Pietraincatenata '06	⟡⟡ 5
● Klèos '06	⟡⟡ 4*
O Kràtos '07	⟡⟡ 4*
● Cilento Aglianico Cenito '03	⟡⟡⟡ 6
O Pietraincatenata '04	⟡⟡⟡ 5
● Cenito '01	⟡⟡ 7
● Cenito '00	⟡⟡ 7
● Cilento Aglianico Cenito '05	⟡⟡ 6
● Cilento Aglianico Cenito '04	⟡⟡ 6
O Pietraincatenata '03	⟡⟡ 5

O Greco di Tufo Novaserra '07	⟡⟡⟡ 4*
● Taurasi Naturalis Historia '04	⟡⟡⟡ 7
O Fiano di Avellino Radici '07	⟡⟡ 4*
● Taurasi Radici Ris. '03	⟡⟡ 6
● Aglianico '06	⟡⟡ 4*
O Fiano di Avellino '07	⟡⟡ 4*
O Fiano di Avellino More Maiorum '06	⟡⟡ 5
● Taurasi Centotrenta Ris. '99	⟡⟡ 6
O Greco di Tufo '07	⟡ 4
O Irpinia Falanghina Morabianca '07	⟡ 4
☉ Lacrimarosa '07	⟡ 4
O Vesuvio Lacryma Christi Bianco '07	⟡ 4
● Vesuvio Lacryma Christi Rosso '07	⟡ 4
O Fiano di Avellino Radici '05	⟡⟡⟡ 4*
O Greco di Tufo Novaserra '06	⟡⟡⟡ 4*
● Taurasi Radici Ris. '01	⟡⟡⟡ 6

Salvatore Molettieri

C.DA MUSANNI, 19B
83040 MONTEMARANO [AV]
TEL. 082763424
www.salvatoremolettieri.it

★ Montevetrano

LOC. NIDO
VIA MONTEVETRANO, 3
84099 SAN CIPRIANO PICENTINO [SA]
TEL. 089882285
www.montevetrano.it

ANNUAL PRODUCTION	50,000 bottles
HECTARES UNDER VINE	11
VITICULTURE METHOD	Conventional

ANNUAL PRODUCTION	30,000 bottles
HECTARES UNDER VINE	5
VITICULTURE METHOD	Conventional

Getting a prize doesn't always mean you've arrived. Take Salvatore Molettieri and his best known wine Taurasi Vigna Cinque Querce. Yes, the '04 has brought Three Glasses back to the estate but we think its real significance lies in the future. And we don't just mean for Salvatore and his modest, hard-working family. We're talking mainly about the future potential of the wine itself. It's already stunning but it could become the quintessence of the DOCG. Everything about it speaks youth from its deep, dark ruby colour onwards through its plummy aromas, its earthy, ashy, mineral resonances, its hints of cocoa powder and cloves. But above all it was the palate and its contrasts that really bowled us over. Almost chewy fruit is enlivened by vibrant acidity and punctuated by an array of tannins that go way beyond all norms for density and continuity. It's simply mind-blowing. The Vigna Cinque Querce Riserva '03 is more approachably enjoyable, although a little excess alcohol on the finish reflected the heat of the year. Irpinia Aglianico Cinque Querce '06 is promising and the lively Ischia Piana '06 is ready.

"A classic is something that never finishes saying what it has to say". We'd like to think it was a bottle of Silvia Imparato's Montevetrano that inspired Italo Calvino because there is no word that better expresses the essence of her creation. At first, Silvia's venture was seen as revolutionary, going as it did beyond traditional concepts of place and style, but now it seems as if the wine has always been there, a fact that may well provide a pointer to future directions for the region to take. Just every time you reread the great masterpieces of literature, you discover something new so too with Montevetrano: every tasting reveals new depths. And who knows how long the latest chapter, the 2006, will be studied and enjoyed? It comes from an abundant but difficult vintage as is obvious from the way the wine remains closed into its earthy and meaty tones, disclosing its deep nuances of ripe blackberry and black pepper only to the most patient. The palate, also introverted, reticent and almost dark, is well anchored in tannins that have more bite than usual but which still leave room for a habitual burst of energy on the finish.

● Taurasi Vigna Cinque Querce '04	🍷🍷🍷	7
● Taurasi Vigna Cinque Querce Ris. '03	🍷🍷	8
● Aglianico Cinque Querce '06	🍷🍷	5
● Ischia Piana '06	🍷🍷	5
○ Greco di Tufo '06	🍷	5
● Taurasi Vigna Cinque Querce '01	🍷🍷🍷	6
● Taurasi Vigna Cinque Querce Ris. '01	🍷🍷🍷	8
● Aglianico Cinque Querce '02	🍷🍷	5
● Taurasi Vigna Cinque Querce '03	🍷🍷	8
● Taurasi Vigna Cinque Querce '00	🍷🍷	6
● Taurasi Vigna Cinque Querce Ris. '00	🍷🍷	7
● Taurasi Vigna Cinque Querce '98	🍷🍷	7
● Taurasi Vigna Cinque Querce Ris. '97	🍷🍷	8

● Montevetrano '06	🍷🍷🍷	8
● Montevetrano '99	🍷🍷🍷	8
● Montevetrano '98	🍷🍷🍷	8
● Montevetrano '97	🍷🍷🍷	8
● Montevetrano '96	🍷🍷🍷	8
● Montevetrano '95	🍷🍷🍷	8
● Montevetrano '93	🍷🍷🍷	8
● Montevetrano '05	🍷🍷🍷	8
● Montevetrano '04	🍷🍷🍷	8
● Montevetrano '03	🍷🍷🍷	8
● Montevetrano '02	🍷🍷🍷	8
● Montevetrano '01	🍷🍷🍷	8
● Montevetrano '00	🍷🍷🍷	8

Pietracupa

C.DA VADIAPERTI, 17
83030 MONTEFREDANE [AV]
TEL. 0825607418
pietracupa@email.it

ANNUAL PRODUCTION   35,000 bottles
HECTARES UNDER VINE   3.5
VITICULTURE METHOD   Conventional

If you telephone Pietracupo and a strange voice responds, declaring he's a cellar worker, you are almost certainly talking to owner Sabino Loffredo on one of his proverbial off days, the sort that can often be sorted out by a good bottle of wine and something to eat. That's Loffredo: take him or leave him. There are no half measures. He tastes incessantly, at his cellar and outside, and his relationship with wine is confrontational, mediated by nerves, not figures. All this comes through in wines that have an almost visceral quality, wines that truly reflect their provenance, wines that, like the greatest, seem to sense the challenges in their making and turn limits into opportunities. Greco di Tufo '07 epitomizes these characteristics and took home Three Glasses, despite the less-than-perfect vintage for this most red-like of Irpinian whites. The hot, dry summer has produced a wine with an open, sunny disposition, giving peach and blueberry aromas that resonate with ash and iodine. The palate is full-on, channelling its appealing, broad initial attack into a flow of vigour and grip, highlighted by a long, oregano and citrus rind finish.

Tenuta Ponte

VIA CARAZITA, 1
83040 LUOGOSANO [AV]
TEL. 082773564
www.tenutaponte.it

ANNUAL PRODUCTION   180,000 bottles
HECTARES UNDER VINE   35
VITICULTURE METHOD   Conventional

Owned by Alessandro Di Stasio and his partners, this winery is named after a small stone bridge (ponte) over the Calore river. It has only been going just over ten years but is already an indispensable part of the regional wine scene. Its success derives from reliable quality combined with amazingly good pricing and its appeal is spreading among both wine lovers and ordinary consumers. Peaking the range this year is the '07 Fiano di Avellino, instantly recognizable by the initial almost gamey hints on the nose before softer, more citrus-like, balsamic tones with orange blossom and fresh mint follow. The highlight of the palate is an iodine tenor that brings grip and adds drive to its subtle but aromatic and persistent flavour. The '07 Greco di Tufo is of similar standing. The nose, suspended between earthy and petrolly notes, is one of the most assertive of the vintage. The palate brings broader, more extractive sensations although loses a little of its grace on the finish. Taurasi '04 has faultless gravity and typicity but seems a touch too immature, both on nose and palate. Coda di Volpe '07 is authoritative.

O Greco di Tufo '07	♟♟♟ 4*
O Fiano di Avellino '07	♟♟ 4*
● Taurasi '04	♟♟ 6
● Quirico '06	♟ 5
O Cupo '05	♟♟♟ 5
O Cupo '03	♟♟♟ 4*
O Greco di Tufo '06	♟♟♟ 4*
O Fiano di Avellino '06	♟♟ 4*
O Fiano di Avellino '05	♟♟ 4*
O Fiano di Avellino '04	♟♟ 4
O Greco di Tufo '05	♟♟ 4*
O Greco di Tufo '04	♟♟ 4
● Taurasi '00	♟♟ 6
● Taurasi '03	♟♟ 6
● Taurasi '01	♟♟ 6

O Fiano di Avellino '07	♟♟ 4*
O Greco di Tufo '07	♟♟ 4*
O Irpinia Coda di Volpe '07	♟♟ 3*
● Taurasi '04	♟♟ 4*
O Falanghina del Beneventano '07	♟ 3
O Fiano di Avellino '06	♟♟ 4*
O Fiano di Avellino '04	♟♟ 4*
● Taurasi '03	♟♟ 5
● Taurasi '01	♟♟ 6
● Taurasi '00	♟♟ 5
O Fiano di Avellino '05	♟♟ 4

Fattoria La Rivolta

C.DA RIVOLTA
82030 TORRECUSO [BN]
TEL. 0824872921
www.fattorialarivolta.com

ANNUAL PRODUCTION 120,000 bottles
HECTARES UNDER VINE 25
VITICULTURE METHOD Certified organic

Is life a dream or does Rivolta's "Dream" (Sogno di Rivolta) improve life? Please excuse us these philosophical musings but they help to convey the calibre of Fattoria La Rivolta's top white. And with Terra di Rivolta '06 still ageing at the time of our tastings – the '05 wasn't considered good enough to market – it is this '07 blend of falanghina, fiano and greco that carries the estate's banner this year. It showed very well with peachskin, tea leaves and tincture of iodine on the nose bringing unique character that sits a little uneasily with the overall sense of fruity softness. The palate has thrust and dynamism and loses out only on a slightly narrow, short finish. Overall, its Two Glasses are well deserved. The aromatic profile of Falanghina del Taburno '07 is more familiar: Aromas of williams pears, citron and broom precede a soft, alluring palate whose iodine notes link its origins to that of the vibrant Coda del Volpe del Taburno and Sannio Fiano, both also '07. Taburno Aglianico '06 is introverted and austere yet has flesh and zip. A couple of bottles in the cellar certainly wouldn't go amiss.

○ Sogno di Rivolta '07	🍷🍷	4*
○ Taburno Falanghina '07	🍷🍷	4*
● Aglianico del Taburno '06	🍷	4
○ Sannio Fiano '07	🍷	4
○ Taburno Coda di Volpe '07	🍷	4
● Aglianico del Taburno Terra di Rivolta Ris. '04	🍷🍷	6
● Aglianico del Taburno Terra di Rivolta Ris. '03	🍷🍷	6
● Aglianico del Taburno '05	🍷🍷	4*
● Aglianico del Taburno Terra di Rivolta Ris. '00	🍷🍷	6
○ Sogno di Rivolta '06	🍷🍷	4*

Rocca del Principe

LOC. ARIANIELLO
VIA ARIANIELLO, 9
83030 LAPIO [AV]
TEL. 0825982435
aurelia65@tele2.it

ANNUAL PRODUCTION 16,000 bottles
HECTARES UNDER VINE 4
VITICULTURE METHOD Conventional

"Terroir" is without doubt one of the most abused words in the wine lexicon. Even so, there are places where this untranslatable word is the key to everything. In Irpinia, in Lapio and within that Arianiello, right in the heart of the Fiano di Avellino zone, is one such spot. More mountain than Mediterranean, Arianello is a place that needs time to release all its energy, a place that makes results like those that Aurelia Fabrizio and her husband Ercole have achieved at their Rocca del Principe estate in just a few vintages a little less unbelievable. As a result, we decided to award it the title of Up-and-Coming Winery of the Year. We welcome them among our Three Glasses winners with an authoritative Fiano di Avellino '07, which sports an authentically mineral profile spanning petrol and smokiness while reflecting citrus and balsamic nuances of pink grapefruit and basil. It is followed by a taut, elegant, multi-faceted palate with wafts of deep saltiness underpinned by full structure while growing towards a long but still very youthful finish.

○ Fiano di Avellino '07	🍷🍷🍷	4*
○ Fiano di Avellino '06	🍷🍷	4*

Ettore Sammarco

VIA CIVITA, 9
84010 RAVELLO [SA]
TEL. 089872774
www.ettoresammarco.it

ANNUAL PRODUCTION	72,000 bottles
HECTARES UNDER VINE	10
VITICULTURE METHOD	Conventional

Last year, we talked about what a revelation it was to taste this estate's wines and this year that new promise has been maintained. The improvement has come about from the commitment and intelligence of determined owner Bartolo Sammarco, as well as his skilled winemaker Fortunato Sebastiano and others. It's been helped by the huge potential of the land, even though this isn't a simple thing to turn to account, requiring careful handling of dozens of plots and growers. The top wine this year, as before, is Selva delle Monache Rosso Riserva, from a traditional blend of aglianico and piedirosso. The '04 has a well-melded, close-knit quality as well as the relaxed gracefulness we so enjoyed last year. There is liquorice, black cherry and tar, reflecting sound aromatic cohesiveness, preceding a tight, semi-full palate that is still in evolution. All the whites are well differentiated by style and blend. From differing proportions of pepella, ginestrella, biancazita and biancolella, they all showed well, taut with a strong saline character, most notably Selva delle Monache Bianco '07.

Tenuta Adolfo Spada

FRAZ. VAGLIE
LOC. FONTANA DI TEANO
81045 GALLUCCIO [CE]
TEL. 0823925709
www.tenutaspada.it

ANNUAL PRODUCTION	80,000 bottles
HECTARES UNDER VINE	30
VITICULTURE METHOD	Conventional

It's not unusual, if not easy, to attract attention with a good range of wines when starting outside the main stream. What is usually much harder is making the passage from outsider to superstar, with wines that can scale the highest heights. But that is what Adolfo Spada has managed, aided by his consultant Riccardo Cotarella. The top wine, Gladius, stands out. This modern-style blend of aglianico and piedirosso garners admiration for the way it consistently marries the expression of its provenance with its stylistic calibration. Now, with the '06, it has reached Three Glass level for the first time. The nose is initially shy but then releases earthy, balsamic scents. The still youthful palate with close-knit but ripe tannins has refreshing acidity to balance out its fruity, glycerine richness. The reds are also good. Sabus '07 is a soft, juicy blend of equal parts of aglianico, piedirosso and montepulciano. Gallicius '06, from aglianico and piedirosso, is nicely earthy but a little raw on the finish.

● Costa d'Amalfi Ravello Rosso Selva delle Monache Ris. '04	♉♉ 5
○ Costa d'Amalfi Ravello Bianco Selva delle Monache '07	♉♉ 4*
○ Costa d'Amalfi Ravello Bianco V. Grotta Piana '07	♉♉ 5
○ Costa d'Amalfi Terre Sarecene Bianco '07	♉♉ 4*
● Costa d'Amalfi Terre Sarecene Rosso '07	♉♉ 4*
● Costa d'Amalfi Ravello Rosso Selva delle Monache '06	♉ 4
● Costa d'Amalfi Ravello Rosso Selva delle Monache Ris. '03	♉♉ 5
○ Costa d'Amalfi Ravello Bianco Selva delle Monache '06	♉♉ 4*
● Costa d'Amalfi Ravello Rosso Selva delle Monache '05	♉♉ 4*

● Gladius '06	♉♉♉ 5
● Sabus '07	♉♉ 4*
● Gallicius Rosso '06	♉ 3
● Gladius '05	♉♉ 5
● Gladius '03	♉♉ 5
● Gladius '04	♉♉ 5
● Gladius '02	♉♉ 4*

Cantina del Taburno

VIA SALA, 16
82030 FOGLIANISE [BN]
TEL. 0824871338
www.cantinadeltaburno.it

ANNUAL PRODUCTION	1,800,000 bottles
HECTARES UNDER VINE	600
VITICULTURE METHOD	Conventional

Our feelings about the Cantina del Taburno continue to swing between enthusiasm and caution. Last year we noted, with some regret, a little dullness on the wines but this year we have nothing to grumble about. The range gets a clear thumbs up. Of course, the co-operative's pathway is eased in years such as this when it can throw down its trump card, Bue Apis, a wine that is practically the symbol of the province's aglianico-based reds. The '04 immediately stood out as one of the best vintages ever. The nose is initially closed and untogether, spanning vegetal and slightly gamey notes, but then opens to reveal a wealth of aromas from cocoa powder to Peruvian bark and cigar tobacco. The elegant, characteristic palate has a glorious fruity sweetness perfectly harmonized by a long, deep finish and enlivened by ripe, luxuriant tannins. As usual, the rest of the range has much to offer value-conscious consumers, especially the '07 Fiano. The first results of trials with a Falanghina Spumante Extra Dry are highly positive.

Terre del Principe

FRAZ. SQUILLE
VIA SS. GIOVANNI E PAOLO, 30
81010 CASTEL CAMPAGNANO [CE]
TEL. 0823867126
www.terredelprincipe.com

ANNUAL PRODUCTION	55,000 bottles
HECTARES UNDER VINE	11
VITICULTURE METHOD	Conventional

This is not the first time that Manuela Piancastelli and Peppe Mancini have won Three Glasses. That was a good number of years ago, when they were working with the Barletta family and brought Vestini Campagnano's Casavecchia top honours. Then the two sides separated and Terre del Principe was born. Now comes the satisfaction of seeing their area's notorious pallagrello nero, which they literally wrenched from oblivion, right in the spotlight. Had they not done so, we might never have seen wines like Ambruco '06, which provides a fascinating mix of character and precision. The nose is fabulous, with citrus, oriental spices and volcanic nuances and the spirited palate is mouthfilling and creamy, revealing a sustained tannic weave. Centomoggia '06 from casavecchia, is not dissimilar, either in style nor quality. Castello delle Femmine '06, from casavecchia and pallagrello, is lighter in weight. As usual the two whites, both '07, are very good, their variety known by all, except the bureaucrats, as pallagrello bianco. Both the barriqued Le Serole version and the unoaked Fontanavigna have vibrancy and complexity of aromas. Neither outshines the other.

Wine	Rating
● Taburno Aglianico Bue Apis '04	▼▼▼ 8
○ Fiano '07	▼▼ 4*
● Aglianico del Taburno Fidelis '05	▼ 4
☉ Albarossa '07	▼ 3
○ Coda di Volpe Amineo '07	▼ 4
○ Falanghina Extra Dry	▼ 4
○ Greco '07	▼ 4
○ Taburno Falanghina '07	▼ 4
○ Taburno Falanghina Folius '06	▼ 5
● Bue Apis '99	♈♈♈ 7
● Bue Apis '00	♈♈♈ 7
● Bue Apis '01	♈♈ 8
● Taburno Aglianico Bue Apis '03	♈♈ 8

Wine	Rating
● Ambruco '06	▼▼▼ 6
● Centomoggia '06	▼▼ 6
○ Fontanavigna Pallagrello Bianco '07	▼▼ 5
○ Le Serole Pallagrello Bianco '07	▼▼ 5
● Castello delle Femmine '06	▼ 4
● Centomoggia '04	♈♈ 6
○ Le Serole Pallagrello Bianco '03	♈♈ 5
● V. Piancastelli '04	♈♈ 7
● Castello delle Femmine '05	♈♈ 4
● Centomoggia '05	♈♈ 6
○ Fontanavigna Pallagrello Bianco '06	♈♈ 5

Terredora

VIA SERRA
83030 MONTEFUSCO [AV]
TEL. 0825968215
www.terredora.com

ANNUAL PRODUCTION	1,200,000 bottles
HECTARES UNDER VINE	180
VITICULTURE METHOD	Conventional

Campania without the serried ranks of Terredora's first-rate wines simply wouldn't be Campania. Not only is it one of the largest producers in the region but every year its broad range spans numerous different types and styles. This year, the icing on the cake is again Greco di Tufo Terre degli Angeli, a cru from Santa Paolina. The '07 has a strongly smoky, balsamic character, its only fall from grace a slightly untidy, tannic finish. But there are several more wines, all comfortably above the Two Glasses threshold and all of them displaying a rich, ripe fruitiness with, crucially, softness throughout. Emblematic here are Fiano di Avellino Terre di Dora '07, Greco di Tufo Loggia della Serra '07 and Coda di Volpe '07, all three offering good value for money. Taurasi Campo Re Riserva '03 is more four-square and edgy with slightly lean tannins; Taurasi Fatica Contadina '03 is more relaxed but also less complex. Both are up against the limits of the year but give a good idea of what could be achieved in more classic vintages.

Urciuolo

FRAZ. CELZI
VIA DUE PRINCIPATI, 9
83020 FORINO [AV]
TEL. 0825761649
www.fratelliurciuolo.it

ANNUAL PRODUCTION	100,000 bottles
HECTARES UNDER VINE	25
VITICULTURE METHOD	Conventional

Describing Urciuolo's wines this year is rather like discussing the result of a football match at half-time where the team is well organized, stays on the ball but hasn't yet managed to get it into the back of the net despite a couple of near misses. Oh, and there are a couple of outstanding players still on the bench. Unravelling our simile, the players waiting to take the field are Fiano di Avellino Faliesi '07 and Taurasi '04, which we'll assess next year, and the near misses came from this tightly knit team's two classics, Fiano di Avellino '07 and Greco di Tufo '07. The former has exemplary style, reflecting both its provenance and that of the estate. The fresh almond and golden delicious apple aromas, given depth by smokiness, are typical of fiano from Forino where soils are looser-grained than in the more famous Lapio and Montefredane crus. Ciro and Antonello Urciolo's touch comes through more on the palate, where fleshiness and extract outweigh depth. Similar considerations apply to the Greco di Tufo, which is sunny yet earthy, slightly uneven in its acidic and mineral timbre but generous in mid palate. But the match isn't over yet.

O Greco di Tufo Terre degli Angeli '07	♛♛	4*
O Coda di Volpe '07	♛♛	4*
O Fiano di Avellino Terre di Dora '07	♛♛	4*
O Greco di Tufo Loggia della Serra '07	♛♛	4*
● Taurasi Campo Re Ris. '03	♛♛	7
● Taurasi Fatica Contadina '03	♛♛	6
O Falanghina '07	♛	4
O Fiano di Avellino Campo Re '06	♛	5
O Irpinia Falanghina '07	♛	4
● Irpinia Aglianico Il Principio '06	♛	5
● Taurasi Pago dei Fusi '03	♛	6
O Fiano di Avellino Terre di Dora '06	♉♉	4*
O Greco di Tufo Loggia della Serra '05	♉♉	4*
O Greco di Tufo Terra degli Angeli '05	♉♉	4*
O Greco di Tufo Loggia della Serra '06	♉♉	4*
O Greco di Tufo Terra degli Angeli '06	♉♉	4*

O Fiano di Avellino '07	♛♛	4*
O Greco di Tufo '07	♛♛	4*
● Aglianico '06	♛♛	3*
O Fiano di Avellino Faliesi '05	♉♉	4*
O Fiano di Avellino Faliesi '04	♉♉	4*
O Greco di Tufo '05	♉♉	4*
● Taurasi '03	♉♉	6
● Taurasi '02	♉♉	6
● Taurasi '01	♉♉	5
O Fiano di Avellino '06	♉♉	4*
O Fiano di Avellino '05	♉♉	4*
O Fiano di Avellino '04	♉♉	4*
O Fiano di Avellino Faliesi '06	♉♉	4*
O Greco di Tufo '06	♉♉	4*
● Taurasi '99	♉♉	6

Vadiaperti

C.DA VADIAPERTI
83030 MONTEFREDANE [AV]
TEL. 0825607270
www.vadiaperti.it

Villa Diamante

VIA TOPPOLE, 16
83030 MONTEFREDANE [AV]
TEL. 0825670014
www.villadiamante.eu

ANNUAL PRODUCTION	50,000 bottles
HECTARES UNDER VINE	8
VITICULTURE METHOD	Conventional

ANNUAL PRODUCTION	10,000 bottles
HECTARES UNDER VINE	2.8
VITICULTURE METHOD	Certified organic

It's party time at Vadiaperti. Not, for once, just to do with Glasses and scores but to celebrate the birth of Roberta Troisi, apple of the eye of mother Irene, father and estate-owner Raffaele, and all the friends and colleagues this tireless character holds in conversation till the early hours. The sense of something new seems to have impacted the wines, too. We had become used to a subtle, rarefied, edgy, austere style in Raffaele's wines but they've now gained a sunnier, more open aspect, more tertiary characters, more hints of skin maceration, with the result that they're fascinating but devilish to interpret. Greco di Tufo '07 is the exemplar. The nose is distinctly old-style Greco, ranging from dried apricot to cereals, and the palate is fat and tannic, still in search of harmony. Similar considerations apply to Coda di Volpe '07, which remains one of the best examples of the variety ever with huge concentration. A bit more freshness would not have come amiss, though. Fiano di Avellino '07 and Greco di Tufo '07 are contradictory wines. Both have seemingly evolved noses but palates of extreme youth.

If Vigna della Congregazione were a soccer player, it would play at number ten, all genius and bad behaviour: the sort that has to make an effort to get into the game but can change its direction from one moment to the next. They can be unwatchable one day and worth the price of the ticket on their own the next. Alright, this gem of a wine from Antoine Gaita doesn't always perform like a true number ten but it still has plenty of loyal fans. It is the archetypal Fiano di Avellino grand cru yet somehow always seems to do well only in even-numbered years. The wine ran true to form in 2006 and a splendid version took Three Glasses. The nose has great individuality with mimosa, citrus peel and balsamic-mineral notes that resemble the smell of a tennis ball, evoking Mosel wines and even more so the clayey, stony soils of its vineyards. The firm, sharply honed, stony palate is shaped by an almost brine-like skeletal purity rather than fleshy richness. In short, it is sheer class and all we can do now is wait and see whether next year's will match it or fall victim to the curse of the odd-numbered years.

○ Greco di Tufo Tornante '07	▼▼	4*
○ Irpinia Coda di Volpe '07	▼▼	4*
○ Falanghina '07	▼▼	4*
○ Fiano di Avellino '07	▼▼	4*
○ Greco di Tufo '07	▼▼	4*
○ Fiano di Avellino Aipierti '05	♈♈	4*
○ Greco di Tufo '05	♈♈	4*
○ Greco di Tufo '04	♈♈	4*
○ Fiano di Avellino '96	♈♈	4
○ Fiano di Avellino '95	♈♈	4
○ Fiano di Avellino '94	♈♈	4
○ Fiano di Avellino '06	♈♈	4*
○ Fiano di Avellino '05	♈♈	4
○ Fiano di Avellino '04	♈♈	4
○ Greco di Tufo '06	♈♈	4*

○ Fiano di Avellino Vigna della Congregazione '06	▼▼▼	5
○ Fiano di Avellino Vigna della Congregazione '04	♈♈♈	5
○ Fiano di Avellino Vigna della Congregazione '05	♈♈	5
○ Fiano di Avellino Vigna della Congregazione '02	♈♈	5

Villa Matilde

s.s. DOMITIANA, 18 KM. 4,700
81030 CELLOLE [CE]
TEL. 0823932088
www.villamatilde.it

ANNUAL PRODUCTION	700,000 bottles
HECTARES UNDER VINE	120
VITICULTURE METHOD	Conventional

There is no doubt that Villa Matilde's performance this year is its best ever. The Avallone family has always been firmly linked with the latter-day re-emergence of Falerno but it is their more recent experiences at Rocca dei Leoni in Benevento province and Tenute d'Altavilla in Irpinia that has brought them wide renown in the region. This year again sees an excellent trio of wines in the finals, including a fabulous '06 Cecubo, from an aristocratic blend of abbuoto, primitivo and piedirosso, with well-defined, pervasive nuances of blackberry and liquorice root. The '06 vintage also very nearly brought Falerno del Massico Bianco Vigna Caracci a third Three Glasses but though full of tropical fruits, it didn't quite hit its usual level of complexity. The '04 Camarato, however, did achieve Three Glasses honours, a longer-than-usual ageing period having brought shimmer and depth, more complete melding, less of a mask from the new oak, a beautifully judged tannicity on the finish and, vitally, an earthy, mineral elegance that leaves no doubt as to its provenance.

Villa Raiano

LOC. SAN MICHELE DI SERINO
VIA NOCELLETTO, 28B
83020 SERINO [AV]
TEL. 0825595663
www.villaraiano.it

ANNUAL PRODUCTION	230,000 bottles
HECTARES UNDER VINE	20
VITICULTURE METHOD	Conventional

For many years, Villa Raiano has been among the top estates in the region and for the fourth year running all its wines came well within the Two Glasses category. Who could ask for more? Well, we could, because we'd like to see at least one wine spark even higher, like a bonus to all that high-level reliability, and while the wines have outstanding precision, richness of fruit and breadth of aroma right across the board, we'd like to see them with a touch of devilment. The '07 Falanghina del Beneventano shows excellently, as usual, with considerable breadth and weight; the easy-going Greco di Tufo '07 has atypical aromas of elderflower, lychee and grapefruit while developing well through the mouth. A yeasty youthfulness holds back the nose on the '07 Fiano di Avellino which nonetheless remains faithful to its habitual soft, relaxed profile despite a slightly unknit finish. The '05 Aglianico Raiano is also excellent. Elegant oaky tones are well integrated into powerful, vibrant fruit that leads to notes of white chocolate, liquorice and black cherry.

● Falerno del Massico Camarato '04	𝖄𝖄𝖄	6
● Cecubo '06	𝖄𝖄	5
○ Falerno del Massico Bianco Vigna Caracci '06	𝖄𝖄	5
○ Eleusi '06	𝖄𝖄	6
○ Falanghina di Roccamonfina '07	𝖄𝖄	4*
○ Falerno del Massico Bianco '07	𝖄𝖄	4*
● Falerno del Massico Rosso '06	𝖄𝖄	4*
○ Fiano di Avellino Tenute di Altavilla '07	𝖄𝖄	4*
○ Falanghina Rocca dei Leoni '07	𝖄	3
● Taurasi Tenute di Altavilla '04	𝖄	6
☉ Terre Cerase Rosato '07	𝖄	4
○ Falerno del Massico Bianco Vigna Caracci '05	𝖄𝖄𝖄	5
● Falerno del Massico Camarato '01	𝖄𝖄𝖄	6
● Falerno del Massico Rosso Vigna Camarato '98	𝖄𝖄𝖄	6
● Falerno del Massico Rosso Vigna Camarato '00	𝖄𝖄𝖄	6

○ Falanghina Beneventano '07	𝖄𝖄	4*
○ Fiano di Avellino '07	𝖄𝖄	4*
○ Greco di Tufo '07	𝖄𝖄	4*
● Raiano '05	𝖄𝖄	5
○ Fiano di Avellino '05	𝖄𝖄	4*
○ Fiano di Avellino '04	𝖄𝖄	4
○ Fiano di Avellino '03	𝖄𝖄	4*
○ Greco di Tufo '06	𝖄𝖄	4*
○ Greco di Tufo '05	𝖄𝖄	4
○ Greco di Tufo '04	𝖄𝖄	4
○ Greco di Tufo '03	𝖄𝖄	4
● Taurasi '01	𝖄𝖄	6
● Taurasi Cretanera Ris. '03	𝖄𝖄	6
● Taurasi Ris. '01	𝖄𝖄	7

OTHER WINERIES

A Casa

LOC. PIANODARDINE
FILANDE, 6
83100 AVELLINO
TEL. 0825626406
www.cantineacasa.it

Enzo Ercolino's new venture is starting on the right foot. Along with his friends and partners, Lavarone, Velardi and Napoli, he has invested heart and soul into it and the objective is to shine. The first reds have yet to appear but the whites are showing well.

O Fiano di Avellino '07	♥♥	4*
O Greco di Tufo '07	♥♥	4*
O Sannio Coda di Volpe '07	♥	4
O Sannio Falanghina '07	♥	4

Aia dei Colombi

C.DA SAPENZE
82034 GUARDIA SANFRAMONDI [BN]
TEL. 0824817384
www.aiadeicolombi.it

The soul of the Pascale siblings' small estate remains primarily white. The range is once more led by Sannio Fiano. The '07 doesn't have the complexity and sense of wholeness of the '06 but majors on fullness and vigour. Guardiolo Falanghina '07 is stylistically similar but more open on the nose.

O Guardiolo Falanghina '07	♥♥	3*
O Sannio Fiano '07	♥♥	4*
● Guardiolo Aglianico '06	♥	4

Alois

LOC. AUDELINO
VIA REGAZZANO
81040 PONTELATONE [CE]
TEL. 0823876710
www.vinialois.it

There has been no backsliding from this winery this year. Indeed, the '07 Pallagrello Bianco Caiatì in particular has improved notably in quality, and has unusual zip for the variety. The reds are fair to good and, vitally, nicely reflect their provenance.

O Pallagrello Bianco Caiatì '07	♥♥	4*
● Cunto '06	♥	5
● Nadhir '07	♥	4
● Trebulanum '06	♥	6

Angelarosa

VIA ARIELLA, 1
83030 SANTA PAOLINA [AV]
TEL. 0825964431
www.angelarosa.it

This is a brilliant debut for this tiny winery located in an area of great suitability and tradition for Greco di Tufo. And it's the Greco that's a knockout, showing masculine and vigorous, with pervasive aromas of grapeskins and ivy, and a warm, multi-layered palate overriding a slightly phenolic finish.

O Fiano di Avellino '07	♥♥	4*
O Greco di Tufo '07	♥♥	4*

Giuseppe Apicella

FRAZ. CAPITIGNANO
VIA CASTELLO SANTA MARIA, 1
84010 TRAMONTI [SA]
TEL. 089856209
www.giuseppeapicella.it

Costa d'Amalfi is one of Campania's up-and-coming wine areas and Giuseppe Apicella is one of its most active protagonists. His energies are mainly concentrated on tintore, the zone's leading variety. Tramonti Rosso '06 seems a little backward but the palate is attractive and long.

O Costa d'Amalfi Tramonti Bianco '07	♥	4*
● Costa d'Amalfi Tramonti Rosso '06	♥	4
● Costa d'Amalfi Tramonti Rosso A' Scippata Ris. '04	♥♥	6

Barone

VIA GIARDINO, 2
84070 RUTINO [SA]
TEL. 0974830463
www.cantinebarone.it

There's a real need for wines like Barone's in a district like Cilento, which has huge but often unexpressed potential. There's even more need for wines that can express its warm, Mediterranean make-up whilst retaining definition and drinkability. Vignolella Fiano '07 is one such.

O Vignolella Fiano '07	♥♥	4*
● Pietralena Aglianico '07	♥	4
⊙ Primula Rosa '07	♥	4

OTHER WINERIES

Boccella

VIA SANT'EUSTACHIO
83040 CASTELFRANCI [AV]
TEL. 082772574
forsebasta@libero.it

Tasting Boccella's first releases is like working your way through a menu full of excellent starters that make you hungrier than ever for the main course. While we wait for satiety from the Taurasi, first made in 2005 and not yet available, the '06 Rasott is again temptingly good.

● Irpinia Aglianico Rasott '06	♟♟	4*
● Irpinia Aglianico Rasott '05	♟♟	4*
○ Irpinia Fiano '06	♟♟	4*

Ca' Stelle

VIA NAZIONALE SANNITICA, 48
82030 CASTELVENERE [BN]
TEL. 0824940232
www.castelle.it

That Campania is gaining status on the Italian wine scene has much to do with estates like this, owned by the Assini siblings. They work very effectively but without hullabaloo and without resorting to special effects yet manage to make fine wines, even from varieties and styles considered minor.

○ Passito Beneventano '05	♟♟	6
● Sannio Barbera '07	♟♟	4*
● Sannio Aglianico Propileo '05	♟	6

I Capitani

VIA BOSCO FAIANO, 15
83030 TORRE LE NOCELLE [AV]
TEL. 0825969182
www.icapitani.com

Slowly does it. And that's exactly what seems to guide developments at I Capitani, where the wines show steady annual improvements rather than impromptu jumps and shifts. So Taurasi again tops their range with the '04, a wine of solidity and tannic rigour.

● Taurasi Bosco Faiano '04	♟♟	5
○ Greco di Tufo Serum '07	♟	4
○ Irpinia Faius '06	♟	4

Alexia Capolino Perlingieri

VIA MARRAIOLI, 58
82037 CASTELVENERE [BN]
TEL. 0824971541
www.capolinoperlingieri.com

There is much that is new and heading for excellence in Campania, and not only in the more eminent zones. One illuminating example is Alexia Capolino Perlingieri's small estate, which has already kicked up a storm with Vignarosa '07, decidedly one of the region's best rosés.

⊙ Sannio Vignarosa '07	♟	4*
○ Sannio Vento '07	♟	4

Castel dei Franci

VIA VALLE
83040 CASTELFRANCI [AV]
TEL. 082772722
www.casteldeifranci.com

It's a case of ups and downs from Antonio Pietro Palma. The wines still lack consistency but the good ones are excellent. This year, it was Taurasi Marchese Brancia '04 that nearly made it to the finals, a wine of a class that brings well-deserved credit to the Castelfranci subzone.

● Taurasi Marchese Brancia '04	♟♟	8
○ Falanghina '07	♟	4
○ Greco di Tufo '07	♟	5
○ Irpinia Coda di Volpe '07	♟	4

Tenuta del Cavalier Pepe

VIA SANTA VARA
83040 LUOGOSANO [AV]
TEL. 082773766
www.tenutacavalierpepe.it

Milena Pepe has made strides in the last couple of years. Her '07 Coda di Volpe Bianco di Bellona is among the best of its type. Making waves among the reds is Sanserino '06, a monovarietal Aglianico which overcomes initial reduction and opens to bring vitality.

○ Irpinia Coda di Volpe Bianco di Bellona '07	♟♟	4*
● Irpinia Sanserino '06	♟♟	4*
○ Fiano di Avellino Refiano '07	♟	4
● Irpinia Aglianico Santo Stefano '06	♟	5

OTHER WINERIES

Az. Agr. Cobellis

LOC. PREVETELUPO
84078 VALLO DELLA LUCANIA [SA]
TEL. 0974 78955
www.aziendaagricolacobellis.it

The new Cobellis estate shows that there is much to discover in Cilento. Our first tastings of Piscriddi, from barbera and aglianico, with two vintages submitted, revealed an attractive compromise between docility and aromatic depth. A lighter hand is needed with the aglianico-only Vigna dei Russi '05.

● Piscriddi '07	♟♟	4
○ Crai '07	♟	4
● Piscriddi '06	♟	4
● Vigna dei Russi '05	♟	4

Colle di San Domenico

S.S. OFANTINA KM 7,500
83040 CHIUSANO DI SAN DOMENICO [AV]
TEL. 0825985423
www.cantinecolledisandomenico.it

The performance by the Violano family's wines this year was their best ever. The wines are always balanced and even but this time round they seem to have gained an extra dose of zip and vitality that makes them considerably more communicative.

● Campi Taurasini Principe '05	♟♟	4*
○ Fiano di Avellino '07	♟♟	4*
○ Greco di Tufo '07	♟♟	4*
● Irpinia Aglianico '06	♟	3

Colli Irpini

LOC. SERRA DI MONTEFUSCO
VIA SERRA (ZONA P.I.P.)
83030 MONTEFUSCO [AV]
TEL. 0825963972
www.montesole.it

Once again there are far too many wines from this colossus, a focal point for anyone looking for everything from Irpinia and Sannio at reasonable prices, for all of them to be listed below. The best of the bunch this year are Simposium Bianco '07, from falanghina, and Sannio Aglianico '06.

● Sannio Aglianico '06	♟♟	3*
○ Simposium Bianco '07	♟♟	4*
○ Greco di Tufo V. Breccia '07	♟	5
○ Sannio Falanghina V. Zampino '07	♟	5

Michele Contrada

C.DA TAVERNA, 31
83040 CANDIDA [AV]
TEL. 0825988434
www.vinicontrada.it

As astute wine lovers know, the most enduring rule in oenology is that there will be an exception. Take Michele and Gerardo Contrada, for instance, proud growers in one of the best areas for Fiano di Avellino. So what bottle of theirs continues to astound us? Greco di Tufo, this year Gaudioso '07.

○ Greco di Tufo Gaudioso '07	♟♟	4*
○ Greco di Tufo Gaudioso '06	♟♟	4*

Corte Normanna

LOC. SAPENZIE, 20
82034 GUARDIA SANFRAMONDI [BN]
TEL. 0824817004
www.cortenormanna.it

This winery is back up to speed, with determination the order of the day. All the wines have regained the character that we so admired a few years back, most notably Sannio Aglianico '06 with its irresistible aromas of rose and pomegranate, and its evenly developing, flavoursome palate.

● Sannio Aglianico '06	♟♟	4*
○ Sannio Falanghina '07	♟	3
○ Sannio Fiano '07	♟	4

De Falco

VIA FIGLIOLA
80040 SAN SEBASTIANO AL VESUVIO [NA]
TEL. 0817713755
www.defalco.it

The impression made by De Falco wines far exceeded what this entry can show. There is a sense of authority throughout the range, deriving from increased precision of style. The two '07 Vesuvio Lacryma Christis are among the best examples of the type ever.

○ Vesuvio Lacryma Christi Bianco '07	♟♟	4*
● Vesuvio Lacryma Christi Rosso '07	♟♟	4*
● Aglianico del Beneventano '06	♟	3
● Penisola Sorrentina Gragnano '07	♟	4

OTHER WINERIES

Della Valle Jappellj

LOC. CASERTA VECCHIA
VIA TIGLIO, 16
81100 CASERTA [CE]
TEL. 0823371731
www.dellavallejappellj.it

Individuality is the message from the Jappellj family, whose wines have now gained an impressive sense of completeness. Extractive strength has been replaced by directness and ease, IGT Canonicato '04, from aglianico, and the San Rocco table wine, from pallagrello nero, exemplifying this.

● Canonicato '04	🍷🍷	5
● San Rocco '04	🍷🍷	5
● Don Alfredo '04	🍷	5

Donna Carmela

V.LE KENNEDY, 41
83030 MONTEFUSCO [AV]
TEL. 0825628030
aziendadonnacarmela@alice.it

This small, new estate nearly leapt onto the leaders' table at its first attempt. Its Fiano di Avellino Borgalanti '07 is a crisp, incisive wine of mountainous character which has an easy-going, citrus-like and smoky nose, and a well-melded, assertive palate.

○ Fiano di Avellino Borgalanti '07	🍷🍷	4*
○ Greco di Tufo '07	🍷🍷	4*
● Irpinia Aglianico '07	🍷	4

Donna Chiara

LOC. PIETRACUPA
VIA STAZIONE
83030 MONTEFALCIONE [AV]
TEL. 3463521354

We shall be hearing more of Donna Chiara wines. Production started only recently but ambition and potential are there in spades. Chiara and Ilaria Petitto are the hub of the estate and their early results augur well. The harmony and restraint of Aglianico Preludio '06 put it at the top of the range.

○ Fiano di Avellino '07	🍷🍷	4*
● Irpinia Aglianico Preludio '06	🍷🍷	4*
● Aglianico '06	🍷	4
○ Greco di Tufo '07	🍷	4

La Dormiente

VIA PEZZE, 2
82030 TORRECUSO [BN]
TEL. 0824872737
www.ladormiente.it

La Dormiente means the sleeper but this small winery with rosé in its soul is anything but, indeed it's all dynamism and movement. The focus is typical Sannio varieties and both the semi-full, multi-faceted Taburno Aglianico '05 and the '07 Falanghina del Beneventano are very successful.

● Aglianico del Taburno '05	🍷🍷	4*
○ Falanghina del Beneventano '07	🍷🍷	3*
● Aglianico '06	🍷	3
○ Taburno Falanghina '07	🍷	3

Cantina Farro

FRAZ. BACOLI - LOC. FUSARO
VIA VIRGILIO, 16/24
80070 NAPOLI
TEL. 0818545555
www.cantinefarro.it

Michele Farro's is a unique voice in the Flegrei area and his winery is back in the Guide in great style, the range led by a Falanghina dei Campi Flegrei '07 of archetypal typicity and backbone. It even outpaced the Falanghina selection Le Cigliate '07, which had more stuffing but less depth.

○ Campi Flegrei Falanghina '07	🍷🍷	4*
○ Campi Flegrei Le Cigliate '07	🍷	4

Cantine Federiciane Monteleone

FRAZ. SAN ROCCO
VIA ANTICA CONSOLARE CAMPANA, 34
80016 MARANO DI NAPOLI [NA]
TEL. 0815764153
www.cantinefedericiane.com

We've missed talking about the Cantine Federiciane wines, which we often used to recommend for those seeking value for money. But they're back, all of them with at least One Glass. Greco di Tufo '07 and Falanghina dei Campi Flegrei '07 lead the short selection listed here.

○ Campi Flegrei Falanghina '07	🍷🍷	4*
○ Greco di Tufo '07	🍷🍷	5
○ Fiano di Avellino '07	🍷	5
● Penisola Sorrentina Gragnano '07	🍷	4

OTHER WINERIES

Benito Ferrara

FRAZ. SAN PAOLO, 14A
83010 TUFO [AV]
TEL. 0825998194
www.benitoferrara.it

Developments in Campanian wine must be truly sensational if an estate like Benito Ferrara has to be relegated to the Other Wineries section. But lovers of Gabriella and Sergio's Greco di Tufo needn't fear its decline. They'll find its habitual richness and slightly tertiary style on the '07.

O Greco di Tufo Vigna Cicogna '07	🍷🍷 5
O Fiano di Avellino '07	🍷 5
O Greco di Tufo '07	🍷 4

Fontanavecchia

VIA FONTANAVECCHIA
82030 TORRECUSO [BN]
TEL. 0824876275
www.fontanavecchia.info

Libero Rillo's wines are good but we would have liked to have seen more from them. Nevertheless, Vigna Cataratte Riserva '05, the estate's most classic wine, showed very well despite the iffy year, with a cedar and tobacco nose, and a particularly good, full palate.

● Aglianico del Taburno V. Cataratte Ris. '05	🍷🍷 5
⊙ Aglianico del Taburno Rosato '07	🍷 4
● Orazio '05	🍷 5
O Taburno Falanghina '07	🍷 3

Macchialupa

FRAZ. SAN PIETRO IRPINO
VIA FONTANA
83020 CHIANCHE [AV]
TEL. 0825996396
www.macchialupa.it

This estate with two Two Glass wines finds itself in the Other Wineries section. That's what happens when quality in a region balloons. But Macchialupa's fans can rest easy. The quality of Angelo Valentino's wines is as high as ever and we're sure he'll soon regain his full entry.

O Fiano di Avellino Le Surte '06	🍷🍷 6
O Greco di Tufo '07	🍷🍷 4*
O Fiano di Avellino '07	🍷 4

Masseria del Procaccia

VIA PROCACCIA, 1
82036 SOLOPACA [BN]
TEL. 0824971366
lcuti@tin.it

Things are bubbling at Solopaca. We're not talking about the fermenting vats but the quality of the wines submitted this year by Masseria del Procaccia. They're immediate and easy to read but never simplistic. The free and easy, creamy Calore '07, from sangiovese, barbera and aglianico, exemplifies the breed.

● Calore '07	🍷🍷 4*
O Falanghina del Beneventano Origini '07	🍷🍷 4*
● Aglianico del Beneventano Tore '07	🍷 4

Masseria Felicia

FRAZ. CARANO
LOC. SAN TERENZANO
81030 SESSA AURUNCA [CE]
TEL. 0823935095
www.masseriafelicia.it

The feeling here is that the best has yet to come. The Falernos are good, recognizably dense, clean and rounded but possibly a bit reined in by slightly excessive extraction. This tends to suppress the fruit when the wines are young while deepening the smoky aromas deriving from their provenance.

● Falerno del Massico Rosso '05	🍷🍷 4*
● Falerno del Massico Rosso Et. Bronzo '05	🍷🍷 6
O Falerno del Massico Bianco Anthologia '07	🍷 4
● Falerno del Massico Rosso Ariapetrina '06	🍷 4

Masseria Frattasi

VIA TORRE VARANI, 15
82016 MONTESARCHIO [BN]
TEL. 0824834392
www.masseriafrattasi.it

The work that Pasquale Clemente is doing in an area that is generally considered marginal in the region's wine geography is highly creditable, as results in the glass confirm. This year we were again seduced by the finesse and mineral thrust of his racy, deep Falanghina di Bonea, the '07.

O Taburno Falanghina di Bonea '07	🍷🍷 4*
O Taburno Falanghina Donna Laura '06	🍷🍷 4*
● Taburno Aglianico di Caudium '06	🍷 4
● Taburno Iovi Tonant Ris. '04	🍷 7

OTHER WINERIES

Michele Moio

V.LE MARGHERITA, 6
81034 MONDRAGONE [CE]
TEL. 0823978017
www.cantinemoio.it

No newcomer stands a chance against Michele Moio when he enters the fray with his primitivo-based Falerno. He's the king. In the last few years, Michele has also been finding his feet with whites and Falerno del Massico Alaora '06, with dried herbs and petrol, has masterful structure and complexity.

O Falerno del Massico Alaora '06	🍷🍷	5
O Falerno del Massico Bianco '07	🍷	4
● Moio 57 '06	🍷	4

La Molara

C.DA PESCO
83040 LUOGOSANO [AV]
TEL. 082778017
www.lamolara.com

A pale ruby-garnet colour; a nose of aromatic herbs and orange peel; a subtle, elegant palate with earthy, biting tannins. Aglianicos like this still exist and Attilio Colucci and Riccardo Morelli deserve double congratulations for a Taurasi '04 that is not just faultless but splendidly traditional.

● Taurasi Santa Vara '04	🍷	6
O Fiano di Avellino Jovis '07	🍷	4
● Naif Rosso '06	🍷	3
● Vigna Claudia '06	🍷	4

Cantina dei Monaci

FRAZ. SANTA LUCIA, 206
83030 SANTA PAOLINA [AV]
TEL. 0825964350
www.cantinadeimonaci.it

It is always wise to take a serious look at Angelo Carpenito and Maria Coppola's wines. Their Greco di Tufo '07 reflects the vintage to a T. The hot summer led to a wine that is less mineral than usual but just as eloquent in its aromas of ripe apple and tea leaves, and full, almost tannic palate.

O Fiano di Avellino '07	🍷🍷	4*
O Greco di Tufo '07	🍷🍷	4*
O Greco di Tufo Decimo Sesto '06	🍷	4
O Greco di Tufo '06	🍷🍷	4*

Mustilli

VIA DEI FIORI, 20
82019 SANT'AGATA DEI GOTI [BN]
TEL. 0823718142
www.mustilli.com

We are pleased to see Mustilli back because we are sure it still has a major part to play in the region's development. The pivotal wine is that classic, Falanghina di Sant'Agata dei Goti, and the '07 has a lovely oregano and apple nose and is just as enticing on the palate.

● Sannio Piedirosso '07	🍷🍷	4*
O Sant' Agata dei Goti Falanghina '07	🍷🍷	4*
● Sannio Aglianico Grifo di Rocca '07	🍷	4
O Sant'Agata dei Goti Falanghina V. Segreta '07	🍷	5

Ocone

LOC. LA MADONNELLA
VIA DEL MONTE, 56
82030 PONTE [BN]
TEL. 0824874040
www.oconevini.it

If you are looking for genuinely artisanal wines, you need look no further than the range from Mimì Ocone. These are wines without frills. They may not be perfect but these wines have a soul. Take, for example, Aglianico del Taburno '04. It's not huge in structure but incisive and sustained.

● Aglianico del Taburno '04	🍷🍷	4*
O Taburno Coda di Volpe '07	🍷🍷	4*
● Aglianico del Taburno V. Pezza la Corte '04	🍷	4
O Taburno Falanghina '07	🍷	4

Gennaro Papa

P.ZZA LIMATA, 2
81030 FALCIANO DEL MASSICO [CE]
TEL. 0823931267
cantinapapa@libero.it

Falerno del Massico Campantuono is no longer the only wine here. It has been joined by Conclave, a primitivo-based IGT, and the '06, the first release, is to some extent on a similar wavelength, centred as it is on a supple roundness, without edges and without excess alcohol.

● Conclave '06	🍷🍷	4*
● Falerno del Massico Primitivo Campantuono '06	🍷🍷	6
● Falerno del Massico Primitivo Campantuono '05	🍷🍷	6

OTHER WINERIES

Perillo

C.DA VALLE, 19
83040 CASTELFRANCI [AV]
TEL. 082772252

We know that Michele Perillo's estate will not stay in the Other Wineries section for long. But this year we are dealing with a cut-down range, given that there is no '04 Taurasi, the wine that tops the list and which has brought this tiny estate to renown well beyond its location.

● Aglianico '04	♟♟	5
○ Coda di Volpe '07	♟♟	5
● Taurasi '03	♟♟	6
● Taurasi '01	♟♟	6

Petilia

LOC. CAMPO FIORITO
C.DA PINCERA
83011 ALTAVILLA IRPINA [AV]
TEL. 0825991696
petilia@interfree.it

Another set of wines like this year's and it will no longer be possible to leave Roberto and Teresa Bruno's estate in the Other Wineries. The pivotal wine is once more Greco di Tufo, one of the best from the '07 vintage, a wine whose main forte is its gunflint, lime and herb nose.

○ Greco di Tufo '07	♟♟	4*
○ Fiano di Avellino '07	♟♟	4*
○ Sannio Falanghina '07	♟♟	3*
○ Greco di Tufo '06	♟♟	4*

Ciro Picariello

VIA MARRONI
83010 SUMMONTE [AV]
TEL. 0825702516
www.ciropicariello.com

Ciro Picariello's tiny estate is heading for the big time. In just two years, it is already making one of the top five Fiano di Avellinos. It's still a touch husky but very pure, almost Mosel-like, in its gooseberry and citron aromas, and it has a mineral strength that comes through mainly on the palate.

○ Fiano di Avellino '06	♟♟	4*
○ Fiano di Avellino '05	♟♟	4*

Azienda Agricola La Pietra di Tommasone

VIA PROVINCIALE FANGO, 98
80076 LACCO AMENO [NA]
TEL. 0813330330
www.tommasonevini.it

This estate is now strengthening its position as one of the most promising on Ischia. While the reds shone last year, this year it's the turn of the whites, led by Terradei '07 from biancolella and forastera, and closely followed by Pithecusa Bianco '07, from fiano and biancolella.

○ Pithecusa Bianco '07	♟♟	4*
○ Terradei '07	♟♟	4*
○ Ischia Biancolella '07	♟	4
● Pignanera '05	♟	7

Il Poggio

VIA DEFENZE, 4
82030 TORRECUSO [BN]
TEL. 0824874068
www.ilpoggiovini.it

This year, Carmine Fusco again presented a range of impressiveley authoritative wines. Taburno Falanghina Vendemmia Tardiva is one of the best of its type, cleverly poised between vivacity and sweetness. Taburno Aglianico '04 is of interest but Coda di Volpe 'O Guerriero '07 falls a little flat.

○ Taburno Falanghina V. T. '07	♟♟	4*
○ Coda di Volpe 'O Guerriero '07	♟	3
● Taburno Aglianico '04	♟	4
○ Taburno Falanghina '07	♟	4

Quintodecimo

VIA SAN LEONARDO
83036 MIRABELLA ECLANO [AV]
TEL. 0825449321
www.quintodecimo.it

It feels as if we're discovering what Luigi Moio is doing in Irpinia by instalments. Since his first Taurasi isn't out yet, we could only judge the whites this year. In any event, we were blown away by Via Del Campo '06, one of the best Falanghinas ever.

○ Via Del Campo Falanghina '06	♟♟	6
○ Fiano di Avellino Exultet '06	♟♟	7

OTHER WINERIES

Andrea Reale

LOC. BORGO DI GETE
VIA CARDAMONE, 75
84010 TRAMONTI [SA]
TEL. 089856144
www.aziendaagricolareale.it

Although they are labelled as IGT, the Reale wines are all made under Costa d'Amalfi DOC precepts and home in on the potential of the tintore variety. Borgo di Gete '06 leads the range. Cardamone is its younger, easier-drinking alter ego. Getis '07 is quite simply Campania's best rosé.

● Borgo di Gete '06	♥♥ 7
● Cardamone '07	♥♥ 5
☉ Getis '07	♥♥ 4*

San Francesco

VIA SOFILCIANO, 18
84010 TRAMONTI [SA]
TEL. 089876748
www.vinitenutasanfrancesco.it

This estate's interpretation of the Costa d'Amalfi Tramonti subzone comes simply delineated: white, red and rosé. The '07 Bianco is delicate and fragrant; the strawberry and pencil lead '06 Rosso is similarly attractive; the '07 Rosato is full of flavour.

○ Costa d'Amalfi Tramonti Bianco '07	♥♥ 4*
☉ Costa d'Amalfi Tramonti Rosato '07	♥♥ 4*
● Costa d'Amalfi Tramonti Rosso '06	♥♥ 4*
○ Costa d'Amalfi Bianco Per Eva '07	♥ 4

Sanpaolo

VIA FERROVIA, 42
83042 ATRIPALDA [AV]
TEL. 0825610307
info@cantineemera.com

This is one of the few wineries in the Tufo area that has good quantities of wines to match their good quality. Again, they showed well. The best of the bunch this year is an enjoyable, extrovert, clean-cut, fresh Fiano di Avellino '07 offering an attractive weave of florality and fruitiness.

○ Fiano di Avellino '07	♥♥ 4*
○ Greco di Tufo '07	♥♥ 4*
○ Falanghina del Beneventano '07	♥ 3
● Taurasi '04	♥ 6

Fattoria Selvanova

VIA SELVANOVA
81010 CASTEL CAMPAGNANO [CE]
TEL. 0823867261
www.fattoriaselvanova.com

No Selvanova wine may have made the finals but the range still showed very well. The most interesting aspect of them is restrained use of oak: Selvanova '04, intense and dense with ripe tannins, benefits particularly from this. The austere, earthy Sopralago '05 is more than just a typical Cabernet.

● Aglianico Selvanova '04	♥♥ 6
● Sopralago '05	♥♥ 5
● Vignantica '06	♥♥ 4*

Cantina Sociale di Solopaca

VIA BEBIANA, 38
82036 SOLOPACA [BN]
TEL. 0824977921
www.cantinasolopaca.it

In the past, we have often been critical of this major co-operative but this time we have only compliments. Solopaca Falanghina '07 is one of the year's choice picks with its irresistible hints of almond and annurca apple. The Spumante Brut, from falanghina, also stands up well.

○ Solopaca Falanghina '07	♥♥ 3*
○ Solopaca Bianco Prima Vigna '07	♥ 1
○ Solopaca Falanghina Spumante Brut	♥ 4

Telaro

LOC. CALABRITTO
VIA CINQUE PIETRE, 2
81045 GALLUCCIO [CE]
TEL. 0823925841
www.vinitelaro.it

Time may pass but the Telaro wines continue to reflect the eclecticism characteristics of Roccamonfina, an area just as suited to producing open, immediate wines as long-livers. The short-term sprinter par excellence is Ciesco Rosso '07, from aglianico and piedirosso, while; the best middle-distancer is Ara Mundi Riserva '05.

● Ciesco Rosso '07	♥♥ 3*
● Galluccio Ara Mundi Ris. '05	♥♥ 5
● Calivierno '06	♥ 5
○ Falanghina di Roccamonfina V.T. '07	♥ 4

OTHER WINERIES

Terranera

VIA SANDRO PERTINI, 13
83010 GROTTOLELLA [AV]
TEL. 0825671455
www.cantineterranera.it

It would have been difficult for the Terranera wines to have repeated last year's splendid showing but they came fairly close. The best is Greco di Tufo Vigne di Tore, a rich, powerful wine with an annurca apple and hazelnut nose.

O Greco di Tufo V. di Tora '07	♥♥ 4*
O Fiano di Avellino V. della Sabina '07	♥ 4
● Taurasi '04	♥ 5

Terre Stregate

VIA MUNICIPIO, 105
82034 GUARDIA SANFRAMONDI [BN]
TEL. 0824864312
www.terrestregate.it

Our admiration We continue to gain admiration for these wines continues to grow. They may not always have perfect definition but they do reflect their provenance and have characterare anything but anonymous. The best example of this is the refreshing Sannio Falanghina Svelato '07 with its pink grapefruit and fresh herbs nose.

O Sannio Falanghina Svelato '07	♥♥ 4*
O Sannio Fiano Genius Loci '07	♥ 4
O Trama '07	♥ 3

Torre Gaia

VIA BOSCO CUPO, 11
82030 DUGENTA [BN]
TEL. 0824978172
www.torregaia.net

You simply can't ignore the wines of Sannio's Torre Gaia, a colossus whose production spans almost all the province's wine types. Below is just a tiny selection of the wines we found to be of note. It's topped by Falanghina Opera '07, all too drinkable despite a hint of terpenes.

O Sannio Falanghina Opera '07	♥♥ 4*
O Solopaca Pagus Cl. '07	♥♥ 4*
O Sannio Fiano Gradualis '07	♥ 4
● Solopaca Cortinolfi Cl. '05	♥ 4

Torricino

LOC. TORRICINO, 5
83010 TUFO [AV]
TEL. 0825998119
www.torricino.com

Stefano Di Marzo should not feel depressed undermined by his estate's relegation tositting with the Other Wineries this year. H because his '07 Greco di Tufo remains faithful to its full, tertiary style and is still incomparable in its aromas of honey, dried fruit and pastry shops and its glorious, fleshy, mouthfilling, warm-finishing palate.

O Fiano di Avellino '07	♥♥ 4*
O Greco di Tufo '07	♥♥ 4*
● Aglianico '06	♥ 4
O Greco di Tufo Raone '06	♥ 4

Antica Masseria Venditti

VIA SANNITICA, 120/122
82037 CASTELVENERE [BN]
TEL. 0824940306
www.venditti.it

There are few growers in Campanian vignerons w who can match Nicola Venditti's style orand his attention to matters of biodiversity and environmental sustainability. We liked best his Solopaca Rosso Bosco Caldaia '04, from aglianico, montepulciano and piedirosso, which combines austerity with lightness of touch.

● Solopaca Rosso Bosco Caldaia '04	♥♥ 5
O Sannio Falanghina Vàndari '07	♥ 4
◉ Sannio Rosato '07	♥ 3
● Sannio Rosso '07	♥ 3

Vestini - Campagnano

FRAZ. SS. GIOVANNI E PAOLO
VIA BARRACCONE, 5
81013 CAIAZZO [CE]
TEL. 0823679087
www.vestinicampagnano.it

There are no fireworks here yet but the large, varied range, which reflects its homeland north of Caserta with individuality, is getting decidedly better. The flagship has always been Casa Vecchia and the '05 has gained grip and verve to partner its typical smokiness.

● Casa Vecchia '05	♥♥ 6
● Kajanero '05	♥♥ 3*
● Connubio '04	♥ 8
O Galluccio Concabianco '07	♥ 4

BASILICATA

 Developments in Basilicata continue apace. Its wine scene has its roots deep in an amazing heritage lavishly endowed with resonant places, wines and ventures: Magna Graecia, Frederick II, Carlo Gesualdo and the rebel heroes of the real Risorgimento, not the official version. All these and more have etched their influence on winemaking in the region, its destiny continually wavering between the opportunities afforded by its wealth of human and natural resources and the restrictions of geography: the region is still, to a great extent, on the sidelines of major communications and money flows. Renovation started only a decade ago but has pervaded the entire wine sector, involving estates large and small, famous names and unknowns, those with huge experience of the terrain and highly ambitious newcomers from outside Basilicata or even the wine sector. This incessant movement of people and ideas renders development in the region uneven, if fascinating. It's more like the syncopated pedalling of a racing cyclist in the mountains than his smooth, regular strokes on the flat. Basilicata's nerve centre is the Vulture zone, where achievements are founded on Aglianico. The health of the denomination derives from its ability to embrace very different approaches and styles, to bring increasing clarity to the characteristics of the various subzones, to launch new producers while bolstering the old stalwarts and to delineate a clear hierarchy with constants and tempting alternatives. It is no coincidence that the situation at the top of the tree is very similar to last year's. The Fucci family's Titolo again took Three Glass honours with the '06, the archetype of an Aglianico del Vulture with maximum – but controlled – power. No less surprising, especially when considering that it's from '05, is a repeat top place for Bisceglia's Gudarrà, a marvel of dynamism and flavour that turned out to be the best wine from the vintage. The third star is Re Manfredi. The '04 overtook Vigna Serpara to grab the crown at Terre degli Svevi and adds yet another award to the Gruppo Italiano Vini collection. Behind this formidable threesome comes the field, all jockeying for position. There are great classics: Rotondo '05 and Don Anselmo '04 from Paternoster, back at the top after a year off, and D'Angelo's Vigna Caselle Riserva '04. There are also wines in more modern style: La Firma '05 from Cantine del Notaio and Tenute Piano Regio '05 from Di Palma. The elegant Basilisco came within a hair of its second consecutive award with the '05, the Macarico wines continue to improve and the bottles from Carbone are a revelation. Developments in Matera are slower, and the province is still without a clear identity, but the wines of Cardillo and Dragone expunge any doubts about its potential.

Basilisco

VIA PIAVE, 35
85022 BARILE [PZ]
TEL. 0972725477
basilisco@interfree.it

ANNUAL PRODUCTION	30,000 bottles
HECTARES UNDER VINE	10
VITICULTURE METHOD	Conventional

The world of wine is full of hackneyed expressions but it also has the ability suddenly to overturn all preconceived ideas. Take, for example, all the debate over the tradition-innovation dichotomy. Discussions can rage for hours between opposing factions and then, in a flash, you realize how senseless it all is. And that flash can often come when you taste wines like Michele Cutolo's Basilisco. Cutolo is a gastroenterologist with a passion for wine who owns ten hectares in the Macarico and Gelosia areas of Barile. With assistance from the skilled Lorenzo Landi he has refined his scented, appetizing Aglianico del Vulture Basilisco into a wine that in a sense squares by marrying a graceful, easy-going silhouette with the taut fibre typical of the variety. The '05 is no exception and almost won Cutolo his second consecutive Three Glasses. All it needed was just a touch more zip on the palate to match its habitual spicy, balsamic, elegant aromatic framework. Teodosio '06 is rather backward: the fruit on the nose is way off balance and the tannins still need to settle.

Bisceglia

C.DA FINOCCHIARO
85024 LAVELLO [PZ]
TEL. 097288409
www.agricolabisceglia.com

ANNUAL PRODUCTION	400,000 bottles
HECTARES UNDER VINE	55
VITICULTURE METHOD	Certified organic

Bisceglia, which has 50 hectares under vine, has taken only a few years to become one of the focal points of Vulture with its consistently fine range. The star is Gudarrà. The '05 earned Three Glasses, as did the '04, but its ascent was almost startling. Despite the fact that the '05 vintage was quite different, and in many ways more complicated to handle than '04, Gudarrà breasted the Three Glass tape having accelerated from tasting to tasting like a great middle-distance runner. As it grew, it became strongly earthy and spicy, these sensations counterpoised by lighter, more floral and citrus-like wafts. It lengthened its stride further on the palate, the supple, racy classiness leading to intensifying flavour with the support of a web of fine-grained, mellow tannins. The style is reflected in the other reds too: the serious, fleshy Tréje '06, made from aglianico, merlot and syrah; and the rounded but not at all heavy Syrah Armille '07. The whites are also very sound. Chardonnay Bosco delle Rose '07 is excellent, fresh and complex while Fiano Labellum '07 brims with the scents of the Mediterranean.

● Aglianico del Vulture Basilisco '05	¶¶	6
● Aglianico del Vulture Teodosio '06	¶	4
● Aglianico del Vulture Basilisco '04	¶¶¶	6
● Aglianico del Vulture Basilisco '01	¶¶¶	6
● Aglianico del Vulture Basilisco '03	¶¶	6
● Aglianico del Vulture Basilisco '02	¶¶	6
● Aglianico del Vulture Basilisco '00	¶¶	6

● Aglianico del Vulture Gudarrà '05	¶¶¶	5
○ Bosco Delle Rose Chardonnay '07	¶¶	4*
● Aglianico del Vulture Terra di Vulcano '06	¶¶	3*
● Armille '07	¶¶	4*
○ Fiano Labellum '07	¶¶	4*
● Tréje '06	¶¶	4*
● Aglianico del Vulture Gudarrà '04	¶¶¶	5*
● Aglianico del Vulture Ris. '01	¶¶	6
● Aglianico del Vulture '03	¶¶	6
● Aglianico del Vulture Terra di Vulcano '03	¶¶	4

Carbone

VIA NITTI, 48
85025 MELFI [PZ]
TEL. 0972237866
www.carbonevini.it

ANNUAL PRODUCTION	45,000 bottles
HECTARES UNDER VINE	18
VITICULTURE METHOD	Conventional

If we hadn't been aware of Luca and Sara Carbone's skills and dedication, we would have been writing here about a revelation. But we can't really call this profile a surprise because we do know about them, and that their grapes come from some of the best sites in Vulture, and that the able Sergio Paternoster is also involved in the winemaking. And so after just two vintages, here they are up among the great and the good of the area with a range of wines comfortably above the Two Glass threshold and a worthy finalist in Aglianico del Vulture 400 Some '06. A luxuriant, abundant nose gives aromas of blackberry shot through with hints of pepper and talc. The palate has a firmer, closer knit style with a uniquely fine salty character, its class revealed by the great creaminess of its tannins. The '06 Stupor Mundi, which we believe was intended as the flagship, is nearly as good. It shares evident savouriness with the Some but has more focus on soft, ripe notes of jam and leather. The well-priced Terra dei Fuochi '06 is slim and graceful.

D'Angelo

VIA PROVINCIALE, 8
85028 RIONERO IN VULTURE [PZ]
TEL. 0972721517
www.dangelowine.com

ANNUAL PRODUCTION	380,000 bottles
HECTARES UNDER VINE	50
VITICULTURE METHOD	Conventional

Donato D'Angelo is one of the people who have brought lustre to the wines of Vulture. Alongside his brother Lucio, who died prematurely in July 2007, he has become known as a specialist in Aglianico in all its incarnations. A man open to experimentation yet firmly anchored in tradition, he has foregrounded the latter in the glorious '04 Vigna Caselle Riserva, one of the best vintages ever of the wine and one which came within a whisker of Three Glasses. Its fascinating tertiary aromas of incense, white pepper and orange peel do not overwhelm the firm yet juicy fruitiness that comes through even more strongly on the palate, a joy of grace and silky tannicity. Donato D'Angelo '06 is decidedly more modern in style but has just as much character, a wealth of strawberry and liquorice leading to a slightly alcoholic finish. Dried flowers, hazelnut and macerated herbs, and an unusually fine piquancy sum up Serra delle Querce '06, made from aglianico and merlot. This year the monovarietal Aglianico Canneto, Valle del Noce and the base Aglianico del Vulture, all from '06, are no more than fair.

● Aglianico del Vulture 400 Some '06	▼▼ 5
● Aglianico del Vulture Stupor Mundi '06	▼▼ 6
● Aglianico del Vulture Terra dei Fuochi '06	▼▼ 4*
● Aglianico del Vulture Stupor Mundi '05	♀♀ 6

● Aglianico del Vulture V. Caselle Ris. '04	▼ 5
● Aglianico del Vulture Donato D'Angelo '06	▼▼ 5
● Serra delle Querce '06	▼▼ 6
● Aglianico del Vulture '06	▼ 4
● Aglianico del Vulture Valle del Noce '06	▼ 6
● Canneto '06	▼ 5
● Aglianico del Vulture V. Caselle Ris. '01	♀♀♀ 4*
● Aglianico del Vulture V. Caselle Ris. '03	♀♀ 5
● Aglianico del Vulture Valle del Noce '05	♀♀ 6
● Aglianico del Vulture Valle del Noce '03	♀♀ 4
● Aglianico del Vulture V. Caselle Ris. '00	♀♀ 4
● Aglianico del Vulture Valle del Noce '04	♀♀ 6
● Canneto '05	♀♀ 5
● Canneto '04	♀♀ 5

Cantine Di Palma

C.DA SCAVONI
85028 RIONERO IN VULTURE [PZ]
TEL. 0972722891
www.cantinedipalma.com

ANNUAL PRODUCTION	130,000 bottles
HECTARES UNDER VINE	15.5
VITICULTURE METHOD	Conventional

As estates evolve and play around with styles, it happens increasingly often that wines designed as base level products outshine those pitched higher. That's what has occurred with the '05 releases of Antonio Di Palma's two fine Aglianico del Vultures, Tenute Piano Regio and Il Nibbio Grigio, which carried away Three Glasses two years earlier. It is likely that time will restore the normal hierarchy, especially since '05 was a difficult vintage, but this year the Tenute Piano Regio has more lustre. Its abundant fruit, clean, succulent and firm, enlivened by a continuous waft of balsam, brought it to within a hair of Three Glasses. Had it won, it would have been one of the most sensational successes ever but even so Antonio deserves huge congratulations, especially when you remember its modest price tag. But don't think that Il Nibbio Grigio is skulking on the sidelines. Its layers of flavour may still be imprisoned by oak pungency and tannins that have not yet harmonized but even now, after a while in the glass, it opens to reveal mineral, spicy vivacity and a mid palate with a wealth of depth and liveliness.

Eubea

VIA ROMA, 209
85028 RIONERO IN VULTURE [PZ]
TEL. 0972723574
www.sacavid.it

ANNUAL PRODUCTION	40,000 bottles
HECTARES UNDER VINE	15
VITICULTURE METHOD	Certified organic

Eubea's two outstanding wines, Ròinos and Covo dei Briganti, continue to switch places at the top of the range. You really can't say which is the chief and which the Indian because both have the style of natural-born winners. They're wines that can bring out the more austere, assertive side of Aglianico del Vulture; wines of great character; wines that don't fit into the standard classic-modern breakdown. Instead, they integrate hints of traditional tertiary characters into a firmly precise whole. This time round, with the '06 vintage, it is Ròinos that pipped its partner at the post, showing deep and eclectic, its vegetality-veined nose spanning aromas from plum to leather. The palate is broad and full of attack, needing just a touch of vibrancy on its slightly drying finish to take top honours. Covo dei Briganti is slightly marred by a touch of overripeness on the light finish but otherwise a nose of liqueur strawberries and geraniums leads to a palate whose acid and mineral backbone just fails to temper an overall impression of softness.

● Aglianico del Vulture Il Nibbio Grigio Et. Nera '05	♼♼ 6
● Aglianico del Vulture Tenuta Piano Regio '05	♼♼ 4*
● Aglianico del Vulture Il Nibbio Grigio Et. Nera '03	♼♼♼ 6
● Aglianico del Vulture Il Nibbio Grigio Et. Nera '04	♼♼ 6
● Aglianico del Vulture Il Nibbio Grigio '02	♼♼ 6
● Aglianico del Vulture Il Nibbio Grigio '00	♼♼ 6
● Aglianico del Vulture Tenuta Piano Regio '04	♼♼ 4*
● Aglianico del Vulture Tenuta Piano Regio '03	♼♼ 4

● Aglianico del Vulture Ròinos '06	♼♼ 8
● Aglianico del Vulture Il Covo dei Briganti '06	♼♼ 6
● Aglianico del Vulture Ròinos '01	♼♼♼ 8
● Aglianico del Vulture Il Covo dei Briganti '04	♼♼ 6
● Aglianico del Vulture Il Covo dei Briganti '03	♼♼ 6
● Aglianico del Vulture Ròinos '04	♼♼ 8
● Aglianico del Vulture Ròinos '03	♼♼ 8
● Aglianico del Vulture Ròinos '02	♼♼ 8

Elena Fucci

C.DA SOLAGNA DEL TITOLO
85022 BARILE [PZ]
TEL. 0972770736
az.elenafucci@tiscali.it

ANNUAL PRODUCTION	16,000 bottles
HECTARES UNDER VINE	6.15
VITICULTURE METHOD	Conventional

If this is modernity then we're all for modernity, "this" being the Fucci family's Titolo. Elena, who has a degree in oenology, brings as much youth to the new enterprise as her father Salvatore brings experience, and the wine they make in tandem reflects not just their hard work and competition but their sharing, fun and friendship. The Three Glass award Titolo takes for the second year running is perhaps one of the year's least surprising results. From the very beginning, the '06 promised great things. Its awesome power is almost off the scale but that muscle is controlled. It's presaged by a nose awash with black cherry, liquorice and printers' ink, punctuated by a rapid change towards pencil lead, black pepper and myrtle leaves. But it's the youthful palate where this small masterpiece of balance really shines. Gentle yet pervasive, it unveils a velvety tannic weave, gaining dynamism from a mineral, balsamic streak that also lends great depth before drawing it to an unexpectedly sober, calm finish.

Macarico

P.ZZA CARACCIOLO, 7
85022 BARILE [PZ]
TEL. 0972771051
www.macaricovini.it

ANNUAL PRODUCTION	22,000 bottles
HECTARES UNDER VINE	5
VITICULTURE METHOD	Natural

If your surname is Botte, which means barrel, and you live in Barile, which means cask, you are predestined to be a winemaker and your estate can only be one of the most promising in the area. The name Macarico comes from one of the best zones for Aglianico del Vulture production, an origin that gives its two wines highly distinctive characteristics. This year the pair were also closer matched than ever before. The better of the two, as usual, is the straight Aglianico del Vulture. The '05 is as generous and stately as ever but doesn't have that rather uneasy complexity which could have shot it to stardom. This may be because the problematic vintage led Botte to push ripeness a bit, the effect coming through mainly on the palate where, despite good structure, there is a rounded start and a slightly drying finish. However, nothing seems to be holding down the '06 Macarì, which is no finalist by accident. Its lesser concentration is well compensated for by a stylishly assertive, fluid, multi-faceted profile, with cinnamon and quinine rounding out younger notes of damp leaves and aromatic herbs.

● Aglianico del Vulture Titolo '06	▼▼▼	6
● Aglianico del Vulture Titolo '05	♈♈♈	6
● Aglianico del Vulture Titolo '02	♈♈♈	6
● Aglianico del Vulture Titolo '04	♈♈	6
● Aglianico del Vulture Titolo '03	♈♈	6
● Aglianico del Vulture Titolo '01	♈♈	6
● Aglianico del Vulture Titolo '00	♈♈	5

● Aglianico del Vulture '05	▼▼	6
● Aglianico del Vulture Macarì '06	▼▼	5
● Aglianico del Vulture Macarì '05	♈♈	5
● Aglianico del Vulture Macarì '04	♈♈	5
● Aglianico del Vulture Macarì '03	♈♈	5
● Aglianico del Vulture '04	♈♈	6
● Aglianico del Vulture '03	♈♈	6

Cantine del Notaio

VIA ROMA, 159
85028 RIONERO IN VULTURE [PZ]
TEL. 0972723689
www.cantinedelnotaio.com

ANNUAL PRODUCTION   110,000 bottles
HECTARES UNDER VINE   27
VITICULTURE METHOD   Certified biodynamic

A day with Gerardo Giuratrabocchetti in his vineyards is a crash course in viticulture. It's become a commonplace that wines are made in the vineyard: the crucial question is how. Gerardo has gone for the biodynamic approach, with great enthusiasm, and he grows aglianico practically exclusively, vinifying it into five different wines depending on when the grapes are picked. La Firma, a wine that is emblematic of the Vulture new wave, comes from a late October picking. The '05 was given longer than usual pre-release bottle ageing and although some over-extraction remained, and there was an excess of new oak, it still went through to the finals. Repertorio '06 is not dissimilar but makes less of an impact. Sigillo '04 suffers a little from a wealth of glyceric fullness, which isn't fully supported by its acid backbone. In the middle of all this Aglianico, however, comes a delightful contrast from L'Autentica, a dried-grape passito from moscato and malvasia bianca that has an easy-going yet penetrating character. It, too, earned a place in the finals.

Paternoster

C.DA VALLE DEL TITOLO
85022 BARILE [PZ]
TEL. 0972770224
www.paternostervini.it

ANNUAL PRODUCTION   150,000 bottles
HECTARES UNDER VINE   30
VITICULTURE METHOD   Certified organic

The Paternoster family has a challenging but gratifying role, embodying the heritage of a glorious past while responding to the challenges of the modern wine scene. In a sense, their renowned Don Anselmo has to do the same. We were impatient to try the '04, a classic vintage of a classic wine, and it showed brilliantly, coming to within an inch of Three Glasses. Aged half in large barrels and half in barriques, only some new, it's a wine that whispers rather than shouts. Anchored in aromas of autumn leaves, undergrowth and damp earth, it gains power from its taut, meaty, austere, straight-down-the-line palate while the tannins make themselves felt but meld into a backdrop of rare harmony and complexity. A similar framework sets off the more incisively powerful Rotondo '05, which has a more international style without trying to be too much of a crowd pleaser. It is another finalist of breed. In fact, this long-standing winery seems to be performing better than ever, an impression confirmed by the brilliant showing of Barigliòtt '07, a lively, irresistibly moreish Aglianico, and the sweet sparkler, Moscato della Basilicata Clivus '07.

● Aglianico del Vulture La Firma '05	♟♟ 7
○ L'Autentica '06	♟♟ 6
● Aglianico del Vulture Il Repertorio '06	♟♟ 5
● Aglianico del Vulture Il Sigillo '04	♟ 7
● Aglianico del Vulture La Firma '00	♟♟♟ 6
● Aglianico del Vulture Il Sigillo '03	♟♟ 7
● Aglianico del Vulture La Firma '04	♟♟ 7
● Aglianico del Vulture La Firma '03	♟♟ 6
● Aglianico del Vulture La Firma '02	♟♟ 6
● Aglianico del Vulture La Firma '01	♟♟ 6
● Aglianico del Vulture Il Repertorio '05	♟♟ 5
● Aglianico del Vulture Il Repertorio '04	♟♟ 5
○ L'Autentica '05	♟♟ 6

● Aglianico del Vulture Don Anselmo '04	♟♟ 7
● Aglianico del Vulture Rotondo '05	♟♟ 6
● Barigliòtt '07	♟♟ 4*
○ Moscato della Basilicata Clivus '07	♟♟ 4
● Aglianico del Vulture Synthesi '05	♟ 4
○ Bianco di Corte '07	♟ 4
● Aglianico del Vulture Don Anselmo '94	♟♟♟ 5
● Aglianico del Vulture Rotondo '98	♟♟♟ 5*
● Aglianico del Vulture Rotondo '01	♟♟♟ 6
● Aglianico del Vulture Rotondo '00	♟♟♟ 6
● Aglianico del Vulture Don Anselmo '03	♟♟ 6
● Aglianico del Vulture Don Anselmo '01	♟♟ 6
● Aglianico del Vulture Don Anselmo '00	♟♟ 6
● Aglianico del Vulture Rotondo '04	♟♟ 6
● Aglianico del Vulture Rotondo '03	♟♟ 6

Terra dei Re

VIA MONTICCHIO S.S. 167 KM 2,700
85028 RIONERO IN VULTURE [PZ]
TEL. 0972725116
www.terradeire.com

ANNUAL PRODUCTION	75,000 bottles
HECTARES UNDER VINE	31
VITICULTURE METHOD	Certified organic

Although nothing from Terra dei Re reached the finals, the overall standard of the wines from the estate owned by the De Sio, Leone and Rabesco families was impressive. With over 30 hectares of vineyards, it has for some time been one of the more prominent Aglianico del Vulture producers. This time, though, it wasn't an Aglianico del Vulture that led the range. That honour went to Pacus '06, made from aglianico with a little pinot nero. An inviting, outgoing nose of red berry fruit, fresh hazelnut and pink pepper with an elegant underlying smokiness gives it great character. The palate doesn't have particularly great impact but offers an intriguing counterplay of delicacy and backbone. More evidence of fine handling of the promising '06 vintage comes from the delicious Aglianico del Vulture Vultur, a base-level wine only in its price. In contrast, the '05 vintage was more complicated than it looked at first and the estate's flagship Aglianico del Vulture Nocte is currently still overwhelmed by oak. The warm, chocolaty Divinus '05 is easier going.

Terre degli Svevi

LOC. PIAN DI CAMERA
85029 VENOSA [PZ]
TEL. 097231263
www.giv.it

ANNUAL PRODUCTION	240,000 bottles
HECTARES UNDER VINE	120
VITICULTURE METHOD	Conventional

Gruppo Italiano Vini is without doubt the most important wine producing company in Italy, both in terms of quantity and quality, and winemaking on its estates is simply impeccable. The huge investments GIV poured into Vulture at the end of the 1990s was one of the first signs that the outside world had recognized the zone's extraordinary and not fully exploited potential. The wines here combine power with great elegance, reflecting the area's strong identity in a robust yet multi-faceted style. Aglianico del Vulture Manfredi '05 is emblematic in this sense. The wine hasn't been this good since 1999 and it deservedly won Three Glasses. Mediterranean scrubland, tar and orange peel shape a nose of rare purity and definition before the palate focuses more on liveliness and flavour than breadth of fruit. The finish goes on for ever. Serpara '04 is more backward. Though concentrated and well-sustained, it's still a little austere. There's further good news from Re Manfredi Bianco '07, from gewürztraminer and müller-thurgau. It is quite simply a fabulously drinkable white.

● Aglianico del Vulture Divinus '05	⚑⚑ 5
● Aglianico del Vulture Vultur '06	⚑⚑ 4*
● Pacus '06	⚑⚑ 4*
● Aglianico del Vulture Nocte '05	⚑ 6
● Aglianico del Vulture Divinus '04	♟♟ 5
● Aglianico del Vulture Divinus '03	♟♟ 5
● Aglianico del Vulture Divinus '01	♟♟ 5
● Aglianico del Vulture Nocte '04	♟♟ 6
● Pacus '05	♟♟ 4*

● Aglianico del Vulture Re Manfredi '05	⚑⚑⚑ 5
● Aglianico del Vulture Vign. Serpara '04	⚑⚑ 6
○ Re Manfredi Bianco '07	⚑⚑ 4*
○ Fonte Luna '07	⚑ 4
⊙ Re Manfredi Rosato '07	⚑ 4
● Aglianico del Vulture Re Manfredi '99	♟♟♟ 5*
● Aglianico del Vulture Vign. Serpara '03	♟♟♟ 5*
● Aglianico del Vulture Re Manfredi '04	♟♟ 5
● Aglianico del Vulture Re Manfredi '03	♟♟ 7
● Aglianico del Vulture Re Manfredi '01	♟♟ 5
● Aglianico del Vulture Re Manfredi '00	♟♟ 5

OTHER WINERIES

Alovini

VIA GRAMSCI, 30
85013 GENZANO DI LUCANIA [PZ]
TEL. 0971776372
www.alovini.it

Tenacious Oronzo Alò's wines express the special character of aglianico grown in the Genzano di Lucania area and can surely only get even better. Armànd '03 reflects the difficulties of a very hot year. Cabànico '04 is a solid, tightly clenched wine and Le Ralle Greco '07 is fair.

● Aglianico del Vulture Armànd '03	♀	4
● Cabànico '04	♀	4
○ Le Ralle Greco '07	♀	3

Camerlengo

VIA T. TASSO, 3
85027 RAPOLLA [PZ]
TEL. 335251885
www.camerlengodoc.com

Sometimes scores and Glasses don't count. They may offer a snapshot of a moment but they can't always reflect a wine's underlying potential. That, we feel, is the situation at Camerlengo, whose wines have fascinating style but need more focus. We back them to find it.

● Aglianico del Vulture Antelio '06	♀	4
● Aglianico del Vulture Camerlengo '06	♀	5

Masseria Cardillo

C.SO UMBERTO, 95
75012 BERNALDA [MT]
TEL. 0835748992
www.masseriacardillo.it

This new venture's great debut brings us an estate that lifts the wines of the province of Matera to new heights. Tittà '05 is an exuberant blend of aglianico and merlot. Vigna Giadì '06 combines sangiovese and primitivo to produce a wine of personality.

● Tittà '05	♀♀	4*
● Vigna Giadì '06	♀♀	3*

Colli Cerentino

VIA MATTEOTTI, 10
85025 RIONERO IN VULTURE [PZ]
TEL. 0972720329
www.collicerentino.com

The wines of this estate, run by Sandro Calabrese, keep on getting better and the best of the range is the clean-cut, tobacco-like, traditional Aglianico del Vulture Dei Colli '05.

● Aglianico del Vulture Dei Colli '05	♀♀	4*
● Aglianico del Vulture Cerentino '05	♀♀	6
● Aglianico del Vulture Masquito '05	♀♀	7

Cantine Cerrolongo

C.DA CERROLONGO, 1
75020 NOVA SIRI [MT]
TEL. 0835536174
www.cerrolongo.it

The Battifarano winery is one of the longest-established in the province of Matera, an area that still has to find a clear identity. They have good whites, like the soft, easy-drinking Matera Greco Le Paglie '07, and unusual blends like Torre Bollita '06, from cabernet sauvignon, syrah and merlot.

○ Matera Greco Le Paglie '07	♀	4
● Torre Bollita '06	♀	4
● Cerrolongo Rosso '06	♀♀	4*

Dragone

LOC. PIETRAPENTA
P.ZZA DEGLI OLMI, 66
75100 MATERA [MT]
TEL. 0835261740
www.dragonevini.it

Matera may have been immortalized by Pasolini and Mel Gibson but it's worth a visit for the wines of Michele Dragone. He makes fine sparkling wines, as exemplified by Matera Metodo Classico Gold Brut. His Matera Primitivo Pietrapenta '05, with its varietal, fleshy, succulent fruitiness, is good.

○ Matera Metodo Classico Gold Brut '07	♀	3
● Matera Opus 199 '05	♀	3
● Matera Primitivo Pietrapenta '05	♀	4
⊙ Ego Sum Rosé	♀♀	4*

OTHER WINERIES

Eleano

C.DA PIAZZOLLA
85028 RIONERO IN VULTURE [PZ]
TEL. 0972722273
www.eleano.it

In a world where praise often goes to wines of impact with more muscle than brain, Eleano wines are a breath of fresh air. Aglianico del Vulture Dioniso '05 is finely nuanced with clean-cut aromas of blood oranges and raspberries, with floral, herbal touches, and a taut, cohesive palate.

● Aglianico del Vulture Dioniso '05	♟♟	4
● Aglianico del Vulture '04	♟	6
○ Ambra Moscato '07	♟	5
● Aglianico del Vulture Pian dell'Altare '03	♟♟	6

Giannattasio

P.ZZA ANGELO BOZZA, 5
85022 BARILE [PZ]
TEL. 0972770571
www.giannattasio.net

The wines from this family-run estate continue to improve. Both those submitted this year scored well over the Two Glasses threshold but the better of the two is the close-knit, intense, lightly oaky Aglianico del Vulture Bramea '06, which is still very young, as is Arcà '05.

● Aglianico del Vulture Arcà '05	♟♟	5
● Aglianico del Vulture Bramea '06	♟♟	4*
● Aglianico del Vulture Arcà '04	♟♟	5

Michele Laluce

VIA ROMA, 21
85020 GINESTRA [PZ]
TEL. 0972646145
www.vinilaluce.it

The assertive, passionate character of the determined Michele Laluce plays a major part in making Vulture so unique and his wines reflect his fiery nature. Leading the range is S'Adatt '05, which has slightly overripe fruit but enlivening clear-cut scents of pencil lead.

● S'Adatt '05	♟	5
● Aglianico del Vulture Zimberno '02	♟♟	5
● S'Adatt '04	♟♟	4*

Lelusi Viticoltori

VIA CROCE, 3
85022 BARILE [PZ]
TEL. 024043805
www.lelusivini.com

Here we have another outsider venturing into Vulture. The Labarbuta siblings come from Milan. Sergio Paternoster helps with the winemaking and two wines were submitted, Aglianico del Vulture Shesh '06 and Aglianico del Vulture Letizia '05. Both have the classic stamp of weight and substance.

● Aglianico del Vulture Letizia '05	♟	6
● Aglianico del Vulture Shesh '06	♟	4
● Aglianico del Vulture Letizia '04	♟♟	6
● Aglianico del Vulture Shesh '05	♟♟	4*

Lucania

LOC. PIAN DI CAMERA
85029 VENOSA [PZ]
TEL. 097231002
grifaicodellalucania@email.it

If you are looking for intense, multi-faceted Aglianico del Vultures, remember this estate's name. Actually, Fabrizio and Cecilia Piccin are rapidly making a name for themselves in the region and wines like Grifalco '06, which also benefits from a good vintage, show why.

● Aglianico del Vulture Grifalco '06	♟♟	4*
● Aglianico del Vulture Damaschito '05	♟♟	5
● Aglianico del Vulture Bosco del Falco '05	♟	5
● Aglianico del Vulture Grifalco '05	♟♟	4*

Cantine Madonna delle Grazie

LOC. VIGNALI
VIA APPIA
85029 VENOSA [PZ]
TEL. 097235704
www.cantinemadonnadellegrazie.it

Incense, pine resin, elegant hints of florality; a well-melded, eloquent palate reinforced by firm, ripe tannins. It doesn't matter if a winery is represented by just one wine when the wine is as good as the Latorraca family's Aglianico del Vulture Bauccio '04, made on their long-standing estate.

● Aglianico del Vulture Bauccio '04	♟♟	5
● Aglianico del Vulture Bauccio '03	♟♟	5

OTHER WINERIES

Tenuta del Portale

LOC. LE QUERCE
85022 BARILE [PZ]
TEL. 0972724691
tenutadelportale@tiscali.it

Filomena Ruppi has over 20 hectares of vines in some of the best sites for Aglianico del Vulture and her three wines are showing significant improvement. They share the same uncompromising vigour but are quite distinct in style. Aglianico del Vulture Riserva '04 is the most classic example.

● Aglianico del Vulture Ris. '04	♟♟	5
● Aglianico del Vulture '06	♟	4
● Aglianico del Vulture Le Vigne a Capanno '06	♟	5

Tenuta Le Querce

C.DA LE QUERCE
85022 BARILE [PZ]
TEL. 0971725102
www.tenutalequerce.com

This is one of the leading wineries in Vulture, its high ambition fuelled by ongoing experimentation and top-ranking winemaking personnel. We could only assess cask samples of the higher-level '06s but we did taste an excellent Aglianico del Vulture Sasso from the same vintage.

● Aglianico del Vulture Sasso '06	♟♟	4*
● Aglianico del Vulture Rosso di Costanza '04	♟♟	6
● Aglianico del Vulture V. della Corona '04	♟♟	8
● Aglianico del Vulture Minorco Sasso '04	♟♟	8

Regio Cantina

LOC. PIANO REGIO
85029 VENOSA [PZ]
TEL. 3346966263
www.regiocantina.it

There are still considerable changes going on at Paolo Zamparelli's winery but the range is already very reliable and rather impressive. It is led by the excellent Aglianico del Vulture Donpà '05, whose tannins are just a touch too firm. Solagna '06 is also interesting.

● Aglianico del Vulture Donpà '05	♟♟	5
● Aglianico del Vulture Solagna '06	♟	3
○ Brinato '07	♟	3
● Aglianico del Vulture Donpà '04	♟♟	5

Taverna

C.DA TAVERNA, 15
75020 NOVA SIRI [MT]
TEL. 0835877083
www.aataverna.com

There is no lack of history or tradition at this small but influential winery, set up in the Taverna district of Nova Siri in 1950. It makes a fair number of wines but our preference goes to the full, linear Aglianico del Vulture '04 with its nuances of cherry and liquorice.

● Aglianico del Vulture '04	♟♟	4*
○ Dry Muscat '07	♟	3
☉ Rosé '07	♟	3
● Aglianico del Vulture '03	♟♟	3*

Cantina di Venosa

LOC. VIGNALI
VIA APPIA
85029 VENOSA [PZ]
TEL. 097236702
www.cantinadivenosa.it

Cantina di Venosa's strengths are consistency of style and reliable quality. No wine is yet truly outstanding but Aglianico del Vulture Il Madrigale di Gesualdo '06 is certainly on the right road, its character meaty and spicy, and its palate warm and full.

● Aglianico del Vulture Carato Venusio Ris. '03	♟♟	7
● Aglianico del Vulture Il Madrigale di Gesualdo '06	♟♟	4*
● Aglianico del Vulture Bali'Aggio '06	♟	3
○ Dry Muscat Terre di Orazio '07	♟	3

Vigne di Mezzo

P.ZZA CARACCIOLO, 7
85022 BARILE [PZ]
TEL. 0972771051
www.vignedimezzo.it

Richness and precision are the characteristics that mark out the bottles from this winery, owned by Campania's famed Feudi di San Gregorio. Typical of the range is the modern-style Aglianico del Vulture Efesto '05, which has cinnamon and cocoa powder, and a mellow tannic weave.

● Aglianico del Vulture Efesto '05	♟♟	5
● Aglianico del Vulture Efesto '04	♟♟	7
● Aglianico del Vulture Efesto '03	♟♟	7

PUGLIA

There are contradictory signs emerging from the Puglian universe, and such is the diversity of its terrains that "universe" is hardly an exaggeration, although overall good things far outweigh the bad. Average quality of the wines, bottled ones at least, is rising and this holds true throughout the region. The number of new estates aiming for high-quality production is also on the increase. By "new" we mean those set up in the last decade and when we talk about "high quality" we mean estates that pay attention to cellar technology and even greater attention to the vineyards: environmental impact, the recovery of ancient varieties and traditional bush training systems, and organic and biodynamic cultivation methods. All these developments are bringing a sense of purpose and the desire to make progress is almost tangible. On the negative side, we appear to be witnessing wobbles at several of the long-standing estates and even more confusion, or so it seems, as regards what constitutes a traditional wine. For the first time in a number of years, not one wine made in this style reached our finals. What instead seem to be engaging wine lovers' enthusiasm are garage wines, incredibly tight-knit products of huge concentration made from low yielding vines and in such small quantities that they are almost unobtainable. Then come the estates which focus more on balance. They take equal care in the vineyards but the direction is towards producing wines of cleanliness, freshness and elegance. This year's award winners included examples of all these schools of thought. It doesn't mean that such a pluralist wine scene will become the norm but we have our fingers hard crossed that it will and that the region will become one where all styles can find their niche, the only requirement being high quality. This year's Three Glass wines include five repeat winners, one comeback and one newcomer. There is also a fairly even division of the spoils among the region's three leading indigenous varieties: primitivo, negroamaro and nero di Troia. It is also worth noting that five of the seven wines are denominated and span the region's most significant DOCs. The repeat winners are Albea's Lui, a monovarietal Nero di Troia; Tormaresca's Negroamaro Masseria Maime; Castello Monaci's Primitivo Artas, all three of these from '06; then Castel del Monte Rosso Vigna Pedale Riserva, a Nero di Troia from Torrevento, and Salice Salentino Rosso Selvarossa Riserva from Due Palme, both '05. The comeback is Accademia dei Racemi's Primitivo di Manduria Zinfandel Sinfarosa '06 and the newcomer is Primitivo di Manduria Es '06, from Gianfranco Fino.

Accademia dei Racemi

via Santo Stasi Primo - Z. I.
74024 Manduria [TA]
tel. 0999711660
www.racemi.it

ANNUAL PRODUCTION 1,200,000 bottles
HECTARES UNDER VINE 150
VITICULTURE METHOD Certified organic

We have often talked about how crucial the "galaxy of estates" managed by Gregory Perrucci is in maintaining local traditions, most notably bush-training of vines, but for the last couple of years we've needed to talk more about the high quality of their products. This year, Three Glasses went to one of the group's landmark wines, Primitivo di Manduria Zinfandel Sinfarosa, the '06. It wasn't released in time for last year's tastings precisely so that it could gain the greater maturity and fullness we so admired. Mediterranean scrubland, black berry fruit and sweet spices dominate the intense, pervasive nose. The palate is full, complex and well structured, with soft tannins and liquorice on the long, deep finish. The '06 Primitivo di Manduria Dunico therefore slots into second place, with appealing black fig and liquorice notes that are attractive but less deep and taut than last year's. Everything else is first-rate too, most notably Torre Guaceto Sum '06, from sussumaniello, whose sweet spice, fig and pomegranate nose is followed by a rich, full, lively palate of good substance and grip.

● Primitivo di Manduria Zinfandel Sinfarosa '06	🍷🍷🍷	5*
● Primitivo di Manduria Dunico Masseria Pepe '06	🍷🍷	6
● Susumaniello Sum Torre Guaceto '06	🍷🍷	5
● Anarkos '07	🍷	3
● Gioia del Colle Joya '07	🍷	3
● Njùru '07	🍷	2*
● Primitivo di Manduria Dunico Masseria Pepe '05	ŸŸŸ	6*
● Primitivo di Manduria Zinfandel Sinfarosa '05	ŸŸ	5
● Primitivo di Manduria Zinfandel Sinfarosa '04	ŸŸ	5
● Primitivo di Manduria Zinfandel Sinfarosa '03	ŸŸ	5
● Susumaniello Sum Torre Guaceto '05	ŸŸ	5

Azienda Vinicola Albano Carrisi

c.da Bosco
72020 Cellino San Marco [BR]
tel. 0831619211
www.albanocarrisi.com

ANNUAL PRODUCTION 425,000 bottles
HECTARES UNDER VINE 65
VITICULTURE METHOD Conventional

Albano Carrisi's wines now seem to have found their level. They're sound, well made and consistently good without anything being truly exceptional. Platone, from 100 per cent negroamaro, continues to top the range. The '05 is a dark ruby, introducing a ripe nose with fruit conserve, cigar tobacco and leather. The palate, too, is very ripe with sweet black berry fruitiness but it finishes a touch flat and needs a bit more zip to make its mark. The '06 Nostalgia, again negroamaro, is not quite as impressive as last year's version. There's balsam and sweet oakiness but we'd have liked to see some more vigour. Salice Salentino '06 showed well, though, proffering a youthful, balsamic, black berry fruit nose and then freshness plus good tannic presence on the palate. Aleatico Passito '07, all coffee and black berry fruit, the warm, subtly vegetal Don Carmelo Rosso '06, and the fresh, floral rosé Mediterraneo '07 are all attractive.

● Platone '05	🍷🍷	8
● Salice Salentino Rosso '06	🍷🍷	4
● Aleatico Passito '07	🍷	5
● Don Carmelo Rosso '06	🍷	4
⊙ Mediterraneo '07	🍷	4
● Nostalgia '06	🍷	5
● Platone '98	ŸŸŸ	8
● Platone '99	ŸŸ	8
● Platone '04	ŸŸ	8
● Platone '02	ŸŸ	8

Cantina Albea

VIA DUE MACELLI, 8
70011 ALBEROBELLO [BA]
TEL. 0804323548
www.albeavini.com

ANNUAL PRODUCTION	300,000 bottles
HECTARES UNDER VINE	40
VITICULTURE METHOD	Conventional

This estate can take its place alongside Italy's best, thanks to the performance of its flagship wine Lui, but more important, and certainly harder to achieve at this level, is the consistency Cantina Albea is beginning to show across the board. This year has brought renewed success, the new '06 vintage of Lui again scooping Three Glasses. The inky black of this monovarietal Nero di Troia is highlighted with purple, leading into floral scents, black berry fruit and sweet spices on a balsamic nose. The surprisingly lively palate is full and fleshy with masses of fruit, plenty of stuffing, tight-knit yet ripe tannins and a deep, long finish. However the rest of the range seemed a little under par. Raro '06, from negroamaro and primitivo, is far too oaky on both nose and palate, and needs a touch more structure. The rosé Petrarosa '07 is a bright pink, has floral aromas and a cohesive palate with ripe fruit and tea leaves but is lightweight and lacks grip. Primitivo Petranera is full of fruit but the vanilla tones are overdone and the palate is a little too sweet.

● Lui '06	▼▼▼	6
● Petranera '06	▼	4
☉ Petrarosa '07	▼	4
● Raro '06	▼	5
● Lui '05	♈♈♈	6
● Lui '04	♈♈	6
● Lui '03	♈♈	6

Francesco Candido

VIA A. DIAZ, 46
72025 SAN DONACI [BR]
TEL. 0831635674
www.candidowines.it

ANNUAL PRODUCTION	2,000,000 bottles
HECTARES UNDER VINE	21
VITICULTURE METHOD	Conventional

We risk repeating ourselves when we discuss Alessandro Candido's wines. But we have to say that the estate is an institution in the region and a beacon for anyone who loves traditionally styled wines, especially if they also like them clean, well made and consistent from year to year. Salice Salentino Riserva La Carta '04 nearly made it to the finals. It's a garnet ruby. The nose is elegant with spices, Mediterranean herbs and a gentle swath of balsam. Its traditional palate is full yet expansive and has an attractive, balsamic, long finish. Similar considerations apply to Cappello di Prete '04, its fig and ripe plum nose highlighted by forest floor nuances and very soft tannin on its palate. It's less complex than previous vintages but attractive and makes for good drinking. Immensum '06, from negroamaro with 30 per cent cabernet sauvignon, gives autumn leaves and tar, with dried fruit on the finish and showed well, despite lacking a touch of zip, as did Cassio Dione '05. From negroamaro and primitivo, it gives Mediterranean scrubland and black berry fruit preceding a clean, lively attractive palate. Everything else is well made.

● Cappello di Prete '04	▼▼	4*
● Cassio Dione '05	▼▼	6
● Immensum '06	▼▼	5
● Salice Salentino La Carta Ris. '04	▼▼	3*
● Duca d'Aragona '01	▼	5
○ Paule Calle '05	▼	5
● Salice Salentino Aleatico '02	▼	5
☉ Salice Salentino Rosato Le Pozzelle '07	▼	3
● Cappello di Prete '03	♈♈	4*
● Immensum '04	♈♈	5*
● Cappello di Prete '01	♈♈	4*
● Cappello di Prete '00	♈♈	4*
● Duca d'Aragona '00	♈♈	5

Cantele

S.P. Salice Salentin
San Donaci km 35,600
73010 Guagnano [LE]
tel. 0832705010
www.cantele.it

ANNUAL PRODUCTION 1,800,000 bottles
HECTARES UNDER VINE 150
VITICULTURE METHOD Conventional

For the first time in some years, this large winery didn't send a wine to the finals but overall quality remains high, revealing that the approach is sound and the winemaking personnel first class. The Teresa Manara line showed well, both the '05 Negroamaro, its vegetal nose lightly infused with tobacco, figs and blackberries, and its lively palate well fruited but slightly green and a touch unexciting, and the zesty, supple '07 Chardonnay, which is consistently one of the region's best whites. Sadly, the year was not of the best for Amativo, the flagship wine, made from a 60-40 blend of primitivo and negroamaro. The '06 has red berry fruit and toasty hints on the nose and an attractively full, extractive palate but lacks the invigorating zestiness of previous vintages. Negroamaro Rosato '07 is spot on. The floral nose has almond and red berry fruit notes and the palate is clean, taut, lively and savoury with a crisply fruity finish. Alticelli '07, a well-made monovarietal Fiano, came in at One Glass. It has sage, spring flowers and fresh citrus on the nose and an attractive, fresh palate of good weight. Everything else is well typed.

● Amativo '06	ŸŸ	5
⊙ Rosato Negroamaro '07	ŸŸ	3*
○ Teresa Manara Chardonnay '07	ŸŸ	4
● Teresa Manara Negroamaro '05	ŸŸ	4
○ Alticelli '07	Ÿ	4
○ Chardonnay '07	Ÿ	3
● Salice Salentino Rosso Ris. '04	Ÿ	3
● Varius '06	Ÿ	4
● Amativo '03	ΥΥΥ	5*
● Amativo '05	ΥΥ	5*
● Amativo '04	ΥΥ	5*
● Amativo '03	ΥΥΥ	5*
● Varius '05	ΥΥ	4*

Giancarlo Ceci

C.da Sant'Agostino
70031 Andria [BA]
tel. 0883564938
www.agrinatura.net

ANNUAL PRODUCTION N.A.
HECTARES UNDER VINE N.A.
VITICULTURE METHOD Certified organic

Giancarlo is the eighth generation of the Ceci family to own this estate. He was one of the first in Puglia to believe in organic farming, which he initiated for his market gardening activities in 1988. Then a few years ago, he started getting serious about winemaking. Success has not taken long. Indeed, the continual advances in the wines' quality and their stylistic precision across the board, plus a finals place for Castel del Monte Rosso Parco Marano '05, which very nearly won Three Glasses, have now enabled us to give him a full entry. The wine is elegant, its floral, fruity aromas shot through with tobacco and spices, and the lively, black berry fruit palate is long, deep and cohesive with clear-cut flavours. The other Castel del Monte, Parco Grande '07, is also admirable. An attractive, easy-drinking wine from nero di Troia, it centres on elegance and fruity freshness, recalling blackberry and blackcurrant in particular. But all the wines impress and we have the sensation that we are seeing the emergence of a new leading player on the Puglian scene.

● Castel del Monte Rosso Parco Marano '05	ŸŸ	4*
● Castel del Monte Rosso Parco Grande '07	ŸŸ	3*
○ Castel del Monte Bianco '07	Ÿ	3
○ Castel del Monte Bianco Chardonnay '07	Ÿ	3
○ Pozzo Sorgente '06	Ÿ	4
● Castel del Monte Rosso Parco Marano '04	ΥΥ	4
○ Pozzo Sorgente '05	ΥΥ	4*

Tenuta Coppadoro

VIA TIBERIO SOLIS, 128
71016 SAN SEVERO [FG]
TEL. 0882242301
www.tenutacoppadoro.it

ANNUAL PRODUCTION	600,000 bottles
HECTARES UNDER VINE	148
VITICULTURE METHOD	Conventional

No wine from this newish estate managed to reach the finals this year but, encouragingly, quality across the range was admirable, which is what consumers like to hear. The only downside in our opinion is that the majority of the wines are too oaky. Radicosa '06, from 100 per cent montepulciano aged in new barriques, has a purple-ruby colour. Oak dominates on the nose, covering the black berry fruit with leather and toasty notes. The palate is extractive, with tight-knit but slightly one-dimensional tannins and a good finish, which provides an additional burst of fruit. The '07 Cotinone, from equal parts of montepulciano, aglianico and cabernet sauvignon, has typical slightly gamey aromas and a palate of good fruit and plentiful substance, but still too much oak. Rosa di Salsola '07, a sort of Puglian Montepulciano Cerasuolo, has fresh, floral aromas and is balanced and mouthfilling. Finally comes the attractive, fruity, well-textured Pescorosso '07, made from aglianico.

D'Alfonso del Sordo

C.DA SANT'ANTONINO
71016 SAN SEVERO [FG]
TEL. 0882221444
www.dalfonsodelsordo.it

ANNUAL PRODUCTION	350,000 bottles
HECTARES UNDER VINE	90
VITICULTURE METHOD	Conventional

The project started in 2001 between the D'Alfonso del Sordo couple and Professor Luigi Moro and the University of Foggia continues to bear fruit. Again one of the wines reached the finals and the whole range now has a stamp of quality and consistency rare in Puglia. Our only quibble is that the wines tend to be over-oaked. We'd like to see wood used differently. This year, it was Doganera '06, from 100 per cent merlot aged in new barriques, which led the field. It's a well-made, lively wine full of fruit, with not just the variety's tobacco and cherry notes but also a typically Mediterranean character. Guado San Leo '06, from nero di Troia only, also did well. Although still too oaky, especially on the nose where chocolate, tobacco and toastiness dominate, it has an already open palate of black berry fruit and a long, attractive finish. Montero '07, from an 80-20 blend of montepulciano and cabernet sauvignon, is every bit as good. The nose has citrus and undergrowth, and the palate is supple: a touch more density and it would be a high-flyer. San Severe Rosato '07 is floral and balsamic while the '07 Rosso is straightforward and well made.

● Cotinone '07	�♀	5
● Radicosa '06	♀♀	6
⊙ Rosa di Salsola '07	♀♀	4*
● Pescorosso '07	♀	4
● Cotinone '05	♀♀♀	5*
● Radicosa '03	♀♀♀	7
● Cotinone '06	♀♀	5
● Cotinone '03	♀♀	5*
● Radicosa '04	♀♀	7
● Radicosa '05	♀♀	7

● Doganera '06	♀♀	6
● Guado San Leo '06	♀♀	6
● Montero '07	♀♀	4*
● Casteldrione '06	♀	3
● Contrada del Santo '06	♀	5
⊙ San Severo Rosato Posta Arignano '07	♀	3
● San Severo Rosso Posta Arignano '07	♀	3
● Guado San Leo '05	♀♀	6
● Cava del Re Cabernet Sauvignon '05	♀♀	6
● Doganera Merlot '05	♀♀	6

Cantina Due Palme

via San Marco, 130
72020 Cellino San Marco [BR]
tel. 0831617909
www.cantineduepalme.it

ANNUAL PRODUCTION	5,000,000 bottles
HECTARES UNDER VINE	2000
VITICULTURE METHOD	Conventional

This large co-operative, run with initiative and determination by Angelo Maci, has now amalgamated a further winery group, consolidating its role as the yardstick for the Salice Salentino denomination as well as the focal point for its many grower members. In fact, Salice Salentino Rosso Selvarossa Riserva earned its second successive Three Glass award with the '05, ensuring a spotlight continues to shine on this long-standing DOC. The wine is a dark, purple-tinged ruby. There are evident violets on the nose, followed by tobacco, black berry fruit and spice. The palate is clean, balanced and lightly balsamic, with a long, deep finish, revealing cardamom, damson and plum. Salice Salentino Bianco Tinaia '07, 100 per cent Chardonnay and strongly varietal, has banana, grapefruit and hints of vanilla on the nose preceding a lively, balanced, supple palate. It's first class, as is Ettamiano '05, a floral, spicy Primitivo with a full, fruity, tight-knit palate. Serre '07, from sussumaniello, is fair enough but needs a bit more length and a touch less sweetness.

Felline - Pervini

via Santo Stasi Primo - Z. I.
74024 Manduria [TA]
tel. 0999711660
www.accademiadeiracemi.it

ANNUAL PRODUCTION	180,000 bottles
HECTARES UNDER VINE	23
VITICULTURE METHOD	Conventional

This estate, run by Gregory Perrucci with help from oenologist Cosimo Spina, is well known for the reliable high quality of its wines, its role in the rebirth of the Manduria zone and in setting new standards for the Primitivo di Manduria DOC. As if that weren't enough, two wines made the finals this year. Primitivo di Manduria Archidamo '06 has red berry fruit, spices and liquorice followed by a taut, zesty palate of good substance and balance with spiciness, tar and black berry fruit. Delicious. Vigna del Feudo '06 is fuller, riper and tighter knit but lacks the zip and almost rakish drinkability of Archidamo. Primitivo Felline Cuvée '06, with its black berry fruit, liquorice and printers' ink nose, and clean, taut palate where bright black berry fruit returns on the long finish, is a very fine wine, as is Primitivo di Manduria Dolce Naturale Primo Amore '04. Here, despite a nose of liqueur cherries and cane sugar, the palate is very much in the house style with plenty of liveliness and flavours of strawberry and cherry jam leading to a nice long finish. The other classics, Bizantino Rosso, Alberello and Segnavento, all '07, are good.

● Salice Salentino Rosso Selvarossa Ris. '05	♟♟♟ 5*
● Ettamiano '05	♟♟ 4
○ Salice Salentino Bianco Tinaia '07	♟♟ 4
● Serre '07	♟ 4
● Salice Salentino Rosso Selvarossa Ris. '04	♟♟♟ 4*
● Salice Salentino Rosso Selvarossa Ris. '03	♟♟ 6
● Salice Salentino Rosso Selvarossa Ris. '01	♟♟ 4
● Salice Salentino Rosso Selvarossa Ris. '00	♟♟ 5

● Primitivo di Manduria Archidamo '06	♟♟ 3*
● Vigna del Feudo '06	♟♟ 5
● Primitivo di Manduria Dolce Natural Primo Amore '04	♟♟ 4
● Primitivo Felline Cuvée '06	♟♟ 4
● Alberello '07	♟ 3
● Bizantino Rosso '07	♟ 3
● Primitivo di Manduria Segnavento '07	♟ 3
● Primitivo di Manduria Archidamo '04	♟♟ 3*
● Primitivo di Manduria Archidamo '03	♟♟ 3*
● Vigna del Feudo '05	♟♟ 5
● Vigna del Feudo '04	♟♟ 5

Gianfranco Fino

LOC. LAMA
VIA FIOR DI SALVIA, 8
74100 TARANTO
TEL. 0997773970
www.gianfrancofino.it

ANNUAL PRODUCTION 6,000 bottles
HECTARES UNDER VINE 3.50
VITICULTURE METHOD Conventional

Much has been said, good and bad, about Gianfranco Fino, as the creator of a Primitivo archetype, in recent years. He founded his estate in 2004 when he acquired a small vineyard with 50-plus-year-old bush-trained vines. Keeping his yields very low, he started to make just one wine, Primitivo di Manduria Es. From its first release, it became a cult wine with wine lovers who espouse artisan ideals and like to see wines pushed to their limits. Quite honestly, at first we weren't totally convinced. We found the sweetness and the alcohol just a bit too much. But then we tasted the '06. It's almost black, purple tinged. The nose is strongly pervasive, full of fruit and nuanced with tobacco and tar. The palate is equally rich and complex, showing cohesive, long and very deep, with crisp black berry fruit. But this time the wine is dry and the alcohol, although plentiful, is controlled. There were no objections to Three Glasses. This year Fino has also launched a Negroamaro, Jo '06. It, too, is from old bush-trained vines, acquired in 2006 this time, and its welcome fullness and sense of provenance means that it falls not far short that of Es.

Fusione

LOC. CASTELLANETA
C.DA CACCAMONE
74011 TARANTO
TEL. 0998493770
a.mani@amonowine.com

ANNUAL PRODUCTION 180,000 bottles
HECTARES UNDER VINE N.A.
VITICULTURE METHOD Conventional

The ethos of this high quality winery, which produces wine from bought-in grapes as well as its own, is primarily to salvage old bush-trained vineyards, to work alongside its growers and help them obtain the best possible grapes, and to ensure high standards of winemaking. Prima Mano '06, made solely from primitivo, nearly reached the finals. A sweet cherry, vanilla and pepper nose leads to a slightly alcoholic, slightly sweet palate that then opens to reveal zestiness but still rather evident tannins before finishing attractively with black berry fruit. The copper-coloured Fiano-Greco has the typical aromatic imprint of Puglian fiano followed by white-fleshed fruit and banana. The palate is clean, balanced and cohesive although it disappoints a little for complexity and length. Overall, it is good, though, as is the intriguing dried-grape A Mano '07, from aleatico. The nose is all toastiness, cocoa powder, coffee and fresh-baked tarts, and the beautifully clean palate has sweet black berry fruit and a fairly zesty finish. The other young wines, the Moscato, Malvasia Rosato and the Negroamaro, are all nicely made.

● Primitivo di Manduria Es '06	♟♟♟	6
● Jo '06	♟♟	6
● Primitivo di Manduria Es '05	♟♟	6
● Primitivo di Manduria Es '04	♟♟	6

○ Fiano - Greco '07	♟♟	3*
● Prima Mano '06	♟♟	5
● A Mano '07	♟	4
⊙ Malvasia Rosato '07	♟	3
○ Moscato '07	♟	3
● Negroamaro '07	♟	3
● Promessa '06	♟♟	3*
● Promessa Negroamaro '05	♟♟	3*

Leone de Castris

VIA SENATORE DE CASTRIS, 26
73015 SALICE SALENTINO [LE]
TEL. 0832731112
www.leonedecastris.com

ANNUAL PRODUCTION	2,500,000 bottles
HECTARES UNDER VINE	250
VITICULTURE METHOD	Conventional

Leone de Castris is a giant in Puglian wine. Even though no wine reached the finals, results in general were formidable. Salice Salentino Rosso Maiana '06, for example, has a nose of black and red berry fruit, tar and liquorice, and a gentle palate of good substance finishing with attractive, ripe black berry fruit. Then there is Salice Salentino Rosso 50° Vendemmia Riserva '05. Its aromas centre more on ash and tobacco, and its palate is less complex but balanced and well textured. The '04 Salice Salentino Rosso Donna Lisa Riserva didn't match the promise of its best vintages. The nose is all red berry fruit, spices and sweet oakiness but the very ripe black berry fruit palate needs a shot more dynamism. But Five Roses '07, both the standard version, its cherry nose nuanced with tea leaves and its lively palate full of crisp fruit; and the long, deep, 64° Anniversario, from over-40-year-old vines, which shows fruit and flowers shot through with pepper spice, are both excellent. The zippy, well-made Copertino Rosso '07, focused on tobacco, pepper and black berry fruit, is also of note. Everything else is as sound as you would expect.

Lomazzi & Sarli

C.DA PARTEMIO, S.S. 7 BR-TA
72022 LATIANO [BR]
TEL. 0831725898
www.vinilomazzi.it

ANNUAL PRODUCTION	1,000,000 bottles
HECTARES UNDER VINE	150
VITICULTURE METHOD	Conventional

With 150 hectares of vineyard, a large cellar being refurbished and annual production exceeding 1,000,000 bottles, Antonio Dimastrodonato's winery is gaining a strong position on the crowded Puglian scene. It's moving in the right direction: renovations in the vineyard, focusing on bush-trained vines, and in the cellar, have coincided with the arrival of top consultants Franco and Marco Bernabei, who have had an impact on the wines. So much so that two of them reached the finals this year, and no doubt the Dimastrodonatos are aiming even higher. Nomas '05 is a refined monovarietal Susumaniello with intense morello cherry and spices, hints of printers' ink, pencil lead and new oak, and a soft, long, mouth-filling palate that ends on blackberry and Mediterranean scrubland. Brindisi Rosso Solise Riserva '05 has elegant oaking, its firm, weighty structure leading to a fruity, balsamic finish. Alongside these two come a harmonious, succulent, oaky Salice Salentino Rosso Irenico '06, a satisfyingly spicy Primitivo Latias '06, a well-structured Imperium Bianco '07, from malvasia bianca and fiano, and an array of simpler but carefully crafted wines.

● Copertino '07	ΨΨ	3*
⊙ Five Roses '07	ΨΨ	4*
⊙ Five Roses Anniversario 64° Anno '07	ΨΨ	4*
● Salice Salentino Rosso 50° Vendemmia Ris. '05	ΨΨ	4*
● Salice Salentino Rosso Donna Lisa Ris. '04	ΨΨ	6
● Salice Salentino Rosso Maiana '06	ΨΨ	3*
● Elo Veni '06	Ψ	4
● Messere Andrea '05	Ψ	5
● Negrino '07	Ψ	4
● Primitivo di Manduria Villa Santera '07	Ψ	4
● Salice Salentino Rosso Donna Lisa Ris. '01	ΨΨΨ	6

● Brindisi Rosso Solise Ris. '05	ΨΨ	4*
● Nomas '05	ΨΨ	6
○ Imperium '06	ΨΨ	4
● Kalòs '06	ΨΨ	3*
● Latias '06	ΨΨ	4*
● Salice Salentino Rosso Irenico '06	ΨΨ	4*
○ Giràle Malvasia Bianca '07	Ψ	2*
○ Partemio '07	Ψ	3
⊙ Solise Rosato '07	Ψ	3
● Nomas '04	ΨΨ	5
● Salice Salentino Rosso Irenico '05	ΨΨ	4*

Alberto Longo

C.DA PADULECCHIA
S.P. 5 LUCERA-PIETRAMONTECORVINO KM 4
71036 LUCERA [FG]
TEL. 0881539057
www.albertolongo.it

ANNUAL PRODUCTION	250,000 bottles
HECTARES UNDER VINE	35
VITICULTURE METHOD	Conventional

Alberto Longo's estate is situated in a
19th-century farmstead. He makes wines
of character and personality, from both
international and indigenous varieties.
Indeed, the wines from nero di Troia are
some of the region's best. Le Cruste '06 is
made solely from that grape, some of the
vines grown on the traditional pagliarello
training system in which they are supported
by bamboo canes strapped together at
their tips. The wine is a deep ruby. The
nose has bitter orange, black damson and
spices while the palate, although not yet
in perfect balance, has plenty of fullness,
great texture and a lively, long finish.
Calcara Vecchia '06 comes from equal
parts of cabernet franc and merlot, and
sees no oak. It has red berry fruits, wild
cherry especially, and tobacco on the nose,
then a clean, uncomplicated, vigorously
supple palate. Just as good is Cacc'e
Mmitte di Lucera '06, from the classic
blend of nero di Troia, montepulciano
and bombino bianco. It's dynamic, even
more supple, clean and attractive. Finally
comes Donnadele '07, an onionskin colour
rosé with aromas of tropical fruit and rose
petals, which is fresh and attractive.

Mille Una

L.GO CHIESA, 11
74020 LIZZANO [TA]
TEL. 0999552638
www.milleuna.it

ANNUAL PRODUCTION	70,000 bottles
HECTARES UNDER VINE	33
VITICULTURE METHOD	Natural

Mille Una continues to oscillate between
the Other Wineries section and a full
profile, its fortunes reflecting the vintage.
To some extent this is no bad thing but
the differences are probably just too great,
especially considering the wines' prices. In
any event, this is very much a "yes" year –
the best ever, we think – with one wine, Tre
Tarante '05, claiming a place in the finals.
It's made from 100 per cent primitivo, from
roughly 70-year-old vines, the oldest on the
property. The nose reveals black fig, pencil
lead and pepper. Its very full, deep palate
is rounded off by sweetness, oakiness
and sensations of fruit conserve. Capitolo
Laureto '05 and Dolce Nero '06 are both
first class. The former is well made and
all too drinkable with fragrant, small black
berry fruit on the nose and a palate that is
attractive, balanced and dynamic despite
having less power than the previous
vintage. Dolce Nero is a dried-grape
passito of good typicity with scents of
liqueur black cherries and cinnamon, and
a palate of Mediterranean scrubland with a
lively, long, chocolate-like finish.

● Cacc'e Mmitte di Lucera '06	♟♟	4
● Calcara Vecchia '06	♟♟	4
☉ Donnadele '07	♟♟	4
● Le Cruste '06	♟♟	5
● Capoposto '06	♟	4
○ Le Fossette '07	♟	4
● Calcara Vecchia '05	♟♟	4*
● Le Cruste '05	♟♟	5
● Le Cruste '04	♟♟	5

● Tre Tarante '05	♟♟	8
● Capitolo Laureto '05	♟♟	8
● Dolce Nero '06	♟♟	8
● Capitolo Laureto '04	♟♟	8
● Tre Tarante '03	♟♟	8

Azienda Monaci

LOC. TENUTA MONACI
73043 COPERTINO [LE]
TEL. 0832947512
www.aziendamonaci.com

ANNUAL PRODUCTION 360,000 bottles
HECTARES UNDER VINE 36
VITICULTURE METHOD Conventional

This is a rather low-key year for Severino Garofano and especially for his top wine Le Braci, which didn't entirely convince us. The negroamaro-only '05 is in a traditional style. Creamy and evolved, it has overripe fruit and the finish lacks both the depth and the zip of previous vintages. However, the '05 Copertino Eloquenzia, from bush-trained vines, showed excellently. In fact, it earned one of the highest scores in the denomination. The colour is pale ruby and a nose of good red berry fruit with smoky hints leads to a cohesive palate with good tannins, good grip, and a nice touch of bitterness on the finish. Aglianico del Vulture Sine Die '05 also stood its ground with scents of printers' ink, tar, dried flowers and ripe black berry fruit; and an open, balanced palate with good texture. But then came another disappointment. After a fine showing last year, the '04 Simpotica, made from negroamaro with small amounts of malvasia nera and montepulciano, is rather vague on the nose and lacks its usual dynamism on the palate.

● Copertino Rosso Eloquenzia '05	🍷🍷	3*
● Le Braci '05	🍷🍷	6
● Aglianico del Vulture Sine Die '05	🍷	5
⊙ Girofle '07	🍷	3
● Simpotica '04		4
● Le Braci '01	🍷🍷🍷	7
● Le Braci '00	🍷🍷🍷	7
● Le Braci '04	🍷🍷	7
● Le Braci '03	🍷🍷	7
● Simpotica '03	🍷🍷	4*
● Copertino Rosso Eloquenzia '04	🍷🍷	3*

Castello Monaci

C.DA MONACI
73015 SALICE SALENTINO [LE]
TEL. 0831665700
www.castellomonaci.it

ANNUAL PRODUCTION 2,200,000 bottles
HECTARES UNDER VINE 150
VITICULTURE METHOD Conventional

Castello Monaci, owned by Gruppo Italiano Vini, has hit the button. This year's wines with their new labels reflect such a rise in quality and such an ability to convey provenance that the winery is something of an example for the region. Artas, a monovarietal Primitivo, now has its second successive Three Glass prize with the '06. It's a garnet-ruby colour. The complex array of aromas, led by figs, pomegranate and plum jam leads into a rich, fruity and dynamic palate through to its long finish. But it's not the only wine to impress. Pilùna '07, also from primitivo, has a lively, floral nose nuanced with black damson, although still with too much vanilla from its oaking, and a youthful, cohesive palate of good texture and a cherry-like finish. Salice Salentino Rosso Aiace Riserva '05 has a deeper, more restrained nose with black berry fruit and tamarind shot through with rhubarb, and a clean, easy-going palate of good length. Medos '07 is a rare example of a wine made solely from malvasia nera di Lecce. It's well-made, uncomplicated, attractive, easy drinking and finishes with zesty red berry fruit. Everything else is well crafted.

● Artas '06	🍷🍷🍷	5
● Medos '07	🍷🍷	4
● Pilùna '07	🍷🍷	4*
● Salice Salentino Aiace Ris. '05	🍷🍷	4
● Campure Metrano '07	🍷	4
⊙ Kreos '07	🍷	4
● Artas '05	🍷🍷🍷	5*
● Artas '04	🍷🍷🍷	5*
● Artas '03	🍷🍷	5*
● Artas '02	🍷🍷	5
● Artas '01	🍷🍷	5*

Morella

VIA PER UGGIANO, 147
74024 MANDURIA [TA]
TEL. 0999791482
azag.morella@libero.it

ANNUAL PRODUCTION	12,000 bottles
HECTARES UNDER VINE	7
VITICULTURE METHOD	Conventional

Small estates like Lisa Gilbee's are more susceptible than others to the fickleness of the weather and growing year. That explains why Lisa's Primitivo selection La Signora wasn't submitted this year, and why none of her wines reached the finals. It doesn't mean that the range isn't excellent for diligent work in both vineyards and cellars ensures wines of consistently good quality. Primitivo Old Vines '06 is a dark ruby. Oak toast meets black cherry and sweet spices on the nose and the palate is sweetly full with good fruit. It simply lacks a little thrust towards the end and has a touch less zip and grip than the '05. The new Primitivo-Negroamaro '06, from a 50-50 blend of the grapes, also showed very well. There is oak again on the broad nose and dark, spicy sensations. The intense palate is still dominated by vanilla, although small black berry fruit, most notably blackberry, emerges on the finish. The clean, supple Primitivo Malbech Terre Rosse '06 also deserves a mention.

Rivera

C.DA RIVERA
S.P. 231 KM 60,500
70031 ANDRIA [BA]
TEL. 0883569501
www.rivera.it

ANNUAL PRODUCTION	1,500,000 bottles
HECTARES UNDER VINE	95
VITICULTURE METHOD	Conventional

Wines from the De Corato family's estate are again outstanding. Some are the modern style while others are traditional and the performance confirms Rivera as one of the most reliable cellars in the region. We start with Puer Apuliae '06, which has a balsamic nose with spices, plum and black damson, and a highly concentrated palate that is still raw and edgy but shows depth and texture. The long finish gives small black berry fruit, blueberries and tobacco. The '05 vintage of the historic Castel del Monte Il Falcone Riserva is more traditional, with ultra-ripe red berry fruit and a cohesive palate dominated by liquorice on the finish. Rupicolo '07, a Castel del Monte from a 70-30 blend of montepulciano and nero di Troia, is particularly successful. It has deep tones of tar, liquorice root, black damson and plum on the nose but the palate is lively, attractive and long. We are also delighted to mention Salice Salentino Rosso '07 which, coming from outside the Castel del Monte zone, demonstrates Rivera's grape selection skills as well as the quality of the winemaking, presenting full of extract framed by crisp fruit and soft tannins.

● Primitivo Negroamaro '06	▼▼ 5
● Primitivo Old Vines '06	▼▼ 6
● Primitivo Malbech Terre Rosse '06	▼ 5
● Primitivo La Signora '05	♈♈ 6
● Primitivo La Signora '04	♈♈ 6
● Primitivo Old Vines '05	♈♈ 6
● Primitivo Old Vines '04	♈♈ 6
● Primitivo Old Vines '03	♈♈ 6

● Castel del Monte Nero di Troia Puer Apuliae '06	▼▼ 7
● Castel del Monte Rosso Il Falcone Ris. '05	▼▼ 5
● Castel del Monte Rosso Rupicolo '07	▼▼ 3*
● Salice Salentino Rosso '07	▼▼ 4*
● Castel del Monte Aglianico Cappellaccio Ris. '05	▼ 4
○ Castel del Monte Bianco Fedora '07	▼ 2
⊙ Castel del Monte Rosé '07	▼ 2*
● Castel del Monte Rosso Violante '07	▼ 4
● Triusco '07	▼ 4
● Castel del Monte Nero di Troia Puer Apuliae '04	♈♈♈ 7
● Castel del Monte Nero di Troia Puer Apuliae '03	♈♈♈ 7
● Castel del Monte Nero di Troia Puer Apuliae '05	♈♈ 7

Tenute Rubino

VIA E. FERMI, 50
72100 BRINDISI
TEL. 0831571955
www.tenuterubino.it

ANNUAL PRODUCTION   800,000 bottles
HECTARES UNDER VINE   200
VITICULTURE METHOD   Conventional

In not time at all, the Rubino family has shot into the lead in the province of Brindisi for both quantity and, significantly, quality. The wines are now shape the zone's history and take their place with the best in Puglia. The two that really shone this year were classics: Visellio '06, from 100 per cent primitivo aged several months in barrique, and Brindisi Jaddico '06, from 85 per cent negroamaro plus malvasia nera and montepulciano. The former has black cherry, pencil lead, tar and oriental spices and a palate of lively fruit, overt but soft tannins and a long, deep finish. Jaddico is clean and elegant with red and black berry fruit. Its palate has texture, structure, good fruit and tight-knit tannins. Sussumaniello Torre Testa '06 fell a little short of expectations, showing a little heaviness and rather raw tannins, despite good concentration and density. This is an important wine for the estate and they even delayed its release by a year to offer a more mature style but it still doesn't seem to have found the shine of earlier vintages. However, the lively, fruit-and-spice Negroamaro is excellent. Everything else is well made.

Cosimo Taurino

S.S. 605
73010 GUAGNANO [LE]
TEL. 0832706490
www.taurinovini.it

ANNUAL PRODUCTION   800,000 bottles
HECTARES UNDER VINE   111
VITICULTURE METHOD   Conventional

The history of winemaking in Puglia over the last 40 years is inextricably linked with that of the Taurino family estate. After the death of Cosimo in 1999, the wines seemed to lose their way and while the family has been trying, we imagine, to regain a more stable set-up, the quality of the wines has not really reflected their fame, although they are still very good. We retasted the '01 vintage of Patriglione, the region's most famous negroamaro-based wine, after a couple of years additional bottle ageing. It shows a garnet ruby with aromas of medicinal herbs, leather, tar, tobacco and liquorice preceding an open palate with fully softened tannins but slightly too little depth and fullness to be a finalist. The negroamaro-only Notarpanaro '04, the estate's other top wine, has an intense nose of black berry fruit and dried figs. The palate is tight knit, with flavours of figs and cherry jam, and a long finish giving spices and dried fruit. The traditional Salice Salentino Rosso Riserva '05 is no more than well styled and is already ready for the corkscrew.

● Brindisi Rosso Jaddico '06	▼▼ 5
● Visellio '06	▼▼ 5
● Negroamaro '06	▼▼ 4*
● Torre Testa '06	▼▼ 6
○ Giancola '07	▼ 4
○ Marmorelle Bianco '07	▼ 3
● Marmorelle Rosso '07	▼ 3
● Primitivo Punta Aquila '07	▼ 4
⊙ Saturnino '07	▼ 3
○ Vermentino '07	▼ 4
● Primitivo Visellio '01	▼▼▼ 5*
● Torre Testa '02	▼▼▼ 6
● Torre Testa '01	▼▼▼ 6
● Primitivo Visellio '05	▼▼ 5
● Primitivo Visellio '04	▼▼ 5
● Torre Testa '04	▼▼ 6
● Torre Testa '03	▼▼ 6

● Notarpanaro '04	▼▼ 4
● Patriglione '01	▼▼ 7
● Salice Salentino Rosso Ris. '05	▼ 5
● Patriglione '94	▼▼▼ 8
● Patriglione '88	▼▼▼ 5
● Patriglione '85	▼▼▼ 5
● A Cosimo Taurino '04	▼▼ 5
● A Cosimo Taurino '03	▼▼ 5
● Notarpanaro '02	▼▼ 5
● Notarpanaro '99	▼▼ 5
● Patriglione '99	▼▼ 8
● Patriglione '95	▼▼ 8

Tormaresca

LOC. TOFANO
C.DA TORRE D'ISOLA
70055 BARI
TEL. 0883692631
www.tormaresca.it

ANNUAL PRODUCTION	2,000,000 bottles
HECTARES UNDER VINE	350
VITICULTURE METHOD	Certified organic

Every year, this estate emerges as one of the best in the Antinori portfolio. Its two properties both had a wine in the finals, Castel del Monte Aglianico Bocca di Lupo '04 from Minervino Murge and the negroamaro-only Masseria Maime '06 from San Pietro Vernotico, the latter soaring to Three Glasses. There are quinine, tar and sweet spices on the nose. The palate is clean, elegant and well constructed with crispy black berry fruit coming out mid palate and a long, deep finish. The Bocca di Lupo has deeper sensations on the nose, with tar, leather and oak, but also black berry fruit, violet and spices preceding a surprisingly refined, open palate with good structure and length. Torcicoda '06, a monovarietal Primitivo, with red berry fruit and undergrowth on the nose, has plenty of fruit but slightly raw tannins on the palate. It's excellent, as is the Chardonnay, Castel del Monte PietraBianca '07. This is still a little too oaky on the nose, with its bread, banana and pastry shop aromas, and the palate is a touch sweet but it has good body, lively peach and apricot flavours and a firm finish. Everything else is well made and well styled.

Torrevento

LOC. CASTEL DEL MONTE
S.P. 234 KM 10,600
70033 CORATO [BA]
TEL. 0808980923
www.torrevento.it

ANNUAL PRODUCTION	2,500,000 bottles
HECTARES UNDER VINE	400
VITICULTURE METHOD	Certified organic

A Three Glass award last year for the flagship Castel del Monte Rosso Vigna Pedale Riserva seems to have given Torrevento extra impetus because the wine did fantastically well and encored the performance this year. Made from 30-plus-year-old nero di Troia vines and traditionally vinified, the '05 has a lively, floral nose with crisp red berry fruit and oriental spices. The clean, cohesive, vigorous yet open palate makes the wine a joy to drink. Kebir '03 is not quite so traditional, being made from equal parts of nero di Troia and cabernet sauvignon aged in barrique. It is excellent, though, ripe red berry fruit leading to a tight-knit, concentrated palate with a quiet, slightly bitterish finish. Similar quality shines through on the '05 Aglianico from the Matervitae line, which has a cherry, red berries and slightly tarry nose, backed up by a lively, fruity palate with good grip. Everything else is attractive and well made, from the appealing, spicy Salice Salentino Rosso Faneros '06 to the floral rosé Matervitae Bombino '07 with its touch of oak, full palate and rose-and-tea leaves finish.

● Masseria Maime '06	▼▼▼ 5
● Castel del Monte Rosso Bocca di Lupo '04	▼▼ 6
○ Castel del Monte Chardonnay PietraBianca '07	▼▼ 5
● Torcicoda '06	▼▼ 5
☉ Calafuria '07	▼ 4
● Fichimori '07	▼ 4
● Neprica Rosso '07	▼ 3
○ Tormaresca Chardonnay '07	▼ 3
● Masseria Maime '05	♈♈♈ 5*
● Masseria Maime '04	♈♈♈ 5*
● Masseria Maime '02	♈♈♈ 5
● Masseria Maime '00	♈♈♈ 5*
● Torcicoda '01	♈♈♈ 5*
● Castel del Monte Rosso Bocca di Lupo '01	♈♈ 5
● Masseria Maime '01	♈♈ 5

● Castel del Monte Rosso V. Pedale Ris. '05	▼▼▼ 4*
● Kebir '03	▼▼ 6
● Matervitae Aglianico '05	▼▼ 4*
☉ Castel del Monte Rosato Primaronda '07	▼ 3
☉ Matervitae Bombino Nero '07	▼ 4
○ Moscato di Trani Dulcis in Fundo '06	▼ 4
● Salice Salentino Rosso Faneros '06	▼ 4
● Castel del Monte Rosso V. Pedale Ris. '04	♈♈♈ 4*
● Castel del Monte Rosso V. Pedale Ris. '01	♈♈ 4*
● Kebir '02	♈♈ 5

Agricole Vallone

via XXV Luglio, 5
73100 Lecce
tel. 0832308041
www.agricolevallone.it

ANNUAL PRODUCTION 525,000 bottles
HECTARES UNDER VINE 170
VITICULTURE METHOD Certified organic

Over the past few years our admiration for traditionally styled Puglian wines has been reflected in the scores awarded and Graticciaia, the Vallone sisters' flagship wine, is often one of the best of the breed. But this year's '04 impressed us less than usual. A pale ruby, with a nose of dried leaves and undergrowth, liquorice and red berry fruit conserve, it reveals a sweet, oxidative palate: traditional for sure, but in need of a bit of stuffing and, in particular, with less sinew on the finish than usual. In short, it's a good wine but nothing to write home about. Salice Salentino Rosso Vereto '06 performed well. It has a cherry red-tinged ruby colour, aromas of spices, incense and red berry fruit, and a clean, open, long palate. Passo delle Viscarde '03, an amber-hued dried-grape passito from an 80-20 blend of sauvignon and malvasia bianca, is appealing, with a caramel-like nose and a well-textured palate resonant of orange blossom, leading to an attractive, candied fruit finish. Everything else is well made.

● Graticciaia '04	🍷🍷	7
● Salice Salentino Rosso Vereto '06	🍷🍷	3*
⊙ Brindisi Rosato V. Flaminio '07	🍷	3
● Brindisi Rosso V. Flaminio '06	🍷	3
○ Passo delle Viscarde '03	🍷	5
● Graticciaia '03	🍷🍷🍷	7
● Graticciaia '01	🍷🍷🍷	7
● Graticciaia '00	🍷🍷	7
● Graticciaia '98	🍷🍷	7
○ Passo delle Viscarde '00	🍷🍷	6

Vetrere

s.da prov. Monteiasi-Montemesola km 16
74100 Taranto
tel. 0995661054
www.vetrere.it

ANNUAL PRODUCTION 180,000 bottles
HECTARES UNDER VINE 37
VITICULTURE METHOD Conventional

Until a few years ago, the Bruni sisters' estate was known mainly for its excellent olive oil but now it's among the region's leaders for wine, too. The range is outstanding and dependably sound. That said, we were hoping to see quality peak even higher but it's slow in coming. Which leaves us with a range of reliable, good wines but no wow factor. The two best this year are Tempio di Giano '07, from negroamaro, offering ripe cherry fruit challenged by oak and vanilla on the nose and a more enjoyably traditional, soft, well-formed palate; and Barone Pazzo '06, from 100 per cent primitivo. The latter has scents of lavender, blackberry and plum, and is an attractive, easy-drinking wine but lacks any great depth or complexity. Lago della Pergola '06, from negroamaro, cabernet and aglianico, showed nicely full and dominated throughout by very ripe black berry fruit laced with hints of tar. Finis Terrae '07, from chardonnay, verdeca and malvasia, is on a par, aromas of flowers and banana being followed by a zippy palate of good length. Crè '07, from fiano minutolo, is intriguing, with wild rose scents and a delicate, supple, aromatic style.

● Barone Pazzo '06	🍷🍷	4
● Tempio di Giano '07	🍷🍷	3*
○ Crè '07	🍷	4
○ Finis Terrae '07	🍷	3
● Lago della Pergola '06	🍷	4
○ Laureato '07	🍷	4
● Livruni '07	🍷	3
● Barone Pazzo '04	🍷🍷	4
● Livruni '06	🍷🍷	3*
⊙ Taranta '06	🍷🍷	3*
⊙ Taranta '05	🍷🍷	3*
● Tempio di Giano '05	🍷🍷	3*

Vinicola Mediterranea

VIA MATERNITÀ INFANZIA, 22
72027 SAN PIETRO VERNOTICO [BR]
TEL. 0831676323
www.vinicolamediterranea.it

ANNUAL PRODUCTION	450,000 bottles
HECTARES UNDER VINE	N.A.
VITICULTURE METHOD	Conventional

In 1997, Vinicola Mediterranea took over the business of the municipal co-operative winery and it now has the capacity to vinify 5,000,000 kilograms of grapes, bottling the best batches of wine. After a couple of years in the Other Wineries section, it has now regained a full entry with a range that is not only very good but also, for the most part, terrific value for money. Squinzano Rosso Il Principe '06 has Mediterranean scrubland and spices on the nose, and a palate of precision with black berry fruit, good stuffing, elegant tannins, and firm acidity giving support to the finish. Salice Salentino Rosso Il Granduca Riserva '04 is centred on blueberry and blackcurrant, showing clean-cut, elegant and floral. The lively Nobile '06, from 100 per cent negroamaro, has a balsam and pencil lead nose, good texture and an attractive, long finish. All gained Two Glasses, as did the very impressive Don Vito '07, from negroamaro and primitivo. This is fruity and spicy, with good acidity to hold up its dynamic finish. Primitivo Dolce Naturale Oblio '06, presenting clean, lively and spicy with ripe cherry, came one slot down.

Conti Zecca

VIA CESAREA
73045 LEVERANO [LE]
TEL. 0832925613
www.contizecca.it

ANNUAL PRODUCTION	2,000,000 bottles
HECTARES UNDER VINE	320
VITICULTURE METHOD	Conventional

The Zecca siblings' winery is one of Puglia's most dependable. Although neither its top wine Nero nor Leverano Riserva Terra were submitted this year, both being left to age further prior to bottling, the range was still more than respectable. Indeed, the Primitivo from the monovarietal range reached the finals for the second year running. This year's '06 has blackberries, oriental spices and oak toast followed by a clean, elegant palate with refined tannicity and a long, black berry finish. Plum, blackberry and oak toast dominate the '05 Negroamaro from the same line, which is rich, full and intense with good backbone. The fruity Salice Salentino Cantalupi Riserva '05 has hints of tar, and a well-textured palate with more black cherry fruit on the finish. Sole '07, from malvasia bianca di Lecce with ten per cent moscato bianco, is an attractively aromatic, long, sweet but not cloying, dried-grape passito with a light citrus tang and an elderflower finish. A fresh, floral, nicely aromatic Fiano '07 and rosé Cantalupi Rosato '07 are also in the Two Glass band. As usual, everything else is good, the Donna Marzia offering particularly good value.

● Don Vito '07	♟♟ 2*
● Nobile '06	♟♟ 3*
● Salice Salentino Rosso Il Granduca Ris. '04	♟♟ 3*
● Squinzano Rosso Il Principe '06	♟♟ 3*
● Primitivo Dolce Natural Oblio '06	♟ 4
● Salice Salentino Rosso Sirio '04	♟♟ 3*

● Primitivo '06	♟♟ 4*
☉ Cantalupi Rosato '07	♟♟ 3*
○ Fiano '07	♟♟ 4*
● Negramaro '05	♟♟ 4
● Salice Salentino Rosso Cantalupi Ris. '05	♟♟ 4*
○ Sole '07	♟♟ 4*
○ Donna Marzia Bianco '07	♟ 2*
● Donna Marzia Negramaro '06	♟ 2*
● Donna Marzia Rosso '06	♟ 2*
○ Luna '07	♟ 4
● Nero '03	♟♟♟ 6
● Nero '02	♟♟♟ 6
● Nero '01	♟♟♟ 6
● Nero '05	♟♟ 6
● Nero '04	♟♟ 6

OTHER WINERIES

Masseria Altemura

C.DA PALOMBARA - SP 69
72028 TORRE SANTA SUSANNA [BR]
TEL. 0831740485
www.masseriaaltemura.it

The Zonin family's Puglia holding continues to turn out good wine but the hoped-for boost into real class hasn't arrived. The best of the range is Negroamaro '06, offering a coffee and chocolate nose followed by a more traditionally soft, open palate. Fiano '07 is clean and nicely aromatic.

● Negroamaro '06	🍷🍷	4
○ Fiano '07	🍷	4
● Sasseo '06	🍷	4

Apollonio

VIA SAN PIETRO IN LAMA, 7
73047 MONTERONI DI LECCE [LE]
TEL. 0832327182
www.apolloniovini.it

Apollonio submitted some older vintages this year alongside its current releases. Most notable was Copertino Rosso Divoto Riserva '01, which has ripe black berry fruit, shot through with still balsamic nuances, and a full, cohesive palate with a tarry finish.

● Copertino Divoto Ris. '01	🍷🍷	6
● Valle Cupa '01	🍷	5

L'Astore Masseria

LOC. L'ASTORE
73020 CUTROFIANO [LE]
TEL. 0836542020
www.lastoremasseria.it

Quality is holding up here. Negroamaro Filimei '07 is first rate. Lively aromas of cherry and black berry fruit lead to a balanced, clean-cut palate with smooth tannins. Argentieri '06 and Massaro Rosa '07, both from negroamaro, are attractive.

● Filimei '07	🍷🍷	4
● Argentieri '06	🍷	5
☉ Il Massaro Rosa '07	🍷	4

Cantine Botromagno

LOC. ZONA PIP
VIA ARCHIMEDE, 22
70024 GRAVINA IN PUGLIA [BA]
TEL. 0803265865
www.botromagno.it

There's the air of the new at the D'Agostino siblings' winery as the cellar makeover a new winemaking consultant start to give the wines a fresh imprint. We await future releases with interest. For now, our best score went to Gravisano '05, a soft, mouthfilling, dried-grape wine from malvasia bianca.

○ Gravisano '05	🍷🍷	5
○ Gravina '07	🍷	3
☉ Silvium '07	🍷	3

Sergio Botrugno

LOC. CASALE
VIA ARCIONE, 1
72100 BRINDISI
TEL. 0831555587
www.vinisalento.com

Botrugno's wines are well made and good quality. Most interesting are the supple, easy-drinking, well-fruited Ottavianello '06 and Brindisi Rosso Arcione '06, which has spices, tobacco and chocolate followed by a lively, long, softly tannic palate.

● Brindisi Rosso Arcione '06	🍷	4
● Ottavianello '06	🍷🍷	4*
● Patrunu Ro Primitivo '06	🍷	2*

C.a.l.o.s.m.

VIA PIETRO SICILIANI, 8
73058 TUGLIE [LE]
TEL. 0833598051
calosm@libero.it

The Calò siblings' wines are well styled and reliably good. Leading the range this year is Villa Valentino Don Carlo '07 from negroamaro with 15 per cent malvasia nera. It's lively, supple, has red berry fruit and a good acid backbone supports the finish.

● Villa Valentino Don Carlo '07	🍷🍷	2*
● Donna Stracca '05	🍷	5
○ Ionia '07	🍷	3
☉ Salmace '07	🍷	3

OTHER WINERIES

Antiche Aziende Canosine
via Sconcordia
70053 Canosa di Puglia [BA]
tel. 3289406102
www.anticheaziendecanosine.it

This estate is skilled at making dried-grape wines and again its Moscato Passito Tharen is one of the region's best sweet wines. Aromas of mixed flower honey and wax lead to a palate of well-judged sweetness, good supporting acidity and a nicely floral finish. Everything else is well made.

O Tharen '06	ŸŸ 5
● Canosa Rosso Pathos Ris. '06	Ÿ 4
● Mherum '06	Ÿ 4

Cantolio Manduria
via per Lecce Km 25
74024 Manduria [TA]
tel. 0999796045
www.cantolio.it

This co-operative submitted a good range of Primitivo di Mandurias. The 14 '06 has red berry fruit, zip and grip and the 15 '05 is balanced and close-knit, with spiciness that ranges from cinnamon to pepper. Dolce Naturale 17.5 '06 focuses more on chocolate, earth and Mediterranean scrubland.

● Primitivo di Manduria 14 '06	ŸŸ 4
● Primitivo di Manduria 15 '05	ŸŸ 4
● Primitivo di Manduria Dolce Natural 17,5 '06	ŸŸ 4

Cefalicchio
c.so San Sabino, 6
70053 Canosa di Puglia [BA]
tel. 0833617601
www.cefalicchio.it

The Rossi siblings' winery is Puglia's most famous biodynamic estate. Leading the range this year are Rosso Canosa '05, with its floral, leather and black berry nose and a long, cohesive palate with acid grip, and the lively, Totila '05, from a 50-50 blend of cabernet sauvignon and nero di Troia.

● Rosso Canosa '05	ŸŸ 2*
● Totila '05	ŸŸ 5
O Moscato di Jalal '07	Ÿ 5

d'Araprì
via Zannotti, 30
71016 San Severo [FG]
tel. 0882227643
www.darapri.it

D'Araprì makes sparkling wines. Gran XXI Cuvée Secolo '02, from 80 per cent bombino bianco and pinot nero, is deep and complex. The bombino bianco Riserva Nobile '04 is soft but structured. The Brut, from bombino bianco and pinot nero, and the Rosé, from montepulciano and pinot nero, are nice.

O d'Araprì Gran Cuvée XXI Secolo '02	ŸŸ 6
O d'Araprì Nobile Ris. '04	ŸŸ 6
O d'Araprì Brut	Ÿ 5
⊙ d'Araprì Brut Rosé	Ÿ 6

De Falco
via Milano, 25
73051 Novoli [LE]
tel. 0832711597
www.cantinedefalco.it

This winery has been part of Puglia's elite for some time. This year, the classic denominations led the field. Squinzano Serre di Sant'Elia '06 is concentrated with dried fig and plum. Salice Salentino Rosso Riserva Falconero '04 has violets and black berry fruit, and great structure.

● Salice Salentino Rosso Falconero Ris. '04	ŸŸ 4
● Squinzano Rosso Serre di Sant'Elia '06	ŸŸ 3*
● Artiglio '05	Ÿ 5
● Salice Salentino Rosso Salore '06	Ÿ 4

Le Fabriche
c.da Le Fabbriche
s.p. Maruggio-Torricella
74020 Maruggio [TA]
tel. 0999738284
www.lefabriche.it

Alessia Perrucci has a knack with primitivo. Medì '06, with aromas of autumn leaves and medicinal herbs, and a clean, lively, open palate, is very well made in a traditional style. Also good is the well-balanced, attractive Primitivo di Manduria '05, which has ripe fruit and good backbone.

● Medì '06	ŸŸ 4
● Primitivo di Manduria '05	Ÿ 5

OTHER WINERIES

Feudi di Terra D'Otranto

VIA ARNEO MARE
73010 VEGLIE [LE]
TEL. 066832448
www.feudidotranto.com

The '07 vintage of the Le Maschere line is more impressive than previous releases. Both the Primitivo and the Syrah are good but the Aglianico is even better, with an elegant nose giving florality and black berry fruit, and a taut, long palate of zip, precision and fine flavour.

● Le Maschere Aglianico '07	♥♥	3*
● Le Maschere Primitivo '07	♥	3
● Le Maschere Syrah '07	♥	3*

Tenute Girolamo

S.DA GIULIANI, 7
74015 MARTINA FRANCA [TA]
TEL. 0804402088
www.tenutegirolamo.it

Good quality has emerged from this estate's first releases. The wines are a bit oaky but reveal great care in the vineyards and winemaking expertise. Pétroma '04, from primitivo and syrah, stands out. It has good grip and length, with pencil lead, black berry fruit and spices.

● Pétroma '04	♥♥	6
○ Iérai Pétrai '06	♥	5
● Pétrakos '04	♥	6

Duca Carlo Guarini

L.GO FRISARI, 1
73020 SCORRANO [LE]
TEL. 0836460288
www.ducacarloguarini.it

This long-standing estate did well this year. We liked Rarum '04, from negroamaro and malvasia nera, one of the region's best dried-grape wines. Aromas of cherry tart and Mediterranean scrubland lead to an attractive, rich palate. Malìa '05, an open, well-fruited Malvasia Nera, is also well made.

● Rarum '04	♥♥	6
○ Ambra '06	♥	5
● Malìa '05	♥	5

Guerrieri

VIA PLAVA, 12
73051 NOVOLI [LE]
TEL. 0832712729
a.guerrieri4@virgilio.it

Only 10,000 bottles are made here but quality is high. We particularly liked Sole Negro '05, a traditionally styled Negroamaro. Liqueur cherries and aromatic herbs on the nose are followed by an open, lively yet cohesive palate with good body and a long, attractive finish.

● Sole Negro '05	♥♥	4
● Le Lombarde '05	♥	3

Paolo Leo

VIA TUTURANO, 21
72025 SAN DONACI [BR]
TEL. 0831635073
www.paololeo.it

This was one of Paolo Leo's lesser years with only Orfeo '06 really up to speed. Its tobacco and ripe plum nose leads to a tight-knit palate of good texture with aromatic herbs, although there's a little over-extraction too. Chardonnay Numen '07 and Salice Salentino Rosso Riserva '03 are pleasant.

● Orfeo '06	♥♥	5
○ Numen '07	♥	5
● Salice Salentino Rosso Ris. '03	♥	4

Cantina Locorotondo

VIA MADONNA DELLA CATENA, 99
70010 LOCOROTONDO [BA]
TEL. 0804311644
www.locorotondodoc.com

Although Locorotondo is traditionally associated with white wine, this year the best wine submitted was Primitivo di Manduria Terre di Don Peppe '06. There's liquorice on the pervasive nose and the palate is deep, cohesive, vibrant and long.

● Primitivo di Manduria Terre di Don Peppe '06	♥♥	6
● Cummerse Rosso '04	♥	4
○ Locorotondo Vign. in Tallinajo '07	♥	4

OTHER WINERIES

Maria Marmo

C.DA COCEVOLA
S.S. 170 CASTEL DEL MONTE KM 9,900
70031 ANDRIA [BA]
TEL. 0883262489
www.tenutacocevola.com

Although their outstanding Vandalo was out of the running this year, as it has been given longer pre-release bottle ageing, the Marmo family still submitted a well-made group of balanced Castel del Montes, with the fresh, attractively fruity Rosato '07, from nero di Troia, leading the range.

⊙ Castel del Monte Rosato '07	♟♟	4
● Castel del Monte Nero di Troia Rosso Cocevola '06	♟	4
○ Castel del Monte Pampanuto '07	♟	4

Masseria Li Veli

S.P. CELLINO-CAMPI, KM 1
72020 CELLINO SAN MARCO [BR]
TEL. 0831617906
www.liveli.it

There are signs that the Falvo family's wines are beginning to make an impact. This year, the negroamaro-only Passamante '07 reached the finals. It's a truly impressive, clean-cut, lively, well-made, balsamic wine with crisp black berry fruit. Salice Salentino Pezzo Morgana '05 is also first rate.

● Passamante '07	♟♟	4*
● Salice Salentino Rosso Pezzo Morgana '05	♟♟	5

Tenute Mater Domini

VIA DEI MARTIRI, 17/19
73012 CAMPI SALENTINA [LE]
TEL. 0832792442
www.tenutematerdomini.it

This estate, owned by the Semeraro family, gains its first entry in the Guide with two wines, both from negroamaro. Marangi Rosso '06 has tobacco, spices and hints of black berry fruit on the nose then a smoky, sweetly fruited palate. Marangi Rosato '07, from free-run must, is fresh and floral.

● Marangi Rosso '06	♟♟	4
⊙ Marangi Rosato '07	♟	3

Menhir

VIA SCARCIGLIA, 16
73027 MINERVINO DI LECCE [LE]
TEL. 0836818191
www.vinimenhirsalento.it

An impressive performance across the board brings Gaetano Marangelli's new estate into the Guide. Two wines stand apart. Salice Salentino Rosso '06, with coffee and ripe cherry notes, is clean, tight-knit, attractive and soft while the negroamaro Numero Zero '06 is spicy, balsamic and balanced.

● Numero Zero '06	♟♟	3*
● Salice Salentino Rosso '06	♟♟	3*
● Trelune '07	♟	3

Cantine Miali

VIA MADONNINA, 1
74015 MARTINA FRANCA [TA]
TEL. 0804303222
www.cantinemiali.com

The wines here, from bought-in grapes, are back on form. We liked Primitivo Campirossi '06, which has a floral and pencil-lead nose, and a lively, cohesive palate with a liquorice finish, as well as the zippy, easy-drinking, blueberry-like Ichore '07, from negroamaro, primitivo and merlot.

● Ichore '07	♟♟	4*
● Primitivo Campirossi '06	♟♟	3*
● Aglianico del Vulture Sepala '04	♟	4
● Primitivo Mater '04	♟	4

Mocavero

C.DA MALLACCA ZUMMARI
73010 ARNESANO [LE]
TEL. 0832327194
www.mocaverovini.it

Mocavero is back in the Guide. The savoury, mineral Negroamaro '06, focused on Mediterranean scrubland, the balsamic Salice Salentino '05, all ripe red berry fruit and pencil lead, well-integrated tannins and a lively finish, and the attractive, floral Tela di Ragno '03 are really good.

● Negramaro '06	♟♟	2*
● Salice Salentino Rosso '05	♟♟	2*
● Tela di Ragno '03	♟♟	5

OTHER WINERIES

Cosimo Palamà

VIA A. DIAZ, 6
73020 CUTROFIANO [LE]
TEL. 0836542865
www.vinicolapalama.com

Improvements continue apace here. The elegant, nicely structured Mavro '06, with its fruity, supple finish, and the spicy, dynamic, firm, clean-cut Albarossa '06, showed really well, as did the youthful but complex Metiusco Rosato '07, full of ripe fruit and one of Puglia's best rosés.

● Mavro '06	♟♟	4
● Salice Salentino Rosso Albarossa '06	♟♟	2*
☉ Metiusco Rosato '07	♟	3

Giovanni Petrelli

VIA VILLA CONVENTO, 33
73041 CARMIANO [LE]
TEL. 0832603051
www.cantinapetrelli.com

Giovanni Petrelli's love for his land and his vineyards is well known and it shows in the wines. The fine Tenuta Scozzi 10,000 '05, from montepulciano and cabernet sauvignon, is balsamic and slightly vegetal with red berry fruit, and has a lively, attractive, easy-drinking palate.

● Tenuta Scozzi 10.000 '05	♟♟	5
● Don Pepè '05	♟	5
● Salice Salentino Rosso Centopietre '06	♟	4

Primis

VIA C. COLOMBO, 44
71048 STORNARELLA [FG]
TEL. 0885433333
www.primisvini.com

The wines remain good here, especially the flagship Crusta '05, from 100 per cent montepulciano. It's a lively, balsamic, spicy wine with black berry fruit and good backbone. The varietal, well-made Sauvignon '07 and Monrose '07, with its notes of wild cherry and green tea leaves, are also good.

● Crusta '05	♟♟	5
☉ Monrose '07	♟	3
○ Sauvignon '07	♟	3

Rasciatano

C.DA RASCIATANO
70051 BARLETTA [BA]
TEL. 0883510999
www.rasciatano.com

Rasciatano is known for its olive oil. Now it has made its wine debut with a very fine Rosso '06 from a 50-30-20 barrique-aged blend of nero di Troia, cabernet sauvignon and merlot, which made the finals. It's soft yet taut, attractive, lively and long, and has spice and forest fruit flavours.

● Rasciatano '06	♟♟	7
☉ Rasciatano Rosè '07	♟	5

Vinicola Resta

VIA MATERNITÀ E INFANZIA, 2
72027 SAN PIETRO VERNOTICO [BR]
TEL. 0831671182
www.vinicolaresta.it

This winery returns to the Guide with a range of well made wines that are cleaner than in recent years. Squinzano '06 has briary fruit nuanced with pepper. The palate is invigorating, close-knit and full of clean fruit. Vigna del Gelso Moro Negroamaro '06 has darker chocolate and chestnut toastiness.

● Squinzano '06	♟♟	4*
● Vigna del Gelso Moro Negroamaro '06	♟♟	4*

Rosa del Golfo

VIA GARIBALDI, 56
73011 ALEZIO [LE]
TEL. 0833281045
www.rosadelgolfo.com

It's definitely been an off-year for Damiano Calò. His more famous rosés suffered as much as the other wines submitted. Vigna Mazzì '06 is as individual as ever but this year its oxidative tones are too marked. The other wines are well styled but there's nothing really exceptional.

○ Bolina '07	♟	4
● Quarantale '05	♟	6
☉ Rosa del Golfo '07	♟	4
○ Vigna Mazzì '06	♟	4

OTHER WINERIES

Cantina Cooperativa di San Donaci

VIA MESAGNE, 62
72025 SAN DONACI [BR]
TEL. 0831681085
www.cantinasandonaci.it

This long-standing co-operative is back in the Guide after a few years' absence with a juicy Salice Salentino Rosso Anticaia '06. Traditional in its ripe, red berry fruit nose, supple structure and soft tannins, it makes for great drinking. Anticaia Riserva '04 is also good but a little evolved.

● Salice Salentino Anticaia '06	¶¶ 3*
● Contrada del Falco '06	¶ 3
● Salice Salentino Anticaia Ris. '04	¶ 4

Santa Barbara

VIA MATERNITÀ E INFANZIA, 23
72027 SAN PIETRO VERNOTICO [BR]
TEL. 0831652749
www.cantinesantabarbara.it

The impression the wines give is that the Giorgiani family is going through a bad patch. Plenty were submitted but few showed really well. The best was the lively, long Squinzano '05, which has a fruity, spicy nose and an attractive, precise palate.

● Squinzano Rosso '05	¶¶ 3*
● Brindisi Rosso '05	¶ 3
● Salice Salentino Rosso '05	¶ 3
● Ursa Major Rosso '01	¶ 5

Santa Lucia

S.DA SAN VITTORE, 1
70033 CORATO [BA]
TEL. 0817642888
www.vinisantalucia.com

The Castel del Montes are back in the limelight here, especially those with nero di Troia. Le More Riserva '06 is particularly good with its slightly smoky, black berry fruit and pomegranate nose, and its nicely textured, well-structured palate. Just a tad more precision of style and it would soar.

● Castel del Monte Le More Ris. '06	¶¶ 6
● Castel del Monte Rosso V. del Melograno '06	¶ 4
O Gazza Ladra '07	¶ 4

Santa Maria del Morige

FRAZ. CARPIGNANA
VIA DEL MARE, KM 2
73044 GALATONE [LE]
TEL. 0833864525
www.santamariadelmorige.com

Annalisa Conserva's wines seem to have found their niche. Cinabro '05 from negroamaro has black berry fruit and hints of printers' ink on the nose, and a zippy, supple palate with blackcurrant and blackberry. Murice Bianco, a rare example of negroamaro vinified as a white wine, is not bad.

● Cinabro '05	¶¶ 4
O Murice Bianco '07	¶ 4

Schola Sarmenti

VIA AVV. P. INGUSCI, 45
73048 NARDÒ [LE]
TEL. 0833567247
www.scholasarmenti.it

Luigi Carlo Marra's wines are some of the most interesting in Nardò and maybe in the whole of Salento. We were particularly struck this year by Critèra '05, from primitivo, where a small red berry fruit and liquorice nose leads to a lively, clean-cut, well-fruited palate.

● Critèra '05	¶¶ 4*
● Armentino '07	¶ 4
● Artetica '05	¶ 6

Setteterre

VIA PER FAGGIANO, 228
74100 TARANTO
TEL. 0994527396
setteterre@hotmail.it

This small estate with bush-trained vines is in the Guide for the first time. Primitivo di Manduria Vigna dell'Ora '07 is excellent: tight-knit, sweetly fruited and tobacco-scented. Vigna dei Mori '07 from negroamaro is almost as good, giving cherry and undergrowth. Prices seem high for a newcomer.

● Primitivo di Manduria V. dell'Ora '07	¶¶ 6
● V. dei Mori '07	¶ 6

OTHER WINERIES

Soloperto

S.S. 7 TER
74024 MANDURIA [TA]
TEL. 0999794286
www.soloperto.it

This, the first winery to be registered as a producer of Primitivo di Manduria, as its back labels recall, is now finding its feet again. We liked Centofuochi '06, a deep, lively Primitivo di Manduria, which is crisply fruity and proffers notes of Mediterranean scrubland.

● Primitivo di Manduria Centofuochi Tenuta Bagnolo '06	🍷🍷 5
● Primitivo di Manduria 14° '06	🍷 2*
● Primitivo di Manduria Mono '05	🍷 5

Azienda Vinicola Terra del Galeso

S.DA VICINALE SALINELLA
74100 TARANTO
TEL. 0997729070
www.terradelgaleso.it

This organic newcomer to the Guide was set up in 2003. The extremely attractive Chierico '05, from primitivo, has a floral, fruity, balsamic nose and a long, lively palate. The chardonnay Bardo '07 has aromas of cedar and camomile flowers, and a savoury, citrus-fruit palate with good backbone.

○ Bardo '07	🍷🍷 3*
● Chierico '05	🍷🍷 4
● Baccanera '06	🍷 4
○ Girotondo '07	🍷 6

Valle dell'Asso

VIA GUIDANO, 18
73024 GALATINA [LE]
TEL. 0836561470
www.valleasso.it

Gino Vallone did not submit his Piromafo this year but his Macàro is right on the ball. This is a sort of Puglian Sherry, made from a blend of the best vintages of aleatico and malvasia aged six years in large old oak barrels. Complex, sweet and long, with dried fruit and figs, it's simply unique.

● Macàro	🍷🍷 6
● Galatina Rosso '06	🍷 3
● Piromàfo '03	🍷🍷 5

Conte Spagnoletti Zeuli

FRAZ. MONTEGROSSO
C.DA SAN DOMENICO, S.P. 231 KM 60,000
70031 ANDRIA [BA]
TEL. 0883569511
www.contespagnolettizeuli.it

We are pleased to see this winery back in the Guide with an excellently made range of Castel del Montes, led by Pezza La Ruca '05, which reached the finals. It's attractive, lively, floral and spicy, and has a soft, balanced palate. Terranera Riserva del Conte '04 is also first rate.

● Castel del Monte Rosso Pezza La Ruca '05	🍷🍷 4*
● Castel del Monte Rosso Terranera Ris. del Conte '04	🍷🍷 6
● Castel del Monte Rosso Il Rinzacco '05	🍷 5

Torre Quarto

C.DA QUARTO, 5
71042 CERIGNOLA [FG]
TEL. 0885418453
www.torrequartocantine.it

The '07 vintage saw the return to form of the two best-known wines, Bottaccia, from nero di Troia, and Tarabuso, from primitivo. The former has blackcurrant and blueberry suffused with oak toast, and a well-made, modern-style palate while Tarabuso is clean-cut and long, with intense black berry fruit.

● Bottaccia '07	🍷🍷 4*
● Tarabuso '07	🍷🍷 4*
○ Nina '07	🍷 3
● Quarto Ducale '05	🍷 4

Vigne & Vini

VIA AMENDOLA, 36
74020 LEPORANO [TA]
TEL. 0995332254
www.vigneevini.it

Both this winery's Primitivo di Mandurias, led by Moi '05, and its negroamaro-based wines, like Schiaccianoci '06, showed well. The latter is spicy, with good body, grip, acid backbone and a long, plummy finish while the Moi is floral with crisp black berry fruit and refined, well-integrated tannins.

● Primitivo di Manduria Moi '05	🍷🍷 4
● Schiaccianoci '06	🍷🍷 4
○ Primadonna '07	🍷 4
● Zinfandel '06	🍷 4

CALABRIA

Now that Calabria has emerged from the dark years of its recent past, the general picture is comforting. Average quality is improving fast and the number of estates submitting wines to our tastings has grown, almost doubling over the past two years. This year in particular is one for the record books. Not only were two wines awarded the coveted Three Glasses but one, Luigi Viola's Moscato Passito '07, was nominated Sweet Wine of the Year. This achievement gives us huge pleasure for several reasons. The first is that we know Luigi Viola and we are sure that his feet will stay firmly on the ground. If anything, he'll probably now work even harder than ever. The second reason is that we gave this affable but firmly determined wine man space in our Guide right from his first releases when he was Moscato's sole producer. We feel we have made our own contribution to realizing Luigi's ideal of saving an ancient, almost forgotten, wine from extinction. Thirdly, we reckon the award might act as a stimulus to the various other youngsters at Saracena who, like Luigi's sons, have decided to stake their future on their homeland and this wine. The other Three Glasses went to Cirò Classico Riserva Duca Sanfelice '05 from the Librandi brothers. It's the first time a Cirò has reached these heights, turning the spotlight onto a winery that has not just brought a group of technical luminaries to Cirò to advise on production but has lavished more energy and funds than practically any other in Italy on raising the profile of its home terrain and grape varieties. We hope that this well-deserved award will also help gaglioppo shrug off the image it has with some as a lesser variety, useful only for making unsophisticated wines. We also have a few promising newcomers to celebrate, in particular the Senatore winery, based in Cirò, which submitted a noteworthy range. Then comes Tenuta Iuzzolini, also in Cirò, and Colacino, whose vineyards lie further south in the Savuto zone, providing company for Gregorio Odoardi. And on the subject of Odoardi, his wines put on another good show even if, unlike in previous years, nothing won Three Glasses. There is good, if slow, progress at Lamezia, although regrettably there is still no single outstanding wine that can stake the area's claim to fame. Things also seem to be on the move in the south of the region. Two dynamic new wineries, Tramontana and Zagarella, situated close to the Strait of Messina, make welcome entries to these pages, as does Malaspina, the only winery in Calabria to be run entirely by women. So it appears that the region's producers are becoming conscious of the potential of their marvellous terrains. At last.

Cantine Lento

via del Progresso, 1
88046 Lamezia Terme [CZ]
tel. 096828028
www.cantinelento.it

ANNUAL PRODUCTION 650,000 bottles
HECTARES UNDER VINE 70
VITICULTURE METHOD Conventional

The Lento family has put a great deal of work into renovating and relaunching their estate. Now everything seems to be in place. Their 70 hectares of vineyard are newly planted and their new 6,000 square-metre cellar is fitted out with modern equipment, all ready to be put to the test with the new vintage. Winemaking is overseen by Lorenzo Landi, whose recommendations have led to a reduction in the number of wines produced. A well-deserved finals place went to Federico II '05, a concentrated, long Cabernet full of fruit, poised beautifully between acidity and sweetness. Contessa Emburga '07, from sauvignon, is also excellent, showing fresh and varietal on the nose followed by a juicy, well-structured palate. The group of Lamezia DOC wines has much to offer. The garnet-ruby '03 Riserva has a fruity, Mediterranean herbs nose and an attractively lively, juicy, long palate. The clean, supple white, Dragone '07, is also well made with a floral nose and a zesty palate. Everything else is sound.

● Federico II '05	🍷🍷	5
○ Contessa Emburga Capsula Rame '07	🍷🍷	4*
● Lamezia Rosso Ris. '03	🍷🍷	5
○ Lamezia Bianco Dragone '07	🍷	4
⊙ Lamezia Rosato Dragone '07	🍷	4
● Lamezia Rosso Dragone '06	🍷	4
● Federico II '99	YY	6
● Federico II '04	YY	5
● Lamezia Rosso Ris. '02	YY	5

Librandi

loc. San Gennaro
s.s. Jonica 106
88811 Cirò Marina [KR]
tel. 096231518
www.librandi.it

ANNUAL PRODUCTION 2,200,000 bottles
HECTARES UNDER VINE 232
VITICULTURE METHOD Conventional

When you work with a dream team of winemakers, viticulturists and researchers, you can be sure that results will come. Over the last decade, Tonino and Nicodemo Librandi have had the services of Mario Fregoni, Donato Lanati, Anna Schneider, Franco Mannini and Andrea Paoletti, who have practically made over the estate. As Nicodemo often says, to be great an estate must always put its terrain and its grape varieties first. He has ensured that this axiom has guided all their labours. There have been endless selections of plants and clones, numerous trial plots, and hundreds of microvinifications, all aimed at identifying the best clones of the indigenous gaglioppo, mantonico, magliocco, greco and arvino. So it's no coincidence that a Cirò, Duca San Felice Riserva '05, has earned Three Glasses for the very first time. The nose is clear cut, brimming with red berry fruit and spice leading into an elegantly succulent, tight-knit palate. Gravello '06, a powerful yet stylish blend of gaglioppo and cabernet, reached the finals, as did the white Efeso '07, which gives minerality and scents of the Mediterranean. But the whole range here is excellent.

● Cirò Rosso Cl. Duca Sanfelice Ris. '05	🍷🍷🍷	4*
○ Efeso '07	🍷🍷	5
● Gravello '06	🍷🍷	6
○ Critone '07	🍷🍷	4*
○ Le Passule '06	🍷🍷	6
● Magno Megonio '06	🍷🍷	5
○ Cirò Bianco '07	🍷	3
⊙ Cirò Rosato '07	🍷	3
● Cirò Rosso Cl. '07	🍷	3
○ Melissa Asylia Bianco '07	🍷	4
● Melissa Asylia Rosso '07	🍷	4
● Gravello '98	YYY	5
● Gravello '05	YYY	5
● Magno Megonio '05	YY	5

G.B. Odoardi

C.DA CAMPODORATO
88047 NOCERA TERINESE [CZ]
TEL. 098429961
odoardi@tin.it

ANNUAL PRODUCTION 300,000 bottles
HECTARES UNDER VINE 95
VITICULTURE METHOD Conventional

Yet again the quality of doctor-wine producer Gregorio Odoardi's wines is reassuringly high. Sadly, he didn't hit gold this year but passion and determination, no matter how strong, don't always suffice when the vintage is a tricky one. Vigna Garrone '05 didn't get further than the finals. Good as it is, it lacks the touch of definition and complexity needed for a Three Glass wine. Vigna Mortilla '05 was another finalist, showing close-knit and juicy with powerful, vibrant fruitiness held in place by a full yet elegant tannic framework. The super-concentrated Polpicello '05 is broad and stylish on the nose and has a well-defined, fleshy, invigorating palate nicely balanced between lively acidity and good fruit. Intense, fruity and with excellently judged oaking, Savuto '06 is not just a highly drinkable prospect but fabulous value for money. Scavigna Bianco '07 is supple and zesty, proffering white-fleshed fruit and aromatic herbs. Odoardi's other white, Pian della Corte '07, is floral and peachy, and has a fresh, mineral palate. Scavigna Rosato '07 is enjoyably easy drinking.

Senatore Vini

LOC. SAN LORENZO
88811 CIRÒ MARINA [KR]
TEL. 096232350
www.senatorevini.com

ANNUAL PRODUCTION 250,000 bottles
HECTARES UNDER VINE 27
VITICULTURE METHOD Conventional

A highly impressive range of wines brings the Senatore family a well-deserved first appearance in the Guide. The estate, which was founded at the start of the last century, comprises four holdings, all in the Cirò DOC area for a total of 27 hectares under vine. One factor distinguishing all the wines submitted was that, although they had a decidedly modern slant, they were well anchored in their terroir and clearly reflected the varieties used. The lively, well-structured, fruity Arcano '06 has aromas of blackberry and cherry, and a richly fruity, succulent palate where tight-knit yet ripe tannins meld well with the alcohol. It is first rate, as is the barrique-aged Bordeaux blend Ethos '06, a concentrated, stylish wine whose forest fruits-like aromas of blackberry and blueberry are shot through with a swath of balsam, and whose long, fleshy palate flaunts clearly defined, elegant tannins. The two whites submitted also showed well, especially Alalei '07, which is varietal, well-structured and has an almondy finish. Silò '06, made from greco and chardonnay, is floral and savoury.

● Savuto Sup. V. Mortilla '05	🍷🍷 5
● Scavigna Vigna Garrone '05	🍷🍷 6
● Savuto '06	🍷🍷 4*
● Scavigna Polpicello '05	🍷🍷 7
○ Scavigna Bianco '07	🍷 4
○ Scavigna Pian della Corte '07	🍷 4
⊙ Scavigna Rosato '07	🍷 3
● Scavigna Vigna Garrone '99	🍷🍷🍷 8
● Scavigna Vigna Garrone '04	🍷🍷🍷 6
● Scavigna Vigna Garrone '03	🍷🍷🍷 6
● Savuto Sup. V. Mortilla '04	🍷🍷 5
● Scavigna Polpicello '03	🍷🍷 7
● Scavigna Polpicello '02	🍷🍷 7
● Scavigna Polpicello '01	🍷🍷 7
● Savuto Sup. V. Mortilla '03	🍷🍷 5

● Cirò Rosso Cl. Arcano '06	🍷🍷 4*
● Ethos '06	🍷🍷 4*
○ Cirò Bianco Alalei '07	🍷 4
⊙ Cirò Rosato Puntalice '07	🍷 4
● Gaglioppo Merlot '06	🍷 4
○ Silò '06	🍷 4

Serracavallo

C.DA SERRACAVALLO
87043 COSENZA
TEL. 098421144
www.viniserracavallo.it

ANNUAL PRODUCTION	41,000 bottles
HECTARES UNDER VINE	25
VITICULTURE METHOD	Conventional

Until about a decade ago, the Stancati family, like many others in Calabria, did not really make the most of the viticultural or commercial possibilities of its estate. Indeed, most of the wine was sold in bulk or passed to other wineries. Then, in the middle of the 1990s, Demetrio, a doctor with an irrepressible passion for making wine, started to make radical changes. He increased the area under vine and expanded the cellar area, equipping it with everything necessary for modern vinification techniques. As a result, from the first appearance of the Serracavallo label, the wines have been distinguished by their modern, elegant styling. Terraccia '06, from magliocco, a wine of considerable power and complexity, reached the final taste-offs. Forest fruit aromas are followed by balsam, coffee and well-integrated oak. The long palate is lively despite its weighty structure, and harmonizes perfectly with the nose. But Sette Chiese '07, from magliocco and cabernet, was not quite as good as expected, probably because of the unprepossessing vintage.

Statti

C.DA LENTI
88046 LAMEZIA TERME [CZ]
TEL. 0968456138
www.statti.com

ANNUAL PRODUCTION	300,000 bottles
HECTARES UNDER VINE	55
VITICULTURE METHOD	Conventional

The Statti siblings own one of the largest, most attractive estates in the region. Although they have been vinifying some wine for ever, it is only in the last five years that they have plunged into full-time winemaking, with the declared aim of boosting their quality profile. And again this year our tastings confirm the trend towards improved quality across the board. Arvino '06, a gaglioppo and cabernet blend, came within an ace of the finals, its nose rendered dense and elegant by oakiness that supports and enhances its fruit. Cauro '06, from gaglioppo, magliocco and cabernet, is equally admirable, warm notes of black berry fruit, coffee and spices leading to a long, tannic palate. The '07 Nosside, from naturally dried mantonico and greco grapes, has also made strides. It's a pleasingly concentrated wine, full of citrus notes, most notably tangerine, kumquat and orange blossom, and its sweetness is well tempered by refreshing acidity. Best of the One Glass wines is I Gelsi Rosso '07, from merlot, cabernet and gaglioppo. Black berry fruit with hints of balsam and tobacco is followed by a well-structured, long palate.

● Terraccia '06	♟♟ 5
● Sette Chiese '07	♟ 4
● Terraccia '04	♟♟ 5
● Terraccia '03	♟♟ 5
● Sette Chiese '05	♟♟ 4*
● Terraccia '02	♟♟ 5

● Arvino '06	♟♟ 4*
● Cauro '06	♟♟ 5
○ Nosside '07	♟♟ 5
● Gaglioppo '07	♟ 3
○ I Gelsi Bianco '07	♟ 2
● I Gelsi Rosso '07	♟ 2
○ Lamezia Bianco '07	♟ 3
○ Lamezia Greco '07	♟ 4
⊙ Lamezia Rosato '07	♟ 3
● Lamezia Rosso '07	♟ 3
○ Mantonico '07	♟ 4
○ Nosside '05	♟♟ 5
● Arvino '05	♟♟ 4*
● Arvino '04	♟♟ 3*
● Cauro '05	♟♟ 5
○ Mantonico '06	♟♟ 4

Tenuta Terre Nobili

LOC. MONTALTO UFFUGO
C.DA CARIGLIALTO
87046 COSENZA
TEL. 0984934005
lidia.matera@libero.it

ANNUAL PRODUCTION	22,000 bottles
HECTARES UNDER VINE	15
VITICULTURE METHOD	Certified organic

Following a couple of years of ups and downs, Lidia Matera's wines seem finally to have regained their gloss, to the extent that her winery has now regained a full entry and we can applaud a fine showing throughout. As well as having full charge of the vineyards, all cultivated on organic principles, Lidia has also been looking after vinification for several years now. So all credit to her for the Two Glass success of Cariglio '07, a Nerello Calabrese full of black berry fruit, cherry, spices and balsamic oak, sensations that are perfectly mirrored on the long, lively, intense palate with its invigorating, juicy fruitiness and its framework of tight-knit, smooth tannins. Alarico '07, from 100 per cent magliocco, is also admirable. An elegant, characterful wine, it has aromas of blueberry, blackcurrant and spices, followed by a soft, succulent, long palate well supported by an enlivening swath of acidity. Santa Chiara '07, from greco, sees no oak and is fresh and floral. Rosato Donn'Eleonò '07 comes from nerello and magliocco. It's full of small red berry fruit aromas and has a supple, zesty palate.

● Alarico '07	▼▼	5
● Cariglio '07	▼▼	5
⊙ Donn'Eleonò '07	▼	4
○ Santa Chiara '07	▼	4

Luigi Viola

VIA ROMA, 18
87010 SARACENA [CS]
TEL. 098134071
www.cantineviola.it

ANNUAL PRODUCTION	7,000 bottles
HECTARES UNDER VINE	3
VITICULTURE METHOD	Certified organic

Luigi Viola's tenacity has finally been repaid. The Moscato made at Saracena, almost forgotten until a few years ago, has returned to the limelight, winning not just the long-awaited Three Glasses but the Sweet Wine of the Year award, too. So all Viola's efforts, all his pluck, not to mention his considerable financial outlay, have brought their rewards. Luigi has shown that it really is possible to make your life's dream come true. His patient, determined approach has also lifted the profile of his homeland. Luigi's wine is more than just aromas and flavours; it is the expression of an indissoluble link with an ancient territory that yields power but is not always generous. Congratulations also to Luigi's three children, who have been with him on this venture and kept him going when things were difficult. After a series of steadily improving wines, it was the '07 that cracked it. The nose is complex and elegant, with candied apricot, dried figs and aromatic herbs. The initial impact on the palate is very attractive, the fruit is juicy and vibrant, and everything is held together by a fresh, very long apricot and peach finish.

○ Moscato Passito '07	▼▼▼	7
○ Moscato di Saracena '05	▼▼	7
○ Moscato di Saracena '04	▼▼	7
○ Moscato di Saracena '03	▼▼	6
○ Moscato Passito '06	▼▼	7
○ Moscato di Saracena '01	▼▼	4
○ Moscato di Saracena '00	▼▼	4

OTHER WINERIES

Umberto Ceratti
via degli Uffizi, 5
89030 Caraffa del Bianco [RC]
tel. 0964956008

The renowned Greco di Bianco DOC made by the Ceratti family is consistently excellent. The '05 has a generous, complex nose with lavender, walnutskin and baked dried figs. The palate is fresh, delicately sweet and recalls prickly pear conserve on the finish.

O Greco di Bianco '05	🍷🍷 5
O Mantonico '05	🍷 5
O Greco di Bianco '04	🍷🍷 5

Roberto Ceraudo
loc. Marina di Strongoli
c.da Dattilo
88815 Crotone
tel. 0962865613
www.dattilo.it

The new DoroBe '01, a dried-grape wine from magliocco, is elegant and intense. Grisara '07, from pecorello, is good, its floral nose giving citrus and iodine, and its palate fresh, fleshy and attractively zesty. Dattilo '05, from magliocco, and the magliocco and cabernet sauvignon Petraro '05 are sound.

● DoroBe '01	🍷🍷 8
O Grisara '07	🍷🍷 5
● Dattilo '05	🍷 5
● Petraro '05	🍷 6

Colacino
via A. Guarasci, 5
87054 Rogliano [CS]
tel. 0984961034
www.colacino.it

Colacino, one of the few Savuto DOC producers, debuted well with the first-rate Vigna Colle Barabba '07, fruity on the nose and soft and succulent on the palate. Amazio '07, from magliocco, is attractive, showing lively, fruity, light-bodied and supple. Quarto '07, from pecorello and malvasia, is good.

● Savuto V. Colle Barabba '07	🍷🍷 4
● Amazio '07	🍷 4
O Quarto '07	🍷 4
● Savuto Sup. Britto '05	🍷 5

Feudo dei Sanseverino
via Vittorio Emanuele, 110
87010 Saracena [CS]
tel. 098121461
www.feudodeisanseverino.it

This year brings another creditable range from this small co-operative. It's led by the nicely complex Moscato Passito '03, which has a nose of candied fruit, citrus and biscuits, all underlain by balsam, and a long, fleshy, invigorating palate.

O Moscato Passito al Governo di Saracena '03	🍷🍷 5
● Gaglioppo '06	🍷 4
O Mastro Terenzio '05	🍷 6

Fattorie Greco
via Magenta, 33
87062 Cariati [CS]
tel. 0983969441
www.igreco.it

Things are improving on the Greco siblings' estate. More wines were submitted this year. The fine Tumà '06, from gaglioppo and calabrese, has good intensity and liveliness. Greco Filù '07 is attractively supple and savoury. Overt florality marks out Riticella '07, made from greco and malvasia.

O Greco Filù '07	🍷🍷 3
● Tumà '06	🍷🍷 4
● Gaglioppo Catà '06	🍷 3
O Riticella '07	🍷 4

Ippolito 1845
via Tirone, 118
88811 Cirò Marina [KR]
tel. 096231106
www.ippolito1845.it

It's been an uncertain year for this long-standing winery. Only the new Gemma del Sole '05, an appealing dessert wine from greco bianco, keeps the flag flying although Mori '06, from gaglioppo and cabernet sauvignon, is attractive with a complex nose and a well-structured, tannic palate.

O Gemma Del Sole Passito '05	🍷🍷 5
● Cirò Rosso Cl. Sup. Colli del Mancuso Ris. '05	🍷 4
● Cirò Rosso Cl. Sup. Liber Pater '06	🍷 3
● I Mori '06	🍷 4

OTHER WINERIES

Iuzzolini

LOC. FRASSÀ
88811 CIRÒ MARINA [KR]
TEL. 0962371326
www.tenutaiuzzolini.it

Iuzzolini is in the Guide thanks to a good showing from the concentrated, nicely complex Paternum '06, from magliocco. Maradea '05, a Cirò Riserva, is also good with small red berry fruit aromas and a gentle, juicy palate. The other DOC wines are sound, as is Artino '07, from magliocco and gaglioppo.

● Paternum '06	🍷🍷 8
● Artino '07	🍷 5
● Cirò Maradea Rosso Cl. Sup. Ris. '05	🍷 5
⊙ Cirò Rosato '07	🍷 3

Azienda Vinicola Malaspina

VIA PALLICA, 67
89063 MELITO DI PORTO SALVO [RC]
TEL. 0965781632
www.aziendavinicolamalaspina.com

The four Malaspina sisters make nice wines, mostly from local grapes. Palika '07, from ansonica and greco, is minerally, well structured and clean. Palikos '05, from nerello and gaglioppo, the full-bodied magliocco and cabernet Patros Pietro '05 and Rosaspina '07, from gaglioppo, are all good.

○ Palika '07	🍷 3
● Palikos '05	🍷 3
● Patros Pietro '05	🍷 5
⊙ Rosaspina '07	🍷 3

Malena

LOC. PETRARO
S.S. JONICA 106
88811 CIRÒ MARINA [KR]
TEL. 096231758
www.malena.it

The Malena estate is a small, family-run affair that retains firm links with its roots and traditions. Cutura del Marchese '05, a blend of gaglioppo and cabernet, is a substantial wine with good structure and clean fruit throughout. It's just a pity that it finishes so short.

○ Cirò Bianco '07	🍷 3
● Cirò Rosso Cl. '06	🍷 3
● Cutura del Marchese '05	🍷 6

Fattoria San Francesco

LOC. QUATTROMANI
88813 CIRÒ [KR]
TEL. 096232228
www.fattoriasanfrancesco.it

The wines here again showed well, especially the characterful Fata Morgana '07, from greco bianco, which gives florality, ripe fruit and mineral scents, and a long, savoury palate. Donna Madda '06, made mainly from gaglioppo, is sound, as is the rest of the range.

○ Fata Morgana '07	🍷🍷 5
⊙ Cirò Rosato Cl. Ronco dei Quattroventi '07	🍷 5
● Cirò Rosso '07	🍷 4
● Donna Madda '06	🍷 5

Santa Venere

LOC. TENUTA VOLTAGRANDE
S.P. 04 KM 10,00
88813 CIRÒ [KR]
TEL. 096238519
www.santavenere.com

Santa Venere wines are consistently good and the potential for even better is high. The elegant, intensely complex Vurgadà '07, from nerello, merlot and gaglioppo, is an easy-drinking, enjoyable wine. Cirò Riserva Federico Scala '05 also impresses, its palate dense, tight knit and well structured.

● Cirò Rosso Cl. Sup. Federico Scala Ris. '05	🍷🍷 5
● Vurgadà '07	🍷🍷 4*
⊙ Cirò Rosato '07	🍷 4
● Cirò Rosso Cl. '07	🍷 4

Luigi Scala

LOC. CASALE SAN VINCENZO
88813 CIRÒ [KR]
TEL. 3495029840
cantinascala@tim.it

Luigi Scala keeps his profile in the Guide with a further range of good-quality wines made in a modern style that still reflects the terroir. We liked best the attractively structured, intense, long Briseo '06, from gaglioppo and magliocco. The Ciròs are also worth uncorking.

● Briseo '06	🍷🍷 4*
○ Cirò Bianco '07	🍷 3
⊙ Cirò Rosato '07	🍷 3
● Cirò Rosso Cl. '06	🍷 3

OTHER WINERIES

Stelitano

C.DA PALAZZI, 1
89030 CASIGNANA [RC]
TEL. 0964913023
stelitano@interfree.it

The Stelitano siblings are among the few making the historic Greco di Bianco but this year proved a slight disappointment as the '06 vintage was not of the best. The wine still showed reasonably well, though, with dried and tropical fruits, and enough fresh acidity to support its sweetness.

O Greco di Bianco '06	♀	6
O Mantonico	♀	6

Terre di Balbia

C.DA MONTINO
87042 ALTOMONTE [CS]
TEL. 048161264
www.terredibalbia.it

Terre di Balbia did very respectably. SerraMonte '05, from magliocco, gaglioppo and sangiovese, is tight knit, fleshy and elegant, its oaking perfectly judged. The lively, fruity Balbium '06, from magliocco and gaglioppo, is also elegant. The '06 vintage of Montino 101, from magliocco, is fair.

● Balbium '06	♀♀	4*
● SerraMonte '05	♀♀	7
● Montino 101 '06	♀	5
● SerraMonte '04	♀♀	7

Tramontana

LOC. GALLICO MARINA
VIA CASA SAVOIA, 156
89139 REGGIO CALABRIA
TEL. 0965370067
www.vinitramontana.it

This estate made a good debut. To Crasì '05, from nerello, cabernet and merlot, is an elegant, fruity wine with tight-knit, fine-grained tannins. The '05 1890, a monovarietal Nerello that reflects its provenance, is also nice. Costa Viola '06, from nerello, cabernet and nocera, is lively and fruity.

● To Crasì '05	♀♀	4*
● 1890 '05	♀	6
O Calabria Bianco '07	♀	4
● Costa Viola '06	♀	4

Val di Neto

FRAZ. CORAZZO
VIA DELLE MAGNOLIE
88831 SCANDALE [KR]
TEL. 096254079
www.cantinavaldineto.com

This winery is coming on. Arkè '06, from aglianico, gaglioppo and greco nero, is well structured, elegant and long. The tight-knit, long Mutrò '06, from gaglioppo and greco nero, appeals with its fruity, balsamic nose. The softly structured Amistà '07, a rosé from gaglioppo, is fresh and supple.

● Arkè '06	♀♀	4
● Melissa Rosso Sup. Mutrò '06	♀♀	5
⊙ Amistà '07	♀	4
O Melissa Bianco Lumia '07	♀	4

F.lli Zagarella

VIA ROMA, 2
89121 REGGIO CALABRIA
TEL. 0965679521
www.aziendazagarella.it

This new estate debuted well. Its best bottle is Terragrande '06, from gaglioppo, merlot and cabernet sauvignon, which has red berry fruit and spice. Alfieri Rosso '06, from malvasia nera, is firm and well defined. Alfieri Bianco '07, from malvasia, inzolia and sauvignon blanc, is fruity and aromatic.

● Terragrande '06	♀♀	4
O Alfieri Bianco '07	♀	4
● Alfieri Rosso '06	♀	4

Vinicola Zito

FRAZ. PUNTA ALICE
VIA SCALARETTO
88811 CIRÒ MARINA [KR]
TEL. 096231853
www.zito.it

Every year, this winery submits a range of well-made territorial wines. Take, for example, Cirò Riserva '04, which has a blackcurrant and blackberry jam nose, and a fruity, tannic, fairly long palate. The vibrant Alceo '06 has a deep, inviting nose and lively tannicity.

● Cirò Rosso Cl. Alceo '06	♀♀	2*
● Cirò Rosso Cl. Ris. '04	♀♀	4
⊙ Cirò Rosato Imerio '07	♀	3
● Cirò Rosso Cl. Krimisà '06	♀	4

SICILY

This year's Sicilian wine scenario is exceptional overall, achieving an all-time record for top award-winning wines with 17 Three Glasses. And there is another important distinction in our Award for Sustainable Viticulture, which went to one of Italy's top agronomist-oenologists, Salvo Foti, the driving force behind Etna's recent viticultural revival. So our check-up of the state of the island's winemaking health shows it to be on top form. Of course, results as brilliant are anything but coincidental and let's not forget that this success is the result of far-sighted regional policy that has involved over two decades of research and experimentation. Nor do should we underestimate the contribution of Sicily's entrepreneurs, who are as dynamic as those in other region in Italy, and who have turned round the island's winemaking in just 20 years. Tomasi di Lampedusa's unchanging Leopard is a less appropriate metaphor nowadays for things Sicilian. A look at the list of winners shows that all the island's best terroirs are represented and that the outstanding district is Etna, an area that was virtually unknown a few years ago. We'll start with the volcano and salute the classic Etna Bianco Superiore Pietramarina, whose '04 vintage is as good as any from recent years. Then there is Cottanera's excellent Etna Rosso '05, now an Etna DOC again, and Biondi's alluring Etna Rosso Outis, from a vineyard in a beautiful landscape, as well as the breathtaking Etna Rosso Prephilloxera La Vigna di Don Peppino '06, from Tenuta Terre Nere. From the Peloritani mountains near Etna is another outstanding '06, Faro Palari, now established as a classic Italian wine. Then there is a list of Nero d'Avolas that collected an astonishing ten awards. This red is conspicuously success in all price bands, in Italy and abroad, so here they are: the Settesoli co-operative in Menfi celebrates its half century with its first Three Glasses for an excellent Carthago '06 from the Mandrarossa line; Planeta's classic Santa Cecilia '06; Cusumano's Sagana '06; Firriato's Harmonium '06; Donnafugata's Milleunanotte '05; Tasca d'Almerita's Rosso del Conte '05; Feudo Principi di Butera's Deliella '05; Morgante's Don Antonio '06; Feudo Maccari's Saia '06, earning its first Three Glasses; and Gulfi repeating last year's success but for its Nerosanloré '05. Sicily isn't just Nero d'Avola and other native varieties that delighted us were the sedately elegant Cerasuolo di Vittoria Classico Vigna Para Para '05 produced by the small Poggio di Bortolone family winery, and Tasca d'Almerita's Chardonnay '06. Sheer magic!

Abbazia Santa Anastasia

C.DA SANTA ANASTASIA
90013 CASTELBUONO [PA]
TEL. 091671959
www.abbaziasantanastasia.it

ANNUAL PRODUCTION	650,000 bottles
HECTARES UNDER VINE	62
VITICULTURE METHOD	Certified organic

Francesco Lena manages his admirable winery with a pioneering approach. This lawyer by trade has over 60 hectares of vines at Castelbuono, in the province of Palermo, where he has created a model winery and stylish country hotel in Roger d'Hauteville's 12th-century lodge, a former abbey and now a splendid 300-hectare estate set between the Madonie mountains and the Tyrrhenian sea. Over the years, Sant'Anastasia wines have earned many plaudits but our man still isn't satisfied. Aided by Riccardo Cotarella, he continues to aim for the stars. Francesco recently converted to organic agriculture, complete with certification, and he's now onto the final, most challenging task, which is to make his viticulture fully biodynamic. This year, we tasted wines that are halfway to his intended objective. He is still finding his feet with the new system so the wines lack their usual definition and the stylistic integrity he's spoiled us with, but it's not a huge issue. We're sure this is a transitional phase and that the winery's trophy cupboard will be adding to its tally of Three Glass awards.

Baglio di Pianetto

VIA FRANCIA
90030 SANTA CRISTINA GELA [PA]
TEL. 0918570002
www.bagliodipianetto.com

ANNUAL PRODUCTION	400,000 bottles
HECTARES UNDER VINE	95
VITICULTURE METHOD	Conventional

Paolo Marzotto presented a fine selection of wines from his two, very different Sicilian estates. The main cellars are set in over 90 hectares of vineyards at Pianetto, a hill location about 20 kilometres from Palermo, which processes its own grapes but also does fermentation and ageing for the company's other wines. The other estate is located in Contrada Baroni, in Val di Noto, the homeland of nero d'Avola, where there are plans to bring terrain under vine to over 60 hectares. The Petit Verdot Chianu Carduni '05, from Pianetto grapes grown at 650 metres, strolled into our taste-offs. It's a distinctly layered wine whose secret is in the fruit. Balsamic on the nose, it's well-structured on the palate with a long, coherent finale. Then there's a fresh firm-bodied Moscato di Noto Ra'is '07 that shows sweet but not cloying and whose complex bouquet is a sequence of floral, citrus and mineral nuances. We'd also mention a very drinkable, satisfying Nero d'Avola '05 for its refined cherry and blackberry notes.

● Litra '06	♟♟	7
● Sens(i)nverso Nero d'Avola '06	♟♟	6
○ Contempo Grillo '07	♟♟	3*
● Montenero '06	♟♟	5
○ Baccante '07	♟	5
● Contempo Nerello Mascalese '07	♟	3
● Contempo Nero d'Avola '07	♟	3
○ Gemelli '07	♟	5
○ Inzolia Contempo '07	♟	3
● Passomaggio '06	♟	4
○ Sinestesia '07	♟	4
○ Zurrica '07	♟	4
● Litra '04	♟♟♟	7
● Litra '01	♟♟♟	8
● Litra '00	♟♟♟	7
● Montenero '04	♟♟♟	5

● Chianu Carduni '05	♟♟	7
○ Moscato di Noto Ra'is '07	♟♟	5
● Nero d'Avola '05	♟♟	4*
● Shymer '06	♟♟	4*
○ Ficiligno '07	♟	4
● Piana dei Cembali '05	♟	6
○ Piana del Ginolfo '07	♟	5
● Ramione '04	♟♟♟	4*
● Piana dei Salici '03	♟♟	5
● Nero d'Avola '04	♟♟	4
● Piana dei Salici '04	♟♟	5
● Ramione '03	♟♟	4
● Ramione '02	♟♟	4
● Shymer '05	♟♟	4

Benanti

VIA G. GARIBALDI, 475
95029 VIAGRANDE [CT]
TEL. 0957893438
www.vinicolabenanti.it

ANNUAL PRODUCTION	180,000 bottles
HECTARES UNDER VINE	44
VITICULTURE METHOD	Conventional

Giuseppe Benanti is one of the most brilliant of Sicily's entrepreneurs. His passion for wine and the land was the driving force that created this leading Italian winery with over 40 hectares of vines, half on Mount Etna and the rest around Pachino. Benanti has worked with his sons Salvino and Antonio, and with oenologist Salvo Foti, to achieve the first-rate range of labels offered today, which represent the best of the two prestigious terroirs. The jewel in the crown is the Etna Bianco Superiore Pietramarina, from pure carricante grown at high altitudes in old vineyards on volcanic slopes. We were entranced by the '04 version, a gleaming straw yellow tinged with green that ushers in layers of floral notes, Mediterranean oils and alluring minerality on the nose, followed by an absolutely symmetrical, fresh, refined palate, making it one of Italy's greatest most cellarable whites. The Etna Rosso Serra della Contessa '05 is deep and austere whereas the fleshy, warm, mouthfilling Nero d'Avola Il Drappo '05 comes from the Pachino vineyards. All the monovarietal wines are captivating, as is the rest of the meticulously produced range.

Vini Biondi

C.SO SICILIA, 20
95039 TRECASTAGNI [CT]
TEL. 0957633933
www.vinibiondi.it

ANNUAL PRODUCTION	20,000 bottles
HECTARES UNDER VINE	14
VITICULTURE METHOD	Conventional

Ciro Biondi, an architect with a passion for winemaking, has breathed new life into his family's historic label. The winery was a successful concern in the Etna district from the late 1800s to the 1950s. Ciro brought back into production the old vines in the municipality of Trecastagni, growing at 700-900 metres on the eastern slope of Etna. Wonderful wines come from these superb vines that are anything from 40 to 50 years old. The looks out as far as the sea and can slope by as much as 50 per cent, requiring a rack-rail system to transport the harvest. We awarded a well-deserved Three Glasses to the lovely Etna Rosso Outis '05, an inviting clear garnet red with deep layers of fruit on the nose, interweaving with elegant mineral and oaky notes that enhance the hint of red berries and Mediterranean herbs. The palate is extremely refined, with full, generous structure and fresh velvety progression, nuanced with tannins and closing slowly on fruit notes. Bianco Outis '06 is fruit-driven with medlar aromas to the fore followed by a well-typed savoury palate that signs of unhurriedly.

O Etna Bianco Sup. Pietramarina '04	🍷🍷🍷	7
● Etna Rosso Serra della Contessa '05	🍷🍷	8
● Il Drappo '05	🍷🍷	6
O Etna Bianco Bianco di Caselle '07	🍷🍷	4*
● Lamorèmio '04	🍷🍷	6
● Majora '05	🍷🍷	7
O Minnella Il Monovitigno '07	🍷🍷	6
● Nerello Cappuccio Il Monovitigno '05	🍷🍷	6
● Nerello Mascalese Il Monovitigno '05	🍷🍷	6
O Edelmio '06	🍷	5
O Etna Bianco Sup. Pietramarina '02	🍷🍷🍷	6
● Etna Rosso Serra della Contessa '04	🍷🍷🍷	8
● Il Drappo '04	🍷🍷🍷	6*

● Etna Rosso Outis '05	🍷🍷🍷	6
O Etna Bianco Outis '06	🍷🍷	5
● Etna Rosso Outis '04	🍷🍷	6
● Outis '03	🍷🍷	5
O Gurna Bianco '05	🍷🍷	5

Calatrasi

C.DA PIANO PIRAINO
90040 SAN CIPIRELLO [PA]
TEL. 0918576767
www.calatrasi.it

ANNUAL PRODUCTION   8,000,000 bottles
HECTARES UNDER VINE 2470
VITICULTURE METHOD   Certified organic

The winery's watchword of "conceiving and producing quality wines that merge authentic territories with innovation" accurately describes this massive operation founded in 1980 by Maurizio Miccichè, with his brother Giuseppe. Over the years, it has expanded and now has three large estates in Puglia, Sicily and Tunisia. For wine consumers worldwide, Calatrasi has become synonymous with fresh, drinkable well-made and affordable wines that neatly reflect the three areas of origin, respecting their territorial traits. Success persuaded this doctor turned winemaker to focus more closely on interpreting the tastes of the wine public and keeping consumers happy. The Terre di Ginestra 651 '06, from nero d'Avola and syrah, made it to our finals. It's spicy, balsamic, richly extracted and flaunts a gratifying tannic weave. D'Istinto Bathéos '07, from nero d'Avola and petit verdot, is also on top form, showing harmonious and mouthfilling with delicious morello cherry and blackberry notes on the nose. Solese Badami '06, a Cabernet Franc, is perky and vibrant. The other wines are good.

Cantina Viticoltori Associati Canicattì

C.DA AQUILATA
92024 CANICATTÌ [AG]
TEL. 0922829371
www.viticultoriassociati.it

ANNUAL PRODUCTION   700,000 bottles
HECTARES UNDER VINE 1000
VITICULTURE METHOD   Conventional

The dynamic, admirable Cantina Viticultori di Canicattì continues to target quality and clock up positive results. It's something of a beacon in the often tricky world of co-operative wineries. We can report that again this year the wines are all drinkable, impeccable, lively and balanced with fragrant fruit, and all reflect the corporate philosophy pursued by the far-sighted president, Alfonso Lo Sardo, oenologist Angelo Molito and consultant winemaker Tonino Guzzo. One wine that went to our taste-offs, just missing Three Glasses, was the Scialo '06, an intense nero d'Avola and syrah blend with refined balsamic notes that shows stylish and leisurely. Not far behind was the inky dark Aynat '06, from pure nero d'Avola, with a larger-than-life personality mingling earthiness, red berries and spice notes before the equally enticing palate displays vibrant but velvety tannins. The deliciously subtle Aquilae Syrah '07 is also first class and we liked all the rest of the range, which is great value for money.

● Terre di Ginestra 651 '06	♟♟ 5
● D'Istinto Bathéos '07	♟ 3*
● D'Istinto Syrah '07	♟ 3*
● Solese Badami '06	♟♟ 4*
O Accademia del Sole Viogner '07	♟ 4
O D'Istinto Chardonnay '07	♟ 3
O D'Istinto Grillo '07	♟ 3
O D'Istinto Ljetas Bianco '07	♟ 2
● D'Istinto Nero d'Avola '07	♟ 3
O Passito di Pantelleria '05	♟ 7
O Terre di Ginestra Catarratto '07	♟ 3
● Terre di Ginestra Nero d'Avola '06	♟ 4
● D'Istinto Magnifico Shiraz '06	♟♟ 5
● Terre di Ginestra 651 '04	♟♟ 6

● Scialo '06	♟♟ 4*
● Aquilae Cabernet Sauvignon '07	♟♟ 3*
● Aquilae Syrah '07	♟♟ 3*
● Aynat '06	♟♟ 5
● Calio '07	♟♟ 4*
O Aquilae Catarratto Inzolia '07	♟ 3
O Aquilae Chardonnay '07	♟ 3
O Aquilae Grillo '07	♟ 3
● Aquilae Merlot '07	♟ 3
● Aquilae Nero d'Avola '07	♟ 3
● Aynat '05	♟♟ 5*
● Aynat '04	♟♟ 4*
● Aquilae Cabernet Sauvignon '04	♟♟ 3*
● Aquilae Merlot '06	♟♟ 3
● Scialo '05	♟♟ 4*

COS

s. p. 3 Agate-Chiaramonte, km 14,300
97019 Vittoria [RG]
tel. 0932876145
www.cosvittoria.it

ANNUAL PRODUCTION	160,000 bottles
HECTARES UNDER VINE	25
VITICULTURE METHOD	Natural

Titta Cilia and Giusto Occhipinti have spent almost 30 years tirelessly developing the Vittoria terroir. The latest stage is the creation of a Cerasuolo Trail, which Giusto will preside and which is set to become a new tool for promoting the designation and associated wineries. At home, the couple stick to their philosophy of a natural vineyard and cellar approach. This year, we're delighted by the characterful inzolia and grecanico Ramì '07, with its pleasing wild flower nose over minerality and cool, zesty palate. The Cerasuolo di Vittoria Classico '06 is another nice bottle, totally true to type, showing perfectly mature and agreeable. The fragrant, minerally Frappato '07 has a fresh, stylish palate profile. The austere ripeness of the Nero d'Avola Contrade Labirinto '04 is intense; the Cerasuolo Pithos '07 is a singular wine, drawing character fròm the clay amphorae where it ferments and adding its own ripe fruit. Although a touch green, the Nero d'Avola Nero di Lupo '06 has subtle varietal aromas. Another Nero d'Avola, the Syre '03, may be over-evolved but still intrigued with its mature, slightly oxidized tones.

Cottanera

loc. Iannazzo
s.p. 89
95030 Castiglione di Sicilia [CT]
tel. 0942963601
www.cottanera.it

ANNUAL PRODUCTION	300,000 bottles
HECTARES UNDER VINE	55
VITICULTURE METHOD	Conventional

After five years out in the cold, the Cambria brothers' winery is back at the top, earning Three Glasses for its elegant nerello mascalese and nerello cappuccino '05 Etna Rosso. The typical garnet-nuanced ruby, with distinct ripe fruit aromas and layered minerality, offers pure symmetry on its firm, complex, well-structured palate, supported by dense, silky tannins. L'Ardenza '06, a monovarietal from Haute Savoie mondeuse vines now perfectly at home on Etna, also strolled into our taste-offs. The enticing deep ruby colour precedes purple and the red berries on the generous nose interweaving nicely with hints of balsam and spice. This chewy, well-structured wine is underpinned by an elegant weave of tannins. The other wine to make the finals was the Grammonte '06, a deep, almost inky, ruby Merlot with purple tinges that presents intense on the nose, where the fruit aromas mingle with cool, stylish vegetal nuances. The tangy palate is layered and well-structured, gliding into a gentle, lingering finish. All the other wines are very good.

● Cerasuolo di Vittoria Classico '06	♙♙ 5
● Contrade Labirinto '04	♙♙ 8
● Frappato '07	♙♙ 4*
O Ramì '07	♙♙ 4*
● Cerasuolo di Vittoria Pithos '07	♙ 5
● Nero di Lupo '06	♙ 4
● Syre '03	♙ 6
● Contrade Labirinto '01	♙♙ 8
● Cerasuolo di Vittoria '05	♙♙ 4
● Cerasuolo di Vittoria Pithos '05	♙♙ 5
● Cerasuolo di Vittoria Venticinquesima Vendemmia '04	♙♙ 4
● Pojo di Lupo '05	♙♙ 4
● Pojo di Lupo '04	♙♙ 4
● Scyri '00	♙♙ 6

● Etna Rosso '05	♙♙♙ 6
● Grammonte '06	♙♙ 5
● L'Ardenza '06	♙♙ 5
● Fatagione '06	♙♙ 5
● Sole di Sesta '06	♙♙ 5
O Barbazzale Bianco '07	♙ 3*
● Barbazzale Rosso '07	♙ 3*
● Fatagione '05	♙♙ 5
● Fatagione '04	♙♙ 5
● L'Ardenza '05	♙♙ 5
● L'Ardenza '04	♙♙ 6
● Grammonte '05	♙♙ 5
● Grammonte '04	♙♙ 6
● Sole di Sesta '05	♙♙ 5
● Sole di Sesta '04	♙♙ 6

★ Cusumano

C.DA SAN CARLO S.S. 113
90047 PARTINICO [PA]
TEL. 0918903456
www.cusumano.it

Marco De Bartoli

C.DA FORNARA SAMPERI, 292
91025 MARSALA [TP]
TEL. 0923962093
www.marcodebartoli.com

ANNUAL PRODUCTION	2,500,000 bottles
HECTARES UNDER VINE	450
VITICULTURE METHOD	Conventional

Alberto and Diego Cusumano's winery is permeated by contemporary spirit, traits, trends and tastes. As it continues its evolution into one of Sicily's best wine producers, its dynamic, youthful fervour infects consumers who appreciate the modern outlook and attractive prices of the fresh, fragrant wines, all made with an eye on the terroir where they originate, and all embodying local traits. We might say that through their products the Cusumanos have updated what is now more or less their corporate motto: "Simplicity, Mediterranean modernity, elegance". This year, we put the Sàgana '06 Nero d'Avola from the Butera vineyard back on the Three Glass podium because it's a subtle, profound, beautifully balanced wine with distinct notes of red berries, spice, earth and pencil lead. Not that the intense Noà '06 nero d'Avola, cabernet sauvignon and merlot blend is any less good, with its incredibly opulent nose and palate. Also excellent, and worthy of their place in taste-offs, are the delicious Benuara '07 nero d'Avola and syrah blend, a bright inzolia Cubìa '07 and the zesty, minerally Angimbé '07, from inzolia and chardonnay.

ANNUAL PRODUCTION	100,000 bottles
HECTARES UNDER VINE	30
VITICULTURE METHOD	Conventional

Sicily's astonishing recent upsurge is due to people like Marco De Bartoli, who challenged old clichés and took their courage in their hands, often paying for mistakes in person. Luckily, Marco made no mistakes or perhaps it would be more precise to say that over the last two decades, decisions that looked risky in a context where most settled for average wines, actually turned out to be trump cards. De Bartoli was one of the figures, possibly the leader, of the Marsala and Pantelleria dessert wine renaissance. He now boasts a series of high-profile labels whose best wines come from these two territories. The Marsala Superiore Oro Dry Vigna La Miccia has redefined the standard for the type, which has two outstanding labels in Superiore Riserva 10 anni and Vecchio Samperi, although this isn't a DOC Marsala. The Passito di Pantelleria Bukkuram '05 is one of the best ever versions of this type and hot on its heels are the Passito di Pantelleria '05 and the Pietranera '07, both from zibibbo only. Grappoli del Grillo '07 is one of this year's most interesting whites and we also liked the Moscato di Sicilia, a sweet wine from raisined grapes.

● Sàgana '06	♟♟♟ 5	○ Marsala Sup. Ris. 10 Anni	♟♟ 7
○ Angimbé '07	♟ 4*	○ Passito di Pantelleria Bukkuram '05	♟♟ 7
● Benuara '07	♟♟ 4*	○ Vecchio Samperi Ventennale	♟♟ 7
○ Cubìa '07	♟♟ 4*	○ Grappoli del Grillo '07	♟♟♟ 5
● Noà '06	♟♟ 5	○ Marsala Sup. Oro Dry V. La Miccia	♟♟ 7
○ Jalé '07	♟♟ 5	○ Passito di Pantelleria '05	♟♟ 6
● Merlot '07	♟♟ 5	○ Pietranera '07	♟♟ 4*
● Nero d'Avola '07	♟♟ 3*	○ Moscato di Sicilia	♟ 3
● Syrah '07	♟♟ 3*	○ Marsala Sup. 10 Anni	♟♟♟ 7
○ Alcamo Bianco '07	♟ 3	○ Grappoli del Grillo '05	♟♟ 5
○ Inzolia '07	♟ 3	○ Passito di Pantelleria Bukkuram '99	♟♟ 7
⊙ Rosato '07	♟ 3	○ Passito di Pantelleria Bukkuram '03	♟♟ 8
● Noà '05	♟♟♟ 5		
● Sàgana '05	♟♟♟ 5		
● Sàgana '04	♟♟♟ 5		

Donnafugata

VIA SEBASTIANO LIPARI, 18
91025 MARSALA [TP]
TEL. 0923724200
www.donnafugata.it

ANNUAL PRODUCTION	2.750,000 bottles
HECTARES UNDER VINE	328
VITICULTURE METHOD	Conventional

Donnafugata may have over 300 hectares under vine and produce almost 3,000,000 bottles but it's still a family winery. Giacomo Rallo began developing this part of his family business in the 1980s, assisted by his wife Gabriella and sons, Antonio and José, to create one of the brightest stars in the Italian wine firmament. The vast range is from three estates at Marsala, Contessa Entellina and Pantelleria, and every label is excellent, thanks in no small measure to consultant oenologist, Stefano Valla. Once again this year, the winery's celebrated Mille e una Notte Nero d'Avola left us in no doubt and grabbed yet another Three Glasses. The '05 is a stylish red of unique concentration, showing fruit-rich, profound and layered with complex balsamic Mediterranean notes, as well as refined tannins. The Ben Ryé '07, a sensual Passito di Pantelleria, also deserves an accolade for its concentrated apricot and aromatic herbs, and honey-sweet, balanced palate. The Tancredi nero d'Avola and cabernet sauvignon blend is excellent but you could say the same of all the other Donnafugata labels.

● Contessa Entellina Milleunanotte '05	♟♟♟	8
● Contessa Entellina Tancredi '06	♟♟	5
○ Passito di Pantelleria Ben Ryé '07	♟♟	8
● Angheli '06	♟♟	5
○ Contessa Entellina Chardonnay La Fuga '07	♟♟	4*
○ Contessa Entellina Chiarandà '06	♟♟	6
○ Contessa Entellina V. di Gabri '07	♟	4
○ Lighea '07	♟	4
● Sedàra '07	♟	4
● Contessa Entellina Milleunanotte '04	♟♟♟	7
● Contessa Entellina Milleunanotte '03	♟♟♟	7
● Contessa Entellina Milleunanotte '02	♟♟♟	7
● Contessa Entellina Milleunanotte '01	♟♟♟	7
● Contessa Entellina Milleunanotte '00	♟♟♟	7
○ Passito di Pantelleria Ben Ryé '06	♟♟♟	7

Duca di Salaparuta - Vini Corvo

VIA NAZIONALE S.S. 113
90014 CASTELDACCIA [PA]
TEL. 091945201
www.duca.it

ANNUAL PRODUCTION	10,000,000 bottles
HECTARES UNDER VINE	139
VITICULTURE METHOD	Conventional

This august Sicilian winery's manager, Carlo Casavecchia, thinks the renowned Duca Enrico isn't quite ready for the market and has decided to hang on to it for another year. While we wait for the '05 star wine to emerge from the new ageing cellar at Casteldaccia, we can console ourselves with what is probably the best-ever version of the Bianca di Valguarnera. We found the '06 vintage of this pure Inzolia to be unbelievably fresh on the nose and palate, thanks to measured use of oak. The fruit is generous and vibrant. The Vajasindi Làvico '05, deep ruby with garnet nuances, is from nerello mascalese with a hint of merlot and throws a nose of spiciness and forest berries before finishing long and austere. The easy-drinking Grillo Kados '07 knocked us off our feet with hints of yellow-fleshed fruit and minerality leading to a supple, zesty palate that signs off nicely with fresh almonds. The other wines we sampled were all enjoyable and, as usual, easy on the wallet.

○ Bianca di Valguarnera '06	♟♟	6
○ Kados '07	♟♟	4*
● Lavico Tenuta Vajasindi '05	♟♟	4*
○ Colomba Platino '07	♟	4
○ Corvo Bianco '07	♟	4
○ Corvo Glicine '07	♟	4
☉ Corvo Rosa '07	♟	4
● Corvo Rosso '06	♟	4
● Corvo Sciaranera '07	♟	4
● Passo delle Mule '06	♟	4
● Triskelè '05	♟	5
● Duca Enrico '03	♟♟♟	7
● Duca Enrico '01	♟♟♟	7

Feudo Maccari

C.DA MACCARI
S. P. PACHINO-NOTO, KM 13,50
96017 NOTO [SR]
TEL. 0931596894
www.feudomaccari.it

ANNUAL PRODUCTION	186,000 bottles
HECTARES UNDER VINE	50
VITICULTURE METHOD	Natural

Antonio Moretti has made a huge commitment to his successful Sicilian winery. As we remember, he had to battle with 70 title deeds to re-assemble the property in its original proportions. Not to mention his long, stubborn recovery of the old bush-trained vines, a system he also preferred for new plantings, despite the size of the winery, which makes it a costly option. Now at long last, Moretti can enjoy the fruits of his dogged toil and after last year's good results, he earned Three Glasses for his elegant Saia '06 Nero d'Avola with its generous, complex nose that opens with the terroir's salt-tinged, mineral nuances before quickly rolling out lively, fresh hints of forest fruits like blackberries, currants and blueberries that become cherry-like on the palate and close with a waft of cigar tobacco. The luscious, richly extracted palate is complex and lingering. In almost a repeat performance, the sun-drenched nero d'Avola, cabernet and syrah Mahâris '06 has intense fruit ushering in firm structure on a palate that retains all its finesse.

Feudo Principi di Butera

C.DA DELIELLA
91033 BUTERA [CL]
TEL. 0934347726
www.feudobutera.it

ANNUAL PRODUCTION	600,000 bottles
HECTARES UNDER VINE	180
VITICULTURE METHOD	Conventional

In wine, as in life, waiting is a dying art. That's bad news, because we miss out on lots of pleasant surprises. So hats off to Gianni Zonin, who paid homage to patience with his Deliella '05, the top Nero d'Avola from his splendid Riesi estate. He left the wine to age longer in bottle and ensured this great red unequalled grace, enhancing its depth and Mediterranean personality. Nose and palate match to perfection and it opens with authority, revealing a silky, compact texture and entrancing length. The Three Glasses are totally deserved and we're in no doubt that the other vineyard selections will be equally gratifying in the future. The excellent Syrah '06 comes with a good cherry preserve aroma, as well as hints of liquorice and a long balsamic note. The ripe, warm Riesi '06, from nero d'Avola with 30 per cent syrah, has the same soft, round palate as the Nero d'Avola '06, and a well-defined varietal nose. The soft, sensual Chardonnay '07 is tinged with dried herb and blossom aromas. Finally, the Insolia '07 is zesty and two other 2006 reds, the Cabernet Sauvignon and the Merlot, are slightly overripe.

● Saia '06	▼▼▼ 5
● Mahâris '06	▼▼ 7
● ReNoto '07	▼▼ 4*
● Mahâris '05	♉♉ 6
● Saia '05	♉♉ 5
● ReNoto '06	♉♉ 4*
● ReNoto '05	♉♉ 4*
● Saia '04	♉♉ 5

● Deliella '05	▼▼▼ 7
● Nero d'Avola '06	▼▼ 4
● Riesi '06	▼▼ 4
● Syrah '06	▼▼ 4
● Cabernet Sauvignon '06	▼ 4
O Chardonnay '07	▼ 4
O Insolia '07	▼ 4
● Merlot '06	▼ 4
● Deliella '02	♉♉♉ 8
● Deliella '00	♉♉♉ 6
O Chardonnay '06	♉♉ 4*
● Nero d'Avola '05	♉♉ 4
● Riesi '05	♉♉ 4*
● Syrah '05	♉♉ 4

Firriato

VIA TRAPANI, 4
91027 PACECO [TP]
TEL. 0923882755
www.firriato.it

ANNUAL PRODUCTION　4,700,000 bottles
HECTARES UNDER VINE　200
VITICULTURE METHOD　Conventional

Vinzia and Salvatore Di Gaetano, the owners of this winery, which became an icon of Sicilian viticulture in just a few years, say that their "products are successful on the international market because they are acknowledged expressions of an ecologically healthy terroir that is above all fertile and thriving". The ingredients of their success, apart from the island's sun and winds, also include total respect for the land in a perspective of healthy, sustainable agriculture, which comes through in the quality of all the wines produced, whether certified or uncertified organic. This year's Three Glasses went to an acknowledged classic, the excellent, firmly structured Harmonium '06, a monovarietal from nero d'Avola, Sicily's quintessential grape. It's a minerally, profound, generous and very drinkable wine. Equally good is the Ribeca '06 nero d'Avola and perricone blend, which is intense, fruit-driven, balsamic and deliciously tannic. The elegant Quater Rosso '06, a blend of nero d'Avola, perricone, frappato and nerello cappuccio, is warm and pervasive. The rest of the range is modern and enjoyable.

Cantine Florio

VIA VINCENZO FLORIO, 1
91025 MARSALA [TP]
TEL. 0923781111
www.cantineflorio.it

ANNUAL PRODUCTION　3,500,000 bottles
HECTARES UNDER VINE　N.A.
VITICULTURE METHOD　Conventional

Florio is a unique label that evokes the Belle Époque saga of Sicily's most admired family, plunging us into a world of Art Nouveau, princes, kings and elegant femmes fatales, the first being none other than the splendid Donna Franca, whose portrait can be seen in Palermo. Florio's lovely old cellars were built in 1832, in the so-called British style of the time, with pointed arches and tufa-based "battuto" floors. Recently and thoughtfully restored, they are a popular stop for wine tourists. And the wines? A superb monovarietal grillo-based Vergine Baglio Florio '97, with a lovely deep, gleaming amber hue and an austere, aristocratic nose nuanced with walnutskin, liquorice and honey, reveals a stunningly fresh, vibrant palate. Then there's the refined malvasia and corinto nero Lipari Passito '07. This cool, poised wine is perhaps the best version ever, interweaving apricot, orange blossom and Mediterranean herbs. Both wines deserved their place at the taste-offs and just missed Three Glasses. The rest of the range is also excellent.

● Harmonium '06	♛♛♛	5*
● Quater Rosso '06	♛♛	5
● Ribeca '06	♛♛	6
○ Altavilla della Corte Grillo '07	♛♛	3*
● Altavilla della Corte Rosso '06	♛♛	4*
● Camelot '06	♛♛	7
○ Chiaramonte Ansonica '07	♛♛	4*
● Chiaramonte Nero d'Avola '06	♛♛	4*
○ Quater Bianco '07	♛♛	5
● Sant'Agostino Rosso Baglio Soria'06	♛♛	5
○ Sant'Agostino Bianco Baglio Soria'07	♛♛	5
● Camelot '01	♛♛♛	7
● Harmonium '03	♛♛♛	5
● Harmonium '02	♛♛♛	6
● Quater Rosso '05	♛♛♛	5

○ Malvasia delle Lipari Passito '07	♛♛	7
○ Marsala Vergine Baglio Florio '97	♛♛	6
○ Marsala Targa 1840 Ris. '99	♛♛	5
○ Marsala Terre Arse '99	♛♛	5
○ Grecale Vino Liquoroso	♛	4
○ Morsi di Luce '06	♛	5
○ Passito di Pantelleria '06	♛	6
○ Marsala Vergine Baglio Florio '94	♛♛	6
○ Marsala Vergine Baglio Florio '90	♛♛	6
○ Malvasia delle Lipari Passito '06	♛♛	6
○ Marsala Sup. Donna Franca Ris.	♛♛	6
○ Marsala Sup. Targa 1840 Ris. '98	♛♛	4
○ Passito di Pantelleria '05	♛♛	6
○ Passito di Pantelleria '04	♛♛	6

Gulfi

C.DA PARTÌA
97010 CHIARAMONTE GULFI [RG]
TEL. 0932921654
www.gulfi.it

ANNUAL PRODUCTION	180,000 bottles
HECTARES UNDER VINE	75
VITICULTURE METHOD	Certified organic

Vito Catania inherited a family tradition and despite being involved in other business interests, he made good use of his passion for wine and vine by setting up a successful winery. Gulfi is named after Chiaramonte Gulfi, east Sicily's balcony in Val Canziria. In little over a decade, Vito and his oenologist, Salvo Foti, have planted a large number of vines around a charming farmhouse, ensuring the best aspect for all of them. Cerasuolo di Vittoria terroir couldn't satisfy Catania's passion for Nero d'Avola so he bought some excellent vineyards at Pachino, the famous vine's area of origin. Applying a textbook density of more than 8,000 vines per hectare, he obtains first-rate wines from his 75 hectares, with the Nerosanloré '05 at the top of the range. It's a dense red bursting with personality and strength, scented with fruit and sea air, and one of the best Nero d'Avolas to be had. The Neromàccarj '05, also named after a district of Pachino, is hot on its heels. But everything, from the Nerobufaleffj '05 to the more straightforward Cerasuolo di Vittoria '07, each label is worth trying.

Marabino

C.DA BUONIVINI
S.P. ROSOLINI - PACHINO KM 8,5
97017 NOTO [SR]
TEL. 3355284101
www.marabino.it

ANNUAL PRODUCTION	150,000 bottles
HECTARES UNDER VINE	30
VITICULTURE METHOD	Conventional

The winery founded through Nello Messina's passion for the terroir of Noto and Pachino forges on. The nero d'Avola legend was born in these vineyards set on white limestone gleaming under the implacable sun of southern Sicily. This is where moscato bianco yields enticing sweet wines like Moscato di Noto della Torre '07, which went to our taste-offs for its alluring profile of citrus and exotic hints of tropical fruit and sugar cane against a mineral backdrop, unfolding into a smooth, persuasive palate that melds sweetness and acidity. The Don Paolo '06, a blend of nero d'Avola and syrah, is very successful with its intense nose of rich sea breeze and spice notes, echoed on a supple, stylish, lingering structure. The well-typed Eloro Archimede '06, is from bush-trained nero d'Avola vines more than 30 years old. We loved its inviting mineral notes and aristocratic leanness. Another more approachable, single-variety Nero d'Avola is the very toothsome Eloro Don Pasquale '07, which oozes varietal fragrance and freshness. We liked the minerality of the Chardonnay Eureka '07 and the drinkable Nero d'Avola Carmen '07.

● Nerosanloré '05	♟♟♟ 6
○ Carjcanti '06	♟♟ 5
● Neromàccarj '05	♟♟ 6
● Nerobufaleffj '05	♟♟ 6
● Nerojbleo '06	♟♟ 4*
● Reseca '04	♟♟ 6
● Cerasuolo di Vittoria '07	♟ 4
● Nerobaronj '05	♟ 6
● Rossojbleo '07	♟ 4
○ Valcanzjria '07	♟ 4
● Neromàccarj '04	♟♟♟ 6
○ Carjcanti '05	♟♟ 5*
● Nerobufaleffj '04	♟♟ 6
● Nerojbleo '05	♟♟ 4*

○ Moscato di Noto Moscato della Torre '07	♟♟ 6
● Don Paolo '06	♟♟ 5
● Eloro Archimede '06	♟♟ 5
● Eloro Don Pasquale '07	♟♟ 4*
● Carmen '07	♟ 3
○ Eureka '07	♟ 4
⊙ Rosa Nera '07	♟ 4
○ Violetta '07	♟ 3
○ Moscato di Noto Moscato della Torre '06	♟♟ 6
○ Moscato di Noto Moscato della Torre '05	♟♟ 6
● Eloro Archimede '04	♟♟ 5
● Eloro Archimede '03	♟♟ 5

Morgante

C.DA RACALMARE
92020 GROTTE [AG]
TEL. 0922945579
www.morgantevini.it

ANNUAL PRODUCTION	340,000 bottles
HECTARES UNDER VINE	60
VITICULTURE METHOD	Conventional

Don Antonio won its seventh Three Glass prize with the '06, which must make this Sicilian red a classic. In his Agrigento winery, Antonio Morgante, and his sons Carmelo and Giovanni, throw themselves into cultivating 60 hectares of nothing but nero d'Avola, assisted by Riccardo Cotarella. The result is 40,000 bottles of their top wine and another whopping 300,000 of basic Nero d'Avola. What's more, we recommend the '07 version of the standard wine for its gorgeous deep ruby with purple highlights, fruit-led fragrances with Mediterranean scrubland, nuanced with vegetality and spice on the nose, nicely full-bodied palate and smooth drinkability. But the top wine is still Don Antonio, with aromas of flawlessly ripe fruit, impressive layering and stylish use of new oak, presenting close-knit, balanced and rich on nose and palate, where well-honed tannins emerge with masterly finesse. The wine signs off with long oak and fruit notes. Finally, both are excellent value for money.

Palari

LOC. SANTO STEFANO BRIGA
C.DA BARNA
98137 MESSINA
TEL. 090630194
www.palari.it

ANNUAL PRODUCTION	50,000 bottles
HECTARES UNDER VINE	7
VITICULTURE METHOD	Conventional

Salvatore Geraci is an architect who multitasks between his day job and his influential winery. He's partnered by eminent consultant oenologist Professor Donato Lanati and we've come to expect classic wines from him every year. The '06 Faro is again a perfect fusion of nerello mascalese and the highland terroir looking out over Messina and the Strait. Here there are not just the two stars, nerello cappuccio and mascalese, but also old vines of nocera, acitana, tignolino, galatena and calabrese, used in small amounts to achieve blends of sheer finesse and elegance. Geraci's dedication is even more laudable considering that a wine of such ancient traditions was on the verge of extinction just 20 years ago. Today, vines are being planted all over the territory and Salvatore is the recognized master. Returning to the '06, the garnet ruby colour, complex nose of red and black berries, and balsamic notes of Mediterranean scrubland and pencil lead, partner a generous layered fresh palate, with round, gentle tannins. The fruit is thoroughly sound and lingers. The same blend of grapes gives the equally good, value for money Rosso del Soprano '06.

● Don Antonio '06	???	5
● Nero d'Avola '07	??	3*
● Don Antonio '03	???	5
● Don Antonio '02	???	5
● Don Antonio '01	???	5
● Don Antonio '00	???	6
● Don Antonio '99	???	5
● Don Antonio '98	???	5

● Faro Palari '06	???	7
● Rosso del Soprano '06	??	5
● Faro Palari '05	???	7*
● Faro Palari '04	???	8
● Faro Palari '03	???	7
● Faro Palari '02	???	7
● Faro Palari '01	???	7
● Faro Palari '00	???	7
● Faro Palari '98	???	7

Passopisciaro

LOC. PASSOPISCIARO
VIA SANTO SPIRITO
95030 CASTIGLIONE DI SICILIA [CT]
TEL. 0578267110
www.passopisciaro.com

ANNUAL PRODUCTION	39,000 bottles
HECTARES UNDER VINE	29
VITICULTURE METHOD	Conventional

Andrea Franchetti is the first of a new wave of Etna wine aficionados who have realized they are winemakers at heart. Back in 2001, Franchetti laid the foundations of the winery here and after a couple of harvests it became a cult amongst wine fans, just as his Tuscan venture did. Our hero preaches his winemaking credo at Castiglione di Sicilia and at Sarteano, where his policy of quality without compromise is applied to the land and to the cellar, with traditional vines and a handful of international grapes involved in a healthy dose of experimentation. Passopisciaro '06 is a homage to its terroir and our tasters decided it was Franchetti's most successful wine. This monovarietal Nerello Mascalese is garnet ruby in colour, with an elegant, intense nose of berry and mineral aromas preceding a palate of unusual finesse and length. It just missed Three Glasses. Franchetti '06 is a forceful fruit-driven Petit Verdot that intrigued us with its refined texture but it wasn't quite as expansive and layered as the previous version. The chardonnay-only Guardiola '07 is tangy, fresh and minerally, in other words a typical Etna white.

Carlo Pellegrino

VIA DEL FANTE, 39
91025 MARSALA [TP]
TEL. 0923719911
www.carlopellegrino.it

ANNUAL PRODUCTION	7,500,000 bottles
HECTARES UNDER VINE	150
VITICULTURE METHOD	Conventional

Now approaching 130 years in business, this distinguished Marsala winery reached the taste-offs with two excellent wines, both from the top of the Duca di Castelmonte range. The first is Passito di Pantelleria Nes, from zibibbo or moscato d'Alessandria, which again has sunny charm in the '06 vintage, with an intense, well-defined nose and generosity on the palate. The second is the refined Tripudium '05, a mature, layered red from a blend of nero d'Avola, cabernet sauvignon and syrah, with a coherent, well-structured palate that signs off crisp and long. The Duca di Castelmonte Gibelè '07, a dry zibibbo, is good news with its cool floral and citrus aromas and gratifying zesty palate. The Dinari del Duca line also performed well with the round, lingering Syrah '06 giving intense aromas; a commendable Grillo '07 shows green almonds on the nose and a nicely balanced palate; the fruity Chardonnay '07 has its well-gauged oak; and the varietal Nero d'Avola '06 is well made. From the special wines, we liked the cleanliness of the Marsala Vergine Soleras Dry.

● Franchetti '06	ΨΨ	8
● Passopisciaro '06	ΨΨ	6
○ Guardiola '07	ΨΨ	6
● Passopisciaro '05	ΨΨ	6
● Passopisciaro '04	ΨΨΨ	6
● Passopisciaro '03	ΨΨ	6
● Passopisciaro '01	ΨΨ	6

○ Duca di Castelmonte Passito di Pantelleria Nes '06	ΨΨ	6
● Duca di Castelmonte Tripudium Rosso '05	ΨΨ	5
○ Duca di Castelmonte Dinari del Duca Grillo '07	ΨΨ	4*
● Duca di Castelmonte Dinari del Duca Syrah '06	ΨΨ	4*
○ Marsala Vergine Soleras Dry	ΨΨ	5
○ Duca di Castelmonte Dinari del Duca Chardonnay '07	Ψ	4
● Duca di Castelmonte Dinari del Duca Nero d'Avola '06	Ψ	4
○ Duca di Castelmonte Gibelè '07	Ψ	4
○ Duca di Castelmonte Passito di Pantelleria Liquoroso '07	Ψ	5
○ Passito di Pantelleria Nes '05	ΨΨ	6
● Tripudium '04	ΨΨ	5

★ Planeta

C.DA DISPENSA
92013 MENFI [AG]
TEL. 091327965
www.planeta.it

ANNUAL PRODUCTION	2,200,000 bottles
HECTARES UNDER VINE	390
VITICULTURE METHOD	Conventional

The Planetas surge on. With fortune on their side and the undoubted flair of cousins Alessio, Francesca and Santi, who are in charge, there is much to celebrate. A splendid Santa Cecilia '06, for instance, an opulent nero d'Avola-only red, garnered the 19th Three Glass prize in less than 15 years' business, not a record many other Italian wineries can approach. Planeta is a very solid operation with 390 hectares under vine in the island's best vineyard terrains from Etna to Noto and Agrigento. Production is in excess of 2,200,000 bottles, successfully exported worldwide, with some first-rate wines that include a succulent, sinewy Merlot '06; the Burdese '06 Bordeaux blend has charisma and staying power; the Fiano Cometa '07 is elegant and minerally; the pervasive Syrah '06 gives spice; and the pulpy Chardonnay '07 has oak with international allure.
The second tier wines, all 2007, are also recommended, from the Alastro white, a chardonnay and grecanico blend, La Segreta Bianco and Rosso to the lovely syrah-based Rosé '07. We also mention the fruity Cerasuolo di Vittoria '07 and the tropical notes in Moscato di Noto '07.

Poggio di Bortolone

LOC. ROCCAZZO
VIA BORTOLONE, 19
97010 CHIARAMONTE GULFI [RG]
TEL. 0932921161
www.poggiodibortolone.it

ANNUAL PRODUCTION	80,000 bottles
HECTARES UNDER VINE	15
VITICULTURE METHOD	Conventional

For three centuries, the Cosenza family has owned Poggio di Bortolone, an 80-hectare estate crossed by the Para Para stream. Before the 1980s, the Cosenzas didn't do much winemaking and their main source of revenue was their olive grove. Then Ignazio Cosenza started to modernize the winery, planting new vines and bottling its first Cerasuolo di Vittoria, now a DOCG. Ignazio's son Pierluigi, or Pigi as he's called at home, a recent agronomy degree under his belt, helps to manage the vineyard and the cellars. This is the first time a Cerasuolo di Vittoria has been awarded Three Glasses in the shape of the nero d'Avola and frappato Vigna Para Para '05, its sheer elegance nuanced with intriguing balsamic and mineral notes before the refined, smoothly pervasive palate perfectly reflects its terroir and tradition. The other wines are good too. All have a fine territorial stamp, especially the aristocratic, intense Syrah Addamanera '04. Two more interesting efforts were the fresh, fruity, affordable Cerasuolo Poggio di Bortolone '06, and the elegant Pigi '04 syrah and cabernet sauvignon mix, which signs off long and silky.

● Santa Cecilia '06	♉♉♉	5
○ Chardonnay '07	♉♉	6
○ Cometa '07	♉♉	6
● Merlot '06	♉♉	5
● Burdese '06	♉♉	5
● Cerasuolo di Vittoria '07	♉♉	4*
● La Segreta Rosso '07	♉♉	3*
○ Moscato di Noto '07	♉♉	6
● Syrah '06	♉♉	5
○ Alastro '07	♉	4
○ La Segreta Bianco '07	♉	3
⊙ Rosé '07	♉	4
● Burdese '05	♉♉♉	5*
● Burdese '03	♉♉♉	5
○ Cometa '05	♉♉♉	5
● Merlot '04	♉♉♉	5

● Cerasuolo di Vittoria V. Para Para '05	♉♉♉	5
● Addamanera '04	♉♉	4*
● Cerasuolo di Vittoria Poggio di Bortolone '06	♉♉	4*
● Pigi Rosso '04	♉♉	6
● Sirka Rosso '03	♉♉	5
● Cerasuolo di Vittoria Contessa Costanza '06	♉	4
● Cerasuolo di Vittoria V. Para Para '04	♀♀	5
● Cerasuolo di Vittoria V. Para Para '03	♀♀	5
● Cerasuolo di Vittoria V. Para Para '02	♀♀	5
● Cerasuolo di Vittoria Poggio di Bortolone '05	♀♀	4*
● Kiron '04	♀♀	6

Pupillo

C.DA LA TARGIA
96100 SIRACUSA
TEL. 0931494029
www.solacium.it

ANNUAL PRODUCTION	125,000 bottles
HECTARES UNDER VINE	24
VITICULTURE METHOD	Conventional

History fills the air at Barone Nino Pupillo's magnificent estate, just outside Siracusa. In the 13th century, Emperor Frederick II actually used to take refuge here, at Solacium castle, when he needed peace, quiet and a bit of hunting. Two striking towers survive from that time, alongside some lesser structures, and now house the winery. However, Pupillo will also leave his mark on history for his 1997 recovery of the more or less abandoned Moscato di Siracusa DOC, of which about half a hectare survived on paper. It took years of trial and error to get there, but he made it, with the support of his daughter Carmela. This year, we were happy to have the moscato bianco-only Solacium '07 in the taste-offs with its sunny golden colour and gentle notes of orange blossom, honey, cinnamon and candied peel. The generous, delicate, lingering palate is the hallmark of a superior wine. Almost as good is the uncomplicated Pollio '07 from moscato bianco, a clean, fresh wine with citrus notes. Confirmation of Pupillo's laudable reliability and continuity is to be found in the zesty, elegant moscato bianco Cyane '0, a mouthfilling, minerally wine.

Cantine Rallo

VIA VINCENZO FLORIO, 2
91025 MARSALA [TP]
TEL. 0923721633
www.cantinerallo.it

ANNUAL PRODUCTION	1,700,000 bottles
HECTARES UNDER VINE	87
VITICULTURE METHOD	Certified organic

Francesco and Andrea Vesco' wine philosophy is, quite simply, to focus on the vineyard. The wines we taste each year offer ample confirmation of the validity of this approach. Even the basic line has a gem in the Grillo '07. It throws a lavish nose of citrus and aromatic herbs, with some upfront aniseed, before the palate nicely offsets freshness with zest. The feisty varietal character of the Nero d'Avola Alaó '05 is expressed in layers of elegant aromas, prominent tannins and a lingering finish. The late-harvest grillo only Aquamadre '07, in its second vintage, expresses clean aromatic notes of pear and tangerine, subtly reprised on the palate. We enjoyed the citrussy notes of the Passito di Pantelleria '06, which gives measured sweetness on a whistle-clean, fresh palate. The Alcamo Carta d'Oro '07 Catarratto is still impeccable for its bright, fragrant fruit and Alcamo Nero d'Avola '07 is equally successful and a pleasure to drink. The other wines are of the usual high standard.

O Moscato di Siracusa Solacium '07	♟♟ 5		● Alaò '05	♟♟ 5
O Cyane '07	♟♟ 4*		O Aquamadre V. T. '07	♟♟ 5
O Moscato di Siracusa Pollio '07	♟♟ 6		O Grillo '07	♟♟ 4*
● Re Federico '07	♟ 4		O Passito di Pantelleria '06	♟♟ 6
O Cyane '06	♟♟ 4*		O Alcamo Carta d'Oro '07	♟ 3
O Cyane '05	♟♟ 4		● Alcamo Nero d'Avola '07	♟ 4
O Cyane '04	♟♟ 4		O Chardonnay '07	♟ 4
O Moscato di Siracusa Pollio '06	♟♟ 6		● Frappato '07	♟ 4
O Moscato di Siracusa Solacium '06	♟♟ 6		O Gruali '06	♟ 5
O Moscato di Siracusa Solacium '05	♟♟ 6		O Müller Thurgau '07	♟ 4
O Moscato di Siracusa Solacium '04	♟♟ 6		● Alcamo Nero d'Avola '06	♟♟ 3*
● Re Federico '04	♟♟ 4		O Aquamadre V. T. '06	♟♟ 5
			● Syrah '06	♟♟ 3

Tenute Rapitalà

C.DA RAPITALÀ
90043 CAMPOREALE [PA]
TEL. 092437233
www.rapitala.it

ANNUAL PRODUCTION	3,400,000 bottles
HECTARES UNDER VINE	175
VITICULTURE METHOD	Conventional

The two main reds from the Gatinais' cellar made the taste-offs, demonstrating the continuity the winery has achieved from its past to its present, under the management of Gigi and Laurent, backed up by the Gruppo Italiano Vini. The close-knit, balsamic Hugonis '05 cabernet sauvignon and nero d'Avola blend has nice chocolate notes and graceful mature fruit. Syrah Solinero '05 has great character, limpid, concentrated aromas and a balanced, lingering structure. The Chardonnay Grand Cru, dedicated to the unforgettable Hugues Bernard, just missed taste-offs so the 2006 vintage has made further progress. Its superb blossom bouquet is lightly veined with the right amount of oak and the palate is luscious and smooth. Nuhar '06, a nero d'Avola and pinot nero blend, continues to fly the flag and has lost none of its intense ripe fruitiness, and signs off cleanly. The grillo and catarratto Piano Maltese Bianco '07 is a fresh, attractive success story and there's a new white. Bouquet '07 is a blend of grillo, sauvignon and viognier that is as good as its name, disclosing a subtle nose and sprightly freshness. The rest of the wines are commendable.

Settesoli

S.S. 115
92013 MENFI [AG]
TEL. 092577111
www.mandrarossa.it

ANNUAL PRODUCTION	20,000,000 bottles
HECTARES UNDER VINE	6500
VITICULTURE METHOD	Conventional

Half a century after its foundation in December 1958, this is a winemaking giant: 2,300 contributing members, 6,500 hectares of vineyards, about 20,000,000 bottles sold annually and turnover exceeding 35,000,000 euros. Our annual tastings suggest laudable average quality and totally reliable production, which can't be faulted technically, in a drinkable contemporary style. These are the excellent results achieved by a far-sighted project that was mapped out years ago by the management of this co-operative winery, inspired by Diego Planeta, its shrewd and dynamic president. Right on cue, Three Glasses were on hand to celebrate the momentous anniversary. The deep, clean Cartagho '06 Nero d'Avola earned out accolade for its luscious chocolate, cherry and nutmeg aromas, smooth, rich palate and lingering polished tannins. Every inch a classy wine. The intense, fruity Bonera '06, a nero d'Avola and cabernet sauvignon blend, is also recommended. We very much enjoyed the elegant Fiano '07, which has subtle citrus and Mediterranean scrubland notes. The rest of the range is interesting and easy on the pocket.

● Hugonis '06	♟♟ 6
● Solinero '06	♟♟ 6
○ Conte Hugues Bernard de la Gatinais Grand Cru '06	♟♟ 5
● Nuhar '06	♟♟ 4*
○ Bouquet '07	♟ 4
● Campo Reale Nero d'Avola '07	♟ 4
○ Casalj '07	♟ 4
○ Cielo d'Alcamo '06	♟ 6
○ Piano Maltese Bianco '07	♟ 4
● Hugonis '01	♟♟♟ 7
● Solinero '03	♟♟♟ 6
● Hugonis '05	♟♟ 6
○ Casalj '06	♟♟ 4
○ Cielo d'Alcamo '05	♟♟ 6
● Solinero '05	♟♟ 6

● Mandrarossa Cartagho '06	♟♟♟ 5
● Bendicò Mandrarossa '06	♟♟ 5
● Bonera Mandrarossa '06	♟♟ 4*
● Cabernet Sauvignon Mandrarossa '07	♟♟ 3*
○ Chardonnay Mandrarossa '07	♟♟ 3*
○ Fiano Mandrarossa '07	♟♟ 3*
○ Furetta Mandrarossa '07	♟♟ 5
○ Grecanico Mandrarossa '07	♟♟ 3*
● Merlot Mandrarossa '07	♟♟ 3*
○ Feudo dei Fiori Mandrarossa '07	♟ 3
● Nero d'Avola Mandrarossa '07	♟ 3
● Syrah Mandrarossa '07	♟ 3*
○ Viogner Mandrarossa '07	♟ 3
● Bonera Mandrarossa '04	♟♟ 4*
● Bendicò Mandrarossa '05	♟♟ 4

Spadafora

VIA AUSONIA, 90
90144 PALERMO
TEL. 091514952
www.spadafora.com

★ Tasca d'Almerita

C.DA REGALEALI
90020 SCLAFANI BAGNI [PA]
TEL. 0916459711
www.tascadalmerita.it

ANNUAL PRODUCTION	260,000 bottles
HECTARES UNDER VINE	100
VITICULTURE METHOD	Conventional

Virzì is a stunning country location and it's the great love of Francesco Spadafora, who opened his winery here 15 years ago. Francesco's energy and commitment have been rewarded with success and his most significant wine is Syrah Sole dei Padri. We voted the 2005 version into taste-offs for its concentrated, intense nose of elegant red berries, spice and beeswax on a balsamic backdrop that ushers in a palate of crisp compact fruit, with smooth upfront tannins and a long, clean finale. This is a great Mediterranean red and we don't think we're sticking our necks out if we predict a great future for it. The Monreale Syrah '07 is far more straightforward, but no less enjoyable for that, with its intense varietal expression and luscious palate. Thumbs up, too, for the Schietto Chardonnay '07, which is fruity and fresh, with well-dosed oak. The zesty, clean aromas of the Schietto Grillo '07 make it appealing. The Don Pietro Bianco '07, a grillo, inzolia and catarratto, blend offers minerality and Mediterranean scrubland. The catarratto and inzolia Monreale Bianco Alhambra '07 is clean and easy drinking.

ANNUAL PRODUCTION	3,000,000 bottles
HECTARES UNDER VINE	460
VITICULTURE METHOD	Conventional

Tasca d'Almerita has been a leading winery for over 30 years but this year's range is unbeatable, with two Three Glass awards to prove it. The Chardonnay was one of the best ever. The '06 is creamy, elegant and concentrated but it's also perfectly balanced, with succulent fruit, and unbelievably easy to drink. It may well be the best so far, by virtue of its upfront varietal traits and perfectly gauged new oak, leading to a long, persuasive finish. Nonetheless, Tasca d'Almerita's star player in recent years has been Rosso del Conte, a mighty red nero d'Avola dedicated to Conte Giuseppe Tasca. The close-knit '05 is deep ruby, with a complex bouquet of well-defined red and black berries fading into light oaky notes of Mediterranean herbs and cedar. The palate is luscious, with a refined, truly symmetrical structure, where the freshness of the fruit is underpinned by acid backbone and ultra-polished tannins. The two champions are flanked by excellent labels like the nero d'Avola and cabernet Cygnus, the Cabernet Sauvignon and the nero d'Avola and merlot Camastra, all 2006 and all extraordinary.

● Sole dei Padri '05	♟♟	7
● Monreale Syrah '07	♟♟	4*
O Schietto Chardonnay '07	♟♟	5
O Schietto Grillo '07	♟♟	4*
O Don Pietro Bianco '07	♟	4
O Monreale Bianco Alhambra '07	♟	3
● Sole dei Padri '04	♟♟	7
● Sole dei Padri '03	♟♟	8
● Sole dei Padri '02	♟♟	8
● Sole dei Padri '01	♟♟	8
● Schietto Syrah '04	♟♟	4
● Schietto Cabernet Sauvignon '05	♟♟	6
● Schietto Cabernet Sauvignon '04	♟♟	6

O Chardonnay '06	♟♟♟	6
● Contea di Sclafani Rosso del Conte '05	♟♟♟	7
● Cabernet Sauvignon '06	♟♟	6
⊙ Almerita Rosé Brut '05	♟♟	6
● Camastra '06	♟♟	5
● Cygnus '06	♟♟	5
O Diamante d'Almerita '07	♟♟	6
● Lamùri '06	♟♟	4
O Regaleali Bianco '07	♟♟	4*
O Tasca d'Almerita Whitaker Grillo '07	♟♟	4
O Contea di Sclafani Nozze d'Oro '07	♟	5
O Leone d'Almerita '07	♟	4
⊙ Regaleali Le Rose '07	♟	4
● Regaleali Nero d'Avola '07	♟	4*
● Contea di Sclafani Rosso del Conte '04	♟♟♟	7

Tenuta delle Terre Nere

C.DA CALDERARA
95036 RANDAZZO [CT]
TEL. 095924002
tenutaterrenere@tiscali.it

ANNUAL PRODUCTION	70,000 bottles
HECTARES UNDER VINE	16
VITICULTURE METHOD	Natural

Marc de Grazia has been involved in the Italian and US wine scenes for years, and he exports some of Italy's most prestigious labels over the Atlantic. A few years back, he was enchanted by the magic of Etna and he set up a winery at Randazzo, recovering old vines and planting new. His approach is to make each vineyard selection according to the various plots where the traditional grapes grow. With his nerello cappuccio and mascalese, and carricante, he has created a range of supremely eminent wines. His 16 hectares under vine produce reds of stunning elegance and complexity, like an Etna Rosso from old vines Prephilloxera La Vigna di Don Peppino '06, which took Three Glasses this year. This stylish, profound wine has extraordinary mineral layers, distinct fruit and subtle, caressing harmonies. There are three more Etna DOCs: the generous, profound and very supple Guardiola '06; a Calderara Sottana '06 with bright notes of red berries and velvety tannins; and the intense, mouthfilling Feudo di Mezzo Quadro delle Rose '06. Finally, Etna Rosato '07 is one of the best rosés in Italy. It's impossible to resist and – sadly – almost impossible to find.

Valle dell'Acate

C.DA BIDINI
97011 ACATE [RG]
TEL. 0932874166
www.valledellacate.it

ANNUAL PRODUCTION	459,000 bottles
HECTARES UNDER VINE	100
VITICULTURE METHOD	Conventional

A few years back, Gaetana Jacono, Tana to her friends, decided to give the family business her best shot. The farm out in the Ragusa countryside produced grew more early produce than grapes so she's to be congratulated for targeting, from her winemaking debut, territory-focused wines like Cerasuolo di Vittoria, currently Sicily's only DOCG. Her other smart intuition was the recovery and promotion of frappato, both productively and commercially. Previously, it had been viewed as a second-tier variety, penalized by trends at the time that demanded full-bodied, structured wine. Her delicious Vittoria Il Frappato '07 continues to distinguish itself for its energy and freshness, making it an enjoyable red for all seasons. But we also noted an excellent performance from the fresh, fruity Cerasuolo di Vittoria '06, a nero d'Avola and frappato blend with gutsy personality. Equally good is the varietal Il Moro '06, a Nero d'Avola with elegant aromas and satisfying harmony on the palate. The Bidis '06, a successful fresh, minerally chardonnay and insolia blend, is a fine balance of structure and acidity.

● Etna Rosso Prephilloxera La V. di Don Peppino '06	▼▼▼ 7
● Etna Rosso Feudo di Mezzo Quadro delle Rose '06	▼▼ 7
● Etna Rosso Guardiola '06	▼▼ 7
☉ Etna Rosato '07	▼▼ 4*
● Etna Rosso Calderara Sottana '06	▼▼ 6
● Etna Rosso Feudo di Mezzo Quadro delle Rose '05	♈♈♈ 7
● Etna Rosso Feudo di Mezzo Quadro delle Rose '04	♈♈♈ 6
● Etna Rosso Calderara Sottana '05	♈♈ 6*
● Etna Rosso Calderara Sottana '04	♈♈ 6
● Etna Rosso Guardiola '05	♈♈ 7
● Etna Rosso Guardiola '04	♈♈ 6

○ Bidis '06	▼▼ 5
● Cerasuolo di Vittoria '06	▼▼ 4
● Il Moro '06	▼▼ 4
● Tanè '05	▼▼ 6
● Vittoria Il Frappato '07	▼▼ 4*
○ Zagra '07	▼▼ 4
● Rusciano '06	▼ 5
○ Vittoria Insolia '07	▼ 3*
● Tanè '04	♈♈ 6
● Tanè '03	♈♈ 6
● Cerasuolo di Vittoria '05	♈♈ 4
● Cerasuolo di Vittoria '03	♈♈ 4
● Il Moro '05	♈♈ 4
● Il Moro '04	♈♈ 4
● Rusciano '05	♈♈ 4

OTHER WINERIES

Tenuta dell'Abate

VIA KENNEDY, 46
93100 CALTANISSETTA
TEL. 0934584188
tenutadellabate@hotmail.com

The stylish Terre del Palco Nero d'Avola '07 has complex aromas, a concentrated palate and signs off long and clean. The Chardonnay '07 has an intense floral nose profile, with fresh zesty fruit. The grassy, inzolia-based Lissandrello '07 is commendable, as is the fruit-led Terre del Palco Grillo Viognier '07.

O Terre del Palco Chardonnay '07	🍷🍷	4
● Terre del Palco Nero d'Avola '07	🍷🍷	4*
O Lissandrello '07	🍷	3
O Terre del Palco Grillo Viognier '07	🍷	4

Abraxas

FRAZ. BUKKURAM
VIA E. ALBANESE, 29
91017 PANTELLERIA [TP]
TEL. 0916116832
www.winesabraxas.com

The selection presented by Abraxas this year is commendable. Passito Abraxas '06 is layered and intense, with a good balance of backbone, fruit and freshness. We were equally happy with the Passito Scirafi, a pure zibibbo, aka moscato d'Alessandria, as are the two well-balanced Kuddias.

O Passito di Pantelleria Abraxas '06	🍷🍷	7
O Passito di Pantelleria Scirafi V. della Fortezza '06	🍷🍷	6
O Kuddia del Gallo '06	🍷	4
O Kuddia delle Ginestre '06	🍷	4

Adragna

VIA REGINA ELENA, 4
91100 TRAPANI
TEL. 092326401
www.classica.it

The stylish Roccagiglio '05 blend of cabernet sauvignon and merlot confirms its superiority, with compact, fresh, lingering fruit. We also like the generous Inzolia '07, which is an admirable combination of fragrance and charm. The impeccable Nero d'Avola '07 is round and vibrant.

O Inzolia '07	🍷🍷	4*
● Roccagiglio '05	🍷🍷	5
● Nero d'Avola '07	🍷	4

AgroArgento

C.DA ANGUILLA
92017 SAMBUCA DI SICILIA [AG]
TEL. 0423860930
www.agroargento.it

The AgroArgento winery, about 60 hectares under vine in the Sambuca di Sicilia countryside, is the brainchild of the Veneto Moretti Polegato and Sicilian Maggio families. We took note of the elegant nero d'Avola, syrah and merlot blend Timoleonte '05, with its cleanliness and impressive backbone.

● Timoleonte '05	🍷🍷	5
O Calancùni '07	🍷	4
● Carrivàli '06	🍷	4

Ajello

C.DA GIUDEO
91025 MAZARA DEL VALLO [TP]
TEL. 091309107
www.ajello.info

This nice Furat '06 blend of nero d'Avola, cabernet sauvignon, merlot and syrah is full and leisurely, with graceful tannins. The winery had some other aces, including a zesty grillo and catarratto Majus Bianco '07, which is cool and agreeable, and the Bizir '07 chardonnay, grillo and inzolia blend.

● Furat '06	🍷🍷	5
O Majus Bianco '07	🍷🍷	4*
O Bizir '07	🍷	5
● Majus Nero d'Avola '06	🍷	4

Alessandro di Camporeale

C.DA MANDRANOVA
90043 CAMPOREALE [PA]
TEL. 092437038
www.alessandrodicamporeale.it

We sent the Syrah Kaid '06 to the taste-offs for its deep aromas of vibrant spice and balsam, followed by crisp, luscious fruit that lingers in the mouth. The fruit and minerals of the Nero d'Avola DonnaTá '07 are right on target and we enjoyed the herbaceous Catarratto Benedè '07.

● Kaid '06	🍷🍷	5
● DonnaTà '07	🍷🍷	4*
O Benedè '07	🍷	4*

OTHER WINERIES

Avide

C.DA MASTRELLA, 346
97013 COMISO [RG]
TEL. 0932967456
www.avide.it

While we wait for the Cerasuolo di Vittoria to mature, there are some excellent 2007 stand-ins from the Hereas. The jolly Syrah is fruit rich, the fragrant Frappato is very drinkable and the fresh Nero d'Avola is true to type. The Vittoria DOC Inzolia Riflessi di Sole '05 is velvety with a delicate mineral note.

● Herea Syrah '07	♥♥	4
○ Vittoria Riflessi di Sole '05	♥♥	5
● Herea Frappato '07	♥	3
● Herea Nero d'Avola '07	♥	3*

Barbera

C.DA TORRENOVA, S.P. 79
92013 MENFI [AG]
TEL. 0925570442
www.cantinebarbera.it

We enjoyed the delicate bouquet and round palate of the Chardonnay Piana del Pozzo '07 and the fleshy, savoury fruit of Menfi Dietro le Case '07 is also to our liking. The merlot, petit verdot and nero d'Avola Coda della Foce '06 lacks last year's focus but is still intense, minerally and fresh.

○ Menfi Chardonnay Piana del Pozzo '07	♥♥	4
● Menfi Coda della Foce '06	♥♥	5
○ Menfi Inzolia Dietro le Case '07	♥♥	4*
● Menfi Azimut '06	♥	4

Vincenzo Bonaccorsi

VIA RE MARTINO, 35
95126 PIEDIMONTE ETNEO [CT]
TEL. 095337134
www.valcerasa.com

The Etna Rosso '05 is excellent. This delicate nerello cappuccio and nerello mascalese blend is a varietal, round and vibrant expression of a weighty territorial wine. On a par is the Etna Bianco '05, from pure carricante. It's a fresh, zesty, mineral wine that is fragrant and intense.

○ Etna Bianco ValCerasa '05	♥♥	4*
● Etna Rosso ValCerasa '05	♥♥	5

Bonavita

LOC. FARO SUPERIORE
C.DA CORSO
98158 MESSINA
TEL. 0902932106
www.bonavitafaro.it

Welcome to this small Messina winery, with just six hectares under vine. Their nerello mascalese, cappuccino and nocera Faro '06 made a good start. It's a complex wine with a plenty of personality, typified by stylish aromas of ripe red berries and brimming with cool minerality.

● Faro '06	♥♥	5

Brugnano

C.DA SAN CARLO - SS 113, KM 307
90047 PARTINICO [PA]
TEL. 0918783360
www.brugnano.it

Antonella Brugnano owns 200 hectares at Castellammare. The easy-drinking Naisi '07, from nero d'Avola and tannat, is fruity with smooth, close-knit tannins. The insolia and viognier blend Kue '07 is a good floral, zesty white. We were intrigued by Honoris Causa '05, a nero d'Avola and syrah blend.

○ Kue '07	♥♥	4*
● Naisi '07	♥♥	4*
● Honoris Causa '05	♥	4

Calabretta

VIA BONAVENTURA, 178
95036 RANDAZZO [CT]
TEL. 0105704857
www.calabretta.net

Venerable bush-trained vines on Etna's north slope, many ungrafted, organic methods and native yeasts all contribute to the lovely hints of liquorice, iron, earth and herbs on the complex nose of the Etna Rosso '99. The palate is long and silky. The '00 is less subtle. Carricante '05 gives pleasing bay leaf.

● Etna Rosso '99	♥♥	5
● Etna Rosso '00	♥♥	5
○ Carricante '05	♥	5
⊙ Etna Rosato '99	♥	5

OTHER WINERIES

Capo Croce - Vini Gancia

C.DA CASTELLAZZO
91027 TRAPANI
TEL. 03489999382
www.gancia.it

The vibrant, generous Addumari '06 is a successful combination of superb cabernet sauvignon and syrah that easily reached our taste-offs. The skills of oenologist Beppe Caviola and agronomist Federico Curtaz are also evident in several other enjoyably concentrated, fresh, fruit-led wines.

● Addumari '06	♟♟	5
● Pulpito '06	♟♟	5
● Nartece '07	♟	4
○ Pulvino '07	♟	4

Caruso & Minini

SALEMI, 3
91025 MARSALA [TP]
TEL. 0923982356
www.carusoeminini.it

We welcome a brilliant debut from this lovely Salemi winery. The syrah, cabernet and nero d'Avola Rosso Riserva '06 is intense and fruity. We also liked the subtle, minerally chardonnay, insolia and catarratto Isula '07, and the Cutaja '06, a syrah, cabernet sauvignon and nero d'Avola mix.

● Delia Novelli		
Terre di Giumara Rosso Ris. '06	♟♟	6
○ Terre di Giumara Isula '07	♟♟	4*
● Terre di Giumara Cutaja '06	♟	4
● Terre di Giumara Syrah '06	♟	4

Castellucci Miano

VIA SICILIA, 1
90029 VALLEDOLMO [PA]
TEL. 0921542385
www.castelluccimiano.it

The wine that ranked best at this year's tasting was the intense, spice-led, lingering Nero d'Avola '06 with its delicious ripe cherry. This dynamic young winery also has other fine products in a range of fragrant, gratifying fruit-led wines of faultless reliability and quality.

● Nero d'Avola '06	♟♟	4*
● Syrah '06	♟♟	4*
○ Catarratto Inzolia '07	♟	4
○ La Masa '07	♟	4

Ceuso

LOC. SEGESTA
C.DA VIVIGNATO
91013 CALATAFIMI [TP]
TEL. 092422836
www.ceuso.it

Ceuso and Fastaia will be spending more time in the cellar so our appointment is postponed. Our congratulations on a bold, wise decision. Scurati Rosso '07 has intense, fleshy fruit and is very drinkable while the agreeable grecanico, grillo and chardonnay Scurati Bianco '07 is zesty and fresh.

● Scurati Rosso '07	♟♟	4*
○ Scurati Bianco '07	♟	4

Tenuta Chiuse del Signore

C.DA CHIUSE DEL SIGNORE
S.P. LINGUAGLOSSA-ZAFFERANA KM. 2
95015 LINGUAGLOSSA [CT]
TEL. 0942611340
www.gaishotels.com

It was a year to remember for Sergio De Luca's winery. The subtle, layered merlot and syrah Serrantico '06 went to our taste-offs for its solid, stylish structure. The Rasule Alte Rosso '07, a nerello mascalese, is also very drinkable and we recommend the Rasule Alte Bianco '07 inzolia and chardonnay blend.

● Serrantico '06	♟♟	6
● Rasule Alte Rosso '07	♟♟	4*
○ Rasule Alte Bianco '07	♟	4

Curto

S.S. 115 ISPICA - ROSOLINI KM 358
97014 ISPICA [RG]
TEL. 0932950161
www.curto.it

Curto gave us another two fine Eloro Nero d'Avolas: a Fontanelle '05 with a subtle nose and textured palate, and the uncomplicated but equally enticing Eloro '05, whose fortes are charm and drinkability. The Ikano '06 mix of nero d'Avola, syrah and merlot is stylish and ripe. The Eos '07 rosé is well-made.

● Eloro Fontanelle '05	♟♟	5
● Eloro Nero d'Avola '05	♟♟	3*
● Curto Ikano '06	♟	4
☉ Eos '07	♟	3

OTHER WINERIES

Gaspare Di Prima

VIA G. GUASTO, 27
92017 SAMBUCA DI SICILIA [AG]
TEL. 0925941201
www.diprimavini.it

The Di Prima family winery is a solid 40-hectare business at Sambuca di Sicilia, not far from Lake Arancio. Their elegant Villamaura Syrah '05 shows depth, texture, subtle aromas and eloquent freshness. The same qualities can be found in the Pepita Rosso '07 syrah and nero d'Avola blend.

● Pepita Rosso '07	🍷🍷 4*
● Villamaura Syrah '05	🍷🍷 6
● Gibilmoro Merlot '06	🍷 4
● Gibilmoro Nero d'Avola '06	🍷 4

Fatascià

VIA MAZZINI, 40
90139 PALERMO
TEL. 091332505
www.fatascia.it

Stefania Lena's wines did well. There's a great Almanera '06 and a ripe, intense Nero d'Avola but we also recommend ·L'Insolente '06, a fruity, balsamic cabernet sauvignon and merlot, the cabernet franc and nero d'Avola Rosso del Presidente '06 and the white Enigma '07 from grillo, grecanico and inzolia.

● Almanera '06	🍷🍷 4*
○ Enigma '07	🍷🍷 4*
● L'Insolente '06	🍷🍷 7
● Rosso del Presidente '06	🍷🍷 5

Feotto dello Jato

C.DA FEOTTO
90048 SAN GIUSEPPE JATO [PA]
TEL. 0918572650
www.feottodellojato.it

One of the flagships from this winery, run by the vibrant Calogero Todaro, is Terre di Giulia '05 from nero d'Avola, merlot and syrah, with striking depth and ripe fruit. Equally good is the intense perricone-only Vigna Curria '04. We also like the chardonnay and inzolia Iris '07 blend.

● Terre di Giulia '05	🍷🍷 5
● Vigna Curria '04	🍷🍷 6
○ Iris '07	🍷 4
○ Sauvignon Blanc '07	🍷 4

Feudi del Pisciotto

LOC. PISCIOTTO
93015 NISCEMI [CL]
TEL. 0577742903
www.castellare.it

Like its Tuscan outposts, this dynamic winery is run by the talented Alessandro Cellai. The Baglio del Sole Nero d'Avola '06 is very pleasant, with hints of damson, black cherry and spice preceding a concentrated, lengthy palate with unobtrusive, close-knit tannins. The other wines are well made.

● Baglio del Sole Nero d'Avola '06	🍷🍷 4*
○ Baglio del Sole Inzolia '07	🍷 3
○ Baglio del Sole Inzolia Catarratto '07	🍷 3

Feudo Arancio

C.DA PORTELLA MISILBESI
92017 SAMBUCA DI SICILIA [AG]
TEL. 0925579000
www.feudoarancio.it

The Mezzacorona group's Sicilian winery offers fresh, fruit-driven wines that stand out for drinkability excellent value for money. The Grillo '07 has noteworthy nuances of yellow peach and melon. The balanced Syrah '06 is delicate and well styled.

○ Grillo '07	🍷🍷 4*
● Merlot '06	🍷 4
● Nero d'Avola '06	🍷 4
● Syrah '06	🍷 4

Feudo di Santa Tresa

S.DA COMUNALE MARANGIO, 35
97019 VITTORIA [RG]
TEL. 0932513126
www.santatresa.it

The appealing monovarietal Nero d'Avola Avulisi '05 is elegant, its rich fruit and spice merging nicely with cool balsam. It also does well on the soft, balanced palate with good length. We also like the nero d'Avola and cabernet Nivuro '06 and the grillo and viognier Rina Ianca '07.

● Avulisi '05	🍷🍷 5
● Cerasuolo di Vittoria '05	🍷 4
● Nivuro '06	🍷 4
○ Rina Ianca '07	🍷 4

OTHER WINERIES

Feudo Montoni

C.DA MONTONI VECCHI
90144 CAMMARATA [AG]
TEL. 091513106
www.feudomontoni.it

Fabio Sireci won't be offering his Vrucara selection this year as he wants it to age a while longer. Aficionados can console themselves with his Nero d'Avola '06, which shows mature and aristocratic on the nose, subtle and stylish on the palate, and possessed of some very round, enticing tannins.

○ Catarratto '07	♈♈	3*
● Nero d'Avola '06	♈♈	4*

Fondo Antico

FRAZ. RILIEVO
VIA FIORAME, 54A
91020 TRAPANI
TEL. 0923864339
www.fondoantico.it

Fondo Antico has about 100 hectares under vine in Marsala and Trapani. There's an interesting Baccadoro '07 from late-harvested grillo with a touch of moscato bianco. It gives quince and citrus on the nose, echoed on the palate. Also nice is the minerally Grillo Parlante '07, a fresh, fleshy Grillo.

○ Baccadoro '07	♈♈	5
○ Grillo Parlante '07	♈♈	4*
● Il Canto di Fondo Antico '05	♈	5
○ Il Coro '06	♈	4

Cantine Foraci

C.DA SERRONI
91026 MAZARA DEL VALLO [TP]
TEL. 0923934286
www.foraci.it

As usual, this cellar gave us good wines, like the rich, powerful Tenute Dorrasita Nero d'Avola '06. We also enjoyed Grillo '07, which is minerally and aromatic on the nose and has a stylish, fresh palate. The rest of the range is interesting and good value for money.

○ Grillo '07	♈♈	3*
● Tenute Dorrasita Nero d'Avola '06	♈♈	5
○ Inzolia Chardonnay '07	♈	3
● Nero d'Avola Satiro Danzante '06	♈	4

Geraci

C.DA TARUCCO, S.P. 12 KM 5,3
90032 BISACQUINO [PA]
TEL. 0918354061
www.tarucco.com

The most interesting wine from Stefano and Antonella Geraci is the layered, minerally and intense blend of chardonnay, grillo and greco dorato Tarucco Colonna '07. But we also like the fresh, zesty Tarucco Chardonnay '07, a gleaming gold wine redolent of pineapple and mango.

○ Tarucco Colonna Bianco '07	♈♈	3*
○ Tarucco Chardonnay '07	♈	4
● Tarucco Syrah '06	♈	5

Tenuta Gorghi Tondi

C.DA SAN NICOLA
91026 MARSALA [TP]
TEL. 0923758210
www.tenutagorghitondi.it

This young, modern Mazara del Vallo winery is worth watching. Keep an eye out for the sprightly, lingering Rajah '07, a pure Zibibbo with agreeable, well-defined notes of lavender and Mediterranean scrubland. The soft, ripe golden Dora '06, from late-harvest grillo, has personality.

○ Oro di Dora '06	♈♈	6
○ Rajah '07	♈♈	4*
○ Coste a Preola Bianco '07	♈	3
○ Kheirè '07	♈	4

Graci

LOC. PASSOPISCIARO
C.DA ARCURIA
95012 CASTIGLIONE DI SICILIA [CT]
TEL. 3487016773
www.graci.eu

We welcome Alberto Aiello Graci's winery to the Guide with a masterly Etna Rosso Quota 600 '06 from selected nerello mascalese grapes. It shows outstanding minerality and concentration, with compact, well-developed fruit. The satisfying pure nerello mascalese Etna Rosso '06 is land-rooted and resolute.

● Etna Rosso Quota 600 '06	♈♈	6
● Etna Rosso '06	♈	6

OTHER WINERIES

Guccione

C.DA CERASA
90100 MONREALE [PA]
TEL. 0916116686
www.guccione.eu

Several of Manfredi and Francesco Guccione's natural wines did well. The '06 vintage brought light minerality and stimulating freshness to the Veruzza and complex, round fruitiness to the oak-aged Lolik. Perricone Arturo di Lanzeria shows promise for its intensity, definition, follow-through and length.

● Arturo di Lanzeria '06	¶¶ 5
○ Loilk '06	¶¶ 4*
○ Veruzza '06	¶¶ 4*
○ Girgis '06	¶ 4

Hauner

LOC. SANTA MARIA
VIA UMBERTO I
98050 LIPARI [ME]
TEL. 0909843141
www.hauner.it

It's thanks to Carlo Hauner senior, founder of the winery, that Malvasia delle Lipari hasn't become extinct. There was a good show from Malvasia Passito Carlo Hauner '05, with its layered nose and lovely balance of acidity and structure. We also liked the Hierà '06, from nero d'Avola, alicante and nocera.

● Hierà '06	¶¶ 4*
○ Malvasia delle Lipari Passito '07	¶¶ 6
○ Malvasia Passito Carlo Hauner '05	¶¶ 7
● Rosso Antonello '04	¶ 5

Cooperativa Placido Rizzotto Libera Terra

VIA PORTA PALERMO, 132
90048 SAN GIUSEPPE JATO [PA]
TEL. 0918577655
www.liberaterra.it

Ethics and taste meet at this laudable venture which farms vineyards confiscated from the Mafia. From a selection of old vines, the Rizzotto Catarratto '07 has crisp fruit, the nero d'Avola and syrah Rosso '07 is very mature and the upfront grillo, catarratto and chardonnay Bianco '07 is fresh-tasting.

○ Centopassi Placido Rizzotto Catarratto '07	¶¶ 3*
● Centopassi Placido Rizzotto Rosso '07	¶¶ 3*
○ Centopassi Placido Rizzotto Bianco '07	¶ 3*

Maggio

S.DA C.LE MARANGIO, 35
97019 VITTORIA [RG]
TEL. 0932984771
www.maggiovini.it

Amongae '05, a nero d'Avola, cabernet sauvignon and merlot blend, did well with its stylish nose and generous, lingering palate. The mature nero d'Avola and frappato Cerasuolo Vigna di Pettineo '06 has intensity, the Nero d'Avola Kalaurisi '06 is very varietal and the organic Cabernet Rasula '06 is austere.

● Amongae '05	¶¶ 4*
● Cerasuolo di Vittoria Vigna di Pettineo '06	¶¶ 5
● Kalaurisi '06	¶ 4
● Rasula Cabernet Sauvignon '06	¶ 4

Masseria Feudo Grottarossa

C.DA GROTTAROSSA
93100 CALTANISSETTA
TEL. 0934856575
www.masseriadelfeudo.it

Francesco and Carolina Cucurullo decided to keep their leading wines, Rosso delle Rose and Haermosa, in the cellar for a few more months so we only tasted basic wines. We had few complaints and liked the perky fruit-forward Syrah '07, which was fresh and vibrant.

● Syrah '07	¶¶ 4*
○ Il Giglio Bianco '07	¶ 3
● Il Giglio Rosso '07	¶ 3

Maurigi

C.DA BUDONETTO
94015 PIAZZA ARMERINA [EN]
TEL. 091321788
www.maurigi.it

Maurigi's most interesting wine this year is the merlot, syrah and pinot noir Saia Grande '05. Elegant, fruit-led and minerally, it has backbone and length. We like the Terre di Sofia '05 Chardonnay, with tropical fruit and summer blossom, the Bacca Bianca blend and the Sauvignon Coste, both 2007s.

● Saia Grande '05	¶¶ 5
○ Terre di Sofia '05	¶¶ 5
○ Bacca Bianca '07	¶ 4
○ Coste all'Ombra '07	¶ 5

OTHER WINERIES

Miceli

C.DA PIANA SCUNCHIPANI, 190
92019 SCIACCA [AG]
TEL. 0923916616
www.miceli.net

The Zibibbo Pantelleria Bianco Yrnm '06 has nice citrus, flowers and minerality and a full, lengthy palate. The mature merlot and cabernet sauvignon Majo San Lorenzo '05 has wafts of sea breeze. The varietal Cabernet Sauvignon '05 is subtle and the grecanico, viognier and gros manseng Baarìa '07 is fresh.

● Majo San Lorenzo '05	�♥	6
○ Moscato di Pantelleria Yrnm '06	♥♥	5
○ Baaria '07	♥	4
● Cabernet Sauvignon '05	♥	5

Salvatore Murana

C.DA KHAMMA, 276
91017 PANTELLERIA [TP]
TEL. 0923915231
www.salvatoremurana.com

The top of the range wines weren't ready so Murana sent us the minerally, aromatic Moscato Turbè '06, from zibibbo, also known as moscato d'Alessandria. We liked the sweet, citrussy, layered Passito Mueggen '06. The Talia '04, a nero d'Avola, merlot and cabernet sauvignon blend, is interesting.

○ Moscato di Pantelleria Turbè '06	♥♥	5
○ Moscato Passito di Pantelleria Mueggen '06	♥♥	7
● Talia '04	♥♥	5
○ Gadì '07	♥	4

Piana dei Cieli

C.DA BERTOLINO - SCIFITELLI
92013 MENFI [AG]
TEL. 092572060
www.pianadeicieli.com

Annalisa and Nino Giambalvo sent us an aromatic Syrah '06 with distinct cherry and pepper preceding full, round fruit that gives the palate gratifying complexity. The lively Nero d'Avola '06 is uncomplicated and fleshy. Chardonnay Pizzo dei Corvi '07, aged partly in oak, has mature notes with nice fruit.

● Nero d'Avola '06	♥♥	4*
● Syrah '06	♥♥	4*
○ Pizzo dei Corvi '07	♥	4

Modica di San Giovanni

C.DA BUFALEFI
96017 NOTO [SR]
TEL. 0931573576
www.olioevinobufalefi.it

A return to the Guide for nero d'Avola specialist Felice Modica's 40-hectare winery near Noto. The non-vintage Dolcenero is a good Nero d'Avola dessert wine with intense forest fruits and dried fig aromas and a sweet but not cloying palate supported by gratifyingly fresh acidity.

● Dolcenero	♥♥	6
● Eloro Arà '05	♥♥	4*

Occhipinti

C.DA FOSSA DI LUPO
S.P. VITTORIA - PEDALINO KM 5,4
97019 VITTORIA [RG]
TEL. 3397383580
www.agricolaocchipinti.it

Arianna looks for "Mediterranean biodiversity" in her wines and has created a vineyard ecosystem, with low intervention in the cellar where natural yeasts set the time scale. The results are refined gamey and spice aromas in the Frappato '06 and sensual minerality in the Nero d'Avola Siccagno '06.

● Frappato '06	♥♥	5
● Siccagno '06	♥♥	5

Riofavara

C.DA FAVARA S.P. 49 ISPICA - PACHINO
97014 ISPICA [RG]
TEL. 0932705130
www.riofavara.it

Massimo and Marianta Padua's winery performed well, above all with Notissimo '07, a Moscato di Noto with a stylish nose of orange blossom and lavender. We also like the typically territorial Sciavè '06, a Nero d'Avola, and the white Marzaiolo '07 blend of inzolia, grecanico and chardonnay.

● Eloro Nero d'Avola Sciavè '06	♥♥	5
○ Marzaiolo '07	♥♥	4*
○ Moscato di Nota Notissimo '07	♥♥	4
● Eloro Nero d'Avola '06	♥	4

OTHER WINERIES

Rudinì

C.DA CAMPOREALE
96018 PACHINO [SR]
TEL. 0931595333
www.vinirudini.it

It's nice to have this Pachino winery back. The summery notes of the Eloro Pachino Saro '06 reflect the terroir. Pachino '05 is subtle, mature and varietal. Moscato di Noto Baroque '07 comes with clean apple and pear nuances and there are pleasing herbaceous notes and minerality in the Espressione '07.

● Eloro Pachino '05	♆♆	4
● Eloro Pachino Saro '06	♆♆	5
○ Espressione Chardonnay '07	♆	4
○ Moscato di Noto Baroque '07	♆	5

Girolamo Russo

LOC. PASSOPISCIARO
VIA REGINA MARGHERITA, 78
95012 CASTIGLIONE DI SICILIA [CT]
TEL. 3283840247
www.girolamorusso.it

A positive debut for a winery dating back to the early half of the last century, with vines aged from 60 to 100 years. The fine minerally Etna Rosso San Lorenzo '06, a nerello mascalese and cappuccino blend went into our finals. The other products, all nerello mascalese and cappuccino blends, are well made.

● Etna Rosso San Lorenzo '06	♆♆	6
● Etna Feudo '06	♆♆	6
● Etna Rosso A Rina '06	♆♆	5

Sallier de la Tour

C.DA PERNICE
90144 MONREALE [PA]
TEL. 092436797
www.sallierdelatour.it

Principe Filiberto's winery strides on. The '05 Merlot confirmed it is the top wine with distinctive varietal fruit aromas. The solid, stylish Cabernet '05 is mature and satisfying, the round Syrah '05 is enjoyable and the well-styled, uncomplicated Nero d'Avola '05 is very drinkable.

● Cabernet '05	♆♆	4*
● Merlot '05	♆♆	4*
● Nero d'Avola '05	♆	4
● Syrah '05	♆	4

Emanuele Scammacca del Murgo

VIA ZAFFERANA, 13
95010 SANTA VENERINA [CT]
TEL. 095950520
www.murgo.it

The Scammacca family runs a tight ship and its reputation for quality is well earned. We're happy with the austere, stylish lines of the Tenuta San Michele '05 Cabernet Sauvignon. The citrussy Etna Bianco '07, with minerals on the nose is refreshing and uncomplicated. The other wines are good.

○ Etna Bianco '07	♆♆	4*
● Tenuta San Michele '05	♆♆	5
● Etna Rosso '06	♆	4
○ Murgo Brut '05	♆	4

Tenuta Scilio di Valle Galfina

C.DA ARRIGO
95015 LINGUAGLOSSA [CT]
TEL. 095932822
www.scilio.com

The intense purplish Etna Rosso '05 is the most persuasive wine with its pleasingly perky fruitiness but the easy-drinking, stylish Etna Rosso Orphéus '01 is worth uncorking. We also enjoyed the Etna Bianco '07.

● Etna Rosso '05	♆♆	4*
● Etna Rosso Orphéus '01	♆♆	5
○ Etna Bianco '07	♆	4

Tenuta di Serramarrocco

LOC. FONTANELLE
C.DA OSPEDALETTO
91100 VALDERICE [TP]
TEL. 063220973
www.serramarrocco.com

The flagship Bordeaux blend '06 is having another year in bottle so for now we recommend the Nero d'Avola Baglio di Serramarrocco '07, which is rounder and less complex than the Nero di Serramarrocco '06 but with its own austere elegance. We also liked the clean, bright fruit in the Grillo del Barone '07.

● Baglio di Serramarrocco '07	♆♆	3*
○ Grillo del Barone '07	♆♆	3*
● Nero di Serramarrocco '06	♆	5

OTHER WINERIES

Solidea

C.DA KADDIUGGIA
91017 PANTELLERIA [TP]
TEL. 0923913016
www.solideavini.it

Giacomo and Solidea D'Ancona sent us three zibibbo-based wines from the grape also called moscato d'Alessandria. These seductive, very drinkable bottles are well up to estate standards. The sensual Passito '07 has apricot notes and its agreeable freshness places it on a par with the other two wines.

O Ilios '07		4*
O Moscato di Pantelleria '07		5
O Passito di Pantelleria '07		6

Tenuta Chiarelli Cuffaro Casale Santa Ida

C.DA CONSORTO
95040 SAN MICHELE DI GANZARIA [CT]
TEL. 0916090065
www.tenutachiarellicuffaro.com

The flagship wine for this new winery supervised by Donato Lanati is a nero d'Avola and petit verdot mix, the deep ruby Euno '06. The well-defined plum and spice notes accompany a lively palate, with tannins that are already round and attractive. Pluzia '07, from chardonnay and viognier, is also good.

● Euno '06		3*
O Pluzia '07		3

Terrelíade

LOC. SILENE
C.DA PORTELLA MISILBESI
92017 SAMBUCA DI SICILIA [AG]
TEL. 0421246281
www.terreliade.com

The Santa Margherita group is getting results at Sambuca, as is clear from their enjoyable, well-made wines. We again enjoyed the breadth of the flagship, the nero d'Avola and syrah Utti Majuri '05. The merlot and nero d'Avola Musia '06 and Feudo Zirtari Rosso '06, from nero d'Avola and syrah, are also good.

● (Utti) Majuri '05		5
● Musìa '06		4*
O Feudo Zirtari Bianco '07		3
● Feudo Zirtari Rosso '06		3

Barone di Villagrande

VIA DEL BOSCO, 25
95025 MILO [CT]
TEL. 0957082175
www.villagrande.it

The wine we liked most was the carricante-only Etna Bianco Superiore '07 for its elegance and minerality. The tasting panel also enjoyed the Fiore '06 carricante and chardonnay blend, the Etna Rosso '05 and the Sciara '04, from merlot and nerello mascalese.

O Etna Bianco Sup. '07		4*
O Fiore '06		5
● Etna Rosso di Villagrande '05		4
● Sciara '04		5

Zenner

VIA PIETRO MASCAGNI, 72
95131 CATANIA
TEL. 0956170728
www.terradellesirene.com

The family's love affair with Noto began 30 years ago and the estate has now grown to six hectares, all old bush-trained vines, with production now managed by Dò Zenner. Terra delle Sirene '06 is still greenish but it has finesse and superb texture as well as full, lingering fruit.

● Terra delle Sirene '06		5
● Terra delle Sirene '04		5

Zisola

C.DA ZISOLA
96017 NOTO [SR]
TEL. 057773571
www.zisola.it

The Mazzei family's Sicilian winery presented just one wine again this year, Zisola '06, a single-variety Nero d'Avola with a stylish nose of berry fruit woven with balsam and minerality. The refreshingly vibrant palate has juicy tannins and perfectly balanced structure and acidity.

● Nero d'Avola '06		4*

SARDINIA

It was a memorable year for Sardinian winemaking. Four of the region's wines earned Three Glasses last year but this time we handed out 12 top accolades. At first glance, this might seem incredible but it underscores the commitment of the sector over the past decade as modernization of wineries has been completed, vineyards replanted and indigenous grape varieties selected. During the 1980s, there were only about 50 producers in Sardinia with less than 30,000 hectares under vine but today the number of independent growers has more than doubled and the 30,000-hectare ceiling is a thing of the past. Much is going on in a region where large and small wineries happily co-exist seeking to bring out the best in the wealth of native grape varieties and typical wines. A brief overview of the winning wines shows Sella & Mosca, Sardinia's best-known producer, out in front. This year, the estate performed better than ever, taking Three Glasses for its stunning '03 Marchese di Villamarina, probably the most captivating Cabernet Sauvignon produced on the shores of the Mediterranean, and the new white Alghero Torbato Terre Bianche Cuvée 161 '07, which bowled us over with its expressive depth and rich mineral character. Antonio Argiolas presented a glorious '04 vintage of Turriga, and came close to repeating the feat with the impressive Korem '06 and the sweet Angialis '05. Top honours also went to another classic, Carignano del Sulcis Superiore Terre Brune '04 by Cantina di Santadi. This winery is also behind one of the new surprises of this edition: Rosso Barrua '05, produced by Agricola Punica, a joint venture with Niccolò Incisa della Rocchetta and Giacomo Tachis, who has driven the modernization of winemaking in the region in more than 20 years as a consultant oenologist. Sardus Pater in Sant'Antioco is one of the finest examples of a modern winery that draws on the area's traditional heritage. Its old bush-trained vineyards along the coast yield a range of impeccable wines whose showpiece is Carignano del Sulcis Arenas '05. Antichi Poderi Jerzu, too, repeated last year's success with its Cannonau di Sardegna Josto Miglior Riserva '05. Other superb Cannonaus came from Giuseppe Gabbas, in the shape of an excellent Dule Riserva '05 and an Arbeskia '05 that was not far behind, and Tenute Soletta, with Cannonau Keramos Riserva '04. Alessandro Dettori again showed what he can do, earning Three Glasses for the deep, complex Dettori Bianco Un Anno Dopo '06. Finally, two well-deserved awards went to Contini's Antico Gregori, no newcomer to the podium, and to another Sardinian gem, Fratelli Porcu's Malvasia di Bosa '05, which we hope will serve as an example to other small growers of the area.

Agricola Punica

LOC. BARRUA
09010 SANTADI [CI]
TEL. 0781950127
www.agripunica.it

ANNUAL PRODUCTION	150,000 bottles
HECTARES UNDER VINE	50
VITICULTURE METHOD	Conventional

Four years have passed since the first release of Barrua from Agricola Punica, a joint venture between Cantina di Santadi and Niccolò Incisa della Rocchetta. That was back in 2002, and even then the carignano, merlot and cabernet blend showed signs of greatness. Over subsequent years, Barrua performed convincingly but without the extra something needed to boost it into the top rank of Italian wines. The 2005 harvest, however, brought several extra somethings: grip, power, finesse and elegance. This great Mediterranean wine has a surprising nose of ripe red fruit, sweet spices and hints of tobacco, which are mirrored on the soft, impeccably balanced palate, where exemplary tannins and the seamless progression assured by a freshness that continues through the agile, dynamic finish. We gave it Three resounding Glasses. This stellar wine is flanked by Montessu, from the same vintage, a second wine from mainly carignano with small amounts of cabernet, merlot and syrah. It is well balanced, although the finish tends to dry the mouth.

★ Antonio Argiolas

VIA ROMA, 56
09040 SERDIANA [CA]
TEL. 070740606
www.argiolas.it

ANNUAL PRODUCTION	2,000,000 bottles
HECTARES UNDER VINE	230
VITICULTURE METHOD	Conventional

You have to admire the consistency of the Argiolas family. We use the word "family" advisedly for it is the key to success. Antonio Argiolas, born in 1906, still oversees business with his sons Franco and Pepetto and their own families. The estate is capably run and has a strong image in Italy and abroad for its range of great-value wines. This year saw the flagship Turriga on top form. The '04 vintage from 85 per cent cannonau with small amounts of carignano, bovale and malvasia nera has an exceptionally complex nose, ranging from peppery sensations to berry fruit. The stylish palate impresses with well-calibrated tannins and a fresh, lingering finish. Korem '06, from bovale, carignano and cannonau, is also excellent, its attractive softness balanced by a perfect tannic weave. Is Solinas '06, from carignano with a little bovale from the estate's Sulcis vineyards, is also captivating. Angialis '05, from late-harvest nasco, almost won Three Glasses for its seductive apricot, honey and candied fruit, sweet but never cloying palate and attractive supporting acidity.

● Barrua '05	♟♟♟	6
● Montessu '05	♟	4
● Barrua '03	♟♟	8
● Barrua '04	♟♟	6

● Turriga '04	♟♟♟	8
○ Angialis '05	♟♟	6
● Is Solinas '06	♟♟	4*
● Korem '06	♟♟	6
● Antonio Argiolas 100 '05	♟♟	6
● Cannonau di Sardegna Costera '07	♟♟	4*
● Monica di Sardegna Perdera '07	♟♟	3*
○ Vermentino di Sardegna Costamolino '07	♟♟	3*
○ Vermentino di Sardegna Is Argiolas '07	♟♟	4*
○ Nuragus di Cagliari S'Elegas '07	♟	3
⊙ Serralori Rosato '07	♟	3
● Turriga '99	♟♟♟	8
● Turriga '98	♟♟♟	8
● Turriga '97	♟♟♟	7
● Turriga '95	♟♟♟	7
● Turriga '02	♟♟♟	8
● Turriga '01	♟♟♟	8
● Turriga '00	♟♟♟	8

Carpante

VIA GARIBALDI, 151
07049 USINI [SS]
TEL. 079380614
info@carpante.it

ANNUAL PRODUCTION	30,000 bottles
HECTARES UNDER VINE	8
VITICULTURE METHOD	Conventional

This winery, founded in 2003, has been operating at Usini in the province of Sassari for five years now. The small estate produces around 30,000 bottles a year, exclusively from the typical grape varieties of the area, particularly cagnulari and vermentino. It was the wines made from vermentino that we liked best. Vermentino di Sardegna Longhera '07 has a complex nose characterized by aromatic thyme and rosemary-like herbs, and delicate citrus notes. The palate displays a pleasant freshness that accompanies it through to the exceptionally clean finish. Vermentino di Sardegna Frinas '07 is simpler but clean and nicely tangy. The best of the reds is Carpante '06, an IGT from cagnulari with small amounts of bovale and pascale. Aromas of ripe red fruit, jam and Mediterranean scrubland dominate the nose while the palate is powerful and tannic, lacking only a little finesse, which it will acquire after a few more months in bottle. The other wines are well made, particularly the heady Cagnulari '07 with its attractive spicy aromas.

Giovanni Cherchi

LOC. SA PALA E SA CHESSA
07049 USINI [SS]
TEL. 079380273
www.vinicolacherchi.it

ANNUAL PRODUCTION	170,000 bottles
HECTARES UNDER VINE	30
VITICULTURE METHOD	Conventional

Giovanni Cherchi is a benchmark for producers around Sassari but not all his vintages are exceptional. Perhaps the work among the rows did not produce the expected results or it might have been the weather – there was rain in the harvest period but 2007 saw a slight drop in quality here and indeed elsewhere in the area. The cellar's top wines include Vermentino di Sardegna Tuvaoes '07, with nice delicacy and an elegant nose. Although attractively fresh on the palate, it lacks the structure of better vintages. Pigalva '07, the other Vermentino di Sardegna, is well typed and subtle on the nose. The single-variety red Cagnulari '07 suffered more than the others from unpredictable weather. It has moderately intense aromas, with notes of ripe red fruit, and is rather light in structure with a slightly bitter finish. Luzzana '06, a blend of cannonau and cagnulari, has a nicely concentrated nose but is still sharpish on the palate but marked acidity, still over-assertive tannins and robust structure make it a good candidate for ageing.

● Carpante '06	¶¶	5
○ Vermentino di Sardegna Frinas '07	¶¶	5
○ Vermentino di Sardegna Longhera '07	¶¶	4*
● Cagnulari '07	¶	4
● Cannonau di Sardegna '06	¶	4
● Lizzos '06	¶	5
● Cagnulari '06	¶¶	4
● Cannonau di Sardegna '05	¶¶	4
● Lizzos '05	¶¶	5

● Luzzana '06	¶¶	5
● Cagnulari '07	¶	4
○ Vermentino di Sardegna Pigalva '07	¶	4
○ Vermentino di Sardegna Tuvaoes '07	¶	4
● Luzzana '02	¶¶	6
● Luzzana '01	¶¶	6
● Soberanu '03	¶¶	8
○ Boghes '06	¶¶	6
● Cagnulari '06	¶¶	5
● Luzzana '05	¶¶	6
● Luzzana '04	¶¶	6

Attilio Contini

VIA GENOVA, 48/50
09072 CABRAS [OR]
TEL. 0783290806
www.vinicontini.it

ANNUAL PRODUCTION	600,000 bottles
HECTARES UNDER VINE	70
VITICULTURE METHOD	Conventional

Paolo Contini's perseverance has led other producers to concentrate their efforts on Vernaccia di Oristano, a delicious ancient wine type. Antico Gregori is an alluring dessert wine created by the skilful blending of great vintages. The complex bouquet is lifted by nuts and almonds before the warm, soft palate reprises toasted hazelnuts and almonds, rounding off with a long finish. It is flanked by a Riserva '88 with a very rich nose but a less intriguing palate. As usual, the red wines are excellent. Nieddera '06 gives blackberry and morello cherry and a soft, full-flavoured palate. Also interesting is Barrile '05, from nieddera and caddiu, which aged in small wood for a year emerging with attractive morello cherry and plum fruit and a soft, warm finish. Cannonau di Sardegna Inu Riserva '05 has a convincingly soft, balsamic palate, Tonaghe '06 is fresher and easy drinking, and Rosso di Contini '07, a cannonau, nieddera and sangiovese blend, is also agreeable. Some of the whites, such as Vermentino di Sardegna Tyrsos '07 and Vermentino di Gallura Elibaria '07, are less interesting but Karmis '07, from vernaccia, is very nice.

Ferruccio Deiana

LOC. SU LEUNAXI
VIA GIALETO, 7
09040 SETTIMO SAN PIETRO [CA]
TEL. 070749117
www.ferrucciodeiana.it

ANNUAL PRODUCTION	378,000 bottles
HECTARES UNDER VINE	62
VITICULTURE METHOD	Certified organic

The '07 vintage was not a great one for Ferruccio Deiana. We look on it as a blip, though. One of Ferruccio's merits is his revival of viticulture in an area that saw almost all of its vine stock grubbed up, and its vineyards abandoned, during the 1980s. Today, the rolling hills of the Parteolla region produce seriously good bottles, such as Ajana '05. This cannonau, carignano and bovale blend gives an appealing nose of red berries and cherry jam, followed by a warm, fresh-tasting palate with youthful tannins. Pluminus '07, from vermentino and nasco, is soft with aromas of ripe white-fleshed fruit. Monica di Sardegna Karel '07 is also interesting, especially on the nose, where alluring notes of jam and morello cherry usher in a balanced palate. Cannonau di Sardegna Sileno '07 is decent, with a full, lingering bouquet and a palate that reveals the assertive acidity and tannins of a young wine. The late-harvest Vermentino di Sardegna Arvali '07 undergoes skin contact that leaves it soft and full, with opulent notes of ripe fruit while Vermentino di Sardegna Donnikalia '07 is simpler and fresher on both nose and palate.

O Vernaccia di Oristano Antico Gregori	♟♟♟ 7
● Barrile '05	♟♟ 7
● Cannonau di Sardegna Inu Ris. '05	♟♟ 5
● Cannonau di Sardegna Tonaghe '06	♟♟ 4*
● Nieddera Rosso '06	♟♟ 4*
O Vernaccia di Oristano Ris. '88	♟♟ 5
O Karmis '07	♟ 4
⊙ Nieddera Rosato '07	♟ 3
● Rosso di Contini '07	♟ 3
O Vermentino di Gallura Elibaria '07	♟ 4
O Vermentino di Sardegna Tyrsos '07	♟ 3
O Pontis '00	♟♟♟ 5
● Barrile '03	♟♟ 7
● Cannonau di Sardegna Inu Ris. '04	♟♟ 5
O Karmis '06	♟♟ 4*
● Nieddera Rosso '05	♟♟ 4*
● Rosso di Contini '06	♟♟ 3*
O Vernaccia di Oristano Ris. '87	♟♟ 5

● Ajana '05	♟♟ 7
O Pluminus '07	♟♟ 7
● Cannonau di Sardegna Sileno '07	♟ 4
● Monica di Sardegna Karel '07	♟ 4
O Vermentino di Sardegna Arvali V.T. '07	♟ 4
O Vermentino di Sardegna Donnikalia '07	♟ 4
● Ajana '02	♟♟♟ 7
● Ajana '04	♟♟ 7
● Ajana '03	♟♟ 7
● Cannonau di Sardegna Sileno '05	♟♟ 4
● Monica di Sardegna Karel '06	♟♟ 4*
O Pluminus '06	♟♟ 7

Tenute Dettori

LOC. BADDE NIGOLOSU
07036 SENNORI [SS]
TEL. 079514711
www.tenutedettori.it

ANNUAL PRODUCTION	55,000 bottles
HECTARES UNDER VINE	18
VITICULTURE METHOD	Natural

Alessandro Dettori's wines seem to court debate. There are those who claim that the range is lacking in all respects, and must be treated as such, while others maintain that these are quite extraordinary bottles. Our position is a little different. We believe Badde Nigolosu has been vitally important for the recovery of a unique region, and has set a valuable example for all Sardinian growers, encouraging them to exploit the potential of traditional grape varieties. However, Dettori's wines are not always perfect. Problems can sometimes arise from his quest for naturalness at all costs, banning chemicals in the vineyards and shunning sulphites, filtration and even steel or temperature control in the cellar. But these wines are eloquent of the land and brim with character and in fact Alessandro's Gravner-style Dettori Bianco 2006 took our Three Glass award this year. This golden Vermentino has aged an extra year in concrete in comparison to the wine released last year and boasts intense aromas of Mediterranean scrubland. In the mouth, it is full, minerally and lightly tannic yet also supple, complex and subtly smoky.

Cantine Dolianova

LOC. SAN'ESU
S.S. 387 KM 17,150
09041 DOLIANOVA [CA]
TEL. 070744101
www.cantinedolianova.com

ANNUAL PRODUCTION	4,000,000 bottles
HECTARES UNDER VINE	1200
VITICULTURE METHOD	Conventional

This winery has stood the test of time, drawing on its impressive 50-year viticultural heritage and 630 member growers who farm 1,200 hectares scattered over the Parteolla area. Output tops 4,000,000 bottles a year. It has also kept pace with the times and conquered markets across the world. Production focuses on traditional wines, although small percentages of international varieties feature in some IGT wines. One of the most interesting is Terresicci '05, a blend of 85 per cent barbera sarda and 15 per cent native varieties, aged in barrique for a year. The nose gives fruity aromas of morello cherry and plum while it's warm, full and round on the palate, with soft, well-calibrated tannins. Montesicci '07, from vermentino, nasco and malvasia, is classy, although not as good as last year. Falconaro '05, from cannonau, carignano and montepulciano, is pleasant. The traditional wines performed well, particularly Monica di Sardegna Arenada '06, with attractive notes of balsam. Also good are the refreshing, well-balanced Vermentino di Sardegna Naeli '07 and Sibiola '07, an alluring rosé blend of sangiovese, barbera, monica and montepulciano.

O Dettori Bianco Un anno dopo '06	▼▼▼	6
O Moscadeddu '06	▼▼	6
● Tenores '05	▼▼	8
● Dettori Rosso '05	▼▼	8
● Renosu Rosso '06	▼▼	3*
● Tuderi '05	▼▼	6
● Dettori Rosso '04	♈♈♈	8
● Tenores '03	♈♈♈	8
● Chimbanta '03	♈♈	6
O Dettori Bianco '06	♈♈	6
● Dettori Rosso '02	♈♈	8
O Moscadeddu '05	♈♈	6
● Ottomarzo '03	♈♈	6
● Tuderi '03	♈♈	6

O Montesicci '07	▼▼	4*
● Terresicci '05	▼▼	6
● Falconaro '05	▼	5
● Monica di Sardegna Arenada '06	▼	3
O Moscato di Cagliari '07	▼	4
⊙ Sibiola '07	▼	3
O Vermentino di Sardegna Naeli '07	▼	4
● Falconaro '04	♈♈	5
● Cannonau di Sardegna Anzenas '05	♈♈	3*
● Falconaro '03	♈♈	5
O Montesicci '06	♈♈	4
O Moscato di Cagliari '06	♈♈	4
● Terresicci '04	♈♈	6

Cantina Sociale Dorgali

VIA PIEMONTE, 11
08022 DORGALI [NU]
TEL. 078496143
www.csdorgali.com

ANNUAL PRODUCTION	1,600,000 bottles
HECTARES UNDER VINE	750
VITICULTURE METHOD	Conventional

The modernization of this co-operative winery is already bearing fruit. Indeed, the wines are starting to express their terroir and their grapes, thanks to hard work in the extensive vineyards, which offer vary greatly in terms of altitude, exposure, soil type and vine-training methods. Another new development is the approach to the flagship wines, which are closely bound up with history and tradition, and whose peak of excellence is Cannonau. We were particularly impressed by Fileri '07, which came within a whisker of Three Glasses for its elegant notes of fruit, oak, vanilla and minerals. Soft, complex, round and coherent in the mouth, it reveals a nice balance of acidity and tannins. Vigna di Isalle '07 is excellent, with an intriguingly fresh, heady, cherry and currant-led nose and a pleasant juicy palate. They emerged from our tastings as some of the best reds from the island in terms of value for money. As for the whites, we liked both Vermentino di Sardegna Isalle '07, with subtle notes of rennet apples, and Calaluna '07, another Vermentino, with a vegetal nose and a fresh, lively palate. The rosé Filieri '07 is also pleasing.

Feudi della Medusa

LOC. SANTA MARGHERITA
POD. SAN LEONARDO, 15
09010 PULA [CA]
TEL. 0709259019
www.feudidellamedusa.it

ANNUAL PRODUCTION	250,000 bottles
HECTARES UNDER VINE	70
VITICULTURE METHOD	Conventional

We already knew that the Siclaris had very clear ideas about what to produce and how to interpret their land. Now that work is drawing to completion, we are witnessing a unique scenario for Sardinia in terms of type and quality of products with a top-level hotel and a winery capable of competing with the world's best. Behind is a hill; in front the vineyards and the sea. The high-quality product range is the result of excellent bases and careful selections, although some go to market too young. Cannonau di Sardegna '06 came dangerously close to our Three Glass award, displaying an elegant fruit and spice nose and a soft, juicy palate. It was a great vintage for both Arrubias '06, from carignano, and Norace '06, a cannonau and syrah blend with a rich nose and young tannins nicely balanced with acidity. Gerione '05 from cagnulari, cabernet and syrah is a red aged in small oak casks but it fell a little short of our expectations. The whites are good: Chardonnay Alba Nora '06, Vermentino di Sardegna Albithia '07 and Sa Perda Bianca '06, from chardonnay and malvasia.

● Filieri Rosso '07	♟♟ 2*
● Cannonau di Sardegna V. di Isalle '07	♟♟ 4*
○ Calaluna '07	♟ 3
☉ Filieri Rosato '07	♟ 3
○ Vermentino di Sardegna Isalle '07	♟ 3
● Cannonau di Sardegna Filieri '06	♟♟ 3*
● Cannonau di Sardegna V. di Isalle '06	♟♟ 4*
● Cannonau di Sardegna Viniola Ris. '04	♟♟ 5
● Filieri Rosso '06	♟♟ 2*
● Fùili '04	♟♟ 5
● Noriolo '05	♟♟ 4

● Cannonau di Sardegna '06	♟♟ 5
● Arrubias '06	♟♟ 6
● Norace '06	♟♟ 6
○ Alba Nora '06	♟ 5
● Gerione '05	♟ 7
○ Sa Perda Bianca '06	♟ 5
○ Vermentino di Sardegna Albithia '07	♟ 4
● Gerione '03	♟♟ 8
● Norace '05	♟♟ 7
● Arrubias '05	♟♟ 7
● Biddas '05	♟♟ 4*
● Cagnulari '05	♟♟ 7
● Cannonau di Sardegna '05	♟♟ 5
● Gerione '04	♟♟ 8
○ Sa Perda Bianca '05	♟♟ 5

Giuseppe Gabbas

VIA TRIESTE, 65
08100 NUORO
TEL. 078433745
ggabbas@tiscali.it

ANNUAL PRODUCTION	70,000 bottles
HECTARES UNDER VINE	13
VITICULTURE METHOD	Conventional

This is a memorable edition of the Guide for Giuseppe Gabbas. After years of sacrifice, investment and experimentation aimed exclusively at quality, the winery has won its first Three Glass award. There are 13 hectares under vine set in one of the finest and loveliest wine areas of Barbagia, between Nuoro, Oliena and Orgosolo. Cannonau is king here, flanked by other traditional varieties like girò, pascale and bovale, and it was the estate's Cannonau di Sardegna Dule Riserva '05, aged in barrique for ten months, took our top honour. The nose opens with vanilla notes, followed by ripe red fruit and morello cherry. Soft tannins on the palate underline the wine's firm structure, fullness and compactness, which are also evident in its long, well-defined finish. Arbeskia '05, from cannonau, pascale, bovale and girò, is also impressive. Aged in barrique for two years, it is still fresh and lively, with notes of balsam and oak, before the palate unfolds soft and warm, with elegant smooth tannins. The youthfully alcoholic Cannonau di Sardegna Lillovè '07 is as captivating as ever, showing fresh on nose and palate. We also liked the dried-grape Avra '05.

Cantina Sociale Gallura

VIA VAL DI COSSU, 9
07029 TEMPIO PAUSANIA [OT]
TEL. 079631241
www.cantinagallura.com

ANNUAL PRODUCTION	1,300,000 bottles
HECTARES UNDER VINE	350
VITICULTURE METHOD	Conventional

We would like to congratulate Dino Addis, the manager of this winery, who has been fighting for the quality of Vermentino for years and again came close to our Three Glass award. A fervent believer in terroir, Dino selects the grapes for each of his wines according to the aspect, altitude and site climate of the vineyard. The result is a excellent range of good-value wines. At our tastings, the whites performed exceptionally well, especially Vermentino di Gallura Superiore Genesi '07, which displays a complex, overwhelming, tropical fruits nose and a fresh, elegant palate. We were also captivated by the wonderfully intense nose and well-balanced palate of Piras '07 and by Canayli '07, which is harmonious, full and pleasant. Almondy notes pervade Gemellae '07 whereas the tangy, uncomplicated Mavriana '07 is more subtle. However, we feel that these seriously good wines need further bottle ageing to express their potential to the full. The range is completed by Karana Nebbiolo '07, Cannonau di Sardegna Templum '07 and Moscato di Tempio, a sweet sparkler.

● Cannonau di Sardegna Dule Ris. '05	♛♛♛	4*
● Arbeskia '05	♛♛	5
● Cannonau di Sardegna Lillové '07	♛♛	4*
● Avra '05	♛	4
● Arbeskia '04	♟♟	5
● Arbeskia '03	♟♟	5
● Arbeskia '02	♟♟	5
● Cannonau di Sardegna Dule Ris. '01	♟♟	4*
● Cannonau di Sardegna Dule Ris. '04	♟♟	4*
● Cannonau di Sardegna Dule Ris. '02	♟♟	4*
● Cannonau di Sardegna Lillové '06	♟♟	4*
● Cannonau di Sardegna Lillové '05	♟♟	4*

○ Vermentino di Gallura Sup. Genesi '07	♛♛	6
● Karana Nebbiolo dei Colli del Limbara '07	♛	3*
○ Moscato di Tempio Pausania '07	♛♛	4*
○ Vermentino di Gallura Gemellae '07	♛♛	3*
○ Vermentino di Gallura Mavriana '07	♛♛	3*
○ Vermentino di Gallura Piras '07	♛♛	3*
○ Vermentino di Gallura Sup. Canayli '07	♛♛	4*
○ Balajana '05	♛	4
☉ Campos '07	♛	3
● Cannonau di Sardegna Templum '07	♛	4
○ Vermentino di Gallura Sup. Genesi '06	♟♟	6
● Dolmen '04	♟♟	5
● Karana Nebbiolo dei Colli del Limbara '06	♟♟	3*
○ Moscato di Tempio Pausania '06	♟♟	4*
○ Vermentino di Gallura Piras '06	♟♟	3*

Cantina del Giogantinu

VIA MILANO, 30
07022 BERCHIDDA [OT]
TEL. 079704163
www.giogantinu.it

ANNUAL PRODUCTION	1,568,000 bottlesv
HECTARES UNDER VINE	320
VITICULTURE METHOD	Conventional

A few years ago, we noted that this winery was showing greater consistency. This year, we ought to point out clear signs of improvement. Well done, then, to the Cantina del Giogantinu, an important co-operative with over 320 hectares of vineyards, much of it bush trained. Our favourite wine was Terra Saliosa '07, a blend of merlot, cabernet and muristellu. On the nose, it gives intense red fruits and delicate vegetality while the palate is soft with well-defined tannins and a fairly long finish. Cannonau di Sardegna Eja '06 is generous and chewy, with a complex nose, and Terra Mala '05, from the indigenous carignano and muristellu varieties, is also interesting. Good whites include the excellent Vermentino di Gallura 12° '07, with mineral notes and an almondy finish, and Vermentino di Gallura Superiore 13° '07, which boasts an exceptionally complex nose and fresh palate. The other wines are well made and nicely balanced.

Antichi Poderi Jerzu

VIA UMBERTO I, 1
08044 JERZU [NU]
TEL. 078270028
www.jerzuantichipoderi.it

ANNUAL PRODUCTION	2,000,000 bottles
HECTARES UNDER VINE	750
VITICULTURE METHOD	Conventional

Ogliastra is leading the revival of Cannonau and credit goes to this winery, which has long been engaged in clonal selection and experimentation. The estate's comprehensive range boasts excellent wines of all types, including an unexpected Vermentino. We thought the best version was Vermentino di Sardegna Lucean Le Stelle '07, which has a fresh, lively palate, but Vermentino di Sardegna Telavè '07 is also nice. But this is a winery that takes pride in its reds and Cannonau di Sardegna Riserva Josto Miglior '05 deservedly took our Three Glass award this year. Made with grapes from an old bush-trained vineyard over 600 metres above sea level, it ages in barrique for a year and for a further 12 months in bottle. On the nose, there is a wealth of red fruit, balsam and subtle vegetal notes while the exceptionally well-balanced palate is full and juicy, with elegant tannins and a long, clean finish. Marghìa '06 is the most captivating of the other Cannonaus, showing impressive fruit and a warm, rounded palate. Riserva '05 Chuerra is softer, with notes of ripe red fruit, while Bantu '07 displays an attractive fresh nose and smooth tannins.

● Terra Saliosa '07	♟♟ 4*
● Cannonau di Sardegna Eja '06	♟♟ 4*
● Terra Mala '05	♟♟ 6
○ Vermentino di Gallura 12° '07	♟♟ 3*
○ Vermentino di Gallura Sup. 13° '07	♟♟ 3*
○ Giogantino Brut '07	♟ 4
● Nastarrè '07	♟ 3
⊙ Nulvàra '07	♟ 3
○ Vermentino di Gallura Lughente '07	♟ 4
○ Lughente V. T. '05	♟♟ 6
○ Vermentino di Gallura Lughente '06	♟♟ 4
○ Vermentino di Gallura Sup. Karenzia '06	♟♟ 5

● Cannonau di Sardegna Josto Miglior Ris. '05	♟♟♟ 5
● Cannonau di Sardegna Marghìa '06	♟♟ 4*
● Akratos '04	♟ 6
● Cannonau di Sardegna Bantu '07	♟ 3
● Cannonau di Sardegna Chuerra Ris. '05	♟ 5
⊙ Cannonau di Sardegna Isara '07	♟ 3
○ Vermentino di Sardegna Lucean Le Stelle '07	♟ 4
○ Vermentino di Sardegna Telavè '07	♟ 3
● Radames '01	♟♟♟ 6
● Akratos '03	♟♟ 5
● Cannonau di Sardegna Josto Miglior Ris. '04	♟♟ 5
● Cannonau di Sardegna Marghìa '05	♟♟ 4*
● Radames '00	♟♟ 6

Alberto Loi

s.s. 125 km 124,200
08040 Cardedu [NU]
tel. 070240866
www.cantina.it/albertoloi

ANNUAL PRODUCTION 240,000 bottles
HECTARES UNDER VINE 63
VITICULTURE METHOD Conventional

The Alberto Loi wine estate, now run by the third generation, is located in Cardedu, a small town near Jerzu. Cannonau is the area's principal grape variety and in fact Jerzu has been designated a specific subzone in the Cannonau DOC. The Loi winery's annual production of around 240,000 bottles is obtained from the grapes of over 60 hectares of vineyards. This year, Cannonau di Sardegna Cardedo Riserva '05 towered head and shoulders above the other wines. It has a nicely complex nose with notes of minerals, ripe red fruit and dried roses leading into a fresh, firm palate with a long, clean finish. Cannonau di Sardegna Riserva '04 is also very good, offering fruit aromas and a soft, concentrated palate. Tuvara '04, a cannonau, carignano and muristellu blend, is rather evolved, as is Astangia '05, from cannonau, carignano, bovale sardo and monica. Finally, we liked Vermentino di Sardegna I Rivoli '07, a very interesting white from the Vitivinicola Cardedu range, with aromas of tropical fruit and a full, tangy palate.

Piero Mancini

loc. Cala Saccaia
07026 Olbia
tel. 078950717
www.pieromancini.it

ANNUAL PRODUCTION 1,400,000 bottles
HECTARES UNDER VINE 100
VITICULTURE METHOD Conventional

The Mancinis have been making wine for over 20 years, rightly convinced of the potential of Vermentino. Their vineyards are situated in various areas of Gallura, at different altitudes and with varying aspects, hence the decision to diversify production with a wide range of wines. Vermentino di Gallura Primo '07 still has young structure and stands out for its concentrated, fruity but fresh aromas, putting on a more rounded performance on the full palate with its caressing mouthfeel. Vermentino di Gallura Cucaione '07 is also impressive. The easiest-drinking wine in the range, it gives alluring tropical fruit and a fresh, full, coherent palate. We were somewhat disappointed by Antiche Cussorgie Bianco '06, from pure vermentino aged in small oak casks for several months. The aromas are evolved, particularly on the nose, although the palate is soft and chewy. Saccaia '06, a red blend of cannonau and cabernet sauvignon, aged in large barrels for around six months, is also nice. While not explosive on the nose, it has a very attractive palate with well-balanced acidity and soft tannins.

● Cannonau di Sardegna Jerzu Cardedo Ris. '05	♥♥ 4*
● Cannonau di Sardegna Ris. '04	♥♥ 4*
● Astangia '05	♥ 5
● Tuvara '04	♥ 6
○ Vermentino di Sardegna I Rivoli '07	♥ 3*
● Cannonau di Sardegna Jerzu Alberto Loi Ris. '03	♀♀ 5
● Cannonau di Sardegna Jerzu Cardedo Ris. '04	♀♀ 4
○ Leila V. T. '05	♀♀ 5

○ Vermentino di Gallura Cucaione '07	♥♥ 4*
○ Vermentino di Gallura Primo '07	♥♥ 5
● Saccaia '06	♥ 4
○ Antiche Cussorgie Bianco '06	♥ 6
● Antiche Cussorgie Rosso '05	♀♀ 6
● Cannonau di Sardegna '05	♀♀ 4*
○ Vermentino di Gallura Saraina '06	♀♀ 5

Masone Mannu

LOC. SU CANALE
SS 199 KM 48
07020 OLBIA
TEL. 078947140
www.masonemannu.com

ANNUAL PRODUCTION 100,000 bottles
HECTARES UNDER VINE 17
VITICULTURE METHOD Conventional

Masone Mannu means "big estate" in Sardinian and over the past few years, the quality of the wines has also increased to match the 17 hectares under vine and annual production of around 100,000 bottles. The vineyards are located in the heart of Gallura, not far from Olbia, and are planted mainly to native grape varieties, concentrating particularly on those best suited to the granite soils of northern Sardinia. Let's take a look at the wines. Mannu '06, available in magnums only, is a blend of cannonau, carignano and muristellu. It's a truly outstanding wine, characterized by a complex nose in which fruity notes mingle with herbaceousness to form a clean, well co-ordinated bouquet that is echoed on the palate. The softness and tannins are in perfect harmony and the wine's remarkable freshness allows it to develop an attractive finish. Entu '06, from carignano and cannonau, is an easier drinking wine, with a nose of wild berries and a supple, juicy palate. Vermentino di Gallura Petrizza '07 is the best of the whites, its soft-textured palate hinting at pear drops. The other wines are well typed and pleasant.

F.lli Pala

VIA VERDI, 7
09040 SERDIANA [CA]
TEL. 070740284
www.pala.it

ANNUAL PRODUCTION 450,000 bottles
HECTARES UNDER VINE 58
VITICULTURE METHOD Conventional

Recently, the wines produced by the Pala brothers have been expanding steadily, making the winery one of the most important in Sardinia. In our tastings, the flagship S'Arai '05, from cannonau, carignano, carignano and barbera sarda, had an extra something that took it through to the finals. Distinctive tobacco and sweet red fruit on the nose precede a palate that opens with softness offset by attractive freshness, while the tannins are combined with good texture. The finish is slightly mouth-drying, perhaps because of the wine's youthfulness, but it still has good continuity through the palate. Essentia '06, from 100 per cent bovale, has distinctive notes of balsam and then a slightly sweet front palate with fresh, full-bodied progression. Moving on to the whites, there was an excellent performance from a Nuragus di Cagliari, obtained from the almost extinct native grape variety of the same name, Sàlnico '07, gives attractive citrus on the nose and a dense, concentrated palate. Vermentino di Sardegna Crabilis '07 is redolent of Mediterranean herbs while the first-rate Silenzi Bianco '07, from vermentino and nuragus, is unbelievably low priced.

● Entu '06	♥♥ 5
● Mannu '06	♥♥ 8
○ Vermentino di Gallura Petrizza '07	♥♥ 4*
○ Ammentu '06	♥ 6
⊙ Rena Rosa '07	♥ 4
○ Vermentino di Gallura Sup. Costarenas '07	♥ 5
○ Ammentu '05	♀♀ 6
● Entu '05	♀♀ 5
● Mannu '05	♀♀ 8
○ Vermentino di Gallura Sup. Costarenas '06	♀♀ 5

● S'Arai '05	♥♥ 6
● Essentija '06	♥♥ 4*
○ Nuragus di Cagliari Sàlnico '07	♥♥ 3*
○ Silenzi Bianco '07	♥♥ 2*
○ Vermentino di Sardegna Crabilis '07	♥ 3
○ Vermentino di Sardegna Stellato '07	♥ 4
○ Entemari '06	♀♀ 5
● Essentija '03	♀♀ 4
● Monica di Sardegna Elima '06	♀♀ 3*
○ Nuragus di Cagliari Sàlnico '06	♀♀ 3*
● S'Arai '04	♀♀ 6
● S'Arai '03	♀♀ 5
● S'Arai '02	♀♀ 5
● S'Arai '01	♀♀ 6
○ Vermentino di Sardegna Stellato '06	♀♀ 4

Pedres

Z. I. SETTORE 7
07026 OLBIA
TEL. 0789595075
www.cantinapedres.it

ANNUAL PRODUCTION	300,000 bottles
HECTARES UNDER VINE	40
VITICULTURE METHOD	Conventional

This all-white estate is run by Giovanni Mancini, with assistance from his offspring. Its 40 hectares of vineyards, located in six sites in upper Gallura, are planted mainly to vermentino, which accounts for almost 80 per cent of the winery's production. A further 12 per cent is planted to moscato and the remainder is local red grapes. This was a bold decision, considering that the winery was founded little more than six years ago. The Mancinis' sacrifices and enthusiasm are yielding excellent results. This year, Vermentino di Gallura Superiore Thilibas '07 stands out from the rest, with a clear fruity nose of apple and pear, a big juicy palate and a long clean finish. Jaldinu '07, the estate's other Vermentino, is only a little less complex. It's pleasant, well balanced and has a citrus finish. The trio is completed by the fresh lively Plebi '07, which is easy drinking but far from banal. We were also impressed by the sparklers. Moscato di Sardegna vaunts concentrated aromas of ripe fruit, with notes of peach and sage. Its delicate, almost velvety palate has a lingering finish. Moscato di Sardegna Assolo is simpler but extremely clean.

O Vermentino di Gallura Sup. Thilibas '07	♔♔	4*
O Moscato di Sardegna	♔♔	4*
O Vermentino di Gallura Jaldinu '07	♔♔	4*
O Vermentino di Gallura Plebi '07	♔♔	4*
O Moscato di Sardegna Assolo	♔	4
O Vermentino di Gallura Plebi '06	♔♔	4

F.lli Porcu

LOC. SU E GIAGU
08019 MODOLO [NU]
TEL. 078535420
fratelliporcu@tiscali.it

ANNUAL PRODUCTION	5,500 bottles
HECTARES UNDER VINE	4
VITICULTURE METHOD	Conventional

The Three Glasses for Malvasia di Bosa '05 reward not just this producer but the entire production area. After numerous unsuccessful attempts to relaunch the wine, other cellars are now quietly releasing their versions. In the Porcu vineyards, quality is the watchword. Young Carlo, who now heads the business, is assisted by his father and uncles. He tends just over four hectares planted to malvsia sardo, although he is also engaged in the attempt to revive the ancient girò variety. The location of the vineyards is excellent, caressed by the sun and the sea breezes on the chalky soils long preferred by local growers. The cellar, too, is equipped with the basic technology required to produce this great wine. Fratelli Porcu keeps yields per hectare low, employs brief skin contact and two years' ageing in steel, even though the production protocol permits ageing in chestnut or oak. It may seem surprisingly straightforward but the result is a wine boasting concentrated aromas of honey and ripe apricots, with hints of almonds and minerals. Entry on the palate is warm, soft and alluring, and the wine displays subtlety, elegance and great complexity.

O Malvasia di Bosa '05	♔♔♔	5
O Malvasia di Bosa '02	♔♔	5
O Malvasia di Bosa '97	♔♔	3*
O Malvasia di Bosa '00	♔♔	5

Cantina Sociale Santa Maria La Palma

LOC. SANTA MARIA LA PALMA
07041 ALGHERO [SS]
TEL. 079999008
www.santamarialapalma.it

ANNUAL PRODUCTION　3,600,000 bottles
HECTARES UNDER VINE　700
VITICULTURE METHOD　Conventional

Although size alone is not sufficient to make a winery great, this is undoubtedly one of the most important operations in north-western Sardinia in terms of both annual production and breadth of range. Among the reds, we were impressed by the interesting cagnulari and cabernet sauvignon-based Alghero Rosso Cabirol '06, now at its second release. Its nose immediately evokes the terroir, with notes of balsam, rockrose and privet, to be followed by a warm, juicy palate. We are no longer surprised at Cannonau di Sardegna Le Bombarde '07, which is unfailingly excellent and offers great value for money. Its balsamic nose and fresh flavours are unmistakable. Alghero Cagnulari '06 is also very convincing, its nice full nose displaying the vegetal and resinous notes characteristic of all the reds of the area. While neither lush nor challenging, the palate is well typed and well balanced. Vermentino di Sardegna I Papiri '07 is uncomplicated and coherent, with fresh aromas and a supple palate, while the rosé Alghero Punta Rosa '07 is pleasant and refreshing.

★ Cantina Sociale di Santadi

VIA CAGLIARI, 78
09010 SANTADI [CI]
TEL. 0781950127
www.cantinadisantadi.it

ANNUAL PRODUCTION　1,700,000 bottles
HECTARES UNDER VINE　606
VITICULTURE METHOD　Conventional

We believe that the most important development to emerge from our tastings this year was not Terra Brune's umpteenth Three Glass award but the overall quality of this leading co-operative, which is a benchmark for both the Sulcis zone and the entire island. Nonetheless, we cannot avoid saying a few words about this classic Carignano del Sulcis. Terre Brune '04 has a concentrated nose of fruity mineral notes and jam. The warm, powerful palate has a nice vein of acidity that sustains it and adds finesse while the aromas of the nose are echoed in the classy finish. Shardana '04 also made it through to our finals, where it performed very well. This carignano and syrah blend has an austere nose characterized by delicate vegetal notes and a juicy, velvety palate with good continuity. We were similarly impressed by two other Carignanos: Rocca Rubia Riserva '05, with soft tannins and a spicy nose, and the juicy, mineral Grotta Rossa '06. From the whites, we were captivated by the complex nose of Nuragus di Cagliari Pedraia '07 and the softness and depth of the sweet Latinia '05, from 100 per cent nasco.

● Alghero Cabirol '06	▼▼	4*
● Alghero Cagnulari '06	▼▼	5
● Cannonau di Sardegna Le Bombarde '07	▼▼	4*
⊙ Alghero Punta Rosa '07	▼	3
○ Vermentino di Sardegna I Papiri '07	▼	4
● Alghero Cagnulari '05	♈♈	5
● Alghero Cagnulari '04	♈♈	5
● Cannonau di Sardegna Le Bombarde '06	♈♈	4*

● Carignano del Sulcis Sup. Terre Brune '04	▼▼▼	8
● Shardana '04	▼▼	6
● Carignano del Sulcis Grotta Rossa '06	▼▼	4*
● Carignano del Sulcis Rocca Rubia Ris. '05	▼▼	5
○ Latinia '05	▼▼	6
○ Nuragus di Cagliari Pedraia '07	▼▼	4*
○ Vermentino di Sardegna Cala Silente '07	▼▼	4*
● Araja '06	▼	4
○ Vermentino di Sardegna Villa Solais '07	▼	3
○ Villa di Chiesa '06	▼	6
● Carignano del Sulcis Sup. Terre Brune '03	♈♈♈	7
● Carignano del Sulcis Sup. Terre Brune '01	♈♈♈	7
● Carignano del Sulcis Sup. Terre Brune '00	♈♈♈	7
○ Latinia '99	♈♈♈	4*

Sardus Pater

VIA RINASCITA, 46
09017 SANT'ANTIOCO [CI]
TEL. 0781800274
www.cantinesarduspater.com

ANNUAL PRODUCTION	500,000 bottles
HECTARES UNDER VINE	300
VITICULTURE METHOD	Conventional

It was a year to remember for this winery, which is part of the Carignano revival. Producers are salvaging the oldest vines, often over 80 years of age in this area and frequently ungrafted. Our Three Glasses went to Carignano del Sulcis Riserva Arenas '05, whose intelligent use of oak imparts delicate vanilla, followed by blackberries and red fruit jam. Well structured and elegant on the palate, it has a long, caressing finish. Kanai '06, the other Carignano Riserva, is also excellent with a complex, intriguing nose of ripe fruit and spices, and a warm, full, enfolding palate. Attractive notes of balsam, freshness and balance are the distinguishing features of the young Carignano del Sulcis Nur '07. This year the fresh, youthful Carignano del Sulcis Is Solus '07 is terrific but Arruga '06 is still too young and needs time to develop in the bottle. Monica di Sardegna Insula '07 offers bay leaf and rosemary-like vegetality and a pleasant fresh palate. Moscato di Cagliari Amentos '07 is another excellent wine while Vermentino di Sardegna Lugore '07 and Carignano del Sulcis Rosato Horus '07 are both pleasant.

● Carignano del Sulcis Arenas Ris. '05	♀♀♀	5*
● Carignano del Sulcis Kanai Ris. '06	♀♀	5
● Carignano del Sulcis Is Solus '07	♀♀	4*
● Carignano del Sulcis Nur '07	♀♀	4*
● Monica di Sardegna Insula '07	♀♀	4*
○ Moscato di Cagliari Amentos '07	♀	5
⊙ Carignano del Sulcis Horus '07	♀	4
● Carignano del Sulcis Sup. Arruga '06	♀	6
○ Vermentino di Sardegna Lugore '07	♀	4
● Carignano del Sulcis Sup. Arruga '04	♀♀	6
● Carignano del Sulcis Is Solus '06	♀♀	4*
● Monica di Sardegna Insula '06	♀♀	4*

Giuseppe Sedilesu

VIA ADUA, 2
08024 MAMOIADA [NU]
TEL. 078456333
giuseppesedilesu@tiscali.it

ANNUAL PRODUCTION	60,000 bottles
HECTARES UNDER VINE	15
VITICULTURE METHOD	Conventional

The landscape around Mamoiada has a rugged beauty, with age-old oak woods, rocks, mountains and very few man-made features. The sparse human traces take the form of magnificent vineyards, planted almost exclusively with bush-trained vines, many of which are very old. The three Sedilesu brothers run the family business with determination. Their winery is temporarily housed in a rented former cheese factory as they await completion of new premises. The current building has a wonderful cellar eight metres high, where the shelves originally used for salting cheeses now serve to raise the barrels and assist gravity racking. Two of the estate's wines reached our finals. Ballutundu Riserva 2005, a magnificent Cannonau, displays deep aromas of Mediterranean scrubland and ripe blackberry before the dense palate reveals impressive minerality and grip, accompanied by good acidity that offsets its impressive concentration. Perda Pintà 2006, from granazza di Mamoiada, is a very distinctive white, brimming with character, whose sole fault is its excessive youth. The other wines are sound, strong and truly reflect the terroir.

● Cannonau di Sardegna Ballutundu Ris. '05	♀♀	7
○ Perda Pintà '06	♀♀	6
● Cannonau di Sardegna Carnevale '06	♀♀	6
● Cannonau di Sardegna Mamuthone '06	♀♀	4*
● Cannonau di Sardegna S'Annada '06	♀	4
● Cannonau di Sardegna Carnevale '03	♀♀	6
● Cannonau di Sardegna Carnevale '01	♀♀	6

★ Tenute Sella & Mosca

LOC. I PIANI
07041 ALGHERO [SS]
TEL. 079997700
www.sellaemosca.com

ANNUAL PRODUCTION	7,000,000 bottles
HECTARES UNDER VINE	550
VITICULTURE METHOD	Conventional

Sella & Mosca put on a memorable show this year. The large estate owned by the Campari group presented us with a more impressive range than ever before, in terms of both quality and consistency. Two wines took our Three Glass award. The first was the now-familiar Alghero Marchese di Villamarina '03, from cabernet sauvignon, which has a spice-laced nose of tobacco and myrtle and thyme balsam, and a rich, well-balanced palate, while the second was Alghero Torbato Terre Bianche Cuvée 161 '07, a great Mediterranean white with a pervasive nose of tropical fruit and a firm, generous, flavoursome palate. The two winners were followed into our finals by Vermentino di Gallura Monteoro '07, which has a mineral and citrus nose, rather like a Mediterranean Riesling, and Alghero Tanca Farrà '04, a cabernet sauvignon and cannonau blend, which showed softer and more complex than in the past. The list ends with Alghero Torbato Terre Bianche '07; the two '07 Vermentino di Sardegnas La Cala and Cala Reale; Alghero Oleandro, a rosé blend of cannonau and cabernet; and Raim '05, from carignano and merlot. All five wines are well made and attractive.

Tenute Soletta

LOC. SIGNOR'ANNA
07040 CODRONGIANOS [SS]
TEL. 079435067
www.tenutesoletta.it

ANNUAL PRODUCTION	100,000 bottles
HECTARES UNDER VINE	15
VITICULTURE METHOD	Conventional

This quality-conscious Codrongianos winery took our Three Glass prize with its Cannonau di Sardegna Riserva Keramos '04, confirming the potential of the variety. The product of the estate's old hillside vineyards and more than 20 days of temperature-controlled maceration, it spends two years in oak and a further six in bottle. Concentrated vanilla mingles with complex florality and spiciness are echoed on the palate, which develops gradually with nicely balanced weight and softness. Corona Majore '05, the other Cannonau Riserva, also did well, displaying a complex nose with vegetal and balsamic notes. Softness on the palate is attenuated by good acidity, lending suppleness and drinkability. Hermes, from dried moscato grapes, also came within a hair's breadth of Three Glasses, the '05 vintage being one of the best from the last decade. Honey and Mediterranean scrubland mingle with aromas of dried flowers before the delightful warm palate unfolds its long, lingering finish. Petalo '07, a rosé cannonau and cabernet blend, and the Vermentino Chimera '07 and barrique-aged Kianos '06 whites, from vermentino and incrocio Manzoni, are all well made.

● Alghero Marchese di Villamarina '03	▾▾▾ 7
○ Alghero Torbato Terre Bianche Cuvée 161 '07	▾▾▾ 4*
● Alghero Tanca Farrà '04	▾▾ 5
○ Vermentino di Gallura Monteoro '07	▾▾ 4*
◉ Alghero Oleandro '07	▾▾ 4*
○ Alghero Torbato Terre Bianche '07	▾ 4
● Cannonau di Sardegna Ris. '05	▾ 4
● Raim '05	▾ 4
○ Vermentino di Sardegna Cala Reale '07	▾ 4
○ Vermentino di Sardegna La Cala '07	▾ 4
● Alghero Marchese di Villamarina '99	▾▾▾ 6
● Alghero Marchese di Villamarina '97	▾▾▾ 6
● Alghero Marchese di Villamarina '95	▾▾▾ 7
● Alghero Marchese di Villamarina '93	▾▾▾ 7
● Alghero Marchese di Villamarina '01	▾▾▾ 7
● Alghero Marchese di Villamarina '00	▾▾▾ 7

● Cannonau di Sardegna Keramos Ris. '04	▾▾▾ 5
● Cannonau di Sardegna Corona Majore Ris. '05	▾▾ 5
○ Hermes '05	▾▾ 5
○ Kianos '06	▾ 5
◉ Petalo Rosato '07	▾ 4
○ Vermentino di Sardegna Chimera '07	▾ 4
○ Dolce Valle Moscato Passito '04	▾▾ 4*
● Cannonau di Sardegna Firmadu '05	▾▾ 4*
● Cannonau di Sardegna Ris. '04	▾▾ 4
○ Kianos '05	▾▾ 5

OTHER WINERIES

6 Mura

Is Pascais, 18
09010 Giba [CA]
tel. 0781964370
www.6mura.com

This promising young Giba winery, founded
by five friends from different walks of life,
produces just one wine, a single-variety
Carignano. The '05 vintage boasts a deep,
elegant palate with caressing, well-knit
tannins and good continuity.

● 6 Mura Rosso '05	🍷🍷	5

Capichera

s.s. Arzachena-Sant'Antonio, km 4
07021 Arzachena [OT]
tel. 078980612
www.capichera.it

The only wine ready in time for our tastings
was Vermentino di Gallura Vigna 'Ngena
2007, so we will reserve judgement on the
rest of the production for next year. The
complex, layered nose is still pervaded by
strong oak notes. Its soft, tangy palate is
potent and nicely textured.

O Vermentino di Gallura Vigna 'Ngena '07	🍷🍷	7
O Capichera Santigaini	🍷🍷	8
O Capichera '05	🍷🍷	8
● Mante'nghja '04	🍷🍷	8

Chessa

via San Giorgio
07049 Usini [SS]
tel. 3283747069
www.cantinechessa.it

This year's results confirmed the quality of
Giovanna Chessa's wines. Lugherra '06,
from cagnulari with cannonau and other
native grapes, has a complex nose and
soft, balanced palate with nice extract.
Vermentino di Sardegna Mattariga '07 and
Kentàles '07, from 100 per cent moscato,
are well made.

● Lugherra '06	🍷🍷	6
O Kentàles '07	🍷	6
O Vermentino di Sardegna Mattariga '07	🍷	5

Cantina di Calasetta

via Roma, 134
09011 Calasetta [CA]
tel. 078188413
www.cantinacalasetta.com

Again this year, we were impressed by
the wines produced by this Calasetta
winery. The pure carignano Maccòri '06 is
outstanding, with a complex nose and a
deep, soft palate. Vermentino di Sardegna
Cala di Seta '07 is also well made, with
citrus aromas and a mineral palate.

● Maccòri '06	🍷🍷	3*
O Vermentino di Sardegna Cala di Seta '07	🍷	3
● Carignano del Sulcis Tupei '06	🍷🍷	4*

Cantina Sociale di Castiadas

loc. Olia Speciosa
09040 Castiadas [CA]
tel. 0709949004
www.cantinacastiadas.com

This Castiadas winery, which produces
mainly Cannonau di Sardegna in the Capo
Ferrato area, did very well. The Riserva '04
has a balsamic nose and a tannic palate
while Rei '04 boasts a complex, lingering
nose followed by a long, well-balanced
palate. The rest of the list is very good.

● Cannonau di Sardegna Capo Ferrato Rei '04	🍷🍷	3*
● Cannonau di Sardegna Capo Ferrato Ris. '04	🍷🍷	5
● Parolto '03	🍷	4
● Sant'Elmo '07	🍷	3

Columbu

via Marconi, 1
08013 Bosa [NU]
tel. 0785373380
www.vinibosa.com

The estate's Malvasia di Bosa '05 had not
been bottled at the time of our tastings
but we sampled Alvarega '07, an IGT from
malvasia. It gives dried fruit on the nose,
with softer, honeyed notes. On the palate
it's sweet, but not cloying, with good
length.

O Alvarega '07	🍷🍷	6
O Malvasia di Bosa '04	🍷🍷	7
O Alvarega '06	🍷🍷	6

OTHER WINERIES

Paolo Depperu

LOC. SAS RUINAS
07025 LURAS [OT]
TEL. 079647314
azienda.depperu@tiscali.it

Once again, we were impressed by Ruinas '07, a Vermentino produced in Gallura by the Depperu brothers, who have opted out of the DOCG. The wine has an intriguing nose, with intense aromas of citrus and tropical fruit. The full, juicy palate has freshness that gives it good balance.

O Ruinas '07	♟♟	5
● Kabaradis '04	♟♟	5
O Ruinas '06	♟♟	5

Vigne Deriu

LOC. SIGNORANNA
07040 CODRONGIANOS [SS]
www.vignederiu.it

This small estate made a fine Guide debut. Cannonau di Sardegna '06 gives a complex nose and velvety palate with well-calibrated tannins. Vermentino di Sardegna '07 has distinctive, geranium and sage-like aromas and an attractive deep palate. Tiu Filuppu '06, from cannonau and cabernet, is a little overripe.

● Cannonau di Sardegna '06	♟♟	4*
O Vermentino di Sardegna '07	♟♟	4*
● Tiu Filippu '06	♟	6

Fradiles

VIA SANDRO PERTINI, 2
08030 ATZARA [NU]
TEL. 3331761683
info@fradiles.it

This small winery concentrates its efforts on the traditional Mandrolisai grapes with satisfying results. We were captivated by Mandrolisai Fradiles '06 and Mandrolisai Antiogu '05, both made from cannonau, bovale and monica. Bagadiu '06, from bovale, is simpler but well made.

● Mandrolisai Antiogu '05	♟♟	5
● Mandrolisai Fradiles '06	♟♟	4*
● Bagadiu '06	♟	4
● Mandrolisai Antiogu '04	♟♟	5

Antonella Ledà d'Ittiri

LOC. ARENOSLI, 29
07100 ALGHERO [SS]
TEL. 3292528891
www.margallo.it

This small Alghero estate boasts six hectares planted to cabernet, merlot and sangiovese. The three varieties are blended to produce Margallò '06, which has vegetal aromas and a juicy, well-balanced palate, although the oak is still overly prominent. Ginjol '06, from mainly merlot, is a touch too simple.

● Ginjol '06	♟	4
● Margallò '06	♟	4

Li Duni

LOC. LI PARISI
07030 BADESI [SS]
TEL. 079585844
www.cantaliduni.it

Li Duni, which grows indigenous grapes only, turned in a good performance. Tajanu '05, a blend of cannonau, bovale, muristellu and cagnulari, has a complex nose and a full, well-sustained palate. Nalboni '04 is also good but Vermentino di Gallura Renabianca Vendemmia Tardiva '06 is too soft.

● Tajanu '05	♟♟	5
● Nalboni '04	♟	3
O Vermentino di Gallura Renabianca V. T. '06	♟	5

Li Seddi

VIA MARE, 29
07030 BADESI [SS]
TEL. 079683052
www.cantinaliseddi.it

Li Seddi, a small Badesi estate, surprised us with a white this year. Vermentino di Gallura Li Pastini '07 has a complex, citrus nose and a tangy, well-sustained palate. Petra Ruja '07, from cannonau, bovale, monica and girò, is also pleasant.

O Vermentino di Gallura Li Pastini '07	♟♟	5
● Petra Ruja '07	♟	4
● Petra Ruja '06	♟♟	4

OTHER WINERIES

Sebastiano Ligios

C.so Europa, 111
07039 Valledoria [SS]
tel. 3296724241
www.cantinaligios.com

In its Guide debut this year, this winery strolled straight into the finals with Cannonau di Sardegna Carammare '05. Fruitiness on the nose is followed by and elegant, well-sustained palate. Campanara '05, from cabernet sauvignon, and Carys '06, a monovarietal syrah, are also well made.

● Cannonau di Sardegna Carammare '05	🍷🍷 4*
● Campanara '05	🍷 5
● Carys '06	🍷 5

Pietro Lilliu

Sardegna, 13
09020 Ussaramanna [VS]
tel. 078395039
lilliupietro@tiscali.it

This year marks the Guide debut of the estate owned by Pietro Lilliu at Ussaramana in central Campidano. Cannonau di Sardegna Dicciosu '05 performed well, giving a complex nose of ripe red fruit with hints of bottled black cherries and then a soft, well-sustained palate with nice freshness.

● Cannonau di Sardegna Dicciosu '05	🍷🍷 5

Cantina Sociale del Mandrolisai

c.so IV Novembre, 20
08038 Sorgono [NU]
tel. 078460113
www.mandrolisai.com

The Mandrolisai co-operative concentrates on local grapes and this year offered an excellent version of Kent'Annos '03, made principally from cannonau and bovale. On the nose it displays elegant notes of ripe red fruit and spices while the well-structured palate has pleasant tannins and good texture.

● Kent'Annos '03	🍷🍷 5
● Kent'Annos '02	🍷🍷 5

Melis

via Santa Suina, 20
09098 Terralba [OR]
tel. 0783851090
melis.vini@tiscali.it

Melis focuses on native grape varieties, particularly the traditional local bovale. Terralba Nabj '05 has good structure, although the oak is still too prominent on the nose. Vermentino di Sardegna localia '07 is simple but clean and pleasant.

● Terralba Nabj '05	🍷🍷 5
○ Vermentino di Sardegna localia '07	🍷 4

Meloni Vini

via Gallus, 79
09047 Selargius [CA]
tel. 070852822
www.melonivini.com

The list performed well, particularly the Cannonaus. Le Sabbie '05 and Le Ghiaie '04, both Cannonau di Sardegnas, are classy wines, the former beings fresher and the latter more structured. Kòsti, from cannonau, monica, bovale, syrah and barbera, and Moscato di Cagliari Donna Jolanda '04, are also very good.

● Cannonau di Sardegna Le Ghiaie '04	🍷🍷 4*
● Cannonau di Sardegna Le Sabbie '05	🍷🍷 4*
● Kòsti '06	🍷🍷 4*
○ Moscato di Cagliari Donna Jolanda '04	🍷🍷 4*

Mesa

loc. Su Baroni
09010 Sant'Anna Arresi [CA]
tel. 0781965057
www.cantinamesa.it

It wasn't a very good year for Mesa but given the estate's potential, we are sure that the wines will soon be back on form. Gioiamia is an interesting classic method Chardonnay Brut. Orodoro, a sweet wine made from moscato and vermentino, and the rosé Rosa Grande '07, from pure carignano, are well made.

○ Gioiamia Brut '07	🍷 6
○ Orodoro	🍷 5
⊙ Rosa Grande '07	🍷 4
● Malombra '05	🍷🍷 7

OTHER WINERIES

Mura

LOC. AZZANIDÒ, 1
07020 LOIRI PORTO SAN PAOLO [OT]
TEL. 078941070
www.vinimura.it

This small but convincing family-run estate offers an excellent Baja '05, from cannonau with a little carignano, that gives complex, lingering notes. The citrussy Vermentino di Gallura Superiore Sienda '07 is interesting and elegant. Cannonau di Sardegna Cortes '07 is uncomplicated but well made.

● Baja '05	♟♟	6
O Vermentino di Gallura Sup. Sienda '07	♟♟	4*
● Cannonau di Sardegna Cortes '07	♟	4

Cantina Sociale Il Nuraghe

S.S. 131 KM 62
09095 MOGORO [OR]
TEL. 0783990285
www.ilnuraghe.it

The Mogoro co-operative's list includes some excellent Cannonaus this year. Cannonau di Sardegna Nero '07 has good structure and softness, with interesting complexity on the nose, and both Cannonau di Sardegna Vignaruja '06 and Cannonau di Sardegna Chio '04 are well executed.

● Cannonau di Sardegna Nero '07	♟♟	4*
● Cannonau di Sardegna Chio '04	♟	6
● Cannonau di Sardegna Vignaruja '06	♟	4

Emidio Oggianu

VIA MARTIRI DELLA LIBERTÀ, 9
08010 MAGOMADAS [OR]
TEL. 0785373345
soggianu@yahoo.it

Emidio Oggianu is a grower from Planargia who owns less than a hectare of vineyards planted with malvasia di Bosa. This year marks his debut in our Guide, with the '05 and '04 vintages. We preferred the latter's soft palate and complex nose with notes of dried fruit and chestnut honey.

O Malvasia di Bosa '04	♟♟	6
O Malvasia di Bosa '05	♟	5

Cantina Sociale di Ogliastra

VIA BACCASERA, 36
08048 TORTOLÌ [NU]
TEL. 0782623228
cantina.ogliastra@tiscali.it

This small but important co-operative at Tortolì in Ogliastro is new to our Guide. Of the two wines we tasted, we preferred Cannonau di Sardegna Su Marchesu '05 for the intensity of its aromas and its well-structured, sustained palate. Cannonau di Sardegna Riserva '04 is warm and full bodied.

● Cannonau di Sardegna Su Marchesu '05	♟♟	3*
● Cannonau di Sardegna Ris. '04	♟	4

Olianas

LOC. PORRUDDU
08030 GERGEI [CA]
TEL. 0558300800
info@tenutacasadei.it

Olianas is an interesting new winery in Gergei, a small municipality in the province of Cagliari. Its Cannonau di Sardegna '06 is excellent, showing a heady nose and a fresh, supple palate. Vermentino di Sardegna '07 is also well made and characterized by distinctive notes of balsam.

● Cannonau di Sardegna '06	♟♟	4*
● Vermentino di Sardegna '07	♟	4

Cantina Cooperativa di Oliena

VIA NUORO, 112
08025 OLIENA [NU]
TEL. 0784287509
www.cantinasocialeoliena.it

This small co-operative winery in Oliena produces Cannonau di Sardegna in the Nepente subzone. Nepente di Oliena '07 has a balsamic nose and a simple yet supple, juicy palate. The alluringly soft Lanaitto '07, from cannonau and other native grape varieties, gives nice Mediterranean scrubland.

● Cannonau di Sardegna Nepente di Oliena '07	♟	4
● Lanaitto '07	♟	3*

OTHER WINERIES

Pedra Majore

VIA ROMA, 106
07020 MONTI [OT]
TEL. 078943185
www.pedramajore.it

We are pleased to confirm that Pedra Majore's decision to concentrate his efforts solely on Vermentino di Gallura was a wise one. Our favourite version was the soft, tangy Superiore Hysonj '07. I Graniti '07 displays an attractively complex nose and Le Conche '07 is simpler but well made.

O Vermentino di Gallura I Graniti '07	❖❖ 4*
O Vermentino di Gallura Sup. Hysonj '07	❖❖ 5
O Vermentino di Sardegna Le Conche '07	❖ 4
O Vermentino di Gallura Sup. Hysonj '06	❖❖ 5

Josto Puddu

VIA SAN LUSSORIO, 1
09070 SAN VERO MILIS [OR]
TEL. 078353329
www.cantinapuddu.it

It was a dessert wine that most impressed us from Josto Puddu's list this year. A blend of nasco, malvasia and moscato, Lunedoro '06 has attractive hazelnut aromas and a nicely sustained palate. The fruity, well-balanced Monica di Sardegna Torremora '06 is also well made.

O Lunedoro '06	❖❖ 6
● Monica di Sardegna Torremora '06	❖ 4
O Vernaccia di Oristano Ris. '02	❖❖ 4

Giampietro Puggioni

VIA NUORO, 11
08024 MAMOIADA [NU]
TEL. 0784203516
www.cantinagiampietropuggioni.it

This year, Cannonau specialist Giampietro Puggioni from Mamoiada offered us an excellent Cannonau di Sardegna Mamuthone '05, with spicy notes and a caressing palate. The pleasant, fresh Cannonau di Sardegna Lakana is simpler but boasts good structure nonetheless.

● Cannonau di Sardegna Mamuthone '05	❖❖ 4*
● Cannonau di Sardegna Lakana '05	❖ 4
● Cannonau di Sardegna Ilisi '04	❖❖ 6

Tenute Silattari

LOC. SILATTARI, 3
08013 BOSA [NU]
TEL. 3339599741
www.silattari.com

The small winery specializes in the production of Malvasia at Bosa. Vendemmia Ottobre '06, from malvasia only, has delicate aromas of peach and Mediterranean herbs. Its sweet, but not cloying, palate gives a slightly almondy finish. Ofelia '06, also from malvasia, is lighter, with hints of lavender.

O Vendemmia Ottobre '06	❖❖ 7
O Ofelia '06	❖ 6

Cantine Surrau

S.P. ARZACHENA - PORTO CERVO
07021 ARZACHENA [OT]
TEL. 078982933
info@vignesurrau.it

This young Gallura winery submitted two good '07 Vermentino di Galluras. The first shows floral, mineral and citrus notes on the nose and is balanced, if not particularly long, on the palate. The Branu version boasts a salty nose and a well-sustained, mineral-veined palate.

O Vermentino di Gallura '07	❖❖ 5
● Cannonau di Sardegna Sincaru '06	❖ 6
O Vermentino di Gallura Branu '07	❖ 5
● Barriu '05	❖❖ 6

Tanca Gioia Carloforte

LOC. GIOIA
09014 CARLOFORTE [CI]
TEL. 3356359329
www.u-tabarka.com

A newcomer to the Guide, this winery concentrates mainly on traditional grape varieties. U Tabarka Roussou '06, from carignano with muristellu and cabernet franc, impressed us with its spicy notes and soft palate. U Tabarka Giancu '07, made from vermentino with a dash of vernaccia, is light but well made.

● U Tabarka Roussou '06	❖❖ 5
O U Tabarka Giancu '07	❖ 5

OTHER WINERIES

Cantina Tondini

LOC. SAN LEONARDO
07023 CALANGIANUS [SS]
TEL. 079661359
cantinatondini@tiscali.it

Cantina Tondini is a promising young estate located in San Leonardo, not far from Calangianus. The best wine on its list is Vermentino di Gallura Superiore Karagnanj '07, with a strikingly complex nose pervaded by tropical fruit. On the palate it shows powerful and tangy with good continuity.

O Vermentino di Gallura Karagnanj '07	♉♉	5
● Taroni '07	♉	4
● Siddaju '04	♉♉	7

Cantina del Vermentino

VIA SAN PAOLO, 1
07020 MONTI [OT]
TEL. 078944012
www.vermentinomonti.it

Cantina del Vermentino scored well at our tastings. Vermentino di Gallura Superiore Aghiloia '07 is fresh, elegant and well sustained. The other two Vermentino di Galluras are also very good: Arakena '06 is concentrated and balanced while Funtanaliras '07 displays pleasant, slightly bitterish notes.

O Vermentino di Gallura Funtanaliras '07	♉♉	5
O Vermentino di Gallura Sup. Aghiloia '07	♉♉	3*
O Vermentino di Gallura Sup. Arakena '06	♉♉	6

Vigne d'Oro

LOC. ISTEDDU
VIA DON LUIGI STURZO, 1
08028 OROSEI [NU]
TEL. 078498216
infovignedoro@tiscali.it

This estate focusing mainly on cannonau-based wines did well at our tastings. Gollei '06, from cannonau with a little carignano and sangiovese, is soft with attractive tannins. Cannonau di Sardegna Lughio '06 and Mirallu '07, also from cannonau with carignano and cabernet, are both interesting.

● Gollei '06	♉♉	4*
● Cannonau di Sardegna Lughio '06	♉	4
● Mirallu '07	♉	5

Cantina Trexenta

V.LE PIEMONTE, 40
09040 SENORBÌ [CA]
TEL. 0709808863
www.cantina-trexenta.it

This winery did very well. Its Cannonau di Sardegna Baione '05 is terrific, with a complex nose and a well-sustained palate. The fresh, fruity Monica di Sardegna Duca di Mandas '06 is great value while the sweet Moscato di Cagliari Simieri '05 and Monica di Sardegna Bingias '05 are also interesting.

● Cannonau di Sardegna Baione '05	♉♉	3*
● Monica di Sardegna Duca di Mandas '06	♉♉	2*
O Moscato di Cagliari Simieri '05	♉♉	4*
● Monica di Sardegna Bingias '05	♉	3*

Cantina Sociale Cooperativa di Vernaccia

LOC. RIMEDIO - VIA ORISTANO, 6A
09170 ORISTANO
TEL. 078333155
www.vinovernaccia.com

The well-established little Vernaccia co-operative gave tangible proof of its importance. The refreshing, scented Terresinis '07, from vernaccia, shows good continuity. Nieddra '06 has an attractively complex nose and a balanced palate. Vermentino di Sardegna Falesia '07 is also well made.

● Nieddera '06	♉♉	4*
O Terresinis '07	♉♉	3*
O Vermentino di Sardegna Falesia '07	♉	3*
O Vernaccia di Oristano '03	♉♉	3*

Villa di Quartu

VIA G. GARIBALDI, 90
09045 QUARTU SANT'ELENA [CA]
TEL. 070826997
www.villadiquartu.com

Villa di Quartu performed admirably in our tastings. Cannonau di Sardegna Parillas '06 is complex with a well-sustained finish. Vermentino di Sardegna Poetho '07 is also impressive, with a fruity nose and a tangy palate. Finally, Cepola Rosso '06, a blend of traditional grapes, is very good.

● Cannonau di Sardegna Parillas '06	♉♉	5
● Cepola Rosso '06	♉♉	5
O Vermentino di Sardegna Poetho '07	♉♉	4*
● Yanna '06	♉	6

PRODUCERS IN ALPHABETICAL ORDER

PRODUCERS BY REGION

PRODUCERS IN ALPHABETICAL ORDER

PRODUCERS BY REGION